Mobile Robotics

Mathematics, Models, and Methods

Mobile Robotics offers comprehensive coverage of the essentials of the field suitable for both students and practitioners. Adapted from the author's graduate and undergraduate courses, the content of the book reflects current approaches to developing effective mobile robots. Professor Alonzo Kelly adapts principles and techniques from the fields of mathematics, physics, and numerical methods to present a consistent framework in a notation that facilitates learning and highlights relationships between topics. This text was developed specifically to be accessible to senior-level undergraduates in engineering and computer science, and includes supporting exercises to reinforce the lessons of each section. Practitioners will value the author's perspectives on practical applications of these principles. Complex subjects are reduced to implementable algorithms extracted from real systems wherever possible, to enhance the real-world relevance of the text.

Alonzo Kelly holds undergraduate degrees in aerospace engineering and computer science, and graduate degrees in robotics. Dr. Kelly worked in the aerospace industry for ten years before returning to academia. As a professor at the Robotics institute at Carnegie Mellon University, he teaches mobile robotics at the graduate and undergraduate levels, conducting research in robot simulation, modeling, controls, position estimation, motion planning, and human interfaces.

Mobile Robotics

Mathematics, Models, and Methods

Alonzo Kelly
Carnegie Mellon University

CAMBRIDGE
UNIVERSITY PRESS

32 Avenue of the Americas, New York NY 10013-2473, USA

Cambridge University Press is part of the University of Cambridge.

It furthers the University's mission by disseminating knowledge in the pursuit of
education, learning and research at the highest international levels of excellence.

www.cambridge.org
Information on this title: www.cambridge.org/9781107031159

First published 2013

A catalogue record for this publication is available from the British Library

Library of Congress Cataloguing in Publication data
Kelly, Alonzo.
Mobile robotics : mathematics, models and methods / Alonzo Kelly.
    pages   cm
Includes bibliographical references and index.
ISBN 978-1-107-03115-9 (hardback)
1. Mobile robots–Textbooks.   I. Title.
TJ211.415.K39   2013
629.8'932–dc23   2013022113

ISBN 978-1-107-03115-9 Hardback

Contents

Preface

Robotics can be a very challenging and very satisfying way to spend your time. A profound moment in the history of most roboticists is the first moment a robot performed a task under the influence of his or her software or electronics. Although a productive pursuit of the study of robotics involves aspects of engineering, mathematics, and physics, its elements do not convey the magic we all feel when interacting with a responsive semi-intelligent device of our own creation.

This book introduces the science and engineering of a particularly interesting class of robots – mobile robots. Although there are many analogs to the field of robot manipulators, mobile robots are sufficiently different to justify their treatment in an entirely separate text. Although the book concentrates on wheeled mobile robots, most of its content is independent of the specific locomotion subsystem used.

The field of mobile robots is changing rapidly. Many specialties are evolving in both the research and the commercial sectors. Any textbook offered in such an evolving field will represent only a snapshot of the field as it was understood at the time of publication. However, the rapid growth of the field, its several decades of history, and its pervasive popular appeal suggest that the time is now right to produce an early text that attempts to codify some of the fundamental ideas in a more accessible manner.

Another indication of timeliness might be the fact that much useful information must be omitted. Many topics, such as perception, are treated only briefly, and others, including legged locomotion, calibration, simulation, human interfaces, and multirobot systems, are omitted completely. The goal of this book is to extract from both the underlying specialties and the depth of mobile robotics research literature a coherent exposition of the concepts, methods, and issues that rise to the forefront in practice, and to represent the core that is unique about this field.

To that end, as much as possible of the material is restricted to two-dimensional wheeled vehicle motion and to structured environments. These assumptions produce a consistent exposition with just enough richness to be relevant and illustrative without overwhelming the reader with details irrelevant to the purpose.

The book follows a logical progression, mimicking the order in which mobile robots are constructed. Each chapter represents a new topic or capability that depends on what came before, and the concepts involved span the fields of numerical methods, signal processing, estimation and control theory, computer vision, and artificial intelligence in that order.

As of this writing, the Mars Science Laboratory Rover named *Curiosity* has recently arrived on Mars. It is our third mobile robotic mission to Mars and the legacy of the last (MER) mission is already historic. This book is not for everyone, but for those who are prepared and motivated, if you master the content of the text you will have a very good idea of what is going on inside the brain of a mobile robot, and you will be well prepared to make one of your own.

CHAPTER 1
Introduction

Figure 1.1 Science Fiction Becomes Fact. Many of the author's generation were introduced to robotics and space travel at the same time when the first *Star Wars* movie appeared in 1977. Little did we suspect that real robots of our own design would drive around on Mars in 1997 for the Pathfinder Mission—only 20 short years later.

Although robot arms that spot weld our cars together have been around for some time, a new class of robots, the mobile robot, has been quietly growing in significance and ability. For several decades now, behind the scenes in research laboratories throughout the world, robots have been evolving to move automatically from place to place. Mobility enables a new capacity to interact with humans while relieving us from jobs we would rather not do anyway.

Mobile robots have recently entered the public consciousness as a result of the spectacular success of the Mars rovers, television shows such as *Battlebots,* and the increasingly robotic toys that are becoming popular at this time.

Mobility of a robot changes everything. The mobile robot faces a different local environment every time it moves. It has the capacity to influence, and be influenced by, a much larger neighborhood than a stationary robot. More important, the world is a dangerous place, and it often cannot be engineered to suit the limitations of the

1

robot, so mobility raises the needed intelligence level. Successfully coping with the different demands and risks of each place and each situation is a significant challenge for even biological systems.

1.1 Applications of Mobile Robots

Every situation in which an animal, human, or vehicle does useful work today is a potential application for a mobile robot. Generally, some of the reasons why it may be a good idea to automate are:

- Better. Manufacturers can improve product quality – perhaps because results are more consistent, easier to measure, or easier to control.
- Faster. Automation can be more productive than alternatives either due to increased rates of production, reduced downtime, or reduced consumption of resources.
- Safer. Sometimes the risk to humans is simply not justified when machines are a viable alterative.
- Cheaper. Using robots can reduce overheads. Robot maintenance costs can be much lower than the equivalent for man-driven vehicles.
- Access. Sometimes, humans cannot even exist at the scales or in the environments in question.

1.2 Types of Mobile Robots

We can classify mobile robots based on such dimensions as their physical characteristics and abilities, the environments for which they are designed, or perhaps the job that they do. Following are some examples of a few different classes of mobile robots.

Figure 1.2 Tug AGV (JBT Corporation, Philadelphia, USA). These laser guided vehicles are used in factories to move materials from place to place.

1.2.1 Automated Guided Vehicles (AGVs)

AGVs are designed to move materials (an application known as *material handling*) in factories, warehouses, and shipping areas in both indoor, and outdoor settings. They may convey automotive parts in manufacturing settings, newsprint in publishing companies, or waste in nuclear power plants.

Early vehicles had guidance systems based on sensing wires embedded in the floor whereas contemporary systems use laser triangulation systems, or inertial systems augmented by occasional magnetic landmarks in the floor.

It is typical for contemporary systems to employ wireless communications to link all vehicles to a central computer responsible for controlling traffic flow. Vehicles are further classified based on whether they pull trailers filled with material (tug-AGV), pick and drop it with forks (forked-AGV) or convey it on an platform on the top of the vehicle (unit load AGV).

Figure 1.3 Straddle Carrier. Used to move containers to and from ships, automated versions of these vehicles are perhaps the largest AGVs in use today.

AGVs are perhaps the most developed market for mobile robots. Companies exist to sell components and controls to many competing vehicle manufacturers, and vehicle manufacturers sometimes compete with each other to sell to value-added systems integrators who assemble a solution for a particular application. In addition to moving material, the loading and unloading of trucks, trains, ships, and planes are potential applications for future generations of vehicles.

1.2.2 Service Robots

Service robots perform tasks that would be considered service industry jobs if they were performed by humans. Some service tasks, like the delivery of mail, food, and medications, are considered to be "light" material handling, and are similar to the job of AGVs. Many service tasks, however, are distinguished by higher levels of intimacy with humans, ranging from coping with crowds to answering questions.

Medical service robots can be used to deliver food, water, medications, reading material, and so on to patients. They can also move biological samples and waste, medical records, and administrative reports from place to place in a hospital.

Surveillance robots are like automated security guards. In some cases, the automated ability to move through an area competently and to simply sense for intruders is valuable. This application was one of early interest to mobile robot manufacturers.

Figure 1.4 Health Care and Surveillance Service Robots. (Left) The Aethon Corp. "Tug" Vehicle is used to move food, linens, records, specimens, and biological waste in hospital settings. (Right) A surveillance robot like Robart might scan a warehouse for unwanted intruders on its regular rounds.

1.2.3 Cleaning and Lawn Care Robots

Other service robots include machines for institutional and home floor cleaning and lawn care. Cleaning robots are used in airports, supermarkets, shopping malls, factories, and so on. They perform such operations as washing, sweeping, vacuuming, carpet shampooing, and trash pickup.

These devices are concerned, not with getting somewhere, or carrying anything, but instead with getting everywhere at least once. They want to cover every part of a particular area of floor in order to clean it.

Figure 1.5 Floor and Lawn Care Service Robots. These kinds of mobile robots care about area coverage. They try to "visit" every place in some predefined area.

1.2.4 Social Robots

Social robots are service robots that are specifically designed to interact with humans and often their main purpose is to convey information or to entertain. Although stationary information kiosks convey information, social robots require mobility for one reason or another.

Figure 1.6 Entertainment and Tour Guide Robots. (Left, Center) The SONY QRIO and AIBO robots dance and play, respectively. (Right) The EPFL tour guide moves from one station to another, often surrounded by people, and it describes museum exhibits.

Some potential applications include answering product location questions in a retail store (grocery, hardware). A robot that delivers hamburgers to kids in a restaurant would be fun. Robot assistants for elderly and infirm individuals could help their owners see (robot seeing-eye dog), move, or remember their medication.

In recent years, SONY Corporation has produced and marketed some impressive robots intended to entertain their owners. The earliest such devices were packaged as "pets." Automated tour guides in museums and expositions can guide customers through a particular set of exhibits.

1.2.5 Field Robots

Field robots perform tasks in the highly challenging "field" conditions of outdoor natural terrain. Almost any type of vehicle that must move about and do useful work in an outdoor setting is a potential candidate for automation. Most things are harder to do outdoors. It's difficult to see in bad weather and it's difficult to decide how to move through complicated natural terrains. It's easy to get stuck, too.

Figure 1.7 Field Robots. Field robots must engage the world exactly as it exists. (Left) Semi-automated fellerbunchers similar to this one have been designed to gather trees. (Right) Automated excavators have been prototyped for mass excavation applications—where large amounts of dirt are loaded over short time periods.

Vehicles that do real work look the way they do for good reasons. Hence, field robots look a lot like their human-driven equivalents. Field robots are often of the form of arms and/or tools (called *implements* in general) mounted on a mobile base. As such, they exemplify a more general case of a mobile robot that not only goes somewhere but also that interacts physically with the environment in some useful way.

In agriculture, real and potential applications include planting, weeding, chemical (herbicide, pesticide, fertilizer) applications, pruning, harvesting and picking fruit and vegetables. In contrast to household grass mowing, large scale mowing is necessary in parks, and on golf courses, and highway medians. The specialized man-driven vehicles used in mowing are good candidates for automation. In forestry, tending nurseries and the harvesting of full grown trees are potential applications.

There are diverse applications in mining, and excavation. Above ground, excavators, loaders, and rock trucks have been automated in open pit mines. Underground, drills, bolting machines, continuous miners, and load-haul-dump (LHD) vehicles have been automated.

1.2.6 Inspection, Reconnaissance, Surveillance, and Exploration Robots

Inspection, reconnaissance, surveillance and explorations robots are field robots that deploy instruments from a mobile platform in order to inspect an area or find or detect something in an area. Often, the best justification for a robot is that the environment is too dangerous to risk using humans to do the job. Clear examples of such environments include areas subject to high radiation levels (deep inside nuclear power plants), certain military and police scenarios (reconnaissance, bomb disposal), and space exploration.

In the energy sector, robots have been deployed to inspect components of nuclear reactors including steam generators, calandria, and waste storage tanks. Robots to inspect high tension power lines, and gas and oil pipelines have been prototyped or deployed. Remotely piloted undersea vehicles are becoming increasingly more autonomous and they and have been used to inspect oil rigs, communications cables on the seabed and even to help find shipwrecks like that of the *Titanic*.

Research into developing the robotic soldier has become particularly intense in recent years. Robotic vehicles are being considered for such missions as reconnaissance and surveillance, troop resupply, minefield mapping and clearing, and ambulance services. Manufacturers of military vehicles are already working hard to get a diverse array of robotic technologies into their products. Bomb disposal is already an established niche market.

In space, several robotic vehicles have now driven autonomously for kilometers over the surface of Mars and the concept of vehicles that maneuver around space stations under thruster power has been on the drawing table for some time.

Figure 1.8 Exploration Robots. (Left) The military robot is intended to explore environments where it may be too unsafe for soldiers. (Right) The Mars Science Laboratory searches for signs of life in the hostile environment on Mars.

1.3 Mobile Robot Engineering

1.3.1 Mobile Robot Subsystems

There are a host of challenges that become instantly obvious when attempting to construct systems exhibiting autonomous mobility. At the lowest level in a conceptual hierarchy of abilities, robots require the capacity of automatic *control*. Doing this involves the sensing of the states of actuators such as steering, speed, or wheel velocities and the precision application of power to those actuators to cause them to exert the correct forces. However, moving around competently requires more than an accelerator, steering and engine that do what they are told – there needs to be a driver. This book is mostly about the construction of such a driver.

Often, the objective is one of *navigation*, to move somewhere in particular or to follow a particular path. Accomplishing that requires a vehicle *state estimation* system that knows where the vehicle is at any time along the way. Navigation and control give a robot the capacity to drive (albeit blindly) from place to place, provided there is nothing in the way – but what if there is something in the way? The need for a capacity to understand the immediate surroundings, known as *perception*, arises in many different contexts ranging from following the road in view, to dodging a fallen tree, to recognizing the object for which the robot has been searching.

Although such an understanding of the environment is one aspect of intelligence, *planning* is another. Planning involves a capacity to predict the consequences of alternative possible courses of action, and a capacity to select the most appropriate one for the present situation. Planning often requires models of both the environment and the vehicle in order to predict how they interact. The former models are called *maps* and they are used to help decide where to go.

Maps may be produced externally to the robot or they may be produced by an onboard *mapping* system that uses the navigation system and the perception system to record salient aspects of what has been seen in its correct relative place. Maps can have other uses besides support of planning. If maps record both what is seen and where it is seen, it becomes possible for the robot to determine its position in the map if it can match what it does see to what it would see if it was in a particular hypothesized position.

1.3.2 Overview of the Text

This book will discuss many aspects of each of these subsystems in the order in which they might be developed, integrated, and tested during the construction of a prototype robot.

Preliminary material in mathematics (Chapter 2), numerical methods (Chapter 3), and physical models (Chapter 4) is presented first and the rest of the text will rely on it heavily. Thereafter incremental aspects of mathematics, models, and methods will be introduced as needed. Chapter 5 presents certain aspects of probability and then a more advanced topic that has special importance in mobile robots – optimal estimation. The problems of knowing where you are and of knowing what is out there are solved more effectively using optimal estimation techniques. State estimation (Chapter 6) is presented next because it produces the most basic feedback necessary for control of mobility. It is also a good introduction to some of the issues that are most peculiar to mobile robots. As we will see, moving is often not so hard compared to the problem of knowing precisely how you have moved or where you are.

The topic of control system design and analysis (Chapter 7) is presented next. Here are the basic techniques that are used to make things move in a controlled and deliberate fashion. Control makes it possible to move at a particular speed, with a particular curvature, or to a particular goal position and heading. It also becomes possible to move any articulations to point sensors, to dig a hole, or to pick up something. When Perception (Chapter 8) is added to this basic moving platform, things get very interesting quickly. Suddenly the mobile system potentially becomes able to look for things, recognize and follow or avoid people, and generally move much more competently in the local area. Such a system can also construct maps on small scales, and plan its motions in those maps based on the results of state estimation.

The topics of Localization and Mapping (Chapter 9) are two sides of the problem of locating objects relative to the robot or locating the robot relative to a map of objects. Once the robot can see objects, it can remember where they are and the associated map can be very useful the next time this or any other robot inhabits the area. The final chapter presents Motion Planning (Chapter 10). When maps are available on a large scale, whether produced by a robot or a human, it becomes possible to do some very intelligent things. Given an accurate map, robots can rapidly compute the best way to get anywhere and they can update that map rapidly as new information is gathered on the move.

1.3.2.1 Layers of Autonomy

For mobile robots, and for us, problems that require deep thought cannot be solved in an instant. There are other problems like avoiding the jaywalking pedestrian, which must be solved in an instant. Yet, it is difficult to be both smart and fast so robots tend to use a hierarchy of perceive-think-act loops in order to allocate resources optimally (Figure 1.9). Higher levels tend to be more abstract and deliberative, whereas lower levels tend to be more quantitative and reactive.

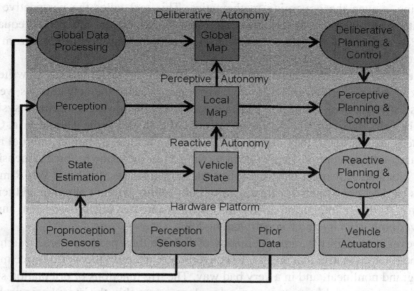

Figure 1.9   Layers of Autonomy. The entire mobile system can be described in terms of three nested perceive-think-act loops.

1.3.2.1.1 Reactive Autonomy. This layer is responsible for controlling the motion of the vehicle with respect to the environment and any required articulations. It typically requires feedback only of the articulation and motion state (position, heading, attitude, velocity) of the vehicle. The content of the book up to the middle of the Control chapter fits in this layer.

1.3.2.1.2 Perceptive Autonomy. This layer is responsible for responding to the immediately perceivable environment. It typically requires feedback of the state of the environment, which is derived from Perception. This layer requires estimates only of short-term relative motion and it tends to use environment models that are valid only locally. Prediction is limited to a few seconds into the future. The content of the book up to the Perception chapter fits in this layer.

1.3.2.1.3 Deliberative Autonomy. This layer is responsible for achieving longer term goals, sometimes called the "mission." This layer requires earth-fixed position estimates and it tends to use environment models that extend over large areas. Prediction may extend arbitrarily far into the future. The content of the book up to Motion Planning chapter fits in this layer.

1.3.3 Fundamentals of Wheeled Mobile Robots

At this point in the history of the field there is no agreed-on list of fundamental concepts that constitute the core a of mobile robotics curriculum. Whereas homogeneous transforms take center stage in any text on robot manipulators, mobility changes everything – even the governing mathematics. This text takes the perspective that the most basic model of a wheeled mobile robot is a kinematic differential equation that is constrained and nonlinear. Most of the content of the text follows from that perspective.

The easiest way to formulate wheeled mobile robot (WMR) models is write the velocity kinematics and to do so in the body frame because the actuators, as well as the sensors, move with the robot. Fluency with ideas of moving coordinate systems makes the velocity kinematics very straightforward to derive in the general case. Once these ideas are mastered, they also play a role in mechanical dynamics, inertial navigation and stability control. However, in moving from the plane to three dimensions, the rate kinematics also get more complicated. In many cases, the basic WMR model requires explicit constraints for treatment of both rolling without slipping and terrain following. At this point, our model has become a differential algebraic system and we will cover both velocity and force driven models.

However, although the rate kinematics of WMRs thus produced are straightforward, the rotation matrix that appears to convert coordinates to the world frame makes the integrand nonlinear, and in a very bad way. The trig functions of orientation states make the problem of driving to a particular place – arguably the most basic problem of all – more formidable than the famous Fresnel integrals, and therefore not solvable in closed form. The elegance of manipulator inverse kinematics is simply not achievable for mobile robots and a host of related problems cannot be solved in closed form – even in the plane. Thus, any time we want to write a relationship between state (pose) and inputs, we have to be content to write an integral, so the text has a lot of integrals in it.

Then computers come to the rescue. The book covers numerical methods because a large number of important problems succumb to a short list of basic numerical methods. Some effort has been expended here to reduce every robotics problem into its associated canonical "method." Nonlinear least squares, for example, is fundamental to both estimation and control and the Kalman filter itself is derived here from weighted least squares. Likewise, the Newton iteration of constrained optimization applies to problems as diverse as terrain following, trajectory generation, consistent map building, dynamic simulation, and optimal control. As for that most basic problem of all? It is a numerical rootfinding problem that Newton's method handles readily once the problem is parameterized. Thus, although we cannot write elegant formulae for fundamental reasons, we can still get the job done in a computer.

Once the basic WMR model is in place we will integrate it, parameterize it, perturb it, take its squared expected value, invert it etc. in multiple ways in order to supply control and estimation systems with the models they need. They need them to provide the feedback and perform the actions necessary for a robot to know where it is and get where it is going. All of this is illustrated using essentially the same basic model of a robot actuated in linear and angular velocity.

Along the way the tools of linear systems theory prove to be powerful. In addition to providing the means to control the robot, these tools allow us to understand the propagation of systematic and stochastic error and therefore to understand the behavior of dead reckoning and to even calibrate the system while it is in operation.

Then the robot opens its eyes and evaluates its options. Once there are options we need optimization to pick the best one, and optimal control supplies the required formalism for both obstacle avoidance in the continuum and global motion planning in discretized world models. The text takes the perspective that Bellman's principle of optimality is the basic strategy needed to search the trajectory continuum. First, we convert the optimal control problem to nonlinear programming to avoid obstacles, follow paths, and execute maneuvers. Then we convert it a second time to a sequential decision process to plan paths on a more global scale using A* and its modern derivatives. When we are done, we will have revealed the mind of an artificial entity endowed with a capacity to navigate intelligently, purposefully, and successfully from one place to another in complicated environments.

It is hard to get all that in one book. Legged robots and humanoids are other fundamentally distinct configurations whose treatment will have to be the subject of other books.

1.3.4 References and Further Reading

There mare many good books on robotics and mobile robotics available on the market today. Here are just some of them.

[1] George A. Bekey, *Autonomous Robots: From Biological Inspiration to Implementation and Control,* MIT Press, 2005.
[2] Greg Dudek and Michael Jenkin, *Computational Principles of Mobile Robotics,* Cambridge University Press 2000.
[3] Joseph L. Jones, Bruce A. Seiger, and Anita M. Flynn, *Mobile Robots: Inspiration to Implementation,* A. K. Peters, 1993.
[4] P. J. McKerrow, *Introduction to Robotics,* Addison-Wesley, 1991.
[5] Ulrich Nehmzo, *Mobile Robots: A Practical Introduction,* Springer, 2003.
[6] Bruno Siciliano and Oussama Khatib (eds.), *Springer Handbook of Robotics,* Springer, 2008.
[7] Roland Siegwart and Illah R. Nourbakhsh, *Introduction to Autonomous Mobile Robots,* MIT Press, 2005.

1.3.5 Exercise

1.3.5.1 Mobility

Comment in one or two sentences for each subsystem on how the goal of mobility requires that a mobile robot have such a subsystem.

- position estimation
- perception
- control
- planning
- locomotion
- power/computing

CHAPTER 2

Math Fundamentals

Figure 2.1 WorkPartner Robot. This robot is designed to not only get to the job, but it can do the job, too. The kinematic and dynamic modelling of this robot illustrates wheeled locomotion and dual-armed manipulation. To control this robot, models of both its mobility and its manipulation capability are needed.

Kinematics is the study of the geometry of motion. Kinematic modelling therefore enjoys a particularly distinguished role as one of the most important analytical tools of mobile robotics. We use kinematics to model the gross motion of the robot body as well as the internal motions of mechanisms associated with suspension, steering, propulsion, implements, and sensors. Kinematic models are employed offline for such diverse purposes as design, analysis, and visualization. Such models are also used online on computers used to interface to robots or on the computers on the robot. Many kinematic models are based on matrices and we will need a few advanced topics on matrices for a few other purposes, so matrices are reviewed first. The tools developed in this section will be used throughout the rest of the book.

2.1 Conventions and Definitions

This chapter will present some aspects of notation that will be unfamiliar to most readers who have not studied advanced dynamics. We do not need advanced dynamics in this book but we do need precise notation. We also need notations powerful enough to handle many concepts from dynamics rather than just homogeneous coordinates applied to points and vectors in space. For these reasons, we will depart from the conventions of many other robotics books and use the notations of physics rather than those of computer graphics. The reader is advised to skim this subchapter first up to Figure 2.7 and the commentary afterward. With that context, a second reading would be more illuminating.

2.1.1 Notational Conventions

It will be necessary in the rest of the text to adhere to a fairly strict set of notational conventions for describing geometry and motion. In most cases, the quantities of interest can be interpreted as properties of a first object that are defined with respect to a second. For example, the velocity of a robot is more precisely a statement about the robot and the ground or floor over which it drives.

2.1.1.1 Unspecified Functions

The most basic interpretation of functional notation is to consider a function $f(\ )$ to be a syntactic mapping of a list of supplied symbols, called the arguments, onto an expression involving those symbols. Thus if $f(x) = x^2 + 6x$, then $f(3) = (3)^2 + 6(3)$ and $f(\text{apple}) = (apple)^2 + 6(apple)$.

The text will present numerous algorithms in an unspecified function notation either for reasons of brevity, to emphasize that the precise form of the function is irrelevant, or because the precise form is too complicated or unknown. The letters $f(\ )$, $g(\ )$ and $h(\ )$ will typically be used for unspecified functions. The appearance of the same letter for a function in two places will not necessarily mean the same function is implied. This convention is common in calculus books because this is the point in mathematics where we discuss transformations of functions, like derivatives, which are independent of the function itself.

Thus in one instance, we may have $f(x) = ax + b$ whereas nearby there appears $f(x) = x^2$. Probability is an extreme case of this convention where $p(X)$ and $p(Y)$ are totally unrelated because the different arguments are intended to indicate different functions, and every probability density function in this and most other books is called $p(\ )$! Hence, this convention is not as new as it may seem.

In such notation, it is important to recognize that the appearance of a symbol in an argument list to a function means that it appears somewhere in the explicit expression of the function. Thus, the expression $f(x, u, t)$ means that all of these arguments will appear explicitly. For example:

$$f(x, u, t) = ax + bu + ct$$

If $f(\ )$ does not explicitly depend on time t, then the expression becomes $f(x, u)$. For example:

$$f(x, u) = ax + bu$$

It is tempting to read the expression $f(x, u)$ from a computational point of view, to mean that if x and u are specified, this constitutes enough information to compute $f(\ )$ but this is true only if the explicit form of $f(\ )$ is known.

As a completely separate matter, it may be the case that either or both of x and u depend on time t. If so, this dependence may be stated or it may be implied, but in any case the expression $f(x, u)$ conveys nothing about whether x or u depend on time or not, or the nature of the dependence. On occasion, when it is important to make this clearer, we may write:

$$f(x(t), u(t))$$

If this is so, it clearly means that $f(\ )$ depends only on time, so we may write:

$$g(t) = f(x(t), u(t))$$

Here, we used $g(\ )$ to make it clearer that the explicit form of $g(\ )$ will certainly be different from the explicit form of $f(\ )$ but note that both functions return the exact same number for their values once t is specified. That is, when one computes $f(x, u)$ from $x(t)$ and $u(t)$, the value returned is that same one that would be returned by computing $g(t)$.

In summary, the statement $y = f(x)$ is a statement that y depends on x in some unspecified manner but we will never write such a statement to mean that y does not depend on u unless there is more context to render such a conclusion a reasonable one. Unspecified functional notation like $f(x)$ is used for indicating that dependencies exist, whereas explicit functional notation like $f(x) = x^2$ is used for specification of the precise nature of dependencies. Neither notation is used to indicate that *other* dependencies do not exist. It may be the case that $f(x)$ is just an abbreviation for $f(x, u)$ but the dependence on u is not relevant to the immediate presentation.

2.1.1.2 Functionals

There is another form of dependence that will be of interest. A *functional* is not the same thing as a function. A functional is a dependence that maps entire functions onto numbers. At times, we will use square brackets to make the distinction clearer. Hence if $J[f]$ means that J is a functional of the function f, then J might such that $J[\sin(x)] = 2$ and $J[ax + b] = b/(2a)$.

Functionals are familiar even if their name is not. Definite integrals are one form of functional because if:

$$J[f] = \int_0^\pi f(x)dx$$

Then $J[\sin(x)] = 2$ and $J[e^x] = e^\pi - 1$ so the integral maps functions onto numbers. Physical quantities like centroids and moments of inertia, and statistical concepts like mean and variance are defined by functionals.

2.1.1.3 Physical Quantities

We will need to represent a physical quantity r, relating two objects a and b, denoted r_a^b. The quantity could be the position, velocity, acceleration, angular velocity, orientation, pose, homogeneous transform, etc. Generally, physical quantities of interest will be asymmetric, so usually:

$$r_a^b \neq r_b^a$$

We will sometimes record our knowledge of the r quantity between a and b by an edge in a graph (Figure 2.2):

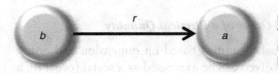

Figure 2.2 Physical Quantity Relating Two Objects. It will sometimes be convenient to use graphs to represent what we know about some objects.

2.1.1.4 Instantiated Quantities

While r denotes the quantity in general, r_a^b means the specific quantity associated with the two named objects. In the second case, we can sometimes think of r as a property of object a but more often context is necessary because the property also depends on the choice of object b:

$$r_a^b \neq r_a^c$$

We read r_a^b as the "r" property of a relative to b. For example, "the" velocity of an object is not defined. Every object has a velocity with respect to every other object in the universe, so it takes two objects, as in v_a^b, to be precise about what the velocity of object a means. Angular velocity can neither be measured relative to a point nor possessed by a point because a point has no orientation and therefore no rate of orientation change. For this reason, points are disqualified as objects for expressing relationships involving orientation or its derivatives.

We will say that a quantity associated with two specific objects is *instantiated*. For example, $v_{car}^{earth} = (10, 20)$ might mean that a car has a velocity relative to the earth surface of 10 mph in the east direction and 20 mph north. Conversely, we will say that a quantity with unspecified objects is *uninstantiated*. For example, $v = (10, 20)$ might mean the property of having a velocity relative to something of 10 mph in the east direction and 20 mph in the north.

2.1.1.5 Frames of Reference and Coordinate Systems

As mentioned above, the velocity of something is only meaningful when expressed relative to something else. That critical something else is known in physics as the *frame of reference* [2]. When we write r_a^b, the object b is the frame of reference. Its role is to serve as the datum or origin with respect to which the property of a is expressed. The thing that distinguishes reference frames from each other is their **state of motion** (linear and angular position, velocity, and acceleration).

Conversely, when we described the uninstantiated velocity $v = (10, 20)$ earlier, it was necessary to refer to the two directions east and north to understand the interpretation of the numbers 10 and 20. These directions are known in physics as the coordinate system. If the directions are changed to west and south, the numbers would have to be changed to −10 and −20 to convey the same meaning. Even the numbers 10 and

20 and the expression "mph" require definition. The numbers are a particular kind of number system and "mph" is a member of the unit system in use. Changing coordinates changes the description but not the underlying relationship. In our conventions, we will denote the fact that north-east (ne) coordinates are used to express the velocity by using the left superscript, thus ^{ne}v. The left superscript will be used on occasion to explicitly specify coordinates.

2.1.1.6 Dimension and Order of a Physical Quantity

Physics distinguishes classes of physical quantities based on dimension and order. Order specifies whether the quantity involved can be expressed as a scalar (order 0), a vector (order 1), a matrix (order 2), and so on. Mass is a scalar; velocity is a vector, and inertia is a matrix. Dimension relates to how many numbers are needed to define the quantity. Velocity in the plane is two-dimensional, whereas inertia in space is a 3×3 matrix.

2.1.1.7 Vectors, Matrices and Tensors

A *matrix* is a set of numbers arranged in a rectangular array. It is a more specialized concept than a simple set because the numbers are sorted in two dimensions and they must form a rectangle. For example:

$$A = \begin{bmatrix} 2 & 3.6 \\ 8 & -4.3 \end{bmatrix}$$

is called a 2×2 matrix because it has 2 *rows* and 2 *columns*. These are the *dimensions* of A. Rectangular matrices, such as a 2×3 matrix, also occur commonly in practice. The matrix A above is square and the numbers 2 and -4.3 are on its *diagonal*. One special square matrix is the identity matrix, which has only ones along its diagonal, and zeros elsewhere:

$$I = \begin{bmatrix} 1 & 0 \\ 0 & 1 \end{bmatrix}$$

Notationally, I is used for any identity matrix regardless of its size. A matrix of the form:

$$\underline{x} = \begin{bmatrix} 2 \\ 8 \end{bmatrix}$$

is sometimes known as a *vector*. Note the $\underline{x}$ is also the first column of A. We will often use such vectors to express a vector quantity from physics, such as force, in a particular coordinate system. Inertia, covariance, and stress are matrix-valued quantities that, just like vectors, change the numbers in the matrix if the coordinate system changes.

Often matrices will be denoted with an uppercase letter and vectors will be underlined. It is conventional to consider most vectors to be matrices of one column rather than one row. Hence, the notational device $\underline{x}^T = [2\ 8]$ is used in most texts to denote the conversion of a column vector to a row vector. The uppercase T superscript is used to denote the *transpose* operation that reflects a matrix around the line that would define the diagonal of a square matrix. As we will see later, a transpose is often necessary to express particular matrix multiplication operations with precision. Note that particular elements in a matrix or vector can be identified by associating indices that amount to defining an integer valued coordinate system with respect to the top left corner. Thus:

$$A[2, 2] = A[2][2] = a_{22} = -4.3$$

Conventionally matrix indices start with 1 in books while they start with 0 in most programming languages and this is a rich source of software bugs. Note that vectors need only a row index – the column index is understood to be 1:

$$\underline{x}[2, 1] = \underline{x}[2] = x_2 = 8$$

Although a vector is a like a line segment and a matrix is like a rectangle, a *tensor* is like a 3D box. It has three dimensions that could be called row, column, and depth. A tensor can be visualized as a stack of matrices. Here are the three "slices" of such a stack:

$$T_1 = \begin{bmatrix} 2 & 3.6 & 7 \\ 8 & -4.3 & 0 \end{bmatrix} \qquad T_2 = \begin{bmatrix} 3 & -5 & 12 \\ 4 & 2 & -1 \end{bmatrix} \qquad T_3 = \begin{bmatrix} 7 & 9.2 & 18 \\ 8 & -4 & 0 & 13 \end{bmatrix}$$

Tensors arise naturally in matrix calculus as well as advanced physics and we will have limited uses for them. This *third-order tensor* has 3 indices, though more are possible. Each element in the tensor has its integer coordinates. For example, if the indices are $[row][col][depth]$ then:

$$T[1, 3, 2] = T[1][3][2] = t_{132} = 12$$

Clearly, matrices and vectors are just tensors of order 2 and 1, respectively, and a scalar is a tensor of order 0.

2.1.2 Embedded Coordinate Frames

2.1.2.1 Objects and Embedded Coordinate Frames

The objects of interest to us will be real physical bodies like wheels and sensors, obstacles, and robots. Generally we will denote these by a single letter, or occasionally a word such as HAND. We will often abstract these bodies by sets of axes that are fixed in the bodies (Figure 2.3) and that move with them to help us track their motion. For example, one convention is to put axes at the robot centroid.

These conceptual embedded sets of axes are fundamental to modelling the motion of rigid bodies. They have two properties of interest. First, because of their association with a real object, they have a state of motion so they can function as reference frames. It is meaningful to ask how something is moving relative to them. Second, three orthogonal axes form the basis of a Cartesian coordinate system so it is meaningful to ask about, for example, the components or projections of a vector onto these axes. Hence, our embedded sets of axes have the properties of a coordinate system.

We will refer to these embedded sets of axes as *coordinate frames* and we will often use them as surrogates for the objects they represent. It will also be convenient at times to embed a coordinate frame in a point with the understanding that its orientation is not meaningful.

2.1.2.2 Coordinate System Independent Quantities

Relationships can be stripped of their coordinate system and remain meaningful. Although the situation is analogous for relationships of all orders, we will concentrate on vectors. Consider the rule for transforming a velocity with respect to frame b into one with respect to frame c:

$$\vec{v}_a^c = \vec{v}_a^b + \vec{v}_b^c \tag{2.1}$$

Here, the important point is that this law holds **regardless of the objects involved**. The letters a, b, c are merely placeholders for any objects we care to use.

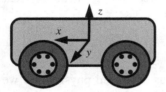

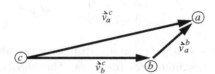

Figure 2.3 Embedded Coordinate Frames. A coordinate frame is embedded in an object. This conceptual object possesses the properties of both a reference frame and a coordinate system.

Figure 2.4 Vector Addition Without Coordinates. Vector addition is defined geometrically so coordinates are not needed to define the operation.

The notation that places a small vector symbol over a letter as in $\vec{v}$ and $\vec{v}_x^y$ is used universally in physics to denote a relationship expressed in **coordinate system independent** form. This is a notational convenience, which is meaningful because all physical laws (such as Equation 2.1) hold **irrespective of the coordinate system in which the relationships involved are expressed**. Addition of vectors in this form is defined geometrically by placing them sequentially in tip to tail fashion as shown in Figure 2.4.

Conversely, an underline and left superscript, such as in the notation ${}^a\underline{v}$, denotes a vector $\vec{v}$ expressed in coordinate system a. If it were expressed in a different coordinate system b, the same vector would have a potentially different representation (different numbers in its associated row vector), and it would be denoted ${}^b\underline{v}$.

2.1.2.3 Free and Bound Transformations

At times it is useful to derive one relationship from another. For example, Equation 2.1 can be regarded as a process that derives v_a^c from v_a^b. The relative velocity of frames b and c (v_b^c) is required to do this. Two classes of transformation (*free* and *bound*) will be of interest to us. They are best illustrated with position vectors as shown in Figure 2.5.

Suppose the position vector $\vec{r}_p^{\,a}$ of the point p is known with respect to frame a. If another frame b is available, at least two mechanisms are available to associate the position of point p with frame b.

In a *bound* transformation to frame b (which treats $\vec{r}_p^{\,a}$ as a *bound* vector) the tail of the vector is moved to frame b to produce the vector $\vec{r}_p^{\,b}$. This is a transformation of reference frame. Conversely, a *free* transformation (which treats $\vec{r}_p^{\,a}$ as a *free* vector) is a more subtle transformation. It leaves the vector alone and merely expresses it in the coordinates of frame b to produce the quantity $^{b}\!r_p^{\,a}$. This is a conversion of coordinates that does not change the definition of the original vector in any way. Some texts call a bound vector a *point* and a free vector is called a *vector*. We will sometimes have to treat the same vector in both ways as just described.

In Figure 2.6, we define the quantity $^{b}\!r_{-p}^{\,a}$ to mean the projections of $\vec{r}_p^{\,a}$ onto the axes of frame b. This can be visualized by freeing $\vec{r}_p^{\,a}$ and moving its tail to frame b before performing the projections as shown in Figure 2.6. The coordinates of the result are:

$$^{b}\!r_{-p}^{\,a} = \begin{bmatrix} x_p^b - x_a^b \\ y_p^b - y_a^b \end{bmatrix} \tag{2.2}$$

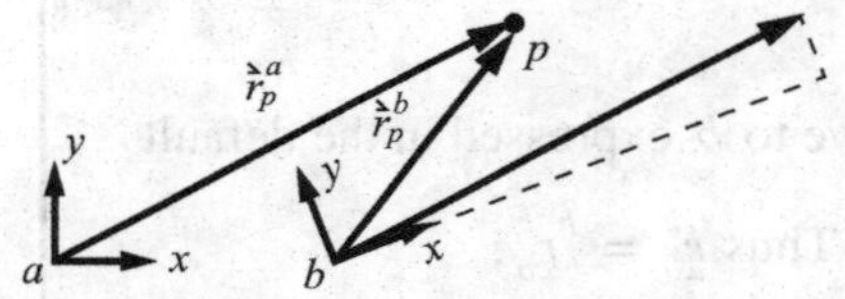

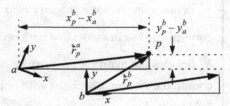

Figure 2.5 Free and Bound Vectors. If the vector $\vec{r}_p^{\,a}$ is bound, the change of reference frame from a to b changes its magnitude and direction to $\vec{r}_p^{\,b}$. If it is free, its tail can be simply moved to the origin of b. This new vector is identical to $\vec{r}_p^{\,a}$ but its expression in the coordinates of b may differ from that of a.

Figure 2.6 Interpretation of $^{b}\!r_{-p}^{\,a}$**.** The coordinates of the result are equivalent to treating $\vec{r}_p^{\,a}$ like a free vector and moving it to the origin of frame b.

2.1.2.4 *Notational Conventions*

The notation that will be used consistently throughout the book can be visualized as follows:

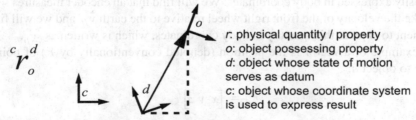

$^{c}\!r_{o}^{\,d}$

r: physical quantity / property
o: object possessing property
d: object whose state of motion serves as datum
c: object whose coordinate system is used to express result

Figure 2.7 Notational Conventions. Letters denoting physical quantities may be adorned by designators for as many as three objects. The right subscript identifies the object to which the quantity is attributed. The right superscript identifies the object whose state of motion is used as datum. The left superscript will identify the object providing the coordinate system in which to express the quantity.

When the coordinate system object is unspecified, it will be the same object as the datum and vice versa. These conventions are summarized in Box 2.1.

Box 2.1: Notation for Physical Quantities

We will use the following conventions for specifying physical quantities:

r_a denotes the scalar r property of object a.

r_n denotes the scalar n-th component of a vector or the n-th entity in a sequence.

r_{ij} denotes the scalar ij-th component of a matrix or the ij-th entity in a sequence of order 2.

$\vec{r}_a$ denotes the vector r property of object a expressed in coordinate system independent form.

$\underline{r}_a$ denotes the vector r property of object a expressed in the default coordinate system associated with object a. Thus $\underline{r}_a = {}^a\underline{r}_a$.

$\vec{r}_a^b$ denotes the vector r property of a relative to b in coordinate system independent form.

$\underline{r}_a^b$ denotes the vector r property of a relative to b expressed in the default coordinate system associated with object b. Thus $\underline{r}_a^b = {}^b\underline{r}_a^b$.

R_a^b denotes the matrix R property of a relative to b expressed in the default coordinate system associated with object b.

${}^c\underline{r}_a^b$ denotes the vector r property of a relative to b expressed in the default coordinate system associated with object c.

These conventions are just complicated enough to capture some of the subtly defined quantities that will be used later. For example, an accelerometer mounted on a robot inherently measures something akin to ${}^b\underline{a}_s^i$ – the acceleration a of the sensor s relative to inertial space i expressed in the robot body b frame. One of the early steps in inertial guidance is to convert this into the acceleration of the body relative to the earth expressed in earth coordinates ${}^e\underline{a}_b^e$. Likewise, wheeled robot kinematics can often be most easily expressed in body coordinates. We will find that an encoder measures something like the velocity of the front right wheel relative to the earth $\vec{v}_{fr}^e$ and we will find it convenient to express this quantity in body coordinates, which is written as ${}^b\underline{v}_{fr}^e$.

An example of a vector is the position (denoted conventionally by r) of point p relative to object a:

$$\underline{r}_p^a = \begin{bmatrix} x & y & z \end{bmatrix}^T$$

If the numbers x, y, and z have values, a coordinate system must have been specified. If they do not have values, it is permissible to write the symbolic form $\underline{r}_p^a$ instead. Sometimes $\underline{r}$ will be written r (without the underline) when it is clear that it is a vector. It is important to recognise that all of these forms are shorthand, but the entity being described is $\underline{r}_p^a$.

2.1.3 References and Further Reading

Few people have thought about notation in recent years because we inherited it from deep thinkers of centuries ago. See Wolfram for some perspectives. Ivey and perhaps other physics texts distinguish reference frames and coordinate systems.

[1] Stephen Wolfram, Mathematical Notation: *Past and Future* (2000), Transcript of a keynote address presented at MathML and Math on the Web: MathML International Conference, October 20, 2000.

[2] Donald G. Ivey, J. N. P. Hume, *Physics: Relativity, Electromagnetism, and Quantum Physics*, Ronald Press, 1974.

2.2 Matrices

2.2.1 Matrix Operations

The reader is assumed to have a basic familiarity with matrix and vector algebra. This section is provided to introduce notation and consolidate more advanced concepts upon which subsequent chapters will rely.

2.2.1.1 Block Notation

It is often convenient to divide a matrix up into blocks. This is denoted as follows:

$$A = \begin{bmatrix} A_{11} & A_{12} \\ A_{21} & A_{22} \end{bmatrix}$$

The division can be arbitrary provided $rows(A_{11}) = rows(A_{12})$ and $cols(A_{11}) = cols(A_{21})$, and so on.

2.2.1.2 Tensor Notation

The notation:

$$A = \begin{bmatrix} a_{ij} \end{bmatrix}$$

means that A is a matrix whose elements are a_{ij} for every allowable pair of indices i and j. The intention is to distinguish this from a set that might be denoted $\{a_{ij}\}$ because the elements of matrices are ordered in 2D and they must form a rectangle.

This notation is very convenient for deriving many results. One main reason for using this notation is that we will have occasional use for arrays with three indices. Such a third-order tensor can be written as:

$$A = \begin{bmatrix} a_{ijk} \end{bmatrix}$$

Representing such higher dimensional objects on paper can be a challenge but, for our purposes, they are nothing more than the multidimensional arrays that all popular computer programming languages provide. We will have only occasional need for tensors of order higher than 3 – and we will never write them out in detail!

2.2.1.3 Basic Operations on Matrices

Operations on matrices are defined only when the operands are *conformable* – meaning when they have appropriate dimensions. Addition and subtraction are defined when the matrices are of the same dimensions, and these operations take place element by element. Scalar multiplication multiplies every element of a matrix of any dimension by the scalar. Thus:

$$A + \frac{1}{2}B = \begin{bmatrix} 2 & 3.6 & 7 \\ 8 & -4.3 & 0 \end{bmatrix} + \frac{1}{2}\begin{bmatrix} 2 & 0 & 0 \\ 0 & 4 & 0 \end{bmatrix} = \begin{bmatrix} 3 & 3.6 & 7 \\ 8 & -2.3 & 0 \end{bmatrix}$$

In contrast to *scalar multiplication* (involving a scalar and a matrix), *matrix multiplication* (involving a matrix and a matrix) is defined when the number of columns of the left operand equals the number of rows of the right. They need not be square.

2.2.1.4 Vector Dot Product

The concept for the multiplication of two matrices is built upon the *dot product* (also called the inner product) operation for vectors. The dot product produces a scalar from two vectors. It is computed as the sum of the element-by-element products of two vectors of the same length:

$$\underline{a} \cdot \underline{b} = \sum_k a_k b_k$$

This is also written as $\underline{a}^T \underline{b}$ – a notation that uses the operation of matrix multiplication as defined next.

2.2.1.5 Matrix Multiplication

Matrix multiplication is defined so that the (i, j) element of the result is the dot product of the ith row of the left argument and the jth column of the right:

$$C = AB = [c_{ij}] = \left[\sum_k a_{ik} b_{kj}\right]$$

Matrix multiplication is not commutative, so the order of the operands matters, and $AB \neq BA$ in general. There are many exceptions to this rule. The simplest is that any square matrix commutes with itself, so $AA = AA$ because switching the order changes nothing in this case. Also, the identity matrix is so-named because it is the identity element under matrix multiplication. When A is square $IA = AI = A$.

2.2.1.6 Vector Cross Product

For completeness, let us briefly consider the vector cross product. It is most useful in three dimensions. If $\underline{a} = [a_x\, a_y\, a_z]^T$ and $\underline{b} = [b_x\, b_y\, b_z]^T$ then:

$$\underline{c} = \underline{a} \times \underline{b} = \begin{bmatrix} a_y b_z - a_z b_y \\ a_z b_x - a_x b_z \\ a_x b_y - a_y b_x \end{bmatrix}$$

This product can be written as a matrix multiplied by a vector $\underline{c} = \underline{a} \times \underline{b} = \underline{a}^{\times}\underline{b}$ where we have used the clever device of defining the matrix-valued skew-symmetric function of the vector $\underline{a}$:

$$\underline{a}^{\times} = \begin{bmatrix} 0 & -a_z & a_y \\ a_z & 0 & -a_x \\ -a_y & a_x & 0 \end{bmatrix}$$

2.2.1.7 Outer Product

The outer product produces a matrix from two vectors:

$$\underline{c} = \underline{a}\underline{b}^T = \begin{bmatrix} a_x b_x & a_x b_y & a_x b_z \\ a_y b_x & a_y b_y & a_y b_z \\ a_z b_x & a_z b_y & a_z b_z \end{bmatrix}$$

2.2.1.8 Block Multiplication

Block multiplication is a convenient high level notation that describes the multiplication operation in terms of component matrices without revealing all of the internal structure. Provided all components are conformable where necessary:

$$A = \begin{bmatrix} A_{11} & A_{12} \\ A_{21} & A_{22} \end{bmatrix} \quad B = \begin{bmatrix} B_{11} & B_{12} \\ B_{21} & B_{22} \end{bmatrix} \quad AB = \begin{bmatrix} (A_{11}B_{11} + A_{12}B_{21}) & (A_{11}B_{12} + A_{12}B_{22}) \\ (A_{21}B_{11} + A_{22}B_{21}) & A_{21}B_{12} + A_{22}B_{22}) \end{bmatrix}$$

2.2.1.9 Linear Mappings

The most common use of matrices and vectors is the use of a matrix as a linear operator that maps vectors onto vectors. The equation:

$$\underline{y} = A\underline{x}$$

occurs throughout applied mathematics. The matrix multiplication operator provides the basic mechanism to express the idea that every element of $\underline{y}$ depends in a linear way on every element in $\underline{x}$. Of course, points are just a particular kind of vector, the displacement vector, so matrices also map points to points.

2.2.1.10 Interpretations of Linear Mappings

Consider the case when matrix A is $m \times n$ so it has m rows and n columns. Note that the length of $\underline{x}$ must equal the length of the rows (i.e., number of columns) of A. Fluency with advanced concepts in linear algebra depends on two equally valid views of the equation $\underline{y} = A\underline{x}$.

One view of this equation is that A is an operator that operates on $\underline{x}$ to produce $\underline{y}$. In this view, the vector $\underline{x}$ is successively projected onto each row of A by computing a dot product, and the output $\underline{y}$ amounts to a list of the magnitudes of these projections (dot products). In this view, the rows of A are a set of axes and the process $\underline{y} = A\underline{x}$ is computing the coordinates of $\underline{x}$ in this coordinate system.

Conversely, note that the length of $\underline{y}$ must equal the length of the columns of A. The equation $\underline{y} = A\underline{x}$ can also be viewed as a process where the vector $\underline{x}$ operates on the matrix A to produce the output $\underline{y}$. In this view, the formula scales every column of A by its corresponding element in $\underline{x}$, adds all the weighted columns up, and produces $\underline{y}$. This process can be visualized as a weighted sum process rather than a projection process and the columns of A are collapsed into a single column as a result.

2.2.2 Matrix Functions

A basic *function* as defined in set theory maps objects of any kind in a set $\mathcal{A}$ to objects of any kind in another set $\mathcal{B}$:

$$f \mid \mathcal{A} \to \mathcal{B}$$

Using this idea, we could define a function mapping each of several atoms to one of several zebras. It turns out that every one of the nine potential combinations where $\mathcal{A}$ is a scalar, vector, or matrix and $\mathcal{B}$ is a scalar, vector, or matrix occurs and is of practical value.

2.2.2.1 Matrix Functions of Scalars and Vectors

It is straightforward to define a matrix-valued function of one or more variables by simply having the elements depend on a variable. For example, a time varying matrix would be written as:

$$A(t) = \begin{bmatrix} a_{11}(t) & a_{12}(t) & \dots \\ a_{21}(t) & a_{22}(t) & \dots \\ \dots & \dots & \dots \end{bmatrix} = \begin{bmatrix} a_{ij}(t) \end{bmatrix}$$

A scalar that depends on a spatial vector is called a scalar *field*. A matrix of such fields would be a matrix-valued function of a vector:

$$A(\underline{x}) = \begin{bmatrix} a_{11}(\underline{x}) & a_{12}(\underline{x}) & \dots \\ a_{21}(\underline{x}) & a_{22}(\underline{x}) & \dots \\ \dots & \dots & \dots \end{bmatrix} = \begin{bmatrix} a_{ij}(\underline{x}) \end{bmatrix}$$

We will have many uses for these in modelling mechanisms.

2.2.2.2 Matrix Polynomials

Matrix-valued functions of matrices are also useful. For square matrices, the result of multiplication is the same size as the original operands. This idea enables us to define the exponentiation (power) function on matrices:

$$A^3 = A(A^2) = (A^2)A = AAA$$

When we combine this notion with scalar multiplication, we can clearly write a matrix polynomial. A matrix "parabola" would be:

$$Y = AX^2 + BX + C$$

Here, X, Y, A, B, C are all matrices; X must be square and A, B, and C must be of the same dimensions and they must have exactly as many rows as X has columns.

2.2.2.3 Arbitrary Functions of Matrices and the Matrix Exponential

The reader may recall that most functions of practical interest can be expressed in terms of a Taylor series. This is an infinite series that can be derived from the derivatives of the function itself. If a function $f(x)$ is known at the origin (or more generally at any x) then its values can be computed everywhere else based only on knowledge of its value and the values of its derivatives at the origin:

$$f(x) = f(0) + x\left\{\frac{df}{dx}\right\}_0 + \frac{x^2}{2!}\left\{\frac{d^2f}{dx}\right\}_0 + \frac{x^3}{3!}\left\{\frac{d^3f}{dx}\right\}_0 + \ldots$$

Now this is relevant to matrices because we just defined polynomials on matrices and the above is just an infinite polynomial. Based on this idea, we can choose to define *almost any function* on matrices.

A very important function of a matrix is the matrix exponential. The ordinary scalar exponential has this expression as a Taylor series:

$$e^x = \exp(x) = 1 + x + \frac{x^2}{2!} + \frac{x^3}{3!} + \ldots$$

Taking the hint, for the square matrix A, the matrix exponential is defined as:

$$\exp(A) = I + A + \frac{A^2}{2!} + \frac{A^3}{3!} + \ldots$$

In practice, the higher-order terms vanish for many situations or the matrix elements are a recognizable series whose limits can be evaluated and an explicit formula for the matrix exponential results.

2.2.3 Matrix Inversion

The inverse A^{-1} of a square matrix A is defined such that $A^{-1}A = I$. We will see later that left and right pseudo inverses of nonsquare matrices can be defined as well. There are explicit formulas for the inverse of a matrix but they become extremely verbose for anything but very small matrices. For a 2×2:

$$A = \begin{bmatrix} a & b \\ c & d \end{bmatrix} \qquad A^{-1} = \left(\frac{1}{ad - cb}\right)\begin{bmatrix} d & -b \\ -c & a \end{bmatrix}$$

This is easy to verify by multiplying AA^{-1} together. The quantity $ad - cb$ appears as a scalar multiplier. The inverse of this matrix exists if and only if this *determinant* is nonzero.

2.2.3.1 Inverting a Linear Mapping

One of the main uses of the matrix inverse is to invert a linear mapping. If $\underline{y} = A\underline{x}$, then multiplying both sides by A^{-1} leads to:

$$A^{-1}\underline{y} = A^{-1}A\underline{x} = \underline{x}$$
$$\underline{x} = A^{-1}\underline{y}$$

This can be thought of as mapping the output vector back to its corresponding input.

2.2.3.2 Determinant

The determinant [5] of a square matrix, denoted $det(A)$ or $|A|$ is a generalization of the vector cross product. It is a scalar function, of particular importance, of a matrix. For a 2×2 matrix:

$$det(A) = \begin{vmatrix} a & b \\ c & d \end{vmatrix} = ad - cb$$

For matrices larger than 3×3, closed form expressions for the determinant become too verbose to use. Luckily, it is rarely necessary to compute a determinant. Nonetheless, we will use it for two of its most basic properties. The determinant expresses the volume of the parallelepiped spanned by the rows of A (Figure 2.8) and this notion carries over to higher dimensions.

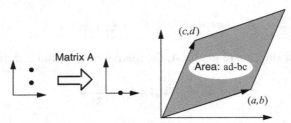

Figure 2.8 Intuition for Determinant. (Left) If both inputs map to the same output, the matrix is not invertible. This situation occurs whenever the output spans less dimensions than the input. (Right) The volume enclosed by the parallelepiped spanned by the rows of the matrix is its determinant.

There are two consequences of this. First, if the volume is zero, it means that when the matrix is interpreted as a linear mapping, information is lost in at least one dimension when a vector is transformed by the matrix. Such lost information means that the input cannot be recovered from the output. In other words, the matrix is not invertible.

Second, notice that:

$$A\begin{bmatrix} 1 \\ 0 \end{bmatrix} = \begin{bmatrix} a \\ c \end{bmatrix} \qquad A\begin{bmatrix} 0 \\ 1 \end{bmatrix} = \begin{bmatrix} b \\ d \end{bmatrix}$$

Just as the rows of A define a volume (area), so do any two vectors if we arrange them as rows of a matrix. In particular, the volume spanned by the transformation of the two unit vectors $[1 \quad 0]^T$ and $[0 \quad 1]^T$ is:

$$\begin{vmatrix} a & c \\ b & d \end{vmatrix} = ad - cb = \begin{vmatrix} a & b \\ c & d \end{vmatrix}$$

This is numerically the same as the determinant of A because $det(A) = det(A^T)$. It's also easy to see that twice the input volume results in twice the output volume. Hence, the determinant provides the scale factor relating an output volume and an input volume of any size. Also, the determinant of a product of two matrices is the product of the individual determinants: $det(AB) = det(A)det(B)$.

2.2.3.3 Rank

The rank of a matrix is the dimension of its largest invertible submatrix. Suppose A is an $n \times n$ matrix. The inverse of A will exist if A is of rank n. An $n \times n$ matrix of rank less than n is said to be *rank deficient* or *singular*. Conversely, if A is of rank n it is said to be *of full rank*, *invertible*, or *nonsingular*. Rank is defined on a nonsquare matrix since it can still have square submatrices which have determinants. In this case, the terms rank deficient or full rank are used.

Several rules about rank are useful. A nonsquare matrix can have a rank no larger than the smaller of its two dimensions. The rank of a matrix product cannot exceed the minimum of the ranks of the two operands.

2.2.3.4 Positivity

A square matrix A is called *positive definite* if:

$$x^T A x > 0 \qquad \forall x \neq 0$$

The quadratic form $x^T A x$ is a scalar and the mapping from x onto this scalar can be visualized as a paraboloid over n dimensions. Positive definite matrices are the matrix equivalent of positive numbers and many operations preserve the positivity property. The sum of two positive definite matrices is positive definite, for example. We will use them to define local minima of functions, and they occur in probability as covariance and in mechanics as inertia.

2.2.3.5 Homogeneous Linear Systems

The special system of linear equations:

$$Ax = 0$$

is called a *homogeneous* system. In the case when A is invertible, the system has a unique and trivial solution given, of course, by:

$$x = A^{-1}0 = 0$$

If A is singular, the system has an infinite number of nonzero solutions.

2.2.3.6 Eigenvalues and Eigenvectors

The vector e is called an *eigenvector* of the square matrix A when it satisfies:

$$Ae = \lambda e$$

for some scalar λ called the *eigenvalue* associated with e. Intuitively, an eigenvector is simply a vector that is not rotated when operated on by A. For such a vector, operation by A is equivalent to simply multiplying the vector by the scalar λ. That is exactly what the definition says.

Note that if (e, λ) satisfies the above, then (ke, λ) is also a solution for any constant k so only the direction of an eigenvector is significant. They are often normalized to unit length by convention. To find the eigenvalues of a matrix, we solve the above condition by rewriting it in the form of:

$$(\lambda I - A)e = 0$$

We know from the rules for homogeneous systems above that this only has a nonzero solution e when:

$$det(\lambda I - A) = 0$$

The most important thing about eigenvectors is the fact that if A is invertible with distinct eigenvalues, then the eigenvectors of A form a basis for $\Re^n$. In other words, every vector $v \in \Re^n$ can be written as a weighted sum of the eigenvectors of A:

$$v = c_1 e_1 + c_2 e_2 + \ldots + c_n e_n$$

2.2.4 Rank-Nullity Theorem

One can associate several subspaces with a given $m \times n$ matrix A $(m < n)$ [3]. When the equation $\underline{y} = A\underline{x}$ is viewed as a weighted sum of the columns of A, it is clear that the set of all possible output vectors $\underline{y}$ is described by all possible weighted combinations of the n columns of A. This set of all such $m \times 1$ vectors $\underline{y}$ is called the *range* or *column space* of A, denoted $C(A)$. Conversely, every vector $\underline{x}$ can be potentially described in terms of its projections on the m rows of A. The rows therefore induce a set of vectors whose projections onto them are nonzero. This set of $n \times 1$ vectors $\underline{x}$ is called the *row space* of A, denoted $\mathcal{R}(A)$.

There are cases where the rows of A do not span all of the n possible dimensions desired – either because there are less than n rows or they are linearly dependent. In this case, there are directions in n dimensions where vectors of any length do not project onto any row of A. It is even possible that there are several such independent directions. The number of such independent directions is called the *nullity* of A. The set of all vectors that satisfy $A\underline{x} = 0$ is called the *nullspace* of A, denoted $\mathcal{N}(A)$.

Vectors in the nullspace are orthogonal to all rows of A, meaning they have no projection onto its rows. The row space and the nullspace are said to be *orthogonal complements* because they are mutually orthogonal. That is, **every** vector in the nullspace is orthogonal to **every** vector in the row space. By the fundamental theorem of linear algebra, their union is $\Re^n$. $\mathcal{R}(A)$ spans at most an m dimensional subspace of $\Re^n$ and

$\mathcal{N}(A)$ spans a subspace of $\mathfrak{R}^n$ of dimension at least $n - m$. In fact, the rank and the nullity of A always sum to n:

$$rank(A) + nullity(A) = n$$

This is known as the *rank-nullity theorem*.

2.2.5 Matrix Algebra

Although simple equations such as $A\underline{x} = \underline{y}$ can be solved by inverting A, it turns out that many of the rules of algebra carry over to matrices with some care. We have already seen that matrix multiplication is not commutative, for example, and that only square matrices are invertible, so there is a need to be mindful of the exceptions.

2.2.5.1 Dividing by a Matrix

We must be careful when "dividing" by a matrix (multiplying by its inverse) to note whether the inverse was left or right multiplied. Thus if A and B are invertible and:

$$AB = CD \tag{2.3}$$

then $B = A^{-1}CD$ whereas $A = CDB^{-1}$.

2.2.5.2 Creation of A Singular Matrix

Suppose $m < n$ and matrix A is $m \times n$ whereas matrix B is $n \times m$ and both are of rank m. The product AB is $m \times m$ and it may be invertible whereas the product BA is $n \times n$ and it definitely is not invertible since its rank is at most m. For example, consider a matrix equation involving the dot product of two $n \times 1$ vectors:

$$\underline{a}^T \underline{x} = b \tag{2.4}$$

where $\underline{a}$ is a vector of constants and $\underline{x}$ contains n unknowns. It is perfectly legitimate to multiply both sides by a row vector $\underline{c}$ to produce:

$$\underline{c}\,\underline{a}^T \underline{x} = \underline{c}b \tag{2.5}$$

Notice also that $\underline{c}\,\underline{a}^T$ is an outer product, and hence, a matrix. We might now be tempted to "solve" for $\underline{x}$ with:

$$\underline{x} = (\underline{c}\,\underline{a}^T)^{-1}\underline{c}b \tag{2.6}$$

Apparently, no rules of matrix algebra have been violated, but in fact, one has. The last equation has tried to invert a singular matrix. Sometimes this occurs in the middle of a computation for reasons that cannot be predicted. In the above case, however, the product $\underline{c}\,\underline{a}^T$ is a rank one matrix, so unless it is 1×1 and not the scalar 0, it cannot be inverted and this was perfectly predictable. Intuitively, Equation 2.3 places a single constraint on the n elements of $\underline{x}$ and it is fundamentally impossible to recover n unknowns from a single constraint.

Although the creation of singular matrices is legitimate and useful, inverting them is not. In general, any matrix product that produces a matrix whose smallest dimension exceeds that of *either* of the operands, will have produced a singular matrix.

2.2.5.3 Blockwise Matrix Elimination

The same principles that are used to eliminate variables in scalar equations can be used to eliminate blocks of equations and invert block matrices. Consider the solution of:

$$\begin{bmatrix} A & B \\ C & D \end{bmatrix} \begin{bmatrix} x_A \\ x_B \end{bmatrix} = \begin{bmatrix} y_A \\ y_B \end{bmatrix}$$

where the structure looks like so:

That is, $dim(A) = n \times n, dim(B) = n \times m, dim(D) = m \times m$ and $dim(C) = m \times n$.

Assuming A is square and invertible, multiplying the first row by the $m \times n$ matrix CA^{-1} reduces the top block to m equations:

$$\begin{bmatrix} C & CA^{-1}B \\ C & D \end{bmatrix} \begin{bmatrix} x_A \\ x_B \end{bmatrix} = \begin{bmatrix} CA^{-1}y_A \\ y_B \end{bmatrix}$$

Now, subtracting the two blocks of m rows produces:

$$(D - CA^{-1}B)x_B = y_B - CA^{-1}y_A$$

In a computer implementation, we could stop here and solve for x_B. Otherwise, the explicit solution for x_B is:

$$x_B = E^{-1}[y_B - CA^{-1}y_A] \tag{2.7}$$

where $E = D - CA^{-1}B$ is called the *Schur complement* of A. In a computer implementation, we would now solve the original first equation for x_A by writing that equation in the form:

$$Ax_A = y_A - Bx_B \tag{2.8}$$

For a closed form result, we substitute into the original first equation and simplify:

$$\begin{aligned} Ax_A + Bx_B &= y_A \\ Ax_A + BE^{-1}[y_B - CA^{-1}y_A] &= y_A \\ Ax_A &= [I + BE^{-1}CA^{-1}]y_A - [BE^{-1}]y_B \\ x_A &= [A^{-1} + A^{-1}BE^{-1}CA^{-1}]y_A - [A^{-1}BE^{-1}]y_B \end{aligned} \tag{2.9}$$

Hence, the inverse is:

$$\begin{bmatrix} A & B \\ C & D \end{bmatrix}^{-1} = \begin{bmatrix} A^{-1} + A^{-1}BE^{-1}CA^{-1} & -A^{-1}BE^{-1} \\ -E^{-1}CA^{-1} & E^{-1} \end{bmatrix} \tag{2.10}$$

Note the special case that occurs often where $B = C^T$ and $D = 0$. Then $E = -CA^{-1}C^T$ and:

$$\begin{bmatrix} A & C^T \\ C & 0 \end{bmatrix}^{-1} = \begin{bmatrix} A^{-1} + A^{-1}C^T E^{-1}CA^{-1} & -A^{-1}C^T E^{-1} \\ -E^{-1}CA^{-1} & E^{-1} \end{bmatrix} \tag{2.11}$$

2.2.5.4 Matrix Inversion Lemma

Alternatively, we could have multiplied the second block of rows by $-BD^{-1}$ and added the two equations. That process produces this result:

$$\begin{bmatrix} A & B \\ C & D \end{bmatrix}^{-1} = \begin{bmatrix} F^{-1} & -F^{-1}BD^{-1} \\ -D^{-1}CF^{-1} & D^{-1} + D^{-1}CF^{-1}BD^{-1} \end{bmatrix} \tag{2.12}$$

where $F = A - BD^{-1}C$ is called the Schur complement of D. By equating the top left submatrices of Equation 2.11 and Equation 2.12, we have:

$$F^{-1} = A^{-1} + A^{-1}BE^{-1}CA^{-1}$$

Substituting for F produces:

$$[A - BD^{-1}C]^{-1} = A^{-1} + A^{-1}B[D - CA^{-1}B]^{-1}CA^{-1} \tag{2.13}$$

Spotlight 2-1 Matrix Inversion Lemma.

Equation 2.13 is known as the *Matrix Inversion Lemma*. This formula is used when A^{-1} is known and it is necessary to compute the inverse of the rank m "correction" to A, which is $[A - BD^{-1}C]^{-1}$. Instead of inverting the $n \times n$ matrix A, one can invert $D - CA^{-1}B$ the *Schur complement* of A, which is $m \times m$. The special case when $m = 1$ is known as the *Sherman-Morrison formula*.

We will have use of the special form when $B = C^T$ and the sign of D is reversed:

$$[C^T D^{-1}C + A]^{-1} = A^{-1} - A^{-1}C^T[CA^{-1}C^T + D]^{-1}CA^{-1} \tag{2.14}$$

2.2.6 Matrix Calculus

It will be necessary in many places to represent derivatives of scalars, vectors, and matrices with respect to each other in every possible combination.

2.2.6.1 Implicit Sum Notation

The notation:

$$\left[c_{ij}\right] = \left[a_{ik}b_{kj}\right] \tag{2.15}$$

is a convenient mechanism to represent operations on tensors, matrices and vectors. By convention, [a], [b], and [c] above are all matrices because they have two indices. They would be denoted A, B, and C in most texts. By convention, if an index is repeated on the right-hand side it is *summed over* its entire range (but the capital sigma summing symbol is omitted) and the index disappears on the left-hand side. Hence, the above expression means the following:

$$C = AB = [c_{ij}] = \left[\sum_k a_{ik}b_{kj}\right]$$

Equation 2.15 is a compact way to represent matrix multiplication. Implicit sum notation is also a very compact specification for a computer program that performs the indicated operations. If [b] was a vector:

$$\left[c_i\right] = \left[a_{ij}b_j\right]$$

the result is a vector. We might interpret this as if the column dimension of the matrix A was *collapsed* by the operation with $\underline{b}$. In this notation, the dot product is:

$$c = \left[a_i b_i\right]$$

(where a is a vector) and the outer product is:

$$\left[c_{ij}\right] = \left[a_i b_j\right]$$

and, in 3D, the cross product is:

$$\left[c_i\right] = \left[\varepsilon_{ijk} a_j b_k\right]$$

Because two indices are repeated, this is a double sum over j and k. The special symbol ε_{ijk} is defined to be:

$$\varepsilon_{ijk} = \begin{matrix} 1: \text{when } (ijk) \in \{(123), (231), (312)\} \\ -1: \text{when } (ijk) \in \{(321), (213), (132)\} \\ 0: \text{otherwise} \end{matrix}$$

2.2.6.2 Compression Operations on Tensors

When two objects of different order are multiplied, the result can be reduced or increased in order. We have already seen that various multiplication operations on vectors can produce, scalars vectors, or matrices. Many operations for matrices can be defined analogously for tensors. In the case of third-order tensors, we can visualize multiplication by a vector to mean a weighted sum of its component matrices. Hence, multiplying such an object a_{ijk} by a vector b_k produces a matrix.

$$\left[c_{ij}\right] = \left[a_{ijk}b_k\right]$$

The operation amounts to a weighted collapsing of the third dimension of tensor A to produce a matrix. This is analogous to how $y = Ax$ is a weighted collapsing of the second dimension of matrix A to produce a vector.

2.2.6.3 Layout Conserving Operations

Differentiation of tensors (and hence the special cases of matrices, vectors and scalars) is defined to be performed on an element-by-element basis. In other words, the derivative of the tensor is the tensor of the derivatives:

$$\frac{\partial}{\partial B} A(B) = \left[\frac{\partial}{\partial B}a_{i\ldots n}(B)\right]$$

for any objects A and B of any order. Hence, we can always take a derivative operation inside a tensor. One consequence of this is that the derivative of anything with respect to a scalar has the same layout as the original object.

2.2.6.4 Derivative of Matrix Product with Respect to a Scalar

Although it is rarely written in texts, the product rule of differentiation applies to matrices. Consider the derivative of a matrix product with respect to a scalar:

$$\frac{\partial}{\partial x} C(x) = \frac{\partial}{\partial x} \{A(x)B(x)\}$$

The general case can be derived from the definition of matrix multiplication. In implicit sum notation:

$$\left[c_{ij}(x)\right] = \left[a_{ik}(x)b_{kj}(x)\right]$$

Each element of the result is the dot product of two vectors. Each dot product is a sum of products of scalars and we know how to differentiate scalar products.

Conveniently, the derivative of a sum is the sum of the derivatives so implicit sum notation can be differentiated to produce more implicit sums. We simply treat the two operands as scalars and the implicit sums take care of themselves:

$$\left[\frac{\partial}{\partial x}c_{ij}(x)\right] = \left[\left(\frac{\partial}{\partial x}a_{ik}(x)b_{kj}(x)\right) + \left(a_{ik}(x)\frac{\partial}{\partial x}b_{kj}(x)\right)\right] \tag{2.16}$$

Which means in matrix notation:

$$\frac{\partial}{\partial x}C(x) = \frac{\partial}{\partial x}\{A(x)B(x)\} = \frac{\partial}{\partial x}\{A(x)\}B(x) + A(x)\frac{\partial}{\partial x}\{B(x)\} \tag{2.17}$$

Extensions to products of three or more matrices are straightforward. Note that the derivation would proceed identically for products of tensors. Clearly, some special cases are the case where A and B are equal, or a transpose pair, and when either of them does not depend on x.

2.2.6.5 Useful Matrix-Scalar Derivatives

The above results permit the derivation of several useful additional results. By Equation 2.16 using t to replace the independent variable x above:

$$\frac{d\{\underline{x}(t)^T A \underline{x}(t)\}}{dt} = \underline{\dot{x}}^T A \underline{x} + \underline{x}^T A \underline{\dot{x}}$$

When A is symmetric, this can be simplified to:

$$\frac{d\{\underline{x}(t)^T A \underline{x}(t)\}}{dt} = 2\underline{x}^T A \underline{\dot{x}}$$

2.2.6.6 Expansion Operations on Tensors

While differentiation with respect to a scalar preserves the order of an object, differentiation with respect to a vector will increase the order of an object. For example, the notation:

$$\left[\frac{\partial}{\partial x_k} y_{ij}(\underline{x})\right]$$

means the tensor whose elements are the derivatives of each element of matrix Y with respect to each element of vector $\underline{x}$. In this case, each element of Y produces an entire vector of derivatives.

2.2.6.7 Derivatives with Respect to a Vector

If $\underline{x}$ is a vector, derivatives taken with respect to it are all partials because there is no longer a single independent variable. Consider the quantity:

$$\frac{\partial Y(\underline{x})}{\partial \underline{x}} = \left[\frac{\partial}{\partial x_k} y_{ij}(\underline{x})\right]$$

The result is a tensor that can be visualized as a cube of numbers formed when the matrix Y is expanded out of the page. Each depth *slice* is associated with a different value of the index k and hence a different element of the vector $\underline{x}$.

Two special cases of this result are when the matrix Y is a scalar and a vector. The first case produces the derivative of a scalar with respect to a vector – the object known as the *gradient vector*:

$$\frac{\partial y(\underline{x})}{\partial \underline{x}} = \left[\frac{\partial}{\partial x_j} y(\underline{x})\right]$$

The second case produces the derivative of a vector with respect to a vector – the *Jacobian matrix*:

$$\frac{\partial \underline{y}(\underline{x})}{\partial \underline{x}} = \left[\frac{\partial}{\partial x_j} y_i(\underline{x})\right]$$

We will have occasional need of the second derivative of a scalar with respect to a vector – the *Hessian matrix*:

$$\frac{\partial^2 y(\underline{x})}{\partial x^2} = \left[\frac{\partial^2 y(\underline{x})}{\partial x_i x_j}\right]$$

Note the special Jacobian matrix when $\underline{y}(\underline{x}) = \underline{x}$:

$$\frac{\partial \underline{x}}{\partial \underline{x}} = \left[\frac{\partial x_i}{\partial x_j}\right] = I$$

Conventionally, both the gradient vector and the Jacobian matrix are laid out on the page as ***expansions along the column dimension*** of the original scalar or vector. This means they are automatically laid out so that they can be multiplied by a column vector.

2.2.6.8 Names and Notation for Derivatives

All combinations of derivatives of (scalars, vectors, matrices) with respect to (scalars, vectors, matrices) are defined and meaningful [4]. In the text, such derivatives will be denoted in one of two ways as outlined in Table 2.1.

Table 2.1 Notation for Derivatives

Symbol	Meaning	Symbol	Meaning
$\frac{\partial y}{\partial x}, y_x$	a partial derivative	$\frac{\partial Y}{\partial x}, Y_x$	a matrix partial derivative
$\frac{\partial \underline{y}}{\partial x}, \underline{y}_x$	a vector partial derivative	$\frac{\partial \underline{y}}{\partial \underline{x}}, \underline{y}_{\underline{x}}$	a Jacobian matrix
$\frac{\partial y}{\partial \underline{x}}, y_{\underline{x}}$	a gradient vector	$\frac{\partial Y}{\partial \underline{x}}, Y_{\underline{x}}$	an order 3 tensor
$\frac{\partial^2 y(x)}{\partial x^2}, y_{xx}$	a Hessian matrix		

The second (subscripted) form will not appear in a context where it can be confused with the notation defined earlier for vectors subscripted by frames of reference. In the very special case where y is a scalar that depends solely on the scalar x, the derivative is a total derivative. Everything else above is a partial derivative. We will tend to use partial derivative notation for everything and rely on context to notice when x is the only independent variable.

2.2.6.9 Derivative of a Matrix Product with Respect to a Vector

Suppose now that $\underline{x}$ is a vector. The product $A(\underline{x})B(\underline{x})$ is a matrix function, say called $C(\underline{x})$, of the vector $\underline{x}$. We know the derivative of this is a tensor but the formula for it requires some interpretation.

Each slice of the tensor can be computed from the result in Equation 2.15 repeated below:

$$\left[\frac{\partial}{\partial x}c_{ij}(x)\right] = \left[\left(\frac{\partial}{\partial x}a_{ik}(x)b_{kj}(x)\right)+\left(a_{ik}(x)\frac{\partial}{\partial x}b_{kj}(x)\right)\right]$$

To get the result for a vector, we simply add one more index to the derivative part:

$$\left[\frac{\partial}{\partial x_l}c_{ij}(\underline{x})\right] = \left[\left(\frac{\partial}{\partial x_l}a_{ik}(\underline{x})b_{kj}(\underline{x})\right)+\left(a_{ik}(\underline{x})\frac{\partial}{\partial x_l}b_{kj}(\underline{x})\right)\right] \tag{2.18}$$

This can be expressed succinctly as:

$$C(\underline{x}) = \frac{\partial\{A(\underline{x})B(\underline{x})\}}{\partial \underline{x}} = \frac{\partial}{\partial \underline{x}}A(\underline{x})B(\underline{x})+A(\underline{x})\frac{\partial}{\partial \underline{x}}B(\underline{x}) \tag{2.19}$$

Spotlight 2-2 Product Rule for Matrix Derivatives.

Derivatives of products of matrices work just like products of scalar-valued functions. Of course the special case when $\underline{x}$ is the scalar x is also covered by this formula.

The expression $\frac{\partial}{\partial x}A(\underline{x})B(\underline{x})$ is a tensor times a matrix, whereas $A(\underline{x})\frac{\partial}{\partial x}B(\underline{x})$ is a matrix times a tensor. Both produce another tensor by multiplying every slice of the tensor by the matrix and stacking the resulting matrices to reconstruct a tensor.

2.2.6.10 Tensor Layout

Tensor and implicit sum notation was introduced in part to hide some severe ambiguities when tensor operations are written out like matrices. Consider the case of differentiation of a matrix with respect to a vector:

$$\frac{\partial Y(\underline{x})}{\partial \underline{x}} = \left[\frac{\partial}{\partial x_k}y_{ij}(\underline{x})\right]$$

The derivative with respect to every element of the vector $\underline{x}$ is a matrix, so the result is a stack of matrices. If we write matrices in the plane of the paper, the only dimension left for stacking the component matrices is the depth dimension – out of the page. The main reason to evaluate such a derivative in the first place is that it will be used to multiply by a small change in the vector $\Delta\underline{x}$ to produce an induced small change in the matrix:

$$\Delta Y = \frac{\partial Y(x)}{\partial\underline{x}}\Delta\underline{x} \qquad (2.20)$$

In the abstract this may seem plausible but when it comes time to write a computer program, some loops over specific indices must be coded, and the above is not as straightforward as it may seem. Indeed, one does **not** multiply every slice of the tensor (a matrix) by the vector using conventional matrix algebra. Consider the implicit sum expression of this result:

$$\left[\Delta y_{ij}\right] = \left[\frac{\partial y_{ij}(x)}{\partial x_k}\Delta x_k\right] \neq \left[\frac{\partial y_{ij}(x)}{\partial x_k}\Delta x_j\right]$$

The small vector $\Delta\underline{x}$ must be multiplied in such a way as to collapse the depth dimension that was created by differentiation. Indeed, there is no guarantee (and certainly no need) for $\Delta\underline{x}$ to have a length equal to the number of columns of Y as would be necessary for a conventional matrix multiplication.

Hence the above really means:

$$\Delta Y = \frac{\partial Y(x)}{\partial\underline{x}}\Delta\underline{x} = \sum_k \frac{\partial Y(x)}{\partial x_k}\Delta x_k$$

The rules for matrix multiplication use the implicit rule that rows of the left operand are aligned with the columns of the right. Once we move to tensors, however, it often becomes necessary to be careful about which dimensions are associated for multiplication. In implicit sum notation, the common letters tell us which dimensions to combine. The above equation can be visualized like so:

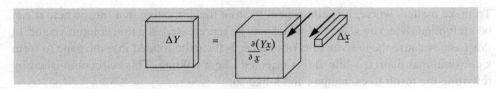

Spotlight 2-3 Tensor Times a Vector.

When a tensor is produced by differentiating a matrix, the "layout" needed to use the tensor with a small $\Delta\underline{x}$ is as shown.

2.2.6.11 Implicit Layout

When we write products involving tensors on paper, it is not necessarily the case that the column dimension collapses in a multiplication. Given that the collapsed dimension is often out of the page, there is no trick like using transpose operations that will make this expression behave according to our conventions for writing matrix products on paper. We will refer to the notation in Equation 2.19 as *implicit layout* and use context to interpret the expression.

When a product is differentiated, the situation is even more complicated. Consider:

$$\underline{y}(\underline{x}) = A(\underline{x})\underline{x}$$

The derivative has two terms, each of which is a tensor. The total differential is:

$$\Delta\underline{y} = \left\{\frac{\partial A(\underline{x})}{\partial \underline{x}}\underline{x} + A(\underline{x})\frac{\partial \underline{x}}{\partial \underline{x}}\right\}\Delta\underline{x}$$

In implicit product notation:

$$\Delta y_i = \left\{\frac{\partial a_{ij}(\underline{x})}{\partial x_k}x_j + a_{ij}(\underline{x})\frac{\partial x_j}{\partial x_k}\right\}\Delta x_k = \{\alpha_{ik}(\underline{x}) + \beta_{ik}(\underline{x})\}\Delta x_k$$

In this case, the vector $\underline{x}$ does collapse the column dimension of the tensor $\partial A(\underline{x})/\partial \underline{x}$ and the columns of the matrix $A(\underline{x})$ collapse with the rows of $\partial\underline{x}/\partial\underline{x}$. The derivative thus formed is a "thick" column, whose depth dimension is collapsed by $\Delta\underline{x}$ to produce the final result – a column vector $\Delta\underline{y}$.

This can be visualized as seen in Figure 2.9.

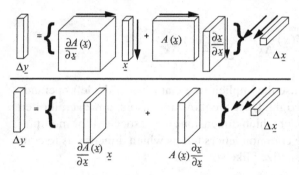

Figure 2.9 A Derivative Tensor. Two intermediate results are "thick" columns that collapse to column vectors when multiplied by a small vector $\Delta\underline{x}$.

To make matters worse, it is convenient to store the derivative in a form where it can be multiplied (later) by some $\Delta\underline{x}$ which can be represented as a true column vector. In this case, because the derivative is of order < 3, it can be rotated into the page to form a conventional matrix, while $\Delta\underline{x}$ is oriented like a column. This is accomplished by rewriting the result to exchange j and k like so:

$$\Delta y_i = \left\{\frac{\partial a_{ik}(\underline{x})}{\partial x_j}x_k + a_{ik}(\underline{x})\frac{\partial x_k}{\partial x_j}\right\}\Delta x_j = \{a_{ij}^1(\underline{x}) + a_{ij}^2(\underline{x})\}\Delta x_j$$

In summary, we will rely on implicit layout whenever tensors are produced by differentiation and the reader will be required to be mindful to produce a consistent explicit layout in computer memory if the equation is ever implemented in software.

2.2.6.12 Useful Matrix-Vector Derivatives

The above results make it possible to compute derivatives of extreme complexity in a computer program without ever having to write an explicit formula. However, for some derivations, it is useful to have a few formulas at hand. The following results are laid out in order to be able to ***multiply the derivative by a column vector*** regardless of how $\underline{x}$ may have appeared in the original expression. By Equation 2.19:

$$\frac{\partial\{A\underline{x}\}}{\partial\underline{x}} = A\frac{\partial}{\partial\underline{x}}(\{\underline{x}\}) = AI = A \tag{2.21}$$

The following are all special cases of this result:

$$\frac{\partial\{\underline{a}^T\underline{x}\}}{\partial\underline{x}} = \underline{a}^T \quad \frac{\partial\{\underline{x}^T\}}{\partial\underline{x}} = \frac{\partial\{\underline{x}^T I\}}{\partial\underline{x}} = I$$

$$\frac{\partial\{\underline{x}^T A\}}{\partial\underline{x}} = A^T \tag{2.22}$$

$$\frac{\partial\{\underline{x}^T\underline{a}\}}{\partial\underline{x}} = \underline{a}^T \quad \frac{\partial\{\underline{x}\}}{\partial\underline{x}} = \frac{\partial\{I\underline{x}\}}{\partial\underline{x}} = I$$

Based on Equation 2.18 when applied to a product of three matrices, we can easily show that:

$$\frac{\partial\{\underline{x}^T A\underline{x}\}}{\partial\underline{x}} = \underline{x}^T A^T + \underline{x}^T A \tag{2.23}$$

When A is symmetric:

$$\frac{\partial\{\underline{x}^T A\underline{x}\}}{\partial\underline{x}} = 2\underline{x}^T A$$

The following is a special case of this result:

$$\frac{\partial\{\underline{x}^T\underline{x}\}}{\partial\underline{x}} = 2\underline{x}^T \tag{2.24}$$

Two useful tricks are worth noting. First, any scalar must equal its transpose so:

$$\underline{y}^T A\underline{x} = \underline{x}^T A\underline{y}$$

Second, it helps to consolidate components that do not depend on the variable. Thus $\underline{y}^T ABCDEF\underline{x}$ is identical in form to $\underline{y}^T A\underline{x}$ above. Also, its derivative with respect to $\underline{x}$ is trivial once you realize that $\underline{y}^T ABCDEF$ is a constant column vector denoted $\underline{a}^T$ in Equation 2.22.

2.2.7 Leibnitz' Rule

We will have a very regular need of a result from calculus for which the reader may have found little use before now. Given any definite integral, Leibnitz' rule states that the derivative of the integral equals the integral of the derivative:

$$\frac{\partial}{\partial \underline{p}}\int_a^b \underline{f}(\underline{x}, \underline{p})dt = \int_a^b \frac{\partial}{\partial \underline{p}}\underline{f}(\underline{x}, \underline{p})dt$$

Spotlight 2-4 Leibniz' Rule.

This rule for differentiating integrals will be used very frequently.

If the variable $\underline{x} = \underline{x}(\underline{p})$ also depends on $\underline{p}$, then we must be careful to take this into account with:

$$\frac{\partial}{\underline{p}}\underline{f}(x, \underline{p}) = \underline{f}_{\underline{x}} \cdot \frac{\partial x}{\partial \underline{p}} + \underline{f}$$

There is a sticky notation issue here. We will have to use $\frac{\partial}{\partial \underline{p}}\underline{f}(\underline{x}, \underline{p})$ to mean the "total" derivative with respect to $\underline{p}$ and $\underline{f}_{\underline{p}}$ to mean the derivative while holding $\underline{x}$ constant.

If either of the limits a or b depend on $\underline{p}$, then this will generate more terms in the derivative but we will not need this case.

2.2.8 References and Further Reading

Strang's book is hands down the most readable book on linear algebra. Poole's book stresses geometric analogy before making the jump to n dimensions. Magnus covers matrix calculus.

[3]   Gilbert Strang, *Introduction to Linear Algebra,* Wellesley-Cambridge, 2009.

[4]   Jan Magnus and Heinz Neudecker, *Matrix Differential Calculus with Applications in Statistics and Econometrics,* 2nd ed., Wiley, 1999.

[5]   David Poole, *Linear Algebra: A Modern Introduction,* 2nd ed., Brooks/Cole, 2006.

2.2.9 Exercises

2.2.9.1 Matrix Exponential

Show that

$$\exp\left\{\begin{bmatrix} 6 & 0 \\ 0 & -2 \end{bmatrix}\right\} = \begin{bmatrix} e^6 & 0 \\ 0 & e^{-2} \end{bmatrix}$$

2.2.9.2 Jacobian Determinant

You probably learned in multivariable calculus that the ratio of volumes in a 2D linear mapping is given by the Jacobian determinant. Consider the matrix:

$$A = \begin{bmatrix} a & b \\ c & d \end{bmatrix}$$

and the vectors $d\underline{x} = \begin{bmatrix} dx & 0 \end{bmatrix}^T$ and $d\underline{y} = \begin{bmatrix} 0 & dy \end{bmatrix}^T$. Using the result for the area of a parallelogram defined by two vectors in Figure 2.6, show that the area formed by the vectors $d\underline{u} = Ad\underline{x}$ and $d\underline{v} = Ad\underline{y}$ is $det(A)dxdy$.

2.2.9.3 Fundamental Theorem and Projections

A matrix P is called a *projection matrix* if it is symmetric and $P^2 = P$ which is called the property of *idempotence*.

(i) What happens if you compute $\underline{p}_1 = P\underline{x}$ and then $\underline{p}_2 = P\underline{p}_1$?

An important projection matrix can be derived from a general $n \times m$ matrix A (where $m < n$) as follows: $P_A = A(A^T A)^{-1} A^T$.

(ii) Show that P_A satisfies both requirements of a projection matrix.

(iii) Note that $\underline{p}_1 = P_A\underline{x}$ must reside in the column space of A. The orthogonal complement Q_A of P_A is defined as $Q_A = I - P_A$. Note that $Q_A P_A = P_A Q_A = 0$. In what subspace does $\underline{q}_1 = Q_A\underline{x}$ reside?

2.2.9.4 Derivative of the Inverse

Suppose a square matrix $A(t)$ depends on a scalar, say t. Differentiate $A^{-1}A$ and find an expression for $\dot{A}^{-1}$.

2.3 Fundamentals of Rigid Transforms

2.3.1 Definitions

2.3.1.1 Transformations

Consider linear relationships between points in 2D. An *affine transformation* [10] is the most general linear transformation possible. In 2D it looks like:

$$\begin{bmatrix} x_2 \\ y_2 \end{bmatrix} = \begin{bmatrix} r_{11} & r_{12} \\ r_{21} & r_{22} \end{bmatrix} \begin{bmatrix} x_1 \\ y_1 \end{bmatrix} + \begin{bmatrix} t_1 \\ t_2 \end{bmatrix} \qquad (2.25)$$

where the r's and t's are constants.

Such a transformation includes all of the following effects: translation, rotation, scale, reflections, and shear. Such a transformation preserves lines, meaning if three points were originally on a line, they will remain on a line after transformation. It is therefore also known as a *collineatory transformation* or a *collinearity*. It may not preserve the distance between two points. Hence, it also may not preserve area or angles between lines. A *homogeneous transformation* is an affine transformation for which: $t_1 = t_2 = 0$:

$$\begin{bmatrix} x_2 \\ y_2 \end{bmatrix} = \begin{bmatrix} r_{11} & r_{12} \\ r_{21} & r_{22} \end{bmatrix} \begin{bmatrix} x_1 \\ y_1 \end{bmatrix} \qquad (2.26)$$

Such a transformation does not include translation but it does include all the others mentioned above. More generally, while the equation $Ax = b$ is said to be linear, the equation $Ax = 0$ is called homogeneous. Another name for these transforms is "projective" transforms and the vectors involved are said to be projective coordinates. Due to their ability to represent the image formation process, they are used in computer vision as extensively as they are in robotics.

An *orthogonal transformation* transforms from one set of rectangular coordinates to another. Its columns are mutually orthogonal and of unit length, so it satisfies the following three constraints.

$$r_{11}r_{12} + r_{21}r_{22} = 0 \qquad r_{11}r_{11} + r_{21}r_{21} = 1 \qquad r_{12}r_{12} + r_{22}r_{22} = 1 \qquad (2.27)$$

Such a transformation preserves the distance between two points, so it is **rigid**. It therefore also preserves lengths, areas, and angles. It does not scale, reflect, or shear. Rotation is the only operation left in the list above.

2.3.2 Why Homogeneous Transforms

The product of a matrix and a vector is another vector; a matrix can be viewed as a mapping from vectors onto other vectors. One view of a matrix is that of an *operator* – a process that maps points onto other points. *Homogeneous or projective* coordinates are those whose interpretation does not change if all of the coordinates are multiplied by the same nonzero number. They are said to be "unique up to a scale factor." 3D Homogeneous coordinates are a method of representing 3D entities by the projections of 4D entities onto a 3D subspace. Following points establish why you would want to use such an awkward construct.

2.3.2.1 The Problem with Translation

Suppose that we multiply the position r of a 3D point by the most general 3X3 matrix and denote the result by r':

$$r' = \begin{bmatrix} x' \\ y' \\ z' \end{bmatrix} = Tr = \begin{bmatrix} t_{xx} & t_{xy} & t_{xz} \\ t_{yx} & t_{yy} & t_{yz} \\ t_{zx} & t_{zy} & t_{zz} \end{bmatrix} \begin{bmatrix} x \\ y \\ z \end{bmatrix} = \begin{bmatrix} t_{xx}x + t_{xy}y + t_{xz}z \\ t_{yx}x + t_{yy}y + t_{yz}z \\ t_{zx}x + t_{zy}y + t_{zz}z \end{bmatrix} \qquad (2.28)$$

This most general transform can represent operators like scale, reflection, rotation, shear, projection. Why? because all of these can be expressed as **constant linear combinations** of the coordinates of the input vector. However, this 3X3 matrix cannot represent a simple addition of a constant vector to another vector like so:

$$r' = r + \Delta r = \begin{bmatrix} x_1 & y_1 & z_1 \end{bmatrix}^T + \begin{bmatrix} \Delta x & \Delta y & \Delta z \end{bmatrix}^T$$

The point r' cannot be represented as a linear combination of the elements of r – because the displacement Δr is independent of r.

2.3.2.2 Introducing Homogeneous Coordinates

The situation can be fixed with a standard trick. In *homogeneous coordinates*, an extra element, w, can be added to each point to represent a kind of *scale factor*:

$$\tilde{r} = \begin{bmatrix} x & y & z & w \end{bmatrix}^T$$

and it is conventional to consider that this 4-vector is "projected" into 3D by dividing by the scale factor:

$$r = \begin{bmatrix} \dfrac{x}{w} & \dfrac{y}{w} & \dfrac{z}{w} \end{bmatrix}^T$$

Points are canonically represented with a scale factor of 1. Thus:

$$\tilde{r} = \begin{bmatrix} \dfrac{x}{w} & \dfrac{y}{w} & \dfrac{z}{w} & 1 \end{bmatrix}^T$$

is a point in homogeneous coordinates. Notationally, $\tilde{r}$ is the (4D) homogeneous point corresponding to its 3D projection r. From now on, we will drop the '~' and use context to distinguish these from each other.

It is also possible to represent a *pure direction* in terms of a point at infinity by using a scale factor of 0. Thus:

$$\tilde{d} = \begin{bmatrix} x & y & z & 0 \end{bmatrix}^T$$

is a direction in homogeneous coordinates. We will see that such objects are free vectors, sometimes called simply "vectors" in the context of homogeneous coordinates.

2.3.2.3 Translation with Homogeneous Transforms

A (3D) matrix in *homogeneous coordinates* is a 4×4 matrix. Using homogeneous coordinates, it is now possible to represent the addition of two position vectors as a matrix operation, thus:

$$r' = r + \Delta r = \begin{bmatrix} x \\ y \\ z \\ 1 \end{bmatrix} + \begin{bmatrix} \Delta x \\ \Delta y \\ \Delta z \\ 1 \end{bmatrix} = \begin{bmatrix} 1 & 0 & 0 & \Delta x \\ 0 & 1 & 0 & \Delta y \\ 0 & 0 & 1 & \Delta z \\ 0 & 0 & 0 & 1 \end{bmatrix} \begin{bmatrix} x \\ y \\ z \\ 1 \end{bmatrix} = Trans(\Delta r)r$$

where $Trans(\Delta r)$ is the homogeneous transform that is equivalent to a translation operator for the translation vector Δr. Homogeneous transforms can also represent somewhat **nonlinear** operations such as perspective projection. They do this by hiding the nonlinearity in the normalization by the scale factor.

2.3.3 Semantics and Interpretations

The whole trick of successful manipulation of homogeneous coordinates is to master the semantics associated with their many interpretations. This section reviews the many ways in which we can conceptualize both what homogeneous transformations are and what they do.

2.3.3.1 Trig Functions

We will henceforth often use a form of shorthand for trig functions in order to render results more readable:

$$s_1 = \sin(\psi_1) \qquad c_{123} = \cos(\psi_1 + \psi_2 + \psi_3)$$

2.3.3.2 Homogeneous Transforms as Operators

Suppose it is necessary to move a point in some manner to generate a new point and express the result in the *same* coordinate system as the original point. The $Trans(\Delta r)$ operator just discussed does this.

The basic *rigid operators* are translation along and rotation about any of the three axes. The four elementary operators in Spotlight 2-5 are sufficient for almost any real problem. The first three rows and columns of each are mutually orthogonal. Operators are identified (here) by an ***upper case first letter***.

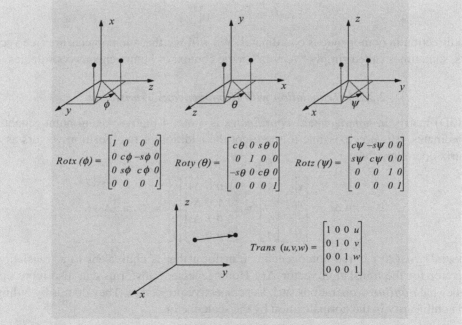

$$Rotx\,(\phi) = \begin{bmatrix} 1 & 0 & 0 & 0 \\ 0 & c\phi & -s\phi & 0 \\ 0 & s\phi & c\phi & 0 \\ 0 & 0 & 0 & 1 \end{bmatrix} \quad Roty\,(\theta) = \begin{bmatrix} c\theta & 0 & s\theta & 0 \\ 0 & 1 & 0 & 0 \\ -s\theta & 0 & c\theta & 0 \\ 0 & 0 & 0 & 1 \end{bmatrix} \quad Rotz\,(\psi) = \begin{bmatrix} c\psi & -s\psi & 0 & 0 \\ s\psi & c\psi & 0 & 0 \\ 0 & 0 & 1 & 0 \\ 0 & 0 & 0 & 1 \end{bmatrix}$$

$$Trans\,(u,v,w) = \begin{bmatrix} 1 & 0 & 0 & u \\ 0 & 1 & 0 & v \\ 0 & 0 & 1 & w \\ 0 & 0 & 0 & 1 \end{bmatrix}$$

Spotlight 2-5 Fundamental Rigid Operators.

If a homogeneous position vector is multiplied by one of these matrices, the result is a new position vector that has been rotated or translated.

2.3.3.3 Example: Operating on a Point

The homogeneous coordinates of the position of a point o at the origin are clearly:

$$o = \begin{bmatrix} 0 & 0 & 0 & 1 \end{bmatrix}^T$$

According to our conventions, the position of point o is r_o but we will use shorthand for this and the unit vectors $i, j,$ and k on occasion. o denotes the position of the origin, and $i, j,$ and k denote the directions of the associated axes.

Figure 2.10 indicates the result of translating a point at the origin along the y axis by 'v' units and then rotating the resulting point by 90° around the x axis.

The order is important because matrix multiplication is not commutative. The grouping is not important because matrix multiplication is associative, so the matrices can be multiplied together before being applied, as a unit, to the point.

Also notice that the initial point, and final result are expressed in terms of the axes of the original coordinate system. Operators have *fixed axis compounding semantics*. Finally, the input was a vector that conceptually started and ended at the origin so its length was zero. It was transformed into a vector that started at the same place but ended elsewhere. It should be clear that the unit scale factor caused this to happen. Hence, *a unit scale factor signifies a bound vector*.

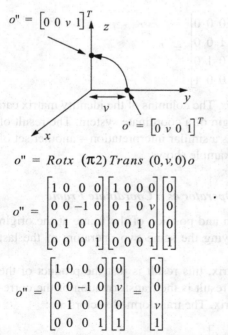

$o'' = \begin{bmatrix} 0 & 0 & v & 1 \end{bmatrix}^T$

$o' = \begin{bmatrix} 0 & v & 0 & 1 \end{bmatrix}^T$

$$o'' = Rotx\ (\pi 2)\ Trans\ (0,v,0)o$$

$$o'' = \begin{bmatrix} 1 & 0 & 0 & 0 \\ 0 & 0 & -1 & 0 \\ 0 & 1 & 0 & 0 \\ 0 & 0 & 0 & 1 \end{bmatrix} \begin{bmatrix} 1 & 0 & 0 & 0 \\ 0 & 1 & 0 & v \\ 0 & 0 & 1 & 0 \\ 0 & 0 & 0 & 1 \end{bmatrix} \begin{bmatrix} 0 \\ 0 \\ 0 \\ 1 \end{bmatrix}$$

$$o'' = \begin{bmatrix} 1 & 0 & 0 & 0 \\ 0 & 0 & -1 & 0 \\ 0 & 1 & 0 & 0 \\ 0 & 0 & 0 & 1 \end{bmatrix} \begin{bmatrix} 0 \\ v \\ 0 \\ 1 \end{bmatrix} = \begin{bmatrix} 0 \\ 0 \\ v \\ 1 \end{bmatrix}$$

$j' = \begin{bmatrix} 0 & 0 & 1 & 0 \end{bmatrix}^T$

$j = \begin{bmatrix} 0 & 1 & 0 & 0 \end{bmatrix}^T$

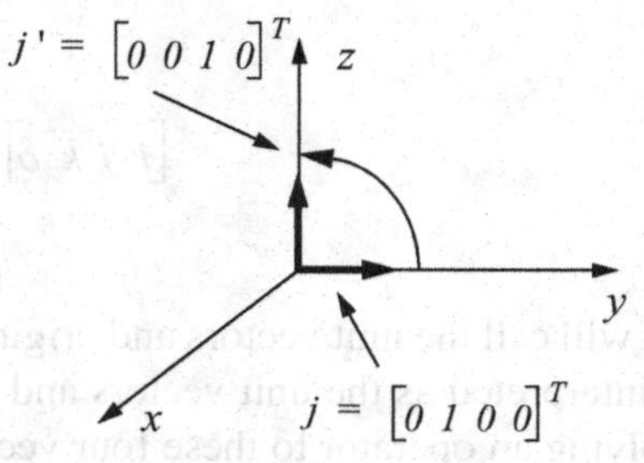

$$j' = Rotx\ (\pi 2)\ Trans\ (0,v,0)j$$

$$j' = \begin{bmatrix} 1 & 0 & 0 & 0 \\ 0 & 0 & -1 & 0 \\ 0 & 1 & 0 & 0 \\ 0 & 0 & 0 & 1 \end{bmatrix} \begin{bmatrix} 1 & 0 & 0 & 0 \\ 0 & 1 & 0 & v \\ 0 & 0 & 1 & 0 \\ 0 & 0 & 0 & 1 \end{bmatrix} \begin{bmatrix} 0 \\ 1 \\ 0 \\ 0 \end{bmatrix}$$

$$j' = \begin{bmatrix} 1 & 0 & 0 & 0 \\ 0 & 0 & -1 & 0 \\ 0 & 1 & 0 & 0 \\ 0 & 0 & 0 & 1 \end{bmatrix} \begin{bmatrix} 0 \\ 1 \\ 0 \\ 0 \end{bmatrix} = \begin{bmatrix} 0 \\ 0 \\ 1 \\ 0 \end{bmatrix}$$

Figure 2.10 Operating on a Point. A point at the origin is translated along the y axis by 'v' units and then rotated the resulting point by 90° around the x axis.

Figure 2.11 Operating on a Direction. The y axis unit vector is translated along the y axis by 'v' units and then rotated by 90° around the x axis.

2.3.3.4 Example: Operating on a Direction

The homogeneous coordinates of the y axis unit vector j are clearly $j = \begin{bmatrix} 0 & 1 & 0 & 0 \end{bmatrix}^T$.
Figure 2.11 indicates the result of translating the y axis unit vector along the y axis by
'v' units and then rotating the resulting point by $90°$ around the x axis. Note that the
translation part of the compound operation has no effect. The result is the z axis unit
vector, so rotation works just as before, so *having a zero scale factor disables translation* and allows us to represent a pure direction. Equivalently, *a zero scale factor
signifies a free vector*.

2.3.3.5 Homogeneous Transforms as Coordinate Frames

The unit vectors of a cartesian coordinate system can be considered to be directions.
The x, y, and z unit vectors can be written as:

$$i = \begin{bmatrix} 1 & 0 & 0 \end{bmatrix}^T$$
$$j = \begin{bmatrix} 0 & 1 & 0 \end{bmatrix}^T$$
$$k = \begin{bmatrix} 0 & 0 & 1 \end{bmatrix}^T$$

These three columns can be grouped together with the homogeneous coordinates of
the origin to form an identity matrix:

$$\begin{bmatrix} i & j & k & o \end{bmatrix} = \begin{bmatrix} 1 & 0 & 0 & 0 \\ 0 & 1 & 0 & 0 \\ 0 & 0 & 1 & 0 \\ 0 & 0 & 0 & 1 \end{bmatrix} = I$$

We will call the unit vectors and origin a *basis*. The columns of the identity matrix can
be interpreted as the unit vectors and the origin of a coordinate system. The result of
applying an operator to these four vectors has a similar interpretation – another set of
unit vectors at a new position – as the next example shows.

2.3.3.6 Example: Interpreting an Operator as a Coordinate Frame

The four vectors representing the orientation and position of the frame at the origin
can be transformed simultaneously by applying the same two operators of the last
example to the identity matrix (Figure 2.12).

Because we started with the identity matrix, this result is just the product of the
original two operators. Each column of this result is the transformation of the corresponding column in the original identity matrix. The transformed vectors are:

$$i' = \begin{bmatrix} 1 & 0 & 0 & 0 \end{bmatrix}^T$$
$$j' = \begin{bmatrix} 0 & 0 & 1 & 0 \end{bmatrix}^T$$
$$k' = \begin{bmatrix} 0 & -1 & 0 & 0 \end{bmatrix}^T$$
$$o' = \begin{bmatrix} 0 & 0 & v & 1 \end{bmatrix}^T$$

That is, because columns of an input matrix are ***treated independently in multiplication***, any number of column vectors can be placed side by side and operated upon as a unit.

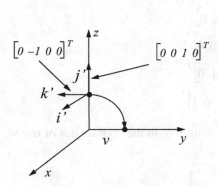

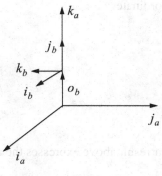

$$I_b^a = Rot\ x\ (\pi 2)\ Trans\ (0,v,0)\ I_a^a$$

$$I' = Rot\ x(\pi 2)\ Trans\ (0,v,0\ I)$$

$$I_b^a = \begin{bmatrix} 1 & 0 & 0 & 0 \\ 0 & 0 & -1 & 0 \\ 0 & 1 & 0 & v \\ 0 & 0 & 0 & 1 \end{bmatrix}$$

$$I' = \begin{bmatrix} 1 & 0 & 0 & 0 \\ 0 & 0 & -1 & 0 \\ 0 & 1 & 0 & 0 \\ 0 & 0 & 0 & 1 \end{bmatrix} \begin{bmatrix} 1 & 0 & 0 & 0 \\ 0 & 1 & 0 & v \\ 0 & 0 & 1 & 0 \\ 0 & 0 & 0 & 1 \end{bmatrix} \begin{bmatrix} 1 & 0 & 0 & 0 \\ 0 & 1 & 0 & 0 \\ 0 & 0 & 1 & 0 \\ 0 & 0 & 0 & 1 \end{bmatrix} = \begin{bmatrix} 1 & 0 & 0 & 0 \\ 0 & 0 & -1 & 0 \\ 0 & 1 & 0 & v \\ 0 & 0 & 0 & 1 \end{bmatrix}$$

Figure 2.12 Operating on a Frame. Each resulting column of this result is the transformation of the corresponding column in the original identity matrix.

Figure 2.13 Conversion of Basis. If a set of 3 orthogonal unit vectors emanating from an origin is called a basis, then a homogeneous transform can be viewed as something which moves a basis rigidly.

It can be shown that the fundamental operators preserve the orthonormality of the first three columns of an input frame. So, the column vectors of any compound fundamental operator are just the homogeneous coordinates of the transformed unit vectors and the origin. That is, every orthonormal matrix can be viewed as the relationship expressing ***how one set of axes is located with respect to another set***. We can use a homogeneous transform to represent the motions of embedded coordinate frames mentioned earlier in the chapter.

We often think of the spatial relationship between two frames in terms of the *aligning operations* – the operations that are applied to the first to move it into coincidence with the second. If you can imagine how to move one frame into coincidence with another, you can write the homogeneous transform corresponding to an arbitrary number of fundamental operations.

2.3.3.7 *Conversion of Basis*

Consider again the two sets of axes above. For important uses later, let us call the original frame 'a' and the transformed one 'b' (Figure 2.13).

We will begin using superscripts and subscripts in the manner outlined earlier in the chapter. Thus o_b^a represents the "origin" property of object b relative to object a. That is, the vector from frame a to frame b – expressed in the coordinates of frame a. By contrast, unit vectors are unit length by definition (and free vectors) so they do not require a right superscript to be meaningful. The quantity i_a^x is equivalent to i_a for any frame x.

Any point of origin is straightforward when "referred to" (expressed in) its own coordinates:

$$i_a^a = i_b^b = \begin{bmatrix} 1 & 0 & 0 & 0 \end{bmatrix}^T$$
$$j_a^a = j_b^b = \begin{bmatrix} 0 & 1 & 0 & 0 \end{bmatrix}^T$$
$$k_a^a = k_b^b = \begin{bmatrix} 0 & 0 & 1 & 0 \end{bmatrix}^T$$
$$^a o_a^a = {}^b o_b^b = \begin{bmatrix} 0 & 0 & 0 & 1 \end{bmatrix}^T$$

Our result above expresses the axes and origin of frame 'b' in the coordinates of frame 'a'.

$$I_b^a = \begin{bmatrix} ^a i_b & ^a j_b & ^a k_b & ^a o_b^a \end{bmatrix}$$

That is, I_b^a converts (equivalently, it expresses) the coordinates of frame 'b's basis to (in) that of frame 'a' and that converted basis is exactly equal to its own columns.

$$I_b^a = \begin{bmatrix} ^a i_b & ^a j_b & ^a k_b & o_b^a \end{bmatrix} I_b^b \qquad I_b^a = \begin{bmatrix} ^a i_b & ^a j_b & ^a k_b & ^a o_b^a \end{bmatrix}$$

2.3.3.8 Homogeneous Transforms as Coordinate and Reference Frame Transforms

So far homogeneous transforms (HTs) have several complementary interpretations:

- move points (operator interpretation)
- re-orient directions (operator interpretation)
- move and orient frames (operator interpretation)
- represent the relationship between coordinate frames (coordinate frame interpretation)
- convert the coordinates of a basis

There is yet another one: *a device to transform coordinates*, and this will be our most common use for them. If HTs can move frames, we can ask about the relationship between the coordinates of any point in each of the two frames involved (original and moved). As before, let the original frame be called 'a' and the transformed one be called 'b'.

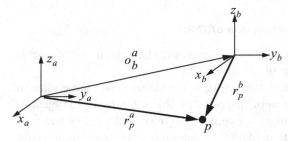

Figure 2.14 Conversion of Coordinates. The black dot represents a point in space. Its coordinates in frame a and frame b are different. A homogeneous transform can be used to convert one set of coordinates to another.

Let the position r_p^b of a general point p be located relative to the origin of frame 'b'. This vector can be written as a weighted sum of the unit vectors and the origin of the 'b' frame thus:

$$r_p^b = x_p^b(^bi_b) + y_p^b(^bj_b) + z_p^b(^bk_b) + {}^bo_b \qquad (2.29)$$

This formula holds regardless of the coordinates in which it is expressed. When the unit vectors of and origin of frame 'b' are also expressed in frame 'b's coordinates, they are trivial:

$$i_b = \begin{bmatrix} 1 & 0 & 0 & 0 \end{bmatrix} \quad etc. \qquad o_b = \begin{bmatrix} 0 & 0 & 0 & 1 \end{bmatrix}$$

The coordinates of p in this frame are written more concisely as:

$$r_p^b = \begin{bmatrix} x^b & y^b & z^b & 1 \end{bmatrix}$$

Sometimes, when there are many unit vectors available, its useful to write the unit vectors explicitly. Consider the problem of how to represent the vector from the origin of frame a to the same point (see Figure 2.14), and express the result in terms of frame 'a's unit vectors and origin. We need only transform the unit vectors of frame 'b' into frame 'a's coordinates and add the vector from the origin of a to that of b:

$$r_p^a = x_p^b(^ai_b) + y_p^b(^aj_b) + z_p^b(^ak_b) + o_b^a$$

We have transformed only the coordinates within which the unit vectors are expressed. They are the same unit vectors, so the scalar weights (x_p^b, y_p^b, z_p^b) are unchanged. However, refer to Figure 2.14 for the meaning of the transformation of the bound vector o_b^a. Because we are adding this vector to r_p^b, the result is now expressed relative to the origin of a. All of the four vectors added above were expressed in the coordinates of a, so the result is now expressed in the coordinates of a. We will therefore denote the result as r_p^a.

Based on our results in the conversion of a basis section above, this can be written as:

$$r_p^a = x_p^b(I_b^a i_b) + y_p^b(I_b^a j_b) + z_p^b(I_b^a k_b) + I_b^a o_b$$

Or more compactly as:

$$r_p^a = I_b^a[x_p^b(^bi_b) + y_p^b(^bj_b) + z_p^b(^bk_b) + {}^bo_b]$$

Substituting from Equation 2.29, we now have proven the capacity of the change of basis matrix to transform the coordinates of any point:

$$r_p^a = I_b^a\, r_p^b$$

2.3.3.9 Converting Coordinate Frame

From now on, we will use the notation T_a^b (T for transform) to denote the change of basis matrix used above. Suppose the 4×4 matrix T_a^b denotes the matrix which transforms a vector from its expression relative to frame 'a' in frame a coordinates to its expression relative to frame 'b' in frame b coordinates. The notation is such that the superscripts and subscripts provide a hint of the result by imagining that the b's cancel:

$$r^a = I^a_b \, r^b$$

Note that multiplying by T^b_a changes the right superscript (and the implied left superscript) of the entity transformed.

2.3.3.10 Converting Coordinates Only

Strictly speaking, the above operation has taken the bound vector r^a_p and transformed it into another bound vector r^b_p. The vectors are "bound" because their definitions depend on the choice of origin, indicated by a right superscript. Mechanically, this occurred because the origin vector, with a unit scale factor was included in the definition in Equation 2.29.

We will occasionally use the notation R^b_a when the transform T^b_a happens to be a rotation matrix. Thus, R^b_a is the same as T^b_a with the last column set to $o = \begin{bmatrix} 0 & 0 & 0 & 1 \end{bmatrix}^T$.

$$R^a_b = \begin{bmatrix} {}^a i_b & {}^a j_b & {}^a k_b & o \end{bmatrix}$$

This matrix performs the rotation part of moving frame b into coincidence with frame a but not the translation part. It can be visualized as a set of axes positioned at the origin of frame b but oriented like frame a. Equivalently, we can imagine that a vector expressed relative to the origin of frame a was unbound and moved to the origin of frame b. The above derivation when modified for a free vector proceeds like so:

$$r^b_p = x^b_p({}^b i_b) + y^b_p({}^b j_b) + z^b_p({}^b k_b) + \underline{0}$$
$$r^a_p = x^b_p({}^a i_b) + y^b_p({}^a j_b) + z^b_p({}^a k_b)$$
$$r^a_p = x^b_p(I^a_b i_b) + y^b_p(I^a_b j_b) + z^b_p(I^a_b k_b)$$
$${}^a r^b_p = R^a_b[x^b_p({}^b i_b) + y^b_p({}^b j_b) + z^b_p({}^b k_b)]$$
$${}^a r^b_p = R^a_b[x^b_p({}^b i_b) + y^b_p({}^b j_b) + z^b_p({}^b k_b) + {}^b o_b]$$
$${}^a r^b_p = R^a_b \, r^b_p$$

The second last step made use of the fact that:

$$R^a_b({}^b o_b) = \begin{bmatrix} 0 & 0 & 0 & 1 \end{bmatrix}^T$$

The matrix R^a_b therefore treats the vector r^p_b like a free vector and converts its coordinates without converting its origin to produce the quantity that we denote by ${}^a r^b_p$.

2.3.3.11 Converting Coordinate Frame of a Displacement

We can represent a displacement (a free vector) in homogeneous coordinates by the difference of two position vectors (bound vectors) expressed relative to the same reference frame. For example:

$$
{}^a r_p^q = r_p^a - r_q^a = \begin{bmatrix} x_p^a \\ y_p^a \\ z_p^a \\ 1 \end{bmatrix} - \begin{bmatrix} x_q^a \\ y_q^a \\ z_q^a \\ 1 \end{bmatrix} = \begin{bmatrix} x_p^a - x_q^a \\ y_p^a - y_q^a \\ z_p^a - z_q^a \\ 0 \end{bmatrix}
$$

It is easy to see that operating on this object with a general homogeneous transform representing translation and rotation will only rotate the object:

$$
T_a^b {}^a r_p^q = T_a^b (r_p^a - r_q^a) = T_a^b r_p^a - T_a^b r_q^a = r_p^b - r_q^b = {}^b r_p^q
$$

So a free vector can be expressed as the **difference between two bound vectors**. In summary, the capacity to change datum can be turned off by either zeroing the origin column in the transform (to produce a rotation matrix) or by zeroing the scale factor in the vector.

2.3.3.12 Operator / Transform Duality

This is the **most important thing** to remember about homogeneous transforms.

Box 2.2: Operator / Transform Duality

The homogeneous transform T_b^a that moves frame 'a' into coincidence with frame 'b' (operator) also converts the coordinates (transform) of points **in the opposite direction** – from frame 'b' to frame 'a':

$$
r_p^a = T_b^a \, r_p^b
$$

The reason for the opposite sense in the interpretation is that moving a point "forward" in a coordinate system is completely equivalent to moving the coordinate system "backward." The reader is strongly encouraged to work through the provided exercises on this topic. Most of kinematics becomes accessible thereafter.

2.3.3.13 Fundamental Transforms

It is easy to show that the inverse of a rotation matrix is equal to its transpose. This is called the property of *orthonormality*. This fact leads to a second set of four matrices, the fundamental transforms, which are the inverses of the operators and which therefore convert coordinates from a to b. These are given in Spotlight 2-6.

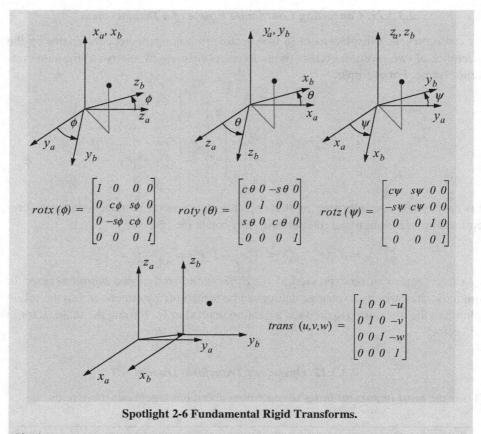

Spotlight 2-6 Fundamental Rigid Transforms.

If a homogeneous vector that is represented in coordinate system a is multiplied by one of these matrices, the result is its representation in coordinate system b.

2.3.3.14 Example: Transforming the Coordinates of a Point

The homogeneous coordinates of the origin o are:

$$o = \begin{bmatrix} 0 & 0 & 0 & 1 \end{bmatrix}^T$$

Figure 2.15 indicates the result of transforming the origin of frame b into the coordinates of frame a where the two frames are related by the same sequence of operators used earlier. Frame b is moved into coincidence with frame a by first rotating frame b by $-90°$ around its x axis to produce the intermediate frame in the figure, and then translating by $-v$ along the z axis *of the intermediate frame*.

Notice that, for transforms, each new transform is interpreted as if it were applied to the last frame in the sequence of frames that ultimately bring the first into coincidence with the last. Transforms have ***moving axis compounding semantics***.

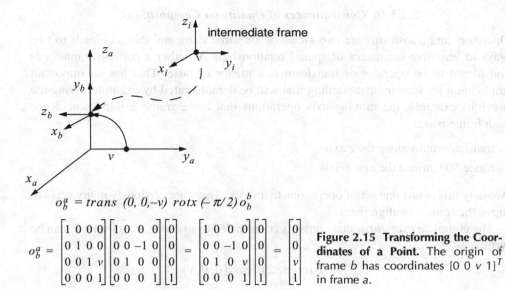

$$o_b^a = trans\ (0,\ 0,-v)\ rotx\ (-\pi/2)\ o_b^b$$

$$o_b^a = \begin{bmatrix} 1 & 0 & 0 & 0 \\ 0 & 1 & 0 & 0 \\ 0 & 0 & 1 & v \\ 0 & 0 & 0 & 1 \end{bmatrix} \begin{bmatrix} 1 & 0 & 0 & 0 \\ 0 & 0 & -1 & 0 \\ 0 & 1 & 0 & 0 \\ 0 & 0 & 0 & 1 \end{bmatrix} \begin{bmatrix} 0 \\ 0 \\ 0 \\ 1 \end{bmatrix} = \begin{bmatrix} 1 & 0 & 0 & 0 \\ 0 & 0 & -1 & 0 \\ 0 & 1 & 0 & v \\ 0 & 0 & 0 & 1 \end{bmatrix} \begin{bmatrix} 0 \\ 0 \\ 0 \\ 1 \end{bmatrix} = \begin{bmatrix} 0 \\ 0 \\ v \\ 1 \end{bmatrix}$$

Figure 2.15 Transforming the Coordinates of a Point. The origin of frame b has coordinates $[0\ 0\ v\ 1]^T$ in frame a.

2.3.3.15 Inverse of a Homogeneous Transform

Essentially all homogeneous transforms that we will use will be structured according to the template in Figure 2.16:

Rotation Matrix	Position Vector
Perspective	Scale

Figure 2.16 Template for a Homogeneous Transform. Every homogeneous transform has the structure shown.

The scale factor will almost always be 1 and the perspective part will be all zeros except when modelling cameras. Under these conditions, it is easy to show by multiplying the inverse by the original matrix, that the inverse is:

$$\begin{bmatrix} R & \underline{p} \\ \underline{0}^T & 1 \end{bmatrix}^{-1} = \begin{bmatrix} R^T & -R^T\underline{p} \\ \underline{0}^T & 1 \end{bmatrix}^{-1} \tag{2.30}$$

This is very useful for converting from a matrix that converts coordinates in one direction to one that converts coordinates in the opposite direction. The opposite direction of "from a to b" is "from b to a." Remember that it is trivial to reverse the sense of a coordinate transform.

2.3.3.16 *Consequences of Duality on Compositions*

Operators and transforms are two views of the same thing and this fact leads to two ways to visualize sequences of spatial relationships. Whether a particular matrix is considered to be operator or transform is a matter of taste. This has an important implication for kinematic modelling that will be demonstrated by example. Using the previous example, the moving axis operations that bring frame a into coincidence with frame b are:

- translate v units along the z axis
- rotate $90°$ around the **new** x axis

Actually this is just one set of operations that work. There are obviously many ways to move the frames to align them.

The complete **transform** that converts coordinates from frame a to frame b can be written as:

$$T_a^b = rotx(\pi/2)trans(0, 0, v)$$

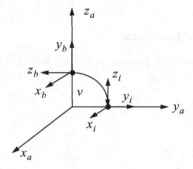

Figure 2.17 Aligning Operations. One way (of many ways) to move frame a into coincidence with frame b is to translate v units along the z axis and then rotate $90°$ around the new x axis.

The $trans(0, 0, v)$ converts coordinates to an intermediate frame called i in Figure 2.17, and then the result of that is converted to frame b by the $rotx(\pi/2)$. The reader probably noticed that the transform matrices look almost identical to the operator matrices. Specifically:

$$rotx(\phi) = Rotx(-\phi)$$
$$roty(\theta) = Roty(-\theta)$$
$$rotz(\psi) = Rotz(-\psi)$$
$$trans(0, 0, v) = Trans(0, 0, -v)$$

In fact, using the above formula for inversion, it's easy to show that they are inverses of each other:

$$
\begin{aligned}
rotx(\phi) &= Rotx(\phi)^{-1} \\
roty(\theta) &= Roty(\theta)^{-1} \quad trans(0, 0, v) = Trans(0, 0, v)^{-1} \\
rotz(\psi) &= Rotz(\psi)^{-1}
\end{aligned}
\tag{2.31}
$$

Therefore, the previous compound transform can be rewritten in terms of operators as:

$$T_a^b = Rotx(-\pi/2)Trans(0, 0, -v)$$

Because this matrix converts coordinates from frame a to frame b, the inverse of this matrix will convert coordinates from frame b to frame a. As was shown earlier, its internal parameters also represent the position and attitude of frame b with respect to frame a. Using the well-known method for inverting a matrix product ($[AB]^{-1} = B^{-1}A^{-1}$), this inverse matrix can be expressed as follows:

$$T_b^a = Trans(0, 0, -v)^{-1}Rotx(-\pi/2)^{-1}$$
$$T_b^a = Trans(0, 0, v)Rotx(\pi/2)$$

Note that, for these matrices, reversing the sign of the argument is equivalent to inverting the matrix, so doing both does nothing:

$$Trans(0, 0, -v)^{-1} = Trans(0, 0, v)$$
$$Rotx(-\pi/2)^{-1} = Rotx(\pi/2)$$

Now our result for the matrix that converts coordinates from b to frame a is:

$$T_b^a = Trans(0, 0, v)Rotx(\pi/2)$$

We have shown that, the transform from b to a can be written in terms of *transforms from right to left* or in terms of *operators in the reverse order*. There are two complementary ways to conceptualize compound transformations. The latter view is traditional in robotics and it will be used from now on.

2.3.3.17 The Semantics of Homogeneous Transforms

Homogeneous transforms are both operators and transforms and they can also be the things that are operated on and transformed. If you have not noticed already, go back and confirm that every one of the five example interpretations was a different interpretation of the same matrix.

2.3.4 References and Further Reading

The first group of references up to Rogers discuss homogeneous transforms in a setting more general than robotics.

[6] James D. Foley and Andris Van Damm, *Fundamentals of Interactive Computer Graphics,* Addison Wesley, 1982.

[7] W. M. Newman and R. F. Sproull, *Principles of Interactive Computer Graphics,* McGraw-Hill, New York, 1979.

[8] E. A. Maxwell, *General Homogeneous Coordinates in Space of Three Dimensions,* Cambridge University Press, 1951.

[9] D. F. Rogers and J. A. Adams, *Mathematical Elements for Computer Graphics,* McGraw-Hill, New York, 1976.

[10] I. M. Vinogradov, *Encyclopedia of Mathematics,* Kluwer, 1988.

2.3.5 Exercises

2.3.5.1 Specific Homogeneous Transforms

What do the following transforms do? If it is not obvious, transform the corners of a square to find out.

$$
\begin{bmatrix} 1 & 0 & 0 & a \\ 0 & 1 & 0 & b \\ 0 & 0 & 1 & c \\ 0 & 0 & 0 & 1 \end{bmatrix}
\begin{bmatrix} a & 0 & 0 & 0 \\ 0 & b & 0 & 0 \\ 0 & 0 & c & 0 \\ 0 & 0 & 0 & 1 \end{bmatrix}
\begin{bmatrix} 1 & 0 & a & 0 \\ 0 & 1 & b & 0 \\ 0 & 0 & 1 & 0 \\ 0 & 0 & 0 & 1 \end{bmatrix}
\begin{bmatrix} 1 & 0 & 0 & 0 \\ 0 & 1 & 0 & 0 \\ 0 & 0 & 1 & 0 \\ 0 & 0 & 1/d & 1 \end{bmatrix}
\begin{bmatrix} 1 & 0 & 0 & 0 \\ 0 & 1 & 0 & 0 \\ 0 & 0 & 0 & 0 \\ 0 & 0 & 0 & 1 \end{bmatrix}
$$

2.3.5.2 Operators and Frames

(i) 2D Homogeneous transforms work just like 3D ones except that a rigid body in 2D has only three degrees of freedom – translation along x or y or rotation in the plane. Consider the transform:

$$
T = \begin{bmatrix} 0 & -1 & 7 \\ 1 & 0 & 3 \\ 0 & 0 & 1 \end{bmatrix}
$$

Recall that the unit vectors and origin of a frame can be represented in its own coordinates as an identity matrix. Let such a matrix represent frame a. Consider the T matrix to be an operator and operate on the unit vectors and origin of frame a expressed in its own coordinates to produce another frame, called b. Write explicit vectors down for the unit vectors and origin of the new frame b. Use a notation that records the coordinate system in which they are expressed.

(ii) Visualization of the New Frame. When a transform is interpreted as an operator, the output vector is expressed in the coordinates of the original frame. Get out some graph paper or draw a grid in your editor with at least 10×10 cells. Draw a set of axes to the bottom left of the paper called frame a. Draw the transformed frame, called b in the right place with respect to frame a based on the above result. Label the axes of both frames with x or y.

(iii) Homogeneous Transforms as Frames. Consider the coordinates of the unit vectors and origin of the transformed frame when expressed with respect to the original frame. Compare these coordinates to the columns of the homogeneous transform. How are they related? Explain why this means homogeneous transforms are also machines to convert coordinates of general points under the same relationship between the two frames involved. HINT: how is a general point related to unit vectors and origin of any frame.

2.3.5.3 Pose of a Transform and Operating on a Point

(i) Solving for the Relative Pose. The parameters of the compound homogeneous transform which relates the frames in question 2.3.5.2 can be found using the techniques of inverse kinematics. Write an expression (in the form of a homogeneous transform with three degrees of freedom (or "parameters" in operator form) $\begin{bmatrix} a & b & \psi \end{bmatrix}^T$ for the general relationship between two rigid bodies in 2D, equate it to the above transform.

(ii) Solve the above expression by inspection for the "parameters."

2.3.5.4 Rigid Transforms

Operating on a general point is no different than operating on the origin.

(i) Operate on the point $p = \begin{bmatrix} 3 & 2 & 1 \end{bmatrix}^T$ with the transform T from Section 2.3.5.2 and write the coordinates p' of the new point. Copy your last figure and draw p and p' on it. Label each.

(ii) How do the coordinates of p' in the new frame (called b) compare to the coordinates of p in the old frame (called a)?

(iii) What property of any two points is preserved when they are operated upon by an orthogonal transform and what does this imply about any set of points?

2.3.5.5 Homogeneous Transforms as Transforms

(i) Transforming a General Point. This exercise is worth extra attention. It illustrates the basic duality of operators and transforms upon which much depends. Copy the last figure including points p and p' on a fresh sheet. Draw the point $q^b = \begin{bmatrix} 4 & 1 & 1 \end{bmatrix}^T$. The notation superscript b means the point has been specified with respect to frame b, so make sure to draw it in its correct position with respect to frame b.

(ii) Write out the multiplication of this point by "the transform" and call the result q^a. Using a different symbol than the one drawn for q^b, draw q^a in its correct position with respect to frame a.

(iii) Earlier, when p was moved to p', p was expressed in frame a and so was p'. Here you expressed q^b in frame b to produce a result q^a expressed in frame a. Now the following is the key point. Discuss how interpreting the input differently (i.e in different coordinates) leads to a different interpretation of the *function of the matrix*.

(iv) How can the function performed on the point p be reinterpreted as a different function applied, instead, to p'?

2.4 Kinematics of Mechanisms

We will distinguish *motions,* which rotate or translate the entire vehicle body from *articulations*, which merely reconfigure the mass of the vehicle without a substantial change in its position or orientation.

2.4.1 Forward Kinematics

Forward kinematics is the process of chaining homogeneous transforms together in order to represent:

- the articulations of a mechanism, or
- the fixed transformation between two frames which is known in terms of (fixed) linear and rotary parameters.

In this process, the joint variables are given, and the problem is to find the transform.

2.4.1.1 Nonlinear Mapping

So, far we have considered transformations and operations of the general form:

$$r' = T(\rho)r$$

and we have used this form to perform essentially linear operations on r because $T(\rho)$ (ρ is a vector of parameters) is considered to be a constant.

Most mechanisms are *not linear* – being composed of one or more rotary degrees of freedom. We can still model them using homogeneous transforms by considering the parameters ρ to be associated with the rotary degrees of freedom and the homogeneous transform $T(\rho)$ to be a *matrix-valued function* of the variables ρ. The problem of forward kinematics is one of understanding the variation in such a homogeneous transform when it is considered to be a function of one or more variables.

In the study of mechanisms, the real world space in which a mechanism moves is often called *task space*. The desired position and orientation of the end of the mechanism are often specified in this space. The term *workspace* is often used to mean the specific volume that can be reached with the end-effector – the reachable task space. However, the mechanism articulations are most easily expressed in terms of angles and displacements along axes. This space is called *configuration space*. Formally, the *configuration space* (C-space) of the system is any set of variables that, when specified, determine the position of every point on an object.

So far, we have studied linear transformations within task space. This section and the following sections will consider the more difficult problem of expressing the relationship between task space and configuration space.

2.4.1.2 Mechanism Models

It is natural to think about the operation of a mechanism in a moving axes sense – because most mechanisms are built that way. That is, the position and orientation of any link in a kinematic chain is dependent on all other joints that come before it in the sequence.

Conventionally, one thinks in terms of moving axis operations applied to frames embedded in the mechanism that move the first frame sequentially into coincidence with all of the others in the mechanism. Then, a sequence of operators is written to represent the mechanism kinematics.

Box 2.3: Forward Kinematic Modelling

The conventional rules for modelling a sequence of connected joints are

- Assign embedded frames to the links in sequence such that the operations that move each frame into coincidence with the next are a function of the appropriate joint variable.
- Write the *orthogonal operator matrices* that correspond to these operations in *left to right order.*

This process will generate the matrix that represents the position and orientation of the last embedded frame with respect to the first, or equivalently, that converts the coordinates of a point from the last to the first.

2.4.1.3 Denavit Hartenberg Convention for Mechanisms

A mechanism is considered to be any collection of joints, either linear or rotary, joined together by links (Figure 2.18). The total number of movable joints is called the number of *degrees of freedom*.

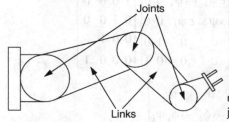

Joints

Links

Figure 2.18 Links versus Joints. Quite often, a mechanism can be viewed as a linear sequence of joints connected by links.

It is conventional in many aspects of robotics to use a ***special product of four fundamental operators as a basic conceptual unit***. The resulting single matrix can represent the most general spatial relationship between two frames of a class of mechanisms called *lower pair mechanisms*. This convention, along with a small number of associated rules for assignment of embedded frames, has come to be called the Denavit-Hartenberg (DH) convention [12].

These special operators can be used in place of the basic orthogonal operators in forward kinematics because they are also orthogonal operators. The set of homogeneous transforms is closed under the operation of composition. For two frames positioned in space, the directions of, say, the z axes of two frames define two lines in 3D space. For nonparallel axes, there is a well-defined measure of the distance between them given by the length of their mutual perpendicular. Let the first frame be called frame k-1 and the second frame k. The first can be moved into coincidence with the second by a sequence of 4 operations:

- rotate around the x_{k-1} axis by an angle ϕ_k
- translate along the x_{k-1} axis by a distance u_k
- rotate around the new z axis by an angle ψ_k
- translate along the new z axis by a distance w_k

Figure 2.19 indicates this sequence graphically.

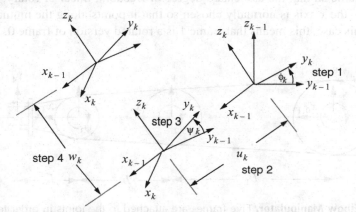

Figure 2.19 Component Operations of a DH Matrix. Attach two frames to two axes in space. Then, the first can be moved into coincidence with the second by a sequence of 4 operations starting at the top right.

The matrix, conventionally called A_k, that converts coordinates from frame k to frame k-1 can be written using the rules for forward kinematic modelling given previously.

$$T_k^{k-1} = Rotx(\phi_k)Trans(u_k, 0, 0)Rotz(\psi_k)Trans(0, 0, w_k)$$

$$T_k^{k-1} = \begin{bmatrix} 1 & 0 & 0 & 0 \\ 0 & c\phi_k & -s\phi_k & 0 \\ 0 & s\phi_k & c\phi_k & 0 \\ 0 & 0 & 0 & 1 \end{bmatrix} \begin{bmatrix} 1 & 0 & 0 & u_k \\ 0 & 1 & 0 & 0 \\ 0 & 0 & 1 & 0 \\ 0 & 0 & 0 & 1 \end{bmatrix} \begin{bmatrix} c\psi_k & -s\psi_k & 0 & 0 \\ s\psi_k & c\psi_k & 0 & 0 \\ 0 & 0 & 1 & 0 \\ 0 & 0 & 0 & 1 \end{bmatrix} \begin{bmatrix} 1 & 0 & 0 & 0 \\ 0 & 1 & 0 & 0 \\ 0 & 0 & 1 & w_k \\ 0 & 0 & 0 & 1 \end{bmatrix}$$

(2.32)

$$A_k = T_k^{k-1} = \begin{bmatrix} c\psi_k & -s\psi_k & 0 & u_k \\ c\phi_k s\psi_k & c\phi_k c\psi_k & -s\phi_k & -s\phi_k w_k \\ s\phi_k s\psi_k & s\phi_k c\psi_k & c\phi_k & c\phi_k w_k \\ 0 & 0 & 0 & 1 \end{bmatrix}$$

Note especially that it has four degrees of freedom although a general 3D relationship between frames has six. This arrangement works because each DH matrix typically models only a single real degree of freedom (dof) while the other three are constant. Mathematically speaking, the DH matrix relates two lines in space, not two frames, so there are only four degrees of freedom if position along each line is immaterial.

This matrix has the following interpretations:

- It will move a point or rotate a direction by the operator which describes how frame k is related to frame k-1.
- Its columns represent the axes and origin of frame k expressed in frame k-1 coordinates.
- It converts coordinates from frame k to frame k-1.

2.4.1.4 Example: 3-Link Planar Manipulator

Coordinate frames are assigned to the center of each rotary joint and the datum angle for each is set to zero as illustrated in Figure 2.20. It is conventional to assign the z axis of a frame so that the associated degree of freedom, linear or rotary, coincides with it. Also, the x axis is normally chosen so that it points along the mutual perpendicular. In this case, this means that frame 1 is a rotated version of frame 0.

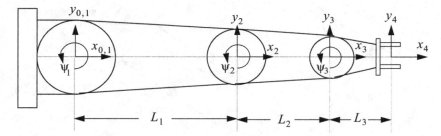

Figure 2.20 Elbow Manipulator. Five frames are attached to the joints in order to track the motions of the three joints and express the offset of the hand from the wrist.

The joint parameters for this manipulator model are indicated in Table 2.2:

Table 2.2 Three-Link Planar Manipulator

Link	ϕ	u	ψ	w
0	0	0	ψ_1	0
1	0	L_1	ψ_2	0
2	0	L_2	ψ_3	0
3	0	L_3	0	0

This table gives the following Denavit-Hartenberg matrices. Their inverses are computed from the inverse formula because they will be useful later:

$$A_1 = \begin{bmatrix} c_1 & -s_1 & 0 & 0 \\ s_1 & c_1 & 0 & 0 \\ 0 & 0 & 1 & 0 \\ 0 & 0 & 0 & 1 \end{bmatrix} A_1^{-1} = \begin{bmatrix} c_1 & s_1 & 0 & 0 \\ -s_1 & c_1 & 0 & 0 \\ 0 & 0 & 1 & 0 \\ 0 & 0 & 0 & 1 \end{bmatrix} A_2 = \begin{bmatrix} c_2 & -s_2 & 0 & L_1 \\ s_2 & c_2 & 0 & 0 \\ 0 & 0 & 1 & 0 \\ 0 & 0 & 0 & 1 \end{bmatrix} A_2^{-1} = \begin{bmatrix} c_2 & s_2 & 0 & -c_2 L_1 \\ -s_2 & c_2 & 0 & s_2 L_1 \\ 0 & 0 & 1 & 0 \\ 0 & 0 & 0 & 1 \end{bmatrix}$$

$$\text{(2.33)}$$

$$A_3 = \begin{bmatrix} c_3 & -s_3 & 0 & L_2 \\ s_3 & c_3 & 0 & 0 \\ 0 & 0 & 1 & 0 \\ 0 & 0 & 0 & 1 \end{bmatrix} A_3^{-1} = \begin{bmatrix} c_3 & s_3 & 0 & -c_3 L_2 \\ -s_3 & c_3 & 0 & s_3 L_2 \\ 0 & 0 & 1 & 0 \\ 0 & 0 & 0 & 1 \end{bmatrix} A_4 = \begin{bmatrix} 1 & 0 & 0 & L_3 \\ 0 & 1 & 0 & 0 \\ 0 & 0 & 1 & 0 \\ 0 & 0 & 0 & 1 \end{bmatrix} A_4^{-1} = \begin{bmatrix} 1 & 0 & 0 & -L_3 \\ 0 & 1 & 0 & 0 \\ 0 & 0 & 1 & 0 \\ 0 & 0 & 0 & 1 \end{bmatrix}$$

The position and orientation of the end effector with respect to the base is given by:

$$T_4^0 = T_1^0 T_2^1 T_3^2 T_4^3 = A_1 A_2 A_3 A_4$$

$$T_4^0 = \begin{bmatrix} c_1 & -s_1 & 0 & 0 \\ s_1 & c_1 & 0 & 0 \\ 0 & 0 & 1 & 0 \\ 0 & 0 & 0 & 1 \end{bmatrix} \begin{bmatrix} c_2 & -s_2 & 0 & L_1 \\ s_2 & c_2 & 0 & 0 \\ 0 & 0 & 1 & 0 \\ 0 & 0 & 0 & 1 \end{bmatrix} \begin{bmatrix} c_3 & -s_3 & 0 & L_2 \\ s_3 & c_3 & 0 & 0 \\ 0 & 0 & 1 & 0 \\ 0 & 0 & 0 & 1 \end{bmatrix} \begin{bmatrix} 1 & 0 & 0 & L_3 \\ 0 & 1 & 0 & 0 \\ 0 & 0 & 1 & 0 \\ 0 & 0 & 0 & 1 \end{bmatrix}$$

$$\text{(2.34)}$$

$$T_4^0 = \begin{bmatrix} c_{123} & -s_{123} & 0 & (c_{123}L_3 + c_{12}L_2 + c_1 L_1) \\ s_{123} & c_{123} & 0 & (s_{123}L_3 + s_{12}L_2 + s_1 L_1) \\ 0 & 0 & 1 & 0 \\ 0 & 0 & 0 & 1 \end{bmatrix}$$

The way you use this is that the last column tells you the (x,y) position of frame 4 with respect to frame 0 and the upper left 2×2 matrix is telling you the angle between frame 4 and frame 0.

2.4.2 Inverse Kinematics

The inverse kinematics problem is that of finding the joint parameters given only the numerical values of the homogeneous transforms that model the mechanism. In other words, it is the problem of determining where to drive the joints in order to get the hand of an arm (or the foot of a leg) in the right place. Hence, it is pretty fundamental to robot control.

2.4.2.1 Existence and Uniqueness

Inverse kinematics usually involves the solution of nonlinear equations. Such equations may have no solution, or a nonunique solution. It has been shown theoretically by Pieper [13], that a six degree of freedom manipulator is always solvable if (not only if) the joint axes of the last three joints intersect at a point. Most manipulators are constructed in this way, so most are solvable.

Any real mechanism has a finite reach, so it can only achieve positions in a region of space known as the *workspace*. Unless the initial transform to be solved is in the workspace, the inverse kinematic problem will have no solution. This manifests itself eventually as some mathematically impossible calculation. For example, inverse sines and cosines of arguments greater than 1 might be encountered. Mechanisms with many rotary joints will often have more than one solution. This problem is known as *redundancy*.

2.4.2.2 Technique

Using the DH convention, a mechanism can be solved more or less one joint at a time. The inverse kinematic problem is solved by rewriting the forward transform in many different ways to attempt to isolate unknowns. Although there are only a few independent relationships, they can be rewritten in many different ways.

Using a three degree of freedom mechanism for example, the forward kinematics can be written in all of these ways by premultiplying or postmultiplying by the inverse of each link transform in turn:

$$
\begin{aligned}
T_4^0 &= A_1 A_2 A_3 A_4 & T_4^0 &= A_1 A_2 A_3 A_4 \\
A_1^{-1} T_4^0 &= A_2 A_3 A_4 & T_4^0 A_4^{-1} &= A_1 A_2 A_3 \\
A_2^{-1} A_1^{-1} T_4^0 &= A_3 A_4 & T_4^0 A_4^{-1} A_3^{-1} &= A_1 A_2 \qquad (2.35) \\
A_3^{-1} A_2^{-1} A_1^{-1} T_4^0 &= A_4 & T_4^0 A_4^{-1} A_3^{-1} A_2^{-1} &= A_1 \\
A_4^{-1} A_3^{-1} A_2^{-1} A_1^{-1} T_4^0 &= I & T_4^0 A_4^{-1} A_3^{-1} A_2^{-1} A_1^{-1} &= I
\end{aligned}
$$

Spotlight 2-7 Mechanism Inverse Kinematics.

The basic process used to isolate unknowns is to rewrite the forward kinematic equations as shown.

These are, of course, redundant specifications of the same set of equations, so they contain no new information. However, they often generate equations that are easy to solve because the DH convention tends to isolate each joint. It is conventional to use the left column of equations, but the right column is easier to follow in our case, so it will be used in our example.

2.4.2.3 Example: 3 Link Planar Manipulator

The process is started by assuming that the forward kinematic solution is known. Names are assigned to each of its elements as follows:

$$T_4^0 = \begin{bmatrix} r_{11} & r_{12} & r_{13} & p_x \\ r_{21} & r_{22} & r_{23} & p_y \\ r_{31} & r_{32} & r_{33} & p_z \\ 0 & 0 & 0 & 1 \end{bmatrix} \tag{2.36}$$

For our example, we know that some of these are zeros and ones, so that the end effector frame is:

$$T_4^0 = \begin{bmatrix} r_{11} & r_{12} & 0 & p_x \\ r_{21} & r_{22} & 0 & p_y \\ 0 & 0 & 1 & 0 \\ 0 & 0 & 0 & 1 \end{bmatrix} \tag{2.37}$$

The first equation is already known:

$$T_4^0 = A_1 A_2 A_3 A_4$$

$$\begin{bmatrix} r_{11} & r_{12} & 0 & p_x \\ r_{21} & r_{22} & 0 & p_y \\ 0 & 0 & 1 & 0 \\ 0 & 0 & 0 & 1 \end{bmatrix} = \begin{bmatrix} c_{123} & -s_{123} & 0 & (c_{123}L_3 + c_{12}L_2 + c_1L_1) \\ s_{123} & c_{123} & 0 & (s_{123}L_3 + s_{12}L_2 + s_1L_1) \\ 0 & 0 & 1 & 0 \\ 0 & 0 & 0 & 1 \end{bmatrix} \tag{2.38}$$

From the (1,1) and (2,1) elements we have:

$$\psi_{123} = \operatorname{atan2}(r_{21}, r_{11}) \tag{2.39}$$

The next equation is:

$$T_4^0 A_4^{-1} = A_1 A_2 A_3$$

$$\begin{bmatrix} r_{11} & r_{12} & 0 & -r_{11}L_3 + p_x \\ r_{21} & r_{22} & 0 & -r_{21}L_3 + p_y \\ 0 & 0 & 1 & 0 \\ 0 & 0 & 0 & 1 \end{bmatrix} = \begin{bmatrix} c_{123} & -s_{123} & 0 & c_1(c_2L_2 + L_1) - s_1(s_2L_2) \\ s_{123} & c_{123} & 0 & s_1(c_2L_2 + L_1) + c_1(s_2L_2) \\ 0 & 0 & 1 & 0 \\ 0 & 0 & 0 & 1 \end{bmatrix} \tag{2.40}$$

$$\begin{bmatrix} r_{11} & r_{12} & 0 & -r_{11}L_3 + p_x \\ r_{21} & r_{22} & 0 & -r_{21}L_3 + p_y \\ 0 & 0 & 1 & 0 \\ 0 & 0 & 0 & 1 \end{bmatrix} = \begin{bmatrix} c_{123} & -s_{123} & 0 & c_{12}L_2 + c_1L_1 \\ s_{123} & c_{123} & 0 & s_{12}L_2 + s_1L_1 \\ 0 & 0 & 1 & 0 \\ 0 & 0 & 0 & 1 \end{bmatrix}$$

From the (1,4) and (2,4) elements:

$$k_1 = -r_{11}L_3 + p_x = c_{12}L_2 + c_1 L_1$$
$$k_2 = -r_{21}L_3 + p_y = s_{12}L_2 + s_1 L_1$$

These can be squared and added to yield:

$$k_1^2 + k_2^2 = L_2^2 + L_1^2 + 2L_2 L_1 (c_1 c_{12} + s_1 s_{12})$$

Or:

$$k_1^2 + k_2^2 = L_2^2 + L_1^2 + 2L_2 L_1 c_2$$

This gives the angle ψ_2 as:

$$\psi_2 = \mathrm{acos}\left[\frac{(k_1^2 + k_2^2) - (L_2^2 + L_1^2)}{2L_2 L_1}\right] \tag{2.41}$$

The result implies that there are two solutions for this angle that are symmetric about zero. These correspond to the elbow up and elbow down configurations. Each solution generates a different value for the other two angles in subsequent steps. Two sets of angles emerge: one for the "elbow up" solution, the other for "elbow down."

Now, before the expressions were reduced to include a sum of angles, they were:

$$k_1 = -r_{11}L_3 + p_x = c_1(c_2 L_2 + L_1) - s_1(s_2 L_2)$$
$$k_2 = -r_{21}L_3 + p_y = s_1(c_2 L_2 + L_1) + c_1(s_2 L_2)$$

With ψ_2 now known, these can be written as:

$$c_1 k_3 - s_1 k_4 = k_1$$
$$s_1 k_3 + c_1 k_4 = k_2$$

This is one of the standard forms that recur in inverse kinematics problems for which the solution is:

$$\psi_1 = \mathrm{atan2}[(k_2 k_3 - k_1 k_4), (k_1 k_3 + k_2 k_4)] \tag{2.42}$$

Finally, the last angle is:

$$\psi_3 = \psi_{123} - \psi_2 - \psi_1 \tag{2.43}$$

2.4.2.4 Standard Forms

There are a few forms of trigonometric equations that recur is most robot mechanisms. The set of solutions described below is sufficient for most applications. One of the most difficult forms, solved by square and add, was presented in the last example. In the following, the letters a, b, and c represent arbitrary known expressions.

2.4.2.4.1 Explicit Tangent. This form generates a single solution because both the sine and cosine are fixed in value (Figure 2.21). It can arise in the last two joints of a three-axis wrist, for example. The equations:

$$a = c_n \qquad\qquad b = s_n$$

have the trivial solution:

$$\psi_n = \text{atan} 2(b, a) \tag{2.44}$$

2.4.2.4.2 Point Symmetric Redundancy. This form generates two solutions that are symmetric about the origin (Figure 2.22). The equation:

$$s_n a - c_n b = 0$$

can be solved by isolating the ratio of the two trig functions. There are two angles in one revolution that have the same tangent so the two solutions are:

$$\psi_n = \text{atan} 2(b, a) \qquad \psi_n = \text{atan} 2(-b, -a) \tag{2.45}$$

Figure 2.21 Explicit Tangent.

Figure 2.22 Point Symmetric.

2.4.2.5 Line Symmetric Redundancy

This case generates two solutions that are symmetric about an axis because the sine or cosine of the deviation from the axis must be constant (Figure 2.23). The sine case will be illustrated.

Figure 2.23 Line Symmetric.

The equation:

$$s_n a - c_n b = c$$

has the solution:

$$\psi_n = \text{atan} 2(b, a) - \text{atan} 2[c, \pm sqrt(r^2 - c^2)] \tag{2.46}$$

where:

$$r = \pm sqrt(a^2 + b^2) \qquad\qquad \theta = \text{atan} 2(b, a)$$

2.4.3 Differential Kinematics

Differential kinematics is the study of the derivatives of kinematic models. These derivatives are called *Jacobians* and they have many uses ranging from:

- resolved rate control
- sensitivity analysis & uncertainty propagation
- static force transformation

2.4.3.1 Derivatives of Fundamental Operators

The derivatives of the fundamental operators with respect to their own parameters will be important. They can be used to compute derivatives of very complex expressions by using the chain rule of differentiation. They are:

$$
\frac{\partial}{\partial u} Trans(u, v, w) = \begin{bmatrix} 0 & 0 & 0 & 1 \\ 0 & 0 & 0 & 0 \\ 0 & 0 & 0 & 0 \\ 0 & 0 & 0 & 0 \end{bmatrix} \qquad \frac{\partial}{\partial \phi} Rotx(\phi) = \begin{bmatrix} 0 & 0 & 0 & 0 \\ 0 & -s\phi & -c\phi & 0 \\ 0 & c\phi & -s\phi & 0 \\ 0 & 0 & 0 & 0 \end{bmatrix}
$$

$$
\frac{\partial}{\partial v} Trans(u, v, w) = \begin{bmatrix} 0 & 0 & 0 & 0 \\ 0 & 0 & 0 & 1 \\ 0 & 0 & 0 & 0 \\ 0 & 0 & 0 & 0 \end{bmatrix} \qquad \frac{\partial}{\partial \theta} Roty(\theta) = \begin{bmatrix} -s\theta & 0 & c\theta & 0 \\ 0 & 0 & 0 & 0 \\ -c\theta & 0 & -s\theta & 0 \\ 0 & 0 & 0 & 0 \end{bmatrix} \qquad (2.47)
$$

$$
\frac{\partial}{\partial w} Trans(u, v, w) = \begin{bmatrix} 0 & 0 & 0 & 0 \\ 0 & 0 & 0 & 0 \\ 0 & 0 & 0 & 1 \\ 0 & 0 & 0 & 0 \end{bmatrix} \qquad \frac{\partial}{\partial \psi} Rotz(\psi) = \begin{bmatrix} -s\psi & -c\psi & 0 & 0 \\ c\psi & -s\psi & 0 & 0 \\ 0 & 0 & 0 & 0 \\ 0 & 0 & 0 & 0 \end{bmatrix}
$$

2.4.3.2 The Mechanism Jacobian

It is natural to ask about the effect of a differential change in joint variables on the position and orientation of the end of the mechanism. A coordinate frame matrix represents orientation indirectly in terms of three unit vectors, so an extra set of equations is required to extract three angles from the rotation matrix. In terms of position, however, the last column of the mechanism model gives the position of the end effector with respect to the base.

Let the configuration of a mechanism have generalized coordinates represented by the vector q, and let the position and orientation, or *pose*, of the end of the mechanism be given by the vector $\underline{x}$:

$$
\underline{x} = \begin{bmatrix} x & y & z & \phi & \theta & \psi \end{bmatrix}
$$

Then, the end effector position is given by:

$$
\underline{x} = \underline{F}(\underline{q})
$$

where the nonlinear multidimensional function $\underline{F}$ comes from the mechanism model.

The *Jacobian matrix* is a multidimensional derivative defined as:

$$J = \frac{\partial \underline{x}}{\partial \underline{q}} = \frac{\partial}{\partial \underline{q}}(\underline{F}(\underline{q})) = \left[\frac{\partial x_i}{\partial q_j}\right] = \begin{bmatrix} \dfrac{\partial x_1}{\partial q_1} & \cdots & \dfrac{\partial x_1}{\partial q_n} \\ \cdots & \cdots & \cdots \\ \dfrac{\partial x_n}{\partial q_1} & \cdots & \dfrac{\partial x_n}{\partial q_n} \end{bmatrix} \tag{2.48}$$

The differential mapping from small changes in $\underline{q}$ to the corresponding small changes in $\underline{x}$ is:

$$d\underline{x} = J d\underline{q} \tag{2.49}$$

The Jacobian also gives velocity relationships via the chain rule of differentiation as follows:

$$\frac{d\underline{x}}{dt} = \left(\frac{\partial \underline{x}}{\partial \underline{q}}\right)\left(\frac{d\underline{q}}{dt}\right) \tag{2.50}$$

which maps joint rates onto end effector velocity.

$$\dot{\underline{x}} = J\dot{\underline{q}} \tag{2.51}$$

Note that this expression is nonlinear in the joint variables, but linear in the joint rates. This fact implies that reducing the joint rates by half reduces the end velocity by exactly half and preserves the direction.

2.4.3.3 Singularity

Redundancy takes the form of *singularity* of the Jacobian matrix in the differential kinematic solution. A mechanism can lose one or more degrees of freedom:

- at points where two different inverse kinematic solutions converge
- when joint axes become aligned or parallel
- when the boundaries of the workspace are reached

Singularity implies that the Jacobian becomes rank deficient and therefore not invertible. At the same time, the inverse kinematic solution tends to fail because axes become aligned. Infinite rates can be generated by resolved rate control laws.

2.4.3.4 Example: Three-Link Planar Manipulator

For the example manipulator, the last column of the manipulator model gives the following two equations:

$$\begin{aligned} x &= (c_{123}L_3 + c_{12}L_2 + c_1L_1) \\ y &= (s_{123}L_3 + s_{12}L_2 + s_1L_1) \end{aligned} \tag{2.52}$$

We also know that the final orientation is:

$$\psi = \psi_1 + \psi_2 + \psi_3 \tag{2.53}$$

These can be differentiated with respect to ψ_1, ψ_2, and ψ_3 in order to determine the velocity of the end effector as the joints move. The solution is:

$$\dot{x} = -(s_{123}\dot{\psi}_{123}L_3 + s_{12}\dot{\psi}_{12}L_2 + s_1\dot{\psi}_1L_1)$$
$$\dot{y} = (c_{123}\dot{\psi}_{123}L_3 + c_{12}\dot{\psi}_{12}L_2 + c_1\dot{\psi}_1L_1) \tag{2.54}$$
$$\dot{\psi} = (\dot{\psi}_1 + \dot{\psi}_2 + \dot{\psi}_3)$$

which can be written as:

$$\begin{bmatrix} \dot{x} \\ \dot{y} \\ \dot{\psi} \end{bmatrix} = \begin{bmatrix} (-s_{123}L_3 - s_{12}L_2 - s_1L_1) & (-s_{123}L_3 - s_{12}L_2) & -s_{123}L_3 \\ (c_{123}L_3 + c_{12}L_2 + c_1L_1) & (c_{123}L_3 + c_{12}L_2) & c_{123}L_3 \\ 1 & 1 & 1 \end{bmatrix} \begin{bmatrix} \dot{\psi}_1 \\ \dot{\psi}_2 \\ \dot{\psi}_3 \end{bmatrix} \tag{2.55}$$

2.4.3.5 Jacobian Determinant

It is known from the implicit function theorem of calculus that the ratio of differential volumes between the domain and range of a multidimensional mapping is given by the Jacobian determinant. This quantity has applications to a technique of navigation and ranging called *triangulation*.

Thus the product of the differentials forms a volume in both configuration space and in task space. The relationship between them is:

$$(dx_1 dx_2 ... dx_n) = |J|(dq_1 dq_2 ... dq_m)$$

2.4.3.6 Jacobian Tensor

At times it is convenient to compute the derivative of a transform matrix with respect to a vector of variables. In this case, the result is the derivative of a matrix with respect to a vector. For example:

$$\frac{\partial}{\partial \underline{q}}[T(\underline{q})] = \left[\frac{\partial T_{ij}}{\partial q_k}\right]$$

This is a third-order tensor. The mechanism model itself is a matrix function of a vector. For example, if:

$$T(\underline{q}) = A_1(q_1)A_2(q_2)A_3(q_3)$$

Then there are three slices of this "Jacobian tensor," each a matrix, given by:

$$\frac{\partial T}{\partial q_1} = \frac{\partial A_1}{\partial q_1}A_2A_3 \qquad \frac{\partial T}{\partial q_2} = A_1\frac{\partial A_2}{\partial q_2}A_3 \qquad \frac{\partial T}{\partial q_3} = A_1A_2\frac{\partial A_3}{\partial q_3}$$

2.4.4 References and Further Reading

Craig's book is perhaps the most popular for teaching robot manipulators. The other two references are classic papers in robot manipulators referenced in the text.

[11] John Craig, *Introduction to Robotics: Mechanics and Control,* Prentice Hall, 2005.

[12] J. Denavit and H. S. Hartenberg, A Kinematic Notation For Lower-Pair Mechanisms Based on Matrices, *ASME Journal of Applied Mechanics,* June 1955, pp. 215–221.

[13] D. Pieper, The Kinematics of Manipulators Under Computer Control, Ph.D. thesis, Stanford University, Stanford, 1968.

2.4.5 Exercises

2.4.5.1 Three Link Planar Manipulator

Every roboticist should code manipulator kinematics at least once. Using your favorite programming environment, code the forward and inverse kinematics for the three-link manipulator. Pick some random angles and draw a figure. Then compute the end effector pose from the angles and verify that the inverse solution regenerates the angle from the pose. What does the second solution look like? If you are ambitious, try a case near singularity, and experiment with the mechanism Jacobian.

2.4.5.2 Pantograph Leg Mechanism

The pantograph is a four-bar linkage that can be used to multiply motion. This one was used on the Dante II robot that ascended and entered an active volcano on Mount Spur in Alaska in 1994. Triangles ABD, ACF, and DEF are all similar. When the actuator pushes the lever down, the leg lifts up by 4 times the distance that the actuator moved.

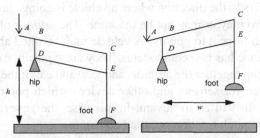

Write the set of "moving axis" operations which will bring frame D into coincidence with frame F. Then, write the 4×4 homogeneous transform T_F^D that converts coordinates from frame F to frame D. Then, write the mechanism Jacobian relating foot extension to actuator extension.

2.4.5.3 Line Symmetric Redundancy

Derive Equation 2.45 using the trig substitution:

$$a = r\cos(\theta) \qquad\qquad b = r\sin(\theta)$$

2.4.5.4 Inverse DH Transform

The general inverse DH transform can be computed for a single mechanism degree of freedom. This transform can be used as the basis of a completely general inverse kinematic solution for robotic mechanisms. The solution can be considered to be the procedure for extracting a joint angle from a link coordinate frame.

"Solve" the DH transform as if it was a mechanism with four degrees of freedom and show that:

$$u_i = p_x \qquad w_i = \sqrt{p_y^2 + p_z^2}$$

$$\psi = \mathrm{atan}2(-r_{12}, r_{11}) \qquad \phi = \mathrm{atan}2(-r_{23}, r_{33})$$

2.4.5.5 SLAM Jacobian

In an algorithm for solving the Simultaneous Localization and Mapping problem in Chapter 9, the pose of a landmark m with respect to the sensor s frame on a robot r is given by:

$$T_m^s = T_r^s T_w^r(\rho_r^w) T_m^w(r_m^w)$$

where ρ_r^w is the pose of the robot and r_m^w is the position of the landmark and two of the transforms depend on these quantities. Using the chain rule applied to matrices, derive expressions for the sensitivity of the left-hand side with respect to small changes in the robot pose, and then with respect to the landmark pose.

2.5 Orientation and Angular Velocity

Although *heading* refers to the direction where a vehicle is going, *yaw* refers to where it is pointing, and the two may or may not be the same. The *attitude* of a vehicle captures its 3D orientation with respect to gravity. A vehicle may be tilted about a forward or a sideways axis, so attitude has two components. They are typically called *roll* and *pitch*. It is convenient to group together the attitude, and yaw and call it the *orientation*.

In a similar manner, for sensors and other devices which point at something, the equivalent angle to roll is often irrelevant. In this case, the yaw rotation is typically called *azimuth* and the pitch rotation is called *elevation*.

We will group position and orientation of the vehicle into a single conceptual unit called the *pose*. In 2D, the pose is $\begin{bmatrix} x & y & \psi \end{bmatrix}^T$ and the orientation is just the yaw. In 3D the pose is $\begin{bmatrix} x & y & z & \phi & \theta & \psi \end{bmatrix}^T$.

2.5.1 Orientation in Euler Angle Form

2.5.1.1 Axis Conventions

In aerospace vehicles, when assigning coordinate frames, the convention is that z points downward. Although this is great for airplanes and satellites (since "down" is a very important direction!), it can be counterintuitive for ground vehicles. The convention used here is that *z points up, y out the left side, and x forward*. This rule has the advantage that the projection of 3D information onto the *x-y* plane is more natural.

The angles yaw, pitch, and roll are conventionally considered to be rotations about vectors out the roof, out the side, and out the front, of the vehicle. If we preserve these names for the attitude and heading, the convention used here *corresponds to a z-y-x Euler angle sequence*. See Figure 2.25 for a summary.

When processing sensor data, it is not advisable to use the homogeneous transforms developed here until you have very carefully determined how to interpret the (angular) outputs of any attitude and heading sensors that are used.

2.5.1.2 Frame Assignment

Some common frames are indicated in Figure 2.24. The *navigation* frame *n*, also known as the *world* frame *w*, is the coordinate frame with respect to which the vehicle position and attitude is ultimately required. Normally, the *z* axis is aligned with the gravity vector; the *y*, or north axis is aligned with the geographic pole; and the *x* axis points east to complete a right-handed system.

The *body* frame *b*, also known as the *vehicle* frame *v* is positioned at the point on the vehicle body that is most convenient and it is considered to be fixed in attitude with respect to the vehicle body. The *positioner* frame *p* is positioned at the point on or near any position estimation system. If the positioner system generates attitude and attitude rates only, this frame is not required because the attitude of the device will also be that of the vehicle; it is a rigid body. For an inertial navigation system (INS), this is typically the center of the inertial measurement unit (IMU) and for a Global Positioning System (GPS) it is the phase center of the antenna (which may be nowhere near the GPS receiver).

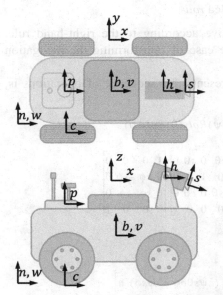

Figure 2.24 Standard Vehicle Frames. Many coordinate frames are commonly used when modelling vehicles.

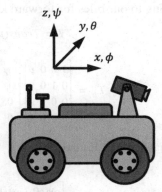

Figure 2.25 Yaw, Pitch, and Roll. These angles are defined in terms of moving axis operations applied to a frame originally fixed to the earth.

The sensor *head* frame *h* is positioned at a convenient point on a sensor head such as the intersection of the two rotary axes, the center of mounting plate, or the optical center of the hosted sensor. At times, a rigid sensor head can and should be defined that tilts the body axes into coincidence with those of the sensor. The *sensor* frame for a video camera is positioned on the optical axis at the center of projection behind the lens or on the image plane. For stereo systems, it is positioned either between both cameras or is associated with the center of projection of the image plane of one of them. For imaging laser rangefinders, it is positioned as the average point of convergence of the rays through all of the pixels in an image for a stationary sensor. The wheel *contact point* frame *c*, is positioned at the point where the wheel touches the ground surface.

2.5.1.3 The RPY Transform

It is usually most convenient to express vehicle attitude in terms of three special angles called *roll*, *pitch*, and *yaw*. A general homogeneous transform, called the RPY transform, can be formed, which is similar in principle to the DH matrix, except that it has three rotations. It can serve to transform between the body frame and all others. There are six degrees of freedom involved, three translations and three rotations, and each can be either a parameter or a variable.

Let two general frames be defined as *a* and *b* and consider the moving axis operations which transform frame *a* into coincidence with frame *b*. **In order,** these are:

- translate along the (x,y,z) axes of frame *a* by (u,v,w) until its origin coincides with that of frame *b*
- rotate about the new *z* axis by an angle ψ called *yaw*
- rotate about the new *y* axis by an angle θ called *pitch*
- rotate about the new *x* axis by an angle ϕ called *roll*

Angles are measured counterclockwise positive according to the right-hand rule. These operations are indicated below for the case of transforming the navigation frame into the body frame.

The forward kinematic transform that represents this sequence of operations is, according to our rules for forward kinematics:

$$T_b^a = Trans(u, v, w)Rotz(\psi)Roty(\theta)Rotx(\phi)$$

$$T_b^a = \begin{bmatrix} 1 & 0 & 0 & u \\ 0 & 1 & 0 & v \\ 0 & 0 & 1 & w \\ 0 & 0 & 0 & 1 \end{bmatrix} \begin{bmatrix} c\psi & -s\psi & 0 & 0 \\ s\psi & c\psi & 0 & 0 \\ 0 & 0 & 1 & 0 \\ 0 & 0 & 0 & 1 \end{bmatrix} \begin{bmatrix} c\theta & 0 & s\theta & 0 \\ 0 & 1 & 0 & 0 \\ -s\theta & 0 & c\theta & 0 \\ 0 & 0 & 0 & 1 \end{bmatrix} \begin{bmatrix} 1 & 0 & 0 & 0 \\ 0 & c\phi & -s\phi & 0 \\ 0 & s\phi & c\phi & 0 \\ 0 & 0 & 0 & 1 \end{bmatrix}$$

The final result is Equation 2.56.

$$T_b^a = \begin{bmatrix} c\psi c\theta & (c\psi s\theta s\phi - s\psi c\phi) & (c\psi s\theta c\phi + s\psi s\phi) & u \\ s\psi c\theta & (s\psi s\theta s\phi + c\psi c\phi) & (s\psi s\theta c\phi - c\psi s\phi) & v \\ -s\theta & c\theta s\phi & c\theta c\phi & w \\ 0 & 0 & 0 & 1 \end{bmatrix} \tag{2.56}$$

Box 2.4: The RPY Transform From Body to World Coordinates

The matrix that converts coordinates between two frames related by a translation and *zyx* Euler angles is given by Equation 2.56. It is used like so:

$$\underline{r}_p^a = T_b^a \underline{r}_p^b$$

It has the following interpretations:

- It rotates and translates points through the operations listed, in the order listed, with respect to the axes of *a*.
- Its columns represent the axes and origin of frame *b* expressed in frame *a* coordinates.
- It converts coordinates from frame *b* to frame *a*.
- It can be considered to be the conversion from a pose vector of the form $\begin{bmatrix} x & y & z & \phi & \theta & \psi \end{bmatrix}^T$ to a coordinate frame.

This matrix will be used extensively throughout the text.

Luckily, most pan/tilt sensor pointing mechanisms are formed from a yaw rotation followed by a pitch and no roll, so these are a degenerate form of the above.

2.5.1.4 Inverse Kinematics for the RPY Transform

The inverse kinematic solution to the RPY transform has at least two uses:

- It gives the angles to which to drive a sensor head, or a directional antenna given the direction cosines of the goal frame.
- It gives the attitude of the vehicle given the body frame axes, which often correspond to the local tangent plane to the terrain over which it moves.

This solution can be considered to be the procedure for *extracting a pose from a coordinate frame*. Each is just a representation for the configuration of a rigid body in space. There are many different ways to get the solution from different elements of the RPY transform.

The one used here is useful for modelling terrain following of a vehicle. Proceeding as for a mechanism, the elements of the transform are assumed to be known:

$$T_b^a = \begin{bmatrix} r_{11} & r_{12} & r_{13} & p_x \\ r_{21} & r_{22} & r_{23} & p_y \\ r_{31} & r_{32} & r_{33} & p_z \\ 0 & 0 & 0 & 1 \end{bmatrix}$$

The premultiplication set of equations will be used. The first equation is:

$$T_b^a = Trans(u, v, w)Rotz(\psi)Roty(\theta)Rotx(\phi)$$

$$\begin{bmatrix} r_{11} & r_{12} & r_{13} & p_x \\ r_{21} & r_{22} & r_{23} & p_y \\ r_{31} & r_{32} & r_{33} & p_z \\ 0 & 0 & 0 & 1 \end{bmatrix} = \begin{bmatrix} c\psi c\theta & (c\psi s\theta s\phi - s\psi c\phi) & (c\psi s\theta c\phi + s\psi s\phi) & u \\ s\psi c\theta & (s\psi s\theta s\phi + c\psi c\phi) & (s\psi s\theta c\phi - c\psi s\phi) & v \\ -s\theta & c\theta s\phi & c\theta c\phi & w \\ 0 & 0 & 0 & 1 \end{bmatrix} \quad (2.57)$$

The translational elements are trivial. Next, from the (1,1) and (2,1) elements:

$$\psi = \text{atan2}(r_{21}, r_{11}) \quad \text{when} \quad c\theta > 0$$

$$\psi = \text{atan2}(-r_{21}, -r_{11}) \quad \text{when} \quad c\theta < 0$$

(2.58)

This implies that yaw can be determined from a vector, that is known to be aligned with the body x axis expressed in the coordinates of frame a. The two solutions emerge because if π is added to the yaw, two other values for pitch and roll will result in the same final configuration. There is clearly a problem when $c\theta = 0$ (i.e., when the vehicle is pitched up or down by 90°). This case is a singularity when the roll and yaw axes become aligned and only the sum of both angles can be determined uniquely.

The second equation (which generates nothing new) is:

$$[Trans(u, v, w)]^{-1}T_b^a = Rotz(\psi)Roty(\theta)Rotx(\phi)$$

$$\begin{bmatrix} r_{11} & r_{12} & r_{13} & 0 \\ r_{21} & r_{22} & r_{23} & 0 \\ r_{31} & r_{32} & r_{33} & 0 \\ 0 & 0 & 0 & 1 \end{bmatrix} = \begin{bmatrix} c\psi c\theta & (c\psi s\theta s\phi - s\psi c\phi) & (c\psi s\theta c\phi + s\psi s\phi) & 0 \\ s\psi c\theta & (s\psi s\theta s\phi + c\psi c\phi) & (s\psi s\theta c\phi - c\psi s\phi) & 0 \\ -s\theta & c\theta s\phi & c\theta c\phi & 0 \\ 0 & 0 & 0 & 1 \end{bmatrix}$$

(2.59)

The next equation is:

$$[Rotz(\psi)]^{-1}[Trans(u, v, w)]^{-1}T_b^a = Roty(\theta)Rotx(\phi)$$

$$\begin{bmatrix} (r_{11}c\psi + r_{21}s\psi) & (r_{12}c\psi + r_{22}s\psi) & (r_{13}c\psi + r_{23}s\psi) & 0 \\ (-r_{11}s\psi + r_{21}c\psi) & (-r_{12}s\psi + r_{22}c\psi) & (-r_{13}s\psi + r_{23}c\psi) & 0 \\ r_{31} & r_{32} & r_{33} & 0 \\ 0 & 0 & 0 & 1 \end{bmatrix} = \begin{bmatrix} c\theta & s\theta s\phi & s\theta c\phi & 0 \\ 0 & c\phi & -s\phi & 0 \\ -s\theta & c\theta s\phi & c\theta c\phi & 0 \\ 0 & 0 & 0 & 1 \end{bmatrix}$$

(2.60)

From the (3,1) and (1,1) elements:

$$\theta = \text{atan2}(-r_{31}, r_{11}c\psi + r_{21}s\psi)$$

(2.61)

This implies that pitch can be determined from a vector known to be aligned with the body x axis expressed in the yawed intermediate frame. Based on the form of Equation 2.60, the arguments of the arctangent are the y and z components of the unit vector of the x axis of the yawed frame expressed in the coordinates of frame a. A good solution for ϕ is also available from the (2,2) and (2,3) elements. However, the solution will be delayed until the next equation so that it can be extracted from a column instead of a row. The next equation is:

$$[Roty(\theta)]^{-1}[Rotz(\psi)]^{-1}[Trans(u, v, w)]^{-1}T_b^a = Rotx(\phi)$$

$$
\begin{bmatrix}
c\theta(r_{11}c\psi + r_{21}s\psi) - r_{31}s\theta & c\theta(r_{12}c\psi + r_{22}s\psi) - r_{32}s\theta & c\theta(r_{13}c\psi + r_{23}s\psi) - r_{33}s\theta & 0 \\
(-r_{11}s\psi + r_{21}c\psi) & (-r_{12}s\psi + r_{22}c\psi) & (-r_{13}s\psi + r_{23}c\psi) & 0 \\
s\theta(r_{11}c\psi + r_{21}s\psi) + r_{31}c\theta & s\theta(r_{12}c\psi + r_{22}s\psi) + r_{32}c\theta & s\theta(r_{13}c\psi + r_{23}s\psi) + r_{33}c\theta & 0 \\
0 & 0 & 0 & 1
\end{bmatrix}
$$

$$
= \begin{bmatrix}
1 & 0 & 0 & 0 \\
0 & c\phi & -s\phi & 0 \\
0 & s\phi & c\phi & 0 \\
0 & 0 & 0 & 1
\end{bmatrix}
$$

(2.62)

From the (2,2) and (2,3) elements:

$$\phi = \text{atan2}(s\theta(r_{12}c\psi + r_{22}s\psi) + r_{32}c\theta, -r_{12}s\psi + r_{22}c\psi)$$

(2.63)

This implies that roll can be derived from a vector known to be aligned with the body y axis expressed in the pitched frame. Based on the form of Equation 2.62, the arguments of the arctangent are the x and z components of the unit vector of the y axis of the yawed frame expressed in the coordinates of frame a.

2.5.2 Angular Rates and Small Angles

2.5.2.1 Euler's Theorem and Axis Angle Representation

According to a theorem of Euler, all rigid body rotations in 3D can be expressed in terms of an axis of rotation and an angle of rotation about that axis. Regardless of what motions moved the body from a starting orientation to a final one, the same motion can always be achieved by a single rotation about a single vector. It is typical to represent this motion in terms of a magnitude and a unit vector, thus:

$$Rot(\phi, \theta, \psi) \leftrightarrow (\hat{\Theta}, \Theta)$$

2.5.2.2 Rotation Vector Representation of Orientation

It is useful to represent the above rotation as a *rotation vector* [15] – a unit vector whose magnitude is scaled to be equal to the magnitude of the desired rotation in radians. Let the vector:

$$\underline{\Theta} = \begin{bmatrix} \theta_x & \theta_y & \theta_z \end{bmatrix}^T$$

(2.64)

represent a rotation in space under this convention. Its magnitude $|\underline{\Theta}|$ is the magnitude of the rotation. Moreover, the unit vector:

$$\hat{\Theta} = \underline{\Theta}/|\underline{\Theta}| \tag{2.65}$$

is the axis of the rotation.

Note especially that the rotation vector is not a true vector. The component-wise addition of two rotation vectors, for instance, *is meaningless*. One special case exception to this rule is when adding a differential rotation. A differential rotation can be added vectorially to another rotation vector to produce the desired composite rotation.

2.5.2.3 Small Angles and Angular Velocity

Let a composite differential rotation around the three orthogonal axes be denoted by a very small rotation vector:

$$d\underline{\Theta} = \begin{bmatrix} d\theta_x & d\theta_y & d\theta_z \end{bmatrix}^T \tag{2.66}$$

The angular velocity $\underline{\omega}$ is defined as the vector about which a body is instantaneously rotating and its magnitude is the magnitude of the orientation rate. If the above rotation takes place over a time period of dt, the angular velocity vector is clearly:

$$\underline{\omega} = \frac{|d\underline{\Theta}|}{dt}\left(\frac{d\underline{\Theta}}{|d\underline{\Theta}|}\right) = \omega d\hat{\underline{\Theta}} = \omega\hat{\omega} \tag{2.67}$$

Thus, for a differentially small period of time, a rotating body rotates through an angle.

$$d\underline{\Theta} = \underline{\omega}dt = \begin{bmatrix} \omega_x & \omega_y & \omega_z \end{bmatrix}^T dt = \begin{bmatrix} d\theta_x & d\theta_y & d\theta_z \end{bmatrix}^T \tag{2.68}$$

Hence, the angular velocity is the time derivative of the rotation vector.

2.5.2.4 Small Angles and Skew Matrices

The rotation operator matrices given earlier can be rewritten to apply to small angles by replacing the trig functions with their first-order approximations. Thus:

$$\sin(\delta\theta) \approx \delta\theta \qquad\qquad \cos(\delta\theta) \approx 1$$

Our rotation operators then become:

$$Rotx(\delta\phi) = \begin{bmatrix} 1 & 0 & 0 & 0 \\ 0 & 1 & -\delta\phi & 0 \\ 0 & \delta\phi & 1 & 0 \\ 0 & 0 & 0 & 1 \end{bmatrix} \quad Roty(\delta\theta) = \begin{bmatrix} 1 & 0 & \delta\theta & 0 \\ 0 & 1 & 0 & 0 \\ -\delta\theta & 0 & 1 & 0 \\ 0 & 0 & 0 & 1 \end{bmatrix} \quad Rotz(\delta\psi) = \begin{bmatrix} 1 & -\delta\psi & 0 & 0 \\ \delta\psi & 1 & 0 & 0 \\ 0 & 0 & 1 & 0 \\ 0 & 0 & 0 & 1 \end{bmatrix}$$

It is traditional to use the symbol d to denote a differential (infinitesimal) quantity whereas δ is used to denote a small but finite quantity (usually an error or perturbation). Also Δ denotes a finite change that may or may not be an error. The d was switched to a δ above because the result will be used in error analysis later. Note that operations using the above transforms are linear in the associated angles. Now define the composite differential rotation:

$$\delta\underline{\Theta} = \begin{bmatrix} \delta\phi & \delta\theta & \delta\psi \end{bmatrix}^T \qquad (2.69)$$

It is easy to show that by multiplying the three above matrices and cancelling second-order terms that the composition reduces, to first order, to:

$$Rotx(\delta\phi)Roty(\delta\theta)Rotz(\delta\psi) = Rot(\delta\underline{\Theta}) = \begin{bmatrix} 1 & -\delta\psi & \delta\theta & 0 \\ \delta\psi & 1 & -\delta\phi & 0 \\ -\delta\theta & \delta\phi & 1 & 0 \\ 0 & 0 & 0 & 1 \end{bmatrix} \qquad (2.70)$$

In fact, the result does not depend on the order in which the rotations are applied. Although rotations through finite angles do not commute in 3D, infinitesimal rotations do.

The last result can be usefully rewritten in terms of the sum of an identity matrix and a skew symmetric matrix.

$$Rot(\delta\underline{\Theta}) = I + [\delta\underline{\Theta}]^\times \qquad (2.71)$$

Where we have defined:

$$Skew(\delta\underline{\Theta}) = [\delta\underline{\Theta}]^\times = \begin{bmatrix} 1 & -\delta\psi & \delta\theta & 0 \\ \delta\psi & 1 & -\delta\phi & 0 \\ -\delta\theta & \delta\phi & 1 & 0 \\ 0 & 0 & 0 & 1 \end{bmatrix} \qquad (2.72)$$

2.5.3 Angular Velocity and Orientation Rates in Euler Angle Form

The roll, pitch, and yaw angles are, as we have defined them, measured about moving axes. Therefore, they are a sequence of *Euler angles*, specifically, the z-y-x sequence of Euler angles. Note that the designation of the sequence depends on the convention for assigning the names of the linear axes. Later, it will be convenient to gather the Euler angles into a vector:

$$\underline{\Psi} = \begin{bmatrix} \phi & \theta & \psi \end{bmatrix}^T$$

Several other vectors of angles will be introduced for various purposes, and we have seen several already, but each will have a distinct name.

The Euler angle definition of vehicle attitude has the disadvantage that the roll, pitch, and yaw angles are *not* the integrals of the quantities that are actually indicated by strapped-down vehicle-mounted sensors such as gyros. The relationship between them is surprisingly complicated, so we will derive it below.

2.5.3.1 Euler Angle Rates from Angular Velocity

The relationship between the rates of the Euler angles and the angular velocity vector is nonlinear and the angles are measured neither about the body axes nor about the navigation frame axes.

The total angular velocity is the sum of three components, each measured about one of the intermediate axes in the chain of rotations that bring the navigation frame into coincidence with the body frame.

$$\underline{\omega}^b = \begin{bmatrix} \dot{\phi} \\ 0 \\ 0 \end{bmatrix} + rot(x, \phi) \begin{bmatrix} 0 \\ \dot{\theta} \\ 0 \end{bmatrix} + rot(x, \phi)rot(y, \theta) \begin{bmatrix} 0 \\ 0 \\ \dot{\psi} \end{bmatrix}$$

$$\underline{\omega}^b = \begin{bmatrix} \omega_x \\ \omega_y \\ \omega_z \end{bmatrix} = \begin{bmatrix} \dot{\phi} - s\theta\dot{\psi} \\ c\phi\dot{\theta} + s\phi c\theta\dot{\psi} \\ -s\phi\dot{\theta} + c\phi c\theta\dot{\psi} \end{bmatrix} = \begin{bmatrix} 1 & 0 & -s\theta \\ 0 & c\phi & s\phi c\theta \\ 0 & -s\phi & c\phi c\theta \end{bmatrix} \begin{bmatrix} \dot{\phi} \\ \dot{\theta} \\ \dot{\psi} \end{bmatrix}$$

(2.73)

This result gives the vehicle angular velocity expressed in the body frame in terms of the Euler angle rates. Notice that when the vehicle is level ($\phi = \theta = 0$), the x and y components of the output due to a body z rotation are zero and the z component of the output is just the yaw rate as expected. This relationship is also very useful in its inverted form. One can verify by substitution that $\omega_z c\phi + \omega_y s\phi = c\theta\dot{\psi}$, and $\omega_y c\phi - \omega_z s\phi = \dot{\theta}$. Hence, we must have:

$$\begin{bmatrix} \dot{\phi} \\ \dot{\theta} \\ \dot{\psi} \end{bmatrix} = \begin{bmatrix} \omega_x + \omega_y s\phi t\theta + \omega_z c\phi t\theta \\ \omega_y c\phi - \omega_z s\phi \\ \omega_y \frac{s\phi}{c\theta} + \omega_z \frac{c\phi}{c\theta} \end{bmatrix} = \begin{bmatrix} 1 & s\phi t\theta & c\phi t\theta \\ 0 & c\phi & -s\phi \\ 0 & \frac{s\phi}{c\theta} & \frac{c\phi}{c\theta} \end{bmatrix} \begin{bmatrix} \omega_x \\ \omega_y \\ \omega_z \end{bmatrix}$$

(2.74)

Box 2.5: Angular Velocity Transformations for zyx Euler Angles

The transformations between the angular velocity in the body frame and the Euler angle rates for zyx Euler angles in both directions are:

$$\underline{\omega}^b = \begin{bmatrix} \omega_x \\ \omega_y \\ \omega_z \end{bmatrix}^b = \begin{bmatrix} 1 & 0 & -s\theta \\ 0 & c\phi & s\phi c\theta \\ 0 & -s\phi & c\phi c\theta \end{bmatrix} \begin{bmatrix} \dot{\phi} \\ \dot{\theta} \\ \dot{\psi} \end{bmatrix} \qquad \begin{bmatrix} \dot{\phi} \\ \dot{\theta} \\ \dot{\psi} \end{bmatrix} = \begin{bmatrix} 1 & s\phi t\theta & c\phi t\theta \\ 0 & c\phi & -s\phi \\ 0 & \frac{s\phi}{c\theta} & \frac{c\phi}{c\theta} \end{bmatrix} \begin{bmatrix} \omega_x \\ \omega_y \\ \omega_z \end{bmatrix}^b$$

These results will be used extensively throughout the text.

2.5.4 Angular Velocity and Orientation Rates in Angle-Axis Form

Angular velocity is most easily defined in terms of the angle-axis representation of 3D rotations.

2.5.4.1 Skew Matrices and Angular Velocity

Recall the skew symmetric matrix formed from a small 3D rotation:

$$Skew(d\underline{\Theta}) = [d\underline{\Theta}]^{\times} = \begin{bmatrix} 0 & -d\theta_z & d\theta_y \\ d\theta_z & 0 & -d\theta_x \\ -d\theta_y & d\theta_x & 0 \end{bmatrix}$$

Hence, the angular velocity also has a skew symmetric matrix representation:

$$\Omega = Skew\left(\frac{d\underline{\Theta}}{dt}\right) = [\underline{\omega}]^{\times} = \begin{bmatrix} 0 & -\omega_z & \omega_y \\ \omega_z & 0 & -\omega_x \\ -\omega_y & \omega_x & 0 \end{bmatrix}$$

2.5.4.2 Time Derivative of a Rotation Matrix

Suppose a rotation matrix expresses the relative orientation of two frames that changes over time. At time instant k, we denote the rotation matrix as R_k^n and we seek an expression for the time rate of change of this matrix. Let the change in the matrix from time instant k to $k+1$ be expressed as a small perturbation as shown in Figure 2.26.

Figure 2.26 Perturbation of a Rotation Matrix. A rotation matrix relating two frames changes by a small amount over a small time period.

Based on Equation 2.71, we can write the composition matrix at time $k+1$ in terms of a small perturbation:

$$R_{k+1}^n = R_k^n R_{k+1}^k = R_k^n[I + [\delta\underline{\Theta}]^{\times}]$$

Now the time derivative of R_k^n is:

$$\dot{R}_k^n = \lim_{\delta t \to 0} \frac{\delta R_k^n}{\delta t} = \lim_{\delta t \to 0} \frac{[R_k^n(t + \delta t) - R_k^n(t)]}{\delta t}$$

Using the immediately preceding result:

$$\dot{R}_k^n = \lim_{\delta t \to 0} \frac{[R_k^n[I + [\delta\underline{\Theta}]^{\times}] - R_k^n]}{\delta t} = \lim_{\delta t \to 0} \frac{R_k^n[\delta\underline{\Theta}]^{\times}}{\delta t} = R_k^n \lim_{\delta t \to 0} \frac{[\delta\underline{\Theta}]^{\times}}{\delta t}$$

We were able to take R_k^n outside the limit because it means the rotation matrix at time step k, rather than the matrix-valued function of k. Now the limit on the right side is just the skew matrix of the angular velocity expressed in the coordinates of frame k because each new perturbation is defined in a moving axis sense with respect to the immediately preceding one. Hence, we can conclude that the time rate of change of a rotation matrix is:

$$\dot{R}_k^n = R_k^n \frac{d[\Theta]^\times}{dt} = R_k^n \Omega_k \tag{2.75}$$

This result holds provided the components of Ω_k are expressed in the coordinates of the moving frame k:

$$\Omega^k = Skew(^k\underline{\omega}_k^n) = \begin{bmatrix} 0 & -\omega_z & \omega_y \\ \omega_z & 0 & -\omega_x \\ -\omega_y & \omega_x & 0 \end{bmatrix} \tag{2.76}$$

2.5.4.3 Direction Cosines from Angular Velocity

It is possible to use the previous result to formulate an extremely useful matrix integral that produces the rotation matrix representation of attitude directly from the angular velocity. Let us assume that the Ω^k matrix is constant over a very small time step. Then, a clever method [14] provides an exact solution for the rotation matrix corresponding to the perturbation $[d\underline{\Theta}]^\times = \Omega^k dt$. Based on Equation 2.75:

$$R_{k+1}^n = R_k^n R_{k+1}^k = R_k^n \int_{t_k}^{t_{k+1}} \Omega^k d\tau = R_k^n \exp\left\{[d\underline{\Theta}]^\times\right\} \tag{2.77}$$

Where we have used:

$$\int_0^t A d\tau = \exp\{At\} \tag{2.78}$$

where A is a constant matrix and $\exp\{At\}$ is the matrix exponential. Conveniently, the skew matrix has a closed form matrix exponential:

$$\exp\left\{\underline{v}^\times\right\} = I + f_1(v)[\underline{v}]^\times + f_2(v)([\underline{v}]^\times)^2 \tag{2.79}$$

Where:

$$f_1(v) = \frac{\sin v}{v} \qquad f_2(v) = \frac{(1 - \cos v)}{v^2} \tag{2.80}$$

Hence the differential angle vector associated with the angular velocity is given by:

$$R_{k+1}^k = I + f_1(d\Theta)[d\underline{\Theta}]^\times + f_2(d\Theta)([d\underline{\Theta}]^\times)^2 \tag{2.81}$$

where dt is the time step, $d\Theta = |d\underline{\Theta}|$, and $d\underline{\Theta} = \underline{\omega} dt$.

2.5.5 References and Further Reading

Jordan's exponential of the skew matrix is presented in his NASA report. The other two references discuss representations of 3D attitude.

[14] J. W. Jordan, An Accurate Strapdown Direction Cosine Algorithm, NASA TN-D-5384, Sept. 1969.

[15] M. D. Shuster, A Survey of Attitude Representations, *Journal of the Astronautical Sciences,* Vol. 41, No. 4, pp. 439–517, 1993.

[16] J. R. Wertz, ed., *Spacecraft Attitude Determination and Control,* Dordrecht, Holland, D. Riedel, 1978.

2.5.6 Exercises

2.5.6.1 Converting Euler Angle Conventions

Suppose that a pose box produces roll ϕ, pitch θ and yaw ψ according to the *zyx* Euler angle sequence. This means the composite rotation matrix to convert coordinates from the body frame to the world frame is given by:

$$
R_b^w = \begin{bmatrix} c\psi & -s\psi & 0 \\ s\psi & c\psi & 0 \\ 0 & 0 & 1 \end{bmatrix} \begin{bmatrix} c\theta & 0 & s\theta \\ 0 & 1 & 0 \\ -s\theta & 0 & c\theta \end{bmatrix} \begin{bmatrix} 1 & 0 & 0 \\ 0 & c\phi & -s\phi \\ 0 & s\phi & c\phi \end{bmatrix}
$$

$$
R_b^w = \begin{bmatrix} c\psi c\theta & (c\psi s\theta s\phi - s\psi c\phi) & (c\psi s\theta c\phi + s\psi s\phi) \\ s\psi c\theta & (s\psi s\theta s\phi + c\psi c\phi) & (s\psi s\theta c\phi - c\psi s\phi) \\ -s\theta & c\theta s\phi & c\theta c\phi \end{bmatrix}
$$

The box is mounted incorrectly on a vehicle with the *y* axis forward and the *x* axis to the right. There is no time to fix it. Using the Euler angle outputs of the box in this configuration, compute the Euler angle outputs that would be generated if it were mounted correctly with the *x* axis forward and *y* pointing to the left. Hint: The RPY matrix relating any two frames is unique regardless of the Euler angle conventions used.

2.5.6.2 Inverse Pose Kinematics Near Singularity

Equation 2.58 cannot be used at or near 90° of pitch. At this point pitch and yaw become synonymous. Derive a special inverse kinematics solution for this case.

2.5.6.3 Exponential of the Skew Matrix

Derive Equation 2.79 and Equation 2.80. Compute $\exp([\underline{v}]^\times)$ by computing powers of $[\underline{v}]^\times$ and noticing the pattern.

2.6 Kinematic Models of Sensors

2.6.1 Kinematics of Video Cameras

Many sensors used on robot vehicles are of the imaging variety. For such sensors, the process of image formation often must be modelled. Typically, the associated transformations are **not linear**, and hence they cannot all be modelled by homogeneous transforms. This section provides the homogeneous transforms and nonlinear equations necessary for modelling such sensors.

2.6.1.1 Perspective Projection

In the case of passive imaging systems, a system of lenses forms an image on an array of sensitive elements called a CCD or *focal plane array*. These systems include traditional video cameras and infrared cameras. The transformation from the sensor frame to the image plane row and column coordinates is the well known perspective projection studied by artists of the Renaissance.

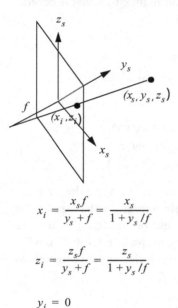

$$x_i = \frac{x_s f}{y_s + f} = \frac{x_s}{1 + y_s / f}$$

$$z_i = \frac{z_s f}{y_s + f} = \frac{z_s}{1 + y_s / f}$$

$$y_i = 0$$

Figure 2.27 Pinhole Camera Model. Its easy to derive the relationship between scene coordinates and image coordinates using similar triangles.

This type of transform is unique in two ways. First, it reduces the dimension of the input vector by one and hence, it discards information. Second, it requires a post normalization step where the output is divided by the scale factor in order to reestablish a unity scale factor.

Although even casual efforts in computer vision will model various imperfections in imaging geometry, we will use the simplest model available. The most basic model of a camera is the pinhole camera model (Figure 2.27), where the focal length of the lens is denoted by f. This ideal camera can be modelled with a homogeneous transform [18]. The transformation can be derived by similar triangles as shown in the figure.

This relationship can then be expressed as a matrix operator relating *scene coordinates* to *image coordinates*.

$$r_i = P^i_s r_s$$

$$
\begin{bmatrix} x_i \\ y_i \\ z_i \\ w_i \end{bmatrix}
=
\begin{bmatrix} 1 & 0 & 0 & 0 \\ 0 & 0 & 0 & 0 \\ 0 & 0 & 1 & 0 \\ 0 & \dfrac{1}{f} & 0 & 1 \end{bmatrix}
\begin{bmatrix} x_s \\ y_s \\ z_s \\ 1 \end{bmatrix}
\qquad
P^i_s =
\begin{bmatrix} 1 & 0 & 0 & 0 \\ 0 & 0 & 0 & 0 \\ 0 & 0 & 1 & 0 \\ 0 & \dfrac{1}{f} & 0 & 1 \end{bmatrix}
\tag{2.82}
$$

Note in particular that all projections into lower dimensions are not invertible. Here, the second row is all zeros, so the matrix is singular. This, of course, is the ultimate source of the difficulty of measuring scene geometry with a single camera. For this reason, this transform is identified by the special capital letter P.

2.6.2 Kinematics of Laser Rangefinders

Kinematics of reflecting a laser beam from a mirror are central to the operation of the many laser rangefinders that scan the laser in two degrees of freedom. There are at least two ways to conceptualize the transformations involved in modelling them:

- In terms of reflections of the laser beam off of mirrors.
- A kind of "mechanism" forward kinematics where we consider the operations on the laser beam to be the mechanism.

It is important, for such sensors, to be aware of and account for *mirror gain*. This is the amount by which the rate of rotation of the laser beam is different from the rate of rotation of the mirror. In the azimuth scanner discussed later in this chapter, for example, the laser beam rotates at twice the rate of the mirror.

2.6.2.1 The Reflection Operator

This approach can be used when the translations of the laser beam can be ignored.
From Snell's law for reflection of a ray:

- The incident ray, the normal to the surface, and the reflected ray, all lie in the same plane.
- The angle of incidence equals the angle of reflection.

From these two rules, a very useful matrix operator can be formulated to reflect a vector off of any surface, given the unit normal to the surface [17]. Consider a vector $\hat{v}_i$, not necessarily a unit vector that impinges on a reflecting surface at a point where the unit normal to the surface is $\hat{n}$. Unless they are parallel, the incident and normal vector define a plane, which will be called the *reflection plane*.

Drawing both vectors in this plane, it is clear that Snell's law (Figure 2.28) can be written in many forms:

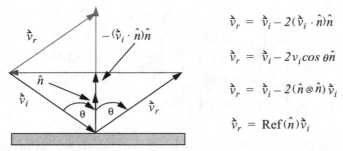

$$\vec{v}_r = \vec{v}_i - 2(\vec{v}_i \cdot \hat{n})\hat{n}$$

$$\vec{v}_r = \vec{v}_i - 2v_i \cos\theta \hat{n}$$

$$\vec{v}_r = \vec{v}_i - 2(\hat{n} \otimes \hat{n})\vec{v}_i$$

$$\vec{v}_r = \text{Ref}(\hat{n})\vec{v}_i$$

Figure 2.28 Snell's Law of Reflection. One way to express the reflection of a vector is to subtract twice its projection onto the surface normal.

This gives us the expression for the matrix reflection operator:

$$\text{Ref}(\hat{n}) = I - 2(\hat{n} \otimes \hat{n}) = \begin{bmatrix} 1 - 2n_x n_x & -2n_x n_y & -2n_x n_z \\ -2n_y n_x & 1 - 2n_y n_y & -2n_y n_z \\ -2n_z n_x & -2n_z n_y & 1 - 2n_z n_z \end{bmatrix} \tag{2.83}$$

Such a matrix implements the famous *Householder transform*. The outer product $(x \otimes y)$ of the normal with itself was used in forming the matrix equivalent. The result is expressed in the same coordinates in which both the normal and the incident ray were expressed. Notice that a reflection is equivalent to a rotation of twice the angle of incidence about the normal to the reflection plane (which is not the normal to the surface). A similar matrix refraction operator can be defined.

In order to model rangefinders, we can use this in the following way. The laser beam will be modelled by a unit vector because the length of the beam is immaterial. The unit vector is operated upon by the reflection operator – one reflection for each mirror – in the sequence in which they are encountered. The ultimate result of all reflections will be expressed in the original coordinate system.

Box 2.6: Kinematic Modelling of Laser Rangefinders

Laser rangefinders can be modelled kinematically as follows:

- Form a 'sensor' coordinate system fixed with respect to the sensor mounting plate and conveniently oriented.
- Write an expression for a unit vector aligned with the beam direction as it leaves the laser diode (the laser generation device).
- Write expression in the sensor frame for the unit normals to the mirrors as functions of the mirror articulation angles.
- Reflect the beam off the mirrors in the order in which they are encountered.
- The result is an expression for the orientation of the beam expressed in terms of the mirror articulation angles.

The results of such an analysis give the orientation of the laser beam as a function of the actuated mirror angles, but it says nothing about where the beam is positioned in space. The precise position of the beam is not difficult to calculate and it is important in the sizing of mirrors. From the point of view of computing kinematics, however, beam position can often be ignored.

2.6.2.2 Example: Kinematics of the Azimuth Scanner

The *azimuth scanner* is a generic name for a class of laser rangefinders with equivalent kinematics (Figure 2.29). In this scanner, the laser beam undergoes the azimuth rotation/reflection first and the elevation rotation/reflection second. One design employs a "polygonal" azimuth mirror and a flat "nodding" elevation mirror. The mirrors move as shown in the figure:

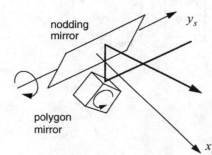

Figure 2.29 **Kinematics of the Azimuth Scanner.** In this kinematic class of devices the transmit beam is rotated in azimuth before elevation.

2.6.2.2.1 Forward Kinematics. A coordinate system called the 's' system is fixed to the sensor with x pointing out the front of the sensor and y pointing out the left side. The beam enters along the negative y_s axis. It reflects off the polygonal mirror which rotates about the x_s axis. It then reflects off the nodding mirror, to leave the housing somewhat aligned with the x_s axis.

First, the beam is reflected from the laser diode about the normal to the polygonal mirror. Computation of the output of the polygonal mirror can be done by inspection – noting that the beam rotates by twice the angle of the mirror because it is a reflection operation. The z-y plane contains both the incident and normal vectors. The datum position of the mirror should correspond to a perfectly vertical beam, so the datum for the mirror rotation angle is chosen appropriately. Consider an input beam $\hat{v}_m$ along the x_s axis and reflect it about the mirror by inspection:

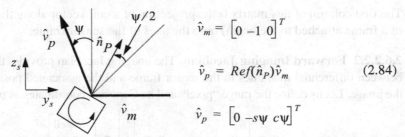

$$\hat{v}_m = \begin{bmatrix} 0 & -1 & 0 \end{bmatrix}^T$$

$$\hat{v}_p = Ref(\hat{n}_P)\hat{v}_m \qquad (2.84)$$

$$\hat{v}_p = \begin{bmatrix} 0 & -s\psi & c\psi \end{bmatrix}^T$$

Notice that this vector is contained within the $y_s - z_s$ plane above. Now this result must be reflected about the nodding mirror. The particular axis of rotation which is equivalent to a reflection is normal to both $\hat{v}_p$ and $\hat{n}_n$. Because $\hat{v}_p$ is not always in the $x_s - z_s$ plane, the y_s axis is not always the axis of rotation.

$$\hat{v}_p = \begin{bmatrix} 0 & -s\psi & c\psi \end{bmatrix}^T$$

$$put \quad \frac{\alpha}{2} = \frac{\pi}{4} - \frac{\theta}{2}$$

$$\hat{n}_n = \begin{bmatrix} s\dfrac{\alpha}{2} & 0 & -c\dfrac{\alpha}{2} \end{bmatrix}^T$$

$$\hat{v}_n = Ref(\hat{n}_n)\hat{v}_p = \hat{v}_p - 2(\hat{v}_p \cdot \hat{n}_n)\hat{n}_n \tag{2.85}$$

$$\hat{v}_n = \begin{bmatrix} 0 \\ -s\psi \\ c\psi \end{bmatrix} + 2c\psi c\frac{\alpha}{2} \begin{bmatrix} s\dfrac{\alpha}{2} \\ 0 \\ -c\dfrac{\alpha}{2} \end{bmatrix} = \begin{bmatrix} 2c\psi c\dfrac{\alpha}{2}\left(s\dfrac{\alpha}{2}\right) \\ -s\psi \\ c\psi - 2c\psi c\dfrac{\alpha}{2}\left(c\dfrac{\alpha}{2}\right) \end{bmatrix} = \begin{bmatrix} c\psi s\alpha \\ -s\psi \\ -c\psi c\alpha \end{bmatrix} = \begin{bmatrix} c\psi s\left(\dfrac{\pi}{2} - \theta\right) \\ -s\psi \\ -c\psi c\left(\dfrac{\pi}{2} - \theta\right) \end{bmatrix}$$

$$\hat{v}_n = \begin{bmatrix} [c\psi c\theta] & -[s\psi] & -[c\psi s\theta] \end{bmatrix}^T$$

This result is summarized in Equation 2.86:

$$\underline{v}_s = \begin{bmatrix} x_s \\ y_s \\ z_s \end{bmatrix} = \begin{bmatrix} Rc\psi c\theta \\ -Rs\psi \\ -Rc\psi s\theta \end{bmatrix} \tag{2.86}$$

Notice that the moving axis operations that take the x_s into coincidence with the beam are a rotation around the y_s axis of θ followed by a rotation around the **new** z_s axis by $-\psi$:

$$R_{beam}^{sensor} = Roty(\theta)Rotz(-\psi) = \begin{bmatrix} c\theta c\psi & s\psi c\theta & s\theta \\ -s\psi & c\psi & 0 \\ -s\theta c\psi & -s\theta s\psi & c\theta \end{bmatrix}$$

The first column of this matrix is the projection of a unit vector along the beam (x axis of a frame attached to the beam) onto the axes of the sensor frame.

2.6.2.2.2 Forward Imaging Jacobian. The imaging Jacobian provides the relationship between differential quantities in the sensor frame and the associated position change in the image. Let us define the range "pixel" and its Cartesian coordinates as follows

$$\underline{v}_i = \begin{bmatrix} R \\ \psi \\ \theta \end{bmatrix} \qquad \underline{v}_s = \begin{bmatrix} x_s \\ y_s \\ z_s \end{bmatrix} = \begin{bmatrix} Rc\psi c\theta \\ -Rs\psi \\ -Rc\psi s\theta \end{bmatrix}$$

Then, the Jacobian is:

$$J_i^s = \frac{\partial \bar{v}^s}{\partial \bar{v}^i} = \begin{bmatrix} \dfrac{\partial x_s}{\partial R} & \dfrac{\partial x_s}{\partial \psi} & \dfrac{\partial x_s}{\partial \theta} \\[2mm] \dfrac{\partial y_s}{\partial R} & \dfrac{\partial y_s}{\partial \psi} & \dfrac{\partial y_s}{\partial \theta} \\[2mm] \dfrac{\partial z_s}{\partial R} & \dfrac{\partial z_s}{\partial \psi} & \dfrac{\partial z_s}{\partial \theta} \end{bmatrix} = \begin{bmatrix} c\psi c\theta & -Rs\psi c\theta & -Rc\psi s\theta \\ -s\psi & -Rc\psi & 0 \\ -c\psi s\theta & Rs\psi s\theta & -Rc\psi c\theta \end{bmatrix} \tag{2.87}$$

2.6.2.2.3 Inverse Kinematics. The forward transform is easily inverted.

$$\begin{bmatrix} R \\ \psi \\ \theta \end{bmatrix} = \begin{bmatrix} \sqrt{x_s^2 + y_s^2 + z_s^2} \\[2mm] \mathrm{atan}\left(-y_s / \sqrt{x_s^2 + z_s^2}\right) \\[2mm] \mathrm{atan}\left(-z_s / x_s\right) \end{bmatrix} = h(x_s, y_s, z_s) \tag{2.88}$$

2.6.2.2.4 Inverse Imaging Jacobian. The imaging Jacobian provides the relationship between differential quantities in the sensor frame and the associated position change in the image. The Jacobian is:

$$v_i = \begin{bmatrix} R \\ \psi \\ \theta \end{bmatrix} = \begin{bmatrix} \sqrt{x_s^2 + y_s^2 + z_s^2} \\[2mm] \mathrm{atan}\left(-y_s / \sqrt{x_s^2 + z_s^2}\right) \\[2mm] \mathrm{atan}\left(-z_s / x_s\right) \end{bmatrix} \qquad v_s = \begin{bmatrix} x_s \\ y_s \\ z_s \end{bmatrix}$$

$$J_s^i = \frac{\partial \bar{v}^i}{\partial \bar{v}^s} = \begin{bmatrix} \dfrac{\partial R}{\partial x_s} & \dfrac{\partial R}{\partial y_s} & \dfrac{\partial R}{\partial z_s} \\[2mm] \dfrac{\partial \psi}{\partial x_s} & \dfrac{\partial \psi}{\partial y_s} & \dfrac{\partial \psi}{\partial z_s} \\[2mm] \dfrac{\partial \theta}{\partial x_s} & \dfrac{\partial \theta}{\partial y_s} & \dfrac{\partial \theta}{\partial z_s} \end{bmatrix} = \begin{bmatrix} \dfrac{x_s}{R} & \dfrac{y_s}{R} & \dfrac{z_s}{R} \\[3mm] \dfrac{x_s}{R^2}\left(\dfrac{y_s}{\sqrt{x_s^2 + z_s^2}}\right) & \dfrac{-\sqrt{x_s^2 + z_s^2}}{R^2} & \dfrac{z_s}{R^2}\left(\dfrac{y_s}{\sqrt{x_s^2 + z_s^2}}\right) \\[3mm] \dfrac{z_s}{x_s^2 + z_s^2} & 0 & \dfrac{-x_s}{x_s^2 + z_s^2} \end{bmatrix}$$

2.6.2.2.5 Analytic Range Image of Flat Terrain. Given the basic kinematic transform, many analyses can be performed. The first is to compute an analytic expression for the range image of a perfectly flat piece of terrain (Figure 2.30).

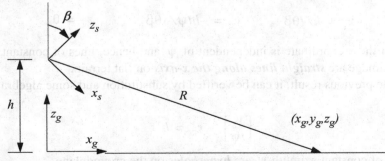

Figure 2.30 Geometry for Determining the Range Image of Flat Terrain. The image produced by an azimuth scanner tilted forward at a known height can be computed in closed form.

Let the sensor fixed "*s*" coordinate system be mounted at a height h and tilted forward by a tilt angle of β. Then, the transform from sensor coordinates to global coordinates is:

$$x_g = x_s c\beta + z_s s\beta$$
$$y_g = y_s$$
$$z_g = -x_s s\beta + z_s c\beta + h$$

If the kinematics are substituted into this, the transform from the polar sensor coordinates to global coordinates is obtained:

$$x_g = (Rc\psi c\theta)c\beta + (-Rc\psi s\theta)s\beta = Rc\theta\beta c\psi$$
$$y_g = -Rs\psi$$
$$z_g = (-Rc\psi c\theta)s\beta - Rc\psi s\theta c\beta + h = h - Rs\theta\beta c\psi$$

Now by setting $z_g = 0$ and solving for R, the expression for R as a function of the beam angles ψ and θ for flat terrain is obtained. This is an analytic expression for the range image of flat terrain under the azimuth transform.

$$R = h/(c\psi s\theta\beta) \tag{2.89}$$

Notice that when R is large $s\theta\beta = h/R$. As a check on the range image formula, the resulting range image is shown in Figure 2.31 for $h = 2.5$, $\beta = 16.5°$, a horizontal field of view of 140°, a vertical field of view of 30°, and a range pixel width of 5 mrads in both directions. It has 490 columns and 105 rows. The intensity edges correspond to contours of constant range of 20 meters, 40 meters, 60 meters, etc.

Figure 2.31 Image of Flat Terrain for the Azimuth Scanner. This image is for a height of 2.5 and a tilt of 16.5°. Image intensity is proportional to range. To aid the visualization, wraparound edges occur at equally spaced ranges.

The curvature of the contours of range is intrinsic to the sensor kinematics and is independent of the sensor tilt. Substituting this range back into the coordinate transform, the coordinates where each ray intersects the groundplane are:

$$x_g = h/t\theta\beta \qquad y_g = -ht\psi/s\theta\beta \qquad z_g = 0 \tag{2.90}$$

Notice that the x coordinate is independent of ψ and hence, lines of constant elevation in the image are **straight lines along the x-axis** on flat terrain.

From the previous result, it can be verified by substitution and some algebra that:

$$\left[\frac{y_g}{t\psi}\right]^2 - x_g^2 = h^2 \tag{2.91}$$

Thus lines of constant azimuth ψ are **hyperbolas** on the groundplane.

2.6.2.2.6 Resolution. The Jacobian of the groundplane transform has many uses. Most important of all, it provides a measure of sensor resolution on the ground plane. Differentiating the previous result:

$$\begin{bmatrix} dx_g \\ dy_g \end{bmatrix} = \begin{bmatrix} 0 & \dfrac{-h}{(s\theta\beta)^2} \\ \dfrac{-h(\sec\psi)^2}{s\theta\beta} & \dfrac{ht\psi c\theta\beta}{(s\theta\beta)^2} \end{bmatrix} \times \begin{bmatrix} d\psi \\ d\theta \end{bmatrix} \tag{2.92}$$

The determinant of the Jacobian relates differential areas:

$$dx_g dy_g = \left[\frac{(h\sec\psi)^2}{(s\theta\beta)^3} \right] d\psi d\theta \tag{2.93}$$

Notice that when R is large and $\psi = 0$, the Jacobian norm is approximately:

$$\left[\frac{(h\sec\psi)^2}{(s\theta\beta)^3} \right] \approx h^2 / \left(\frac{h}{R}\right)^3 = R^2 / \left(\frac{h}{R}\right) \tag{2.94}$$

Thus, the pixel density on the ground is proportional to the cube of the range.

2.6.2.2.7 Azimuth Scanning Pattern. The scanning pattern is shown in Figure 2.32 with a 10 m grid superimposed for reference purposes. Only every fifth pixel is shown in azimuth to avoid clutter.

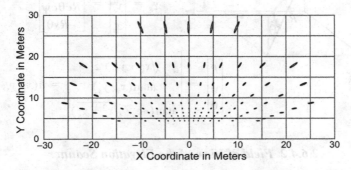

Figure 2.32 Azimuth Scanning Pattern. Pixels both spread and increase in size rapidly with distance from the scanner. The arrangements of the ellipses suggests the hyperbolas (opening to the sides) derived in the text.

2.6.3 References and Further Reading

Bass covers radiometry including the reflection operator whereas Hausner presents geometry from a linear algebra perspective. Hartley is one book that presents the pinhole camera model.

[17] Michael Bass, Virendra N. Mahajan, Eric Van Stryland, *Handbook of Optics: Design, Fabrication, and Testing; Sources and Detectors; Radiometry and Photometry*, McGraw-Hill, 2009.

[18] Richard Hartley and Andrew Zisserman, *Multiple View Geometry in Computer Vision*, Cambridge University Press, 2003.

[19] Melvin Hausner, *A Vector Space Approach to Geometry*, Dover, 1998.

2.6.4 Exercises

2.6.4.1 Kinematics of the Elevation Scanner

The *elevation scanner* is the kinematic dual of the azimuth scanner. For this canonical configuration, the roles of the mirrors are reversed, and the order in which the beam encounters them is reversed as shown below.

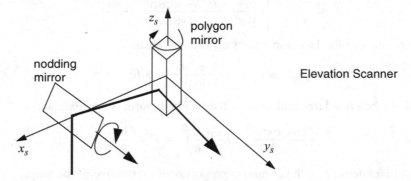

Show that the forward and inverse kinematics are given by:

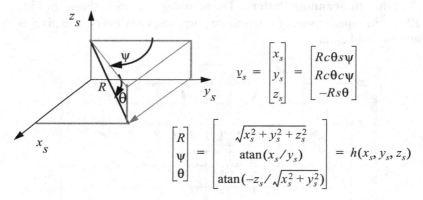

$$\underline{v}_s = \begin{bmatrix} x_s \\ y_s \\ z_s \end{bmatrix} = \begin{bmatrix} Rc\theta s\psi \\ Rc\theta c\psi \\ -Rs\theta \end{bmatrix}$$

$$\begin{bmatrix} R \\ \psi \\ \theta \end{bmatrix} = \begin{bmatrix} \sqrt{x_s^2 + y_s^2 + z_s^2} \\ \mathrm{atan}(x_s/y_s) \\ \mathrm{atan}(-z_s/\sqrt{x_s^2 + y_s^2}) \end{bmatrix} = h(x_s, y_s, z_s)$$

2.6.4.2 Field of View of the Elevation Scanner

Compute the expression for the range image of flat terrain for the elevation scanner and show that lines of constant elevation in the image are arcs on the ground whereas lines of constant azimuth are radial lines on the ground.

2.7 Transform Graphs & Pose Networks

2.7.1 Transforms as Relationships

Recall that an orthogonal homogenous transform encodes a rigid spatial relationship between two frames – which can be visualized as two rigid bodies in the correct relative configuration. We can think of the transform as encoding the generic property. For example, given our usual conventions for axes and angles, the 2D transform:

$$T = \begin{bmatrix} c\dfrac{\pi}{3} & -s\dfrac{\pi}{3} & 3 \\[2mm] s\dfrac{\pi}{3} & c\dfrac{\pi}{3} & 7 \\[2mm] 0 & 0 & 1 \end{bmatrix}$$

encodes the property of "being positioned 3 units to the right, 7 units above, and rotated 60° with respect to something."

We can also instantiate (create a specific instance of) this generic relationship, by supplying two objects that have this property. Let's imagine a vision system fixed with respect to a robot hand that can compute where the box is relative to the hand (Figure 2.33).

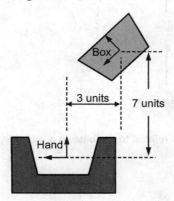

Figure 2.33 Instance of a Geometric Relationship. The box is 7 units above, 3 units to the right, and rotated 60° with respect to the hand.

We symbolize an instantiated relationship like this with the notation T^{hand}_{box}. Contrast that with the generic notation for the uninstantiated relationship:

$$Rot\left(\frac{\pi}{3}\right)Trans(3, 7)$$

The matrices are the same but the first conveys the objects involved and the second tells us something about the relationship itself. We don't normally need both at the same time. Note that the property is directional. The box has this property with respect to the hand. The hand has a different (but related) relationship with respect to the object. T^{box}_{hand} has different numbers in it.

It is useful to represent this relationship in a graph structure like so [23].

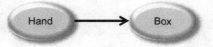

The words *graph* and *network* are synonymous. The direction of the arrow is the author's preference (because the pose is interpreted in this direction) but consistency is all that matters. This is read to mean that the pose of the box is known with respect to the hand.

Now, by measuring joint angles and performing forward kinematics, we may know where the hand is with respect to the robot base (Figure 2.34). The base may be fixed to a mobile robot, and so on.

Imagine that the frames Base, Hand, and Object are connected by rigid links when their relative pose is known. Intuitively, ***everything is known with respect to everything else***. In particular, the transform relating the Box to the Base (dotted arc in the figure) is computable as follows:

$$T^{base}_{box} = T^{base}_{hand} T^{hand}_{box}$$

despite the fact there is no such arc in the original network.

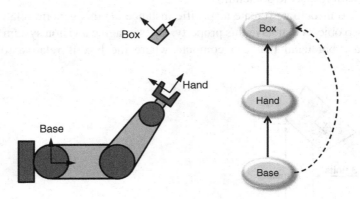

Figure 2.34 Compound Geometric Relationships. The hand is related to the base in a manner similar to the relationship between the box and the hand.

2.7.1.1 Topology

Topology is the study of the properties of shapes that are invariant to deformations. Here, it's about the connectedness of things. Connectedness is transitive. If Hand is connected to Base and Box is connected to Hand, then Box is connected to Base. A path exists in networks between connected nodes. A network is *fully connected* when there is a path between every pair of nodes.

2.7.1.2 Nonlinear Graphs

In more complicated cases, the network of relationships is more tree-like (Figure 2.35). Here, the World is the root node. In order to implement a visual tracking algorithm, it would be desirable to predict the pose of the Corner with respect to the

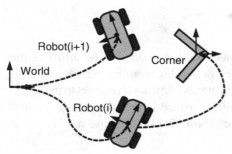

Figure 2.35 Transform Tree. This transform graph is a tree. This complicated yet acyclic configuration occurs commonly.

Robot at time step $i + 1$. For such problems, it is sometimes useful to imagine that a robot "stamps" a set of axes on the floor at certain times. Then you can talk about where it "was" in addition to where it is.

2.7.1.3 Poses and Transforms

The 3D RPY homogeneous transform has six degrees of freedom:

$$T_b^a = \begin{bmatrix} c\psi c\theta & (c\psi s\theta s\phi - s\psi c\phi) & (c\psi s\theta s\phi + s\psi s\phi) & u \\ s\psi c\theta & (s\psi s\theta s\phi + c\psi c\phi) & (s\psi s\theta s\phi - c\psi s\phi) & v \\ -s\theta & c\theta s\phi & c\theta c\phi & w \\ 0 & 0 & 0 & 1 \end{bmatrix}$$

Its common to collect them into a pose "vector" thus:

$$\rho_b^a = \begin{bmatrix} u & v & w & \phi & \theta & \psi \end{bmatrix}$$

These are two different representations of the same underlying concept.

Although the transform T_b^a for a given pose is uniquely defined, the pose for a given transform is not unique – in two ways. First, there are twelve possible Euler angle conventions because there are three ways to choose the first rotation, two for the second, and the choice of fixed or moving axis semantics. Second, for any convention, there are redundant solutions for the same RPY transform.

Another complexity is the fact that poses themselves are not vectors in the linear algebra sense. It never makes sense to add two sets of finite Euler angles but direct addition of finite and infinitesimal Euler angles is legitimate. The closest thing, for 3D rotations, to the way that traditional vectors add is the multiplication of the transforms that encode two relative poses. For example, the transformation composition:

$$T_c^a = T_b^a T_c^b$$

is something like:

$$\rho_c^a = \rho_b^a + \rho_c^b$$

In reality, if we define $\rho(T)$ as the process for producing a pose from a transform and $T(\rho)$ as the reverse, then:

$$\rho_c^a = \rho[T(\rho_b^a) T(\rho_c^b)]$$

This equivalence between a homogeneous transform and its parameters clearly generalizes to all parametrized matrices, not just the RPY matrix.

2.7.2 Solving Pose Networks

The process of ordering superscripts and subscripts to generate cancellations is equivalent to finding a path in a network. For example, if you want:

$$T_d^a = T_b^a T_c^b T_d^c \tag{2.95}$$

This can be represented as a three edge graph relating frames *a* and *d* (Figure 2.36):

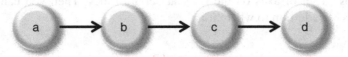

Figure 2.36 Linear Network. This is a visual representation of Equation 2.95.

So, if a path exists in a network between two frames, it is possible to determine the relative pose between the two frames (Box 2.7).

Box 2.7: Solving Pose Networks

It is possible to write by inspection kinematic equations of arbitrary complexity given a pose network. Some rules for writing equations from pose networks are as follows:

- Write down what you know. Draw the frames involved in a roughly correct spatial relationship. Draw edges for known relationships.
- Find the (or a) path from the start (superscript) to the end (subscript).
- Write operator matrices in left to right order as the path is traversed.
- Invert any transforms whose arrow is followed in the reverse direction.
- Substitute all known constraints.

This process will generate the matrix that represents the position and orientation of the last embedded frame with respect to the first, or equivalently, that converts the coordinates of a point from the last to the first.

2.7.2.1 Automation

It is clearly possible to automate this. Given a graph data structure with poses stored as edge attributes, one can write a function in software called `getTransform(Frame1, Frame2)`, which finds the path and returns the transform.

2.7.2.2 Example: Picking Up a Pallet

A robot fork truck is equipped with a vision system that can find the front of a pallet. Let's find the formula for the relative pose between the present pose of the robot and the new pose required to pick up the pallet. Assume the robot must line up the fork tips with the pallet holes and that the camera reads the position of the fork base with respect to the pallet.

First, let the frames on the forktruck be denoted as shown in Figure 2.37. The transforms between all pairs of these are considered known.

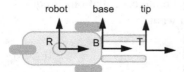

Figure 2.37 ForkTruck Frames. The robot frame is placed in a convenient place for control. The tip and base frames are defined to simplify picking up loads.

Now, we need to draw two forktrucks (one "here" and one "there") and a pallet in roughly the right places. The tip frame "there" is to be lined up with the face of the pallet (P) as shown in Figure 2.38. Following the process described earlier, all known transforms are drawn in a network sketch in Figure 2.38:

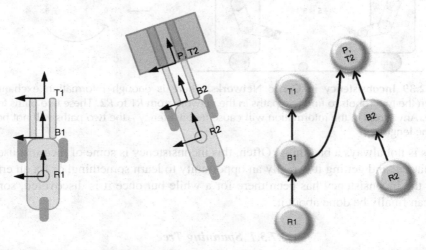

Figure 2.38 Kinematic Placement Problem. Where must $R2$ be relative to $R1$ if the tip frame ($T2$) is to be aligned with the pallet (P)?

Now, the path from $R1$ to $R2$ can be read off by inspection:

$$T_{R2}^{R1} = T_{B1}^{R1} T_P^{B1} T_{T2}^P T_{B2}^{T2} T_{R2}^{B2}$$

To get a more usable form, we substitute all known constraints. Notice that we are requiring the second tip frame to be lined up with the pallet face, so:

$$T_{T2}^P = I$$

Also, the transforms for the frames attached to the robot are (for this robot) fixed. Hence:

$$T_{B1}^{R1} = T_B^R \qquad T_{R2}^{B2} = \left(T_B^R\right)^{-1} \qquad T_{B2}^{T2} = \left(T_T^B\right)^{-1}$$

Substituting all this in gives the solution:

$$T_{R2}^{R1} = T_B^R T_P^B \left(T_T^B\right)^{-1} \left(T_B^R\right)^{-1} \tag{2.96}$$

This "sandwich" of one or more transforms between forward and inverse pairs is a common occurrence. Later in Section 2.5 of Chapter 7, we will see how to take this answer and make a steering function out of it to accomplish the required motion.

2.7.3 Overconstrained Networks

When we add edges to a fully connected network, we create the potential for (and almost always the fact of) inconsistency (Figure 2.39). The network becomes *cyclic*.

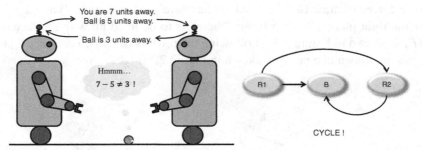

Figure 2.39 Inconsistency in Cyclic Networks. There is enough information exchanged between the two robots to find two paths in the network from *R*1 to *R*2. These two paths form a cycle. Any errors in the information will cause inconsistency – the two paths will not be of the same length.

This is not always a bad thing. Often, this inconsistency is some of the most useful information, and getting it is really an opportunity to learn something, or fix an error. Often, the inconsistency has been there for a while but once it is discovered, something can finally be done about it.

2.7.3.1 Spanning Tree

For a cyclic network, the concept of a spanning tree (Figure 2.40) is fundamental. In a spanning tree, each node (except an arbitrarily chosen root node) is assigned one and only one parent:

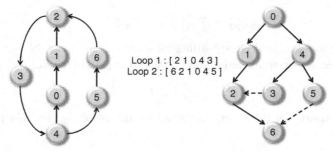

Figure 2.40 Spanning Tree. If node 0 is chosen arbitrarily as the root, the spanning tree to the right is generated. The two leftover edges mean that the graph has two independent cycles in it.

Once the spanning tree is constructed, two important statements become true:

- There is now a ***unique acyclic*** path between any two nodes in the tree.
- Any edge in the original network, but not in the tree, closes an independent loop that is a member of the *cycle basis* encoded by the tree.

No matter how complicated the network gets, you can always find a unique path between two nodes by choosing a root and building a spanning tree. The path is just that from the start node to the root to the end node. This is easy to generate if the edges in the spanning tree point to each node's ancestor.

2.7.3.2 Cycle Basis

The cycle basis is a set of independent loops in a network. Notice that if there are N nodes, then the spanning tree contains $N - 1$ edges. If there are E edges in the original network, then there must be:

$$L = E - (N - 1) = E - N + 1$$

independent loops. This will be important later for building sparse maps and sparse mosaics efficiently.

2.7.4 Differential Kinematics Applied to Frames in General Position

This section considers the problem of expressing the differential kinematics of pose networks from the perspective of how small perturbations in one pose affect others when various constraints apply.

Recall that, in the plane, the matrix denoted as follows:

$$T^i_j = \begin{bmatrix} c\psi^i_j & -s\psi^i_j & a^i_j \\ s\psi^i_j & c\psi^i_j & b^i_j \\ 0 & 0 & 1 \end{bmatrix}$$

encodes the relationship between two frames in "general position." It is useful to visualize such a relationship by drawing frame j at a positive displacement in x and y and at a positive rotation angle with respect to frame i.

Similarly, we will find it useful to place a third frame in general position with respect to frame j as shown in Figure 2.41.

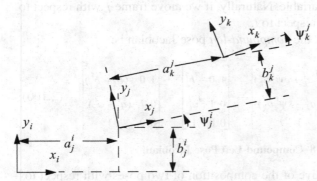

Figure 2.41 Coordinate Frames in General Position. Three coordinate frames are shown which are in general position with respect to each other. All elements of the poses relating the frames are positive in the figure.

2.7.4.1 Pose Composition

The pose of frame k with respect to frame i can be extracted from the compound transform:

$$T^i_k = \begin{bmatrix} c\psi^i_j & -s\psi^i_j & a^i_j \\ s\psi^i_j & c\psi^i_j & b^i_j \\ 0 & 0 & 1 \end{bmatrix} \begin{bmatrix} c\psi^j_k & -s\psi^j_k & a^j_k \\ s\psi^j_k & c\psi^j_k & b^j_k \\ 0 & 0 & 1 \end{bmatrix} = \begin{bmatrix} c\psi^i_k & -s\psi^i_k & c\psi^i_j a^j_k - s\psi^i_j b^j_k + a^i_j \\ s\psi^i_k & c\psi^i_k & s\psi^i_j a^j_k + c\psi^i_j b^j_k + b^i_j \\ 0 & 0 & 1 \end{bmatrix} \quad (2.97)$$

Let us introduce the following notation for relative poses:

$$\underline{\rho}^i_j = \begin{bmatrix} a^i_j & b^i_j & \psi^i_j \end{bmatrix}$$

which is read as the pose of frame j expressed in frame i coordinates. Reading the result directly from Equation 2.97, the relative pose relating frame i and k is:

$$a_k^i = c\psi_j^i a_k^j - s\psi_j^i b_k^j + a_j^i$$

$$b_k^i = s\psi_j^i a_k^j + c\psi_j^i b_k^j + b_j^i \tag{2.98}$$

$$\psi_k^i = \psi_j^i + \psi_k^j$$

This result can be considered to be the formula that defines the operation of pose composition. We denote this with '*' as follows:

$$\underline{\rho}_k^i = \underline{\rho}_j^i * \underline{\rho}_k^j \tag{2.99}$$

For the three poses that appear in this result, it is legitimate to ask what happens to a first pose if a second is changed slightly and a third remains fixed. Because there are three ways to choose the first, and then two ways to choose the second, six such poses can be defined. Let $\underline{\rho}_k^i$ be called the *compound* pose, then $\underline{\rho}_j^i$ will be called the *left* pose and $\underline{\rho}_k^j$ is the *right* pose of the composition.

2.7.4.2 Compound-Left Pose Jacobian

Imagine that the relationship between frame k and frame j (*right*) is fixed but that between frame j and i (*left*) is variable. Naturally, if we move frame j with respect to i, then frame k also moves with respect to i.

Differentiating Equation 2.98, the *compound-left* pose Jacobian is:

$$J_{ij}^{ik} = \frac{\partial \underline{\rho}_k^i}{\partial \underline{\rho}_j^i} = \begin{bmatrix} 1 & 0 & -(s\psi_j^i a_k^j + c\psi_j^i b_k^j) \\ 0 & 1 & (c\psi_j^i a_k^j - s\psi_j^i b_k^j) \\ 0 & 0 & 1 \end{bmatrix} = \begin{bmatrix} 1 & 0 & -{}^i b_k^j \\ 0 & 1 & {}^i a_k^j \\ 0 & 0 & 1 \end{bmatrix} = \begin{bmatrix} 1 & 0 & -(b_k^i - b_j^i) \\ 0 & 1 & (a_k^i - a_j^i) \\ 0 & 0 & 1 \end{bmatrix} \tag{2.100}$$

Spotlight 2-8 Compound-Left Pose Jacobian.

General solution for the derivative of the composition of two poses with respect to the left pose of the composition. Both forms are useful – depending on which information is readily available.

The last form was based on Equation 2.2 for free vectors. A *left-compound* pose Jacobian can clearly be defined which is the inverse of this one.

2.7.4.3 Compound-Right Pose Jacobian

Imagine now that the relationship between frame j and frame i is fixed but that between frame k and j is variable. Naturally, if frame k moves with respect to frame j, it also moves with respect to frame i.

We can express the *compound-right* pose Jacobian as:

$$J_{jk}^{\;ik} = \frac{\partial \underline{\rho}_k^i}{\partial \underline{\rho}_k^j} = \begin{bmatrix} c\psi_j^i & -s\psi_j^i & 0 \\ s\psi_j^i & c\psi_j^i & 0 \\ 0 & 0 & 1 \end{bmatrix} \qquad (2.101)$$

Spotlight 2-9 Compound-Right Pose Jacobian.

General solution for the derivative of the composition of two poses with respect to the right pose of the composition.

A *right-compound* pose Jacobian can be defined, which is the inverse of this one.

2.7.4.4 Right-Left Pose Jacobian

We can also fix the relationship $\underline{\rho}_k^i$ and compute the relative sensitivity of the other two. Let us rewrite Equation 2.98 to isolate $\underline{\rho}_k^j$:

$$\begin{bmatrix} a_k^i - a_j^i \\ b_k^i - b_j^i \end{bmatrix} = \begin{bmatrix} c\psi_j^i & -s\psi_j^i \\ s\psi_j^i & c\psi_j^i \end{bmatrix} \begin{bmatrix} a_k^j \\ b_k^j \end{bmatrix} \Rightarrow \begin{bmatrix} a_k^j \\ b_k^j \end{bmatrix} = \begin{bmatrix} c\psi_j^i & s\psi_j^i \\ -s\psi_j^i & c\psi_j^i \end{bmatrix} \begin{bmatrix} a_k^i - a_j^i \\ b_k^i - b_j^i \end{bmatrix} = \begin{bmatrix} c\psi_j^i & s\psi_j^i \\ -s\psi_j^i & c\psi_j^i \end{bmatrix} \begin{bmatrix} {}^i a_k^j \\ {}^i b_k^j \end{bmatrix} \qquad (2.102)$$

$$\psi_k^i - \psi_j^i = \psi_k^j \qquad\qquad \psi_k^j = \psi_k^i - \psi_j^i$$

Now if $\underline{\rho}_j^i$ is varied, the *right-left* pose Jacobian – of the right pose with respect to the left pose – is the derivative of Equation 2.102:

$$\substack{jk \\ ij} = \frac{\partial \underline{\rho}_k^j}{\partial \underline{\rho}_j^i} = \begin{bmatrix} -\begin{bmatrix} c\psi_j^i & s\psi_j^i \\ -s\psi_j^i & c\psi_j^i \end{bmatrix}\begin{bmatrix} -s\psi_j^i & c\psi_j^i \\ -c\psi_j^i & -s\psi_j^i \end{bmatrix}\begin{bmatrix} a_k^j \\ {}^i b_k^j \end{bmatrix} & \\ \begin{bmatrix} 0 & 0 \end{bmatrix} & -1 \end{bmatrix} = -\begin{bmatrix} \begin{bmatrix} c\psi_j^i & s\psi_j^i \\ -s\psi_j^i & c\psi_j^i \end{bmatrix}\begin{bmatrix} -s\psi_i^j & -c\psi_i^j \\ c\psi_i^j & -s\psi_i^j \end{bmatrix}\begin{bmatrix} a_k^j \\ {}^i b_k^j \end{bmatrix} & \\ \begin{bmatrix} 0 & 0 \end{bmatrix} & 1 \end{bmatrix}$$

$$J_{ij}^{\;jk} = \frac{\partial \underline{\rho}_k^j}{\partial \underline{\rho}_j^i} = -\begin{bmatrix} c\psi_j^i & s\psi_j^i & -b_k^j \\ -s\psi_j^i & c\psi_j^i & a_k^j \\ 0 & 0 & 1 \end{bmatrix} \qquad (2.103)$$

Spotlight 2-10 Right-Left Pose Jacobian.

General solution for the derivative of the right pose of a composition of two poses with respect to the left pose if the composition remains fixed.

Clearly an equivalent *left-right* pose Jacobian can be defined, which is the inverse of this one.

2.7.4.5 Compound-Inner Pose Jacobian

The most general case is that of the partial derivative of the composite pose of a sequence with respect to an arbitrary pose in the sequence. Consider Figure 2.42:

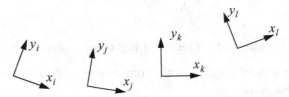

Figure 2.42 Setup For the Compound Inner Pose Jacobian. Four coordinate frames are shown that are in general position with respect to each other. We are interested in the differential change in $\underline{\rho}_l^i$ associated with a differential change in $\underline{\rho}_k^j$.

The Jacobian of $\underline{\rho}_l^i$ with respect to $\underline{\rho}_k^j$ is, by the chain rule, the product of a compound-left and compound-right Jacobian:

$$
J_{jk}^{il} = \frac{\partial \underline{\rho}_l^i}{\partial \underline{\rho}_k^j} = \left(\frac{\partial \underline{\rho}_l^i}{\partial \underline{\rho}_k^i}\right)\left(\frac{\partial \underline{\rho}_k^i}{\partial \underline{\rho}_k^j}\right) = J_{ik}^{il} \; J_{jk}^{ik}
$$

$$
J_{jk}^{il} = \frac{\partial \underline{\rho}_l^i}{\partial \underline{\rho}_k^j} = \begin{bmatrix} 1 & 0 & -(b_l^i - b_k^i) \\ 0 & 1 & (a_l^i - a_k^i) \\ 0 & 0 & 1 \end{bmatrix} \begin{bmatrix} c\psi_j^i & -s\psi_j^i & 0 \\ s\psi_j^i & c\psi_j^i & 0 \\ 0 & 0 & 1 \end{bmatrix}
\tag{2.104}
$$

$$
J_{jk}^{il} = \frac{\partial \underline{\rho}_l^i}{\partial \underline{\rho}_k^j} = \begin{bmatrix} c\psi_j^i & -s\psi_j^i & -{}^ib_l^k \\ s\psi_j^i & c\psi_j^i & {}^ia_l^k \\ 0 & 0 & 1 \end{bmatrix} = \begin{bmatrix} c\psi_j^i & -s\psi_j^i & -(b_l^i - b_k^i) \\ s\psi_j^i & c\psi_j^i & (a_l^i - a_k^i) \\ 0 & 0 & 1 \end{bmatrix}
$$

Spotlight 2-11 Compound-Inner Pose Jacobian.

General solution for the derivative of the composition of any number poses with respect to an arbitrary pose in the middle of the composition.

The result involves the rotation matrix from j to i, and the vector joining k to l expressed in the coordinates of i. Note that when $i = j$, the right half is identity and we get the compound-left pose Jacobian J_{ik}^{il}. When $k = l$, the left half is identity and we get the compound-right pose Jacobian J_{jk}^{ik}. Hence, all of the six pose Jacobians mentioned earlier are special cases of this one. An inverse of this Jacobian can be defined, which is the inverse of the above matrix, and the rules for inverting a product of two matrices can produce it readily.

There is a second way to compute this Jacobian by varying the intermediate pose in the chain rule. This way produces a product of a compound right and a compound left pose Jacobian:

$$J^{il}_{jk} = \frac{\partial \rho^i_l}{\partial \rho^j_k} = \left(\frac{\partial \rho^i_l}{\partial \rho^j_k}\right)\left(\frac{\partial \rho^j_k}{\partial \rho^j_k}\right) = J^{il}_{jl} \, J^{jl}_{jk}$$

$$J^{il}_{jk} = \frac{\partial \rho^i_l}{\partial \rho^j_k} = \begin{bmatrix} c\psi^i_j & -s\psi^i_j & 0 \\ s\psi^i_j & c\psi^i_j & 0 \\ 0 & 0 & 1 \end{bmatrix} \begin{bmatrix} 1 & 0 & -(b^j_l - b^j_k) \\ 0 & 1 & (a^j_l - a^j_k) \\ 0 & 0 & 1 \end{bmatrix} \tag{2.105}$$

$$J^{il}_{jk} = \frac{\partial \rho^i_l}{\partial \rho^j_k} = \begin{bmatrix} c\psi^i_j & -s\psi^i_j & -^ib^k_l \\ s\psi^i_j & c\psi^i_j & ^ia^k_l \\ 0 & 0 & 1 \end{bmatrix} = \begin{bmatrix} c\psi^i_j & -s\psi^i_j & -(b^i_l - b^i_k) \\ s\psi^i_j & c\psi^i_j & (a^i_l - a^i_k) \\ 0 & 0 & 1 \end{bmatrix}$$

Consider the case of trying to compute a series of such Jacobians when the adjacent frames move along the sequence. Let $j = n$ and $k = n + 1$. Then the formula is:

$$J^{il}_{jk} = \frac{\partial \rho^i_l}{\partial \rho^n_{n+1}} = \begin{bmatrix} c\psi^i_n & -s\psi^i_n & -(b^i_l - b^i_{n+1}) \\ s\psi^i_n & c\psi^i_n & (a^i_l - a^i_{n+1}) \\ 0 & 0 & 1 \end{bmatrix}$$

The upper left 4×4 is the rotation matrix R^a_n and the third column depends on the position $\underline{x}^a_{n+1}$. Both are components of T^a_i). They can be computed recursively as follows:

$$T^a_{n+1} = T^a_n T^n_{n+1}$$

2.7.4.6 Inverse Pose Jacobian

Sometimes, the pose in a pose network is known in the opposite sense from which we want it and it is not convenient to invert it. Consider above the Jacobian of ρ^i_l with respect to ρ^j_i – that is, with respect to the inverse of the left pose ρ^i_j of the composition. By the chain rule:

$$\frac{\partial \rho^i_l}{\partial \rho^j_i} = \left(\frac{\partial \rho^i_k}{\partial \rho^j_i}\right)\left(\frac{\partial \rho^i_j}{\partial \rho^j_i}\right)$$

Because the left part is known, finding a solution is tantamount to finding the quantity $\partial \rho^i_j / \partial \rho^j_i$. We will call this the *inverse pose Jacobian*. This is the derivative of the elements of a pose with respect to the elements of its own inverse.

In order to compute the Jacobian we need a formula for ρ^i_j in terms of its own inverse in order to differentiate it. Based on the inverse of a homogeneous transform, we can express a pose in terms of its own inverse. Consider the formula for the inverse of the 2D homogeneous transform T^j_i:

$$T^j_i = \begin{bmatrix} c\psi^j_i & -s\psi^j_i & a^j_i \\ s\psi^j_i & c\psi^j_i & b^j_i \\ 0 & 0 & 1 \end{bmatrix} \qquad (T^j_i)^{-1} = T^i_j = \begin{bmatrix} c\psi^j_i & s\psi^j_i & -c\psi^j_i a^j_i - s\psi^j_i b^j_i \\ -s\psi^j_i & c\psi^j_i & s\psi^j_i a^j_i - c\psi^j_i b^j_i \\ 0 & 0 & 1 \end{bmatrix}$$

The elements of this inverse matrix encode the pose $\underline{\rho}_j^i$ but this pose is expressed in terms of the components of $\underline{\rho}_i^j$.

$$a_j^i = -c\psi_i^j a_i^j - s\psi_i^j b_i^j$$
$$b_j^i = s\psi_i^j a_i^j - c\psi_i^j b_i^j \tag{2.106}$$
$$\psi_j^i = -\psi_i^j$$

Differentiating leads to:

$$\frac{\partial \underline{\rho}_j^i}{\partial \underline{\rho}_i^j} = \begin{bmatrix} -c\psi_i^j & -s\psi_i^j & s\psi_i^j a_i^j - c\psi_i^j b_i^j \\ s\psi_i^j & -c\psi_i^j & c\psi_i^j a_i^j + s\psi_i^j b_i^j \\ 0 & 0 & -1 \end{bmatrix} = \begin{bmatrix} -(R_i^j)^T & -(\dot{R}_i^j)^T \underline{\rho}_i^j \\ \underline{0}^T & -1 \end{bmatrix}$$

$$\text{where} \qquad (\dot{R}_i^j)^T = \frac{d(R_i^j)^T}{d\psi_i^j} = \frac{d}{d\psi_i^j}\begin{bmatrix} c\psi_i^j & -s\psi_i^j \\ s\psi_i^j & c\psi_i^j \end{bmatrix} \tag{2.107}$$

$$\text{or} \quad \frac{\partial \underline{\rho}_j^i}{\partial \underline{\rho}_i^j} = \begin{bmatrix} -c\psi_i^j & -s\psi_i^j & s\psi_i^j a_i^j - c\psi_i^j b_i^j \\ s\psi_i^j & -c\psi_i^j & c\psi_i^j a_i^j + s\psi_i^j b_i^j \\ 0 & 0 & -1 \end{bmatrix} = -\begin{bmatrix} c\psi_i^j & s\psi_i^j & -b_j^i \\ -s\psi_i^j & c\psi_i^j & a_j^i \\ 0 & 0 & 1 \end{bmatrix}$$

Spotlight 2-12 Inverse Pose Jacobian.

General solution for the derivative of a 2D pose with respect to the elements of its own inverse.

The structure is remarkably similar to a rigid transform. However, this matrix is a Jacobian. Also, because $(R_i^j)^T = R_j^i$, this expression can be easily rewritten in terms of the elements of $\underline{\rho}_j^i$.

2.7.5 References and Further Reading

Smith is a classic robotics reference on networks of spatial relationships. Paul presents transform graphs (pose networks) in the context of robotics. Kavitha is one source on the cycle basis. Bosse and Kelly are two papers in robotics that use graphs to construct maps.

[20] M. Bosse, P. Newman, J. Leonard, M Soika, W. Feiten, and S. Teller. An Atlas Framework for Scalable Mapping, in Proceedings of the IEEE International Conference on Robotics and Automation (ICRA), September 2003.

[21] T. Kavitha, C. Liebchen, K. Mehlhorn, D. Michail, R. Rizzi, T. Ueckerdt, and K. Zweig, Cycle Bases in Graphs: Characterization, Algorithms, Complexity, and Applications, *Computer Science Review*, Vol. 3, No. 4, pp 19

[22] A. Kelly and R. Unnikrishnan, Efficient Construction of Globally Consistent Ladar Maps using Pose Network Topology and Nonlinear Programming, Proceedings of the 11th International Symposium of Robotics Research (ISRR '03), November, 2003.

[23] R. P. Paul, Robot Manipulators: *Mathematics, Programming, and Control,* MIT Press, 1981.

[24] R. Smith, M. Self, and P. Cheeseman. Estimating Uncertain Spatial Relationships in robotics, in I. Cox and G. Wilfong, eds., *Autonomous Robot Vehicles,* pp. 167–193. Springer-Verlag, 1990.

2.7.6 Exercises

2.7.6.1 Pose Jacobians from the Jacobian Tensor

Consider again four frames in general position.

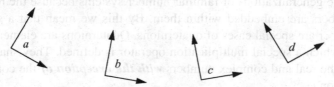

There is another way to get pose Jacobians that extends easily to 3D. Recall that the Jacobian Tensor is a third-order tensor – a cube of numbers, like an array with three indices. For 2D problems, the tensor $\partial T/\partial \rho$ is a set of three matrices that can be written:

$$\frac{\partial T}{\partial \rho} = \left\{ \frac{\partial T}{\partial x}, \frac{\partial T}{\partial y}, \frac{\partial T}{\partial \theta} \right\}$$

Hence, each "slice" of this Jacobian is a matrix and that matrix is the derivative of each element of T with respect to one of the parameters of ρ.

The homogeneous transform relating the total transform above to the three component transforms is:

$$T_d^a = T_b^a T_c^b T_d^c$$

The Jacobian tensor $\partial T_d^a / \partial \rho_c^b$ encodes the elements of the pose Jacobian J_{bc}^{ad}. Using the chain rule (which applies to tensors of any order) it can be expressed as:

$$\frac{\partial T_d^a}{\partial \rho_c^b} = (T_b^a)\left(\frac{\partial T_c^b}{\partial \rho_c^b}\right)(T_d^c)$$

Write out as much of $\partial T_d^a / \partial \rho_c^b$ as you need to and extract the elements of J_{bc}^{ad} to show that the same result is obtained as that in the text.

2.8 Quaternions

Quaternions were invented by the Irish mathematician William Rowan Hamilton [30] in the late 1890s in a quest to provide a vector analogy to the operation of (scalar) division [28].

Quaternions are the only way to solve some problems – like the problem of generating regularly spaced 3D angles [26]. They are the simplest way to solve other problems.

Some problems in registration for example, can be solved in closed form. They are also the fastest way to solve some problems. Although the quaternion remains relatively obscure, even in most branches of engineering, it is nonetheless particularly effective for the representation and manipulation of 3D rotations. Our primary motivation for studying them here is implementing the *quaternion loop* in an inertial navigation system. It may update vehicle attitude perhaps 1,000 times a second.

Like homogeneous transforms, quaternions can function as objects or as operators. As operators, they can represent rotations, translations, affine transformations and projections – everything that a Homogeneous transform can represent. As objects, quaternions are generalizations of familiar number systems because the reals and the complex numbers are embedded within them. By this we mean that a scalar and a complex number are special cases of quaternions. Quaternions are elements of a vector space on which a special multiplication operator is defined. They share all of the properties of the real and complex numbers **with the exception of** the commutativity of multiplication.

2.8.1 Representations and Notation

Many different notations are in use for quaternions. It is convenient at different times to visualize quaternions in different ways:

- complex numbers
- four-vectors in matrix algebra.
- the "sum" of a scalar and a three-vector
- polynomials in the variables (i, j, k)

It is even useful to switch back and forth between different views of the same quaternion.

2.8.1.1 Tuples and Polynomials

We will use a tilde over a symbol ($\tilde{q}$) to denote that it is a quaternion. Hamilton liked to represent quaternions as four-tuples like so:

$$\tilde{q} = (q_0, q_1, q_2, q_3) \tag{2.108}$$

Quaternions can also be viewed as *hypercomplex* numbers with one real and three imaginary parts:

$$\tilde{q} = q_0 + q_1 i + q_2 j + q_3 k \tag{2.109}$$

where (i, j, k) are called the *principal imaginaries*. In this form, they can be manipulated **as if they were polynomials** in the variables (i, j, k). Compare this notation with standard complex numbers of the form

$$\tilde{q} = q_0 + q_1 i$$

For quaternions, as for complex numbers, the number $a + bi$ is just notation for the ordered pair (a, b) and we will never ask for $a + bi$ to be simplified by actually adding these things together. The sum is considered to be the simplest form because the components themselves cannot be added. The sum does, however, have a mnemonic function when the law of distribution is invoked. So we treat the sum notationally like a real sum, but it can never be simplified.

2.8.1.2 Scalar Plus Vector, Exponential of a Vector

Alternately, some people write quaternions as the sum of a traditional scalar and a traditional three-vector. Indeed, the terms *scalar* and *vector* were originally coined to distinguish these two parts of a quaternion:

$$\tilde{q} = q + \vec{q}$$
$$where: \quad q = q_0$$
$$and: \quad \vec{q} = q_1 i + q_2 j + q_3 k$$

Henceforth, note that q, $\vec{q}$, and $\tilde{q}$ denote a scalar, a vector, and a quaternion. Others write quaternions as an ordered pair of real and complex parts:

$$\tilde{q} = (q, \vec{q}) \tag{2.110}$$

Note that q means neither $|\vec{q}|$ nor $|\tilde{q}|$ here. The reader should also be wary that some authors use $\tilde{q} = (\vec{q}, q)$ and this convention will change any results that depend on the order. In particular, it changes the definition of the matrix equivalent multiplication operator $(\tilde{p}^{\times})$ defined below. It also means that quaternion software libraries will depend on the ordering convention used to lay out a quaternion in memory. Here we assume they are stored as expressed in Equation 2.108.

By analogy to the exponential notation of complex numbers $z = e^{i\theta}$, mathematicians have often used exponential notation for quaternions. Thus:

$$\tilde{q} = \exp\left(\frac{1}{2}\theta\vec{w}\right)$$

means the quaternion for a rotation by the angle θ about the axis $\vec{w}$.

2.8.2 Quaternion Multiplication

It is likely that the reader is already familiar with as many as four "products" defined on vectors. Scalar multiplication is defined so that $k\vec{v}$ changes the length of the vector $\vec{v}$ but not its direction. The dot (or "scalar") product $\vec{a} \cdot \vec{b}$ produces a scalar from two vectors. The vector (or "cross") product $\vec{a} \times \vec{b}$ produces a vector from two vectors. The outer product is the matrix product ab^T and it produces a matrix from two vectors.

2.8.2.1 Products of Imaginaries

The quaternion product is, in fact, a fifth vector product. If we want to treat quaternions as polynomials in (i, j, k), then an expression like:

$$\tilde{p}\tilde{q} = (p_0 + p_1 i + p_2 j + p_3 k)(q_0 + q_1 i + q_2 j + q_3 k)$$

must multiply out to be the sum of all the elements in Table 2.3.

Table 2.3 Quaternion Multiplication

	q_0	$q_1 i$	$q_2 j$	$q_3 k$
p_0	$p_0 q_0$	$p_0 q_1 i$	$p_0 q_2 j$	$p_0 q_3 k$
$p_1 i$	$p_1 q_0 i$	$p_1 q_1 i^2$	$p_1 q_2 ij$	$p_1 q_3 ik$
$p_2 j$	$p_2 q_0 j$	$p_2 q_1 ji$	$p_2 q_2 j^2$	$p_2 q_3 jk$
$p_3 k$	$p_3 q_0 k$	$p_3 q_1 ki$	$p_3 q_2 kj$	$p_3 q_3 k^2$

For this product to be a quaternion, the terms like i^2 and jk must somehow turn into scalars, or singletons in the imaginaries (i, j, k). In fact, the "rules" that apply are as seen in Table 2.4.

Table 2.4 Quaternion Multiplication Table

	i	j	k
i	-1	k	-j
j	-k	-1	i
k	j	-i	-1

These are a consequence of the more compact rule $i^2 = j^2 = k^2 = ijk = -1$. In the table, the off-diagonal elements are the same rules associated with the vector cross product and the diagonal elements are the extension of the rule for complex numbers. Self multiplication of the principle imaginaries does not follow the rules for the cross product because $i \times i = 0$ whereas $ii = -1$. The imaginaries act as real vectors in pairs and as complex numbers when acting alone.

2.8.2.2 *Matrix Equivalent of Multiplication*

Based on the above table, we can express the quaternion product in terms of a 4×4 matrix reminiscent of the matrix representation of $\omega \times$:

$$\tilde{p}\tilde{q} = \begin{bmatrix} p_0 & -p_1 & -p_2 & -p_3 \\ p_1 & p_0 & -p_3 & p_2 \\ p_2 & p_3 & p_0 & -p_1 \\ p_3 & -p_2 & p_1 & p_0 \end{bmatrix} \begin{bmatrix} q_0 \\ q_1 \\ q_2 \\ q_3 \end{bmatrix} = \tilde{p}^{\times}\tilde{q} \qquad (2.111)$$

We will interpret a right superscript "$\times$" on a quaternion to mean the above matrix. It is skew symmetric when $p_0 = 0$. The notation is intended to suggest that quaternion rotation is similar to the vector cross product – the other product that produces a vector from two vectors. We can also define the matrix that represents a right multiplication by q with a left superscript:

$$\tilde{p}\tilde{q} = \begin{bmatrix} q_0 & -q_1 & -q_2 & -q_3 \\ q_1 & q_0 & q_3 & -q_2 \\ q_2 & -q_3 & q_0 & q_1 \\ q_3 & q_2 & -q_1 & q_0 \end{bmatrix} \begin{bmatrix} p_0 \\ p_1 \\ p_2 \\ p_3 \end{bmatrix} = {}^{\times}\tilde{q}\tilde{p} \qquad (2.112)$$

2.8.3 Other Quaternion Operations

As we saw above, operations like addition and multiplication are defined as if quaternions were polynomials in the imaginaries. This section further explores the implications of these definitions.

2.8.3.1 Quaternion Product in Alternative Notations

Ways to write the product of two quaternions depend on the notation used but all are equivalent. In hypercomplex number form:

$$\tilde{p}\tilde{q} = (p_0 + p_1 i + p_2 j + p_3 k)(q_0 + q_1 i + p_2 j + p_3 k)$$
$$\tilde{p}\tilde{q} = (p_0 q_0 - p_1 q_1 - p_2 q_2 - p_3 q_3) + (\ldots)i + \ldots$$

In scalar-vector form, this same result can presumably be written as follows:

$$\tilde{p}\tilde{q} = (p + \vec{p})(q + \vec{q})$$
$$\tilde{p}\tilde{q} = pq + p\vec{q} + q\vec{p} + \vec{p}\vec{q}$$

The first three terms are easy to interpret. The last term can be written in terms of both the dot and cross products:

$$\vec{p}\vec{q} = (\vec{p} \times \vec{q}) - (\vec{p} \cdot \vec{q})$$

Thus, the quaternion product can be thought of as a superset of all of these operations. It is convenient to summarize this result like so:

$$\tilde{p}\tilde{q} = (pq - \vec{p} \cdot \vec{q}) + (p\vec{q} + q\vec{p} + \vec{p} \times \vec{q}) \qquad (2.113)$$

The first bracketed term is the scalar part and second is the vector part. At this point, the reader will need to be clear that all of the following pieces of notation mean something distinct:($\tilde{p}\tilde{q}$, pq, $\vec{p}\vec{q}$, $\vec{p} \cdot \vec{q}$, $p\vec{q}$, $\vec{p} \times \vec{q}$, $\vec{p} \cdot \vec{q}$).

2.8.3.2 Non-Commutativity

Because the cross product in Equation 2.113 does not commute, the quaternion product also does not commute. In general:

$$\tilde{p}\tilde{q} \neq \tilde{q}\tilde{p}$$

2.8.3.3 Quaternion Addition

Quaternion addition follows the same pattern as complex numbers, vectors, and polynomials – we add them element by element:

$$\tilde{p} + \tilde{q} = (p_0 + q_0) + (p_1 + q_1)i + (p_2 + q_2)j + (p_3 + q_3)k$$

2.8.3.4 Distributivity

A very important property is that of distributivity:

$$(\tilde{p} + \tilde{q})\tilde{r} = \tilde{p}\tilde{r} + \tilde{q}\tilde{r}$$
$$\tilde{p}(\tilde{q} + \tilde{r}) = \tilde{p}\tilde{q} + \tilde{p}\tilde{r}$$

Many derivations involving quaternions become easy due to this property.

2.8.3.5 Quaternion Dot Product & Norm

We can define a dot product on quaternions (not to be confused with the quaternion product) as the scalar component of the quaternion product in Equation 2.113:

$$\tilde{p} \cdot \tilde{q} = pq + \vec{p} \cdot \vec{q}$$

This is just the sum of pairwise products. Given this, the quaternion norm (equivalent of length) is defined as:

$$|\tilde{q}| = \sqrt{\tilde{q} \cdot \tilde{q}}$$

2.8.3.6 Unit Quaternions

A quaternion whose norm is 1 is called a *unit quaternion*. Note that the product of two unit quaternions is a unit quaternion so unit quaternions constitute a subgroup of general quaternions.

2.8.3.7 Quaternion Conjugate

As for complex numbers, the conjugate of a quaternion is formed by reversing the sign of the complex part:

$$\tilde{q}^* = q - \vec{q}$$

Based on Equation 2.113, several things cancel in the quaternion product with the conjugate leaving:

$$\tilde{q}\tilde{q}^* = (qq + \vec{q} \cdot \vec{q}) = \tilde{q} \cdot \tilde{q} \qquad (2.114)$$

which is the same result as the dot product. This gives us a second way to get the norm of a quaternion:

$$|\tilde{q}| = \sqrt{\tilde{q}\tilde{q}^*} \qquad (2.115)$$

2.8.3.8 Quaternion Inverse

More important, Equation 2.115 is a quaternion product (not a dot product) which produces a scalar, and a scalar is a legitimate quaternion. By definition, the multiplicative inverse of a quaternion (or anything else) is the thing which, when multiplied by it, produces unity:

$$\tilde{q}\,\tilde{q}^{-1} = 1$$

Given that for a general $\tilde{q}$:

$$\tilde{q}\,\tilde{q}^{*}/|\tilde{q}|^{2} = 1$$

we have the multiplicative inverse of a quaternion as:

$$\tilde{q}^{-1} = \tilde{q}^{*}/|\tilde{q}|^{2} \tag{2.116}$$

This result was the original point of quaternions. It effectively defines the process of dividing one vector by another.

2.8.3.9 Conjugate of the Product

The product of two conjugates is the same as conjugate of the product in the opposite order. This is useful in several proofs:

$$\tilde{p}^{*}\tilde{q}^{*} = (p - \vec{p})(q - \vec{q}) = (pq + \vec{p}\cdot\vec{q}) + (-p\vec{q} - q\vec{p} + \vec{p}\times\vec{q})$$
$$(\tilde{q}\tilde{p})^{*} = [(q + \vec{q})(p + \vec{p})]^{*} = [(qp + \vec{q}\cdot\vec{p}) + (q\vec{p} + p\vec{q} + \vec{q}\times\vec{p})]^{*}$$
$$(\tilde{q}\tilde{p})^{*} = [(qp + \vec{q}\cdot\vec{p}) + (-q\vec{p} - p\vec{q} - \vec{q}\times\vec{p})]\text{the same thing}$$

That is:

$$(\tilde{q}\tilde{p})^{*} = \tilde{p}^{*}\tilde{q}^{*} \tag{2.117}$$

2.8.4 Representing 3D Rotations

3D rotations can be represented conveniently in terms of unit quaternions. The unit quaternion:

$$\tilde{q} = \cos(\theta/2) + \hat{w}\sin(\theta/2) \tag{2.118}$$

can be interpreted to represent a rotation operator in 3D by the angle θ about the (unit vector) axis $\hat{w}$. Note that $\hat{w}$ is now being interpreted as a vector in 3D rather than a hypercomplex number.

The above provides the conversion from axis-angle $(\theta, \hat{w})$ notation to quaternion. Clearly, the inverse is:

$$\theta = 2\, atan2(|\vec{q}|, q)$$
$$\hat{w} = \vec{q}/|\vec{q}| \tag{2.119}$$

Taking the negative $-\tilde{q}$ represents the same rotation (opposite direction about the negative vector) whereas taking the conjugate $\tilde{q}^*$ produces the inverse rotation (like the inverse of a rotation matrix).

2.8.4.1 Rotating a Vector

Let us "augment" or "quaternize" a vector $\vec{x}$ by making it the vector part of an associated quaternion:

$$\tilde{x} = 0 + \vec{x}$$

This vector can be operated on by a unit quaternion thus:

$$\tilde{x}' = \tilde{q}\tilde{x}\tilde{q}^* \tag{2.120}$$

and this result will always have a zero scalar part like the original $\tilde{x}$.

Finally, because rotation is accomplished by a quaternion product, and because quaternion products are associative, it follows that compound rotation operations are formed by multiplying the two unit quaternions:

$$\tilde{x}'' = \tilde{p}\tilde{x}'\tilde{p}^* = (\tilde{p}\tilde{q})\tilde{x}(\tilde{q}^*\tilde{p}^*) \tag{2.121}$$

Using the earlier result for the product of two conjugates, we have shown that the product $(\tilde{p}\tilde{q})$ rotates a vector first by $\tilde{q}$ and then by $\tilde{p}$.

2.8.4.2 Rotation Matrix Equivalent

Of course, we know that a matrix can also implement a general 3D rotation operator. Therefore, there must be a way to compute the matrix from the quaternion and vice versa. For the quaternion:

$$q = q_0 + q_1 i + q_2 j + q_3 k$$

The equivalent 3D rotation matrix is:

$$R = \begin{bmatrix} 2[q_0^2 + q_1^2] - 1 & 2[q_1 q_2 - q_0 q_3] & 2[q_1 q_3 + q_0 q_2] \\ 2[q_1 q_2 + q_0 q_3] & 2[q_0^2 + q_2^2] - 1 & 2[q_2 q_3 - q_0 q_1] \\ 2[q_1 q_3 - q_0 q_2] & 2[q_0 q_1 + q_2 q_3] & 2[q_0^2 + q_3^2] - 1 \end{bmatrix} \tag{2.122}$$

This is tedious but easy to show if you are organized in your algebra by expanding $\tilde{q}\tilde{x}\tilde{q}^*$ and collecting like terms. The inverse problem is also solvable. Suppose we have the matrix:

$$R = \begin{bmatrix} r_{11} & r_{12} & r_{13} \\ r_{21} & r_{22} & r_{23} \\ r_{31} & r_{32} & r_{33} \end{bmatrix}$$

We can equate this to the last result and solve for the quaternion elements:

$$
\begin{aligned}
r_{13} + r_{31} &= 4q_1 q_3 & r_{21} + r_{12} &= 4q_1 q_2 & r_{32} + r_{23} &= 4q_2 q_3 \\
r_{13} - r_{31} &= 4q_0 q_2 & r_{21} - r_{12} &= 4q_0 q_3 & r_{32} - r_{23} &= 4q_0 q_1
\end{aligned}
\tag{2.123}
$$

If one of the q_i is known, the rest can be determined from these equations. We can find one q_i from combinations of the diagonal elements:

$$
\begin{aligned}
r_{11} + r_{22} + r_{33} &= 4q_0^2 - 1 & -r_{11} + r_{22} - r_{33} &= 4q_2^2 - 1 \\
r_{11} - r_{22} - r_{33} &= 4q_1^2 - 1 & -r_{11} - r_{22} + r_{33} &= 4q_3^2 - 1
\end{aligned}
\tag{2.124}
$$

These equations assume the original quaternion was a unit quaternion but the general solution is not much harder to derive. In practice any of these can be zero, so the largest of these is computed and used to find the others using the earlier equations. We determine only one q_i using the second set to get the signs right. The sign of any one q_i can be assigned arbitrarily because the negative of a quaternion represents the same rotation.

2.8.4.3 Derivatives and Integrals

The derivative of a quaternion with respect to a scalar on which its elements depends, such as time, is defined as:

$$
\frac{d\tilde{q}}{dt} = \frac{dq}{dt} + \frac{d\vec{q}}{dt}
\tag{2.125}
$$

Quaternions can be integrated just like vectors as well:

$$
\int_0^t \frac{d\tilde{q}}{dt}\, dt = \int_0^t \frac{dq}{dt}\, dt + \int_0^t \frac{d\vec{q}}{dt}\, dt
\tag{2.126}
$$

2.8.5 Attitude and Angular Velocity

In applications, we can adorn quaternions with frame names just as we did for poses. Thus the unit quaternion $\tilde{q}_b^n$ represents the attitude of the body frame relative to the navigation frame. This means the operator that is applied to the unit vectors of the navigation frame in order to move them into coincidence with the body frame. Recall that the angles in a rotation matrix have the same semantics.

2.8.5.1 Time Derivative of the Attitude Quaternion

We can express the time rate of change of this quaternion using first principles. For the time varying unit quaternion:

$$
\tilde{q}(t) = \cos\frac{\theta(t)}{2} + \hat{w}\sin\frac{\theta(t)}{2}
$$

We can express its new value a short time later at $t + \Delta t$ by a composition with a differential unit quaternion $\tilde{p}$ that accomplishes the rotation from t to $t + \Delta t$:

$$\tilde{q}(t + \Delta t) = \tilde{p}\tilde{q}(t)$$

where:

$$\tilde{p} = \cos\frac{\Delta\theta}{2} + \hat{u}\sin\frac{\Delta\theta}{2}$$

From first principles:

$$\frac{d\tilde{q}}{dt} = \lim_{\Delta t \to 0}\left[\frac{\tilde{q}(t + \Delta t) - \tilde{q}(t)}{\Delta t}\right] = \lim_{\Delta t \to 0}\left[\frac{\tilde{p}\tilde{q}(t) - \tilde{q}(t)}{\Delta t}\right]$$

The *identity quaternion* is simply $\tilde{i} = (1, 0, 0, 0)$. Using it, we can factor out the original quaternion:

$$\frac{d\tilde{q}}{dt} = \lim_{\Delta t \to 0}\left[\frac{\tilde{p} - \tilde{i}}{\Delta t}\right]\tilde{q}(t) = \frac{d\tilde{p}}{dt}\tilde{q}(t) \tag{2.127}$$

where we also used the fact that $\lim_{\Delta t \to 0}\Delta\tilde{p} = \tilde{i}$ to recognize $\dfrac{d\tilde{p}}{dt}$.

Substituting for $\Delta\tilde{q}$ and writing the Taylor series for the cosine

$$\frac{d\tilde{p}}{dt} = \lim_{\Delta t \to 0}\left[\frac{\left(1 - \dfrac{\Delta\theta^2}{4} + \ldots\right) + \hat{u}\sin\dfrac{\Delta\theta}{2} - \tilde{i}}{\Delta t}\right]$$

Now the terms $\Delta\theta^2$, and so on, are vanishingly small in the limit $\Delta\theta^2 \to 0$ and $\sin\Delta\theta/2 \to \Delta\theta/2$, so this is:

$$\frac{d\tilde{q}}{dt} = \lim_{\Delta t \to 0}\left[\frac{(1 - \ldots) + \hat{u}\dfrac{\Delta\theta}{2} - \tilde{i}}{\Delta t}\right] = \lim_{\Delta t \to 0}\left[\frac{\hat{u}\dfrac{\Delta\theta}{2}}{\Delta t}\right] = \frac{1}{2}\lim_{\Delta t \to 0}\left[\frac{\Delta\theta}{\Delta t}\right]\hat{u}$$

But, by definition, the angular velocity of the body frame, expressed in navigation coordinates is:

$$\tilde{\omega}_n = \lim_{\Delta t \to 0}\left[\frac{\Delta\theta}{\Delta t}\right]\hat{u}$$

Therefore, we have the very elegant result for the time derivative of the unit quaternion:

$$\frac{d\tilde{q}(t)}{dt} = \frac{1}{2}\tilde{\omega}_n(t)\tilde{q}(t) \tag{2.128}$$

The product on the right-hand side is a quaternion product and the angular velocity quaternion $\tilde{\omega}_n(t)$ is a "quaternized" vector in fixed (navigation) coordinates:

$$\tilde{\omega}_n(t) = (0 + \omega_1 i + \omega_2 j + \omega_3 k)$$

2.8.5.2 Time Derivative for Strapdown Sensing

If the angular velocity is known in body coordinates (i.e., sensors mounted on some vehicle), then for the same $\tilde{q}(t)$ that we are differentiating:

$$\tilde{\omega}_n(t) = \tilde{q}(t)\tilde{\omega}_b(t)\tilde{q}(t)^*$$

Which leads immediately to (note the analogy with Equation 2.75):

$$\frac{d\tilde{q}(t)}{dt} = \frac{1}{2}\tilde{q}(t)\tilde{\omega}_b(t) \tag{2.129}$$

2.8.5.3 Quaternion Attitude From Angular Velocity

Based on the above, the attitude of a vehicle can be generated from:

$$\tilde{q}(t) = \frac{1}{2}\int_0^t \tilde{q}(t)\tilde{\omega}_b(t)dt \tag{2.130}$$

So it is trivial computationally to convert body-fixed angular velocity $\tilde{\omega}_b$ into a quaternion rate $d\tilde{q}/dt$, which can be integrated rapidly and then converted to Euler angle attitude at any desired time.

For highest accuracy, it is convenient to write the above in the following form:

$$\tilde{q}_{k+1}^n = \tilde{q}_{k+1}^k\tilde{q}_k^n = \frac{1}{2}\int_{t_k}^{t_{k+1}} \tilde{q}_k^n\tilde{\omega}_k dt = \frac{1}{2}\int_{t_k}^{t_{k+1}} (^\times\tilde{\omega}_b)\, dt\; \tilde{q}_k^n = \exp\left\{ ^\times[\delta\Theta] \right\}\tilde{q}_k^n$$

We exploited Equation 2.79 once again in the quaternion case because the matrix equivalent of quaternion multiplication is skew symmetric. We have defined:

$$^\times[\delta\Theta] = \frac{1}{2}(^\times\tilde{\omega}_b)\, dt = \frac{1}{2}\begin{bmatrix} 0 & -\omega_x & -\omega_y & -\omega_z \\ \omega_x & 0 & \omega_z & -\omega_y \\ \omega_y & -\omega_z & 0 & \omega_x \\ \omega_z & \omega_y & -\omega_x & 0 \end{bmatrix}dt$$

Recalling that any skew symmetric matrix has a closed form matrix exponential, we have:

$$\tilde{q}_{k+1}^k = \exp\left\{ ^\times[\delta\Theta] \right\} = I + f_1(\delta\Theta)\, ^\times[\delta\Theta] + f_2(\delta\Theta)(^\times[\delta\Theta])^2 \tag{2.131}$$

Where:

$$f_1(\delta\Theta) = \frac{\sin\delta\Theta}{\delta\Theta} \qquad f_2(\delta\Theta) = \frac{(1-\cos\delta\Theta)}{\delta\Theta^2} \tag{2.132}$$

Where dt is the time step, $d\Theta = |\delta\Theta|$, and $\delta\Theta = \frac{1}{2}\omega dt$.

In this case, unlike for the rotation vector:

$$({}^{\times}[\delta\tilde{\Theta}])^2 = -(\delta\Theta)^2 I$$

So:

$$f_2(d\Theta)({}^{\times}[\delta\tilde{\Theta}])^2 = \frac{(1-\cos\delta\Theta)}{\delta\Theta^2}(\delta\Theta^2 I) = (\cos\delta\Theta - 1)I$$

So:

$$\tilde{q}^k_{k+1} = \cos\delta\Theta[I] + f_1(\delta\Theta)\,{}^{\times}[\delta\tilde{\Theta}]$$

Which can be written:

$$\tilde{q}^k_{k+1} = \cos\delta\Theta[I] + \sin\delta\Theta[(\,{}^{\times}[\tilde{\omega}_b])/|\tilde{\omega}_b|] \qquad (2.133)$$

2.8.6 References and Further Reading

Horn covers quaternions briefly in his book and his listed paper develops a closed form solution for registering points. Funda and also Pervin discuss the role of the quaternion in robotics. Hamilton's actual book can still be found in libraries. Eves is a somewhat tutorial source.

[25] B. K. P. Horn, Closed-Form Solution of Absolute Orientation Using Unit Quaternions, Journal of the Optical Society of America, Vol. 4, No. 4, pp. 629–642, Apr. 1987.

[26] B. K. P. Horn, *Robot Vision,* pp. 437-438, MIT Press / McGraw-Hill, 1986.

[27] Janez Funda and Richard P. Paul, A Comparison of Transforms and Quaternions in Robotics, *IEEE Transactions on Robotics and Automation,* pp. 886–891, 1988.

[28] E Pervin, and J Webb, Quaternions in Computer Vision and Robotics, *Technical Report* CMU-CS-82-150.

[29] H. Eves, *Foundations and Fundamental Concepts of Mathematics,* 3rd ed., Dover, 1997.

[30] W. R. Hamilton, *Elements of Quaternions,* Chelsea, New York, 1969.

2.8.7 Exercises

2.8.7.1 *Quaternion Multiplication Table*

Hamilton is said to have scratched the essence of his multiplication table into a stone bridge in Dublin. The essence of the table is very brief:

$$i^2 = j^2 = k^2 = ijk = -1$$

Show that the remaining contents of the entire multiplication table in the text follows from this formula. Recall that quaternion multiplication is not commutative and this is because products of the imaginary elements do not commute ($ij \neq ji$ etc.). However, products of imaginaries and scalars (like -1) do commute, so that $(-i)j = i(-j)$.

2.8.7.2 Rotation of a Vector

The real part of a quaternion product does not change if the order of the product is reversed. Prove as succinctly as you can that the rotation of a quaternized vector must have zero scalar part.

2.8.7.3 Integration of Quaternion Angular Velocity

Represent the initial orientation of a vehicle by the unit quaternion:

$$\tilde{q}(t) = \tilde{q}(t) = \cos\frac{\theta(t)}{2} + \hat{w}\sin\frac{\theta(t)}{2} = \begin{bmatrix} 1 & 0 & 0 & 0 \end{bmatrix}$$

Show that the following formula

$$\tilde{q}(t) = \frac{1}{2}\int_0^t \tilde{q}(t)\tilde{\omega}_b(t)dt$$

correctly increments the yaw of a vehicle by an angle of ωdt after the expiration of a differential time period of length dt.

CHAPTER 3
Numerical Methods

Figure 3.1 Urban Search and Rescue (USAR) Robots. When nature strikes in the form of earthquakes, hurricanes and so on, USAR robots can be deployed to search the rubble. Numerical methods are the basis of almost all of the algorithms used to make them easier for the operator to use, or even to endow the robots with a little intelligence of their own.

A large number of problems in mobile robotics can be reduced to a few basic problem formulations. Most problems reduce to some mixture of optimizing something, solving simultaneous linear or nonlinear equations, or integrating differential equations. Well-known numerical methods exist for all of these problems and all are accessible as black boxes in both software applications and general purpose toolboxes. Of course offline toolboxes cannot be used to control a system in real time and almost any solution benefits from exploiting the nature of the problem, so it is still very common to implement numerical algorithms from scratch for many real time systems.

The techniques described in this section will be referenced in many future places in the text. These techniques will be used to compute wheel velocities, invert dynamic models, generate trajectories, track features in an image, construct globally consistent maps, identify dynamic models, calibrate cameras, and so on.

3.1 Linearization and Optimization of Functions of Vectors

Perhaps paradoxically, linearization is the fundamental process that enables us to deal with nonlinear functions. The topics of linearization and optimization are closely

116

linked because a local optimum of a function coincides with special properties of its linear approximation.

Box 3.1. Notation for Numerical Methods Problems

The following notational conventions will be used consistently throughout the text in order to elucidate how most problems reduce to a need for a few fundamental algorithms:

$\underline{x}^{*} = \text{argmin}\,[f(\underline{x})]$	optimization problem
$\text{optimize:}_{\underline{x}}\quad f(\underline{x})$	optimization problem
$\underline{g}(\underline{x}) = \underline{b}$	level curve of $\underline{g}(\ )$
$\underline{c}(\underline{x}) = \underline{0}$	rootfinding, constraints
$\underline{z} = \underline{h}(\underline{x})$	measurement of state
$\underline{r}(\underline{x}) = \underline{z} - \underline{h}(\underline{x})$	residual

---

3.1.1 Linearization

3.1.1.1 Taylor Series of Functions of Vectors

The basic scalar Taylor series for a scalar function of a scalar was discussed in Section 2.2.2.3 of Chapter 2. That result can be rewritten in terms of an expansion about an arbitrary point rather than about the origin:

$$f(x + \Delta x) = f(x) + \Delta x \left\{ \frac{df}{dx} \right\}_x + \frac{\Delta x^2}{2!} \left\{ \frac{d^2 f}{dx^2} \right\}_x + \frac{\Delta x^3}{3!} \left\{ \frac{d^3 f}{dx^3} \right\}_x + \dots$$

Here, the derivatives involved are the first, second, and third total derivatives. This idea can be expanded to scalar functions of a vector. In implicit layout form (see Section 2.2.6.10 of Chapter 2):

$$f(\underline{x} + \Delta \underline{x}) = f(\underline{x}) + \Delta \underline{x} \left\{ \frac{\partial f}{\partial \underline{x}} \right\}_{\underline{x}} + \frac{\Delta \underline{x}^2}{2!} \left\{ \frac{\partial^2 f}{\partial \underline{x}^2} \right\}_{\underline{x}} + \frac{\Delta \underline{x}^3}{3!} \left\{ \frac{\partial^3 f}{\partial \underline{x}^3} \right\}_{\underline{x}} + \dots$$

The derivatives involved are the gradient vector, the Hessian matrix and a third-order tensor derivative. For a vector-valued function of a vector:

$$\underline{f}(\underline{x} + \Delta \underline{x}) = \underline{f}(\underline{x}) + \Delta \underline{x} \left\{ \frac{\partial \underline{f}}{\partial \underline{x}} \right\}_{\underline{x}} + \frac{\Delta \underline{x}^2}{2!} \left\{ \frac{\partial^2 \underline{f}}{\partial \underline{x}^2} \right\}_{\underline{x}} + \frac{\Delta \underline{x}^3}{3!} \left\{ \frac{\partial^3 \underline{f}}{\partial \underline{x}^3} \right\}_{\underline{x}} + \dots$$

Now the derivatives involved are a Jacobian matrix, a third-order tensor, and a fourth-order tensor.

3.1.1.2 Taylor Remainder Theorem

The above results, if truncated at the cubic term, would be called Taylor polynomials of third-degree $T_3(\Delta x)$. For the scalar forms of the theorem, it can be shown that:

$$f(x + \Delta x) = T_n(\Delta x) + R_n(\Delta x)$$

where the remainder or truncation error is given by:

$$R_n(\Delta x) = \frac{1}{n!} \int_x^{(x+\Delta x)} (x - \zeta)^n \left\{ \frac{\partial^{(n)} f}{\partial x^n} \right\}_\zeta d\zeta$$

In other words, provided the n-th derivative is bounded, the error in the Taylor series is a term of order Δx^{n+1}. Hence, if Δx is small, the error approaches zero for large enough n. It is easy to generalize this result to the other two cases above.

3.1.1.3 Linearization

The practical utility of the remainder theorem is that we can say with some confidence that a series of any order is a good enough approximation to a given function provided Δx is small enough. In particular, most techniques in numerical methods are based on first-order approximations to nonlinear functions. For example the *first-order approximation*:

$$\underline{f}(\underline{x} + \Delta \underline{x}) = \underline{f}(\underline{x}) + \Delta \underline{x} \left\{ \frac{\partial \underline{f}}{\partial \underline{x}} \right\}_{\underline{x}}$$

is said to be accurate *to first order* – meaning that the error in the approximation is a term that is second order, also known as *quadratic*, in $\Delta \underline{x}$. We will use the term *linearization* to mean the approximation of a function to first order, that is, by a linear Taylor polynomial.

3.1.1.4 Gradients and Level Curves and Surfaces

Consider a scalar-valued function of a vector $g(\underline{x})$. If $\underline{x}$ is $n \times 1$, the set of solutions to:

$$g(\underline{x}) = b \quad \underline{x} \in \Re^n$$

for some constant b forms an $n - 1$ dimensional subspace of $\Re^n$ called a *level surface*. Let the set of solutions to the above constraint be parameterized locally by a parameter s to produce the surface $\underline{x}(s)$. Each element of the vector $\underline{x}(s)$ is a *level curve*. By the chain rule, the derivative of g with respect to the parameter s is:

$$\frac{\partial g(\underline{x}(s))}{\partial s} = \frac{\partial g}{\partial \underline{x}} \frac{\partial \underline{x}}{\partial s}^T = \frac{\partial b}{\partial s} = \underline{0}^T$$

We can conclude that the gradient $\partial g / \partial \underline{x}$ is **normal to the level curves of** g. The vector $\partial \underline{x} / \partial s$ is tangent to the level curve. In general, the gradient of any scalar function of a vector is directed orthogonally to its level curves.

3.1.1.5 Example

For example, if

$$g(\underline{x}) = x_1^2 + x_2^2 = R^2$$

The gradient is:

$$\frac{\partial g}{\partial \underline{x}} = 2 \begin{bmatrix} x_1 & x_2 \end{bmatrix}$$

Then parameterize the level curve (a circle) with:

$$x(s) = \begin{bmatrix} \cos(\kappa s) & \sin(\kappa s) \end{bmatrix}^T$$

where κ is $1/R$. Therefore, the tangent vector is:

$$\frac{\partial \underline{x}}{\partial s} = \begin{bmatrix} -\kappa \sin(\kappa s) & \kappa \cos(\kappa s) \end{bmatrix} = \kappa \begin{bmatrix} -x_2 & x_1 \end{bmatrix}$$

which is orthogonal to $\partial g / \partial \underline{x}$ as their dot product will show.

3.1.1.6 Jacobians and Level Surfaces

When g is of higher dimension, the set of solutions to:

$$g(x) = \underline{b} \qquad \underline{x} \in \Re^n \qquad \underline{g} \in \Re^m$$

for some constant $\underline{b}$ forms an $n - m$ dimensional subspace of $\Re^n$, which is called a *level surface*. Let the set of solutions to the above constraints be parameterized locally by a parameter vector $\underline{s}$ to produce the surface $\underline{x}(\underline{s})$. Each element of $\underline{x}(s)$ is a *level curve*.

By the chain rule, the derivative of g with respect to these parameters is:

$$\frac{\partial \underline{g}(x(\underline{s}))}{\partial \underline{s}} = \frac{\partial \underline{g}}{\partial \underline{x}} \frac{\partial \underline{x}}{\partial \underline{s}}^T = \frac{\partial \underline{b}}{\partial \underline{s}} = [0]$$

The derivative $\partial g / \partial \underline{x}$ is m rows, each of which is an n dimensional gradient of one of the elements of g and $\partial x / \partial \underline{s}$ is the set of m row vectors in n dimensions that are tangent to the level surface. We can conclude that every row of the Jacobian, that is, the gradient of every element of the vector $g(\underline{x})$, is normal to all of the tangents to the level surface $\underline{x}(\underline{s})$. This is clearly also true for any linear combination of the tangents. The set of all such linear combinations is called the *tangent plane*. The result means that the tangent plane lies in the nullspace of the constraint Jacobian.

3.1.2 Optimization of Objective Functions

Suppose we desire to optimize $f(\underline{x})$ by choosing one or more values of $\underline{x}$ which are optimal:

$$optimize_{\underline{x}} \quad f(\underline{x}) \qquad \underline{x} \in \Re^n \tag{3.1}$$

Above, $f(\ )$ is a scalar-valued function of a vector. It is called the *objective* function in general, the *utility* function when it is to be maximized, and the *cost* function when it is to be minimized. Note that f can be maximized by minimizing $-f$ so we will treat all problems as minimization problems for consistency.

Perhaps the most important question affecting the difficulty of an optimization problem is the question of *convexity*. Intuitively, a convex (concave) function has the property that the function itself is uniformly on or below (above) any line segment between any two values in its domain (Figure 3.2).

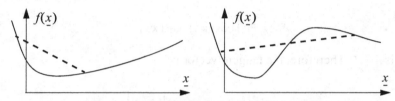

Figure 3.2 Convex and Nonconvex Functions. The function on the left is convex. It is below any line joining two points on the curve. The function on the right is not convex.

Any solution $\underline{x}^*$ to this optimization problem must have the property that all values of $f(\underline{x})$, over the entire range of possible values of $\underline{x}$, are not lower than $f(\underline{x}^*)$. Such a point $\underline{x}^*$ is called a *global minimum*. Unless the objective function is convex or the problem can be converted into one which is convex, finding the global minimum can be quite difficult to do. Another form of minimum is a *local minimum*. In this case, we define a neighborhood of $\underline{x}^*$ and require that the objective not decrease relative to $f(\underline{x}^*)$ anywhere in this neighborhood. For an objective with several local minima, the one that is found depends on the initial guess that is used in such algorithms.

One potential technique for finding a global minimum is *sampling*. If the local minima for enough initial guesses are computed, there is a good chance one of them will be the global minimum – provided the sampling is dense enough (Figure 3.3).

Based on the observation that a global minimum is also a local minimum, at least on unbounded domains, the search for a local minimum is, in some sense, a more fundamental problem.

3.1.2.1 First-Order (Necessary) Conditions on Local Extrema

We will concentrate therefore on finding points which satisfy the weaker condition of being local minima. We have seen that, for small enough neighborhoods, a function can be well approximated by a first-order Taylor series. Consider the change in $f(\ )$ that occurs after moving a small amount $\Delta \underline{x}$ away from the minimum in an arbitrary

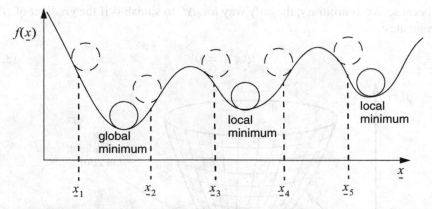

Figure 3.3 Dense Sampling to Find the Global Minimum. The local minimum that results from a choice of initial guess can be visualized as the valley into which a ball placed at that position would roll. Above, the leftmost local minimum is the global minimum and it can be found by solving for a large number of local minima.

direction:

$$\Delta f = f(\underline{x}^* + \Delta \underline{x}) - f(\underline{x}^*) = f(\underline{x}^*) + \left\{ \frac{\partial f(\underline{x}^*)}{\partial x} \right\} \Delta \underline{x} - f(\underline{x}^*) = f_{\underline{x}}(\underline{x}^*) \Delta \underline{x}$$

where $f_{\underline{x}}(\underline{x}) = \partial f(\underline{x})/\partial x$ is called the *objective gradient*. To avoid unwieldy partial derivative notation, the remainder of this section will use a single subscript to denote a first derivative (of a scalar or vector) and a double subscript to denote a second derivative. Strictly speaking, $f(\underline{x}^*)$ is a constant vector whose derivative vanishes, because $\underline{x}^*$ is a constant, so our compact abuse of notation (which will be used extensively below) really means:

$$\underline{f}_{\underline{x}}(\underline{x}^*) \equiv \frac{\partial \underline{f}(\underline{x}^*)}{\partial \underline{x}} \equiv \frac{\partial \underline{f}(\underline{x})}{\partial \underline{x}} \Bigg|_{\underline{x} = \underline{x}^*}$$

If $\underline{x}^*$ is a local minimum point, then we must require $\Delta f \geq 0$ for arbitrary perturbations $\Delta \underline{x}$:

$$\Delta f = f_{\underline{x}}(\underline{x}^*) \Delta \underline{x} \geq 0 \qquad \forall \Delta \underline{x}$$

Imagine that a particular $\Delta \underline{x}$ causes an increase in $f(\ )$. If this is so, clearly the perturbation $-\Delta \underline{x}$ will cause an equivalent decrease by moving in the opposite direction, so the only way for this first order approximation to $f(\underline{x})$ to have been expanded about a local minimum is if the change in the objective vanishes:

$$\Delta f = f_{\underline{x}}(\underline{x}^*) \Delta \underline{x} = 0 \qquad \forall \Delta \underline{x} \tag{3.2}$$

Now, because $\Delta \underline{x}$ is arbitrary, the only way for Δf to vanish is if the gradient of $f(\ )$ itself vanishes:

$$f_{\underline{x}}(\underline{x}^*) = \underline{0}^T \qquad\qquad (3.3)$$

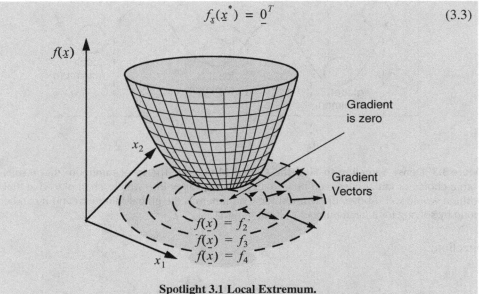

Spotlight 3.1 Local Extremum.

The gradient vector of $f(\underline{x})$ is always orthogonal to the level curves of $f(\underline{x})$ and it vanishes at a local extremum.

Under such conditions, the first-order behavior of a perturbation in any direction in $\mathfrak{R}^n$ satisfies:

$$f(\underline{x}^* + \Delta \underline{x}) = f(\underline{x}^*) + f_{\underline{x}}(\underline{x}^*)\Delta \underline{x} = f(\underline{x}^*) \qquad \forall \Delta \underline{x} \qquad\qquad (3.4)$$

3.1.2.2 Second-Order (Sufficient) Conditions on Local Extrema

Under the assumption that the above first-order condition is satisfied, we can write the second-degree Taylor polynomial for $f(\ )$ in implicit layout format as:

$$f(\underline{x} + \Delta \underline{x}) = f(\underline{x}) + \frac{\Delta \underline{x}^2}{2!}\left\{\frac{\partial^2 f}{\partial \underline{x}^2}\right\}_{\underline{x}}$$

When we enforce vector-matrix layout conventions, and denote the derivative as the Hessian matrix $f_{\underline{xx}}$ that it is, this becomes:

$$\Delta f = f(\underline{x} + \Delta \underline{x}) - f(\underline{x}) = f(\underline{x}) + \frac{1}{2}\Delta \underline{x}^T f_{\underline{xx}}(\underline{x})\Delta \underline{x}$$

Now the condition of local optimality is:

$$\Delta f = \frac{1}{2}\Delta \underline{x}^T f_{\underline{xx}}(\underline{x})\Delta \underline{x} \geq 0 \qquad \forall \Delta \underline{x}$$

This requirement that $\Delta \underline{x}^T f_{\underline{x}\underline{x}}(\underline{x})\Delta\underline{x} \geq 0$ is the requirement that $f_{\underline{x}\underline{x}}(\underline{x})$ be positive semidefinite. This is the second-order necessary condition for a local minimum. If $f_{\underline{x}\underline{x}}(\underline{x})$ is positive definite then $\Delta\underline{x}^T f_{\underline{x}\underline{x}}(\underline{x})\Delta\underline{x} > 0$ and this is a sufficient condition for guaranteeing a local minimum.

3.1.2.3 Feasible Perturbations

Consider a general set of m nonlinear constraints

$$\underline{c}(\underline{x}) = \underline{0} \quad \underline{c} \in \Re^m \quad \underline{x} \in \Re^n \tag{3.5}$$

Any point that satisfies these constraints is said to be *feasible* and the set of all such points is called the *feasible set*. Suppose we know the location $\underline{x}'$ of a feasible point. Let's examine the behavior of the feasible set near this point. Consider a *feasible perturbation* $\Delta\underline{x}$ – one which remains feasible to first order. Expanding the constraints in a Taylor series around $\underline{x}'$:

$$\underline{c}(\underline{x}' + \Delta\underline{x}) = \underline{c}(\underline{x}') + \underline{c}_{\underline{x}}(\underline{x}')\Delta\underline{x} + \ldots$$

The Jacobian matrix $\underline{c}_{\underline{x}}$ is $m \times n$ and therefore it is typically nonsquare. We will at least assume that this matrix is of rank m from now on, but if it is not, we can always redefine m to be the number of linearly independent rows and there must always be at least one. Now, if this perturbation moves in a feasible direction, the constraints are still satisfied to first order, so we have:

$$\underline{c}(\underline{x}' + \Delta\underline{x}) = \underline{c}(\underline{x}') + \underline{c}_{\underline{x}}(\underline{x}')\Delta\underline{x} = \underline{0}$$

Since $\underline{c}(\underline{x}') = \underline{0}$, we can conclude that:

$$\underline{c}_{\underline{x}}(\underline{x}')\Delta\underline{x} = \underline{0} \tag{3.6}$$

for a feasible perturbation.

3.1.2.4 Constraint Nullspace and Tangent Plane

Some interpretation of this last conclusion is illuminating. It helps to remember that the constraint Jacobian $\underline{c}_{\underline{x}}(\underline{x}')$ is $m \times n$. Its rows constitute a set of gradient vectors in $\Re^n$ (evaluated at $\underline{x}'$) of the m scalar quantities $\{c_1(\underline{x}), c_2(\underline{x})\ldots c_m(\underline{x})\}$ corresponding to each constraint. Every element of the zero column on the right side of Equation 3.6 was computed from a dot product of a row of $\underline{c}_{\underline{x}}$ and the perturbation. So, this condition on a feasible perturbation means that the vector $\Delta\underline{x}$ must be orthogonal to *all* of the rows of the constraint Jacobian. The set of all such vectors is called the *constraint tangent plane*:

$$N(\underline{c}_{\underline{x}}) = \{\Delta\underline{x}: \quad \underline{c}_{\underline{x}}(\underline{x}')\Delta\underline{x} = \underline{0}\}$$

which is also known more generally as the nullspace of the constraint Jacobian. Conversely, all vectors in the row space of $\underline{c}_{\underline{x}}$ are orthogonal to the tangent plane and they constitute the disallowed directions for perturbations. This concept can be visualized as shown in Spotlight 3.2.

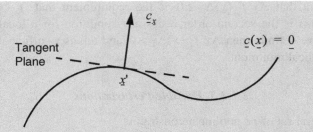

Spotlight 3.2 Constraint Tangent Plane.

The tangent plane to the constraints $\underline{c}(x) = \underline{0}$ is the set of all vectors that are perpendicular to the constraint Jacobian denoted as $\underline{c}_x$. If the feasible set were a curve in 3D, the tangent plane would be a line and the normal vector in the figure could be rotated around the line while remaining tangent to the line and therefore normal to the constraint curve. In doing so, it sweeps through the row space of the constraint Jacobian.

Box 3.2. Conditions for Optimality and Feasibility

For the scalar-valued objective function $f(\underline{x})$...

The necessary condition for a local optimum at $\underline{x}^*$ is that the gradient with respect to $\underline{x}$ vanish at that point:

$$f_{\underline{x}}(\underline{x}^*) = \underline{0}^T$$

The sufficient condition for a local minimum at $\underline{x}^*$ is that the Hessian be positive definite:

$$\frac{1}{2}\Delta\underline{x}^T f_{\underline{xx}}(\underline{x})\Delta\underline{x} > 0 \qquad \forall \Delta\underline{x}$$

For the set of constraint functions $\underline{c}(x) = \underline{0}$, if $\underline{x}'$ is a feasible point (i.e. $\underline{c}(\underline{x}') = \underline{0}$, then the new point $\underline{x}'' = \underline{x}' + \Delta\underline{x}$ is also feasible (to first order) if the state change $\Delta\underline{x}$ is confined to the constraint tangent plane.

$$\underline{c}_{\underline{x}}(\underline{x}')\Delta\underline{x} = \underline{0}$$

3.1.3 Constrained Optimization

Many problems can be expressed in terms of a scalar-valued function of many variables which is to be optimized while satisfying constraints. When the unknowns are points, parameters, or vectors, this type of problem is called (interchangeably) either *constrained optimization* or *nonlinear programming*. The most general expression of a constrained optimization problem that we will need is:

$$\begin{aligned}
\text{optimize:}_{\underline{x}} \quad & f(\underline{x}) & \underline{x} \in \Re^n \\
\text{subject to:} \quad & \underline{c}'mp(\underline{x}) = \underline{0} & \underline{c} \in \Re^m
\end{aligned} \qquad (3.7)$$

where $f(\ )$ is the objective function and $\underline{c}(\ )$ contains the constraints. More general problems incorporate inequality constraints like $\underline{c}(x) \leq \underline{0}$ as well. Still more general problems allow $\underline{x}$ to be an unknown function or even the time varying state vector $\underline{x}(t)$ of a system that is controlled by another time-varying input $\underline{u}(t)$. Such *variational* optimization problems will be discussed later in the text.

If the constraints are not present, the problem is called *unconstrained optimization*. If the objective is not present, the problem will be called *constraint satisfaction*. At times, the approaches to solving each of three classes of problem are quite different.

If $\underline{x}$ is $n \times 1$, then typically $\underline{c}$ is $m \times 1$ with $m < n$. If m and n were equal, then the feasible set could be reduced to a few roots of $\underline{c}(\ )$ or even a single point. In the latter case, there would be nothing to optimize.

3.1.3.1 First-Order Conditions on a Constrained Local Optimum

The constrained optimization problem is quite difficult because $\underline{c}(\ )$ imposes some constraints on $\underline{x}$ and we must search the remaining degrees of freedom to find the optimum of $f(\ )$. Let us once again imagine that we have found a local optimum $\underline{x}^*$. In order to solve our problem it must be both feasible and locally minimal. Consider the first-order conditions that must apply for it to be a constrained local minimum.

This and all subsequent discussions will assume the Jacobian is of full rank for brevity. Because $\underline{c}(\ )$ imposes only m constraints on a vector in $\Re^n$, there are $n - m$ unconstrained degrees of freedom left in the tangent plane. Based on Equation 3.6, if the point $\underline{x}^*$ is feasible, a feasible perturbation $\Delta \underline{x}$ must satisfy:

$$\underline{c}_x(\underline{x}^*)\Delta \underline{x} = \underline{0} \qquad \forall \Delta \underline{x} \text{ feasible}$$

At a constrained minimum, we cannot invoke Equation 3.3 and require that the gradient itself vanish because there is no guarantee that such a point would be feasible. In this constrained case, we *define* a local minimum to mean that the change in the objective $f(\ )$ must vanish only for feasible perturbations from a feasible point. We can still argue based on the above equation that if a particular $\Delta \underline{x}$ is feasible then $-\Delta \underline{x}$ must also be feasible. So, if $\Delta \underline{x}$ causes an increase in $f(\ )$, then $-\Delta \underline{x}$ will cause a decrease. This conclusion contradicts the assumption of a local minimum. Hence, we can conclude that the change in the objective must vanish for any feasible perturbation:

$$f_x(\underline{x}^*)\Delta \underline{x} = 0 \qquad \forall \Delta \underline{x} \text{ feasible}$$

Unlike in the unconstrained case, the perturbation $\Delta \underline{x}$ here is constrained to lie in the constraint tangent plane. Now this last condition requires the objective gradient to be perpendicular to an arbitrary vector in the tangent plan. The set of all vectors in the tangent plane is $N(\underline{c}_x)$ and the set of all vectors orthogonal to an arbitrary vector in $N(\underline{c}_x)$ is its orthogonal complement, the rowspace $R(\underline{c}_x)$. Therefore, the objective gradient must lie in $R(\underline{c}_x)$.

The objective gradient $f_x(\underline{x}^*)$ is a vector in $\Re^n$ whereas $R(\underline{c}_x)$ is of dimension m. Every vector in $R(\underline{c}_x)$ can be written as a weighted sum of the rows of $\underline{c}_x$, that is as

$\underline{\lambda}^T \underline{c}_x$ for some $1 \times m$ vector of constants $\underline{\lambda}^T$. We conclude that the objective gradient must be of the form given in Spotlight 3.3.

$$f_{\underline{x}}(\underline{x}^*) = \underline{\lambda}^T \underline{c}_{\underline{x}}(\underline{x}^*) \qquad (3.8)$$

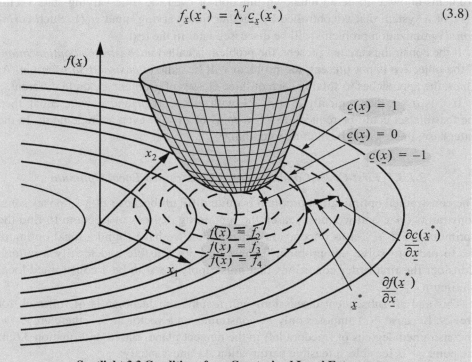

Spotlight 3.3 Conditions for a Constrained Local Extremum.

The gradient vector of $f(\underline{x})$ is orthogonal to the level curves of $f(\underline{x})$ and it is also orthogonal to those of $\underline{c}(x)$. The extremum occurs when the gradient of $f(\underline{x})$ is normal to the level curve $\underline{c}(x) = \underline{0}$ (which is otherwise known as the constraints).

Because $\underline{\lambda}$ is unknown, we can change its sign without loss of generality and then transpose the above to produce the following n equations in the $n + m$ unknowns in $\underline{x}$ and $\underline{\lambda}$:

$$f_{\underline{x}}^T(\underline{x}^*) + \underline{c}_{\underline{x}}^T(\underline{x}^*)\underline{\lambda} = \underline{0}$$

Recall that there are m constraints $\underline{c}(\underline{x}) = \underline{0}$ so, in total, there are now enough conditions on the collected unknowns in $\underline{x}$ and $\underline{\lambda}$ to solve the system. The first order necessary conditions for a constrained local minimum are therefore:

$$f_{\underline{x}}^T(\underline{x}^*) + \underline{c}_{\underline{x}}^T(\underline{x}^*)\underline{\lambda} = \underline{0}$$
$$\underline{c}(\underline{x}^*) = \underline{0} \qquad (3.9)$$

It is customary to define a scalar-valued function called the *Lagrangian* thus:

$$l(\underline{x}, \underline{\lambda}) = f(\underline{x}) + \underline{\lambda}^T \underline{c}(\underline{x}) \qquad (3.10)$$

Under this definition, the necessary conditions take the compact form:

$$\frac{\partial l(\underline{x}, \underline{\lambda})}{\partial \underline{x}}^T = \underline{0} \qquad \frac{\partial l(\underline{x}, \underline{\lambda})}{\partial \underline{\lambda}}^T = \underline{0} \qquad (3.11)$$

3.1.3.2 Solving Constrained Optimization Problems

There are four basic methods available for solving such problems with a computer:

- Substitution: In rare cases, it is possible to substitute the constraints into the objective and reduce the problem to an unconstrained optimization problem.
- Descent: An initial guess for the solution is continuously refined by moving in the tangent plane to progressively lower values of $f(\ )$ until the refined guess arrives at a minimum.
- Lagrange Multipliers: The necessary conditions are linearized and solved iteratively.
- Penalty Function: The constraints are added to the objective function so that their dissatisfaction increases the objective and then the combined objective is minimized as an unconstrained problem.

Following sections investigate a few closed-form examples and numerical methods are presented in Section 3.3.2.

3.1.3.3 Unconstrained Quadratic Optimization

The simplest unconstrained optimization problem is that of optimization of a vector quadratic form. Consider the quadratic function of a vector:

$$minimize:_{\underline{x}} \quad f(\underline{x}) = \frac{1}{2} \underline{x}^T Q \underline{x} \quad \underline{x} \in \Re^n$$

where Q is a symmetric positive definite matrix. This continuous scalar-valued function of a vector must possess a gradient vector and we know that a local extremum will occur at any point for which the gradient is zero. Like a parabola in one dimension, a quadratic cost function has a single extremum. Setting the derivative to the zero vector:

$$f_{\underline{x}} = \underline{x}^T Q = \underline{0}^T$$

Transposing leads to $Q\underline{x} = \underline{0}$. This is a homogenous system of linear equations. Because Q is symmetric and positive definite, all of its eigenvalues are positive and it is nonsingular. Therefore, the minimizer of this quadratic form is the origin:

$$\underline{x}^* = Q^{-1}\underline{0} = \underline{0}$$

In retrospect, given that $\underline{x}^T Q \underline{x} > 0$, $\underline{x} \neq \underline{0}$ for a positive definite Q, this result is obvious. A more general case is a kind of vector "parabola":

$$minimize:_{\underline{x}} \quad f(\underline{x}) = \frac{1}{2} \underline{x}^T Q_{xx} \underline{x} + \underline{b}^T \underline{x} + \underline{c} \qquad (3.12)$$

Setting the derivative to zero:

$$f_{\underline{x}} = \underline{x}^{*T}Q + \underline{b}^T = \underline{0}^T$$

Transposing and moving the constant to the other side:

$$Q\underline{x}^* = -\underline{b}$$

So the minimum occurs at:

$$\underline{x}^* = -Q^{-1}\underline{b} \qquad (3.13)$$

For comparison, the minimum of the scalar parabola $f(x) = (1/2)ax^2 + bx + c$ occurs at $x^* = -(b/a)$. The most general case is to ask for the minimizer of a form with linear terms and a constant:

$$minimize:_{\underline{x}} f(\underline{x}) = \frac{1}{2}\underline{x}^T Q_{xx}\underline{x} + \underline{c}^T Q_{cx}\underline{x} + \underline{x}^T Q_{xc}\underline{c} + \underline{c}^T Q_{cc}\underline{c} \qquad (3.14)$$

for some constant vector $\underline{c}$ and arbitrary matrices Q_{cx} etc. In this case the solution is:

$$\underline{x}^* = -Q^{-1}(Q_{cx} + Q_{xc}^T)\underline{c} \qquad (3.15)$$

3.1.3.4 Linearly Constrained Optimization: Substitution

Another canonical problem is the minimization of the simplest interesting multivariable objective function (quadratic) subject to the simplest multivariable constraint (linear). Consider the problem:

$$\begin{aligned} minimize:_{\underline{x}} \; f(\underline{x}) &= \frac{1}{2}\underline{x}^T Q\underline{x} \qquad \underline{x} \in \Re^n \\ subject\ to:\ \ G\underline{x} &= \underline{b} \qquad\qquad \underline{b} \in \Re^m \end{aligned} \qquad (3.16)$$

The matrix G is not square, for if it was, and it was invertible, there would be a unique solution to the constraints, a singleton feasible set, and nothing to optimize. This problem is quite difficult because G imposes some constraints on $\underline{x}$ and we must search the remaining degrees of freedom to find the extremum.

However, the case with linear constraints can be solved by substitution. Let us partition the unknowns like so:

$$\underline{x} = \begin{bmatrix} \underline{x}_1^T & \underline{x}_2^T \end{bmatrix}^T \qquad \begin{matrix} \underline{x}_1 \in \Re^m \\ \underline{x}_2 \in \Re^{n-m} \end{matrix}$$

Then, in block notation, the constraints become:

$$\begin{bmatrix} G_1 & G_2 \end{bmatrix} \begin{bmatrix} \underline{x}_1 \\ \underline{x}_2 \end{bmatrix} = \underline{b}$$

G_1 is square $m \times m$. If G_1 is invertible, and $\underline{x}_2$ is known, we can write:

$$G_1\underline{x}_1 + G_2\underline{x}_2 = \underline{b}$$

$$G_1\underline{x}_1 = \underline{b} - G_2\underline{x}_2$$

$$\underline{x}_1 = G_1^{-1}[\underline{b} - G_2\underline{x}_2] = \underline{b}_1 - G_3\underline{x}_2$$

Hence, on the assumption that the variables are chosen such that G_1 is invertible, $\underline{x}_1$ can be computed from $\underline{x}_2$. Note that G_3 and $\underline{b}_1$ are known. Substituting this into the objective function produces an unconstrained problem in the $n - m$ free unknowns in $\underline{x}_2$ of the following form:

$$f(\underline{x}) = \frac{1}{2}\underline{x}_2^T Q_{xx}\underline{x}_2 + \underline{b}_1^T Q_{bx}\underline{x}_2 + \underline{x}_2^T Q_{xb}\underline{b}_1 + \underline{b}_1^T Q_{bb}\underline{b}_1 \qquad (3.17)$$

This is now identical to the unconstrained problem solved above.

3.1.3.5 Linearly Constrained Optimization: Penalty Function

Consider again the previous problem:

$$\begin{aligned} minimize:_{\underline{x}} \ f(\underline{x}) &= \frac{1}{2}\underline{x}^T Q\underline{x} \qquad \underline{x} \in \mathfrak{R}^n \\ subject \ to: \ G\underline{x} &= \underline{b} \qquad\qquad \underline{b} \in \mathfrak{R}^m \end{aligned} \qquad (3.18)$$

but consider the situation where the constraints are not exactly satisfied. In this case, we could form a residual vector:

$$\underline{r}(\underline{x}) = G\underline{x} - \underline{b} \qquad \underline{r} \in \mathfrak{R}^m$$

Now, this can be converted to a scalar cost by computing its magnitude $\underline{r}^T(\underline{x})\underline{r}(\underline{x})$ or, slightly more generally, the weighted magnitude $\underline{r}^T(\underline{x})R\underline{r}(\underline{x})$ for some symmetric positive definite matrix R. If this cost function is added to the original objective we have the new unconstrained problem:

$$minimize:_{\underline{x}} \ f(\underline{x}) = \frac{1}{2}\underline{x}^T Q\underline{x} + \frac{1}{2}\underline{r}^T(\underline{x})R\underline{r}(\underline{x}) \qquad \underline{x} \in \mathfrak{R}^n$$

The minimizer is computed as follows:

$$f_{\underline{x}} = \underline{x}^T Q + \underline{r}^T(\underline{x})R\frac{\partial \underline{r}(\underline{x})}{\partial \underline{x}} = \underline{0}^T$$

$$f_{\underline{x}} = \underline{x}^T Q + (\underline{x}^T G^T - \underline{b}^T)RG = \underline{0}^T$$

$$\underline{x}^T Q + \underline{x}^T G^T RG = \underline{b}^T RG$$

$$\{Q + G^T RG\}\underline{x} = G^T R\underline{b}$$

Which gives the solution as:

$$\underline{x} = \{Q + G^T RG\}^{-1} G^T R\underline{b} \qquad (3.19)$$

The relative magnitudes of R and Q will give rise to a tradeoff between them. High values of R can be used to force the constraints to be satisfied to high accuracy at the expense of placing less emphasis on minimizing the true objective. The penalty function technique can be a powerful way to quickly compute an answer that is good enough while avoiding the complexity of computing a truly constrained optimum.

3.1.4 References and Further Reading

Both of these books are good sources on linearization and sufficient and necessary conditions for optimality.

[1] P. E. Gill, W. Murray, and M. H. Wright, *Practical Optimization,* Academic Press, 1981.
[2] D. G. Luenberger, *Linear and Nonlinear Programming,* 2nd ed., Addison Wesley, Reading, MA, 1989.

3.1.5 Exercises

3.1.5.1 Taylor Remainder Theorem

Write a Taylor series for the function $y = \cos(x)$ for second and fourth order. Use each series to compute an approximation to $\cos(\pi/8)$ interpreted as $\cos(0 + \pi/8)$. That is, expand the series about the origin. Compute the error in the approximation. Use the derivatives of $\cos(x)$ and powers of x to approximate a bound on the remainder. Does the Taylor remainder theorem seem to work? Recall that derivatives of all orders for this function are bounded by unity.

3.1.5.2 Substitution vs. Constrained Optimization

Consider the problem:

$$\begin{aligned} \text{minimize:}_x \quad & f(\underline{x}) = f(x, y) = x^2 + y^2 \\ \text{subject to:} \quad & x + y - 1 = 0 \end{aligned}$$

Develop some intuition for the operation of constrained optimization. Sketch the objective function as a surface $z = f(x, y)$ with the x axis pointing downward to the left and the y axis pointing to the right. Draw the constraint plane projected on the x-y plane. What does the intersection of the objective and the constraint plane look like? Solve the optimization problem first using substitution then a second time using the necessary conditions (three equations) of constrained optimization. What does it mean in this case that the objective gradient is a linear combination of the constraint gradients (i.e., is in the nullspace of the constraints) and what is the value of the Lagrange multiplier at the minimum?

3.1.5.3 Closed Form Unconstrained Quadratic Optimization

Derive the minimizer of the most general matrix quadratic form:

$$\text{minimize:}_{\underline{x}} \qquad f(\underline{x}) = \frac{1}{2}\underline{x}^T Q_{xx}\underline{x} + \underline{c}^T Q_{cx}\underline{x} + \underline{x}^T Q_{xc}\underline{c} + \underline{c}^T Q_{cc}\underline{c}$$

for some constant vector $\underline{c}$.

3.2 Systems of Equations

3.2.1 Linear Systems

Of course, a numerical method for inverting a matrix amounts to a technique for solving square systems of linear equations of the form:

$$z = Hx \tag{3.20}$$

The solution is immediate if one can calculate the inverse:

$$x = H^{-1}z \tag{3.21}$$

and if the inverse exists. In practice, however, matrices are rarely inverted explicitly because it turns out that there are techniques that are somewhat more efficient and more numerically stable for solving such equations.

3.2.1.1 Square Systems

The reader is probably familiar with Gaussian or Gauss-Jordan elimination – basic techniques used to invert a matrix in a computer. They amount to repeated application of basic reduction techniques akin to how one would solve the problem on paper by elimination of variables. Briefly, consider three linear equations of the form:

$$a_{11}x_1 + a_{12}x_2 + a_{13}x_3 = y_1$$
$$a_{21}x_1 + a_{22}x_2 + a_{23}x_3 = y_2 \tag{3.22}$$
$$a_{31}x_1 + a_{32}x_2 + a_{33}x_3 = y_3$$

This is of the form $Ax = y$. If we multiply the second equation by a_{31}/a_{21} we produce:

$$a_{31}x_1 + \left(\frac{a_{31}}{a_{21}}\right)a_{22}x_2 + \left(\frac{a_{31}}{a_{22}}\right)a_{23}x_3 = \left(\frac{a_{31}}{a_{23}}\right)y_2$$

This new equation has the same coefficient for x_1 as the third equation. Subtracting it from the third equation produces a new equation with x_1 eliminated because its coefficient becomes 0. An important theorem of linear algebra states that if we replace the third equation with this new equation, the solution to the new system is the same as the original system. The new system becomes:

$$a_{11}x_1 + a_{12}x_2 + a_{13}x_3 = y_1$$
$$a_{21}x_1 + a_{22}x_2 + a_{23}x_3 = y_2$$
$$a_{32}^{(1)}x_2 + a_{33}^{(1)}x_3 = y_3^{(1)}$$

The superscript (1) means these coefficients are new ones resulting from the computations which replace the old ones. By multiplying the first equation by a_{21}/a_{11}, the same set of operations can now be performed on the first and second equations to eliminate x_1 from the second equation:

$$a_{11}x_1 + a_{12}x_2 + a_{13}x_3 = y_1$$
$$a_{22}^{(1)}x_2 + a_{23}^{(1)}x_3 = y_2^{(1)}$$
$$a_{32}^{(1)}x_2 + a_{33}^{(1)}x_3 = y_3^{(1)}$$

Finally, the same process can be applied to the second and third equation to eliminate x_2:

$$a_{11}x_1 + a_{12}x_2 + a_{13}x_3 = y_1$$
$$a_{22}^{(1)}x_2 + a_{23}^{(1)}x_3 = y_2^{(1)}$$
$$a_{33}^{(2)}x_3 = y_3^{(2)}$$

The last equation can now be solved for x_3. Once it is known, we can move $a_{23}^{(1)}x_3$ to the other side of the second equation. Then, the second last equation can be solved for x_2. Continuing in this manner, we can solve for x_1 once the other two variables are known.

Notice that this process clearly generalizes to larger systems of equations. It is a completely general algorithm in the sense that the coefficients in the matrix A can be arbitrary. A robust implementation of these ideas requires detection of singular matrices and techniques to deal with nearly singular matrices.

3.2.1.2 Left Pseudoinverse of an Overdetermined System

If, for the system:

$$z = Hx \tag{3.23}$$

the x vector is $n \times 1$ and the z vector is $m \times 1$, then the H matrix must be $m \times n$. When $m \neq n$ the system is nonsquare and it is not clear what it means to solve the system. The theory of constrained optimization that was presented earlier is adequate to derive the so-called *pseudoinverses* of nonsquare matrices which solve such problems.

When $m > n$ then the system is said to be *overdetermined* and, unless the right number of equations are redundant, there are insufficient unknowns in x to satisfy the m constraints. Quite often, the z vector represents measurements that depend on x as specified in H but the measurements are corrupted by errors.

In this case, the original equations cannot be satisfied exactly. It is useful to define the *residual* vector:

$$r(x) = z - Hx \tag{3.24}$$

We can regard the residual vector as a function of x and we can write its squared magnitude as the scalar-valued quadratic form:

$$f(x) = \frac{1}{2}r^T(x)r(x)$$

The one-half coefficient is introduced to eliminate a 2, which would otherwise occur in later expressions. The problem of finding the value of x, which minimizes this expression is known as the *least squares* problem. Substituting for the definition of the residual, this is:

$$f(\underline{x}) = \frac{1}{2}(\underline{z} - H\underline{x})^T(\underline{z} - H\underline{x})$$

It is instructive to use the product rule of differentiation to express the gradient of this scalar with respect to $\underline{x}$:

$$f_{\underline{x}} = -(\underline{z} - H\underline{x})^T H$$

This gradient will vanish at any local minimum, so setting this derivative to zero (and transposing) produces:

$$H^T(\underline{z} - H\underline{x}^*) = \underline{0} \tag{3.25}$$

This system of equations is often called the *normal equations* because they require the residual at the minimizer to be orthogonal (normal) to the *column space* of H (row space of H^T) because the dot product of every row of H^T with the residual is zero. Writing this in the form of a standard linear system of equations gives:

$$H^T H \underline{x}^* = H^T \underline{z} \tag{3.26}$$

Solving this square linear system of equations, allows the explicit computation of the unique minimizer:

$$\underline{x}^* = (H^T H)^{-1} H^T \underline{z}$$

The matrix:

$$H^+ = (H^T H)^{-1} H^T \tag{3.27}$$

is known as the *left pseudoinverse* because when it is multiplied by H on the left:

$$H^+ H = (H^T H)^{-1} H^T H = I_n \qquad\qquad m > n$$

This form is used when $m > n$. In practice the left pseudoinverse is not usually explicitly computed. Rather, Equation 3.26 is solved as a linear system of equations.

3.2.1.3 Right PseudoInverse of an Underdetermined System

When $m < n$, there are less constraints than there are unknowns and potentially an entire set of solutions exists that satisfy the constraints. In such cases, when a unique solution is desired to an underdetermined system, the most basic technique used is to introduce a *regularizer* (cost function) to rank all members of the set of solutions. Then, we seek the minimizer under this ranking. It turns out that if the cost function is simply the magnitude of the solution vector:

$$f(\underline{x}) = \frac{1}{2}\underline{x}^T \underline{x}$$

an elegant solution results. Let us formulate a constrained optimization problem like so:

$$\text{optimize:}_x \quad f(\underline{x}) = \frac{1}{2}\underline{x}^T\underline{x} \qquad \underline{x} \in \Re^n$$

$$\text{subject to:} \quad \underline{c}(\underline{x}) = \underline{z} - H\underline{x} = \underline{0} \quad \underline{z} \in \Re^m$$

We now form a quantity called the *Lagrangian*:

$$l(\underline{x}, \underline{\lambda}) = \frac{1}{2}\underline{x}^T\underline{x} + \underline{\lambda}^T(\underline{z} - H\underline{x})$$

The first necessary condition is:

$$l_{\underline{x}}(\underline{x}, \underline{\lambda})^T = \underline{x} - H^T\underline{\lambda} = \underline{0} \Rightarrow \underline{x} = H^T\underline{\lambda}$$

Substitute this into the second necessary condition:

$$l_{\underline{\lambda}}(\underline{x}, \underline{\lambda})^T = \underline{z} - H\underline{x} = \underline{0}$$

$$\underline{z} - HH^T\underline{\lambda} = \underline{0} \tag{3.28}$$

$$HH^T\underline{\lambda} = \underline{z}$$

The solution is:

$$\underline{\lambda} = (HH^T)^{-1}\underline{z}$$

Now, substitute this back into the first condition to get:

$$\underline{x} = H^T\underline{\lambda} = H^T(HH^T)^{-1}\underline{z} \tag{3.29}$$

The matrix:

$$H^+ = H^T(HH^T)^{-1} \tag{3.30}$$

is known as the *right pseudoinverse* because when it is multiplied by H on the right:

$$HH^+ = HH^T(HH^T)^{-1} = I_m \qquad m < n$$

This form is used when $m < n$. In practice the right pseudoinverse is not usually explicitly computed. Rather, Equation 3.28 is solved as a linear system of equations and the result is substituted into the left half of Equation 3.29.

3.2.1.4 About the Pseudoinverse

Note that both the left and right pseudoinverses reduce to the ordinary matrix inverse when $m = n$. Both expressions require H to be of full rank and they ultimately invert a square matrix whose size is the smaller of the two dimensions of H.

The notation H^+ for the pseudoinverse is not ambiguous because its form depends on the dimensions of the coefficient matrix H. The pseudoinverse is computable provided a matrix inverse is computable and this means the H matrix must have full rank.

3.2.1.5 *Weighted PseudoInverses*

For the left pseudoinverse, it is possible to introduce a symmetric weight matrix R to produce a weighted cost function. For example:

$$f(\underline{x}) = \frac{1}{2}\underline{r}^T(\underline{x})R^{-1}\underline{r}(\underline{x})$$

An easy way to derive the solution is transformation. Assuming R^{-1} is symmetric positive definite, we define it as the square of D:

$$R^{-1} = D^TD$$

The transformed unweighted objective is:

$$f(\underline{x}) = \frac{1}{2}\underline{r}^T(\underline{x})D^TD\underline{r}(\underline{x}) = \frac{1}{2}\underline{r}'^T(\underline{x})\underline{r}'(\underline{x})$$

This substitution allows us to define a new residual vector:

$$\underline{r}' = D\underline{r} = D(\underline{z} - H\underline{x}) = D\underline{z} - DH\underline{x} = \underline{z}' - H'\underline{x}$$

Where we have defined a new $\underline{z}' = D\underline{z}$ and a new coefficient matrix $H' = DH$. The problem is now in unweighted form and its solution is the given by the left pseudoinverse:

$$\underline{x}^* = (H'^TH')^{-1}H'^T\underline{z}'$$

In terms of the original H matrix, the solution becomes:

$$\underline{x}^* = (H^TD^TDH)^{-1}H^TD^TD\underline{z}$$

Remembering the factoring of the weight matrix $R^{-1} = D^TD$, we arrive at:

$$\underline{x}^* = (H^TR^{-1}H)^{-1}H^TR^{-1}\underline{z} \qquad (3.31)$$

The equivalent solution for the underconstrained case is given in Box 3.3.

Box 3.3. Matrix Pseudoinverses

The pseudoinverse solves the nonsquare linear system:

$$\underline{z} = H\underline{x} \qquad \underline{x} \in \Re^n \qquad \underline{z} \in \Re^m$$

For the overconstrained problem $m > n$ with weight matrix R, we solve:

$$\text{optimize:}_{\underline{x}}\, f(\underline{x}) = \frac{1}{2}\underline{r}^T(\underline{x})R^{-1}\underline{r}(\underline{x}) \qquad \text{where:} \qquad \underline{r}(\underline{x}) = \underline{z} - H\underline{x}$$

and the solution uses the left pseudoinverse:

$$\underline{x}^* = (H^TR^{-1}H)^{-1}H^TR^{-1}\underline{z}$$

For the underconstrained problem $m < n$ with weight matrix R, we solve

$$\text{optimize:}_{\underline{x}}\, f(\underline{x}) = \frac{1}{2}\underline{x}^TR^{-1}\underline{x} \qquad \text{subject to:} \qquad \underline{c}(\underline{x}) = \underline{z} - H\underline{x} = \underline{0}$$

and the solution uses the right pseudoinverse:

$$\underline{x}^* = RH^T(HRH^T)^{-1}\underline{z}$$

3.2.2 Nonlinear Systems

The problem of solving nonlinear equations can always be converted to a problem of finding roots of a nonlinear function because, if $\underline{g}(\ )$ is nonlinear in $\underline{x}$, the problem of solving:

$$\underline{g}(\underline{x}) = \underline{b} \qquad \underline{x} \in \Re^n, \quad \underline{g} \in \Re^n \tag{3.32}$$

is equivalent to solving:

$$\underline{c}(\underline{x}) = \underline{g}(\underline{x}) - \underline{b} = \underline{0} \tag{3.33}$$

This problem arises most often when the vector $\underline{x}$ represents a set (often denoted in the text as $\underline{p}$) of unknown parameters.

3.2.2.1 Newton's Method

The most basic technique used to solve nonlinear equations is to *linearize* them. That is, to find a local linear approximation and to use this in some clever way. In the case of rootfinding, linearization takes the form of Newton's method (also known as the Newton-Raphson method).

For any linear system, the first derivative is a constant. Here, because $\underline{g}(\underline{x})$ is not linear in $\underline{x}$, it follows that the Jacobian:

$$\underline{c}_x = \frac{\partial \underline{c}(\underline{x})}{\partial \underline{x}} = \frac{\partial \underline{g}(\underline{x})}{\partial \underline{x}} = \underline{g}_x \tag{3.34}$$

depends on $\underline{x}$. This means that any local linear approximation to $\underline{g}(\underline{x})$ and hence to $\underline{c}(\underline{x})$ will depend on the locality – the specific value of $\underline{x}$ used. We say that the system is "linearized about" this specific value of $\underline{x}$.

Consider now the solution of:

$$\underline{c}(\underline{x}) = 0$$

Suppose we have a guess for a solution and we want to refine the guess. Let us write an expression for a linear approximation to the value of $\underline{c}$ at some small perturbation $\Delta\underline{x}$ from its present value. By Taylor's theorem applied to vector-valued functions:

$$\underline{c}(\underline{x} + \Delta\underline{x}) = \underline{c}(\underline{x}) + \underline{c}_x\Delta\underline{x} + \ldots \tag{3.35}$$

If we require that this perturbed point be a root of the linear approximation, then we require that $\underline{c}(\underline{x} + \Delta\underline{x}) = \underline{0}$, which leads to the following system of linear equations:

$$\underline{c}_x\Delta\underline{x} = -\underline{c}(\underline{x}) \tag{3.36}$$

The basic Newton iteration is:

$$\Delta\underline{x} = -\underline{c}_x^{-1}\underline{c}(\underline{x}) = -\underline{c}_x^{-1}[\underline{g}(\underline{x}) - \underline{b}] \tag{3.37}$$

This is the precise change which, when added to $\underline{x}$ will produce a root of the linearization of $\underline{c}(\underline{x})$. It is often wise to move only a fraction $\alpha < 1$ of the distance computed by the Newton step in order to avoid very large jumps when $\underline{c}_x$ is small. The basic iteration then becomes:

$$\underline{x}_{k+1} = \underline{x}_k - \alpha \underline{c}_x^{-1} \underline{c}(\underline{x}) \tag{3.38}$$

Newton's method can be understood by analogy to the scalar case. In Figure 3.4, each line extends from the last estimate of the root at the slope of the curve at that point. Such lines progressively cross the x axis closer and closer to the root.

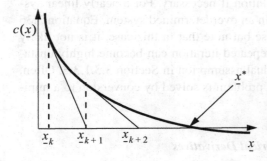

Figure 3.4 Root of The Linearization. The local linearization is a line and Newton's method finds the root of successive lines, rapidly approaching the root of the nonlinear function $c(\ )$.

Of course, many pathologies can complicate this simple picture (Figure 3.5). Nonlinear functions can have many roots and the problem may be posed in terms of finding all roots, any root, or a specific root. A radius of convergence can be defined for each root as the region within which any initial guess will converge to the associated root.

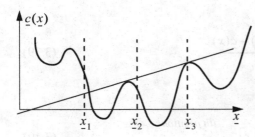

Figure 3.5 Pathologies in Rootfinding. Starting at $\underline{x}_1$ will produce a different root than starting at $\underline{x}_2$. Small changes in a starting point near $\underline{x}_3$ will produce different answers and there is a high risk that the next iteration may have jumped to a point closer to an entirely different root.

At an extremum of $\underline{c}(\underline{x})$, the Jacobian is not invertible and some other mechanism must be used to tweak the estimate off the extremum – and different tweaks will potentially lead to a different root. Near an extremum, the Newton step can produce a very large jump in the estimate.

The most basic defenses against such issues are ensuring a good initial estimate, ensuring that the function is moving closer to zero in each iteration, and limiting the size of the change in $\underline{x}$.

Newton's method converges quadratically. This means that eventually, when the function is locally well approximated by a multidimensional parabola, each successive deviation from the true root is squared, and hence dramatically reduced, in each iteration. In rootfinding, a straightforward way to terminate the search is to stop when $\underline{c}(\underline{x})$ is sufficiently close to zero.

3.2.2.2 Non Square Nonlinear Systems of Equations

Non square Jacobians occasionally arise in practice in rootfinding problems. In an underdetermined system, relatively few constraints must be satisfied by a large number of variables. For example, this situation occurs when there are more calibration parameters than necessary to explain the observed independent errors. It also occurs in loop closure in mapping where a sequence of perhaps a thousand poses may need to form a closed loop.

In the nonsquare Jacobian case, Equation 3.36 can be solved with the right pseudoinverse and iterated to improve the solution if necessary. For a nearly linear system, few iterations should be necessary. In an overdetermined system, Equation 3.36 can be solved using the left pseudoinverse but note that in this case, it is not likely that all constraints can be satisfied and repeated iteration can become highly unstable. See the discussion on the small residual assumption in Section 3.3.1.3.3. Often, the overdetermined nonlinear constraints problem is solved by conversion to a minimization problem.

3.2.2.3 Numerical Derivatives

Although it is sometimes possible to compute an explicit formula for the Jacobian of a system, it is not unusual for the formula to be complicated and relatively expensive to compute. In many cases, it is simpler and less error prone to differentiate numerically. The technique is so easy to code in a computer that it is also an excellent way to check an implementation of a closed-form derivative.

To differentiate, compute the constraint vector $\underline{c}$ one additional time, at a slightly perturbed location, for each element of $\underline{x}$:

$$\frac{\partial \underline{c}}{\partial x_i} = \frac{\underline{c}(\underline{x} + \Delta \underline{x}_i) - \underline{c}(\underline{x})}{\Delta x_i} \tag{3.39}$$

where the **vector** $\Delta \underline{x}_i$ in the numerator is:

$$\Delta \underline{x}_i = \begin{bmatrix} 0 & 0 & \dots & \Delta x_i & \dots & 0 & 0 \end{bmatrix}^T \quad \overset{ith\ position}{} \tag{3.40}$$

This is a numerical approximation for the ith column of $\underline{c}_x$. If we collect all of these columns together, we have the Jacobian $\underline{c}_x$.

3.2.3 References and Further Reading

Although Golib is a classic reference, Trefethen is a more tutorial source for the same material. Press is a well-known source written for the practitioner.

[3]   Gene H. Golib, and Charles F., *Matrix Computations,* Johns Hopkins, 1996.
[4]   Loyd N. Trefethen, and David Bau III, *Numerical Linear Algebra*, Society for Industrial and Applied Mathematics, 1997.
[5]   W. Press, B. Flannery, S. Teukolsky, and W. Vetterling, *Numerical Recipes in C,* Cambridge University Press, Cambridge, 1988.

3.2.4 Exercises

3.2.4.1 Normal Equations

Solve the following overdetermined system of the form $H\underline{x} = \underline{z}$:

$$\begin{bmatrix} 1 & 2 \\ 2 & 4 \\ 3 & 9 \end{bmatrix} \begin{bmatrix} x \\ y \end{bmatrix} = \begin{bmatrix} 4 \\ 5 \\ 6 \end{bmatrix}$$

with the normal equations and show that

$$H^T(\underline{z} - H\underline{x}^*) = \underline{0}$$

3.2.4.2 Weighted Right PseudoInverse

Consider again the underconstrained minimization problem whose solution is the right pseudoinverse:

$$optimize:_{\underline{x}} \quad f(\underline{x}) = \frac{1}{2}\underline{x}^T\underline{x} \qquad \underline{x} \in \mathfrak{R}^n$$

$$subject\ to: \quad \underline{c}(\underline{x}) = \underline{z} - H\underline{x} = \underline{0} \quad \underline{z} \in \mathfrak{R}^m$$

Consider the weighted cost function $f(\underline{x}) = \frac{1}{2}\underline{x}^T R^{-1}\underline{x}$. We can always redo the derivation in this case but, instead, use the technique of section Figure 3.2.1.4 to derive the solution to the weighted version of the underconstrained problem.

3.2.4.3 Newton's Method

Consider the cubic polynomial expressed in factored form:

$$y = (x-a)(x-b)(x-c)$$

Its roots are clearly (a, b, c). Using your favorite programming environment, plot this polynomial for the convenient distinct roots $(1 - 1, 0, 1)$. Then choose initial guesses not to far from the mean and execute a few iterations of Newton's method. Consider these three cases. The case $x_0 = 0.2$; $\alpha = 1$ should work correctly. Note how many significant figures become correct per iteration. However, the case $x_0 = 0.5$; $\alpha = 1$ should jump initially away from the nearest root. Reducing the step size to the case $x_0 = 0.5$; $\alpha = 0.3$ should fix the problem.

3.2.4.4 Numerical Derivatives

The function $y(x) = e^x$ is particularly convenient for this exercise because $y'(x) = e^x$ as well. Compute the numerical derivative of $y(x)$ at the point $x = 1$ for forward steps of $dx = 10^{-n}$; $n = 2, 3, \ldots$ until a numerical division by zero occurs. The point of computing failure will depend on the precision of your computer. Use this formula that computes every component explicitly:

$$y(x) \approx \frac{y(x + dx) - y(x)}{(x + dx) - x}$$

Because $y'(1) = y(1) = e$ is the correct answer, the error is straightforward to compute. Plot the error on a logarithmic horizontal scale. Explain what you see.

3.3 Nonlinear and Constrained Optimization

3.3.1 Nonlinear Optimization

The problem of maximizing a function can always be converted to one of minimizing another by using the transformation:

$$argmax\{f(x)\} = argmin\{-f(x)\} \tag{3.41}$$

so it is expedient to consider all problems to be of one form or the other. Many problems of interest will involve minimization of error or "cost" so we will consider minimization problems only.

We have seen in Section 3.1.3.3 that unconstrained quadratic optimization problems can be solved in closed form. In this section, we consider the more general nonlinear optimization problem.

$$\underset{\underline{x}}{minimize:} \quad f(\underline{x}) \qquad \underline{x} \in \Re^n \tag{3.42}$$

Notice that $f(\underline{x})$ is a scalar. Although this may seem to be unnecessarily restrictive, note that at a minimum we must have the condition that the objective is "below" its value at all other places and all straightforward ways to define this for a vector amount to computing its magnitude or its projection onto a vector. All of these operations amount to converting the objective to a scalar.

Fundamental techniques for solving such problems step through the domain of the objective, producing a series of estimates for the extremum. In doing so, they produce a series of samples of the objective and they enforce the descent condition:

$$f(\underline{x}_{k+1}) < f(\underline{x}_k)$$

by controlling both the length and the direction of the step.

3.3.1.1 Line Search in a Descent Direction

The most basic approach to a minimization problem is iterative *line search*. The process is to start from an initial guess and search in a particular direction $\underline{d}$ in order to reduce the value of the objective. This process converts the problem to a one dimensional minimization problem:

$$\underset{\alpha}{minimize:} \; f(\underline{x} + \alpha\underline{d}) \qquad \alpha \in \Re^1 \tag{3.43}$$

It is essentially always possible to ensure that the direction chosen is a *descent direction* so the search can be restricted to positive values of α. Ideally, a true minimum is computed for each successive direction $\underline{d}$ but this is not usually worth the effort. In practice a few trial steps are tried and the best of these is returned as the approximate solution for that direction.

Consider the scalar function of step length given by the linearization of $f(\underline{x})$:

$$\hat{f}(\alpha\underline{d}) = f(\underline{x}) + f_x \cdot \alpha\underline{d} \qquad (3.44)$$

Convergence in line search is guaranteed provided each step satisfies the *sufficient decrease* condition [10] and the algorithm favors large steps over small ones. The condition specifies that each iteration must reduce the objective by a fraction η_{min}: $0 < \eta_{min} < 1$ of the amount predicted by this linear approximation:

$$\eta = \frac{f(\underline{x}) - f(\underline{x} + \alpha\underline{d})}{\hat{f}(0) - \hat{f}(\alpha\underline{d})} > \eta_{min} \qquad (3.45)$$

In order to converge quickly, we would prefer the step size to be the largest α that satisfies this test. One strategy for achieving this is *backtracking*. The technique starts with the step that would be used normally, and then it tries:

$$\alpha_{k+1} = (2^{-i})\alpha_k : i = 0, 1, 2, \ldots$$

The details are provided in Algorithm 3.1:

```
00   algorithm lineSearch()
01       x ← x₀  // initial guess
02       η_min ← const ∈ [0, 1/4]
03       α_last ← α₀
04       while(true)
05           d ← findDirection(x)
06           α ← α_last × 4  // or α ← 1  for Newton step
07           while (true)
08               η ←   (see Equation 3.45)
09               if( η > η_min ) break
10               α ← α ÷ 2
11           endwhile
12           x ← x + αd ; α_last ← α
13           if(finished()) break
14       endwhile
15       return
```

Algorithm 3.1 Line Search in a Descent Direction with Backtracking. The algorithm searches repeatedly in a descent direction.

A slight improvement is to replace line 06 with a routine that fits a cubic polynomial to the last two values of the objective and its gradient. The true minimizer of this cubic can be used instead of the last value of α.

3.3.1.1.1 Termination. The function finished() at line 13 was left unspecified to be presented here. Unlike in the case of rootfinding, the magnitude of the objective $f(\underline{x})$ is not known at the extremum solution. Instead, the line search algorithm terminates when the changes in the value of the objective become sufficiently small. If the gradient is computed, as discussed next, a test for a small gradient magnitude can also be used for termination.

3.3.1.1.2 Gradient Descent. Also known as *steepest descent*, this technique uses the gradient of the objective to compute the descent direction. Of course the objective can be approximated by a degree one Taylor polynomial:

$$f(\underline{x} + \Delta \underline{x}) \approx f(\underline{x}) + f_{\underline{x}} \Delta \underline{x}$$

Hence, the change in the objective is the projection of the step $\Delta \underline{x}$ onto the gradient vector. The projection is minimized when they are antiparallel and the cosine of the angle between them is -1. Hence, the direction of maximum decrease is the negative of the gradient:

$$\underline{d}^T = -f_{\underline{x}} \tag{3.46}$$

The gradient descent technique has the advantage of being very simple to implement. Its robustness depends on the robustness of the line search used. The disadvantage is that it is not particularly fast.

3.3.1.1.3 Newton Direction. Rootfinding techniques can be used to solve optimization problems because the gradient vanishes at a local minimum. The basic technique is to consider the linearization, not of $f(\underline{x})$, but of its gradient, and require that the gradient vanish after taking a step $\Delta \underline{x}$:

$$f_{\underline{x}}(\underline{x} + \Delta \underline{x}) \approx f_{\underline{x}}(\underline{x}) + \Delta \underline{x}^T f_{\underline{xx}} = \underline{0}^T \tag{3.47}$$

Recall that the symmetric $f_{\underline{xx}}$ is called the Hessian. Rewriting the condition:

$$f_{\underline{xx}} \Delta \underline{x} = -f_{\underline{x}}^T \tag{3.48}$$

The solution (assuming a full rank Hessian) to this is:

$$\Delta \underline{x} = -f_{\underline{xx}}^{-1} f_{\underline{x}}^T \tag{3.49}$$

and this solution can be used as a descent direction in line search. Alternatively, we could have approximated the objective by a paraboloid derived from a second-order Taylor series. Then we could have found its minimizer to get the same result. Therefore, the magnitude of the step is also very likely to be very close to correct when the objective is well approximated by a second-degree polynomial. The use of the curvature information in the Hessian makes Newton's method proceed more directly to the solution than gradient descent.

Although this algorithm converges quadratically, the algorithm is rarely used in this precise form. Slight modifications of the algorithm are used instead. One reason is the fact that the Newton step may not be a descent direction if the Hessian (or its approximation) is not positive definite. Another is that the Hessian may be expensive to compute or simply not available. Algorithms based on approximations to the Hessian are called *quasi-Newton* methods.

3.3.1.2 Trust Region Technique

Line search techniques choose a direction to move from first principles, and then they choose a step length. Conversely, the *trust region* technique first enforces a maximum stepsize and then uses this to constrain the choice of direction. The direction is found by solving an auxiliary constrained optimization problem for an approximation to $f(\underline{x})$. For a second-degree approximation, the gradient and the Hessian are used. The problem is to solve for the step $\Delta \underline{x}$ where its length is restricted by a trust region radius ρ_k. In implicit layout, the problem is expressed:

$$optimize:_{\Delta \underline{x}} \quad \hat{f}(\Delta \underline{x}) = f(\underline{x}) + f_{\underline{x}}\Delta \underline{x} + f_{\underline{x}\underline{x}}\frac{\Delta \underline{x}^2}{2} \quad \Delta \underline{x} \in \Re^n$$

$$subject\ to: \quad \underline{g}(\Delta \underline{x}) = \Delta \underline{x}^T \Delta \underline{x} \leq \rho_k^2 \tag{3.50}$$

We have not covered inequality constraints in optimization problems. Nonetheless, it can be shown that the solution to this problem is the solution to the linear system of equations:

$$(f_{\underline{x}\underline{x}} + \mu I)\Delta \underline{x}^* = -f_{\underline{x}}^T \tag{3.51}$$

for some value of $\mu \geq 0$ that renders the matrix on the left-hand side positive definite. Notice how this seems to fix a major issue with the Newton step. Large values of μ occur when the objective is not locally well approximated by a quadratic. In this case, the algorithm approaches choosing the gradient as the descent direction.

Also note that:

$$\mu \cdot (|\Delta \underline{x}| - \rho_k) = 0 \tag{3.52}$$

So, when $\mu = 0$, the solution is a local minimum inside the trust region. When $\mu \neq 0$, the solution occurs on the boundary of the trust region. These points are provided for information, without derivation.

The trust region is adapted based on the ratio of actual and predicted reduction of the objective:

$$\eta = \frac{f(\underline{x}) - f(\underline{x} + \Delta \underline{x})}{\hat{f}(\underline{0}) - \hat{f}(\Delta \underline{x})} \tag{3.53}$$

In fact, this is the trust region formulation of the very popular Levenberg-Marquardt algorithm. The algorithm proceeds as shown in Algorithm 3.2:

```
00    algorithm Levenberg-Marquardt()
01    x ← x_0 // initial guess
02    Δx_max ← const
03    ρ_max ← const
04    ρ ← ρ_0 ∈ [0, ρ_max]
05    η_min ← const ∈ [0, 1/4]
06    while(true)
07        solve Equation 3.51 for Δx
08        compute η using Equation 3.53
09        if(η < η_min)then Δx ← 0
10        x ← x + Δx // step to new point
11        if(η < 1/4 ) ρ ← ρ/4 // decrease trust
12        else if(η > 3/4 and |Δx|= ρ )
13            ρ ← min(2ρ, ρ_max) // increase trust
14        endif
15        if(finished()) break
16    endwhile
17    return
```

Algorithm 3.2 Levenberg-Marquardt. This is a popular optimization algorithm based on the trust region technique.

One form of termination condition is based on the norm of the update for some threshold ε:

$$\|\Delta \underline{x}\| < \varepsilon$$

3.3.1.3 Nonlinear Least Squares

Recall that the solution to the linear least squares problem involves the left pseudoinverse. Consider the problem of recovering the values of n parameters $\underline{x}$ based on m observations $\underline{z}$ that depend on the parameters in a nonlinear way:

$$\underline{z} = \underline{h}(\underline{x}) \qquad \underline{z} \in \Re^m, \underline{x} \in \Re^n, m > n \tag{3.54}$$

If there is noise in the measurements, these equations will not be satisfied exactly. Define the residual as usual:

$$\underline{r}(\underline{x}) = \underline{z} - \underline{h}(\underline{x}) \tag{3.55}$$

Where $\underline{z}$ is the actual measurements and $\underline{h}(\underline{x})$ represents the measurements that would be predicted based on a particular value of the parameters. From this we can define an objective function based on a weighted squared residual:

$$f(\underline{x}) = \frac{1}{2}\underline{r}^T(\underline{x})W\underline{r}(\underline{x}) \tag{3.56}$$

In practice, the weight matrix W can be obtained as the inverse of the covariance matrix of the measurements $\underline{z}$:

$$W = R^{-1} = Exp(\underline{z}\underline{z}^T)^{-1} \tag{3.57}$$

and it is often set to the identity matrix if the measurements deserve equal weight.

3.3.1.3.1 Derivatives. Unlike in linear least squares, there is no closed-form solution to this problem. Rather the objective must be linearized and some algorithm must be iterated from an initial guess of the parameters. The Jacobian of this objective for symmetric W is a product of the residuals with their own gradient. By the chain rule:

$$f_{\underline{x}} = f_{\underline{r}} \cdot \underline{r}_{\underline{x}} = \underline{r}^T(\underline{x})W \cdot \underline{r}_{\underline{x}} \tag{3.58}$$

Note that the following can be substituted throughout this section:

$$\underline{r}_x = -\underline{h}_x \qquad \underline{r}_{\underline{xx}} = -\underline{h}_{\underline{xx}}$$

The Hessian is:

$$f_{\underline{xx}} = \underline{r}_x^T W \underline{r}_x + \underline{r}_{\underline{xx}} W \underline{r}(\underline{x}) \tag{3.59}$$

where the second term contains the tensor $\underline{r}_{\underline{xx}}$. These derivatives can be provided to any Newton-type minimization algorithm, such as Levenberg-Marquardt.

3.3.1.3.2 Gauss-Newton Algorithm for Small Residuals. Recall that, for this problem as defined, the only reason that the residuals are not zero is noise in the observations. In many cases, this means it is valid to assume that the residuals $r_i(\underline{x})$ are small and the entire (complicated, expensive) second term $\underline{r}_{xx}W\underline{r}(\underline{x})$ of the Hessian can be neglected. Also, the first term is easy to calculate because it involves only the Jacobian that would be computed for a first-order approximation anyway. It is therefore common to use the Hessian approximation:

$$f_{xx} \approx \underline{r}_x^T W \underline{r}_x \tag{3.60}$$

When this approximation is used, the algorithm is called the Gauss-Newton algorithm. Under this approximation, the Newton step becomes:

$$\Delta\underline{x} = -f_{xx}^{-1} f_x^T = -[\underline{r}_x^T W \underline{r}_x]^{-1} \underline{r}_x^T W \underline{r}(x) \tag{3.61}$$

3.3.1.3.3 Rootfinding to a Minimum. We have already seen that rootfinding applies to minimization problems because the gradient vanishes at a minimum. However, for least squares problems, the objective itself ***nearly*** vanishes at a minimum, too. It is tempting to linearize Equation 3.55 and try to solve for the "root" of the overdetermined system of equations. In doing so we would arrive at Equation 3.36 in this form:

$$\underline{r}_x \Delta\underline{x} = -r(x)$$

and solve it iteratively using the left pseudoinverse:

$$\Delta\underline{x} = -[\underline{r}_x^T \underline{r}_x]^{-1} \underline{r}_x^T r(\underline{x})$$

Unfortunately, this only works when the predicted residual is large relative to the true minimum. As the minimum is approached, the root of the linear approximation can jump arbitrarily far from the correct answer.

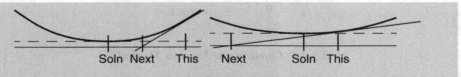

Soln   Next   This   Next   Soln   This

Spotlight 3.4 Rootfinding to a Minimum.

When the present residual is large relative to the solution residual, a rootfinding approach works reasonably well. However, as the solution is approached, the iteration can jump arbitrarily far away – just when it was getting close to the answer. Line search is a necessity for minimization problems.

This technique can work if the update $\Delta\underline{x}$ is treated as a descent direction in a standard line search. However, this is not a new idea because when $W = I$ is substituted into Equation 3.60, we get:

$$\Delta\underline{x} = -[\underline{r}_x^T \underline{r}_x]^{-1} f_x^T = -[\underline{r}_x^T \underline{r}_x]^{-1} \underline{r}_x^T r(\underline{x}) \tag{3.62}$$

Hence, for small residuals, the Newton step of the inverse Hessian times the gradient reproduces the pseudoinverse and the two approaches are equivalent. The descent direction for rootfinding to a minimum is the same as the one used in a minimization approach based on the small residuals approximation to the Hessian. Whether the problem is considered a rootfinding problem or a minimization problem, the key thing is to ensure that the movement along the descent direction is guarded to prevent instability near the minimum.

3.3.2 Constrained Optimization

Recall that the constrained optimization problem is formulated as Equation 3.7:

$$\begin{aligned} optimize:_x \quad & f(\underline{x}) & \underline{x} \in \Re^n \\ subject\ to: \quad & \underline{c}(\underline{x}) = \underline{0} & \underline{c} \in \Re^m \end{aligned} \tag{3.63}$$

The first-order conditions for a minimum were given as Equation 3.9:

$$\begin{aligned} f_{\underline{x}}^T + c_{\underline{x}}^T \underline{\lambda} &= \underline{0} & n\ eqns \\ \underline{c}(\underline{x}) &= \underline{0} & m\ eqns \end{aligned} \tag{3.64}$$

These give a total of $n + m$ (generally nonlinear) equations in the $n + m$ variables comprising $(\underline{x}^*, \underline{\lambda}^*)$. There are as many equations as unknowns, so provided they are independent, they determine, at least locally, a unique solution.

More compactly, the constraints can be adjoined to the performance index to form the Lagrangian:

$$l(\underline{x}, \underline{\lambda}) = f(\underline{x}) + \underline{\lambda}^T \underline{c}(\underline{x}) \tag{3.65}$$

Then, the first-order conditions can be written as:

$$\begin{aligned} l_{\underline{x}}^T &= \underline{0} & n\ eqns \\ l_{\underline{\lambda}}^T &= \underline{0} & m\ eqns \end{aligned} \tag{3.66}$$

3.3.2.1 Constrained Newton Method

It should not be surprising by now that the first step to formulate a numerical algorithm for a nonlinear problem is linearization. To generate a constrained version of Newton's method, the necessary conditions are linearized about a point where they are not satisfied, and they are required to be satisfied on perturbation. The ultimate result of the derivation is:

$$\begin{bmatrix} l_{\underline{xx}} & c_{\underline{x}}^T \\ c_{\underline{x}} & 0 \end{bmatrix} \begin{bmatrix} \Delta \underline{x} \\ \Delta \underline{\lambda} \end{bmatrix} = - \begin{bmatrix} l_{\underline{x}}^T \\ \underline{c}(\underline{x}) \end{bmatrix} \tag{3.67}$$

Where $l_{xx} = f_{xx} + \underline{\lambda}^T c_{xx}$ and $l_x = f_x + \underline{\lambda}^T c_x$. Note that this is a square system where the matrix on the left hand side serves the same purpose as the Hessian in Equation 3.48 so its solution is a descent direction that can be used in line search. A diagonal matrix can also be added as in Equation 3.51 to solve this system using a trust region approach. Each iteration solves for the composite vector of unknowns $[\Delta \underline{x}^T \underline{\lambda} \Delta^T]^T$. An efficient method for inverting matrices in the form of this Hessian was covered in Section 2.5.3 on block matrices in Chapter 2.

3.3.2.1.1 Initial Estimates for the Lagrange Multipliers. While it is possible to imagine a process to guess the initial estimate for $\underline{x}$, it seems much more difficult to choose an initial estimate for $\underline{\lambda}$. One effective scheme is to solve the n first-order conditions. These are overconstrained in $\underline{\lambda}$ so the left pseudoinverse (of $\underline{c}_{\underline{x}}^T$) applies:

$$\underline{\lambda}_0 = -[\underline{c}_{\underline{x}} \underline{c}_{\underline{x}}^T]^{-1} \underline{c}_{\underline{x}} f_{\underline{x}}^T \tag{3.68}$$

The result represents the best fit solution for projecting the objective gradient onto the rowspace of the constraint Jacobian.

3.3.2.1.2 Constrained Gauss Newton Formulation. Consider the constrained optimization problem with a quadratic objective as it occurs in nonlinear least squares:

$$\begin{aligned} \textit{minimize:} \quad & f(\underline{x}) = \frac{1}{2} \underline{r}(\underline{x})^T \underline{r}(\underline{x}) \\ \textit{subject to:} \quad & \underline{g}(\underline{x}) = \underline{b} \end{aligned} \tag{3.69}$$

Here, the first and second derivatives of the Lagrangian are of the form:

$$\begin{aligned} l_{\underline{xx}} &= f_{\underline{xx}} + \underline{\lambda}^T \underline{g}_{\underline{xx}} = \underline{r}_{\underline{x}}^T \underline{r}_{\underline{x}} + \underline{\lambda}^T \underline{g}_{\underline{xx}} \\ l_{\underline{x}} &= f_{\underline{x}} + \underline{\lambda}^T \underline{g}_{\underline{x}} = \underline{r}^T(\underline{x}) \underline{r}_{\underline{x}} + \underline{\lambda}^T \underline{g}_{\underline{x}} \end{aligned}$$

Where a small residuals assumption was used in the first equation.

3.3.2.2 Penalty Function Approach

In the *penalty function* methods, the constraints are absorbed into the objective function. For example, we can compute a cost from the constraints by squaring the constraint residual $\underline{c}(x)$ and then we can solve the following unconstrained problem repeatedly:

$$f_k(\underline{x}) = f(\underline{x}) + \frac{1}{2} w_k \underline{c}(\underline{x})^T W \underline{c}(\underline{x}) \tag{3.70}$$

for progressively increasing values of the weight w_k. In this way, a constrained optimization problem can be converted to an equivalent unconstrained one. Many constraints are "soft" in practice, and the weight w_k can be used to tradeoff the degree to which more optimization is to be permitted at the expense of violating the original constraints. One of the main other advantages of the penalty function approach is the reduction of the number of equations from $n + m$ to n.

3.3.2.3 Projected Gradient Methods

The projected gradient methods are among the most straightforward numerical techniques available for solving constrained optimization problems. As the problem has been posed, the unknown vector x, of dimension n, is underconstrained by the m constraints. The previous constrained Newton technique searches in the $n + m$ dimensional space where both the parameters and the Lagrange multipliers are considered the unknowns. On the other hand, the m constraints can in principle be used to reduce the number of unknown parameters to n, which can then be used to optimize the objective. Similarly, the m Lagrange multipliers are overconstrained by the n necessary conditions, so we can choose to determine their values in a best fit sense. Then, we can reduce the objective by iterating over the remaining $n - m$ free variables. This is the principle behind the reduced gradient methods. There are other methods in this class but the one that will be discussed here has been called *reduced gradient projection* or simply *gradient descent*.

3.3.2.3.1 Parameter Partitioning. Begin by partitioning the parameters in $\underline{x}$ into two sets that will be called the dependent $\underline{x}$, and the independent $\underline{u}$ variables, where the dependence will be created by the constraints:

$$\underline{x} = [\underline{x}, \underline{u}] \tag{3.71}$$

Let there be m dependent variables in new $\underline{x}$ and therefore there are $n - m$ independent ones in $\underline{u}$. **Henceforth in this section**, $\underline{x}$ denotes the dependent variables only. The notation is intended to be analogous to states and inputs in control theory. The elements of $\underline{x}$ are dependent in the sense that once the elements of $\underline{u}$ are chosen, the elements of $\underline{x}$ are determined by satisfaction of the constraints.

3.3.2.3.2 Satisfying the Constraints. With the variables partitioned, the constraint equations take the form:

$$\underline{c}(\underline{x}, \underline{u}) = \underline{0} \tag{3.72}$$

Let us suppose that in a particular iteration, an estimate $(\underline{x}_k, \underline{u}_k)$ is available. We will use the dependent variables to satisfy the constraints, while allowing the independent ones to be free.

Linearizing the constraints and holding the independent variables constant leads to:

$$\underline{c}(\underline{x} + \Delta \underline{x}, \underline{u}) = \underline{c}(\underline{x}, \underline{u}) + \underline{c}_{\underline{x}}(\underline{x}, \underline{u})\Delta \underline{x} = \underline{0} \tag{3.73}$$

This Jacobian is square and invertible by assumption, so the change in dependent variables required to satisfy the constraints to first order is:

$$\Delta \underline{x} = -\underline{c}_{\underline{x}}(\underline{x}, \underline{u})^{-1}\underline{c}(\underline{x}, \underline{u}) \tag{3.74}$$

This equation can be used iteratively to move a point near the constraint surface back onto the constraint surface (to first order).

3.3.2.3.3 Optimality Conditions. Let us define the objective gradients $f_{\underline{x}}(\underline{x}, \underline{u}) = \partial f / \partial \underline{x}$ and $f_{\underline{u}}(\underline{x}, \underline{u}) = \partial f / \partial \underline{u}$ and adopt similar notation for the constraints and the Lagrangian. The optimality conditions can be partitioned into two sets based on the partitioning of $\underline{x}$:

$$
\begin{aligned}
f_{\underline{x}}^T(\underline{x}, \underline{u}) + \underline{g}_{\underline{x}}^T(\underline{x}, \underline{u})\underline{\lambda} = \underline{0} \quad m \text{ eqns} \\
f_{\underline{u}}^T(\underline{x}, \underline{u}) + \underline{g}_{\underline{u}}^T(\underline{x}, \underline{u})\underline{\lambda} = \underline{0} \quad n\text{-}m \text{ eqns}
\end{aligned}
\tag{3.75}
$$

These optimality conditions are an overdetermined system with respect to the m multipliers. Given that the dependent variables were just corrected and there are m of them, let us choose to satisfy the first set of optimality conditions exactly with the m multipliers:

$$\underline{\lambda} = -\underline{c}_x^T(\underline{x}, \underline{u})^{-1} f_x^T(\underline{x}, \underline{u}) \tag{3.76}$$

At this point there are $n - m$ optimality conditions left to solve in the second set and an equal number of "independent" parameters in $\underline{u}$. So far, because the parameters were not changed, the constraints are still satisfied and the first (m) optimality conditions are still satisfied.

The second optimality condition will not be satisfied in general at this point, but its right-hand side is, of course, the gradient of the Lagrangian with respect to the dependent variables. Therefore, it provides a descent direction, called the *reduced gradient*, with respect to the remaining independent variables that can be used to reduce its value:

$$l_u(\underline{x}, \underline{u}) = f_u(\underline{x}, \underline{u}) + \underline{\lambda}^T \underline{c}_u(\underline{x}, \underline{u}) \tag{3.77}$$

where the multipliers are given by Equation 3.76 and the dependent variables were computed by iterating on Equation 3.74. Line search can be conducted to determine a local minimum in this direction.

3.3.2.3.4 Line Search in the Tangent Plane. When a step of $\Delta \underline{u}$ is made in order to reduce the Lagrangian, it will in general violate the constraints. The total differential of the constraints is:

$$\Delta \underline{c} = \underline{c}_x(\underline{x}, \underline{u}) \Delta \underline{x} + \underline{c}_u(\underline{x}, \underline{u}) \Delta \underline{u} \tag{3.78}$$

For the constraints to be satisfied to first order $\Delta \underline{c} = 0$ while taking the step of $\Delta \underline{u}$ above, we must adjust the dependent variables by:

$$\Delta \underline{x} = -\underline{c}_x(\underline{x}, \underline{u})^{-1} \underline{c}_u(\underline{x}, \underline{u}) \Delta \underline{u} \tag{3.79}$$

and this completes the algorithm.

3.3.2.3.5 The Complete Algorithm. The complete algorithm starts with an initial guess for the solution and iterates on Equation 3.74 until it satisfies the constraints (Algorithm 3.3). Then Equation 3.76 and Equation 3.77 are used to find the multipliers

```
00   algorithm reducedGradient()
01      x ← x₀ // initial guess
02      u ← u₀ // initial guess
03      while(not converged)
04         while(not converged)
05            x_{k+1} ← x_k − c_x(x, u)⁻¹ c(x, u) // Newton step
06         endwhile
07         λ ← −c_x(x, u)⁻¹ f_x^T(x, u) // x is now feasible
08         l_u(x, u) ← f_u(x, u) + λ^T c_u(x, u) // reduced gradient
09         u ← lineSearch(l_u(x, u)) // optimal point
10      endwhile
11      return
```

Algorithm 3.3 Reduced Gradient. This technique solves constrained optimization problems by following a constrained gradient. The line search algorithm should execute Equation 3.79 at every tentative step to keep the constraints satisfied to first order. In this way, the line search stays near the constraints.

and the resulting Lagrangian gradient with respect to the independent variables. Line search is conducted in this direction for a local minimum and the process is repeated until the conditions for a local minimum are achieved.

3.3.2.3.6 Degenerate Forms. Note that when there is no objective function, then the optimality condition does not apply and there are no Lagrange multipliers. The first iteration is used in order to find a feasible point. With minor modifications, all cases for the relationship between the number of constraints m and unknowns n can be accommodated by using the appropriate pseudoinverse in each iteration.

On the other hand, when there are no constraints, all points are feasible. The optimality condition degenerates to:

$$f_{\underline{x}}(\underline{x}, \underline{u}) = \underline{0}^T \tag{3.80}$$

and again there are no Lagrange multipliers. In this case, only the second last equation is needed (where $\underline{u}$ now equals $\underline{x}$) and there are exactly as many equations as unknowns.

3.3.3 References and Further Reading

Whereas Marquardt is the original source for the famous algorithm, Madsen is a more tutorial source. Madsen and Mangasarian and Nocedal are good texts on nonlinear programming.

[6] Stephen Boyd and Lieven Vandenberghe, *Convex Optimization,* Cambridge University Press, 2004.

[7] Kaj Madsen, Hans Bruun Nielsen, and Ole Tingleff, *Methods for Non-Linear Least Squares Problems* (2nd ed.), Informatics and Mathematical Modelling, Technical University of Denmark, DTU, 2004.

[8] Olvi L. Mangasarian, *Nonlinear Programming,* McGraw-Hill 1969, reprinted by SIAM.

[9] Donald Marquardt, An Algorithm for Least-Squares Estimation of Nonlinear Parameters, *SIAM Journal on Applied Mathematics,* pp. 431–441, 1963.

[10] Jorge Nocedal and Stephen J. Wright, *Numerical Optimization,* Springer, 1999.

3.3.4 Exercises

3.3.4.1 Approximate Paraboloid

The Newton direction can be derived by writing a second-order Taylor series for the objective f to produce a paraboloid that approximates the local shape of the objective. Write an expression for this paraboloid and find an expression for its minimum. Compare with Equation 3.49.

3.3.4.2 Levenberg-Marquardt

Argue why large values of μ make the algorithm tend toward gradient descent. How does the length of the step vary as μ is increased?

3.3.4.3 Small Residuals

Using your favorite programming environment, use Newton's method to "minimize" the objective $y(x) = x^2 + \varepsilon$ from an initial guess of $x = 0.5$. Take a fraction

$\alpha = 0.4$ of the Newton step in each iteration. Set $\varepsilon = 0$ initially to get it working. Then, set $\varepsilon = 0.015$ and perform 40 iterations of Newton's method. Near what value of the objective does the estimate jump away from the root and start toward it again. Comment on whether this process terminates for an arbitrary objective function and how robust it is.

3.3.4.4 Constrained Newton's Method

Derive Equation 3.67, which again is:

$$\begin{bmatrix} l_{xx} & c_x^T \\ c_x & 0 \end{bmatrix} \begin{bmatrix} \Delta x \\ \Delta \lambda \end{bmatrix} = - \begin{bmatrix} l_x^T \\ c(x) \end{bmatrix}$$

3.3.4.5 Eigenvectors as Optimal Projections

Form the matrix (math font) V whose rows are two arbitrary vectors (math font, underlined) v_1 and (math font, underlined) v_2 in the plane. Use constrained optimization to show that the unit vector that maximizes the sum of its squared projections into both vectors is an eigenvector of (math font) V^{TV}.

3.4 Differential Algebraic Systems

One of the more sophisticated ways to predict the motion of a mobile robot is to simulate its dynamics. Doing so turns out to be quite difficult. There are several reasons for this: the equations are differential, they are nonlinear, they are subject to constraints, and the constraints are also nonlinear.

This section will develop the *augmented formulation* of velocity kinematics and of Lagrange's dynamics. In this formulation, constraints remain separate and explicit. As a result, the infeasible velocities and constraint forces also remain explicit, and this information can be very useful. For example, knowing the required constraint forces makes it possible to ascertain if the terrain can provide the needed friction to generate the required constraint force.

The augmented formulation can be implemented in a manner that is both highly efficient and completely general. A good implementation can compute the motion of any system of rigid bodies whose motions are controlled by known inputs and constraints. Many general purpose dynamics modelling systems are based on this formulation because it permits bodies and the constraints between them to be combined arbitrarily within the limits of physical realism.

3.4.1 Constrained Dynamics

Differential equations augmented by algebraic constraints are known as DAEs (differential-algebraic equations). The essential structure of such problems is a constraint satisfaction problem embedded inside a differential equation problem. Once the differential equation is computed, it is then integrated numerically one time step, and the whole process repeats. It is important that the integrations be performed well. The next subchapter will present methods for doing so.

3.4.1.1 Augmented Systems

An *augmented system* is a differential equation with explicit constraints. Unlike in the case of constrained optimization, it is not clear what it means to constrain a differential equation. Consider the problem of integrating a linear first-order differential equation whose n states are subject to $m < n$ algebraic constraints:

$$\dot{\underline{x}} = \underline{f}(\underline{x}, \underline{u})$$
$$\underline{c}(\underline{x}) = \underline{0} \tag{3.81}$$

The vector $\underline{u}$ refers to a set of system inputs that can be manipulated in order to control the system trajectory to some degree. Likewise, a second-order augmented system might look like the following:

$$\ddot{\underline{x}} = \underline{f}(\underline{x}, \dot{\underline{x}}, \underline{u})$$
$$\underline{c}(\underline{x}, \dot{\underline{x}}) = \underline{0} \tag{3.82}$$

In constrained optimization, the objective has a large number of degrees of freedom to be searched for a solution. The constraints may limit them somewhat but there is still some space left to search for an optimum. Here, the differential equation has no degrees of freedom left to constrain because once the inputs and initial state are specified, the differential equation has a unique solution already. If constraints are imposed, they will almost certainly be inconsistent with the state trajectory, already completely determined by the differential equation, and there will be no solution. One or the other equation has to be wrong!

In fact, the interpretation of a DAE is that *the differential equation is partially wrong*. At each time step, only the component of the state derivative that is consistent with the constraints is allowed to advance the state to the next time step. In practice, what this means is that there are other inputs to the system $\underline{u}_{cons}$ whose magnitudes are not known but they are known to act in such a way as to enforce constraints. The most famous use of this idea is Lagrange's formulation of dynamics, but the technique is applicable in general to DAEs, including those describing robot motion in the plane or over uneven terrain.

3.4.1.2 Linear Constraints

If the constraints above were linear (of the form $G\underline{x} = \underline{b}$), we could partition the states into m dependent ones $\underline{x}_d$ and $n - m$ independent ones $\underline{x}_i$ as we did in Section 3.3.2.3. Linear constraints could then be partitioned as:

$$\begin{bmatrix} G_i & G_d \end{bmatrix} \begin{bmatrix} \underline{x}_i \\ \underline{x}_d \end{bmatrix} = \underline{b}$$

By assumption G_d is $m \times m$ and invertible so we can multiply by G_d^{-1} to produce:

$$G_d^{-1} G_i \underline{x}_i + \underline{x}_d = G_d^{-1} \underline{b}$$

Therefore, we can substitute the constraints in the form of $\underline{x}_d = G_d^{-1}(\underline{b} - G_i \underline{x}_i)$ into the differential equation to produce a reduced order unconstrained system. For the first-order system, this would be of the form $\dot{\underline{x}}_i = \tilde{f}(\underline{x}_i, \underline{u})$. Unfortunately, most cases of interest to us will have nonlinear constraints.

3.4.1.3 Sequential Approach for Nonlinear Constraints

For nonlinear constraints, a potential solution approach would be to solve both differential and constraint equations in a sequential manner by integrating the unconstrained differential equation first, and then enforcing the constraints after every time step. For the first-order system, the unconstrained increment to the state would be:

$$\underline{x}_{k+1} = \underline{x}_k + \Delta\underline{x}_k = \underline{x}_k + \underline{f}(\underline{x}, \underline{u})\Delta t$$

This new state could then be returned to the constraint surface $\underline{c}(\underline{x}) = \underline{0}$ using a root-finding algorithm by solving the constraints for the nearest root given the initial guess of $\underline{x}_{k+1}$. This approach will produce a state change $\Delta\underline{x}_k$ confined to a feasible direction and the infeasible component of the state derivative $\dot{\underline{x}}$ will have been removed.

3.4.1.4 Projection Approach for Nonlinear Constraints

A second approach is to project the state derivative itself onto the constraint tangent plane in order to remove its component normal to the tangent plane. For the $n \times 1$ state change $\Delta\underline{x}$ to be feasible to first order, it would have to be in the constraint tangent plane, and hence orthogonal to all m rows of the constraint gradient:

$$\underline{c}_x \Delta\underline{x} = \underline{c}_x \underline{f}(\underline{x}, \underline{u})\Delta t = \underline{0} \tag{3.83}$$

If the state change $\Delta\underline{x}$ is not in the tangent plane, we can try to remove the component normal to it so that the constraints remain satisfied to first order. Let us write the state change in terms of an *infeasible* component $\Delta\underline{x}_\perp$ which is normal to the tangent plane and a *feasible* component $\Delta\underline{x}_\parallel$ within the tangent plane:

$$\Delta\underline{x} = \Delta\underline{x}_\perp + \Delta\underline{x}_\parallel$$

Now, the constraints will not be satisfied in general by the state change, so there is a residual $\underline{r}$:

$$\underline{c}_x \Delta\underline{x} = \underline{c}_x (\Delta\underline{x}_\perp + \Delta\underline{x}_\parallel) = \underline{r}$$

But, by definition $\Delta\underline{x}_\parallel$ satisfies the constraints to first order, so $\underline{c}_x \Delta\underline{x}_\parallel = \underline{0}$. Substituting, this of course means that the constraint residual is due solely to component orthogonal to the tangent plane:

$$\underline{c}_x \Delta\underline{x} = \underline{c}_x \Delta\underline{x}_\perp = \underline{r} \tag{3.84}$$

Now any component strictly orthogonal to the tangent plane can be written as a weighted sum of the constraint gradients:

$$\Delta\underline{x}_\perp = \underline{c}_x^T \underline{\lambda}\Delta t \tag{3.85}$$

It is convenient to scale $\Delta\underline{x}_\perp$ by Δt as written. Because $\underline{\lambda}$ is unknown, this merely redefines these unknown weights. The above can now be substituted into Equation 3.84 to produce:

$$\underline{c}_x \Delta\underline{x}_\perp = \underline{c}_x \underline{c}_x^T \underline{\lambda}\Delta t = \underline{r} = \underline{c}_x \Delta\underline{x}$$

Solving for $\underline{\lambda}$ gives:

$$\underline{\lambda} = [\underline{c}_x \underline{c}_x^T]^{-1} \underline{c}_x \frac{\Delta \underline{x}}{\Delta t} \tag{3.86}$$

The infeasible state change is then given by Equation 3.85. Upon substituting the above, into it, it becomes:

$$\Delta \underline{x}_\perp = \underline{c}_x^T [\underline{c}_x \underline{c}_x^T]^{-1} \underline{c}_x \Delta \underline{x} \tag{3.87}$$

Note that the matrix:

$$P_C = A[A^T A]^{-1} A^T$$

is an operator that performs a projection onto the column space of A (see Exercise 2.2.9.3 of Chapter 2). Here the operator produces the projection onto the columns of $\underline{c}_x^T$—which are the rows of the constraint Jacobian—also known as the constraint gradients. Having produced $\Delta \underline{x}_\perp$, we can now compute the feasible state change:

$$\Delta \underline{x}_\| = \Delta \underline{x} - \Delta \underline{x}_\perp = \Delta \underline{x} - P_C \Delta \underline{x} = (I - P_C)\Delta \underline{x} = P_N \Delta \underline{x}$$

where the matrix P_N projects the state change directly into the constraint tangent plane. The constants $\underline{\lambda}$ provide the projections of $\Delta \underline{x}$ onto the disallowed directions. They are therefore the same construct as the *Lagrange multipliers* used in constrained optimization. In this approach, the constrained state derivative $P_N \Delta \underline{x} = P_N \underline{f}(\underline{x}, \underline{u})\Delta t$ is computed automatically.

3.4.2 First- and Second-Order Constrained Kinematic Systems

With the context of the last section, we are now in a position to present principled techniques for solving DAEs. Here, we will consider the motion of the system without regard to the forces which cause it. That is, we consider *kinematic* models of first and second order where driving velocities and accelerations are known.

3.4.2.1 Augmented First-Order Systems

A third approach to solving Equation 3.81 is to leave the infeasible state change in the form of Equation 3.85, and substitute this into the differential equation. The infeasible component can then be removed from the state change with:

$$\Delta \underline{x}_\| = \underline{f}(\underline{x}, \underline{u})\Delta t - \Delta \underline{x}_\perp = \underline{f}(\underline{x}, \underline{u})\Delta t - \underline{c}_x^T \underline{\lambda} \Delta t \tag{3.88}$$

Now, notice that if Equation 3.83 and Equation 3.88 are divided by Δt and passed to the limit as $\Delta t \to 0$, there results:

$$\begin{aligned} \underline{\dot{x}} + \underline{c}_x^T \underline{\lambda} &= \underline{f}(\underline{x}, \underline{u}) \\ \underline{c}_x \underline{\dot{x}} &= \underline{0} \end{aligned} \tag{3.89}$$

In this equation, $\underline{\dot{x}}$ is really $\underline{\dot{x}}_\|$, the feasible component of the state derivative. Note that the matrix $\underline{c}_x$ is used in two complementary ways above. In the first equation, it supplies disallowed directions in order to find the *infeasible velocities* $\underline{c}_x^T \underline{\lambda}$. In the second, it supplies the same disallowed directions in order to find the *feasible velocities* $\underline{\dot{x}}$. These velocities are orthogonal to each other because:

$$[\underline{c}_x^T \underline{\lambda}]^T \underline{\dot{x}} = \underline{\lambda}[\underline{c}_x \underline{\dot{x}}] = \underline{0}$$

3.4.2.2 Solving the Equations of Motion

Equation 3.89 is of a special form we have seen before, and it is easily solved by block elimination:

$$\begin{bmatrix} I & \underline{c}_x^T \\ \underline{c}_x & 0 \end{bmatrix} \begin{bmatrix} \underline{\dot{x}} \\ \underline{\lambda} \end{bmatrix} = \begin{bmatrix} \underline{f}(\underline{x}, \underline{u}) \\ \underline{0} \end{bmatrix} \tag{3.90}$$

This new set of equations is an ***unconstrained*** set of differential equations in the augmented unknowns $(\underline{\dot{x}}, \underline{\lambda})$. Unlike in the case of constrained optimization, the multipliers here are functions of time (i.e., we need to solve for new ones every iteration during integration). They represent the projections of the infeasible component of the unconstrained state change onto the constraint gradients.

To solve the system, we multiply the first equation by $\underline{c}_x$ to produce:

$$\underline{c}_x \underline{\dot{x}} + \underline{c}_x \underline{c}_x^T \underline{\lambda} = \underline{c}_x \underline{f}(\underline{x}, \underline{u})$$

But by the second equation $\underline{c}_x \underline{\dot{x}} = \underline{0}$ so this becomes:

$$\underline{c}_x \underline{c}_x^T \underline{\lambda} = \underline{c}_x \underline{f}(\underline{x}, \underline{u})$$
$$\underline{\lambda} = (\underline{c}_x \underline{c}_x^T)^{-1} \underline{c}_x \underline{f}(\underline{x}, \underline{u})$$

Substituting this back into the first equation produces:

$$\underline{\dot{x}} + \underline{c}_x^T (\underline{c}_x \underline{c}_x^T)^{-1} \underline{c}_x f(\underline{x}, \underline{u}) = f(\underline{x}, \underline{u})$$
$$\underline{\dot{x}} = [I - \underline{c}_x^T (\underline{c}_x \underline{c}_x^T)^{-1} \underline{c}_x] f(\underline{x}, \underline{u}) \tag{3.91}$$

The nullspace projection matrix has appeared again.

$$P_N(\underline{c}_x^T) = I - \underline{c}_x^T (\underline{c}_x \underline{c}_x^T)^{-1} \underline{c}_x \tag{3.92}$$

Spotlight 3.5 Nullspace Projection Matrix.

For a holonomic constraint, as defined in Section 3.4.2.3, this equation removes all components of the state derivative that are inconsistent with the constraints.

This new differential equation is an unconstrained one that satisfies the constraints at each timestep. A second-order system subject to such constraint would be solved in an analogous manner after differentiating the constraint twice as described below.

3.4.2.3 Holonomic Constraints

Another view of the key operation that occurred at Equation 3.83 is that the constraint was differentiated with respect to time. A vector constraint equation of the form:

$$\underline{c}(\underline{x}) = \underline{0}$$

is called a *holonomic* constraint. Differentiating it with respect to time leads to:

$$\underline{\dot{c}}(\underline{x}) = \underline{c}_x \underline{\dot{x}} = \underline{0} \tag{3.93}$$

which is the second half of Equation 3.89. The matrix $\underline{c}_x \cong \partial \underline{c} / \partial \underline{x}$ is the now familiar constraint Jacobian. Evidently, for any such constraint, the state derivative must be orthogonal to the constraint gradient. In other words, if the differential equation involves $\underline{\dot{x}}$, a holonomic constraint implies that $\underline{\dot{x}}$ must be constrained as well, and the differentiated constraint specifies precisely how.

Now compare Equation 3.81 and Equation 3.89. Something important has changed in this transformation that eliminated the need to solve the constraints explicitly. As the derivation showed, enforcing differentiated constraints merely enforces them to first order. Therefore, in a numerical integration routine, finite time steps will allow the constraint residuals to drift slowly away from zero. Mechanisms to solve this constraint drift problem will be presented in the context of force driven systems in the next section.

One might ask at this point why it is useful to differentiate constraints if the solution is less accurate than enforcing constraints directly. First note that whether enforcing nonlinear constraints with rootfinding or by differentiating them, the constraint gradients are needed in either case. Differentiated constraints, however, are uniquely able to provide the constrained state derivatives upon which accurate differential equation solvers like Runge-Kutta depend.

When holonomic constraints are used in second-order systems, they imply constraints on the second derivative which can be derived by differentiating again. Doing so leads to:

$$\underline{\ddot{c}}(\underline{x}) = \underline{c}_{xt} \underline{\dot{x}} + \underline{c}_x \underline{\ddot{x}} = \underline{0} \tag{3.94}$$

where $\underline{c}_{xt} \cong \partial^2 \underline{c} / \partial \underline{x} \partial t$ is a matrix representing the time derivative of the constraint Jacobian. If Equation 3.82 were subject to such constraints, the problem can be transformed in this way to the following matrix form:

$$\begin{bmatrix} I & \underline{c}_x^T \\ \underline{c}_x & 0 \end{bmatrix} \begin{bmatrix} \underline{\ddot{x}} \\ \underline{\lambda} \end{bmatrix} = \begin{bmatrix} \underline{f}(\underline{x}, \underline{u}) \\ -\underline{c}_{xt} \underline{\dot{x}} \end{bmatrix} \tag{3.95}$$

3.4.2.4 Nonholonomic Constraints

Another form of constraint is of the form:

$$\underline{c}(\underline{x}, \underline{\dot{x}}) = \underline{0}$$

Differentiated holonomic constraints like Equation 3.93 are of this form. Often however, intrinsic velocity constraints arise which are not derived from holonomic constraints on state. Often such velocity constraints cannot be reduced to holonomic constraints either, in which case they are called *nonholonomic*. See Chapter 4 for more on nonholonomic constraints.

Often, nonholonomic constraints occur in this special form:

$$\underline{c}(\underline{x}, \underline{\dot{x}}) = \underline{w}(\underline{x})\underline{\dot{x}} = \underline{0} \tag{3.96}$$

for some weight vector $\underline{w}(\underline{x})$ which depends on the state. For first-order systems, the weight vector $\underline{w}(\underline{x})$ is already a disallowed direction so **the constraint does not need to be differentiated** to be used. One simply uses $\underline{w}(\underline{x})$ in place of $\underline{c}_{\underline{x}}$ in both places in Equation 3.90.

When the constraint is not of the above special form, then it will need to be differentiated for both first and second-order systems. The first derivative of a nonholonomic constraint is of the form:

$$\underline{\dot{c}}(\underline{x}, \underline{\dot{x}}) = \underline{c}_x\,\underline{\dot{x}} + \underline{c}_{\underline{\dot{x}}}\,\underline{\ddot{x}} = \underline{0} \tag{3.97}$$

For a first-order system, one way to use this result is to ignore the second-order term $\underline{c}_{\underline{\dot{x}}}\,\underline{\ddot{x}}$. It can also be moved to the right-hand side and computed numerically from the last two iterations as a backward difference of $\underline{\ddot{x}}$. For a second-order system, one can move $\underline{c}_x\underline{\dot{x}}$ to the right-hand side in a manner similar to what we did in Equation 3.95.

3.4.3 Lagrangian Dynamics

This section will present a numerical approach to Lagrangian dynamics. There are several distinct formulations of Lagrangian dynamics from a computational perspective but here again, we will use the augmented formulation with explicit constraints. The Lagrangian formulation of dynamics is very relevant to wheeled mobile robots because of the constraints that apply to wheels.

In mechanics, dynamics is distinguished from kinematics by the appearance of true forces and mass properties in the models used. A mechanical dynamics model differs from our second-order kinematic model only in this respect.

3.4.3.1 Equations of Motion

When the coordinates $\underline{x}$ of a system of bodies are absolute (inertial), the equations of motion take a simple form. To simplify matters, we will restrict our attention to motions in the plane but the extension to 3D is very straightforward in these coordinates. Let the coordinates of rigid body i be given by:

$$\underline{x}_i = \begin{bmatrix} x_i & y_i & \theta_i \end{bmatrix}^T$$

Assuming no viscous forces (which would appear in the form $V_i\,\underline{\dot{x}}_i$), the motion of this body is governed by Newton's 2nd Law:

$$M_i\underline{\ddot{x}}_i = \underline{F}_i^{ext} + \underline{F}_i^{con}$$

where M_i is the mass-inertia matrix, $\ddot{\underline{x}}_i$ is the acceleration in absolute coordinates, $\underline{F}_i^{ext}$ is the externally applied forces and torques in the absence of constraints and $\underline{F}_i^{con}$ is the constraint forces (and torques). See Figure 3.6 for an example of the difference between applied and constraint forces.

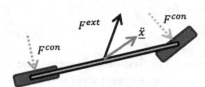

Figure 3.6 Applied and Constraint Forces. For the bicycle, constraint forces are generated to oppose the applied force and prevent motion in the disallowed directions (those of wheel slip). The net force (parallel to acceleration) is therefore not in the direction of the applied force.

If the reference point on the body is the center of mass, then the mass-inertia matrix takes the form:

$$M_i = \begin{bmatrix} m_i I & 0 \\ 0 & J_i \end{bmatrix}$$

where m_i is the mass of body i, I is a 2×2 identity matrix and J_i is the polar moment of inertia about the center of mass. For a system of n bodies, n such matrix equations form a block diagonal system:

$$M\ddot{\underline{x}} = \underline{F}^{ext} + \underline{F}^{con} \tag{3.98}$$

Assuming the mass-inertia matrix is known and the external forces are known, there are n unknown accelerations which can be integrated to determine the motion once they are known. If there are c constraint forces, then these comprise c additional unknowns, so c more equations are needed to solve this system. The needed extra equations can be generated by considering the constraints that these unknown forces impose on the motion.

3.4.3.2 Differentiated Constraints

For holonomic constraints, consider again Equation 3.94 and define:

$$\underline{F}_d = -\underline{c}_{xt}\,\dot{\underline{x}}$$

Then Equation 3.94 can be witten as:

$$\underline{c}_x\,\ddot{\underline{x}} = \underline{F}_d \tag{3.99}$$

The expression $\underline{F}_d$ acts as a kind of pseudoforce that makes the differentiated constraint look like Newton's 2nd law. Such pseudoforces should not be confused with the actual constraint forces that are related to the multipliers as described below.

Similarly, for the nonholonomic constraint in Equation 3.97, define:

$$\underline{F}_d = -\underline{c}_x\,\dot{\underline{x}}$$

Then Equation 3.97 becomes:

$$c_{\ddot{x}}\, \ddot{x} = F_d \tag{3.100}$$

Both kinds of differentiated constraints are written as a matrix times $\ddot{x}$ equals another matrix times $\dot{x}$. To form the system equations we group all these differentiated constraints in either the form of Equation 3.99 or the form of Equation 3.100 together to produce a system of c constraints with a coefficient matrix known as the *system Jacobian C*:

$$C\, \ddot{x} = F_d \tag{3.101}$$

Notice that the F_d vector seems to act as a force that keeps the constraints satisfied – even if the system is moving but there are no applied external forces.

Note that whenever velocities are differentiated in order to produce accelerations *for use in dynamics*, the derivatives must often be carried out in an inertial frame because $\ddot{x}$ must be inertially referenced in dynamics to relate it to real forces. See Chapter 4 for more on inertial frames.

3.4.3.3 Lagrange Multipliers

Reusing the trick from constrained dynamics earlier, we will write the constraint forces in terms of arbitrary projections onto the disallowed directions encoded in the rows of the constraint Jacobian.

$$F_i^{con} = -C^T \lambda \tag{3.102}$$

In this context, the physical interpretation is that the constraint forces are being required to do no work. This is known as the *principle of virtual work*. Intuitively, each row of C (or column of C^T) is a normal to a constraint hypersurface indicating a prohibited direction. The above expresses the constraint force as a weighted sum of all prohibited directions. Restricting the constraint force to this set of vectors is the minimum amount of restriction necessary to ensure that its dot product with any *feasible* displacement in the constraint tangent plane will be zero.

This virtual work principle solves the difficult problem of determining the unknown constraint force magnitudes because the value of λ_i determines the magnitude of the associated constraint force. Namely, for constraint i, associated with the ith column of C^T, the constraint force is

$$F_i^{con} = -\lambda_i C_i^T \tag{3.103}$$

These Lagrange multipliers have the same function as they do in constrained optimization. They are unknown weights of a set of vectors that span the rowspace of the constraint Jacobian.

3.4.3.4 Augmented System

Now Equation 3.98 written for all bodies becomes:

$$M\ddot{x} + C^T \lambda = F^{ext} \tag{3.104}$$

Combining with Equation 3.101 yields the system:

$$\begin{bmatrix} M & C^T \\ C & 0 \end{bmatrix} \begin{bmatrix} \ddot{\underline{x}} \\ \underline{\lambda} \end{bmatrix} = \begin{bmatrix} \underline{F}^{ext} \\ \underline{F}_d \end{bmatrix} \tag{3.105}$$

Spotlight 3.6 Augmented Form of Lagrangian Dynamics.

In this standard form of the matrix differential equation, the accelerations and multipliers form the adjoined unknowns.

We have seen matrices of this format in constrained optimization and in constrained dynamics.

3.4.3.5 Solving the Equations of Motion

Once the constraints are formulated, the C matrix and the $\underline{F}_d$ pseudoforces are known. An explicit inverse for matrices in the form of Equation 3.105 was provided in Chapter 2. From Equation 2.6 in Chapter 2

$$\underline{\lambda} = (CM^{-1} C^T)^{-1} (CM^{-1} \underline{F}^{ext} - \underline{F}_d) \tag{3.106}$$

In practice, this inverse would not be explicitly computed. A simultaneous linear equation solver would be used. Comparison with Equation 3.86 reveals that $\underline{\lambda}$ appears to be the projections of the applied force (and derived pseudoforce) onto the constraint nullspace. Under certain conditions [11] this system can be solved in linear time. Once $\underline{\lambda}$ is known, the accelerations can be computed from Equation 2.7 in Chapter 2:

$$\ddot{\underline{x}} = M^{-1}(\underline{F}^{ext} - C^T \underline{\lambda}) \tag{3.107}$$

Once these are known, the equations are integrated one time step and the entire process repeats.

3.4.3.6 Conjugate Gradient for Ill-Conditioned Systems

In wheeled mobile robots, it is not unusual for the matrix $(CM^{-1} C^T)$, which is inverted to find the multipliers, to become ill-conditioned. This can occur when multiple constraint gradients become nearly parallel or otherwise dependent. In such a case, just as we do in least squares, we can seek the solution for $\underline{\lambda}$ of least residual norm:

$$\underline{\lambda}^* = \operatorname{argmin} \left\| CM^{-1} C^T \underline{\lambda} - F \right\|_2 \tag{3.108}$$

Given the symmetric structure of the coefficient matrix, an efficient and stable method to do this is the *conjugate gradient algorithm*, which is provided in Figure 3.4.

The algorithm solves the linear system $A\underline{x} = \underline{b}$ when A is symmetric and positive definite. It proceeds by generating n directions which are mutually conjugate and then expressing the solution in terms of its projections onto these directions. Recall that two vectors $\underline{d}_1$ and $\underline{d}_2$ are said to be A-*orthogonal*, or *conjugate* with respect to A if:

$$\underline{d}_1^T A \underline{d}_2 = 0 \tag{3.109}$$

It can be shown that a set of n such vectors forms a basis of $\mathfrak{R}^n$ so any n vector can be written as a linear combination of them. If so, then the solution $\underline{x}^*$ to the original linear system can be written in terms of them:

$$\underline{b} = A(\alpha_0 \underline{d}_0 + \dots + \alpha_{n-1} \underline{d}_{n-1}) \tag{3.110}$$

The CG algorithm proceeds by solving for the αs and the $\underline{d}$s one at a time.

3.4.3.6.1 Finding the α by Minimization. The solution to the original problem can be viewed in terms of an equivalent minimization problem for the quadratic form:

$$y = \underline{x}^T A \underline{x} - \underline{b}^T \underline{x} + c$$

because setting its derivative to zero reproduces the original linear system. Suppose we have an estimate for the solution $\underline{x}_{k-1}$ and we choose a particular direction $\underline{d}_k$ and conduct a line search in this direction to minimize the function:

$$y(\alpha) = y(\underline{x}_{k-1} + \alpha_k \underline{d}_k)$$

to get a new estimate:

$$\underline{x}_k = \underline{x}_{k-1} + \alpha_k \underline{d}_k \tag{3.111}$$

Now $y(\underline{x})$ is an n dimensional paraboloid and the above curve $y(\alpha_k)$ is a parabola with a unique minimizer where its derivative vanishes:

$$\frac{dy}{d\alpha_k} = \frac{dy}{d\underline{x}} \frac{d}{d\alpha_k}(\underline{x}) = (A\underline{x}_k - \underline{b})^T \underline{d}_k = \underline{r}_k^T \underline{d}_k = 0$$

The residual $\underline{r}_k$ is clearly also the gradient of $y(\underline{x}_k)$:

$$\underline{r}_k = \underline{b} - A\underline{x}_k \tag{3.112}$$

We conclude that the correct value of α_k is the one where the residual at the new point is normal to the direction. If CG produces a different value of α_k, the solution will not be minimum. We can solve for α_k:

$$[A(\underline{x}_{k-1} + \alpha_k \underline{d}_k) - \underline{b}]^T \underline{d}_k = 0$$

$$[\underline{r}_{k-1} + \alpha_k A\underline{d}_k]^T \underline{d}_k = 0$$

Which gives:

$$\alpha_k = -\underline{r}_{k-1}^T \underline{d}_k / \underline{d}_k^T A \underline{d}_k \tag{3.113}$$

3.4.3.6.2 New Directions. Now a new direction must be conjugate to the old one. Suppose that we try a new direction of the form:

$$\underline{d}_{k+1} = -\underline{r}_k + \beta_k \underline{d}_k \tag{3.114}$$

This has index $k + 1$ because it will be the first step in the loop. If it is conjugate then we must have:

$$\underline{d}_{k+1}^T A \underline{d}_k = 0 \Rightarrow (-\underline{r}_k + \beta_k \underline{d}_k)^T A \underline{d}_k = 0$$

Which gives:

$$\beta_k = \underline{r}_k^T A \underline{d}_k / \underline{d}_k^T A \underline{d}_k \tag{3.115}$$

The algorithm proceeds by computing $\underline{d}_k$, α_k, $\underline{x}_k$, $\underline{r}_k$, then β_k. This is done n times or until the residual is small enough to stop early. It can be shown that when the $\underline{d}$ s are conjugate, the $\underline{r}$ s are orthogonal to the $\underline{d}$ s, and to each other. As a consequence the expressions for the α s and β s simplify:

$$\alpha_k = \frac{\underline{r}_{k-1}^T \underline{r}_{k-1}}{\underline{d}_k^T A \underline{d}_k} \qquad \beta_k = \frac{\underline{r}_k^T \underline{r}_k}{\underline{r}_{k-1}^T \underline{r}_{k-1}} \tag{3.116}$$

3.4.3.6.3 Algorithm. The complete algorithm is provided in Algorithm 3.4.

```
00   algorithm conjugateGradient()
01       i ← 0 ; r ← b − Ax ; d ← r ; δ_new ← r^T r
02       while( i < n and δ_new < tol )
03           q ← Ad ; α ← δ_new / d^T q ; x ← x + αd
04           r ← r − αq  // equivalent to r ← b − Ax
05           δ_old ← δ_new ; δ_new ← r^T r ; β ← δ_new / δ_old
06           d ← r + βd ; i ← i + 1
07       endwhile
08       return
```

Algorithm 3.4 Conjugate Gradient. Up to n conjugate search directions are generated. An efficient technique is used for updating the residuals that avoids a matrix multiply. The result is the final value of x.

3.4.4 Constraints

This section presents more pragmatics of enforcing constraints as well as a the constraints used to connect bodies together in rigid or articulated manner.

3.4.4.1 Constraint Trim

The process of differentiating the constraints has the unfortunate side effect that the computation will attempt to hold the constraints constant rather than necessarily at zero. Over time, numerical errors will often allow the constraints to become violated as a result. There are a few techniques for managing this issue but the most straightforward is to enforce differentiated constraints directly, in their original undifferentiated form, during the integration process.

The first derivative of a holonomic constraint takes the form $\underline{c}_x \dot{\underline{x}} = \underline{0}$ and many forms of nonholonomic constraints, before differentiation, take the form $\underline{w}(x)\dot{\underline{x}} = 0$. An arbitrary combination of such constraints is therefore of the form $C \dot{\underline{x}} = \underline{0}$ for some constraint matrix C. Once the second derivative of state $\ddot{\underline{x}}$ is computed using Equation 3.107, the problem of computing the state can be viewed as another constrained dynamics problem of lower order. Let $\underline{f}(t)$ be the state derivative computed by solving the second-order system, however it is accomplished:

$$\underline{f}(t) = \underline{f}(0) + \int_0^t \ddot{\underline{x}}(t)dt \tag{3.117}$$

The related constrained first-order system is:

$$\dot{\underline{x}} = \underline{f}(t)$$
$$C \dot{\underline{x}} = \underline{0}$$

Recall from Equation 3.91 that the constrained first derivative takes the form:

$$\dot{\underline{x}} = [I - C^T(CC^T)^{-1}C]\underline{f}(t)$$

This procedure can be used to project the state derivative onto the nullspace of the constraints before it is integrated.

In a similar manner, if there are any holonomic constraints, these can be enforced in original form by numerical rootfinding after this Equation 3.117 is integrated. Or, drift controllers can be used as described in Section 3.4.4.2.

3.4.4.2 Drift Controllers

Although the constraints can be numerically enforced in each iteration, another way to deal with the *drift-off* phenomenon [12] is to generate a restoring force based on the error in the original (undifferentiated) constraint. This approach is better suited to those nonlinear constraints that cannot be resolved adequately in a single iteration of constraint trim.

The constraint pseudoforce $\underline{F}_d$ can be augmented with what amounts to a closed loop proportional control system. A small restoring force is generated by this controller that is proportional to the constraint error. For a holonomic or nonholonomic constraint:

$$\underline{F}_d \leftarrow \underline{F}_d - k_p \, \underline{c}(\underline{x})$$
$$\underline{F}_d \leftarrow \underline{F}_d - k_p \, \underline{c}(\underline{x}, \dot{\underline{x}}) \qquad (3.118)$$

For $k_p > 0$, this extra term will drive the constraints back to the level curve at zero if they drift. If the time step is Δt then:

$$k_p = \frac{\tau}{\Delta t} \qquad (3.119)$$

will generate a restoring force that tends to reduce the error to zero with a time constant of τ. If the constraint error has a dc component, an integral term can be added which integrates the constraint error.

The timestep and velocity of the system matters not only for the accuracy of the integration but also for the constraint loops. At some point, the loop bandwidth becomes insufficient relative to the step sizes and the model ceases to work correctly. Therefore, once a model is tuned for one step size, it may not work well at a very different step size unless the tuning is adaptive to the change.

Another consequence of the differentiated constraints is that it is not possible to directly change the configuration of the system by manipulating the states or velocities because it creates dissatisfied constraints. A good constraint loop may permit some direct manipulation but the correct way to effect configuration changes is applied forces. For example, the best way to steer a wheel is to apply an external torque around the axis of its pin joint.

3.4.4.3 Maintaining System Kinetic Energy

For finite time steps, constraint pseudoforces may have small components that are not orthogonal to the level curves of the constraints so they may add to or subtract from system total energy. These small errors may not matter if the model is actively controlled by forces, but a passive system placed in an initial state will accelerate or decelerate slowly without compensation for this effect.

For motion in the plane (orthogonal to gravity), all energy is kinetic. The system kinetic energy is:

$$T = \frac{1}{2}\underline{\dot{x}}^T M \underline{\dot{x}} \qquad (3.120)$$

The total change in energy expected over a time step Δt based on the external forces is:

$$\Delta T = Q^{ext}\underline{\dot{x}}\Delta t \qquad (3.121)$$

and, of course this would be zero if there were no applied forces. Suppose that there is an error δT in the change in system energy:

$$\delta T = \Delta T_{act} - \Delta T \qquad (3.122)$$

Either the external forces or the system velocities could be modulated to try to resolve this error but there may be less forces than velocities, so let us choose to adjust the velocities slightly.

The energy error is a scalar and the velocity is a vector so this an underconstrained problem. The linearized relationship between a change in energy and velocity is given by the gradient of energy with respect to velocity:

$$\delta T = \underline{\dot{x}}^T M(\Delta \underline{\dot{x}}) \qquad (3.123)$$

So, the gradient of kinetic energy with respect to velocity is the system momentum:

$$T_{\underline{\dot{x}}} = \underline{\dot{x}}^T M = \underline{L}^T \qquad (3.124)$$

Equation 3.123 is underdetermined so there are multiple solutions. The smallest velocity change required to explain the energy error is given by the right pseudoinverse:

$$\Delta \underline{\dot{x}} = (T_{\underline{\dot{x}}} T_{\underline{\dot{x}}}^T)^{-1} T_{\underline{\dot{x}}}^T \delta T = \left(\frac{\underline{L}^T}{\underline{L}^T \underline{L}}\right)\delta T \qquad (3.125)$$

This is a vector in the direction of the gradient $\underline{L}^T$ scaled by the scalar $\delta T/(\underline{L}^T\underline{L})$.

In practice, there will be numerical errors in this calculation as well, so it is prudent to integrate the energy error over time and to base an integral controller on the above result:

$$\Delta \underline{\dot{x}} = [k_i]\left(\frac{\underline{L}^T}{\underline{L}^T \underline{L}}\right)\int_0^t \delta T dt \qquad (3.126)$$

The constant $k_i = 1/\tau_i$ is a tunable integral gain that drives the system energy error to zero over time. This "energy loop" should be much slower than (order of magnitude slower time constant) the constraint loop so that they do not interfere with each other.

3.4.4.4 Initial Conditions

Another consequence of differentiated constraints is a need for accurate initial conditions. In the absence of constraint trim, the constraints can only stay at zero if they start at zero. Therefore, it is critical that the initial conditions provided satisfy the constraints exactly. Any initial errors in the constraints will lead to errors in the constraint gradients, which will create constraint forces that do work and change the system total energy – even when there are no applied external forces.

At least two approaches to mitigate this issue are available. First, the model can be started from a zero energy state, which is guaranteed to satisfy the constraints. Then applied forces can be used to activate it. An alternative is to regard the initial conditions as a guess and then use constraint trim and enforce all constraints to numerical precision.

3.4.4.5 Basic Rigid Body Constraints

The most basic planar vehicle can be constructed from a body to which some steerable and fixed wheels are connected. For this reason, this section will present rigid and rotary constraints in the plane.

3.4.4.5.1 Rigid Constraint. Consider the case of two bodies denoted i and j constrained to move together as one (Figure 3.7). We want to express the constraint in terms of the poses of their centers of mass in the inertial frame w, denoted $\underline{\rho}_i^w$ and $\underline{\rho}_j^w$. The constraint can be expressed informally in terms of pose composition as follows:

$$\underline{\rho}_i^j = \underline{\rho}_w^j * \underline{\rho}_i^w = (\underline{\rho}_j^w)^{-1} * \underline{\rho}_i^w = const$$

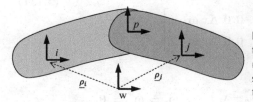

Figure 3.7 Two Bodies in General Pose. These two bodies i and j have poses known with respect to the world frame w and various constraints could act between them. Frame p is at the pivot point when the constraint is rotary.

This is a constraint of the form:

$$g(\underline{x}) = const \tag{3.127}$$

It can be treated the same as homogeneous constraints because the constant does not affect the gradient:

$$\underline{c}(\underline{x}) = g(\underline{x}) - const = \underline{0} \tag{3.128}$$

The gradient contains two elements:

$$C_{\underline{\rho}_i} = \frac{\partial \underline{\rho}_i^j}{\partial \underline{\rho}_i^w} \qquad\qquad C_{\underline{\rho}_j} = \frac{\partial \underline{\rho}_i^j}{\partial \underline{\rho}_j^w} \tag{3.129}$$

It is left as an exercise to show that:

$$
\begin{array}{cc}
\qquad\qquad \text{Posn i} & \qquad \text{Posn j} \\
\underline{c}_{\underline{x}} = \begin{bmatrix} \dots & c\theta & s\theta & 0 & \dots & -c\theta & -s\theta & y_i^j & \dots \\ \dots & -s\theta & c\theta & 0 & \dots & s\theta & -c\theta & -x_i^j & \dots \\ \dots & 0 & 0 & 1 & \dots & 0 & 0 & -1 & \dots \end{bmatrix} \\[4pt]
\underline{c}_{\underline{xt}} = \begin{bmatrix} \dots & -\omega s\theta & \omega c\theta & 0 & \dots & \omega s\theta & -\omega c\theta & 0 & \dots \\ \dots & -\omega c\theta & -\omega s\theta & 0 & \dots & \omega c\theta & \omega s\theta & 0 & \dots \\ \dots & 0 & 0 & 0 & \dots & 0 & 0 & 0 & \dots \end{bmatrix}
\end{array}
\tag{3.130}
$$

where $\theta = \theta_j^w$ and $\omega = \dot{\theta}$.

3.4.4.5.2 Rotary Joint. Consider a rotary joint (i.e., the front wheel of a bicycle viewed from above) whose axis of rotation is the z axis. Let p denote a reference frame attached to the point of rotation. The constraints for the rotary joint can be expressed as the first two elements of the equation:

$$\underline{\rho}_p^w - \underline{\rho}_p^w = 0$$

$$\underline{\rho}_i^w * \underline{\rho}_p^i - \underline{\rho}_j^w * \underline{\rho}_p^j = 0$$

It is left as an exercise to show that:

$$
\begin{array}{cc}
\qquad\qquad \text{Posn i} & \qquad \text{Posn j} \\
\underline{c}_{\underline{x}} = \begin{bmatrix} \dots & 1 & 0 & -\Delta y_i & \dots & -1 & 0 & \Delta y_j & \dots \\ \dots & 0 & 1 & \Delta x_i & \dots & 0 & -1 & -\Delta x_j & \dots \end{bmatrix} \\[4pt]
\underline{c}_{\underline{xt}} = \begin{bmatrix} \dots & 0 & 0 & -\Delta x_i \omega_i & \dots & 0 & 0 & \Delta x_j \omega_j & \dots \\ \dots & 0 & 0 & -\Delta y_i \omega_i & \dots & 0 & 0 & \Delta y_j \omega_j & \dots \end{bmatrix}
\end{array}
\tag{3.131}
$$

where:

$$\Delta x_i = (x_p^w - x_i^w) \qquad \Delta x_j = (x_p^w - x_j^w) \qquad \omega_i = \omega_i^w = \dot{\theta}_i^w$$
$$\Delta y_i = (y_p^w - y_i^w) \qquad \Delta y_j = (y_p^w - y_j^w) \qquad \omega_j = \omega_j^w = \dot{\theta}_j^w$$

3.4.5 References and Further Reading

Featherstone is a source for dynamics adapted to the problems of robotics. Pars is a source for nonholonomic constraints in analytical dynamics. The rest of these references were discussed in the text.

[11] D. Baraff, *Linear-Time Dynamics Using Lagrange Multipliers,* In proceedings SIGGRAPH, 1996, New Orleans.

[12] J. Baumgarte, Stabilization of Constraints and Integrals of Motion in Dynamical Systems, *Computer Methods in Applied Mechanics and Engineering,* Vol. 1, pp. 1–16, 1972.

[13] Roy Featherstone, *Rigid Body Dynamics Algorithms,* Springer, 2007.

[14] Ahmed Shabana, *Computational Dynamics,* 2nd ed., Wiley, 2001.

[15] L. A. Pars, *A Treatise on Analytical Dynamics,* Wiley, New York, 1968.

[16] Jonathan Shewchuk, An Introduction to the Conjugate Gradient Method Without the Agonizing Pain, CMU-SCS Technical Report, 1994.

3.4.6 Exercises

3.4.6.1 Solving Constrained Dynamics Matrix Equations

Solve Equation 3.104 using substitution. Solve first for $\ddot{\underline{x}}$ and substitute this result into the second equation and then solve for the multipliers. Why not solve the second equation for $\ddot{\underline{x}}$? It looks easier.

3.4.6.2 Preparation for Runge Kutta

The use of a good integration routine like Runge Kutta makes a major difference in the performance of dynamic simulations. As we will see in the next subchapter, the equations must be of state space form:

$$\dot{\underline{x}}(t) = \underline{f}(\underline{x}(t), \underline{u}(t), t)$$

Write the constrained dynamics solution for the adjoined state vector $\underline{x}(t) = [\dot{\underline{x}}^T \underline{x}^T]^T$ in state space form.

3.4.6.3 Rigid Constraint

Derive Equation 3.130. The Jacobian J_{ρ_i} is a right pose Jacobian whereas J_{ρ_j} is the product of a left pose Jacobian and an inverse pose Jacobian.

3.4.6.4 Rotary Constraint

Derive Equation 3.131. The Jacobians for both bodies are left pose Jacobians. Use only their first two rows.

3.4.6.5 Conjugate Gradient

Show that:

(i) When A is positive definite, conjugate vectors form a basis for $\mathfrak{R}^n$. That is if $\alpha_0 \underline{d}_0 + \ldots + \alpha_{n-1} \underline{d}_{n-1} = \underline{0}$, then $\alpha_k = 0$ for all k.

(ii) Use Equation 3.109, Equation 3.111, Equation 3.112, and Equation 3.114 to show that, because $\underline{r}_k^T \underline{d}_k = 0$ we must also have $\underline{r}_k^T \underline{d}_{k-1} = 0$ and $\underline{r}_k^T \underline{r}_{k-1} = 0$.

(iii) Use the last result and substitute Equation 3.114 into Equation 3.113 to produce the left result in Equation 3.116. Then substitute that result into Equation 3.115 and multiply Equation 3.111 by A and add $\underline{b} - \underline{b}$. Combine these results to produce the right result in Equation 3.116.

3.5 Integration of Differential Equations

Mobile robot models occur in the form of differential equations describing the evolution of the state derivatives over time. Hence, the basic mechanism for computation of the state itself is one of integration.

3.5.1 Dynamic Models in State Space

A particularly general way to express the model of a robot is like so:

$$\dot{\underline{x}}(t) = f(\underline{x}(t), \underline{u}(t), t) \tag{3.132}$$

where $\underline{x}(t)$ is called the *state vector* and $\underline{u}(t)$ is an optional *input*. This form of model will be used commonly later. The system model must be placed in this form for the Runge-Kutta algorithm discussed below, so we will use it for all presented integration methods to maintain consistency.

Given such a model, the state at any point in time can be obtained by computing:

$$\underline{x}(t) = \underline{x}(0) + \int_0^t f(\underline{x}(t), \underline{u}(t), t)dt \tag{3.133}$$

This expression is somewhat more complicated than an integral of an unforced differential equation whose terminal state depends only on the initial conditions. Equation 3.133 is, in fact, a mapping from a vector-valued function $\underline{u}(t)$ to another vector $\underline{x}(t)$ and every distinct input function produces a potentially different terminal state. We say that the state is a *functional* over $\underline{u}(t)$, and denote it with square brackets thus:

$$\underline{x}(t) = \mathcal{J}[\underline{u}(t)] \tag{3.134}$$

By this we mean that the entire time signal $\underline{u}(t)$ must be known in order to determine the terminal state. If this concept seems foreign to the reader, it may be helpful to recall that any scalar integral produces a number, which is the area under a curve, and the entire curve must be known to compute the area. Even the most basic of integrals is a functional.

3.5.2 Integration of State Space Models

This section presents basic and more sophisticated ways to integrate the state equations.

3.5.2.1 Euler's Method

Consider a nonlinear differential equation of the form:

$$\dot{\underline{x}}(t) = \underline{f}(\underline{x}, \underline{u}, t)$$

It seems reasonable to project the state forward in time by writing a first-degree Taylor series in time:

$$\underline{x}(t + \Delta t) = \underline{x}(t) + \underline{f}(\underline{x}, \underline{u}, t)\Delta t \qquad (3.135)$$

where terms of second and higher degree were neglected. In a computer, this would be implemented in discrete time:

$$\underline{x}_{k+1} = \underline{x}_k + \underline{f}(\underline{x}_k, \underline{u}_k, t_k)\Delta t_k \qquad (3.136)$$

This technique, known as Euler's method, works well enough when the first degree approximation is a good one. However, if the neglected higher degree terms are non negligible, errors will occur.

By the remainder theorem, the error in a single step is related to the magnitude of the first neglected term – the second derivative. Furthermore, if there is an error in $\underline{x}_k$ there will be two sources of error in $\underline{x}_{k+1}$: the error in $\underline{x}_k$ and the truncation error in the series.

3.5.2.1.1 Example. The basic differential equation governing the motion of a point along a planar curve is:

$$\frac{d\underline{x}}{ds} = \frac{d}{ds}\begin{bmatrix} x \\ y \\ \theta \end{bmatrix} = \begin{bmatrix} \cos\theta \\ \sin\theta \\ \kappa \end{bmatrix} = \underline{f}(x, u, s) \qquad (3.137)$$

where the input u is the curvature κ, and distance s replaces time. Its integral is:

$$\begin{bmatrix} x(s) \\ y(s) \\ \theta(s) \end{bmatrix} = \begin{bmatrix} x(0) \\ y(0) \\ \theta(0) \end{bmatrix} + \int_0^s \begin{bmatrix} \cos\theta(s) \\ \sin\theta(s) \\ \kappa(s) \end{bmatrix} ds$$

Its discrete version is:

$$\begin{bmatrix} x \\ y \\ \theta \end{bmatrix}_{k+1} = \begin{bmatrix} x \\ y \\ \theta \end{bmatrix}_k + \begin{bmatrix} \cos\theta \\ \sin\theta \\ \kappa \end{bmatrix}_k \Delta s \qquad (3.138)$$

Consider the constant curvature trajectory given by:

$$\kappa(s) = \kappa_0 = 1$$

The computed solution is plotted in Figure 3.8 for a large step size Δs. The result is even more surprising when you consider that the computed curvatures and headings

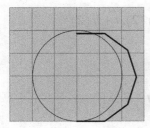

Figure 3.8 Euler's Method. The error grows dramatically as the step size increases.

are perfectly accurate functions of distance. All of the error is due to integration. The figure is suggestive of the reason. Although the heading at each step is a correct function of distance, it is changing continuously around the circle whereas the heading remains fixed along each approximating line segment.

3.5.2.2 Midpoint Method

If a neglected second derivative is a cause of errors, it seems advisable to try to include a second-degree term so that the errors will be third-order. A second-degree Taylor series is:

$$\underline{x}(t + h) \approx \underline{x}(t) + \underline{f}(\underline{x}, \underline{u}, t)h + \frac{d\underline{f}(\underline{x}, \underline{u}, t)}{dt} \frac{h^2}{2} \tag{3.139}$$

Where $h = \Delta t$ is used to be consistent with many other writings. Note that this can be written as:

$$\underline{x}(t + h) \approx \underline{x}(t) + \left\{ \underline{f}(\underline{x}, \underline{u}, t) + \frac{d\underline{f}(\underline{x}, \underline{u}, t)}{dt} \frac{h}{2} \right\} h \tag{3.140}$$

and the part in braces is clearly the first-degree Taylor series for the first derivative $\dot{\underline{x}}(t)$, evaluated at the midpoint of the time step, because:

$$\underline{f}[\underline{x}(t + h/2), \underline{u}(t + h/2), t + h/2] \approx \underline{f}(\underline{x}, t) + \frac{d\underline{f}(\underline{x}, \underline{u}, t)}{dt} \frac{h}{2}$$

The second derivative $d\underline{f}(\underline{x}, \underline{u}, t)/dt$ could be computed with the chain rule but the resulting Jacobian is typically expensive to compute. Consider instead approximating the time derivative with a finite difference by inverting this formula:

$$\frac{d\underline{f}(\underline{x}, \underline{u}, t)}{dt} \frac{h}{2} \approx \underline{f}[\underline{x}(t + h/2), \underline{u}(t + h/2), t + h/2] - \underline{f}(\underline{x}, t)$$

Substituting this into Equation 3.127 above causes the derivative $\dot{\underline{x}}(t)$ to cancel to produce:

$$\underline{x}(t + h) \approx \underline{x}(t) + h\underline{f}[\underline{x}(t + h/2), \underline{u}(t + h/2), t + h/2] \tag{3.141}$$

Now, the value of $\underline{x}$ at the midpoint can also be approximated with Equation 3.139 applied to the half step:

$$\underline{x}(t + h/2) \approx \underline{x}(t) + \underline{f}(\underline{x}, \underline{u}, t)(h/2)$$

The final result is:

$$\underline{x}(t + h) \approx \underline{x}(t) + h\underline{f}[\underline{x}(t) + \underline{f}(\underline{x}, \underline{u}, t)(h/2), \underline{u}(t + h/2), t + h/2]$$

Which can be written as:

$$\underline{k} = h\underline{f}(\underline{x}, \underline{u}, t)$$
$$\underline{x}(t + h) \approx \underline{x}(t) + h\underline{f}[\underline{x}(t) + \underline{k}/2, \underline{u}(t + h/2), t + h/2]$$

Instead of doing a full step, the algorithm first performs a half step based on the initial estimate of the derivative to produce the midpoint $\underline{k}$ of the time step as shown in Figure 3.9. Then a better estimate of the time derivative is computed at the midpoint, and this better estimate is used to start over and advance the full step with a first-order Taylor series.

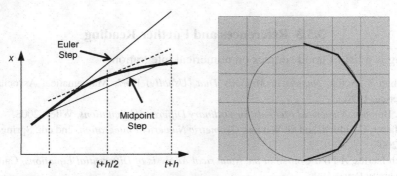

Figure 3.9 Midpoint Method. By taking a half step and evaluating the time derivative there, the midpoint step reduces the integration error to third order.

This algorithm is called the *midpoint algorithm* and it is accurate to second order. In Figure 3.9, the maximum integration error over the half circle is reduced from 0.6 to 0.03 using this method.

3.5.2.3 Runge Kutta

The midpoint method is an instance of the Runge-Kutta method that is accurate to second order (i.e., its error is third-order). Higher-degree methods can be derived using the same techniques. The most popular is accurate to fourth order, and the equations are:

$$
\begin{aligned}
\underline{k}_1 &= h\underline{f}(\underline{x}, \underline{u}, t) \\
\underline{k}_2 &= h\underline{f}[\underline{x}(t) + \underline{k}_1/2, \underline{u}(t + h/2), t + h/2] \\
\underline{k}_3 &= h\underline{f}[\underline{x}(t) + \underline{k}_2/2, \underline{u}(t + h/2), t + h/2] \\
\underline{k}_4 &= h\underline{f}[\underline{x}(t) + \underline{k}_3, \underline{u}(t + h), t + h] \\
\underline{x}(t + h) &= \underline{x}(t) + \underline{k}_1/6 + \underline{k}_2/3 + \underline{k}_3/3 + \underline{k}_4/6
\end{aligned}
$$
(3.142)

Spotlight 3.7 Runge Kutta Integration.

These magic formulae can produce orders of magnitude better solutions than Euler's method.

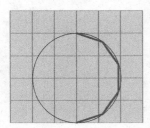

Figure 3.10 Runge Kutta. Errors are a factor of 300 smaller than the midpoint method.

This algorithm is extremely useful for performing odometry, and for implementing dynamic predictions for the purpose of either motion planning or model identification. The state derivative does not usually depend explicitly on time, so the third argument of $\underline{f}\,(\_)$ can often be dropped. Note carefully how time dependent inputs are treated.

3.5.3 References and Further Reading

Following is a list of good sources on numerical integration.

[17] Forman S. Acton, *Numerical Methods That (Usually) Work,* Mathematical Association of America, 1990.

[18] J. C. Butcher, *Numerical Methods for Ordinary Differential Equations,* Wiley, 2008.

[19] E. Hairer, C Lubich, and G. Wanner, *Geometric Numerical Integration,* 2nd ed., Springer, Berlin, 2006.

[20] Arieh Iserles, *A First Course in the Numerical Analysis of Differential Equations,* Cambridge University Press, 1996.

3.5.4 Exercises

3.5.4.1 Midpoint Algorithm for Odometry

Show that for the system in Equation 3.137, the midpoint algorithm reduces to:

$$
\underline{x}(s + \Delta s) = \begin{bmatrix} x(s) \\ y(s) \\ \theta(s) \end{bmatrix} + h \begin{bmatrix} \cos[\theta(s) + \kappa \Delta s / 2] \\ \sin[\theta(s) + \kappa \Delta s / 2] \\ \kappa(s) \end{bmatrix}
$$

Does this provide an improvement if the curvature is constant and why?

3.5.4.2 Euler's Method versus Runge Kutta

Implement the Runge Kutta algorithm on the constant curvature arc shown in Figure 3.8. For a step size $ds = 0.63$, How many thousand times better is the error than it was for Euler's method? Than the Midpoint algorithm?

CHAPTER 4

Dynamics

Figure 4.1 Soccer Robots. Robot soccer is tons of fun, and the robots move fast—as the blurred parts of the image show. Doing a good job controlling high speed robots requires knowledge of their dynamics.

The equations that describe the motion of wheeled mobile robots (WMRs) are very different from those that describe manipulators because they are differential rather than algebraic, and often underactuated and constrained. Unlike manipulators, the simplest models of how mobile robots move are nonlinear differential equations. Much of the relative difficulty of mobile robot modelling can be traced to this fact.

This section explores dynamics in two different senses of the term. Dynamics in mechanics refers to the particular models of mechanical systems that are used in that discipline. These tend to be second-order equations involving forces, mass properties, and accelerations. In control theory, dynamics refers to any differential equations that describe the system of interest.

4.1 Moving Coordinate Systems

The fact that mobile robot sensors are fixed to the robot and move with them has profound implications. On the one hand, it is the source of nonlinear models in Kalman filters. On the other, it is the source of nonholonomic wheel constraints. This section concentrates on a third effect – the fact that the derivatives of many vector quantities of interest depend on the motion of the robot.

173

4.1.1 Context of Measurement

Suppose a state policeman uses his radar gun to measure your car's motion of 30 meters/second (70 mph) on your way to work. Suppose he pulls you over and says "You were going southbound at 30 m/s. That's 5 mph over the limit." The correct interpretation of his measurement requires considerable context. The expression of any measurement in physics generally requires: a unit system (e.g., meters, seconds), a number system (e.g., base 10 weighted positional), a coordinate system (e.g., directions north, east), a reference frame to which the measurement is ascribed (e.g., your car), and a reference frame with respect to which the measurement is made (e.g., the radar gun).

Although the idea of a number system and a unit system are probably familiar to the reader, the distinction between a coordinate system and a reference frame may not be. As discussed in Section 2.1.1.5 in Chapter 2, these are not only not the same thing; in fact, they have nothing to do with each other.

4.1.1.1 Coordinate Systems

Coordinate systems are like language. They are **conventions for the representation** of physical quantities. The traditional Cartesian system in 3D represents a vector quantity by its projections onto three orthogonal axes. The Euler angle representation of attitude is defined in terms of rotations about those axes in a specific order. Polar coordinates are an alternative to Cartesian ones. Mathematical laws alone govern the conversion of a representation from one coordinate system to another coordinate system. However, a conversion of coordinates does not change the magnitude or direction of the physical quantity being represented – it only changes the way it is described.

In the speeding ticket example, the coordinate system can be described as an orthogonal right-handed Cartesian coordinate system where three directions are defined. The direction called *north* is aligned with the projection of the Earth's instantaneous spin axis onto the locally level plane. The direction called *up* is aligned with the direction of gravity. North and up are distinct everywhere but the poles. The direction called *east* is determined from the other two such that $north \times up = east$. North and east have no meaning at the poles.

4.1.1.2 Reference Frames

Imagine two observers with sensors ready to take measurements. The observers have different states of motion – meaning they have a different position or orientation, linear or angular velocity, or linear or angular acceleration. A *reference frame* is a **state of motion**, and it is convenient to associate it with a real physical body with such a state of motion. We need this concept because a physical phenomenon, when observed from one frame of reference, may or may not look the same when observed from a second frame of reference.

In the speeding ticket example, the reference frames are (1) your car and (2) the policeman's radar gun. The speed measurement of the radar gun was that *of* the car **with respect to** the gun (which happened to be fixed to the Earth). The car does not have a unique velocity because it depends on who is measuring it. While it was driving down the road, the road was attached to the Earth, which was moving around the Sun. If the policeman was on the Sun, the car velocity measurement would have been a whopping 30 km/sec – about 3600 times faster. Imagine the fine!

The distinction between coordinate systems and reference frames is crucial to understanding the laws of physics. In fact, the laws of physics hold *regardless* of the coordinate system in which they are expressed. This statement is called the *principle of relativity*. However, reference frames matter crucially. The laws of physics hold *only* in the reference frames to which they apply (e.g. Newton's laws hold only in inertial reference frames).

4.1.2 Change of Reference Frame

Two frames are called *equivalent* with respect to a measurement when the measurement is the same in both frames. If they are not equivalent, a method of converting between the frames of reference is often available. The *laws of physics* are necessary to convert among frames of reference (i.e., to predict a measurement made by one observer from those of another). In the speeding ticket example, given the velocity of the car on the Earth, one can compute its velocity with respect to the Sun.

4.1.2.1 Mutually Stationary Frames

Two frames of reference are shown – an apartment building a and a house h. A particle p is in motion above the buildings. The motion of the particle can be expressed with respect to either of the two mutually stationary frames (Figure 4.2).

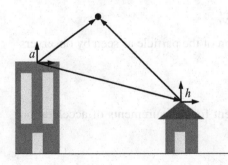

Figure 4.2 Mutually Stationary Frames. Observers in the two buildings will agree on the velocity of the particle but not on its position vector.

Because the buildings (the frames of reference) are not in motion with respect to one another, the position vector $\vec{r}_p^{\,a}$ can be expressed in terms of $\vec{r}_p^{\,h}$ by a constant offset vector $\vec{r}_h^{\,a}$.

$$\vec{r}_p^{\,a} = \vec{r}_p^{\,h} + \vec{r}_h^{\,a} \tag{4.1}$$

If this expression is differentiated, the derivative of the constant disappears.

$$\vec{v}_p^{\,a} = \vec{v}_p^{\,h} \tag{4.2}$$

So observers in either building equipped with appropriate sensors would measure the same velocity of this particle. Hence mutually stationary frames of reference are equivalent for measurements of velocity of a particle, and its time derivatives.

4.1.2.2 The Galilean Transformation

Consider two frames of reference, a fighter aircraft f and a control tower t. The fighter is translating at a constant velocity $\vec{v}_f^{\,t}$ with respect to the tower. Consider particle p, located by the position vectors $\vec{r}_p^{\,t}$ and $\vec{r}_p^{\,f}$ (Figure 4.3).

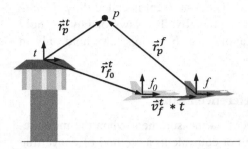

Figure 4.3 Frames Moving at Constant Velocity. Observers in the tower and airplane will agree on the acceleration of the particle but not on its velocity vector.

Let us assume that the airplane was at position $\vec{r}_{f0}^{\,t}$ relative to the tower at $t = 0$. This vector is a constant.

Assuming constant velocity, the relationship between the two position vectors at any time t can be expressed as follows.

$$\vec{r}_p^{\,t} = \vec{r}_p^{\,f} + \vec{r}_{f0}^{\,t} + \vec{v}_f^{\,t} \cdot t$$

The first time derivative of this equation relates the velocity of the particle as seen by an observer **in the control tower** to the velocity of the particle as seen by an observer **in the airplane**.

$$\vec{v}_p^{\,t} = \vec{v}_p^{\,f} + \vec{v}_f^{\,t}$$

The second time derivative relates the acceleration of the particle as seen by observers in the two frames of reference.

$$\vec{a}_p^{\,t} = \vec{a}_p^{\,f}$$

Hence uniformly translating frames are equivalent for measurements of acceleration of a particle and its time derivatives.

4.1.2.3 Rotating Frames: Coriolis Equation

Consider next two frames of reference which are rotating with respect to each one another at some **instantaneous** angular velocity $\vec{\omega}$, (of the second w.r.t. the first). Two observers in such relative rotation will disagree on the derivative of **any vector**. That they disagree is easy to see if we imagine that the vector is fixed with respect to one observer. In that case, the other will see a moving vector due to the relative rotation of the two frames.

It can be convenient to imagine that the two frames have coincident origins but this is not necessary in the case of free vectors like displacement, velocity, force etc. We will call the first frame *fixed* and the second *moving* – though this is completely arbitrary. We will indicate derivatives measured in the first frame by an f subscript to a pair of braces ( ) and those measured in the second by an m subscript. Suppose $\vec{u}$ is any vector (position, velocity, acceleration, force) and $\vec{\omega}$ is the instantaneous angular velocity of the moving frame w.r.t. the fixed one. It is a tedious but straightforward exercise to show that the relationship between the derivatives measured by the two observers is given by:

$$\left(\frac{d\vec{u}}{dt}\right)_f = \left(\frac{d\vec{u}}{dt}\right)_m + \vec{\omega} \times \vec{u} \qquad (4.3)$$

Spotlight 4.1 Coriolis Equation.

One must be very careful when using this equation to keep the reference frames straight. It is used to relate different time derivatives of the *same vector* computed by two observers in relative rotational motion. The left hand side is said to be the derivative computed (or measured) "in" the fixed frame.

An alternative notation for such derivatives is

$$\frac{d}{dt}\bigg|_x u = \left(\frac{du}{dt}\right)_x \qquad (4.4)$$

Despite the fundamental importance of this equation [2][3], it seems to have no standard name. In navigation, it is sometimes called the *Coriolis Equation*. In physics, it is sometimes called the *Transport Theorem*.

A simple example of the use of the formula is to consider a vector of constant magnitude that is rotating relative to a "fixed" observer. If we imagine a moving observer that is moving with the vector, then:

$$\left(\frac{d\vec{u}}{dt}\right)_m = 0$$

and the law reduces to:

$$\left(\frac{d\vec{u}}{dt}\right)_f = \vec{\omega} \times \vec{u} \qquad (4.5)$$

Again, $\vec{u}$ is an arbitrary vector quantity. If it represents the position vector $\vec{r}$ from a fixed observed at a center of rotation to any particle, then the law provides the velocity $\vec{v}_{fixed}$ of the particle with respect to the fixed observer:

$$\vec{v}_{fixed} = \left(\frac{d\vec{r}}{dt}\right)_f = \vec{\omega} \times \vec{r} \qquad (4.6)$$

4.1.2.4 Velocity Transformation Under General Relative Motion

Application of the Coriolis equation to two frames separated in space leads to more general results. Let the two frames also have an **instantaneous** relative position of $\vec{r}_m^f$. Suppose an observer **in the moving frame** measures the position $\vec{r}$, velocity $\vec{v}$, and acceleration $\vec{a}$ of an object, and we wish to know what another observer **in the fixed** *frame* would measure for the motion of the same object. The situation is depicted in Figure 4.4.

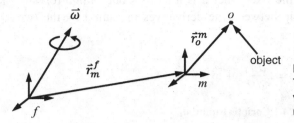

Figure 4.4 Frames in General Motion. Two observers are in general motion with respect to each other and both measure the motion of the object.

Clearly, the positions add by simple vector addition:

$$\vec{r}_o^f = \vec{r}_m^f + \vec{r}_o^m$$

The time derivative computed in the fixed frame is:

$$\frac{d}{dt}\bigg|_f (\vec{r}_o^f) = \frac{d}{dt}\bigg|_f (\vec{r}_m^f + \vec{r}_o^m) = \frac{d}{dt}\bigg|_f (\vec{r}_m^f) + \frac{d}{dt}\bigg|_f (\vec{r}_o^m)$$

Now we can apply the Coriolis equation to the second term on the right to get the general velocity transformation:

$$\vec{v}_o^f = \vec{v}_m^f + \vec{\omega}_m^f \times \vec{r}_o^m + \vec{v}_o^m \tag{4.7}$$

Here, $\vec{v}_o^f$ is the velocity of the object with respect to the fixed observer $\vec{v}_m^f$ is the linear velocity of the moving observer with respect to the fixed one, $\vec{\omega}_m^f$ is the angular velocity of the moving observer with respect to the fixed one, $\vec{r}_o^m$ is the position of the object relative to the moving observer, and $\vec{v}_o^m$ is the velocity of the object with respect to the moving observer. We have used the fact that, for any frames x and y, by definition:

$$\frac{d}{dt}\bigg|_x (\vec{r}_y^x) = \vec{v}_y^x \tag{4.8}$$

The result means that the fixed observer sees two components of velocity in addition to the velocity measured by the moving observer. Namely: $\vec{v}_m^f$ and $\vec{\omega}_m^f \times \vec{r}_o^m$. This result will be the basis of wheeled mobile robot kinematic analysis.

4.1.2.5 Acceleration Transformation Under General Relative Motion

Differentiating the velocity relation in the fixed frame leads to:

$$\frac{d}{dt}\bigg|_f (\vec{v}_o^f) = \frac{d}{dt}\bigg|_f (\vec{v}_m^f + \vec{\omega}_m^f \times \vec{r}_o^m + \vec{v}_o^m)$$

Which is:

$$\frac{d}{dt}\bigg|_f (\vec{v}_o^f) = \frac{d}{dt}\bigg|_f (\vec{v}_m^f) + \frac{d}{dt}\bigg|_f (\vec{\omega}_m^f \times \vec{r}_o^m) + \frac{d}{dt}\bigg|_f (\vec{v}_o^m) \tag{4.9}$$

Lets take each element in sequence. The left-hand side of Equation 4.9 is by definition:

$$\frac{d}{dt}\bigg|_f (\vec{v}_o^{\,f}) = \vec{a}_o^{\,f}$$

The first term on the right-hand side of Equation 4.9 is by definition:

$$\frac{d}{dt}\bigg|_f (\vec{v}_m^{\,f}) = \vec{a}_m^{\,f}$$

The second term on the right-hand side of Equation 4.9 is complicated. First by the chain rule, we have:

$$\frac{d}{dt}\bigg|_f (\vec{\omega}_m^{\,f} \times \vec{r}_o^{\,m}) = \frac{d}{dt}\bigg|_f (\vec{\omega}_m^{\,f}) \times \vec{r}_o^{\,m} + \vec{\omega}_m^{\,f} \times \frac{d}{dt}\bigg|_f (\vec{r}_o^{\,m}) \tag{4.10}$$

The first term on the right-hand side of Equation 4.10 is:

$$\frac{d}{dt}\bigg|_f (\vec{\omega}_m^{\,f}) \times \vec{r}_o^{\,m} = \vec{\alpha}_m^{\,f} \times \vec{r}_o^{\,m}$$

The second term on the right-hand side of Equation 4.10, switching the frame of differentiation, is:

$$\vec{\omega}_m^{\,f} \times \frac{d}{dt}\bigg|_f (\vec{r}_o^{\,m}) = \vec{\omega}_m^{\,f} \times \left[\frac{d}{dt}\bigg|_m (\vec{r}_o^{\,m}) + \vec{\omega}_m^{\,f} \times \vec{r}_o^{\,m} \right]$$

Which is:

$$\vec{\omega}_m^{\,f} \times \frac{d}{dt}\bigg|_f (\vec{r}_o^{\,m}) = \vec{\omega}_m^{\,f} \times [\vec{v}_o^{\,m} + \vec{\omega}_m^{\,f} \times \vec{r}_o^{\,m}] = \vec{\omega}_m^{\,f} \times \vec{v}_o^{\,m} + \vec{\omega}_m^{\,f} \times [\vec{\omega}_m^{\,f} \times \vec{r}_o^{\,m}]$$

The third term on right-hand side of Equation 4.9 is:

$$\frac{d}{dt}\bigg|_f (\vec{v}_o^{\,m}) = \frac{d}{dt}\bigg|_m (\vec{v}_o^{\,m}) + \vec{\omega}_m^{\,f} \times \vec{v}_o^{\,m} = \vec{a}_o^{\,m} + \vec{\omega}_m^{\,f} \times \vec{v}_o^{\,m}$$

Putting all of the rewrites of Equation 4.9 together gives the general acceleration transformation:

$$\vec{a}_o^{\,f} = \vec{a}_m^{\,f} + \vec{\alpha}_m^{\,f} \times \vec{r}_o^{\,m} + \vec{\omega}_m^{\,f} \times [\vec{\omega}_m^{\,f} \times \vec{r}_o^{\,m}] + 2\vec{\omega}_m^{\,f} \times \vec{v}_o^{\,m} + \vec{a}_o^{\,m} \tag{4.11}$$

Notationally, $\vec{a}_o^{\,f}$ is the acceleration of the object relative to the fixed observer and $\vec{a}_o^{\,m}$ is that relative to the moving observer. The remaining four terms are terms measured by the fixed observer but not by the moving one. They are so famous that they have names. The Einstein acceleration $\vec{a}_m^{\,f}$ is that of the moving frame relative to the fixed. The Euler acceleration is $\vec{\alpha}_m^{\,f} \times \vec{r}_o^{\,m}$ and the Centripetal acceleration is $\vec{\omega}_m^{\,f} \times [\vec{\omega}_m^{\,f} \times \vec{r}_o^{\,m}]$. The Coriolis acceleration is $2\vec{\omega}_m^{\,f} \times \vec{v}_o^{\,m}$,

This result is the basic formula needed for inertial navigation. The main results related to change of reference frames are summarized in Box 4.1.

Box 4.1 Rules for Transformations of Derivatives of Vectors

For two observers called fixed and moving, the Coriolis equation relates time derivatives of the same vector.

$$\left(\frac{d\vec{u}}{dt}\right)_f = \left(\frac{d\vec{u}}{dt}\right)_m + \vec{\omega} \times \vec{u}$$

For arbitrary relative motion of the observers, the transformation of their measurements is given by Equation 4.11, Equation 4.12, and Equation 4.13.

$$\vec{r}_o^f = \vec{r}_m^f + \vec{r}_o^m \tag{4.12}$$

$$\vec{v}_o^f = \vec{v}_m^f + \vec{\omega}_m^f \times \vec{r}_o^m + \vec{v}_o^m \tag{4.13}$$

$$\vec{a}_o^f = \vec{a}_m^f + \vec{\alpha}_m^f \times \vec{r}_o^m + \vec{\omega}_m^f \times [\vec{\omega}_m^f \times \vec{r}_o^m] + 2\vec{\omega}_m^f \times \vec{v}_o^m + \vec{a}_o^m \tag{4.14}$$

4.1.3 Example: Attitude Stability Margin Estimation

The use of inertial sensing in advanced vehicle controls is commonplace in automotive engineering. One form of advanced control is governing to prevent loss of attitude stability. Stability in this context refers to keeping the vehicle upright and in contact with the terrain. It can be defined for roll, pitch, or yaw. The attitude *stability margin* is defined as proximity to rollover or tipover and it can be estimated in order to take action if the present motion is, or is close to being, unsafe.

Attitude stability is important for vehicles that lift heavy loads, turn at speed, or operate on sloped terrain. Many vehicles do one or more of these things. Examples of such vehicles are forklifts and lift trucks; commercial outdoor vehicles in mining, forestry, agriculture; and military vehicles. For a robot, knowledge of stability margin can be used to control it by choosing speed, articulation or trajectory.

One definition of attitude stability margin relates to the angle of the net force acting at the center of gravity (cg). Computing it requires knowledge of the location of the cg, the geometry of the convex polygon formed by the wheel contact points with the terrain, the attitude of the vehicle with respect to the local gravity field, and the inertial forces being experienced due to accelerated motion. The gravity and inertial forces can be measured at once by a sensor called an accelerometer.

4.1.3.1 Proximity to Wheel Liftoff

Before a vehicle rolls or tips, some of its wheels have to leave the ground, so preventing wheel liftoff will prevent a loss of stability. It turns out that liftoff is relatively easy to predict. Rather than measure forces at the wheels, there is a simpler way that is more fundamental.

Wheel liftoff can be predicted by measuring the direction of the vector sum of inertial and gravitational forces acting at the center of gravity and comparing it to the polygon

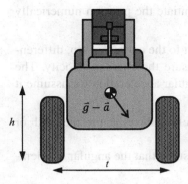

h

$\vec{g} - \vec{a}$

t

Figure 4.5 Attitude Stability Margin. The vehicle is viewed from the rear and it is in a hard left turn. Roll stability margin is zero, and the wheels on the inside of the turn (left) are about to lift off.

formed by the wheel contact points. Figure 4.5 shows a simple case for vehicle rollover. The central issue is the direction of the net noncontact force vector acting at the cg – and whether it causes an unbalanced moment about any tipover axis. We can define the *specific force* as the vector acceleration minus the acceleration due to gravity:

$$\vec{t} = \vec{a} - \vec{g} \tag{4.15}$$

An *accelerometer* can be used to predict the behavior of a pendulum. It indicates the direction in which a pendulum would point if it were free to swing. In the figure, a pendulum positioned at the cg would point in the direction shown. This means we can measure attitude stability margin by simply placing a two-axis accelerometer at the cg.

4.1.3.2 Acceleration Transformation

Unfortunately, it is not convenient or even necessarily possible to place a sensor at the cg. The cg may be embedded in the structure, or the vehicle may articulate mass, and thereby move the cg over time. The practical solution to the problem is to place the accelerometer in any convenient place and then transform its readings to produce what a hypothetical sensor at the cg would read [1].

Let us define a sensor frame s, the cg frame c, and we can assume for this problem that a frame fixed to the earth is inertial i. We can use Equation 4.14 to solve the problem. Let the fixed frame be the inertial frame, the moving frame be the sensor frame, and the object frame be the cg frame. Then by merely substituting the subscripts and superscripts we get:

$$\vec{a}_c^i = \vec{a}_s^i + \vec{\alpha}_s^i \times \vec{r}_c^s + \vec{\omega}_s^i \times [\vec{\omega}_s^i \times \vec{r}_c^s] + 2\vec{\omega}_s^i \times \vec{v}_c^s + \vec{a}_c^s \tag{4.16}$$

Subtracting gravity $\vec{g}$ from both sides produces the virtual and the real specific forces that would be read by the 2-axis accelerometers.

4.1.3.3 Computational Requirements

In addition to the readings $\vec{a}_s^i$ from the real sensor, computing the readings of a hypothetical sensor requires that we know all of the following:

$(\vec{r}_c^s, \vec{v}_c^s, \vec{a}_c^s)$: the translational motion of the cg with respect to the sensor. This is nonzero on an articulating vehicle, and we would need articulation sensors (encoders, string pots) to measure the positions. Then we would have to differentiate the position numerically once to get velocity and once again to get acceleration.

$(\vec{\omega}_s^i, \vec{a}_s^i)$: the rotational motion of the sensor with respect to the earth. A gyro, differential wheel speeds, or steering angle encoder can measure the angular velocity. The data would be differentiated numerically to get the angular acceleration (or assume it is zero).

Note that the position, velocity, or attitude of the vehicle with respect to the earth or inertial space is not required anywhere.

For a typical vehicle whose cg is fixed, if we also assume that the angular acceleration $\vec{\alpha}_s^i$ can be neglected, the result is simply:

$$\vec{a}_c^i = \vec{a}_s^i + \vec{\omega}_s^i \times [\vec{\omega}_s^i \times \vec{r}_c^s] \tag{4.17}$$

Hence stability margin can be computed if angular rate sensors are added and the position of the cg relative to the sensor is known.

4.1.4 Recursive Transformations of State of Motion

This section will develop the kinematic equations of mobile robots in their general recursive form in 3D. Equation 4.12, Equation 4.13, and Equation 4.14 may be used to model the effects of arbitrary articulations between sequences of reference frames. One simply replaces frame f with frame k and frame m with frame $k + 1$. For two adjacent frames in the sequence, the transformations are:

$$\vec{r}_o^k = \vec{r}_{k+1}^k + \vec{r}_o^{k+1}$$

$$\vec{v}_o^k = \vec{v}_{k+1}^k + \vec{\omega}_{k+1}^k \times \vec{r}_o^{k+1} + \vec{v}_o^{k+1} \tag{4.18}$$

$$\vec{a}_o^k = \vec{a}_{k+1}^k + \vec{\alpha}_{k+1}^k \times \vec{r}_o^{k+1} + \vec{\omega}_{k+1}^k \times [\vec{\omega}_{k+1}^k \times \vec{r}_o^{k+1}] + 2\vec{\omega}_{k+1}^k \times \vec{v}_o^{k+1} + \vec{a}_o^{k+1}$$

Now that we have introduced numeric superscripts, it is important to remember that the o subscript stands for object rather than frame 0 (zero).

4.1.4.1 Conversion to Coordinatized Form

Computer implementation of the equations will require that the physical vector quantities involved be *coordinatized* – expressed in a particular coordinate system. This is accomplished with the skew-symmetric matrix equivalent of the cross product. Once a coordinate system is chosen for expressing both $\vec{\omega}$ and $\vec{u}$, we have:

$$\vec{\omega} \times \vec{u} \Rightarrow \underline{\omega} \times \underline{u} = [\underline{\omega}]^{\times}\underline{u} = -[\underline{u}]^{\times}\underline{\omega}$$

where:

$$[\underline{u}]^{\times} \cong \begin{bmatrix} 0 & -u_z & u_y \\ u_z & 0 & -u_x \\ -u_y & u_x & 0 \end{bmatrix}$$

Also, we can write the transport theorem in matrix form:

$$\left(\frac{d\underline{u}}{dt}\right)_f = \left(\frac{d\underline{u}}{dt}\right)_m + [\underline{\omega}]^\times \underline{u} \tag{4.19}$$

Using this matrix, we can rewrite Equation 4.18:

$$\underline{r}_o^k = \underline{r}_{k+1}^k + \underline{r}_o^{k+1}$$

$$\underline{v}_o^k = \left[I \mid -[\underline{r}_o^{k+1}]^\times\right]\begin{bmatrix} \underline{v}_{k+1}^k \\ \underline{\omega}_{k+1}^k \end{bmatrix} + \underline{v}_o^{k+1} \tag{4.20}$$

$$\underline{a}_o^k = \left[I \mid -[\underline{r}_o^{k+1}]^\times\right]\begin{bmatrix} \underline{a}_{k+1}^k \\ \underline{\alpha}_{k+1}^k \end{bmatrix} + \left[[\underline{\omega}_{k+1}^k]^{\times\times} \mid 2[\underline{\omega}_{k+1}^k]^\times \mid I\right]\begin{bmatrix} \underline{r}_o^{k+1} \\ \underline{v}_o^{k+1} \\ \underline{a}_o^{k+1} \end{bmatrix}$$

We are also using the notation $[\underline{u}]^{\times\times} = [\underline{u}]^\times[\underline{u}]^\times$. Let a semicolon in a vector mean vertical concatenation of its component vectors. Then, define:

$$\underline{\rho} \cong \left[\underline{r} \; ; \; \underline{v} \; ; \; \underline{a}\right] \qquad \underline{x} \cong \left[\underline{r} \; ; \; \underline{v} \; ; \; \underline{\omega} \; ; \; \underline{a} \; ; \; \underline{\alpha}\right]$$

Equation 4.20 can then be written as a single matrix equation of the form:

$$\underline{\rho}_o^k = H(\underline{\rho}_o^{k+1})\underline{x}_{k+1}^k + \Omega(\underline{x}_{k+1}^k)\underline{\rho}_o^{k+1} \tag{4.21}$$

and we could even substitute $\underline{x}_i^j$ for $\underline{\rho}_i^j$ because the elements of $\underline{\rho}$ are a subset of those of $\underline{x}$. This form is useful for computer simulation purposes and it represents the general case.

Typically the quantities $\underline{x}_{k+1}^k$ represent the internal articulations of a mechanism and $\underline{\rho}_o^k$ represents the partial solutions generated at each stage of the recursion for successive "moving observers" along the kinematic chain. The choice of the letter H is based on the use of these equations as measurement models in state estimation where $\underline{\rho}_o^k$ is the measurements and $\underline{x}_{k+1}^k$, and so on is the state. The matrix Ω captures the dependence of centrifugal and Coriolis apparent forces on angular velocity.

If acceleration is not required for the task at hand, one can redefine:

$$\underline{\rho} \cong \left[\underline{r} \; ; \; \underline{v}\right] \qquad \underline{x} \cong \left[\underline{r} \; ; \; \underline{v} \; ; \; \underline{\omega}\right]$$

and Equation 4.21 becomes:

$$\underline{\rho}_o^k = H(\underline{\rho}_o^{k+1})\underline{x}_{k+1}^k + \underline{\rho}_o^{k+1} \tag{4.22}$$

so $\Omega(\underline{x}_{k+1}^k)$ vanishes and $H(\underline{\rho}_o^{k+1})$ loses two columns.

4.1.4.2 General Recursive Transforms in Matrix Form

Consider just the velocity component of Equation 4.20:

$$\underline{v}_o^k = \left[I \mid -[\underline{r}_o^{k+1}]^\times\right]\begin{bmatrix} \underline{v}_{k+1}^k \\ \underline{\omega}_{k+1}^k \end{bmatrix} + \underline{v}_o^{k+1} \tag{4.23}$$

We will denote this as:

$$\underline{v}_o^k = H(\underline{r}_o^{k+1})\dot{\underline{x}}_{k+1}^k + \underline{v}_o^{k+1} \tag{4.24}$$

where $H(\underline{r}_o^{k+1})$ and $\dot{\underline{x}}_{k+1}^k$ are defined for this case as they occur in Equation 4.22.

Now consider just the acceleration component of Equation 4.20:

$$\underline{a}_o^k = \begin{bmatrix} I & -[\underline{r}_o^{k+1}]^\times \end{bmatrix} \begin{bmatrix} \underline{a}_{k+1}^k \\ \underline{\alpha}_{k+1}^k \end{bmatrix} + \begin{bmatrix} [\underline{\omega}_{k+1}^k]^{\times\times} & 2[\underline{\omega}_{k+1}^k]^\times \end{bmatrix} \begin{bmatrix} \underline{r}_o^{k+1} \\ \underline{v}_o^{k+1} \end{bmatrix} + \underline{a}_o^{k+1} \tag{4.25}$$

We will denote this as:

$$\underline{a}_o^k = H(\underline{r}_o^{k+1})\ddot{\underline{x}}_{k+1}^k + \Omega(\underline{\omega}_{k+1}^k)\underline{\rho}_o^{k+1} + \underline{a}_o^{k+1} \tag{4.26}$$

where $H(\underline{r}_o^{k+1})$, $\dot{\underline{x}}_{k+1}^k$, $\ddot{\underline{x}}_{k+1}^k$, $\Omega(\dot{\underline{x}}_{k+1}^k)$ and $\underline{\rho}_o^{k+1}$ are defined for this case as they occur in Equation 4.24.

4.1.4.3 The Articulated Wheel

We turn now to a useful specific case of sufficient complexity for most practical problems. Let n be the maximum value of $k + 1$ for a particular system. In the case of $n = 2$, there are two intermediate frames in the pose network relating frame 0 to the object. In this case, the velocity transformations in Equation 4.24 take the form:

$$\underline{v}_o^0 = H(\underline{r}_o^1)\dot{\underline{x}}_1^0 + \underline{v}_o^1$$
$$\underline{v}_o^1 = H(\underline{r}_o^2)\dot{\underline{x}}_2^1 + \underline{v}_o^2$$

Substituting the second into the first produces:

$$\underline{v}_o^0 = H(\underline{r}_o^1)\dot{\underline{x}}_1^0 + H(\underline{r}_o^2)\dot{\underline{x}}_2^1 + \underline{v}_o^2 \tag{4.27}$$

In the case of $n = 2$, the acceleration transformations in Equation 4.26 take the form:

$$\underline{a}_o^0 = H(\underline{r}_o^1)\ddot{\underline{x}}_1^0 + \Omega(\underline{\omega}_1^0)\underline{\rho}_o^1 + \underline{a}_o^1$$
$$\underline{a}_o^1 = H(\underline{r}_o^2)\ddot{\underline{x}}_2^1 + \Omega(\underline{\omega}_2^1)\underline{\rho}_o^2 + \underline{a}_o^2 \tag{4.28}$$

Substituting the second into the first produces:

$$\underline{a}_o^0 = H(\underline{r}_o^1)\ddot{\underline{x}}_1^0 + \Omega(\underline{\omega}_1^0)\underline{\rho}_o^1 + H(\underline{r}_o^2)\ddot{\underline{x}}_2^1 + \Omega(\underline{\omega}_2^1)\underline{\rho}_o^2 + \underline{a}_o^2 \tag{4.29}$$

Figure 4.6 shows a case of moderate complexity where a wheel, possibly steered, possibly suspended, is attached to the body. We will work with the pose network at the bottom of the figure, meaning the arrows represent the key poses of interest. Frame c is the wheel contact point. The s frame is introduced for convenience to represent the typical case in the top view where a wheel is steered around an axis offset from the wheel contact point. In the side view, we can imagine that s refers to the suspension.

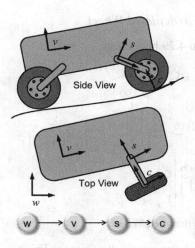

Figure 4.6 Frames for Kinematic Modelling. Frames for vehicle, steer/suspension and contact point are shown.

In either case, the main point is that we will allow some frame s to move arbitrarily with respect to frame v.

If the wheel were **both** suspended and offset-steered, we might need two distinct frames. In the general case, there could even be a few more levels of articulation between the body frame and the wheel contact point.

4.1.4.4 Velocity Transforms For the Articulated Wheel

The kinematic transformations that apply to this case have already been developed above. Let frame 0 be the world frame w and frame 1 be the vehicle body frame v. Let the object frame o be the wheel contact point c and frame 2 be the suspension or steering frame s.

Under these substitutions Equation 4.27 becomes:

$$
\underline{v}_c^w = H(\underline{r}_c^v)\underline{\dot{x}}_v^w + H(\underline{r}_c^s)\underline{\dot{x}}_s^v + \underline{v}_c^s
$$

$$
\underline{v}_c^w = \left[I \mid -[\underline{r}_c^v]^\times \right] \begin{bmatrix} \underline{v}_v^w \\ \underline{\omega}_v^w \end{bmatrix} + \left[I \mid -[\underline{r}_c^s]^\times \right] \begin{bmatrix} \underline{v}_s^v \\ \underline{\omega}_s^v \end{bmatrix} + \underline{v}_c^s \qquad (4.30)
$$

Spotlight 4.2 Velocity Kinematics: Articulated Wheel.

This equation is valid for arbitrary 3D relationships between all the frames. This form describes the case of a single degree of articulation between the vehicle frame and the (possibly moving) contact point.

We will call this the **articulated wheel velocity equation.** If more frames were introduced to be able to capture the effect of nested articulations, the derivation would proceed similarly. The important point is to establish a pose graph relating the world and contact point frames through whatever number of intermediate frames is necessary to isolate individual degrees of articulation freedom. The result is simply the sum of the effects of motion, articulation, and rolling contact.

4.1.4.5 Acceleration Transforms for the Articulated Wheel

Using the same substitutions of frame names, Equation 4.29 becomes:

$$\underline{a}_c^w = H(\underline{r}_c^v)\,\underline{\ddot{x}}_v^w + \Omega(\underline{\omega}_v^w)\underline{\rho}_c^v + H(\underline{r}_c^s)\,\underline{\ddot{x}}_s^v + \Omega(\underline{\omega}_s^v)\underline{\rho}_c^s + \underline{a}_c^s$$

$$\underline{a}_c^w = \left[\, I \mid -[\underline{r}_c^v]^\times \,\right]\begin{bmatrix}\underline{a}_v^w \\ \underline{\alpha}_v^w\end{bmatrix} + \left[\,[\underline{\omega}_v^w]^{\times\times} \mid 2[\underline{\omega}_v^w]^\times\,\right]\begin{bmatrix}\underline{r}_c^v \\ \underline{v}_c^v\end{bmatrix}$$

$$+ \left[\, I \mid -[\underline{r}_c^s]^\times \,\right]\begin{bmatrix}\underline{a}_s^v \\ \underline{\alpha}_s^v\end{bmatrix} + \left[\,[\underline{\omega}_s^v]^{\times\times} \mid 2[\underline{\omega}_s^v]^\times\,\right]\begin{bmatrix}\underline{r}_c^s \\ \underline{v}_c^s\end{bmatrix} + \underline{a}_c^s \qquad (4.31)$$

Spotlight 4.3 Acceleration Kinematics: Articulated Wheel.

This equation is valid for arbitrary 3D relationships between all the frames. This form describes the case of a single degree of articulation between the vehicle frame and the (possibly moving) contact point.

We will call this the ***articulated wheel acceleration equation.*** The combined result is again the sum of the effects of motion, articulation, and rolling contact.

4.1.5 References and Further Reading

Goldstein is a classic reference in mechanics, and Gregory is a more tutorial source. Diaz-Calderon is the source of the vehicle rollover example.

[1]   A. Diaz-Calderon and A. Kelly, On-line Stability Margin and Attitude Estimation for Dynamic Articulating Mobile Robots, *The International Journal of Robotics Research,* Vol. 24, No. 10, pp. 845–866, 2005.

[2]   Herbert Goldstein, Charles P. Poole, and John L. Safko, *Classical Mechanics*, 3rd ed., Addison-Wesley, 2002.

[3]   Douglas Gregory, *Classical Mechanics: An Undergraduate Text,* Cambridge, 2006.

4.1.6 Exercises

4.1.6.1 Coriolis Equation

Let $\hat{i}_m$ denote the unit vector directed along the x axis of a moving coordinate system. Its magnitude is fixed by definition at unity, so its time derivative as seen by a fixed observer must be directed orthogonal (i.e., it can only rotate, not elongate) to $\hat{i}_m$. Show using first principles that its time derivative is, in fact

$$\left.\frac{d}{dt}\right|_f (\hat{i}_m) = \vec{\omega} \times \hat{i}_m$$

Then use linearity of the cross product to derive the Coriolis equation for any vector of constant magnitude and then for any vector at all.

4.1.6.2 Velocity Field on a Rigid Body

When the objects being observed are points on a robot vehicle, their velocities relative to an observer on the robot $\vec{v}_o^m$ vanish. Then, if w represents the fixed world frame and v represents the moving vehicle frame, the velocity transformation takes the form:

$$\vec{v}_o^w = \vec{v}_v^w + \vec{\omega}_v^w \times \vec{r}_o^v$$

(i) Show, for a rigid body moving in the plane, that the linear velocity vector on a line between any two points varies linearly with the displacement vector between the two points.

(ii) Does the angle of the velocity vector vary linearly. Does the tangent of the angle?

4.2 Kinematics of Wheeled Mobile Robots

This section begins the modelling the wheeled mobile robot (WMR) as a differential algebraic equation. Recall that this is a differential equation subject to constraints. In the case of WMRs subject to non-slip constraints, the first-order (velocity) kinematics takes the form:

$$\dot{\underline{x}} = f(\underline{x}, \underline{u})$$
$$w(\underline{x}) \, \dot{\underline{x}} = 0 \tag{4.32}$$

In this section, we will primarily consider the case where the constraints are satisfied by construction by assuming that the wheel motions are already consistent with rigid body motion. In this case, the second equation above can be ignored. We will also choose $\underline{x}(t)$ to be the linear and angular velocity of the body (vehicle frame) and the inputs will be wheel velocities. In this way, the first equation also becomes simpler – it is merely a transformation of velocities according to the rules presented in the last subchapter.

This subchapter will express the equations of motion in body coordinates. This approach will also eliminate the vehicle position and orientation from consideration entirely and render the models in simplest form. This means that the results of this subchapter are completely valid in 3D because the body velocity can be converted to an arbitrary world frame before it is integrated to generate a trajectory.

4.2.1 Aspects of Rigid Body Motion

This section will remind the reader of some important concepts from mechanics upon which much of the subchapter is based.

4.2.1.1 Instantaneous Center of Rotation

Suppose a *particle p* is executing a pure rotation about a point in the plane. Clearly, because its trajectory is a circle, its position vector $\vec{r}_p$ relative to the center of that circle is given by:

$$\vec{r}_p = r(\cos(\psi)\hat{i} + \sin(\psi)\hat{j})$$

where ψ is the angle that $\vec{r}_p(t)$ makes with respect to the chosen x axis. Because r is fixed, the particle velocity is merely:

$$\vec{v}_p = r\omega(-\sin(\psi)\hat{i} + \cos(\psi)\hat{j})$$

Note that the velocity vector is always orthogonal to $\vec{r}_p$. It is easy to show that this is equivalent to:

$$\vec{v}_p = \vec{\omega} \times \vec{r}_p$$

And note especially that the magnitudes are related by:

$$v_p = r_p\omega \tag{4.33}$$

Now consider, instead of a particle, a *rigid body* executing a general motion in the plane (Figure 4.7). A basic theorem of mechanics shows that all rigid body motions in the plane can be considered to be a rotation about some point – the instantaneous center of rotation (ICR). To see this, define the ratio r that relates the linear and angular velocity of some point on the body with respect to some world frame thus:

$$r = v_p^w / \omega \qquad v_p^w = r\omega$$

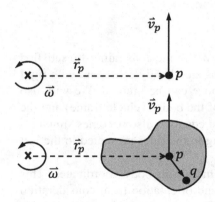

Figure 4.7 Pure Rotation and Instantaneous Center of Rotation. All planar motions can be described as a pure rotation about an instantaneous center of rotation. (Top) A particle undergoing pure rotation. (Bottom) Every particle on this body is in pure rotation about the ICR.

With reference to Equation 4.33, the equation immediately above describes the motion of the point on the body if it were rotating about a point positioned r units along the normal to the instantaneous velocity vector. In vector terms:

$$\vec{v}_p^{\,icr} = \vec{\omega} \times \vec{r}_p^{\,icr}$$

In such a case, r is called the *radius of curvature* because the curvature of the point's trajectory is $\kappa = 1/r$. That is true for one point on the body. Consider a neighboring point q. The position vector to q can be written as:

$$\vec{r}_q^{\,icr} = \vec{r}_p^{\,icr} + \vec{r}_q^{\,p}$$

Taking time derivatives in a frame fixed to the world:

$$\left.\frac{d}{dt}\right|_w (\vec{r}_q^{\,icr}) = \left.\frac{d}{dt}\right|_w (\vec{r}_p^{\,icr}) + \left.\frac{d}{dt}\right|_w (\vec{r}_q^{\,p})$$

But the last derivative can be rewritten in terms of a derivative computed in the body frame:

$$\left.\frac{d}{dt}\right|_w (\vec{r}_q^p) = \left.\frac{d}{dt}\right|_b (\vec{r}_q^p) + \vec{\omega} \times \vec{r}_q^p = \vec{\omega} \times \vec{r}_q^p$$

Hence the derivative is:

$$\vec{v}_q^{icr} = \vec{v}_p^{icr} + \vec{\omega} \times \vec{r}_q^p$$

Substituting for the velocity of p relative to its ICR:

$$\vec{v}_q^{icr} = \vec{\omega} \times \vec{r}_p^{icr} + \vec{\omega} \times \vec{r}_q^p = \vec{\omega} \times (\vec{r}_p^{icr} + \vec{r}_q^p) = \vec{\omega} \times \vec{r}_q^{icr}$$

Remarkably, the motion of an arbitrary other point q on the body is also a pure rotation about the ICR! We have shown that ***all particles on a rigid body*** move in a manner that can be instantaneously described as a ***pure rotation about a point*** that we called the ICR.

4.2.1.2 Jeantaud Diagrams

Now let the rigid body be a vehicle. Note that fixing just the (distinct) directions of the linear velocity of two points will often fix the position of the ICR. If the directions are not distinct, the magnitudes of the velocities are required. If the magnitudes of parallel velocities are the same, the ICR is at infinity and the vehicle is travelling in a straight line.

When steering, we typically try to reduce or eliminate wheel skid (and the associated energy losses) by actuating all wheels in order to be consistent with a single instantaneous center of rotation. If all wheels are consistent, any two steer angles, and one velocity can be used to predict the motion.

A *Jeantaud Diagram* extends the inner normals to the velocities at the wheels until they meet at the ICR. Consider the case of 4 wheel steer in Figure 4.8:

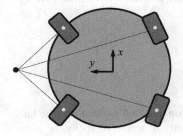

Figure 4.8 Jeantaud Diagram. When the wheels are set to a steering configuration that is consistent with rigid body motion, the wheels do not slip. In this configuration their axles all point to the same instantaneous center of rotation.

This vehicle, with four steered wheels, can move in any direction without changing its heading. Such designs are extremely maneuverable. They can even spin about any point within the vehicle envelope. However, if there are limits on steer angles, there is a forbidden region where the instantaneous center of rotation (ICR) cannot lie.

4.2.1.3 Rolling Contact

Wheels normally have up to two degrees of freedom (steer and drive) with respect to the vehicle to which they are attached. When a wheel rolls over terrain, a typical abstraction is to define a single point, the *contact point*, which is **both** on the wheel and on the terrain. The fact that it is on both means the wheel and terrain touch at this point.

The contact point moves arbitrarily over the terrain but, on flat terrain, it is fixed with respect to the wheel center. The nominal relationship between wheel angular velocity and the linear velocity of the contact point is shown in Figure 4.9. The qualifier *nominal* was used because the real situation is more complicated.

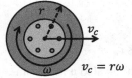

Figure 4.9 Wheel Linear and Angular Velocity. Assuming a point contact at the precise bottom of the wheel, and a known radius, the linear and angular velocity of a wheel are related as shown.

The contact point is an idealization in several respects. First, when the terrain is not flat, the contact point may move with respect to the wheel center. Second, neither wheels nor terrain are perfectly rigid so a finite region of the wheel surface, the *contact patch*, is in contact. The contact point can be defined in this case as a particular kind of centroid of the contact patch. Now that the reader is aware of the assumptions, we will henceforth adopt the contact point idealization.

The contact point can be used to define the natural coordinate system for expressing constraints. The normal to the terrain at the contact point defines a direction in which the wheel velocity, relative to the terrain, must be zero. The wheel velocity must be confined to the terrain tangent plane.

4.2.1.4 Rolling Without Slipping

Moreover, if any component of wheel velocity is oriented along the projection of the wheel lateral axis onto the terrain tangent plane, it means the wheel is slipping in that direction because it cannot roll in that direction. Consider a wheeled vehicle rolling without slipping in the plane (Figure 4.10).

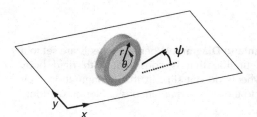

Figure 4.10 Non-slip Rolling Motion. The lateral component of wheel velocity is zero under non-slip conditions.

One way to express the idea that wheels cannot (or are not supposed to) move sideways is to write a constraint equation.

The constraint of "rolling without slipping" means that $\dot{x}$ and $\dot{y}$ of the wheel must be consistent with the direction of rolling – they are not independent. In mathematics terms, the dot product of the wheel velocity vector $[\dot{x}\dot{y}]^T$ with the *disallowed direction* $[\sin\psi - \cos\psi]^T$ must vanish:

$$\dot{x}\sin\psi - \dot{y}\cos\psi = 0 \qquad\qquad (4.34)$$

If we define the wheel configuration vector:

$$\underline{x} = \begin{bmatrix} x & y & \psi & \theta \end{bmatrix}^T \tag{4.35}$$

and the weight vector:

$$\underline{w}(\underline{x}) = \begin{bmatrix} \sin\psi & -\cos\psi & 0 & 0 \end{bmatrix} \tag{4.36}$$

The constraint is then of the form:

$$\underline{w}(\underline{x})\dot{\underline{x}} = 0 \tag{4.37}$$

Constraints in this precise form are called *Pfaffian* constraints. More generally, in Lagrangian dynamics, this type of constraint is classified as *nonholonomic* because it cannot be rewritten in the form:

$$c(\underline{x}) = 0 \tag{4.38}$$

Naturally, the process to remove $\dot{\underline{x}}$ in favor of $\underline{x}$ would be integration – but the expression cannot be integrated to generate the above form. The integral would be:

$$\int_0^t \underline{w}(\underline{x})\dot{\underline{x}}dt = \int_0^t (\dot{x}\sin\psi(t) - \dot{y}\cos\psi(t))dt$$

That is as far as we can go. The integrals of sine functions of anything more complicated than a quadratic polynomial in time have no closed form solution. The latter are the famous *Fresnel integrals* but we will have no need for them.

4.2.2 WMR Velocity Kinematics for Fixed Contact Point

This section considers two questions that are central to estimation and control of mobile robots:

- Forward Kinematics: How do measured motions of the wheels translate into equivalent motions of the robot?
- Inverse Kinematics: How do desired motions of the robot translate into equivalent motions of the wheels?

The problem will reveal difficulties in terms of nonlinearity and overdetermined equations. Nonetheless, the techniques presented here are more than adequate for both driving and estimating the state of WMRs in many circumstances.

Consider again an articulated wheel as shown in Figure 4.11. To accommodate a more general case, we allow a single degree of articulation between the vehicle and contact point frames. The frames of reference w, v, s, and c were defined in Section 4.1.4.3. The c frame has the same orientation as the steer frame.

Throughout this section we will make the *fixed contact point assumption*. Although the wheel contact point is a point that moves on both the wheel and the floor, it is fixed with respect to the steer frame. If the terrain is locally convex under all wheels, this means the contact points will be at the "bottom" of the wheels as viewed from the vehicle frame.

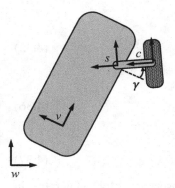

Figure 4.11 Frames for WMR Kinematics. The four frames necessary for the relation of wheel rotation rates to vehicle speed and angular velocity.

4.2.2.1 Inverse Kinematics

The **inverse** kinematics problem, relevant to control, is that of determining the wheel velocities given the velocity of the body. Given the linear $\underline{v}_v^w$ and angular $\underline{\omega}_v^w$ velocity of the vehicle frame with respect to the world frame, the linear velocity of the wheel contact point can be computed. The solution to this problem is a special case of the articulated wheel equation presented as Equation 4.30. Substituting $\underline{v}_s^v = \underline{v}_c^s = \underline{0}$ gives:

$$\underline{v}_c^w = \underline{v}_v^w - [\underline{r}_c^v]^{\times}\underline{\omega}_v^w - [\underline{r}_c^s]^{\times}\underline{\omega}_s^v \qquad (4.39)$$

Spotlight 4.4 Inverse Kinematics: Offset Wheel Equation.

The relationship between the linear velocity of the contact point and the motions of the vehicle (v) and articulation (s) frames for an offset wheel.

We will call this the **offset wheel equation**. It applies to an articulated wheel whose contact point is fixed with respect to the body frame. To use this result for an offset wheel, we need to know rate of steering rotation $\underline{\omega}_s^v$ with respect to the vehicle. This is usually measurable or otherwise known to be zero if there is no steering rotation. The other vectors $\underline{r}_c^v$ and $\underline{r}_c^s$ are known vehicle dimensions.

In the special case where the s and c frames are coincident $\underline{r}_c^s = \underline{0}$ and this reduces even further to:

$$\underline{v}_c^w = \underline{v}_v^w - [\underline{r}_c^v]^{\times}\underline{\omega}_v^w \qquad (4.40)$$

Spotlight 4.5 Inverse Kinematics: Wheel Equation.

The relationship between the linear velocity of the contact point and the motions of the vehicle (v) frame for a non-offset wheel.

4.2.2.1.1 Wheel. . . . Wheel Steering Control. Controlling a wheel involves steering it and driving it around its axle. For steering, doing so in a kinematically correct fashion based on Equation 4.39 seems surprisingly difficult. The wheel steer angle γ must be chosen such that the x axis of the c frame is aligned with the wheel velocity vector. Equivalently, the wheel velocity in the y direction of the contact point frame must vanish. Once this is so, the steer rate $\underline{\omega}_s^v$ is predetermined to be the time derivative of the necessary steer angle. The component of $\underline{r}_c^v$ expressing the steer offset $\underline{r}_c^s$ must also

be consistent and all three of these quantities must be consistent with $\underline{v}_c^w$, which is also unknown. In other words, everything other than gross motion and the position of the steer frame, is unknown.

The solution to this dilemma is to recognize (a) that we need only the direction of the wheel velocity to steer correctly; (b) that the direction of the c frame velocity with respect to the world must always be parallel to that of the s frame if the link joining them is rigid; and (c) that the velocity of the s frame is completely determined by the velocity of the vehicle frame. That is, we can solve the problem recursively by propagating the known quantities $\underline{v}_v^w$ and $\underline{\omega}_v^w$ as far as possible up the kinematic chain to the wheel.

The steer frame velocity is given by:

$$\underline{v}_s^w = \underline{v}_v^w - [\underline{r}_s^v]^\times \underline{\omega}_v^w \tag{4.41}$$

When this is expressed in vehicle coordinates, the angle of the contact point velocity with respect to the vehicle body is:

$$\gamma = \operatorname{atan2}[(\,{}^v\underline{v}_s^w)_y, (\,{}^v\underline{v}_s^w)_x] \tag{4.42}$$

The wheel can be steered to this angle, and it will then roll without lateral slipping. Recall once again a critical aspect of notation. The notation ${}^c\underline{v}_a^b$ means the velocity of frame a with respect to frame b (i.e $\underline{v}_a^b$) expressed in the coordinates of frame c. Above, the velocity ${}^v\underline{v}_s^w$ is that of the steer/suspension frame with respect to the world, expressed in vehicle coordinates.

4.2.2.1.2 Wheel Speed Control. Once the steer angle is known, the steering rate becomes known from differentiation, and the geometry of the whole kinematic chain becomes known. We could compute the component of $\underline{v}_c^w$ along the x axis of the c frame but we already know the y component is zero, so we can simply compute the magnitude of the velocity. Furthermore, we can compute it in any coordinates. In the vehicle frame, the contact point velocity is computed as:

$$ {}^v\underline{v}_c^w = {}^v\underline{v}_v^w - [\underline{r}_c^v]^\times {}^v\underline{\omega}_v^w - [R_s^v \underline{r}_c^s]^\times {}^v\underline{\omega}_s^v \tag{4.43}$$

The wheel translational speed is then:

$$v_c^w = \sqrt{(\,{}^v\underline{v}_c^w)_x^2 + (\,{}^v\underline{v}_c^w)_y^2} \tag{4.44}$$

This can be converted to angular velocities of the wheel (about its axle) using:

$$\omega_{wheel} = v_c^w / r_{wheel} \tag{4.45}$$

where r_{wheel} is the wheel radius. The sign of the wheel angular velocity may need to be adjusted depending on the conventions in effect for the positive sense of rotation.

4.2.2.2 Forward Kinematics

Now, consider the opposite problem. The **forward** kinematics problem, relevant to estimation, is that of determining the velocity of the body given the wheel velocities.

Suppose we have measurements of wheel angular velocities ω_k and steer angles γ_k and we want to determined the linear and angular velocity of the vehicle.

4.2.2.2.1 Wheel Sensing. Typically, the wheel angular velocity and steer angles are sensed more or less directly. Under this assumption, the linear velocities of the wheels are derived by inverting Equation 4.45:

$$v_k = r_k \omega_k \tag{4.46}$$

Assuming no slip, the wheel velocity components are directed along the x axis of the contact point frame. In the body frame, they are:

$$(v_k)_x = v_k \cos(\gamma_k) \qquad\qquad (v_k)_y = v_k \sin(\gamma_k)$$

4.2.2.2.2 Multiple Wheels. Usually, there are three unknowns in the body velocity $(\underline{v}_v^w, \underline{\omega}_v^w)$ and measurements provide only two constraints (γ_k, v_k) per wheel. Therefore, we need at least two sets of wheel measurements in general to determine the motion of the vehicle frame. However, the problem then becomes overdetemined with at least four conditions on three unknowns. Steer axes cannot be perfectly aligned in practice, so a best fit solution is needed, which tolerates the potential inconsistency in the measurements.

Consider again the offset wheel equation. Writing it in vehicle coordinates:

$$\underline{v}_c^{v\,w} = \underline{v}_v^{v\,w} - [\underline{r}_c^v]^\times \underline{\omega}_v^{v\,w} - [R_s^v \underline{r}_c^s]^\times \underline{\omega}_s^{v\,v} \tag{4.47}$$

Spotlight 4.6 Offset Wheel Equation in Vehicle Coordinates.

This formula will be the basis of all WMR kinematic models derived later.

The last term was written in steer frame coordinates before converting to vehicle coordinates using the rotation matrix R_s^v. To get R_s^v, we need to know the steer angle γ. Note that $\underline{r}_c^v$ also depends on the steer angle γ. This is of the form:

$$\underline{v}_c^{v\,w} = H_c^v(\gamma) \begin{bmatrix} \underline{v}_v^{v\,w} \\ \underline{\omega}_v^w \end{bmatrix} + Q_c^s(\gamma) \,\underline{\omega}_s^{v\,v} \tag{4.48}$$

If we knew the vehicle frame velocities, we could write Equation 4.47 for each wheel in order to compute the velocity of each wheel contact point in one matrix equation. Stacking all equations together and grouping the first two terms together produces a matrix equation of the form:

$$\underline{v}_c^{v\,w} = H_c^v(\gamma)\dot{\underline{x}}_v^w + Q_c^s(\gamma)\dot{\gamma} \tag{4.49}$$

Because the left-hand side and the steer angles are known, this is a set of simultaneous equations constraining the vehicle linear and angular velocity $\dot{x}_v^w$ that can be solved using any suitable method, including the pseudoinverse:

$$\dot{x}_v^w = [H_c^v(\gamma)^T H_c^v(\gamma)]^{-1} H_c^v(\gamma)^T [\underline{v}_c^w - Q_c^s(\gamma)\dot{\gamma}] \tag{4.50}$$

This solution produces the linear and angular velocities that are most consistent (in a least squares sense) with the measurements even if the measurements do not agree. The results are summarized in Box 4.2.

Box 4.2 WMR Forward Kinematics: Offset Wheels

Offset wheel equations for all wheels can be grouped together to produce

$$\underline{v}_c^w = H_c^v(\gamma)\,\dot{\underline{x}}_v^w + Q_c^s(\gamma)\,\dot{\gamma}$$

where each pair of rows of H_c^v and Q_c^s comes from an offset wheel equation expressed in body coordinates, $\underline{v}_c^w$ is the wheel velocities, $\dot{\underline{x}}_v^w$ is the linear and angular velocity of the vehicle, and γ is the steer angles.

The inverse mapping (for two or more wheels) can be computed with:

$$\dot{\underline{x}}_v^w = [H_c^v(\gamma)^T H_c^v(\gamma)]^{-1} H_c^v(\gamma)^T [\underline{v}_c^w - Q_c^s(\gamma)\dot{\gamma}]$$

For nonoffset wheels H_c^v simplifies, and Q_c^s disappears.

4.2.3 Common Steering Configurations

This section provides examples of velocity kinematics for a few important cases. The problem is expressed as 2D in the instantaneous terrain tangent plane.

4.2.3.1 Differential Steer

The case of differential steer is easy (Figure 4.12).

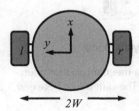

Figure 4.12 Differential Steer. In this very simple configuration, there are two fixed wheels that are unable to steer.

4.2.3.1.1 Inverse Kinematics. Let the two wheel frames be called l and r for left and right. Let the *forward* velocity be v_x and the angular velocity be ω. The dimensions are:

$$\underline{r}_r^v = \begin{bmatrix} 0 & -W \end{bmatrix}^T \qquad \underline{r}_l^v = \begin{bmatrix} 0 & W \end{bmatrix}^T \tag{4.51}$$

Written in the body frame, Equation 4.40 for each wheel reduces to two scalar equations for the velocities in the x direction:

$$\begin{bmatrix} v_r \\ v_l \end{bmatrix} = \begin{bmatrix} v_x + \omega W \\ v_x - \omega W \end{bmatrix} = \begin{bmatrix} 1 & W \\ 1 & -W \end{bmatrix} \begin{bmatrix} v_x \\ \omega \end{bmatrix} \tag{4.52}$$

where v_x is the velocity of the robot center in the x direction and ω is the angular velocity in the z direction. The equation for the wheel velocities in the *sideways* direction vanishes (when expressed in body coordinates), if we assume that the wheels cannot move sideways. Essentially, this constraint is being substituted into the kinematics to eliminate one unknown. We are therefore able to solve for the (normally 3 dof) motion using only two measurements.

4.2.3.1.2 Forward Kinematics. In body coordinates, the constraints for two wheels generate two scalar equations. Equation 4.52 is easy to invert:

$$\begin{bmatrix} v_x \\ \omega \end{bmatrix} = \frac{1}{2W} \begin{bmatrix} W & W \\ 1 & -1 \end{bmatrix} \begin{bmatrix} v_r \\ v_l \end{bmatrix} = \frac{1}{2} \begin{bmatrix} 1 & 1 \\ \dfrac{1}{W} & -\dfrac{1}{W} \end{bmatrix} \begin{bmatrix} v_r \\ v_l \end{bmatrix} \tag{4.53}$$

This case was a special one as the equations were not overdetermined.

4.2.3.2 Ackerman Steer

This is the configuration of the ordinary automobile.

We can model this vehicle by just two wheels as described to the right in Figure 4.13. This is called the *bicycle model*.

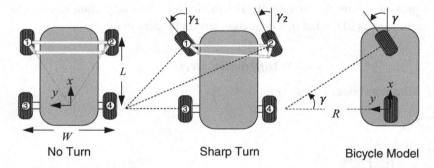

No Turn   Sharp Turn   Bicycle Model

Figure 4.13 Ackerman Steer. The two front wheels are connected by a mechanism that maintains consistent steering angles. In this way, wheel slip is minimized. The difference between left and right steering angles increases with path curvature.

4.2.3.2.1 Inverse Kinematics. In this case, it is convenient to place the vehicle frame at the center of the rear axle. Let the forward velocity of the vehicle frame be denoted v_x and the angular velocity is ω. The position vector to the front wheel is:

$$\underline{r}_f^v = \begin{bmatrix} L & 0 \end{bmatrix}^T \tag{4.54}$$

So, the cross product matrix is:

$$[\underline{r}_f^v]^\times = \begin{bmatrix} 0 & -(\underline{r}_f^v)_z & (\underline{r}_f^v)_y \\ (\underline{r}_f^v)_z & 0 & -(\underline{r}_f^v)_x \\ -(\underline{r}_f^v)_y & (\underline{r}_f^v)_x & 0 \end{bmatrix} = \begin{bmatrix} 0 & 0 & 0 \\ 0 & 0 & -L \\ 0 & L & 0 \end{bmatrix}$$

For the inverse kinematics in the body frame, Equation 4.47 reduces to:

$$\underline{v}_f^{\,v\,w} = \underline{v}_v^{\,v\,w} - [\underline{r}_c^{\,v}]^\times \,\underline{\omega}_{\underline{v}^w} \Rightarrow v_f = \begin{bmatrix} v_x & \omega L \end{bmatrix}^T \tag{4.55}$$

If we define $\underline{\dot{x}}_v^w = \begin{bmatrix} v_x & \omega \end{bmatrix}^T$ this is of the form $\underline{v}_f^{\,v\,w} = H_c^v \, \underline{\dot{x}}_v^w$:

$$\begin{bmatrix} v_{fx} \\ v_{fy} \end{bmatrix} = \begin{bmatrix} 1 & 0 \\ 0 & L \end{bmatrix} \begin{bmatrix} v_x \\ \omega \end{bmatrix} \tag{4.56}$$

H_c^v does not depend on the steer angle in this case because there is no steer axis offset. The velocity vector of the front wheel is oriented with respect to the body at an angle $\gamma = \operatorname{atan2}(\omega L, v_x)$ or:

$$\tan(\gamma) = \frac{\omega L}{v_x} = \kappa L = \frac{L}{R} \tag{4.57}$$

where R is the instantaneous radius of curvature. This result relating curvature to steer angle could have been derived by geometry from the figure. An equivalent formula for curvature can be generated for any two wheels of a vehicle that are not slipping.

4.2.3.2.2 Forward Kinematics. For this configuration, H_c^v in Equation 4.48 became a diagonal matrix, decoupling the effects of linear and angular velocity controls, due to the choice of the rear wheel for the vehicle reference point. This makes the inverse kinematics particularly trivial.

$$\begin{bmatrix} v_x \\ \omega \end{bmatrix} = \begin{bmatrix} 1 & 0 \\ 0 & L \end{bmatrix}^{-1} \begin{bmatrix} v_{fx} \\ v_{fy} \end{bmatrix} = \begin{bmatrix} v_{fx} \\ v_{fy}/L \end{bmatrix} \tag{4.58}$$

4.2.3.3 Generalized Bicycle Model

It should be clear from the discussion of the ICR that any wheeled vehicle whose wheels roll without slipping moves in a manner that can be described by just two wheels with the same ICR as the original vehicle. Consider the generalized bicycle model (Figure 4.14).

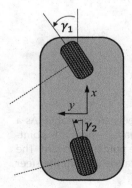

Figure 4.14 Generalized Bicycle Model. Any vehicle whose wheels roll without slipping can be modelled by just two wheels.

4.2.3.3.1 Inverse Kinematics. The model is simpler if the body frame is placed on one of the wheels but this is not always possible so the wheel positions are defined more generally. The wheel positions are:

$$\underline{r}_1^v = \begin{bmatrix} x_1 \ y_1 \end{bmatrix}^T \qquad \underline{r}_2^v = \begin{bmatrix} x_2 \ y_2 \end{bmatrix}^T \tag{4.59}$$

So, the cross product matrix for wheel i is:

$$[\underline{r}_i^v]^\times = \begin{bmatrix} 0 & 0 & y_i \\ 0 & 0 & -x_i \\ -y_i & x_i & 0 \end{bmatrix}$$

The wheel velocities are then given by Equation 4.47, which reduces to:

$$\underline{v}_i^w = \underline{v}_v^w - [\underline{r}_i^v]^\times \, \underline{\omega}_{v^w}^v$$

$$v_i = \begin{bmatrix} (V_x - \omega y_i) & (V_y + \omega x_i) \end{bmatrix}^T$$

Gathering the equations for both wheels:

$$\underline{v}_c^w = H_c^v \, \underline{\dot{x}}_v^w$$

$$\begin{bmatrix} v_{1x} \\ v_{1y} \\ v_{2x} \\ v_{2y} \end{bmatrix} = \begin{bmatrix} v_x - \omega y_1 \\ v_y + \omega x_1 \\ v_x - \omega y_2 \\ v_y + \omega x_2 \end{bmatrix} = \begin{bmatrix} 1 & 0 & -y_1 \\ 0 & 1 & x_1 \\ 1 & 0 & -y_2 \\ 0 & 1 & x_2 \end{bmatrix} \begin{bmatrix} v_x \\ v_y \\ \omega \end{bmatrix} \tag{4.60}$$

4.2.3.3.2 Forward Kinematics. This case requires the general solution for nonoffset wheels:

$$\underline{\dot{x}}_v^w = [(H_c^v)^T (H_c^v)]^{-1} (H_c^v)^T \underline{v}_c^w$$

4.2.3.4 Four Wheel Steer

This is the case of 4 independently steerable wheels. Subject to any limits on steer angles, this vehicle configuration is very maneuverable. It can turn in place and it can drive in any direction while facing another direction (Figure 4.15).

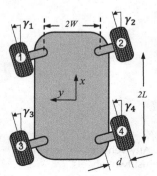

Figure 4.15 4-Wheel Steer. All four wheels are steerable. As a result, it can drive in any direction no matter where it is pointing. This figure suggests driving left while pointing forward. The wheel contact points are offset by a distance d from the steer centers.

A related configuration is *double Ackerman*. In this case, there is an Ackerman mechanism at both the front and the rear and the vehicle can turn through smaller radii than single Ackerman as a result.

4.2.3.4.1 Inverse Kinematics. For the four wheel steer configuration. Let the wheel frames be identified by numbers as shown. The centers of their contact points are assumed to be in the center of their vertical projections. Let the **forward** velocity of the vehicle frame be denoted v_x and the angular velocity is ω. The steer center position vectors are of the form $r^v_{sk} = [x_k \ y_k]^T$.

In detail:

$$r^v_{s1} = \begin{bmatrix} L & W \end{bmatrix}^T \quad r^v_{s2} = \begin{bmatrix} L & -W \end{bmatrix}^T \quad r^v_{s3} = \begin{bmatrix} -L & W \end{bmatrix}^T \quad r^v_{s4} = \begin{bmatrix} -L & -W \end{bmatrix}^T \quad (4.61)$$

The contact point offsets in the body frame depend on the steer angles. They are of the form $r^{sk}_{ck} = [a_k \ b_k]^T$. In detail:

$$r^{s1}_{c1} = d\begin{bmatrix} -s\gamma_1 & -c\gamma_1 \end{bmatrix}^T \quad r^{s2}_{c2} = d\begin{bmatrix} s\gamma_2 & c\gamma_2 \end{bmatrix}^T$$
$$r^{s3}_{c3} = d\begin{bmatrix} -s\gamma_3 & -c\gamma_3 \end{bmatrix}^T \quad r^{s4}_{c4} = d\begin{bmatrix} s\gamma_4 & c\gamma_4 \end{bmatrix}^T \quad (4.62)$$

Written in the body frame, Equation 4.47 for each wheel reduces to four equations of the form:

$$v^w_c = v^w_v - [r^v_c]^\times \omega^w_v - [r^s_c]^\times \omega^v_s$$

$$\begin{bmatrix} v_{ix} \\ v_{iy} \end{bmatrix} = \begin{bmatrix} 1 & 0 & -(y^v_{si} + b_i) \\ 0 & 1 & (x^v_{si} + a_i) \end{bmatrix} \begin{bmatrix} v_x \\ v_y \\ \omega \end{bmatrix} + \begin{bmatrix} -b_i \\ a_i \end{bmatrix} \dot{\gamma}_i \quad (4.63)$$

Filling in all the matrices gives:

$$\begin{bmatrix} v_{1x} \\ v_{1y} \end{bmatrix} = H^v_{c1} \dot{x}^w_v + Q^s_{c1} \dot{\gamma} = \begin{bmatrix} 1 & 0 & -(y_1 + b_1) \\ 0 & 1 & x_1 + a_1 \end{bmatrix} \dot{x}^w_v + \begin{bmatrix} -b_1 & 0 & 0 & 0 \\ a_1 & 0 & 0 & 0 \end{bmatrix} \dot{\gamma}$$

$$\begin{bmatrix} v_{2x} \\ v_{2y} \end{bmatrix} = H^v_{c2} \dot{x}^w_v + Q^s_{c2} \dot{\gamma} = \begin{bmatrix} 1 & 0 & -(y_2 + b_2) \\ 0 & 1 & x_2 + a_2 \end{bmatrix} \dot{x}^w_v + \begin{bmatrix} 0 & -b_2 & 0 & 0 \\ 0 & a_2 & 0 & 0 \end{bmatrix} \dot{\gamma}$$

$$\begin{bmatrix} v_{3x} \\ v_{3y} \end{bmatrix} = H^v_{c3} \dot{x}^w_v + Q^s_{c3} \dot{\gamma} = \begin{bmatrix} 1 & 0 & -(y_3 + b_3) \\ 0 & 1 & x_3 + a_3 \end{bmatrix} \dot{x}^w_v + \begin{bmatrix} 0 & 0 & -b_3 & 0 \\ 0 & 0 & a_3 & 0 \end{bmatrix} \dot{\gamma} \quad (4.64)$$

$$\begin{bmatrix} v_{4x} \\ v_{4y} \end{bmatrix} = H^v_{c4} \dot{x}^w_v + Q^s_{c4} \dot{\gamma} = \begin{bmatrix} 1 & 0 & -(y_4 + b_4) \\ 0 & 1 & x_4 + a_4 \end{bmatrix} \dot{x}^w_v + \begin{bmatrix} 0 & 0 & 0 & -b_4 \\ 0 & 0 & 0 & a_4 \end{bmatrix} \dot{\gamma}$$

Stacking all equations together leads to:

$$v^w_c = H^v_c(\gamma) \dot{x}^w_v + Q^s_c(\gamma) \dot{\gamma} \quad (4.65)$$

where:

$$\dot{\underline{x}}_v^w = \begin{bmatrix} v_x & v_y & \omega \end{bmatrix}^T \qquad \dot{\underline{\gamma}} = \begin{bmatrix} \dot{\gamma}_1 & \dot{\gamma}_2 & \dot{\gamma}_3 & \dot{\gamma}_4 \end{bmatrix}^T$$

$$\underline{v} = \begin{bmatrix} v_{1x} & v_{1y} & v_{2x} & v_{2y} & v_{3x} & v_{3y} & v_{4x} & v_{4y} \end{bmatrix}^T$$

$$H_c^v(\underline{\gamma}) = \begin{bmatrix} 1 & 0 & -(y_1 + b_1) \\ 0 & 1 & x_1 + a_1 \\ 1 & 0 & -(y_2 + b_2) \\ 0 & 1 & x_2 + a_2 \\ 1 & 0 & -(y_3 + b_3) \\ 0 & 1 & x_3 + a_3 \\ 1 & 0 & -(y_4 + b_4) \\ 0 & 1 & x_4 + a_4 \end{bmatrix} \qquad Q_c^s(\underline{\gamma}) = \begin{bmatrix} -b_1 & 0 & 0 & 0 \\ a_1 & 0 & 0 & 0 \\ 0 & -b_2 & 0 & 0 \\ 0 & a_2 & 0 & 0 \\ 0 & 0 & -b_3 & 0 \\ 0 & 0 & a_3 & 0 \\ 0 & 0 & 0 & -b_4 \\ 0 & 0 & 0 & a_4 \end{bmatrix} \qquad (4.66)$$

The steer angles and steer rates $\dot{\underline{\gamma}}$ would be known in an estimation or control context, so the above solution computes the velocities of the wheels based on this information.

4.2.3.4.2 Forward Kinematics. The inverse solution follows the general case described in Section 4.2.2.2.2:

$$\dot{\underline{x}}_v^w = [H_c^v(\underline{\gamma})^T H_c^v(\underline{\gamma})]^{-1} H_c^v(\underline{\gamma})^T [\underline{v}_c^w - Q_c^s(\underline{\gamma})\dot{\underline{\gamma}}] \qquad (4.67)$$

This solution produces the linear and angular velocities that are most consistent with the measurements, even if the measurements are mutually inconsistent.

4.2.4 References and Further Reading

Much of the content of this section deviates significantly in formulation from the literature for tutorial reasons. The paper by B. d'Andrea-Novel is an early source for the expression of Pfaffian constraints in mobile robots and they are also covered in the book by Murray. Alexander and also Muir present the use of the constraints to generate kinematic models. Campion classifies WMRs based on their degree of constraint.

[4] J. C. Alexander and J. H. Maddocks, On the Kinematics of Wheeled Mobile Robots, *The International Journal of Robotics Research,* Vol. 8, pp. 15–27, 1989.

[5] B. d'Andrea-Novel, G. Bastin, and G. Campion, Modelling and Control of Non Holonomic Wheeled Mobile Robots, in Proceedings of 1991 International Conference on Robotics and Automation, pp. 1130–1135, Sacramento, CA, April 1991.

[6] G. Campion, G. Bastin and B. d'Andrea-Novel, Structural Properties and Classification of Kinematic and Dynamic Models of Wheeled Mobile Robots, *IEEE Transactions on Robotics and Automation,* Vol. 12, No. 1, pp. 47-62, 1996.

[7] P. F. Muir and C. P. Neuman, Kinematic Modeling of Wheeled Mobile Robots, Journal of Robotic *Systems,* Vol. 4, No. 2, pp. 281–333, 1987.

[8] R. M. Murray, Z. Li, and S. S. Sastry, *A Mathematical Introduction to Robotic Manipulation,* CRC Press, 1994.

[9] A. Kelly and N. Seegmiller, A Vector Algebra Formulation of Mobile Robot Velocity Kinematics, in *Proceedings of Field and Service Robots,* 2012.

4.2.5 Exercises

4.2.5.1 Detecting Wheel Slip from Encoders

A wheeled mobile robot has four wheels – each instrumented by an encoder. It moves on a perfectly flat floor. How might you determine if there is wheel slip?

4.2.5.2 Feasible Commands under Steering Limits

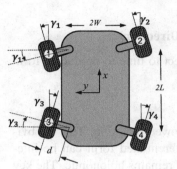

Consider a four-wheel steer car under the restriction that the lateral vehicle velocity component must always vanish. Derive the relationship between linear and angular velocity in a turn at the point where the steering limits are reached for the inside wheels.

4.2.5.3 Steering an Offset Wheel

For an offset wheel, the steering and driving control problems are related because the required axle rotation rate depends on the steer angle. As we did for the nonoffset case, to get the steer angle, impose the constraint that the y component of the wheel velocity with respect to ground should vanish in wheel coordinates. In other words $(^c_w \underline{v}_c)_y = 0$.

Rewrite Equation 4.40 by substituting $\overset{v}{\vec{r}}_c = \overset{v}{\vec{r}}_s + \overset{s}{\vec{r}}_c$, move the steer frame velocity to the left-hand side, use $\underline{\omega}^w_c = (\underline{\omega}^w_v + \underline{\omega}^v_c)$ and then express the result in the contact point frame where the non-slip constraint is easy to express. Impose the constraint and show that:

$$(v_x + \omega_y r_z)c\gamma + (v_y - \omega_y r_z)s\gamma = \omega_z r_y$$

4.3 Constrained Kinematics and Dynamics

This section now considers the case of explicit constraints on the motion of the wheeled mobile robot. Recall again the form of the model:

$$\dot{\underline{x}} = f(\underline{x}, \underline{u})$$
$$w(\underline{x})\,\dot{\underline{x}} = 0 \tag{4.68}$$

We shall see that this form of model occurs both in control/modelling contexts and in estimation contexts.

There are two main reasons for expressing constraints and two different types of constraints that arise. We have already seen that the lateral motion of a wheel is typically constrained by $\vec{v}_c \cdot \hat{y}_c = 0$. This type of constraint, in some sense, moves with the robot because the disallowed direction $\hat{y}_c$ is fixed in the wheel frame. This type of constraint is *nonholonomic*, and it can be expressed abstractly as:

$$\underline{c}(\underline{x}, \dot{\underline{x}}) = \underline{0}$$

where $\underline{x}$ is the position and orientation of the robot.

The second constraint of interest is terrain contact. At the speeds of most contemporary robots, ballistic motion (where the only force on the vehicle is gravity) does not occur. Instead, vehicles move in a 3 degree of freedom subspace of the 6 degree of freedom world because they remain in contact with some supporting surface, neither rising above nor sinking into the terrain. This type of constraint is *holonomic*, and it can be expressed abstractly as:

$$\underline{c}(\underline{x}) = 0$$

4.3.1 Constraints of Disallowed Direction

A holonomic constraint can be differentiated with respect to time to produce a form that looks like a nonholonomic one:

$$\underline{c}_x \dot{\underline{x}} = 0$$

where the constraint gradient $\underline{c}_x$ functions like a disallowed direction. This is obviously also of the form $\underline{c}(x, \dot{x}) = 0$. However, this differentiated form can be integrated to produce the original holonomic constraint so it remains holonomic. The key distinction is whether the constraint involving $\dot{x}$ is a total derivative of a simpler form, or not. In any case, it is useful to know that holonomic and nonholonomic constraints have the same form when the former is differentiated.

4.3.1.1 Velocity Constraints for Fixed Contact Point

As we saw earlier, the condition of rolling without slipping is a Pfaffian constraint expressed mathematically in terms of a direction $\vec{w}$ in which wheel velocity is not permitted to have a component:

$$\vec{w}_c \cdot \vec{v}_c^w = 0 \tag{4.69}$$

Once a coordinate system is chosen for expressing the vectors, this can be written in matrix form:

$$\underline{w}_c^T \underline{v}_c^w = 0 \tag{4.70}$$

The disallowed direction was also known as the Pfaffian weight vector $\vec{w}_c$ earlier. Its magnitude is usually irrelevant but it is assumed to be fixed when differentiating. This constraint can be converted to a constraint on vehicle state by simply substituting the rate kinematics from Equation 4.30:

$$\underline{w}_c^T \underline{v}_c^w = \underline{w}_c^T H(\underline{r}_c^v)\dot{\underline{x}}_v^w + \underline{w}_c^T H(\underline{r}_c^s)\dot{\underline{x}}_s^v + \underline{w}_c^T \underline{v}_c^s = 0 \tag{4.71}$$

This is the general 3D case for an articulated wheel on arbitrary terrain. To use this form, it is necessary to compute wheel contact point based on the terrain geometry in each iteration.

We will now elaborate a more detailed expression for the special case of a wheel contact point fixed in the vehicle frame. The second half of Equation 4.30 provides a more detailed expression for $\underline{v}_c^w$ in terms of vehicle motion and articulations. For a fixed contact point, the last two terms (i.e. $\underline{v}_c^v$) vanish. This case will occur when three conditions are met: the contact point is fixed on the wheel ($\underline{v}_c^s = \underline{0}$), the s frame is fixed with respect to the v frame ($\underline{v}_s^v = \underline{0}$), and the wheel offset is zero ($\underline{r}_c^s = \underline{0}$). Under these conditions, the contact point velocity reduces to:

$$\underline{v}_c^w = H_c^v \, \underline{\dot{x}}_v^w = \begin{bmatrix} I & | & -[\underline{r}_c^v]^\times \end{bmatrix} \begin{bmatrix} \underline{v}_v^w & | & \underline{\omega}_v^w \end{bmatrix}^T = \underline{v}_v^w - [\underline{r}_c^v]^\times \underline{\omega}_v^w \tag{4.72}$$

Substituting this into Equation 4.70 produces:

$$\underline{w}_c^T(\underline{v}_v^w - [\underline{r}_c^v]^\times \underline{\omega}_v^w) = 0 \tag{4.73}$$

For notational convenience, let us define the *Pfaffian radius* $\underline{\rho}_c$. It is the projection of rotation-induced wheel motion onto the disallowed direction:

$$\underline{\rho}_c^T = \underline{w}_v^T[\underline{r}_c^v]^\times \tag{4.74}$$

Then the velocity constraint can be written in any convenient coordinates in matrix form as follows:

$$\underline{w}_c^T \underline{v}_v^w - \underline{\rho}_c^T \underline{\omega}_v^w = 0 \tag{4.75}$$

This expression, valid in 3D for an articulated wheel with a contact point fixed in the vehicle frame, requires any motion in the disallowed direction due to the translational velocity $\underline{v}_v^w$, to be cancelled by that due to rotational velocity $\underline{\omega}_v^w$.

4.3.1.2 Differentiated Velocity Constraints for Fixed Contact Point

We will also have need shortly of an expression for the time derivative of a velocity constraint. In particular, we will need to differentiate Equation 4.69 in the world frame. Let us choose any moving frame m in which $\vec{w}_c$ is constant and differentiate:

$$\frac{d}{dt}\bigg|_w (\vec{w}_c \cdot \vec{v}_c^w) = \vec{w}_c \cdot \frac{d}{dt}\bigg|_w \vec{v}_c^w + \frac{d}{dt}\bigg|_w \vec{w}_c \cdot \vec{v}_c^w$$

Invoking the Transport Theorem, the derivative of the velocity constraint is:

$$\vec{w}_c \cdot \vec{a}_c^w + (\vec{\omega}_m^w \times \vec{w}_c) \cdot \vec{v}_c^w = 0 \tag{4.76}$$

Let us define the *Pfaffian rate* $\dot{\vec{w}}_c = (\vec{\omega}_m^w \times \vec{w}_c)$. In matrix form:

$$\underline{\dot{w}}_c^T = \left[[\underline{\omega}_m^w]^\times \underline{w}_c \right]^T = -\underline{w}_c^T[\underline{\omega}_m^w]^\times \tag{4.77}$$

Then Equation 4.76 becomes in matrix form:

$$\underline{w}_c^T \underline{a}_c^w + \underline{\dot{w}}_c^T \underline{v}_c^w = 0 \tag{4.78}$$

This could also have been produced by differentiating Equation 4.69. Substituting Equation 4.30 and Equation 4.31 into this produces:

$$\underline{w}_c^T(\underline{a}_c^w = H(\underline{r}_c^v) \, \underline{\ddot{x}}_v^w + \Omega(\underline{\omega}_v^v)\underline{\rho}_c^v + H(\underline{r}_c^s) \, \underline{\ddot{x}}_s^v + \Omega(\underline{\omega}_s^v)\underline{\rho}_c^s + \underline{a}_c^s)$$
$$+ \underline{\dot{w}}_c^T(H(\underline{r}_c^v)\underline{\dot{x}}_v^w + H(\underline{r}_c^s)\underline{\dot{x}}_s^v + \underline{v}_c^v) = 0 \tag{4.79}$$

This is the general 3D case for an articulated wheel on arbitrary terrain. To use this form, it is necessary to compute wheel contact points based on the terrain geometry in each iteration.

We will now elaborate a more detailed expression for the special case of a wheel contact point fixed in the vehicle frame. Equation 4.31 provides a detailed expression for $\underline{a}_c^{w'}$ in terms of vehicle motion and articulations. For a fixed contact point, the last three terms (i.e., $\underline{a}_c^v$) of Equation 4.31 vanish and because $\underline{v}_c^v = 0$, the expression for $\underline{a}_c^w$ reduces to:

$$\underline{a}_c^w = \underline{a}_v^w - [\underline{r}_c^v]^\times \underline{\alpha}_v^w + [\underline{\omega}_v^w]^{\times\times} \underline{r}_c^v$$

Substituting this into the first term in Equation 4.77 while recalling the definition of Pfaffian radius $\underline{\rho}_c$ gives:

$$\underline{w}_c^T \underline{a}_c^w = \underline{w}_c^T \underline{a}_v^w - \underline{\rho}_c^T \underline{\alpha}_v^w + \underline{w}_c^T [\underline{\omega}_v^w]^{\times\times} \underline{r}_c^v \tag{4.80}$$

Substituting Equation 4.71 into the second term of Equation 4.77 produces:

$$\dot{\underline{w}}_c^T \underline{v}_c^w = \dot{\underline{w}}_c^T (\underline{v}_v^w - [\underline{r}_c^v]^\times \underline{\omega}_v^w) = \dot{\underline{w}}_c^T \underline{v}_v^w - \dot{\underline{\rho}}_c^T \underline{\omega}_v^w \tag{4.81}$$

Where we defined the *Pfaffian radius rate (transposed):*

$$\dot{\underline{\rho}}_c^T = \dot{\underline{w}}_c^T [\underline{r}_c^v]^\times \tag{4.82}$$

Now, rewriting all of Equation 4.78, using Equation 4.80 and Equation 4.81, we have:

$$\underline{w}_c^T \underline{a}_v^w - \underline{\rho}_c^T \underline{\alpha}_v^w + \underline{w}_c^T [\underline{\omega}_v^w]^{\times\times} \underline{r}_c^v + \dot{\underline{w}}_c^T \underline{v}_v^w - \dot{\underline{\rho}}_c^T \underline{\omega}_v^w = 0 \tag{4.83}$$

This result, valid in 3D for an articulated wheel with a contact point fixed in the vehicle frame, will allow us to differentiate constraints relevant to a mobile robot in order to implement second-order DAE models.

4.3.1.3 Example: Terrain Contact Using a Disallowed Direction

Terrain following is a holonomic constraint on pose. We could, however, prevent wheel motion in the (disallowed) direction along the terrain normal. As we saw with differentiated constraints in Chapter 3, this is not entirely equivalent to forcing the wheel to contact the terrain. Nonetheless, we will see that there are advantages to using differentiated constraints. This case also makes a good example.

Let the wheels of a vehicle be un-suspended so that $\dot{\underline{x}}_s^v = 0$. Let the terrain be locally convex at the wheels so that $\underline{v}_c^s \approx 0$. Then, if the ith surface normal at the wheel contact point is denoted $\hat{n}_i$. we can use Equation 4.75 by substituting $\underline{w}_c^T = \underline{n}_i^T$:

$$\underline{n}_i^T \underline{v}_v^w + \underline{\rho}_i^T \underline{\omega}_v^w = 0 \tag{4.84}$$

When the terrain is flat, we have $\hat{n}_i \parallel \vec{\omega}$ and therefore $\underline{\rho}_i^T \underline{\omega}_v^w = 0$ so the constraints reduce to the statement that the vehicle velocity should have no component directed along the surface normal. That is, $\underline{n}_i^T \underline{v}_v^w = 0$. Consider the motion of a 2D vehicle confined to the elevation plane (Figure 4.16). It has two wheels of radius r and it maintains contact with a terrain surface given by $z = \zeta(x)$ while moving with known velocity v. The velocity equations are:

$$\dot{x} = vc\theta \qquad \dot{z} = -vs\theta$$

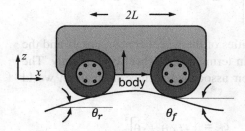

Figure 4.16 Constrained Kinematics Example. The vehicle moves over the terrain while both wheels remain in contact. The state derivative at all times remains confined to the constraint tangent plane.

where the state vector is $\underline{x} = \begin{bmatrix} x & z & \theta \end{bmatrix}^T$ and positive pitch is nose down. Let the body frame be positioned at the center of the body at the height of the wheels. Let the body be of length $2L$.

4.3.1.3.1 Explicit Contact Constraints. The first method of solution differentiates the contact constraints to produce velocity constraints. The line from the center of the wheel to the contact point on the bottom of the wheel is oriented along the terrain normal. Therefore, the coordinates of the contact points are:

$$x_f = x + Lc\theta - rs\theta_f \qquad x_r = x - Lc\theta - rs\theta_r$$
$$z_f = z - Ls\theta - rc\theta_f \qquad z_r = z + Ls\theta - rc\theta_r$$

In standard form, the terrain contact constraints are:

$$\underline{c}(\underline{x}) = \begin{bmatrix} \zeta(x_f) - z_f \\ \zeta(x_r) - z_r \end{bmatrix} = \begin{bmatrix} 0 \\ 0 \end{bmatrix}$$

The constraint Jacobian (with respect to $\begin{bmatrix} x & z & \theta \end{bmatrix}^T$) is therefore, using the notation $t\theta = \tan(\theta)$:

$$C_{\underline{x}} = \begin{bmatrix} \dfrac{\partial \zeta(x_f)}{\partial x_f} \dfrac{\partial x_f}{\partial x} & -1 & \dfrac{\partial \zeta(x_f)}{\partial x_f} \dfrac{\partial x_f}{\partial \theta} + Lc\theta \\ \dfrac{\partial \zeta(x_r)}{\partial x_r} \dfrac{\partial x_r}{\partial x} & -1 & \dfrac{\partial \zeta(x_r)}{\partial x_r} \dfrac{\partial x_r}{\partial \theta} - Lc\theta \end{bmatrix} = \begin{bmatrix} -t\theta_f & -1 & (-t\theta_f(-Ls\theta) + Lc\theta) \\ -t\theta_r & -1 & (-t\theta_r(Ls\theta) - Lc\theta) \end{bmatrix} \qquad (4.85)$$

4.3.1.3.2 Disallowed Directions. This method uses the formula for disallowed directions of wheel velocities. Equation 4.84 adapted to the elevation plane, expressed in world coordinates, is:

$$\begin{bmatrix} n_x & n_z & \rho_i \end{bmatrix} \begin{bmatrix} v_x & v_z & \omega \end{bmatrix}^T = 0$$

Note that $\vec{\omega}$ is oriented into the page. The Pfaffian radius is $\underline{\rho}_i^T = [\underline{n}_i^T [\underline{r}_i^v]^\times]$ in this case. When motion is confined to the elevation plane $n_z = 0$, and $z_c^v = 0$, so this is:

$$\underline{\rho}_i^T = \left[\begin{bmatrix} n_x & n_y & 0 \end{bmatrix} \begin{bmatrix} 0 & 0 & y_i^v \\ 0 & 0 & -x_i^v \\ -y_i^v & x_i^v & 0 \end{bmatrix} \right] = \begin{bmatrix} 0 & 0 & (n_x y_i^v - n_y x_i^v) \end{bmatrix}$$

When $\underline{v}_c^s = 0$ as we have assumed, the velocities of the wheel contact points and the wheel centers are the same so we can work in terms of the wheel centers only. The position vectors of the wheel centers and their associated surface normals in world coordinates are:

$$\underline{r}_f = \begin{bmatrix} Lc\theta & -Ls\theta \end{bmatrix}^T \qquad\qquad \underline{r}_r = \begin{bmatrix} -Lc\theta & Ls\theta \end{bmatrix}^T$$
$$\hat{n}_f = \begin{bmatrix} s\theta_f & c\theta_f \end{bmatrix}^T \qquad\qquad \hat{n}_r = \begin{bmatrix} s\theta_r & c\theta_r \end{bmatrix}^T$$

So the Pfaffian radii $\underline{\rho}_i^T$ are:

$$\underline{\rho}_f^T = \begin{bmatrix} 0 & 0 & -(Ls\theta s\theta_f + Lc\theta c\theta_f) \end{bmatrix}$$
$$\underline{\rho}_r^T = \begin{bmatrix} 0 & 0 & (Ls\theta s\theta_r + Lc\theta c\theta_r) \end{bmatrix}$$

So, the constraints $\underline{n}_i^T \underline{v}_v^w - \underline{\rho}_i^T \underline{\omega}_v^w = 0$ are:

$$\begin{bmatrix} s\theta_f & c\theta_f & (Ls\theta s\theta_f + Lc\theta c\theta_f) \\ s\theta_r & c\theta_r & -(Ls\theta s\theta_r + Lc\theta c\theta_r) \end{bmatrix} \begin{bmatrix} v_x & v_y & \omega \end{bmatrix}^T = \begin{bmatrix} 0 \\ 0 \end{bmatrix}$$

Only the directions of the constraint Jacobian rows matters. Dividing each equation by the constant $-c\theta_f$ or $-c\theta_r$ respectively reproduces Equation 4.85.

4.3.1.3.3 Numerical Result. Suppose that $L = 1$ and $\theta = 0$. Suppose the slope at the rear wheel is $\zeta_x(x_r) = -0.1$ and at the front wheel it is $\zeta_x(x_f) = 0.2$. The constraint Jacobian is:

$$c_{\underline{x}} = \begin{bmatrix} -t\theta_f & -1 & (-t\theta_f(-Ls\theta) + Lc\theta) \\ -t\theta_r & -1 & (-t\theta_r(Ls\theta) - Lc\theta) \end{bmatrix} = \begin{bmatrix} -t\theta_f & -1 & L \\ -t\theta_r & -1 & -L \end{bmatrix} = \begin{bmatrix} -0.2 & -1 & 1 \\ 0.1 & -1 & -1 \end{bmatrix}$$

The constraint projection is:

$$P_C = c_{\underline{x}}^T (c_{\underline{x}} c_{\underline{x}}^T)^{-1} c_{\underline{x}} = \begin{bmatrix} 0.0244 & 0.0488 & -0.1463 \\ 0.0488 & 0.9976 & 0.0073 \\ -0.1463 & 0.0073 & 0.9780 \end{bmatrix}$$

If the unconstrained applied derivative is:

$$f(\underline{x}, \underline{u}) = \begin{bmatrix} 1 & 1 & 0 \end{bmatrix}^T$$

Then the constrained derivative is:

$$\dot{\underline{x}} = [I - P_C]f(\underline{x}, \underline{u}) = \begin{bmatrix} 0.9268 & -0.0463 & 0.1390 \end{bmatrix}^T$$

The instantaneous velocity of the body frame is therefore directed downward at an angle:

$$\theta = \text{atan}\left(\frac{0.0463}{0.9268}\right) = 0.05$$

This is half of the sum of the two terrain tangents as would be expected from the geometry. To check, we will compute the solution intuitively. The velocities of the wheel centers are:

$$\vec{v}_f = \vec{v} + \vec{\omega} \times \vec{r}_f$$
$$\vec{v}_r = \vec{v} + \vec{\omega} \times \vec{r}_r$$

When terrain following is enforced, the x and z components of the wheel center velocities are dependent on the instantaneous terrain slope at their contact points. Rewriting the first equation in world coordinates based on what is known:

$$\begin{bmatrix} v_{fx} \\ -v_{fx}t\theta_f \end{bmatrix} = \begin{bmatrix} v_x \\ v_z \end{bmatrix} - \omega \begin{bmatrix} 0 \\ L \end{bmatrix}$$

This is two equations in the two unknowns v_{fx} and ω. From the first equation $v_{fx} = v_x$ so the second equation becomes:

$$-v_x t\theta_f = v_z - \omega L \Rightarrow \omega = \frac{(v_z + v_x t\theta_f)}{L}$$
$$\omega = (-0.0463 + 0.9268(0.2)) = 0.1390$$

This is the same as the value computed by the nullspace projection technique.

4.3.2 Constraints of Rolling Without Slipping

Another type of disallowed direction constraint occurs in nonholonomic form when wheels roll without slipping. This section develops this type of constraint into a form suitable for modelling WMRs as a differential algebraic system.

4.3.2.1 Rolling Constraints in the Plane

Consider the problem of modelling the motion of a WMR confined to the plane. Let a wheel be located arbitrarily with respect to a vehicle frame as shown in Figure 4.17. Suppose there are no articulations. Also, the contact point does not translate with respect to the wheel so $\vec{v}_c^s = 0$ but it may rotate. Under these conditions, Equation 4.75 applies directly but we will attempt to express it in more detail in both body-fixed and ground-fixed coordinates. Let the contact point for the i th wheel be designated as i.

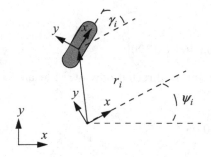

Figure 4.17 Wheel Model. The non-slip condition for a wheel requires the velocity component in the lateral direction to vanish.

4.3.2.1.1 Pfaffian Constraint in Body Frame. The disallowed direction $\vec{w}_c$ is $\hat{y}_i$ in this case. The position vector of the wheel is $\underline{r}_i^v = [x_i^v \ y_i^v]^T$. In body coordinates, the two unit vectors of the i frame are:

$$\hat{x}_i = \begin{bmatrix} c\gamma_i \ s\gamma_i \end{bmatrix}^T \qquad \hat{y}_i = \begin{bmatrix} -s\gamma_i \ c\gamma_i \end{bmatrix}^T$$

Then, the Pfaffian radius $\underline{\rho}_i^T = [\hat{y}_i^T [\underline{r}_i^v]^\times]$ is:

$$\underline{\rho}_i^T = \left[\begin{bmatrix} -s\gamma \ c\gamma \ 0 \end{bmatrix} \begin{bmatrix} 0 & 0 & y_i^v \\ 0 & 0 & -x_i^v \\ -y_i^v & x_i^v & 0 \end{bmatrix} \right] = \begin{bmatrix} 0 \ 0 \ (c\gamma x_i^v + s\gamma y_i^v) \end{bmatrix} = \begin{bmatrix} 0 \ 0 \ -(\vec{r}_i^v \cdot \hat{x}_i) \end{bmatrix}$$

So, Equation 4.75 is:

$$\underline{w}_c^T \underline{v}_v^w - \underline{\rho}_c^T \underline{\omega}_v^w = 0$$

$$\begin{bmatrix} -s\gamma_i \ c\gamma_i \end{bmatrix} \begin{bmatrix} v_x \ v_y \end{bmatrix}^T - \begin{bmatrix} 0 \ 0 \ -(\vec{r}_i^v \cdot \hat{x}_i) \end{bmatrix} \underline{\omega}_v^w = 0 \qquad (4.86)$$

Denoting the vehicle state as $[v_x \ v_y \ \omega]^T$, the constraint in body coordinates is:

$$\begin{bmatrix} -s\gamma_i \ c\gamma_i \ (\underline{r}_i \cdot \hat{x}_i) \end{bmatrix} \begin{bmatrix} v_x \ v_y \ \omega \end{bmatrix}^T = 0 \qquad (4.87)$$

4.3.2.1.2 Pfaffian Constraint in Inertial Frame. It will also be important for later to express the non-slip constraint in the world frame. In this frame, the two unit vectors of the c frame are:

$$\hat{x}_i = \begin{bmatrix} c\psi\gamma_i \ s\psi\gamma_i \end{bmatrix}^T \qquad \hat{y}_c = \begin{bmatrix} -s\psi\gamma_i \ c\psi\gamma_i \end{bmatrix}^T$$

where $c\psi\gamma = \cos(\psi + \gamma)$ etc. Now the constraint is:

$$\begin{bmatrix} -s\psi\gamma_i \ c\psi\gamma_i \ (\underline{r}_i \cdot \hat{x}_i) \end{bmatrix} \begin{bmatrix} v_x \ v_y \ \omega \end{bmatrix}^T = 0 \qquad (4.88)$$

Spotlight 4.7 Planar Pfaffian Constraint In Inertial Frame.

In this form, the constraint at the wheel is transformed into a constraint on the inertial velocities of the vehicle frame.

4.3.2.2 *Example: Modelling a Velocity-Driven Bicycle*

Consider the model of a bicycle shown in Figure 4.18. This system is described by the first order model:

$$\dot{x} = \underline{f}(\underline{x}, \underline{u}) = \underline{u}$$
$$\underline{c}_r(\underline{x}, \dot{\underline{x}}) = \underline{w}_r(\underline{x}) \, \dot{\underline{x}} = 0 \qquad (4.89)$$
$$\underline{c}_f(\underline{x}, \dot{\underline{x}}) = \underline{w}_f(\underline{x}) \, \dot{\underline{x}} = 0$$

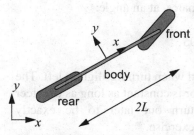

Figure 4.18 Bicycle Model. A simplified planar bicycle can be considered to consist of three rigid bodies. The *x* axis of the body frame is aligned with the direction of the rear wheel.

Although a rigid body has three degrees of freedom in the plane, this vehicle can only move instantaneously in one degree of freedom due to nonholonomic constraints at the wheels.

4.3.2.2.1 Model in Body Coordinates. We will formulate the model first in body coordinates. The position vectors to the wheels in body coordinates are:

$$\underline{r}_r = \begin{bmatrix} -L & 0 \end{bmatrix}^T \qquad \underline{r}_f = \begin{bmatrix} L & 0 \end{bmatrix}^T \qquad (4.90)$$

Based on Equation 4.87, the constraints are therefore:

$$\underline{c}_r(\underline{x}, \dot{\underline{x}}) = \underline{w}_r(\underline{x}) \, \dot{\underline{x}} = \begin{bmatrix} 0 & 1 & -L \end{bmatrix} \begin{bmatrix} v_x & v_y & \omega \end{bmatrix}^T = 0$$
$$\underline{c}_f(\underline{x}, \dot{\underline{x}}) = \underline{w}_f(\underline{x}) \, \dot{\underline{x}} = \begin{bmatrix} -s\gamma & c\gamma & Lc\gamma \end{bmatrix} \begin{bmatrix} v_x & v_y & \omega \end{bmatrix}^T = 0 \qquad (4.91)$$

Using the notation of Section 3.4.2.1 of Chapter 3, the constraint Jacobian is:

$$\underline{c}_{\dot{x}} = \begin{bmatrix} 0 & 1 & -L \\ -s\gamma & c\gamma & Lc\gamma \end{bmatrix} \qquad (4.92)$$

For an arbitrary input velocity $\underline{u}$ expressed in body coordinates, Equation 4.91 provides the component that is consistent with the constraints:

$$\dot{\underline{x}} = [I - \underline{c}_{\dot{x}}^T (\underline{c}_{\dot{x}} \underline{c}_{\dot{x}}^T)^{-1} \underline{c}_{\dot{x}}] \, \underline{u}$$

Suppose that $L = 1$ and $\gamma = 0.1$ as shown. Then, the constraint projection is:

$$P_C = \underline{c}_{\dot{x}}^T (\underline{c}_{\dot{x}} \underline{c}_{\dot{x}}^T)^{-1} \underline{c}_{\dot{x}} = \begin{bmatrix} 0.005 & -0.050 & -0.050 \\ -0.050 & 0.997 & -0.0025 \\ -0.050 & -0.0025 & 0.997 \end{bmatrix}$$

If the unconstrained applied derivative in body coordinates is:

$$\underline{f}(\underline{x}, \underline{u}) = \underline{u} = \begin{bmatrix} 1 & 0 & 0 \end{bmatrix}^T$$

Then the constrained derivative is:

$$\underline{\dot{x}} = [I - P_C]\underline{f}(\underline{x}, \underline{u}) = \begin{bmatrix} 0.995 & 0.050 & 0.050 \end{bmatrix}^T$$

This is integrated for one time step, and the process is repeated. The instantaneous velocity *of the body frame* is directed, in body coordinates, at an angle:

$$\theta = \text{atan}\left(\frac{0.097}{0.980}\right) = 0.05$$

so it is directed slightly to the left as would be expected when turning slightly left. The velocity was computed in the body frame, so this vector is constant as long as the steer angle is unchanged. The angle θ above will turn out later to be exactly $\theta = \text{atan}[(\tan(\gamma))/2]$ and its derivation is left as an exercise.

Note that if the body frame is moved to the rear wheel (by changing the third row of $\underline{c}_x$ appropriately), the constrained solution then becomes:

$$\underline{\dot{x}} = [I - P_C]\underline{f}(\underline{x}, \underline{u}) = \begin{bmatrix} 0.9975 & 0.0 & 0.050 \end{bmatrix}^T$$

The curvature of the path of the rear wheel is then is given by:

$$\kappa = \omega/V = \frac{0.050}{0.9975} = 0.050167$$

This agrees exactly with $\kappa = \tan(\gamma)/2L$, which is the solution obtained by solving Equation 4.57 for $\kappa = 1/R$.

4.3.2.2.2 Model in World Coordinates. Luckily, the dot product $\underline{r}_i \cdot \hat{x}_i$ in Equation 4.88 can be computed in any coordinates so the above result for it is still valid. We merely have to change the expressions for $\hat{y}_c$ and reinterpret the velocities in the state to be in world coordinates. Then, the constraints are:

$$\begin{aligned} \underline{c}_r(\underline{x}, \underline{\dot{x}}) = \underline{w}_r(\underline{x}) \, \underline{\dot{x}} = \begin{bmatrix} -s\psi & c\psi & -L \end{bmatrix} \begin{bmatrix} v_x & v_y & \omega \end{bmatrix}^T = 0 \\ \underline{c}_f(\underline{x}, \underline{\dot{x}}) = \underline{w}_f(\underline{x}) \, \underline{\dot{x}} = \begin{bmatrix} -s\psi\gamma & c\psi\gamma & Lc\gamma \end{bmatrix} \begin{bmatrix} v_x & v_y & \omega \end{bmatrix}^T = 0 \end{aligned} \tag{4.93}$$

The constraint Jacobian is now:

$$\underline{c}_x = \begin{bmatrix} -s\psi & c\psi & -L \\ -s\psi\gamma & c\psi\gamma & Lc\gamma \end{bmatrix} \tag{4.94}$$

4.3.2.3 Example: Implementing the Velocity-Driven Bicycle

Pseudocode for the world frame model is provided in Algorithm 4.2. A closed form solution to even this simplest of constrained vehicle dynamics problems is very tedious, so the reader is encouraged to experiment with this model in a computer. The model starts the vehicle at the origin with a velocity initially directed along the x axis.

The constraints were solved explicitly to determine the correct initial heading and angular velocity that is exactly consistent with this. A simple Euler integration technique is used. As it is provided, there is no change to steering so the vehicle will drive in a circle. A good test case for this example is $\Delta t = 0.1$, $\gamma = 0.1$.

In order to facilitate comparison with the Lagrangian bicycle model presented later, the solution is computed in a two step process:

$$\underline{\lambda} = (CC^T)^{-1} C\underline{u}$$
$$\underline{\dot{x}} = (\underline{u} - C^T\underline{\lambda})$$

```
00    algorithm VelocityDrivenBicycle()
01    L ← 1 ; γ ← 0.1 ; ψ₀ ← −atan[(tan(γ))/2]
```

$$02 \quad x \leftarrow \begin{bmatrix} 0 & 0 & \psi_0 \end{bmatrix} ; v_x \leftarrow 1 ; \dot{x} \leftarrow \begin{bmatrix} v_x & 0 & -v_x \sin\frac{(\psi_0)}{L} \end{bmatrix}$$

```
03    Δt ← 0.01 ; t_max ← 2π/ẋ(3)
04    for( t ← 0 ; t < t_max ; t ← t + Δt )
```

$$05 \quad \psi \leftarrow x(3) ; C \leftarrow C_{\dot{x}} \leftarrow \begin{bmatrix} -s\psi & c\psi & -L \\ -s\psi\gamma & c\psi\gamma & Lc\gamma \end{bmatrix} ;$$

$$06 \quad \hat{v} \leftarrow \begin{bmatrix} \dot{x}(1) & \dot{x}(2) \end{bmatrix}^T ; \hat{v} \leftarrow \hat{v}/|\hat{v}|$$

$$07 \quad f_x \leftarrow f_x(t) ; \text{// or just 1;} \ u \leftarrow f_x\hat{v} ;$$

$$08 \quad \lambda \leftarrow (CC^T)^{-1}(Cu)$$
$$09 \quad \dot{x} \leftarrow (u - C^T\lambda)$$
$$10 \quad x \leftarrow x + \dot{x}\Delta t$$

```
11    endfor
12    return
```

Algorithm 4.1 First-Order Model of a Single Body Bicycle. This model can be coded quickly and once debugged will drive the vehicle in a circle. Try steering it by setting $\gamma = \cos(2\pi t/t_{max})$.

4.3.3 Lagrangian Dynamics

The Lagrangian formulation of vehicle dynamics is particularly useful for wheeled mobile robots because, unlike in the more common Newton-Euler formulation of dynamics, the (generally unknown) constraint forces are computed automatically. Although it is simpler, the Newton-Euler formulation does not work until the constraint forces are known and the mechanism to find them is the principle of virtual work. The general numerical methods framework was presented in Section 3.4.3 of Chapter 3. Recall from Equation 3.105 that the formulation is a constrained dynamic system of second order (i.e., involving accelerations):

$$\begin{bmatrix} M & C^T \\ C & 0 \end{bmatrix} \begin{bmatrix} \underline{\ddot{x}} \\ \underline{\lambda} \end{bmatrix} = \begin{bmatrix} \underline{F}^{ext} \\ \underline{F}_d \end{bmatrix}$$

This section presents the peculiarities of Lagrangian dynamics applicable to wheeled mobile robots.

4.3.3.1 Differentiated Rolling Constraints in the Plane

It will be necessary to use an expression for the time derivative (in world coordinates) of the rolling without slipping constraint. Equation 4.83 applies to the case of the bicycle in Figure 4.18 if we choose the moving frame m in the Pfaffian rate definition to be the s frame fixed to the wheel. Under these conditions, two key components of Equation 4.83 ($\underline{w}_i$ and $\underline{\rho}_i$) were derived above for the velocity constraint:

$$\underline{w}_c^T = \hat{y}_i = \begin{bmatrix} -s\psi\gamma_i & c\psi\gamma_i \end{bmatrix}^T \qquad \underline{\rho}_i^T = \begin{bmatrix} 0 & 0 & -(\overset{\scriptscriptstyle v}{r}_i \cdot \hat{x}_i) \end{bmatrix}$$

The other two remaining key components are:

$$\dot{\underline{w}}_c^T = -\underline{w}_c^T[\underline{\omega}_m^w]^\times = \begin{bmatrix} -s\psi\gamma_i \\ c\psi\gamma_i \\ 0 \end{bmatrix}^T \begin{bmatrix} 0 & \omega_s^w & 0 \\ -\omega_s^w & 0 & 0 \\ 0 & 0 & 0 \end{bmatrix} = -\omega_s^w \begin{bmatrix} c\psi\gamma_i \\ s\psi\gamma_i \\ 0 \end{bmatrix}^T$$

$$\dot{\underline{\rho}}_c^T = \dot{\underline{w}}_c^T[\underline{r}_c^v]^\times = -\begin{bmatrix} \omega_s^w c\psi\gamma_i \\ \omega_s^w s\psi\gamma_i \\ 0 \end{bmatrix}^T \begin{bmatrix} 0 & 0 & y_i^v \\ 0 & 0 & -x_i^v \\ -y_i^v & x_i^v & 0 \end{bmatrix} = -\omega_s^w \begin{bmatrix} 0 \\ 0 \\ (\overset{\scriptscriptstyle v}{r}_i \cdot \hat{y}_i) \end{bmatrix}$$

Also, $\underline{\omega}_v^w \perp \underline{r}_c^v$ so where $\omega \cong |\underline{\omega}_v^w|$:

$$\underline{w}_c^T[\underline{\omega}_v^w]^\times[\underline{\omega}_v^w]^\times \underline{r}_c^v = -\underline{w}_c^T\omega^2 \underline{r}_c^v = -\omega^2 \begin{bmatrix} -s\psi\gamma_i & c\psi\gamma_i & 0 \end{bmatrix} \underline{r}_c^v = -\omega^2(\underline{r}_i \cdot \hat{y}_i)$$

It is useful to write Equation 4.83 in this form

$$\underline{w}_c^T\underline{a}_v^w - \underline{\rho}_c^T\underline{\alpha}_v^w = \dot{\underline{\rho}}_c^T\underline{\omega}_v^w - \dot{\underline{w}}_c^T\underline{v}_v^w - \underline{w}_c^T[\underline{\omega}_v^w]^{\times\times}\underline{r}_c^v$$

Then it becomes:

$$\begin{bmatrix} -s\psi\gamma_i \\ c\psi\gamma_i \\ (\underline{r}_i \cdot \hat{x}_i) \end{bmatrix}^T \begin{bmatrix} a_x \\ a_y \\ \alpha \end{bmatrix} = \omega_s^w \begin{bmatrix} \omega_s^w c\psi\gamma_i \\ \omega_s^w s\psi\gamma_i \\ -(\underline{r}_i \cdot \hat{y}_i) \end{bmatrix}^T \begin{bmatrix} v_x \\ v_y \\ \omega \end{bmatrix} + \omega^2(\underline{r}_i \cdot \hat{y}_i) \tag{4.95}$$

But $\omega_s^w = \omega + \dot{\gamma}$ so this reduces to:

$$\begin{bmatrix} -s\psi\gamma_i \\ c\psi\gamma_i \\ (\underline{r}_i \cdot \hat{x}_i) \end{bmatrix}^T \begin{bmatrix} a_x \\ a_y \\ \alpha \end{bmatrix} = \begin{bmatrix} (\omega + \dot{\gamma}_i)c\psi\gamma_i \\ (\omega + \dot{\gamma}_i)s\psi\gamma_i \\ -\dot{\gamma}_i(\underline{r}_i \cdot \hat{y}_i) \end{bmatrix}^T \begin{bmatrix} v_x \\ v_y \\ \omega \end{bmatrix} \tag{4.96}$$

Spotlight 4.8 Planar Pfaffian Constraint Differentiated In Inertial Frame.

In this form, the differentiated constraint at the wheel is transformed into a constraint on the inertial accelerations of the vehicle frame.

4.3.3.2 Example: Modelling a Force-Driven Bicycle

A dynamic model of a bicycle is just difficult enough to illustrate some concepts but just easy enough to avoid some difficult pitfalls. Consider again the model of a bicycle shown in Figure 4.18. To simplify matters, we will treat the bicycle as a single body and ignore the mass of the wheels while still imposing non-slip constraints. The front wheel will be allowed to articulate, and the effect of this on the constraint will be captured in the form of the steering rate $\dot{\gamma}$.

The equations of motion are of the form:

$$M\ddot{x} = \underline{F}^{ext} + \underline{F}^{con}$$

$$\begin{bmatrix} m & 0 & 0 \\ 0 & m & 0 \\ 0 & 0 & I \end{bmatrix} \begin{bmatrix} a_x \\ a_y \\ \alpha \end{bmatrix} = \begin{bmatrix} F_x \\ F_y \\ \tau \end{bmatrix}^{ext} + \begin{bmatrix} F_x \\ F_y \\ \tau \end{bmatrix}^{con} \tag{4.97}$$

where the reference point is the center of mass and I is the polar moment of inertia. These equations only take this simple diagonal form when the reference point is chosen to be the center of mass.

The position vectors to the wheels are computed in Equation 4.90 and the constraints in Equation 4.94. By Equation 4.96, the constraint derivatives are:

$$\begin{bmatrix} -s\psi & c\psi & -L \\ -s\psi\gamma & c\psi\gamma & Lc\gamma \end{bmatrix} \begin{bmatrix} a_x \\ a_y \\ \alpha \end{bmatrix} = \begin{bmatrix} \omega c\psi & \omega s\psi & 0 \\ (\omega+\dot{\gamma})c\psi\gamma & (\omega+\dot{\gamma})s\psi\gamma & \dot{\gamma}Ls\gamma \end{bmatrix} \begin{bmatrix} v_x \\ v_y \\ \omega \end{bmatrix} \tag{4.98}$$

Using the notation of Section 3.4.3 of Chapter 3, the relevant Jacobians are:

$$\underline{c}_x = - \begin{bmatrix} \omega c\psi & \omega s\psi & 0 \\ (\omega+\dot{\gamma})c\psi\gamma & (\omega+\dot{\gamma})s\psi\gamma & \dot{\gamma}Ls\gamma \end{bmatrix} \qquad \underline{c}_{\dot{x}} = \begin{bmatrix} -s\psi & c\psi & -L \\ -s\psi\gamma & c\psi\gamma & Lc\gamma \end{bmatrix}$$

Once these Jacobians are computed, the rest of the computation for the state update is as follows:

$$\underline{F}_d = - C_{\dot{x}} \, \underline{\dot{x}}$$
$$\underline{\lambda} = (CM^{-1} C^T)^{-1} (CM^{-1} \underline{F}^{ext} - \underline{F}_d)$$
$$\underline{\ddot{x}} = M^{-1}(\underline{F}^{ext} - C^T \underline{\lambda})$$

This result is integrated one time step, and the process is repeated. Many of the matrices depend on the state so they will change in every iteration.

4.3.3.3 Example: Implementing the Force-Driven Bicycle

Pseudocode for this model is provided in Algorithm 4.2.

It has much in common with the first-order bicycle model in Algorithm 4.1. As described in Section 3.4.4.1 of Chapter 3, the constraint trim projection that occurs at line 11 is an excellent technique to recover the information when differentiating constraints.

```
00   algorithm LagrangeBicycle()
01   m ← I ← L ← 1; γ ← 0.1; ψ₀ ← −atan[(tan(γ))/2]
```

$$02 \quad x \leftarrow \begin{bmatrix} 0 & 0 & \psi_0 \end{bmatrix}; \; v_x \leftarrow 1; \; \dot{x} \leftarrow \begin{bmatrix} v_x & 0 & -v_x \sin\dfrac{(\psi_0)}{L} \end{bmatrix}$$

$$03 \quad \Delta t \leftarrow 0.01; \; M \leftarrow diag\left(\begin{bmatrix} m & m & I \end{bmatrix}\right); \; t_{max} \leftarrow 2\pi/\dot{x}(3)$$

$$04 \quad M^{-1} \leftarrow inverse(M))$$

```
05   for( t ← 0 ; t < t_max ; t ← t + Δt )
```

$$06 \quad \psi \leftarrow x(3) \,; \; C \leftarrow C_{\dot{x}} \leftarrow \begin{bmatrix} -s\psi & c\psi & -L \\ -s\psi\gamma & c\psi\gamma & Lc\gamma \end{bmatrix}; \; \omega \leftarrow \dot{x}(3)$$

$$07 \quad C_x \leftarrow -\begin{bmatrix} \omega c\psi & \omega s\psi & 0 \\ (\omega + \dot{\gamma})c\psi\gamma & (\omega + \dot{\gamma})s\psi\gamma & \dot{\gamma}Ls\gamma \end{bmatrix}$$

$$08 \quad \hat{v} \leftarrow \begin{bmatrix} \dot{x}(1) & \dot{x}(2) \end{bmatrix}^T; \; \hat{v} \leftarrow \hat{v}/|\hat{v}|$$

$$09 \quad f_x \leftarrow f_x(t) \,; \text{ // or just } 0; \; F^{ext} \leftarrow f_x\hat{v}; \; F_d \leftarrow -C_x\dot{x}$$

$$10 \quad \lambda \leftarrow (CM^{-1}C^T)^{-1}(CM^{-1}F^{ext} - F_d)$$

$$11 \quad \ddot{x} \leftarrow M^{-1}(F^{ext} - C^T\lambda)$$

$$12 \quad \dot{x} \leftarrow \dot{x} + \ddot{x}\Delta t \,; \; \dot{x} \leftarrow [I - C^T(CC^T)^{-1}C]\,\dot{x}$$

$$13 \quad x \leftarrow x + \dot{x}\Delta t$$

```
14   endfor
15   return
```

Algorithm 4.2 Lagrangian Model of a Single Body Bicycle. This model can be coded quickly and once debugged will drive the vehicle in a circle.

It immediately removes any motion that violates the undifferentiated constraints. This technique makes drift compensation for the associated constraints unnecessary. A good test case for this example is $\Delta t = 0.1$, $\gamma = 0.1$. The path under these conditions is highly accurate and the constraint error is negligible. However, without a better integration technique like Runge-Kutta, system energy is not well preserved.

A more complicated model gives the wheels mass and connects them to the body with constraints. The front wheel is connected to the body with a pin joint, and the rear wheel is rigidly attached. Three equations like Equation 4.97 are stacked to produce nine. The rigid constraint imposes 3 constraints, and the pin joint imposes 2 for a total of 5. The two wheel nonholonomic constraints now take a much simpler form and raise the total degree of constraint to 7. The remaining two degrees of freedom are the steer angle of the front wheel and the more-or-less forward velocity of the vehicle.

4.3.3.4 Actual Constraint Forces at the Wheels

Two sets of forces are called *equipollent* if they have the same resultant about a point. The constraint forces computed by the multipliers are forces and moments acting at the cg that enforce constraints. These are transformations of the ***real*** forces acting at the wheels. Consider the problem of computing those real forces for the bicycle in the last example.

If a real constraint force acted along the disallowed $\hat{y}_i$ axis direction of the wheel, the equipollent force acting at the origin of the body frame would be:

$$\begin{bmatrix} F_x \\ F_y \end{bmatrix}_i^b = \begin{bmatrix} c\psi\gamma & -s\psi\gamma \\ s\psi\gamma & c\psi\gamma \end{bmatrix} \begin{bmatrix} 0 \\ f_i \end{bmatrix} = f_i \begin{bmatrix} -s\psi\gamma \\ c\psi\gamma \end{bmatrix}$$

Likewise, the moment of this wheel force around the body frame origin would be:

$$\tau_i^b = \underline{r}_i \times f_i\,\hat{y}_i = f_i(\underline{r}_i \times \hat{y}_i) = f_i(\underline{r}_i \times (\hat{z}_i \times \hat{x}_i)) = f_i(\underline{r}_i \cdot \hat{x}_i)\hat{z}_i$$

Therefore, the total force and moment acting at the body frame caused by this real constraint force is:

$$\begin{bmatrix} F_x & F_y & \tau \end{bmatrix}_i^b = f_i \begin{bmatrix} -s\psi\gamma & c\psi\gamma & \underline{r}_i \cdot \hat{x}_i \end{bmatrix} = f_i\, \underline{c}(\underline{x}) \tag{4.99}$$

We can conclude that the Pfaffian constraint vector $\underline{c}(\underline{x})$ produces the equipollent force and moment, acting at the body frame, of a real constraint force acting at the wheel. Recall that, in a Lagrangian formulation, the constraint forces are given by $\underline{F}^{con} = -C^T\lambda$ where C is the coefficient of $\ddot{\underline{x}}$ in the differentiated constraint. In the case of a wheel constraint, the rows of C are the Pfaffian weight vectors $\underline{w}(\underline{x})$. The constraint force, in general, acts in a direction orthogonal to the constraint surface expressed in the coordinates of the state vector, so they are equivalent to forces acting at the origin of the body frame.

The real constraint forces are applied at the wheels, and we would, at times, like to know their magnitudes. We saw in Equation 4.99 that the equipollent force acting at the body frame, of a real wheel constraint force has magnitude $f_i\,\underline{c}(\underline{x})$. Therefore, the sum of the equipollent forces of m wheels would be:

$$\underline{F}^{con} = \begin{bmatrix} \underline{c}_1(\underline{x}) & \underline{c}_2(\underline{x}) & \cdots & \underline{c}_m(\underline{x}) \end{bmatrix} \begin{bmatrix} f_1 & f_2 & \cdots & f_m \end{bmatrix}^T = C^T\underline{f}$$

Clearly, the Lagrange multipliers are equal to the **negative magnitudes of the real constraint forces** acting at the wheels. Once these forces are known, it is tempting to use them to implement a simpler Newton-Euler formulation, but, of course, this is exactly what the constrained dynamics formulation does anyway.

4.3.3.5 Allowing Wheel Slip

Although the nominal constraint on a wheel is zero slip, the constraints in a constrained dynamics formulation can be anything at all. If it is important to model the slippage of a wheel, it is tempting to write a constraint of the form:

$$g(\underline{x}, \dot{\underline{x}}) = v_y(\underline{x}, \dot{\underline{x}}, \underline{u})$$

for some arbitrary lateral wheel velocity function $v_y(\underline{x}, \dot{\underline{x}}, \underline{u})$ that may depend on the state and/or inputs. Of course, this is easily placed in standard form with:

$$c(\underline{x}, \dot{\underline{x}}, \underline{u}) = g(\underline{x}, \dot{\underline{x}}) - v_y(\underline{x}, \dot{\underline{x}}, \underline{u}) = 0$$

So, allowing the wheels to slip is easy. For example, the magic tire model [10] expresses how the lateral force on a tire is proportional to the slip angle for small slip angles:

$$f = (kv_y)/v_x$$

In this model, slip velocity is proportional to lateral force. Because the lateral force is the negative Lagrange multiplier, we can write:

$$v_y = -(1/k)fv_x = -k_c\lambda v_x$$

Then, we substitute for v_x at the wheel by inspiring from Equation 4.88 and exchanging $\hat{y}_i$ for $\hat{x}_i$:

$$v_y = -k_c\lambda v_x = -k_c\lambda \left[c\psi\gamma_i \ s\psi\gamma_i \ (\underline{r}_i \cdot \hat{y}_i) \right] \left[v_x \ v_y \ \omega \right]^T$$

Then the gradient of this component of the constraint is:

$$\underline{c}_x = \left[c\psi\gamma_i \ s\psi\gamma_i \ (\underline{r}_i \cdot \hat{y}_i) \right]$$

Rather than introduce a dependence on the multipliers into the constraint, it is simpler to use the values of the multipliers from the last cycle of the computations. For the bicycle example, setting $k_c = 0.5$ increases the radius of the circle by 25%. This is easiest to show in the first-order model where a differentiated constraints is not needed. In that case, the multipliers are velocities rather than forces.

4.3.3.6 Redundant and Inconsistent Constraints

In constrained differential equations, the removal of the disallowed components of the state derivative occurs in the augmented state equation:

$$M\ddot{\underline{x}} = \underline{F}^{ext} - C^T\underline{\lambda}$$

The term $C^T\lambda$ is both the infeasible component of the applied forces and the constraint forces (acting at the body origin). For the wheels, the constraints themselves take the form $\underline{w}(\underline{x}) \cdot \dot{\underline{x}} = 0$ for each wheel.

When these equations are stacked together they form the system $C\dot{\underline{x}} = \underline{0}$. With n degrees of freedom, when $n-1$ wheels are aligned as they should be, a constraint tangent plane exists, and the constraints $C\dot{\underline{x}} = \underline{0}$ have a nontrivial solution that lies in their nullspace. In this case, the matrix $CM^{-1} \ C^T$ used to compute the multipliers has full rank of $m = n-1$ and it is invertible. Bicycles in the plane have $n-1 = 2$ wheels so we used one in Algorithm 4.1. Properly constrained systems have constraints that do no work, and they will move forever, while respecting the constraints, at constant total energy if there are no applied forces. However, when there are more than two wheels in the plane, two complexities often arise, as presented below.

4.3.3.6.1 Redundant Constraints. Steerable wheels may become instantaneously aligned. Also, it is very typical for many vehicles, including cars, to have wheels that are aligned by design (Figure 4.19). In the plane, if a single *redundant* constraint is added to an otherwise well-formed set of constraints, the matrix C becomes both square and rank deficient. The matrix $CM^{-1} \ C^T$ is then no longer invertible.

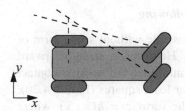

Figure 4.19 Automobile Model. Unless the two front wheels are turned to consistent angles, the three lines of velocity constraint do not cross at a single point, and no velocities are feasible.

It is possible to detect and remove redundant constraints and to solve the reduced order system, but it is simpler to use the conjugate gradient algorithm to solve the system for the multipliers because it easily tolerates redundant constraints.

4.3.3.6.2 Inconsistent Constraints. If a *non-redundant* constraint is added to a bicycle, a different problem occurs. For example, unless the two front wheels of a car are steered in precisely the right way (Figure 4.19), the wheel constraints overconstrain the velocity, and they prevent any motion. In this case, the nullspace of the constraints disappears.

Two simple solutions are to (a) eliminate constraints until a nullspace is generated, and (b) fix the Jeantaud diagram by computing a unique best fit ICR using least squares on the lines normal to the wheels. Perhaps the most principled approach is to find the "closest" approximation C^* to C which has a rank of exactly $n - 1$. This problem can be solved using the singular value decomposition according to the Eckart–Young theorem. The details will be omitted here, but the principle is to factor C and then strike all singular values beyond the $n - 1$ largest and reconstruct the new C as C^*. Based on exercise 3.3.4.5, the eigenvectors associated with the $n-1$ largest eigenvalues of C^{TC} will be the closest approximation.

4.3.4 Terrain Contact

We have seen that terrain contact can be treated as a disallowed direction, normal to the terrain, for wheel velocity. However, later content has argued that all differentiated constraints are subject to drift. We have also seen that direct enforcement of constraints is ultimately needed to resolve drift. All this means that it is important to formulate terrain contact as a true holonomic constraint.

In rough terms, the terrain contact constraint is a constraint placed on the attitude and altitude of the vehicle that requires that all the wheels remain in contact. In 3D, real vehicles typically have more than the three wheels strictly necessary to support their weight stably, and the relationships involved are nonlinear. Hence the problem is of the form:

$$\underline{c}(\underline{x}) = \underline{0}$$

where $\underline{x} = [z \; \theta \; \phi]$. There are four or more such constraints. The rest of the vehicle pose is the position and yaw ($[x \; y \; \psi]^T$), and straightforward approaches assume this information is known. Given that the problem is overconstrained, satisfaction of all constraints is impossible in general. Instead, the terrain contact must be formulated as yet another optimization problem. A viable approach is to fit a plane to the four points under the wheels and then extract attitude and altitude from the plane. This section presents two techniques inspired by such an approach.

4.3.4.1 Least Residual Terrain Following

For an overdetermined system' terrain contact is not possible without some form of suspension that introduces extra degrees of freedom. However, a straightforward approach that still avoids modelling a suspension is to minimize the squared contact residuals by adjusting the unknown states with nonlinear least squares (Figure 4.20). Suppose there are four wheels. The constraint is of the form $\underline{z} = h(\underline{x}_f, \underline{x})$ where $\underline{z} = [z_1 \ z_2 \ z_3 \ z_4]^T$ is the terrain elevations at the assumed pose and the state has been divided into a fixed part $\underline{x}_f = [x \ y \ \psi]$ and a part that is to be optimized $\underline{x} = [z \ \theta \ \phi]^T$.

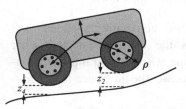

Figure 4.20 Simple Model for Terrain Following. The altitude error of the contact points of the wheels is shown. Minimizing the norm of the error for all 4 wheels is a nonlinear least squares problem.

The terrain contact optimization problem is then of the form:

$$\begin{aligned} minimize:_{\underline{x}} \quad & f(\underline{x}) = \frac{1}{2}\underline{r}^T\underline{r} \\ where: \quad & \underline{r}(\underline{x}) = \underline{z} - h(\underline{x}_f, \underline{x}) \\ & z_i = (R_b^w \underline{r}_i^b)_z - \rho \end{aligned} \qquad (4.100)$$

Here, $\underline{r}_i^b$ is the position of the center point of wheel i expressed in body coordinates, $(R_b^w \underline{r}_i^b)_z$ means its z coordinate in world coordinates, and ρ is the wheel radius. Consistency with notation everywhere else requires us to tolerate the use of $\underline{r}$ for residual as well. This is an unconstrained optimization problem that can be solved using nonlinear least squares.

Clearly, even for rigid terrain, the wheel contact points are not necessarily on the bottoms of the wheels and a vertical measure of proximity (or penetration) will be incorrect if the terrain slope is high. A better solution is to search the periphery of the wheel and compute a maximum signed deviation normal to the wheel surface (Figure 4.21).

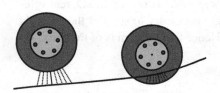

Figure 4.21 Computing Wheel Contact Points. For the sampled terrain model shown, the distance above or inside the surface can be computed as the local minimum or maximum perpendicular distance from the wheel surface. Knowing the terrain normals (contact normals) at these extrema is also very useful for force driven models.

4.3.4.1.1 Minimum Energy Terrain Following. The functions of a suspension system include enhancing traction by keeping all wheels in contact with the ground, controlling attitude on uneven terrain, and damping bumps and oscillations. Only three constraints are required to fix the three degrees of freedom of roll, pitch, and altitude.

However, many vehicles have 4 wheels or more. If the terrain is not locally flat, a vehicle with no suspension will be unable to keep all four in contact with the ground. This is both a mathematics issue and a mechanical issue.

In terms of mathematical modelling, there are insufficient constraints to determine attitude if every wheel is suspended. Nature typically solves such problems by minimizing energy and we can do the same in this case (Figure 4.22).

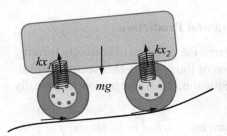

Figure 4.22 Modelling a Spring Suspension. If each wheel is attached to the chassis with a spring, the static attitude can be predicted from the terrain shape and the minimum energy principle.

Suppose all wheels are attached to the vehicle with spring-damper systems. Doing so introduces 4 more degrees of freedom, and converts an overconstrained (4 > 3) problem into an underconstrained (4 < 7) one. The ambiguity can be resolved by requiring that the suspension systems remain in the minimum energy configuration.

Let $\underline{x} = [x_1\ x_2\ x_3\ x_4]^T$ represent the deflections of the four springs, all of spring constant k. We will consider the quasi-static case where velocities are so small that the dampers exert no forces. Then, the vertical components of the forces kx_i in the springs can be written as:

$$^w\!f_i = [R_b^w(\theta, \phi)kx_i]_z$$

The constraint that the vehicle weight must be supported is:

$$^w\!f_1 + {}^w\!f_2 + {}^w\!f_3 + {}^w\!f_4 = mg$$

So far, nothing has been written to require that the wheels follow the terrain. Given a suspension, it is now reasonable to assume that all four can touch the terrain. One way to do this is to enforce four wheel contact constraints of the form used in the last section:

$$\underline{c}(\underline{x}) = \underline{z} - h(\underline{x}_f, \underline{x}) = \underline{0}$$

The problem is then of the form:

$$
\begin{aligned}
minimize_{\underline{x}}:\quad & f(\underline{x}) = \frac{1}{2}\underline{x}^T\underline{x}\\
subject\ to:\quad & (^w\!f_1 + {}^w\!f_2 + {}^w\!f_3 + {}^w\!f_4 = mg)\\
& \underline{c}(\underline{x}) = \underline{z} - h(\underline{x}_f, \underline{x}) = \underline{0}
\end{aligned}
\qquad (4.101)
$$

This is a constrained optimization problem that can be solved using constrained nonlinear least squares. Another option is to move the second constraint to the objective with a diagonal weight matrix like $\underline{c}^T K \underline{c}$. This approach amounts to treating the contact points like another set of "springs" that resist both wheels penetrating the terrain and wheels above the terrain. Because this second set of springs represent constraints, they must be very stiff relative to the real ones in the suspension. The weight support constraint is necessary in some form in general to prevent all springs going to zero deflection to minimize the energy.

Highly terrainable vehicles may have an articulated degree of freedom specifically designed into the suspension mechanism to allow all four wheels to remain in contact with the terrain.

4.3.5 Trajectory Estimation and Prediction

All of this subchapter up to this point has considered the problem of correctly forming the differential equations that describe the motion of the system. This section considers the process of integrating that differential equation. Such integration is typically performed for one of two purposes:

- estimating state in odometry, Kalman filter system models, and more generally in pose estimation of any kind.
- predicting state in predictive control or in motion simulators.

In estimation, measurements of wheel speeds and steer angles or transmission speed, and so on, are used to compute the linear and angular velocity. This information is then integrated to determine the present position and orientation of the vehicle. Conversely, in control, commands in the form of wheel speeds and steer angles or throttle etc. are provided and these are used to compute the linear and angular velocity. This information is again integrated to determine the present position and orientation of the vehicle that is predicted to occur.

Many of the models produced before this point in the subchapter have manipulated velocities expressed in body coordinates. Doing so has been a useful way to suppress detail. However, models of wheeled mobile robot are ultimately nonlinear for the simple reason that the actuators are carried on the vehicle. This fact implies that velocities (whether actuation signals or measurements) must ultimately be transformed to earth-fixed coordinates before they are integrated. The trajectory followed in the world can only be computed by integrating in the world frame. Therefore, this section will explicitly consider the conversion of velocity information to world coordinates before it is integrated.

4.3.5.1 Trajectory Heading, Yaw, and Curvature

Consider any vehicle moving in the plane. In order to describe its motion, it is necessary to choose a reference point – the origin of the vehicle frame. This reference point is a particle moving along a path in space.

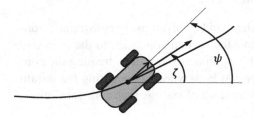

Figure 4.23 Distinguishing Heading from Yaw. Yaw is where a vehicle is pointing whereas heading is the direction of the velocity vector.

The *heading* ζ is the angle formed by the path tangent with some specified datum direction fixed to the Earth. Conversely, the yaw ψ of the vehicle body, is the angle formed by the forward looking axis of the vehicle body with an earth fixed datum. These two angles may be related or completely independent of each other. Some vehicles must go where they are pointed and some need not. Even in the first case, it is only true for some points on the vehicle. Even for those points, if we allow lateral wheel slip to occur, these two angles are not the same.

Curvature κ is a property of the 2D path followed by the vehicle reference point – regardless of the orientation of the vehicle during the motion:

$$\kappa = \frac{d\zeta}{ds} \tag{4.102}$$

where s is distance along the path. Furthermore, the *radius of curvature* is defined as the reciprocal of curvature:

$$R = 1/\kappa \tag{4.103}$$

The time derivative $\dot{\zeta}$ is precisely the rate of change of heading. This can be equal to the angular velocity, but it may have no relationship to angular velocity for a given vehicle or a given motion. Some vehicles can move in any direction (linear velocity) while orienting themselves arbitrarily (angular velocity). The rotation rate of the tangent vector to the path can be obtained from the chain rule of differentiation using the speed v as follows:

$$\dot{\zeta} = \frac{d\zeta}{ds}\frac{ds}{dt} = \kappa v \tag{4.104}$$

4.3.5.2 Fully Actuated WMR in the Plane

Many inverse models presented so far have ultimately produced the linear and angular velocity of the vehicle based on wheel measurements, and later control sections will produce the same information in a prediction context based on the control inputs. If we ignore the details of the actuation scheme, a somewhat generic 2D model of vehicle motion can be written by treating it like any other rigid body. We place a body frame at the reference point at some orientation on the vehicle.

In the general case of a fully actuated vehicle (whose velocity commands have three degrees of freedom), we can write:

$$\frac{d}{dt}\begin{bmatrix} x(t) \\ y(t) \\ \psi(t) \end{bmatrix} = \begin{bmatrix} \cos\psi(t) & -\sin\psi(t) & 0 \\ \sin\psi(t) & \cos\psi(t) & 0 \\ 0 & 0 & 1 \end{bmatrix} \begin{bmatrix} v_x(t) \\ v_y(t) \\ \dot{\psi}(t) \end{bmatrix} \tag{4.105}$$

Spotlight 4.9 Kinematic Differential Equation of Generic Planar Vehicle.

This is the most basic model of a robot vehicle moving in a plane – which may be the terrain tangent plane. We will call it the generic planar vehicle model. The matrix converts coordinates from the body frame to the tangent plane frame

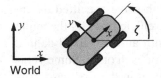

Figure 4.24 Generic 2D Velocity Kinematics. Provided the velocity, curvature, and heading used are those of the reference point, the same model applies to all vehicles in the plane.

where the state vector $[x\ y\ \psi]^T$ is the position and yaw of the vehicle with respect to some world frame. This model is nonlinear because the heading state occurs inside the trig functions in the rotation matrix.

A similar model can be written if heading $\zeta(t)$ is the orientation state. In this case though, the lateral velocity is zero by definition of heading, so the model becomes:

$$\frac{d}{dt}\begin{bmatrix} x(t) \\ y(t) \\ \zeta(t) \end{bmatrix} = \begin{bmatrix} \cos\zeta(t) & -\sin\zeta(t) & 0 \\ \sin\zeta(t) & \cos\zeta(t) & 0 \\ 0 & 0 & 1 \end{bmatrix} \begin{bmatrix} v_x(t) \\ 0 \\ \dot{\zeta}(t) \end{bmatrix} \qquad (4.106)$$

where the state vector $[x\ y\ \zeta]^T$ is the position and heading of the vehicle with respect to some world frame. The rightmost vector containing $v_x(t)$ is no longer expressed in the body frame, but rather a frame aligned with the velocity vector.

4.3.5.3 Underactuated WMR in the Plane

Many wheeled vehicles are underactuated as a consequence of the fact that lateral motion of wheels is not actuated. Suppose that the vehicle reference point is placed at the center of the rear axles and the front wheels steer like a car. On the assumption that the wheels are not slipping, the vehicle velocity must be oriented in the forward direction. Under these conditions, heading and yaw are synonymous $\zeta(t) = \psi(t)$ and

$$v_x(t) = v \qquad\qquad v_y(t) = 0$$

After substituting Equation 4.104 as well, the system differential equation becomes:

$$\frac{d}{dt}\begin{bmatrix} x(t) \\ y(t) \\ \psi(t) \end{bmatrix} = \begin{bmatrix} \cos\psi(t) & 0 \\ \sin\psi(t) & 0 \\ 0 & 1 \end{bmatrix} \begin{bmatrix} v(t) \\ \kappa(t)v(t) \end{bmatrix} \qquad (4.107)$$

Then its integral becomes simply:

$$\begin{bmatrix} x(t) \\ y(t) \\ \psi(t) \end{bmatrix} = \begin{bmatrix} x(0) \\ y(0) \\ \psi(0) \end{bmatrix} + \int_0^t \begin{bmatrix} \cos\psi(t) \\ \sin\psi(t) \\ \kappa(t) \end{bmatrix} v(t)dt \qquad (4.108)$$

Notice that the equations have a very special decoupled form that permits *back substitution* without further manipulation. The yaw $\psi(t)$ can be completely determined from the curvature and velocity independently from the other two states. Once it is known, the position coordinates $[x(t)\ y(t)]^T$ can be computed.

Of special importance is the fact that two inputs control three outputs. For this reason, the system is called *underactuated*. This formula is not really a solution because the integrals have to be worked out given the inputs $[v(t)\ \kappa(t)]^T$, and often that will turn out to be **impossible** to do in closed form. In discrete time, the equations for Euler integration take the recursive form:

$$\psi_{k+1} = \psi + v_k \kappa_k \Delta t$$
$$x_{k+1} = x_k + v_k c \psi_k \Delta t$$
$$y_{k+1} = y_k + v_k s \psi_k \Delta t$$

$$(4.109)$$

This is very close now to actual computer code. Note that curvature is integrated once to get heading and heading is integrated once to get position – meaning curvature is effectively integrated twice. It will turn out for this reason that small changes in curvature can accumulate to relatively large changes in position after being passed through the integrals.

4.3.5.4 Fully Actuated WMR in 3D

Let us assume that the attitude (θ, ϕ) (not the yaw) and the altitude z are determined by the terrain contact constraints. The position (x, y) and yaw ψ are not constrained. We will assume that the vehicle does not slip. In the body frame, our basic kinematic model in the 3 dof subspace of the local terrain tangent plane would be written (based on Equation 4.105) as:

$$\frac{d}{dt}\begin{bmatrix} x(t) \\ y(t) \\ \beta(t) \end{bmatrix} = \begin{bmatrix} v_x(t)c\psi(t) - v_y(t)s\psi(t) \\ v_x(t)s\psi(t) + v_y(t)c\psi(t) \\ v(t)\kappa(t) \end{bmatrix}$$

$$(4.110)$$

where $v = \sqrt{v_x^2 + v_y^2}$. Unlike in Equation 4.105, the rates above are expressed in body coordinates – for a reason. The angular velocity $\dot{\beta}$ is the z component of the angular velocity expressed in the body frame:

$$\dot{\beta} = ({}^v\underline{\omega}{}^w_v)_z$$

The attitude changes in general at every time step, so these equations can be converted to world coordinates in each computational step and integrated there. The robot rotates, instantaneously, about *its* vertical axis in 3D and it moves, instantaneously in the direction it is headed in 3D. A diagram representing such a 3D model for abstract curvature-velocity actuation is as follows:

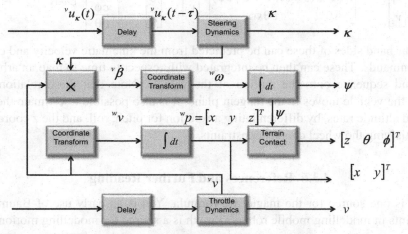

Figure 4.25 Ideal Kinematic Motion Prediction over Rigid Rolling Terrain. This velocity-driven model captures the effects of delays, actuator dynamics, terrain following, and 3D effects.

Of course, the last subchapter provided the means to convert any kind of wheel steering and drive configuration to curvature and speed, so the above model is quite general.

4.3.5.4.1 Coordinate Transforms. Two coordinate transformations are referenced in the diagrams. Based on Equation 2.56, the linear velocity in the body frame is converted to the world frame with:

$$^w\underline{v}_w^w = Rotz(\psi)Roty(\theta)Rotx(\phi)\,{}^v\underline{v}_v^w$$

$$^w\begin{bmatrix} v_x \\ v_y \\ v_z \end{bmatrix}_v^w = \begin{bmatrix} c\psi c\theta & (c\psi s\theta s\phi - s\psi c\phi) & (c\psi s\theta c\phi + s\psi s\phi) \\ s\psi c\theta & (s\psi s\theta s\phi + c\psi c\phi) & (s\psi s\theta c\phi - c\psi s\phi) \\ -s\theta & c\theta s\phi & c\theta c\phi \end{bmatrix}\,{}^v\begin{bmatrix} v_x \\ v_y \\ v_z \end{bmatrix}_v^w$$

Based on Equation 4.74, the angular velocity in the body frame is converted to the Euler angle rates with:

$$\begin{bmatrix} \dot{\phi} \\ \dot{\theta} \\ \dot{\psi} \end{bmatrix} = \begin{bmatrix} 1 & s\phi t\theta & c\phi t\theta \\ 0 & c\phi & -s\phi \\ 0 & \dfrac{s\phi}{c\theta} & \dfrac{c\phi}{c\theta} \end{bmatrix}\,{}^v\begin{bmatrix} \omega_x \\ \omega_y \\ \omega_z \end{bmatrix}_v^w$$

The assumption that the vehicle moves instantaneously in the tangent plane means that in body coordinates, the constraints are:

$$\underline{c}(\underline{x}) = {}^v\begin{bmatrix} v_z \\ \omega_x \\ \omega_y \end{bmatrix}_w^v = \underline{0} \tag{4.111}$$

This gives the result as:

$$^w\begin{bmatrix} v_x \\ v_y \\ v_z \end{bmatrix}_v^w = \begin{bmatrix} c\psi c\theta & (c\psi s\theta s\phi - s\psi c\phi) \\ s\psi c\theta & (s\psi s\theta s\phi + c\psi c\phi) \\ -s\theta & c\theta s\phi \end{bmatrix}\,{}^v\begin{bmatrix} v_x \\ v_y \end{bmatrix}_v^w \quad \begin{bmatrix} \dot{\phi} \\ \dot{\theta} \\ \dot{\psi} \end{bmatrix} = \begin{bmatrix} c\phi t\theta \\ -s\phi \\ \dfrac{c\phi}{c\theta} \end{bmatrix}\,{}^v[\omega_z]_v^w \tag{4.112}$$

The right-hand sides of these can be predicted from the kinematic velocity and curvature commands. These can then be integrated with respect to time to map an arbitrary command sequence onto the motion of the vehicle. Note that these relationships assume the vehicle moves in the tangent plane. It is also possible to estimate the attitude and altitude rates, by differentiating a solution for pitch, roll, and the z coordinate after satisfying the wheel contact constraints.

4.3.6 References and Further Reading

Bakker is one source for the magic tire formula. Yun is an early use of Baumgarte constraints in modelling mobile robots. Tarokh is a source for modelling motion over uneven terrain and Choi discusses compatibility of motion with the constraint tangent plane. Sidek is a recent source for incorporating slip into Lagrangian models.

[10] E. Bakker, H. B. Pacejka, and L. Lidner, A New Tyre Model with an Application in Vehicle Dynamics Studies, SAE paper 890087, 1989.

[11] B.J. Choi and S.V. Sreenivasan, Gross Motion Characteristics of Articulated Mobile Robots with Pure Rolling Capability on Smooth Uneven Surfaces, *IEEE Transactions on Robotics and Automation,* Vol. 15, No. 2, pp. 340–343, 1999.

[12] Naim Sidek and Nilanjan Sarkar, Dynamic Modeling and Control of Nonholonomic Mobile Robot with Lateral Slip, Third International Conference on Systems (ICONS 2008), pp. 35–40, 2008.

[13] Mahmoud Tarokh and G. J. McDermott, Kinematics Modeling and Analyses of Articulated Rovers, in *IEEE Transactions on Robotics,* Vol. 21, No. 4, pp. 539–553, 2005.

[14] X. Yun and N. Sarkar, Unified Formulation of Robotic Systems with Holonomic and Nonholonomic Constraints, *IEEE Transactions on Robotics and Automation,* Vol. 14, pp. 640–650, Aug. 1998.

4.3.7 Exercises

4.3.7.1 *Pfaffian Wheel Constraints*

Recall the basic geometry of a wheel constraint from Figure 4.6. The basic constraint equation is written in Pfaffian form in world coordinates as:

$$\left[(\hat{y}_i^w)_x \ (\hat{y}_i^w)_y \ (\hat{x}_i^w \cdot \underline{r}_i) \right] \left[{}^w v_x \ {}^w v_y \ \omega \right]^T = 0$$

where the subscript i indicates wheel i. Or, in terms of the steer angles and body frame yaw:

$$\left[-s\psi\gamma_i \ c\psi\gamma_i \ (\underline{r}_i \cdot \hat{x}_i) \right] \left[{}^w v_x \ {}^w v_y \ \omega \right]^T = 0$$

Provide a geometric interpretation for the set of all points (x, y) for which the third component of the Pfaffian weight vector (which is $(\underline{r}_i \cdot \hat{x}_i)$) for a given wheel is constant. Find an explicit formula for the set of all of such points (x, y).

4.3.7.2 *Initialization of the Generalized Bicycle*

The bicycle example did not derive the equations for the initial conditions. Consider the more general case of the generalized bicycle comprised of two wheels in arbitrary configuration. In this more general case, two wheel constraints are:

$$\begin{bmatrix} -s_1 & c_1 & r_1 \\ -s_2 & c_2 & r_2 \end{bmatrix} \begin{bmatrix} v_x \\ v_y \\ \omega \end{bmatrix} = \underline{0}$$

Where the wheel orientations in the world frame are:

$$\psi_1 = \psi + \gamma_1$$
$$\psi_2 = \psi + \gamma_2$$

Use the two constraints to eliminate the angular velocity (actually $L\omega$) and generate a constraint on the two components of linear velocity. Then, use the available degree of freedom to set the y component of linear velocity to zero, and determine the initial orientation ψ of the vehicle which is consistent with a linear velocity oriented along the x axis. Assuming that the wheel constraints are independent, confirm the formula $\psi_0 = -\mathrm{atan}[(\tan(\gamma))/2]$ used in the simulation.

4.3.7.3 Kinematic Bicycle Model

The net forces and torques acting at the cg of a bicycle model are guaranteed by the constraint equations to not cause motions that violate the constraints. Because the velocities are time integrals of the accelerations, this means that the linear and angular accelerations must act precisely in the directions of allowed linear and angular velocities.

If one is willing to assume that the net forces and torques acting at the cg are known (or controllable), then it is a very simple matter to integrate them to produce linear and angular velocities and integrate again to compute the bicycle motion without ever resorting to computing the constraint forces.

Write the two constraints for a bicycle in the body frame and determine the direction of allowed linear velocity. When the front wheel steer angle is nonzero, what is the relationship between applied forces and torques?

4.3.7.4 Differentiating Constraints Using Moving Coordinates

For the geometry of the bicycle with both wheels positioned on the x axis of the body frame, differentiate the constraint:

$$(\vec{v} + \vec{\omega} \times \vec{\rho}) \cdot \hat{y} = 0$$

with respect to time using moving coordinate systems to show that:

$$\vec{a} \cdot \hat{y} + \alpha\rho - \omega(\vec{v} + \vec{\omega} \times \vec{\rho}) = 0$$

Where $\vec{a}$ is the linear acceleration and α is the angular acceleration. Assume no steer rate. Compare the result to Equation 4.98.

4.3.7.5 Basic Terrain Following

A simple way to avoid the issue of overconstraint in terrain contact is to average the roll of the front wheels with the rear and to average the pitch of the left wheels with the right. Write out the equations based on known elevations of the terrain under the wheels.

4.4 Aspects of Linear Systems Theory

Although manipulators can often be usefully modelled by (algebraic) kinematic equations, wheeled mobile robots are best modelled by nonlinear differential equations.

Furthermore, the perturbative dynamics of such models apply to odometry error propagation. For these reasons, we need to review some concepts from systems theory.

4.4.1 Linear Time Invariant Systems

Many systems of interest behave in a manner which is described by a linear time invariant ordinary differential equation (ODE) thus:

$$\frac{d^{(n)}y}{dt^n} + a_{n-1}\frac{d^{(n-1)}y}{dt^{n-1}} + \ldots + a_1\frac{d}{dt}(y) + a_0 y = u(t) \tag{4.113}$$

The main thing to note about such an equation is that it establishes a relationship between $y(t)$ and its time derivatives. Even in the case when $u(t)$ is not present, the fact that $y(t)$ has a certain value at one time possibly means that its time derivative is nonzero – which means that it will be in a different state in a moment, for which a different state derivative may apply. This equation therefore describes a system that is potentially in motion for all time.

We call $u(t)$ the *forcing function*, the *input*, or the *control* depending on the context. The casting of the forcing function as an "input" in differential equations is the viewpoint of control theory. In the engineering discipline of controls, we presume that we have control over some of the quantities that govern system behavior. With the addition of these inputs, such systems are referred to as *forced* systems, although the inputs can be any physical quantity – they are not restricted to just forces.

A system that changes over time like this is called *dynamical* and there are many instances from physics that will be familiar to most readers. However, we will investigate them initially from a more abstract perspective.

4.4.1.1 First Order System

Perhaps the simplest dynamical system is the first-order system whose behavior is governed by:

$$\tau\frac{dy}{dt} + y = u(t) \tag{4.114}$$

Such a system is known as a *first-order system*, a *first-order filter*, or a *first-order lag*. The constant τ is known as the *time constant*. It is very illuminating and useful to approximate the ODE by a difference equation:

$$\frac{\tau}{\Delta t}(y_{k+1} - y_k) + y_{k+1} = u_{k+1}$$

Rewriting:

$$y_{k+1} = y_k + \frac{\Delta t}{\tau}(u_{k+1} - y_{k+1})$$

Note that this takes perhaps one line of code to turn into a computer program in almost any language. The result means that the output at the next time step is increased by a fraction of the distance-to-go (i.e., the difference between the input and the output). The system continues to move toward the input reference at a rate proportional to the remaining difference. It behaves correctly for changing inputs.

4.4.1.2 Step Response

Although a solution can be computed for an arbitrary input, it is useful to describe the behavior for a few illustrative cases in order to compare different systems to each other for standard inputs. Two such solutions are the *impulse response* to a shock at $t = 0$ and the *step response* to a constant input applied for $t \geq 0$.

The above system (Equation 4.114) can be solved in closed form using the theory of linear ordinary differential equations with constant coefficients. Because any solution to the unforced system (i.e., with $u(t) = 0$) can be added to a solution to the forced system (i.e., with $u(t) \neq 0$) to create a new solution, the general solution is the sum of the solutions to each case.

For the unforced case, we need a solution that preserves its form under differentiation in order for a weighted sum of its derivatives to vanish. Therefore, because exponentials have this characteristic, one assumes a solution of the form:

$$y(t) = e^{st} \tag{4.115}$$

for an unknown constant s. Substituting this into Equation 4.114 produces:

$$e^{st}(\tau s + 1) = 0 \tag{4.116}$$

We see that the roots of the *characteristic equation* $\tau s + 1 = 0$ play a central role. The root in this case is $s = -1/\tau$, so the unforced solution is of the form:

$$y(t) = ae^{-t/\tau} \tag{4.117}$$

where a is a coefficient whose value can be determined by considering the initial conditions.

For the forced solution, we need a function that is similar in form to $u(t)$. For a step input, $u(t)$ is the constant u_{ss} (ss for steady state), then a solution of the form $y(t) = y_{ss}$ (also a constant) also satisfies the ODE.

A complete solution proceeds by assuming a solution of the form:

$$y(t) = ae^{-t/\tau} + y_{ss}$$

If the system starts at $y(0) = 0$ then we have $a = -y_{ss}$ so the final solution is:

$$y(t) = y_{ss}(1 - e^{-t/\tau})$$

Now an interpretation for the time constant is available. When $t = \tau$ the system has moved a fraction of $1 - 1/e$ or 63% of the way to the terminal state.

Note briefly that if $\tau < 0$ in Equation 4.114, then the root $s = -1/\tau$ is positive. In that case, Equation 4.117 implies that the output will increase exponentially. Such a system is called *unstable*.

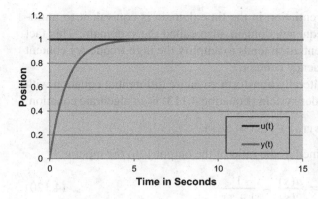

Figure 4.26 First-Order   Step Response. The system approaches the desired terminal state asymptotically.

4.4.1.3 Laplace Transform

The Laplace transform is an extremely powerful tool for analyzing dynamical systems. For the arbitrary function of time $y(t)$, the transform, denoted $y(s)$ is defined as:

$$y(s) = \mathcal{L}[y(t)] = \int_0^\infty e^{-st}y(t)dt \qquad (4.118)$$

The variable $s = \sigma + j\omega$ is a complex number and the kernel function e^{-st} is a damped sinusoid because:

$$e^{-st} = e^{-\sigma t}e^{-j\omega t} = e^{-\sigma t}[\cos(\omega t) - j\sin(\omega t)]$$

For a particular value of s, the transform is computing the projection (function dot product) of $y(t)$ with a damped sinusoid, and $y(s)$ encodes the dot product for every value of s.

In practice, one rarely computes this integral. Instead, the transforms (and their inverses) for all commonly encountered functions are available in tables, so one merely looks them up. Because the integral (as well as multiplication by a scalar) of a vector and a matrix are defined, the Laplace transform of a vector and a matrix are defined as expected. For a vector:

$$\underline{y}(s) = \mathcal{L}[\underline{y}(t)] = \int_0^\infty e^{-st}\underline{y}(t)dt$$

4.4.1.4 Transfer Functions

For our purpose, the most valuable property of the Laplace transform is its capacity to convert various compositions of dynamical systems into products of polynomials from which the dominant behavior of a system can be extracted easily. This property emerges from the following property of the transform:

$$\mathcal{L}[\dot{y}(t)] = s\mathcal{L}[y(t)] - y(0) = sy(s) - y(0) \qquad (4.119)$$

where $y(0)$ means the initial condition on y when $t = 0$ rather than when $s = 0$. It is traditional to ignore this initial condition in the transfer function defined below so this permits our abuse of notation where a lowercase y is used for both the time and Laplace domain.

According to this result, differentiation in the time domain is equivalent to multiplication by s in the complex frequency domain, also called the s, domain. This fact also encodes the result that differentiation tends to amplify the high frequency content of signals more than the low frequency content.

Using this result, we can now literally transform an entire differential equation with ease. The transform of our first-order system (Equation 4.113) is an algebraic equation:

$$\tau s y(s) + y(s) = u(s)$$

The transfer function $T(s)$ is defined as the ratio of the output y to the input u:

$$T(s) = \frac{u(s)}{y(s)} = \frac{1}{1 + \tau s} \tag{4.120}$$

Note particularly that the *characteristic polynomial* has appeared in the denominator of the transfer function. It is easy to show that it always will. It is also easy to see that an n-th order ODE will generate an n-th order characteristic polynomial and it will therefore have n roots. The roots of the characteristic polynomial are called the *poles* of the system. It can be shown that the associated system is unstable unless all roots of the characteristic polynomial have negative real parts.

4.4.1.5 Block Diagrams

It is convenient to represent either the original ODE or its Laplace transform as a block diagram like so:

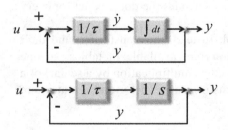

Figure 4.27 Block Diagram for a First-Order System. This type of diagram is a standard tool in dynamical systems analysis and design. The upper one is in the time domain and the lower in the s domain.

Note how the diagram was cleverly drawn with u as the input and y as the output and how $\dot{y}$ is computed from y per the differential equation and then integrated to produce y again. This feedback loop is intrinsic to the differential equation because the state and its derivatives are explicitly related to each other. Wherever $\dot{y}$ occurs it is integrated and fed to wherever y is needed.

We have a special interest in a block diagram of the following form:

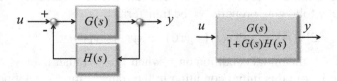

Figure 4.28 Block Diagram Algebra. The right diagram is equivalent to the left.

As the figure suggests, the diagram can be simplified to eliminate the closed loop. The output state can be written as:

$$y(s) = G(s)(u(s) - H(s)y(s))$$

$$y(s)(1 + G(s)H(s)) = G(s)u(s)$$

Therefore, the transfer function is:

$$T(s) = \frac{G(s)}{1 + G(s)H(s)}$$

Note especially that this formula, applied to Figure 4.28 with $G(s) = 1/\tau s$ and $H(s) = 1$, reproduces Equation 4.120, so the equivalent block diagram for a first order system is Figure 4.29:

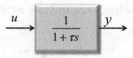

Figure 4.29 Equivalent Block Diagram for a First-Order System. This diagram is equivalent to the one in Figure 4.27.

4.4.1.6 Frequency Response

The *frequency response* is the *gain* of the transfer function as a function of frequency. To compute it, we relate the magnitude $|T(\omega)|$ of the transfer function to the real frequency ω by substituting $s = j\omega$ and then compute its magnitude:

$$T(j\omega) = \frac{u(j\omega)}{y(j\omega)} = \frac{1}{1 + \tau(j\omega)}$$

$$|T(j\omega)| = \frac{1}{|1 + \tau(j\omega)|} = \frac{1}{\sqrt{1 + (\tau\omega)^2}}$$

The power implied by this magnitude is plotted below in Figure 4.30. Plotting in units of dB (decibels) corresponds to taking the base 10 logarithm of amplitude and multiplying by 20. Note that at a frequency of $1/\tau$, the output has fallen by 3 dB (i.e., to half) of its maximum value. The gain also falls off at its maximum rate beyond this point.

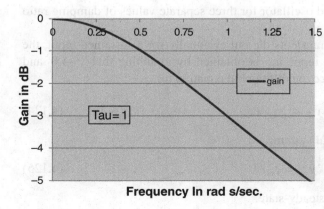

Figure 4.30 Frequency Response a First-Order System. This type of diagram is also a standard tool in dynamical systems analysis and design. The gain is typically quoted in decibels.

4.4.1.7 The Second-Order System

Perhaps the simplest mechanical system that is just complicated enough to exhibit all interesting behaviors for our purpose is the damped mass-spring system. Suppose a mass is attached to a wall via a spring and a damper as shown in Figure 4.31.

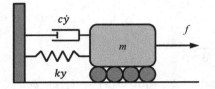

Figure 4.31 A Damped Mass-Spring System. The applied force is opposed by the spring and the damper.

Let an external force f be applied in the positive sense. Given that the spring exerts an opposing force proportional to the deflection y and the damper exerts an opposing force proportional to the deflection rate $\dot{y}$, we can write Newton's second law as follows:

$$m\ddot{y} = f - c\dot{y} - ky \tag{4.121}$$

where c is the *damping coefficient* and k is the *spring constant*. This is a second-order linear differential equation also known simply as a *second-order system*. It can be rewritten in a more familiar form as:

$$\ddot{y} + \frac{c}{m}\dot{y} + \frac{k}{m}y = \frac{f}{m} \tag{4.122}$$

In a context more general than mechanics, a second order system is also known as a *damped oscillator* and written as:

$$\ddot{y} + 2\zeta\omega_0\dot{y} + \omega_0^2 y = u(t) \tag{4.123}$$

where ζ is called the *damping ratio* and ω_0 is called the *natural frequency*.

4.4.1.8 Step Response

The step response of the damped oscillator for three separate values of damping ratio is shown below in Figure 4.32.

On the assumption that the transients die out eventually for a sustained input, the output corresponding to a step input u_{ss} is obtained by assuming that $\ddot{y} \to 0$ and $\dot{y} \to 0$. These assumptions reduce the differential equation to:

$$y_{ss} = u_{ss}/\omega_0^2 \tag{4.124}$$

Or, for the equivalent mechanical system:

$$y_{ss} = f_{ss}/k \tag{4.125}$$

where the subscript ss denotes steady-state.

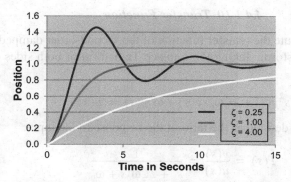

Figure 4.32 Step Response of Second-Order System. The natural frequency ω_0 controls the frequency of oscillation when the system is underdamped $\zeta < 1$. The overdamped system $\zeta > 1$ does not oscillate but its rise time is slow. The critically damped system $\zeta = 1$ rises rapidly and does not oscillate.

4.4.1.9 Closed Form Solution to the Second-Order System

The second-order system can be solved in closed form using the theory of linear ordinary differential equations with constant coefficients. For the unforced case, one assumes a solution of the form:

$$y(t) = e^{st} \tag{4.126}$$

for an unknown constant s. Substituting this into Equation 4.123 produces:

$$e^{st}(s^2 + 2\zeta\omega_0 s + \omega_0^2) = 0 \tag{4.127}$$

Once again, we see that the roots of the *characteristic equation* $(s^2 + 2\zeta\omega_0 s + \omega_0^2)$ play a central role. The two roots are given by the quadratic equation:

$$s = \frac{-2\zeta\omega_0 \pm \sqrt{4\zeta^2\omega_0^2 - 4\omega_0^2}}{2} = -\zeta\omega_0 \pm \omega_0\sqrt{(\zeta^2 - 1)} \tag{4.128}$$

Or, most simply:

$$s = \omega_0(-\zeta \pm \sqrt{\zeta^2 - 1}) \tag{4.129}$$

The roots are complex conjugate pairs when $\zeta^2 < 1$ and, under these conditions, the system oscillates. The critical damping condition $\zeta = 1$ corresponds to a double real root. This occurs when the imaginary components of the roots disappear, which is to say when the *discriminant* $\zeta^2 - 1$ vanishes.

A complete solution proceeds by assuming a solution of the form:

$$y(t) = ae^{s_1 t} + be^{s_2 t}$$

and solving for the constants a and b that satisfy the initial conditions.

A solution to the forced system can then be found by assuming a solution of similar form to $u(t)$. Clearly, Equation 4.124 is a solution to the forced system. In Figure 4.32, the behavior is clearly a sum of both of these solutions. The oscillations eventually die out and the system stabilizes at the steady-state position.

4.4.1.10 Transfer Function

It is illustrative to compute the transfer function of the second-order damped oscillator using the Laplace Transform. Taking the Laplace Transform of both sides of the differential equation:

$$s^2 y(s) + 2\zeta\omega_0 s y(s) + \omega_0^2 y(s) = u(s)$$

The transfer function is defined as the ratio of the response to the input:

$$T(s) = \frac{y(s)}{u(s)} = \frac{1}{s^2 + 2\zeta\omega_0 s + \omega_0^2}$$

Again the characteristic equation has appeared in the denominator of the transfer function.

4.4.1.11 Solution to the Linear State Equations: Scalar Case

So far, the differential equations encountered have had constant coefficients. Cases with time varying coefficients are also very important. For this section, the output variable y will be written as x for comparison with a later result. Consider the scalar, linear, time varying differential equation:

$$\dot{x}(t) = f(t)x(t) + g(t)u(t)$$

The general solution can be derived by defining the integrating function:

$$\phi(t, t_0) = \exp\left[\int_{t_0}^{t} f(\tau)d\tau\right] \tag{4.130}$$

and using it in the general solution as follows:

$$x(t) = \phi(t, t_0)x(t_0) + \int_{t_0}^{t} \phi(t, \tau)g(\tau)u(\tau)d\tau \tag{4.131}$$

The reader might have seen this result in the form:

$$\dot{x}(t) = f(t)x(t) + g(t) \quad p(t) = e^{\int f(\tau)d\tau} \quad x(t) = \int p(t)g(t)dt \tag{4.132}$$

When $f(\tau)$ is constant (independent of time), then:

$$\phi(t, t_0) = \exp[f \cdot (t - t_0)] = e^{f \cdot (t - t_0)}$$

which is the ordinary exponential function.

4.4.2 State Space Representation of Linear Dynamical Systems

Recall the system representation in terms of a vector differential equation that was used earlier for numerical integration algorithms:

$$\dot{\underline{x}}(t) = \underline{f}(\underline{x}(t), \underline{u}(t), t) \tag{4.133}$$

This form will be shown to be more general than the LTI ODE but it includes it as a special case. This form is known as the *state space* representation of the system. Formally, the *state* of a system is a minimal set of variables that permit the prediction of future state given the inputs and time. Informally, the elements of the state are the same as the elements of the initial conditions needed to solve the governing differential equations. If you need to know the initial velocity to predict system behavior, then velocity is a state. The state space representation turns out to be particularly powerful and we will use it throughout the book.

4.4.2.1 Conversion of an ODE to State Space

For the moment, consider the state space representation in its linear form. It is a straightforward matter to convert an LTI ODE of any order to state space form. Recall that initial conditions are required for all $n - 1$ derivatives including 0, so this is a strong hint that the state space form is simply a vector of all of the derivatives, but the highest, in the equation. For brevity, consider the second-order case:

$$\frac{d^2 y}{dt^2} + a_1 \frac{dy}{dt} + a_0 y = u(t)$$

Choose the state variables to be:

$$x_1(t) = y(t)$$
$$x_2(t) = \dot{y}(t) = \dot{x}_1(t)$$

Now, rewrite the second of these and the original ODE in the following form:

$$\dot{x}_1(t) = x_2(t)$$
$$\dot{x}_2(t) = -a_1 x_2(t) - a_0 x_1(t) + u(t)$$

This can be written in the vector form:

$$\frac{d}{dt} \begin{bmatrix} x_1 \\ x_2 \end{bmatrix} = \begin{bmatrix} 0 & 1 \\ -a_0 & -a_1 \end{bmatrix} \begin{bmatrix} x_1 \\ x_2 \end{bmatrix} + \begin{bmatrix} 0 \\ 1 \end{bmatrix} u(t) \tag{4.134}$$

Which is of the form:

$$\dot{x}(t) = Fx(t) + Gu(t)$$

The general case for arbitrary n can be derived similarly using the above process. Note that an LTI ODE will always produce a sparse F matrix with all of the original coefficients arranged in the bottom row, so an arbitrary F matrix can represent something more general than this.

4.4.2.2 General Linear Dynamical Systems

The continuous-time, linear, lumped-parameter dynamical system is one of the most generally useful representations of applied mathematics. Although not as expressive as the nonlinear case, the linear system has the advantage that general solutions exist. It is used to represent some real or imagined process whose behavior can be captured in a time-varying vector.

Many variations on the theme are used, but for the moment, we will be interested in the form that also has an output vector $y(t)$ that is derived from the state in a linear way. In continuous time, this representation is of the form:

$$\dot{\underline{x}}(t) = F(t)\underline{x}(t) + G(t)\underline{u}(t)$$
$$\underline{y}(t) = H(t)\underline{x}(t) + M(t)\underline{u}(t)$$

(4.135)

This system can be represented with a block a diagram like Figure 4.33.

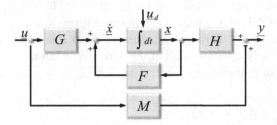

Figure 4.33 State Space Model. Such a block diagram represents the equations describing the behavior of a linear multivariable dynamical system.

These equations will be called the linear *state equations*. Note that the first is a differential equation and the second is not. The process or system is described by the time varying *state* $\underline{x}(t)$ of the system. The matrix $F(t)$, the *system dynamics matrix*, determines the unforced response of the system. The input vector $\underline{u}(t)$ captures any forcing functions that are mapped onto the state vector through the *control (or input) distribution matrix* $G(t)$.

The second equation comes into play more often for us because we will be interested in the process by which various sensory devices can be used to observe the system state. In that case, the *output vector* $y(t)$ may be denoted as the measurement vector $\underline{z}(t)$. It captures the information that is obtained from the sensors and the *measurement matrix* $H(t)$ models the process by which the measurements are related to the underlying state $\underline{x}(t)$. On occasion, it will be necessary to model the manner by which the input $\underline{u}(t)$ is also observed indirectly through the transformation $M(t)$.

The special case where the coefficient matrices are not time dependent is the theoretically important "constant coefficient" case. Note that the equations are still linear even in the time dependent case given above, because the matrices do not depend on the state.

4.4.2.3 Solution to the Linear State Equations: Vector Case

Consider now the problem of deriving an explicit solution to the linear state equations:

$$\dot{\underline{x}}(t) = F(t)\underline{x}(t) + G(t)\underline{u}(t)$$

(4.136)

Consider a time varying matrix function, called the *transition matrix*, defined as the matrix direct mapping (or *transition*) of states from one time τ to any other time t:

$$\underline{x}(t) = \Phi(t, \tau)\underline{x}(\tau)$$

Another property, often considered the definition, is that it, and hence all of its columns, satisfies the unforced state equation:

$$\frac{d}{dt}\Phi(t, \tau) = F(t)\Phi(t, \tau) \quad \Phi(t, t) = I \tag{4.137}$$

Often, the transition matrix depends only on the time difference $t - \tau$ rather than the specific times involved. In the constant coefficient case, the transition matrix takes the elegant form of the exponential of the constant dynamics matrix:

$$\Phi(t, \tau) = e^{F(t - \tau)} \tag{4.138}$$

Note that if the time difference is small enough (i.e., $t - \tau = \Delta t$), then we may be able to assume that $F(t - \tau)$ is approximately constant and truncate a Taylor series at the linear term:

$$\Phi(t, \tau) \approx I + F\Delta t \tag{4.139}$$

For longer time differences, writing a few terms of the exponential series often generates recognizable series in each element of the matrix partial sum, and the general form for each term can be generated by inspection. At other times, higher powers of F conveniently vanish anyway.

In the time dependent coefficient case, $\Phi(t, \tau)$ is known to exist but it may not be easy to find. One special case is important though. The matrix equivalent of Equation 4.130 is:

$$\Psi(t, \tau) = \exp\left(\int_{\tau}^{t} F(\tau)d\tau\right) \tag{4.140}$$

When this matrix commutes with the dynamics matrix (its own derivative):

$$\Psi(t, \tau)F(t) = F(t)\Psi(t, \tau)$$

then it is the transition matrix for $F(t)$. It will also be convenient to define another special matrix product, that we will call the *input transition matrix*:

$$\Gamma(t, \tau) = \Phi(t, \tau)G(\tau)$$

Knowing the transition matrix is tantamount to solving the linear system because the solution to the general linear, time varying system is:

$$\underline{x}(t) = \Phi(t, t_0)\underline{x}(t_0) + \int_{t_0}^{t}\Gamma(t, \tau)\underline{u}(\tau)d\tau \tag{4.141}$$

Spotlight 4.10 Vector Superposition Integral.

General solution to the linear dynamical system.

Compare this with Equation 4.131. Because G is already known, when $\Phi(t, \tau)$ is found, this integral completely describes the behavior of the system. In other texts, this equation is called the *matrix superposition integral*. We will call it the *vector superposition integral* in order to clarify its relationship to an equivalent integral that will be used later for covariance matrices.

4.4.2.4 Stability

Basic stability is a property of the unforced system and hence, a property of $F(t)$. For the time invariant autonomous system $\dot{x}(t) = Fx(t)$, it is intuitive that if any eigenvalue λ is positive, then its eigenvector e is a direction with an unfortunate property. If $x(t) = ke$ for some $k > 0$, then $\dot{x}(t) = \lambda x(t)$ by the definition of an eigenvector. So if the state vector is ever directed along this eigenvector, it will be trapped in that direction and grow (or shrink) in magnitude indefinitely depending on the sign of the eigenvalue. A time invariant system with positive eigenvalues is clearly unstable. Conversely, the basic stability condition is the condition that all eigenvalues must have negative real parts.

4.4.2.4.1 Stability in the Sense of Lyapunov. A general definition of stability that applies to linear and nonlinear systems applies to the state at the origin. The origin $x(t_1) = 0$ is *stable in the sense of Lyapunov* if for any t_1 and every real number $\varepsilon > 0$, we can choose some $\delta > 0$ that is as small as we please, such that if $\|x(t_1)\| < \delta$ then $\|x(t_2)\| < \varepsilon$ for all $t_2 > t_1$. In other words, $x(t_2)$ can be kept arbitrarily close to the origin provided that $x(t_1)$ can also. In even other words, for every start state, there is an envelope that the system will never exceed.

4.4.2.4.2 Effect of Transition Matrix on Stability. When we turn our attention to the time varying system where $F(t)$ depends on time, the eigenvectors will change over time as well. In this case, we can turn to the transition matrix to develop conditions for stability. The basic property of the transition matrix can be written as:

$$x(t_2) = \Phi(t_1, t_2)x(t_1)$$

Hence, it transitions the state at t_1 to the state at t_2 via matrix multiplication. Clearly if $x(t_1)$ is bounded and the norm of the transition matrix is bounded, then $x(t_2)$ will be bounded as well. The norm of the transition matrix can be no larger than the largest eigenvalue, hence:

$$\|\Phi(t_1, t_2)\| = max_i(\lambda_i)$$

It can be easily shown that if the transition matrix norm is bounded, the system is stable in the sense of Lyapunov.

4.4.2.5 Transfer Function of a Linear System

In the time invariant case, the transfer function of the linear system can be derived easily. Take the Laplace transform of Equation 4.135 when F and G do not depend on time:

$$s\,x(s) = Fx(s) + Gu(s)$$

Hence $x(s)[sI - F] = Gu(s)$ so, we can conclude $x(s) = [sI - F]^{-1}Gu(s)$. Substitute this into the Laplace transform of the output equation to yield:

$$y(s) = Hx(s) + Mu(s) = \{H[sI - F]^{-1}G + M\}u(s)$$

The transfer function is the "ratio" of output to input or more generally, the operator which, when applied to $u(s)$ will produce $y(s)$. Under such an interpretation, we have the result:

$$T(s) = H[sI - F]^{-1}G + M \qquad (4.142)$$

4.4.3 Nonlinear Dynamical Systems

Let us return now to the nonlinear case. With the addition of an output equation, the nonlinear dynamical system takes the form:

$$\dot{x}(t) = f(\underline{x}(t), \underline{u}(t), t)$$
$$\underline{y}(t) = \underline{h}(\underline{x}(t), \underline{u}(t), t)$$

4.4.3.1 Solutions Of Nonlinear Dynamical Systems

Although a lot is known about the solution to linear systems – particularly in the constant coefficient case – general results for the nonlinear case are not available. Indeed, unlike in the linear case, there is no guarantee that an explicit solution to such nonlinear differential equations exists at all. Practical numerical solutions are available, however, by direct integration of the first equation:

$$\underline{x}(t) = \underline{x}(0) + \int_0^t \underline{f}(\underline{x}(\tau), \underline{u}(\tau), \tau)d\tau \qquad (4.143)$$

Because the nonlinear case subsumes the linear one, any conclusions that apply to the above system will apply to linear systems.

4.4.3.2 Relevant Properties of Nonlinear Dynamical Systems

Mobile robot dynamics are typically nonlinear and, at times, they have some very special properties as outlined below.

4.4.3.2.1 Homogeneity. When the nonlinear dynamics satisfy:

$$\underline{f}[\underline{x}(t), k \times \underline{u}(t)] = k^n \times f[\underline{x}(t), \underline{u}(t)] \qquad (4.144)$$

for some constant k, the system is said to be homogeneous of degree n with respect to $\underline{u}(t)$. Homogeneity implies that $u(t)$ must occur inside $f(\ )$ solely in the form of a factor of its nth power:

$$\underline{f}[\underline{x}(t), \underline{u}(t)] = \underline{u}^n(t)g(\underline{x}(t)) \qquad (4.145)$$

As a result, all terms of the Taylor series of $f(\ )$ over $\underline{u}(t)$ of order less than n vanish. When they do it has important implications.

4.4.3.2.2 Drift-Free. Systems that are homogeneous to any nonzero degree with respect to their inputs are drift-free. Their *zero input response* is zero, so they can be stopped instantly by nulling the inputs:

$$\underline{u}(t) = 0 \Rightarrow \underline{\dot{x}}(t) = 0 \tag{4.146}$$

It is not necessarily the case that $f(\ )$ is independent of the states (i.e., the system has no dynamics) because the states may be multiplied by the inputs in order to create homogeneity.

4.4.3.2.3 Reversibility and Monotonicity. Systems of odd degree homogeneity are odd with respect to $\underline{u}(t)$ and hence *reversible* because they can be driven precisely back over their original trajectory by simply reversing the input signal $\underline{u}(t)$ in time.

$$\underline{u}_2(t) = -\underline{u}_1(\tau - t) \Rightarrow \underline{f}_2(t) = -\underline{f}_1(\tau - t)$$

Systems of even degree homogeneity are even with respect to $\underline{u}(t)$ and *monotone* because the sign of the state derivative is invariant under changes in the inputs.

$$\underline{u}_2(t) = -\underline{u}_1(t) \Rightarrow \underline{f}_2(t) = \underline{f}_1(t)$$

4.4.3.2.4 Regularity. Suppose a system is homogeneous with respect to a particular input $u_i(t)$ that can be written as the time rate of some other parameter such as s. Then, it can be divided by the input without creating a singularity:

$$\frac{f[\underline{x}(t), \underline{u}(t)]}{u_i(t)} = \frac{f[\underline{x}(t), \underline{u}(t)]}{(ds)/(dt)} = finite \tag{4.147}$$

In this case, a change of variable becomes possible and the system can be written in the form:

$$\frac{d}{ds}\underline{x}(s) = \tilde{f}[\underline{x}(s), \underline{u}(s)] \tag{4.148}$$

Borrowing a term from differential geometry, such well-behaved systems are referred to here as *regular*.

4.4.3.2.5 Motion Dependence. A regular system can be readily studied from a geometric perspective by analyzing the geometry of its response without regard to time. We will refer to such systems as *motion dependent*. This distinction will be important in odometry because the influence of inertially derived sensor errors (inertial navigation) continues to grow when motion stops, whereas that of sensor errors for terrain relative indications (odometry) does not.

4.4.4 Perturbative Dynamics of Nonlinear Dynamical Systems

It is generally possible to produce a "linearized" version of a nonlinear system that applies to small perturbations about a *reference trajectory* (i.e., a solution for a given input).

Let us consider again the nonlinear system:

$$\underline{\dot{x}}(t) = \underline{f}(\underline{x}(t), \underline{u}(t), t) \tag{4.149}$$

Assume that a nominal input $\underline{u}(t)$ and the associated nominal solution $\underline{x}(t)$ are known. That is, they satisfy Equation 4.149 (and can be generated numerically even for nonlinear systems). They constitute our reference trajectory. Suppose now that a solution is desired for a slightly different input.

$$\underline{u}'(t) = \underline{u}(t) + \delta\underline{u}(t)$$

We will call $\underline{u}'(t)$ the "perturbed input," and $\delta\underline{u}(t)$ the "input perturbation." These are both entire functions of time. Let us designate the solution associated with this input as follows:

$$\underline{x}'(t) = \underline{x}(t) + \delta\underline{x}(t)$$

This expression amounts to a definition of the state perturbation $\delta\underline{x}(t)$ as the difference between the perturbed and the nominal state. The time derivative of this solution is clearly the sum of the time derivatives of the nominal solution and the perturbation. This slightly different solution also, by definition, satisfies the original state equation, so we can write:

$$\underline{\dot{x}}'(t) = \underline{\dot{x}}(t) + \delta\underline{\dot{x}}(t) = \underline{f}[\underline{x}(t) + \delta\underline{x}(t), \underline{u}(t) + \delta\underline{u}(t), t]$$

An approximation for $\delta\underline{x}(t)$ will generate an approximation for $\underline{x}'(t)$. We can get this approximation from the Taylor series expansion as follows:

$$\underline{f}[\underline{x}(t) + \delta\underline{x}(t), \underline{u}(t) + \delta\underline{u}(t), t] \approx \underline{f}[\underline{x}(t), \underline{u}(t), t] + F(t)\delta\underline{x}(t) + G(t)\delta\underline{u}(t)$$

where the two new matrices are the Jacobians of $\underline{f}$ with respect to the state and input – evaluated on the nominal trajectory:

$$F(t) = \left.\frac{\partial}{\partial\underline{x}}\underline{f}\right|_{\underline{x},\underline{u}} \qquad G(t) = \left.\frac{\partial}{\partial\underline{u}}\underline{f}\right|_{\underline{x},\underline{u}}$$

At this point, we have:

$$\underline{\dot{x}}(t) + \delta\underline{\dot{x}}(t) = \underline{f}(\underline{x}(t), \underline{u}(t), t) + F(t)\delta\underline{x}(t) + G(t)\delta\underline{u}(t)$$

Finally, by cancelling out the original state equation, a linear system is produced that approximates the behavior of the perturbation.

$$\delta\underline{\dot{x}}(t) = F(t)\delta\underline{x}(t) + G(t)\delta\underline{u}(t) \qquad (4.150)$$

Spotlight 4.11 Linear Perturbation Equation.

Expresses first-order dynamic behavior of systematic error for linear and nonlinear dynamical systems.

A transition matrix for the linearized dynamics must exist because it is linear, so the first order propagation of systematic error in a dynamical system is a solved problem once the transition matrix is computed. All of the solution techniques for linear systems, including Equation 4.141, can now be applied to determine the behavior of this perturbation:

$$\delta \underline{x}(t) = \Phi(t, t_0)\delta \underline{x}(t_0) + \int_{t_0}^{t} \Gamma(t, \tau)\delta \underline{u}(\tau)d\tau \qquad (4.151)$$

Spotlight 4.12 Vector Superposition Integral.

General solution for the first-order dynamic behavior of systematic error for linear and linearized dynamical systems.

By the same technique, the output equation:

$$\underline{y}(t) = \underline{h}(\underline{x}(t), \underline{u}(t), t)$$

can be linearized to produce:

$$\delta \underline{y}(t) = H(t)\delta \underline{x}(t) + M(t)\delta \underline{u}(t)$$

Where:

$$H(t) = \frac{\partial}{\partial \underline{x}}\underline{h}\bigg|_{\underline{x},\,\underline{u}} \qquad\qquad M(t) = \frac{\partial}{\partial \underline{u}}\underline{h}\bigg|_{\underline{x},\,\underline{u}}$$

4.4.4.1 Example: Fully Actuated WMR in the Plane

Recall that the instantaneous velocity transform for a fully actuated WMR in the plane is given by:

$$\frac{d}{dt}\begin{bmatrix} x(t) \\ y(t) \\ \theta(t) \end{bmatrix} = \begin{bmatrix} c\theta(t) & -s\theta(t) & 0 \\ s\theta(t) & c\theta(t) & 0 \\ 0 & 0 & 1 \end{bmatrix}\begin{bmatrix} V_x(t) \\ V_y(t) \\ \omega(t) \end{bmatrix} \qquad (4.152)$$

where $\theta(t)$ is the heading or yaw. The state vector is $\underline{x}(t) = [x(t)\ y(t)\ \theta(t)]^T$ and the input vector $\underline{u}(t) = [V_x(t)\ V_y(t)\ \omega(t)]^T$ is expressed in the body frame.

The state Jacobian is:

$$F(t) = \frac{\partial \underline{\dot{x}}}{\partial \underline{x}} = \begin{bmatrix} 0 & 0 & -[s\theta(t)V_x(t) + c\theta(t)V_y(t)] \\ 0 & 0 & [c\theta(t)V_x(t) - s\theta(t)V_y(t)] \\ 0 & 0 & 0 \end{bmatrix} = \begin{bmatrix} 0 & 0 & -\dot{y}(t) \\ 0 & 0 & \dot{x}(t) \\ 0 & 0 & 0 \end{bmatrix}$$

The input Jacobian is:

$$G(t) = \frac{\partial \underline{\dot{x}}}{\partial \underline{u}} = \begin{bmatrix} c\theta(t) & -s\theta(t) & 0 \\ s\theta(t) & c\theta(t) & 0 \\ 0 & 0 & 1 \end{bmatrix}$$

Define the matrix integral:

$$\chi(t, \tau) = \int_\tau^t F(\tau)d\tau = \int_\tau^t \begin{bmatrix} 0 & 0 & -\dot{y}(t) \\ 0 & 0 & \dot{x}(t) \\ 0 & 0 & 0 \end{bmatrix} d\tau = \begin{bmatrix} 0 & 0 & -\Delta[y(t, \tau)] \\ 0 & 0 & \Delta[x(t, \tau)] \\ 0 & 0 & 0 \end{bmatrix}$$

where we have defined notation for the *history point displacements*:

$$\Delta x(t, \tau) = [x(t) - x(\tau)] \qquad \Delta y(t, \tau) = [y(t) - y(\tau)]$$

These provide the displacements from a point on the trajectory at time τ to the point at time t. Based on $\chi(t, \tau)$, the integrating function is:

$$\Psi(t, \tau) = \exp\left(\int_\tau^t F(\tau)d\tau\right) = \exp\left(\begin{bmatrix} 0 & 0 & -\Delta[y(t, \tau)] \\ 0 & 0 & \Delta[x(t, \tau)] \\ 0 & 0 & 0 \end{bmatrix}\right) = \begin{bmatrix} 1 & 0 & -\Delta y(t, \tau) \\ 0 & 1 & \Delta x(t, \tau) \\ 0 & 0 & 1 \end{bmatrix} \tag{4.153}$$

This simplification occurs because:

$$\exp\chi = I + \chi + \frac{\chi^2}{2} + \dots$$

and all powers of χ beyond the first vanish. χ is said to be *nilpotent* to degree 2 and this fact is related to the fact that Equation 4.152 is drift-free. Finally, note that $\Psi F = F\Psi = F$, which establishes that:

$$\Psi(t, \tau) = \Phi(t, \tau)$$

is the transition matrix of the linear system. The *input transition matrix* is:

$$\Gamma(t, \tau) = \Phi(t, \tau)G(\tau) = \begin{bmatrix} c\theta(t) & -s\theta(t) & -\Delta y(t, \tau) \\ s\theta(t) & c\theta(t) & \Delta x(t, \tau) \\ 0 & 0 & 1 \end{bmatrix} \tag{4.154}$$

This fact allows us to write immediately from Equation 4.141:

$$\delta\underline{x}(t) = \begin{bmatrix} 1 & 0 & -y(t_0) \\ 0 & 1 & x(t_0) \\ 0 & 0 & 1 \end{bmatrix} \delta\underline{x}(t_0) + \int_{t_0}^t \begin{bmatrix} c\theta(t) & -s\theta(t) & -\Delta y(t, \tau) \\ s\theta(t) & c\theta(t) & \Delta x(t, \tau) \\ 0 & 0 & 1 \end{bmatrix} \delta\underline{u}(\tau)d\tau \tag{4.155}$$

Spotlight 4.13 Perturbation Dynamics for Generic Planar Vehicle.

General solution for the state perturbation trajectory $\delta\underline{x}(t)$, which occurs in response to the input perturbation trajectory $\delta\underline{u}(t)$.

The matrices are computed from the elements of the reference trajectory $\underline{x}(t)$, so one must first solve the nonlinear system for the reference trajectory before the perturbation trajectory can be computed.

4.4.5 References and Further Reading

Thornton is one of many classical mechanics texts that treats the damped oscillator. Luenberger is a very readable introduction to linear systems. Brogan covers the material on the transition matrix that is used here. Gajic and many Kalman filter texts cover linearization as it is presented here.

[15] Stephen T. Thornton, and Jerry B. Marion, *Classical Dynamics of Particles and Systems,* Brooks/Cole, 2004.
[16] William L. Brogan, *Modern Control Theory,* Prentice Hall, 1991.
[17] Zoran Gajic, *Linear Dynamic Systems and Signals,* Prentice Hall, 2003.
[18] David G. Luenberger, *Introduction to Dynamic Systems: Theory, Models, & Applications,* Wiley, 1979.

4.4.6 Exercises

4.4.6.1 Simulator For Dynamical Systems

It is worth the time of anyone who has not done it before to write a simple simulation program to integrate Equation 4.123 for a step input to reproduce Figure 4.32. Write a finite difference approximation to the differential equation. Using your favorite spreadsheet or programming language, integrate it for zero initial conditions and a step input for the three values of damping ratio.

4.4.6.2 Damped Oscillator

For the damped oscillator in Equation 4.123:
 (i) Based on the content in Section 4.4.2.1, write the state space form of the differential equation. It will involve 2×2 matrices.
 (ii) The basic stability condition that the real parts of all eigenvalues be negative sounds very similar to the condition on the poles of the transfer function, and for good reason. Using the state space representation of the damped oscillator that you just developed, show that the eigenvalues of the dynamics matrix F must be the same as the poles of the system.

4.4.6.3 Transition Matrix

Consider the homogeneous linear state space system:

$$\dot{\underline{x}}(t) = F\underline{x}(t)$$

Note that when $\underline{x}(t) \in \mathfrak{R}^n$, all possible initial conditions can be written as a weighted sum of any n linearly independent vectors:

$$\underline{x}(t_0) = a\underline{x}_1(t_0) + b\underline{x}_2(t_0) + c\underline{x}_3(t_0) + \ldots = U(t_0)\begin{bmatrix} a & b & c & \ldots \end{bmatrix}^T$$

where $U(t_0)$ is the matrix whose columns are the n linearly independent vectors. If $\underline{x}_i(t)$ is the solution corresponding to $\underline{x}_i(t_0)$, show that any two solution vectors to the system are related by a matrix

$$\underline{x}(t) = \Phi(t, t_0)\underline{x}(t_0)$$

4.4.6.4 Perturbative Dynamics

The common pendulum is an unforced second-order nonlinear dynamical system described by:

$$\frac{d^2 x}{dt^2} = \frac{g}{l}\sin(x)$$

where x is the angle the pendulum makes with the vertical, g is the acceleration due to gravity, and l is the length of the pendulum. Transform this system to a state space nonlinear system of order 2. Set $g = l = 10$. Integrate the nonlinear system with a time step of 0.01 seconds from initial conditions of $x(t_0) = 1$ and $\dot{x}(t_0) = 0$. Next perturb the initial conditions by adding $\delta x = 0.1$ to the initial angle, resolve the system and plot the difference between the two solutions. Finally, derive the linearized error dynamics:

$$\delta\dot{\underline{x}} = F(\underline{x})\delta\underline{x}$$

Solve this system and show that it approximates the difference between the two solutions extremely well.

4.5 Predictive Modeling and System Identification

Mobile robots must use predictive models in order to predict the consequences of candidate actions. Generally, many processes must be modelled. The propagation of information through the system must be modelled because it takes time to perceive, think, and act, and often the robot is moving during all of those stages.

The physics of executing the chosen action must also be modelled because the mapping from input to response is complicated and the final result of interest (e.g. coming to a stop) may occur many seconds into the future after the command has been executed fully. Ultimately, the environment must react and exert forces back on the vehicle to cause it alter its trajectory. Whether and to what degree the environment will do that depends on many factors.

4.5.1 Braking

The braking performance of a vehicle will depend on the terrain and the inputs. Of course, sometimes a vehicle may brake because it is time to come to a stop, or to change direction, and braking can be needed to slow down on a slope. Braking can also be a last resort response indicating that something unexpected or unwanted has occurred. Potential reasons for this situation may be failure to recognize an obstacle until it was too late, dynamic obstacles that moved onto the path, lead vehicles that have slowed unexpectedly, or failure to follow the intended trajectory accurately enough.

4.5.1.1 Braking to Avoid Collision

The stopping distance in a braking maneuver depends on initial speed, terrain material, and slope. A vehicle must look for obstacles beyond the stopping distance in order to have enough space to stop before hitting them. Effective braking to avoid a collision therefore requires precise knowledge of the time and space required to stop.

Consider the vehicle to be moving at some known velocity V at the point where the brakes are applied. Assume that the brakes are applied instantly, that propulsive forces are removed instantly, and the vehicle enters a sliding mode of friction. We will assume that the vehicle is translating, so that a particle model will suffice.

On a free body diagram (Figure 4.34) the external forces are the forces of gravity and friction. If θ is the instantaneous pitch angle, and there is no roll, the magnitude of the normal force is given by $F_n = mgc\theta$, so the frictional force is:

$$f = \mu_s F_n = \mu_s mgc\theta \qquad (4.156)$$

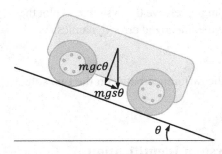

Figure 4.34 Free Body Diagram for a Braking Car. Vehicle going downhill. Weight acts downward and friction acts tangentially.

Note particularly that the normal and frictional forces are coupled, so a heavier vehicle generates a higher friction force. The component of gravity $F_t = mgs\theta$ also acts to induce motion.

4.5.1.2 Stopping Distance on Slopes

To compute the stopping distance, let the work done by the external forces equal the initial kinetic energy. Let the initial velocity be v. Recall that work is simply the product of force and distance and for a fixed pitch angle the forces are evidently constant. Both the downward component of gravity and friction do work.

$$\frac{1}{2}mv^2 = (\mu_s mgc\theta - mgs\theta)s_{brake} \qquad (4.157)$$

Solving:

$$s_{brake} = \frac{v^2}{2g(\mu_s c\theta - s\theta)} = \frac{v^2}{2\mu_{eff}g} \qquad (4.158)$$

Considering the level ground case when $\theta = 0$, the quantity in brackets in the denominator acts as an "effective" coefficient of friction:

$$\mu_{eff} = (\mu_s c\theta - s\theta) \qquad (4.159)$$

As the downslope (positive pitch) angle increases, braking distance increases dramatically (Figure 4.35). Clearly, there is a critical angle beyond which gravity overcomes friction. This is when $\mu_s c\theta - s\theta = 0$. That is, when:

$$\tan\theta = \mu_s \qquad (4.160)$$

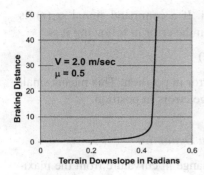

Figure 4.35 Stopping Distance Versus Slope. A critical angle exists beyond which stopping is impossible.

For the parameters used above, this critical angle is around 25°.

4.5.2 Turning

A vehicle turns by causing the terrain to exert a turning moment that causes a yaw angular velocity. The moment can be generated by controlling wheel steer angles that map fairly directly onto curvature, or it can be generated by altering wheel speeds in differential or skid steering in order to cause an angular velocity.

Of particular interest here is the integrated effect of steering commands. We will consider a simple case. Equation 4.108 provides the trajectory followed in the plane by a vehicle actuated in velocity and curvature. Once again, the equation is:

$$\begin{bmatrix} x(t) \\ y(t) \\ \psi(t) \end{bmatrix} = \begin{bmatrix} x(0) \\ y(0) \\ \psi(0) \end{bmatrix} + \int_0^t \begin{bmatrix} \cos\psi(t) \\ \sin\psi(t) \\ \kappa(t) \end{bmatrix} v(t)dt \qquad (4.161)$$

This is a simple approximation for an automobile.

4.5.2.1 Actuator Dynamics in Kinematic Steering

Actuators don't move at infinite speeds and, in particular, there are practical limits on the first and second derivatives of wheel steer angles. Consider a very simple bicycle model of a car. Suppose that the steering wheel angle (and the wheel "steer angle" α) satisfy an inequality constraint:

$$\dot{\alpha} \leq \dot{\alpha}_{max}$$

Any real actuator does not achieve maximum speed in an instant either so the second derivative is likely to be limited as well:

$$\ddot{\alpha} \leq \ddot{\alpha}_{max}$$

Such limits have a significant impact on the capacity of a car-like vehicle to change direction quickly. If we assume that α is small, and $L = 1$ in Equation 4.57 then, the curvature is simply:

$$\kappa(t) = \alpha(t)$$

Hence, the derivatives of κ will be limited as well. If a command signal $\alpha_r(t)$ is issued that the system does not execute perfectly, then the error in following it is:

$$\delta\alpha(t) = \alpha_r(t) - \alpha(t)$$

This error is integrated twice before it becomes an error in position. This means small errors in steer angle will quickly accumulate into large errors in position.

4.5.2.2 Example: Reverse Turn Dynamics

The worst case aggressive turn is an instantaneous change in curvature from the maximum positive to the maximum negative. Consider such a "reverse turn" for a vehicle whose maximum steer angle rate of 30°/sec. and rate derivative permits acceleration from 0 to the maximum rate in 1/4 sec. Integrating the true dynamics in Equation 4.161 gives the results shown in Figure 4.36:

This example provides a clear argument of the need for prediction. If such a robot did not have such a model and decided to turn right to avoid the obstacle, the unmodelled slow steering response would actually cause a collision at any speed over 5.0 m/s. The correct decision at such speeds is to continue turning left and avoid the obstacle on the left.

Now, consider the response to different steering commands at the same speed, say 5.0 m/s. The same dynamic model used in the last graph gives the result in Figure 4.37. In any attempt to change the sign of curvature and turn right, it clearly takes about 10 meters of motion before the steering actuator even reaches the halfway point and curvature reverses sign. Due to the doubly integrated effect of curvature tracking error, many of these issues can become significant even at speeds well below 5.0 m/s. It can be advisable for autonomy to reason in terms of linear curvature polynomials, called *clothoids*, instead of constant curvature arcs for these reasons. These curves are a better approximation of the path followed when curvature rate is limited.

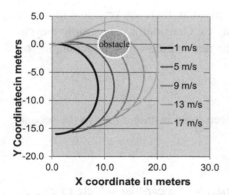

Figure 4.36 Constant Speed Reverse Turn. Response to a command to turn hard right is illustrated at various operating speeds.

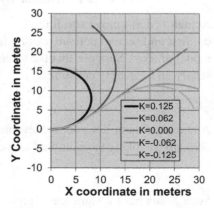

Figure 4.37 Constant Speed Partial Reverse Turn. Response to various curvature commands at 5.0 m/s speed is illustrated.

4.5.2.3 Example: Swerving

A swerve maneuver turns quickly in order to move a small amount laterally. It can be a better option than stopping for avoiding obstacles at high speed because it requires less distance – meaning obstacles do not need to be seen so far ahead.

Two limits on lateral acceleration of similar form can be defined based on excessive side slip and wheel liftoff during a turn. On a flat level road, if the vehicle is about to slip sideways, its lateral acceleration will reach its maximum value right before lateral slipping occurs. At that point the lateral frictional force is of magnitude $f = \mu mg$ so:

$$a_{ss} = \mu g$$

where μ is the lateral sliding friction. Likewise, assuming a flat level road, wheel lift-off (which precedes rollover) will occur when:

$$a_{roll} = \left(\frac{t}{2h}\right)g$$

where t is the wheel track and h is the height of the center of gravity. At all times, the lateral acceleration of a turning vehicle is given by:

$$a_{lat} = \frac{v^2}{R} = \kappa v^2$$

Substituting into both expressions for limits on acceleration and solving for curvature leads to:

$$\kappa_{ss} = \mu(g/v^2) \qquad\qquad \kappa_{roll} = \left(\frac{t}{2h}\right)(g/v^2)$$

Clearly, the most stringent curvature limit is associated with the smaller of μ and the quantity $T/2h$, which is known as the *static stability factor* (SSF) (see section Section 4.5.3).

The curvature limit derived above is the sharpest turn that can be executed in order to swerve around an obstacle (and then swerve back to the original heading). At highway speeds, this curvature will be very small and it will possible to steer to this curvature in a fraction of a second. The associated trajectory will be an arc of a circle that can be approximated well by substituting null initial conditions and a constant velocity and curvature into Equation 4.162 and assuming that the yaw angle remains small:

$$\begin{bmatrix} x(t) \\ y(t) \\ \psi(t) \end{bmatrix} = \begin{bmatrix} s \\ (\kappa s^2)/2 \\ \kappa s \end{bmatrix} \tag{4.162}$$

For a fixed curvature and a given lateral offset y, the distance required to achieve the offset is:

$$s_{ss}^{\;2} = (2y)/\kappa = [(2y)/(\mu g)]v^2 = 4y[v^2/(2\mu g)] = 4ys_{brake} \tag{4.163}$$

where a sliding threshold for curvature was used. Clearly, the required distance is proportional to the lateral offset and the square root of the braking distance. It is also linear in velocity when written as:

$$s_{ss} = v\sqrt{[(2y)/(\mu g)]} \tag{4.164}$$

Substituting a speed of 60 mph (32 m/sec), $\mu = 0.5$, and $y = 2.5m$ gives 32 meters range. For comparison, the braking distance at this speed is 100 meters.

4.5.3 Vehicle Rollover

Vehicle *rollover* occurs when a vehicle rolls onto its side or even its roof. Although a small number of vehicles have been designed to recover from such a catastrophe, almost all will not, so avoiding rollover is the only practical approach to maintaining safety and operation in most cases. The factors that cause rollover come down to the effects of gravity and the other forces acting on the vehicle. Some of those other forces depend on the maneuver that the vehicle may be executing. Geometry and mass properties also play a role.

4.5.3.1 Causes of Rollover

Although slow-moving indoor mobile robots are typically not at significant risk of rolling over, indoor industrial trucks that lift loads onto high shelves certainly are. Outdoor field robots are also at risk when operating on slopes, lifting loads, or during forceful interactions with the environment. Automobiles are also at risk when turning, due to their high speeds.

Rollover incidents can be induced by the terrain and not much can be done to avoid them if they cannot be predicted. Examples include a car sliding sideways into a rigid short obstacle, a field robot driving its high wheels over a rock when on a slope, or a fork truck colliding its lift mast or load with the arch over a doorway.

Rollover may be *maneuver-induced* by turning too sharply for the present speed or, equivalently, by driving too fast for the present curvature. An incident be also be induced by stopping too quickly while going down a slope or turning too sharply on a slope.

4.5.3.2 Forms of Instability

It is useful to distinguish the point of wheel liftoff (which is potentially reversible) from the state where the vehicle has already rolled so far that complete rollover becomes inevitable. The second case is both more serious and harder to predict because it requires knowledge of the inertia of the vehicle. The first case is a more conservative test and it is easier to predict and detect. For this reason, we will concentrate on wheel liftoff rather than rollover.

4.5.3.3 Static Case

For a static vehicle, the physics are relatively easy. Consider a rectangular vehicle on a slope as shown in Figure 4.38. Assume that the vehicle and its suspension are rigid, and that the forces shown represent both the front and rear wheels.

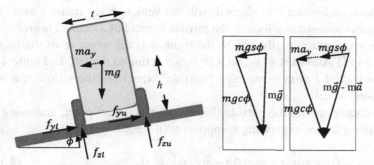

Figure 4.38 Rollover Physics. (Left) Front view. Vehicle is on flat (not level) slope. When it is not moving, the vector ma_y is not present. (Center) The components of the weight and acceleration resolved into body coordinates. (Right) Addition of the inertial force vector.

The subscripts l and u designate "lower" and "upper" wheels. For this rigid body to be in equilibrium, the required force balances are:

$$f_{z_u} + f_{z_l} = mg\cos\phi \qquad f_{y_u} + f_{y_l} = mg\sin\phi$$
$$\text{(4.165)}$$

For rotational equilibrium, the sum of the moments around any axis must cancel. It is clever to choose the lower wheel contact point and sum moments around it:

$$f_{z_u} t + mg\sin\phi h = mg\cos\phi\frac{t}{2} \qquad \text{(4.166)}$$

Now, imagine that the slope slowly continues to increase. Intuitively, the forces on the lower wheel increase and those on the upper wheel decrease in order to counteract the increasing tendency increasing tendency to roll over. However, at some point, the force on the upper wheel(s) goes to zero. This is also the point where the weight vector points directly at the line between the two lower wheels because the moment of the weight was causing the upper wheel reaction. At this instant, the moment balance becomes:

$$mg\sin\phi h = mg\cos\phi\frac{t}{2} \qquad \text{(4.167)}$$

Therefore, the slope at which liftoff is imminent is given by:

$$\tan\phi = \frac{t}{2h} \qquad \text{(4.168)}$$

This is a well-known result in vehicle manufacturing. The quantity $t/(2h)$ is known as the *static stability factor*. Clearly, it is the tangent of the static tipping angle. Furthermore, if the *wheel track* t is known, and the slope can be adjusted (safely) until liftoff, the cg height can be determined precisely by solving for h.

4.5.3.4 Dynamic Case

The dynamic case is a little more complicated. Let the same vehicle be executing a sharp left turn on the inclined plane. Assume that there is no roll acceleration (i.e., a steady turn). We will use D'Alembert's law to convert the problem to a simpler equivalent statics problem. The resultant inertial force ma_y will be assumed to act parallel to the groundplane, and hence it is aligned with the vehicle body frame y axis. This assumption amounts to assuming locally flat terrain, instead of a banked turn.

Although the acceleration really acts to the right, it is the negative of the inertial force that is used in D'Alembert's law, so it is drawn acting to the left. In Figure 4.38, we replace the subscript l with o meaning "outside" wheel and the subscript u with i meaning "inside" wheel.

Summing moments around the outside (lower) wheel contact point, and using the vehicle body frame axes for expressing components of forces, we have:

$$f_{z_i} t + ma_y h + mgs\phi h - mgc\phi \frac{t}{2} = 0 \qquad (4.169)$$

solving for the lateral acceleration in g's, we have:

$$\frac{a_y}{g} = \left[\frac{t}{2}c\phi - hs\phi - \frac{tf_{z_i}}{mg} \right] / h \qquad (4.170)$$

Once again, liftoff commences when the vertical reaction on the inside wheel vanishes. At this point, groundplane forces cannot counteract the moment tending to tip the vehicle toward the outside of the turn. Setting $f_{z_i} = 0$ leads to the threshold on lateral acceleration where rollover begins to occur:

$$\frac{a_y}{g} = \left[\frac{t}{2}c\phi - hs\phi \right] / h \qquad (4.171)$$

Rewriting gives:

$$\frac{a_y + gs\phi}{gc\phi} = \frac{t}{2h} \qquad (4.172)$$

Once again, this result can be interpreted in terms of the direction of the resultant non-contact force. The vector *specific force* given by:

$$\vec{f} = \vec{g} - \vec{a} \qquad (4.173)$$

represents the direction that a pendulum at the center of gravity would point if allowed to swing freely. When this vector points at the outside wheel contact points, the inside wheel begins to lift off. The static case is just a special case of this result. Note that lowering the cg, widening the wheel track, reversing the slope, or decreasing the acceleration (slowing down or turning less sharply), will increase stability. On flat ground, some vehicles cannot rollover during cornering – the wheels will slip sideways first.

4.5.3.5 Stability Pyramid

The wheel configurations of vehicle need not be rectangles, but the theory presented above generalizes to arbitrary shapes [20]. The basic issue is whether the net noncontact force acting at the center of gravity (cg) remains within the *stability pyramid* (Figure 4.39). This is the pyramid formed with the wheel contact points with the cg at the apex.

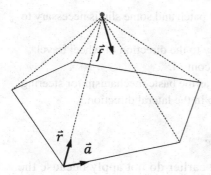

Figure 4.39 Stability Pyramid. The most general case for arbitrary wheel configurations.

The wheels need not be in the same plane. Each line between adjacent wheels is a potential tipover axis because when a rigid vehicle lifts off, only two adjacent wheels stay in contact. If $\vec{a}$ is a vector directed counterclockwise as viewed from above along a potential tipover axis, and if $\vec{r}$ is any vector from any point on that axis directed to the cg, then:

$$\vec{M} = \vec{r} \times \vec{f} \qquad (4.174)$$

is the moment of the specific force about the axis. Furthermore, the quantity

$$\vec{M} \bullet \vec{a} \qquad (4.175)$$

is positive when the vehicle experiences an unbalanced moment and it is zero at the point of liftoff. The remaining angle before liftoff occurs is a kind of *stability margin*. This formulation applies to the total inertial acceleration whether it is caused by turning or braking or any other maneuver.

4.5.3.6 Stability Control

A mobile robot can use the above theory reactively if it knows or can measure its present net specific force. Corrective measures such as slowing down could then be taken. If the robot articulates mass, the cg itself must be computed online and this will require other measurements of articulations and masses. Using these techniques, a robot can implement reactive stability control in relatively little hardware and software.

The theory can be used predictively as well. If the shape of the upcoming terrain can be measured, attitude (and hence gravity in the body frame) can be predicted and acceleration can be predicted from the inputs. If such calculations determine the stability margin is too small, the robot can choose a more stable option, like slowing down or turning less sharply. This process fits easily into model predictive control algorithms.

4.5.4 Wheel Slip and Yaw Stability

The fundamental design concept of a wheel is to replace sliding friction with rolling friction by having the wheel roll around its axle and not slip in the orthogonal direction. Despite this ideal concept, there are several reasons why wheels do slip in practice:

- The terrain may not be able to generate the (shear) forces necessary either due to surface properties (e.g., ice) or material properties (e.g., powdery sand).

- The wheel contact point is not a point, but a contact patch and some slip is necessary to avoid tearing the wheel or tire apart.
- The steerable axles may not be aligned orthogonally to the direction of wheel travel over the terrain due to inadequacies in the steering control.
- Lateral wheel forces may be intended in the design as the basic mechanism for steering the vehicle, and such forces will generate some slip in the lateral direction.

4.5.4.1 Slip Angle

When wheels slip, the simple kinematics derived earlier do not apply because the velocity vectors of the wheels no longer satisfy the non slip assumptions. However, it is still the case that the wheels have a velocity and the vehicle is still a rigid body. When wheels slip, the vehicle velocity may differ in either magnitude or direction from what would be predicted based on wheel angular velocities and non slip models.

The *slip angle* of an automobile is defined as the angle between the direction in which the vehicle points (yaw) and the direction it is moving (heading). The slip angle of a tire is defined similarly based on the direction the tire is pointing. In Figure 4.23, the slip angle of the vehicle is:

$$\beta = \psi - \zeta \tag{4.176}$$

Alternatively, the slip angle can be computed from the lateral v_y and longitudinal v_x components of the velocity vector resolved into the body frame:

$$\beta = \mathrm{atan2}(v_y, v_x) \tag{4.177}$$

4.5.4.2 Generalized Velocity Error

The slip angle concept can be generalized to any form of vehicle if we define it as the angle between the intended velocity $\underline{v}$ and the actual one $\underline{\dot{x}}$:

$$\beta = \mathrm{acos}[(\underline{\dot{x}} \cdot \underline{v})/(|\underline{\dot{x}}||\underline{v}|)] \tag{4.178}$$

More generally, a rigid body has three degrees of freedom of motion when confined to the local terrain tangent plane. The perturbed differential equations of motion for the most general possible wheel slip situation is:

$$\begin{bmatrix} \dot{x} \\ \dot{y} \\ \dot{\psi} \end{bmatrix} = \begin{bmatrix} c\psi & -s\psi & 0 \\ s\psi & c\psi & 0 \\ 0 & 0 & 1 \end{bmatrix} \left(\begin{bmatrix} v_x \\ v_y \\ \omega \end{bmatrix} + \begin{bmatrix} \delta v_x \\ \delta v_y \\ \delta \omega \end{bmatrix} \right) \tag{4.179}$$

Which is of the form:

$$^{w}\dot{\underline{\rho}} = R(\psi)(\underline{v} + \delta \underline{v}) \tag{4.180}$$

4.5.4.3 Modelling Skidding and Slipping

The instantaneous values of the perturbation (slip) velocities will depend on the intrinsic mechanical properties of the terrain and the wheels and the forces exerted by the terrain on the wheels. These things in turn depend on:

- the speed and curvature of the vehicle trajectory (inertial forces)
- terrain moisture content and temperature (e.g., mud)
- the instantaneous direction of gravity in the body frame (terrain slope)
- suspension state and related load transfer effects

Although the full physics of wheel terrain interaction and vehicle dynamics are quite complicated, a simple model is better than none at all. For example, on flat level gravel, a particular skid steered vehicle produces steady slip velocities that depend on speed and curvature more-or-less linearly.

Lateral slip is on the order of a few percent of forward velocity, for example. Such a model is of the form:

$$\delta \underline{v} = A \underline{\dot{\rho}} \tag{4.181}$$

A more refined model is nonlinear in state. It reflects, for example, the fact that the sign of longitudinal slip is invariant to the sign of curvature, and the fact that lateral slip depends on lateral acceleration – the product ωv:

$$\delta \underline{v} = h(\underline{\dot{\rho}}) \tag{4.182}$$

4.5.4.4 Compensating for Slip in a Model Predictive Controller

If the desired state velocities are known, it is possible to solve Equation 4.180 for the commanded velocities that produce the desired output:

$$\underline{v} = R^{-1}(\psi) \, {}^{w}\underline{\dot{\rho}} - \delta \underline{v} = \underline{\dot{\rho}} - \delta \underline{v} \tag{4.183}$$

Essentially, this means that the projected slips should be removed from the desired state velocities $\underline{\dot{\rho}}$ (these are expressed in the body frame) to compute the compensated inputs. If the vehicle wheels are actuated directly, this result can be fed to the vehicle kinematics inverse model to produce the wheel speeds that should be commanded.

Given a linear slip model, the above controller becomes linear in the state:

$$\underline{v} = \underline{\dot{\rho}} - A \underline{\dot{\rho}} = (I - A) \underline{\dot{\rho}} \tag{4.184}$$

If the slip model is nonlinear, we can set up a numerical rootfinding problem:

$$g(\underline{\dot{\rho}}) = \underline{\dot{\rho}} - h(\underline{\dot{\rho}}) = \underline{0} \tag{4.185}$$

4.5.4.5 Yaw Stability Control

By contrast to rollover, another way in which a vehicle may lose control is loss of yaw stability. In this case, the wheels are slipping to such an excessive degree that it becomes difficult or impossible to control the heading of the vehicle. The vehicle may fail, to some degree, to turn when requested or the rear wheels may slip laterally to cause more turning than desired.

Both predictive and reactive remedies are potentially available. The associated skidding of the vehicle may be predicted and avoided based on slip prediction models in a model predictive controller. Also, numerous mechanisms to measure slip or yaw rate error based on speed or wheel encoders, or based on a gyro, may indicate when yaw control is failing. In such a case, brakes or individual wheel controls can be used to generate a restoring moment to prevent further undue slip.

4.5.5 Parameterization and Linearization of Dynamic Models

One technique that we will use many times in subsequent chapters is to parameterize a differential equation and then linearize it with respect to the parameters. We will use this basic technique to discover how to drive a robot to a precise place, to follow prescribed paths, and/or to avoid obstacles along the way. We will also use it to calibrate odometry and dynamic models of vehicles.

4.5.5.1 Linearization of State Space Models w.r.t. Parameters

Consider a state space model of the system that depends on some parameters:

$$\dot{\underline{x}} = \underline{f}(\underline{x}, \underline{u}, \underline{p}, t) \tag{4.186}$$

In practice, state space models almost always depend on some parameters. For mobile robots, these parameters may be wheel radii, coefficients of friction, or moments of inertia. In such a case, we can write the model in the form:

$$\dot{\underline{x}}(t) = \underline{f}(\underline{x}(t), \underline{u}(t), \underline{p}, t) \tag{4.187}$$

At times, we will be interested in the question of how the state derivative changes when the parameters of the above state equation change. The first-order relationship between them is the Jacobian matrix:

$$\frac{\partial \dot{\underline{x}}(t)}{\partial \underline{p}} = \frac{\partial}{\partial \underline{p}} \underline{f}(\underline{x}(t), \underline{u}(t), \underline{p}, t) \tag{4.188}$$

A naive, and incorrect, solution for this Jacobian is obtained by simply differentiating the functional form of $\underline{f}(\ )$ wherever a parameter appears. For example if:

$$\dot{x} = 2ax + 3b$$

Then, one might expect that $\partial \dot{x}(t) / \partial b = 3$. However, when computing the Jacobian, it is important to note that if $\underline{f}(\ )$ depends, by assumption, on $\underline{p}$, this means that $\dot{\underline{x}}$ and therefore $\underline{x}$ also depends on $\underline{p}$. In the most general case, $\underline{u}$ depends on $\underline{p}$ as well. Therefore, the correct Jacobian is:

$$\frac{\partial \dot{\underline{x}}(t)}{\partial \underline{p}} = \underline{f}_x \underline{x}_p + \underline{f}_u \underline{u}_p + \underline{f}_p \tag{4.189}$$

The Jacobians $\underline{f}_x$, $\underline{f}_u$, $\underline{f}_p$, and $\underline{u}_p$ can be obtained in a straightforward manner from the explicit function forms of these quantities. In order to get $\underline{x}_p$, note that:

$$\frac{\partial \underline{\dot{x}}(t)}{\partial \underline{p}} = \frac{\partial}{\partial \underline{p}}\left(\frac{d}{dt}\underline{x}(t)\right) = \frac{d}{dt}\left(\frac{\partial \underline{x}(t)}{\partial \underline{p}}\right) = \frac{d}{dt}(\underline{x}_p) = \underline{\dot{x}}_p(t)$$

This means that $\underline{x}_p$ can be obtained by integration with respect to time, once the other derivatives are known. The initial conditions are normally zero because the initial state does not depend on the parameters. The Jacobian of the state equation with respect to parameters in the state equation actually requires the computation of an integral of the derivative of that same Jacobian. We will use this device, and related ones, for differentiating integrals, in many places in the text.

4.5.5.2 Linearization of Integrals of State Space Models w.r.t. Parameters

A similar result to the last one can be obtained for an integral of the state space model. Clearly, for the parameterized state equations used above, the state at any time is given by:

$$\underline{x}(t) = \underline{x}(0) + \int_0^t \underline{f}(\underline{x}(t), \underline{u}(t), \underline{p}, t)dt \tag{4.190}$$

The process to compute this Jacobian is the process to compute the derivative of an integral. According to Leibnitz' rule, one simply moves the derivative inside the integral sign and then integrates the derivative of the integrand $\underline{f}(\ )$. Assuming zero initial conditions:

$$\frac{\partial \underline{x}(t)}{\partial \underline{p}} = \int_0^t \frac{\partial}{\partial \underline{p}}\underline{f}(\underline{x}(\underline{p}, t), \underline{u}(\underline{p}, t), t)dt \tag{4.191}$$

As we saw in the last section, the derivative of this integrand is:

$$\frac{\partial}{\partial \underline{p}}\underline{f}(\underline{x}(\underline{p}, t), \underline{u}(\underline{p}, t), t) = \underline{f}_x\underline{x}_p + \underline{f}_u\underline{u}_p + \underline{f}_p$$

The left-hand side is a "total" derivative with respect to the parameter **vector** for which there seems to be no accepted notation, whereas the quantity $\underline{f}_p$ is a partial derivative taken by holding $\underline{x}$ and $\underline{u}$ constant. Now we have:

$$\frac{\partial \underline{x}(t)}{\partial \underline{p}} = \underline{x}_p(t) = \int_0^t (\underline{f}_x\underline{x}_p + \underline{f}_u\underline{u}_p + \underline{f}_p)dt \tag{4.192}$$

Spotlight 4.14 Jacobian of System Response w.r.t. Model Parameters.

This integral provides the change in the state of the system that is caused by a small change in the parameters in the system differential equation.

The result is merely Equation 4.189 integrated over time. Of course, the quantity on the left-hand side also appears inside the integral on the right. In practice, the problem can be solved numerically by using the previous value(s) of $\underline{x}_p(t)$ to compute the next. This self reference can be eliminated in a general solution when the dynamics are linear. It is also possible to simply differentiate the integral numerically with respect to the parameters as described in Section 2.2.3 of Chapter 3.

4.5.5.3 Input Parameterization of State Space Models

A particularly useful way to parameterize a state space model is to parameterize the inputs. In general, we can write:

$$\underline{u}(t) = \underline{u}(\underline{p}, t) \tag{4.193}$$

For some arbitrary parameter vector $\underline{p}$. For example, if the input vector is curvature as in Equation 3.126 of Chapter 3, we might express it as a polynomial:

$$\underline{u}(\underline{p}, t) = \kappa(\underline{p}, t) = a + bt + ct^2 \tag{4.194}$$

where the parameters are $\underline{p} = [a\ b\ c]^T$. The key observation is that this device establishes a mapping between a vector of parameters and an entire function of time. Once the parameters are known, the entire curvature *signal* becomes known. Furthermore, if this input function is used to drive a state space model, then a particular and entire state trajectory is generated as well, so we can write:

$$\underline{x}(t) = \underline{x}(0) + \int_0^t \underline{f}(\underline{x}(\underline{p}, t), \underline{u}(\underline{p}, t), t)dt = \underline{g}(\underline{p}, t) \tag{4.195}$$

In other words, we have converted the functional in Equation 3.122 in Chapter 3 to a function. This expression establishes a mapping from a value of the parameter vector $\underline{p}$ and time to the resulting state at that time.

4.5.5.4 Path Integral Linearization With Respect to Parameters of Inputs

Given the above parameterized integral, it now becomes possible to investigate the first-order behavior of the integral with respect to small changes in the parameters. Consider the Jacobian matrix:

$$\frac{\partial \underline{x}(t)}{\partial \underline{p}} = \underline{x}_p(t) = \frac{\partial \underline{g}(\underline{p}, t)}{\partial \underline{p}} \tag{4.196}$$

This is a matrix-valued function of time that maps a small change in the parameters $\Delta \underline{p}$ onto the associated change in the terminal state $\Delta \underline{x}(t)$ computed by the integral. This is a special case of Equation 4.192, so we may write:

$$\frac{\partial \underline{x}(t)}{\partial \underline{p}} = \underline{x}_p(t) = \int_0^t (f_x \underline{x}_p + f_u \underline{u}_p)dt \tag{4.197}$$

There are situations in which the system dynamics are linear and, in that case, an integral expression is available that depends only on the inputs. In that case, the path integral is of the form:

$$\underline{x}(t) = \underline{x}(0) + \int_0^t \underline{f}(\underline{u}(\underline{p}, t))dt = \underline{g}(\underline{p}, t) \tag{4.198}$$

Then the path is linearized with:

$$\frac{\partial \underline{x}(t)}{\partial \underline{p}} = \underline{x}_p(t) = \int_0^t (\underline{f}_u \underline{u}_p) dt \tag{4.199}$$

4.5.5.5 Relaxation of Input Parameterized Paths

The previous result is a very basic mechanism to drive a robot to a desired terminal state. One simply writes:

$$\underline{x}(t_f) = \underline{g}(\underline{p}, t_f) \tag{4.200}$$

where the integral nature of $g(\ )$ is suppressed for clarity. This equation is simply a rootfinding problem that can be solved with Newton's method and the means to compute the needed Jacobian was presented above. This procedure is called *path relaxation* because as the parameter $\underline{p}$ changes from iteration to iteration, the path geometry will be changing all along its length.

4.5.5.6 Cost Integral Linearization With Respect to Parameters of Inputs

In other cases, the integral of the path will be a more arbitrary integral, perhaps one intended to evaluate a path by assigning a scalar cost. For example, the total squared curvature on a path might be represented as a line integral:

$$J(s) = \int_0^s L(\underline{x}(\underline{p}, s), \underline{u}(\underline{p}, s), s) ds \tag{4.201}$$

This is a kind of double integral because $\underline{x}(\ )$ is itself computed as an integral. This cost integral can be linearized using Leibnitz' rule:

$$\frac{\partial J(s)}{\partial \underline{p}} = J_p(s) = \int_0^s \frac{\partial}{\partial \underline{p}} L(\underline{x}(\underline{p}, s), \underline{u}(\underline{p}, s), s) ds \tag{4.202}$$

Which can be written as:

$$g(\underline{p}, s) = J_p(s) = \int_0^s (L_x \underline{x}_p + L_u \underline{u}_p) ds \tag{4.203}$$

Now the problem of finding the least cost path is:

$$\underline{p}^* = \operatorname{argmin}[\underline{g}(\underline{p}, s)] \tag{4.204}$$

This is an optimization problem that can be solved using any of the optimization techniques described in Chapter 3.

4.5.6 System Identification

The predicted motion of the vehicle in all of the more realistic maneuvers described above depends on parameters that characterize the vehicle (time constants, center of gravity) or the environment (coefficient of friction) or both (slip ratio). Such parameters can never be known precisely and even if they could, many will change over time.

Yet, the accuracy with which a mobile robot predicts its own actions is important, so the question of how such parameters can be determined is important.

The determination of the correct values of system parameters is known as *calibration* in general and as *system identification* in the case of dynamic models. This section will present techniques for system identification for mobile robots.

4.5.6.1 Fundamental Principle

Suppose the system is a nonlinear multivariate system:

$$\dot{x} = \underline{f}(\underline{x}, \underline{u}, \underline{p}, t)$$
$$\underline{y} = \underline{h}(\underline{x}, \underline{u}, \underline{p}, \underline{q}, t)$$

(4.205)

for some unknown parameter vectors $\underline{p}$ and $\underline{q}$. The basic identification process is one of comparing the results of a system model with measurements of the system itself in an attempt to refine estimates of parameters used in the model (Figure 4.40).

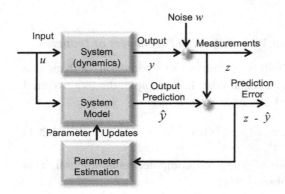

Figure 4.40 Simplified System Identification Block Diagram. The parameters of the system model are progressively fine-tuned in an attempt to null the error of the model.

The inputs $\underline{u}$ may be measured or specified depending on whether the digital part of the system is being identified as well. The state $\hat{x}$ may be either measured or predicted based on the inputs and the state equation, and the outputs $\hat{y}$ are measured.

An *online* identification system is one that uses normal operating input-output signals and that identifies the model in real time. An offline system uses stored data that was collected earlier, and it may use specially designed test signals.

4.5.6.2 Equation Error Approach

A classical approach to system identification is to try to adjust the parameters to make the system model consistent. Sometimes the output equation is something relatively trivial like $\underline{y} = \underline{x}$ because the state can be observed with (noisy) measurements. The *equation error formulation* forms a residual based on the system differential equation for some number of time steps. For such a system, the state equation alone is calibrated.

In this case, it is possible to take measurements of the inputs $\underline{u}$, the state $\underline{x}$, and the state derivative $\dot{x}$ at each time step k and form residuals that can be written as:

$$\underline{r}_k(\underline{p}) = \dot{x}_k - \underline{f}(x_k, \underline{u}_k, \underline{p}, t_k)$$

(4.206)

All of the equations for each observation can be stacked to form a residual vector $\underline{r}(\underline{p})$:

$$\underline{r} = \underline{\dot{x}} - \underline{f}(\underline{p}) \tag{4.207}$$

The measurements will likely be noisy, and the model may be somewhat incorrect, so this will not have an exact solution. It may be underdetermined or overdetermined depending on how much data is collected and how independent the measurements are.

The unknown parameters can be estimated by using the above Jacobian and solving the minimization problem:

$$\underline{p} = \text{argmin}[\underline{r}^T(\underline{p})\underline{r}(\underline{p})] \tag{4.208}$$

Doing so will require that Equation 4.207 be linearized with respect to the parameters:

$$\underline{r}_{\underline{p}} = -\partial \underline{f}/\partial \underline{p}$$

Based again on Equation 4.189, this is:

$$\frac{\partial \underline{f}}{\partial \underline{p}} = \frac{\partial \underline{\dot{x}}(t)}{\partial \underline{p}} = \underline{f}_x \underline{x}_{\underline{p}} + \underline{f}_u \underline{u}_{\underline{p}} + \underline{f}_{\underline{p}} \tag{4.209}$$

The Jacobians $\underline{f}_x$, $\underline{f}_u$, $\underline{f}_{\underline{p}}$, and $\underline{u}_{\underline{p}}$ can be obtained in a straightforward manner. To get $\underline{x}_{\underline{p}}$, note that Equation 4.209 is merely the expression for $\underline{\dot{x}}_{\underline{p}}$, so $\underline{x}_{\underline{p}}$ can be obtained by integration:

$$\underline{x}_{\underline{p}}(t) = \underline{x}_{\underline{p}}(t_0) + \int_{t_0}^{t} (\underline{f}_x \underline{x}_{\underline{p}} + \underline{f}_u \underline{u}_{\underline{p}} + \underline{f}_{\underline{p}})dt \tag{4.210}$$

4.5.6.3 Example: Identification of a Time Constant

Suppose that a wheel speed servo is a proportional controller whose gain is unknown. The proportional gain k_p is related to the time constant with:

$$\tau = 1/k_p$$

We know that the differential equation describing this system is:

$$\dot{x} = f(x, u, p, t) = k_p(u - x) \tag{4.211}$$

Where both x and u have units of velocity rather than position. The equation error formulation is to form numerous residuals:

$$r_k = \dot{x}_k - k_p(u_k - x_k) = \dot{x}_k - H_k k_p$$

However, in this case, it is convenient to rewrite this simply as:

$$z_k = \dot{x}_k = k_p(u_k - x_k) = H_k k_p$$

Although one such observation is enough to find the single parameter, a more accurate solution will result from overdetermining the solution. Multiple such observations are of the form:

$$\underline{z} = H k_p$$

where each row of the Jacobian H is the scalar $u_k - x_k$. Because this is now a linear overdetermined system of equations, the solution can be obtained from the left pseudoinverse:

$$k_p = H^+ \underline{z}$$

4.5.6.4 Output Error Approach

The *output error approach* is based on forming residuals of the output equation. Recalling p and q in Equation 4.205, define the composite parameter vector for the system to be:

$$\underline{\rho} = \left[\underline{p}^T \; \underline{q}^T \right]^T \tag{4.212}$$

Even if it is possible to measure the state, the parameters p may only be obtainable if the state is predicted as well. The state is predicted by integrating the state equation:

$$\underline{x}(t) = \underline{x}(t_0) + \int_{t_0}^{t} \underline{f}(\underline{x}, \underline{u}, \underline{\rho}, t) dt$$

Residuals are formed based on the outputs:

$$\underline{r}_k(\underline{\rho}) = \underline{y}_k - \underline{h}(\underline{x}_k, \underline{u}_k, \underline{\rho}, t) \tag{4.213}$$

Multiple such measurements will produce a vector of residuals:

$$\underline{r} = \underline{y} - \underline{h}(\underline{\rho}) \tag{4.214}$$

which can be processed in a nonlinear least squares problem to find the minimizing parameters as in the equation error formulation.

In a manner similar to the equation error formulation, the output equation is linearized with respect to the parameters as follows:

$$\underline{h}_{\underline{\rho}} = \underline{h}_x \underline{x}_{\underline{\rho}} + \underline{h}_u \underline{u}_{\underline{\rho}} + \underline{h}_{\underline{\rho}} \tag{4.215}$$

and all Jacobians are straightforward except $\underline{x}_{\underline{\rho}}$, which must be obtained from numerical integration of the gradient of the state equations as was done in the equation error method:

$$\underline{x}_{\underline{\rho}}(t) = \underline{x}_{\underline{\rho}}(t_0) + \int_{t_0}^{t} [\underline{f}_{\underline{x}} \underline{x}_{\underline{\rho}} + \underline{f}_{\underline{u}} \underline{u}_{\underline{\rho}} + \underline{f}_{\underline{\rho}}] dt \tag{4.216}$$

Then, the identification problem can be posed as the following nonlinear least squares problem:

$$\underline{\rho} = \operatorname{argmin}[\underline{r}^T(\underline{\rho})\underline{r}(\underline{\rho})]$$

Because the state is predicted in this case, it depends on the initial conditions $\underline{x}_0 = \underline{x}(t_0)$. If the initial conditions are not known precisely, they can be added to the parameter vector and estimated. The Jacobian of state with respect to the initial conditions can be obtained from Equation 4.216 which becomes:

$$\underline{x}_{\underline{x}_0}(t) = \underline{x}_{\underline{x}_0}(t_0) + \int_{t_0}^{t} \underline{f}_{\underline{x}} \underline{x}_{\underline{p}} \, dt$$

because $\underline{u}_{\underline{x}_0} = 0$ and $\underline{f}_{\underline{x}_0} = 0$.

4.5.6.5 Integrated Equation Error Formulation

The *integrated equation error* (IEE) formulation is a nonstandard formulation that is very similar to the equation error formulation except that:

- it forms residuals based on the state, the integral of the state equation, and
- it predicts over longer periods of time than one time step.

This formulation is used because it is well suited to identification of predictive models, or situations where measurements of state occur too infrequently or intermittently for differentiation to be viable.

Is this formulation, assuming the state is measurable, we form residuals from the present measured state and the state that would be predicted by the present model given the state a few moments ago and inputs that have been generated since then:

$$\underline{e}_k = \underline{x}_k - \left(\underline{x}_{k-n} + \int_{t_{k-n}}^{t_k} \underline{f}(\underline{x}, \underline{u}, \underline{p}, t) \, dt \right) \tag{4.217}$$

The measurements in this case consist of the two states, $\underline{x}_k$ and $\underline{x}_{k-n}$, and the inputs are assumed to be known. The residuals are linearized with respect to the unknown parameters thus:

$$\frac{\partial \underline{e}_k}{\partial \underline{p}} = \int_{t_{k-n}}^{t_k} (\underline{f}_{\underline{x}} \underline{x}_{\underline{p}} + \underline{f}_{\underline{u}} \underline{u}_{\underline{p}} + \underline{f}_{\underline{p}}) \, dt$$

4.5.6.6 Example: Identifying Odometry Models

This example applies the IEE formulation to the problem of calibrating odometry. An odometry system is a process that integrates a differential equation that depends on some unknown parameters. For example, Equation 4.53 can be substituted into Equation 6.20 in Chapter 6, to produce this differential equation for differential heading odometry:

$$\frac{d}{dt} \begin{bmatrix} x(t) \\ y(t) \\ \theta(t) \end{bmatrix} = \begin{bmatrix} V(t)\cos\theta(t) \\ V(t)\sin\theta(t) \\ \omega(t) \end{bmatrix} = \begin{bmatrix} c\theta & 0 \\ s\theta & 0 \\ 0 & 1 \end{bmatrix} \begin{bmatrix} v(t) \\ \omega(t) \end{bmatrix} = \begin{bmatrix} c\theta & 0 \\ s\theta & 0 \\ 0 & 1 \end{bmatrix} \begin{bmatrix} 1 & 1 \\ 1/W & -1/W \end{bmatrix} \begin{bmatrix} v_r \\ v_l \end{bmatrix}$$

Which is:

$$
\underline{\dot{x}} = \begin{bmatrix} \dot{x} \\ \dot{y} \\ \dot{\theta} \end{bmatrix} = \begin{bmatrix} c\theta & c\theta \\ s\theta & s\theta \\ 1/W & -1/W \end{bmatrix} \begin{bmatrix} v_r \\ v_l \end{bmatrix}
$$

where $\underline{p} = W$ and $u = \begin{bmatrix} v_r & v_l \end{bmatrix}^T$. Assuming that initial conditions are known, we can write:

$$
\begin{bmatrix} x(t) \\ y(t) \\ \theta(t) \end{bmatrix} = \begin{bmatrix} x(0) \\ y(0) \\ \theta(0) \end{bmatrix} + \int_0^t \begin{bmatrix} (v_r + v_l)c\theta \\ (v_r + v_l)s\theta \\ (v_r - v_l)/W \end{bmatrix} dt
$$

We can use Equation 4.214 to linearize this with respect to the wheel track W in order to calibrate its value. As an alternative we can also differentiate it numerically by integrating the terminal position twice with two slightly different values of W:

$$
\underline{x}_W(t) \approx \frac{1}{\Delta W}[\underline{x}(W + \Delta W, t) - \underline{x}(W, t)]
$$

Note that while the position coordinates (x, y) seem independent of W, they depend on θ and θ depends on W so they do as well. Although the example has a single parameter, any number of parameters can be identified when the system is *observable* as described later in the text.

4.5.6.7 Example: Identification of Wheel Slip

This is an example in which the inputs also depend on parameters. Suppose for the moment that a vehicle is operating on a level flat surface. Suppose further that the amount of slip can be characterized as a deviation between the predicted vehicle velocity and the true velocity. Suppose the state equations are the general fully actuated case for velocity inputs and motion in a plane.

$$
\frac{d}{dt} \begin{bmatrix} x \\ y \\ \psi \end{bmatrix} = \begin{bmatrix} c\psi & -s\psi & 0 \\ s\psi & c\psi & 0 \\ 0 & 0 & 1 \end{bmatrix} \begin{bmatrix} v_x \\ v_y \\ \omega \end{bmatrix} \tag{4.218}
$$

4.5.6.7.1 Perturbative Dynamics Formulation. This formulation models the prediction error as if it were caused by an input perturbation:

$$
\underline{u}(t) = \underline{u}(t) + \delta\underline{u}(t) \tag{4.219}
$$

One advantage of this approach is the fact that it assumes nothing about the form of the state equations because any inputs can be perturbed in this way. A second advantage of this approach is that we can use perturbative dynamics in order to produce a general solution integral which can then be linearized. The solution integral acts as the observation prediction because it predicts the error in the state. The general solution will make it possible to compute the needed Jacobian incrementally online even as the parameters are changing.

For now, let the "parameters" be the slip rates:

$$\underline{p} = \delta \underline{u}(t) = \begin{bmatrix} \delta v_x & \delta v_y & \delta \omega \end{bmatrix}^T \tag{4.220}$$

We already know that the linearized error dynamics propagate according to:

$$\delta \underline{x}(t) = F \delta \underline{x}(t) + G \delta \underline{u}(t) \tag{4.221}$$

Furthermore the transition matrix for this system is known and the deviation in predicted state due to the slip velocities is given by Equation 4.155:

$$\delta \underline{x}(t) = \begin{bmatrix} 1 & 0 & -y(t_0) \\ 0 & 1 & x(t_0) \\ 0 & 0 & 1 \end{bmatrix} \delta \underline{x}(t_0) + \int_{t_0}^{t} \begin{bmatrix} c\psi(t) & -s\psi(t) & -\Delta y(t, \tau) \\ s\psi(t) & c\psi(t) & \Delta x(t, \tau) \\ 0 & 0 & 1 \end{bmatrix} \delta \underline{u}(\tau) d\tau \tag{4.222}$$

This expression can be interpreted as a prediction of the deviation in the state $\delta x(t)$ from some nominal model, which is due to a slip velocity of $\delta \underline{u}(t)$.

On the assumption that the input perturbations are constants, we can take the Jacobian of the left hand side of Equation 4.221 with respect to the "parameters" $\delta \underline{u}$. This gives:

$$\delta \underline{x}(t) = H(t) \delta \underline{u} \tag{4.223}$$

where $H(t)$ is the integral of the input transition matrix from Equation 4.154:

$$H(t) = \int_{t_0}^{t} \Gamma(t, \tau) d\tau = \int_{t_0}^{t} \begin{bmatrix} c\psi(t) & -s\psi(t) & -\Delta y(t, \tau) \\ s\psi(t) & c\psi(t) & \Delta x(t, \tau) \\ 0 & 0 & 1 \end{bmatrix} d\tau \tag{4.224}$$

Although the original state equations were nonlinear, the perturbative dynamics were linear and they therefore produce a linear measurement function. Given an observation of a difference between a predicted state and a measured state, we can use the above Jacobian to form a linearized observation:

$$\underline{x}_{meas}(t) - \underline{x}_{pred}(t) = H \delta \underline{u}(t) \tag{4.225}$$

where $\underline{x}_{pred}(t)$ is produced by integrating Equation 4.218 assuming that there are no perturbations. Since there are three equations here and three unknowns, the problem can be solved by inverting H to produce the slip rates that best explain the observed residual.

If the initial conditions are not known precisely, they can be added to the parameter vector and the Jacobian is immediate – the transition matrix:

$$H_{\delta \underline{x}_0} = \frac{\partial \underline{z}}{\partial \delta \underline{x}_0} = \Phi(t, t_0) \tag{4.226}$$

In this case, one observation will not be enough to resolve the all the parameters. When several observations are stacked together, they form an overdetermined system of equations which can be solved for the best fit parameters by minimizing the squared residual using the pseudoinverse:

$$\underline{p} = H^+ \underline{z} \tag{4.227}$$

4.5.6.7.2 Nonlinear Dynamics Formulation. The above formulation can be generated using nonlinear system theory as well. Assume it is possible to measure the state directly, and let the "parameters" be the three slip velocities used above. The nonlinear system model is:

$$\frac{d}{dt}\begin{bmatrix} x \\ y \\ \psi \end{bmatrix} = \begin{bmatrix} c\psi & -s\psi & 0 \\ s\psi & c\psi & 0 \\ 0 & 0 & 1 \end{bmatrix}\begin{bmatrix} v_x + \delta v_x \\ v_y + \delta v_y \\ \omega + \delta\omega \end{bmatrix} \tag{4.228}$$

where the right-hand side is $\underline{f}(\underline{x}, \underline{u}, \underline{p}, t)$ for this problem.

The residuals will be observed as the difference between the predicted state $\hat{\underline{x}}_k = h(\underline{p})$ and the observed state $\underline{x}_k$:

$$\underline{e}_k = \underline{x}_k - \hat{\underline{x}} \tag{4.229}$$

The prediction equation is the integral of the state equation:

$$\hat{\underline{x}}_k = h(\underline{p}) = \underline{x}_0 + \int_{t_0}^{t} \begin{bmatrix} c\psi & -s\psi & 0 \\ s\psi & c\psi & 0 \\ 0 & 0 & 1 \end{bmatrix}\begin{bmatrix} v_x + \delta v_x \\ v_y + \delta v_y \\ \omega + \delta\omega \end{bmatrix} dt \tag{4.230}$$

We can linearize this with respect to the parameters by writing:

$$h_{\underline{p}} = h_{\underline{p}}(t_0) + \int_{t_0}^{t} (\underline{f}_x \underline{x}_{\underline{p}} + \underline{f}_u \underline{u}_{\underline{p}} + \underline{f}_{\underline{p}}) dt \tag{4.231}$$

where $\underline{u}_{\underline{p}} = I$ because the inputs include the parameters in an additive fashion, $\underline{f}_{\underline{p}} = 0$ and:

$$\underline{f}_x = F = \begin{bmatrix} 0 & 0 & -\dot{y} \\ 0 & 0 & \dot{x} \\ 0 & 0 & 0 \end{bmatrix} \qquad \underline{f}_u = G = \begin{bmatrix} c\psi & -s\psi & 0 \\ s\psi & c\psi & 0 \\ 0 & 0 & 1 \end{bmatrix}$$

The measurement Jacobian cannot yet be written because $\underline{x}_{\underline{p}}$ is unknown. However, $\underline{x}_{\underline{p}} = h_{\underline{p}}$ in this case, so when this is implemented numerically, the last value(s) of $\underline{x}_{\underline{p}}$ is used to compute the next value of $h_{\underline{p}}$. Thus, we have:

$$h_{\underline{p}} = \underline{x}_{\underline{p}} = \underline{x}_{\underline{p}}(t_0) + \int_{t_0}^{t} \left(\begin{bmatrix} 0 & 0 & -\dot{y} \\ 0 & 0 & \dot{x} \\ 0 & 0 & 0 \end{bmatrix}\underline{x}_{\underline{p}} + \begin{bmatrix} c\psi & -s\psi & 0 \\ s\psi & c\psi & 0 \\ 0 & 0 & 1 \end{bmatrix} \right) dt$$

This gradient can be computed in this way but note that the integral implies that the gradient must satisfy the linear matrix differential equation:

$$\frac{d}{dt}\underline{x}_{\underline{p}}(t) = F(t)\,\underline{x}_{\underline{p}}(t) + G(t)$$

For this particular $F(t)$ and $G(t)$, we already know the transition matrix, so the general solution is:

$$\underline{h}_{\underline{p}}(t) = \underline{x}_{\underline{p}}(t) = \Phi(t,t_0)\underline{x}_{\underline{p}}(t_0) + \int_{t_0}^{t}\Gamma(t,\tau)dt$$

If we assume null initial conditions $\underline{x}_{\underline{p}}(t_0) = 0$, this is the same result obtained for the perturbative dynamics formulation. This result was obtained by computing the gradient of the nonlinear dynamics rather than by linearizing the dynamics first.

If the initial conditions are not known precisely, then we can add them to the parameter vector. The inputs do not depend on the initial conditions, so Equation 4.231 becomes:

$$\underline{h}_{\underline{x}_0} = \underline{x}_{\underline{x}_0}(t_0) + \int_{t_0}^{t}\left(\begin{bmatrix} 0 & 0 & -\dot{y} \\ 0 & 0 & \dot{x} \\ 0 & 0 & 0 \end{bmatrix}\underline{x}_{\underline{x}_0}\right)dt \qquad (4.232)$$

This gradient can be computed in this way but note that the integral implies that the gradient must satisfy the linear matrix differential equation:

$$\frac{d}{dt}\underline{x}_{\underline{x}_0}(t) = F(t)\underline{x}_{\underline{x}_0}(t) \qquad (4.233)$$

For this particular $F(t)$ with no inputs ($G(t) = 0$), we already know the transition matrix, so the solution is:

$$\underline{h}_{\underline{x}_0}(t) = \underline{x}_{\underline{x}_0}(t) = \Phi(t,t_0)\underline{x}_{\underline{x}_0}(t_0) = \Phi(t,t_0)$$

because $\underline{x}_{\underline{x}_0}(t_0) = I$. Once again, this is the same result obtained for the perturbative dynamics formulation. However, the derivation was performed to demonstrate how the solution can be found even when the transition matrix is unknown.

In general, although the system may be nonlinear, the gradient of the state equations must be a linear matrix differential equation whose transition matrix is the same as the linearized dynamics of the original state equations.

Given that the gradient must satisfy a linear matrix differential equation, the transition matrix must exist and it can be computed numerically by solving the system:

$$\frac{d}{dt}\Phi(t,t_0) = F\Phi(t,t_0) \qquad \Phi(t_0,t_0) = I$$

It therefore is no coincidence that this is exactly what Equation 4.232 is computing. Also, Equation 4.233 permits us to recognize $\underline{x}_{\underline{x}_0}(t)$ as the transition matrix itself.

4.5.6.7.3 Slip Surfaces. The above formulation assumes that the slip rates are independent of the trajectory followed and this is not likely to be the case. Even the simplest useful models of slip express slip as a fraction of the velocity, for example.

In a more general case, the slip relationship can be regarded as a function of the state and the parameters:

$$\delta\underline{u}(t) = \delta\underline{u}(\underline{u}, \underline{p}) \tag{4.234}$$

This formulation permits the system to learn an entire slip field over all of input space. While it assumes the parameters are constants, it no longer assumes that the inputs are constants. Hence, it applies to arbitrary trajectories. The measurement Jacobian under these conditions is:

$$H = \frac{\partial\delta\underline{x}(t)}{\partial\underline{p}} = \int_0^t \Gamma(t, \tau)\frac{\partial\delta\underline{u}(\underline{u}, \underline{p})}{\partial\underline{p}} \, d\tau \tag{4.235}$$

This equation will be nonlinear in the parameters if the derivative of Equation 4.234 is nonlinear in them. If there are more than three parameters, it is underdetermined and it may be necessary to accumulate multiple observations before trying to solve for the parameters.

This formulation can also be used to learn the slip surfaces online using an algorithm called a Kalman filter which will be described later. Also, while this formulation was developed for identifying wheel slip, the same mathematics apply to the problem of odometry calibration when the parameters are geometric things like wheel track and wheel radii or errors like biases or scale factors in the sensors.

4.5.7 References and Further Reading

Gillespie and Wong are two books on ground vehicle dynamics. Papadopoulos developed the stability margin technique presented here. Raol is one of many texts on system identification. The integrated equation error technique presented here comes from the paper by Seegmiller.

4.5.7.1 Books

[19] Thomas Gillespie, *Fundamentals of Vehicle Dynamics,* Society of Automotive Engineers, 1992.

4.5.7.2 Papers

[20] E. G. Papadopoulos, D. A. Rey, The Force-Angle Measure of Tipover Stability Margin for Mobile Manipulators, *Vehicle System Dynamics*, Vol. 33, pp 29–48, 2000.

[21] J. R. Raol, G. Girija, J. Singh, *Modelling and Parameter Estimation of Dynamic Systems,* IEEE Control Series 65.

[22] J. Y. Wong, *Theory of Ground Vehicles,* Wiley, 1993.

[23] Neal Seegmiller, Forrest Rogers-Marcovitz, Greg Miller and Alonzo Kelly, A Unified Perturbative Dynamics Approach to Online Vehicle Model Identification, Proceedings of International Symposium on Reading Review, 2011.

4.5.8 Exercises

4.5.8.1 *Effect of Weight on Stopping Distance.*

Derive the stopping distance on flat terrain. Do heavier vehicles take more time or distance to stop?

4.5.8.2 *A Rough Braking Heuristic for Slopes*

Derive a rule of thumb for the factor by which braking distance increases when the slope changes by a small amount.

4.5.8.3 *Stopping Distance on Rolling Terrain*

Outline how to compute stopping distance when the pitch angle varies with distance.

4.5.8.4 *Total Derivative of a Differential Equation*

Solve the differential equation $\dot{x} = 2ax + 3b$ from zero initial conditions. Then differentiate the result with respect to b and show that $\partial \dot{x}(t)/\partial b = 3$ is only true when $t = 0$.

CHAPTER 5
Optimal Estimation

Figure 5.1 Tour Guide Robots. The challenges of dealing with lots of people blocking the views of the walls inspired the application of Bayesian estimation techniques for localizing the robot.

Uncertainty is a catch-all term that refers to any and all of the different ways in which the sensors, models, and actuators of a robot do not behave ideally. Sensors rarely give exact and noise-free measurements, environmental models rarely capture all information that matters, and a wheel that does not slip has never been built. As is the case for so many other human capabilities, we rarely notice our own competence dealing with noisy, missing, and conflicting information. This chapter covers some elementary concepts of random processes and then presents classical techniques that can be used to make robots more competent in our uncertain world.

Uncertainty models can be applied to many forms of error, whether the errors are random or systematic, temporal or spatial. Every measurement has some amount of random noise impressed on it as a matter of basic thermodynamics. Modelling that noise can lead to systems of considerably higher performance. Such performance improvements may lead to improved safety, availability, and robustness.

5.1 Random Variables, Processes, and Transformation

5.1.1 Characterizing Uncertainty

Uncertainty and error are related in the sense that the magnitudes of true errors are typically unknown. By distinguishing different types of error, we can be better equipped to tolerate each type.

5.1.1.1 Types of Uncertainty

Measurements may be modelled by a general additive error model such as:

$$x_{meas} = x_{true} + \varepsilon \tag{5.1}$$

The notation $\hat{x}$ (pronounced "x hat") is sometimes used to denote an estimate of x_{true} and it will be used in this way here. In this case, we write:

$$\hat{x} = x_{true} + \varepsilon \tag{5.2}$$

In general, ε may be zero, a constant, or a function. It may be deterministic (systematic), stochastic (random) or a combination of both. We will generally assume that the random component of ε is *unbiased* (i.e., has a mean of zero). Often that assumption is somewhat justified if most systematic error (i.e., the mean of the distribution of ε) has been removed through calibration. Of course, ε is also **unknown**. Otherwise we would just subtract it from the measurement to produce the correct answer.

Some classes of error include:

- When the error is occasionally very far off from the true value, it's called an *outlier*.
- When the error follows a deterministic relationship, we often call it a systematic error. Calibration or model errors are examples of systematic error. A slope and/or offset error are typically defined for linear models.
- When the error possesses a random distribution, it may be called *noise*, but random errors in *scale factors* (slopes) and *biases* (offsets) are also defined.

It is important to not confuse the unknown with the random. Errors may be unknown but systematic. Random error models may be useful for approximating unknown quantities but they are not the same thing.

Suppose we measure the rotation rate of a wheel with both a typical wheel encoder and an ideal sensor. Figure 5.2 illustrates several types of errors that might occur.

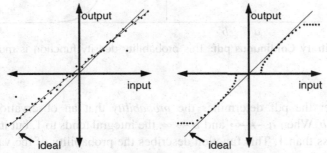

Figure 5.2 Forms of Error in Real Measurements. (Left) Bias and scale error, and two outliers. (Right) Nonlinearity, deadband, and saturation.

For the rightmost case in the figure, ignoring the outliers, we might model the errors as follows:

$$\varepsilon = a + b\theta + N(\mu, \sigma)$$

where N represents the *normal* or *Gaussian* probability distribution function. Notice that the unknowns include parameters of both systematic (a, b) and stochastic (μ, σ) processes.

5.1.1.2 Tolerating and Removing Uncertainty

We can remove some systematic error through the process of calibration. To do calibration you generally need:

- A *model* for the systematic components of ε. This model must be based on knowledge of the expected behavior.
- A set of *observations* from a reference that has the accuracy you want to achieve.
- An *estimation process* that computes the best fit parameters of the model that matches the observations.

We can remove some random error and outliers by the process of *filtering*. Also, if two measurements at different times or in different places are correlated, the correlated part of the error can be removed by *differential observation*. In this way, if two measurements are corrupted by the same constant value, observations of their difference (or the difference of both observations) will not include the error.

5.1.2 Random Variables

A random variable (or random vector, if there are several treated as a unit) may be continuous or discrete. A continuous one can be described in terms of its *probability density* function (pdf). An arbitrary pdf may look like Figure 5.3.

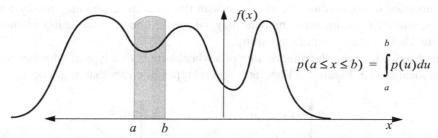

$$p(a \leq x \leq b) = \int_a^b p(u)\,du$$

Figure 5.3 Arbitrary Continuous pdf: This probability density function is multimodal (has several bumps).

The area under the pdf determines the *probability* that an observation of x falls between a and b. When $a \to -\infty$ and $b \to \infty$, the integral tends to 1, but it is otherwise positive and less than 1. This function describes the probability of the various potential outcomes for a *single* random event.

A critical point on notation must be made. Unlike in most other places in mathematics, the $p(\ )$ in $p(A)$ and $p(B)$ are not necessarily the same function – as we would interpret $f(\ )$ to mean in $f(x)$ and $f(y)$. Read $p(A)$ to mean an **unspecified** probability function rather than a specific one and $p(B)$ is, in general, a completely different function. For probability notation, the focus is on the arguments to the function rather than the function name.

A discrete random variable can be described in terms of its *probability mass function* (pmf). An arbitrary one may look like Figure 5.4.

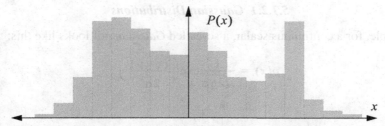

Figure 5.4 Arbitrary Discrete pmf: This probability mass function is multimodal (i.e., it has several bumps).

In like manner to the continuous case:

$$P(a \leq x \leq b) = \sum_i P(x_i) \tag{5.3}$$

This expresses, for example, the probability that a thrown die will read either 3 or 4 or 5. It is important that the potential outcomes be mutually exclusive if you want to write a sum. We use an upper case P in the discrete case.

Two dimensional and higher dimensionality pdf's will be important to us. For example, consider a representation of a 2D pdf in terms of the density of the points in the plane (Figure 5.5).

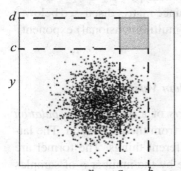

Figure 5.5 Sampling a 2D pdf: These points are sampled from a 2D Gaussian distribution.

In this case, the *joint* pdf is a scalar function of a vector:

$$p(a \leq x \leq b \wedge c \leq y \leq d) = \int_c^d \int_a^b p(u, v) du dv \tag{5.4}$$

and there are also *conditional* pdf's such as:

$$p(a \leq x \leq b \mid y) = \int_a^b p(u, y) du / \int_{-\infty}^{\infty} p(u, y) du \tag{5.5}$$

which fix one or more coordinates and treat them as known values.

5.1.2.1 Gaussian Distributions

For example, for a continuous scalar, a so-called *Gaussian* pdf looks like this:

$$p(x) = \frac{1}{\sqrt{2\pi}\sigma} \exp\left(-\frac{(x-\mu)^2}{2\sigma^2}\right)$$

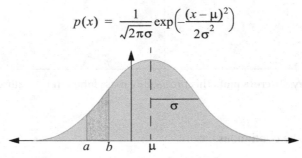

Figure 5.6 Gaussian Distribution. This is the famous "bell curve" – the most commonly used pdf.

The parameters μ and σ are the mean and standard deviation defined below. In n dimensions we have:

$$p(\underline{x}) = \frac{1}{(2\pi)^{n/2}\sqrt{|C|}} \exp\left(-\frac{[\underline{x}-\underline{\mu}]^T C^{-1}[\underline{x}-\underline{\mu}]}{2}\right) \tag{5.6}$$

Spotlight 5.1 Multidimensional Gaussian and Mahalanobis Distance.

The Gaussian distribution in n dimensions. The exponent $[\underline{x}-\underline{\mu}]^T C^{-1}[\underline{x}-\underline{\mu}]$ is called the *Mahalanobis distance* (MHD). C is the covariance matrix discussed below, and $|C|$ is its determinant. Note the similarity of this (multidimensional) exponent to the exponent in the scalar case in Figure 5.6.

5.1.2.2 Mean and Variance of a Random Variable

We must always be careful to distinguish the *parameters* of a theoretical *population* distribution from the *statistics* of a *sampling* distribution from the population. The latter can be used to estimate the former, but they are different things. The former are computed using knowledge of the pdf. The latter divide by the number n of samples somewhere in their formulas.

The *expected* value or *expectation* of the function $h(x)$ is its weighted average where the pdf provides the weighting function:

$$
\begin{aligned}
Exp[h(x)] &= \int_{-\infty}^{\infty} h(x)p(x)dx & &\text{\textit{scalar-scalar continuous}}\\
Exp[\underline{h}(x)] &= \int_{-\infty}^{\infty} \underline{h}(x)p(x)dx & &\text{\textit{vector-scalar continuous}}\\
Exp[\underline{h}(\underline{x})] &= \int_{-\infty}^{\infty} \underline{h}(\underline{x})p(\underline{x})d\underline{x} & &\text{\textit{vector-vector continuous}}\\
Exp[\underline{h}(x)] &= \sum_{i=1}^{n} \underline{h}(\underline{u}_i)P(\underline{u}_i) & &\text{\textit{vector-vector discrete}}
\end{aligned}
\tag{5.7}
$$

Note especially that the expectation is a functional (i.e., a moment), so you need the entire distribution $p(x)$ to find it. The notation for the integral of a vector valued differential such as dx means a volume integral over all dimensions of x. If the whole distribution is known, it is possible to compute all kinds of "moments." Mean and variance are two important moments.

Expectation is a (definite) integral, so it has these properties:

$$Exp[k] = k$$

$$Exp[kh(x)] = kExp[h(x)] \tag{5.8}$$

$$Exp[h(x) + g(x)] = Exp[h(x)] + Exp[g(x)]$$

The *population mean* is the expected value of the trivial function $g(x) = x$. This is basically the centroid of the distribution.

$$\mu = Exp[x] = \int_{-\infty}^{\infty} [xp(x)]dx \qquad \textit{scalar continuous}$$

$$\underline{\mu} = Exp(\underline{x}) = \int_{-\infty}^{\infty} \underline{x}p(\underline{x})d\underline{x} \qquad \textit{vector continuous} \tag{5.9}$$

$$\underline{\mu} = Exp[\underline{x}] = \sum_{i=1}^{n} \underline{x}_i P(\underline{x}_i) \qquad \textit{vector discrete}$$

Note that this is not the most likely value of x, which is determined by the mode of the distribution – the point at which the pdf or pmf is maximum. So "expected" value is a very misleading name for the mean. For a bimodal distribution, the expected value may be very unlikely to occur as shown in Figure 5.7.

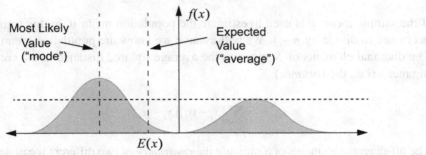

Figure 5.7 Multimodal Distribution. The mean and the most likely value are very different in this case.

A Gaussian distribution is unimodal and the mean and maximum likelihood estimate (most likely value) of x are the same.

The *population variance* of a distribution for a scalar random variable is the expected value of the squared deviation from the mean $g(x) = (x-\mu)^2$:

$$\sigma_{xx} = \int_{-\infty}^{\infty} [(x-\mu)^2 \cdot p(x)]dx \tag{5.10}$$

Note the alternate notation for variance $\sigma^2(x)$. Also, the *standard deviation* is *defined* as the square root of variance:

$$\sigma_x = \sigma(x) = \sqrt{\sigma_{xx}} \tag{5.11}$$

The *population covariance* is the expected value of the outer product (a matrix) of two deviation vectors:

$$\Sigma_{\underline{xx}} = E([\underline{x} - \underline{\mu}][\underline{x} - \underline{\mu}]^T) = \int_{-\infty}^{\infty} [\underline{x} - \underline{\mu}][\underline{x} - \underline{\mu}]^T p(\underline{x}) d\underline{x} \quad continuous$$

$$\Sigma_{\underline{xx}} = E([\underline{x} - \underline{\mu}][\underline{x} - \underline{\mu}]^T) = \sum_{i=1} [\underline{x} - \underline{\mu}][\underline{x} - \underline{\mu}]^T P(\underline{x}) \quad discrete \tag{5.12}$$

5.1.2.3 Sampling Distributions and Statistics

Statistics are quantities computed from a sample of measurements that can be used to estimate the parameters of the population from which the sample was taken. Samples are not normally continuous, so we will deal only with discrete values.

The *sample mean* is:

$$\underline{\bar{x}} = \frac{1}{n} \sum_{i=1}^{n} \underline{x} \tag{5.13}$$

The *sample covariance* is:

$$S_{\underline{xx}} = \frac{1}{n} \sum_{i=1}^{n} [\underline{x} - \underline{\mu}][\underline{x} - \underline{\mu}]^T \tag{5.14}$$

If the sample mean $\underline{\bar{x}}$ is used to estimate the population mean $\underline{\mu}$ in this formula, it is necessary to divide by $n - 1$. We will assume we know the population mean for now. The diagonal elements of S measure the average squared distance to the corresponding mean (i.e., the *variance*)

$$s_{ii} = \frac{1}{n} \sum_{i=1}^{n} [x_i - \mu_i][x_i - \mu_i] . \tag{5.15}$$

The off-diagonal elements of S measure the *covariance* of two different mean deviations.

$$s_{ij} = \frac{1}{n} \sum_{i=1}^{n} [x_i - \mu_i][x_j - \mu_j] \tag{5.16}$$

If these elements are zero, we say that the variables involved are *uncorrelated*.

5.1.2.4 Computation of Sample Statistics

It can be very important in practice to know how to compute mean and covariance continuously on the fly.

The *batch methods* assume that all data is available at the beginning:

$$\text{mean} \qquad \bar{\underline{x}} = \frac{1}{n}\sum_{i=1}^{n} \underline{x}$$

$$\text{covariance} \qquad S = \frac{1}{n}\sum_{i=1}^{n} [\underline{x} - \underline{\mu}][\underline{x} - \underline{\mu}]^{T} \qquad (5.17)$$

The *recursive methods* keep a running tally and add one point at a time as necessary. These are related to the Kalman filter:

$$\text{mean} \qquad \bar{\underline{x}}_{k+1} = \frac{(k\bar{\underline{x}}_k + \underline{x}_{k+1})}{(k+1)}$$

$$\text{covariance} \qquad S_{k+1} = \frac{kS_k + [\underline{x}_{k+1} - \underline{\mu}][\underline{x}_{k+1} - \underline{\mu}]^{T}}{(k+1)} \qquad (5.18)$$

The *calculator methods* update statistical accumulators when data arrives and then compute the statistics on demand at any time:

$$\text{mean} \qquad \underline{T}_{k+1} = \underline{T}_k + \underline{x}_{k+1} \qquad \qquad \text{when data arrives}$$

$$\bar{\underline{x}}_{k+1} = \frac{\underline{T}_{k+1}}{(k+1)} \qquad \qquad \text{when result necessary}$$

$$(5.19)$$

$$\text{covariance} \quad Q_{k+1} = Q_k + [\underline{x}_{k+1} - \underline{\mu}][\underline{x}_{k+1} - \underline{\mu}]^{T} \; \text{when data arrives}$$

$$S_{k+1} = \frac{Q_k}{(k+1)} \qquad \qquad \text{when result necessary}$$

It can be a bad idea to compute standard deviation (not variance) recursively because it requires a square root – which is expensive. Also, these intuitive algorithms are not very robust to round off errors.

5.1.2.5 *Why Use a Gaussian to Model Uncertainty*

In general, the mean and covariance are the first and second moments of an arbitrary pdf. Use of these alone to characterize a real pdf is a form of linear assumption. This linear assumption happens to correspond to the use of a Gaussian because its higher moments are all zero. Many real noise signals follow a Gaussian distribution anyway. By the Central Limit Theorem, the sum of a number of independent variables has a Gaussian distribution *regardless* of their individual distributions.

5.1.2.6 *Contours of Constant Probability Density*

In one dimension, for a Gaussian distribution, consider the probability contained within a symmetric interval on the *x* axis (Figure 5.8).

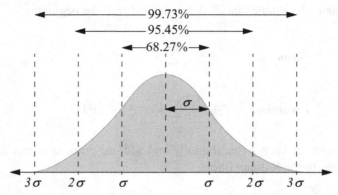

Figure 5.8 Contours of Constant Probability: 1D. For a one-dimensional Gaussian, a random event has a 99.73% chance of falling within 3 sigma of the mean.

In general, these contours of constant exponent in the Gaussian are *n-ellipsoids* because $p(\underline{x})$ is constant when the exponent (the *Mahalanobis distance*) is a constant k that depends on the probability p.

$$(\underline{x} - \underline{\mu})^T \Sigma^{-1} (\underline{x} - \underline{\mu}) = k^2(p) \tag{5.20}$$

and this can be shown to be the equation of an ellipse in n dimensions. We can only plot an ellipse in 2D, so we can remove all but two corresponding rows and columns from Σ, then for a probability p ellipse in 2D:

$$k^2(p) = -2ln(1 - p) \tag{5.21}$$

Figure 5.9 shows some *concentration ellipsoids*. They get the name because most of the probability is concentrated inside them.

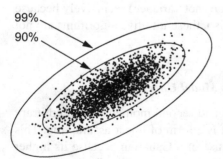

Figure 5.9 Contours of Constant Gaussian Exponent: 2D. A point has the indicated probability of falling within each ellipse.

The covariance matrix is diagonal when it is expressed in a set of rectangular coordinates coincident with the major and minor axes of the elliptical distribution that it represents. Let these axes be given (with respect to the system in which the covariance is expressed) by the columns of a rotation matrix R. Then, the covariance matrix can be converted to a diagonal matrix with a *similarity transformation*:

$$\Sigma^{-1} = RD^{-1}R^T \tag{5.22}$$

The diagonal values of D are the eigenvalues of Σ and the columns of R are its eigenvectors. The ellipse given by Σ has these properties:

- It is centered at the mean $\hat{\underline{x}}$.
- It has major and minor axes coinciding with the columns of R.
- It has elongations along each axis proportional to the square roots of the corresponding diagonal elements of D.

5.1.3 Transformation of Uncertainty

We can use the covariance matrix to represent the "spread" of data to get an idea of how much uncertainty exists in measurements. However, it is often the case that we cannot measure the quantity of interest directly and it must be inferred from the measurements. This fact leads to the question of how we can understand the uncertainty in those inferences. One way to pose the question is to imagine the measurements and inferences as random variables and to ask how the distributions of one relate to the other when they are constrained to follow some transformation rule.

5.1.3.1 Linear Transformation of the Mean and Covariance

Suppose that we know the mean of some distribution of a random variable $\underline{x}$ and we want to compute the mean of the distribution of a linear function of $\underline{x}$:

$$\underline{y} = F\underline{x} \tag{5.23}$$

Because expectation is an integral over $\underline{x}$, and F is assumed to be independent of $\underline{x}$, it can be taken outside the integral.

$$\mu_y = Exp(F\underline{x}) = FExp(\underline{x}) \tag{5.24}$$

In other words:

$$\mu_y = F\mu_x \tag{5.25}$$

Suppose further that we know the covariance of $\underline{x}$ above and we want to compute the covariance of $\underline{y}$. Once again, because F is assumed to be independent of $\underline{x}$, it can be taken outside the covariance integral. In other words:

$$\Sigma_{yy} = Exp(F\underline{x}\underline{x}^T F^T) = FExp(\underline{x}\underline{x}^T)F^T \tag{5.26}$$

Therefore, the covariance of $\underline{y}$ is:

$$\Sigma_{yy} = F\Sigma_{xx}F^T \tag{5.27}$$

5.1.3.2 Example: Variance of a Sum of Random Variables

Consider the problem of finding the variance of a sum of random variables. This problem will be important later in models of error in dead reckoning. Let there be n random variables x_i each of which has a variance of $\sigma_{x_i}^2$. Let us define a new random variable y as the sum of all of these.

$$y = \sum_{i=1}^{n} x_i$$

If all of the original variables are uncorrelated then:

$$\Sigma_{\underline{x}} = \text{diag}\left[\sigma_{x_1}^2 \ \sigma_{x_2}^2 \ \cdots \ \sigma_{x_n}^2\right] = \begin{bmatrix} \sigma_{x_1}^2 & 0 & 0 & 0 \\ 0 & \sigma_{x_2}^2 & 0 & 0 \\ 0 & 0 & \cdots & 0 \\ 0 & 0 & 0 & \sigma_{x_n}^2 \end{bmatrix}$$

If we arrange all the x: in a column vector $\underline{x}$, and cleverly define a vector of ones:

$$F = \begin{bmatrix} 1 & 1 & \cdots & 1 \end{bmatrix}$$

Then $y = F\underline{x}$ and our transformation rule for the linear case now tells us:

$$\sigma_y^2 = F\Sigma_{\underline{xx}}F^T = \sum_{i=1}^{n} \sigma_{x_i}^2 \tag{5.28}$$

So the variance of a sum of n uncorrelated scalar random variables is the sum of their respective variances. In the special case where all of the variances are equal to the same value σ_x^2:

$$\sigma_y^2 = n\sigma_x^2 \tag{5.29}$$

5.1.3.3 Example: Variance of an Average of Random Variables

Consider the problem of finding the average of some random variables. This problem will be important later in models of measurement processing. Let there be n random variables x_i each of which has a variance of $\sigma_{x_i}^2$. Let us define a new random variable y as the average of all of these.

$$y = \frac{1}{n}\sum_{i=1}^{n} x_i$$

Now we will use a scaled vector of ones:

$$F = \frac{1}{n}\begin{bmatrix} 1 & 1 & \cdots & 1 \end{bmatrix}$$

Then $y = F\underline{x}$ again and if the variables are uncorrelated, we have:

$$\sigma_y^2 = J\Sigma_{\underline{xx}}J^T = \frac{1}{n^2}\sum_{i=1}^{n} \sigma_{x_i}^2 \tag{5.30}$$

So the variance of an average of n uncorrelated scalar random variables is the sum of their respective variances divided by n^2. In the special case in which all of the variances are equal to the same value σ_x^2:

$$\sigma_y^2 = \frac{1}{n}\sigma_x^2 \tag{5.31}$$

This means something very important happens when we divide a sum of random variables by their number. Not dividing by n increases variance of the sum relative to that of a single element added whereas dividing by n reduces its variance. From a mathematics perspective the variance of the sum grows with n whereas dividing the sum by n introduces a new factor of $1/n^2$ into the variance that counteracts the growth in the former case. These basic facts have far reaching implications. Intuitively, averaging reduces "noise" but it does so by overwhelming a more basic tendency for the error in a sum to actually increase noise.

5.1.3.4 Coordinate Transformations

It is often the case that the transformation from measurements to the quantity of interest is a coordinate system transformation. Suppose we know the covariance matrix of a measurement of a point expressed in one frame (because it's easy to express or measure there) and we want to express it in another (because we need to use it there).

Let the transformation of coordinates from frame a to frame b be:

$$^b\underline{x} = R^a\underline{x} + \underline{t}$$

Then the transformed measurement and its covariance are:

$$\begin{aligned}
^b\mu_{\underline{x}} &= R^a\mu_{\underline{x}} + \underline{t} \\
^b\Sigma_{\underline{xx}} &= R^a\Sigma_{\underline{xx}}R^T
\end{aligned} \tag{5.32}$$

Note especially that such a transformation will introduce off-diagonal nonzero entries into the covariance matrix. These elements indicate that the new distribution is correlated. This means that the covariance ellipse is not principally oriented in coordinate system b if it was principally oriented in coordinate system a (Figure 5.10).

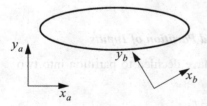

Figure 5.10 Diagonal Covariance Matrix. For data that is spread as indicated in the ellipse, the covariance would be diagonal if expressed in the coordinates of frame a. Not so for b.

5.1.3.5 Nonlinear Transformations

More generally, let us imagine a case where we know the uncertainty in $\underline{x}$ and want to compute the uncertainty in a nonlinear function of $\underline{x}$.

$$\underline{y} = \underline{f}(\underline{x})$$

Let us write any particular value of $\underline{x}$ in terms of its deviation from some reference value $\underline{x}'$:

$$\underline{x} = \underline{x}' + \underline{\varepsilon}$$

We can use the Jacobian to linearly approximate $\underline{y}$ with a truncated Taylor series as follows:

$$\underline{y} = f(\underline{x}) = f(\underline{x}' + \underline{\varepsilon}) \approx f(\underline{x}') + J\underline{\varepsilon} \tag{5.33}$$

Now the mean of $\underline{y}$ is:

$$\mu_{\underline{y}} = Exp(\underline{y}) \approx Exp[f(\underline{x}') + J\underline{\varepsilon}] = Exp[f(\underline{x}')] + Exp(J\underline{\varepsilon}) \tag{5.34}$$

Now $\underline{x}'$ is not random, so the first part of the right side of Equation 5.34 is:

$$Exp[f(\underline{x}')] = f(\underline{x}')$$

When we choose the reference value $\underline{x}'$ to be the mean μ_x (i.e., $\underline{x}' = \mu_x$) and we assume that the error $\underline{\varepsilon}$ is *unbiased* (has a mean of zero), the second half of Equation 5.34 simplifies to:

$$Exp(J\underline{\varepsilon}) = J Exp(\underline{\varepsilon}) = 0$$

We conclude that, based on a first order approximation to $f(\ )$ the mean of $\underline{y}$ is:

$$\mu_{\underline{y}} = Exp(\underline{y}) = f(\mu_x) \tag{5.35}$$

If we define $\underline{y}' = f(\underline{x}')$, then from Equation 5.33, to first-order $\underline{y} - \underline{y}' = J\underline{\varepsilon}$, so the covariance of the transformed variable $\underline{y}$ is:

$$\Sigma_{\underline{y}\underline{y}} = Exp([\underline{y} - \underline{y}'][\underline{y} - \underline{y}']^T) = Exp(J\underline{\varepsilon}\underline{\varepsilon}^T J^T)$$

Which is:

$$\Sigma_{\underline{y}\underline{y}} = J\Sigma_{\underline{x}\underline{x}}J^T \tag{5.36}$$

Note that the linear case of the last section is just a special case of this where the Jacobian was the transformation matrix.

5.1.3.6 Covariance of an Uncorrelated Partition of Inputs

Let a function $f(\ )$ depend on a vector $\underline{x}$ that we have decided to partition into two smaller vectors of possibly different length:

$$\underline{y} = f(\underline{x}) \qquad \underline{x} = \begin{bmatrix} \underline{x}_1 & \underline{x}_2 \end{bmatrix}^T$$

Let us also partition the covariance Σ_{xx} and Jacobian J_x:

$$J_x = \begin{bmatrix} J_1 & J_2 \end{bmatrix} \qquad \Sigma_{xx} = \begin{bmatrix} \Sigma_{11} & \Sigma_{12} \\ \Sigma_{21} & \Sigma_{22} \end{bmatrix}$$

where the block covariance matrices are $\Sigma_{ij} = Exp(\underline{x}_i \underline{x}_j^T)$. Then, the covariance of $\underline{y}$ is:

$$\Sigma_{yy} = J_x \Sigma_{xx} J_x^T \qquad\qquad \Sigma_{yy} = \begin{bmatrix} J_1 & J_2 \end{bmatrix} \begin{bmatrix} \Sigma_{11} & \Sigma_{12} \\ \Sigma_{21} & \Sigma_{22} \end{bmatrix} \begin{bmatrix} J_1^T \\ J_2^T \end{bmatrix}$$

Let us make the assumption that $\underline{x}_1$ and $\underline{x}_2$ are *uncorrelated* meaning $\Sigma_{ij} = 0$ when $(i \neq j)$. In this case:

$$\Sigma_{12} = \Sigma_{21} = [0] \qquad \therefore \quad \Sigma_{yy} = \begin{bmatrix} J_1 & J_2 \end{bmatrix} \begin{bmatrix} \Sigma_{11} & 0 \\ 0 & \Sigma_{22} \end{bmatrix} \begin{bmatrix} J_1^T \\ J_2^T \end{bmatrix}$$

Note that the size of the input matrix on the right is determined by the length of the parameters $\underline{x}$, but the size of the output matrix is determined by the size of $\underline{y}$. The result can be interpreted as the sum of the two input covariances transformed by the relevant Jacobians.

$$\Sigma_y = J_1 \Sigma_{11} J_1^T + J_2 \Sigma_{22} J_2^T \tag{5.37}$$

This result merely means that the total covariance of $\underline{y}$ can be considered to be a literal sum of contributions of both of the uncorrelated inputs.

Box 5.1 Formulae For Transformation of Uncertainty

For the following nonlinear transformation relating random vector $\underline{x}$ to random vector $\underline{y}$:

$$\underline{y} = \underline{f}(\underline{x})$$

The mean and covariance of $\underline{y}$ are related to those of $\underline{x}$ by:

$$\mu_y = \underline{f}(\mu_{xx}) \qquad\qquad \Sigma_{yy} = J \Sigma_{xx} J^T$$

Remember that, when using this result, unless all derivatives beyond J vanish (unless the original mapping really was linear), the result is a linear approximation to the true mean and covariance.

When $\underline{x}$ can be partitioned into two uncorrelated components, then:

$$\Sigma_{yy} = J_1 \Sigma_{11} J_1^T + J_2 \Sigma_{22} J_2^T$$

5.1.3.7 Example: Transforming Uncertainty from Image to Groundplane in the Azimuth Scanner

The coordinates in x need not be cartesian coordinates as they were in the last example. Consider how to convert uncertainty from the polar coordinates of a laser rangefinder to the cartesian coordinates of the groundplane.

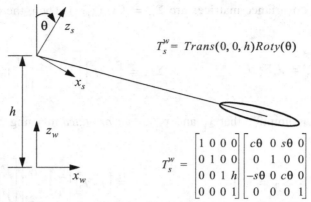

$$T_s^w = Trans(0, 0, h)Roty(\theta)$$

$$T_s^w = \begin{bmatrix} 1 & 0 & 0 & 0 \\ 0 & 1 & 0 & 0 \\ 0 & 0 & 1 & h \\ 0 & 0 & 0 & 1 \end{bmatrix} \begin{bmatrix} c\theta & 0 & s\theta & 0 \\ 0 & 1 & 0 & 0 \\ -s\theta & 0 & c\theta & 0 \\ 0 & 0 & 0 & 1 \end{bmatrix}$$

Figure 5.11 Transforming Uncertainty in the Azimuth Scanner. The coordinate transform from sensor to world coordinates is the first step. Note that the sensor tilt angle is negative in the figure.

First, consider converting coordinates from polar range, azimuth, elevation (i) to a sensor-fixed (s) cartesian frame (Figure 5.12).

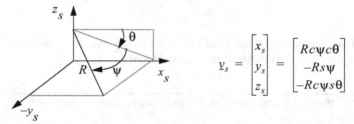

$$\underline{v}_s = \begin{bmatrix} x_s \\ y_s \\ z_s \end{bmatrix} = \begin{bmatrix} Rc\psi c\theta \\ -Rs\psi \\ -Rc\psi s\theta \end{bmatrix}$$

Figure 5.12 Azimuth Scanner Sensor to Image Transform. This converts from polar coordinates to sensor-fixed Cartesian coordinates.

Consider representing the uncertainty in range and the two scanning angles in terms of the diagonal matrix:

$$\Sigma_i = \begin{bmatrix} \sigma_{RR} & 0 & 0 \\ 0 & \sigma_{\theta\theta} & 0 \\ 0 & 0 & \sigma_{\psi\psi} \end{bmatrix}$$

Here we have implicitly made an assumption that our errors are uncorrelated (as well as unbiased) in the natural (polar) frame of reference because we used a diagonal matrix. Note that every covariance matrix is positive definite, so it is diagonalizeable. Therefore, there is some coordinate system within which the associated variables are uncorrelated. Whether or not two quantities are correlated depends on the choice of coordinates.

Recall that the Jacobian of the transform to the sensor frame is:

$$J_i^s = \begin{bmatrix} c\psi c\theta & -Rs\psi c\theta & -Rc\psi s\theta \\ -s\psi & -Rc\psi & 0 \\ -c\psi s\theta & Rs\psi s\theta & -Rc\psi c\theta \end{bmatrix}$$

Hence:

$$\Sigma_s = J_i^s \Sigma_i (J_i^s)^T$$

The transformation from this to the groundplane frame w involves the RPY transform and the location of the sensor on the vehicle. Let this homogeneous transform be called T_s^w. A simplified version was given above for the case when the vehicle is level and its control point is directly beneath the sensor. This part of the problem is identical to Equation 5.32, so using only the contained rotation matrix R_s^w:

$$\Sigma_w = R_s^w \Sigma_s (R_s^w)^T$$
$$\Sigma_w = R_s^w J_i^s \Sigma_i (J_i^s)^T (R_s^w)^T$$

5.1.3.8 Example: Computing Attitude from a Terrain Map

This is a case where the Jacobian is not square. We can use the last result to get uncertainty of elevation in a terrain map. Using this, we can compute uncertainty in predicted vehicle attitude.

Many forms of hazards that present themselves to a vehicle can be interpreted in terms of a gradient operator over some support length. For example, static stability involves estimation of vehicle pitch and roll under an assumption of terrain following. In the case of pitch, the appropriate length is the vehicle wheelbase. In the case of roll, the appropriate length is the vehicle width.

Consider the problem of estimation of the slope angle of the terrain in a particular direction over a certain distance (Figure 5.13). The distance L represents the separation of the wheels. Let the slope angle (positive downward) be represented in terms of its tangent, thus:

$$\theta = \frac{(z_r - z_f)}{L}$$

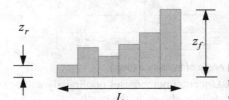

Figure 5.13 Terrain Slope from Elevations. The front and rear wheels are in contact with the indicated points.

The two elevations can be considered to be a two-vector whose covariance is:

$$\Sigma_{zz} = \begin{bmatrix} \sigma_f^2 & o \\ 0 & \sigma_r^2 \end{bmatrix}$$

Under our uncertainty propagation techniques, the covariance $\Sigma_{\theta\theta}$ of the computed pitch angle is a scalar. It can be computed from the covariance Σ_{zz} of the elevations as:

$$\Sigma_{\theta\theta} = J \Sigma_{zz} J^T$$

where J is, in this case, the gradient vector of pitch with respect to the elevations.

$$J = \begin{bmatrix} \dfrac{\partial \theta}{\partial z_f} & \dfrac{\partial \theta}{\partial z_r} \end{bmatrix} = \begin{bmatrix} \dfrac{1}{L} & -\dfrac{1}{L} \end{bmatrix}$$

The uncertainty in pitch is therefore simply:

$$\sigma_\theta^2 = \frac{1}{L^2}[\sigma_f^2 + \sigma_r^2]$$

This simple formula permits an assessment of confidence in predicted pitch at any point.

5.1.3.9 Example: Range Error in Rangefinders

We have up to now assumed that the variances in sensor readings are constants. It is often more realistic to express them as functions of something else – especially the sensor readings themselves. For laser rangefinders, the received laser radiation intensity is inversely proportional to the fourth power of the measured range (from the *radar equation*). Also, the range noise can be expected to depend on the received intensity and the local terrain gradient because there is a range distribution within that footprint. One reasonable model of all this is to express range uncertainty in terms of the intensity signal ρ, the range R, and the beam incidence angle α (Figure 5.14).

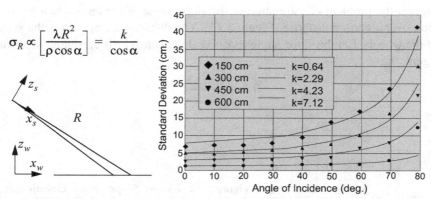

$$\sigma_R \propto \left[\frac{\lambda R^2}{\rho \cos \alpha} \right] = \frac{k}{\cos \alpha}$$

Figure 5.14 Laser Rangefinder Uncertainty Analysis. Uncertainty increases nonlinearly with range and intensity. The model was verified experimentally as shown in the graph.

5.1.3.10 Example: Stereo Vision

In the case of stereo vision, a completely different model for range error applies. We use the term *depth* instead of range because it is measured normally rather than radially. There are several ways to formulate this problem. Matthies [3] considers the image plane coordinates the independent variables whereas we will use their difference (called *disparity*) here.

Consider the geometry of two cameras with parallel image planes Figure 5.15. The basic stereo triangulation formula for perfectly aligned cameras is quoted below. It

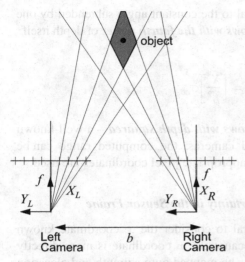

Left Camera $\qquad$ b $\qquad$ Right Camera

Figure 5.15 Range Uncertainty Versus Range in Stereo Vision. The footprints of corresponding pixels increases quickly with range.

can be derived simply from the principle of similar triangles.

$$\frac{Y_L}{X_L} = \frac{Y_L}{X} = \frac{y_l}{f} \qquad \frac{Y_R}{X_R} = \frac{Y_R}{X} = \frac{y_r}{f}$$

Therefore:

$$Y_L - Y_R = \frac{X[x_l - x_r]}{f}$$

This gives the relationship between disparity d and depth X:

$$b = \frac{Xd}{f} \qquad\qquad X = \frac{bf}{d}$$

$$(5.38)$$

Uppercase letters signify scene (3D) quantities whereas lowercase signify image plane quantities.

Once stereo matching is performed, the depth coordinate can be determined from the disparity d of each pixel. Then the y and z coordinates come from the known unit vector through each pixel that is given by the camera kinematic model. It will be useful at times to define disparity as the tangent of an angle thus:

$$\delta = \frac{d}{f} = \frac{b}{X}$$

because this hides the dependence of disparity on focal length of the lens. Then, the basic triangulation equation becomes:

$$X = \frac{b}{\delta}$$

Thus, if $s_{\delta\delta}$ is the uncertainty in disparity, then the uncertainty in depth is:

$$\sigma_{xx} = J\sigma_{\delta\delta}J^T$$

where the Jacobian in this case is simply the scalar:

$$J = \frac{\partial X}{\partial \delta} = \frac{-b}{\delta^2}$$

If we take the disparity uncertainty to be equal to the constant angle subtended by one pixel, then it's clear that the depth variance **grows with the fourth power** of depth itself:

$$\sigma_{xx} = \left[\frac{b^2}{\delta^4}\right]\sigma_{\delta\delta} = \left[\frac{X^4}{b^2}\right]\sigma_{\delta\delta}$$

and hence the standard deviation of depth **grows with depth squared** – a well-known and important result. For perfectly aligned cameras, the computed range can be applied to either camera model provided the appropriate pixel coordinates are used.

5.1.3.11 Example: Stereo Uncertainty in the Sensor Frame

Unlike the case for rangefinders, it is natural to consider the x coordinate known instead of the true 3D range to an object because the x coordinate is more directly related to disparity. Let the image coordinates be mapped onto azimuth and elevation angles as shown in Figure 5.16:

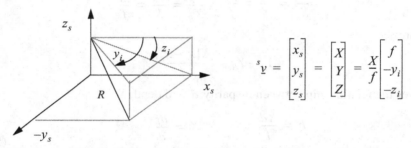

$$^s\underline{y} = \begin{bmatrix} x_s \\ y_s \\ z_s \end{bmatrix} = \begin{bmatrix} X \\ Y \\ Z \end{bmatrix} = \frac{X}{f}\begin{bmatrix} f \\ -y_i \\ -z_i \end{bmatrix}$$

Figure 5.16 Stereo Vision Image to Sensor Transform. This is how to convert depth and pixel coordinates into a 3D point in the sensor frame.

The imaging Jacobian provides the relationship between differential quantities in the sensor frame and the associated position change in the image. The Jacobian is:

$$J_i^s = \begin{bmatrix} \partial x_s/\partial X & \partial x_s/\partial y_i & \partial x_s/\partial z_i \\ \partial y_s/\partial X & \partial y_s/\partial y_i & \partial y_s/\partial z_i \\ \partial z_s/\partial X & \partial z_s/\partial y_i & \partial z_s/\partial z_i \end{bmatrix} = \frac{1}{f}\begin{bmatrix} f & 0 & 0 \\ -y_i & -X & 0 \\ -z_i & 0 & -X \end{bmatrix}$$

If we consider that the **only** sensor error is the depth measurement, the uncertainty in the sensor frame is:

$$\Sigma_s = J_i^s\sigma_{yy}J_i^{sT} = \left[\frac{X^4}{b^2}\right]\sigma_{\delta\delta}$$

Multiplying out and cancelling small terms leads to:

$$\Sigma_s \approx \left[\frac{X^4}{f^2b^2}\right]\Sigma_{\delta\delta}\begin{bmatrix} f^2 & 0 & 0 \\ 0 & X^2 & 0 \\ 0 & 0 & X^2 \end{bmatrix}$$

5.1.4 Random Processes

Recall that a *random variable* is a single (may be vector-valued) value chosen at random from a theoretical collection of all possible points called a *population*. Conversely, the *random process* (random sequence, random signal) is a function chosen at random from a theoretical collection of all possible functions of time called an *ensemble*. Usually, the statistical variation of the ensemble of functions at any time is considered known. For a random process, when a single "outcome" is chosen, a whole function results – not just one value.

Exactly which signal is chosen is a random variable, and therefore the value of the chosen function at any time **across all experiments** is a random variable. The values of the signal from sample to sample **may or may not** be random and if so, may or may not be independent. Some examples include:

* Turn on a gyroscope and measure its bias. It is a constant, but unknown value until measured, because they are all different.
* Measure the voltage from a wall socket at a random time. The frequency is 60 Hz. The peak amplitude may slowly vary from time to time. The phase is a uniformly distributed random variable because it depends on exactly when it was measured.
* Flip a coin 100 times. This is a uniformly distributed binary random signal.
* Measure the cosmic background radiation from the big bang. This is a fairly random signal.

5.1.4.1 Random Constant

Consider for example a random constant process generated by turning on a gyroscope and plotting its bias. The biases of all gyroscopes manufactured follow some sort of distribution. To be sure, the bias for any particular gyroscope could be plotted on, an oscilloscope and it would produce (something like) the signal in Figure 5.17:

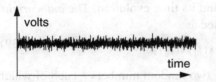

Figure 5.17 Bias of a Gyroscope Selection Random Process. Any randomly chosen gyroscope will have a noisy nonzero resting output.

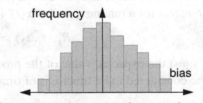

Figure 5.18 Histogram of Gyro Biases. A histogram of a set of trials of gyroscopes.

Although there is a slight random variation, the output is essentially constant and nonzero. Suppose, however, several people buy several gyros at the same time, connect them to an oscilloscope, wait ten seconds, and record the output value. The values of the biases at t = 10 seconds could be plotted in a histogram to produce something like Figure 5.18.

This distribution is the probability distribution of the associated random constant process at t = 10 seconds. In this case, while any member of the *ensemble* of functions is mostly deterministic in time, the **choice** of the function is random.

In general, there may be a family of related functions of time where some important parameter varies randomly – a family of sinusoids of random amplitude, for instance. Even though there is no way to predict which function will be chosen, it may be known that all functions are related by a single random parameter and from this knowledge, it is possible to compute the distribution for the process as a function of time.

5.1.4.2 Random Process Attributes

It is important to be familiar with certain attributes of random signals that are outlined below.

5.1.4.2.1 Bias, Stationarity, Ergodicity and Whiteness. A random process is *unbiased* if its expected (i.e., average) value is zero for all time. A random process is said to be *stationary* if the distribution of values of the functions in the ensemble does not vary with time. Conceptually, a movie of the histogram above for the gyroscopes for each second of time would be a still picture. An *ergodic* random process is one where time averaging is equivalent to ensemble averaging – which is to say that everything about the process can be discovered by watching a single function for all time, or by watching all signals at a single instant. This is related to the way that a Fourier or Taylor series can predict the value of a function anywhere if its respective coefficients are known at a single point. A *white* signal is one that contains all frequencies.

Fluency with these concepts requires the ability to think about a random process in three different ways: in terms of its probability distribution; in terms of it evolution over time; and in terms of its frequency content. These different views of the same process will be discussed in the next sections, as well as methods for converting back and forth between them.

5.1.4.2.2 Correlation Function. Correlation is a way of thinking about both the probability distributions of a random process and its time evolution. The *autocorrelation function* for a random process $x(t)$ is defined as:

$$R_{xx}(t_1, t_2) = Exp[x(t_1)x(t_2)] \tag{5.39}$$

so it's just the expected value of the product of two random numbers – each of which can be considered to be functions of time. The result is a function of both times. Let:

$$x_1 = x(t_1) \qquad x_2 = x(t_2)$$

then the autocorrelation function is, by definition of expectation:

$$R_{xx}(t_1, t_2) = \int\limits_{-\infty}^{\infty} \int\limits_{-\infty}^{\infty} x_1 x_2 f(x_1, x_2) dx_1 dx_2 \tag{5.40}$$

where $f(x_1, x_2)$ is the joint probability distribution.

The autocorrelation function gives the "tendency" of a function to have the same sign and magnitude (i.e., to be *correlated*) at two different times. For smooth functions it is expected that the autocorrelation function would be highest when the two times are close because a smooth function changes little in a short time. This idea can be expressed formally in terms of the frequency content of the signal, and conversely, the autocorrelation function says a lot about how smooth a function is. Equivalently, the autocorrelation function specifies how fast a function can change, which is equivalent to saying something about the magnitude of the coefficients in its Taylor series, or its Fourier series, or its Fourier transform. All of these things are linked.

5.1.4.2.3 Cross-Correlation Function. The *crosscorrelation function* relates two different random processes in an analogous way:

$$R_{xy}(t_1, t_2) = E[x(t_1)y(t_2)] \qquad (5.41)$$

For a *stationary process* the correlation function is dependent only on the difference $\tau = t_1 - t_2$. When the processes involved are unbiased, the correlation functions give the variance and covariance of the indicated random variables. This is easy to see by considering the general formula for variance and setting the mean to zero. Thus, for stationary unbiased processes, the correlation functions *are* the variances and covariances expressed as a function of the time difference:

$$R_{xx}(\tau) = \sigma_{xx}^2(\tau) \qquad R_{xy}(\tau) = \sigma_{xy}^2(\tau) \qquad (5.42)$$

Also, for stationary unbiased processes, setting the time difference to zero recovers the traditional variance of the associated random variable:

$$\sigma_{xx}^2 = R_{xx}(0) \qquad \sigma_{xy}^2 = R_{xy}(0) \qquad (5.43)$$

5.1.4.2.4 Power Spectral Density. The *power spectral density* is just the Fourier transform (denoted here by F) of the autocorrelation function, thus:

$$S_{xx}(j\omega) = F[R_{xx}(\tau)] = \int_{-\infty}^{\infty} R_{xx}(\tau)e^{-j\omega\tau}d\tau \qquad (5.44)$$

The power spectral density is a direct measure of the frequency content of a signal, and hence, of its power content. Of course, the inverse Fourier transform yields the autocorrelation back again.

$$R_{xx}(\tau) = \frac{1}{2\pi} \int_{-\infty}^{\infty} S_{xx}(j\omega)e^{j\omega\tau}d\omega \qquad (5.45)$$

Similarly, the *cross power spectral density* function is the Fourier transform of cross-correlation:

$$S_{xy}(j\omega) = F[R_{xy}(\tau)] = \int_{-\infty}^{\infty} R_{xy}(\tau)e^{-j\omega\tau}d\tau \qquad (5.46)$$

5.1.4.3 The Random Walk

The *random walk* is one of the simplest and most important random processes. We will see that it is fundamental to the definition of stochastic integrals.

5.1.4.3.1 Unit Impulse Function. The Dirac delta $\delta(t)$, or *unit impulse function*, is a generalized function that is defined in terms of its relation to other functions when it is integrated with them. In particular, we need only one property, which is:

$$\int_{-\infty}^{\infty} f(t)\delta(t-T)dt = f(T)$$

Thus, the unit impulse has the property that it returns the value of the function being integrated (i.e., $f(t)$) at the time when the delta function argument is zero.

5.1.4.3.2 White Noise. White noise is defined as a stationary random process whose power spectral density function is constant (Figure 5.19). That is, it contains all frequencies of equal amplitude. If the constant *spectral amplitude* is A, then the corresponding autocorrelation function is given by the inverse Fourier transform of a constant, which is the Dirac delta.

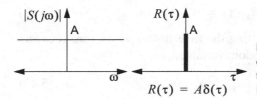

$$R(\tau) = A\delta(\tau)$$

Figure 5.19 Spectral Amplitude and Autocorrelation of White Noise. White noise contains all frequencies. It is a mathematical idealization that does not exist in nature.

Such an autocorrelation function means that the value of a white noise signal at some instant of time tells us absolutely nothing about its value at any other time. This is because it is possible for white noise to jump around at "infinite" frequency.

5.1.4.3.3 White Noise Process Covariance. Let the white unbiased Gaussian random process $x(t)$ have power spectral density S_p. Then the variance is:

$$\sigma_{xx}^2 = R_{xx}(0) = \frac{1}{2\pi}\int_{-\infty}^{\infty} S_p\delta(t)e^{j\omega\tau}d\omega = S_p\delta(0) = S_p \tag{5.47}$$

Thus the variance of a white noise process is numerically **equal to its spectral amplitude**. However, the integral was over frequency, so a change in units occurs to remove "per unit frequency (Hz^{-1}) to produce σ_{xx}^2 in units of squared amplitude.

5.1.4.3.4 Random Walk Process Covariance. Now suppose that the white noise process is associated with the time derivative $\dot{x}$ of the real variable of interest. Thus:

$$\sigma_{\dot{x}\dot{x}}^2 = S_p \tag{5.48}$$

An interesting question in this case is: what are σ_{xx}^2, $\sigma_{x\dot{x}}^2$, and σ_{xx}^2? These quantities can be derived from first principles. Notice that the value of x at any time must be, by definition, the integral of $\dot{x}$. Then, the variance must be:

$$\sigma_{xx}^2 = E(x^2) = E\left[\int_0^t \dot{x}(u)du \int_0^t \dot{x}(v)dv\right] \tag{5.49}$$

This can be written easily as a double integral since the variables of integration are independent thus:

$$\sigma_{xx}^2 = E\left[\int_0^t\int_0^t \dot{x}(u)\dot{x}(v)dudv\right] \tag{5.50}$$

The trick is to interchange the order of expectation and integration:

$$\sigma_{xx}^2 = \int_0^t\int_0^t E[\dot{x}(u)\dot{x}(v)]dudv \tag{5.51}$$

Now the inner integrand is just the autocorrelation function, which, for white noise is the Dirac delta scaled by spectral amplitude, so, the variance is:

$$\sigma_{xx}^2 = \int_0^t\int_0^t S_p\delta(u-v)dudv = \int_0^t S_p dv = S_p t \tag{5.52}$$

Spotlight 5.2 Random Walk Process.

The variance of the integral of a white noise process grows linearly with time. Also, the standard deviation grows with the square root of time.

The process $x(t)$ is the random walk. Its time derivative $\dot{x}(t)$ at any instant is a white noise process.

5.1.4.3.5 ARW and Noise Density of Gyros.
The angle random walk (ARW) $\dot{\sigma}_\theta$ of a gyro is a measure of the magnitude (standard deviation) of noise present in the angular velocity measurement, but it is expressed in terms of the slope (with respect to time) of the random walk that it produces. The noise magnitude is assumed to be more or less constant. Therefore, we know that it will give rise to a computed angle whose variance will grow linearly with time:

$$\sigma_{\theta\theta} = \dot{\sigma}_\theta^2 \times t \tag{5.53}$$

The units of $\dot{\sigma}_\theta^2$ must be squared angle per unit time. Therefore, the units of $\dot{\sigma}_\theta$ are angle per square root time. The notation $\dot{\sigma}_\theta$ is therefore awkward because this quantity has square root time units and it is not a true time derivative. It is also conventional to express the "square root time" unit as a time unit divided by a square root time unit. Using degrees and secs for example:

$$\frac{deg}{\sqrt{sec}} = \frac{deg}{sec/(\sqrt{sec})} = \frac{deg}{sec\sqrt{Hz}}$$

ARW, when expressed in the units of rightmost form is called the *noise density*. The square of the noise density is the *power spectral density* and it has units of angle per unit time squared per unit frequency, or $\deg^2/(\sec^2 \cdot Hz)$. The reader will encounter these terms often in device spec sheets.

Random walks of good gyros are typically under a few degrees in an hour, so these are units that are intuitive for comparison purposes. A useful conversion is:

$$\frac{deg}{hr\sqrt{Hz}} = \frac{deg}{hr/(\sqrt{sec})} = \frac{deg}{hr}\sqrt{sec} = \frac{deg}{hr}\sqrt{\frac{hr}{3600sec}} = \left(\frac{1}{60}\right)\frac{deg}{\sqrt{hr}}$$

So we divide $\deg/(hr\sqrt{Hz})$ by 60 to get $\deg/\sqrt{hr}$. Thus a spectral density of 7.5 deg/hr-rt(Hz) is equivalent to an angle random walk of 0.125 deg/rt(hr). A *rate random walk* can be defined for an accelerometer that is the equivalent of the angle random walk but its velocity variance grows linearly with time.

5.1.4.3.6 Integrated Random Walk Process Covariance. If the second derivative of $x(t)$ with respect to time is a white process, then the variance in $x(t)$ is:

$$\sigma_{xx}^2 = E(x^2) = E\left[\int_0^t \dot{x}(u)du \int_0^t \dot{x}(v)dv\right] \tag{5.54}$$

The velocities come from accelerations.

$$\sigma_{xx}^2 = E(x^2) = E\left[\int_0^t\left(\int_0^u \ddot{x}(u)du\right)du \int_0^t\left(\int_0^v \ddot{x}(v)dv\right)dv\right] \tag{5.55}$$

The derivation of the correct result requires the stochastic calculus discussed later. For now, we quote the result simply as:

$$\sigma_{xx}^2 = \frac{S_p t^3}{3} \tag{5.56}$$

Thus the variance grows with the cube of time. This process, the double integral of a white noise (for example, an acceleration), is called an *integrated random walk*. This process is a good model for the variance in a position estimate that is computed by integrating noisy acceleration twice.

5.1.5 References and Further Reading

Ross is a good elementary text in probability whereas Papoulis is a more authoritative reference. The material here on random processes in based on Brown. Duda is a good source on random vectors, uncertainty transformation, and the multivariate (vector) Gaussian distribution.

[1] R. G. Brown and P. Y. C. Hwang, *Introduction to Random Signals and Applied Kalman Filtering,* Wiley, 1997.

[2] R. O. Duda and P. E. Hart, *Pattern Classification and Scene Analysis,* Wiley, 1973.

[3] L. Matthies and Steven Shafer, Error Modeling in Stereo Navigation, *IEEE Journal of Robotics and Automation,* Vol. RA-3, No. 3, pp. 239–250, June 1987.

[4] Athanasios Papoulis and S. Unnikrishna Pillai, *Probability Random Variables and Stochastic Processes,* McGraw-Hill, 2001.

[5] S. Ross, *A First Course in Probability,* Prentice Hall, 2002.

5.1.6 Exercises

5.1.6.1 *Correlation of GPS Measurements*

The errors in GPS measurements of position are correlated over short time periods. Suppose your robot GPS system provides position estimate with error x_1 at time t_1 and position estimate with error x_2 at time t_2. The correlation of the errors $Exp[x_1 x_2^T]$ is known. Rederive Equation 5.37 with no assumptions of decorrelation and then provide a formula for the covariance of the relative position measurement:

$$\Delta \underline{x} = \underline{x}_2 - \underline{x}_1$$

5.1.6.2 *Probability Distribution of Discrete Random Variables*

Use any programming language or spreadsheet you prefer that has a capacity to generate Gaussian random variables of unit variance. Plot a normalized histogram of at least 1,000,000 Gaussian random numbers by separating its elements into bins of width 0.5 spanning the values from –4 to +4. Use the width of the bins to normalize the probability mass function so that it has an area of unity under it. Adjust the number of bins and see what happens to the distribution.

5.1.6.3 *Random Processes*

A sequence is an ordered set. Produce at least 200 normalized (variance = 1, mean = 0) random sequences of length 400 or more; 200 random sequences of length 400 is 80,000 random numbers. Separate them into 200 sequences of 400 numbers each. For the rest of this question, suppose that position in the sequence is equivalent to time.

 (i) Plot 3 representative sequences on one graph using different colors or symbols for each sequence. Plot them as functions of time.

(ii) The variance of a random process is a function of time where the value of the variance at any time is the variance of then values in all sequences at that same point in time. The variance is computed across the sequences. Suppose we want the variance at time $t = 6$. You take the values of each of the random sequences at $t = 6$ (there will be 200 such numbers if you have 200 sequences) and compute the variance of this sample of values. Then you do the same at $t = 7$, and so on.

On a separate graph, plot the variance of the 200 sequences as a function of time. This variance is a single function of time. Interpret the results in terms of smoothness and general trends (i.e., how does the variance change with time?).

(iii) What happens to the process variance curve when you increase the number of sequences from 200 to as much as your computer can handle?

(iv) Now produce a second set of 200 sequences where each is the integral (sum) of the associated original sequence. Each of these integrated sequences is called a *random walk*. Intuitively, imagine that the original sequences represent velocity measurements (for a stationary vehicle) and your job is to compute the positions (in one dimension) which correspond to each noisy velocity sequence. Plot 3 representative random walk sequences on one graph using different colors or symbols for each sequence.

(v) On a separate graph, plot the variance of the 200 random walk sequences as a function of time. Interpret the results in terms of smoothness and general trends (i.e., how does the variance change with time?). What limits can be placed on the deviation from the origin at the end of the integrated sequence?

(vi) Consider the expected behavior of the variance of the random walk as a function of time and comment on whether your results fit.

5.2 Covariance Propagation and Optimal Estimation

Our transformation rules give us all the tools necessary to compute the uncertainty associated with an estimate, derived from measurements, of a continuously changing quantity. For reasons of computational efficiency, continuous estimation is performed with *recursive* algorithms. A recursive algorithm is one that computes a new estimate from the last estimate and the new measurement, while making no reference to any earlier measurements. Uncertainty can also be computed recursively.

This section will develop various means to compute a new estimate of system state $\hat{\underline{x}}_k$ and its uncertainty P_k by considering the result at any point to be a function of the last *estimate* $\hat{\underline{x}}_{k-1}$, its uncertainty P_{k-1}, and the current *measurement* $\underline{z}_k$ and its uncertainty R_k.

5.2.1 Variance of Continuous Integration and Averaging Processes

This section will use our rules for transforming uncertainty to derive the behavior of certain continuous random processes from a time series perspective.

5.2.1.1 Variance of a Continuous Summing Process

Consider the earlier result in Equation 5.29 for the variance of a sum of random variables with the same distribution. In our new notation, the output y becomes the state estimate $\hat{x}$ and the input x becomes the measurement z. In this notation, the result is:

$$\sigma_x^2 = n\sigma_z^2 \tag{5.57}$$

We can imagine the summing process as a continuous process where measurements are added one by one. The number of elements in the sum $n = t/\Delta t$ is proportional to time, so Equation 5.58 implies that the variance of the sum will be linear in time.

Likewise, the standard deviation will grow with the square root of time, initially growing rapidly and then levelling off as time evolves (Figure 5.20). This levelling off behavior arises from the fact that truly random errors tend to cancel each other if enough of them are added.

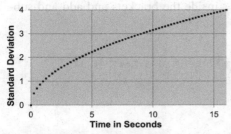

Figure 5.20 Standard Deviation of a Continuous Sum. The standard deviation grows with the square root of time.

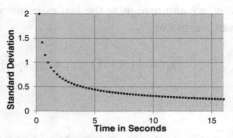

Figure 5.21 Standard Deviation of a Continuous Average. The standard deviation decreases with the square root of time.

5.2.1.2 Recursive Integration

The integration process is easy to convert to recursive form. The summing process can be written recursively as:

$$\hat{x}_k = \sum_{i=1}^{k} z_i = \sum_{i=1}^{k-1} z_i + z_k = \hat{x}_{k-1} + z_k \tag{5.58}$$

The uncertainty propagation can be written recursively as:

$$\sigma_k^2 = \sum_{i=1}^{k} \sigma_z^2 = \sum_{i=1}^{k-1} \sigma_z^2 + \sigma_z^2 = \sigma_{k-1}^2 + \sigma_z^2 \tag{5.59}$$

5.2.1.3 Variance of a Continuous Averaging Process

Consider the earlier result in Equation 5.31 for the variance of an average of random variables with the same distribution. In our new notation, the result is:

$$\sigma_x^2 = \frac{1}{n}\sigma_z^2 \tag{5.60}$$

As for the sum earlier, we can imagine the averaging process as a continuous process where measurements are added one by one. The number of elements in the sum $n = t/\Delta t$ is again proportional to time, so Equation 5.61 implies that the variance will decrease inversely with respect to time.

Likewise, the standard deviation will decrease with the inverse square root of time (Figure 5.21), initially decreasing rapidly and then leveling off as time evolves. This behavior arises from the fact that the errors in the measurements are being averaged away.

5.2.1.4 Recursive Averaging

The averaging process is less easy to convert to recursive form. It can be written as:

$$\hat{x}_k = \frac{1}{k}\sum_{i=1}^{k} z_i = \frac{1}{k}\left(\sum_{i=1}^{k-1} z_i + z_k\right) = \frac{1}{k}\left(\frac{k-1}{k-1}\sum_{i=1}^{k-1} z_i + z_k\right)$$

Now, we can recognize the last estimate $\hat{x}'_{k-1}$ inside the brackets and add and subtract one more:

$$\hat{x}_k = \frac{1}{k}[(k-1)\hat{x}_{k-1} + z_k] = \frac{1}{k}[(k-1)\hat{x}_{k-1} + \hat{x}_{k-1} + z_k - \hat{x}_{k-1}]$$

This simplifies to:

$$\hat{x}_k = \hat{x}_{k-1} + \frac{1}{k}(z_k - \hat{x}_{k-1})$$

The difference between the current measurement and the last measurement $z_k - \hat{x}_{k-1}$ is known as the *innovation*. When k is large, the innovation is progressively downweighted and z_k has less and less effect on the answer.

One straightforward way to interpret this formulation is that the old estimate votes "k" times for its value and the new measurement votes once for its value. It is instructive to rewrite the result as:

$$\hat{x}_k = \hat{x}_{k-1} + K(z_k - \hat{x}_{k-1}) \tag{5.61}$$

where K will be recognized later as serving the role of the *Kalman gain*. Note that, in this simple case, it is simply the reciprocal of the time step k and it could be precomputed.

Now for the recursive covariance result. Let σ_z^2 be the variance of a single measurement z_k. Once again, the variance after k measurements is:

$$\sigma_k^2 = \frac{1}{k^2}\sum_{i=1}^{k}\sigma_z^2 = \frac{1}{k}\sigma_z^2$$

First, note that:

$$\sigma_k^2 = \frac{\sigma_z^2}{k} \Rightarrow \frac{1}{\sigma_k^2} = \frac{k}{\sigma_z^2} = \frac{k-1}{\sigma_z^2} + \frac{1}{\sigma_z^2}$$

Which means:

$$\frac{1}{\sigma_k^2} = \frac{1}{\sigma_{k-1}^2} + \frac{1}{\sigma_z^2}$$

Hence the accumulation of variance in an averaging process can be considered to follow a reciprocal addition rule like conductances in electric circuits.

Also note that:

$$\sigma_k^2 = \frac{\sigma_z^2}{k} \qquad\qquad \sigma_{k-1}^2 = \frac{\sigma_z^2}{k-1}$$

So:

$$\frac{\sigma_k^2}{\sigma_{k-1}^2} = \frac{k-1}{k} \Rightarrow \sigma_k^2 = \left(\frac{k-1}{k}\right)\sigma_k^2 = \left(1 - \frac{1}{k}\right)\sigma_k^2$$

Which means:

$$\sigma_{k+1}^2 = (1-K)\sigma_k^2 \tag{5.62}$$

where $K = 1/k$ as it did in the average formula. Each new iteration reduces the variance to $1 - K$ of its former value. Equation 5.61 and Equation 5.62 form a recursive filter that is applicable when the uncertainty of all measurements is equal.

The major advantages of recursive filters are:

- They require virtually no memory because there is no longer a need to store all previous measurements.
- They spread the computation out over time so that each new estimate requires only a few operations.
- They provide an answer, not only at the end of the measurement sequence, but at every point during the processing of the sequence.

5.2.1.5 Example: Inertial Sensor Performance Characterization

The Allan Variance $\sigma_A^2(\tau)$ is an empirical measure of the stability of clocks and inertial sensors. Its computation is a procedure that can be performed readily on a sensor, once it is purchased, in order to assess several important error characteristics. It can be computed for accelerometers and gyros but the following presentation will concentrate on gyros.

Suppose that a long series of data from a stationary sensor is collected. The process is to divide the data into bins of elapsed time τ. Define $\bar{y}_k(\tau)$ to be the average of all of the sensor readings in bin k:

$$\bar{y}_k(\tau) = \frac{1}{m} \sum_{i=0}^{m} y[t_0(k) + i\Delta t]$$

The Allan Variance is 1/2 the sample variance of, the differences between, averages of consecutive bins:

$$\sigma_A^2(\tau) = \frac{1}{2(n-1)} \sum_{k=0}^{n} (\bar{y}_{k+1}(\tau) - \bar{y}_k(\tau))^2$$

The square root of Allan Variance is called Allan Deviation. If we suppose that both $\bar{y}_k(\tau)$ and $\bar{y}_{k+1}(\tau)$ are random variables of some variance $\sigma^2(\tau)$, then the variance of the difference is given by:

$$Var[\bar{y}_{k+1}(\tau) - \bar{y}_k(\tau)] = \sigma^2(\tau) + \sigma^2(\tau) = 2\sigma^2(\tau)$$

Furthermore, if $\bar{y}_k(\tau)$ and $\bar{y}_{k+1}(\tau)$ contain a slowly changing bias, it cancels out in the difference, so the sample mean of the difference vanishes. In this case, the Allan variance is computing the sample variance of a random variable whose variance is $2\sigma^2(\tau)$ and then dividing by 2. Hence it is computing an estimate of $\sigma^2(\tau)$.

It is conventional to compute Allan Variance for a very large range of bin widths τ and to plot the results as a function of τ on a log-log scale. A typical Allan Deviation graph for a gyro looks like the following:

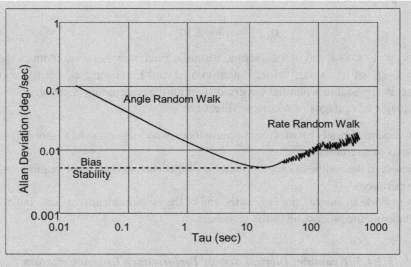

Spotlight 5.3 Allan Deviation Plot.

Such a plot for an inertial sensor provides much useful information about its performance – notably the angle random walk and the bias stability.

5.2.1.5.1 Angle Random Walk Region. Note that the initial trend is toward lower deviation as the bin size increases. In this region, the bias is slowly changing and the Allan Deviation is dominated by the random noise in the sensor output. It was argued above that the Allan Variance is estimating the variance of the bin averages if bias is changing slowly. If the noise density for the sensor is $\dot\sigma_\theta^2$, then the variance of the bin averages would be expected to decrease with the square root of time:

$$\sigma_{\bar{y}} = \dot\sigma_\theta / (\sqrt{\tau})$$

Such a relationship will have a slope of $-1/2$ on a log-log plot. Indeed, this is exactly what we typically see on such a plot, as we do above.

Of course, we can solve for the noise density:

$$\dot\sigma_\theta = \sigma_{\bar{y}}\sqrt{\tau}$$

and therefore we can read the noise density off the graph at any point on the region of the graph where the slope is $-1/2$. This is done by multiplying the Allan Deviation by the square root of the bin width. The easiest place to do this above is when $\tau = 1$ and the units of τ are consistent with those of $\sigma_{\bar{y}}$. From the graph we have:

$$\dot\sigma_\theta = \sigma_{\bar{y}}(1)\frac{deg}{\sec}\sqrt{1\sec} = 0.015\frac{deg}{\sqrt{\sec}}$$

5.2.1.5.2 Rate Random Walk Region. At the far right of the graph, the bin sizes are very large and the time durations are relatively long. On this time scale, the sensor noise is being averaged effectively to zero, but the sensor bias is no longer constant for all of τ and the bin average becomes a measure of average bias. Whether and how much the average sensor bias rises and falls from one bin to the next is effectively a random variable and the deviations $y_{k+1} - y_k$ which are squared in the Allan Variance formula, begin to increase with τ rather than decrease as they did in the angle random walk region. This region of unstable sensor bias in called the rate random walk region.

5.2.1.5.3 Bias Stability Region. Given the above two regions of the curve, it should be clear that there will be a blending point in the middle of them where one effect gives way to the other. At the precise middle of this region the decrease in bin average variance due to noise will be balanced by the increase in bin average variance due to bias changes. This region where they cancel will have a slope of zero and it is the point where the sensor bias can be measured best. At this point, the maximum amount of noise averaging is occurring before the bias itself begins to change. Sensor manufacturers typically quote the bin average variation at this point as the *bias stability*. This value represents the best case for the error to be expected in active bias estimation. On the graph above, the bias stability is 0.005 deg/sec.

5.2.2 Stochastic Integration

This section extends our understanding of random walk phenomena to the case of random vectors and continuous time. We will call this more general case *stochastic integration*. It is often necessary to perform stochastic integration whenever the system being measured is in motion.

Moreover, some measurements cannot reduce uncertainty. They can only slow down its growth rate. This phenomenon occurs when one has measurements of one or more time derivatives of a quantity of interest and the state is then computed by integrating a differential equation. As in the case of the random walk, it is possible to compute the time evolution of the uncertainty in the state given the uncertainty in the measurements that were used.

5.2.2.1 Discrete Stochastic Integration

We can use the result in Equation 5.37 to propagate covariance in a continuous integration process. Let us identify the output y with the next estimate $\underline{x}_{i+1}$ of some state vector. Let the inputs $\underline{x}_1$ and $\underline{x}_2$ correspond respectively to the last estimate of state $\underline{x}_i$ and the present inputs $\underline{u}_i$. Our integration process is then expressed as:

$$\underline{x}_{i+1} = f(\underline{x}_i, \underline{u}_i) \tag{5.63}$$

We can linearize this nonlinear difference equation to express the evolution in errors in the state given errors in the inputs:

$$\delta\underline{x}_{i+1} = \Phi_i\delta\underline{x}_i + \Gamma_i\delta\underline{u}_i \tag{5.64}$$

Because this is now linear, we can immediately write the covariance propagation equation if we assume the state and input errors are uncorrelated:

$$P_{i+1} = \Phi_i P_i \Phi_i^T + \Gamma_i Q_i \Gamma_i^T \tag{5.65}$$

This is merely a use of the covariance propagation result from Equation 5.37 when applied to a difference equation:

$$\Sigma_{i+1} = J_x \Sigma_i J_x^T + J_u \Sigma_u J_u^T \tag{5.66}$$

5.2.2.2 Example: Dead Reckoning with Odometer Error Only

Consider a case in which vehicle position is generated by adding together tiny displacement vectors in a process called *dead reckoning*. Assume that displacement lengths are measured by a noisy sensor but their directions are known perfectly. This process can be formulated in terms of two vectors, the current position x_i and the current measurements u_i, which when combined generate the new position x_{i+1} (Figure 5.22).

Let the state at step i be $\underline{x}_i = [x_i \; y_i]^T$ and the measurement vector is $\underline{u}_i = [l_i \; \psi_i]^T$. The dynamics of the system are expressed in the discrete time difference equation that is nonlinear in the inputs:

$$\underline{x}_{i+1} = f(\underline{x}_i, \underline{u}_i) = \begin{bmatrix} x_i + l_i \cos(\psi_i) \\ y_i + l_i \sin(\psi_i) \end{bmatrix} = \begin{bmatrix} 1 & 0 \\ 0 & 1 \end{bmatrix} \begin{bmatrix} x_i \\ y_i \end{bmatrix} + \begin{bmatrix} c_i & -l_i s_i \\ s_i & l_i c_i \end{bmatrix}$$

The Jacobians are:

$$\Phi_i = \frac{\partial \underline{x}_{i+1}}{\partial \underline{x}_i} = \begin{bmatrix} 1 & 0 \\ 0 & 1 \end{bmatrix} \qquad G_i = \frac{\partial \underline{x}_{i+1}}{\partial \underline{u}_i} = \begin{bmatrix} c_i & -l_i s_i \\ s_i & l_i c_i \end{bmatrix}$$

For perfect heading, the uncertainty in the current position and measurements is:

$$P_i = \begin{bmatrix} \sigma_{xx} & \sigma_{xy} \\ \sigma_{yx} & \sigma_{yy} \end{bmatrix}_i \qquad\qquad Q_i = \begin{bmatrix} \sigma_l^2 & 0 \\ 0 & 0 \end{bmatrix}$$

So, for uncorrelated error (i.e., if the error in the new measurements has nothing to do with the current position). The error in the new position can be written as:

$$P_{i+1} = \Phi_i P_i \Phi_i^T + G_i Q_i G_i^T \tag{5.67}$$

Expanding the last term:

$$P_{i+1} = P_i + \begin{bmatrix} c_i^2 \sigma_l^2 & c_i s_i \sigma_l^2 \\ c_i s_i \sigma_l^2 & s_i^2 \sigma_l^2 \end{bmatrix}$$

This result gives the uncertainty of the new position estimate. Note that the off diagonal terms will remain zero for motion along either axis. Also, the diagonal terms are always positive and their sum (the "*total*" uncertainty) increases monotonically.

In simulating such a system along a slowly turning path (Figure 5.23), the covariance grows without bound. Also, the ellipses turn to the right more slowly than the path, because they remember the contributions of all past measurements, and remain pointing mostly upward.

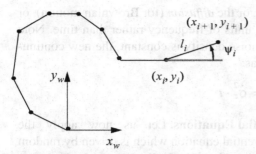

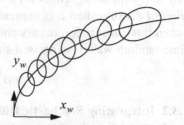

Figure 5.22 Setup for Computing Uncertainty of Odometry. Measurements of distance and angle are available for dead reckoning position as shown.

Figure 5.23 Variance Growth in Odometry. The ellipses represent contours of constant 99% probability. At any point, the right answer should be inside the ellipse 99% of the time.

5.2.2.3 *Continuous Stochastic Integration*

Historically, the continuous time version of Equation 5.65 turned out to be far more difficult to formulate than it may appear at first glance, and the complete resolution required the invention of a branch of mathematics called *stochastic calculus*. The discussion so far has been structured to avoid some thorny issues. For example, the discussion of random walks avoided the issue of how one integrates white noise by reverting to Fourier Transforms. This section will now address those thorny issues.

5.2.2.3.1 Variance of a Continuous Random Walk. Consider how we might develop an expression for the variance of a continuous random walk process. Recall from Equation 5.57 that the discrete time version of the random walk variance is:

$$\sigma_x^2 = n\sigma_z^2$$

If we now substitute for the number of time steps with $n = t/\Delta t$, this becomes:

$$\sigma_x^2(t) = (\sigma_z^2 t)/\Delta t$$

Now as $\Delta t \to 0$ above, we may naturally conclude that $\sigma_x^2 \to \infty$. Thus, the variance of this and all similar "integrals" becomes infinite. The issue can be made a little more real by noticing the trend in Spotlight 5.3 as τ is decreased beyond the left margin in the random walk region.

There are two resolutions to this problem. From an engineering perspective, the problem lies in the assumption that σ_z^2 can be independent of the sampling period Δt. Any real process that generates noise will have a reduced variance if sampled faster because, for a process to do otherwise requires infinite power. For an idealized noise generation process of finite power, we require that the variance depend on the sampling time such that:

$$\frac{d\sigma_x^2}{dt} = \dot{\sigma}_x^2 = finite$$

This would occur if $\sigma_z^2(\Delta t) = \dot{\sigma}_z^2(t)\Delta t$ by which we mean that the variance of the noise will increase linearly with sampling period. Most important is the fact that $\dot{\sigma}_x^2$ is simply the slope of the random walk produced. Under this form of noise source:

$$\sigma_x^2(t) = (\sigma_z^2 t)/\Delta t = \int_0^t \frac{\dot{\sigma}_z^2(t)\Delta t}{\Delta t} dt = \int_0^t \dot{\sigma}_z^2(t) dt$$

We call $\dot{\sigma}_z^2(t)$ the *noise density* for a sensor, or the *diffusion* (for Brownian motion), or the *spectral density* when it is expressed in units of frequency rather than time. Note that when this substitution occurs and the noise density is constant, the new continuous time random walk is expressed simply as:

$$\sigma_x^2(t) = \dot{\sigma}_z^2 \cdot t$$

5.2.2.3.2 Integrating Stochastic Differential Equations.

Let us now apply the above ideas to define the concept of a differential equation which is driven by random noise. First, we reinterpret the state perturbation $\delta \underline{x}(t)$ in the linear perturbation equation (Equation 4.150) as a random variable:

$$\delta \underline{\dot{x}}(t) = F(t)\delta \underline{x}(t) + G(t)\delta \underline{u}(t) \tag{5.68}$$

and define the covariances:

$$Exp(\delta \underline{x}(t)\delta \underline{x}(t)^T) = P(t)$$
$$Exp(\delta \underline{u}(t)\delta \underline{u}(\tau)^T) = Q(t)\delta(t-\tau) \tag{5.69}$$

The delta function $\delta(t-\tau)$ is used to indicate that the input noise $\delta \underline{u}(t)$ is uncorrelated in time, or *white*. We might be tempted to use the solution provided in Equation 4.141 and write:

$$\delta \underline{x}(t) = \Phi(t, t_0)\delta \underline{x}(t_0) + \int_{t_0}^{t} \Gamma(t, \tau)\delta \underline{u}(\tau)d\tau \tag{5.70}$$

but it is not clear what is meant by the continuous integral of a white noise signal that appears on the right-hand side. The branch of mathematics known as *stochastic calculus* was invented to rigorously define such quantities. For our purposes, it is enough to know that the equation is rewritten as:

$$\delta \underline{x}(t) = \Phi(t, t_0)\delta \underline{x}(t_0) + \int_{t_0}^{t} \Gamma(t, \tau)d\underline{\beta}(\tau) \tag{5.71}$$

where $d\underline{\beta}(\tau) = \delta \underline{u}(\tau)d\tau$ is a differential element of a random walk. The result is then the solution to the original stochastic differential equation. Thus, while the derivative of a white noise signal cannot be defined in a rigorous sense, its integral can. Henceforth, we will treat a continuous white noise process as a noise source whose integral is a random walk.

5.2.2.3.3 Variance From a Stochastic Differential Equation.

With this understanding, we can now derive a very useful result. The covariance of the state can be derived by taking the expectation of the outer product of Equation 5.71:

$$Exp[\delta \underline{x}(t)\delta \underline{x}(t)^T] = Exp[\Phi(t, t_0)\delta \underline{x}(t_0)\delta \underline{x}(t_0)\Phi(t, t_0)^T] +$$

$$Exp\left[\int_{t_0}^{t}\Gamma(t, \zeta)\delta \underline{u}(\zeta)d\zeta\left(\int_{t_0}^{t}\Gamma(t, \xi)\delta \underline{u}(\xi)d\xi\right)^T\right]$$

The two cross terms were omitted because the resulting random walks will be independent of the initial conditions.

Now there is nothing uncertain about the matrices in this equation so the expectations can be taken inside the integral to produce:

$$Exp[\delta\underline{x}(t)\delta\underline{x}(t)^T] = \Phi(t, t_0)P(t_0)\Phi(t, t_0)^T +$$

$$\int_{t_0}^{t}\int_{t_0}^{t}\Gamma(t, \tau)Exp[\delta\underline{u}(\tau)\delta\underline{u}(\xi)^T]\Gamma(\tau, \xi)^T d\xi d\tau$$

Now we can substitute for Q from Equation 5.71:

$$P(t) = \Phi(t, t_0)P(t_0)\Phi(t, t_0)^T + \int_{t_0}^{t}\int_{t_0}^{t}\Gamma(t, \tau)Q(\tau)\delta(\xi - \tau)\Gamma(\tau, \xi)^T d\xi d\tau$$

If we choose to integrate with respect to ξ first, its integral disappears with the delta function:

$$P(t) = \Phi(t, t_0)P(t_0)\Phi(t, t_0)^T + \int_{t_0}^{t}\Gamma(t, \tau)Q(\tau)\Gamma(t, \tau)^T d\tau \qquad (5.72)$$

Spotlight 5.4 Matrix Superposition Integral.

General solution for the first-order behavior of the covariance of random error for linear and linearized dynamical systems. Compare this with Spotlight 4.12.

We now have a matrix integral equation that provides the time evolution of the variance of the stochastic differential equation defined in Equation 5.69. The original equation was itself the linearization of a fairly arbitrary system model. This result provides the answer, to first order, for how the variance of any nonlinear dynamical system behaves if it is excited by random noise.

This is a remarkable result. We will find it is key to characterizing the error dynamics of dead reckoning systems.

5.2.2.3.4 Linear Variance Equation. Consider now the question of whether we can differentiate the variance integral to produce a matrix differential equation for the covariance matrix. Recall that $\Phi(t, \tau) \approx I + F\Delta t$ when the time difference $\Delta t = t - \tau$ is small.

Therefore, to first order:

$$\Gamma(t, \tau) = \Phi(t, \tau)G(t) = (I + F(t)\Delta t)G(t) = G(t)$$

Substituting above gives:

$$P(t + \Delta t) = (I + F(t)\Delta t)P(t)(I + F(t)\Delta t)^T + \int_{t}^{t+\Delta t} G(t)Q(t)G(t)^T dt$$

The first part can be rewritten to first order as:

$$P(t + \Delta t) = P(t) + F(t)\Delta t P(t) + P(t)F(t)\Delta t + \int\limits_{t}^{t+\Delta t} G(t)Q(t)G(t)^T dt$$

Now we can move $P(t)$ to the other side, divide by Δt and take the limit as $\Delta t \to 0$ to produce the analog of Equation 4.138 for random errors, known as the *linear variance equation*:

$$\dot{P}(t) = F(t)P(t) + P(t)F(t)^T + G(t)Q(t)G(t)^T \qquad (5.73)$$

Spotlight 5.5 Linear Variance Equation.

Governs the first-order continuous time propagation of random error for linear and linearized dynamical systems. Compare this with Spotlight 4.11.

This equation is the basis of uncertainty propagation in the continuous time Kalman filter.

5.2.2.3.5 Discrete Time Equivalents of Continuous White Noise. Based on the above result, for small values of Δt and for slowly varying $G(t)$ and $Q(t)$, the relationship between the spectral density matrix Q and the equivalent discrete time covariance matrix is:

$$Q_k \cong G(t_k)Q(t_k)G(t_k)^T \Delta t$$

The equivalent calculation for discrete measurement noise of variance R_k, comes to the opposite conclusion about what to do with Δt. Any real device will do its best to reduce noise in its outputs by filtering and the longer the time period between samples, the more filtering that can be performed. The measurement relationship for a system can be written as:

$$\underline{z} = H\underline{x}(t) + \underline{v}(t) \qquad \underline{v} \sim N(0, R)$$

where the measurement covariance is:

$$Exp[\underline{v}(t)\underline{v}(\tau)^T] = R\delta(t - \tau) \qquad (5.74)$$

Consider the outcome of averaging for a short period Δt:

$$\underline{z}_k = \frac{1}{\Delta t}\int\limits_{t_{k-1}}^{t_k} [H\underline{x}(t) + \underline{v}(t)]dt = H_k\underline{x}_k + \frac{1}{\Delta t}\int\limits_{t_{k-1}}^{t_k} \underline{v}(t)dt$$

So the discrete noise is:

$$\underline{v}_k = \frac{1}{\Delta t}\int\limits_{t_{k-1}}^{t_k} \underline{v}(t)dt$$

and the variance is:

$$R_k = Exp[\underline{v}_k\underline{v}_k^T] = \frac{1}{\Delta t^2}\int\limits_{t_{k-1}}^{t_k}\int\limits_{t_{k-1}}^{t_k} Exp[\underline{v}(u)\underline{v}(v)^T]dudv = \frac{1}{\Delta t^2}\int\limits_{t_{k-1}}^{t_k}\int\limits_{t_{k-1}}^{t_k} R\delta(u - v)dudv$$

which gives the result:

$$R_k = \frac{R}{\Delta t} \tag{5.75}$$

The interpretation is that a filtered (averaging) sensor produces an output with half the variance if sampled half as quickly.

5.2.3 Optimal Estimation

This section addresses the problem of producing an optimal estimate from a continuous sequence of measurements. As we saw in averaging, certain calculations can produce a net reduction in uncertainty. In this section we will generalize this process to include any number of measurements related in arbitrary ways to any number of states. The process of getting the best overall estimate is called *estimation* and the tools used are called *estimators*.

5.2.3.1 Maximum Likelihood Estimation of a Random Vector

Consider again the problem of optimally estimating state from a set of measurements. Among many difficult issues is the question of how to compute such an estimate when the measurements do not have the same uncertainty. Another difficulty occurs when the measurements are related only indirectly to the state.

The estimation problem is now generalized as follows:

- The *state* $\underline{x} \in \mathfrak{R}^n$ and *measurements* $\underline{z} \in \mathfrak{R}^m$ are now vectors.
- The measurements relate to the state by a measurement matrix H.
- The measurements are assumed to be corrupted by a random noise vector $\underline{v}$ of known covariance $R = Exp(\underline{v}\underline{v}^T)$:

$$\underline{z} = H\underline{x} + \underline{v} \qquad \underline{v} \sim N(0, R) \tag{5.76}$$

The notation $N(0, R)$ means a normal distribution with zero mean and covariance. We will assume for now that there are more measurements than there are states, so $m > n$.

Of course, the innovation associated with measurements is exactly the corrupting noise $\underline{z} - H\underline{x} = \underline{v}$, so the innovation is, by assumption, an unbiased Gaussian. Recall that the *conditional probability* $p(\underline{z}|\underline{x})$ represents the probability of observing a particular measurement $\underline{z}$, given that the true state is $\underline{x}$. Since the innovation is Gaussian, the conditional probability that the true state is $\underline{x}$ given only the knowledge that a particular measurement $\underline{z}$ was observed, is given by:

$$p(\underline{z}|\underline{x}) = \frac{1}{(2\pi)^{m/2}|R|^{1/2}} \exp\left[-\frac{1}{2}(\underline{z} - H\underline{x})R^{-1}(\underline{z} - H\underline{x})^T\right] \tag{5.77}$$

One definition of an optimal estimate is the value of the state that best explains the measurements. The above exponential function will be maximized when the quadratic form in the exponent is minimized. Thus, the *maximum likelihood estimate* (MLE) of the state is:

$$\hat{\underline{x}}^* = \underset{\underline{x}}{argmin} \left(\frac{1}{2}(\underline{z} - H\underline{x})R^{-1}(\underline{z} - H\underline{x})^T \right) \tag{5.78}$$

This is the well-known weighted least squares problem. Assuming that the system is overdetermined, we know from Equation 3.31 that the solution is given by the weighted left pseudoinverse:

$$\hat{\underline{x}}^* = (H^T R^{-1} H)^{-1} H^T R^{-1} \underline{z} \tag{5.79}$$

We have shown that, when the corrupting noise is Gaussian, the maximum likelihood estimate of the state is the solution to a weighted least squares problem where the weight is the inverse covariance of the measurements. In this way, measurements that are most uncertain are weighted least in the cost function.

5.2.3.1.1 Covariance of the MLE Estimate. Clearly, the above result is merely a function mapping $\underline{z}$ onto $\hat{\underline{x}}^*$, so if we define:

$$J_{\underline{z}} = (H^T R^{-1} H)^{-1} H^T R^{-1}$$

Then the covariance of the result is $\Sigma_{xx} = J_{\underline{z}} \Sigma_{zz} J_{\underline{z}}^T$ but $\Sigma_{zz} = R$ and $H^T R^{-1} H$ is symmetric so this simplifies as follows:

$$\Sigma_{xx} = J_{\underline{z}} \Sigma_{zz} J_{\underline{z}}^T = (H^T R^{-1} H)^{-1} H^T R^{-1} R R^{-1} H (H^T R^{-1} H)^{-1}$$

$$\Sigma_{xx} = J_{\underline{z}} \Sigma_{zz} J_{\underline{z}}^T = (H^T R^{-1} H)^{-1} H^T R^{-1} H (H^T R^{-1} H)^{-1}$$

From which we get the elegant result:

$$\Sigma_{xx} = (H^T R^{-1} H)^{-1} \tag{5.80}$$

Spotlight 5.6 Covariance of the Least Squares Solution.

This is very useful for computing the variance of the least squares solution from the covariance of the measurements.

Note that by assumption $\hat{\underline{x}}^*$ is shorter than $\underline{z}$ because it is an overdetermined system. It is not possible to invert this relationship to determine R from Σ_{xx}.

5.2.3.2 Recursive Optimal Estimation of a Random Scalar

Consider again the problem of averaging multiple measurements, but now allow the uncertainty of the measurements to be unequal. Suppose we wish to process a continuous series of measurements in an optimal fashion – meaning the best possible estimate of system state is to be produced at each iteration. There are many ways to derive a solution to this problem, but we will use a technique that reuses earlier results while enhancing our intuition for how the solution operates.

Consider the problem of incorporating a single measurement. In this case, we can use the above result to derive the new MLE given a prior MLE and a new measurement, provided the variances of both are known. Let the present state be denoted x of covariance σ_x^2. The measurement is denoted z of covariance σ_z^2. Let us pretend that a second measurement occurs which happens to produce the present state estimate with the same covariance. These two measurements can now be combined in the least squares sense to determine the new optimal estimate x' and its uncertainty.

The measurement relationship is:

$$
\begin{bmatrix} z \\ x \end{bmatrix} = \begin{bmatrix} 1 \\ 1 \end{bmatrix} x'
$$

We will assume the new measurement and old state have uncorrelated errors, but this assumption is easy to relax. The weighted least squares solution from Equation 5.80 for $H = \begin{bmatrix} 1 & 1 \end{bmatrix}^T$ and $R = \mathrm{diag}\,[\sigma_z^2\ \sigma_x^2]$ is:

$$
x' = (H^T R^{-1} H)^{-1} H^T R^{-1} z = \left(\begin{bmatrix} 1 & 1 \end{bmatrix} \begin{bmatrix} \dfrac{1}{\sigma_z^2} & 0 \\ 0 & \dfrac{1}{\sigma_x^2} \end{bmatrix} \begin{bmatrix} 1 \\ 1 \end{bmatrix} \right)^{-1} \begin{bmatrix} 1 & 1 \end{bmatrix} \begin{bmatrix} \dfrac{1}{\sigma_z^2} & 0 \\ 0 & \dfrac{1}{\sigma_x^2} \end{bmatrix} z
$$

Which is:

$$
x' = \left(\left[\frac{1}{\sigma_z^2} + \frac{1}{\sigma_x^2} \right] \right)^{-1} \left[\frac{1}{\sigma_z^2} z + \frac{1}{\sigma_x^2} x \right] \tag{5.81}
$$

And the uncertainty of the new estimate is:

$$
\sigma_{x'}^2 = (H^T R^{-1} H)^{-1} = \left(\left[\frac{1}{\sigma_z^2} + \frac{1}{\sigma_x^2} \right] \right)^{-1} \tag{5.82}
$$

Notice that the new estimate is merely a weighted average and the new uncertainty can be generated through addition of reciprocals:

$$
\frac{1}{\sigma_{x'}^2} = \frac{1}{\sigma_z^2} + \frac{1}{\sigma_x^2} \tag{5.83}
$$

5.2.3.3 Example: Estimating Temperature from Two Sensors

The following example, adapted from the first chapter of [18], shows how weighted averaging can be used to produce a progressively more refined estimate of a scalar using measurements of differing precision. An ocean-going robot is responsible for measuring water temperature in the Antarctic. It has two different sensors.

Suppose that an initial measurement $z_1 = 4$ is made of the temperature of a component and the measurement has some uncertainty that we represent by its variance $\sigma_{z1}^2 = 2^2$. If the distribution of errors was Gaussian, then the conditional probability $p(x|z_1)$ would be centered at the measurement as shown in Figure 5.24. Based on only this information, the best estimate of the temperature is the measurement itself:

$$
\hat{x}_1 = z_1
$$

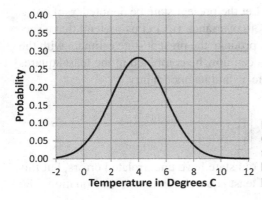

Figure 5.24 Conditional Probability Given Only the First Measurement. The most likely temperature is the point of maximum probability: which is the value of the measurement itself: 4° C.

And the best estimate of its uncertainty is that of the measurement:

$$\sigma_1^2 = \sigma_{z1}^2$$

Now, suppose that another measurement $z_2 = 6$ was produced at the same time as the first with variance $\sigma_{z1}^2 = (1.5)^2$. This measurement was produced by a better sensor and it produced a somewhat different measurement. The conditional probability for just this measurement is narrower in uncertainty and it is centered elsewhere (Figure 5.25).

The obvious question is what is the best estimate of the temperature and its uncertainty after incorporating this new information. Application of Equation 5.81 and Equation 5.83 produces the new estimate $x' = 5.28$ with a variance of $\sigma_{x'}^2 = (1.2)^2$. The new estimate is closer to the more precise second measurement and its uncertainty is smaller than either of the measurements used to produce it. The distribution which corresponds to this new estimate is shown in Figure 5.26.

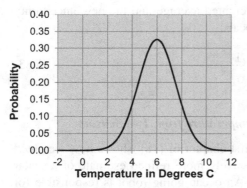

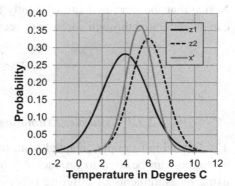

Figure 5.25 Conditional Probability Given Only the Second Measurement. For this measurement, the most likely temperature is 6°.

Figure 5.26 Conditional Probability Given Both Measurements. The optimal estimate for these measurements is 5.28°.

5.2.3.4 Recursive Optimal Estimation of Random Vector

Now, suppose that we wish to combine vector measurements to estimate a vector state. We can use the same trick as before where we try to write the new solution in terms of the last by pretending to have a pseudomeasurement of the prior estimate. The measurements relationship is:

$$\begin{bmatrix} \underline{z} \\ \underline{x} \end{bmatrix} = \begin{bmatrix} H \\ I \end{bmatrix} \underline{x}'$$

where the prior estimate $\underline{x}$ appears as a measurement and the new estimate $\underline{x}'$ appears as the new unknown state. Let $\underline{z}$ have covariance R and the prior estimate $\underline{x}$ has covariance P. We will assume the new measurement and old state have uncorrelated errors, but this assumption is easy to relax. The system is definitely overdetermined if there are any real measurements at all. The weighted left pseudoinverse solution is:

$$\underline{x}' = (H^T R^{-1} H)^{-1} H^T R^{-1} \underline{z}$$

$$\underline{x}' = \left(\begin{bmatrix} H \\ I \end{bmatrix}^T \begin{bmatrix} R & 0 \\ 0 & P \end{bmatrix}^{-1} \begin{bmatrix} H \\ I \end{bmatrix} \right)^{-1} \begin{bmatrix} H \\ I \end{bmatrix}^T \begin{bmatrix} R & 0 \\ 0 & P \end{bmatrix}^{-1} \underline{z} \tag{5.84}$$

Invert the covariance matrix:

$$\underline{x}' = \left(\begin{bmatrix} H \\ I \end{bmatrix}^T \begin{bmatrix} R^{-1} & 0 \\ 0 & P^{-1} \end{bmatrix} \begin{bmatrix} H \\ I \end{bmatrix} \right)^{-1} \begin{bmatrix} H \\ I \end{bmatrix}^T \begin{bmatrix} R^{-1} & 0 \\ 0 & P^{-1} \end{bmatrix} \underline{z} \tag{5.85}$$

Simplifying the quadratic form:

$$\underline{x}' = (H^T R^{-1} H + P^{-1})^{-1} \begin{bmatrix} H^T R^{-1} & P^{-1} \end{bmatrix} \begin{bmatrix} \underline{z} \\ \underline{x} \end{bmatrix}$$

Then, multiplying out the other matrices produces:

$$\underline{x}' = (H^T R^{-1} H + P^{-1})^{-1} (P^{-1} \underline{x} + H^T R^{-1} \underline{z}) \tag{5.86}$$

Note how this result seems to be computing a weighted average of the measurements and the state where each is weighted by its own inverse covariance divided by the total covariance.

5.2.3.4.1 Efficient State Update.

The result of Equation 5.87 can be used in this form but note that it requires the inversion of an $n \times n$ matrix. Often $m \ll n$. The result can be converted to a form that inverts an $m \times m$ matrix by using the matrix inversion lemma (Equation 2.14 of Chapter 2).

$$[C^T D^{-1} C + A]^{-1} = A^{-1} - A^{-1} C^T [CA^{-1} C^T + D]^{-1} CA^{-1}$$

$$[H^T R^{-1} H + P^{-1}]^{-1} = P - PH^T [HPH^T + R]^{-1} HP \tag{5.87}$$

Substituting:

$$\underline{x}' = (P - PH^T [HPH^T + R]^{-1} HP)(P^{-1} \underline{x} + H^T R^{-1} \underline{z})$$

To avoid clutter, define $S = [HPH^T + R]$. Then, this becomes:

$$\underline{x}' = (P - PH^T S^{-1} HP)(P^{-1}\underline{x} + H^T R^{-1}\underline{z})$$

Then, multiplying this out produces four terms:

$$\underline{x}' = \underline{x} - PH^T S^{-1} H\underline{x} + PH^T R^{-1}\underline{z} - PH^T S^{-1} HP(H^T R^{-1}\underline{z})$$

Factoring common terms from the front and back of the last two parts:

$$\underline{x}' = \underline{x} - PH^T S^{-1} H\underline{x} + PH^T [I - S^{-1} HPH^T] R^{-1}\underline{z}$$

Then, the trick is to add and subtract $S^{-1} R$ inside the square brackets:

$$\underline{x}' = \underline{x} - PH^T S^{-1} H\underline{x} + PH^T [I - S^{-1} HPH^T + S^{-1} R - S^{-1} R] R^{-1}\underline{z}$$

And then, noting the definition of S, this simplifies to:

$$\underline{x}' = \underline{x} - PH^T S^{-1} H\underline{x} + PH^T [S^{-1} R] R^{-1}\underline{z}$$

Now, we define the Kalman gain:

$$K = PH^T S^{-1} = PH^T [HPH^T + R]^{-1} \tag{5.88}$$

And the result reduces to:

$$\underline{x}' = \underline{x} + K(\underline{z} - H\underline{x}) \tag{5.89}$$

The form $\underline{z} - H\underline{x}$, is again, called the *innovation* – the difference between the current measurement and the measurement that **would have been** predicted based on the current state estimate. Furthermore, the quantity $S = HPH^T + R$ in the Kalman gain is called the *innovation covariance*. Based on our knowledge of how Jacobians transform uncertainty, it is clear that it is aptly named, for this is the uncertainty of the quantity $\underline{z} - H\underline{x}$.

Some interpretation of this result is in order. Substituting the gain formula into the state update equation and multiplying by PP^{-1} produces:

$$\underline{x}' = P[P^{-1}\underline{x} + H^T S^{-1}(\underline{z} - H\underline{x})]$$

So it is clear that the Kalman filter is computing a weighted average (weighted by the inverse covariance) of the innovation and the prior estimate. If the innovation is based on a high quality measurement, it will be assigned a higher weight and vice versa.

5.2.3.4.2 Covariance Update. In a recursive estimation context, we would also like to know the covariance of this new estimate after having incorporated the measurement. It is possible to compute the Jacobians of Equation 5.89 with respect to $\underline{z}$ and $\underline{x}$ and then substitute into Equation 5.37, but there is a more direct method. By substituting Equation 5.85 into Equation 5.80, we immediately get:

$$P' = (H^T R^{-1} H + P^{-1})^{-1} \tag{5.90}$$

and we used the matrix inversion lemma above to show:

$$[H^T R^{-1} H + P^{-1}]^{-1} = P - PH^T [HPH^T + R]^{-1} HP = P - KHP$$

From which we can conclude:

$$P' = (I - KH)P \tag{5.91}$$

Equation 5.89 and Equation 5.91 and those they depend on constitute the famous *Kalman filter* [7]. This result is the optimal estimate, under our assumptions, of the state given the previous state and its uncertainty and a measurement and its uncertainty.

Several points are worth noting. First, the new covariance seems to be the old one with a certain amount subtracted. So, uncertainty appears to be decreased by this operation. Second, the estimate of covariance does not depend at all on the measurements, whereas the estimate of state certainly depends on the covariance when the Kalman gain is computed. Third, the prior estimate of state provides sufficient constraint on the process to admit the processing of a single scalar measurement. In other words, it is not at all necessary to accumulate a total measurement vector of length n – even a single scalar measurement can be incorporated.

5.2.3.4.3 Example: Covariance Update for Direct Measurements.

In the case in which $H = I$ (Equation 5.86) is computing exactly the weighted estimate:

$$\underline{x}' = (R^{-1} + P^{-1})^{-1}(P^{-1}\underline{x} + R^{-1}\underline{z}) \tag{5.92}$$

and the covariance update in the form of Equation 5.91 is:

$$P' = (R^{-1} + P^{-1})^{-1}$$

Note in particular that this can be written as:

$$(P')^{-1} = (R^{-1} + P^{-1})$$

This establishes the idea that the inverse covariance, also known as the *information matrix*, adds directly.

Suppose that an initial estimate of the state exists and it has covariance:

$$P_0 = \begin{bmatrix} 10 & 0 \\ 0 & 10 \end{bmatrix}$$

A measurement is processed with covariance $R_1 = diag\,[10\ 1]$ suggesting high precision in the y coordinate. The updated state covariance is:

$$P_1 = (R_1^{-1} + P_0^{-1})^{-1} = \left[\begin{bmatrix} 10 & 0 \\ 0 & 10 \end{bmatrix}^{-1} + \begin{bmatrix} 10 & 0 \\ 0 & 1 \end{bmatrix}^{-1} \right]^{-1} = \begin{bmatrix} 5 & 0 \\ 0 & 0.9 \end{bmatrix}$$

Another measurement is processed with covariance $R_2 = diag\,[1\ 10]$ suggesting high precision in the x coordinate. The updated state covariance is:

$$P_2 = (R_2^{-1} + P_1^{-1})^{-1} = \left[\begin{bmatrix} 5 & 0 \\ 0 & 0.9 \end{bmatrix}^{-1} + \begin{bmatrix} 1 & 0 \\ 0 & 10 \end{bmatrix}^{-1} \right]^{-1} = \begin{bmatrix} 0.83 & 0 \\ 0 & 0.83 \end{bmatrix}$$

Subsequent measurements have covariances of $R_3 = diag\,[1\ 0.1]$ and $R_4 = diag\,[0.1\ 0.1]$.

Recall that contours of constant Gaussian probability are contours of the quadratic form in the exponent of the Gaussian. Such contours are ellipses so it is possible to represent covariance in 2D as an ellipse of appropriate dimensions and orientation. Figure 5.27 uses this device to represent the evolution of covariance in this example.

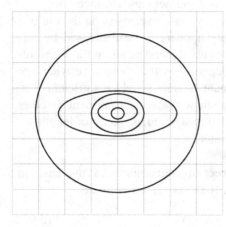

Figure 5.27 Variance Reduction Kalman Filtering. A sequence of measurements increases in precision by an order of magnitude in y and then in x. The state covariance reduces size along the same axis as the direction of highest precision of the measurement until the covariance ellipse is a tiny circle.

5.2.3.5 Nonlinear Optimal Estimation

When the measurement relationships are nonlinear, it is still possible to use nonlinear optimization theory to produce an optimal estimate. Let the measurements z be indirectly related to the state vector x by a nonlinear function and corrupted by a random noise vector v of known covariance R:

$$z = h(x) + v \qquad R = Exp(vv^T)$$

Perhaps it is not a surprise to learn that nonlinear least squares can be used to derive the solution and it looks exactly like what we have used so far – with one exception. We replace the measurement matrix of the linear case with the *measurement Jacobian* defined as follows:

$$H = \frac{\partial}{\partial x}[h(x)]\Big|_x$$

When the Jacobian is evaluated at the current state estimate, the filter is called an *Extended Kalman Filter* (EKF). If it is evaluated on some reference trajectory it is known as a *Linearized Kalman Filter*. Unlike the linear filter, the EKF is not necessarily optimal and it can misbehave in various ways. Even if the measurement noises are perfectly Gaussian, their impact the state estimate will not be (due to the nonlinearity in the measurement function), but the EKF will not account for this.

Unlike in the linear filter, the covariance estimates do depend on the state in the sense that the Jacobians depend on the state. This fact leads to the possibility that, if the state estimate is sufficiently incorrect, the Jacobians will likewise be incorrect, which will lead to incorrect covariances and even more incorrect state estimates. This potential divergence behavior is a main cause of brittleness of the EKF. Nonetheless the EKF is one of the workhorses of several branches of engineering, including guidance, computer vision, and robotics.

Many measurement relationships in mobile robots are nonlinear. For the EKF, the measurement Jacobian evaluates to the measurement matrix in the special case of linearity anyway. So we will use only the extended Kalman filter from now on.

5.2.4 References and Further Reading

The material here on stochastic integration is based on Stengel. Gelb is a readable reference on Kalman filtering.

[6] A. Gelb, *Applied Optimal Estimation*, MIT Press, 1974.
[7] Kalman, R. E., A New Approach to Linear Filtering and Prediction Problems, *Journal of Basic Engineering,* pp. 35–45, March 1960.
[8] Robert F. Stengel, *Optimal Control and Estimation,* Dover, 1994.

5.2.5 Exercises

5.2.5.1 Nonlinear Uncertainty Transformation

Consider the polar to cartesian coordinate transformations $x = r\cos(\theta)$ and $y = r\sin(\theta)$. Generate two sequences of at least 400 Gaussian random numbers ε_{θ_k} and ε_{r_k} taken from distributions with a zero mean and standard deviations of 0.3 rads and 0.01 meters respectively.

(i) *Monte Carlo* analysis is the name for the process of computing the derived sequences:

$$x_k = (r + \varepsilon_{r_k})\cos(\theta + \varepsilon_{\theta_k}) \qquad y_k = (r + \varepsilon_{r_k})\sin(\theta + \varepsilon_{\theta_k})$$

and computing their distributions directly. Plot the derived sequences x_k and y_k produced by applying the above transformation to the original polar coordinate sequences computed at the *reference point* $r = 1$ and $\theta = 0.0$. Plot x versus y.

(ii) Mean Transformation. The Kalman Filter uses the reference point itself as the estimate of the mean of the distribution. The mean of the distribution of the random vector $\rho = [r \ \theta]^T$ is zero by construction. We now investigate the mean of the distribution of the random vector $\underline{x} = [x \ y]^T$. Compute the mean (a 2D vector) of the derived sequence (that is, the mean of the derived (x, y) data sequence) and compare it to the (x, y) coordinates of the reference point. Look closely at the x coordinate mean and its error relative to the y coordinate mean. What happens if you increase the angle variance more (to 0.9)? Explain the result intuitively based on the distribution in the graph. Under what circumstances, in general, is the mean of $f(x)$ equal to $f( )$ of the mean of x? You may assume that the range and angle noises are not correlated.

(iii) Using our rules for linear uncertainty transformation (i.e., Jacobians), compute the formulas for the covariance of the vector $\underline{x} = [x \ y]^T$ given the covariance of the vector $\rho = [r \ \theta]^T$ and then plug in the noises on the polar coordinate measurements to compute the numeric variances of x and y at the reference point. Draw a 99% ellipse (an ellipse whose principal axes are 3 times the associated standard deviation) positioned at the reference point on a copy of the earlier x–y graph and comment on how well or poorly it fits the distribution of the samples and why.

5.2.5.2 *Joseph form of Covariance Update*

The Joseph form of the covariance update is sometimes used because its symmetric form provides a level of insurance that the state covariance will remain positive definite and the filter will not diverge. It takes the form:

$$P' = (I - KH)P(I - KH)^T + KRK^T$$

Compute the Jacobians of Equation 5.89 with respect to $\underline{z}$ and $\underline{x}$ and then substitute into Equation 5.37 to produce the Joseph form.

5.2.5.3 *Alternative Derivation of Covariance Update*

Multiply out the Joseph form and isolate the common term $(HPH^T + R)$. Then substitute the formula for the Kalman gain to recover the covariance update:

$$P' = (I - KH)P$$

5.2.5.4 *Alternative form of Kalman Gain*

Take the Kalman gain in the form $K = PH^T[HPH^T + R^{-1}]$ and pre-multiply by $P'P'^{-1}$. Then substitute for P'^{-1} from Equation 5.90 and simplify to produce the form $K = P'H^TR^{-1}$.

5.3 State Space Kalman Filters

This section generalizes the Kalman filter of the last section to state space form in order to permit the estimation of the state of a system in motion. The Kalman filter (KF) was invented by R. E. Kalman in the 1960s [7]. It is an algorithm for recursively estimating the state of a dynamic system based on the use of noisy measurements. The algorithm is used throughout robotics in such applications as perception, localization, control, state estimation, data association, calibration, and system identification.

5.3.1 Introduction

Recall that a linear systems model, or *state space model* of a random process is of the form:

$$\begin{aligned}\dot{\underline{x}} &= F\underline{x} + G\underline{w} \\ \underline{z} &= H\underline{x} + \underline{v}\end{aligned} \qquad (5.93)$$

Both the measurements and the system dynamic model are assumed to be corrupted by noise (Figure 5.28). In both cases, the noises are assumed to be unbiased, and

Gaussian. Unless special measures for colored noise are taken, the filter also assumes that the noises are white.

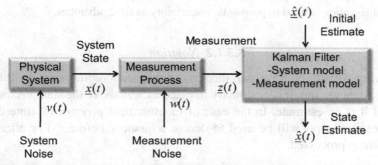

Figure 5.28 Kalman Filter. The filter stochastically models both the system and the measurement process.

The system model is a matrix linear differential equation. The *state vector* is any set of quantities sufficient to completely describe the unforced motion of the system. Given the state at any point in time, the state at any future time can be determined from the control inputs and the state space model. Time may be considered continuous or discrete and models of one form can be converted to the other.

The state space form of the filter has these additional abilities:

- It can predict system state independent of measurements.
- It can easily use measurements that are derivatives of required state variables. In this way, dead reckoning calculations can be incorporated directly into the projection step.
- It is a natural formulation for processing redundant measurements of the same state or states and for integrating dead reckoning and triangulation.
- It can explicitly account for modeling assumptions and disturbances in a more precise way than just "noise." It can be used to model error correlations among states or over time.
- It can calibrate parameters in real time and it can model frequency response of sensors in a natural way.
- Its forward measurement models make it straightforward to compensate for dynamic effects.
- The correlations that are accumulated in the state covariance make it possible to remove the effects of historical errors from all affected states.

5.3.1.1 Need for State Prediction

Measurements are assumed to be available at least on an intermittent basis, and they may constrain only part of the entire state vector. When they are available, the algorithm is used to update the state and its covariance. Let subscripts denote time, and consider the state and measurements of the system at the present (time t_k) and when the last estimate was computed (time t_{k-1}). Consider the last state $x_{k-1} = x(t_{k-1})$ and the most recent measurement $z_k = z(t_k)$.

Not all of the difference between x_1 and z_2 is due to error in the state estimate because the system will have moved and $x_2 \neq x_1$. The solution to this problem is to compute x_2

somehow from x_1 and then compare z_2 to the predicted state x_2. To do so, a model of system dynamics is needed to perform the prediction and it will be necessary to estimate the error of the prediction process too. For these time periods between measurements, stochastic integration is used to propagate uncertainty as time advances.

5.3.1.2 Notation

The following notation will be used throughout this section. Subscripts will be used, as above, to denote time. It is customary to place a carat above the state vector ($\hat{x}_k$) to denote that it is an estimate. In the case of measurement processing, time does not change, so superscripts will be used to denote a quantity before (–) or after (+) the measurement is processed.

5.3.1.3 Discrete System Model

The continuous time model presented above is convenient for analysis but it is not amenable to direct computer implementation. Modern implementations are usually implemented digitally in discrete time. If time is considered to be discrete, the system is described in the following form:

$$\hat{\underline{x}}_{k+1} = \Phi_k \hat{\underline{x}}_k + G_k \underline{w}_k$$
$$\underline{z}_k = H_k \underline{x}_k + \underline{v}_k$$

(5.94)

The names and sizes of the vectors and matrices are defined in Table 5.1.

Table 5.1 Kalman Filter Quantities

Object	Size	Name	Comment
$\hat{\underline{x}}_k$	$n \times 1$	state vector estimate at time t_k	
Φ_k	$n \times n$	transition matrix	relates $\underline{x}_k$ to $\underline{x}_{k+1}$ in the absence of a forcing function
G_k	$n \times n$	process noise distribution matrix	transforms the $\underline{w}_k$ vector into the coordinates of $\underline{x}_k$
$\underline{w}_k$	$n \times 1$	disturbance sequence or process noise sequence	white, known covariance structure
$\underline{z}_k$	$m \times 1$	measurement at time t_k	
H_k	$m \times n$	measurement matrix or observation matrix	relates $\underline{x}_k$ to $\underline{z}_k$ in the absence of measurement noise
$\underline{v}_k$	$m \times 1$	measurement noise sequence	white, known covariance structure

The covariance matrices for the white sequences are:

$$E(\underline{w}_k \underline{w}_i^T) = \delta_{ik} Q_k \qquad E(\underline{v}_k \underline{v}_i^T) = \delta_{ik} R_k \qquad E(\underline{w}_k \underline{v}_i^T) = 0, \forall (i, k)$$

The vanishing cross covariance in the last expression reflects the assumption in the derivation in Section 5.2.3.4 that the measurement and state have uncorrelated errors.

The symbol δ_{ik} denotes the Kronecker delta function. It is 1 when $i = j$ and 0 otherwise. Hence, the above means that we assume that process and measurement noise sequences are uncorrelated in time (white) and uncorrelated with each other.

5.3.1.4 Transition Matrix

In order to implement the Kalman filter, a continuous time system model must be converted to a discrete one, and the key to doing this is the transition matrix. See Section 4.4.2.3 of Chapter 4 for more on the transition matrix. Even when the system dynamics matrix $F(t)$ is time varying, we can use the transition matrix to write:

$$\underline{x}_{k+1} = \Phi_k \underline{x}_k \tag{5.95}$$

Recall that when the F matrix is constant, the transition matrix is given by the matrix exponential:

$$\Phi_k = e^{F\Delta t} = I + F\Delta t + \frac{(F\Delta t)^2}{2!} + \ldots \tag{5.96}$$

Even when $F(t)$ is time varying, provided Δt is much smaller than the dominant time constants in the system, the following two-term approximation is sufficient:

$$\Phi_k \approx e^{F\Delta t} \approx I + F\Delta t \tag{5.97}$$

In Kalman filters, the transition matrix is typically only used to propagate state for very short periods of time between measurements, so the above approximation is very useful.

5.3.1.5 Predictive Measurement Models That Underdetermine State

Notice that the measurement model is also predictive in the sense that it expresses what measurements would be expected given the present state. Very often, it is much easier to predict the measurement from the state than vice versa because $m < n$ so the reverse problem in underdetermined. The filter is able to use underdetermined measurements of state and it automatically inverts the underdetermined measurement relationship to update the entire state vector. For example, if a single range measurement is available, the filter can use it to attempt to estimate two position coordinates or even more. It is often possible to, under assumptions necessary for other reasons, process measurements one at a time and avoid matrix inversion completely.

5.3.2 Linear Discrete Time Kalman Filter

The state space Kalman filter propagates *both* the state and its covariance forward in time, given an initial estimate of the state.

5.3.2.1 Filter Equations

The linear KF equations are divided into two groups as shown in Box 5.2. The first two equations are the system model and the last three are the proper KF.

Box 5.2 Linear Kalman Filter

The Kalman filter equations for the linear system model are as follows:

System	$\hat{\underline{x}}_{k+1} = \Phi_k \hat{\underline{x}}_k$	*predict state*
Model	$P_{k+1} = \Phi_k P_k \Phi_k^T + G_k Q_k G_k^T$	*predict covariance*
	$K_k = P_k^- H_k^T [H_k P_k^- H_k^T + R_k]^{-1}$	*compute Kalman gain*
Kalman	$\hat{\underline{x}}_k^+ = \hat{\underline{x}}_k^- + K_k[\underline{z}_k - H_k \hat{\underline{x}}_k^-]$	*update state estimate*
Filter	$P_k^+ = [I - K_k H_k]P_k^-$	*update its covariance*

5.3.2.2 Time and Updates

It is important to distinguish the passage of time from the arrival of measurements because the equations are **not** run all at once. Except in the forced formulation discussed later, the system model runs at high frequency in order to project the system state forward in time. It proceeds based solely on a measurement of time. The KF, on the other hand, is run when measurements are available and intermittent measurements are acceptable. Whenever a measurement is available, it is processed **after** the state has been predicted for that cycle by the system model (Figure 5.29).

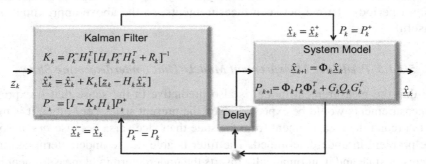

Figure 5.29 Distinguishing Time from Updates. The KF runs whenever a measurement arrives. The System Model runs as fast as may be required to control numerical error in the integration process.

5.3.2.3 The Uncertainty Matrices

The Q_k matrix models the uncertainty that corrupts the system model whereas the R_k matrix models the uncertainty associated with the measurement. The developer must provide these matrices based on knowledge of the system and sensors involved. Q_k acts like the time derivative of P_k causing it to grow between measurements to reflect uncertain motion of the system. R_k encodes the relative quality of the sensors. Its contents will normally be different for different sensors and the contents may depend on the measurement itself or on other measurements.

Finally, the P_k matrix gives the total uncertainty of the state estimate as a function of time. This matrix is mostly managed by the filter itself but the developer must provide its initial conditions P_0. In some cases, the value of P_0 must be determined very carefully. At all times, the Kalman gain acts as a weighting mechanism that boosts or attenuates the proportion of the innovation that is applied to the state estimate based on the relative magnitudes of P_k and R_k.

5.3.2.4 Observability

Situations may arise in which there are not enough measurements in the entire sensor suite to predict the system state over the long term. These are called *observability* problems and they often give rise to the diagonal elements of P_k that are growing with time. Observability is a property of the entire model including both the system and the measurement model, so it changes every time the sensors change.

Formally, a system is observable if the initial state can be determined by observing the output for some finite period of time. Consider the discrete, nth order, constant coefficient linear system for which there are m measurements:

$$\underline{x}_{k+1} = \Phi \underline{x}_k$$
$$\underline{z}_k = H\underline{x}_k \quad k = 0, m-1$$

The sequence of the first n measurements can be written as:

$$\underline{z}_0 = H\underline{x}_0$$
$$\underline{z}_1 = H\underline{x}_1 = H\Phi\underline{x}_0$$
$$\dots$$
$$\underline{z}_{n-1} = H\underline{x}_{n-1} = H(\Phi)^{n-1}\underline{x}_0$$

These equations can be stacked together to produce the system:

$$\underline{z} = \Xi^T \underline{x}_0 \quad \text{or} \quad \underline{z}^T = \underline{x}_0^T \Xi$$

If the initial state $\underline{x}_0$ is to be determined from this sequence of measurements then, the following matrix must have rank n:

$$\Xi = \left[H^T \middle| \Phi^T H^T \middle| \dots (\Phi^T)^{n-1} H^T \right] \tag{5.98}$$

Observability problems can often be fixed by reducing the number of state variables, or by adding additional sensors, or by adding pseudomeasurements (fake measurements) to impose constraints on non observable quantities.

5.3.3 Kalman Filters for Nonlinear Systems

The filter formulation presented earlier is based on a linear system model and it is therefore not applicable in situations when either the system model or the measurement relationships are nonlinear. Consider an exact nonlinear model of a system as follows:

$$\underline{\dot{x}} = \underline{f}(\underline{x}, t) + \underline{g}(\underline{w}, t)$$
$$\underline{z} = \underline{h}(\underline{x}, t) + \underline{v}(t) \tag{5.99}$$

Where f, g, and h are vector-valued nonlinear functions and $\underline{w}$ and $\underline{v}$ are white noise processes with zero crosscorrelation. Let the actual trajectory be written in terms of a reference trajectory $\underline{x}_r(t)$ and an error trajectory $\delta\underline{x}(t)$ as follows:

$$\underline{x}(t) = \underline{x}_r(t) + \delta\underline{x}(t) \tag{5.100}$$

By substituting this back into the model and approximating $f(\ )$ and $h(\ )$ by their Jacobians evaluated at the reference trajectory, we produce:

$$\delta\underline{\dot{x}} = \frac{\partial f}{\partial \underline{x}}(\underline{x}_r, t)\delta\underline{x} + \frac{\partial g}{\partial \underline{w}}(\underline{x}_r, t)\underline{w}(t)$$

$$\underline{z} - h(\underline{x}_r, t) = \frac{\partial h}{\partial \underline{x}}(\underline{x}_r, t)\delta\underline{x} + \underline{v}(t) \tag{5.101}$$

By defining the usual Jacobians this becomes:

$$\delta\underline{\dot{x}} = F(t)\delta\underline{x} + G(t)\underline{w}(t)$$

$$\underline{z} - h(\underline{x}_r, t) = H(t)\delta\underline{x} + \underline{v}(t) \tag{5.102}$$

This is a new dynamical system whose states are the errors in the original states and whose measurements are the innovations of the measurements relative to the reference trajectory. Many different forms of KF can be defined based on this distinction between the error trajectory and the reference trajectory. A filter whose states contain the actual states of interest is called a *total state* or a *direct* filter. Conversely, one whose states are the errors in the actual states of interest is called an *error state* or *indirect* filter.

5.3.3.1 Direct versus Indirect Filters

The advantage of a direct filter is that it computes an optimal estimate of the states of interest. However, there are serious drawbacks. Often, the states of interest change very quickly and if these are provided to the rest of the system by the KF, it means the KF must run very quickly. Often, it simply is not feasible to run the KF as fast as the application requires.

An even greater problem with the direct formulation is the fact that the models of most systems of interest are nonlinear, so the linear system model upon which the KF algorithm is based cannot be generated. Due to the above issues, it is often advisable to use an indirect filter formulation except in those cases where the states are changing slowly and a linear model of the total state dynamics is adequate.

For any indirect formulation: (a) the state vector is the deviation from the reference trajectory (the error state), (b) the measurements are the innovations (measurements less predictions of measurements).

5.3.3.2 Linearized versus Extended Kalman Filters

Among indirect formulations, two forms can be distinguished based on the reference trajectory used in the measurement function $h(\underline{x}_r)$. The *linearized* filter is a *feedforward* configuration as shown below where the reference trajectory is **not** updated to reflect the error estimates computed by the filter (Figure 5.30).

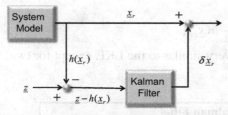

Figure 5.30 Feedforward (Linearized) Kalman Filter. The computed errors are added to the reference trajectory at the output but are not fed back to the system model.

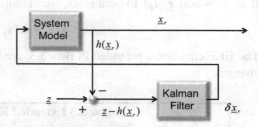

Figure 5.31 Feedback (Extended) Kalman Filter. The computed errors are fed back to the system model in order to alter the reference trajectory.

Such a filter can be difficult to use for extended missions because the reference trajectory may eventually diverge to the point where the linear assumption is no longer valid across the variation in the state vector. However, it can be a good choice when the reference trajectory really is known beforehand because a known reference trajectory provides a degree of insurance against divergence.

In the *extended* Kalman filter (EKF), the trajectory error estimates are used to update the reference trajectory as time evolves. This approach has the advantage that it is more applicable to extended missions. The extended filter can be visualized in a *feedback* configuration as shown in (Figure 5.31).

5.3.3.3 *Extended Kalman Filter*

The extended Kalman filter (EKF) is probably the simplest filter that is general enough to be of use in many applications. The EKF is an error state filter but it is possible to express its operation in terms of the state variables themselves rather than the error states.

Based on Equation 5.102, the discrete time linearized system is:

$$\delta\dot{\underline{x}}_k = F_k\delta\underline{x} + G_k\underline{w}_k$$
$$\underline{z}_k - h(\underline{x}_r(t_k), t_k) = H_k\delta\underline{x}_k + \underline{v}_k \tag{5.103}$$

The discrete time state update equation is:

$$\delta\hat{\underline{x}}_k^+ = \delta\hat{\underline{x}}_k^- + K[\underline{z}_k - h(\underline{x}_r(t_k), t_k) - H_k\delta\hat{\underline{x}}_k^-]$$

Now, if we associate the last two terms in the brackets rather than the first two, we can define the predicted measurement to be the sum of the ideal measurement at the reference state and the deviation computed to first order by the Jacobian of $h(\underline{x}_r, t)$.

$$h(\hat{\underline{x}}_k^-) = h(\underline{x}_r(t_k), t_k) + H_k\delta\hat{\underline{x}}_k^-$$

Then the innovation is the difference between the predicted measurement and the actual measurement:

$$\delta\underline{z}_k = \underline{z}_k - h(\hat{\underline{x}}_k^-)$$

Under this substitution, the state update equation can be written as:

$$\delta\hat{\underline{x}}_k^+ = \delta\hat{\underline{x}}_k^- + K[\underline{z}_k - h(\hat{\underline{x}}_k^-)]$$

If we now add $\underline{x}_r(t_k)$ to both sides, we obtain:

$$\hat{\underline{x}}_k^+ = \hat{\underline{x}}_k^- + K[\underline{z}_k - h(\hat{\underline{x}}_k^-)]$$

The EKF equations, provided in Box 5.3, are very similar to the LKF, except for two changes:

Box 5.3 Extended Kalman Filter

The Extended Kalman filter equations are as follows:

System
Model

$$\hat{\underline{x}}_{k+1} = \phi_k(\hat{\underline{x}}_k) \qquad\qquad \text{\textit{predict state}}$$

$$P_{k+1} = \Phi_k P_k \Phi_k^T + G_k Q_k G_k^T \quad \text{\textit{predict covariance}}$$

$$K_k = P_k^- H_k^T [H_k P_k^- H_k^T + R_k]^{-1} \quad \text{\textit{compute Kalman gain}}$$

Kalman
Filter

$$\hat{\underline{x}}_k^+ = \hat{\underline{x}}_k^- + K_k[\underline{z}_k - h(\hat{\underline{x}}_k^-)] \qquad \text{\textit{update state estimate}}$$

$$P_k^+ = [I - K_k H_k]P_k^- \qquad\qquad \text{\textit{update its covariance}}$$

The usual conversion to the discrete time model has been performed and the following Jacobians are defined:

$$F_k = \frac{\partial \underline{f}}{\partial \underline{x}}(\hat{x}_k^-) \qquad G_k = \frac{\partial \underline{g}}{\partial \underline{w}}(\hat{x}_k^-) \qquad H_k = \frac{\partial h}{\partial \underline{x}}(\hat{x}_k^-)$$

The Jacobian G_k is defined for convenience to permit a transformation of the driving noises.

5.3.3.3.1 State Transition for Nonlinear Problems. The first change relative to the LKF is the state propagation. Due to the nonlinearity of the system differential equation, the state propagation equation is written as:

$$\hat{\underline{x}}_{k+1} = \phi_k(\underline{x}_k)$$

This expression is intended to mean whatever process is used to integrate the system dynamics. One simple method is Euler integration:

$$\underline{x}_{k+1} = \underline{x}_k + f(\underline{x}_k, t_k)\Delta t \tag{5.104}$$

5.3.3.3.2 The Measurement Conceptualization in the EKF. The second change relative to the LKF is the innovation calculation. The measurement prediction calculation $h(\hat{x}_k^-)$ is considered to be part of the EKF and the innovation is also computed as part of its operation. All of this happens in the state update equation:

$$\hat{\underline{x}}_k = \hat{\underline{x}}_k^- + K_k[\underline{z}_k - h(\hat{\underline{x}}_k^-)] \tag{5.105}$$

5.3.3.3.3 Uncertainty Propagation for Nonlinear Problems. Uncertainty propagation is also subtly changed. Although the filter was reshaped to make it appear to be a total state filter, it is important to recognize that the uncertainty propagation is based on the error dynamics of Equation 5.103. The transition matrix Φ_k is that of the linearized dynamics, induced by the system Jacobian F. One way to compute it is to use Equation 5.97.

5.3.3.4 Complementary Kalman Filters

The Complementary Kalman filter (CKF) is, in a sense, the opposite of the EKF because it does not compute the total state dynamics inside the filter. It gets its name from a concept in signal processing where two (or more) filters that are complementary can be used to remove noise without distorting the signal. In the CKF, the linearized system dynamics are used explicitly to propagate the error states. The filter equations are therefore those of the linearized Kalman filter (LKF) provided in Box 5.4. These are very similar to the EKF, except for the use of error states and error measurements.

Box 5.4 Linearized Kalman Filter

The Linearized Kalman filter equations are as follows:

System	$\delta \hat{\underline{x}}_{k+1} = \Phi_k \delta \hat{\underline{x}}_k$	*predict state*
Model	$P_{k+1} = \Phi_k P_k \Phi_k^T + G_k Q_k G_k^T$	*predict covariance*
	$K_k = P_k^- H_k^T [H_k P_k^- H_k^T + R_k]^{-1}$	*compute Kalman gain*
Kalman	$\delta \hat{\underline{x}}_k^+ = \delta \hat{\underline{x}}_k^- + K_k [\delta \underline{z}_k]$	*update state estimate*
Filter	$P_k^+ = [I - K_k H_k] P_k^-$	*update its covariance*

The error measurement $\delta \underline{z}_k$ is computed from the innovation $\underline{z}_k - h(\underline{x}_r(t_k), t_k)$ as follows:

$$\delta \underline{z}_k = [(\underline{z}_k - h(\underline{x}_r(t_k), t_k)) - H_k \delta \hat{\underline{x}}_k^-]$$

but the innovation is computed outside the filter. This means the LKF does not incorporate a model of the measurement process. The "complement" of the linearized filter is an system dynamics model also implemented outside the LKF, so the LKF also has no model of the total state dynamics. The CKF is then a trivial synthesis of the entire state vector from the reference trajectory and the "errors":

$$\hat{\underline{x}}_k = \hat{\underline{x}}_r(t_k) + \delta \hat{\underline{x}}_k \tag{5.106}$$

Note the errors are defined in this case as the quantities added to the reference trajectory to produce the true one.

The external system model can be implemented based on knowledge of the forcing function (the true inputs to the system) or based on a set of redundant sensors that are used to compute a reference trajectory. An example of the former is to use commanded speed and curvature for a mobile robot.

An example of the latter is to consider the output of an inertial navigation system (INS) to be the reference trajectory. Here, the complementary approach is advantageous because the INS sensors can typically respond to very rapid changes in total state whereas the errors in the inertial navigation states are known to change relatively slowly. Such a filter is typically configured to estimate the errors in the INS sensors as well as the errors in position, velocity, and attitude.

A complementary filter can be constructed that is feedforward or feedback. Since the total state dynamics (i.e., system model) are external, the error state estimation can run at a different rate, typically slower, than the system model. In the feedback case, some or all error states are transferred to the system model on a regular basis and the error states are then immediately reset to zero to reflect the fact that the reference trajectory has been redefined to remove all presently known errors. The covariance propagation in the LKF in unchanged after such a reset.

5.3.3.5 Deterministic Inputs

Yet another way to achieve the benefits of a complementary filter formulation is to incorporate deterministic inputs (also known as the forcing function) into the filter formulation. Consider the case of a nonlinear system model:

$$\dot{\underline{x}} = f(\underline{x}, \underline{u}, t) + g(\underline{w}, t) \tag{5.107}$$

In a complementary filter, the external system model would be used to integrate this equation after the noise term is removed. For the EKF, deterministic inputs are used in the projection step. Assuming Euler integration, such an approach would be implemented as:

$$\hat{\underline{x}}_{k+1} = \phi_k(\hat{\underline{x}}_k) = \hat{\underline{x}}_k + f(\underline{x}, \underline{u}, t)\Delta t$$

Often, it is difficult to obtain an accurate nonlinear system model but there is another alternative. Any high rate sensors can be treated as inputs rather than sensors. If this is done, the state will respond instantly to their unfiltered inputs. Such rapid response comes at the risk of passing bad data into the algorithm so it may be necessary to pre-filter these measurements, at least for outliers, before they are provided to the EKF.

Depriving the EKF of such measurements may require that the state vector be reduced to remove any associated states. Also, it may be advisable to use the Q matrix to represent some degree of uncertainty in the deterministic inputs or in the removed states. We can rewrite the covariance update as:

$$P_{k+1} = \Phi_k P_k \Phi_k^T + \Psi_k U_k \Psi_k^T + G_k Q_k G_k^T$$

Where:

$$\Psi_k = \frac{\partial f}{\partial \underline{u}}(\hat{x}_k) \qquad\qquad U_k = Exp[\delta\underline{u}\delta\underline{u}^T]$$

Often, it will turn out that $\Psi_k = G_k$ and the Q matrix can have its values increased to model the errors in deterministic inputs as if they were additional driving noises.

The EKF with deterministic inputs is essentially equivalent to the complementary filter while being simpler to implement. It incorporates all of the benefits of generality to the nonlinear case, straightforward automatic treatment of error transfer to the total state, and rapid response to high frequency inputs so it will be our preferred formulation from now on.

5.3.4 Simple Example: 2D Mobile Robot

This section develops one of the simplest quite useful Kalman filters for a real robot. This example depends on a substantial amount of preparation that has been developed in preceding chapters. However because the first job of a mobile robot is awareness of its own motion, that is perhaps appropriate.

5.3.4.1 System and Measurement Model

Consider a mobile robot moving in the plane as shown in Figure 5.32. Let the state vector include the position and orientation of the robot and its linear and angular velocity:

$$\underline{x} = [x \ y \ \psi \ v \ \omega]^T \tag{5.108}$$

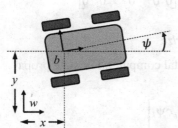

Figure 5.32 2D Mobile Robot. Illustrates the simplest case for a mobile robot Kalman Filter.

We will assume that the lateral velocity is zero by design when expressed in the body frame, so the velocity has but one component. Furthermore, this model also implicitly assumes no wheel slip because such slip will generate lateral velocity even for a vehicle whose actuators nominally cannot produce it.

Suppose that direct measurements are available of both the linear (from a transmission encoder) and the angular velocities (from a gyro):

$$\underline{z} = [z_e \ z_g]^T \tag{5.109}$$

Contemporary (and affordable) fiber optic gyros perform so well that this option is far better than computing heading rate from more than one wheel. It is often better than using a compass to directly measure heading because compasses are subject to significant systematic error that cannot be modelled well in practice.

An encoder intrinsically measures a rotation proportional to distance travelled s. This reading can be converted either into the change in distance Δs since the last read, or velocity by dividing that change by the change in time Δt. We will assume the latter for simplicity.

Although the angular velocity of every point on a rigid body is the same, the linear velocity varies with position, if there is any rotation. It may be necessary to account for the position of the velocity sensor, or more precisely the position of the point whose velocity is being measured.

Having revealed the issue, we will now assume that the encoder is at the body frame origin for simplicity. The system model describes the dynamics of the situation (if any):

$$\dot{x} = \frac{dx}{dt} = f(x, t) \Rightarrow \frac{d}{dt}\begin{bmatrix} x & y & \psi & v & \omega \end{bmatrix}^T = \begin{bmatrix} vc\psi & vs\psi & \omega & 0 & 0 \end{bmatrix}^T \quad (5.110)$$

This is a constant velocity model but the constant velocity assumption is being made only in the system model. It governs only the state propagation between measurements. The measurements will change the velocity to reflect the real motion.

Note that even this simple model is nonlinear because of the trigonometric functions of the heading ψ – which is a state. The Jacobian $F = \partial \dot{x}/\partial x$ of this model will therefore be needed. It is:

$$F = \begin{bmatrix} \partial\dot{x}/\partial x & \partial\dot{x}/\partial y & \partial\dot{x}/\partial\theta & \partial\dot{x}/\partial v & \partial\dot{x}/\partial\omega \\ \partial\dot{y}/\partial x & \partial\dot{y}/\partial y & \partial\dot{y}/\partial\theta & \partial\dot{y}/\partial v & \partial\dot{y}/\partial\omega \\ \partial\dot{\theta}/\partial x & \partial\dot{\theta}/\partial y & \partial\dot{\theta}/\partial\theta & \partial\dot{\theta}/\partial v & \partial\dot{\theta}/\partial\omega \\ \partial\dot{v}/\partial x & \partial\dot{v}/\partial y & \partial\dot{v}/\partial\theta & \partial\dot{v}/\partial v & \partial\dot{v}/\partial\omega \\ \partial\dot{\omega}/\partial x & \partial\dot{\omega}/\partial y & \partial\dot{\omega}/\partial\theta & \partial\dot{\omega}/\partial v & \partial\dot{\omega}/\partial\omega \end{bmatrix} = \begin{bmatrix} 0 & 0 & -vs\psi & c\psi & 0 \\ 0 & 0 & vc\psi & s\psi & 0 \\ 0 & 0 & 0 & 0 & 1 \\ 0 & 0 & 0 & 0 & 0 \\ 0 & 0 & 0 & 0 & 0 \end{bmatrix} \quad (5.111)$$

5.3.4.2 Discretize and Linearize

The equations cannot be used in the above form in a digital computer. For state propagation, we will use the linear approximation:

$$x_{k+1} \approx x_k + f(x, t)\Delta t \Rightarrow \begin{bmatrix} x_{k+1} \\ y_{k+1} \\ \psi_{k+1} \\ v_k \\ \omega_k \end{bmatrix} \approx \begin{bmatrix} x_k \\ y_k \\ \psi_k \\ v_k \\ \omega_k \end{bmatrix} + \begin{bmatrix} v_k c\psi_k \\ v_k s\psi_k \\ \omega_k \\ 0 \\ 0 \end{bmatrix} \Delta t_k \quad (5.112)$$

For coding convenience, this can be written in terms of a pseudo "transition matrix," thus:

$$x_{k+1} \approx \hat{\Phi} x_k \Rightarrow \hat{\Phi} \approx \begin{bmatrix} 1 & 0 & 0 & c\psi\Delta t & 0 \\ 0 & 1 & 0 & s\psi\Delta t & 0 \\ 0 & 0 & 1 & 0 & \Delta t \\ 0 & 0 & 0 & 1 & 0 \\ 0 & 0 & 0 & 0 & 1 \end{bmatrix} \quad (5.113)$$

But this is not an exact solution as it would be in the linear case. For the state covariance propagation equation, we use:

$$P_{k+1}^- = \Phi_k P_k \Phi_k^T + G_k Q_k G_k^T$$

$$\Phi_k \approx I + F\Delta t \Rightarrow \Phi_k \approx \begin{bmatrix} 1 & 0 & -vs\psi\Delta t & c\psi\Delta t & 0 \\ 0 & 1 & vc\psi\Delta t & s\psi\Delta t & 0 \\ 0 & 0 & 1 & 0 & \Delta t \\ 0 & 0 & 0 & 1 & 0 \\ 0 & 0 & 0 & 0 & 1 \end{bmatrix} \quad (5.114)$$

If the matrices Φ and Φ_k are confused in the implementation, it is not an easy bug to find. This completes the idealized system model part of the filter.

5.3.4.3 Initialization

We still have to specify the initial conditions x_0 and P_0 and the system disturbance model. The former is straightforward. For P_0 one must be very careful. If P_0 is set to a zero matrix, it indicates perfect confidence in the initial state. It is easy to show that all measurements will be ignored under these circumstances, so such a filter will report the initial conditions – forever. It is sometimes practical to set P_0 to some diagonal matrix whose elements represent reasonable estimates of the errors in the initial state estimate.

$$P_0 = diag\left[\sigma_{xx} \; \sigma_{yy} \; \sigma_{\psi\psi} \; \sigma_{vv} \; \sigma_{\omega\omega}\right]$$

The notation $diag[\quad]$ means the diagonal *matrix* whose diagonal is specified inside the square braces.

5.3.4.4 System Disturbances

For the system disturbances, we would like the term $G_k Q_k G_k^T$ to account for the errors in the 2D world assumption (e.g., floor roughness), the lack of wheel slip assumption (implicit in the model) and the constant velocity assumption (violated during accelerations) among others. Let the system disturbances adapt to the time step:

$$Q_k = diag[k_{xx}, k_{yy}, k_{\psi\psi}, k_{vv}k_{\omega\omega}]\Delta t$$

This part governs the growth of error between time steps. We interpret k_{xx} and k_{yy} to be aligned with the forward and lateral vehicle axes respectively – in order to permit asymmetric disturbances to be expressed in the body frame. The notation is intended to convey that these are constants whose values must be determined by the designer.

The process noise distribution matrix is identity except for the mapping between velocity variables in the robot frame and the global frame. That part involves a familiar rotation matrix:

$$G = \begin{bmatrix} c\psi & -s\psi & 0 & 0 & 0 \\ s\psi & c\psi & 0 & 0 & 0 \\ 0 & 0 & 1 & 0 & 0 \\ 0 & 0 & 0 & 1 & 0 \\ 0 & 0 & 0 & 0 & 1 \end{bmatrix} \tag{5.115}$$

5.3.4.5 Measurement Model

The available measurements so far are the speed encoder, and a gyro. Each measurement model is derived below.

5.3.4.5.1 Transmission Encoder. A transmission encoder, if positioned at the vehicle reference point (origin of body frame), is a fairly direct measurement of vehicle velocity

(Figure 5.33). The measurement model and its Jacobian are:

$$z_e = v \quad H_e = \frac{\partial z_e}{\partial \underline{x}} = \begin{bmatrix} 0 & 0 & 0 & 1 & 0 \end{bmatrix}$$

Note the convention of expressing the measurement in terms of the present value of the state. This is a forward model.

Now consider the question of the uncertainty. Generally if $R(t)$ represents a continuous measurement uncertainty matrix, the discrete time matrix which produces the same behavior is given by Equation 5.75 as $R_k = R(t)/\Delta t_e$ where Δt_e represents the time elapsed between measurements. However, an encoder is a counter (an integrator) whose error increases with the distance integrated. We can express a variance that is proportional to distance as a distance dependent random walk. In continuous time terms:

$$\dot{R}_e = \dot{\sigma}_{ee} = \alpha |v|$$

This is easily converted to discrete time by multiplying by the time increment Δt_e:

$$R_e = \sigma_{ee} = \alpha |\Delta s|$$

Such an error model would make the variance in the associated computed distance grow linearly with the length of the distance increments between samples.

5.3.4.5.2 Gyro. For a gyro the measurement model and its Jacobian are:

$$z_g = \omega \quad H_g = \frac{\partial z_g}{\partial \underline{x}} = \begin{bmatrix} 0 & 0 & 0 & 0 & 1 \end{bmatrix}$$

This is typically an averaging sensor so we can express the variance in terms of its angle random walk $\dot{\sigma}_{gg}$:

$$\dot{R}_g = \dot{\sigma}_{gg}/\Delta t_g$$

where Δt_g is the time elapsed between gyro measurements.

5.3.4.5.3 Wheel Encoders. An alternative to the gyro and transmission encoder is the measurement of the speeds and/or steer angles of some or all of the wheels. Consider a single wheel on a vehicle that has two degrees of rotational freedom (roll and steer) as shown in Figure 5.34. Assume the body frame is chosen such that it cannot have a sideways velocity, though this is an easy assumption to relax.

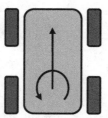

Figure 5.33 Sensing Model. To make things easiest, we will assume the linear and angular velocity of the body frame can be measured directly.

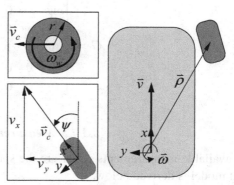

Figure 5.34 Measurements of Wheel Rotation and Steer. This figure defines symbols for the derivation of the wheel encoder measurement model.

Let $\vec{\rho}$ be the position vector of the wheel relative to the body frame and let $\vec{\omega}$ denote the angular velocity which, is assumed to be directed vertically in the body frame. Several kinds of measurements may be available from instrumented wheels. Let a *fixed* wheel be permitted to rotate about a single axis – the one associated with forward motion. A *free* wheel may rotate about a vertical axis as well as the axis associated with forward motion. Either of these two degrees of freedom may be powered or not and either may be instrumented or not.

It is simplest to formulate the measurements in the body frame. The velocity of the wheel contact point relative to the world is given by:

$$\vec{v}_c = \vec{v} + \vec{\omega} \times \vec{\rho} = v\hat{i} + \omega\hat{k} \times (\rho_x \hat{i} + \rho_y \hat{j})$$

$$\vec{v}_x = (v - \omega\rho_y)\hat{i} \qquad \vec{v}_y = (\omega\rho_x)\hat{j}$$

5.3.4.5.4 Steer Angle. The available measurements are inverses of these relationships. We will assume that the wheel is not slipping laterally. Let σ denote the tangent of the steer angle γ. This is a measurement of the ratio of angular to linear velocity and hence is a measure of curvature just as is the Ackerman steer angle. The steer angle of the wheel is:

$$\gamma = \text{atan}(\sigma) = \text{atan}(v_y / v_x)$$

Needed derivatives of the tangent are:

$$\frac{\partial\sigma}{\partial v} = -\frac{\omega\rho_x}{(v - \omega\rho_y)^2} = -v_y / (v_x^2) \qquad \frac{\partial\sigma}{\partial\omega} = \frac{\rho_x}{(v - \omega\rho_y)} = v_y / (\omega v_x)$$

Its Jacobian therefore is:

$$\frac{\partial\theta}{\partial v} = \frac{\partial\theta}{\partial\sigma}\frac{\partial\sigma}{\partial v} = \left(\frac{1}{1 + \sigma^2}\right)\left(\frac{-v_y}{v_x^2}\right) = -\left(\frac{1}{\omega\rho_x}\right)\left(\frac{\sigma^2}{1 + \sigma^2}\right)$$

$$\frac{\partial\theta}{\partial\omega} = \frac{\partial\theta}{\partial\sigma}\frac{\partial\sigma}{\partial\omega} = \left(\frac{1}{1 + \sigma^2}\right)\left(\frac{v_y}{\omega v_x}\right) = \left(\frac{1}{\omega}\right)\left(\frac{\sigma}{1 + \sigma^2}\right)$$

5.3.4.5.5 Free Wheel Velocity. A free wheel will rotate (more or less) automatically about the body z axis by the necessary steer angle due to the action of friction. Its measurement relationship in radians is:

$$\omega_w = \frac{1}{r}(\sqrt{v_x^2 + v_y^2}) = \frac{1}{r}[\sqrt{(v - \omega\rho_y)^2 + (\omega\rho_x)^2}]$$

$$\frac{\partial\omega_w}{\partial v} = \frac{1}{r}\left(\frac{2v_x}{2v}\right) = \frac{1}{r}\cos(\gamma)$$

$$\frac{\partial\omega_w}{\partial\omega} = \frac{1}{r}\left(\frac{2v_x(-\rho_y) + 2v_y(\rho_x)}{2v}\right) = \frac{1}{r}(\cos(\gamma)(-\rho_y) + \sin(\gamma)(\rho_x)) = -(\,^{w}\vec{\rho})_y / r$$

Where $(\,^{w}\vec{\rho})_y$ is the component of the wheel position vector along the y axis of the wheel frame. This is a measurement that responds to both the linear and angular velocity of the vehicle but they cannot be distinguished from a single measurement. The filter will automatically distinguish linear and angular velocity when two or more wheel velocities are measured.

5.3.4.5.6 Fixed Wheel Velocity. A fixed wheel will not rotate automatically about the body z axis. Its measurement relationship in radians is its projection onto the wheel forward axis:

$$\omega_w = \hat{\underline{v}}_c \cdot \hat{i}_w = v_x/r = \frac{1}{r}(v - \omega\rho_y)$$
$$\frac{\partial\omega_w}{\partial v} = \frac{1}{r} \qquad \frac{\partial\omega_w}{\partial\omega} = \frac{-\rho_y}{r}$$

Again, this is a measurement that responds to both the linear and angular velocity of the vehicle but they cannot be distinguished from a single measurement. The filter will automatically distinguish linear and angular velocity when two or more wheel velocities are measured.

5.3.4.6 Incorporating a Map

This filter is actually still not very useful. The problem is that it does only *dead reckoning* calculations because we only have measurements related to linear and angular velocity. As we saw in stochastic integration, any process that only integrates velocities generates unbounded error growth in position and orientation. The practical solution is as ancient as the problem. We use a *map*. Different kinds of maps are discussed later but localization maps are used to help robots navigate.

Suppose that a map is available that tells us the more or less precise locations of some set of "landmarks" (distinctive, localized features in the environment). Suppose further that the robot has a sensor that can measure the range and direction of the landmarks relative to itself.

In general, the landmark may be an object of some size that possesses an orientation. Let us associate a model frame (subscript m) with the landmark. Let both the robot and model frames be known in the world frame and let the sensor frame be known in the robot frame. Let there be a detection point frame (d subscript) on each landmark. The detection frame coordinates are known and constant in the model frame. The situation now is as shown in Figure 5.35.

5.3.4.6.1 Forced Formulation. Before presenting landmark processing, we will first change the treatment of the other measurements. The velocity states were included in the state vector of the previous example in order to illustrate concepts and present measurement and uncertainty models. However, it is a valid design to treat the associated measurements from the encoder and gyro as deterministic inputs $\underline{u}$ rather than as measurements $\underline{z}$. Doing so requires that errors in these measurements be modelled with the Q matrix rather than the R matrix but the system will be more responsive as a result. A disadvantage is that only the landmark measurements are filtered, but provided the velocity inputs have reasonableness checks in place, this is a practical solution.

The only measurements that need to be processed in this design are the landmarks so the state vector is smaller:

$$\underline{x} = \begin{bmatrix} x & y & \psi \end{bmatrix}$$

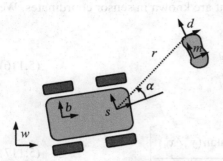

Figure 5.35 Frames for Formulating Landmark Observations. A sensor mounted on the vehicle might be able to measure the bearing and/or range to a landmark in the map.

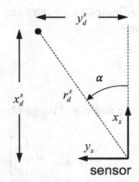

Figure 5.36 Sensor Geometry. The sensor measures range and bearing to the landmark.

This formulation turns out to be the equivalent of simply striking all rows and columns associated with velocities from all the earlier matrices. The state model is:

$$\underline{x}_{k+1} \approx \underline{x}_k + f(x, u, t)\Delta t \;\Rightarrow\; \begin{bmatrix} x_{k+1} \\ y_{k+1} \\ \psi_{k+1} \end{bmatrix} \approx \begin{bmatrix} x_k \\ y_k \\ \psi_k \end{bmatrix} + \begin{bmatrix} v_k c\psi_k \\ v_k s\psi_k \\ \omega_k \end{bmatrix} \Delta t_k$$

This runs at the rate the velocities are measured. In matrix form this is:

$$\underline{x}_{k+1} \approx \hat{\Phi}\underline{x}_k + Gu_k \Rightarrow \hat{\Phi} \approx \begin{bmatrix} 1 & 0 & 0 \\ 0 & 1 & 0 \\ 0 & 0 & 1 \end{bmatrix} \qquad G \approx \begin{bmatrix} c\psi_k \Delta t_k \\ s\psi_k \Delta t_k \\ 0 \end{bmatrix}$$

The system Jacobian is now:

$$F = \frac{\partial \underline{\dot{x}}}{\partial \underline{x}} = \begin{bmatrix} \partial\dot{x}/\partial x & \partial\dot{x}/\partial y & \partial\dot{x}/\partial\theta \\ \partial\dot{y}/\partial x & \partial\dot{y}/\partial y & \partial\dot{y}/\partial\theta \\ \partial\dot{\theta}/\partial x & \partial\dot{\theta}/\partial y & \partial\dot{\theta}/\partial\theta \end{bmatrix} = \begin{bmatrix} 0 & 0 & -vs\psi \\ 0 & 0 & vc\psi \\ 0 & 0 & 0 \end{bmatrix}$$

This gives for the matrix Φ_k:

$$\Phi_k \approx I + F\Delta t = \begin{bmatrix} 1 & 0 & -vs\psi\Delta t \\ 0 & 1 & vc\psi\Delta t \\ 0 & 0 & 1 \end{bmatrix}$$

There are no longer measurement models for the encoder or gyro. The models for landmark observations, presented below, are quite difficult but they are worth the effort. They amount to the difference between a robot that always knows its location and one that gets progressively more lost.

5.3.4.6.2 Observer and Jacobian. It is common for noncontact navigation sensors to measure either bearings to landmarks, or ranges, or both. Let the x axis of the sensor point forward as shown in Figure 5.36. For the moment, assume that the coordinates (x_d, y_d) of the detection point are known in sensor coordinates. We can write:

$$\cos \alpha = x_d^s / r_d^s$$
$$\sin \alpha = y_d^s / r_d^s$$

(5.116)

Hence, the angle and range observations are:

$$z_{sen} = \begin{bmatrix} \alpha \\ r_d^s \end{bmatrix} = f(\underline{r}_d^s) = \begin{bmatrix} \text{atan}\,(y_d^s / x_d^s) \\ \sqrt{(x_d^s)^2 + (y_d^s)^2} \end{bmatrix}$$

(5.117)

The Jacobian of these observations with respect to the detection point in sensor referenced coordinates ($\underline{r}_d^s$) is:

$$H_{sd}^z = \frac{\partial \underline{z}}{\partial \underline{r}_d^s} = \begin{bmatrix} H_s^\alpha \\ H_s^r \end{bmatrix} = \begin{bmatrix} \dfrac{1}{(r_d^s)^2}\begin{bmatrix} -y_d^s & x_d^s \end{bmatrix} \\ \dfrac{1}{r_d^s}\begin{bmatrix} x_d^s & y_d^s \end{bmatrix} \end{bmatrix} = \begin{bmatrix} \dfrac{1}{r_d^s}\begin{bmatrix} -s\alpha & c\alpha \end{bmatrix} \\ \begin{bmatrix} c\alpha & s\alpha \end{bmatrix} \end{bmatrix}$$

(5.118)

5.3.4.6.3 Sensor Referenced Observation. The sensor referenced pose of the detection point can be written in terms of a series of transformations that transform the detection pose from model, to world, to body, to sensor coordinates. Using pose composition notation:

$$\underline{\rho}_d^s = \underline{\rho}_b^s * \underline{\rho}_w^b * \underline{\rho}_m^w * \underline{\rho}_d^m$$

(5.119)

We will be interested in the variation of this quantity with respect to variations in the robot pose $\underline{\rho}_b^w$, which is known as the state vector $\underline{x}$ in the filter formulation just described. When the feature is a point we will use $\underline{r}_d^m = \begin{bmatrix} x & y \end{bmatrix}^T$ instead of $\underline{\rho}_d^m = \begin{bmatrix} x & y & \psi \end{bmatrix}^T$ and $\underline{r}_d^s$ instead of $\underline{\rho}_d^s$.

   Later in the text, we will see that it is possible to also find the landmark positions in a process known as SLAM. For that purpose, we will also derive here the variation of the above quantity with respect to the landmark pose $\underline{\rho}_m^w$. In order to simplify the computations, the above will be rewritten in three steps, so that the Jacobian can be developed using the chain rule:

$$\underline{\rho}_d^s = \underline{\rho}_b^s * \underline{\rho}_d^b \qquad \underline{\rho}_d^b = \underline{\rho}_w^b * \underline{\rho}_d^w \qquad \underline{\rho}_d^w = \underline{\rho}_m^w * \underline{\rho}_d^m$$

(5.120)

It is possible to use a product of an inner pose Jacobian and an inverse pose Jacobian but we want to isolate and reuse the quantity H_{bd}^{sd}. Define four more Jacobians besides H_{sd}^z:

$$H_{bd}^{sd} = \frac{\partial \underline{\rho}_d^s}{\partial \underline{\rho}_d^b} \qquad H_w^b = \frac{\partial \underline{\rho}_d^b}{\partial \underline{\rho}_d^w} \qquad H_x^{bd} = \frac{\partial \underline{\rho}_d^b}{\partial \underline{\rho}_b^w} \qquad H_m^w = \frac{\partial \underline{\rho}_d^w}{\partial \underline{\rho}_m^w}$$

(5.121)

The subscript x will refer to the pose $\underline{\rho}_b^w$ while emphasizing that this particular pose is the robot state in which we are mostly interested. We will be interested in two Jacobians composed of the above four. First, the Jacobian of the observation with respect to the robot pose:

$$H_x^z = \left(\frac{\partial z}{\partial \underline{\rho}_d^s}\right)\left(\frac{\partial \underline{\rho}_d^s}{\partial \underline{\rho}_d^b}\right)\left(\frac{\partial \underline{\rho}_d^b}{\partial \underline{\rho}_b^w}\right) = H_{sd}^z H_{bd}^{sd} H_x^{bd} \tag{5.122}$$

Second, the Jacobian of the observation with respect to the landmark pose:

$$H_{wm}^z = \left(\frac{\partial z}{\partial \underline{\rho}_d^s}\right)\left(\frac{\partial \underline{\rho}_d^s}{\partial \underline{\rho}_d^b}\right)\left(\frac{\partial \underline{\rho}_d^b}{\partial \underline{\rho}_d^w}\right)\left(\frac{\partial \underline{\rho}_d^w}{\partial \underline{\rho}_m^w}\right) = H_{sd}^z H_{bd}^{sd} H_{wd}^{bd} H_{wm}^{wd} \tag{5.123}$$

5.3.4.6.4 Body To Sensor. Consider the pose network in Figure 5.37. The Jacobian $\partial \underline{\rho}_d^s / \partial \underline{\rho}_d^b$ relating the sensor referenced and body referenced observations is the inverse of $\partial \underline{\rho}_d^b / \partial \underline{\rho}_d^s$ – which, according to the graph, is a compound-right pose Jacobian that is easy to invert (because it is a rotation matrix).

Therefore:

$$\frac{\partial \underline{\rho}_d^b}{\partial \underline{\rho}_d^s} = \begin{bmatrix} c\psi_s^b & -s\psi_s^b & 0 \\ s\psi_s^b & c\psi_s^b & 0 \\ 0 & 0 & 1 \end{bmatrix} \quad H_{bd}^{sd} = \left(\frac{\partial \underline{\rho}_d^b}{\partial \underline{\rho}_d^s}\right)^{-1} = \frac{\partial \underline{\rho}_d^s}{\partial \underline{\rho}_d^b} = \begin{bmatrix} c\psi_s^b & s\psi_s^b & 0 \\ -s\psi_s^b & c\psi_s^b & 0 \\ 0 & 0 & 1 \end{bmatrix} \tag{5.124}$$

The last row and column are omitted for a point feature.

5.3.4.6.5 World to Body. Consider the pose network in Figure 5.38. In this, case we are interested in two Jacobians. First, the Jacobian of the body referenced detection point with respect to the world referenced one is $\partial \underline{\rho}_d^b / \partial \underline{\rho}_d^w$. This is the inverse of $\partial \underline{\rho}_d^w / \partial \underline{\rho}_d^b$ – a compound-right pose Jacobian according to the above figure.

Figure 5.37 Pose Network For Body to Sensor Jacobian. This network of three frames will be used to define pose Jacobians.

Figure 5.38 Pose Network For World to Body Jacobian. This network of three frames will be used to define pose Jacobians.

Therefore:

$$\frac{\partial \underline{\rho}_d^w}{\partial \underline{\rho}_d^b} = \begin{bmatrix} c\psi_b^w & -s\psi_b^w & 0 \\ s\psi_b^w & c\psi_b^w & 0 \\ 0 & 0 & 1 \end{bmatrix} \quad H_{wd}^{bd} = \left(\frac{\partial \underline{\rho}_d^w}{\partial \underline{\rho}_d^b}\right)^{-1} = \frac{\partial \underline{\rho}_d^b}{\partial \underline{\rho}_d^w} = \begin{bmatrix} c\psi_b^w & s\psi_b^w & 0 \\ -s\psi_b^w & c\psi_b^w & 0 \\ 0 & 0 & 1 \end{bmatrix}$$

The last row and column are omitted for a point feature. Next, the derivative of the body referenced detection point with respect to the robot pose in the world is

$\partial \underline{\rho}_d^b / \partial \underline{\rho}_b^w$ – which is a right-left pose Jacobian. Immediately we can write:

$$H_x^{bd} = \frac{\partial \underline{\rho}_d^b}{\partial \underline{\rho}_b^w} = -\begin{bmatrix} c\psi_b^w & s\psi_b^w & -y_d^b \\ -s\psi_b^w & c\psi_b^w & x_d^b \\ 0 & 0 & 1 \end{bmatrix} \tag{5.125}$$

The last row is omitted for a point feature. The importance of landmarks and maps is the fact that the associated measurements project directly onto the position states – they tell the robot where it is without any integrations. This is evident from the nonzero elements in the first two columns of this measurement Jacobian. The variation of the range and bearing measurements with the velocity states is zero, so it was not written.

5.3.4.6.6 Model to World. Consider the pose network in Figure 5.39. The Jacobian $\partial \underline{\rho}_d^w / \partial \underline{\rho}_m^w$ relating the world referenced and model referenced observations is a compound-left pose Jacobian.

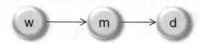

Figure 5.39 Pose Network For Model to World Jacobian. This network of three frames will be used to define pose Jacobians.

Therefore:

$$H_{wm}^{wd} = \frac{\partial \underline{\rho}_d^w}{\partial \underline{\rho}_m^w} = \begin{bmatrix} 1 & 0 & -(y_d^w - y_m^w) \\ 0 & 1 & (x_d^w - x_m^w) \\ 0 & 0 & 1 \end{bmatrix} \tag{5.126}$$

The last row and column are omitted for a point feature because such a feature has no orientation.

5.3.4.6.7 Point Features. For point features, the complete measurement model is the point version ($\underline{r}_d^s$ rather than $\underline{\rho}_d^s$) of Equation 5.119 as shown in Box 5.5.

Box 5.5 Measurement Models and Jacobians for Making and Using Maps

The complete measurement model is the point version of Equation 5.119:

$$\underline{r}_d^s = T_b^s * T_w^b(\underline{\rho}_b^w) * T_m^w(\underline{r}_m^w) * \underline{r}_d^m$$

$$z_{sen} = f(\underline{r}_d^s) = \begin{bmatrix} \operatorname{atan}(y_d^s/x_d^s) - \pi/2 \\ \sqrt{(x_d^s)^2 + (y_d^s)^2} \end{bmatrix}$$

$$H_x^z = \left(\frac{\partial z}{\partial \underline{\rho}_d^s}\right)\left(\frac{\partial \underline{\rho}_d^s}{\partial \underline{\rho}_d^b}\right)\left(\frac{\partial \underline{\rho}_d^b}{\partial \underline{\rho}_b^w}\right) = H_{sd}^z H_{bd}^{sd} H_x^{bd}$$

$$H_{wm}^z = \left(\frac{\partial z}{\partial \underline{\rho}_d^s}\right)\left(\frac{\partial \underline{\rho}_d^s}{\partial \underline{\rho}_d^b}\right)\left(\frac{\partial \underline{\rho}_d^b}{\partial \underline{\rho}_d^w}\right)\left(\frac{\partial \underline{\rho}_d^w}{\partial \underline{\rho}_m^w}\right) = H_{sd}^z H_{bd}^{sd} H_{wd}^{bd} H_{wm}^{wd}$$

These are the main formulas needed to use, or to use and update, a map of landmarks for bearing or range measurements or both.

This result gives the predicted sensor readings z_{sen} given the landmark position r_m^w and the robot pose ρ_b^w. The first Jacobian is used to determine the robot position from the landmarks and the second is used to determine the landmark positions from the robot pose. We will see later that both can be done at once.

5.3.4.6.8 Measurement Uncertainty. Finally, the measurement uncertainty can be assumed in the simplest case to be constant and uncorrelated:

$$R = \begin{bmatrix} \sigma_{\alpha\alpha} & 0 \\ 0 & \sigma_{rr} \end{bmatrix} \qquad (5.127)$$

This type of sensor is usually neither integrated nor averaged. A fixed amount of time is allocated to take an image and it has no relationship to vehicle speed.

5.3.4.7 Data Association

The filter will form innovations based on predicted sensor readings, so the immediate implementation question is which landmark should be used to form the predictions. Kalman filters are not very robust to a mistake in this part of the processing. One mis-association can cause a large error in state whose uncertainty is underestimated and that can cause a chain reaction of more misassociations and complete failure of the system. Data association must be done well.

Normally, landmark identification information is not in the data stream from the sensors, though there are exceptions, so landmark identification must be inferred. Clearly, it is possible to pick the landmark that is closest to the estimated position of the end of the ray to the landmark, but this turns out to be a fairly ineffective approach in several situations.

A somewhat intuitive way to proceed is to examine the *innovation covariance:*

$$S = HPH^T + R \qquad (5.128)$$

This is computed inside the filter already in the Kalman Gain calculation. It represents the covariance of the innovation. Recall the innovation is:

$$\Delta\underline{z} = \underline{z}_k - h(\underline{x}_k^-)$$

The uncertainty in this prediction involves both the state estimate uncertainty and the measurement uncertainty. In fact, we derived back in Equation 5.37 the result that proves Equation 5.128 is the innovation covariance. To use it, we need some multi dimensional sense of scaled deviation from the mean. Recall the Mahalanobis distance (MD):

$$d = \sqrt{\Delta\underline{z}^T S^{-1} \Delta\underline{z}} \qquad (5.129)$$

This represents deviation from the mean, reduced to a single dimension of "length" in measurement space, in units of standard deviation. If the innovations are Gaussian distributed, then d^2 is Chi-square distributed [10] where the number of degrees of freedom of the Chi-square distribution is the dimension of $\Delta\underline{z}$. The *validation gate* technique compares the magnitude of d^2 to confidence thresholds extracted from this distribution. Table 5.2 provides a few values for confidence thresholds (on d^2 not d).

Table 5.2 Chi Square Validation Gates

Degrees of Freedom	95% confidence gate	99% confidence gate
1	5.02	7.87
2	7.38	10.60
3	9.35	12.38
4	11.14	14.86

Based on this table, assuming two degrees of freedom in $\Delta \underline{z}$, we can design a fairly robust data association procedure. A potential association of a measurement to a landmark can be rejected if:

- It has a $d > 3$, or . . .
- If $d \leq 3$, there is second candidate association with a $d < 6$. This case means there is too close a match to be sure which landmark is being imaged.
- Apparent readings from the matched landmark are not stable for several cycles.

One good way to diagnose errors in implementation is to plot the MD for a particular sensor as a function of time. If the actual errors are significantly smaller than the variance (MD < about 3), the filter is overestimating the error in the measurements and not using them optimally. If the actual errors are larger than the variance (MD > about 3) then the filter is underestimating the error in the measurements and relying on them too much. The latter case often leads quickly to divergence.

5.3.5 Pragmatic Information for Kalman Filters

This section presents several aspects of applied optimal estimation that are of high relevance to practitioners.

5.3.5.1 State Vector Augmentation

A Kalman filter assumes that the errors being modelled stochastically are unbiased. We have seen that random errors can accumulate in the state estimate at a rate proportional to the square root of time. However, it is not hard to see that a deterministic scale error in velocity measurement will cause a position error that grows linearly with time. When significant systematic errors exist, and the important measurements are infrequent, underestimated error present in the P matrix can lead to divergence.

Under appropriate sensing, the Kalman filter formulation provides a mechanism known as state vector augmentation, that permits unknown systematic parameters to be identified in real time. Incorrect values for such parameters are a major source of systematic errors, so this form of calibration removes the associated systematic errors.

5.3.5.1.1 Modelling Nonwhite Noise Sources. The technique also permits the modelling of nonwhite (time correlated) noise sources. Suppose the measurement noise $\underline{v}$ in the continuous time model below is correlated:

$$\dot{\underline{x}} = F\underline{x} + G\underline{w}$$
$$\underline{z} = H\underline{x} + \underline{v}$$

Oftentimes it is possible to model the correlated measurement noise by passing uncorrelated white noise $\bar{w}_1$ through a system with linear dynamics (i.e., by filtering it) thus:

$$\dot{\underline{v}} = E\underline{v} + \underline{w}_1$$

Using this model, the correlated component of noise can be considered to constitute a random element in the state vector. This element is added to the existing states to form the *augmented* state vector $\begin{bmatrix} x & \upsilon \end{bmatrix}^T$. Then, the new system model becomes:

$$\frac{d}{dt}\begin{bmatrix} x \\ \upsilon \end{bmatrix} = \begin{bmatrix} F & 0 \\ 0 & E \end{bmatrix}\begin{bmatrix} x \\ \upsilon \end{bmatrix} + \begin{bmatrix} G & 0 \\ 0 & I \end{bmatrix}\begin{bmatrix} w \\ w_1 \end{bmatrix}$$

The measurement equation becomes:

$$\underline{z} = \begin{bmatrix} H & I \end{bmatrix}\begin{bmatrix} x \\ \underline{v} \end{bmatrix}$$

5.3.5.1.2 Parameter Identification. Unknown system parameters can be modelled as deterministic new state variables with this technique. The (scalar) state differential equation for one new constant state x_i is:

$$\dot{x}_i = 0$$

The measurement matrices H of all sensors are updated to reflect the presence of a new state. The basic operation of the filter is to project the measurement residual onto the states, so it will determine a value for this constant and even allow it to vary slowly with time.

5.3.5.1.3 Example: Encoder Scale Factor Calibration. Suppose that we want to calibrate the scale factor used on the transmission encoder in order to compensate in real time for wheel slip – or simply to calibrate the average wheel radii. We can put the scale factor in a new augmented state vector. The process defines a new scale factor state, call it k, and adds it to the state vector:

$$\underline{x} = \begin{bmatrix} x & y & \psi & v & \omega & k \end{bmatrix}$$

It might be convenient to think of k as a number close to unity that converts correct velocity to nominal velocity from the encoder. The system model is largely unchanged because it depends on the real velocity state. However, there is one extra state equation for the new state that expresses that we expect it to be constant:

$$\dot{k} = 0$$

The measurement model for encoder is the one place where this new state appears because it is associated with this senor only:

$$z_e = kv \qquad H_e = \frac{\partial z_e}{\partial \underline{x}} = \begin{bmatrix} 0 & 0 & 0 & k & 0 & v \end{bmatrix}$$

Provided there is at least one other sensor that gives information directly or indirectly (e.g., landmarks) about velocity, the filter will be able to determine the scale factor based on processing the encoder residuals.

The system can start with the initial conditions $k(t_0) = 1$ and a high enough value in the associated place in P_0 to tell the system that there is low confidence in this value for the scale factor. As the vehicle drives, the processing of encoder readings will project some of the residual onto the scale factor and some onto the velocity. Furthermore, the errors in the other sensor will be unbiased so they will quickly remove any misallocations of encoder residuals to velocity errors. The KF will quickly find the value of k that best explains the bias in the residuals and the bias will disappear.

Provided the value in Q associated with k is nonzero, the system will continue to update scale factor continuously. This means that wheel slip can be calibrated as if it was a scale factor error. A similar formulation can be used to learn wheel radii, wheelbase, wheel track, etc.

5.3.5.2 Special Treatment of Measurements

The following few points relate to special circumstances when processing measurements.

5.3.5.2.1 Pseudomeasurements. Although it is possible to incorporate constraints directly into the formulation of a KF, there is also a simpler approach that is quite useful. Suppose we have a constraint equation of the form:

$$\underline{c}(\underline{x}) = \underline{h}(\underline{x}) = \underline{0}$$

We could try to rewrite the system dynamics by substituting this so that the constraint is satisfied implicitly. However, this is not always easy to do as we saw in Lagrange dynamics. Often it is simpler to write a measurement model of the form:

$$\underline{z} = \underline{h}(\underline{x})$$

Then we can regularly generate a fake measurement, call it a *pseudomeasurement*, with a value of 0 and present it to the KF as if it was real. The processing will proceed exactly as if a sensor existed that measured the constraint residual, and it will force the states to comply with the constraint in an optimal fashion. This is one way, for example, to enforce a no wheel slip or low wheel slip constraint on a system that otherwise assumes that lateral velocities are possible.

In some cases, pseudomeasurements should be generated only under special conditions. A *zero velocity update* or *zupt*, is a powerful pseudomeasurement that can be used to help determine sensor biases in inertial navigation. The KF is told that the true velocity is zero and if the state is not, the KF will explain the difference in terms of sensor biases, and hence remove them.

5.3.5.2.2 Measurement Latency. In situations where different measurements arrive subject to different latencies, the question of how to align them in time arises. The simplest solution is to maintain a measurement queue, sort it by time tags if necessary, and then continue to process measurements as necessary to compute the state a few moments in the past. At the other end of the complexity scale, memory of recent states and measurements would allow a reset to an earlier state and reprocessing of subsequent measurements if a highly delayed measurement arrives after others that were not delayed.

5.3.5.2.3 Coordinate Transforms to Sensor Frames. It is virtually never the case that sensors are positioned and aligned with the robot coordinate frame so most measurement models incorporate a compensation for sensor positioning. We saw this issue when landmarks were added to the map based filter earlier. For velocities and accelerations, transformations based on the Coriolis equation are required.

Typically, measurements cannot reasonably be packaged to arrive synchronously. For example, Doppler readings may not be available as frequently as encoder readings because they are already filtered. GPS measurements may not be generated faster than 2-20 Hz whereas inertial systems can be 100 times faster than this.

5.3.5.2.4 Angle Arithmetic. Whenever angles are added or subtracted in the filter, it is imperative that the result be converted to a canonical representation that does not include an extra cycle of the unit circle. Otherwise the filter will fail catastrophically. This issue potentially occurs twice in the state update $\hat{x}_k = \hat{\underline{x}}_k + K_k[\underline{z}_k - h(\hat{\underline{x}}_k)]$. If the measurement is an angle, then angle arithmetic occurs when the innovation is computed in the subtraction above. If the state is an angle, then angle arithmetic occurs when the state is updated in the addition.

For example, suppose that the measured bearing to a landmark is 181° and the predicted bearing is –181°. These two angles are actually only 2° apart. A straightforward difference will produce an innovation of 362° which will produce 181 times the correct change in the state. Clearly, all additions and subtractions of angles must be normalized immediately. Such computations also occur in the system model when the state is updated based on an angular velocity state.

5.3.5.3 Delayed State Filter Formulation

There are situations in which a sensor inherently produces differential quantities and it would be inconvenient or incorrect to divide by the time difference to produce a time derivative. A visual odometry system will produce differential quantities, for example, and it may be a difficult matter to determine the time between measurements if a processor with a clock does not receive the measurements with repeatable delay.

The more general case of differential measurements is to suppose we have a measurement that depends on both the present state and the previous state:

$$z_k = H_k x_k + H_m x_{k-1} + \upsilon_k$$

This is not in the standard form we require for a Kalman filter. It is tempting to try to fix this by simply putting both states in a single state vector. Then the measurement becomes:

$$z_k = \begin{bmatrix} H_k & H_m \end{bmatrix} \begin{bmatrix} x_k \\ x_{k-1} \end{bmatrix} + \upsilon_k = H_{km} x_{km} + \upsilon_k$$

Now it seems we have returned to the usual case except that the state vector would have doubled in length. However, a dependence of a measurement on a delayed state introduces a dependence on the errors in the delayed state and that violates a fundamental assumption of the Kalman filter as it was derived earlier.

To see the problem, and closely following [1], we solve the state equation for the delayed state:

$$x_{k-1} = \Phi_{k-1}^{-1} x_k - \Phi_{k-1}^{-1} w_{k-1}$$

and substitute into the measurement model:

$$z_k = H_k x_k + J_k x_{k-1} + \upsilon_k$$

$$z_k = H_k x_k + J_k[\Phi_{k-1}^{-1} x_k - \Phi_{k-1}^{-1} w_{k-1}] + \upsilon_k$$

$$z_k = [H_k + J_k\Phi_{k-1}^{-1}]x_k + [-J_k\Phi_{k-1}^{-1} w_{k-1} + \upsilon_k]$$

This is now in the correct form where the new effective measurement Jacobian is:

$$H_k^{eff} = H_k + J_k\Phi_{k-1}^{-1} \tag{5.130}$$

Note how the last term in square brackets above makes it clear that the error in the measurement will be correlated with that in the delayed state. The covariance matrix of this new effective noise term is:

$$R_k^{eff} = Exp[(-J_k\Phi_{k-1}^{-1} w_{k-1} + \upsilon_k)(-J_k\Phi_{k-1}^{-1} w_{k-1} + \upsilon_k)^T]$$

The quantity in square brackets expands into four terms and two cancel because w_{k-1} and v_k are uncorrelated by assumption. Therefore:

$$R_k^{eff} = J_k\Phi_{k-1}^{-1} Q_{k-1} \Phi_{k-1}^{-1T} J_k^T + R_k \tag{5.131}$$

The correlation is captured in the cross covariance:

$$C_k^{eff} = Exp[(w_{k-1})(-J_k\Phi_{k-1}^{-1} w_{k-1} + \upsilon_k)^T]$$

Again, due to our assumptions, this simplifies to:

$$C_k^{eff} = -Q_{k-1}\Phi_{k-1}^{-1T} J_k^T \tag{5.132}$$

Noting that:

$$P_k^- = Q_{k-1} + \Phi_{k-1}P_{k-1}\Phi_{k-1}^T$$

This matrix can be used in a more general KF that allows correlated measurement and process noise. It can be derived by returning to Equation 5.83 and including the above cross covariance denoted as C:

$$\underline{x}' = \left(\begin{bmatrix} H \\ I \end{bmatrix}^T \begin{bmatrix} R & C \\ C^T & P \end{bmatrix}^{-1} \begin{bmatrix} H \\ I \end{bmatrix} \right)^{-1} \begin{bmatrix} H \\ I \end{bmatrix}^T \begin{bmatrix} R & 0 \\ 0 & P \end{bmatrix}^{-1} \underline{z}$$

The result of solving this more general case is only slightly more complicated than the standard filter:

$$K_k = (P_k^- H_k^T + C_k)[H_k P_k^- H_k^T + R_k + H_k C_k + C_k^T H_k^T]^{-1}$$

$$P_k = (I - K_k H_k)P_k^- - K_k C_k^T \tag{5.133}$$

It is possible to eliminate the inversion of the transition matrix in the computation of C with more manipulation.

5.3.5.4 Sequential Measurement Processing

It can be shown that if concurrent measurements are uncorrelated, they can still be processed one at a time to produce the same result as processing them as a vector measurement. Doing so allows modular software implementations that adapt in real time to the presence or absence of measurements at any particular time step. This technique has computational advantages as well because inverting two matrices of order $n/2$ is much cheaper than inverting one of order n.

The state equations can be run at whatever rate the rest of the system requires while measurements are incorporated at whatever rate they are generated by the sensors. The basic algorithm is given below in Algorithm 5.1:

```
00    algorithm estimateState()
01        predict state with x̂_{k+1} = Φ_k x̂_k
02        predict covariance with P_{k+1} = Φ_k P_k Φ_k^T + G_k Q_k G_k^T
03        for each sensor
04            if(sensor has measurement z available)
05                kalmanFilter(z)
06    return
07    algorithm kalmanFilter(z)
08        compute predicted measurement h(x)
09        compute Jacobian H(x)
10        compute innovation z − h(x)
11        compute Kalman gain K_k = P_k^- H_k^T [H_k P_k^- H_k^T + R_k]^{-1}
12        update state x̂_k^+ = x̂_k^- + K_k[z_k − H_k x̂_k^-]
13        update covariance P_k^+ = [I − K_k H_k]P_k^-
14        return
```

Algorithm 5.1 Pseudocode for a Kalman Filter that Adapts to Measurement Availability. Measurements are processed independently whenever they are available.

5.3.5.5 Measurements Related to a Single State

It is not unusual to find that most processing is spent computing the uncertainty matrices, and the Kalman gain, and in inverting and multiplying matrices. When the measurement Jacobian projects onto a single state, as it does in our simple robot example for the transmission encoder and gyro, then some efficiencies are available.

5.3.5.5.1 Kalman Gain. The matrix Kalman gain equation for an EKF is:

$$K_k = P_k^- H_k^T [H_k P_k^- H_k^T + R_k]^{-1}$$

Let a single measurement arrive for integration with the state estimate. Then, the R matrix is a scalar:

$$R = [r]$$

Let the measurement project onto a single state whose index is s with a coefficient of unity. Then the H matrix is a row vector with a single unit element in the sth position:

$$H = \begin{bmatrix} 0 & 0 & 0 & 0 & 0 & 1 & 0 & 0 & 0 & 0 \end{bmatrix}$$

The expression $P_k^- H_k^T$ is the sth column of P_k^- and the expression $H_k P_k^- H_k^T$ is the (s, s) element of P_k^-. Define:

$$p = P_{ss}$$

Based on all of the above, the Kalman gain is a column vector equal to a constant times the sth column of P_k^-:

$$K = \left(\frac{1}{p + r}\right) P(:, s)$$

Here we are using MATLAB colon notation where a colon indicates the range of the associated index. In this notation, $A(i, :)$ is the ith row of A and $A(:, j)$ is the jth column.

5.3.5.5.2 Uncertainty Propagation.
The matrix uncertainty propagation equation for an EKF is:

$$P = [I - (KH)]P$$

This can be computed many times faster as:

$$P = P - K(HP)$$

and this rewrite is valid regardless of the form of the measurement matrix H. Further simplification is possible in the case of a single scalar measurement. Let a single measurement arrive for integration with the state estimate. Again, let the measurement project onto a single state whose index is s with a coefficient of unity. The expression HP is then the sth row of P_k^-. Reusing the last result, the expression KHP is simply a constant times the outer product of the sth column and the sth row of P_k^-:

$$KHP = \left(\frac{1}{p + r}\right) P(:, s) P(s, :)$$

5.3.6 Other Forms of the Kalman Filter

Since the Kalman Filter was originally published a large number of useful variants have been developed. The Joseph form is guaranteed numerically to preserve positive definiteness of the state covariance. Various square root forms of the filter are more numerically stable than the standard form. The information filter is very popular in robotics due to its relative efficiency for some operations. The unscented filter performs correct nonlinear propagation of the mean and it can lead to much more consistent estimates and reduced risk of divergence. The technique of covariance intersection is a technique for data fusion that is advantageous when correlations are unknown. The iterated Kalman filter uses iteration to compute more precise intermediate and final results. Cascaded and federated filters are architectural approaches to integrating systems with other Kalman filters in them. The sliding window filter is useful for visual motion estimation.

5.3.7 References and Further Reading

Grewal is one of a few overall first texts on Kalman filters. Farrel is one source for comparison of various filter architectures. Bar-Shalom is a source for tests on the reasonableness of the innovation based on Chi-squared tests.

[9] Jay Farrell and Matthew and Barth, *The Global Positioning System and Inertial Navigation*, McGraw-Hill, 1998.

[10] Yaakov Bar-Shalom and Xiao-Rong LI, *Estimation and Tracking: Principles, Techniques, and Software*, YBS Publishing, 1993.

[11] Mohinder S. Grewal and Angus P. Andrews, *Kalman Filtering: Theory and Practice using MATLAB*, 2nd ed., Wiley, 2001.

5.3.8 Exercises

5.3.8.1 Velocity Measurements

There are several situations in which a speed or rotation sensor is placed somewhere on a vehicle but its output is best interpreted as the velocity of somewhere else.

(i) A rotary encoder is mounted on a small disk attached to a fender over a wheel. It functions as a small wheel that rolls on the vehicle wheel. The disk remains in contact with the wheel and rotates as the wheel spins but in the opposite direction. The ratio of disk radius to wheel radius converts the disk speed to wheel speed. What position vector (of the sensor relative to the body frame) should be used? The disk? The wheel hub? The wheel contact point? Does it matter and why?

(ii) A transmission encoder is mounted such that it measures the output of a rear axle differential. Therefore it will indicate a quantity proportional to the average angular velocity of the two wheels. Under what two conditions does it also measure the average of the two wheel linear velocities.

(iii) A transmission encoder on a double Ackerman steer vehicle indicates the magnitude of the velocity of the geometric center point between the four wheels but its direction is not fixed in the body frame because the front and rear steer angles are not necessarily equal. A gyro is available to measure the angular velocity. Is there enough information to determine the direction of the velocity in the vehicle frame?

5.3.8.2 Wheel Radius Identification for Differential Steer

Recall that a differential steer vehicle has a left and a right wheel, and often a caster at the third point of contact with the ground. Write the measurement relationships for the left and right wheel angular velocities in terms of the linear and angular velocity of the vehicle, including the dependence on wheel radii.

(i) Can wheel radii be distinguished from lateral offsets of the wheels?

(ii) Are measurements of the forward linear velocity and the angular velocity adequate to observe the wheel radii? If not, what measurements can be added to create an observable system?

5.3.8.3 System Model in 3D

A pose estimation Kalman filter for 3D motion is formulated for observability reasons to *explicitly* assume that:

• the vehicle translates only along the body x axis
• the vehicle rotates only around the body z axis

In this model, the state variables are $\underline{x} = \begin{bmatrix} x & y & z & v & \phi & \theta & \psi & \dot{\beta} \end{bmatrix}^T$ where v is the projection of the vehicle velocity onto the body x axis, and $\dot{\beta}$ is the projection of the vehicle angular velocity onto the body z axis. Using Equation 2.56 and Equation 2.74 from Chapter 2, formulate the system model, and its Jacobians.

5.4 Bayesian Estimation

The famous Bayes', Theorem (or Rule) [12] is a result of remarkable generality and power. In robotics, it represents a much more general technique for performing optimal estimation than the Kalman filter. Unlike the Kalman filter, the Bayesian approach can work with arbitrary probability distributions rather than Gaussians. It can operate on distributions that are multimodal and it can produce results of the same multimodal character. In position estimation for example, the Bayesian approach has the power to compute a probability field over the entire workspace of the robot. Such a field can capture subtle cues in even highly ambiguous environments in order to eventually determine where the robot is located.

5.4.1 Definitions

Let A and B be two events whose probability we wish to investigate. For now, let them be discrete variables. Suppose, for example, A takes on the value of the color of a randomly selected jelly bean. We will denote by $P(A)$ the probability that event A occurs. That is, the probability that the proposition that A occurred is true. By definition $0 \leq P(A) \leq 1$ for any event A. We will denote by $\overline{A}$ the proposition that event that A did not occur. From the definition of probability, we have:

$$P(\overline{A}) = 1 - P(A)$$

The *odds* of event A, denoted $O(A)$ is the ratio of the number of times we expect A to occur to the number of times we expect it not to occur. That is:

$$O(A) = \frac{P(A)}{P(\overline{A})} = \frac{P(A)}{1 - P(A)} = \frac{1 - P(\overline{A})}{P(\overline{A})}$$

The odds of heads in a coin toss are $1/1$ (written as 1:1) whereas the odds of getting a red jelly bean in a balanced bag of red, green, and blue ones is 1:2. Thus, given either $P(A)$, $P(\overline{A})$, or $O(A)$, we can always recover the other two unambiguously.

5.4.1.1 Two Random Variables

For two random variables we have the probability of *either* occurring as:

$$P(A \vee B) = P(A) + P(B) - P(A \wedge B) \tag{5.134}$$

where the last term removes any double counting. The symbol $\vee$ means "or" and the symbol $\wedge$ means "and." When A and B are propositions that a random object is in the indicated set, the need for the third term becomes clear. Consider Figure 5.40 where the experiment involves selecting a point in the rectangle at random and imagine that probability is proportional to the area of each region.

If the two events are *mutually exclusive*, we have:

$$P(A \vee B) = P(A) + P(B) \tag{5.135}$$

This would occur if the circles did not overlap. When the events A and B are *independent* of each other, we can easily compute the probability of *both* occurring:

$$P(A \wedge B) = P(A) \cdot P(B) \tag{5.136}$$

Rearranging the last result two ways leads to:

$$P(A) = \frac{P(A \wedge B)}{P(B)}$$

$$P(B) = \frac{P(A \wedge B)}{P(A)}$$

For a continuous random variable x, the equivalent of the *probability mass function (pmf)* $P(A)$ is the *probability density function (pdf)* $p(x)$. The density function produces a probability when integrated over a region of some kind:

$$P(a < x < b) = \int_a^b p(x)dx$$

Notationally, we will use an uppercase P when the domain is discrete whereas a lowercase p means the domain is continuous. We will refer to both types of functions as *distributions*.

5.4.1.2 Conditional Probability

Consider Figure 5.42 a few pages ahead. When the circles overlap, a point in A has a finite probability of also being in B and vice versa. When there are two variables, we can talk about the probability of A occurring given that B has occurred. This *conditional probability* is denoted $P(A|B)$ and is read as the probability that event A occurs on the assumption event B occurs. This is a central notion when applied to robotics because sensors can be modelled as random processes that produce measurements given that the robot is in a certain state.

When the two variables are mutually independent, the conditional probability reduces to the "unconditional" one:

$$P(A|B) = P(A)$$

because A is, in fact, not at all dependent on B. For example, exclusivity is an extreme form of dependence. If A and B are mutually exclusive, then $P(A|B)$ is zero. B being true forces A not to be true.

For the dependent case, suppose, for instance, that knowledge that event B has occurred, somehow alters our estimate of the probability of A. For example, one is more likely to get a full coffee cup from a particular server at the local diner. When one variable is fixed, the remaining probability must be complementary whatever its value. That is:

$$P(A|B) + P(\neg A|B) = 1$$

for any value of B. However $P(A|B) + P(A|\neg B)$ can be anything from 0 to 2 in general.

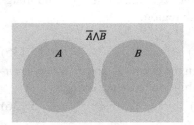

Figure 5.40 Venn Diagram. Such diagrams are an intuitive way to visualize sets and associated probabilities.

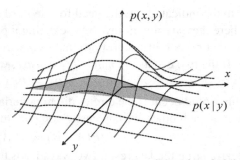

Figure 5.41 Joint Versus Conditional Probability. The conditional probability is essentially a slice through the joint probability surface.

5.4.1.3 Interpretations

Conditional probability can be used to model several situations.

5.4.1.3.1 Staged Experiment. In a staged experiment, one variable is sampled before another. For example, suppose that $P(B)$ means the probability of selection of a particular barrel of jelly beans. Then $P(A)$ might mean the probability that a red bean is selected from *any* barrel. In which case, $P(A|B)$ would denote the probability of selecting a red bean from the *specific* barrel denoted as B.

5.4.1.3.2 Slice of Joint PDF. Consider discrete random variables. The meaning of $P(A|B)$ is very different from the meaning of the *joint* probability mass function $P(A, B)$. The latter means the probability of each possible pair (A, B). Similarly, for continuous random variables, $p(x, y)$ is a surface and $p(x|y)$ is a slice through that surface at a particular value of y, which has been renormalized (scaled) to contain an area of unity (Figure 5.41).

This clarifies what we mean by conditional probability. The variable y ceases to be considered random – because its value has become known. The new distribution $p(x|y)$ then depends on it deterministically.

5.4.1.3.3 An Estimation Process. Switching now to continuous random variables, let us identify A with the state of a system denoted x and identify B with a measurement denoted z. Then, the typical probability densities we will encounter are as follows:

- $p(x)$ means the probability of the system being in state x.
- $p(z)$ means the probability that a particular measurement is observed.
- $p(x|z)$ means the probability of the system being in the state x *given that* the measurement z is observed.
- $p(z|x)$ means the probability of a measurement being observed *given that* the state is x.
- $p(x, z)$ means the probability of the system being in a state *and* measurement z is observed.

The density $p(x|z)$ is used to estimate the state of the system by tracking the probability of every possible state in a very explicit manner. It is common to use the prior probability $p(x)$ to represent our present state of knowledge and the density $p(z)$ to represent new evidence or information of some kind. Also, we can view $p(x|z)$ as representing diagnostic knowledge whereas $p(z|x)$ often has a causal connotation – and it is often easier to obtain. For example, the connection between causal probability models and forward sensing models is a close one.

5.4.1.4 Total Probability and Marginalization

If we have a set of mutually exclusive events $B_1 \ldots B_n$, then the probability of event A given that one (unknown one) of them occurs is computed by:

$$P(A|B_1 \ldots B_n) = P(A|B_1)P(B_1) + P(A|B_2)P(B_2) + \ldots + P(A|B_n)P(B_n)$$

This is a version of the *total probability theorem*. In the continuous case, we have:

$$p(x|a < z < b) = \int_a^b p(x|z)p(z)dy$$

We can imagine that this process is "integrating out" the z dimension of the distribution, projecting all of the associated volume onto the plane containing the x axis. This is called *marginalization*. This resulting distribution, reduced in dimension relative to the original, is called the *marginal* distribution. Any distribution that ignores a parameter on which the true probability depends is a marginal version of a higher dimensional one.

5.4.2 Bayes' Rule

Consider again the Venn diagram in Figure 5.42. Suppose that we know that B has occurred. This statement means that a randomly selected point has fallen somewhere in the circle labelled B. Suppose we want to know the probability that A has also occurred. Clearly, **given that** B has occurred, A can only occur **now** when $A \wedge B$ occurs. Hence, the probability that A occurs given that B has occurred is the ratio of two rightmost areas in the figure:

$$P(A|B) = \frac{P(A \wedge B)}{P(B)} \tag{5.137}$$

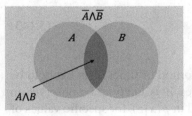

Figure 5.42 Venn Diagram for Visualizing Bayes' Rule. If a random point falls inside circle B, what is the probability it is also in A?

This is known as *Bayes' Rule*, and we will be using it extensively from now on in this section. Arguing symmetrically when the point falls somewhere in A, we also have

$$P(B|A) = \frac{P(A \wedge B)}{P(A)} \tag{5.138}$$

From that, we can conclude by eliminating the common expression $P(A \wedge B)$:

$$P(A) \times P(B|A) = P(B) \times P(A|B) \tag{5.139}$$

We often rewrite this to get another common form of Bayes' Rule:

$$P(A|B) = \frac{P(B|A)}{P(B)} \times P(A) \tag{5.140}$$

Spotlight 5.7 Bayes' Rule.

Bayes' Rule involves an inversion of the roles of A and B in the conditional probabilities. We call $P(A)$ the *a priori* or prior probability of event A – it is the probability of A based on no knowledge of B. The quantity $P(A|B)$ is called the *a posteriori* or posterior probability. It is the probability of A after the information B has been acquired.

We will use our estimator notation hereafter. It takes the form:

$$p(x|z) = \frac{p(z|x)}{p(z)} \times p(x)$$

$$P(X|Z) = \frac{P(Z|X)}{P(Z)} \times P(X) \tag{5.141}$$

5.4.2.1 Normalization

It is often convenient to use the total probability theorem to compute the marginal distribution $p(z)$ that appears in the denominator from the other two distributions on the right-hand side of Bayes' Rule:

$$p(z) = \int_{-\infty}^{\infty} p(z|x)p(x)dx = \int_{-\infty}^{\infty} p(z, x)dx$$

$$P(Z) = \sum_{\text{all } x} P(Z|X)P(X) = \sum_{\text{all } x} P(X \wedge Z) \tag{5.142}$$

Then, Bayes' Rule relates the conditional to the joint and prior probability:

$$p(x|z) = \frac{p(z, x)}{p(z)}$$

$$P(X|Z) = \frac{P(X \wedge Z)}{P(Z)} \tag{5.143}$$

This last form of Bayes' Rule is computing the proportion of times Z is likely to be observed in state X relative to the proportion of times Z is likely to be observed in any state. Note that, even though we may be interested in $p(x|z)$ for specific values of x and z, the computation of the denominator in Equation 5.142 requires that $p(x)$ be known for all values of x.

For example, consider barrels of jelly beans. The joint probability $P(X \wedge Z)$ represents the probability that both Z will be observed **and** the state is X (not that Z will be observed *given* the state is X). The probability of getting a green jelly bean "that came from the first barrel" is different from the probability of getting a green one, "given that it came from" the first barrel. The first case allows the barrel to be selected randomly and computes the probability that it will be the first one.

Note that many documents define the normalizing function:

$$\eta(z) = \frac{1}{p(z)} \quad \text{or} \quad \eta(Z) = \frac{1}{P(Z)}$$

5.4.2.2 Example: Museum Tour Guide

Thomas is a museum tour guide robot named in honor of the originator of the powerful estimation theory it uses in its operations. Thomas must cope with high levels of background noise, ambiguous human behavior, noisy imprecise perception sensing, and a motion control and estimation system that is of unusually low quality. However, despite these challenges, Thomas is well prepared (can invert a conditional probability distribution) and it has a keen mind (powerful processor).

The first problem facing our robot is to estimate whether anyone has entered the room to determine if it should initiate a greeting behavior. For brevity, let us use the values of the variables to tell us which variables we mean. Thus:

$$P(X = \text{visitor}) \leftrightarrow P(vis)$$
$$P(X = \neg visior) \leftrightarrow P(\neg vis)$$
$$P(Z = \text{motion}) \leftrightarrow P(mot)$$
$$P(Z = \neg\ motion) \leftrightarrow P(\neg\ mot)$$

5.4.2.2.1 Prior on X. The room is empty 90% of the time this early in the morning:

$$P(\neg vis) = 0.9$$

So the prior probability of the room being occupied is:

$$P(vis) = 0.1$$

Thus our prior can be summarized in Table 5.3.

Table 5.3 Prior on X

X	$P(X)$
vis	0.1
$\neg vis$	0.9

5.4.2.2.2 Sensor Model. The robot has a sonar sensor array and it is configured during downtime as a motion detector. It uses scan differencing to sense motion. There is a large fan nearby generating noise in the ultrasound range that corrupts the sonar measurements. Therefore, the probability that the sonars will register motion at the right time is high but not unity:

$$P(mot|vis) = 0.7$$

Clearly, the probability of not registering motion under these conditions must therefore be:

$$P(\neg\, mot | vis) \;=\; 0.3$$

This nontrivial probability of false negatives is also, in part, due to the paintings on the wall at which many visitors stare while standing still. In a shopping mall, with the same fan noise, $P(\neg\, mot | vis)$ would be lower (and $P(mot | vis)$ would be correspondingly higher). This analysis points out how many factors influence the probabilities and some ways in which they are related to each other.

We will also need to know the probability of detecting motion when the room is not occupied (caused by falsely registering the fan noise as a visitor):

$$P(\, mot | \neg vis) \;=\; 0.6$$

That is not much lower than the case of a real visitor because it is a pretty noisy fan. Thus our sensor model can be summarized in Table 5.4.

Table 5.4 Sensor Model $P(Z|X)$

		Z	
		mot	$\neg mot$
X	*vis*	0.7	0.3
	$\neg vis$	0.6	0.4

5.4.2.2.3 Process First Measurement. Now suppose the sensor generates a first motion reading Z_1. The goal is to compute the posterior $P(X|Z_1)$ which provides the probability of the room being in any state given the sensor reading. Let's use the rule in this form:

$$P(X|Z_1) \;=\; \frac{P(Z_1|X)}{P(Z_1)} \times P(X)$$

Normally, we would not compute the result for both values of Z_1 because a particular Z_1 will have been measured. However, for later use, both are provided in Table 5.5 which simply multiplies each row of the sensor model by the scalar in the corresponding row of the prior.

Table 5.5 First Unnormalized PMF $[P(Z_1|X) \times P(X)]$

		Z_1	
		mot	$\neg mot$
X	*vis*	(0.7)(0.1)	(0.3)(0.1)
	$\neg vis$	(0.6)(0.9)	(0.4)(0.9)

Next, we compute the normalizer for Z_1 using this pmf table by summing the appropriate column:

$$P(Z_1) \;=\; \sum_{\text{all } x} P(Z_1|X)P(X)$$

Normally, we would not compute the result for both values of Z_1 but for later use, both are provided in the Table 5.6:

Table 5.6 Normalizer $P(Z_1)$

Z_1	$P(Z_1)$
mot	0.61
$\neg mot$	0.39

The second value could have been derived from the first because $P(\neg mot) = 1 - P(mot)$ but this complement rule is only useful for binary variables. The posterior is again computed by dividing each column of the unnormalized pmf table by its associated normalizer:

$$P(X|Z_1) = \frac{[P(Z_1|X) \times P(X)]}{P(Z_1)}$$

The result, again for both values of Z_1, is in Table 5.7:

Table 5.7 First Posterior $P(X|Z_1)$

		Z_1	
		mot	$\neg mot$
X	vis	0.11	0.08
	$\neg vis$	0.89	0.92

The second row could be derived from the first, but only in the case of a binary state variable. The table tells us that if the sensor reads motion, the probability of a visitor is bumped from 0.1 to 0.11 whereas if it reads no motion, the probability is dropped from 0.1 to 0.08. Presumably, a succession of positive or negative readings would eventually drive the probability to 1 or 0, respectively, if the first result was used as the prior for a second sensor reading. This case is discussed next.

5.4.3 Bayes' Filters

A continuous stream of measurements can be processed in an iterative fashion with a Bayes', Filter [17]. Suppose now that we conduct an experiment where a lot of measurements are taken. This section addresses this case in stages.

5.4.3.1 Two Sequential Measurements

Suppose that two measurements are taken sequentially. Using subscripts to denote time, we can write of the first measurement:

$$P(X|Z_1) = \frac{P(Z_1|X)}{P(Z_1)} \times P(X) \tag{5.144}$$

When a second measurement Z_2 is available, we can use Bayes' Rule again with $P(X|Z_1)$ serving as the prior probability:

$$P(X|Z_1, Z_2) = \frac{P(Z_2|X, Z_1)}{P(Z_2|Z_1)} P(X|Z_1) \tag{5.145}$$

Following standard notation in robotics, we are using the notation A, B instead of $A \wedge B$. In practice, it is expedient to use the *Markov assumption* that Z_2 is independent of Z_1 **when X is known**. This means that:

$$P(Z_2|X, Z_1) = P(Z_2|X)$$

So the rule becomes:

$$P(X|Z_1, Z_2) = \frac{P(Z_2|X)}{P(Z_2|Z_1)} P(X|Z_1) \tag{5.146}$$

We **cannot** conclude that the measurements are independent of each other when the state is not known with:

$$P(Z_2|Z_1) = P(Z_1)P(Z_2) \quad \text{No!}$$

In fact, the true relationship $P(Z_2|Z_1)$ has already been specified by specifying the sensor model $P(Z|X)$ and the most recent estimate $P(X|Z_1)$:

$$P(Z_2|Z_1) = \sum_{\text{all } x} P(Z_2|X, Z_1)P(X|Z_1) = \sum_{\text{all } x} P(Z_2|X)P(X|Z_1)$$

5.4.3.2 Two Consecutive Measurements

Suppose that two independent measurements are taken at the same time and the data is to be processed in one "batch." In this case, both measurements switch sides of the conditioning bar in Bayes' Rule at the same time:

$$P(X|Z_1, Z_2) = \frac{P(Z_1, Z_2|X)}{P(Z_1, Z_2)} P(X) \tag{5.147}$$

Now if events Z_1 and Z_2 are independent we can write:

$$P(Z_1, Z_2|X) = P(Z_1|X)P(Z_2|X)$$
$$P(Z_1, Z_2) = P(Z_1)P(Z_2) \tag{5.148}$$

So that the batch form of the update rule takes the form:

$$P(X|Z_1, Z_2) = \left[\frac{P(Z_1|X)}{P(Z_1)}\right]\left[\frac{P(Z_2|X)}{P(Z_2)}\right]P(X)$$

Now we can apply the original form of Bayes' Rule (Equation 5.141) to invert both conditional probabilities on the right to get:

$$P(X|Z_1, Z_2) = \left[\frac{P(X|Z_1)}{P(X)}\right]\left[\frac{P(X|Z_2)}{P(X)}\right]P(X) \tag{5.149}$$

5.4.3.3 Example: Museum Tour Guide (Second Measurement)

The second measurement can be processed using this more general rule. The goal now is to compute the posterior $P(X|Z_1, Z_2)$, providing the probability of being in any state given the sequence of **both** sensor readings. Lets use this form:

$$P(X|Z_1, Z_2) = \frac{P(Z_2|X)}{P(Z_2|Z_1)} P(X|Z_1)$$

Now, the conditional probability $P(Z_2|X)$ is just the same sensor model if Z_2 is from the same sensor. Normally, we would not compute the result for all possible values of the sequence Z_1, Z_2 but Table 5.8 computes both, at least for the case where Z_2 is the second motion reading or the second nonmotion reading in a row. Table 5.8 simply multiplies each row of the sensor model by the scalar in the corresponding row of the joint probability $P(X, Z_1)$ computed from the first reading.

Table 5.8 Second Unnormalized PMF $[P(Z_2|X) \times P(X|Z_1)]$

		Z_1, Z_2	
		mot^2	$\neg mot^2$
X	vis	0.08	0.02
	$\neg vis$	0.53	0.37

Next, we compute the normalizer for $Z_2|Z_1$ using this joint distribution table by summing the appropriate column:

$$P(Z_2|Z_1) = \sum_{\text{all } x} P(Z_2|X) P(X|Z_1)$$

Normally, we would not compute the result for all possible values of the sequence Z_1, Z_2 but Table 5.9 computes both the case where Z_2 is the second motion reading or the second nonmotion reading in a row (Table 5.9). The table is unchanged from last time to two significant figures.

Table 5.9 Normalizer $P(Z_2|Z_1)$

Z_1, Z_2	$P(Z_2|Z_1)$
mot^2	0.61
$\neg mot^2$	0.39

The posterior is again:

$$P(X|Z_1, Z_2) = \frac{[P(Z_2|X) \times P(X|Z_1)]}{P(Z_2|Z_1)}$$

This is computed by dividing each column of the unnormalized table by its associated normalizer. The result, again for both values of Z_2, is in Table 5.10.

Table 5.10 Second Posterior $P(X|Z_1, Z_2)$

		Z_1, Z_2	
		mot^2	$\neg mot^2$
X	vis	0.13	0.06
	$\neg vis$	0.87	0.94

The table means that if the sensor reads motion twice, the probability of a visitor in the room is raised from 0.1 to 0.13 whereas if it reads no motion twice, the probability is dropped from 0.1 to 0.06.

If this process is repeated the numbers continue to change as shown in Figure 5.43. At any point in time, the estimate of the state of the room can be obtained from the maximum likelihood estimate – the state of highest probability – the higher of $P(vis|Z_{1,n})$ and $P(\neg vis|Z_{1,n})$. Given the prior probabilities we started with, it takes about 15 straight indications of motion before the room would be determined to have a visitor under this rule. This is because the sensor model says that the sensor is barely able to extract the signal from the noise and the prior model says it's highly unlikely that there is a visitor in the first place. Successive measurements of motion and no motion would drive the probabilities up and down accordingly.

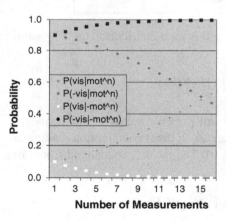

Figure 5.43 Bayesian Visitor Detection. The graph shows the behavior of the Bayesian visitor detection algorithm with respect to initial assumptions about room occupancy. Two cases are shown – where the motion detector repeatedly indicates motion and repeatedly does not indicate motion. Its takes 16 consecutive measurements of detected motion to overturn the prior estimate that the room is empty.

5.4.3.4 Multiple Sequential Measurements

The previous result is straightforward to generalize. If we denote all of the evidence obtained so far as:

$$Z_{1...n} = Z_1, Z_2, ..., Z_n$$

Then Equation 5.145 can be written in general in the recursive form:

$$P(X|Z_{1...n}) = \frac{P(Z_n|X, Z_{1...(n-1)})}{P(Z_n|Z_{1...(n-1)})} P(X|Z_{1...(n-1)})$$

And if we invoke the Markov assumption, we have:

$$P(X|Z_{1...n}) = \left[\frac{P(Z_n|X)}{P(Z_n|Z_{1...(n-1)})}\right]P(X|Z_{1...(n-1)}) \qquad (5.150)$$

Where the denominator is:

$$P(Z_n|Z_{1...(n-1)}) = \sum_{\text{all } x} P(Z_n|X, Z_{1...(n-1)})P(X|Z_{1...(n-1)})$$

Using the Markov assumption again, this is:

$$P(Z_n|Z_{1...(n-1)}) = \sum_{\text{all } x} P(Z_n|X)P(X|Z_{1...(n-1)}) \qquad (5.151)$$

Box 5.6 Recursive Bayesian Update

Here are the formulae necessary for updating a conditional probability density recursively based on a stream of measurements. The new measurement is incorporated with:

$$P(X|Z_{1...n}) = \left[\frac{P(Z_n|X)}{P(Z_n|Z_{1...(n-1)})}\right]P(X|Z_{1...(n-1)})$$

Where the normalizer is:

$$P(Z_n|Z_{1...(n-1)}) = \sum_{\text{all } x} P(Z_n|X)P(X|Z_{1...(n-1)})$$

The recursion can be unwound by substituting each earlier estimate into the next to give this result:

$$P(X|Z_{1...n}) = \left\{\prod_{k=1}^{n}\left[\frac{P(Z_k|X)}{\sum_{\text{all } x} P(Z_n|X)P(X|Z_{1...(n-1)})}\right]\right\}P(X) \qquad (5.152)$$

The big pi symbol $\prod$ means a product just like the big sigma $\sum$ means a sum. However, in practice we use these equations recursively as discussed next.

5.4.3.5 Multiple Simultaneous Measurements

It is easy to generalize the earlier result for two simultaneous measurements. If there are n measurements available at once, all switch sides of the conditioning bar in Bayes' Rule at the same time:

$$P(X|Z_{1...n}) = \frac{P(Z_{1...n}|X)}{P(Z_{1...n})}P(X)$$

Now if all of the events Z_1 through Z_n are independent we can write:

$$P(Z_{1\ldots n}|X) = P(Z_1|X)P(Z_2|X)\ldots P(Z_n|X)$$

$$P(Z_{1\ldots n}) = P(Z_1)P(Z_2)\ldots P(Z_n)$$

So that the batch form of the update rule takes the form:

$$P(X|Z_{1\ldots n}) = \left[\frac{P(Z_1|X)}{P(Z_1)}\right]\left[\frac{P(Z_2|X)}{P(Z_2)}\right]\ldots\left[\frac{P(Z_n|X)}{P(Z_n)}\right]P(X)$$

Once again, we can apply the original form of Bayes' Rule (Equation 5.141) to invert all conditional probabilities on the right to get:

$$P(X|Z_{1\ldots n}) = \left[\frac{P(X|Z_1)}{P(X)}\right]\left[\frac{P(X|Z_2)}{P(X)}\right]\ldots\left[\frac{P(X|Z_n)}{P(X)}\right]P(X) \qquad (5.153)$$

Spotlight 5.8 Batch Bayesian Update.

This is the formula necessary for updating a conditional probability density based on a batch of simultaneous independent measurements.

5.4.3.6 Standard Form of Bayes' Filter

It is traditional to define the "belief function":

$$Bel(X_n) = P(X|Z_{1\ldots n})$$

and the normalizer:

$$\eta(Z_{1\ldots n}) = \{P(Z_n|Z_{1\ldots(n-1)})\}^{-1}$$

In practice only the actual measurement sequence is processed and η is a scalar rather than a function of every possible sequence $Z_{1,n}$. Reviewing the last examples will show that there were three loops over the state involved. If the dependencies are analyzed, it's clear that the first two can be combined. Under these definitions, the Bayesian estimation algorithm is given in Algorithm 5.2.

```
01    algorithm BayesFilter(Bel(X),Z)
02    η⁻¹ ← 0
03    for all x
04        Bel'(X) ← P(Zₙ|X) · Bel(X)
05        η⁻¹ ← η⁻¹ + Bel'(X) //accumulate normalizer
06    endfor
07    for all x do Bel'(X) ← η⁻¹ · Bel'(X) // normalize
08    return Bel'(x)
```

Algorithm 5.2 Bayes' Filter. The Bayesian Filter continues to incorporate evidence into the belief function. At any time the belief function can be used to compute the best estimate of associated state.

5.4.4 Bayesian Mapping

If our museum robot decides to move around, maybe to greet the visitor, it may need to keep track of the objects (people, display cases) around it. Bayesian filtering can be used to build a map of the environment that includes the transient objects as well as the persistent ones. Sometimes a robot is equipped with a map of the environment before it moves. Other times it has to make the map, at least once by driving around for the first time. When the environment is dynamic, it may continue to map on a regular basis. For this section, we will assume that the robot is competent to determine its position and orientation and it will try to construct a map of the museum using its very noisy sonar range sensors.

5.4.4.1 Evidence Grids

Occupancy grids are a form of *evidence* (also called *certainty*) grid. They are a discretized representation of a robot's environment where each cell contains a probability of being occupied, say, by a wall, a fixture, or a moving object. In addition to tracking evidence over time, they maintain a field of probability over space. In essence, each cell in the grid is an individual Bayesian filter.

Evidence grids were originally proposed as a mechanism for dealing with the poor angular resolution of sonar range measurements. It is difficult to construct a high resolution world model for a robot by using a sonar sensor because of the wide beamwidth of such devices. For example, in the following figure, the bearing of the object cannot be determined from a single range reading (Figure 5.44).

In principle, however, if two range readings were available from two different vantage points, the intersection of the two circles of constant range centered at the sensor positions would pinpoint the object (Figure 5.45). However, real objects are not points, and it may be necessary to discover not only the location of an object, but its spatial extent as well.

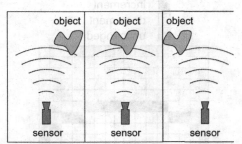

Figure 5.44 Sonar Angular Resolution. The object reflecting the sound energy permits a determination of its range. Its bearing cannot be resolved because all three cases shown generate the same range reading.

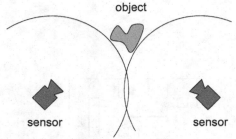

Figure 5.45 Range Triangulation. Two range readings from different vantage points can constrain the object position.

It turns out that the above idea can also be exploited to recover the object's extent. The basic idea is that each sensor reading supplies some degree of constraint on the position and extent of the object, and the union of all such constraints represents the most likely state of the object. In general, the environment is not composed only of objects but a probabilistic field such as an evidence grid can represent arbitrary information.

5.4.4.2 Banks of Bayesian Filters

We will confine our discussion to evidence grids that are used to encode the probability that a certain cell is occupied. By adopting such a probabilistic model, it is possible to recover remarkably detailed descriptions of the world from low resolution sensors such as sonars and radars.

In the implementation of an evidence grid mapping algorithm, two ingredients are necessary – a sensor model, and an update rule. Each time that a sensor reading is obtained, the sensor model is used to specify which cells within the field of view are to be updated, and it specifies the certainty value to be merged with the value currently in the map at that location. The update rule then specifies the algorithm to be used to perform the merging.

Four different solutions to mapping the museum hall in Figure 5.46 will be presented below in order of increasing sophistication. This space is 16 meters on a side. In all runs, a simulated sonar ring consisting of 32 sonars is used. This large number of sonars makes it more likely that a return will be received at all vehicle poses in a highly reflective environment. Vehicle motion between each set of 32 readings is limited to 0.25 meters.

5.4.4.2.1 Solution 1: Ideal Sensor with Accumulation Update Rule. If we had an ideal sonar sensor, it would return exactly the range to the first reflecting surface along each ray and it would be insensitive to the angular position of the objects and walls within the field of view. The readings from such a sensor contain two pieces of information: first, that there is an object somewhere at the measured range and second, that there is no object at any shorter range.

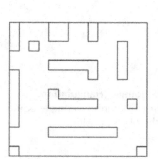

Figure 5.46 Museum Hallway. This 2D world where black lines represent solid walls viewed from above is the ground truth for the following experiments.

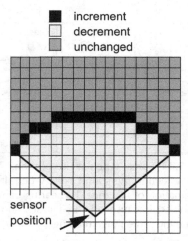

Figure 5.47 Intuitive Sensor Model. A range reading is evidence of an object or objects at the indicated range positioned somewhere along an arc as wide as the sensor beam.

In this first algorithm (Figure 5.47), we will process a wedge of area whose range and angular span matches that of the sensor reading. Each grid cell inside the wedge will be updated to incorporate the evidence encoded in the sonar reading. We will accumulate a number of "votes" in the cells in the grid that are also inside the wedge. When a cell is voted to be occupied, we will increase its value by one. Similarly, we will decrease its value by one when it is voted unoccupied. Such a sensor model is shown below as a grid encoding the votes for each cell.

As a practical matter, the number of votes in a cell is limited between 0 and 10. One sensor beamwidth is used as the angular span of the sonar wedge. The results of this approach are given below in (Figure 5.48). The quality of the map is far from perfect. Corner reflections cause the wall positions to be poorly localized and the low fidelity of the update rule causes some cells that were originally considered occupied to be subsequently considered unoccupied.

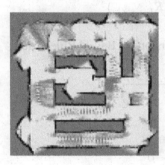

Figure 5.48 Results for Intuitive Model. Sharp corners are poorly defined but the overall map is recognizable.

5.4.4.2.2 Solution 2: Ideal Sensor with Bayesian Update Rule. In order to improve the update rule, we might consider extending the maximum number of votes toward infinity because this would eliminate the loss of information associated with limiting the number of votes to the finite range of 0 through 10. The same thing can be achieved by employing a floating point representation of occupancy. If we use a floating point number between 0 and 1, we can use it to represent a probability of occupancy. Let $P(occ)$ denote the probability that a cell is occupied. We can then use Bayes' Rule to merge sonar measurements. Let us also assume that the probabilities of any pair of cells are independent which is to say that:

$$P(occ[x_i, y_i] | occ[x_j, y_j]) = P(occ[x_i, y_i]) \qquad i \neq j$$

Under this assumption we can imagine a bank of Bayesian Filters, one in each cell in the map, each doing its own thing regardless of its neighbors. Let X denote the state of occupancy of the cell and Z denotes the sonar measurement generated at some unspecified robot position. Since X has only two possible values (occupied and not occupied), and one can be determined from the other, a single $P(occ)$ is enough information to remember in each cell. Further, let r_k denote the range measurement at time step k and $R_{1, k}$ denote all of the range measurements so far.

Recall Equation 5.151 and Equation 5.152:

$$P(X|Z_{1...n}) = \left[\frac{P(Z_n|X)}{P(Z_n|Z_{1...(n-1)})} \right] P(X|Z_{1...(n-1)})$$

$$P(Z_n|Z_{1...(n-1)}) = \sum_{\text{all } x} P(Z_n|X) P(X|Z_{1...(n-1)})$$

(5.154)

Rewriting this in our new notation:

$$P(occ|R_{1...k}) = \left[\frac{P(r_k|occ)}{P(r_k|R_{1...(k-1)})}\right]P(occ|R_{1...(k-1)})$$

$$P(r_k|R_{1...(k-1)}) = \sum_{\text{all } x} P(r_k|X)P(X|R_{1...(k-1)})$$

The normalizer is just the sum of two products for each update. Nonetheless, a nice trick can be used to eliminate the normalizer in the denominator. For the other value of the state we have:

$$P(\overline{occ}|R_{1...k}) = \left[\frac{P(r_k|\overline{occ})}{P(r_k|R_{1...(k-1)})}\right]P(\overline{occ}|R_{1...(k-1)})$$

Now, the denominators are the same, so we can divide both versions of Bayes' Rule to get:

$$\frac{P(occ|R_{1...k})}{P(\overline{occ}|R_{1...k})} = \left[\frac{P(r_k|occ)}{P(r_k|\overline{occ})}\right]\frac{P(occ|R_{1...(k-1)})}{P(\overline{occ}|R_{1...(k-1)})}$$

Recalling the definition of the odds ratio:

$$O(occ|R_{1...k}) = O(r_k|occ) \cdot O(occ|R_{1...(k-1)}) \tag{5.155}$$

This is an extremely efficient update rule where the new odds of occupancy is just the previous odds multiplied by the odds of the measurement conditioned on occupancy. Odds are infinite at certain truth, zero at certain falseness, and unity at 50% probability.

We will use this rule as follows. Initially the quantity stored in the cell is $O(occ)$, the prior odds of occupancy before any range readings are taken. This could be set to 1, meaning unknown, but a better estimate is available, namely, the odds corresponding to the average density of known cells in the world. This can be estimated as some multiple of the world perimeter divided by the world area – both expressed in cells. For our world, a value of 0.05 is used.

The sensor model $O(r_k|occ)$ remains to be determined. For an ideal sensor, we would expect that the probability of occupancy would be around 1 if the cell is within a cell width of range r_k, and zero otherwise. If the range to the cell exceeds the measured range, it is consistent to assume it is occluded by a closer cell, so its value is left unchanged. That is:

$$P(r_k|occ) = \begin{bmatrix} 0.5, \, range(cell) > r_k \\ 1.0, \, range(cell)=r_k \\ 0.0, \, range(cell) < r_k \end{bmatrix}$$

As a practical matter, cells outside the beamwidth are left unchanged. The probabilities above are also reduced from 1.0 to 0.9 and raised from 0.0 to 0.1 to avoid divisions by zero. The result of using such a model is given in Figure 5.49. The background color is closer to reality this time as a result of correct initialization of the map. Corner reflections continue to cause problems.

Figure 5.49 Results for Bayesian Estimator, Ideal Sensor Model. Bayes rule seems to do a somewhat better job but corners are still not resolved well.

Figure 5.50 Results for Bayesian Estimator, Gaussian Sensor Model. Encoding the knowledge that detected objects are less likely to be positioned far from the beam center leads to a more accurate map.

5.4.4.2.3 Solution 3: Gaussian Sensor with Bayesian Update Rule.

In order to improve the performance for corner reflectors, we must encode the idea that cells in the center of the beam are far mode likely to reflect enough energy to cause their range to be read, as more beam energy is concentrated in the beam center. In this solution, we allow $P(r_k|occ)$ to decay smoothly as the cell position strays from the measured range and from the beam center axis. Let r_k be the measured range. Let ρ be the range to a cell, and let θ be the bearing of the cell relative to the beam center. Let σ_r and σ_θ be the appropriate scaling factors for decay of the probability of occupancy as any cell moves away from the measured range and the beam center.

Under all these specifications, a polar coordinate sensor model can be given by:

$$P(r_k|occ) = \begin{bmatrix} 0.5, \rho > r_k \\ 0.99\,exp\left[-\frac{1}{2}\left(\frac{\theta}{\sigma_r}\right)^2\right], (\rho - r_k) < \sigma_r \\ 0.05, otherwise \end{bmatrix}$$

We use 0.5 beyond the measured range to ensure that the value there is left unchanged. The wedge interior is set to the a priori probability of occupancy.

The results of such a model are given in Figure 5.50.

5.4.4.2.4 Solution 4: Gaussian Sensor Map with Bayesian Update Rule.

The evidence grid formalism can also be used to merge together two maps resulting from two different sensors, or to sequentially merge sonar readings that have been converted to map form. We will now investigate the second of these two. The primary difference between this approach and the approach of solutions 2 and 3 is that instead of dealing with the quantity $p(occ|r_k)$, we deal with its relative $p(r_k|occ)$. The major advantage of this approach is that it does not assume that the values of each cell are independent of each other (and they certainly are not in reality).

Recall that the batch form of the Bayesian update rule for two independent measurements (Equation 5.149) takes the form:

$$P(X|Z_1, Z_2) = \left[\frac{P(X|Z_1)}{P(X)}\right]\left[\frac{P(X|Z_2)}{P(X)}\right]P(X)$$

If we identify X with the new estimate of occupancy, Z_1 with the latest estimate of the evolving map, and Z_2 with the map resulting from the latest sensor reading, we have:

$$P(occ|R_{1\ldots k}) = P(occ|R_{1\ldots(k-1)}) \times P(occ|r_k)/P(occ)$$

This is similar to the sequential rule, with two important differences.

First, we use the quantity $P(occ|r_k)$ not $P(r_k|occ)$. This is an evidence grid of the same semantic form as the grid that models the world. To use this, we must position the sensor map over the grid and use its values to update the cells in the map that it overlaps. It's important to make sure that each cell in the grid is touched only once in this process. The prior map $p(occ|R_{k-1})$ has the same form as before.

Second, the term $p(occ)$ arises as a normalizer. This is the prior probability of a cell being occupied, which can be approximated by the average occupied cell density. Notice that when the incoming map cell $P(occ|r_k)$ has this value, the grid remains unchanged, so this is the value that contains no information. The grid is initially set to this value, which we take to be 0.05.

The sensor map $p(occ|r_k)$ could be developed based on driving around the hall and learning the average map that corresponds to each possible range reading. We will construct it from first principles based on intuitive arguments. First define the functions:

$$p_1 = \begin{bmatrix} 0.05\,exp\left[-\frac{1}{2}\left(\frac{\rho - r_k}{\sigma_r}\right)\right] - 0.05(\rho < r_k) \\ 0.0, \rho > r_k \end{bmatrix} \qquad p_2 = 0.95\,exp\left[-\frac{1}{2}\left(\frac{\rho - r_k}{\sigma_r}\right)^2\right]$$

Using the normalized variable $(\rho - r_k)/\sigma_r$, the sum of these functions is shown in Figure 5.51. Next, we account for the fact that longer range readings are more prone to be multiple reflections with the following:

$$\sigma_r = 2 \times \left(\frac{r_k}{R_{max}}\right)^2$$

where R_{max} is the sensor maximum range.

Next, we allow the height of the peak and the depth of the trough to decay with range to account for the fact that information is less certain at higher range as follows:

$$p_3 = exp\left[-6\frac{r_k}{R_{max}}\right]$$

Finally, we allow the whole distribution to decay with angular offset from the beam center as follows:

$$p_4 = exp\left[-\frac{\theta}{\theta_{3dB}}\right]$$

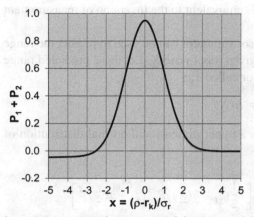

Figure 5.51 Inverted Sensor Model. This model is of the semantic form $P(occ|r_k)$ – the map that corresponds to a sensor reading. The value 0.5 is added later to ensure that it is not negative.

Figure 5.52 Results for Bayesian Estimator, Dependent Sensor Model. This model is produced based on merging a map that depends on the range readings $P(occ|r_k)$ with the underlying world model.

where θ_{3dB} is the nominal beamwidth of the sensor. The resulting unnormalized distribution is given by:

$$p(occ|r_k) = (p_1 + p_2) \times p_3 \times p_4 + 0.05$$

It can be normalized by sampling everywhere within its bounds and dividing by the volume under the probability surface. Such a model achieves the result in Figure 5.52.

5.4.5 Bayesian Localization

The dual problem to mapping is localization. On the assumption that a map is available, our museum robot can use Bayesian estimation to locate itself. This problem has the same flavor as Kalman filtering in the sense that there are two parts to the problem – using the map to generate a pose fix, and accounting for motion in between fixes. This section will present basic Bayesian approaches to these two problems.

The goal of Bayesian localization is to produce and maintain a discrete belief field $P(\underline{X}, R_{1,k-1})$ that encodes the probability that the robot is in each potential pose $\underline{X}$ in the environment. The belief field is updated whenever new measurements r_k from the sonars arrive and when new commands $\underline{U}_k$ are executed by to the robot.

5.4.5.1 Map-Based Localization

The power of Bayesian estimation becomes clear when it is used to localize a robot in a map. Let the robot be equipped with a ring of $m = 16$ sonars that measure ranges in all directions more or less at once. Let the vector of range readings be represented as an $m \times 1$ vector called $\underline{z}_k$. Then, the belief field is denoted $P(\underline{X}, \underline{Z}_{1,k})$.

Although it is difficult to imagine how to compute the belief field, Bayes' Rule allows us to solve the problem in terms of a much simpler problem. We need only generate the sensor model $P(\underline{z}_k, \underline{X})$ and the mechanism of Bayesian estimation will do the rest for us. This inversion process is equivalent to the inversion of measurement models in Kalman filters.

Given a map of the environment, a sensor simulator can be used to predict the range readings that would be generated from a given robot pose $\underline{X}$. Let these predicted range readings be represented as an $m \times 1$ vector called $\hat{\underline{z}}_k$:

$$\hat{\underline{z}}_k = \underline{h}(\underline{X})$$

Then a reasonable model of the sensor is a hyper dimensional normal distribution of the form:

$$p(\underline{z}_k|\underline{X}) = \frac{1}{(2\pi)^{m/2}|R|^{1/2}} \exp\left[-\frac{1}{2}(\underline{z}_k - \underline{h}(\underline{X}))R^{-1}(\underline{z}_k - \underline{h}(\underline{X}))^T\right]$$

Spotlight 5.9 Sensor Model for Map Based Localization.

This distribution estimates the probability of obtaining a certain sensor reading based on the weighted squared residual with respect to the predicted image.

where R captures the expected covariance of the range readings. Note that although we have assumed Gaussian errors for the sensor for simplicity, this distribution could be anything in general. Furthermore, even under such a sensor model, the computed belief field will have peaks at all places where the robot is likely to be based on the evidence so far, and lower values elsewhere.

5.4.5.2 Motion Modelling

In contrast to pose fix measurements, which decrease uncertainty, actions undertaken by robots often increase uncertainty. Indeed, when the robot moves between sonar measurements, the belief field should degrade in the sense that small regions of high confidence will become larger regions of somewhat lower confidence. Nonetheless, it is computationally expensive to update the robot pose based on sonar measurements so significant motion between pose fixes may be necessary.

We can model the effects of motion (more generally, or actions) in the Bayesian framework by treating them as another kind of evidence. In practice, a robot typically has sensors to measure wheel rotations, speed, or angular velocity, and so on, which can measure the results of executing motions, but these sensors are also imperfect. We will work in terms of general inputs $\underline{U}_k$ with the understanding that these may represent either computed inputs or measured responses.

Recall from the last section, the sensor model of the form $P(\underline{Z}_{1,k}|\underline{X})$ provides the pmf of sensor readings conditioned on the state. To model actions, we would like to determine a new state conditioned on both the input executed and the last state. Thus, the conditional probability:

$$P(\underline{X}_k|\underline{X}_{k-1}, \underline{U}_{k-1})$$

might provide the pmf we are seeking. It means the probability of ending up in state $\underline{X}_k$ given that the input $\underline{U}_{k-1}$ was executed and the previous state was $\underline{X}_{k-1}$.

Such models can capture the behavior of dynamical systems in a probabilistic framework – capturing the idea that no intended actions are executed perfectly. The net effect of executing an input can be obtained by marginalization over the previous state. This takes the form of the convolution integral or sum:

$$p(\underline{x}_k|\underline{u}_{1...k}) = \int_{\text{all } \underline{x}_{k-1}} p(\underline{x}_k|\underline{x}_{k-1}, \underline{u}_{1...(k-1)})p(\underline{x}_{k-1})d\underline{x}_{k-1}$$

$$P(\underline{X}_k|\underline{U}_{1...k}) = \sum_{\text{all } \underline{X}_{k-1}} P(\underline{X}_k|\underline{X}_{k-1}, \underline{U}_{1...(k-1)})P(\underline{X}_{k-1})$$

This sum is evaluated over all the places from which the last motion could have started – weighted by their probabilities. Here, the Markov assumption takes the reasonable form of assuming that the probability of a transition depends solely on the last action, rather than the entire sequence of actions, so the motion models become:

$$p(\underline{x}_k|\underline{u}_{1...k}) = \int_{\text{all } \underline{x}_{k-1}} p(\underline{x}_k|\underline{x}_{k-1}, \underline{u}_{k-1})p(\underline{x}_{k-1})d\underline{x}_{k-1}$$

$$P(\underline{X}_k|\underline{U}_{1...k}) = \sum_{\text{all } \underline{X}_{k-1}} P(\underline{X}_k|\underline{X}_{k-1}, \underline{U}_{k-1})P(\underline{X}_{k-1})$$

Spotlight 5.10 Conditional Action Model.

The belief function over states is based on the transition probabilities $p(\underline{x}_k|\underline{x}_{k-1}, \underline{u}_{k-1})$ and the prior $p(\underline{x}_{k-1})$.

The intuition for this process is to imagine moving probability mass from each possible prior pose $\underline{X}_{k-1}$, to a new pose $\underline{X}_k$ weighted by the probability of being in that prior pose. In that case, there is an outer loop over all $\underline{X}_k$ and an inner loop over all possible $\underline{X}_{k-1}$. It is equally valid to view the process as one of moving the entire belief field by the commanded motion and then smoothing the result to incorporate motion uncertainty. In that case, there is an outer loop over all $\underline{X}_{k-1}$ and an inner loop over all possible $\underline{X}_k$. The domain of the marginalization can be limited in practice to some region beyond which the prior probability of robot occupancy is vanishingly small (Figure 5.53).

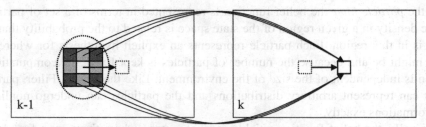

Figure 5.53 Bayesian Motion Models. The probability of ending up in a particular terminal state after an action is related to every place the robot could have started from, the probability that the robot was in that place, and the probability that the action would result in the particular terminal state.

5.4.5.3 Bayesian Filters with Actions

In the most general case, a system is presented with a stream of both sensor data $Z_{1,n}$ and action data $U_{1,n}$. Let D_n represent a piece of information of either kind. Then, the a more general Bayes' Filter is shown in Algorithm 5.3.

```
00   algorithm BayesFilterWithActions(Bel(X),D)
01     η⁻¹ ← 0
02     if D is a perceptual data item Z
03        for all X
04             Bel'(X) ← P(Zₙ|X) · Bel(X)
05             η⁻¹ ← η⁻¹ + Bel'(X)
06        endfor
07        for all X do Bel'(X) ← η⁻¹ · Bel'(X)
08     else if D is an action data item U
09        for all X do Bel'(X) ←  ∑  P(Xₙ|Xₙ₋₁, Uₙ)P(Xₙ₋₁)
10     endif                       all Xₙ₋₁
11     return Bel'(x)
```

Algorithm 5.3 Bayes Filter with Actions. When the inputs to the filter include actions, a separate update rule is used.

5.4.5.4 Other Forms of Bayesian Filter

Some of the advantages of the Bayesian filter relative to the Kalman filter are its capacity to process non-Gaussian distributions, to represent multiple hypotheses, and its nonreliance on initial conditions. A Bayesian filter can automatically discover where the robot is, based on no initial conditions, and this capacity can be important in some circumstances. On the other hand, a properly tuned Kalman filter can be much more accurate when its assumptions are valid, and it demands much less memory, and much less computation.

Each cell in the data structure used to represent the belief field represents a hypothesis for where the robot could be, and given some desired resolution of such hypotheses, the computation associated with the Bayes' Filter grows rapidly with the scale of the environment representation. Intuitively, it seems that much of the computation in a Bayes' Filter is in some sense wasted on updating highly unlikely hypotheses whose associated belief function is very low. One way to save computation would be to simply not update these hypotheses. There are several practical variations on this idea.

In the *particle filter* the belief function is represented in terms of a set of particles whose density in a given region of the state space is related to the probability that the robot is in this region. Each particle represents an explicit hypothesis for where the robot might be and because the number of particles is kept fixed, the computational burden is independent of the size of the environment. Like the Bayes' Filter, particle filters can represent arbitrary distributions and the particles can undergo nonlinear transformations exactly.

Typically, the belief function quickly reaches a stage where there are a few dominant hypotheses whose probability is high and the robot must be in or near one of these places. In such a case, the belief function can be well approximated by a weighted sum of Gaussian distributions – one of each having a probability peak that corresponds to a dominant hypothesis. This is called a *mixture of Gaussians* representation. A special case is the case where there is only one such Gaussian and this case corresponds to the Kalman filter itself.

5.4.6 References and Further Reading

Maybeck is a classic reference on Bayesian methods. Thrun is probably the first comprehensive text on probabilistic methods applied to robotics covering many relevant techniques including unscented, particle, and Bayesian filters. Pearl is a source devoted to recursive Bayesian estimation. Jazwinsky is an early source for Bayesian filtering before robotics adopted it. The certainty grid example is based heavily on Moravec. The Bayesian localization example is inspired by Burgard.

[12] Reverend Thomas Bayes (1702–1761), Essay Toward Solving a Problem in the Doctrine of Chances, in *Landmark Writings in Western Mathematics 1640–1940,* I. Grattan-Guinness, ed., Elsevier, 2005.

[13] W. Burgard, D. Fox, D. Hennig, and T. Schmidt, Estimating the Absolute Position of a Mobile Robot Using Position Probability Grids, in Proceedings of the Fourteenth *National Conference on Artificial Intelligence* (AAAI-96), pp. 896–901, 1996.

[14] Hans Moravec, Sensor Fusion in Certainty Grids for Mobile Robots, *AI Magazine,* 1988.

[15] J. Pearl, *Probabilistic Reasoning in Intelligent Systems: Networks of Plausible Inference,* Morgan Kaufmann, San Mateo, CA, 1988.

[16] S. Thrun, W. Burgard, and D. Fox, *Probabilistic Robotics*, MIT Press, 2005.

[17] A. H. Jazwinsky, *Stochastic Processes and Filtering Theory,* Academic Press, New York, 1970.

[18] P. Maybeck, *Stochastic Models, Estimation, and Control*, Academic Press, 1982.

5.4.7 Exercises

5.4.7.1 Bayes' Theorem

Seattle gets measurable rain 150 days per year. When it does rain, it is predicted correctly 90% of the time. However, even when it does not rain, rain is still predicted 30% of the time. Rain is predicted for tomorrow. What is the probability that it will actually rain?

5.4.7.2 Independence and Correlation

Consider two real-valued random variables x and y of joint distribution $p(x, y)$. Their covariance is by definition:

$$cov(x, y) = Exp[(x - Exp[x])(y - Exp[y])]$$

The marginal distribution of x is given by:

$$p(x) = \int_{\text{All } y} p(x, y) dy$$

Show that:

$$cov(x, y) = Exp[xy] - Exp[x]Exp[y]$$

Based on this result, show that their covariance is zero (i.e., they are uncorrelated) if they are independent.

CHAPTER 6

State Estimation

Figure 6.1 The "Boss" Autonomous Car. Boss is one of the six robots that finished the entire 2007 DARPA Urban Challenge course. The challenge was a test of driving in city streets with other robots and cars. Boss and most of its competition used very high performance inertial and satellite navigation systems.

The most basic necessity of a mobile robot is the capacity to measure its own motion. For otherwise, how could it determine which way to go or whether it ever got there? In the plane, the *pose* of the robot is defined as the position and orientation coordinates (x, y, ψ) of some distinguished reference frame on the body. In some cases, velocities or higher derivatives or perhaps articulations are desired and this more general problem is referred to as *state estimation*. Determining the exact pose of the robot is not usually a practical goal. The best that can be done is to estimate pose so it is common to refer to the problem of localization as *pose estimation*. Much of the theory of estimation is directly applicable.

For any element of the robot pose, an important distinction relates to the question of whether available measurements project onto the pose itself or onto any of its time derivatives. In the former case, algebraic equations relate the pose to the measurements and the technique is classified as triangulation. In the latter case, differential equations relate the pose to the measurements and the technique is classified as dead reckoning. The errors that occur in these two fundamental techniques behave in very different ways.

6.1 Mathematics of Pose Estimation

Robots need pose estimation in order to control their gross motions through their environments. Pose estimation is also important in map making because the robot needs to know where it is in order to put objects in the right place in the map. The orientation

370

components of pose are also important because only a system that can decide which way to move can move toward a goal. Furthermore, a robot needs to know its attitude in order to predict the slope of terrain in view and assess the present degree of danger of tipping over.

This section presents some basic theory of error propagation, which is fundamental to our understanding of the challenges of pose estimation.

6.1.1 Pose Fixing Versus Dead Reckoning

All ways of estimating robot pose can be divided into two categories (Figure 6.2). In typical cases, the process of *fixing* position (or pose) is based on some combination of triangulation or trilateration, whereas the process of *dead reckoning* position (or pose) is based on the mathematical process of integration.

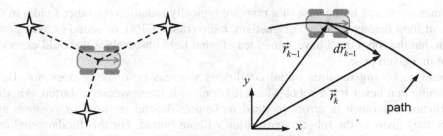

Figure 6.2 Pose Fixing versus Dead Reckoning. Although fixing position uses measurements that project directly onto the states of interest, dead reckoning uses measurements that project onto their time derivatives, providing only differential updates.

In pose fixing, the state is related to the measurements by algebraic/transcendental equations. In this case, a generally nonlinear system of equations is solved in order to navigate. In dead reckoning (DR), the state is related to the measurements by differential equations and they are integrated in order to navigate. In both cases, the observation relationships involved are kinematic (i.e., involving only linear and angular displacements and their derivatives, not mass or force, etc.).

The measurements used for pose estimation can be related to linear or angular position and orientation states or any of their derivatives. Thus, a gyro output can be integrated to get an angle and acceleration can be integrated to get velocity. A more unusual example is trilateration of velocity from Doppler range rates. Whether or not sufficient measurements exist is the question of *observability* discussed in Section 5.3.2.4 of Chapter 5.

6.1.1.1 Complementarity

In terms of the behavior of errors, dead reckoning and pose fixing are fundamental opposites in every way. This is, in fact, good news, because it means they can complement each other very well in a practical sense. Table 6.1 summarizes the differences between the two approaches to pose estimation.

The most significant differences are that pose fixing requires a capacity to predict a measurement given a pose – in other words, a map, whereas dead reckoning does not.

Table 6.1 Differences Between Techniques

Attribute	Dead Reckoning	Pose Fixing
Process	Integration	Nonlinear System Solvers
Initial Conditions	Required	Not required
Errors	(Often) Time Dependent	Position Dependent
Update Frequency	Determined by Required Accuracy	Determined only by the application
Error Propagation	Dependent on Previous Estimates	Independent of Previous Estimates
Requires a map.	No	Yes

The measurements in the case of a map are typically radiation (or other fields) in the form of light (cameras, lidar), magnetism, radio (radar, GPS), or sound or even gravitation, but the robot must have some idea of what field observables it should expect to sense in a given pose.

Dead reckoning requires initial conditions whereas pose fixing does not. Dead reckoning can never tell a robot where it is unless it knew where it started. Another significant difference is errors in dead reckoning depend on time or position and hence they grow as the robot moves, often without bound. For this fundamental reason, most practical systems use some form of pose fixing to aid the dead reckoning components of the pose estimation system.

6.1.2 Pose Fixing

Triangulation and trilateration techniques are perhaps as ancient as civilization itself. *Triangulation* generally refers to solving a triangle of some form using measurements of lengths or angles whereas *trilateration* is a similar technique where distances alone are measured. We will refer to them both as pose fixing. The general process is solution of simultaneous constraint equations in which navigation variables appear as unknowns. The robot position is a point where all constraints are satisfied. The measurements used are usually bearings or ranges to landmarks but there are many fields available to sense in order to fix position.

This section will analyze the performance of pose fixing systems. This analysis is performed in order to understand some fundamentals. It is typically not the case in practice that explicit constraint equations are solved. Rather, the optimal estimation techniques covered in Chapter 5 are used instead.

6.1.2.1 Revisiting Nonlinearly Constrained Systems

The general problem of solving nonlinear equations is one of finding roots of simultaneous constraint equations:

$$\underline{c}(\underline{x}) = \underline{0} \tag{6.1}$$

There are no useful existence or uniqueness theorems for such problems so there is no guarantee from a mathematics perspective that a solution exists or that it is unique.

There can be issues with the independence of the constraint equations and whether or not they over or underconstrain the solution. This section will mostly be concerned with the conditioning of the equations – that is, how the constraints modulate the error in the measurements to produce the error in the pose estimate. In most situations, significant benefits derive from the best possible pose solution so approximations are not typically considered acceptable.

The following sections will present some examples of pose fixing systems in the plane. These examples are chosen to illustrate concepts in cases that are easy to visualize, and whose solutions are geometrically intuitive. The situation in higher dimensions only becomes intuitive in the context of these simpler cases.

6.1.2.1.1 Explicit Case. Suppose we have the minimum number of measurements required to determine 2D pose – three. In rare situations, we can write an explicit formula to determine the state $\underline{x} = \begin{bmatrix} x & y & \psi \end{bmatrix}^T$ from the measurements $\underline{z} = \begin{bmatrix} z_1 & z_2 & z_3 \end{bmatrix}^T$:

$$x = f_1(z_1, z_2, z_3)$$
$$y = f_2(z_1, z_2, z_3)$$
$$\psi = f_3(z_1, z_2, z_3)$$

Which is of the form:

$$\underline{x} = f(\underline{z})$$

This system is trivial to solve. We simply evaluate the function $f(\ )$ at the measurement vector to ascertain the state.

6.1.2.1.2 Implicit Case. The implicit case is the inverse situation in which measurements can be predicted given the state:

$$z_1 = h_1(x, y, \psi)$$
$$z_2 = h_2(x, y, \psi)$$
$$z_3 = h_3(x, y, \psi)$$

In a Kalman filter, this is just the measurement equation:

$$\underline{z} = h(\underline{x})$$

We can solve this system, for example, with nonlinear least squares. Linearizing:

$$\Delta\underline{z} = H\Delta\underline{x}$$

Even when there are not three measurements, this system can be solved iteratively with the pseudoinverse:

$$\Delta\underline{x} = (H^T H)^{-1} H^T \Delta\underline{z} \quad \textit{overdetermined}$$
$$\Delta\underline{x} = H^T (HH^T)^{-1} \Delta\underline{z} \quad \textit{underdetermined}$$

We have seen how to use the measurement covariance R as a weight matrix, and of course a Kalman filter will solve these equations essentially automatically given the measurement Jacobian H.

6.1.2.2 Example 1: Bearing Observations With Known Yaw

Suppose that a vehicle can measure the bearings of landmarks with respect to itself and it has a sensor for measuring vehicle yaw ψ_v. The yaw measurement constrains orientation, and the bearings constrain position. By adding the observed bearings of the landmarks to the heading angle, the ground-referenced bearings ψ_1 and ψ_2 to the landmarks are determined (Figure 6.3).

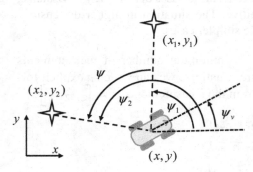

Figure 6.3 Bearing Observations with Known Yaw. The vehicle can measure the bearing to two landmarks and it has a way to measure its yaw angle.

The constraint equations for this configuration are:

$$\tan\psi_1 = \frac{\sin\psi_1}{\cos\psi_1} = \frac{y_1 - y}{x_1 - x} \qquad \tan\psi_2 = \frac{\sin\psi_2}{\cos\psi_2} = \frac{y_2 - y}{x_2 - x}$$

These two simultaneous equations in the unknowns (x, y) can be written as:

$$\begin{aligned} (x_1 - x)s_1 &= (y_1 - y)c_1 \\ (x_2 - x)s_2 &= (y_2 - y)c_2 \end{aligned} \Rightarrow \begin{bmatrix} -s_1 & c_1 \\ -s_2 & c_2 \end{bmatrix}\begin{bmatrix} x \\ y \end{bmatrix} = \begin{bmatrix} -s_1 x_1 + c_1 y_1 \\ -s_2 x_2 + c_2 y_2 \end{bmatrix} = \begin{bmatrix} b_1 \\ b_2 \end{bmatrix} \tag{6.2}$$

where again $s_1 = \sin(\psi_1)$, and so on. This system always has a solution except when the coefficient matrix on the left has a vanishing determinant. This case occurs when:

$$-s_1 c_2 + s_2 c_1 = 0 \Rightarrow \sin(\psi_2 - \psi_1) = 0 \Rightarrow \psi = n\pi \tag{6.3}$$

This is an example of constraint *degeneracy*. There is no solution in this case because the constraints are not independent. Physically, this situation occurs when the robot is positioned anywhere on the line that joins the landmarks, whether it is between them or not. Pragmatic design rules can be derived from this example. The landmarks should be placed to avoid having the robot operate along the line between them. If this cannot be avoided, a third landmark can be used to generate an extra constraint.

6.1.2.3 Example 2: Bearing Observations with Unknown Yaw

If there is no yaw sensor, a third landmark can be used to create a third constraint (Figure 6.4). In this case, we use true (vehicle relative) bearings and the constraint

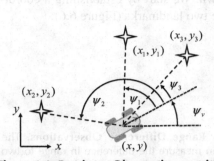

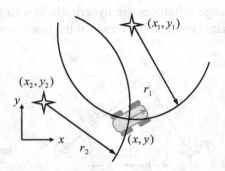

Figure 6.4 Bearing Observations with Unknown Yaw. The vehicle can measure bearings to three landmarks.

Figure 6.5 Range Observations. The vehicle can measure range to two landmarks. Yaw cannot be determined.

equations are:

$$\tan(\psi_v + \psi_1) = \frac{\sin(\psi_v + \psi_1)}{\cos(\psi_v + \psi_1)} = \frac{y_1 - y}{x_1 - x}$$

$$\tan(\psi_v + \psi_2) = \frac{\sin(\psi_v + \psi_2)}{\cos(\psi_v + \psi_2)} = \frac{y_2 - y}{x_2 - x} \tag{6.4}$$

$$\tan(\psi_v + \psi_3) = \frac{\sin(\psi_v + \psi_3)}{\cos(\psi_v + \psi_3)} = \frac{y_3 - y}{x_3 - x}$$

6.1.2.4 Example 3: Circular Constraints

When the measurements are ranges to landmarks, the constraint contours are circles centered at the landmarks. The yaw of the vehicle cannot be determined from ranges alone unless ranges to two points on the vehicle are being measured (Figure 6.5). The constraint equations for this case are:

$$r_1 = \sqrt{(x - x_1)^2 + (y - y_1)^2}$$

$$r_2 = \sqrt{(x - x_2)^2 + (y - y_2)^2} \tag{6.5}$$

These can be solved using a nonlinear equation solver like Levenberg-Marquardt. Doing so is much easier if the last known position is a good initial guess for the solution. When the landmarks are unique, the constraints are unique. However, there may no solution or two solutions to the two constraints. In the latter case, a rough estimate can perhaps be used to eliminate the incorrect solution. Intuitively, when the robot is near the line between the landmarks, the two solutions are close together and an initial guess may converge to the wrong answer.

6.1.2.5 Example 4: Hyperbolic Constraints

Marine radio navigation systems like LORAN and OMEGA are (or were) based on a system that allowed shipboard radio receivers to measure phase differences or time of flight in order to derive range differences to pairs of landmarks. Contours of constant range difference are hyperbolae as will be shown. We start by establishing a coordinate system at the center of the line between the two landmarks (Figure 6.6).

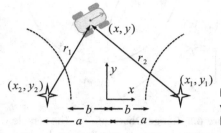

Figure 6.6 Range Difference Observations. The vehicle can measure the difference in range to two landmarks. Yaw cannot be determined.

A hyperbola is precisely the contour of constant range difference. From the figure, imagine placing the vehicle at the origin. Then, it is clear that this constant range difference is $2b$.

We can derive the equation of the hyperbola as follows:

$$r_1 - r_2 = 2b$$

$$\sqrt{(x+a)^2 + y^2} - \sqrt{(x-a)^2 + y^2} = 2b$$

$$\sqrt{(x+a)^2 + y^2} = 2b + \sqrt{(x-a)^2 + y^2} \tag{6.6}$$

$$b^2 - ax = -b\sqrt{(x-a)^2 + y^2}$$

$$\frac{x^2}{b^2} - \frac{y^2}{(a^2 - b^2)} = 1$$

The second last result was obtained by squaring both sides and simplifying. The last result was obtained by squaring again, cancelling the term $2ab^2x$, gathering terms in x and then dividing by $(a^2 - b^2)$.

6.1.3 Error Propagation in Triangulation

This section investigates the relationship between errors in the measurements used to generate a pose fix and the errors in the resultant solution.

6.1.3.1 First-Order Response to Systematic Errors

Determining the effect of systematic error involves the same mathematics used to solve the nonlinear problem by linearization. We can investigate the response to perturbations (the solution error caused by measurement error) with the Jacobian matrix:

$$\delta \underline{x} = \left(\frac{\partial \underline{x}}{\partial \underline{z}}\right) \delta \underline{z} = J \delta \underline{z} \tag{6.7}$$

In the fully determined explicit case of the form $\underline{x} = \underline{f}(\underline{z})$, the linearization is:

$$\begin{bmatrix} \delta x \\ \delta y \\ \delta \theta \end{bmatrix} = \begin{bmatrix} \partial f_1/\partial z_1 & \partial f_1/\partial z_2 & \partial f_1/\partial z_3 \\ \partial f_2/\partial z_1 & \partial f_2/\partial z_2 & \partial f_2/\partial z_3 \\ \partial f_3/\partial z_1 & \partial f_3/\partial z_2 & \partial f_3/\partial z_3 \end{bmatrix} \begin{bmatrix} \delta z_1 \\ \delta z_2 \\ \delta z_3 \end{bmatrix} \tag{6.8}$$

Typically, the Jacobian is a function of the vehicle position and, for this reason, it behaves differently in different positions.

Conversely, for the indirect case, we have:

$$\delta \underline{z} = \left(\frac{\partial \underline{z}}{\partial \underline{x}} \right) \delta \underline{x} = H \delta \underline{x} \tag{6.9}$$

Assuming that the measurements determine or overdetermine the state, the best fit error in the state is given by the left pseudoinverse:

$$\delta \underline{x} = \left(H^T H \right)^{-1} H^T \delta \underline{z} \tag{6.10}$$

6.1.3.2 Geometric Dilution of Precision

Based on Equation 5.80, the covariance of the above position is given by:

$$Exp[\delta \underline{x} \delta \underline{x}^T] = \left(H^T R^{-1} H \right)^{-1}$$

where $R = Exp[\delta \underline{z} \delta \underline{z}^T]$ is the covariance of the measurements. Therefore the matrix $\left(H^T H \right)^{-1}$ represents the covariance of the pose error when the measurement errors are of unit magnitude. It is desirable to have a single number which characterizes whether or not the observation geometry is favorable. This *geometric dilution of precision* (GDOP) – is, roughly speaking, the ratio of state error "magnitude" to measurement area "magnitude." There are two standard ways to "size" a covariance matrix – its trace and its determinant. With reference to Equation 6.10, the GDOP is defined in satellite navigation as [6]:

$$GDOP = \sqrt{trace[(H^T H)^{-1}]} = \sqrt{\sigma_{xx} + \sigma_{yy} + \sigma_{\theta\theta}} \tag{6.11}$$

However, we will use an even simpler approach. We will define a *dilution of precision* for square H based on the determinant:

$$DOP = \sqrt{det[(H^T H)^{-1}]} = \sqrt{det[H^{-1}]det[H^{-T}]}$$

Which simplifies to:

$$DOP = det[H^{-1}] = \frac{1}{det[H]} \tag{6.12}$$

6.1.3.2.1 Mapping Theory. Recall from multidimensional integral calculus that there is often a need to transform differential volumes from one set of coordinates to another (Figure 6.7). It is well known in the context of multidimensional mapping that the

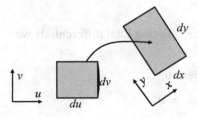

Figure 6.7 Mapping from R^m to R^n: The input area in (u, v) space maps onto the output area in (x, y) space.

ratio of differential areas (volumes) in the domain (input) and range (output) of such a mapping is given by the Jacobian determinant.

Now H is the measurement Jacobian, so when DOP is defined by Equation 6.12, we know immediately that it relates differential volumes in pose and measurement space:

$$DOP = \|\delta\underline{x}\| / \|\delta\underline{z}\| \tag{6.13}$$

For a 3D case, $\|\delta\underline{x}\| = \delta x_1 \delta x_2 \delta x_3$ and $\|\delta\underline{z}\| = \delta z_1 \delta z_2 \delta z_3$. DOP is the measurement error gain or attenuation factor. In rough terms, the precision of the fix $\delta\underline{x}$ is the precision of the measurements $\delta\underline{z}$ multiplied by the DOP provided "precision" is defined in a manner consistent with the definition of DOP:

$$\|\delta\underline{x}\| = \left|\left(\frac{\partial\underline{x}}{\partial\underline{z}}\right)\right| \|\delta\underline{z}\| = |J| \|\delta\underline{z}\| \tag{6.14}$$

The statement is only true for differential volumes, so the limit of the DOP as measurement error tends to zero is the (explicit) Jacobian determinant:

$$\lim_{\delta\underline{z}\to 0} DOP = \frac{\|\delta\underline{x}\|}{\|\delta\underline{z}\|} = |J| = \frac{1}{|H|} \tag{6.15}$$

Box 6.1 Computing Dilution of Precision

In the limit of small measurement errors, the DOP in pose fixing is the determinant of the explicit Jacobian J and it is also the reciprocal of the determinant of the (implicit) measurement Jacobian H.

We used the properties of determinants to relate DOP to H. This result gives us a method to evaluate the geometry of any pose fixing situation.

Note that the fix error depends on both measurement error and the DOP, so large DOP is not necessarily irrecoverable. Good sensors can overcome poor conditioning in theory. The range of DOP is $0 < \text{DOP} < \infty$ and very high DOP values can occur when the measurement Jacobian H is near singularity. The DOP varies smoothly over space like $|J|$ so we can visualize a DOP scalar field over pose space. We can also visualize DOP in 2D with contour graphs like Figure 6.9.

6.1.3.2.2 Implicit DOP. There is a clever way to evaluate DOP because only $|J|$ is required, rather than J itself. This technique has its roots in the implicit function theorem of calculus. Most often, real constraint equations are implicit because most measurement models are nonlinear, J is either difficult or impossible to find. However, we can compute DOP anyway. Consider two nonlinear constraints on 4 variables:

$$F(x, y, z, w) = 0$$
$$G(x, y, z, w) = 0$$

These define two implicit functions $z(x, y)$ and $w(x, y)$. Taking total differentials we can write:

$$F_x\delta x + F_y\delta y + F_z\delta z + F_w\delta w = 0$$
$$G_x\delta x + G_y\delta y + G_z\delta z + G_w\delta w = 0$$

These can be considered to be two simultaneous linear equations for δz and δw in terms of δx and δy:

$$[f_x]\delta\underline{x} = -[f_z]\delta\underline{z}$$

$$\begin{bmatrix} F_x & F_y \\ G_x & G_y \end{bmatrix} \begin{bmatrix} \delta x \\ \delta y \end{bmatrix} = -\begin{bmatrix} F_z & F_w \\ G_z & G_w \end{bmatrix} \begin{bmatrix} \delta z \\ \delta w \end{bmatrix}$$

So:

$$\begin{bmatrix} \delta z \\ \delta w \end{bmatrix} = -\begin{bmatrix} F_z & F_w \\ G_z & G_w \end{bmatrix}^{-1} \begin{bmatrix} F_x & F_y \\ G_x & G_y \end{bmatrix} \begin{bmatrix} \delta x \\ \delta y \end{bmatrix}$$

Using the rules for determinant of product and inverse:

$$|H| = \begin{vmatrix} F_x & F_y \\ G_x & G_y \end{vmatrix} / \begin{vmatrix} F_z & F_w \\ G_z & G_w \end{vmatrix} = \frac{\|f_x\|}{\|f_z\|}$$

Alternatively, we could solve in the other direction:

$$\begin{bmatrix} \delta x \\ \delta y \end{bmatrix} = -\begin{bmatrix} F_x & F_y \\ G_x & G_y \end{bmatrix}^{-1} \begin{bmatrix} F_z & F_w \\ G_z & G_w \end{bmatrix} \begin{bmatrix} \delta z \\ \delta w \end{bmatrix}$$

To give:

$$|J| = \begin{vmatrix} F_z & F_w \\ G_z & G_w \end{vmatrix} / \begin{vmatrix} F_x & F_y \\ G_x & G_y \end{vmatrix} = \frac{\|f_z\|}{\|f_x\|}$$

So, we can get the DOP without even explicitly computing J.

6.1.3.3 First-Order Response to Random Errors

When the input errors are random, we can use our uncertainty transformation formulas to compute the covariance in the state. For the implicit case:

$$\delta\underline{z} = H\delta\underline{x}$$

The measurement covariance is clearly:

$$C_{\underline{z}} = HC_{\underline{x}}H^T$$

Provided the measurement matrix determines or overdetermines the state, this can be inverted (see Equation 5.80) to produce the covariance of the state from the covariance of the measurements:

$$C_{\underline{x}} = (H^T C_{\underline{z}}^{-1} H)^{-1}$$

6.1.3.4 Example 6.1: Bearing Observations With Known Yaw

Recall that the constraint equations for this case are as shown in Figure 6.8. We can determine the DOP using our formula for the implicit functions $x(\psi_1, \psi_2)$ and $y(\psi_1, \psi_2)$:

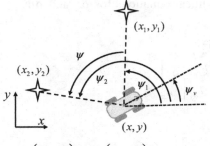

$$(x_1 - x)s_1 = (y_1 - y)c_1$$
$$(x_2 - x)s_2 = (y_2 - y)c_2$$

Figure 6.8 Bearing Observations with Known Yaw and Equations. The vehicle can measure the bearing to two landmarks and it has a way to measure its yaw angle.

$$F(x, y, \psi_1, \psi_2) = 0$$
$$G(x, y, \psi_1, \psi_2) = 0$$

which is:

$$s_1(x_1 - x) - c_1(y_1 - y) = 0$$
$$s_2(x_2 - x) - c_2(y_2 - y) = 0$$

Writing total differentials:

$$F_x \delta x + F_y \delta y + F_{\theta_1} \delta \psi_1 + F_{\theta_2} \delta \psi_2 = 0$$
$$G_x \delta x + G_y \delta y + G_{\theta_1} \delta \psi_1 + G_{\theta_2} \delta \psi_2 = 0$$

This gives the Jacobian determinant as:

$$|J| = \begin{vmatrix} F_{\psi_1} & F_{\psi_2} \\ G_{\psi_1} & G_{\psi_2} \end{vmatrix} \Big/ \begin{vmatrix} F_x & F_y \\ G_x & G_y \end{vmatrix} \qquad \begin{aligned} \text{Let:} \\ \Delta x_1 &= (x_1 - x) \\ \Delta y_1 &= (y_1 - y) \end{aligned} \quad \text{etc.}$$

$$|J| = \begin{vmatrix} c_1 \Delta x_1 + s_1 \Delta y_1 & 0 \\ 0 & c_2 \Delta x_2 + s_2 \Delta y_2 \end{vmatrix} \Big/ \begin{vmatrix} -s_1 & c_1 \\ -s_2 & c_2 \end{vmatrix}$$

Multiplied out, this is:

$$|J| = \frac{[c_1 \Delta x_1 + s_1 \Delta y_1][c_2 \Delta x_2 + s_2 \Delta y_2]}{\sin(\psi_2 - \psi_1)}$$

Noting that $c_1 \Delta x_1 + s_1 \Delta y_1 = r_1$, and so on, the above result is simply:

$$|J| = \frac{r_1 r_2}{\sin(\psi)}$$

The main conclusions to be drawn are summarized in Box 6.2.

A *contour diagram* shows a collection of level curves of the constraints that are equally spaced in constraint value. When they are equally spaced in this way, the size of any region bounded by level curves is an indication of the DOP at its center. A complete contour diagram for this case is shown in Figure 6.9.

> **Box 6.2 Dilution of Precision for Bearing Measurements**
>
> For the case of bearing observations with known yaw, the DOP is given by:
>
> $$|J| = \frac{r_1 r_2}{\sin(\psi)}$$
>
> The DOP is infinite at points on the line between landmarks and it is large nearby. DOP grows in any case with the square of distance from the landmarks. Large distance also tends to also make the subtended angle of the landmarks small, further increasing DOP.

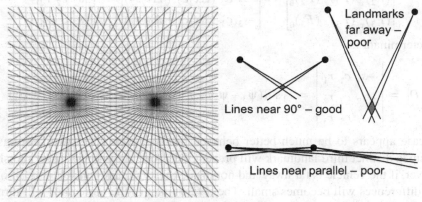

Figure 6.9 Contour Diagram for Bearing Observations: The size of the areas between level curves is proportional to DOP.

6.1.3.5 Example 6.2: Bearing Observations with Unknown Yaw

Consider again the measurement equations for this case shown in Figure 6.10.

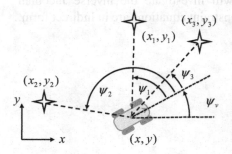

Figure 6.10 Bearing Observations with Unknown Yaw and Equations: The vehicle can measure bearings to three landmarks.

Letting $\beta_1 = \psi_v + \psi_1$ and $c_1 = \cos(\beta_1)$ and so on, these can be written as:

$$F_1(x, y, \psi, \psi_1, \psi_2, \psi_3) = 0$$
$$F_2(x, y, \psi, \psi_1, \psi_2, \psi_3) = 0$$
$$F_3(x, y, \psi, \psi_1, \psi_2, \psi_3) = 0$$

$$\tan(\psi_v + \psi_1) = \frac{\sin(\psi_v + \psi_1)}{\cos(\psi_v + \psi_1)} = \frac{y_1 - y}{x_1 - x}$$

$$\tan(\psi_v + \psi_2) = \frac{\sin(\psi_v + \psi_2)}{\cos(\psi_v + \psi_2)} = \frac{y_2 - y}{x_2 - x}$$

$$\tan(\psi_v + \psi_3) = \frac{\sin(\psi_v + \psi_3)}{\cos(\psi_v + \psi_3)} = \frac{y_3 - y}{x_3 - x}$$

Which is:

$$\Delta x_1 s_1 - \Delta y_1 c_1 = 0$$
$$\Delta x_2 s_2 - \Delta y_2 c_2 = 0$$
$$\Delta x_3 s_3 - \Delta y_3 c_3 = 0$$

Inspiring from the last case, problems will occur when the matrix in the denominator of the expression for $|J|$ has a zero determinant. The denominator D is:

$$\begin{bmatrix} (F_1)_x & (F_1)_y & (F_1)_\theta \\ (F_2)_x & (F_2)_y & (F_2)_\theta \\ (F_3)_x & (F_3)_y & (F_3)_\theta \end{bmatrix} = \begin{bmatrix} -s_1 & c_1 & (\Delta x_1 c_1 + \Delta y_1 s_1) \\ -s_2 & c_2 & (\Delta x_2 c_2 + \Delta y_2 s_2) \\ -s_3 & c_3 & (\Delta x_3 c_3 + \Delta y_3 s_3) \end{bmatrix} = \begin{bmatrix} -s_1 & c_1 & r_1 \\ -s_2 & c_2 & r_2 \\ -s_3 & c_3 & r_3 \end{bmatrix}$$

The determinant is:

$$|D| = \begin{vmatrix} -s_1 & c_1 & r_1 \\ -s_2 & c_2 & r_2 \\ -s_3 & c_3 & r_3 \end{vmatrix} = r_1 \sin(\psi_3 - \psi_2) + r_2 \sin(\psi_1 - \psi_3) + r_3 \sin(\psi_2 - \psi_1)$$

This case appears to be much better behaved because even when two bearings are lined up, a distinct third landmark will prevent the above determinant from vanishing. However, if the vehicle is far away and not inside the landmark constellation all of the angle differences will becomes small. The determinant of the numerator will turn out to be the product $r_1 r_2 r_3$ leading to high error growth with range. In retrospect, there is more information in a third bearing than in a measurement of absolute heading because it constrains position along the line between the other two landmarks.

6.1.3.6 Example 6.3: Circular Constraints

Once again, the constraint equations for this case are shown in Figure 6.11. To get the DOP here, we will use a useful trick. We will investigate the inverse Jacobian $H = J^{-1}$ instead of the Jacobian because the constraint equations are in indirect form.

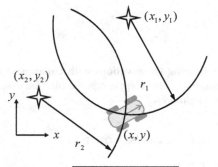

$$r_1 = \sqrt{(x - x_1)^2 + (y - y_1)^2}$$

$$r_2 = \sqrt{(x - x_2)^2 + (y - y_2)^2}$$

Figure 6.11 Range Observations and Equations: The vehicle can measure range to two landmarks. Yaw cannot be determined.

Take total differentials:

$$\delta r_1 = \frac{(x - x_1)}{r_1}\delta x + \frac{(y - y_1)}{r_1}\delta y$$

$$\delta r_2 = \frac{(x - x_2)}{r_2}\delta x + \frac{(y - y_2)}{r_2}\delta y$$

Then, the determinant is:

$$\left|J^{-1}\right| = \begin{vmatrix} \dfrac{x - x_1}{r_1} & \dfrac{y - y_1}{r_1} \\[2ex] \dfrac{x - x_2}{r_2} & \dfrac{y - y_2}{r_2} \end{vmatrix}$$

Note that the cross product in the plane is often written exactly in terms of this determinant, so the result is:

$$\left|J^{-1}\right| = \frac{\vec{r}_1 \times \vec{r}_2}{|\vec{r}_1||\vec{r}_2|} = \sin(\psi)$$

where ψ is the angle between the two vectors from the landmarks to the vehicle. The conclusions that can be drawn from this result are summarized in Box 6.3.

Box 6.3 Dilution of Precision for Range Measurements

For the case of range observations, the DOP is given by:

$$|J| = \frac{1}{\sin(\psi)}$$

DOP is again infinite on the line between the landmarks. There is no explicit variation with range, but there is an implicit one because (ψ decreases with increased range from the landmarks).

The contour diagram for this case is provided in Figure 6.12.

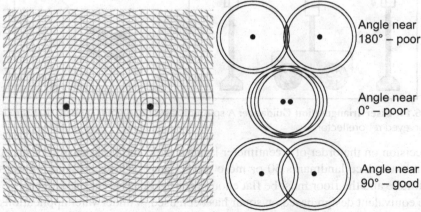

Angle near
180° – poor

Angle near
0° – poor

Angle near
90° – good

Figure 6.12 Contour Diagram for Range Observations: The size of the areas between level curves is proportional to DOP.

6.1.3.7 Example 4: Hyperbolic Constraints

The contour diagram for hyperbolic constraints (for two transmitter pairs) reveals a very favorable configuration from the point of view of DOP (Figure 6.13).

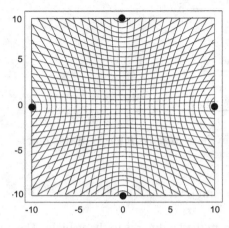

Figure 6.13 Contour Diagram for Range Difference Observations: DOP is best near the origin and it increases with distance from either axis. There are no singularities except at infinity but clearly DOP becomes poor after leaving the region between the landmarks.

6.1.4 Real Pose Fixing Systems

The Global Positioning System is a range trilateration system that will be presented in a later section. Other options exist for robots that are confined to indoor spaces or finite regions.

6.1.4.1 Retroreflector Triangulation

Systems that measure bearings to multiple landmarks have often been used in practice (Figure 6.14). Often the radiation source resides on the robot and the landmarks are passive retro-reflectors that reflect received energy right back to its source. For indoor mobile robots, laser triangulation based on retroreflectors is a common technique in autonomous guided vehicle (AGV) applications.

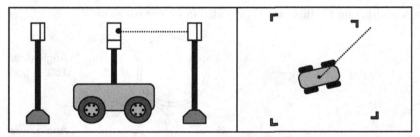

Figure 6.14 Laser Triangulation Guidance: A spinning laser head emits a beam that is reflected from surveyed retroreflectors.

Fix precision on the order of a centimeter is achievable and the focussed beam makes it feasible to place landmarks 50 or more meters apart. This configuration does not give altitude and the floor must be flat enough for the beam to hit the reflectors.

The equivalent design based on sonar has been used in underwater applications and radar systems have been developed for outdoor applications – which must work even in bad weather and dusty conditions when a laser beam would not be detectable.

A simple implementation of bearing triangulation can be achieved with no more equipment than a camera and recognizable (and surveyed) features in the environment in view. An omnidirectional camera may be best for this purpose and retroreflectors and a light source co-located with the camera will increase reliability. Robot orientation can often be measured to higher precision if a camera on the robot is imaging the environment rather than a camera in the environment imaging the robot.

6.1.4.2 Radio Trilateration

Range trilateration could be achieved in the above configuration by emitting omnidirectional pulses of energy and measuring the times for all returns. It would not be obvious which reflector returned the energy but good tracking data association techniques could resolve ambiguities when dead reckoning is also used.

In practice, radio navigation tends to have the power source located at the landmarks in order to serve many vehicles operating in a given area while avoiding radio interference issues. In this case, the simplest configuration to understand is one where synchronized transmitters emit a signal at the same time in all directions. Receivers on the vehicles will receive the signals at different times depending on the ranges from each transmitter and the time difference will correspond to the range difference used in hyperbolic navigation.

Synchronization to nanosecond precision would be required to enable fix precisions on the order of 30 cm. For the LORAN-C marine radio navigation system, secondary transmitters wait to receive the signal of the primary and then emit their signals after a fixed delay. In this way, the signals themselves are used to synchronize the transmitters. Because the primary transmitter is shared, two secondary transmitters with different delays are enough to generate two hyperbolic constraints. LORAN-C was decommissioned in North America in 2010, having been obsoleted by GPS, but custom radio navigation systems may still have their merits in special circumstances.

6.1.5 Dead Reckoning

As was the case for pose fixing, *dead reckoning* techniques are ancient. The first mariner to estimate position beyond sight of land by projecting position along the present course was performing dead reckoning. We will use the term to apply to all calculations that integrate derivatives to compute states of interest.

Position can be reckoned from measurements of differential position:

$$\vec{r} = \vec{r}(0) + \int_0^t d\vec{r} = \vec{r}(0) + \int_0^t \vec{v}dt \tag{6.16}$$

Position can also be reckoned from measurements of velocity or acceleration.

$$\vec{r} = \vec{r}(0) + \int_0^t \left[\vec{v}(0) + \int_0^t \vec{a}dt \right] dt = \vec{r}(0) + \vec{v}(0)t + \int_0^t \int_0^t \vec{a}dtdt \tag{6.17}$$

Likewise, one can integrate differential angles or angular velocity to compute orientation.

$$\psi = \psi(0) + \int_0^t d\psi = \psi(0) + \int_0^t \dot{\psi}dt \tag{6.18}$$

Detailed treatment of angular velocity in 3D and its relationship to Euler angle rates was presented in Section 2.5.3 of Chapter 2. The continuous integrals presented above become discrete sums in practice. In pure (unaided) dead reckoning, any error present in an old estimate is preserved in subsequent estimates so sensor and numerical errors play a much larger role in governing system performance.

6.1.5.1 Canonical Cases for Odometry

The mathematics of dead reckoning can be similar or even identical to the mathematics of motion prediction in control or in simulation. We will restrict our attention for the moment to the process of dead reckoning position and orientation from measurements of linear and/or angular velocity. We will call such a process *odometry* but the term is borrowed (and altered) from automotive engineering where its definition is restricted to the use of wheel rotations to measure distance travelled. A better term might be *odometric dead reckoning*.

In all cases of dead reckoning, the governing equations are of the form:

$$\dot{\underline{x}}(t) = f[\underline{x}(t), \underline{u}(t), \underline{p}]$$

Where, as usual, the state $\underline{x}(t)$ depends on some inputs $\underline{u}(t)$ and parameters $\underline{p}$. In the case of odometry, we might also be able to directly or indirectly measure the inputs. In such a case, the measurements $\underline{z}(t)$ will satisfy a model of the form:

$$\underline{z}(t) = h[\underline{x}(t), \underline{u}(t), \underline{p}]$$

We will restrict our attention mostly to planar motion because that is already difficult enough for the following analysis, but dead reckoning in 3D can be accomplished using the terrain following models provided in Chapter 4. We will also assume that there is nominally no wheel slip but such slip can be regarded as one form of error in the analysis that follows, and explicit models of slip can always be added.

A few generic cases are useful to distinguish. For now, we will adopt the assumption that the vehicle moves in the direction in which it is pointed (Figure 6.15). Not all vehicles move this way and we have already seen how to model such vehicles as well.

The following subsections define three important cases of odometry, distinguished in terms of how the heading angle is computed.

6.1.5.1.1 Direct Heading. If a direct measurement of heading from, for example, a compass, is available, the vehicle dynamics can be expressed as:

$$\frac{d}{dt}\begin{bmatrix} x(t) \\ y(t) \end{bmatrix} = \begin{bmatrix} v(t)\cos\psi(t) \\ v(t)\sin\psi(t) \end{bmatrix} \tag{6.19}$$

Heading is not considered a state in this model because there is no need to integrate to measure it. The state and input vectors are therefore:

$$\underline{x}(t) = \begin{bmatrix} x(t) & y(t) \end{bmatrix}^T \qquad \underline{u}(t) = \begin{bmatrix} v(t) & \psi(t) \end{bmatrix}^T$$

The measurement model is trivial:

$$\underline{z}(t) = \underline{u}(t) = \begin{bmatrix} v(t) & \psi(t) \end{bmatrix}^T$$

Figure 6.15 Coordinates for Odometry. The state to be estimated is the robot pose and zero initial conditions occurs when the world and robot frames are aligned.

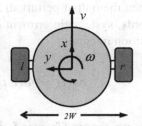

Figure 6.16 Differential Heading Odometry. The difference in rotation rates of left and right wheels indicates angular velocity.

As always, the input can be considered to be a command signal, a command measurement, or feedback of actual motion depending on the context.

6.1.5.1.2 Integrated Heading. Given a measurement of the rate of heading from, for example, a gyro, the vehicle dynamics can be expressed as:

$$\frac{d}{dt}\begin{bmatrix} x(t) \\ y(t) \\ \psi(t) \end{bmatrix} = \begin{bmatrix} v(t)\cos\psi(t) \\ v(t)\sin\psi(t) \\ \omega(t) \end{bmatrix} \tag{6.20}$$

Where the state and input vectors are:

$$\underline{x}(t) = \begin{bmatrix} x(t) & y(t) & \psi(t) \end{bmatrix}^T \qquad \underline{u}(t) = \begin{bmatrix} v(t) & \omega(t) \end{bmatrix}^T$$

and the measurement equation is, again, trivial.

6.1.5.1.3 Differential Heading. An important special case of integrated heading that we saw in Chapter 4 is the case where there is no gyro but the differential speeds of two wheels constrain the heading rate (Figure 6.16). The state equation is the same but the measurement equation is:

$$\begin{bmatrix} v_r(t) \\ v_l(t) \end{bmatrix} = \begin{bmatrix} 1 & W \\ 1 & -W \end{bmatrix}\begin{bmatrix} v(t) \\ \omega(t) \end{bmatrix} \tag{6.21}$$

or:

$$\underline{z}(t) = H\underline{u}(t)$$

6.1.5.2 Error Dynamics in Odometry

Fortunately, there is a mechanism that can be used like the Jacobian matrix in pose fixing to express the relationship between errors in odometry sensing and their effects on the errors in computed pose. However, because odometry models are differential equations, the relevant matrices will be integrals evaluated over the path followed.

6.1.5.2.1 Error Propagation Integrals. We saw in Chapter 4 that the vector superposition integral expresses the general solution for the linearized or "perturbative" dynamics of any system. If we interpret the input perturbations $\delta\underline{u}(\tau)$ as sensor errors, then the output perturbations $\delta\underline{x}(t)$ represent the errors in computed pose. In other words, systematic error in dead reckoning propagates according to the vector superposition integral:

$$\delta\underline{x}(t) = \Phi(t, t_0)\delta\underline{x}(t_0) + \int_{t_0}^{t}\Gamma(t, \tau)\delta\underline{u}(\tau)d\tau \tag{6.22}$$

Similarly, we saw in Chapter 5 that presenting white Gaussian noise to a system as input will generate an output state whose variance, to first order, is given by the matrix superposition integral. If we interpret the noisy input as random sensor error of variance $Q(\tau)$, then the associated random error in computed pose has a variance $P(t)$ given by the matrix superposition integral:

$$P(t) = \Phi(t, t_0)P(t_0)\Phi^{T}(t, t_0) + \int_{t_0}^{t}\Gamma(t, \tau)Q(\tau)\Gamma^{T}(t, \tau)d\tau \tag{6.23}$$

It is important to note that this last formula does not give the pose error that is expected in a single experiment. It gives the variance of pose errors that would be expected if the same experiment was repeated many times.

6.1.5.2.2 Input Transition Matrix. Let us define $G(\tau)$ as the systematic error distribution matrix and $L(\tau)$ as the random noise distribution matrix. The product of the transition matrix and the appropriate distribution matrix will be called the *input transition matrix,* a non-standard term:

$$\Gamma(t, \tau) = \Phi(t, \tau)G(\tau) \qquad \Gamma(t, \tau) = \Phi(t, \tau)L(\tau)$$

Based on the above two integrals, this matrix governs the propagation of both systematic and random error in odometry. This fact is investigated below.

6.1.5.2.3 Moments of Error. We will see that integrals of the columns of $\Gamma(t, \tau)$, and of outer products of its columns, are the canonical error propagation modes. First note that the product $\Gamma\delta\underline{u}$ can be interpreted as a weighted sum of the columns of the matrix. In particular:

$$\Gamma\delta\underline{u} = \sum_{i}\underline{\gamma}_i\delta u_i$$

where $\underline{\gamma}_i$ is the ith column of $\Gamma(t, \tau)$ and the elements δu_i are the individual input error sources. Substituting into Equation 6.22 and exchanging the order of integration and summation leads to:

$$\delta\underline{x}(t) = \Phi(t, t_0)\delta\underline{x}(t_0) + \sum_{i}\left[\int_{t_0}^{t}\underline{\gamma}_i\delta u_i d\tau\right] \tag{6.24}$$

This result means that the total error in pose is the sum of the contributions of each input error source where each contribution is an integral over the path or a *moment,* which depends on the trajectory followed.

Next, note that the matrix quadratic form $\Gamma Q \Gamma^T$ can be interpreted as a weighted sum of matrices where each is an outer product of the one row of the left operand and one column of the right. In particular:

$$\Gamma Q \Gamma^T = \sum_i (\underline{\gamma}_i \underline{\gamma}_j^T q_{ij})$$

where the elements $\underline{\gamma}_i \underline{\gamma}_j^T$ are outer product matrices formed from the two indicated columns of the input transition matrix, and the elements q_{ij} are the individual covariance of the input error sources.

Substituting into Equation 6.23 and exchanging the order of integration and summation leads to:

$$P(t) = \Phi(t, t_0) P(t_0) \Phi^T(t, t_0) + \sum_i \sum_j \left[\int_{t_0}^{t} (\underline{\gamma}_i \underline{\gamma}_j^T q_{ij}) d\tau \right] \tag{6.25}$$

The same sum of moments interpretation applies but now the moments are matrix-valued. If the input errors sources are constant, the moments can be interpreted literally as geometric properties of the trajectory as outlined in Box 6.4.

Box 6.4 Error Propagation in Odometry

The pose errors experienced by odometry systems are dependent on the path followed. Systematic sensor errors in odometry give rise to systematic pose errors whose magnitudes are a weighted superposition of the sensor errors. The weights are vector-valued line integrals of the columns of the input transition matrix:

$$\delta \underline{x}(t) = \Phi(t, t_0) \delta \underline{x}(t_0) + \sum_i \delta u_i \left| \int_{t_0}^{t} \underline{\gamma}_i(t, \tau) d\tau \right|$$

Likewise random sensor errors in odometry give rise to random pose errors whose covariance is a weighted superposition of the sensor covariances. The weights are matrix-valued line integrals of outer product matrices formed from the columns of the input transition matrix:

$$P(t) = \Phi(t, t_0) P(t_0) \Phi^T(t, t_0) + \sum_i \sum_j q_{ij} \left| \int_{t_0}^{t} \underline{\gamma}_i(t, \tau) \underline{\gamma}_i^T(t, \tau) d\tau \right|$$

6.1.5.2.4 Numerical Evaluation of Error Dynamics. When the transition matrix is not available in closed form, it can be computed numerically as discussed in Section 4.5.6 of Chapter 4. For systematic error, a full nonlinear solution can be implemented by integrating the nonlinear dynamics with a perturbative input and subtracting the unperturbed input. An approximate solution can be obtained by integrating the linearized dynamics.

For random error, a nonlinear solution requires Monte Carlo techniques, which require significant computation. An approximate solution can be obtained by integrating the linear variance equation numerically and this technique is adequate for many practical purposes.

6.1.5.3 Example: Error Propagation in Integrated Heading Odometry

The use of path moments to characterize error dynamics will be illustrated on this case. The integrated heading case is described by this system:

$$\frac{d}{dt}\begin{bmatrix} x(t) \\ y(t) \\ \psi(t) \end{bmatrix} = \begin{bmatrix} v(t)\cos\psi(t) \\ v(t)\sin\psi(t) \\ \omega(t) \end{bmatrix}$$

The linearized dynamics equations for the fully actuated WMR were computed in Section 4.4.4.1 of Chapter 4. The above system is a special case with no lateral velocity input. Hence the transition matrix and input transition matrix are:

$$\Phi(t, \tau) = \begin{bmatrix} 1 & 0 & -\Delta y(t, \tau) \\ 0 & 1 & \Delta x(t, \tau) \\ 0 & 0 & 1 \end{bmatrix} \quad \Gamma(t, \tau) = \begin{bmatrix} c\psi(t) & -s\psi(t) & -\Delta y(t, \tau) \\ s\psi(t) & c\psi(t) & \Delta x(t, \tau) \\ 0 & 0 & 1 \end{bmatrix}$$

The second column of $\Gamma(t, \tau)$ must be deleted for the case of no lateral velocity input. Recall the definitions of the *history point displacements* from Section 4.4.4.1 of Chapter 4:

$$\Delta x(t, \tau) = [x(\tau) - x(t)] \qquad \Delta y(t, \tau) = [y(\tau) - y(t)]$$

6.1.5.3.1 Error Propagation. Substituting these matrices into the general solution in Equation 6.22 gives the expression for the general solution for the propagation of systematic error in integrated heading odometry

$$\delta \underline{x}(t) = \begin{bmatrix} 1 & 0 & -y(t) \\ 0 & 1 & x(t) \\ 0 & 0 & 1 \end{bmatrix} \delta \underline{x}(0) + \int_0^t \begin{bmatrix} c\psi & -\Delta y(t, \tau) \\ s\psi & \Delta x(t, \tau) \\ 0 & 1 \end{bmatrix} \begin{bmatrix} \delta v(\tau) \\ \delta \omega(\tau) \end{bmatrix} d\tau \qquad (6.26)$$

This result has the intuitive interpretation shown in Figure 6.17.

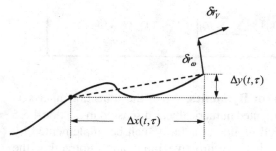

Figure 6.17 Superposition Integral. The vector superposition integral takes every error that has ever happened, projects its effects forward to the present time, and adds the results of all such errors together in superposition. The vectors $\delta \vec{r}_v$ and $\delta \vec{r}_\omega$ are incremental errors caused by linear and angular velocity errors that occurred at time τ.

The matrix relating input systematic errors occurring at time τ to their later effect at time t is:

$$d\begin{bmatrix} \delta x(t) \\ \delta y(t) \\ \delta \psi(t) \end{bmatrix} = \begin{bmatrix} c\psi & -\Delta y(t, \tau) \\ s\psi & \Delta x(t, \tau) \\ 0 & 1 \end{bmatrix} \begin{bmatrix} \delta v(\tau) \\ \delta \omega(\tau) \end{bmatrix} d\tau$$

So, the solution is simply adding up the effect of the entire history of input errors on the present pose error. In moment form, the solution integral is:

$$\delta \underline{x}(t) = \underline{IC}_d + \int_0^t \underline{\gamma}_v(\tau) \delta v d\tau + \int_0^t \underline{\gamma}_\omega(\tau) \delta \omega d\tau$$

where:

$$\underline{IC}_d = \begin{bmatrix} 1 & 0 & -y(t) \\ 0 & 1 & x(t) \\ 0 & 0 & 1 \end{bmatrix} \delta \underline{x}(0) \qquad \underline{\gamma}_v(\tau) = \begin{bmatrix} c\psi & s\psi & 0 \end{bmatrix}^T$$

$$\underline{\gamma}_\omega(\tau) = \begin{bmatrix} -\Delta y(t, \tau) & \Delta x(t, \tau) & 1 \end{bmatrix}^T$$

The complete result in moment form is:

$$\delta \underline{x}(t) = \underline{IC}_d + \int_0^t \begin{bmatrix} c\psi \\ s\psi \\ 0 \end{bmatrix} \delta V d\tau + \int_0^t \begin{bmatrix} -\Delta y(t, \tau) \\ \Delta x(t, \tau) \\ 1 \end{bmatrix} \delta \omega d\tau \tag{6.27}$$

Now consider random error. The general solution for the propagation of random error in integrated heading odometry is:

$$P(t) = IC_s + \int_0^t \begin{bmatrix} c\psi & -\Delta y(t, \tau) \\ s\psi & \Delta x(t, \tau) \\ 0 & 1 \end{bmatrix} \begin{bmatrix} \sigma_{vv} & \sigma_{v\omega} \\ \sigma_{v\omega} & \sigma_{\omega\omega} \end{bmatrix} \begin{bmatrix} c\psi & -\Delta y(t, \tau) \\ s\psi & \Delta x(t, \tau) \\ 0 & 1 \end{bmatrix}^T d\tau$$

Where the effect of initial conditions is:

$$IC_s = \begin{bmatrix} 1 & 0 & -y(t) \\ 0 & 1 & x(t) \\ 0 & 0 & 1 \end{bmatrix} \begin{bmatrix} \sigma_{xx}(0) & \sigma_{xy}(0) & \sigma_{x\theta}(0) \\ \sigma_{xy}(0) & \sigma_{yy}(0) & \sigma_{y\theta}(0) \\ \sigma_{x\theta}(0) & \sigma_{y\theta}(0) & \sigma_{\theta\theta}(0) \end{bmatrix} \begin{bmatrix} 1 & 0 & -y(t) \\ 0 & 1 & x(t) \\ 0 & 0 & 1 \end{bmatrix}^T$$

In moment form, as defined in Section 6.1.5.2.3, this is:

$$P(t) = IC_s + \int_0^t [\Gamma_{v\omega}(\tau) + \Gamma_{\omega v}(\tau)]\sigma_{v\omega} d\tau + \int_0^t \Gamma_{vv}(\tau)\sigma_{vv} d\tau + \int_0^t \Gamma_{\omega\omega}(\tau)\sigma_{\omega\omega} d\tau$$

where we have defined notation for certain outer product matrices:

$$
\Gamma_{vv}(\tau) = \begin{bmatrix} c\psi \\ s\psi \\ 0 \end{bmatrix} \begin{bmatrix} c\psi \\ s\psi \\ 0 \end{bmatrix}^T = \begin{bmatrix} c^2\psi & c\psi s\psi & 0 \\ c\psi s\psi & s^2\psi & 0 \\ 0 & 0 & 0 \end{bmatrix}
$$

$$
\Gamma_{v\omega}(\tau) = \Gamma_{\omega v}^T(\tau) = \begin{bmatrix} c\psi \\ s\psi \\ 0 \end{bmatrix} \begin{bmatrix} -\Delta y \\ \Delta x \\ 1 \end{bmatrix}^T = \begin{bmatrix} -c\psi\Delta y & c\psi\Delta x & c\psi \\ -s\psi\Delta y & s\psi\Delta x & s\psi \\ 0 & 0 & 0 \end{bmatrix}
$$

$$
\Gamma_{\omega\omega}(\tau) = \begin{bmatrix} -\Delta y \\ \Delta x \\ 1 \end{bmatrix} \begin{bmatrix} -\Delta y \\ \Delta x \\ 1 \end{bmatrix}^T = \begin{bmatrix} \Delta y^2 & -\Delta x\Delta y & -\Delta y \\ -\Delta x\Delta y & \Delta x^2 & \Delta x \\ -\Delta y & \Delta x & 1 \end{bmatrix}
$$

Assuming uncorrelated inputs $\sigma_{v\omega} = 0$, the complete result in moment form is:

$$
P(t) = IC_s + \int_0^t \begin{bmatrix} c^2\psi & c\psi s\psi & 0 \\ c\psi s\psi & s^2\psi & 0 \\ 0 & 0 & 0 \end{bmatrix} \sigma_{vv} d\tau + \int_0^t \begin{bmatrix} \Delta y^2 & -\Delta x\Delta y & -\Delta y \\ -\Delta x\Delta y & \Delta x^2 & \Delta x \\ -\Delta y & \Delta x & 1 \end{bmatrix} \sigma_{\omega\omega} d\tau \qquad (6.28)
$$

6.1.5.3.2 Error Models. Getting concrete results from the above equations requires both the input errors and the trajectory followed to be specified. Let the systematic error model be a constant scale error on the velocity (encoder) and a constant bias error on the angular velocity (gyro):

$$
\delta v = \delta v_v \times v
$$

$$
\delta\omega = const
$$

where the notation means:

$$
\delta v_v = \frac{\partial}{\partial v}(\delta v)
$$

Let the random error model be a distance-dependent random walk for linear velocity and a constant covariance for angular velocity.

$$
\sigma_{vv} = \sigma_{vv}^{(v)}|v| \qquad\qquad \sigma_{\omega\omega} = const \qquad\qquad \sigma_{v\omega} = 0
$$

Now the general solution for this systematic error model on any trajectory is:

$$
\delta\underline{x}(t) = \underline{IC}_d + \delta v_v \int_0^s \begin{bmatrix} c\psi \\ s\psi \\ 0 \end{bmatrix} ds + \delta\omega \int_0^t \begin{bmatrix} -\Delta y \\ \Delta x \\ 1 \end{bmatrix} d\tau
$$

Assuming that the input errors are uncorrelated, the general solution for the covariance of random error for this error model on any trajectory is:

$$
P(t) = IC_s + \sigma_{vv}^{(v)} \int_0^s \begin{bmatrix} c^2\psi & c\psi s\psi & 0 \\ c\psi s\psi & s^2\psi & 0 \\ 0 & 0 & 0 \end{bmatrix} ds + \sigma_{\omega\omega} \int_0^t \begin{bmatrix} \Delta y^2 & -\Delta x\Delta y & -\Delta y \\ -\Delta x\Delta y & \Delta x^2 & \Delta x \\ -\Delta y & \Delta x & 1 \end{bmatrix} d\tau
$$

Note especially that the moment integrals are now functions solely of the shape of the trajectory followed. The trajectory must be specified in order to compute them.

6.1.5.3.3 Interpretation. The last two results contain a lot of information. Ignoring initial conditions for simplicity, notice first of all that the response to velocity scale error is not dependent on the path because the moment can be evaluated in closed form:

$$\delta \underline{r}(t) = \delta v_v \int_0^s \begin{bmatrix} c\psi \\ s\psi \end{bmatrix} ds = \delta v_v \begin{bmatrix} x(t) \\ y(t) \end{bmatrix} = \delta v_v \underline{r}(t) \tag{6.29}$$

where the position vector is $\underline{r}(t) = \begin{bmatrix} x(t) & y(t) \end{bmatrix}^T$. Intuitively such an error simply scales the entire path. One important implication is that the effects of velocity scale error vanish, to first order, on returning to the origin.

Now, consider the response to gyro bias.

$$\delta \underline{x}(t) = \delta \omega \int_0^t \begin{bmatrix} -\Delta y \\ \Delta x \\ 1 \end{bmatrix} d\tau = \delta \omega \int_0^t \begin{bmatrix} -[y(\tau) - y(t)] \\ [x(\tau) - x(t)] \\ 1 \end{bmatrix} d\tau = \delta \omega t \begin{bmatrix} y(t) - \bar{y}(t) \\ -(x(t) - \bar{x}(t)) \\ 1 \end{bmatrix}$$

Heading error is linear in time: $\delta\psi(t) = \delta\omega t$. Position error is more complicated. The effect is proportional to time and to deviation from a point that we will call the *dwell centroid* defined by:

$$\bar{\rho}(t) = \begin{bmatrix} \bar{x}(t) \\ \bar{y}(t) \end{bmatrix} = \frac{1}{t} \int_0^t \begin{bmatrix} x(\tau) \\ y(\tau) \end{bmatrix} d\tau$$

This point is analogous to the centroid of a plane curve except that it is weighted by time rather than arc length. It represents the center of the entire trajectory in a particular sense. The effect of gyro bias on position error is then given by:

$$\delta \underline{r}(t) = \delta\omega t \times [\underline{r}(t) - \bar{\rho}(t)] \tag{6.30}$$

where the vector $\delta\underline{\omega}$ is directed out of the plane and the product $\delta\omega t$ is the heading angle that results from integrating the bias for the elapsed time. Error caused by gyro bias is therefore directed orthogonally to the line to the dwell centroid and it cancels, to first order, on returning there.

Ignoring initial conditions and correlations, and rearranging the diagonal of the covariance into a vector, the impact of random velocity error is given by:

$$\begin{bmatrix} \sigma_{xx} \\ \sigma_{yy} \\ \sigma_{\psi\psi} \end{bmatrix} = \sigma_{vv}^{(v)} \int_0^s \begin{bmatrix} c^2\psi \\ s^2\psi \\ 0 \end{bmatrix} ds = \sigma_{vv}^{(v)} \int_0^s \begin{bmatrix} c\psi dx \\ s\psi dy \\ 0 \end{bmatrix}$$

In this case the differential ds is unsigned and the integrands happen to be as well. Clearly, the position covariance matrix has a trace given by:

$$\sigma_{rr} = \sigma_{xx} + \sigma_{yy} = \sigma_{vv}^{(v)} \int_0^s \left[c^2\psi + s^2\psi \right] ds = \sigma_{vv}^{(v)} s \tag{6.31}$$

So the total covariance of the position error is proportional to the distance travelled regardless of the shape of the path. Further analysis reveals that the major axis of the covariance ellipse is directed along the dominant direction of travel.

Once again ignoring initial conditions and correlations, and rearranging the diagonal of the covariance into a vector, the impact of random gyro error is given by:

$$
\begin{bmatrix} \sigma_{xx} \\ \sigma_{yy} \\ \sigma_{\psi\psi} \end{bmatrix} = \sigma_{\omega\omega} \int_0^t \begin{bmatrix} \Delta y^2 \\ \Delta x^2 \\ 1 \end{bmatrix} d\tau = \sigma_{\omega\omega} \int_0^t \begin{bmatrix} [y(\tau) - y(t)]^2 \\ [x(\tau) - x(t)]^2 \\ 1 \end{bmatrix} d\tau
$$

The heading variance is linear in time: $\sigma_{\psi\psi} = \sigma_{\omega\omega} t$. Position variance is even more complicated. The trace is given by:

$$
\sigma_{rr} = \sigma_{xx} + \sigma_{yy} = \sigma_{\omega\omega} \int_0^t \left[\Delta x^2 + \Delta y^2 \right] d\tau
$$

Notice that:

$$
[x(\tau) - x(t)]^2 = x^2(t) - 2x(t)x(\tau) + x^2(\tau)
$$

Hence, the total variance has three terms:

$$
\sigma_{xx} = \sigma_{\omega\omega} \left\{ x^2(t) \int_0^t d\tau - 2x(t) \int_0^t \left[x(\tau) \right] d\tau + \int_0^t \left[x^2(\tau) \right] d\tau \right\}
$$

If we choose the origin to be at the dwell centroid, then the middle integral vanishes and we are left with:

$$
\sigma_{xx} = \sigma_{\omega\omega} t \left\{ x_{\bar\rho}^2(t) + \frac{1}{t} \int_0^t \left[x_{\bar\rho}^2(\tau) \right] d\tau \right\}
$$

Performing the same derivation for σ_{yy} leads to the following expression for the total variance in dwell-centroid-relative coordinates:

$$
\sigma_{rr} = \sigma_{\omega\omega} t \left\{ r_{\bar\rho}^2(t) + \frac{1}{t} \int_0^t \left[r_{\bar\rho}^2(\tau) \right] d\tau \right\}
$$

Now let us define the squared *dwell radius:*

$$
\rho_{\bar\rho}^2(t) = \frac{1}{t} \int_0^t \left[r_{\bar\rho}^2(\tau) \right] d\tau
$$

This is the time averaged squared radius from the dwell centroid. The total result for the impact of gyro random error is:

$$
\sigma_{rr} = \sigma_{\omega\omega} t [r_{\bar\rho}^2(t) + \rho_{\bar\rho}^2(t)] \tag{6.32}
$$

So there is a component due to instantaneous squared radius from the dwell centroid and another component due to average squared radius. These results are summarized below in Box 6.5.

Box 6.5: Error Propagation in Integrated Heading Odometry

Integrated heading odometry is defined as the process of dead reckoning position and orientation from measurements of linear and angular velocity. For such a system, if velocity measurements have a scale error and angular velocity measurements have a bias, errors propagate as follows.

$$\delta \underline{r}(t) = \delta v_v \underline{r}(t)$$

The effect of velocity scale error is proportional to the position vector and is independent of path shape.

$$\delta \psi(t) = \delta \omega t$$

Heading error due to gyro bias grows linearly in time.

$$\delta \underline{r}(t) = \delta \underline{\omega} t \times [\underline{r}(t) - \bar{\underline{\rho}}(t)]$$

Position error caused by gyro bias is proportional to time and radius from the dwell centroid, directed normally.

If velocity measurements contain random errors proportional to distance and gyro measurements contain random noise, errors propagate as follows:

$$\sigma_{rr} = \sigma_{vv}^{(v)} s$$

Total position covariance is proportional to distance travelled and is independent of path shape.

$$\sigma_{\psi\psi} = \sigma_{\omega\omega} t$$

Heading variance due to gyro noise grows linearly in time.

$$\sigma_{rr} = \sigma_{\omega\omega} t [r_\rho^2(t) + \rho_\rho^2(t)]$$

Position variance caused by gyro noise is proportional to time and both instantaneous and average squared radius from the dwell centroid.

6.1.5.3.4 Insights. Odometry errors exhibit many interesting behaviors. Response to input errors is always the (path-dependent) sum of one moment for each error source. Response to initial conditions (initial pose errors) is always path-independent. These two properties are inherited from differential equations.

Systematic odometry error is not linear in distance, at least not in the crosstrack direction. The effects of several sources of error will vanish to first order at special points on the trajectory, and this property can hide errors if it is misunderstood.

For velocity scale errors, the path will be the wrong size but the right shape – so the estimate of a closed path will still close regardless of scale error. The effects of gyro bias errors vanish at the dwell centroid of the trajectory. Every path has a dwell centroid but symmetric paths have an obvious one.

The response to random gyro bias error is not monotone increasing. The dependence in the instantaneous dwell radius implies that returning to the dwell centroid will reduce, but perhaps not eliminate any accumulated error.

6.1.6 Real Dead Reckoning Systems

Inertial navigation is a very effective form of dead reckoning, which will be presented later. Whereas inertial navigation systems are typically purchased, odometry systems are typically implemented from scratch. In either case, a common strategy is to implement the dead reckoning equations as the projection step in a Kalman filter.

Heading errors typically dominate the long-term performance of odometry systems. High-quality gyros are affordable and they will typically outperform any heading solution based on measuring differential wheel velocities. The wheel velocities will still be needed to indicate linear velocity though. When rotational speeds are relatively high, the frequency of the computations and the sophistication of the numerical integration will matter. Runge Kutta is not difficult to implement and it is far more accurate than Euler's method. However, the effects of wheel slip may render such accurate mathematics irrelevant unless the actual slip is modelled well.

The general mathematical approach to describing the kinematic relationships between wheel motions and vehicle motion was presented in Chapter 4. Wheels may be passive or active and active wheels may be steerable, driven, or both. Measurements of wheel steer angles are roughly equivalent to measurements of path curvature. If more than the minimum measurements are available, body motion will be overdetermined and some form of optimization is necessary to produce an estimate.

In addition to sensor errors, nonmodeled wheel slip is an error in the system model itself. Wheel deformation must always occur anyway because a wheel contact patch is not a discrete point. Such effects change the effective dimensions of the vehicle, for dead reckoning purposes, by moving the wheel contact points to off-nominal positions. Odometry systems can be calibrated to recover the best estimate of wheel radii, wheelbase, wheel track, and so on, using the system identification techniques presented in Chapter 4.

6.1.7 References and Further Reading

This subchapter is based on the two papers by Kelly. The material in Bowditch related to pilotage inspired the work in triangulation. The papers by Borenstein and Chong inspired the work on dead reckoning.

[1] J. Borenstein and L. Feng, Correction of Systematic Odometry Error in Mobile Robots, in *Proceedings of the International Conference on Intelligent Robots and Systems*, Pittsburgh, PA, August 5–9, 1995.

[2] Nathaniel Bowditch, *The American Practical Navigator*, Bethesda, MD, National Imagery and Mapping Agency, 2002.

[3] K. S. Chong and L. Kleeman, Accurate Odometry and Error Modelling for a Mobile Robot, *Proceedings of International Conference on Robotics and Automation*, Albuquerque, New Mexico, April 1997.

[4] A. Kelly, Linearized Error Propagation in Vehicle Odometry, *The International Journal of Robotics Research*, Vol. 23, No. 2, pp. 179–218, 2004.

[5] A. Kelly, Precision Dilution in Mobile Robot Position Estimation, in Proceedings of Intelligent Autonomous Systems, Amsterdam, 2003.

[6] George M. Siouris, *Aerospace Avionic Systems*, Academic Press, 1993.

6.1.8 Exercises

6.1.8.1 Influence of Angles of Lines of Position in Kalman Filtering

Suppose a rangefinder was used to locate features in the environment. For this particular rangefinder, the uncertainty in the angle of the beam can be ignored relative to the uncertainty in range. Consider the covariance matrices given below, which correspond to three measurements of landmark locations that have already been converted to some global coordinate system:

$$C_1 = \begin{bmatrix} 100 & 0 \\ 0 & 1 \end{bmatrix} \qquad C_2 = \begin{bmatrix} 100 & 0 \\ 0 & 1 \end{bmatrix} \qquad C_3 = \begin{bmatrix} 1 & 0 \\ 0 & 100 \end{bmatrix}$$

Combine C1 and C2 according to the Kalman filter covariance update formula (i.e., the linear measurement case with identity observation matrix). Combine C1 and C3. Draw equiprobability ellipses to indicate the original matrices and the combined result.

How is the effect of the angle between different observations of the same landmark automatically factored in by the Kalman filter? How much difference does the angle make in the length of the major axis of the resulting equiprobability ellipse?

In answering this question, you will need, the following matrix identity:

$$A = \begin{bmatrix} a & b \\ c & d \end{bmatrix} \qquad A^{-1} = \left(\frac{1}{ad - cb} \right) \begin{bmatrix} d & -b \\ -c & a \end{bmatrix}$$

6.1.8.2 Uncertainty in Aided Dead Reckoning

Suppose that an odometer provides readings every 1/100th of a mile but that an additional sensor can detect when a mile marker is passed. Plot the expected development of magnitude of state uncertainty versus distance for 5 miles when extremely precise detection of mile markers is merged with the dead reckoned state.

6.1.8.3 Error Dynamics in One Dimension

Use the odometry error propagation modelling process based on the transition matrix to compute the error dynamics of the random walk and the integrated random walk. An integrated random walk is a system whose acceleration is white noise. The velocity of such a system is a single integral of white noise, and hence a random walk. The position of such a system is a double integral of white noise and hence an integrated random walk. Drive a dynamic system (a differential equation) with an acceleration input and then compute the variance in position and velocity which results from a constant variance in acceleration.

Let the system state vector be $\underline{x}(t) = \begin{bmatrix} x(t) & v(t) \end{bmatrix}^T$ and the input "vector" is $u(t) = \begin{bmatrix} a(t) \end{bmatrix}$. The system dynamics is given by:

$$\frac{d}{dt} \begin{bmatrix} x(t) \\ v(t) \end{bmatrix} = \begin{bmatrix} v(t) \\ a(t) \end{bmatrix}$$

Compute the transition matrix for this system and then use the matrix convolution integral and solve it in closed form.

6.1.8.4 Hyperbolic Navigation

Consider the four beacon square hyperbolic navigation system indicated in the figure:

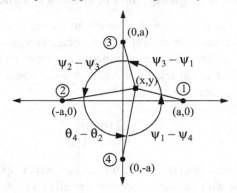

Recall that in hyperbolic navigation, the difference of the ranges to two landmarks are directly measured (say, by a phase difference). Hence, one measurement is produced from each pair of landmarks. The geometry above is the simplest example that can be used to determine position in the plane.

(i) If the measurements $z = [(r_2 - r_1)\ (r_4 - r_3)]^T$ are the range differences generated at the present position $x = [x\ y]^T$ from the horizontal landmark pair and the vertical landmark pair, show that the (inverse) DOP for this configuration is given by:

$$\left|\frac{\partial z}{\partial x}\right| = \sin(\psi_4 - \psi_2) + \sin(\psi_3 - \psi_1) + \sin(\psi_1 - \psi_4) + \sin(\psi_2 - \psi_3)$$

$$\|H^{-1}\| = s\psi_{42} + s\psi_{31} + s\psi_{14} + s\psi_{23}$$

where the angles ψ_i are the angles that the ray from landmark i to the present position makes with the x axis.

(ii) What is the DOP at the origin? At infinity in any direction?

(iii) How does the structure of the inverse DOP change if the landmarks are in general position (positioned arbitrarily)?

6.2 Sensors For State Estimation

This section presents various sensors that are applicable to mobile robot articulation and pose estimation. There are three categories, articulation, field, and inertial. Articulation sensors measure angles and displacements of robot mechanisms. Alternatively, basic sensors for measuring attitude on the Earth, such as *compasses and inclinometers,* rely on the Earth's fields (magnetic and gravitational). Inertial sensors such as *accelerometers and gyroscopes (gyros)* are based on inertial principles.

6.2.1 Articulation Sensors

Whereas articulation sensors are critical to manipulators, they are less important to mobile robots. There are a large number of different types of sensors available for use in motion control applications. Just a few are encoders, resolvers, synchros, Hall effect devices, linear variable differential transformers (LVDTs), and position sensitive devices (PSDs).

This section will present the basics of just the most common wheel rotation sensor – the optical encoder. Encoders are used to measure wheel rotations or drive shaft rotations for purposes of motion control or navigation and they can be important for the measurement of the attitude of sensors and sensor heads that scan or are pointed.

6.2.1.1 Optical Encoders

Optical encoders (Figure 6.18) provide a measurement of the rotation of a shaft that exits the sensor housing. The basic principle is a mechanical *light chopper*. A grating (sheet of glass with regularly spaced holes in it) is fixed to the moving half of the mechanism. As the grating rotates past a phototransmitter (laser diode), which is fixed to the stationary part of the device, a photodetector (photodiode) is alternately exposed and shielded from the light source so that it produces a pulse for every hole in the grating that passes.

The pulses from the detector are counted in the interface circuitry, which then outputs a measurement of the total rotation. In mobile robots, so-called *quadrature* encoders are typically used. In these, a second emitter/detector pair is offset from the first by 1/4 of a hole width. This pair generates a second signal that is 90° out of phase relative to the first. Resolution is improved by a factor of 4 and the direction of motion can be determined from the two pulse streams. Resolutions of 1000 to 10000 pulses per revolution (ppr) are typical.

For the measurement of wheel rotation, high accuracy rotation measurement is usually not justified because wheels slip on the surface anyway. If the encoder is used as feedback for motor control purposes, it is very important to realize that any *backlash* in the gearbox will not be measured if the encoder is placed on the motor shaft. Sometimes this is necessary for control purposes. In that case, one solution is to put another encoder on the output of the gearbox.

6.2.1.2 Absolute Encoders

For perception sensor pointing applications, it is usually important to know the absolute angle of the perception sensor. Figure 6.18 is a type of *incremental encoder*. It is not an absolute device because it only indicates changes in angle. The record of motion stored in the counter will be lost when power to the sensor is shut off. The only way to use it as an absolute sensor is to drive it physically to a home position when it is turned on. When this is undesirable, an absolute encoder can be used.

If the disk is instead printed with n concentric traces of slots and n transmitters and receivers are arranged radially, the device can be used to measure absolute angle to n bits precision. Encoders up to 26 bits of precision are available. Incremental encoders can be converted to absolute in a few ways. Some use index pulses that occur once per turn and some save their state when powered off.

6.2.1.3 Linear Encoders

Encoders are also available for measuring linear motion. Some, called *string encoders* are based on attaching a spool of thin cable to the shaft. Of course, a rack and pinion mechanism can be used to convert a rotary encoder to a linear one as well.

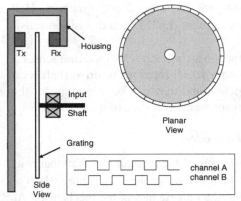

Figure 6.18 Optical Encoder. Light shines through holes in the disk when the shaft is rotated. External signal processing counts the pulses to indicate rotary position.

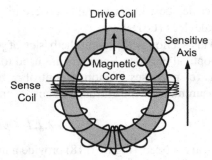

Figure 6.19 Fluxgate Magnetometer. The device compares the difference in drive current needed to saturate the core in both directions. The difference is proportional to the ambient field. Using three such devices permits the measurement of the field vector in 3D.

6.2.2 Ambient Field Sensors

6.2.2.1 Compasses and Magnetometers

A magnetic *compass* is a device that measures the direction of the ambient magnetic field. Such devices often occur on mobile robots in the form of a *magnetometer* which measures the magnitude of the local magnetic field in one or more directions (Figure 6.19).

6.2.2.1.1 Earth's Magnetic Field. The flow of the Earth's electrically conducting fluid core is believed to be the cause a weak global magnetic field whose strength is on the order of 1 gauss. By contrast, a magnet in a child's toy can be as strong as several hundred gauss. The *geographic north pole* is the point where the spin axis of the Earth pierces its surface and this is the true definition of north for navigation purposes.

The ambient field is nominally directed toward north but the Earth's magnetic field is not even close to being aligned with true north. The *magnetic variation* is the angle between the local field and geographic north and it can be surprisingly large. For example, the east coast of the United States is 15° east of north in variation.

6.2.2.1.2 Magnetic Deviation. Changes in variation are usually fairly small over a short distance so it may seem reasonable to use a magnetometer to measure changes in heading. Unfortunately, there are other effects that make doing so difficult. Magnetic metals and electromagnets (e.g., motors) produce their own fields, which add to the ambient Earth-generated field, changing its direction, and the degree of change depends on proximity to the source of corruption. Furthermore some sources will be on the robot so that the field at any point will be the vector sum of an Earth-fixed field and a robot-fixed field.

The effects of all these extra fields are called the compass *deviation*. Although deviation is complicated the main issue is that it varies over time in an unpredictable manner. The most basic requirement of any navigational field is that it be predictable and the ambient magnetic field fails the test, so it is of little use on mobile robots.

Magnetometers are used occasionally as an aid to other devices like gyros, but the errors in those devices must already be large before a magnetometer can be of much assistance.

6.2.2.2 Inclinometers

An inclinometer is an instrument that nominally indicates the direction gravity (Figure 6.20). For example, a pendulous device measure the angle of deflection of a proof mass in order to indicate the direction of gravity.

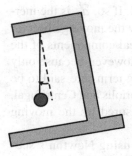

Figure 6.20 Pendulous Inclinometer. The device permits a proof mass to move under the influence of gravity and measures the angle of deflection to determine attitude. An orthogonal pair can measure pitch and roll angles.

Inexpensive devices have bandwidths on the order or 2 Hz, meaning they cannot accurately indicate attitude angles that change faster than this. A faster device implements a *rebalance loop* that prevent the sensor from responding too drastically to its inputs. A servo loop prevents motion and the effort required to prevent motion becomes a measure of the motion that would have occurred otherwise.

Although the principle is both simple and elegant, an inclinometer is another sensor that is of little use in most applications. The issue is that the device really indicates a quantity called *specific force* and not the direction of gravity at all. Imagine what happens if the device is accelerated to the right. Then it becomes clear that it is also sensitive to acceleration. So a robot using the device would think it is tilted when it is merely accelerating.

This issue is not a trivial one. It touches the heart of what is so difficult about measuring motion well with inertial sensors. The next section will provide the background necessary to resolve this problem in order to implement inertial navigation.

6.2.3 Inertial Frames of Reference

Simply put, an inertial frame is one in which Newton's laws hold. Such a frame of reference is any frame that is not rotating with respect to the stars, and that is free to move under the influence of gravitation. This is statement of a physical law as proposed by physicists and as verified in experimentation. It has very little to do with mathematics although we can use mathematics to manipulate it effectively. All of Newton's laws hold **only** in inertial frames. For the famous second law $f = ma$, two points are worth emphasis. First, the forces comprising f are those of contact (electrostatic), gravitation, nuclear and electromagnetic phenomena. There are no other forces in nature. The acceleration a is the *inertial* acceleration. Only an observer in an inertial frame observes motion according to Newton's second law, so an inertial measure of acceleration is the one that must be used in that law.

6.2.3.1 Apparent Forces

Recall the basic acceleration transformation from Equation 4.14 of Chapter 4:

$$\vec{a}_o^f = \vec{a}_o^m + \vec{a}_m^f + 2\vec{\omega}_m^f \times \vec{v}_o^m + \vec{\alpha}_m^f \times \vec{r}_o^m + \vec{\omega}_m^f \times [\vec{\omega}_m^f \times \vec{r}_o^m] \qquad (6.33)$$

Solving for the acceleration of the object relative to the moving frame:

$$\vec{a}_o^m = \vec{a}_o^f - (\vec{a}_m^f + 2\vec{\omega}_m^f \times \vec{v}_o^m + \vec{\alpha}_m^f \times \vec{r}_o^m + \vec{\omega}_m^f \times [\vec{\omega}_m^f \times \vec{r}_o^m]) \qquad (6.34)$$

Let us for the moment assume that the "fixed" frame f is inertial. If so, $\vec{a}_o^f$ is the inertial acceleration of the object o and the acceleration observed by the moving observer includes the four extra terms in the brackets. These terms are real components of the acceleration that would be measured by the moving observer. However, because only $\vec{a}_o^f$ can be explained in terms of applied forces, these remaining terms are said to be associated with *apparent forces*, and they are given names like Coriolis and Centrifugal, and so on, but they are not real forces. The acceleration measured by the moving observer is real but the apparent forces are not.

Such conjured forces are necessary only if one insists on using Newton's second law in a noninertial frame of reference. That may seem like a bad idea anyway but the practical matter is that observers, and more specifically sensors, do not usually get to choose their frame of reference. They measure what they measure and if their motion affects what they measure, those effects must be compensated somehow.

Now the central points are these. First, the surface of the Earth is not an inertial frame of reference due to its rotation about its axis once per day. Second, inertial sensors respond to inertially referenced motion. Robots using inertial sensors to measure their accelerations while operating on the surface of the Earth are not measuring their accelerations relative to the Earth. Therefore, the acceleration measurements will need to be compensated for any apparent forces in order to measure motion relative to the Earth.

6.2.3.2 Noninertial Earth-Fixed Frame of Reference

Consider a brick sitting on a table at the equator, and two different observers learning Newton's laws (Figure 6.21). One observer is fixed to the surface of the Earth. From this point of view, the weight of the brick is cancelled by the reaction of the table.

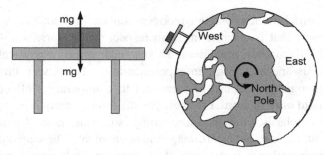

Figure 6.21 Real Forces. (Left) An Earth-fixed observer believes that the brick on the table is stationary. (Right) A stars-fixed observer sees the brick and table rotating in a giant circle once per day. For which observer does $f = ma$?

Because the sum of forces is zero, no acceleration takes place and Newton's laws are apparently satisfied. The Earth-fixed observer writes:

$$\sum \vec{F} = \vec{R} + m\vec{g} = 0 \tag{6.35}$$

Conversely a stars-fixed observer looking down on the North Pole and hovering over the Earth observes the table rotating at constant speed. From that point of view, there must be a difference between the reaction and the force of gravitation to explain the acceleration causing the brick to move in a circle:

$$\sum \vec{F} = \vec{R} + \vec{G} = m\vec{a} \tag{6.36}$$

This case illustrates the precise issue. Both formulae cannot be correct unless the real forces are different for each observer and the real forces are not different. The correct analysis is the perspective of the stars fixed observer because it is that observer, not the Earth-fixed one, for whom Newton's laws hold. If the table is at the equator, the difference between the two forces must equal $\Omega^2 R$ where Ω is the rotation of the Earth and R is the radius of the Earth. That works out to 3.5 milli-g, which seems small, but we will see that it is not small if it's integrated twice over time. For the Earth-fixed observer, we will see that $m\vec{g}$ is not just the force of gravitation on the mass. Indeed $m\vec{g} = \vec{G} - m\vec{a}$ so the two formulas are the same.

The "constant" g is, in fact, neither constant nor entirely a real force. It includes the centrifugal apparent force that is due to the rotation of the Earth. Hence, while Equation 6.35 is correct if g is suitably interpreted, it is not a direct expression of Newton's second law where the quantity $m\vec{g}$ is interpreted as a real force. It is Equation 6.36 rewritten to hide the effects of (latitude dependent) apparent forces. Those effects can be ignored in most cases but not in all.

6.2.3.2.1 Effect of Earth's Rotation. Sensitive instruments fixed to the surface of the Earth can easily detect its rotation with respect to the stars. If the brick were replaced with a 3 axis gyroscope, the gyroscope would register the rotation rate of the Earth around a locally horizontal north-pointing axis, aligned with the Earth's spin. If the output of the gyro were compensated by subtracting the Earth rate, it would read rotation rates relative to the Earth.

The Earth rotates wrt the stars about once a mean solar day whereas a sidereal day is 364/365 of solar day (4 minutes shorter) (Figure 6.22).

6.2.4 Inertial Sensors

Accelerometers and gyroscopes are of fundamental importance to the measurement of motion because they form the basis of inertial navigation. Decades ago, the

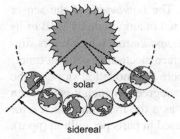

Figure 6.22 Sidereal Day. The sidereal day is slightly shorter than the solar day. Due to its circular motion around the sun, the Earth must rotate slightly farther than 360° with respect to the stars each day to return the Sun to the same position in the sky. Arrows indicate motion of Earth during each type of day.

implementation of highly accurate inertial navigation for large aerospace vehicles required the sensors to be mounted on a stable platform in order to insulate the sensitive devices from the rotational dynamics of the vehicle. The rotations required to keep the platform level were then a measure of the rotation of the vehicle.

Modern systems, however, are known as *strapdown* systems because the sensors are literally fixed to the structure of the vehicle and they undergo the same motion that the vehicle does. This modern approach has several implications. Strapdown systems need no stable table so they are much smaller. Tracking the potentially high rotation rates requires significant computation. Sensors require higher dynamic ranges as well. Some modern sensors use rebalance loops to enhance dynamic range. This section will briefly discuss small strapdown sensors that are not cost prohibitive. These sensors are most likely to be relevant to a mobile robot.

6.2.4.1 Inertial Sensor Performance

The engineering of inertial sensors is often focussed on such attributes as accuracy, environmental effects, cost, robustness, and size.

6.2.4.1.1 Accuracy. A useful model of sensor performance is:

$$f_{meas} = kf_{true} + b + w_{noise} \qquad (6.37)$$

where the key performance parameters include *scale factor k*, *bias b*, and noise w_{noise}. The best that can be done with noise is to average it and all optimal estimation systems do so as a basic aspect of their operation. We saw earlier how the Allan variance graph reveals the basic noise characteristics of an inertial sensor and the figures of merit are known as angle random walk (for gyros) and velocity random walk (for accelerometers).

6.2.4.1.2 Bias and Scale Factor. Definitions of bias and scale factor errors are further refined into components that can be compensated easily and those that cannot. *Turn-on bias* refers to the value of the bias magnitude when the sensor is first powered on and it can be further divided into a constant and a random component. *Bias repeatability* refers to the variation of turn-on bias. This can be important for systems that must perform special initialization processing. *In-run bias stability* refers to the random variation that occurs during operation. It may be less than bias repeatability because, for example, in-run temperature is more stable than turn-on temperature.

Bias stability refers to the best possible variation of in-run bias if the sensor is optimally modelled. All of the above variations on bias can be defined for scale factor errors as well and all may be quoted as functions of temperature or time.

6.2.4.1.3 Bandwidth, Linearity and Dynamic Range. The *bandwidth* of the sensor refers to the frequency at which an input signal is attenuated in amplitude by 3 dB of its unattenuated value (Figure 4.30). It is often confused with *update rate* which refers simply to the number of frames of data produced by the interface electronics per unit time.

Whereas scale factor error refers to the situation where the modelled slope of the input-output curve is incorrect, *nonlinearity* refers to the degree to which it is not even a straight line (Figure 5.2). Nonlinearity is often quoted as a the maximum such error magnitude divided by the full scale output, perhaps expressed in parts per million (ppm).

Saturation is an extreme form of nonlinearity that will occur when the dynamic range of the device is exceeded.

6.2.4.1.4 Alignment and Cross Coupling. It is typically the case that each sensitive axis is slightly sensitive to inputs that are nominally orthogonal to it. This phenomenon may be due to alignment errors of the whole package, of a single axis, or it may be intrinsic to the device.

6.2.4.1.5 Environmental Sensitivity. Inertial sensors are generally sensitive to environmental effects including temperature, shock, and vibration. The term *g-dependent bias* refers to the sensitivity of a gyro to acceleration. *Cross coupling errors* arise when a sensor that is designed to be sensitive to motion along one axis is also somewhat sensitive to motion in an orthogonal direction.

6.2.4.2 Accelerometers

The situation in the brick-on-table example (Figure 6.21) is somewhat more complex. If the brick were replaced with an accelerometer, it would not measure just the 3.5 milli-g mentioned above. It would measure essentially 1 g because "accelerometers" do not measure acceleration. A more complicated form of compensation is necessary to produce the acceleration of the device relative to the surface of the Earth as described below.

6.2.4.2.1 Operating Principle. All accelerometers operate on the principle of measuring the relative displacement of a small mass attached to the instrument case by an elastic, viscous, or electromagnetic restraint (Figure 6.23). A transducer returns a signal proportional to the displacement of the proof mass. Typically, the mass is only allowed a single degree of freedom, which may be either linear or rotary.

6.2.4.2.2 Specific Force. The indicated deflection of the elastic restraint is directly influenced by the ***tension in the spring*** – and that tension is a response to the vector ***sum*** of acceleration and gravity acting along the sensitive axis of the device. Writing Newton's second law for the proof mass:

$$\vec{T} + \vec{W} = m\vec{a}^i \tag{6.38}$$

where $\vec{a}^i$ is the inertial acceleration and $\vec{W}$ is the weight of the mass. Solving for the applied force and dividing by the proof mass gives:

$$\vec{t} = \frac{\vec{T}}{m} = \vec{a}^i - \frac{\vec{W}}{m} \tag{6.39}$$

The classical substitution $\vec{W} = m\vec{g}$ where $\vec{g}$ is the "acceleration due to gravity" has deliberately not been performed because we will want to understand this substitution in more detail.

We call the applied nongravitational force $\vec{T}$ divided by the proof mass magnitude the *specific force* $\vec{t}$. Note especially that specific force output includes the magnitude of the local gravitational force $\vec{W}$. The equation is a vector sum and the sign of the gravitational force is reversed because a gravity field pointing down is the equivalent, by Einstein's principle of equivalence, to an acceleration directed upward.

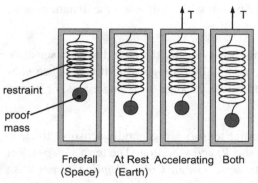

Freefall   At Rest Accelerating Both
(Space)   (Earth)

Figure 6.23 Accelerometer Principle. Out in space, moving freely under the influence of gravitation, the device produces no output. When at rest on Earth or when accelerating upward in space at 1 g, the device produces an output of 1 g. When accelerating upward at 1 g near the surface of the Earth, the device outputs 2 g.

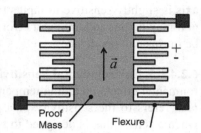

Proof   Flexure
Mass

Figure 6.24 In-Plane MEMS Accelerometer. A large number of comb fingers are placed so as to increase the net capacitance of the device. An applied force causes deflection of the flexures and hence changes in the finger gaps.

6.2.4.2.3 MEMS Accelerometers.
MEMS (Micro ElectroMechanical Systems) technology has advanced dramatically in the last decade. MEMS inertial sensors apply semiconductor design and fabrication principles to the construction of microscopic mechanical systems that vibrate and deflect in order to sense motion. MEMS accelerometers are already very well established. There are several design categories. One that is easy to understand is the in-plane (lateral) mass displacement design (Figure 6.24). In this case, a proof mass is mounted on flexures and permitted to deflect under acceleration in such a way as to change the gaps between comb fingers, and hence the overall capacitance between all pairs of fingers.

Vibratory versions of this principle cause the proof mass to oscillate in the plane of the wafer and the application of external acceleration can be sensed as a change in the resonant frequency of the device. As of this writing, these sensors have biases on the order of 1 mg and noise densities on the order of 10 mg/rt-Hz. Technology continues to improve and sensors significantly better than this have also been demonstrated.

6.2.4.3 Gyroscopes

Gyroscopes are devices that are used to measure angular velocity and the laws of physics are such that they can only do so with respect to an inertial frame of reference. As is the case for accelerometers, a wide variety of sensor technologies exist.

6.2.4.3.1 Mechanical Gyroscope.
The most basic gyroscope, or *gyro*, configuration is the original mechanical gyroscope – a spinning rotor. A rotor is a mass exhibiting rotational symmetry. Such geometry is necessary by the law of conservation of angular momentum to keep the spin axis fixed in inertial space – the natural rotational motion of asymmetric bodies is tumbling, not spinning.

This property of *rigidity* of the spin axis gives rise to a second property called *precession* that governs how the gyro responds to applied torques trying to rotate its spin axis (Figure 6.25).

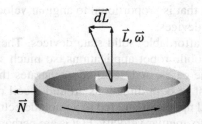

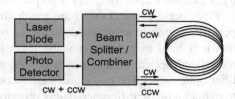

Figure 6.25 Gyro Precession Principle. The response to a torque applied orthogonal to the input axis is a rotation around the third axis orthogonal to the other two. In this case, the gyro rotates around an axis out of the page.

Figure 6.26 Fiber Optic Gyroscope. Two counterotating beams are combined after many circuits around a fiber optic coil. The Sagnac effect gives rise to a phase shift, which is magnified by the number of turns in the coil.

Consider Euler's equation applied to a spinning rotor:

$$\vec{N} = \frac{d\vec{L}^i}{dt} = \frac{d(I^i\vec{\omega})}{dt}$$

where $\vec{N}$ is the applied torque, $\vec{L}^i$ is the angular momentum with respect to inertial space, I^i is the inertia tensor expressed in an inertial frame and $\vec{\omega}$ is the angular velocity of the rotor. As the figure shows, the formula implies that any **changes** in momentum $d\vec{L}^i$, and hence (for symmetric bodies) any changes in angular velocity, must be aligned with the applied torque $\vec{N}$. This means that the response of the rotor to a torque applied normal to the spin axis is to rotate its angular velocity about an axis that is normal to both the spin axis and the applied torque.

6.2.4.3.2 Dynamically Tuned Gyros.
Mechanical gyros have been refined over decades of engineering in order to reduce drift rates and improve reliability and life. One form of mechanical gyro that is relevant to mobile robots is the dynamically tuned gyro (DTG). These are similar to a bare rotor above but two pairs of flexible pivots are used to form a kind of universal joint that suspends the rotor around a shaft that spins with the rotor. At a particular rotational speed of the spin axis, the stiffness of the pivots essentially vanishes and the device functions in a near ideal fashion. DTGs have been very successful in the first generation of strapdown inertial systems. They are low cost, small (a few cc's in volume), rugged sensors with bias stabilities under 1°/hr and ARW around 0.1°/rt-hr. Sensors with bias stabilities as low as 0.01°/hr can be constructed.

6.2.4.3.3 Optical Gyroscopes.
Contemporary optical gyroscopes fall into two categories: the ring laser gyro and the fiber optic gyro. Both are based on a measurement principle called the Sagnac effect that mixes two counterotating beams of light in order to extract a signal that is proportional to angular velocity (Figure 6.26). In effect, when the device rotates around its sensitive axis, photons rotating on one direction experience a longer path length and those in the other direction experience a shortened path length. When the two beams are mixed, measurable interference occurs if it is amplified significantly.

In the case of the ring laser gyro (RLG), the "ring" in which the beams are travelling is fixed with a lasing medium and the ring itself is also a laser. When the two beams are combined, a beat frequency is created that is proportional to angular velocity. RLGs are expensive, very high performance devices.

Fiber optic gyros (FOGs) are much simpler, affordable, solid state devices. Their performance is more than adequate for most mobile robot applications, so much so that it is hard to justify not using them in some cases. A laser diode generates the modulated optical signal, which is split and sent in both directions around a coil of fiber optic cable. The two signals are recombined upon exit and fed to a photodetector to extract a phase difference that is proportional to angular velocity. FOGs are perhaps the highest performance technology that is placed on mobile robots today. Bias stabilities are on the order of 1°/ hr with very low ARW around 1 mrad/rt-hr.

6.2.4.3.4 MEMS gyros. Some very good MEMS gyroscopes are based on the comb drive tuning fork principle developed at Draper labs and licensed to many manufacturers (Figure 6.27). The fundamental principle is to induce a velocity of a mass in one direction and then sense the movement in an orthogonal direction that is caused by the Coriolis force when the device is rotated. Of course, a proof mass cannot be translated very far inside a sensor housing, so practical devices are based on vibrating the proof mass using sinusoidal drive velocities.

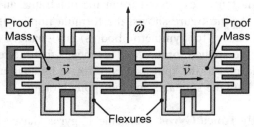

Figure 6.27 MEMS "Tuning Fork" Gyro. In this case, the comb fingers operate as tiny electrostatic motors inducing the required oscillations. Darker areas are fixed with respect to the instrument housing. Lighter areas nominally oscillate left and right out of phase. If the sensor is rotated around the vertical axis of the page, the two proof masses will oscillate into and out of the page due to the induced Coriolis force. Capacitor plates above and below each of the masses are used to sense the out of plane motion.

Using the Coriolis acceleration term from Equation 4.14 allows us to conclude that the apparent force acting on a translating mass m as observed in the frame of reference of the moving sensor itself is given by:

$$\vec{f}_{cor} = m(2\vec{\omega}_m^f \times \vec{v}_o^m) \tag{6.40}$$

If the device is driven by a sinusoidal force, any rotation around an orthogonal axis will cause a sinusoidal orthogonal motion. The designation *tuning fork* is used because two proof masses are used that are driven to oscillate precisely out of phase with each other.

The induced motion is sensed capacitively or piezoelectrically (for quartz gyros) and the signal is demodulated to produce turn rate. Contemporary (i.e., as of publication) *tactical grade* gyros have bias stabilities on the order of 1°/hr and an ARW around 0.1° /rt-hr.

6.2.4.4 Inertial Measurement Units

An inertial measurement unit (IMU) is an arrangement of accelerometers and gyroscopes into a compact package intended for the purpose of measuring linear and angular motions in all three directions at the same time. For vehicles that operate on uneven, nonflat surfaces, an IMU will typically be required to correctly measure their attitude. Whereas three gyros are nominally all that is required to measure orientation, the capacity of accelerometers to indicate the direction of gravity turns out to be a very important method for removing accumulated attitude error.

Some sources of error are unique to IMU configurations. The sensitive axes cannot be arranged perfectly, so alignment errors may need attention in some cases. Likewise, the position and orientation of the IMU on the vehicle may need to be well calibrated. Orientation is important for processing perception data and the linear velocity and acceleration of the IMU will differ from those of the vehicle frame unless the IMU is placed exactly at the origin of the body frame and this is typically not possible or convenient.

Small inexpensive IMUs that combine the sensors mentioned above are becoming very common. Many come configured for computer interfacing. A very small IMU based entirely on quartz components was announced in the 1990s. Consumer applications have driven the development of small low performance IMUs with serial data interfaces.

Contemporary small IMUs achieve three axis sensitivity either by combining in-plane and out-of-plane sensors or by physically mounting them in a 3D configuration. A single chip containing three gyros has already been produced and a single chip with three accelerometers has also been produced. The development of a complete IMU on a single chip seems to be an inevitable outcome in the very near future if it has not happened already.

6.2.5 References and Further Reading

Bornstein is a source specifically concentrating on sensors for robotics. Barbour is a recent source for information on inertial sensors. Dyer is a comprehensive and recently update survey of sensors of all kinds including modern inertial sensors. Kissell is one example of a source on instrumentation for process control. El-Sheimy is perhaps the earliest use of Allan variance to characterize MEMS sensor performance. The related IEEE standard is quoted below.

[7] N. Barbour, Inertial Navigation Sensors, NATO RTO Lecture Series-232, Advances in Navigation Sensors and Integration Technology, Oct. 2003.

[8] J. Bornstein, H. R. Everett, and L. Feng, Where Am I? Sensors and Methods for Autonomous Mobile Robot Positioning, University of Michigan Report, 1996.

[9] Stephen A. Dyer, Survey of Instrumentation and Measurement, Wiley, 2001.

[10] N. El-Sheimy, H. Hou, and X. Niu, Analysis and Modeling of Inertial Sensors Using Allan Variance," IEEE Transactions on Instrumentation and Measurement, Vol. 57, No. 1, pp. 140–149, 2008.

[11] Thomas E. Kissell, Industrial Electronics: Applications for Programmable Controllers, Instrumentation and Process Control, and Electrical Machines and Motor Controls, 3/E, Prentice-Hall, 2003.

[12] IEEE Std 952-1997, Guide and Test Procedure for Single Axis Interferometric Fiber Optic Gyros, IEEE, 1997, p. 63.

6.2.6 Exercises

6.2.6.1 Accelerometers

An accelerometer is bolted to the floor of an elevator. Initially, the elevator is at rest and the accelerometer output is 1g. Describe the magnitude of the output of the device when:

(i) The elevator falls freely without friction under the influence of the gravity field it is in.
(ii) The elevator accelerates in air under the influence of gravity until it reaches its terminal velocity.
(iii) The elevator travels at constant speed determined by its terminal velocity.

6.2.6.2 Sagnac Effect

Although optical measurement of inertial translation is impossible (see the famous Michelson-Morely experiment), optical measurement of inertial rotation, paradoxically, is possible. The Sagnac effect, on which optical gyros are based, is such a small effect that it was considered an academic curiosity until ways to amplify it were found. The principle is that physical rotation of a ring interferometer gives rise to an apparent path length difference for two counter-rotating coherent beams of light.

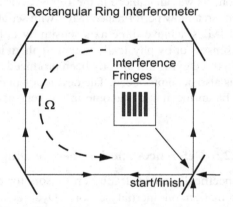

Rectangular Ring Interferometer

There are three intuitive ways to understand the effect: difference in path length, difference in time of transit, or a Doppler frequency shift. Either causes a relative phase shift of the two beams, which in turn causes interference when they are recombined after the transit. Although Einstein's relativity is needed to understand these devices well, an intuitive derivation of the path length difference provides the right answer. Compute the transit time difference and then the path length difference for a ring 0.1 meter in radius rotating at a speed of 1 °/ second. Show that the Sagnac effect gives about 1/100 nanometers ($1 \times 10^{-11} m$) of deviation. A sheet of paper is about 10 million of these "centi-nanometers" thick!

6.3 Inertial Navigation Systems

6.3.1 Introduction

Inertial navigation in some form is of fundamental importance to mobile robots operating on nonflat terrain. Although mobile robots need to know their attitude for safety reasons, they especially need attitude to correctly process perception sensor data. Attitude cannot be measured well during acceleration with accelerometers (inclinometers) due to the equivalence principle, so compensation for apparent forces is required. Doing so requires gyroscopes anyway because the apparent forces depend on angular velocity. Once accelerometers and gyroscopes are included in the pose estimation sensor suite, it becomes a matter of software to extract all of their value in the form of an inertial navigation solution. In this way, naive approaches to the problem are driven toward a complete inertial solution.

The strengths of inertial navigation are profound. It requires no infrastructure so it applies to missions of unlimited excursion. It can be used anywhere where gravity is known and it has already been used on the scale of the solar system. It is jamproof because it needs no external communication and it exhibits perfect stealth because it radiates nothing. This "box" that simply knows where it is, is an impressive piece of technology, particularly when we compare it with the global infrastructure necessary for satellite navigation.

The weaknesses of inertial navigation are those of dead reckoning. It requires initial conditions and these are not always easy to acquire. Also, when no other sensors are used, errors grow in an essentially unbounded fashion with time. This section will develop the mathematics of inertial navigation from first principles and present a simple estimation system.

6.3.2 Mathematics of Inertial Navigation

The fundamental idea of inertial navigation is to measure the acceleration of the vehicle in each of three orthogonal directions and to integrate twice with respect to time to compute position. If one tries strapping three accelerometers to a vehicle and double integrating their outputs, it will quickly become clear that this does not work. Furthermore, it is striking just how wrong this naive concept is. There are three things wrong with this concept.

First, accelerometers measure the wrong quantity. Specific force is not acceleration ($\vec{f} \neq \vec{a}$) so the effect of gravity has to be removed from the accelerometer readings. Second, the acceleration component of specific force is measured with respect to the wrong reference frame. An inertial frame of reference is not the Earth ($\vec{a}_v^i \neq \vec{a}_v^e$), so apparent forces must be removed. Third, the accelerations are represented in the wrong coordinate system. A body fixed coordinate system is not Earth fixed $^v\bar{a}_e^v \neq {}^e\bar{a}_e^v$, so all readings must be converted to an Earth-fixed coordinate system before they are integrated. The next several pages will address these issues in sequence.

6.3.2.1 First Fix: Convert Specific Force to Acceleration

An accelerometer is a specific force transducer because the calibrated restraint responds to force in the spring (which is not the net force on the mass). We can solve Equation 6.39 for the inertial acceleration to express it in terms of the specific force and gravitational force as follows:

$$\vec{a}^i = \frac{\vec{T}}{m} + \frac{\vec{W}}{m} = \vec{t} + \vec{w} \tag{6.41}$$

At this point, (if gravitation is known), it is possible to convert the specific force into inertial acceleration, so that it can be integrated. Explicit knowledge of the gravitational field strength is required at every position of the vehicle. Inertial navigation is only viable when this field is known (or known to be insignificant). Otherwise, gravitational forces will be confused with inertial acceleration. For example, a vertically oriented accelerometer on a table will "think" it is accelerating upward at 1 g.

6.3.2.2 Second Fix: Remove Apparent Forces

A moving vehicle with sensors mounted on it amounts to a moving reference frame. In such a strapdown configuration, the accelerometers will experience apparent forces due to both the rotation of the Earth and the rotation of the vehicle, as described earlier. The equations of inertial navigation are essentially the acceleration transformation developed in Equation 4.14 with the specific force equation above substituted into it.

Let there be three frames of reference of interest. An inertial frame, denoted i is positioned at the center of the Earth but is not rotating with respect to the stars. The Earth frame, denoted e, is also positioned at the center of the Earth but it rotates with the Earth. The vehicle frame, denoted v is positioned at the center of the accelerometer triad in the IMU and it rotates with them.

Let $\vec{r}_v^x$, $\vec{v}_v^x$, and $\vec{a}_v^x$ be the position vector, velocity, and acceleration of the vehicle measured with respect to the frame x. We will formulate the equations so that they can be integrated easily in the Earth frame.

A vehicle frame integration would be more appropriate for vehicles that move on a global scale – due to the associated simplicity of extracting latitude and longitude. Equation 4.14 of Chapter 4 is:

$$\vec{a}_o^f = \vec{a}_o^m + \vec{a}_m^f + 2\vec{\omega}_m^f \times \vec{v}_o^m + \vec{\alpha}_m^f \times \vec{r}_o^m + \vec{\omega}_m^f \times [\vec{\omega}_m^f \times \vec{r}_o^m] \tag{6.42}$$

Let the object frame o be identified with the vehicle frame v. Let the moving frame m be identified with the Earth frame e. Let the fixed frame f be identified with the inertial frame i. Then $\vec{a}_m^f = \vec{a}_e^i = 0$ and $\vec{\alpha}_m^f = \vec{\alpha}_e^i = 0$ and this substitution of frame names gives:

$$\vec{a}_v^i = \vec{a}_v^e + 2\vec{\omega}_e^i \times \vec{v}_v^e + \vec{\omega}_e^i \times [\vec{\omega}_e^i \times \vec{r}_v^e] \tag{6.43}$$

Let the constant rotation of the Earth with respect to inertial space be given by $\vec{\omega}_e^i = \vec{\Omega}$. Moving Earth-referenced acceleration to the left-hand side gives:

$$\vec{a}_v^e = \vec{a}_v^i - 2\vec{\Omega} \times \vec{v}_v^e - \vec{\Omega} \times (\vec{\Omega} \times \vec{r}_v^e) \tag{6.44}$$

Substituting the specific force equation (Equation 6.41) gives:

$$\vec{a}_v^e = \vec{t} - 2\vec{\Omega} \times \vec{v}_v^e + \vec{w} - \vec{\Omega} \times (\vec{\Omega} \times \vec{r}_v^e) \tag{6.45}$$

The quantity $\vec{w} - \vec{\Omega} \times (\vec{\Omega} \times \vec{r}_v^e)$ is known as *gravity* and denoted $\vec{g}$ as discussed below. The following is one of the most convenient forms of the equation of motion of the vehicle. We will consider it to be **the** equation of inertial navigation.

$$\vec{a}_v^e = \left(\frac{d\vec{v}_v^e}{dt}\right)_e = \vec{t} - 2\vec{\Omega} \times \vec{v}_v^e + \vec{g} \qquad (6.46)$$

Spotlight 6.1 Inertial Navigation: Part 1.

This is the basic equation of inertial navigation. Gravity and the Coriolis force are subtracted from specific force.

The quantity $\vec{a}_v^e = (d\vec{v}_v^e)/dt\big|_e$ means the derivative of $\vec{v}_v^e$ as it would be measured by an Earth-fixed observer. We need this derivative to be the Earth-fixed one in order to be able to integrate it.

Equation 6.46 is solved for the quantities of interest by integrating them. The equations are only valid if they are integrated in the Earth frame (meaning in any coordinate system fixed in the Earth frame):

$$\vec{v}_v^e = \int_0^t [\vec{t} - 2\vec{\Omega} \times \vec{v}_v^e + \vec{g}] dt\big|_e + \vec{v}_v^e(t_0) \qquad \vec{r}_v^e = \int_0^t \vec{v}_v^e dt\big|_e + \vec{r}_v^e(t_0) \qquad (6.47)$$

Spotlight 6.2 Inertial Navigation: Part 2.

Acceleration is integrated twice to get velocity and then position.

The notation $\int dt\big|_x$ is intended to be the opposite of $d/dt\big|_x$. Just as a vector derivative subtracts finite vectors to produce a differential one, a vector integral adds differential vectors to produce a finite one. The sums and differences can be accomplished computationally using any coordinate system. However, only the derivative $(d\vec{v}_v^e)/dt\big|_e$ is $\vec{a}_v^e$ and only the integral $\int \vec{v}_v^e dt\big|_e$ is $\vec{r}_v^e$.

These equations can be solved for the unknown position, and velocity, given a model of the Earth's acceleration due to gravity $\vec{g}$, the Earth's sidereal rate of rotation $\vec{\Omega}$, the specific forces $\vec{t}$ from the accelerometers, and the initial position $\vec{r}_v^e(t_0)$ and velocity $\vec{v}_v^e(t_0)$.

6.3.2.2.1 Vector Formulation of Inertial Navigation. These equations remove centrifugal and Coriolis forces and then they perform two integrations incorporating initial conditions (Figure 6.28):

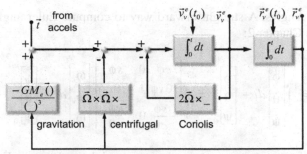

Figure 6.28 Inertial Navigation. The basic equations of inertial navigation are illustrated in coordinate system independent terms.

6.3.2.2.2 Gravity and Gravitation. *Gravity* is defined as the force per unit mass required to keep a test mass in the same position relative to the Earth. *Gravitation*, however, is the force that's proportional to the masses of interacting bodies as expressed by Newton's law of gravitation:

$$\vec{W} = \frac{\vec{w}}{m} = -\left[\frac{GM_e}{\left|\vec{r}_v^e\right|^3}\vec{r}_v^e\right]$$

An object fixed to the surface of the Earth experiences a centrifugal force as viewed from a reference frame spinning with the Earth. Due to this apparent force, a plumb bob at mid latitudes on the surface of the Earth does not point toward its center but is rather displaced slightly toward the equator (Figure 6.29).

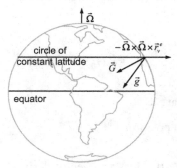

Figure 6.29 Gravity and Gravitation. A plumb bob on the surface of the Earth experiences an apparent centrifugal force that varies with latitude. Only at the equator and the poles does gravity point toward the center of the Earth. Only at the poles does the apparent force vanish.

Gravity therefore depends on latitude. It also depends on the precise shape and mass distribution of the Earth. For this reason, it is important to use the correct local value for gravity, and it can be obtained from tables or a formula.

6.3.2.3 Third Fix: Adopt Coordinate Systems

In order to integrate the equations of motion, all vector quantities must first be expressed in an Earth-fixed coordinate system. Although the vectors $\vec{g}$ and $\bar{\Omega}$ are already known in the Earth frame, the vectors $\vec{t}$ and $\bar{\omega}$ are being measured in the vehicle frame. Inertial navigation systems use gyroscopes to measure the angular velocity of the vehicle and then integrate it to produce the orientation information necessary to convert coordinates. The associated computations may proceed at 500 Hz or even faster.

6.3.2.3.1 Euler Angles. A straightforward way to compute Euler angles is based on Equation 2.74 in Chapter 2:

$$\begin{bmatrix}\phi\\\theta\\\psi\end{bmatrix} = \int_0^t\begin{bmatrix}\dot\phi\\\dot\theta\\\dot\psi\end{bmatrix}dt + \begin{bmatrix}\phi\\\theta\\\psi\end{bmatrix}_0 = \int_0^t\begin{bmatrix}c\phi & 0 & s\phi\\ t\theta s\phi & 1 & -t\theta c\phi\\ -\frac{s\phi}{c\theta} & 0 & \frac{c\phi}{c\theta}\end{bmatrix}\begin{bmatrix}\omega_x\\\omega_y\\\omega_z\end{bmatrix}dt + \begin{bmatrix}\phi\\\theta\\\psi\end{bmatrix}_0 \tag{6.48}$$

The precise transformation to appear in the integrand depends on the Euler angle conventions in effect, but the above assumes a z-y-x sequence. Let us define for later, the matrix that converts coordinates from the vehicle frame angular velocity to Euler angle rates:

$$\mathcal{R}_v^n = \begin{bmatrix} c\phi & 0 & s\phi \\ t\theta s\phi & 1 & -t\theta c\phi \\ -\dfrac{s\phi}{c\theta} & 0 & \dfrac{c\phi}{c\theta} \end{bmatrix} \tag{6.49}$$

6.3.2.3.2 Direction Cosine Matrix. An alternative is to work in terms of the rotation matrix R_v^e itself. To generate the direction cosine matrix expressing the rotation matrix from the vehicle to the navigation frame, based on Equation 2.76 in Chapter 2, one computes:

$$\begin{aligned} \delta\Theta &= \omega\delta t & \delta\Theta &= \left|\underline{\delta\Theta}\right| \\ f_1(\delta\Theta) &= \frac{\sin\delta\Theta}{\delta\Theta} & f_2(\delta\Theta) &= \frac{(1-\cos\delta\Theta)}{\delta\Theta^2} \\ R_{k+1}^k &= I + f_1(\delta\Theta)[\underline{\delta\Theta}]^\times + f_2(\delta\Theta)\left([\underline{\delta\Theta}]^\times\right)^2 \\ R_{k+1}^n &= R_k^n R_{k+1}^k \end{aligned} \tag{6.50}$$

Spotlight 6.3 Jordan's Orientation Update.

This is an exact and very efficient mechanism to update orientation in the form of a direction cosine matrix based directly on the angular velocity.

6.3.2.3.3 Attitude Quaternion. Equivalently, based on Equation 2.132 in Chapter 2, a quaternion encoding attitude can be updated directly from angular velocity with:

$$\begin{aligned} \delta\Theta &= \omega\delta t & \delta\Theta &= \left|\underline{\delta\Theta}\right| \\ \tilde{q}_{k+1}^k &= \cos\delta\Theta[I] + \sin\delta\Theta\left[\left(^\times[\tilde{\omega}_b]\right)/|\vec{\omega}_b|\right] \\ \tilde{q}_{k+1}^n &= \tilde{q}_{k+1}^k \tilde{q}_k^n \end{aligned} \tag{6.51}$$

6.3.2.3.4 Earth Rate Compensation. If the frequency of aiding is such that the effects of Earth rate $\overrightarrow{\Omega}$ will matter, the above computations will need to be augmented to subtract Earth rate from the sensed angular velocity after it has been converted from Earth-fixed coordinates to the body frame:

$$^v\underline{\omega}_v^e = {}^v\underline{\omega}_v^i - R_e^v R_i^e \underline{\Omega}_e^i$$

If the Earth-fixed coordinate system e in use is locally level, the expression of Earth rate will depend on the latitude via R_i^e. It will depend on the azimuth (yaw) as well but the component oriented around the local vertical is often the only important component and that component is independent of azimuth. Attitude will be determined from gravity sensed by the accelerometers anyway.

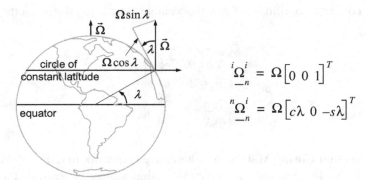

$${}^{i}\underline{\Omega}_{n}^{i} = \Omega\begin{bmatrix} 0 & 0 & 1 \end{bmatrix}^{T}$$

$${}^{n}\underline{\Omega}_{n}^{i} = \Omega\begin{bmatrix} c\lambda & 0 & -s\lambda \end{bmatrix}^{T}$$

Figure 6.30 Earth Rate Compensation. The expression of earth rate in both a geocentric and a tangent plane North, East, Down (NED) coordinate system is shown. The projection onto the local vertical is the component that must be removed for precision work if no other aiding does so already.

6.3.2.3.5 Position and Velocity. The inertial navigation equation is then implemented as:

$$\underline{v}_{v}^{e} = \int_{0}^{t}[R_{v}^{e}\underline{t} + \underline{g} - 2\underline{\Omega} \times \underline{v}_{v}^{e}]dt + \underline{v}_{v}^{e}(t_{0}) \tag{6.52}$$

Position is then computed from the velocity as follows:

$$\underline{r}_{v}^{e} = \int_{0}^{t}\underline{v}_{v}^{e}dt + \underline{r}_{v}^{e}(t_{0}) \tag{6.53}$$

More precise methods for computing both of these states are available in the publications of Savage [14][15].

6.3.3 Errors and Aiding in Inertial Navigation

Inertial navigation is rarely used alone because it is still dead reckoning and subject to nominally unbounded error growth. If other sensors besides the IMU are used, they are called *aiding* sensors, and the system is called an *aided inertial navigation system*. Inertial navigation used without aiding sensors is called *free inertial*. This section characterizes the errors that occur in an INS.

6.3.3.1 Error Propagation in Free Inertial Mode

It is natural to question whether all of the correction terms in the navigation equations are necessary as some are very small in magnitude. They are more necessary than intuition may suggest because the double integration of acceleration that occurs in an INS gives rise to an extreme sensitivity to small errors in acceleration.

For a vehicle at the equator, moving eastward at a velocity of 10 meters per second, and accelerating at 0.1 g, Table 6.2 gives the magnitude of each term:

Table 6.2 Navigation Equation Term Magnitudes

Term Name	Expression	Nominal Value
specific force	$\vec{f}$	0.1 g
gravitational	$\vec{g}$	1.0 g
centrifugal	$\vec{\Omega} \times \vec{\Omega} \times \vec{r}_v^e$	3.5×10^{-3} g
Coriolis	$2\Omega \times \vec{v}_v^e$	1.5×10^{-4} g

It may seem that the last two terms can be neglected. However, the process of integration multiplies acceleration by the square of time. After 1 hour, neglecting the Coriolis term will generate just under 9.5 kilometers of accumulated position error. Likewise, neglecting the centrifugal term will generate 220 km of accumulated error if the vehicle drives continuously for an hour. These effects also do not account for the fact that the Earth itself rotates 15° an hour and the gyros will measure this rotation and bend the computed trajectory by an amount that depends on latitude.

Vehicles such as aircraft and submarines move around on the global scale so their inertial systems must model the curvature of the Earth and the rotation of the gravity vector due to large excursions over the surface. In free inertial mode, it can be shown that recomputing gravity as a function of position converts the error growth rate from quadratic in time to an oscillatory behavior with a period of 84 minutes. Hence, it has a stabilizing effect and it bounds horizontal error. The cost of this effect is that it has a corresponding destabilizing effect on vertical error, converting it to a very undesirable exponential growth. For limited excursion vehicles like mobile robots that model the Earth as locally flat, a quadratic error model is more appropriate.

6.3.3.2 Aided Inertial Mode

How much the above compensation terms matter in practice depends strongly on the availability of other aiding sensors and on the accuracy requirements. Extra sensors can often remove these cumulative errors, but it is also very valuable to be able to reduce pose errors as much as possible for as long as possible in situations where aiding sensors like satellite navigation are unavailable.

Of course, accelerometers and gyros are not ideal and accelerometers with 1 milli-g of bias and gyros with 10°/hr bias are not uncommon as of publication. This means that even if the compensation terms are used, there may still be sensor errors whose equivalent effects are even worse and aiding sensors are still desirable in order to remove the effects of such errors.

Some of the aiding sensors that are relevant to mobile robots include such position fixes as satellite navigation (GPS), landmarks, and all other forms of map aids. Velocity aids include odometry, wheel/track speed, and zero velocity updates (Zupts). Zupts are pseudomeasurements of zero velocity that are produced when the system knows it is stationary – even if some sensors are still reading motion.

Mobile robots can usually perform occasional zero velocity updates and some form of odometry is typically available. Both of these aiding sources can be used to bound the magnitude of velocity errors and resolve sensor biases. The net effect of velocity aiding is to convert the error dynamics from that of free inertial to that of odometry. Hence, the analyses provided in Section 6.1.5 for odometry systems apply to velocity aided inertial navigation systems.

6.3.3.3 *Initialization*

When GPS or other map-based pose fixes are available, obtaining the initial position is easy. However, the initialization of an INS is not an easy matter in the general case. For mobile robots, navigation relative to any locally level frame of reference is usually adequate, and the initial position can often be used as the origin of the frame – so the initial position is defined to be the origin. If global position is unknown, it may still be useful to directly provide the system with its latitude. Once latitude is known, gravity is known from an ellipsoid model. However, knowledge of longitude as well will permit use of more accurate tables of gravity.

Computing initial attitude is one reason why knowing local gravity is important. The correct value includes the correct value for the latitude-dependent centrifugal term. Any remaining disagreement between the predicted accelerometer readings and the actual ones will be caused by both errors in attitude and biases in the accelerometers. A milli-g accelerometer turn-on bias causes a milliradian error in computed attitude, so provided the biases are small, an excellent initial attitude can be generated. A second reason for desiring accurate local gravity is the fact that it is fixed in the Earth frame whereas errors in the z accelerometer are fixed in the vehicle frame. Gravity errors will appear as accelerometer biases that move around in the vehicle frame when vehicle attitude changes.

Knowing absolute north-relative yaw may not matter unless Earth rate terms are used, so it can often be set to zero in those cases. Initial north-relative yaw is very difficult to determine without inferring it from a sequence of pose fixes. If knowing absolute yaw does matter, it is possible in principle to average the gyro outputs when the system is stationary in order to resolve yaw from the projection of Earth rate into the vehicle frame (called *gyrocompassing*). Typically, however, the gyros are not good enough for this process because their turn-on biases must be a very small fraction of Earth rate in order to resolve it.

6.3.3.4 *Kalman Filters for INS*

The Kalman filter was adopted quickly by the guidance community after it was invented. The typical formulation of the filter for an INS includes states for the errors in the gyros and accelerometers as well as the position, velocity, and orientation of the INS.

In such a formulation, regular pose fixes make it possible to resolve the biases of all of the sensors. Even regular zupts or velocity measurements make it possible to resolve some or all of the errors in the accelerometers and the attitude gyros in a Kalman filter. With velocity aiding, however, the bias of the azimuth gyro only becomes observable under sufficiently dynamic conditions.

The typical formulation of an INS filter is a feedback complementary one, but we will use the more straightforward EKF with deterministic inputs and error states.

6.3.3.4.1 State Model. The state vector contains 15 elements divided into 5 subvectors as follows:

$$\underline{x} = \left[\underline{\Psi} \ \delta^v \underline{\omega} \ {}^n \underline{r} \ {}^n \underline{v} \ \delta^v \underline{f} \right]^V \tag{6.54}$$

The notation M^V (capital V) for matrix M appends all columns of matrix M to form a column vector. $\underline{\Psi}$ is the Euler angle orientation, ${}^n \underline{r}$ is the position, and ${}^n \underline{v}$ is the velocity of the vehicle with respect to the navigation frame. The other two groups are error states associated with the gyros $\delta^v\omega$ and the accelerometers $\delta^v f$. These are expressed in the vehicle frame because the sensors are strapdown. To be more precise, these are in IMU coordinates but we assume the IMU is aligned with the vehicle axes.

The navigation equations provided earlier constitute the system model of the Kalman filter. The origin of the navigation frame is defined here as the position at which the INS was turned on. The accelerometers and gyros are considered to be deterministic inputs in order to track high frequency motions, so the inputs are $\underline{u} = \begin{bmatrix} ^v\omega & ^v f \end{bmatrix}^V$.

When the system model is executed, the error estimates, forming the $\underline{x}$ part of $f(\underline{x}, \underline{u})$ are subtracted from these inertial sensor readings, forming the $\underline{u}$ part. The system differential equation is given in Equation 6.55. Note that R_v^n and $\tilde{R}_v^n$ and very different matrices.

$$\dot{x} = \begin{bmatrix} \mathfrak{R}_v^n({}^v\omega - \delta^v\omega - R_n^{v} {}^n\Omega) \\ 0 \\ \underline{v} \\ R_v^n({}^v f - \delta^v f) - 2{}^n\Omega \times {}^n\underline{v} + {}^n\underline{g} \\ 0 \end{bmatrix} \tag{6.55}$$

6.3.3.4.2 Linearization.
The system Jacobian is given in Equation 6.56. The Jacobian $\partial\Psi/\partial\Psi$ can neglect the Earth rate term which significantly complicates the expression. Both $\partial\Psi/\partial\Psi$ and $\partial^n\underline{v}/\partial\Psi$ can be computed by considering the vector $^v\Psi$ and $^v\underline{v}$ to be constant, multiplying them by the coordinate conversion matrix that depends on Ψ and differentiating the resultant vector.

$$F = \begin{bmatrix} \dfrac{\partial\dot{\Psi}}{\partial\Psi} & -\mathfrak{R}_v^n & 0 & 0 & 0 \\ 0 & 0 & 0 & 0 & 0 \\ 0 & 0 & 0 & I & 0 \\ \dfrac{\partial^n\dot{v}}{\partial\Psi} & 0 & 0 & -2{}^n\underline{\Omega}^\times & -R_v^n \\ 0 & 0 & 0 & 0 & 0 \end{bmatrix} \tag{6.56}$$

In order to associate disturbances with the deterministic inputs, the input Jacobian is defined with respect to the concatenation of the deterministic inputs $\begin{bmatrix} ^v\omega & ^v f \end{bmatrix}^V$ and the error states $\begin{bmatrix} \delta^v\underline{\omega} & \delta^v f \end{bmatrix}^V$ in that order:

$$G = \begin{bmatrix} \mathfrak{R}_v^n & 0 & 0 & 0 \\ 0 & 0 & I & 0 \\ 0 & 0 & 0 & 0 \\ R_v^n & 0 & 0 & 0 \\ 0 & 0 & I & 0 \end{bmatrix}$$

6.3.3.4.3 Uncertainty Propagation. On this basis, the uncertainty propagation equation is:

$$P_{k+1} = \Phi_k P_k \Phi_k^T + G_k Q_k G_k^T$$

where Q_k is a diagonal matrix whose elements are the magnitudes of the variances of the four disturbances:

$$Q_k = diag \left[\sigma_{\underline{\omega}}^2 \ \sigma_{\underline{f}}^2 \ \sigma_{\delta\omega}^2 \ \sigma_{\delta\underline{f}}^2 \right]^V \Delta t$$

This particular formulation of an INS Kalman filter is also useful for incorporating visual odometry measurements [16].

6.3.4 Example: Simple Odometry-Aided Attitude and Heading Reference System

An Attitude and Heading Reference System (AHRS) is a degenerate form of an inertial navigation system, using much of the same components. It typically indicates orientation only. If attitude gyros are not present, an input of velocity relative to the Earth can be used with an azimuth gyro to compensate the accelerometers for apparent forces. A simple version of this device uses a strapped down two axis accelerometer to measure attitude and a fiber optic gyro for determining heading.

The difficulty in distinguishing acceleration from gravity makes it difficult to determine attitude. However, one solution is to use externally-provided earth-relative velocity information to estimate the instantaneous inertial forces acting on the accelerometers and then remove them to produce gravity expressed in the body frame. The attitude of the vehicle can be determined by solving for the transformation that converts the measured gravity vector into the known Earth-relative gravity vector.

6.3.4.1 Navigation Equations in Body Frame

Recall the basic inertial navigation equation (Equation 6.46):

$$\vec{a}_v^e = \left(\frac{d\vec{v}_v^e}{dt} \right)_e = \vec{t} - 2\vec{\Omega} \times \vec{v}_v^e + \vec{g}$$

In order to implement an AHRS, it will turn out to be useful to express this basic derivative in the body frame so that it will not be necessary to know the vehicle orientation. By the Coriolis equation:

$$\left(\frac{d\vec{v}_v^e}{dt} \right)_v = \left(\frac{d\vec{v}_v^e}{dt} \right)_e + \vec{\omega}_v^e \times \vec{v}_v^e$$

Define the strapdown angular velocity of the vehicle (measured by the gyros) as follows:

$$\vec{\omega} = \vec{\omega}_v^i = \vec{\omega}_v^e + \vec{\omega}_e^i = \vec{\omega}_v^e + \vec{\Omega}$$

Substituting into the inertial navigation equation gives a form that can be integrated in the body frame:

$$\left(\frac{d\vec{v}_v^e}{dt}\right)_v = \vec{t} - (\vec{\omega} + \vec{\Omega}) \times \vec{v}_v^e + \vec{g} \qquad (6.57)$$

Spotlight 6.4 AHRS Measurement Model.

This model gives a quantity that can be integrated in the vehicle frame rather than the Earth frame. This is perfect for strapdown sensing.

The quantity $(d\vec{v}_v^e / dt)_v$ means the derivative of $\vec{v}_v^e$ as computed by a vehicle fixed observer. Once the integration is performed, the result is expressed in a vehicle-fixed coordinate system. An inertial navigation solution could proceed from here by converting the velocity to Earth fixed coordinates and integrating it, but we have another use for this result.

The Earth rate $\vec{\Omega}$ can be neglected relative to the vehicle rotation rates for this application. Then, the equation becomes:

$$\left(\frac{d\vec{v}_v^e}{dt}\right)_v = \vec{t} - \vec{\omega} \times \vec{v}_v^e + \vec{g} \qquad (6.58)$$

We can solve this for gravity:

$$\vec{g} = \left(\frac{d\vec{v}_v^e}{dt}\right)_v - \vec{t} + \vec{\omega} \times \vec{v}_v^e$$

For strapdown sensing, if we have an indication of vehicle velocity in the body frame, all of the vectors on the right are known in the vehicle frame if we assume that velocity $\vec{v}_v^e$ and angular velocity $\vec{\omega}$ are directed along the x and z axes respectively of the vehicle frame. The expression $(d\vec{v}_v^e / dt)_v$ can be generated by numerical differentiation of the velocity vector expressed in vehicle coordinates (i.e., the time derivative of the odometer). When velocity is constant in the body frame, this term is zero, but when accelerating forward, this term captures the effect on the accelerometers that was described earlier as the reason inclinometers are not useful. Likewise, if the vehicle is turning, the Coriolis term captures the sideways swing of a pendulum that would be measured by the accelerometers. Writing the formula in body coordinates:

$$R_w^v {}^w\underline{g} = \frac{d(^v\underline{v}_v^e)}{dt} - {}^v\underline{t} + {}^v\underline{\omega} \times {}^v\underline{v}_v^e = {}^v\underline{g}_{meas}$$

The frame w is a locally level frame whose yaw is the same as the vehicle. In this way the rotation matrix R_w^v depends only on attitude.

6.3.4.2 Solving for Attitude

The last expression can be solved for the attitude angles embedded in this rotation matrix since g is known in world coordinates. The rotation matrix that converts coordinates from the vehicle frame to the w frame is:

$$R_v^w = Roty(\theta)Rotx(\phi) = \begin{bmatrix} c\theta & 0 & s\theta \\ 0 & 1 & 0 \\ -s\theta & 0 & c\theta \end{bmatrix}\begin{bmatrix} 1 & 0 & 0 \\ 0 & c\phi & -s\phi \\ 0 & s\phi & c\phi \end{bmatrix} = \begin{bmatrix} c\theta & s\theta s\phi & s\theta c\phi \\ 0 & c\phi & -s\phi \\ -s\theta & c\theta s\phi & c\theta c\phi \end{bmatrix}$$

Therefore its transpose converts in the opposite direction and the expression for gravity in the vehicle frame is:

$$\underline{g}_{meas}^v = R_w^v \,{}^w\underline{g} = \begin{bmatrix} g_x \\ g_y \\ g_z \end{bmatrix} = \begin{bmatrix} c\theta & 0 & -s\theta \\ s\theta s\phi & c\phi & c\theta s\phi \\ s\theta c\phi & -s\phi & c\theta c\phi \end{bmatrix}\begin{bmatrix} 0 \\ 0 \\ g \end{bmatrix} = g\begin{bmatrix} -s\theta \\ c\theta s\phi \\ c\theta c\phi \end{bmatrix}$$

Hence, the vehicle attitude is:

$$\tan\theta = s\theta/c\theta = -g_x/(\sqrt{g_y^2 + g_z^2})$$

$$\tan\phi = s\phi/c\phi = g_y/g_z$$

If there is no z accelerometer, we can use:

$$g^2 = g_x^2 + g_y^2 + g_z^2$$

Substituting:

$$\tan\theta = -g_x/(\sqrt{g_y^2 + g_z^2}) = -g_x/(\sqrt{g^2 - g_x^2})$$

$$\tan\phi = g_y/g_z = g_y/(\sqrt{g^2 - g_x^2 - g_y^2})$$

6.3.4.3 Solving for Yaw

It is tempting, once the attitude is known, the try to determine the yaw angle by integrating the component of the yaw gyro that is aligned with the local vertical. However, recall from Equation 2.74 that:

$$\begin{bmatrix} \dot\phi \\ \dot\theta \\ \dot\psi \end{bmatrix} = \begin{bmatrix} \omega_x + \omega_y s\phi t\theta + \omega_z c\phi t\theta \\ \omega_y c\phi - \omega_z s\phi \\ \omega_y \dfrac{s\phi}{c\theta} + \omega_z \dfrac{c\phi}{c\theta} \end{bmatrix} = \begin{bmatrix} 1 & s\phi t\theta & c\phi t\theta \\ 0 & c\phi & -s\phi \\ 0 & \dfrac{s\phi}{c\theta} & \dfrac{c\phi}{c\theta} \end{bmatrix}\begin{bmatrix} \omega_x \\ \omega_y \\ \omega_z \end{bmatrix}$$

So the yawrate is given by:

$$\dot\psi = \frac{s\phi}{c\theta}\omega_y + \frac{c\phi}{c\theta}\omega_z$$

It seems that it requires two gyros to compute the yawrate given the attitude angles. At high roll angles $s\phi$ is of significant magnitude, the vehicle y axis approaches vertical, and rotation around y (ω_y) projects onto yawrate.

Yet, it seems like we should be able to estimate heading with just one gyro and two accelerometers, because they all relate to three more or less orthogonal rotations. We can get ω_y from the inverse (Equation 2.73 in Chapter 2) of the above transformation:

$$\begin{bmatrix} \omega_x \\ \omega_y \\ \omega_z \end{bmatrix} = \begin{bmatrix} \dot{\phi} - s\theta\dot{\psi} \\ c\phi\dot{\theta} + s\phi c\theta\dot{\psi} \\ -s\phi\dot{\theta} + c\phi c\theta\dot{\psi} \end{bmatrix} = \begin{bmatrix} 1 & 0 & -s\theta \\ 0 & c\phi & s\phi c\theta \\ 0 & -s\phi & c\phi c\theta \end{bmatrix} \begin{bmatrix} \dot{\phi} \\ \dot{\theta} \\ \dot{\psi} \end{bmatrix}$$

The second line is:

$$\omega_y = c\phi\dot{\theta} + s\phi c\theta\dot{\psi}$$

Substituting into the expression for $\dot{\psi}$:

$$\dot{\psi} = \frac{s\phi}{c\theta}(c\phi\dot{\theta} + s\phi c\theta\dot{\psi}) + \frac{c\phi}{c\theta}\omega_z = \left(\frac{s\phi}{c\theta}c\phi\dot{\theta} + s\phi s\phi\dot{\psi}\right) + \frac{c\phi}{c\theta}\omega_z$$

Gathering common terms:

$$\dot{\psi}(1 - s^2\phi) = \dot{\psi}(c^2\phi) = \frac{s\phi}{c\theta}c\phi\dot{\theta} + \frac{c\phi}{c\theta}\omega_z$$

Thus, we can determine yawrate if we differentiate the pitch angle:

$$\dot{\psi} = \frac{s\phi}{c\theta c\phi}\dot{\theta} + \frac{1}{c\theta c\phi}\omega_z$$

In discrete time, we only need to difference the pitch angle:

$$\Delta\psi = \left(\frac{1}{c\theta c\phi}\right)(s\phi\Delta\theta + \omega_z\Delta t)$$

This result was based on the assumption that the dominant component of the angular velocity was directed along the body z axis.

6.3.5 References and Further Reading

There are many good books on inertial navigation. A very recent and good source is Titterton. The two papers by Savage are fairly definitive expositions of implementation of navigation algorithms. The Euler angle formulation presented is based on Tardiff.

[13] D. H. Titterton and J. L. Weston, *Strapdown Inertial Navigation Technology*, 2nd ed., AIAA, 2004.

[14] Paul G. Savage, Strapdown Inertial Navigation Integration Algorithm Design Part 1: Attitude Algorithms, *Journal of Guidance, Control, and Dynamics*, Vol. 21, No. 1, January–February 1998.

[15] Paul G. Savage, Strapdown Inertial Navigation Integration Algorithm Design Part 2: Velocity and Position Algorithms, *Journal of Guidance, Control, and Dynamics*, Vol. 21, No. 2, March–April, 1998.

[16] J. P. Tardiff, M. George, M. Laverne, A. Kelly, A. Stentz, *A New Approach to Vision Aided Inertial Navigation*, IEEE/RSJ International Conference on Intelligent Robots and Systems, pp. 4161–4168, 2010.

6.3.6 Exercises

6.3.6.1 Naive Inertial Navigation

Suppose a vehicle at the equator is stationary and integrating its accelerometers to get its position. Compute the magnitude in km of the position error that would be observed after one minute if the local value of gravitation was correctly used but the centrifugal term in the inertial navigation equations was neglected.

6.3.6.2 Simple Error Analysis of Inertial Navigation

Many errors in an INS oscillate with the Schuler period of 84 minutes. Compute this behavior from first principles. Consider a single error source – accelerometer bias. The basic navigation equation in vector form – inertial acceleration expressed in terms of the specific force indicated by the accelerometers $\vec{a}$, and gravitation $\vec{g}$ is:

$$\vec{a} = \frac{d^2}{dt^2}\vec{r} = \vec{t} + \vec{g} \qquad (6.59)$$

We will use the technique of perturbative analysis. A hypothetical perturbative error is applied to the sensed specific force and the effect of this on the system output is investigated. Let the indicated specific force include an error denoted $\delta\vec{t}$, and let it cause errors in the computed position and gravitation denoted by $\delta\vec{r}$ and $\delta\vec{g}$. This is accomplished through the substitutions:

$$\vec{t}_i = \vec{t}_t + \delta\vec{t} \qquad \vec{r}_i = \vec{r}_t + \delta\vec{r} \qquad \vec{g}_i = \vec{g}_t + \delta\vec{g} \qquad (6.60)$$

Where the subscripts i and t represent indicated and true quantities. Substituting this back into the original equation and cancelling out the original equation yields.

$$\frac{d^2}{dt^2}\delta\vec{r} = \delta\vec{t} + \delta\vec{g} \qquad (6.61)$$

This is the differential equation which describes the propagation of errors from the accelerometer to the position and gravity computations. However, the gravitational force depends on the position.

$$\vec{g} = -\frac{GM}{r^3}\vec{r} = -\frac{GM}{(\vec{r}\cdot\vec{r})^{3/2}}\vec{r} \qquad (6.62)$$

Take the total differential of Equation 6.62 with respect to radius. Substitute it into Equation 6.61. Place a coordinate system at the center of the Earth and consider a reference trajectory so that $x = y = 0$ and $z = r = R$. Then show that horizontal error oscillates with the Schuler period and vertical error is exponential.

6.3.6.3 Kalman Filter

Formulate a Kalman filter for the AHRS described earlier based on the first two lines of Equation 6.57 and the last line of Equation 2.73 in Chapter 2.

6.3.6.4 Inertial Navigation Filtering

Compute the Jacobians $\partial\underline{\Psi}/\partial\underline{\Psi}$ and $\partial^n\underline{v}/\partial\underline{\Psi}$ necessary in Equation 6.56.

6.4 Satellite Navigation Systems

6.4.1 Introduction

Satellite navigation complements inertial navigation very nicely due to its capacity to provide a regular fix on the position of a vehicle anywhere on the planet. It has been called the "next utility" – similar in availability, quality, and scope of coverage to electric power and telephones. Though relatively new, satellite navigation has already revolutionized several industries including shipping, surveying, and perhaps all resource industries.

There are presently two separate complete constellations of navigation satellites in orbit. The Global Positioning System (GPS) satellites were developed by the U.S. Department of Defense. The GLONASS satellites were launched by the Soviet Union. Other systems are in development as of this writing in Europe, Japan, China, and India. GPS and GLONASS are virtually identical for our purposes and many navigation systems use both sets of satellites. To remain brief, this section will only present GPS.

There are many GPS signals and many ways of using them. Accuracies can vary from millimeters to a few tens of meters depending on many factors including receiver cost, signals used, satellites in view, vehicle dynamics, and the availability of any augmentation systems.

6.4.2 Implementation

A constellation of satellites in Earth orbit transmits very weak signals over the entire surface of the Earth. Small radio receivers are able to receive the satellite transmissions, and without transmitting anything themselves, they can compute their position on the globe. This architecture makes it possible for any number of receivers to operate simultaneously. Although the equipment to use the signals must be purchased, use of the GPS signals is cost-free.

6.4.2.1 Satellites and Ground Stations

The GPS satellite constellation consists of 24 (or more) satellites in six circular orbits of 11,000 miles in amplitude (Figure 6.31). Satellite motions repeat exactly twice per sidereal day.

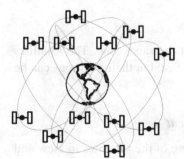

Figure 6.31 GPS Constellation. Twenty-four satellites are present in six circular orbits.

Satellite visibility is the primary factor affecting GPS availability. Satellites are typically visible at 10° above the horizon and higher and there are always at least four visible above this angle in the absence of buildings, and so on, that occlude the signal.

Eleven ground stations are in operation as of this writing and more are planned. Many act as GPS receivers that collect data from all satellites and transmit the data to the master control station where it is processed to compute accurate ephemeris (orbit) and clock data. Once the corrections to the clocks and orbital data are computed, they are retransmitted to the satellites from three of the ground stations. The satellites will eventually send the data to all receivers and in this way the entire system remains highly accurate.

6.4.2.2 Signals

The GPS signals are modulated carrier signals. The civilian carriers are designated L1 (1575.42 MHz, 19 cm wavelength), and L2 (1227.60 MHz, 24 cm wavelength). There are three modulation signals called the C/A code, the Y code, and the *navigation message*. The first two of these are pseudorandom noise (PRN) codes that mimic random numbers but are, in fact, completely predictable. The use of PRN codes permits the use of small antennae and even handheld receivers.

The coarse acquisition (C/A) code is on the L1 carrier, is basically a 1023 bit binary number that is unique to each satellite and is retransmitted every millisecond. The particular codes used have very low cross correlations so that it is easy to distinguish one satellite from another.

The much longer and much more precise Y code, transmitted on both carriers, is for exclusive military use. The use of both carriers permits atmospheric delay to be measured. Satellite flight path information is called the *ephemeris data*. The navigation message includes the system time, accurate ephemeris for the transmitting satellite and less accurate ephemeris for all the others.

6.4.2.3 Receiver Operation

The most basic operation of a GPS receiver is code correlation to recover the *pseudorange* time delay. Each receiver duplicates the satellite PRN codes internally in order to match them with received signals. In this way, the systems operates like setting a wristwatch based on a recognizable radio signal whose true time of transmission is known. The correlation is computed as a function of time delay and it peaks at the correct delay. GPS time is so accurate that some receivers function solely as precision time or frequency standards.

6.4.3 State Measurement

GPS receivers are able to listen to multiple satellites at the same time. The satellites function as known landmarks and they are moving very fast, but their positions can be predicted to very high precision.

6.4.3.1 Position Measurement

Receivers operate by measuring the range to four or more of the satellites in view and then performing trilateration on the signals. Intuitively, we can think of each measured range defining a circle around the associated satellite and the receiver is at the location where the circles intersect. In order to keep the predictions of their positions accurate, the satellites also transmit their locations on a regular basis.

Range is measured as the wave speed multiplied by the *time of flight* – the time it takes for the signals to leave the satellites and arrive at the receiver. As we will see, neither the wave speed nor the time are known perfectly.

6.4.3.2 Time Measurement

The measurement of the time of flight must be very accurate because radio travels at the speed of light. It takes about 68 milliseconds for the signals to travel from the satellites to the receiver. Yet, a time error on the order of 45 nanoseconds would consume the entire 15 meter error budget of the most basic GPS receiver. One whole second of clock error will cause a range error equal to the distance to the moon!

The satellites use very accurate atomic clocks based on cesium oscillators. These atomic clocks are synchronized with the GPS ground stations to the nearest nanosecond or so. Receivers, on the other hand, use cheap crystal oscillators in their clocks, so they are very inaccurate. Clock error causes range measurement errors so range measurements are called *pseudoranges* (Figure 6.32).

The GPS system uses an ingenious technique to avoid the expense of placing a highly accurate clock in each receiver. Because the satellites are synchronized to a nanosecond, the receiver clock error is common to all range calculations and this *user clock bias* can be treated as a fourth unknown. Accordingly, receivers need to track at least four satellites to produce a position fix. Figure 6.28 illustrates the equivalent process in 2D. In this case it would normally take two ranges to fix position but the clock bias can be resolved with a third pseudorange.

The equations that describe the trilateration constraints are quite simply:

$$
\begin{aligned}
r1 &= \sqrt{(x-x1)^2 + (y-y1)^2 + (z-z1)^2} + c\Delta t \\
r2 &= \sqrt{(x-x2)^2 + (y-y2)^2 + (z-z2)^2} + c\Delta t \\
r3 &= \sqrt{(x-x3)^2 + (y-y3)^2 + (z-z3)^2} + c\Delta t \\
r4 &= \sqrt{(x-x4)^2 + (y-y4)^2 + (z-z4)^2} + c\Delta t
\end{aligned}
\tag{6.63}
$$

Spotlight 6.5 Basic GPS Measurement Model.

Pseudoranges are the Cartesian distance to the satellites corrupted by clock errors.

6.4.3.3 Wave Speed Prediction and Measurement

While the speed of light is fixed in a vacuum, it varies (slows down) in a medium if one is present. For GPS, the deviation of wave speed with atmospheric conditions is significant enough to matter. Two methods are used to determine wave speed. First, mathematical models of atmospheric delay can be used to predict effective wave speed. The satellites broadcast the delay model coefficients. Second, it is possible to measure atmospheric effects by observing the (frequency dependent) differential delay on two different frequencies. A known dependence of delay on frequency then permits the absolute delay to be computed.

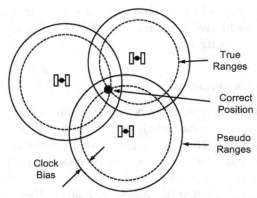

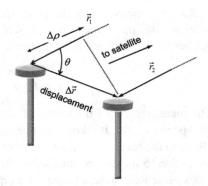

Figure 6.33 GPS Measurement of Orientation. The range difference to two antenna provides the cosine of the angle between the displacement vector and the line to the satellite.

Figure 6.32 GPS Pseudoranges and Clock Bias. The clock bias is the common error in all pseudoranges. When it is removed, all the circles meet at one point.

6.4.3.4 Velocity Measurement

There are several ways in principle to measure velocity using GPS but the highest accuracy approach is to measure the Doppler frequency shift of the signals. The frequency shift observed will be proportional to the range rate (the time derivative of range) and it will in turn depend on the velocity of the satellite, the velocity of the surface of the Earth due to the Earth's spin, and the velocity of the vehicle over the Earth.

As difficult as this sounds, it is already the case that every GPS receiver must search over time delay and frequency shift just to match the radio signals. Systems which measure velocity to an accuracy of 1 cm/sec using the carrier phase rate have been produced. A rough sense for the mathematics can be obtained by differentiating Equation 6.63 to convert four range rate observations into geocentric Cartesian velocity.

6.4.3.5 Orientation Measurement

If two or more antennae are fixed to a rigid vehicle, it is possible to extract orientation information (Figure 6.33). Good sources of absolute yaw measurements are rare so this is an important aspect of GPS. Yaw measurement is accomplished by measuring the carrier phases at the antennae and converting the results to differential range. The differential range $\Delta\rho$ gives the projection of the antenna displacement vector Δr onto the line to the satellite in question:

$$\Delta\rho = \Delta r \cos\theta$$

If three distinct satellites are in view, each provides an independent projection of the antenna displacement vector onto a different axis. The resulting three linear equations can be solved for the displacement vector $\overrightarrow{\Delta r}$ in geocentric coordinates.

$$\Delta\rho_1 = \Delta r \cos\theta_1 = (\overrightarrow{\Delta r} \cdot \hat{r}_1)/|\hat{r}_1|$$
$$\Delta\rho_2 = \Delta r \cos\theta_2 = (\overrightarrow{\Delta r} \cdot \hat{r}_2)/|\hat{r}_2|$$
$$\Delta\rho_3 = \Delta r \cos\theta_3 = (\overrightarrow{\Delta r} \cdot \hat{r}_3)/|\hat{r}_3|$$

$$\begin{bmatrix} \hat{r}_{1x} & \hat{r}_{1y} & \hat{r}_{1z} \\ \hat{r}_{2x} & \hat{r}_{2y} & \hat{r}_{2z} \\ \hat{r}_{3x} & \hat{r}_{3y} & \hat{r}_{3z} \end{bmatrix} \begin{bmatrix} \Delta x \\ \Delta y \\ \Delta z \end{bmatrix} = \begin{bmatrix} \Delta\rho_1 \\ \Delta\rho_2 \\ \Delta\rho_3 \end{bmatrix}$$

6.4.3.6 Geodetic Coordinate Systems

The topic of coordinate systems that are used to express position on the Earth is a complicated one with a long history. For our purposes, it is enough to know that one convenient (x, y, z) coordinate system used in GPS processing is the WGS-84 Earth-centered Earth-fixed (ECEF) system as shown in Figure 6.34. Its origin is positioned at the mass center of gravity of the Earth (so that satellite orbits are easy to express in these coordinates). Its z axis pierces the geographic north pole (through which the Earth's spin axis points). The equator is defined by the plane whose normal is the spin axis, whose center is the origin.

The ECEF x axis goes through the Greenwich meridian (where longitude is defined to be $0°$). It pierces the Earth on the equator in the Atlantic ocean just south of Ghana, Africa. The y axis passes through the $90°$ East meridian on the equator in the Indian ocean just west of Singapore.

Furthermore, the satellite positions are often available in latitude and longitude. Although the Earth is nominally a sphere, it is 21 km lower in radius at the poles than at the equator. For this reason, a reference ellipsoid is defined in the WGS84 convention, which approximates the shape of the Earth by a flattened sphere. For the reference ellipsoid, longitude has the same definition but latitude is redefined as the angle that the local vertical makes with the equatorial plane (Figure 6.34).

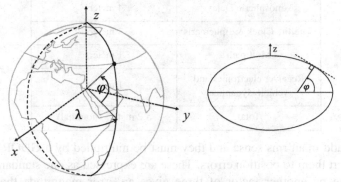

Figure 6.34 WGS-84 ECEF Coordinate System and Geodetic Latitude. An Ellipsoid is fit to the true shape of the Earth and latitude is redefined as shown.

For this choice of coordinates, the relationship between latitude-longitude-altitude and ECEF coordinates is:

$$x = (R_n + h)\cos\varphi\cos\lambda$$
$$y = (R_n + h)\cos\varphi\sin\lambda \qquad (6.64)$$
$$z = ((1 - e^2)R_n + h)\sin\varphi$$

Spotlight 6.6 Lat-Long to ECEF in WGS-84.

These formulae convert from latitude and longitude to the ECEF system where the pseudoranges can be computed.

where h is the altitude above the ellipsoid, $e = 0.081819191$ is the *eccentricity* of the ellipse and R_n is the *longitude radius of curvature* defined in terms of *geodetic longitude* as:

$$R_N = \frac{a}{\sqrt{1 - (e \sin \varphi)^2}} \tag{6.65}$$

and a = 6378.137 km is the equatorial radius of the Earth.

6.4.4 Performance

GPS requires line of sight to the satellites in order to receive the signals, so it cannot be used effectively under dense forest canopy and it cannot be used at all underground or underwater. It also tends to be fairly unreliable around tall buildings – as many urban motorists have already discovered.

6.4.4.1 Sources of Error

Because the raw observation of a receiver is a pseudorange, the analysis of GPS errors starts with the errors in the pseudoranges. Table 6.3 presents the typical magnitude of pseudorange errors caused by various sources.

Table 6.3 Pseudorange Error Sources (1 sigma)

Error Source	Nominal Value
Atmospheric Delays	4 meters
Satellite Clock & Ephemeris	3 meters
Multipath	1 meters
Receiver electronics and vehicle dynamics	1 meters
Total	5.2 meters (nominal)

These errors add in an rms sense and they must be multiplied by a GDOP of 4 to 6 in order to convert them to position errors. These are expressed as one standard deviation, so multiplying by another factor of three gives an error magnitude that would be exceeded only 1% of the time if the errors were truly Gaussian.

6.4.4.1.1 Atmospheric Delay. Atmospheric delay (also called "group" delay) can be as large as 30 meters if not compensated at all but basic compensation removes most of it. It varies with time and position of both the receiver and satellite and it is therefore different for each satellite at any time.

The ionospheric portion of group delay is caused by charged particles and it varies by a factor of at least 15 with variations in time of day, latitude, elevation angle and solar magnetic activity. It cannot be modelled very well so it must be measured to be removed. The tropospheric portion of group delay is caused by water content. It varies by a factor of 10 with elevation angle but it is easy to model effectively.

6.4.4.1.2 Multipath. Multipath errors occur when the radio signal arrives through a reflected non-line-of-sight path.

In the scenario in Figure 6.35, the change in path length is given by:

$$\Delta L = c \Delta t \approx 2h \sin \theta$$

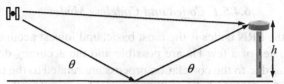

Figure 6.35 GPS Multipath Error. The same signal received along two different paths causes destructive interference at the antenna.

The lengthened path of the secondary signal causes it to be out of phase with the direct signal and it destructively interferes with the direct signal. Multipath errors are substantial above large bodies of water but multipath usually accounts for less than 1 meter pseudorange error. It is more pronounced when the antenna is close to a reflecting surface.

6.4.4.1.3 Geometric Dilution of Precision. The GDOP of range trilateration was discussed earlier in this chapter. The GDOP of a GPS measurement usually has a magnitude from 4 to 6 but it can be as high as 20 near the poles where all satellites are always at the horizon. Recall that the pseudorange error magnitude is converted to position error magnitude by multiplying by the GDOP. In this way the 5 meters pseudorange error in Table 6.3 can be associated with a 1 sigma position error of 20–30 meters or even more.

6.4.4.2 Measures of Accuracy

There are enough definitions of GPS accuracy to make the question of interpreting a specification a tricky one. It can be defined in 2D or in 3D, with or without GDOP included. Various statistics are used and once the meaning of the number is understood, the context of aiding sources, differential aids, area augmentation, vehicle dynamics, and averaging must be understood.

In 2D, the drms (*distance rms*) accuracy metric is the standard deviation of the radial error (the vector sum of the x and y horizontal error). Likewise, 2drms is simply twice the drms value. 68% of errors should be less than drms in magnitude and 95% of measurements should be less than 2drms in magnitude.

Circular Error Probable (CEP) is defined as the deviation from the mean that contains 1/2 the errors on average.

$$CEP \approx 0.83 \times DRMS \tag{6.66}$$

Variations include horizontal, vertical, and spherical error probable. Many of these concepts assume that the error is unbiased and Gaussian. Otherwise, precision and accuracy would have to be distinguished as well to account for the bias.

When comparing receivers, it is important to understand how many satellites are being tracked at a time because more satellites lead to reduced errors. It is also important to understand what signals are being processed, and in what manner, as described in the following section on modes of operation.

6.4.5 Modes of Operation

Receivers can process the GPS signals in various ways and basic tradeoffs exist between the averaging time, the accuracy, and the excursion over which it applies. It is possible to remove many errors by averaging over long periods of time. Although this is a viable technique in surveying applications, it has limited applicability to mobile robots – unless the robot is stationary surveying landmarks or other features of interest.

6.4.5.1 Coded and Codeless Modes

The correlation of the PRN codes is the most basic, and lowest accuracy, form of GPS operation. Update rates of a few Hz are possible and the accuracy depends on which codes are used. Error due to the correlation process are related to the pulse wavelength of the PRN codes. The C/A code has a 300 meter pulse wavelength and the P code is an order of magnitude smaller at 30 meter pulse wavelength.

Codeless modes of operation track the phase of the L1 (19 cm wavelength) and L2 (24 cm wavelength) carrier signals. Because these wavelengths are three orders of magnitude smaller than the PRN pulses, relative accuracies on the order of centimeters are possible.

6.4.5.2 Code Phase Differential GPS

The dominant sources of error are related to atmospheric delays and clock and ephemeris data.

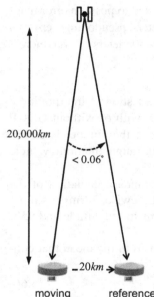

20,000km

< 0.06°

_20km_

moving
receiver

reference
receiver

Figure 6.36 Geometry of Differential GPS. The angle between the two receivers is very small so the atmospheric effects are similar.

Differential GPS is a technique that exploits the fact that the atmospheric delays are essentially the same for two receivers that are close to each other on the surface of the Earth (Figure 6.36), and of course, ephemeris and satellite clock data are the same everywhere. If the position of one receiver (known as the *reference set* or *base station*) is known (or considered the origin), the errors in its GPS solution can be computed and provided to any moving receiver nearby. The moving receiver then simply subtracts the error from its solution to improve its accuracy.

Better yet, the pseudorange errors of individual satellites will be mostly common to the two receivers and they can be computed at the reference location. For maximum accuracy, the reference receiver should be an "all in view" receiver that computes pseudorange errors for every satellite in view. Then the moving receiver can remove the pseudorange errors of whatever satellites it is tracking. Such corrections can be useful up to 1000 miles away from the reference receiver. three to five meter accuracy is possible up to 20 Km away by communicating pseudorange errors while tracking the C/A code.

If differential GPS is performed in real time then a radio link is necessary to communicate the corrections. This link creates another opportunity for signal occlusion. Radio repeaters can be used in that case to (re)transmit corrections. For real time use, accuracy degradation occurs if the correction data takes more than 60 seconds to arrive at the moving station.

6.4.5.3 Carrier Phase Differential GPS

If the base station and the receiver are both tracking carrier phases, the base station can transmit its phase measurements as well and this data will permit the moving receiver to track the carrier phases from the satellites. This technique is known as real-time kinematic (RTK) GPS. It is possible to achieve accuracies on the order of 2 cm plus 2 ppm (2 cm for every 10 km) of the excursion from the base station.

6.4.5.4 GPS Augmentation

Code phase GPS corrections are valid over large distances and they can be interpolated between reference stations. This fact creates the possibility of having base stations broadcast corrections over very large distance on behalf of all users. Many such correction services are available today.

The Wide Area Augmentation System (WAAS) was developed by the U.S. Federal Aviation Administration to make GPS accurate enough for aircraft to use. It uses a network of base stations that compute correction data and transmit it to communication satellites every few seconds. The satellites then retransmit the data all over the continental U.S. The European equivalent system is called EGNOS.

Some augmentation systems, such as STARFIRE and STARFIX, are proprietary and providers charge a fee for use of the data. Accuracies on the order of 5 cm are achievable.

GPS corrections are also being streamed over the internet, radio, and cellphone data networks by continuously operating reference stations (CORS). As of 2010, most of these 1500 or more base stations are operated by the National Geodetic Survey in the U.S. The base stations operate continuously and the data is made available for public use. Such data is often archived and made available for days afterward. Archived data makes is possible to compute highly accurate solutions (after a delay) without having to use a radio data link when the original GPS measurements were taken, so it is an excellent way to produce ground truth motion data for a robot in postprocessing.

6.4.6 References and Further Reading

GPS is evolving rapidly so recent sources are to be preferred. Kaplan is a thorough reference, recently updated. Langley has written many accessible yet authoritative articles on GPS. Strang covers the mathematics in tutorial style. For estimation related to GPS, see Farrell or Grewal.

[17] Jay A. Farrell, *Aided Navigation*, McGraw-Hill, 2008.

[18] M. H. Grewal, L. R. Weill, and A. P. Andrews, *Global Positioning Systems, Inertial Navigation and Integration,* Wiley, 2001.

[19] E. Kaplan and C. Egardy, eds., *Understanding GPS: Principles and Applications,* 2nd ed., Artech House, 2006.

[20] Richard P. Langley, The Mathematics of GPS, *GPS World,* pp. 45–50, July 1991.

[21] Richard P. Langley, Time, Clocks, and GPS, *GPS World*, pp. 38–42, Nov. 1991.

[22] Richard P. Langley, The Mathematics of GPS, *GPS World*, pp. 45–50, July 1991.

[23] Richard P. Langley, Why Is the GPS Signal So Complex?, *GPS World*, pp. 56–59, May 1990.

[24] Gilbert Strang and Kai Borre, *Linear Algebra*, Geodesy and GPS, SIAM 1997.

6.4.7 Exercises

6.4.7.1 PRN Code Correlation

Generate a random sequence of binary digits of length 26 digits. Compute its autocorrelation (with a shifted version of itself) for a few displacements to the left and the right. Interpret the zeros as −1 when computing the products of corresponding signal values. Observe the sharpness of the peak at zero shift.

Repeat with many different signals. Add some digital noise (flip a few bits) and observe the robustness of the peak location to noise. Experiment with longer codes and higher levels of noise.

6.4.7.2 GPS Solution via Nonlinear Least Squares

One Tue Aug 16, 2011 at 9:41 pm, you are in Pittsburgh at geodetic coordinates (lat-long-height) (40.363, −79.867, 234 m). You observe the following 4 NAVSTAR GPS satellites that are presently in view.

GPS Satellites in View over Pittsburgh

Satellite Number	Latitude (deg)	Longitude (deg)	Height (km)	Vicinity
38	48.25	−49.72	19948	St. Johns, Canada
56	53.53	−84.33	20270	Monsonee, Canada
64	18.11	−91.38	20125	Villahermosa, Mexico
59	20.9	−118.73	20275	La Paz, Mexico

Using Equation 6.64, find the ECEF coordinates of yourself and each satellite and then compute the true ranges to the 4 satellites. This gives you to solution the problem you are about to set up. Your position should be (856,248.27, −4,790,966.00, 4,108,931.67). Now, create an artificial GPS fix problem by corrupting your ECE coordinates by +5 km in all directions. Based on this initial guess (which is 5 km in error) compute the pseudoranges that would be predicted from the satellite positions and a predicted user clock bias of +15 microsecs (equivalent to about 5 km). Use the speed of light in vacuum. These incorrect initial coordinates and clock bias form the initial guess of the state. The corrupted pseudoranges constitute the measurements.

Next, solve the problem that your car GPS solves when you turn it on. Linearize Equation 6.63 with respect to the states $(x, y, z, \Delta t)$ at the initial guess and perform one or more iterations of nonlinear least squares. You should be able to recover your coordinates in McKeesport, Pittsburgh to 1 meter (3 nanosecond) accuracy in a single iteration.

CHAPTER 7
Control

Control is the process of converting intentions into actions. We use control to move the robot with respect to the environment but also to articulate sensor heads, arms, grippers, tools, and implements. Dynamic models are useful in control for purposes of analysis but they are also used explicitly in refined implementations.

Figure 7.1 Kiva Systems Unit Load Robot. This robot is used to bring the racks in the distribution center to the order picking personnel. Feedforward terms in its controller turned out to be very important to its performance.

7.1 Classical Control

The main objective of a control system is to provide the inputs necessary at the hardware level that will generate the desired motions. This section describes the methods used to implement the reactive autonomy layer that was initially described in Chapter 1.

7.1.1 Introduction

There are many motivations for the use of controllers on mobile robots:

- Real hardware ultimately responds to forces, energy, power, etc, whereas we are usually concerned with positions and velocities etc. Controllers map between the two.

435

- Measurements can be used to measure what the system is doing, thereby reject disturbances, and even alter the dynamics of the system in some favorable manner.
- Models of the system can be used to elaborate a terse description of the desired motion into the details necessary to make it happen.

A generic block diagram that describes most cases of interest to us is presented in Figure 7.2.

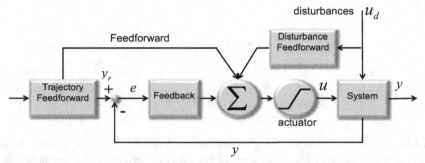

Figure 7.2 Generic Controller Block Diagram. This diagram summarizes most cases of interest.

7.1.1.1 Controller Signals

In Figure 7.2, y_r is called the *reference signal*. It specifies what the controlled system is supposed to do whereas the *output signal y* specifies what it is doing. The signal u is the *input* – the component of the system input that we can control whereas u_d represents *disturbances* – those system inputs that we cannot control. Friction and wind are examples of disturbances.

The actuator that drives the system could be exerting a force or controlling a fuel flow rate but one way or another it will be changing the state of motion of the system. The limiter curve inside the actuator symbol is used to indicate that it has an output that is limited in magnitude in some way.

The difference $e = y_d - y$ is known as the *error signal*. Note the order of the two components in the formula. Reversing a sign in a control system can be disastrous, so it can be important to get the signs right and to have safety measures to take over if a mistake happens anyway.

7.1.1.2 Controller Elements

When the reference input to a controller is constant with respect to time, it is called the *set point*, and the controller is called a *regulator*. Controllers that try to follow a time varying reference input are called *servos*.

The term *feedback* control refers to a class of techniques that measure the response of the system and actively compensate for any deviations from the desired behavior. We use feedback control for a number of reasons, and most or all will occur in any application. Overall, feedback can reduce the negative effects of all of the following effects on system behavior.

- parameter changes
- modelling errors
- unwanted inputs (disturbances)

Feedback can also modify the transient behavior of a system and it can be used to reduce the effects of measurement noise.

Two other components of interest are the feedforward components. These are predictive elements that anticipate the response of the system to provided inputs or measured disturbances. Then they use those predictions to improve the system behavior. The following sections will elaborate the contents of the boxes labelled feedback and feedforward.

The *controlled variable* is the same thing as the reference signal. In a mobile robot, the quantity being controlled might represent articulations of the body that change its shape or gross motions of the whole body that move it about. Examples of articulation variables include wheel velocities, steer angles, throttles, brakes, and sensor pan/tilt mechanisms. This kind of control may rely on internal motion prediction or feedback. Examples of mobility variables include the pose and velocity of the entire robot. This kind of control may rely on bodily motion prediction or feedback.

7.1.1.3 Controller Hierarchy

Most real controllers for complex systems exhibit hierarchical structure. For a mobile robot, a hierarchy of control problems can be defined. Although there is no definitive hierarchy, one hierarchy that captures many of relevant ideas is Figure 7.3. Each layer in the hierarchy is implemented by supplying the reference signals (commands) to the immediately subordinate layer and often each layer generates composite feedback for the layer above.

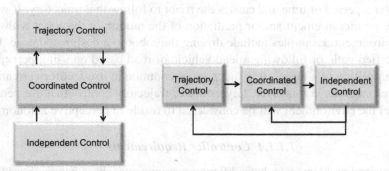

Figure 7.3 A Controller Hierarchy. Left: Higher levels produce the reference signals for lower levels. Right: The equivalent block diagram is a cascade configuration.

7.1.1.3.1 Independent Control. The independent control level is also known as the single input single output (SISO) level. It is concerned with directing the motions of a single degree of freedom and it may rely on sensing associated with that single degree of freedom but it is typically accomplished with no knowledge of what other degrees of freedom may be doing. Furthermore, this layer typically reacts simply to the current (and past) error signal and any prediction is limited to the computation of error derivatives.

Controllers at this level are connected directly to actuators such as engine throttles, electric motors, and hydraulic valves. There is usually a calibration required, which maps the computed output onto the quantity actuated. Basic kinematic transforms may be required to convert coordinates in minor ways. The methods of classical control are adequate to implement this layer.

7.1.1.3.2 Coordinated Control. The coordinated control level is also known as the multi input, multi output (MIMO) level or multivariable control. This layer accomplishes instantaneous control of the entire vehicle considered as one entity. Coordinated control attempts to keep the independent axes of control both consistent and synchronized so that their net effect is the desired behavior. It may rely on composite feedback generated from several components and it may perform multiple transformations of commands and feedback. The methods of modern state space control are often used to implement this layer.

An example of such a controller is one that controls the linear and angular velocity of the vehicle by commanding the velocities of four wheels (Figure 7.4) based on the methods described in Section 4.2 of Chapter 4. Feedback from the four wheels is converted to feedback on linear and angular velocity before the state error vector is formed.

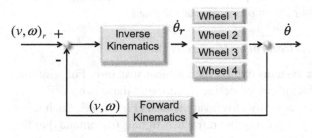

Figure 7.4 Coordinated Controller for WMR. Four wheels are controlled in order to produce the desired linear and angular velocity. Individual wheel speed servos operate independently.

7.1.1.3.3 Trajectory Control. The trajectory control level considers and entire trajectory over a period of time and causes the robot to follow that trajectory. It will normally rely on measurement and/or prediction of the motion of the robot with respect to the environment. Examples include driving the robot to a designated pose, following a specified path, or following a lead vehicle or road based on using perception to derive the position of a target. It is much more common to use feedforward and optimal control methods in this layer. Layers above trajectory control that use perception to interpret the environment will be considered to reside in perceptive autonomy.

7.1.1.4 Controller Requirements

Different control problems may have different requirements whose nature drives the controller design. If it is necessary to move a precise distance or move to a precise location, then position control may be the best approach. Sometimes achieving the precise endpoint is critical. For certain problems where maneuverability is reduced or highly constrained, the path cannot be controlled anyway because the end state predetermines the path. On occasion only some of the coordinates of the endpoint must be achieved precisely.

Sometimes, following a specified path is very important. In some such cases, the component of error along the path (*alongtrack*) can be ignored and only the *crosstrack* error orthogonal to the path matters. This enables a decoupled approach where speed is controlled independently from crosstrack error.

Velocity control is often used to achieve gross motions between resting positions. However, velocity control can be important in situations in which a process, like lawn care or floor cleaning, depends on precise control of velocity.

7.1.2 Virtual Spring-Damper

As a simple example, suppose that it is necessary to control the position of a mass using applied forces. The motion is governed by the differential equation:

$$\ddot{y} = u(t) \tag{7.1}$$

The damped mass spring system of Section 4.4.1.7 of Chapter 4 has the advantage that there is a clear mapping between the steady-state response of the system and the applied input. For an unconstrained mass, there is no obvious way to determine an input $u(t)$ control (function of time) that will drive the system to some desired terminal state y_{ss}.

One idea is to introduce measurements of the position $y(t)$ and velocity $\dot{y}(t)$ of the mass and create artificial constraints. Given measurements, it becomes possible to compute an input of the form:

$$u(t) = \frac{f}{m} - \frac{c_c}{m}\dot{y} - \frac{k_c}{m}y \tag{7.2}$$

where artificial springs k_c and dampers c_c have been introduced **computationally**. Substituting this into Equation 7.1 reproduces the equation of the damped mass-spring system:

$$\ddot{y} + \frac{c_c}{m}\dot{y} + \frac{k_c}{m}y = \frac{f}{m} \tag{7.3}$$

This system is indicated in Figure 7.5. The process of adding sensors to measure the behavior of the system is known as *feedback* control. It is also conventional to refer to Equation 7.1 as the *open-loop* system and Equation 7.3 as the *closed-loop* system.

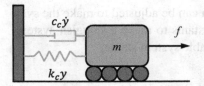

Figure 7.5 A Computationally Damped Mass-Spring System. The applied force is opposed by a virtual spring and damper.

This closed-loop system will behave exactly like a damped mass-spring system and it will settle at the terminal state f/k derived in Equation 4.125 in Chapter 4. Initially, the term f/m will exceed the other two because both y and $\dot{y}$ will be small, but as the system starts to move, the virtual damper will begin to put the "brakes" on and the virtual spring will increasingly oppose all deviation from the origin. After the transients pass, the damper will exert no force. Then, the virtual spring force and the applied force will cancel at one particular equilibrium location.

7.1.2.1 Stability

The poles for the above system will be the same as they were for the real system:

$$s = \omega_0(-\zeta \pm \sqrt{\zeta^2 - 1})$$

The roots are complex numbers in general and the associated solutions are known to be exponentials. The imaginary parts of the roots lead to oscillatory behaviors and the real parts modulate the amplitude up or down as time advances, based on whether their signs are positive or negative. The solutions to the unforced system are therefore damped sinusoids in general. If the roots have negative real parts, the oscillations will die out over time and the system is said to be *stable*. Otherwise the oscillations will increase in amplitude without bound and the system is said to be *unstable*.

For our virtual damped mass-spring system, the stability condition requires that $\zeta\omega_0 > 0$, which is to say that the damping coefficient c for the mechanical system is positive in sign. Intuitively, this means that as long as friction acts to oppose motion, the mechanical system will come to rest in the absence of a time varying forcing function.

7.1.2.2 Pole Placement

Consider now the case where we want to change the behavior of a real damped mass-spring system:

$$\ddot{y} + \frac{c}{m}\dot{y} + \frac{k}{m}y = u(t) \tag{7.4}$$

The approach is similar. We add sensors for position and velocity and the control becomes:

$$u(t) = \frac{f}{m} - \frac{c_c}{m}\dot{y} - \frac{k_c}{m}y \tag{7.5}$$

Substituting back into the differential equation produces:

$$\ddot{y} + \frac{(c + c_c)}{m}\dot{y} + \frac{(k + k_c)}{m}y = \frac{f}{m} \tag{7.6}$$

We see that the gains in the feedback control system can be adjusted to make the system have any coefficients we desire. There are constants to make a sluggish system fast, a fast system sluggish, or even to make an unstable system stable.

7.1.2.3 Error Coordinates and Dynamics

In Equation 7.3, the y coordinate was defined as deviation from the origin in order to be consistent with the case of a real spring. However, it is often more convenient to shift coordinates to that of an explicit deviation from desired behavior. It is convenient to define the *error signal* as the difference between the reference position y_r and the present position:

$$e(t) = y_r(t) - y(t)$$

Substituting for the present position and its derivatives in Equation 7.3:

$$[\ddot{y}_r - \ddot{e}] + \frac{c_c}{m}[\dot{y}_r - \dot{e}] + \frac{k_c}{m}[y_r - e] = \frac{f_r}{m}$$

Where f_r means the force exerted to achieve the steady position y_r. For a constant desired input $\ddot{y}_r = \dot{y}_r = 0$. Moving the desired position above to the right side:

$$[-\ddot{e}] + \frac{c_c}{m}[-\dot{e}] + \frac{k_c}{m}[-e] = \frac{f_r}{m} - \frac{k_c}{m}[y_r]$$

But according to Equation 7.4, $f_r - k_c y_r = 0$ for a constant input, so the right side vanishes and the left side can then be multiplied by -1 to obtain:

$$\ddot{e} + \frac{c_c}{m}\dot{e} + \frac{k_c}{m}e = 0$$

So, the differential equation in error coordinates for a constant input is the same as the unforced damped oscillator. This suggests that a control computed in error coordinates would have the same effect as the control computed in Equation 7.5. Consider:

$$u(t) = \frac{c_c}{m}\dot{e} + \frac{k_c}{m}e \tag{7.7}$$

Substitute this into Equation 7.1 to produce:

$$\ddot{y} = \frac{c_c}{m}\dot{e} + \frac{k_c}{m}e = \frac{c_c}{m}[\dot{y}_r - \dot{y}] + \frac{k_c}{m}[y_r - y]$$

But $\dot{y}_r = 0$ and $k_c y_r = f_r$ so this becomes:

$$\ddot{y} + \frac{c_c}{m}\dot{y} + \frac{k_c}{m}y = \frac{f_r}{m} \tag{7.8}$$

which is Equation 7.3. We have shown that measurements of position and velocity can be used to implement a control in error coordinates to cause an unconstrained mass to behave like a damped oscillator.

7.1.3 Feedback Control

Equation 7.7 can be rewritten in more common notation as:

$$u(t) = k_d\dot{e} + k_p e \tag{7.9}$$

The constant k_d is known as the *derivative gain* and its associated control term functions as a virtual damper. The constant k_p is known as the *proportional gain* and its associated control terms functions as a virtual spring. This controller is supplied with a desired position y_r and it uses measurements to compute the error signal, and its derivative. The response to a constant input is to drive the system to the desired position y_r.

This situation can be visualized as follows:

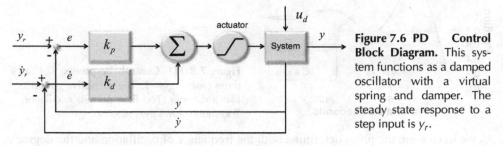

Figure 7.6 PD Control Block Diagram. This system functions as a damped oscillator with a virtual spring and damper. The steady state response to a step input is y_r.

The figure shows a second input to the control, the derivative of the desired state $\dot{y}_r$, which is used to form the error derivative. This signal may be desirable if such a measurement is available. An alternative is to simply differentiate the error signal $e(t)$ that is computed from the measurements of $y(t)$.

The equivalent block diagram in the frequency domain for this system is as follows in Figure 7.7:

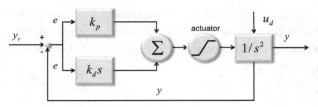

Figure 7.7 PD Control Block Diagram in Frequency Domain. This is the equivalent of Figure 7.6 in the frequency domain.

The closed loop transfer function is:

$$T(s) = \frac{H}{1 + GH} = \frac{(1/s^2)(k_d s + k_p)}{1 + (1/s^2)(k_d s + k_p)} = \frac{k_d s + k_p}{s^2 + k_d s + k_p}$$

According to Equation 7.7, for a unit mass:

$$k_d = 2\zeta\omega_0 \qquad\qquad k_p = \omega_0^2$$

So, the oscillator parameters are related to the gains as follows:

$$\omega_0 = \sqrt{k_p} \qquad\qquad \zeta = \frac{k_d}{2\sqrt{k_p}}$$

$$(7.10)$$

The closed loop poles are:

$$s = -\zeta\omega_0 \pm \omega_0\sqrt{(\zeta^2 - 1)} = -\frac{k_d}{2} \pm \frac{1}{2}\sqrt{(k_d^2 - 4k_p)}$$

$$(7.11)$$

The system is critically damped when $\zeta = 1$, which is when $k_p = 1$ and $k_d = 2$. In this case, there is a repeated real pole at $x = -1$ and the mass will move to the desired position in about 5 seconds as shown in Figure 7.8.

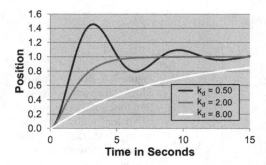

Figure 7.8 PD Control Response. For all three cases $k_p = 1$. The derivative gain acts like a damper. Too little permits oscillation. Too much slows the response.

As we have seen, the poles determine both the frequency of oscillation and the degree of damping. They also govern stability or instability. Furthermore note that although an explicit input is present that is trying to drive the system in a particular way, the transient responses in Figure 7.8, are governed almost entirely by the poles. In mechanical terms, the input force may control where the system ends up but the spring and damper decide how it gets there.

7.1.3.1 Root Locus

Given an explicit formula for the poles, it is possible to plot their trajectories in the complex plane as the derivative gain k_d varies. As shown in Figure 7.9, they start out at ± 1 on the imaginary axis when $k_d = 0$. Here, the system is purely oscillatory due to the lack of damping. As k_d increases, the imaginary part (and hence the frequency of oscillation) decreases and the real part becomes more and more negative indicating increased damping. At $k_d = 2$, they meet at -1 on the real axis. This is the point of critical damping. Thereafter as the derivative gain increases, they move in opposite directions on the real axis. The one that moves to the right achieves the origin only when $k_d = \infty$.

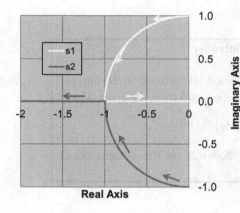

Figure 7.9 PD Root Locus Plot. The trajectory of the two system are shown as the derivative gain varies.

7.1.3.2 Performance Characteristics

Several characteristics of the controlled system response to a step input are defined.

- The 90% *rise time* is the time required to achieve 90% of the final value. For the three responses in Figure 7.8, these are 1.7, 3.9, and 18.2 seconds.
- The *time constant* is the 63% rise time.
- The *percent overshoot* is the overshoot amplitude divided by the final value, converted to a percent. It is 45.7% for the first response and zero for the others.
- The 2% *settling time* is the time required for the system to settle to within 2% of its final value. Typically this is about four time constants.
- The *steady-state error* is the remaining error after all transients have faded.

7.1.3.3 Derivative Term Issues

The derivative term will amplify noise and it can lead to erratic behavior if the signal to noise ratio of the error signal is low. In such cases, it may be advisable to low pass filter the derivative signal to remove frequencies that are beyond the capacity of the real system to produce. In Figure 7.6, a measurement of the velocity was assumed so that it would be unnecessary to differentiate the error signal. This is a good solution in practice when it is feasible to use such a sensor. Note that since $e(t) = y_r(t) - y(t)$, then $\dot{e}(t) = \dot{y}_r(t) - \dot{y}(t)$.

So, provided the velocity input is consistent with the position (i.e., it really is the derivative of the reference position), and provided the sensor does measure velocity, the velocity error is equal to the derivative of the position error.

7.1.3.4 PID Control

The proportional term in the PD controller is used to react to the present value of the error signal. Likewise, the derivative term is used to react to predicted future errors because a positive error rate means that the error is increasing. Given this interpretation in terms of present and future errors, it is natural to wonder whether memory of past errors is of any use. It turns out that it does and the result is very well known:

Box 7.1: PID Controller

The PID controller is the workhorse of industrial automation. It requires no system model because it simply forms a control from the error signal:

$$u(t) = k_d\dot{e} + k_p e + k_i\int e(t)dt$$

How the closed loop system behaves depends on the system being controlled.

The constant k_i is called the *integral gain*. Integral gain is useful in situations where a steady-state error would otherwise exist.

Suppose that the mass is resting on a rough surface so that a small amount of static friction f_s exists. Then Equation 7.9 becomes:

$$\ddot{y} + \frac{c_c}{m}\dot{y} + \frac{k_c}{m}y = \frac{f_r + f_s}{m} \tag{7.12}$$

The friction force will act so as to oppose the applied force. The steady-state solution is:

$$y_{ss} = \left(\frac{f_r + f_s}{k_c}\right)$$

See Figure 7.10. Let f_s be set to 0.5 for our unit mass, with $y_d = 1$ as in Figure 7.8. Use a $k_p = 1$ and $k_d = 2$ for critical damping of the loop without the integral. If $k_i = 0$ the system settles to the position of $y_{ss} = 1.05$. However, with $k_i = 0.2$, the system settles to $y_{ss} = 1.0$. The mechanism that achieves this is the fact that an error of persistent sign causes the integral term to continue to grow with time until it eventually generates enough control effort to overwhelm the friction.

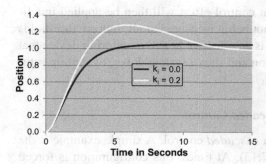

Figure 7.10 Response of PID Controller with Plant Friction. The friction in the system prevents a PD controller from converging to the correct steady state value. The additional of an integral term in the controller resolves the issue.

In this case, the $k_i = 0.2$ system rises to roughly the correct output in 5 seconds as it did for the PD loop.

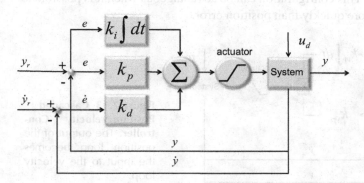

Figure 7.11 PID Controller Block Diagram. An integral term was added to the PD controller. This PID controller can also remove steady-state error.

The equivalent block diagram for this system is as follows in Figure 7.12:

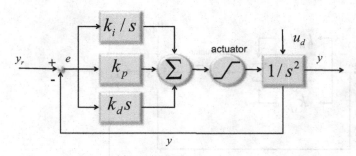

Figure 7.12 PID Controller Block Diagram in Frequency Domain. This is the equivalent of Figure 7.11 in the frequency domain.

The closed loop transfer function is:

$$T(s) = \frac{H}{1+GH} = \frac{(1/s^2)(k_d s + k_p + k_i/s)}{1 + (1/s^2)(k_d s + k_p + k_i/s)} = \frac{k_d s^2 + k_p s + k_i}{s^3 + k_d s^2 + k_p s + k_i}$$

7.1.3.5 Integral Term Issues

The growth of the integral term is known as *windup*. It is often advisable to limit its growth because it has the capacity to apply maximum control effort for an extended period. A broken wire to a feedback sensor, for example, could cause the integrator value to grow indefinitely, and maximum control effort will then be applied indefinitely because the effects of outputs are not being measured at all. Indeed, thresholds on the magnitudes of the three PID terms is an effective health monitoring device that can be used to detect uncommanded motion and shut a system down, by cutting actuator power, in the case of failure.

7.1.3.6 Cascaded Control

Another typical control configuration is a *cascaded* control. A simple example is the cascaded position-velocity loop (Figure 7.13). At times, this configuration is forced upon the user because the device being controlled includes a velocity loop in its basic design. Typically the inner velocity loop runs much faster than the outer position loop, but this is not necessary. This configuration can be advantageous when it is possible to remove velocity error more quickly than position error.

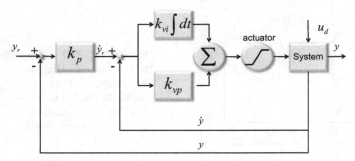

Figure 7.13 Cascaded Position-Velocity Controller. The output of the position loop becomes the input to the velocity loop.

The equivalent block diagram for this system is as follows:

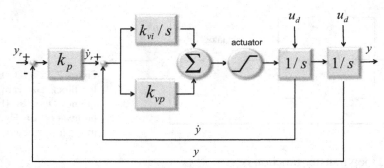

Figure 7.14 Cascaded Position-Velocity Controller in Frequency Domain. This is the equivalent of Figure 7.13 in the frequency domain.

The closed loop transfer function for the inner velocity loop is:

$$T_v(s) = \frac{H_v}{1 + G_v H_v} = \frac{(1/s^2)(k_{vp}s + k_{vi})}{1 + (1/s^2)(k_{vp}s + k_{vi})} = \frac{k_{vp}s + k_{vi}}{s^2 + k_{vp}s + k_{vi}}$$

Hence, the closed loop transfer function of the outer position loop is:

$$T(s) = \frac{H}{1 + GH} = \frac{(1/s)k_p T_v(s)}{1 + (1/s)k_p T_v(s)} = \frac{k_p[k_{vp}s + k_{vi}]}{s^3 + k_{vp}s^2 + [k_{vi} + k_p k_{vp}]s + k_p k_{vi}}$$

For $k_{vi} = 0$, this becomes:

$$T(s) = \frac{k_p k_{vp}}{s^2 + k_{vp}s + k_p k_{vp}}$$

For $k_{vp} = 2$, $k_p = 0.5$, there is a repeated real pole at -1:

$$s = \frac{-k_{vp} \pm \sqrt{k_{vp}^2 - 4k_p k_{vp}}}{2} = \frac{-2 \pm \sqrt{4-4}}{2} = -1$$

So, this system is critically damped and it achieves a target position exactly as do PD and PID loops discussed earlier (Figure 7.15).

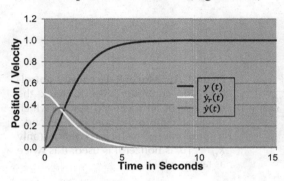

Figure 7.15 Response of a Cascade Controller. This controller responds exactly like a PD controller. Position and velocity are plotted on the same vertical scale.

For any of the above controllers, the speed with which the goal is achieved is determined mostly by the maximum magnitude of the force that can be applied to the mass. For the gains used above, the maximum force exerted was of unit magnitude. Of course, if the gains are increased, the applied forces will increase proportionally, the mass will accelerate and decelerate proportionally faster, and the goal will be achieved faster.

Many mobile robot control systems are cascades because a cascade is a hierarchy of loops. Hierarchy turns out to be a natural structure for real systems composed of multiple computers, running multiple algorithms at different rates.

7.1.4 Model Referenced and Feedforward Control

One of the drawbacks of the controller presented so far is the violent initial reaction to the error generated by a step input. This reaction creates momentum, which potentially causes overshoot later. It seems that it can only be removed by reducing the gains and accepting a more sluggish response. Note, however, that the instantaneous jump in position, which is encoded in a step input, is an unrealistic goal for the response of any finite mass acted upon by a finite force.

7.1.4.1 Model Referenced Control

When the reference trajectory contains such infeasible motions, it can be advantageous to compute a new reference that terminates at the same place but involves feasible or at least "less infeasible" motions. A step input tells the system where to go but it's so infeasible that it provides no guidance on how to get there.

On the other hand, if the system is guided on a more-or-less feasible trajectory to the goal, the performance tradeoffs can become more favorable. This simple approach makes it possible to raise the gains beyond the original ones while also improving response. This device can be viewed as the creation of a new reference input or as the use of a model of a *reference system* that responds in a more reasonable way (Figure 7.16).

In this form of control, errors in the feedback loop are computed with respect to the new reference trajectory. In the following example, the reference trajectory is a position ramp that moves directly to the goal at fixed velocity. Although this is also infeasible, it is less infeasible than a step.

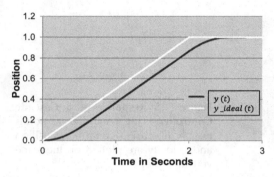

Figure 7.16 Model Referenced Controller. This controller tries to track the response of an idealized system which drives straight to the goal in 2 seconds. A proportional velocity control (only $k_d = 10$ is nonzero) is used. It is twice as fast as a PID.

A commonly used reference model is the trapezoidal velocity profile. This would be used when both acceleration and velocity have some maximum limit.

7.1.4.2 Limitations of Feedback-Only Controls

Although it is the case that PID and cascade control configurations form a large fraction of all installed systems, the use of feedback alone suffers from several severe limitations.

7.1.4.2.1 Delayed Response to Errors. Even though it is quite possible to predict many of the errors in a feedback control system, a pure feedback system must wait until they occur before it can respond to them. In the case of a servo, for example, a rise in the reference input will cause the system output to be too low in subsequent iterations if the control signal is not raised immediately as well.

7.1.4.2.2 Coupled Response. The response to disturbances (and modelling errors, and noise) and the response to the reference signal is computed by the same mechanism – error feedback. However, as we have seen in model-referenced control, it can be very effective to manipulate response to the reference independently from the response to errors. In the recent example, the position ramp was the response to the step input and the proportional velocity servo was the response to errors.

7.1.4.3 Feedforward Control

The term *feedforward* control is introduced to distinguish it from feedback. Any term which appears in the output signal from a controller that does not involve measurements of the controlled system is a feedforward term. Feedforward terms may involve measurements of other things – like disturbances for example, or they may involve models of the system and use no measurements at all.

Clearly one reference trajectory of interest is the fastest one. It is easy to show that the feedback controllers described earlier are not optimal. For example, an open-loop control can easily move the mass to the goal position much faster (in fact, in 2 seconds instead of 5). Furthermore, it can be done with zero overshoot.

In the earlier example of the unit mass, for zero initial conditions, and a constant applied force, the position is given by:

$$y(t) = \frac{1}{2}\left(\frac{f}{m}\right)t^2$$

If the maximum force that can be applied is f_{max}, the time required to travel to position y_r is:

$$t = \sqrt{2\frac{m}{f_{max}}y_r}$$

However, if the maximum force is applied for this entire duration, the mass will have a high velocity at the reference position and an overshoot will occur. In order to come to a stop at the reference position, the force must be reversed at the midpoint of the trajectory – which occurs at the halfway position.

$$t_{mid} = \sqrt{\frac{m}{f_{max}}y_r}$$

For a unit mass and the same maximum value $f_{max} = 1$ that limited the feedback controllers in the previous examples, this gives simply $t_{mid} = 1$. The complete control is:

$$u_{bb}(t) = \begin{bmatrix} f_{max} \text{ if } t < t_{mid} \\ -f_{max} \text{ if } t_{mid} < t < 2t_{mid} \\ 0 \text{ otherwise} \end{bmatrix} \tag{7.13}$$

The response of this controller is shown below in Figure 7.17.

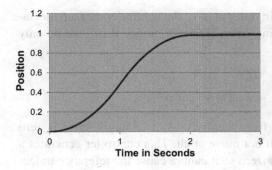

Figure 7.17 Response of A Bang-Bang Controller. This controller applies maximum positive and then maximum negative force for exactly the correct durations to arrive at the goal as fast as possible with no overshoot.

The goal is achieved in 2 seconds with zero overshoot! With a result like this, it seems reasonable to wonder about the value of feedback. From one perspective, feedback underperforms, does not remove errors quickly, is potentially unstable, and requires extra sensors. So, why bother with it at all?

The answer is that feedback has its role, too. Feedback does remove errors that cannot be removed with feedforward. For example, if the mass value used for the above control was slightly incorrect, or if there was (unmodelled) friction in the system that opposed the applied force, the above result would come to a stop before or after the goal and stay there.

7.1.4.4 Feedforward with Feedback Trim

Ideally then, the outputs from the feedback portion of the controller should be as small as possible and their function should be solely to remove errors measured with respect to an intended response trajectory. Conversely, the feedforward terms should ideally be precomputed inputs that cause the system to follow the reference trajectory exactly based on the best model available. Achieving these goals involves three steps:

- reconfiguring the controller to generate the reference trajectory
- causing that trajectory to be executed
- removing any errors that occur with feedback

Notice that the model referenced control example was a constant velocity reference trajectory. The actuator is a force actuator so this trajectory requires no feedforward force at steady-state. In general, an explicit feedforward term is required to cause a reference trajectory to be followed without feedback. Such a feedforward controller has two components:

- The *trajectory generator* specifies the reference trajectory.
- The reference *model follower* generates the feedforward inputs that cause the reference trajectory to be executed. Typically, doing so involves computing the derivatives of the reference trajectory.

For example, the optimal reference trajectory (associated with the input specified by Equation 7.13) is computed as:

$$y_r(t) = \int_0^t \int_0^t u_{bb}(t)dtdt \tag{7.14}$$

This can be fed to a feedback controller in order to have the controller measure deviation from the reference as the true tracking error. However, notice that if we do only this the PD controller becomes:

$$e(t) = y_r(t) - y(t)$$
$$u(t) = u_{fb}(t) = k_p e(t) + k_d \dot{e}(t)$$

where $u_{fb}(t)$ denotes the input derived from feedback. At $t = 0$, the error is zero so the control is zero and the system will not move at all. This controller generates a signal only when the tracking error is nonzero so it cannot cause the reference trajectory to be executed.

To create the motion in the reference trajectory, we need to add a feedforward term of magnitude $u_{bb}(t)$, which is independent of the error. This term will drive the system based solely on time:

$$u(t) = u_{bb}(t) + u_{fb}(t) = \begin{bmatrix} f_{max} \text{ if } t < t_{mid} \\ -f_{max} \text{ if } t_{mid} < t < 2t_{mid} \\ 0 \text{ otherwise} \end{bmatrix} + k_i \int_0^t e(t)dt + k_d \dot{e}(t) \quad (7.15)$$

Note that the feedforward term $u_{bb}(t)$ does not depend on measurements or errors (which depend on measurements), so it is generated regardless of the state of the system. It is the feedback terms which monitor the state of the system and try to null the tracking error. The response of this controller in the presence of friction equal to up to 10% of the applied force is shown in Figure 7.18.

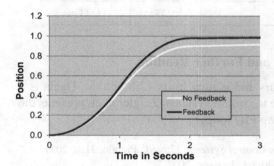

Figure 7.18 Response of a Bang-Bang Controller with Feedback Trim. This controller augments the same open loop (feedforward) term of the last figure with feedback trim in order to overcome significant friction.

7.1.4.5 Trajectory Generation from Reference Models

The problem of computing an intended response trajectory from a reference model involves inverting the model dynamics. For example, driving a mass to a particular position could be expressed in terms of generating the input trajectory $u(t)$, that when integrated twice, will place the mass at the desired terminal state y_r with zero velocity and acceleration. That is, to solve:

$$y_r(t_f) = \int_0^{t_f} \int_0^{t_f} \ddot{y}(u(t), t) dt dt = y_f$$

$$\dot{y}_r(t_f) = \ddot{y}_r(t_f) = 0$$

(7.16)

for an input trajectory $u(t)$ and terminal time t_f. Zero initial conditions were also assumed. This problem is known as *trajectory generation,* and any trajectory that satisfies the model is said to be *feasible.* Note that if any of y, $\dot{y}$ or $\ddot{y}$ are known as a function of time, the other two can be generated by differentiation or integration and once all three are known, the input $u(t)$ can then be found from the system model. We will discuss methods for solving the trajectory generation problem later in the context of steering control.

7.1.4.6 Feedback Versus Feedforward

We are now in a position to present the relative merits of feedback and feedforward. As Table 7.1 suggests, the two approaches to control are as complementary as dead reckoning and triangulation are to state estimation.

Table 7.1 Feedback vs. Feedforward

	Feedback	Feedforward
Removes Unpredictable Errors and Disturbances	(+) yes	(−) no
Removes Predictable Errors and Disturbances	(−) no	(+) yes
Removes Errors and Disturbances Before They Happen	(−) no	(+) yes
Requires Model of System	(+) no	(−) yes
Affects Stability of System	(−) yes	(+) no

7.1.5 References and Further Reading

Dorf has been a popular text for 30 years and is now in its 12th edition. Ogata is a highly regarded book for a first exposure to control systems. Zeigler et al. presents the famous Zeigler-Nichols method for tuning PID loops.

[1] Richard Dorf and Robert Bishop, *Modern Control Systems,* 12th ed., Prentice Hall, 2011.

[2] K. Ogata, *Modern Control Engineering,* 4th ed., Pearson, 2002.

[3] J. G. Ziegler and N. B. Nichols, Optimum Settings for Automatic Controllers, *Transactions of the ASME*, Vol. 64, pp. 759–768, 1942.

7.1.6 Exercises

7.1.6.1 Computational Spring and Damper

Using your favorite programming environment implement a one dimensional finite difference model of the motion of a unit mass m responding to an applied force $u(t)$. The model to produce $y(t)$ from $u(t)$ is simply a double integral. Now change the input to be that described in Equation 7.2. Rerun the simulation and reproduce Figure 7.8. Comment on how using feedback alters the dynamics of a system.

7.1.6.2 Stability

Show using Equation 7.11 that when $k_p \geq 0$ the damped oscillator PD loop is stable when $k_d \geq 0$. What happens when $k_p < 0$?

7.1.6.3 Root Locus

Taking inspiration from how Figure 7.9 was computed, fix $k_d = 1$ and plot the root locus diagram as k_p varies from 0 to 2.

7.1.6.4 Transfer Function For Cascade Controller

Provide the details of the transfer function derivation for the cascade controller shown in Figure 7.14.

7.2 State Space Control

State space control, also known as *modern* control is a technique that tries to control the entire state vector of the system as a unit by exposing and examining the states of the system. This view of the problem turns out to have major advantages (Figure 7.19).

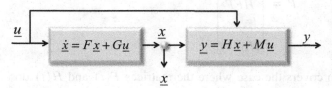

Figure 7.19 State Space. The entire system state is assumed to be available, at least for analysis. The output vector y consists of measurements of the states.

7.2.1 Introduction

We have already seen the state space equations in their linear form in Equation 4.135.

$$
\begin{aligned}
\dot{x}(t) &= F(t)\underline{x}(t) + G(t)\underline{u}(t) \\
y(t) &= H(t)\underline{x}(t) + M(t)\underline{u}(t)
\end{aligned}
\tag{7.17}
$$

Let $\underline{x}$ be $n \times 1$ and $\underline{u}$ be $r \times 1$ and y be $m \times 1$ and the rules of matrix multiplication will then fix the size of all of the matrices. When these equations are viewed from a control perspective, we address the question of what inputs $\underline{u}(t)$ will create a desired behavior.

7.2.1.1 Controllability

Perhaps the most basic question to ask in any control context is whether the system can be made to behave as desired. The system is said to be *completely controllable* if for any initial state $\underline{x}(t_1)$ there exists a control function $\underline{u}(t)$ that drives the system to any final state $\underline{x}(t_2)$ in finite time. If the time interval $t_2 - t_1$ can be made as small as desired for any t_1, the system is said to be *totally controllable*.

For a time invariant system where the matrices F and G do not depend on time, and F is $n \times n$ and G is $n \times r$, the system is *totally controllable* if and only if the $n \times nr$ matrix:

$$
Q = [G|FG|FFG|...F^{n-1}G]
$$

is of full rank. This condition covers the case where the matrices $F(t)$ and $G(t)$ do depend on time if Q loses rank only at isolated points in time.

7.2.1.2 Observability

The system is said to be *completely observable* if for any initial state $\underline{x}(t_1)$, it is possible to completely determine that initial state from knowledge of the system input $\underline{u}(t)$ and output functions $\underline{y}(t)$ on a finite interval $[t_1, t_2]$ where $t_2 > t_1$. If the time interval $t_2 - t_1$ can be made as small as desired for any t_1, the system is said to be *totally observable*.

For a time invariant system where the matrices F and H do not depend on time, and F is $n \times n$ and H is $m \times n$, the system is *totally observable* if and only if the $mn \times n$ matrix:

$$P = \begin{bmatrix} H \\ HF \\ HFF \\ \cdots \\ HF^{n-1} \end{bmatrix}$$

is of full rank. This condition covers the case where the matrices $F(t)$ and $H(t)$ do depend on time if P loses rank only at isolated points in time.

7.2.2 State Space Feedback Control

Two options exist for feedback control laws in state space. The first is to use the system state, known as *state feedback*, and the second is to use the output, known as *output feedback*. It can be argued that only the latter is relevant in applications because only the output is accessible by definition. However, one can at times measure the entire state or reconstruct it so full state feedback is still an important special case.

7.2.2.1 State Feedback

A state feedback control law is of the form:

$$\underline{u}(t) = W\underline{v}(t) - K\underline{x}(t)$$

where $\underline{v}(t)$ is a new reference input (assumed to contain at least as many rows as $\underline{u}$) to the closed loop system that is acted upon by the feedforward model W. The gain matrix K is assumed to be constant.

Upon substitution, the new linear system becomes:

$$\underline{\dot{x}} = [F - GK]\underline{x} + GW\underline{v}$$
$$\underline{y} = [H - MK]\underline{x} + MW\underline{v}$$

This is of the same form as the original system but, of course, all of the matrices have changed (Figure 7.20). It is easy to show that the controllability of the system is unaltered if W is of full rank. Observability is potentially altered and it could even be lost completely if $H = MK$.

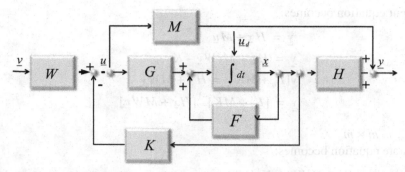

Figure 7.20 State Feedback. The state is fed back and combined with a feedforward term to generate a new input to the system.

7.2.2.2 Eigenvalue Assignment for State Feedback

In the context of state space representations, the pole placement problem is called *eigenvalue assignment*. The stability question and system behavior in general rests on the eigenvalues of the new dynamics matrix $F - GK$. The new characteristic equation is:

$$det(\lambda I - F + GK) = 0$$

It can be shown that provided the original system is controllable, the eigenvalues of the system can be placed arbitrarily using some constant, real-valued, gain matrix K. This is similar to the earlier result for the damped oscillator. If the gains can independently determine every coefficient of the characteristic polynomial, then any polynomial, and hence any roots can be generated.

7.2.2.3 Output Feedback

An output feedback control law is of the form:

$$\underline{u}(t) = W\underline{v}(t) - K\underline{y}(t)$$

where $\underline{v}(t)$ is a new reference input (assumed to contain at least as many rows as $\underline{u}$) to the closed loop system that is acted upon by the feedforward model W (Figure 7.21). The gain matrix K is assumed to be constant.

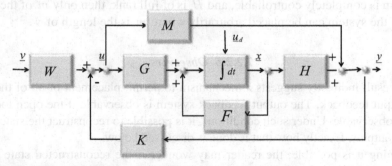

Figure 7.21 Output Feedback. The output is fed back and combined with a feedforward term to generate a new input to the system.

The output equation becomes:

$$\underline{y} = H\underline{x} + M\underline{u}$$
$$\underline{y} = H\underline{x} + M(W\underline{v} - K\underline{y})$$
$$\underline{y}[I_m + MK] = H\underline{x} + MW\underline{v}$$
$$\underline{y} = [I_m + MK]^{-1}[H\underline{x} + MW\underline{v}]$$

where I_m is $m \times m$.

The state equation becomes:

$$\dot{\underline{x}} = F\underline{x} + G(W\underline{v} - K\underline{y})$$
$$\dot{\underline{x}} = F\underline{x} + G(W\underline{v} - K[I_m + MK]^{-1}[H\underline{x} + MW\underline{v}])$$
$$\dot{\underline{x}} = [F - GK[I_m + MK]^{-1}H]\underline{x} + G(I_r - K[I_m + MK]^{-1}M)W\underline{v}$$
$$\dot{\underline{x}} = [F - GK[I_m + MK]^{-1}H]\underline{x} + G[I_r + KM]^{-1}W\underline{v}$$

where I_r is $r \times r$. The last step used the matrix inversion lemma:

$$I_r - K[I_m + MK]^{-1}M = [I_r + KM]^{-1}$$

In summary, the new linear system becomes:

$$\dot{\underline{x}} = [F - GK[I_m + MK]^{-1}H]\underline{x} + G[I_r + KM]^{-1}W\underline{v}$$
$$\underline{y} = [I_m + MK]^{-1}[H\underline{x} + MW\underline{v}]$$

This is of the same form as the original system but, of course, all of the matrices have changed. It is easy to show that the controllability of the system is unaltered if W is of full rank and $[I_r + KM]^{-1}$ is of full rank. Unlike for state feedback, observability is preserved.

7.2.2.4 Eigenvalue Assignment for Output Feedback

The stability question and system behavior in general rests on the eigenvalues of the new dynamics matrix $F - GK[I_m + MK]^{-1}H$. It can be shown that provided the original system is completely controllable, and H is of full rank, then only m of the eigenvalues of the system can be placed arbitrarily where m is the length of $\underline{y}$.

7.2.2.5 Observers

The last result indirectly suggests a mechanism to permit placement of all of the poles using output feedback. The output feedback system is observable if the open loop system was observable. Under such conditions, it is possible to reconstruct the state vector from the outputs. Exactly how that is done is discussed below.

Assuming it is possible, the reader may wonder if the reconstructed state can be used instead of the output to convert output feedback to state feedback. Indeed, this is the case. The system to reconstruct the state is called an *observer* (Figure 7.22).

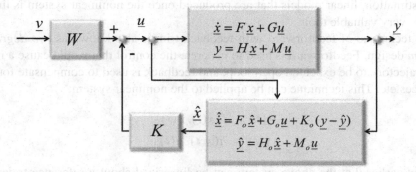

Figure 7.22 Reconstructed State Feedback. An observer is used to reconstruct the state and convert output feedback to state feedback.

As shown in the figure, an observer is a kind of copy of the system that knows the dynamics and is provided with both the inputs and the outputs. Let the observer produce an estimate of the output based on its estimate of state.

$$\hat{\underline{y}} = H_o \hat{\underline{x}} + M_o \underline{u}$$

The observer dynamics are driven by one extra input – the output prediction error:

$$\frac{d}{dt} \hat{\underline{x}} = F_o \hat{\underline{x}} + G_o \underline{u} + K_o (\underline{y} - \hat{\underline{y}})$$

Where K_o is some gain matrix yet to be determined. If the observer dynamics matrices F_o and G_o are exactly equal to those of the system, then the above can be subtracted from the real system dynamics to produce:

$$\frac{d}{dt}(\underline{x} - \hat{\underline{x}}) = F(\underline{x} - \hat{\underline{x}}) - K_o(\underline{y} - \hat{\underline{y}})$$

This is clearly of the form of a linear system whose "state" is the error in the reconstructed state and whose "output" is the error in the output. The error in the output is known because $\hat{\underline{y}}$ is predicted from the predicted state and $\underline{y}$ is by definition the available signal from the sensors.

Clearly, an observer is of the same mathematical form as a controller and we can ask about whether the error in $\hat{\underline{x}}$ is "controllable." When it is totally controllable, the state estimate can be made equal to the state itself in an arbitrarily short period of time, in theory. In practice the measurements are not available continuously and both the measurements and the matrices are not known perfectly so the solution converges more slowly and it is never perfect.

Many mobile robots use reconstructed state feedback from time to time because not all states are measurable. For example, position and orientation states can sometimes only be generated by integrating linear and angular velocities. The Kalman filter is an observer.

7.2.2.6 *Control of Nonlinear State Space Systems*

Given the observation that most robots are nonlinear systems, the reader may wonder why linear systems theory is of any relevance. As we saw in numerical methods and in state estimation, linear models that are produced once the nonlinear system is linearized are very valuable tools.

The technique of feedforward with feedback trim is also known as *two degree of freedom* design. Feedforward is used to generate the control that would cause a reference trajectory to be executed open loop, and feedback is used to compensate for disturbances etc. This technique can be applied to the nonlinear system:

$$\dot{\underline{x}}(t) = \underline{f}(\underline{x}(t), \underline{u}(t))$$
$$\underline{y}(t) = \underline{h}(\underline{x}(t), \underline{u}(t))$$

We saw earlier that the above system can be linearized about a reference trajectory $\underline{x}_r(t)$ to produce the linearized error dynamics:

$$\delta\dot{\underline{x}}(t) = F(t)\delta\underline{x}(t) + G(t)\delta\underline{u}(t)$$
$$\delta\underline{y}(t) = H(t)\delta\underline{x}(t) + M(t)\delta\underline{u}(t)$$

where F, G, H, M are the appropriate Jacobians.

Assume for the moment that some trajectory generation process can be designed to produce the input $\underline{u}_r(t)$ that generates a feasible reference trajectory (one that satisfies the nonlinear system dynamics). Under such conditions, a state space controller can be configured to perform feedback compensation based on the linearized error dynamics.

7.2.3 Example: Robot Trajectory Following

This section applies state space control concepts to the problem of causing a robot to follow a specified path.

7.2.3.1 Representing Robot Trajectories

It will shortly be necessary to represent an entire motion of a robot as a continuous vector-valued signal. In order to avoid duplication later, this section will lay out two options that apply in different circumstances.

Let the state vector of a robot vehicle moving in 2D be $\underline{x} = \begin{bmatrix} x & y & \psi \end{bmatrix}^T$. Then, a state space trajectory would be the vector-valued function $\underline{x}(t)$. Suppose the inputs $\underline{u} = \begin{bmatrix} \kappa & v \end{bmatrix}^T$ to the robot are velocity and curvature. This is the first way to represent a trajectory because the trajectory follows from the inputs. Assuming that the velocity is always directed forward in the body frame, we already know that a nonlinear state space model of the system, in both differential and integral form is:

$$\frac{d}{dt}\begin{bmatrix} x \\ y \\ \psi \end{bmatrix} = \begin{bmatrix} \cos\psi \\ \sin\psi \\ \kappa \end{bmatrix} v \qquad \begin{bmatrix} x(t) \\ y(t) \\ \psi(t) \end{bmatrix} = \begin{bmatrix} x(0) \\ y(0) \\ \psi(0) \end{bmatrix} + \int_0^t \begin{bmatrix} \cos\psi \\ \sin\psi \\ \kappa \end{bmatrix} V \, dt \qquad (7.18)$$

It is significant that the velocity can be factored from every element on the right-hand side of the differential form. We can change the independent variable from time to distance by just dividing by velocity because:

$$\frac{dx}{dt} \bigg/ v = \frac{dx}{dt} \bigg/ \frac{ds}{dt} = \frac{dx}{ds} \tag{7.19}$$

Now, we can write the system dynamics in the form:

$$\frac{d}{ds}\begin{bmatrix} x \\ y \\ \psi \end{bmatrix} = \begin{bmatrix} \cos\psi \\ \sin\psi \\ \kappa \end{bmatrix} \qquad \begin{bmatrix} x(s) \\ y(s) \\ \psi(s) \end{bmatrix} = \begin{bmatrix} x(0) \\ y(0) \\ \psi(0) \end{bmatrix} + \int_0^t \begin{bmatrix} \cos\psi \\ \sin\psi \\ \kappa \end{bmatrix} ds \tag{7.20}$$

This is the second form – where the velocity input has been eliminated. It is an implicit specification of some curve whose shape is determined by a single input – curvature. This fact is known as the *Fundamental Theorem of Plane Curves*. The curvature is assumed to be a specified function of distance.

The explicit conversion from time to distance-based derivatives in a computer can be problematic if the velocity is ever zero along the time trajectory. However, the singularity can be removed by avoiding the computation until the vehicle moves again.

7.2.3.2 Example: Robot Trajectory Following

Suppose a trajectory generator has produced a reference trajectory $[\underline{u}_r(t), \underline{x}_r(t)]$. Suppose further that the system output is equal to the state (i.e., assume we can measure $\begin{bmatrix} x & y & \psi \end{bmatrix}^T$) so the output equation can be ignored.

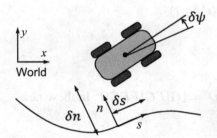

Figure 7.23 Trajectory Following. In 2D for a vehicle, full state feedback means measuring x and y and heading error.

7.2.3.2.1 Linearization and Controllability. The linearized dynamics based on linearizing Equation 7.18 are of the form:

$$\frac{d}{dt}\begin{bmatrix} \delta x \\ \delta y \\ \delta\psi \end{bmatrix} = \begin{bmatrix} 0 & 0 & -vs\psi \\ 0 & 0 & vc\psi \\ 0 & 0 & 0 \end{bmatrix}\begin{bmatrix} \delta x \\ \delta y \\ \delta\psi \end{bmatrix} + \begin{bmatrix} c\psi & 0 \\ s\psi & 0 \\ 0 & 1 \end{bmatrix}\begin{bmatrix} \delta v \\ \delta\kappa \end{bmatrix} \tag{7.21}$$

A conversion of coordinates to the body frame as shown in Figure 7.23 will simplify the derivation. Multiply Equation 7.21 by the rotation matrix that converts from the world frame to the body frame:

$$\begin{bmatrix} c\psi & s\psi & 0 \\ -s\psi & c\psi & 0 \\ 0 & 0 & 1 \end{bmatrix} \begin{bmatrix} \delta\dot{x} \\ \delta\dot{y} \\ \delta\dot{\psi} \end{bmatrix} = \begin{bmatrix} c\psi & s\psi & 0 \\ -s\psi & c\psi & 0 \\ 0 & 0 & 1 \end{bmatrix} \begin{bmatrix} 0 & 0 & -vs\psi \\ 0 & 0 & vc\psi \\ 0 & 0 & 0 \end{bmatrix} \begin{bmatrix} \delta x \\ \delta y \\ \delta\psi \end{bmatrix} + \begin{bmatrix} c\psi & s\psi & 0 \\ -s\psi & c\psi & 0 \\ 0 & 0 & 1 \end{bmatrix} \begin{bmatrix} c\psi & 0 \\ s\psi & 0 \\ 0 & 1 \end{bmatrix} \begin{bmatrix} \delta v \\ \delta\kappa \end{bmatrix}$$

$$\begin{bmatrix} c\psi & s\psi & 0 \\ -s\psi & c\psi & 0 \\ 0 & 0 & 1 \end{bmatrix} \begin{bmatrix} \delta\dot{x} \\ \delta\dot{y} \\ \delta\dot{\psi} \end{bmatrix} = \begin{bmatrix} 0 & 0 & 0 \\ 0 & 0 & v \\ 0 & 0 & 0 \end{bmatrix} \begin{bmatrix} \delta x \\ \delta y \\ \delta\psi \end{bmatrix} + \begin{bmatrix} 1 & 0 \\ 0 & 0 \\ 0 & 1 \end{bmatrix} \begin{bmatrix} \delta v \\ \delta\kappa \end{bmatrix}$$

(7.22)

Now, define the perturbative positions and velocities in the body frame thus:

$$\delta\underline{x}(t) = R\delta\underline{s}(t) = \begin{bmatrix} c\psi & -s\psi & 0 \\ s\psi & c\psi & 0 \\ 0 & 0 & 1 \end{bmatrix} \begin{bmatrix} \delta s \\ \delta n \\ \delta\psi \end{bmatrix} \quad \delta\underline{\dot{x}}(t) = R\delta\underline{\dot{s}}(t) = \begin{bmatrix} c\psi & -s\psi & 0 \\ s\psi & c\psi & 0 \\ 0 & 0 & 1 \end{bmatrix} \begin{bmatrix} \delta\dot{s} \\ \delta\dot{n} \\ \delta\dot{\psi} \end{bmatrix}$$

where δs and δn are the errors in the instantaneous direction of travel (alongtrack) and orthogonal to it (crosstrack). Substituting these into Equation 7.22 gives:

$$\begin{bmatrix} \delta\dot{s} \\ \delta\dot{n} \\ \delta\dot{\psi} \end{bmatrix} = \begin{bmatrix} 0 & 0 & 0 \\ 0 & 0 & V \\ 0 & 0 & 0 \end{bmatrix} \begin{bmatrix} \delta s \\ \delta n \\ \delta\psi \end{bmatrix} + \begin{bmatrix} 1 & 0 \\ 0 & 0 \\ 0 & 1 \end{bmatrix} \begin{bmatrix} \delta v \\ \delta\kappa \end{bmatrix}$$

(7.23)

because the rotation matrices cancel each other to become the identity. The speed V appears because the crosstrack error rate $\delta\dot{n}$ caused by heading error $\delta\theta$ is proportional to speed. This system is linear and it is even time invariant when the speed is constant. This result is of the form:

$$\delta\underline{\dot{s}}(t) = F(t)\delta\underline{s}(t) + G(t)\delta\underline{u}(t)$$

where

$$\underline{s} = \begin{bmatrix} s & n & \psi \end{bmatrix}^T$$

The test for controllability is based on the matrix $Q = [G|FG|FFG|]$. In these new coordinates:

$$Q = \begin{bmatrix} 1 & 0 & 0 & 0 & 0 & 0 \\ 0 & 0 & 0 & v & 0 & 0 \\ 0 & 1 & 0 & 0 & 0 & 0 \end{bmatrix}$$

There are three nonzero columns and they clearly point in different directions. This system is controllable.

7.2.3.2.2 State Feedback Control Law.
A state feedback control law is of the form:

$$\delta\underline{u}(t) = -K\delta\underline{s}(t)$$

where K is 2×3. To simplify the derivation, let us choose to have three nonzero gains based on the intuition that steering can remove crosstrack and heading error and speed can remove alongtrack error. Thus:

$$K = \begin{bmatrix} k_s & 0 & 0 \\ 0 & k_n & k_\theta \end{bmatrix}$$

and the control is:

$$\begin{bmatrix} \delta v \\ \delta \kappa \end{bmatrix} = \begin{bmatrix} k_s & 0 & 0 \\ 0 & k_n & k_\psi \end{bmatrix} \begin{bmatrix} \delta s \\ \delta n \\ \delta \psi \end{bmatrix} = \begin{bmatrix} k_s(\delta s) \\ k_n(\delta n) + k_\psi(\delta \psi) \end{bmatrix}$$

The total control includes the feedforward terms as well as the feedback terms:

$$\underline{u}(t) = \underline{u}_r(t) + \delta \underline{u}(t) = \underline{u}_r(t) - \begin{bmatrix} k_s & 0 & 0 \\ 0 & k_n & k_\psi \end{bmatrix} \begin{bmatrix} \delta s \\ \delta n \\ \delta \psi \end{bmatrix} \qquad (7.24)$$

Spotlight 7.1 Two Degree of Freedom Path Follower.

Because a heading error will cause an increasing or decreasing crosstrack according to Equation 7.23, the heading error is essentially the crosstrack error rate. Under this interpretation, the control amounts to a proportional control on alongtrack error and a PD control on crosstrack error.

7.2.3.2.3 Behavior. The operation of this controller can be understood by examining the behavior when different terms are added. First, an open loop controller simply executes the reference curvature trajectory. As shown in Figure 7.24, an initial pose error will not be removed but the path followed will probably have the correct shape.

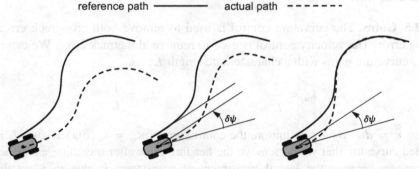

reference path ——————— actual path - - - - - - -

Figure 7.24 Path Follower Behavior. Three cases are illustrated. (Left) Open loop does not compensate for errors. (Center) Heading compensation fixes heading but not position errors. (Right) Pose compensation tries to remove all errors.

The speed feedback term simply speeds up when the vehicle is lagging its desired position etc. It is possible to omit this term and then the system will tolerate speed errors while trying to remove the others. If so, it is a good idea to reformulate the reference trajectory to depend on the measured distance thus:

$$u_r(s) = \kappa(s_{measured})$$

This will cause the control to try to achieve the desired curvature at the present position on the path even if the vehicle is ahead of or behind schedule.

If only the heading feedback term is included, the actual path will be deformed as necessary to achieve the correct heading but crosstrack error will not be nulled. Addition of the crosstrack error term causes all errors to be removed.

7.2.3.2.4 Eigenvalue Placement. The closed loop perturbative system dynamics matrix is:

$$F - GK = \begin{bmatrix} 0 & 0 & 0 \\ 0 & 0 & v \\ 0 & 0 & 0 \end{bmatrix} - \begin{bmatrix} 1 & 0 \\ 0 & 0 \\ 0 & 1 \end{bmatrix} \begin{bmatrix} k_s & 0 & 0 \\ 0 & k_n & k_\psi \end{bmatrix} = - \begin{bmatrix} k_s & 0 & 0 \\ 0 & 0 & -v \\ 0 & k_n & k_\psi \end{bmatrix}$$

The characteristic polynomial is:

$$det(\lambda I - F + GK) = \begin{vmatrix} \lambda + k_s & 0 & 0 \\ 0 & \lambda & -v \\ 0 & k_n & \lambda + k_\psi \end{vmatrix}$$

$$det(\lambda I - F + GK) = (\lambda + k_s)(\lambda)(\lambda + k_\psi) + (k_n)(v)(\lambda + k_s)$$

$$det(\lambda I - F + GK) = (\lambda + k_s)(\lambda^2 + \lambda k_\psi + k_n v)$$

$$det(\lambda I - F + GK) = (\lambda^3 + \lambda^2(k_\psi + k_s) + \lambda(k_n v + k_s k_\psi) + k_s k_n v)$$

Because the eigenvalues depend on the coefficients and because all the coefficients can be adjusted independently by changing the gains, the eigenvalues can be placed anywhere we like.

7.2.3.2.5 Gains. The curvature control is used to remove both crosstrack error and heading error. The velocity control is used to remove alongtrack error. We can relate the two curvature gains with a characteristic length L:

$$k_n = \frac{2}{L^2} \qquad\qquad k_\psi = \frac{1}{L}$$

Because $\kappa = d\psi/ds$ by definition, the control term $\delta\kappa_\psi = k_\theta(\delta\psi) = \delta\psi/L$ is the sustained curvature that would remove the heading error after travelling a distance L. Furthermore, because the lateral movement at a distance L due to a rotation is $\delta n = L d\psi$, the control term $\delta\kappa_n = k_n(\delta n) = 2\delta n/L^2$ rotates through an angle of magnitude $2\delta n/L$ over a distance of L in order to remove the crosstrack error. Because the average heading over that period of time is only half the total change, the factor of 2 is introduced. The gain k_s tries to remove the velocity error after the time period of $\tau_s = 1/k_s$. These intuitions can be used to set reasonable values for the gains.

This simple example also illustrates the typical need for an observer in certain mobile robot applications. The measurements required to compute the path following errors are not easy to obtain. Measurements of linear and angular velocity are relatively common, but measurements of position and orientation take more work.

One way to get them is to integrate the linear and angular velocity by dead reckoning. Another way to get them is to use a receiver for the radio signals of a satellite navigation system.

7.2.4 Perception Based Control

Visual servoing [5] is an instance of perception-based control – the use of a perception sensor to form error signals in a control loop. It is a very important technology for mobile robots because it is a means for generating high quality feedback on the pose error of the system. It can be used on a manipulator to grasp an object. It can be used on mobile robots in order to move within reach of a viewed object such as, for example, an electrical outlet that will be used for charging the batteries.

In some cases, the sensor is moving, as would be the case for a sensor on the front of a forktruck. In others, the sensor is stationary and it views the motion of the robot. An example is a ceiling camera used to localize a mobile robot. In some cases, both the camera and the object are moving. Examples include a mobile robot following a person, or tracking other cars on the road, or a torso-mounted sensor used to precisely localize the hand of a manipulator. In all cases, the important elements are that an error can be measured and that some degrees of freedom of motion can be controlled to reduce the error.

7.2.4.1 Error Coordinates

As shown in Figure 7.25, one approach is to form errors in image space by comparing the present image (whether it is color, intensity, or range) to a reference image that defines what the robot would see if it was in the correct configuration.

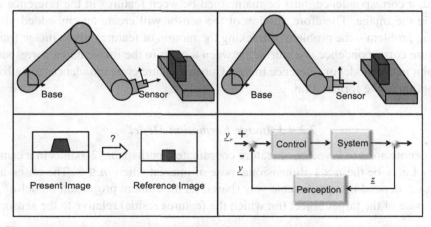

Figure 7.25 Image-Based Visual Servoing. This is a moving sensor configuration for a manipulator. The sensor is a camera and errors are formed in image space.

In some cases, the pixels in the present image may be compared directly to those in a reference image. It is more likely in practice that just the image coordinates of various features in the image, like corners or line segments, will be compared to a model of the object in view in order to form errors.

Another formulation uses the imagery to explicitly calculate the pose of the sensor relative to the object in view Figure 7.26. An error is then computed in pose coordinates that corresponds directly to the difference between where the sensor is and where it should be. For a manipulator, an inverse kinematics calculation might be used to determine the desired joint angles. For a mobile robot, a trajectory generator might be used to produce a reference trajectory for a controller to follow.

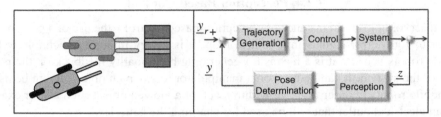

Figure 7.26 Pose Based Visual Servoing. This is a moving sensor configuration for a mobile robot. The sensor could be a lidar and errors are formed in pose space.

Of course, a detailed implementation might convert the sensor pose error into a vehicle pose error before invoking trajectory generation.

7.2.4.2 Visual Servoing

This section will develop some of the details of a feature-based visual servo that ignores the detailed dynamics of the system and develops a basic geometric approach. Later in Chapter 9, the details of pose determination, visual tracking, correspondence, and so on, will be presented.

Regardless of the coordinates used to express the error, if a feature based approach is used, a correspondence must be maintained between features in the reference and those in the image. Therefore, motion of the sensor will create an embedded visual tracking problem – the problem of tracking the motion of features in the image frame. A feature correspondence is a pairing between a point in the image and a corresponding point in the model or reference image. Correct feature correspondences are a basic assumption in the formulation.

7.2.4.3 Image Formation Model

Let z denote an $m \times 1$ vector of feature coordinates (perhaps $n/2$ points in a camera image). Let x be the $n \times 1$ dimensional pose of interest where $n \leq 6$. The observable features z depend in a predictable way (based on the camera projection model $h(\_)$) on the pose of the target object (on which the features reside) relative to the sensor:

$$z = h(x(t)) \qquad (7.25)$$

We will require that $\underline{h}$ impose at least n independent constraints on $\underline{x}$. Hence $m \geq n$ and the Jacobian of $\underline{h}$ will be nonsingular by assumption.

The reference image or feature vector $\underline{z}_r$ must be specified manually or derived from a recorded reference image. The goal of the system is to drive the feature error $\underline{z}_r - \underline{z}$ to zero in order to cause the system to acquire the reference pose (vehicle) or configuration (manipulator) $\underline{x}_r$ which is associated with the reference image.

7.2.4.4 Controller Design

The time derivative of Equation 7.25 is:

$$\dot{\underline{z}} = \left(\frac{\partial h}{\partial \underline{x}}\right)\left(\frac{\partial \underline{x}}{\partial t}\right) = H(t)\,\underline{v}(t) \tag{7.26}$$

where the measurement Jacobian H, is called the *interaction matrix* [4] in this context. It relates the sensor-object velocity (derivatives of pose elements) to the velocities of features in the image. By definition, it also relates small changes in pose to small changes in feature location:

$$\Delta \underline{z} = H\Delta \underline{x} \tag{7.27}$$

This relationship could, for example, be solved with the left pseudoinverse H^+:

$$\Delta \underline{x} = H^+ \Delta \underline{z}$$

If we now interpret $\Delta \underline{z}$ to be the feature error vector, then:

$$\Delta \underline{x} = H^+[\underline{z}_r - \underline{z}]$$

Dividing by a small Δt and passing to the limit produces:

$$\underline{v} = H^+ \frac{d}{dt}[\underline{z}_r - \underline{z}] \tag{7.28}$$

This is now a relationship between pose error rate and feature error rates, which can be used to drive the system to remove the pose error. Suppose we would like the commanded velocity $\underline{v}$ to be consistent with nulling the error in τ (alternately $1/\lambda$) seconds. Then, we can set the feature error rate to be:

$$\frac{d}{dt}[\underline{z}_r - \underline{z}] = -\frac{[\underline{z}_r - \underline{z}]}{\tau} = -\lambda[\underline{z}_r - \underline{z}]$$

Substituting this into Equation 7.28, and rearranging gives:

$$\underline{v}_c = -\lambda H^+[\underline{z}_r - \underline{z}] \tag{7.29}$$

Spotlight 7.2 Visual Servoing.

This is merely a proportional controller with a gain $K_p = \lambda = 1/\tau$, which will drive the observed feature errors exponentially to zero.

Returning to Equation 7.26 and substituting the control gives the closed loop system dynamics:

$$\dot{\underline{z}} = H\underline{v}_c(t) = -\lambda HH^+[\underline{z}_r - \underline{z}] \qquad (7.30)$$

Now because the feature error is $\underline{e} = \underline{z}_r - \underline{z}$, we can write for a constant reference image:

$$\dot{\underline{e}} = \frac{d}{dt}[\underline{z}_r - \underline{z}] = \dot{\underline{z}}$$

Substituting this into Equation 7.30 produces the system error dynamics:

$$\dot{\underline{e}} = \dot{\underline{z}} = -\lambda H(t)H(t)^+[\underline{z}_r - \underline{z}] = A(t)\underline{e}$$

For the feature error vector $\underline{e}$ and the system dynamics matrix A. As we saw earlier, stability depends on the eigenvalues of this time varying matrix. The real parts of all eigenvalues must be negative throughout the trajectory for the system to converge to a solution. It is important that the pseudoinverse exist, so $H^T H$ must not become singular.

7.2.5 Steering Trajectory Generation

This section presents a relatively simple method for the generation of reference trajectories for mobile robots. We often think of this problem in terms of generating steering functions but there is an equivalent (but easier) problem of generating velocity functions. This section will concentrate on the steering trajectory generation problem.

A capacity to generate the precise open loop control needed to drive somewhere is highly enabling (Figure 7.27). We saw earlier that it is advisable to provide a controller with a feasible reference signal in order to decouple the response to true errors from the specification of the desired motion. Most vehicles are underactuated, so it is often is not good enough to steer "generally toward" some goal position. As the forktruck trajectory shows, knowledge of the nonholonomic constraints may mean that the vehicle must start by turning right in order to ultimately achieve a goal pose to its left.

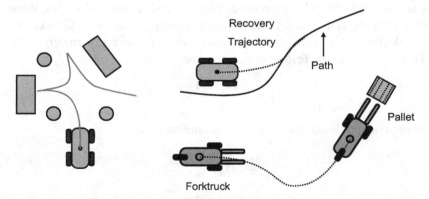

Figure 7.27 Uses For Trajectory Generation. (Top) Corrective trajectories in high speed path following reacquire the path at the correct heading and curvature. (Left) Precision maneuvers allow the robot to turn around competently in a cluttered space. (Bottom) In order to pick up the pallet, the forktruck must arrive at precisely the right position and heading with zero curvature.

7.2.5.1 Problem Specification

By *trajectory generation,* we mean the problem of generating an entire control function $\underline{u}(t)$, which corresponds to some desired state trajectory $\underline{x}(t)$. Oftentimes, the term *path* is used interchangeably with trajectory but we will distinguish them. Here, *path* will refer to motions specified in terms of geometry only, with no indication of the speed of motion.

The trajectory generation problem can be posed as a two-point boundary value problem. The boundary conditions are typically the constraints that we care the most about: to start somewhere in particular and end up somewhere in particular (Figure 7.28):

$$\underline{x}(t_0) = \underline{x}_0 \quad \underline{x}(t_f) = \underline{x}_f \tag{7.31}$$

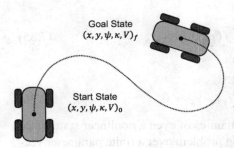

Goal State
$(x, y, \psi, \kappa, V)_f$

Start State
$(x, y, \psi, \kappa, V)_0$

Figure 7.28 Trajectory Generation Problem. The initial and final state are given. The problem is to find an input consistent with all of these constraints, the system dynamics, and bounds on the inputs.

The system dynamics are also a kind of constraint:

$$\dot{\underline{x}} = f(\underline{x}, \underline{u}) \tag{7.32}$$

Although every $\underline{u}(t)$ generates some $\underline{x}(t)$, which can be found by integrating the dynamics, there are potentially many $\underline{x}(t)$ for which there is no corresponding $\underline{u}(t)$. This situation may occur for mathematical existence reasons, physics reasons, or practical power related reasons. If no $\underline{u}(t)$ exists for a given $\underline{x}(t)$ the state trajectory is called *infeasible.*

Let a *trajectory* be a representation of a motion confined to some time interval. This could be a specification of the state vector (a state trajectory) over an interval $\{\underline{x}(t) | (t_0 < t < t_f)\}$ or it could be a specification of the input (an input trajectory) over an interval $\{\underline{u}(t) | (t_0 < t < t_f)\}$.

Both forms can be visualized as the trajectory followed by the tip of a vector in some space. In a feedforward control system, the first is the reference trajectory given to the feedback controller and the second is the feedforward control signal passed directly to the output.

7.2.5.2 Formulation as a Rootfinding Problem

The reader may want to refer to Section 7.2.3.1 while reading this section. A search process that searches the function continuum of all possible input signals $\underline{u}(t)$ is not feasible in a computer. Any practical implementation must approximate this search in some manner. One effective way to do so, parameterization, is presented here.

Let us assume that the space of all input functions $\underline{u}(t)$ can be expressed as a family of functions that depend on some parameters.

$$\underline{u}(t) \rightarrow \underline{\tilde{u}}(\underline{p}, t) \tag{7.33}$$

This is plausible because we know that if we pick any function, it can be well approximated, for example, by a truncated Taylor series and enough parameters can make the approximation arbitrarily good. Hence the space of all vectors of Taylor coefficients is a good approximation to the space of all continuous functions.

Now, because the input is completely determined by the parameters and the state is completely determined by the input, the dynamics become:

$$\underline{\dot{x}}(t) = \underline{f}[\underline{x}(\underline{p}, t), \underline{\tilde{u}}(\underline{p}, t), t] = \underline{\tilde{f}}(\underline{p}, t) \tag{7.34}$$

The boundary conditions then become:

$$\underline{g}(\underline{p}, t_0, t_f) = \underline{x}(t_0) + \int_{t_0}^{t_f} \underline{\tilde{f}}(\underline{p}, t)dt = \underline{x}_b \tag{7.35}$$

which is conventionally written as:

$$\underline{c}(\underline{p}, t_0, t_f) = \underline{g}(\underline{p}, t_0, t_f) - \underline{x}_b = 0 \tag{7.36}$$

In other words, the problem of inverting the dynamics of even a nonlinear state space system can be easily converted into a rootfinding problem over a finite parameter vector. This is a very significant fact that we will exploit in several ways.

7.2.5.3 Steering Trajectory Generation

Let us move now to the specific problem of generating a steering trajectory. For this problem, it is convenient to express the trajectory in terms of curvature $u(\underline{p}, s) \rightarrow \kappa(\underline{p}, s)$ expressed as a function of distance s. We can also take the initial distance to be 0. The unknowns are then reduced to:

$$\underline{q} = \left[\underline{p}^T \; s_f \right]^T$$

where s_f is the terminal distance and it is also regarded as unknown.

It should be clear that if the input $\kappa(\underline{p}, s)$ has n parameters, we can vary them in order to satisfy up to n constraints. Of all possible functions with parameters, polynomial curvature functions have a long history in mobile robotics and the simplest polynomial is a constant. It is not too hard to compute the unique constant curvature arc $\kappa(s) = a$, which goes through a required point (Figure 7.29).

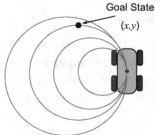

Goal State

(x,y)

Figure 7.29 Arc Trajectory Generation. By imagining a family of arcs emanating from the vehicle, its clear that there must be one that goes through any point.

Note that once a and s_f are fixed by the choice of goal point, the heading and curvature that result are dependent on the final position and are entirely beyond our control. If one is willing to join two arcs together and require that they have the same radius, up to three constraints can be satisfied with the three parameters (a, s_1, s_2). Such a trajectory might be named an *s-curve* primitive.

One historically popular curve is the *clothoid*, which is of the form:

$$\kappa(s) = a + bs \tag{7.37}$$

For the clothoid, curvature is simply a linear function of distance. Its representation in the complex plane is called the *Cornu Spiral* (Figure 7.30).

One clothoid has three degrees of freedom (a, b, s_f). This is still not enough for most mobile robot trajectories. Let the state vector consist of the position, orientation, and curvature. To achieve a general terminal posture, we still must satisfy five constraints. The initial position and heading can be mapped to the origin. Then, the remaining constraints include an initial curvature $\kappa(0) = \kappa_0$ and an entire terminal state $\underline{x}s_f = \begin{bmatrix} x_f & y_f & \psi_f & \kappa_f \end{bmatrix}$.

So, we would need at least two more parameters than a clothoid to be able to satisfy five constraints. We could chain two clothoids together. Conversely, one curve with five degrees of freedom (a, b, c, d, s_f) is a cubic curvature polynomial:

$$\kappa(s) = a + bs + cs^2 + ds^3 \tag{7.38}$$

Let this class of functions (which includes arcs and clothoids as special cases) be called the *polynomial spirals*. This is a pretty good choice of trajectory representation because it is compact and completely general. By the Taylor remainder theorem, a long enough polynomial can represent any input we will care about. As shown in (Figure 7.31), a cubic polynomial spiral can drive anywhere in the plane.

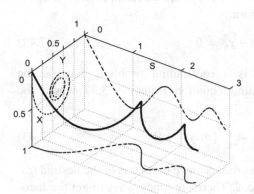

Figure 7.30 Cornu Spiral. The projection onto the complex plane is the plane trajectory which results from a linearly varying curvature input. The curvature polynomial coefficients are $a = 1$, $b = \pi$.

Figure 7.31 Expressiveness of the Polynomial Spiral. The figure shows trajectories which acquire all points on a grid of positions – each with a number of different headings.

It is also possible to compute heading given curvature in closed form:

$$\psi(s) = as + \frac{b}{2}s^2 + \frac{c}{3}s^3 + \frac{d}{4}s^4 + \psi_0 \tag{7.39}$$

7.2.5.4 Numerical Formulation

Once again, there are five constraints to satisfy (κ_0, x_f, y_f, ψ_f, κ_f). The constraint on initial curvature can be satisfied by setting $a = \kappa_0$. The four remaining parameters are denoted as:

$$\underline{q} = \begin{bmatrix} b & c & d & s_f \end{bmatrix}^T \tag{7.40}$$

Now, we have four equations to satisfy with the four remaining parameters:

$$\kappa(\underline{q}) = \kappa_0 + bs_f + cs_f^2 + ds_f^3 = \kappa_f$$

$$\psi(\underline{q}) = \kappa_0 s_f + \frac{b}{2}s_f^2 + \frac{c}{3}s_f^3 + \frac{d}{4}s_f^4 = \psi_f$$

$$x(\underline{q}) = \int_0^{s_f} \cos\left[\kappa_0 s + \frac{b}{2}s^2 + \frac{c}{3}s^3 + \frac{d}{4}s^4\right]ds = x_f \tag{7.41}$$

$$y(\underline{q}) = \int_0^{s_f} \sin\left[\kappa_0 s + \frac{b}{2}s^2 + \frac{c}{3}s^3 + \frac{d}{4}s^4\right]ds = y_f$$

Spotlight 7.3 Trajectory Generation as Rootfinding.

The basic problem of driving a vehicle to a terminal state comes down to solving these integro-algebraic equations for the desired parameters $\underline{q} = \begin{bmatrix} b & c & d & s_f \end{bmatrix}^T$.

Some of these are integrals, and they cannot be solved in closed form. However, this is still just a set of nonlinear equations of the form:

$$\underline{c}(\underline{q}) = \underline{g}(\underline{q}) - \underline{x}_b = 0 \tag{7.42}$$

where $\underline{x}_b = \begin{bmatrix} x_f & y_f & \psi_f & \kappa_f \end{bmatrix}$. Clearly, this is a rootfinding problem that can be addressed with Newton's method. Rewriting equation Equation 3.37 where the parameters $\underline{q}$ are the unknowns:

$$\Delta\underline{q} = -\underline{c}_q^{-1}\underline{c}(\underline{q}) = -\underline{c}_q^{-1}[\underline{g}(\underline{q}) - \underline{x}_b] \tag{7.43}$$

This formula is iterated until convergence to produce the parameters of the desired trajectory. This is how Figure 7.31 was produced. There are fancy ways to get the Jacobian but numerical differentiation as outlined in Section 3.2.2.3 of Chapter 3 is often sufficient or even preferred. In the latter case, it is important to make sure the integration is accurate enough so that the changes computed in the numerator of the derivative are due to the parameter perturbation – not to round off.

7.2.5.5 *Scaling Issues*

Scaling of the Jacobian can be an issue in practice. Jacobian entries with respect to coefficients of higher powers of s tend to be large, whereas others are small. One solution is to scale the curve down so that $s \approx 1$, solve the problem on the unit circle, and then scale the solution back.

Another solution is to redefine the parameters. For a four parameter vector $q = \begin{bmatrix} b & c & d & s_f \end{bmatrix}^T$, a new set of parameters can be defined which are the curvatures at equally separated points on the path:

$$\kappa_1 = \kappa_0 + b\left(\frac{s_f}{3}\right) + c\left(\frac{s_f}{3}\right)^2 + d\left(\frac{s_f}{3}\right)^3$$

$$\kappa_2 = \kappa_0 + b\left(\frac{2s_f}{3}\right) + c\left(\frac{2s_f}{3}\right)^2 + d\left(\frac{2s_f}{3}\right)^3$$

$$\kappa_3 = \kappa_0 + b(s_f) + c(s_f)^2 + d(s_f)^3$$

These three equations can be inverted in closed form. In the more general case, the technique produces a set of equations that relate the curvatures to the original parameters.

$$\underline{\kappa} = \begin{bmatrix} \kappa_1 \\ \kappa_2 \\ \kappa_3 \\ s_f \end{bmatrix} = \begin{bmatrix} \kappa_0 \\ \kappa_0 \\ \kappa_0 \\ 0 \end{bmatrix} + \begin{bmatrix} \left(\frac{s_f}{3}\right) & \left(\frac{s_f}{3}\right)^2 & \left(\frac{s_f}{3}\right)^3 & 0 \\ \left(\frac{2s_f}{3}\right) & \left(\frac{2s_f}{3}\right)^2 & \left(\frac{2s_f}{3}\right)^3 & 0 \\ (s_f) & (s_f)^2 & (s_f)^3 & 0 \\ 0 & 0 & 0 & 1 \end{bmatrix} \begin{bmatrix} b \\ c \\ d \\ s_f \end{bmatrix} = \underline{\kappa}_0 + S\underline{q}$$

The matrix can be inverted numerically. In Newton's method, one can simply make the substitution:

$$\underline{c}_\kappa = \frac{\partial \underline{c}}{\partial \underline{\kappa}} = \frac{\partial \underline{c}}{\partial \underline{q}} \frac{\partial \underline{q}}{\partial \underline{\kappa}} = \frac{\partial \underline{c}}{\partial \underline{\kappa}} S^{-1}$$

and then work in terms of the new parameters $\underline{\kappa}$.

7.2.5.6 *Extensions*

The above formulation is quite general – based on inverting the system dynamics. If the dynamic model is a 3D terrain following model, the algorithm will work as is with the new dynamic model. In the absence of disturbances and modelling errors, it would cause the vehicle to drive over rolling hills and end up precisely at the desired terminal state. In practice, the terrain may not have an analytic representation, which means the dynamic model will necessarily involve a numerical integration.

It's straightforward to connect multiple trajectories, impose continuity constraints, and solve the associated system of equations for the composite parameter vector. This technique can be useful when the length of the trajectory exceeds the limits of numerical stability. Generation of speed trajectories proceeds in an analogous manner given a model of how the vehicle speed will change in response to inputs and terrain.

7.2.6 References and Further Reading

Chaumette and Hutchinson are two tutorial sources on visual servoing. Corke is an entire book devoted to the subject. Wonham first showed that the closed loop eigenvalues of any controllable system can be assigned arbitrarily using state feedback and Davis showed similarly that m poles can be placed with output feedback. The content on steering trajectory generation is based directly on Nagy. It was inspired by the early work of Horn and the paper by Kanayama.

[4] F. Chaumette and S. Hutchinson, Visual Servo Control, Part I: Basic Approaches, *IEEE Robotics and Automation Magazine,* Vol. 13, No. 4, pp. 82–90, December 2006.

[5] P. Corke, *Visual Control of Robots: High Performance Visual Servoing,* John Wiley & Sons, New York, 1996.

[6] E. J. Davison, On Pole Assignment in Linear Systems with Incomplete State Feedback, *IEEE Transactions on Automatic Control,* Vol. 15, No. 15, pp. 348–351, 1970.

[7] B. K. Horn, The Curve of Least Energy, *ACM Transactions on Mathematical Software,* Vol. 9, No. 4, pp. 441–460, 1983.

[8] S. Hutchinson, G. D. Hager, and P. Corke, Visual Servoing: A Tutorial. *IEEE Transactions on Robotics and Automation,* Vol. 12, No. 5, pp. 651–670, 1996.

[9] Y. Kanayama and B. Hartman, Smooth Local Planning for Autonomous Vehicles, in *Proceedings of International Conference on Robotics and Automation,* 1989.

[10] B. Nagy and A. Kelly, Trajectory Generation for Car-Like Robots Using Cubic Curvature Polynomials, Field and Service Robots 2001 (FSR 01), Helsinki, Finland, 2001.

[11] W. M. Wonham, On Pole Assignment in Multi-Input Controllable Linear Systems, *IEEE Transactions on Automatic Control,* Vol. 12, pp. 660–665, 1967.

7.2.7 Exercises

7.2.7.1 Arc and Clothoid Trajectory Generation

Suppose that a mobile robot controller provides for only arc trajectories. It will drive the vehicle a specific distance with the provided curvature and then come to a stop. Provide formulas for the *curvature* (left turn is positive) and *signed distance* (backward is negative) required to move to a point along an arc. [Hints: Recall the equation of a circle not at the origin and recall the radian definition of angle measure.] Consider degenerate cases and singularities. Think of how a car steering wheel turns to interpret the sign of curvature when driving backward. The sign of curvature does not change if the steering wheel angle is the same, whether you drive forward or backward. Provide a table showing how the sign of the curvature and the sign of the length vary with the signs of both coordinates (x, y) of the point (all four cases).

7.2.7.2   Forward Solution for a Clothoid Trajectory

An arc trajectory is a trivial curvature "polynomial" in the form of a constant:

$$\kappa = a$$

Using arcs in practice often requires the assumption that the trajectory starts from a stopped position so that a vehicle can change curvature before it begins to move.

Notice that, using an arc, the heading at which the terminal point is achieved is not controllable – it is predetermined by the position. One way to add another parameter to generate this missing heading degree of freedom, is to use "clothoid" trajectories – which are of the form:

$$\kappa = a + bs$$

On the assumption that the robot stops at both the start and the end of the trajectory, there is no need to constrain the initial or terminal curvatures (i.e., the wheels can be turned while the robot is stopped to change curvature). Under such assumptions, this curve becomes a somewhat practical trajectory.

Write one polynomial and two integral equations that must be satisfied in order to achieve a terminal pose (position and heading). The opinion of many eminent mathematicians is that these integrals cannot be integrated in closed form so waste only a little time trying. Once you give up, notice that by adding one more term to the curvature (from arc to clothoid) the problem changed from pretty trivial to impossible. This problem must be solved numerically.

7.3 Optimal and Model Predictive Control

This chapter begins with a survey of theoretical results in variational optimization that form the theoretical underpinnings of a good part of the rest of the book. The basics of feedback control were covered in earlier chapters. There, we learned the value of a feasible reference trajectory and we saw one method of generating them. If the reference trajectory generator operates online, it typically generates a solution that starts at the present time and predicts the state trajectory for some finite horizon into the future. Just like disturbance feedforward, prediction creates the capacity to remove errors before they have occurred in the sense that there is freedom to select the input that is predicted to produce the desired output despite the disturbances that can be predicted.

Except in the trivial case of the bang-bang control, earlier discussion of control has also not addressed the question of how an optimal reference input might be generated. Techniques do exist to compute optimal inputs for control problems. When prediction and optimal control are combined, a system is created that can behave intelligently in the sense of carefully considering the consequences of actions and making good decisions on how to proceed.

7.3.1 Calculus of Variations

Variational optimization is a generalization of parameter optimization where the problem is framed in terms of solving for an entire unknown function, usually a function of time. When we note that the motion of a mobile robot through space is a function of time, the connection to mobile robots is clear. This class of problem exhibits all of the same issues as parameter optimization problems while introducing a few more. In particular, solution functions may have to satisfy constraints to be deemed *feasible*, and the objective may or may not be *convex*. If it is not convex, solution techniques will have to contend with local minima and the quest for a global minimum will be more difficult.

The quest for a distinguished function can be framed in terms of an optimization problem. Consider the optimization problem:

$$\text{minimize: } \underset{\underline{x}(t)}{} \quad J[\underline{x}, t_f] = \phi(\underline{x}(t_f)) + \int_{t_0}^{t_f} L(\underline{x}, \underline{\dot{x}}, t)dt$$

$$\text{subject to: } \underline{x}(t_0) = \underline{x}_0 \quad ; \quad \underline{x}(t_f) = \underline{x}_f \text{ (when } \phi(\underline{x}(t_f)) \text{ is absent)}$$

(7.44)

There are many variations on this theme. One important variation replaces time t with arc length s and it specifies a search for an optimal path instead of a trajectory.

The objective function is composed of two parts. The *endpoint cost function* $\phi[x(t_f)]$ associates a cost with the terminal state, whereas the integral term (called the *Lagrangian*) computes a cost for the entire trajectory. The second line specifies boundary conditions. If the terminal state is specified as a boundary condition, the endpoint cost is constant and not needed. In some cases relevant to mobile robots, neither is present.

The scalar valued objective function $J[\underline{x}, t_f]$ is, in fact, not a function. It is a function of a function, known as a *functional*. The square brackets in the notation $J[\underline{x}, t_f]$ are sometimes used to denote functionals. J is a functional because it is based on a definite integral.

For specified values of t_0 and t_f, the integrand $L(x) = \sin(x)$ would produce some number, whereas $L(x) = ax^2 + bx + c$ would produce a different number. Indeed, even $L(x) = ax^2 + bx + c + 1$ produces a different number, so J also depends on any parameters used to specify the function L.

7.3.1.1 Euler Lagrange Equations

The posed optimization problem is a quest for an unknown function. It turns out that any solution to the problem must satisfy a particular differential equation that defines the unknown function implicitly.

Suppose a solution $x^*(t)$ has been found. In order to investigate the behavior of the functional in the neighborhod of the solution, consider adding a small perturbation $\delta x(t)$ (called a *variation* in this context) to the solution. Consider the value of J when evaluated at this perturbed function.

$$J[\underline{x}^* + \delta\underline{x}] = \phi(\underline{x}^*(t_f)) + \int_{t_0}^{t_f} L(\underline{x}^* + \delta\underline{x}, \underline{\dot{x}}^* + \delta\underline{\dot{x}}, t)dt$$

Assuming ϕ is not present, we will require that the initial and terminal boundary constraints remain satisfied, thus:

$$\underline{x}^*(t_0) + \delta\underline{x}(t_0) = \underline{x}_0 \qquad \underline{x}^*(t_f) + \delta\underline{x}(t_f) = \underline{x}_f$$

This means that the perturbations must vanish at the endpoints, we must have:

$$\delta\underline{x}(t_0) = \underline{0} \qquad \delta\underline{x}(t_f) = \underline{0}$$

The second set of conditions will be absent if ϕ is present in the objective. Now, we can approximate L by its first-order Taylor series over $\underline{x}$ and $\underline{\dot{x}}$:

$$L(\underline{x}^* + \delta\underline{x}, \underline{\dot{x}}^* + \delta\underline{\dot{x}}, t) \approx L(\underline{x}^*, \underline{\dot{x}}^*, t) + L_{\underline{x}}(\underline{x}^*, \underline{\dot{x}}^*, t)\delta\underline{x} + L_{\underline{\dot{x}}}(\underline{x}^*, \underline{\dot{x}}^*, t)\delta\underline{\dot{x}}$$

The perturbed objective then becomes:

$$J[\underline{x}^* + \delta\underline{x}] = \phi(\underline{x}^*(t_f)) + \int_{t_0}^{t_f} (L(.) + L_{\underline{x}}(.)\delta\underline{x} + L_{\underline{\dot{x}}}(.)\delta\underline{\dot{x}})dt$$

where the shorthand $(.) = (\underline{x}^*, \underline{\dot{x}}^*, t)$ was used. Note that the third term can be integrated by parts because:

$$\int_{t_0}^{t_f} (L_{\underline{\dot{x}}}(.)\delta\underline{\dot{x}})dt = L_{\underline{\dot{x}}}(.)\delta\underline{x}\Big|_{t_0}^{t_f} - \int_{t_0}^{t_f} \left(\frac{d}{dt}L_{\underline{\dot{x}}}(.)\delta\underline{x}\right)dt$$

Based on the boundary conditions, the first part is zero. The perturbed objective can now be written (ignoring the small term $L(.)\delta t$) as:

$$J[\underline{x}^* + \delta\underline{x}] = \phi(\underline{x}^*(t_f)) + \int_{t_0}^{t_f} L(.)dt + \int_{t_0}^{t_f} \left(L_{\underline{x}}(.) - \frac{d}{dt}L_{\underline{\dot{x}}}(.)\right)\delta\underline{x}dt$$

Notably, $\delta\underline{x}$ is now a common factor in the second integrand. This is the same as:

$$J[\underline{x}^* + \delta\underline{x}] = J[\underline{x}^*] + \int_{t_0}^{t_f} \left(L_{\underline{x}}(.) - \frac{d}{dt}L_{\underline{\dot{x}}}(.)\right)\delta\underline{x}dt \qquad (7.45)$$

Now, for $J[\underline{x}^*]$ to be a local minimum at the "point" in function space $\underline{x}^*$, the integral in Equation 7.45 must vanish to first order. Because $\delta\underline{x}(t)$ is an arbitrary feasible function of time, the only way that the integrand can vanish is if:

$$L_{\underline{x}}(.) - \frac{d}{dt}L_{\underline{\dot{x}}}(.) = 0 \qquad (7.46)$$

Spotlight 7.4 Euler Lagrange (E-L) Equations.

This vector differential equation must be satisfied (necessary condition) by any solution to the optimization problem posed in Equation 7.44. The equation is solved subject to the boundary conditions $\underline{x}(t_0) = \underline{x}_0$ and $\underline{x}(t_f) = \underline{x}_f$ (when $\phi(\underline{x}(t_f))$ is not present in the objective).

7.3.1.2 Transversality Condition

For many problems in mobile robots, t_f is free. Also, it is common that the problem is specified in terms of derivatives with respect to arc length s and the path length s_f

is free. In these cases, the condition for stationarity of J with respect to t_f (or s_f) must also be added. These quantities are parameters rather than functions, so a straightforward parameter derivative supplies the necessary conditions:

$$\frac{d}{dt_f}J[\underline{x}, t_f] = [\dot{\phi}(\underline{x}(t)) + L(\underline{x}, \dot{\underline{x}}, t)]_{t = t_f} = 0 \qquad (7.47)$$

This is known as the *transversality condition*.

7.3.1.3 Example: Lagrangian Dynamics

Lagrangian dynamics is formulated as a search for trajectories of least *action*. The action of a system is defined as the time integral of the (physical) Lagrangian defined as:

$$L(\underline{x}, \dot{\underline{x}}, t) = T - U$$

where T is the kinetic energy and U is the potential energy. The Euler Lagrange equations are:

$$\frac{d}{dt}L_{\dot{\underline{x}}}(\underline{x}, \dot{\underline{x}}, t) = L_{\underline{x}}(\underline{x}, \dot{\underline{x}}, t)$$

For a particle moving in space, the kinetic energy is:

$$T = \frac{1}{2}\dot{\underline{x}}^T m \dot{\underline{x}}$$

The gravitational potential energy is:

$$U = -m\underline{g}^T \underline{x}$$

Assuming no potential energy, the Lagrangian partial derivatives are:

$$L_{\dot{\underline{x}}}(\underline{x}, \dot{\underline{x}}, t) = m\dot{\underline{x}} \qquad\qquad L_{\underline{x}}(\underline{x}, \dot{\underline{x}}, t) = m\underline{g}$$

Therefore, the Euler-Lagrange equations are:

$$m\ddot{\underline{x}} = m\underline{g}$$

This is Newton's second law of motion and it implies that the body will fall toward the center of the gravity field.

7.3.2 Optimal Control

The optimal control problem is a generalization of the calculus of variations. Here, the Lagrangian depends not on the state $\underline{x}$ and its time derivative $\dot{\underline{x}}$ but rather on the state $\underline{x}$ and a vector of inputs $\underline{u}$. We are presumed to have some degree of control over the values of the inputs and hence of the behavior of the system. The relationship between the state and the inputs is our familiar state space model of the system.

For our purpose, the optimal control problem can be expressed in the following form due to Bolza:

$$\text{minimize:}_{\underline{x}(t)} \quad J[\underline{x}, \underline{u}, t_f] = \phi(\underline{x}(t_f)) + \int_{t_0}^{t_f} L(\underline{x}, \underline{u})dt$$

$$\text{subject to:} \quad \dot{\underline{x}} = f(\underline{x}, \underline{u}) \quad ; \quad \underline{u} \in U \tag{7.48}$$

$$\underline{x}(t_0) = \underline{x}_0 \ ; \ \underline{x}(t_f) = \underline{x}_f \ \text{(when } \phi(\ ) \text{ absent)} \ ; \ t_f \ \text{free}$$

Spotlight 7.5 Optimal Control Problem in Bolza Form.

In many ways, the basic problem that a robot faces – of deciding where to go and how to get there – comes down to this.

Both the state and input are functions of time. There are many variations on this theme. The objective function is composed of two parts. The endpoint cost function $\phi[x(t_f)]$ associates a cost with the terminal state, whereas the integral term (again called the *Lagrangian*) computes a cost for the trajectory that reached the final state.

The second and third lines specify the constraints. These include at least the system state space dynamics and the boundary conditions. At times, the terminal state is constrained to lie in some reachable region of state space. If the terminal state is specified as a boundary condition, the endpoint cost is constant and not needed. In some cases relevant to mobile robots, neither is present. Likewise, the input $\underline{u}(t)$ is sometimes restricted to lie in some set of admissible inputs U.

7.3.2.1 Minimum Principle

One technique that is available to solve the optimal control problem is the minimum (or maximum) principle due to Pontryagin and colleagues [20]. In a manner that is analogous to that of solving constrained parameter optimization problems, we can define the scalar-valued *Hamiltonian* function:

$$H(\underline{\lambda}, \underline{x}, \underline{u}) = L(\underline{x}, \underline{u}) + \underline{\lambda}^T f(\underline{x}, \underline{u}) \tag{7.49}$$

The time-varying vector $\underline{\lambda}(t)$ is known as the *costate vector* and, as the notation suggests, its function is analogous to that of the Lagrange multipliers. The minimum principle states that, on the minimum cost trajectory, the Hamiltonian achieves the minimum possible value for any valid control:

$$H(\underline{\lambda}^*, \underline{x}^*, \underline{u}^*) \leq H(\underline{\lambda}^*, \underline{x}^*, \underline{u}) \quad ; \quad \underline{u} \in U \tag{7.50}$$

When $\underline{u}$ is unrestricted, this global optimum (necessary and sufficient) condition can be replaced by a local (necessary) condition by requiring that the Hamiltonian be stationary. Based on a derivation similar to the one provided above for the Euler-Lagrange equations, one can derive the first-order conditions for optimality. Under the minimum principle, the necessary conditions for an optimum solution $(\underline{x}^*, \underline{u}^*)$ are that $\underline{\lambda}(t)$ exists and:

$$\dot{\underline{x}} = \frac{\partial H}{\partial \underline{\lambda}} = f(\underline{x}, \underline{u})$$

$$\dot{\underline{\lambda}}^T = -\frac{\partial H}{\partial \underline{x}} = -L_x(\underline{x}, \underline{u}) - \underline{\lambda}^T f_{\underline{x}}(\underline{x}, \underline{u})$$

$$\frac{\partial}{\partial \underline{u}} H(\underline{\lambda}, \underline{x}, \underline{u}) = \underline{0}$$

$$\underline{x}(t_0) = \underline{x}_0 \quad \underline{x}(t_f) = \underline{x}_f \quad \underline{\lambda}(t_f) = \phi_{\underline{x}}(\underline{x}(t_f))$$

(7.51)

Spotlight 7.6 Euler Lagrange (E-L) Equations for Optimal Control.

This is the form of the E-L equations that form the necessary conditions for the optimal control problem outlined earlier.

In this case, the equations are once again known as the *Euler-Lagrange equations*. The transversality condition for a free final time is:

$$\frac{d}{dt_f} J[\underline{x}, t_f] = [\dot{\phi}(\underline{x}(t)) + \underline{\lambda}^T f(\underline{x}, \underline{u}) + L(\underline{x}, \dot{\underline{x}})]_{t = t_f} = 0 \qquad (7.52)$$

The minimum principle produces a set of simultaneous coupled differential equations that can be solved using various numerical procedures. The initial state and the final costate are constrained in the boundary conditions so this is a 2 point boundary value problem.

7.3.2.2 Dynamic Programming

Dynamic programming is a significant result in optimization theory that takes a somewhat different view of the optimal control problem. Rather than trying to find the state trajectory, it produces the optimal value of the cost function for all possible initial conditions. Its basis is the principle of optimality (Box 7.2).

Box 7.2: Principle of Optimality

Bellman's *dynamic programming* method is based on the principle of optimality, which states that:

- An optimal policy has the property that whatever the initial state and initial decision are, the remaining decisions must constitute an optimal policy with regard to the state resulting from the first decision.

This is a statement of the obvious fact that an optimal solution to the whole problem must be composed of a first step and an optimal solution to the remaining problem.

7.3.2.3 Value Function

Let us define a *value function*, also called the optimal *cost to go* or the *optimal return function*, $V[\underline{x}(t_0), t_0]$ which is equal to the cost of the optimal path extending from

$x(t_0)$ to the desired terminal state:

$$V[\underline{x}(t_0), t_0] = J^*[\underline{x}, \underline{u}] = min_u\{J[\underline{x}, \underline{u}]\} = min_u\left\{\phi[x(t_f)] + \int_{t_0}^{t_f} L(\underline{x}, \underline{u}, t)dt\right\} \quad (7.53)$$

We will see later that the optimal control $\underline{u}^*(t)$ can be generated from the value function, and, of course it will depend on the initial state. The resulting control $\underline{u}^*(x, t)$ is then expressed in the form of a feedback control law. By contrast, the solution computed from the minimum principle is an open loop control that is optimal only if the system does not deviate from the designated trajectory.

7.3.2.4 Hamilton-Jacobi-Bellman Equation

For continuum optimization problems, the principle of optimality leads to a differential equation that is satisfied by an optimal trajectory. Consider the question of what control should be applied for a short period of time Δt at the beginning of the optimal path. By the principle of optimality, we must have:

$$V[\underline{x}(t), t] = min_u\{V[\underline{x}(t + \Delta t), t] + L(\underline{x}, \underline{u}, t)\Delta t\} \quad (7.54)$$

In words, the value function at time t must be equal to its value at time $t + \Delta t$ plus the cost of moving from $\underline{x}(t)$ to $\underline{x}(t + \Delta t)$ under the control for which the sum of the two is minimum. The inside of the right-hand side can be rewritten using the Taylor series as:

$$V[\underline{x}(t + \Delta t), t + \Delta t] = V[\underline{x}(t), t] + V_x[\underline{x}(t)]\Delta \underline{x} + \dot{V}[\underline{x}(t), t]\Delta t$$

$$V[\underline{x}(t + \Delta t), t + \Delta t] = V[\underline{x}(t), t] + V_x f(\underline{x}, \underline{u}, t)\Delta t + \dot{V}[\underline{x}(t), t]\Delta t$$

Substitute this into Equation 7.54 to get:

$$V[\underline{x}(t), t] = min_u\{V[\underline{x}(t), t] + V_x f(\underline{x}, \underline{u}, t)\Delta t + \dot{V}[\underline{x}(t), t]\Delta t + L(\underline{x}, \underline{u}, t)\Delta t\}$$

Now, $V[\underline{x}(t), t]$ does not depend on $\underline{u}$ by definition so neither does $\dot{V}$. These can be taken outside the minimization, whereupon $V[\underline{x}(t), t]$ cancels from both sides and Δt cancels for all remaining terms to leave:

$$\dot{V}[\underline{x}(t), t] = min_u\{V_x f(\underline{x}, \underline{u}, t) + L(\underline{x}, \underline{u}, t)\} \quad (7.55)$$

Spotlight 7.7 Hamilton Jacobi Bellman (HJB) Equation.

This expresses the principle of optimality in a time continuous case. It specifies an objective function on the right-hand side, which, when minimized, produces the time derivative of the value function. All of our algorithms in motion planning will be based on the discrete time version of this equation.

At times, it is convenient to denote the objective being minimized as the *Hamiltonian:*

$$H(\underline{x}, \underline{u}, V, t) = V_x f(\underline{x}, \underline{u}, t) + L(\underline{x}, \underline{u}, t)$$

Clearly, the quantity V_x plays the role of the costate vector in the calculus of variations and this is no accident because on an optimal trajectory:

$$V_x[\underline{x}^*(t), t] = \underline{\lambda}^*(t)$$

When $\underline{u}$ is unrestricted, we can differentiate the objective with respect to $\underline{u}$ to produce the following differential equation:

$$H_{\underline{u}}(\underline{x}, \underline{u}, V, t) = V_x f_{\underline{u}}(\underline{x}, \underline{u}, t) + L_{\underline{u}}(\underline{x}, \underline{u}, t) = 0 \qquad (7.56)$$

The boundary condition comes from Equation 7.48:

$$V[\underline{x}(t_f), t_f] = \phi(\underline{x}(t_f)) \qquad (7.57)$$

7.3.2.5 Example: LQR Control

A famous result in optimal control deals with the case in which a linear system must be controlled to optimize a quadratic objective. The system must be driven near to a null terminal state by using acceptable control effort and maintaining an acceptable magnitude of the state along the way. Consider the linear system:

$$\dot{\underline{x}} = F(t)\underline{x} + G(t)\underline{u}$$

It is initially in state $\underline{x}_0$ and the goal is to drive the system near to the state $\underline{x}_f = \underline{0}$ at the terminal time. A quadratic objective can be written like so:

$$J[\underline{x}, \underline{u}, t_f] = \frac{1}{2}\underline{x}^T(t_f)S_f\underline{x}(t_f) + \frac{1}{2}\int_{t_0}^{t_f}(\underline{x}^T Q(t)\underline{x} + \underline{u}^T R(t)\underline{u})dt \qquad (7.58)$$

where S_f and $Q(t)$ are positive semidefinite, and $R(t)$ is positive definite. Suppressing the time dependence in the notation, the Hamiltonian is:

$$H = \frac{1}{2}(\underline{x}^T Q\underline{x} + \underline{u}^T R\underline{u}) + \underline{\lambda}^T(F\underline{x} + G\underline{u})$$

The Euler Lagrange equations from Equation 7.51 are:

$$\dot{\underline{\lambda}} = -\frac{\partial H}{\partial \underline{x}}^T = -Q\underline{x} - F^T\underline{\lambda}$$

$$\frac{\partial}{\partial \underline{u}}H(\underline{\lambda}, \underline{x}, \underline{u}) = R\underline{u} + G^T\underline{\lambda} = \underline{0}$$

The second line produces.

$$\underline{u} = -R^{-1}G^T\underline{\lambda} \qquad (7.59)$$

Substituting this into the state space model and repeating the first line above leads to:

$$\begin{bmatrix} \dot{\underline{x}} \\ \dot{\underline{\lambda}} \end{bmatrix} = \begin{bmatrix} F & -GR^{-1}G^T \\ -Q & -F^T \end{bmatrix}\begin{bmatrix} \underline{x} \\ \underline{\lambda} \end{bmatrix} \qquad (7.60)$$

The boundary conditions are:

$$\underline{x}(t_0) = \underline{x}_0 \qquad \underline{\lambda}(t_f) = \phi_x(\underline{x}(t_f)) = S_f\,\underline{x}(t_f)$$

So, the Euler Lagrange equations reduce to a linear two-point boundary value problem. Kalman [15] solved this problem using a technique called the *sweep method*. The terminal boundary constraint must hold for any value of t_f so it must hold for all time. Thus, we may write:

$$\underline{\lambda}(t) = S(t)\underline{x}(t) \tag{7.61}$$

Substituting this into the second part of Equation 7.60 yields:

$$\dot{\underline{\lambda}} = \dot{S}\underline{x} + S\dot{\underline{x}} = -Q\underline{x} - F^T S\underline{x}$$

Now, substituting for $\dot{\underline{x}}$ from the first part of Equation 7.60 and reusing Equation 7.61 yields:

$$\dot{S}\underline{x} + S(F\underline{x} - GR^{-1}G^T\underline{\lambda}) = -Q\underline{x} - F^T S\underline{x}$$
$$\dot{S}\underline{x} + S(F\underline{x} - GR^{-1}G^T S\underline{x}) = -Q\underline{x} - F^T S\underline{x}$$
$$(\dot{S} + SF + F^T S - SGR^{-1}G^T S + Q)\underline{x} = \underline{0}$$

Because $\underline{x}(t) \neq \underline{0}$, we can conclude that the following must hold:

$$-\dot{S} = SF + F^T S - SGR^{-1}G^T S + Q \tag{7.62}$$

This matrix differential equation is called the *Ricatti* equation. We have seen it in its discrete time form as the uncertainty propagation equation for P in the Kalman filter. Because all the matrices but S are known, it can be integrated (or "swept") backward in time from the terminal boundary constraint $S(t_f) = S_f$ to compute the matrix S. Once $S(t_0)$ is known, the initial costate $\underline{\lambda}(t_0)$ can be determined from the initial state $\underline{x}(t_0)$ with $\underline{\lambda}(t_0) = S(t_0)\underline{x}(t_0)$ and then the state trajectory can be solved by forward integration of the coupled Euler Lagrange equations.

Often, we are more interested in the optimal state feedback control that has been derived here. Once $S(t)$ is known, we can substitute for $\underline{\lambda}$ in Equation 7.59 to produce the optimal control:

$$\underline{u} = -R^{-1}G^T\underline{\lambda} = R^{-1}G^T S\underline{x} \tag{7.63}$$

Spotlight 7.8 Optimal Control for the LQR Problem.

This is the optimal way to drive a system to a terminal state under quadratic costs for state and control effort.

Although it may seem to be irrelevant to drive a system to the zero state, it is easy to drive it anywhere else given the above solution. Also, the LQR solution is applicable to feedback trim where it can be used to provide optimal linearized feedback to augment open loop control of a nonlinear system.

7.3.3 Model Predictive Control

As we will see later, mobile robots fundamentally need predictive models for planning purposes. When such models are suitable, they can also be used for predictive control. A control approach that is based on using a system model to predict the results of candidate inputs is called a *model predictive control* approach. Typically, the prediction is performed only for a short period of time known as the *prediction horizon* and it is common to compute an optimal solution over this finite horizon. One advantage of this approach is that the model, and hence the controller, can be changed online to adapt to varying conditions.

7.3.3.1 Receding Horizon Control

In *receding horizon control*, the optimal control problem is solved iteratively. At each step, starting at time t_k, the control $\underline{u}^*(.)$ is executed for a short period of time called the *control horizon* and then a new optimal control problem is solved starting at the state $\underline{x}(t_{k+1})$ that results from execution of the last input.

Receding horizon control has been successfully used in the process control industry to control relatively slow processes. However, when system dynamics are relatively fast, or nonlinear, or stability is critical, this method of control can be more difficult to use. Receding horizon control is particularly relevant to mobile robot obstacle avoidance where the limited range of perception sensing combined with the vehicle speed create an effective time and space horizon beyond which less is known about the state of the environment.

An important result from inverse optimal control states that under certain conditions, any state feedback control of the form $\underline{u} = K\underline{x}$ can be realized by appropriate choice of the cost function in a receding horizon optimal controller of the form.

$$J[\underline{x}, \underline{u}, t_f] = \frac{1}{2}\underline{x}^T(t_f)S_f\underline{x}(t_f) + \frac{1}{2}\int_{t_0}^{t_f}(\underline{x}^T Q(t)\underline{x} + \underline{u}^T R(t)\underline{u})dt$$

In a more general context, the cost function can be written as:

$$J[\underline{x}, \underline{u}, t_f] = V(\underline{x}_f, \underline{u}) + \frac{1}{2}\int_{t_0}^{t_f}L(\underline{x}, \underline{u})dt$$

It is known that the stability of a receding horizon control system depends rather critically on the length of the time horizon $t_f - t_0$ and on the properties of the terminal cost $V(\underline{x}_f, \underline{u})$. Ideally, the terminal cost is the value function for the infinite horizon problem, in which case certain stability guarantees can be made.

7.3.3.2 Model Predictive Path Following

Because present errors have already occurred, trying to remove them is only useful if they are indicative of future errors that have not occurred yet. One issue with the feedback controller presented in Section 7.2.3.2 is that the vehicle may decide to turn left because it is right of the path only to discover that the path was about to turn right to meet the vehicle anyway. In this case, turning left will actually increase the crosstrack error. Clearly, prediction of future error is a good strategy in this case.

In path following, the availability of an explicit representation of the shape of the desired path, for all time, permits a computation of a corrective curvature in a more predictive fashion. That is, the position error at some point in the future can be predicted, and a corrective curvature command can be issued now to prevent it (Figure 7.32).

7.3.3.2.1 Crosstrack Error As Objective, No Model. The simplest form of model predictive control is to compute the objective at a single point x_f ahead of the vehicle:

$$J[\underline{x}, \underline{u}, t_f] = V(\underline{x}_f, \underline{u}) = (x(t_f) - x_f)^2 + (y(t_f) - y_f)^2$$

$$t_f = L/v$$

where v is the present vehicle speed, (x_f, y_f) is the closest point on the path to the predicted terminal state, and L is the length of the line segment to that terminal state (Figure 7.32).

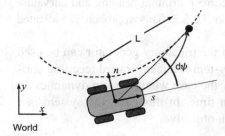

Figure 7.32 Pure Pursuit Path Following. Of all possible constant curvature trajectories, the one which meets the path at the horizon distance is optimal.

World

If the control is restricted to constant curvature arcs $u_\kappa(t) = const$, the optimal control is the curvature u_κ which rotates the vehicle through the angle $\delta\psi$ between the current vehicle heading and the heading of the line toward the lookahead point on the path.

$$u_\kappa^* = \delta\psi/L \tag{7.64}$$

The quantity $1/L$ acts like a proportional gain and the controller can also be viewed as a kind of feedback controller where the corrective heading change $\delta\psi$ is considered to be an error in the current heading. In practice, tuning the lookahead distance L can be difficult. When it's too large, following is poor and when its too small, the system can easily become very unstable.

7.3.3.2.2 Crosstrack Error As Objective, Model Predictive Trajectory Generation. One mechanism that causes instability is overcompensation by the steering controller when it is given infeasible references to follow. The stability of the above controller can be enhanced by switching to a model predictive approach that is aware of how steering control responds in terms of latency and rate limits (Figure 7.33). A simple approach is to sample the space of all possible commanded curvatures and to model how the steering control will respond. Then, the sample that minimizes the objective is chosen.

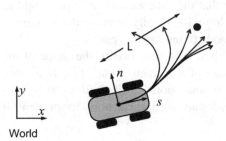

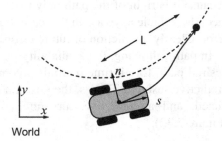

Figure 7.33 Sampled Model Predictive Path Following. A steering response simulator is used to choose the input that is predicted to have smallest crosstrack error.

Figure 7.34 Trajectory Generation Path Following. A steering response simulator is used to choose the input that is predicted to have smallest crosstrack error.

7.3.3.2.3 Pose Error as Objective, Model Predictive Trajectory Generation. A clear problem with the use of crosstrack error as the objective is the fact that the vehicle may arrive at the correct lookahead point with the wrong heading so it will necessarily incur following error immediately thereafter. One way to fix this problem is to generate a feasible trajectory to the lookahead point that has the correct terminal heading and curvature using the trajectory generator described in Section 7.2.5.3. This approach is indicated in Figure 7.34.

The problem can be expressed in two ways. If the trajectory generator can be used to achieve the lookahead state $\underline{x}_f$ precisely, the system is a feedforward receding horizon controller. It can be more robust to allow for the case where system dynamics do not permit acquisition of the lookahead state in time. In this case, the system is a receding horizon model predictive controller with objective:

$$J[\underline{x}, \underline{u}, t_f] = V(\underline{x}_f, \underline{u}) = \delta\underline{x}_f^T S \delta\underline{x}_f$$

$$\delta\underline{x}_f = \underline{x}(t_f) - \underline{x}_f$$

$$t_f = L/v$$

Even this approach has a few problems. The most obvious is that it will cut corners because it does not care about any predicted errors that occur before the lookahead point. This behavior can be improved by adding an integral term to the objective.

7.3.4 Techniques for Solving Optimal Control Problems

One approach to solving optimal control problems is to use dynamic programming. In this case, the optimal return function is generated and the optimal trajectory can then be found by following its gradient from start state to the terminal state. In practice, it is common to integrate the discrete version of the HJB equation, known as the *Bellman* equation to determine the optimal return function. Dynamic programming problems are often solved backward by a *backward induction*, moving from the terminal state, backward in time, to the start.

Much of the forth coming discussion of motion planning is based on the dynamic programming formulation, so it will be discussed later where it is used. The rest of this section is restricted to approaches to solving optimal control problems that are based on manipulating the objective and the constraints. It should not be surprising that there are two basic techniques available. They are similar to the two basic approaches for solution of parameter optimization problems. The objective can be minimized directly or this can be accomplished indirectly by finding a stationary point.

7.3.4.1 Optimization over Function Spaces

7.3.4.1.1 Sampling and Hilbert Spaces. Optimal control problems are a quest for an unknown function. A *function space* is a set of all possible functions of a given type. Typical controls are of the form $u\colon \mathcal{R} \to \mathcal{R}^m$ because they map the scalar time t onto the real-valued m-vector $\underline{u}$. It turns out that a function in a function space can, under certain conditions, be related to a point in an infinite dimensional vector space called a *Hilbert space* (Figure 7.35).

A very useful mechanism for visualizing optimal control problems is to imagine both the control and state trajectories to be points in such infinite dimensional spaces. Once the reader accepts this idea, the relationship between optimal control and parameter optimization becomes clearer.

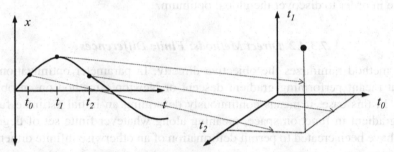

Figure 7.35 Notion of a Hilbert Space. Three samples of an arbitrary function of time span $\mathcal{R}^3$. n samples will span $\mathcal{R}^n$. In the limit, the continuous function $x(t)$ maps to a point in $\mathcal{R}^\infty$.

Consider three samples of the scalar function $x(t)$ at 3 times $t_0 = 0$, $t_1 = 1$ and $t_2 = 2$, which correspond to the time interval from 0 to 2 seconds. Define the sampled values of $x(t)$ as $x_k = x(t_k)$. Clearly, if there are no restrictions on $x(t)$, all possible values of the vector $\underline{x}_2 = \begin{bmatrix} x_0 & x_1 & x_2 \end{bmatrix}^T$ form a 3D vector that will span $\mathcal{R}^3$. As the point $\underline{x}_2$ moves around, its time continuous counterpart deforms from one function to another. For example, movement of the point along the t_1 axis, raises the value of x_1.

A continuous function will naturally place restrictions on how adjacent samples can move relative to each other $x(t)$. If instead, we choose to produce 201 samples over the 2 seconds, the vector $\underline{x}_{201} = \begin{bmatrix} x_0 & x_1 & \dots & x_{200} \end{bmatrix}^T$ would span $\mathcal{R}^{201}$. Passing to the limit as $n \to \infty$, we see that the vector $\underline{x}_\infty$ spans $\mathcal{R}^\infty$ and it is equivalent to the function space in the sense that a one-to-one correspondence exists between every continuous function and some point in $\mathcal{R}^\infty$. We will sometimes briefly refer to a function of time as a "point" in a function space to invoke this notion. Time samples are only one way to produce a point representation in $\mathcal{R}^\infty$. The coefficients of any infinite series representation of a function form an equally valid point representation in $\mathcal{R}^\infty$.

7.3.4.1.2 Convexity and Sampling. Once armed with the notion of a function space, an arbitrary function can be viewed as a very long parameter vector and many of the important concepts of parameter optimization carry over to optimal control. In particular, the question of convexity is central. Objectives that are functionals may be nonconvex just like functions. If the objective functional admits more than one local minimum then it may be difficult to find the global minimum using local methods alone.

7.3.4.1.3 Continuum and Sampling Methods. Continuum optimization approaches have the advantage that local regions can be searched at arbitrary density and the search can benefit from the information encoded in the derivatives of the objectives and the constraints. However, a given initial guess function ("point") will typically lead to a particular local minimum that may not be the global one.

Therefore, it can be important to sample multiple initial guesses in an intelligent fashion. Sampling mechanisms can achieve relative immunity to local minimum issues at the cost of extra computation. If the minima are dense in function space, even this technique may fail.

A combined approach that searches the continuum from many initial guesses can be a powerful mechanism that computes precise local minima in many places in function space in order to discover the global optimum.

7.3.4.2 Direct Methods: Finite Differences

A *direct* method minimizes the objective directly. In parameter optimization problems, that meant performing gradient descent or Newton's method on an objective function. In this case, it means continuously deforming an initial estimate function along a gradient in function space, meaning along whatever finite set of degrees of freedom have been created to permit deformation of an otherwise infinite dimensional vector.

A very basic technique is finite differences. We substitute for $\underline{u}(t)$ a set of N equally spaced samples $\underline{u}(k)$. The boundary conditions are easy to express as $\underline{x}(0) = \underline{x}_0$. The dynamic model is then converted to a difference equation with:

$$\underline{x}(k+1) = \underline{x}(k) + f(\underline{x}(k), \underline{u}(k))\Delta t$$

The objective becomes:

$$J = \phi(\underline{x}(n)) + \sum_{k=0}^{N-1} L(\underline{x}(k), \underline{u}(k), k)\Delta t$$

This is a parameter optimization problem where the control vector history $\underline{u}(.)$ constitutes the Nm unknowns and there are Nn degrees of freedom in the state vector history $\underline{x}(.)$. For $n > m$, there is room for optimization. The objective is subject to the equality constraints given by the boundary conditions and the discrete system model. Given an initial guess of the inputs $\underline{u}(.)$, the system model can be integrated to produce $\underline{x}(.)$. Then, J can be computed. Gradient descent can be applied by numerically differentiating J with respect to $\underline{u}(.)$ while holding $\underline{x}(.)$ constant, then moving in the descent direction, and iterating again. Many more techniques, including indirect methods based on determining the costate sequence $\underline{\lambda}(k)$ are covered in [13].

7.3.4.3 Indirect Methods: Shooting Method

An *indirect* method finds a solution for the necessary conditions. In parameter optimization problems, that meant linearizing and solving simultaneous nonlinear equations that were generated by setting derivatives to zero. In this case, it means solving the Euler-Lagrange equations – a set of simultaneous differential equations with boundary conditions.

Start   End

Figure 7.36 Shooting Method. This method for solving boundary value problems searches through initial conditions to find solutions which satisfy the terminal boundary values. If multiple feasible solutions are found, the best can be chosen.

If all initial conditions of an n-th order unforced ODE are specified, the evolution of the solution over time is completely determined. Similarly, a total of n boundary conditions imposed with some at the start point and others at the end would typically determine a unique solution. Hence, some boundary conditions must remain unspecified for optimization to be possible. There must be at least two (typically there are an infinite number of) functions that satisfy the imposed boundary conditions. In this case, the purpose of the objective is to enable selection of the best among them.

One class of techniques are called *shooting* methods (Figure 7.36). By analogy to aiming a canon, these methods search for values of the unspecified initial conditions for a solution that satisfies both the differential equation and the terminal constraints. If there are several, an optimum can often be found.

7.3.4.4 Penalty Function Approach

The penalty function approach to optimization can be useful in variational optimization as well. Recall that in this approach the constraints are converted to a cost function and not satisfied directly. The approach typically reduces the order of the problem, leading to a simpler, more efficient formulation. In the case of optimal control, the simplest example is the use of the endpoint cost function $\phi[x(t_f)]$ instead of a terminal boundary condition.

7.3.5 Parametric Optimal Control

This section builds on Section 7.2.5.2 and Section 7.2.5.3 which introduced parametric trajectory representations for the purpose of trajectory generation. In broad terms, these techniques are related to the *method of undetermined coefficients* in differential equations and the *Rayleigh-Ritz* method for solving optimal control problems.

7.3.5.1 Conversion to Constrained Optimization

Consider now the problem of converting the optimal control problem into an optimization over a finite length parameter vector. Recall from Section 7.2.5.2 that the space of all inputs can be converted to depend on a parameter vector $\underline{p}$, thus:

$$\underline{u}(t) \rightarrow \tilde{\underline{u}}(\underline{p}, t) \tag{7.65}$$

The system dynamics then become:

$$\dot{\underline{x}}(t) = \underline{f}[\underline{x}(\underline{p}, t), \underline{u}(\underline{p}, t), t] = \tilde{\underline{f}}(\underline{p}, t) \tag{7.66}$$

and the boundary conditions then become:

$$\underline{g}(\underline{p}, t_0, t_f) = \underline{x}(t_0) + \int_{t_0}^{t_f} \tilde{\underline{f}}(\underline{p}, t)dt = \underline{x}_b \tag{7.67}$$

which is conventionally written as:

$$\underline{c}(\underline{p}, t_0, t_f) = \underline{g}(\underline{p}, t_0, t_f) - \underline{x}_b = 0 \tag{7.68}$$

The performance index becomes:

$$\tilde{J}(\underline{p}, t_f) = \tilde{\phi}(\underline{p}, t_f) + \int_{t_0}^{t_f} \tilde{L}(\underline{p}, t)dt \tag{7.69}$$

The whole optimal control problem has now been converted to a constrained parameter optimization problem:

$$\underset{\underline{p}}{minimize:} \quad \tilde{J}(\underline{p}, t_f) = \tilde{\phi}(\underline{p}, t_f) + \int_{t_0}^{t_f} \tilde{L}(\underline{p}, t)dt \tag{7.70}$$

$$subject\ to: \quad \underline{c}(\underline{p}, t_0, t_f) = 0 \ ; \ t_f \ free$$

7.3.5.2 First-Order Response to Parameter Variation

The standard approach to solving nonlinear equations is to linearize. The objective and the constraints must be linearized in order to implement a numerical solution.

Note the following property of partial derivatives:

$$\frac{\partial}{\partial \underline{p}}(\dot{\underline{x}}) = \frac{\partial}{\partial \underline{p}}\left(\frac{\partial \underline{x}}{\partial t}\right) = \frac{\partial}{\partial t}\left(\frac{\partial \underline{x}}{\partial \underline{p}}\right) \tag{7.71}$$

The parameter Jacobian of the time derivative is equal to the time derivative of the parameter Jacobian. Therefore, we can differentiate the system dynamics $\dot{\underline{x}}(t) = \tilde{f}(\underline{p}, t)$ with respect to the parameters to get:

$$\frac{\partial}{\partial \underline{p}} \dot{\underline{x}}(t) = \left[\frac{\partial \dot{\underline{x}}}{\partial \underline{p}}\right] = F(\underline{p}, t)\frac{\partial \underline{x}}{\partial \underline{p}} + G(\underline{p}, t)\frac{\partial \underline{u}}{\partial \underline{p}} \tag{7.72}$$

Where we have defined the usual system Jacobians:

$$F = \frac{\partial \dot{\underline{x}}}{\partial \underline{x}} = \frac{\partial \underline{f}}{\partial \underline{x}} \qquad\qquad G = \frac{\partial \dot{\underline{x}}}{\partial \underline{u}} = \frac{\partial \underline{f}}{\partial \underline{u}}$$

We can now compute the Jacobian of the terminal state by integrating this auxiliary differential equation:

$$\frac{\partial \underline{x}_f}{\partial \underline{p}} = \int_{t_0}^{t_f}\left[F(\underline{p}, t)\frac{\partial \underline{x}}{\partial \underline{p}} + G(\underline{p}, t)\frac{\partial \underline{u}}{\partial \underline{p}}\right]dt \tag{7.73}$$

In practice, it may be more straightforward to differentiate the integral in Equation 7.67. Likewise, the objective can be differentiated:

$$\frac{\partial}{\partial \underline{p}}\tilde{J}(\underline{p}) = \frac{\partial}{\partial \underline{p}}\tilde{\phi}(\underline{p}, t_f) + \int_{t_0}^{t_f}\left\{\frac{\partial}{\partial \underline{x}}L(\underline{p}, t)\frac{\partial \underline{x}}{\partial \underline{p}} + \frac{\partial}{\partial \underline{u}}L(\underline{p}, t)\frac{\partial \underline{u}}{\partial \underline{p}}\right\}dt \tag{7.74}$$

These results are different forms of Leibnitz rule – which states that the derivative of the integral is the integral of the derivative.

7.3.5.3 Necessary Conditions

Often it is convenient to change the independent variable from time to distance. Let the initial distance s_0 be zero and absorb the final distance into the parameter vector, thus:

$$\underline{q} = [\underline{p}^T, s_f]^T \tag{7.75}$$

Now the problem can be written as:

$$\begin{aligned} \text{minimize:}_{\underline{q}} \quad & J(\underline{q}) = \phi(\underline{q}) + \int_0^{s_f}L(\underline{q})ds \\ \text{subject to:} \quad & \underline{c}(\underline{q}) = 0 \;\; ; \;\; s_f \quad \text{free} \end{aligned} \tag{7.76}$$

As we have seen, the solution to such a problem is obtained with Lagrange Multipliers. We define the Hamiltonian (known as the Lagrangian in constrained optimization):

$$H(\underline{q}, \lambda) = J(\underline{q}) + \lambda^T \underline{c}(\underline{q}) \tag{7.77}$$

Let there be p+1 parameters (including s_f) and n constraints (boundary conditions). The necessary conditions for a constrained optimum are:

$$\frac{\partial}{\partial \underline{q}} H(\underline{q}, \underline{\lambda}) = \frac{\partial}{\partial \underline{q}} J(\underline{q}) + \underline{\lambda}^T \frac{\partial}{\partial \underline{q}} \underline{c}(\underline{q}) = \underline{0}^T \quad \text{(p+1 eqns)}$$

$$\frac{\partial}{\partial \underline{\lambda}} H(\underline{q}) = \underline{c}(\underline{q}) = \underline{0} \qquad \text{(n eqns)}$$

(7.78)

This is a set of $n + p + 1$ simultaneous equations in the $n + p + 1$ unknowns in $\underline{q}$ and $\underline{\lambda}$. Based on the derivation of the constrained Newton method in Equation 3.67, the required iteration can be written immediately as:

$$\begin{bmatrix} \frac{\partial^2 H}{\partial \underline{q}^2}(q, \lambda) & \frac{\partial}{\partial \underline{q}} g(q)^T \\ \frac{\partial}{\partial \underline{q}} g(q) & 0 \end{bmatrix} \begin{bmatrix} \Delta \underline{q} \\ \Delta \underline{\lambda} \end{bmatrix} = \begin{bmatrix} -\frac{\partial}{\partial \underline{q}} H(q, \lambda)^T \\ -g(q) \end{bmatrix}$$

(7.79)

Spotlight 7.9 Newton Iteration for Parametric Optimal Control.

By parameterizing the inputs, the optimal control problem can be converted to a constrained optimization problem that can be solved using numerical methods.

After specifying some initial guesses for $\underline{q}$ and $\underline{\lambda}$, each iteration produces a new descent direction that can be used to update them both until convergence is achieved.

7.3.5.4 Example: Path Following with Parametric Optimal Control

In the last path following example in Section 7.3.3.2, it was noted that adding an integral term would potentially reduce the tendency to cut corners. If only the lookahead point on the control horizon is used, the vehicle will head directly for it as shown in Figure 7.37.

Adding an integral to the objective gives:

$$J[\underline{x}, \underline{u}, t_f] = \delta \underline{x}_f^T S \delta \underline{x}_f + \int_{t_0}^{t_f} \delta \underline{x}^T(t) Q \delta \underline{x}(t) dt$$

$$\delta \underline{x}(t) = \underline{x}(t) - \underline{x}_{path}(t)$$

$$t_f = L/v$$

This formulation of the control can be converted to parametric form to solve for the feasible trajectory of any shape which best matches the desired path. It is straightforward to add a (parametric) velocity control as well that will adjust speed to keep pace if the desired path has timing requirements. Such a speed control could benefit from and exploit any 3D terrain information and a model of the propulsion system.

7.3.5.5 Example: Adaptive Horizon Path Following

A potential improvement to the previous approach is to use the exact trajectory generator to acquire a sampling of lookahead points in the spirit of keeping the terminal time t_f free. The prediction horizon that optimizes an objective is then used. The objective is designed to trade off the control effort of aggressive maneuvers against the integrated crosstrack error that occurs with no control effort.

$$J[\underline{x}, \underline{u}, t_f] = \delta \underline{x}_f^T S \delta \underline{x}_f + \int_{t_0}^{t_f} (\delta \underline{x}^T(t) Q \delta \underline{x}(t) + \underline{u}^T(t) R \underline{u}(t)) dt$$

$$\delta \underline{x}(t) = \underline{x}(t) - \underline{x}_{path}(t) \qquad t_f \text{ is } free$$

This case corresponds to boundary conditions that are functions rather than constants and optimal control theory accommodates this case. This approach is indicated in Figure 7.38.

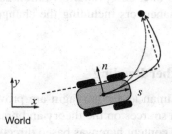

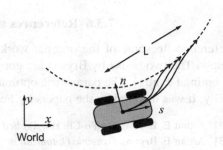

Figure 7.37 Parametric Optimal Control Path Following. The integral term in the objective discourages the corner cutting that results from having only an endpoint cost in the objective (dotted arc). The parametric search space allows essentially all inputs to be searched – leading to a result (solid line) that best approximates the infeasible path (dashed line).

Figure 7.38 Adaptive Horizon Path Following. A sampling of horizons is used to optimize an objective that trades control effort against integrated crosstrack error.

7.3.5.6 Example: Model Predictive Following of Intricate Maneuvers

Of course, there are situations, such as operation in cluttered environments where the target trajectory is discontinuous in the plane because it requires changes in direction, and so on. However, when a sequence of maneuvers such as this is parameterized by time or distance, there is no discontinuity. Suppose that there are three trajectories to be followed that are separated by a change in direction (Figure 7.39).

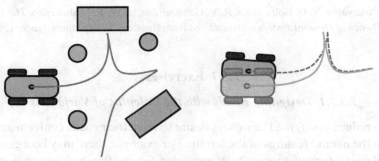

Figure 7.39 Intricate Maneuver Following. (Left) An intricate three step maneuver is necessary to turn around and avoid the obstacles. (Right) The parameter vectors of a sequence of maneuvers are adjoined to solve the composite problem. The controller optimizes the response right through the discontinuity of velocity.

The trajectory that results from any choice of parameters is:

$$\underline{x}(t) = \underline{x}(t_0) + \int_0^{t_1} f(\underline{x}, \underline{u}(\underline{p}_1, t))dt \qquad (t_0 < t < t_1)$$

$$\underline{x}(t) = \underline{x}(t_1) + \int_{t_1}^{t_2} f(\underline{x}, \underline{u}(\underline{p}_2, t))dt \qquad (t_1 < t < t_2)$$

$$\underline{x}(t) = \underline{x}(t_2) + \int_{t_2}^{t_3} f(\underline{x}, \underline{u}(\underline{p}_3, t))dt \qquad (t_2 < t < t_3)$$

By concatenating the three parameter vectors into one, an optimum solution can be found that evaluates error throughout the three maneuvers including the changes in direction.

7.3.6 References and Further Reading

References to some of the original works by Bellman and Pontryagin are provided below. The two books by Bryson are good tutorial sources on the theory and practice of optimal control. The parametric optimal control content here was based directly on Kelly. It was inspired by the papers by Fernandez and Reuter.

[12] Arthur E. Bryson and Yu-Chi Ho, *Applied Optimal Control,* Taylor and Francis, 1975.

[13] Arthur E. Bryson, *Dynamic Optimization,* Addison-Wesley, 1999.

[14] C. Fernandes, L. Gurvits, and Z. X. Li, A Variational Approach to Optimal Nonholonomic Motion Planning, IEEE International Conference on Robotics and Automation, pp. 680–685, Sacramento, 1991.

[15] R. E. Kalman, Towards a Theory of Difficulty in the Computation of Optimal Controls, in *proceedings 1964 IBM Symposium on Computing and Control,* 1966.

[16] A. Kelly and B. Nagy, Reactive Nonholonomic Trajectory Generation via Parametric Optimal Control, *International Journal of Robotics Research,* Vol. 22, pp. 583–601, 2003.

[17] D. E. Kirk, *Optimal Control Theory, An Introduction,* Prentice Hall, 1970.

[18] J. Reuter, Mobile Robot Trajectories with Continuously Differentiable Curvature: An Optimal Control Approach, in *Proceedings of the IEEE/RSJ Conference on Intelligent Robots and Systems,* Victoria, BC, Canada, 1998.

[19] R. E. Bellman, *Dynamic Programming,* Princeton University Press, Princeton, NJ, Dover, 2003.

[20] L. S. Pontryagin, V. G. Boltyanskii, R. V. Gamkrelidze, and E. F. Mishchenko, *The Mathematical Theory of Optimal Processes* (translated from Russian), Wiley-Interscience, 1962.

7.3.7 Exercises

7.3.7.1 Designing Roads with the Calculus of Variations

In order to reduce costs, road designers desire to have their roads conform as far as is possible to the natural features of the terrain. For example, there may be a good reason to route a road segment to start at a particular (x_0, y_0, θ_0) and end at a particular (x_f, y_f, θ_f). Among all of the possible roads that join these two poses, it is desirable to choose the shape that is easiest to drive. As we have seen for Ackerman steering, when a car drives on a road at constant speed, the gradient of the curvature κ_s is roughly proportional to the rate $\dot{\alpha}$ at which the steering wheel needs to be turned. Therefore, one way to specify the most drivable road is the one whose integrated steering rate is lowest:

$$minimize: \quad J[\underline{x}, s_f] = \int_{s_0}^{s_f} (\kappa_s)^2 ds$$

$$subject\ to: \quad \underline{x}(s_0) = \underline{x}_0 \quad ; \quad \underline{x}(s_f) = \underline{x}_f$$

The state variables for this system are $\underline{x} = \begin{bmatrix} x & y & \theta & \kappa \end{bmatrix}$. Show using the Euler Lagrange equations that the optimal curves for road segments are clothoids – curves whose curvature varies linearly with arc length.

7.3.7.2 Optimal Control of an Integrator

Suppose that a one-dimensional system is driven in velocity (i.e., $\dot{x}(t) = u(t)$) from $x(t_0) = 0$ to $x(t_1) = 1$. Using the minimum principle, for $u(t)$ unrestricted, find the optimal control and the optimal trajectory for the performance criterion:

$$J = \frac{1}{2} \int_{t_0}^{t_f} (x^2 + u^2) dt$$

7.4 Intelligent Control

This section begins the presentation of elements at the level of the perceptive auton-omy layer in Figure 1-9 presented in Chapter 1. Intelligent control means control that is aware of the surroundings of the vehicle. Once a capacity to perceive the environ-ment is available, it leads to a need for a predictive process that predicts the interac-tions of the vehicle with the sensed elements in the environment. Like classical control, intelligent control incorporates knowledge of dynamics. Like motion plan-ning, it incorporates prediction and may incorporate several kinds of search in order to assess options.

It is perhaps not a surprise that intelligent control can be formulated in optimization terms. Fundamentally, there are many options for what to do and each may have its good and bad points. The problem is much like trajectory generation and it can be for-mulated similarly except that now we will introduce elements from the environment into the constraints and the objectives.

7.4.1 Introduction

The need for intelligent control in robotics is fundamental. By assumption the envi-ronment is only partially known so it must be measured on the move. These facts have broad implications on the formulation of intelligent control.

7.4.1.1 Intelligent Predictive Control

The limitations of real sensors and the motion of the robot lead to a need for approaches to control that are perceptive, predictive, and reactive all at once. The basic argument for this conclusion follows.

- Perceptive: The system must be perceptive simply because it must measure salient aspects of its external environment.
- Predictive: Robot latencies and momentum imply that it takes time for the results of actions to take place. Hence, once the robot is moving, it becomes necessary to predict the results of actions in order to correctly understand their consequences. Dynamic objects in the scene also require prediction for related reasons.
- Reactive: Prediction is effective only for short periods of time. Sensors have limited effective range and elements of the environment may occlude each other anyway. Robots can only perceive their immediate surroundings and once they move, information becomes obsolete quickly. The environment must be sensed at high frequency in order understand the situation and react to what is learned in a timely fashion.

7.4.1.1.1 Generic Intelligent Control Loop. The generic intelligent controller, therefore, performs the following tasks on a continuous basis:

- Consider "all" or many options for proceeding through space while predicting motion sufficiently accurately.
- For each option, consider the manner in which the volume of the vehicle interacts with the matter in the environment.
- Eliminate those options that are definitely or probably going to cause damage and/or mission failure.
- If any options remain, pick the best from the perspective of mission execution. Execute it and return to the first step.
- Otherwise, execute a predefined exception action.

Clearly, this procedure is easy to express in the form of model predictive control (MPC). Recall that MPC is merely an optimal control algorithm with limited prediction that is executed on a regular basis. The next section will develop the optimal control formulation and the rest of this section will present many details of implementation.

7.4.1.2 Formulation as Optimal Control

In optimization terms, each possible action (path, trajectory, maneuver) $\underline{x}(t)$ can have a certain relative merit, utility, or cost J associated with it. For example, slamming on the brakes might be discouraged relative to a gentle turn, and some paths may go where the robot wants to go while others do not. More generally, paths might be evaluated based on their risk level, predicted following or speed error, or proximity to a goal.

Candidate motions can also be evaluated based on their satisfaction of hard constraints. Obstacles may be formulated as forbidden regions $\underline{x}(t) \notin O$ whose traversal violates constraints. Other important constraints are the feasibility of the motion (satisfaction of $\underline{\dot{x}} = f(\underline{x}, \underline{u}, t)$) and the desire to maintain roll and yaw stability at all times.

One simple formulation is to associate a cost/utility score with each motion and to impose a constraint of not colliding with obstacles. As is typically the case, however, many considerations can be expressed usefully either as objectives/costs or as constraints. As opposed to constraints, obstacles may be formulated as regions whose traversal have an associated cost $L(x, u, t)$ in unstructured environments. Furthermore, candidate motions can be evaluated against a constraint expressing whether they terminate at a goal $x(t_f) \in G$.

7.4.1.2.1 Optimal Control Formulation. We can express the above statements in the form of an optimal control problem:

$$optimize: \quad J[x, t_f] = \phi(x_f) + \int_{t_0}^{t_f} L(x, u, t)dt$$

$$subject\ to: \quad x(t_0) \in S \quad x(t_f) \in G \qquad (7.80)$$

$$\dot{x} = f(x, u, t) \quad ; \quad u \in U$$

$$x(t) \notin O$$

The (normally singleton) set S defines possible start states and G is the set of goals. The set U defines all feasible inputs and O is the set of states that collide with obstacles. We normally care only about the shape of the path, so distance can be a more useful parameter than time – as in $x(s)$.

$$optimize: \quad J[x, s_f] = \phi(x_f) + \int_{s_0}^{s_f} L(x, u, s)ds$$

$$subject\ to: \quad x(s_0) \in S \quad x(s_f) \in G$$

$$\dot{x} = f(x, u, s) \quad ; \quad u \in U$$

$$x(s) \notin O \qquad u \in U$$

$$(7.81)$$

In this case, the integral in the objective function is a line integral. This is the connection between continuum optimization theory and the common practice of summing costs along a discretely represented path in order to evaluate it.

7.4.1.2.2 Encoding the Mission in the Objective. The function of the objective is to cause appropriate behavior to emerge while granting authority to lower levels to decide which action to execute. The definition of the "mission" may impart differing levels of responsibility to the intelligent controller. Sometimes the objective is to stay on a specific path and there are only two options – to keep going or to stop. Contemporary AGVs operate in this way in factories. A robot might have the additional authority to modulate its speed. A following behavior is a special case of this type of objective.

The robot might have the authority to avoid obstacles provided it returns as quickly as possible to the prescribed path. It might be given a set of (potentially ordered) wayoints that it is required to visit, but it might have complete authority to plan the paths used between them. The robot might be required to cover an area (e.g., mow the grass) or even to search for something, run from something, or chase something.

7.4.1.2.3 Multiple Goals. When multiple goals are to be satisfied at once, some mechanism may be needed to break ties or otherwise choose between them. One obvious issue is the potential that two goals will disagree on what to do. One approach is to evaluate multiple goals separately and choose which goal is to be allowed to influence vehicle behavior at each instant. This approach fails in a *limit cycle* when pursuing a second goal undoes the work accomplished while recently trying to achieve the first and vice versa.

Consider the case when a path following goal coexists with obstacle avoidance. This architecture would be used when a nominally safe path is known a priori. A simple approach is to do what is necessary to follow the path precisely subject to an occasional veto and drastic action imposed by obstacle avoidance.

A variation is to use obstacle avoidance as an inequality constraint – as a safety threshold. In this case, the process is to choose the maneuver with the highest utility score (path following) that still has an acceptable safety score (obstacle avoidance).

Multiple goals may interfere with each other in other ways besides disagreement. For example, obstacle avoidance maneuvers can cause unusually large path following errors, which may induce instability or nonconvergence in path following.

7.4.2 Evaluation

This section considers the computation of the integrand $L(\underline{x}, \underline{u}, s)$ and its integral in Equation 7.81. For now, we will consider that this integrand can represent a collision test with discrete obstacles or a travel cost computation in a cost field. For now, let $\underline{x}(s)$ denote whatever coordinates are convenient for assessing obstacle intersections or traversal costs. In either case, the cost associated with the robot being in a particular place typically depends, in general, on the entire volume occupied by the robot – because any part of it may collide.

For binary obstacles, computing $L[\underline{x}(s)]$ involves volumetric (or area) intersection calculations.

$$L[\underline{x}(s)] = \bigcap_V \{o(x, y, z) \cap v(x, y, z)\} \qquad (7.82)$$

The notation is intended to suggest intersection computed over the entire volume of the vehicle. o is the obstacle binary field and v is the vehicle binary field. For a cost field, computing $L(\underline{x}(s))$ involves volumetric (or area) cost integrals:

$$L[\underline{x}(s)] = \int_V c(x, y, z) dV \qquad (7.83)$$

Where c is the cost field.

7.4.2.1 Cost of a Configuration

Literally, an *obstacle* is an impediment to motion. It does not need to stop the robot – just impede its motion. Obstacles may be characterized in familiar terms as steps and slopes that cannot be climbed or descended easily, or as ice or mud for which traction is difficult even if the geometry is not. Dense branches may be impenetrable because of opposing forces on the nose of the vehicle.

Although it is convenient to think of obstacles as regions of space, the robot interaction with an obstacle may depend on precisely what part drives into or over it:

- Point hazards: no part of the vehicle can drive over a 20-foot-tall tree.
- Wheel hazards: wheels cannot drive over a hole – but the undercarriage can.
- Pose hazards: a slope may risk rollover if oriented orthogonal to the grade but not if oriented parallel (going up or downhill).

Having recognized that the representation problem is more complex than labelling regions, we will nonetheless assume in the following that it is a valid approximation.

In the case of a cost field, the basic calculation of the cost of a configuration is a volume integral, sometimes known as cost *convolution*. At some point in the computation, we must account for the width and length of the vehicle (Figure 7.40). In the general case, the height matters as well because overhanging obstacles occur in factories, warehouses, forests, and homes (tables).

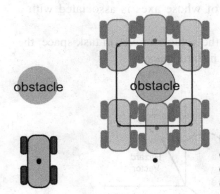

Figure 7.40 Cost Convolution. Because the robot occupies volume, the region occupied by its reference point for which obstacle interaction occurs is considerably larger than the obstacle.

When the environment is known and static, the cost field can be preconvolved with the vehicle offline to create a representation that is much more efficient to use.

7.4.2.2 Cost of a State

Many situations to be avoided depend on more than just the vehicle pose. For example, rollover propensity relates to lateral acceleration and obstacle impact force depends on at least speed. This section considers costs $L(\underline{x}, \underline{u}, s)$ that are more correctly expressed as functions of the entire state $\underline{x}$.

7.4.2.2.1 Types of State Dependent Hazards. A more general concept than an obstacle is a *hazard*. A hazard is any situation or state of motion that places the robot at risk of failing to achieve its mission. Hazards include:

- *Loss of control*: Yaw instability occurs when the vehicle skids and loses the capacity to control its angular velocity around the vertical axis. Sliding may occur on an upslope when traction is lost or on a downslope when the slope is too steep to brake effectively.

- **Loss of contact:** Rollover around a longitudinal (roll) or lateral (pitch) axis may temporarily or permanently take the vehicle off its wheels. Ballistic motion is a complete loss of contact. *High centering* refers to contact of the undercarriage with the terrain. It may permanently lift all wheels off the ground. Driving the front wheels into holes (*negative obstacles*) can cause high centering.
- **Loss of traction:** Wet or frozen surfaces may cause extreme wheel slip. Entrapment hazards are regions that a robot can enter, deliberately or otherwise, but then will be unable to leave.
- **Collisions:** Interactions with obstacles that cause damage. Wheels may collide frontally or laterally. Frontal, side and undercarriage collisions with the body are possible.
- **Risks:** Unquantified situations that are risky because they are unknown. Driving over terrain that has not been completely characterized by perception is a hazardous behavior.

7.4.2.2.2 Hazard Space. Although obstacle costs are easily formulated as scalar quantities, complex environments, and ambitious maneuvers may require a more refined approach. Many situations present multiple hazards at once and the cost of occupying a state at an instant must fuse several considerations at once. It is useful to imagine a hyperdimensional *hazard space* each of whose axes is associated with a particular hazardous condition.

As Figure 7.41 shows, we can imagine that as the vehicle moves in task space, the tip of some kind of hazard vector sweeps through hazard space.

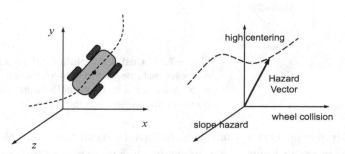

Figure 7.41 Mapping States onto Hazards. Any state space trajectory induces an associated hazard space trajectory.

7.4.2.2.3 Consistent Hazards Units. In order to make a meaningful choice between alternative trajectories, it is the designer's task to formulate a consistent unit system that corresponds more or less to the severity level of the conditions represented. In some cases, a natural concept of magnitude may exist. For example, it may be reasonable to consider $20°$ pitch to be twice as severe as $10°$ with $30°$ as the upper tolerable limit. In the case of slopes, use of stability margin accounts for the added effect of acceleration if necessary.

Once all dimensions of hazard space have been reduced to consistent units, the length of this hazard vector becomes meaningful. The ultimate goal of dimensional consistency is to cause the correct choice between alternatives to emerge. For example, if $20°$ pitch is worse than a 5 cm gap between undercarriage and terrain, the robot should take the path that risks high centering rather than traverse the slope.

7.4.2.3 Cost of a Path

Once all configurations and/or states on a trajectory or path have an associated cost, an optimal control formulation computes the cost of the trajectory or path by integrating along its length

Spotlight 7.10 Cost of a Path.

The computation of the cost of a candidate path comes down to a line integral over a cost field $L(\underline{x}, \underline{u}, s)$.

$$J[\underline{x}, s_f] = \phi(\underline{x}_f) + \int_{s_0}^{s_f} L(\underline{x}, \underline{u}, s)ds \qquad (7.84)$$

The first term in Equation 7.84 can represent the cost of the place at the end of the trajectory. It might be the estimated cost for the rest of the path to the ultimate goal.

Costs must be consistent across space for the correct behavior to emerge. Once again, the goal is to cause the correct behavior in terms of the choices that the robot makes. Ultimately, $L[\underline{x}(s)]$ represents the cost per unit distance, perhaps in units of energy or risk, associated with occupying state $\underline{x}(s)$. If $L = 11$ then the system would instead choose a path ten times longer of average cost $L = 1$.

7.4.2.4 Models Used in Objectives and Constraints

In order to compute the cost of a path, we need to compute the cost of a point (state, configuration) on the path. Evaluating constraint compliance also requires computations over robot configurations. In order to perform these computations, it is necessary to model aspects of both the environment and the vehicle. Such models may be used in either objective functions or constraints or both (Table 7.2).

Table 7.2 Model Uses.

	Attribute Used to Generate a Motion	Attribute Used in a Constraint	Attribute Used in Objective Function
Vehicle Model	State (for motion prediction)	volume of vehicle (for collision constraints)	power consumption, wheel slip, maneuver aggressiveness
Environment Model	Terrain shape or mechanical properties.	volume of obstacles (for collision constraints)	proximity to obstacles

7.4.3 Representation

This section addresses the representations that are needed to compute objectives and constraints in intelligent controllers. Intelligent controllers need to transform scene information into representations that enable effective decision making. The transformation of raw environmental sensor information into scene models is the job of perception. Perception is presented in a later chapter. In this section, we will use an environmental model that was produced by perception in conjunction with representations of vehicle states and motion in order to assess the relative merits and risks of candidate motions.

7.4.3.1 Representing Motions

Some data structure is needed to encode the motions that are being evaluated in intelligent control. This section presents some important aspects of the design.

7.4.3.1.1 Motion Constraints. Some constraints on motion, such as limited curvature or curvature rate can be represented kinematically:

$$|\kappa(s)| < \kappa_{max} \qquad\qquad |\dot{\kappa}(s)| < \dot{\kappa}_{max} \qquad\qquad (7.85)$$

Oftentimes though, mobility constraints can only be represented as differential equations because they cannot be integrated:

$$\dot{\underline{x}} = f(\underline{x}, \underline{u}, t) \qquad\qquad (7.86)$$

At times it may be expedient to reduce computation by imposing artificial limits on motions. For example, a controller might search only lines and point turns for a differential steer robot. Let paths that satisfy such constraints be called *feasible*, whereas others are called *infeasible*.

7.4.3.1.2 Representation of Paths and Trajectories. We will occasionally distinguish representations of motion parameterized by time and space. We will call $\underline{x}(t)$ a *trajectory,* whereas $\underline{x}(s)$ is a *path*. At least two options for representing motions are the input history $\underline{u}(t)$ or the associated state trajectory $\underline{x}(t)$. There is a long list of tradeoffs associated with either choice but the most basic one is that input histories are inherently feasible whereas state trajectory are expressed conveniently in ground fixed coordinates. Other options are special cases of these two. A sequence of curvatures κ_k is just a sampled input history $\underline{u}(t)$, whereas an ordered sequence of grid cells or waypoints (x_k, y_k) is a sampled form of $\underline{x}(s)$.

7.4.3.1.3 Compactness and Completeness of Motion Representations. It can be valuable to have a path representation that is both compact and complete. A compact representation minimizes the amount of data that needs to be communicated between processes or computers and it can constitute a mechanism to provide more information than merely the desired present input or state to a controller. Predictive controllers, for example, need to know the future trajectory to perform their optimizations. Compact representations may also lead to processing efficiencies because there are less things to modify to change a path.

There are also occasions where it is important to store trajectories in some offline representation. For AGVs, clothoids, lines, and arcs are a common library of trajectory shapes. Complex shapes can always be approximated by a sequence of simpler ones but it can be advantageous to be able to express more arbitrary motions in a single primitive (Figure 7.42).

When trajectories are used for planning purposes, the search for the best solution will only be a complete search if all feasible motions can be expressed in the representation used. The lack of a complete representation can lead to non-intelligent behavior.

In obstacle avoidance (a short term form of planning), for example, the search for a safe trajectory must ideally include all possible motions (Figure 7.42) or the controller may not find the obvious solution in certain cases.

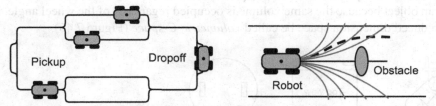

Figure 7.42 Compactness and Completeness in Path Representations. (Left) AGV guidepaths can be represented as a sequence of trajectories rather than a large set of points or poses. (Right) The problem of avoiding the obstacle and staying on the road is solvable – but solution is not in the space of arcs. Only a compound turn (left, then right) will work.

For a car, curvature polynomials are an example of a compact and (nearly) complete representation of steering inputs. Speed or acceleration inputs can be expressed similarly.

7.4.3.2 Representing Configurations

Cost computations may require knowledge of the volume or area occupied by the vehicle. When the environment is known and static, it is possible to represent obstacles as a cost field or as subsets or regions over a special set of coordinates. In this case, it is possible to precompute volumetric intersections and thereby make tests for obstacle intersection much less computationally expensive.

A *configuration* of an object is a specification of the position of every point on the object with respect to a desired fixed frame of reference. A *configuration space*, or *C-space*, is the space of all configurations of the object. Informally, C-space [22] can be thought of as a set of generalized coordinates that completely determine the configuration.

7.4.3.2.1 C-Space Obstacles. In the context of motion planning and control, C-space is often contrasted with *work space,* which is merely the space of all points in cartesian 3D. A vehicle can be represented as a point in C-space, whereas it occupies volume in work space, and this is the key distinction. Conceptually every point in C-space can be checked to see if the associated configuration intersects an obstacle, and if so, the point is identified as part of a *C-space obstacle*. Doing so transforms the problem of evaluating the motion of a volume to that of evaluating the motion of a point. It permits the expression of the problem in terms of the properties of a path in C-space rather than a swept volume in task space.

7.4.3.2.2 C-Space Dimension. The number of variables required to specify the robot configuration in the general case is the dimension of the C-space. To get the dimension of C-space:

- Start by adding the number of spatial dof of each rigid body comprising the object.
- Then, impose the constraints of articulation and contact (including terrain following).

While formally, radial symmetries matter in order to fix every particle, they do not matter for computing swept volume or detecting intersection, so the dimension of the coordinate system used can be lower than that of C-space in the event of radial symmetries. For example, the rotation angle of a wheel does not affect whether it collides with an object because the same volume is occupied regardless of the wheel angle. Let this reduced dimension space be called *volumetric C-space* (Figure 7.43).

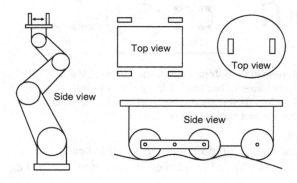

Figure 7.43 Volumetric C-Space Dimension. Due to articulations and symmetries, determining the dimension of volumetric C-space requires a little analysis. Clockwise from the manipulator, the required dimensions for the four robots are 5, 3, 2, and 5.

Computational complexity of path collision checking is directly related to the dimension of volumetric C-space and the complexity of the obstacles. Therefore, at times, it can be valuable to mimic symmetry and approximate a robot shape (say, by a circle) in order to reduce the dimension of the space.

7.4.3.3 Representing the Environment

Once a point on a candidate path is selected for consideration and the configuration of the robot is specified, the calculations will require references to the environmental model. This section presents some aspects of the design of a representation of cost associated with occupying different places in the environment. Some of the more important discriminators for the design of a representation include the dynamic range of cost and spatial dimensions, memory requirements, the efficiency of intersection calculations and the availability of cost gradient information.

7.4.3.3.1 Set and Field Representations. One of the most basic options is whether to represent relevant aspects of the environment as sets (e.g., regions or objects) or as fields. A set representation maps a label or index like "obstacle" onto regions of space. Typically, a cost (or binary obstacle flag) is associated explicitly or implicitly with each region and cost is considered to be uniform within the region. The members of the set may be point-valued or region-valued but in either case a position and shape for each member must be derived if volumetric intersection calculations are to be performed. The shape information could be encoded as a volume or a boundary. Sets can be very efficient when the environment has simple structure. For example, a simple list of obstacles and their positions and radii is very effective for representing moving objects.

Conversely, a field representation maps points in space onto labels or directly onto costs. Such a representation uses a raster (array) over space where each element encodes a cost and perhaps other useful information (e.g., altitude). Every point in the space has an associated cost or label (Figure 7.44). When large regions are represented at high resolution, a raster can require significant memory.

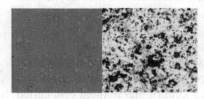

Figure 7.44 Set and Field Representations. Left: A set of polygonal obstacles can be stored as a list of lists of edges. Right: A scalar cost field can be stored as an array.

7.4.3.3.2 Shape Representations. For robots and discrete objects in the world (e.g., furniture), it is typical to use boundary representations (B-reps) rather than interior (volume) representations. Most sensors measure anyway. Volumetric intersection cannot occur without boundary intersection so intersection tests can be performed in either case. During motion simulation planning, the depth of penetration can be as useful as the volume of intersection as a measure of how in admissible a candidate motion is.

7.4.3.3.3 Obstacles versus Free Space. The most basic information required to compute collision (shape intersection) is volumetric information. Whether volumes or surfaces are used, it may be better to express obstacles or free space explicitly and leave the other implicit. In an *occupancy* representation, the environment is expressed in terms of subsets of space that are occupied and not to be collided with. At times, it is best to represent the dual of occupancy and represent *free space* – the sets that are unoccupied (Figure 7.45).

7.4.3.3.4 Sampled versus Continuum . When sets are used, a continuum representation of objects is often used as well. For example, sequences of simple curves, such as polynomials, can be used to represent obstacle boundaries. Continuous representations can be highly efficient in simple environments. For example, for polygonal obstacles and polygonal robots, collisions can be computed efficiently by intersecting line segments. In such a representation computational complexity depends on the number of objects (or pieces of their boundaries).

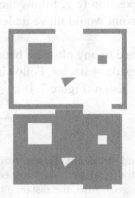

Figure 7.45 Duality of Occupied and Free Space. One or the other may be better in different situations.

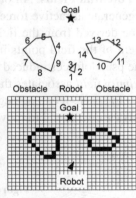

Figure 7.46 Compare Continuum and Sampled Representations. Top: Line intersections can be checked very quickly. Bottom: Boundaries are represented as occupied cells in a regular array.

Although fields are conceptually one continuum representation, they are often represented in sampled form. This can be the best alternative in complex environments whose continuous representation would use unreasonable amounts of memory. In this case, computational complexity tends to depend on the resolution of the representation (Figure 7.46).

7.4.3.3.5 Hierarchy and Quadtrees. In sampled representations, a computational complexity dependent on resolution leads to a desire to represent details only when necessary. A useful approach to reducing memory is a kind of hierarchical grid called a quadtree (octree in 3D). These are represented as a tree of filled, unfilled and partially filled nodes where only the partially filled ones at each level are elaborated (Figure 7.47).

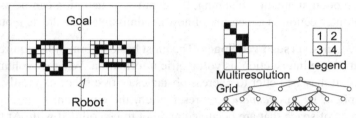

Figure 7.47 Octree Representation. (Left) Whereas the grid of Figure 7.46 required 24 × 36 = 864 cells, this one requires 8 + 5 + 18 + 21 = 47 cells. (Right) Octrees are implemented as tree containing filled, unfilled, and partially filled cells. Only partially filled cells have children.

7.4.3.4 Derived Spatial Representations

Once the basic geometric or cost information is encoded, it can be useful to derive other information from it. One motivation for doing so may be that the derived information is computed once rather than every time a collision check is performed.

7.4.3.4.1 Potential Fields. An obstacle *potential field* can be derived in which goal positions generate attractive forces and obstacles generate repulsive forces [21]. Controls can be derived from the field at the present position (e.g. follow the gradient). The gradient of the field points in the direction a point would move under the influence of the pseudoforces induced by the potential.

A *proximity field* associates the minimum distance to any obstacle boundary with every point in space. It can be negative for points inside obstacles. Following the gradient in this case will tend to move a point out of collision (Figure 7.48).

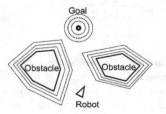

Figure 7.48 Potential and Proximity Fields. Attractive and repulsive potentials at the goal and start respectively can direct a point toward the goal. Also, the distance to the nearest obstacle surface can be used as a derived potential field whose gradient directs a point away from obstacles.

A *navigation function* [23] is a special field whose gradient at all times points in the direction of the optimal solution to the goal. These are produced as a by-product of many motion planning algorithms.

7.4.3.4.2 Voronoi Diagrams. The *Voronoi diagram* (see Figure 10-11 in chapter 10) is another useful derived representation [24]. It can be thought of as a subspace formed from the local maxima of the proximity field. Points in the Voronoi diagram are equidistant from two or more obstacles and closer to no others so these points are, in a sense, the safest roadways through a space.

7.4.3.4.3 C-Space Obstacles. When the environment is known and static, and obstacles are represented discretely, boundaries of obstacles in the environment can be converted offline to equivalent obstacle boundaries in C-space.

For every point on the boundary of an obstacle, every configuration of the robot that can be in contact with that point is computed and the union of such points is the boundary of the C-space obstacle (Figure 7.49).

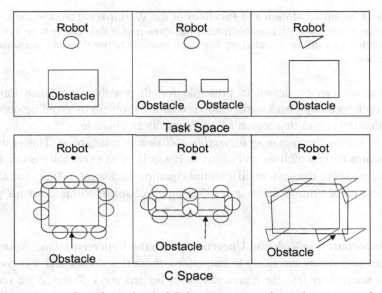

Figure 7.49 C-Space Obstacles. A kind of sliding contact produces the C-space obstacle for a given robot and obstacle pair. The rightmost case is a constant heading slice of C-space. The union of all such slices is the 3D shape in C-space.

The set of all such points is the boundary of the associated C-space obstacle. A C-space obstacle is a property of both the robot shape and the obstacle shape. In C-space, collisions can be detected by asking if the robot reference point is inside a C-space obstacle.

7.4.3.4.4 Partitions of State Space and Work Space. In analogy to C-space obstacles, useful partitions of state space and workspace exist as well. For a finite time period, the *time limited reachable state space* [25] is the set of all states that can be reached with at least one input function $\underline{u}(t)$. The corresponding set of all points in the workspace that can be reached by some part of the vehicle can be called the *reachable workspace*. Conversely, the set of points in the workspace that cannot be avoided can be called the *committed workspace* and the set difference is the avoidable workspace. Obstacles in the avoidable workspace can be avoided whereas those in the committed workspace cannot.

For example, if turning is the only avoidance trajectory permitted, given a zero curvature initial state and very low forward speed, these regions for an automobile are indicated in Figure 7.50.

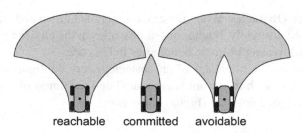

reachable   committed   avoidable

Figure 7.50   Committed Motion and Partitions of the Workspace. Points in the committed region must be driven over. All possible futures put some part of the vehicle here. Points in the avoidable region can still be avoided. At least one possible future does not put some part of the vehicle here.

Such a diagram can be drawn in principle for all possible avoidance trajectories including options that go backward. One view of the problem of avoiding obstacles is to ensure that the committed region never intersects an obstacle.

A related idea is the *region of inevitable collision* in state space. This is the set of all initial states from which an entry into an obstacle must eventually occur [26]. To compute it, we solve the system differential equation backward in time, for all points on obstacles, to determine those states that intersect *some* obstacle for *all* possible controls.

7.4.3.4.5 Incorporating Risk and Uncertainty into the Representation.

Systems that reason about uncertainty are likely to outperform those that do not and it is possible to incorporate uncertainty into the representation in limited ways. Some of the sources of uncertainty include:

- Assessments of hazards are not accurate.
- Obstacles may be incorrectly located relative to the vehicle.
- Motion control may not do what was intended.

These considerations suggest that closer predicted proximity to obstacles implies heightened risk. Some potential ways to reduce risk are to use a deliberately oversized vehicle when assessing collisions in continuous cost fields. Binary obstacle regions in the workspace or C-space can also be oversized equivalently to achieve the same goal and cost fields can be filtered so blur the cost function in a similar manner. The magnitude of spatial uncertainty due to pose error, wheel slip, and so on, can be predicted based on techniques presented earlier.

7.4.4 Search

The solution to the intelligent control problem, as we have formulated it, still rests on a process that considers multiple alternatives and picks the best. This section considers the question of how to compute a useful solution in practice.

Ideally, all alternatives are considered in the search process but, because the search space is a continuum, doing so is not feasible in finite time. Typically, any search process will generate discrete samples to both be tested for all constraints and have an objective value computed. There are a large number of considerations to take into account when designing this sampling process.

7.4.4.1 Sampling, Discretization, and Relaxation

One way to visualize the space of all possible trajectories is to consider the space of all possible inputs $u(t)$. Practical methods for searching this function space include discrete sampling and parameterization and relaxation can be a very effective approach when used alone or in addition to sampling.

7.4.4.1.1 Input Discretization and Parameterization. Consider input discretization first and assume that the inputs are curvature and speed. Suppose the objective function is to be computed for 40 time steps Δt into the future, and suppose there are 10 possible signal levels. If there are no constraints in the time derivatives of the input signals, then there are 10^{40} unique curvature, and as many unique speed signals. For some sense of the magnitude of this number, the age of the universe is 434×10^{15} seconds. Even if amplitude changes are limited to one step, there are $10 \times 3^{39} = 405 \times 10^{16}$ unique signals. Clearly, this kind of discretization is only feasible for few time steps and signal levels.

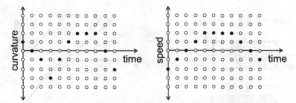

Figure 7.51 Input Discretization. If time and amplitude are discretized, the number of unique possible signals can be very large.

Numerous options for parameterization can be generated based on splines and curves used in other applications. A simple technique is to approximate input signals by their Taylor series and search in the space of the series coefficients. This technique was used in trajectory generation earlier. The coefficients can be discretized to generate the required samples.

7.4.4.1.2 Sampling and Relaxation. Sampling techniques have the advantage that solutions are not necessarily drawn to the same local minima, but they can be very inefficient when obstacles are dense or the objective function has many local minima. Conversely, path relaxation techniques can exploit gradient information for

more efficient search, but they can only find the nearest local minimum. A good
approach in complex scenes is to sample for multiple initial guesses that are supplied to a relaxation routine.

7.4.4.2 *Constraint Ordering*

In artificial intelligence, when multiple constraints must be satisfied in a search process, an *ordering heuristic* is a rule for which constraints are to be imposed in what
order. In some cases, one order may be much more efficient than another. It is typically more efficient to impose the most limiting constraint first because it eliminates
more options in one step rather than two.

In intelligent control, a similar problem must be solved because there are multiple
constraints that apply. The two most prevalent constraints are admissibility (avoiding
obstacles) and feasibility (satisfying a dynamic model). If these constraints are
imposed sequentially, two choices exist:

- Find admissible paths and then check for feasibility.
- Find feasible paths and then check for admissibility.

This choice relates to a choice of the coordinates in which to express motion alternatives. Feasible trajectories are easy to find in input space and admissible ones are easy
to find in state space.

7.4.4.2.1 Search Coordinates. Its not always easy or even possible to construct trajectories in state space $x(t)$ and then try to compute the inputs $u(t)$ which correspond
to them. The input $u(t)$ often does not exist because the feasible subspace of state
space is relatively small (Figure 7.52).

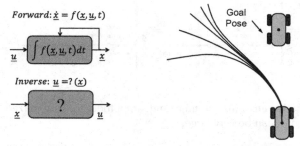

Figure 7.52 Inverse Models. Inverse models do not exist for arbitrary terminal states since not
all states are reachable. The time limited reachable state space for the car for these initial conditions does not include driving forward because the steering column takes time to move.

In general the path followed by a vehicle depends on the shape of the terrain as well as
the inputs.

Dynamics can sometimes be ignored if the vehicle moves slowly and the mobility
of the vehicle is artificially limited to simple geometric primitives that can be inverted
(Figure 7.53). This approach assumes that the inputs required to generate the primitive
trajectories can be found to sufficient accuracy.

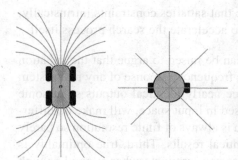

Figure 7.53 Expressing Alternative Motions in State Space. Almost any vehicle can be driven by considering only arcs. A differentially steered vehicle can be driven by considering compositions of point turns and line segments.

7.4.4.2.2 Environmental Constraints and Guidance.

On the basis of the above analysis, it seems that sampling options in input space is a good idea because feasibility is a very limiting constraint. However, there are times when certain constraints expressed in state space are even more limiting than dynamic feasibility. When following a road (or a specified path of any kind), it is effective to search only trajectories that are consistent with staying on the road because a uniform sampling in input space is likely to produce few or no options that are appropriate [27]. This approach focuses the search and reduces wasted computation.

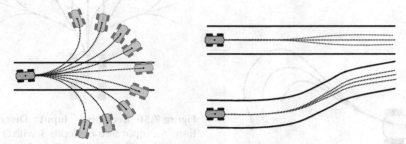

Figure 7.54 Path Constraints. Sometimes there is value in limiting maneuverability artificially to respect or exploit environmental structure. Right: Uniform sampling in curvature produces no valid paths. Left: Sampling endpoints on the road produces multiple valid options.

Such a search can be conducted by first sampling points on the road at a fixed forward distance, and then using a trajectory generator to invert the system dynamic model. Roads are designed to be drivable so, in this case, it is likely that a solution will exist.

A road or a path can be considered to be prior guidance information expressed in state space. Other forms of guidance may exist. A navigation function may be provided by a global path planner, for example. In such a case, a similar approach can be followed by orienting path samples along the gradient of the supplied navigation function (Figure 7.55).

7.4.4.3 Efficient Search

Whenever the search is highly constrained due to any combination of path constraints, a cluttered environment, or dynamics, the efficiency of the search will matter more because there are fewer trajectories that satisfy all constraints. Whereas the above discussion tried to search in a subspace that satisfies constraints intrinsically, a relative few other techniques are available to accelerate the search process itself.

7.4.4.3.1 Mitigating Effects. Several points can be raised to argue that the situation is not as bad as Figure 7.51 suggests. First, the frequency response of any real system will ultimately cause distinct inputs to produce nearly identical outputs so at some point more samples, at least if they are expressed in input space, will make no difference. Second, the environmental representation is always of finite resolution so barely distinct trajectories are likely to produce identical results. Third, true optimality is often not a requirement and the search process can terminate when a good enough solution is found.

7.4.4.3.2 Reusing Computations. A few techniques are available for reusing computations. As Figure 7.56 suggests, a recursive path structure can reduce the total length of trajectories tested significantly. Such a recursive structure is also amenable to the use of dynamic programming.

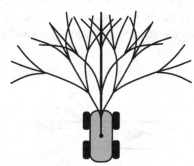

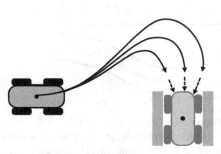

Figure 7.55 Navigation Function Guidance. The corridor is a tight squeeze and only trajectories that end within a small pose region will allow the vehicle to fit.

Figure 7.56 Recursive Input Discretization. An input tree of depth 3 with 3 alternatives produces this set of trajectory samples for zero initial conditions. Note that this recursive structure also reduces computation because path segments are shared. There are only 39 unique segments but the total length of all of the distinct paths is equivalent to testing 81 segments.

Another technique remembers the indices of all trajectories whose vehicle swaths pass through a given cell in the environment model. This idea uses precomputed lookup tables in a manner similar to [28]. The search for admissible trajectories is then conducted in the environment model by eliminating all trajectories that pass through obstacles.

7.4.4.3.3 Exploiting Committed Motion. At high speeds the region of state space that the robot is committed to travelling is relatively large and any effort spent searching for obstacles in this region is arguably a waste of time. Given a choice, it is a better use of time to scan for obstacles in the avoidable region (Figure 7.50) of state space because there will still be time to do something about it. In other words, concentrating on detecting this type of failure may cause it to occur. The robot should instead prevent it.

By a similar argument, we can conclude that excessive lookahead is also not efficient. Computational constraints will force a limit on lookahead – on how far forward in space or time prediction can extend. Only imminent dangers must be assessed because less imminent ones can be assessed later. Therefore, the avoidable region needs to be scanned only out to some finite horizon.

7.4.4.4 Search Space Design

The population from which the samples tested in intelligent control are derived comprises the search space. This section presents a few other trade-offs and desirable characteristics.

7.4.4.4.1 Mutual Separation. The continuum nature of the true search space leads to the conclusion that a complete search is impossible but the layout of a discrete search space can affect the likelihood that an admissible solution will be found. In the absence of any other information, it is best when samples are well separated in task space [29]. In Figure 7.54, for example, samples which span the width of the lane at a regular spacing are optimal from the point of view of avoiding unknown obstacles. Conversely, if all samples are to the left of the lane, an obstacle in this position will eliminate all options when the admissibility test is applied.

In a more general case, it is advantageous if samples span the space of those motions which satisfy all constraints. For the road example, this was easy to achieve with a trajectory generator. When there are no such guidance constraints the search space of Figure 7.56 is a better option than an equivalent number of constant curvature commands. The terminal pose has three degrees of freedom but an arc has only two so the terminal heading is completely dependent on the terminal position. In other words, if the only way to navigate obstacles is an S curve, an arc-based search space may never find it.

7.4.4.4.2 Completeness. It may seem that testing arcs at high enough frequency is an effective approach to search because any curve can be approximated well by short arcs. However, the momentum of the vehicle requires that the trajectory be safe for an interval of time in the future. There is no guarantee that executing half an unsafe trajectory will reveal another safe option later (Figure 7.57).

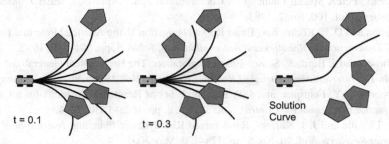

Figure 7.57 Incomplete Search. Although an S curve solution exists, searching arcs quickly will not generate it. (Left) No arc is entirely safe throughout its length, so the vehicle slows down. (Center) Again, no arc is safe. (Right) If an S curve was in the original search space, it would have been selected for execution.

7.4.4.4.3 Robustness to Control Uncertainty via Persistence. Controls will not be executed perfectly due to unmodelled latency, other model errors, or disturbances. Hence, future robot states will not be predicted perfectly, so a solution with little margin for error may disappear from future search spaces, if the search space is relatively sparse and it lacks persistence over time (Figure 7.58).

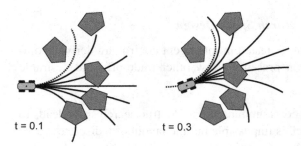

$t = 0.1$ $t = 0.3$

Figure 7.58 Non Robust Control. In the second iteration, the vehicle has drifted to the right of the desired path. A new set of test trajectories rooted at the actual pose of the robot no longer contains a solution.

This problem is not necessarily as serious as it may seem. Although the risk of driving through a tight corridor is fundamental, the simple device of fixing the search space to the ground rather than to the robot will produce the desired persistence of the solution. Each new search iteration is started from the nearest intended state rather than the actual state. When trajectories are generated from the actual robot position, control errors are forgotten and the search space moves to the new position. When they are generated from the intended robot position, the initial control error is not nulled and lower levels of control will continue to try to reject the disturbances that caused the error. A special case of this approach is to replan from the next fork in the search space in Figure 7.56 once the robot gets close.

Another approach to achieving robustness is relaxation. If the initial search space can be deformed slightly to avoid obstacles, it is likely to regenerate an earlier solution.

7.4.5 References and Further Reading

These references have been used in this subchapter.

[21] O. Khatib, Real-Time Obstacle Avoidance for Manipulators and Mobile Robots, *IEEE International Conference on Robotics and Automation,* Vol. 5, No. 1, pp. 90–8, 1985.

[22] T. Lozano Perez, Spatial Planning: A Configuration Space Approach, IEEE *Transaction on Computers,* Vol. 100, No. 2, 1983.

[23] E. Rimon and D. E. Koditschek, Exact Robot Navigation Using Artificial Potential Functions, *IEEE Transaction on Robotics and Automation,* Vol. 8, No. 5, pp. 501–517, 1992.

[24] H. Choset, and J. Burdick, Sensor-Based Exploration: The Hierarchical Generalized Voronoi Graph. *The International Journal of Robotics Research,* Vol. 19, pp. 96–125, February 2000.

[25] P. Soueres, J.-Y. Fourquet, and J.-P. Laumond, Set of Reachable Positions for a Car, IEEE *Transactions on Automatic Control,* Vol. 39, No. 8, pp. 1626–1630, 1994.

[26] S. M. LaValle and J. J. Kuffner, Randomized Kinodynamic Planning, *International Journal Robotics Research,* Vol. 20, No. 5, pp. 378–400, May 2001.

[27] T. Howard, C. Green, and A. Kelly, State Space Sampling of Feasible Motions for High Performance Mobile Robot Navigation in Highly Constrained Environments, *International Symposium on Field and Service Robots, 2007.* Vol. 25, No. 6–7, 2008.

[28] C. Schlegel, Fast Local Obstacle Avoidance Under Kinematic and Dynamic Constraints for a Mobile Robot, in *Proceedings of the International Conference on Intelligent Robots and Systems,* Victoria, BC, Canada, October 1998.

[29] C. Green and A. Kelly, Toward Optimal Sampling in the Space of Paths, *13th International Symposium of Robotics Research,* 2007.

7.4.6 Exercises

7.4.6.1 Configuration Space

Draw the Configuration Space obstacle due to the two polygons shown in the figure below. Assume that the polygon on the left is mobile and the one on the right is stationary. Use the bottom left corner as the representative point of the triangle. Give dimension of each side of the polygon that describes the C-Space obstacle. Rotate the triangle by 90° and repeat the above.

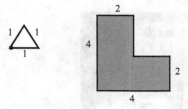

7.4.6.2 Path Separation

Using your favorite spreadsheet or programming environment, demonstrate the dependence of success in obstacle avoidance on the mutual separation of the paths searched. Generate two sets of nine paths of length 10 m based on the clothoid parameters in the following tables:

Table 1: Arcs

	1	2	3	4	5	6	7	8	9
a	-0.2	-0.15	-0.1	-0.05	0.0	0.05	0.1	0.15	0.2
b	0.0	0.0	0.0	0.0	0.0	0.0	0.0	0.0	0.0

Table 2: Clothoids

	1	2	3	4	5	6	7	8	9
a	-0.2	-0.2	-0.13	-0.05	0.0	0.05	0.13	0.2	0.2
b	0.0	0.05	0.0	0.0	0.0	0.0	0.0	-0.05	0.0

For each set, generate 50 obstacles of unit radius at random positions in the range $0 < x < 10$ and $-(7.5 < y < 7.5)$ and determine if at least one of the nine trajectories in the set does not intersect any obstacles. Do this 10 times for both path sets and note the average success rate in finding a safe path through a random obstacle field. Draw the path sets to see the difference between them. Try to explain your results.

CHAPTER 8

Perception

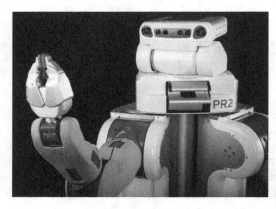

Figure 8.1 Willow Garage PR2 Robot. The robot includes a lidar in its body and a structured light system in its head. It has cameras in its forearms and sensors in its grippers.

This section describes the methods used to implement the perceptive autonomy layer that was initially described in Chapter 1. Perception is the process of understanding the environment based on measurements. Often the process involves the construction of models that are subsequently interpreted and improved or expanded. Although localization may enable mobility, it is environmental perception that enables a system to respond intelligently to what is out there – even when it differs from any expectations. Oftentimes, sufficiently intelligent behaviors emerge naturally based only on perception. Later, in Chapter 10, we will see that an ability to predict the future is sometimes necessary too.

Perception is a rapidly expanding area because it has many applications beyond robotics. For this reason, because space is limited, and because there are already many textbooks that concentrate on perception, this section will present only the bare essentials and only those that are most applicable to mobile robots.

8.1 Image Processing Operators and Algorithms

Perception and state estimation have a lot in common. Whereas state estimation estimates the state of the robot, perception estimates the state of the environment.

Although states estimation tends to deal with signal variation over time, perception tends to deal with signal variation over space.

State estimation commonly uses several forms of mathematics:

- kinematics: for expressing the relationships between fixed frames on the robot and between the robot and those objects with respect to which it moves.
- probability and statistics: to express probability of different outcomes.
- moving reference frames: for understanding and exploiting the indications of inertial sensors.

While perception uses at least the first two of these, it also uses *signal processing* to suppress noise, enhance edges, match and align signals, and many more things.

From a mathematics point of view, it is useful to recall that imagery is fundamentally a *field* over image coordinates – meaning that it is a mapping from a vector onto a scalar or a vector. A greyscale image can be represented by the image intensity function $I(x, y)$, a color image by the vector-valued color function $\underline{I}(x, y)$ and a range image by the range function $R(x, y)$. Both cameras and imaging rangefinders may be configured as 1D signals or 2D signals, but 1D cameras are not commonly used. In any case, the signals are, of course, **discrete** in both the position coordinates (x, y) and in amplitude I (or R).

8.1.1 Taxonomy of Computer Vision Algorithms

A large number of computer vision algorithms have found good use in mobile robot applications, but they cannot all be presented in this text. Those that are presented here can be organized into three categories.

- *Image Processing:* Algorithms that operate on pixels without much regard for what they represent. These tend to operate directly on the raw input data at the level of individual pixels or windows of pixels including those that create and process arbitrary shapes in an image.
- *Geometric Computer Vision:* Algorithms that focus on inferring shape or motion or both or on constructing models or maps. These tend to focus on understanding spatial relationships, on localization of objects in the scene, or on relative motion of the sensor and of objects.
- *Semantic Computer Vision:* Algorithms that recognize or reason about the nature of objects or parts of the scene, and algorithms that try to understand or interpret the content of the scene. Such algorithms tend to use artificial intelligence and machine learning techniques to perform such actions as *object recognition* and *scene understanding*.

8.1.1.1 Image Processing Algorithms

When signal processing is applied to images it is often called *image processing*. We will mostly deal with either appearance data (which comes from cameras of various kinds) or geometry data (which comes from imaging range sensors). Some of the important algorithms include:

- *Edge Detection* (high pass filtering): extracts spatial derivatives of image data. The "edges" found in this way often define the boundaries of objects.

- *Smoothing* (low pass filtering): removes "noise" in images. This is very useful for those algorithms that are sensitive to noise.
- *Segmentation*: finds connected regions in images. These often correspond to objects in the scene.
- *Feature Detection*: finds lines, interesting points, corners etc. These can signify (arbitrary) landmarks, corners in rooms, etc that are useful for position estimation and calibration purposes.
- *Optical Flow*: approximates the velocity of many or of all pixels in an image.

Most of these algorithms are presented later in this chapter.

8.1.1.2 Geometric Computer Vision

These algorithms tend to perform additional processing in addition to more fundamental image processing. Some of the more important algorithms include:

- *Shape Inference*: Although there are numerous methods to infer shape, the most important algorithm by far is computational stereo vision.
- *Feature Tracking*: Tracks the position of points, lines, corners, etc from image to image in order to infer apparent motion.
- *Visual Odometry*: When the sensor moves in a mostly stationary scene, feature tracking can be used to infer sensor motion.
- *Structure From Motion (SFM)*: It is possible to infer shape and motion at the same time. Visual odometry and SFM are similar when cameras are used.

Most of these algorithms are presented in Chapter 9 of the text.

8.1.1.3 Semantic Computer Vision

These algorithms tend to perform additional processing in addition to more fundamental image processing and/or geometric computer vision. They tend to involve prior knowledge, and sophisticated probabilistic models or search processes or both. Some of the more important algorithms include:

- *Pixel Classification*: assigns each pixel to one of a number of "classes" such as road, rock, bush, grass, yellow paint, and so on. This is clearly useful for picking out the road for road following and obstacles for obstacle avoidance.
- *Object Detection*: searches the scene to detect one or more instances of a specified object.
- *Object Recognition*: classifies or labels objects that may be people, other robots, refuse, landmarks, and so on, for a long list of purposes.
- *Obstacle Detection*: classifies or evaluates objects or regions of the scene in terms of difficulty of traversal or tendency to impede motion of the vehicle.
- *Place Recognition*: labels the present position of the sensor based on earlier experience.
- *Scene Understanding*: interpreting the content or activity in the scene to extract semantic meaning.

Most of these algorithms are presented in Chapter 9.

8.1.2 High Pass Filtering Operators

The presentation will now return to the first category presented in the last section, image processing, and discuss several topics related to detecting edges and features, filtering, and segmentation.

Operators designated as *high pass filters* are applied to signals to enhance the high frequency information and suppress the low frequencies. Such operations are useful when the high frequency information is the dominant signal of interest. However, when noise contains high frequency information, it will be amplified by such operators as well.

8.1.2.1 First Derivatives in 1D

First derivatives can identify where the image data is locally changing. Such regions are often called *edges* if they are points in a signal or one dimensional contours in an image. In implementation, signal processing is always performed on discrete signals, so derivative operators take the form of *finite difference* operators.

Compare the *forward difference* operator to the *backward difference* for an arbitrary signal $y(x)$:

$$\left.\frac{dy}{dx}\right|_{fwd} \sim \frac{y(x + \Delta x) - y(x)}{\Delta x} \qquad \left.\frac{dy}{dx}\right|_{bwd} \sim \frac{y(x) - y(x - \Delta x)}{\Delta x} \tag{8.1}$$

A *central difference* can also be defined which is the average of the forward difference and the backward difference:

$$\left.\frac{dy}{dx}\right|_{cen} = \frac{1}{2}\left[\left.\frac{dy}{dx}\right|_{fwd} + \left.\frac{dy}{dx}\right|_{bwd}\right] = \frac{y(x + \Delta x) - y(x - \Delta x)}{2\Delta x} \tag{8.2}$$

We can visualize this operator, and other operators, in terms of an array of scalar weights that is applied at every point in the image (Figure 8.2).

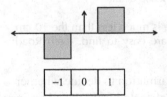

Figure 8.2 Central Difference Mask. This mask, applied everywhere in an image, computes the gradient.

8.1.2.2 Image Operators as Masks

Such a vector (or array) of scalar weights $m(x)$ has many names. It has been called a *stencil*, *template*, *kernel*, or *mask*. We can consider such a mask to be simply another scalar field. At times it can even be another signal or image. In this (first derivative) case, it is an abstract signal derived from a basic operator of mathematics. This first derivative mask is a 1×3 array. We will see others that are 3×3 later. The size of the mask is known as its *support*. More generally the support of a mask or function is the size of the region over which it is nonzero.

To apply the operator at a given pixel, we perform a ***vector dot product*** everywhere with the discrete version of the signal $y(i)$:

$$y'(i) = \sum_{k \in \{-1, 0, 1\}} m(k)y(i+k) \tag{8.3}$$

In the signal $y(i)$, for a 1×3 operator, the region consisting of the signal positions $i-1$, i, and $i+1$ is called the *neighborhood* of i. Each mask has an implicit origin – one cell which is the cell to be associated with a particular pixel in the image, in order to apply the mask to the neighborhood of the pixel.

In the case of a 2D mask, we perform a matrix dot product – element by element multiplication, followed by adding all the products together. If all of the weights in the mask are normalized to a sum near unity, the magnitudes of the output signal will be similar to those of the input. Otherwise, the output may need to be rescaled in a second pass over the output signal. Sometimes a second pass is desirable if the scale is supposed to depend on the signal itself.

When it is desired in implementation to overwrite storage for the input signal with the output signal, care must be taken to avoid overwriting the input while it is still being used. A common way to accomplish this is to store the output in a separate data structure until all of the input signal is processed.

8.1.2.3 Example: First Derivative of 1D Range Data

A lidar sensor that is pointed slightly down at a city roadway with sidewalks produces elevation data shown to the left in Figure 8.3.

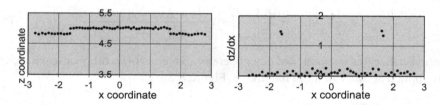

Figure 8.3 Roadway Edge Detection. Because the 1.0 cm noise is much less than the 10 cm range edge, the drop and subsequent rise in the range data are easy to find. (Left) Road Height. (Right) Derivative Magnitude.

Perhaps an autonomous city bus would want to use this information to decide whether a pedestrian is on the sidewalk or not. The sidewalk can be detected from the edges in the range data that signify where it rises from the roadway. The central difference is used to detect *edges* in the range data in the right figure. Evidently the road is about 3.6 units wide.

8.1.2.4 First Derivatives of 2D Intensity Data

In a 2D image, the intensity $I(x, y)$ gradient at a point is given by the vector:

$$\nabla I(x, y) = \frac{\partial}{\partial x}I(x, y)\hat{i} + \frac{\partial}{\partial y}I(x, y)\hat{j} \tag{8.4}$$

For real (discrete) imagery, this operator can be approximated by using finite differences for each component:

$$\frac{\partial}{\partial x}I(x, y) \sim \frac{I(x + \Delta x, y) - I(x, y)}{\Delta x} \quad \frac{\partial}{\partial y}I(x, y) \sim \frac{I(x, y + \Delta y) - I(x, y)}{\Delta y} \quad (8.5)$$

The gradient image can be interpreted as a derived image and visualized as two component images $\partial I(x, y)/\partial x$ and $\partial I(x, y)/\partial y$. Or it can be viewed as a magnitude image and an angle image. In 2D, a famous central difference operator is the Sobel operator. An example is provided in Figure 8.4.

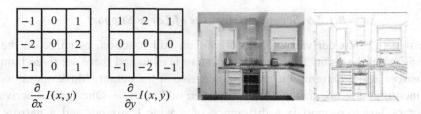

Figure 8.4 Sobel Operator. This is perhaps the simplest useful edge detector. The right image is the Sobel output for the kitchen scene. Each output pixel is an approximation of the gradient magnitude at the corresponding place in the input image. Vertical edges such as those in this image can be useful for localization.

The Sobel operator is one of support 3×3, which produces a vector-valued output. A more sophisticated edge detector [10] finds those points that are a local maximum of the first derivative in the gradient direction. The next section provides an alternative way to do that.

8.1.2.5 Second Derivatives in 1D

Second derivatives are useful for at least two reasons. First derivatives (edges) are locally highest (or lowest) when the second derivatives are zero. Also, the second derivative of a signal contains all information except the mean (bias) and the linear deviation from the mean (scale), so the operator produces an image that is somewhat invariant to lighting variations.

Second derivatives can be computed in discrete signals as second differences – that is, differences of first differences. Based on earlier definitions:

$$\frac{d^2 y}{dx^2} \sim \frac{1}{\Delta x}\left[\frac{dy}{dx}\bigg|_{fwd} - \frac{dy}{dx}\bigg|_{bwd}\right] \quad (8.6)$$

This expands to:

$$\frac{d^2 y}{dx^2} \sim \frac{1}{\Delta x}\left[\frac{y(x + \Delta x) - y(x)}{\Delta x} - \frac{y(x) - y(x - \Delta x)}{\Delta x}\right]$$

$$\frac{d^2 y}{dx^2} \sim \frac{y(x + \Delta x) - 2y(x) + y(x - \Delta x)}{(\Delta x)^2} \quad (8.7)$$

Which can be expressed as a 1×3 mask vector $\begin{bmatrix} 1 & -2 & 1 \end{bmatrix}$ (Figure 8.5).

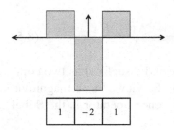

Figure 8.5 Second Difference Mask. This mask, applied everywhere in a signal, computes the second derivative in the x direction.

8.1.2.6 Second Derivatives of Large Support

Notice that the first derivative operator was an odd function, negative on the left and positive on the right. The second derivative is even and there are three humps – two positive at the extremities, and one negative at the center. Mask operators can be defined that are any size and they are often odd or even. One second derivative operator of larger support is a difference of a wide Gaussian and a narrow one (Figure 8.6).

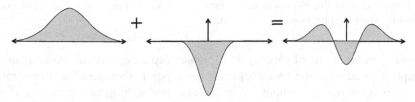

Figure 8.6 Difference of Gaussian Mask. This mask extends over many pixels so it appears as a smooth function. It performs a second derivative operation on the scale of the wider Gaussian.

8.1.2.7 Derivatives as Robust Comparisons

Note that if $y(x)$ has the Taylor series about the origin of a neighborhood:

$$y(x) = a + bx + \frac{1}{2}cx^2 + \frac{1}{3!}dx^3 + \dots$$

Then its first derivative is:

$$y'(x) = b + cx + \frac{1}{2}dx^2 + \dots$$

So the first derivative removes the local bias a of the neighborhood. Two neighborhoods that differ only in a will have the same first derivative.

Its second derivative is:

$$y''(x) = c + dx + \dots$$

So the second derivative removes the local bias a and local scale b of the image so two neighborhoods which differ only in a and b will have the same second derivative. This is useful when two images patches that are to be compared are illuminated differently.

8.1.2.8 Second Derivatives in 2D

A few types of multidimensional 2nd derivatives are important. First, consider the Hessian matrix of a scalar spatial signal $z(x, y)$, which is:

$$\frac{\partial^2 z}{\partial x^2} = \begin{bmatrix} \partial^2 z/\partial x^2 & \partial^2 z/\partial x \partial y \\ \partial^2 z/\partial x \partial y & \partial^2 z/\partial y^2 \end{bmatrix} \tag{8.8}$$

The trace of this matrix is called the Laplacian (a scalar). It is again defined for a scalar spatial signal:

$$\nabla^2 z = \frac{\partial^2 z}{\partial x^2} + \frac{\partial^2 z}{\partial y^2} \tag{8.9}$$

This operator can be implemented as the algebraic sum of two second difference kernels applied at right angles to each other at the central pixel. The mask in this case is shown in Figure 8.7.

0	1	0
1	−4	1
0	1	0

Figure 8.7 Laplacian Mask. This mask, applied everywhere in an image, computes the trace of the Hessian, known as the Laplacian.

8.1.2.9 Statistical Normalization in 1D

Statistical normalization is the basis for computing the normalized correlation between two signals. As we will see later, this is an important technique for performing signal matching. The mean of a signal f computed at time t over an interval of width T centered at t is:

$$f_{mean}(t) = \frac{1}{T} \int_{(t-T/2)}^{(t+T/2)} f(\tau) d\tau \tag{8.10}$$

The rms value of this signal over the interval is:

$$f_{rms}(t) = \sqrt{\frac{1}{T} \int_{(t-T/2)}^{(t+T/2)} [f(\tau)]^2 d\tau} \tag{8.11}$$

It is convenient to define the standard deviation of a signal as:

$$f_{std}(t) = \sqrt{\frac{1}{T} \int_{(t-T/2)}^{(t+T/2)} [f(\tau) - f_{mean}(t)]^2 d\tau} \tag{8.12}$$

Thus, the normalized signal (for the defined interval T) can be defined:

$$\tilde{f}(t) = \frac{f(t) - f_{mean}(t)}{f_{std}(t)} \tag{8.13}$$

8.1.2.10 Image Sum Notation

Following sections will begin the practice of using discrete sum notation to replace continuous integrals. For images, double sums are common. To avoid overly complicated looking double sums, let the following shorthand denote a sum where the dummy index i varies symmetrically about 0 over a defined interval h:

$$\sum_{i \in h} f = \sum_{i = -h/2}^{i = h/2} f \tag{8.14}$$

At various points, the letters x, i, u, and w may be used to represent the horizontal (column) coordinate in an image or matrix. Likewise, y, j, v, and h represent the vertical (row) coordinate.

8.1.2.11 Statistical Normalization in 2D

In discrete 2D imagery, the local mean can be defined over a rectangular neighborhood of size $w \times h$ thus:

$$\mu(x, y) = \frac{1}{wh} \sum_{i \in w} \sum_{j \in h} I(x + i, y + j) \tag{8.15}$$

Likewise, the variance of the neighborhood is defined as:

$$\sigma^2(x, y) = \frac{1}{(wh - 1)} \sum_{i \in w} \sum_{j \in h} \{I(x + i, y + j) - \mu(x, y)\}^2 \tag{8.16}$$

and the standard deviation is its square root:

$$\sigma(x, y) = \sqrt{\sigma^2(x, y)} \tag{8.17}$$

The normalized image is defined as:

$$\tilde{I}(x, y) = \frac{I(x, y) - \mu(x, y)}{\sigma(x, y)} \tag{8.18}$$

The normalized output image contains, at the location corresponding to each input pixel, its normalized deviation from the mean of its local neighborhood. This operator removes bias (mean) and then scales the deviation from the mean by the neighborhood average deviation (standard deviation). This operator is not well behaved if the denominator is small but usually, in the context of signal alignment and matching, it would not be advisable to match a signal with no variation in it anyway. The operator emphasizes the "texture" or "edginess" of the image (Figure 8.8).

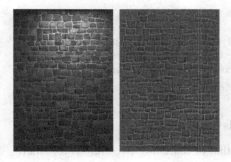

Figure 8.8 Normalization. Like a second derivative, a normalization removes most of the bias and scale differences in an image to emphasize local variation only. Both bright and dark areas in the original (left) are removed (right).

8.1.3 Low Pass Operators

Operators designated as *low pass filters* are applied to signals to enhance the low frequency information and suppress the high frequencies. These are useful when the low frequency information is the signal of interest. When there is high frequency noise present in the signal, low pass filters tend to reduce the significance of those high frequencies. As we saw in estimation, merely adding random numbers corrupted by uncorrelated random noise produces a sum with less noise. Similarly, in signal processing, whereas derivatives enhance high frequencies, integrals enhance low frequencies so low pass operators tend to involve integrals.

8.1.3.1 Average Filtering

The simplest way to filter out high frequencies is to replace every signal value by the average of the neighborhood around it. For an operator of width three pixels, the mask would look like Figure 8.9. There are very efficient ways to compute this kind of average across an entire signal (or image) by reusing computations (see Exercise 8.1.8.3). When it is desirable to filter an image multiple times over varying mask sizes, recursive image "pyramids" are sometimes defined. Such a pyramid is a set of output images, where each layer of the pyramid is half as large as the layer below it. Each higher layer is a filtered version of the layer below that replaces each 2×2 neighborhood in the input with a single pixel in the output.

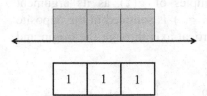

Figure 8.9 Average Mask (Box Filter). This mask, applied everywhere in a signal, computes the local average at every point.

8.1.3.2 Gaussian Filtering

The averaging filter presented in Section 8.1.3.1 gives all points in the mask window equal weight. Intuitively, it might be better to weight signal values close to the center of the neighborhood more highly. We might like a mask that is shaped like a Gaussian (Figure 8.10). Notice that the operators presented so far have the following properties: integrals are even and unimodal, first derivatives are odd and bimodal, second derivatives are even and trimodal.

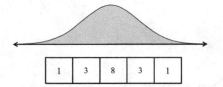

Figure 8.10 Gaussian Mask. This mask, applied everywhere in a signal, computes the local average at every pixel. Numeric values are illustrative only (nearest integers).

8.1.4 Matching Signals and Images

Another basic operation in image processing is that of matching two signals together. Signal matching has many motivations:

- Detection. Determining if an instance of an object appears in the image.
- Recognition. Labelling objects in an image with their correct names.
- Registration/mosaicking. Joining together two partial views to produce a larger view.
- Tracking. Determining the displacement that a known region has undergone as a result of parallax or motion.

The mathematical expression for signal matching is very similar to operating with a mask.

8.1.4.1 Convolution

Formally, the *convolution* of two signals $f(t)$ and $g(t)$ is the integral of the continuous dot product of the function $f(t)$ and a reflected and displaced version of $g(t)$. Mathematically, it is expressed as:

$$(f*g)(t) = \int_0^t f(\tau)g(t-\tau)d\tau \tag{8.19}$$

Convolution is typically defined as an integral over an interval extending from $-\infty$ to ∞ but in our work, the function $g(t)$ will always have finite support, so the integral can be restricted to its support region and still produce the correct result.

As the dummy variable of integration τ advances from 0 to t, samples of the function $f(\tau)$ are generated in the usual manner for an integral. However, the other function in the integrand $g(t-\tau)$ generates samples of $g(\tau)$ as its argument advances from t toward 0. Therefore, the function $g(\ )$ is sampled in the opposite direction. Equivalently it is reflected about the vertical axis through the origin and sampled in the same direction (Figure 8.11).

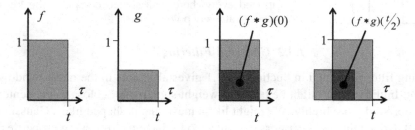

Figure 8.11 Convolution. The convolution of two functions at time t is the area under their product in their region of overlap.

8.1.4.2 Correlation

Whereas the convolution operation is important in Fourier analysis of signals, the term is sometimes used in robotics to mean a more straight forward operation, called *correlation*. Correlation does not reflect the function $g(t)$. We saw autocorrelation and crosscorrelation earlier in the context of random processes. The cross-correlation of two signals is defined as their product over an interval:

$$(f \times g)(t) = \int_0^t f(\tau)g(t + \tau)d\tau \qquad (8.20)$$

Just like convolution, the correlation of two signals is a function of t. The relationship to image processing is that $g(\ )$ can be considered the operator mask whereas $f(\ )$ is the operand or image. Changes in the variable t (or x or y in the spatial domain) correspond to moving the operator over the image whereas changes in the limits of τ correspond to moving around in the mask.

The integral corresponds to multiplying the image $f(\ )$ by the corresponding weights $g(\ )$ in the operator and adding up the products. Based on earlier discussion this means that the mechanism described earlier for applying a mask to an image is to compute the correlation with the mask at each point in the image.

8.1.4.3 Correlation in 2D

According to our definition of normalization in Equation 8.18, the normalized signal correlation can be defined as the integral:

$$(\tilde{f} \times \tilde{g})(t) = \int_0^t \tilde{f}(\tau)\tilde{g}(t + \tau)d\tau \qquad (8.21)$$

In continuous 2D imagery, the integral becomes a double integral:

$$(\tilde{f} \times \tilde{g})(x, y) = \iint f(u, v)g(x + u, y + v)dudv \qquad (8.22)$$

In discrete 2D imagery, the (double) integral becomes a double sum:

$$(\tilde{F} \times \tilde{G})(x, y) = \frac{1}{wh} \sum_{i \in w} \sum_{j \in h} \tilde{F}(i, j)\tilde{G}(x + i, y + j) \qquad (8.23)$$

Masks can also be parts of images. The above form is often used to match regions in two images against each other by searching a region of (x, y) for the best match (Figure 8.12).

(oversized)

Figure 8.12 Template Correlation. If resources are available to compute correlation everywhere, it can be used to find the occurrence of the center image in the left one. The peak in the correlation signal occurs at the location of the closest match. As shown, the technique can be used by a robot to locate a plug in order to plug itself in to charge its batteries.

Correlation with the exact signal that is to be found is known as a *matched filter*. It is the best available way to reject noise. For this reason it is used in stereo vision, in feature tracking, in surface alignment, and even in GPS signal processing.

8.1.4.4 Sums of Differences

Whereas a correlation based signal alignment maximizes a match criterion, an alternative view is to minimize differences. The *sum of squared differences* between two signals is defined as:

$$SSD(f, g)(t) = \int_0^t [f(\tau) - g(t + \tau)]^2 d\tau \qquad (8.24)$$

For a discrete 2D image, this becomes:

$$SSD(F, G)(x, y) = \frac{1}{wh} \sum_{i \in w} \sum_{j \in h} [\tilde{F}(i, j) - \tilde{G}(x + i, y + j)]^2 \qquad (8.25)$$

This operation can be viewed as the squared residual between two images, as the squared volume between two surfaces or as the Euclidean distance between signals viewed as vectors, or between images viewed as matrices. An alternative called *sum of absolute differences* is sometimes preferred to the above:

$$SAD(f, g)(t) = \int_0^t |f(\tau) - g(t + \tau)| d\tau \qquad (8.26)$$

For a discrete 2D image, this becomes:

$$SAD(F, G)(x, y) = \frac{1}{wh} \sum_{i \in w} \sum_{j \in h} |\tilde{F}(i, j) - \tilde{G}(x + i, y + j)| \qquad (8.27)$$

Minimizing the SSD can be shown to be equivalent to maximizing the correlation.

8.1.5 Feature Detection

Features, also known as "interest" points, are points, curves, or regions in an image that are distinguished in order to do something useful. Often features are used as a form of semantic compression that extracts the useful content in an image and represents it minimally. The word "feature" is used in a broad range of contexts, including:

- Points with high texture in images.
- Points where lines intersect in images.
- Points of high curvature in range images.
- Regions like edges, lines, and shapes in images.
- Regions of constant curvature in range imagery.
- Regions of constant depth in sonar data.

The problems of edge detection and (point) feature detection are closely related. In both we hope to find places in imagery where there are discontinuities in the signal. Conversely, regions are often places where some local property is not changing.

Extracting features can be valuable because they are:

- Persistent from image to image, and hence trackable.
- Relatively rare in the image, and hence a good way to distill the scene to a few pieces of data.
- Known to be well distributed, giving a good basis for triangulation.
- Relatively distinct, which creates a potential to use them for recognition.

When features are used for geometric reasoning, we care mostly about their positions in the image. When they are used for classification and recognition, attributes like length, texture, curvature, and so on, are more important.

8.1.5.1 Detecting Features to Track in Imagery

For motion inference, it is often sufficient to assume that the scene is *textured*, meaning that there are regions where intensity changes rapidly across the image. A widely used way to compress an image for motion inference is to concentrate on those places in an image where there seems to be a lot of texture, and there are algorithms that find such places (Figure 8.13).

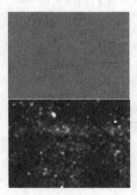

Figure 8.13 Texture Scores. Bright spots in the bottom image are regions of high texture in the top image. The linear features do not cause a strong response.

Consider the Harris corner and edge detector [11]. Let ∇x and ∇y denote the image intensity gradient in the x and y directions at a point in the image. In this detector, each pixel is evaluated for texture by first computing, over a region around the pixel, a weighted (by $w(x, y)$) covariance of the gradient vectors:

$$ H = \begin{bmatrix} \sum w(x, y) \nabla x \nabla x & \sum w(x, y) \nabla x \nabla y \\ \sum w(x, y) \nabla x \nabla y & \sum w(x, y) \nabla y \nabla y \end{bmatrix} \tag{8.28} $$

The eigenvalues of this matrix provide the weighted average gradient magnitudes in the two principle directions of variation. If only one eigenvalue is large, the region is an edge, if both are high, it is called a "corner" – although it could be any arrangement of pixels with high frequency content in both directions. Figure 8.13 shows a derived image whose intensity is proportional to the product of the eigenvalues. Of course, this approach will also detect true corners (Figure 8.14) because they have bidirectional texture.

Figure 8.14 Harris Corner Detector. The Harris "corner" detector identifies features with high gradients in both directions. These are likely to be stable from image to image and hence, good candidates for matching and/or tracking.

In practice, the eigenvalue computation is often avoided for efficiency and one computes the scalar quantity:

$$R = det(H) - k \cdot Trace(H)^2 \qquad (8.29)$$

for $k \sim 0.05$. An entire image of R values can be produced. Then the corners are found by finding those points that have both a large value of R and that are also local maxima of R. Local maxima can be found by requiring that such a point be higher in R value than all of its neighbors in a surrounding region. This is how Figure 8.14 was produced. The Sobel operator was used for the gradients, and a Gaussian weighting function of unit standard deviation was used.

8.1.5.2 Finding Corners in Range Data

Lidar scans of indoor scenes (Figure 8.15) have a lot of right angles in them. These features can be useful for computing ego motion (visual odometry) or for map-based guidance.

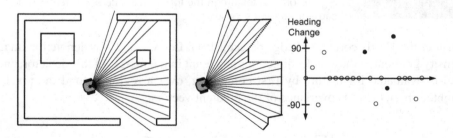

Figure 8.15 Scanning Lidar in Indoor Scene. Planar lidar scans are rich in geometric information. Occluding edges (dotted) give rise to erroneous curvatures.

A simple edge (corner) finding technique is based on the curvature. This is particularly effective in environments that are composed mostly of lines. However, a straightforward arctangent of adjacent range pixel endpoints is not always a measurement of a real angle in the scene. Occluding edges can occur if there are large depth continuities associated with object boundaries. These can masquerade as real surfaces or they may be real.

8.1.6 Region Processing

Another class of algorithms concentrates on the dual of edges – regions of relatively uniform properties. Although features possess position and perhaps orientation attributes, regions possess shape attributes. Some of the well-known algorithms include:

- *Segmentation*: Extracts regions of pixels that are similar in some way. In many cases (in both intensity and range imagery), these regions often correspond to objects.
- *Growing and Thinning*: Shrink and expand regions. Useful for cleanup of small errors.
- *Splitting and Merging*: Can be used to find canonical descriptions of objects. Also, this is a good way to find the largest object possible of a given type.
- *Medial Axis and Grassfire Transforms*: A family of operations that are extremely efficient at finding the skeleton and range contours of an arbitrary shape.
- *Moment and Invariant Computations*: Abstract regions into a few numbers that are often invariant to scale and sometimes perspective transformation. These provide convenient metrics to compare shapes for recognition purposes.
- *Histogramming and Thresholding*: Compute statistics to find the natural boundaries between pixel classes. These shrink an image into a small number of possible "colors."

8.1.6.1 Segmentation: Appearance Imagery

The famous "blob-coloring" algorithm of computer vision finds regions in imagery whose component pixels are "similar" [1]. In this case "color" means a distinct label for a region, rather than a true color. For appearance imagery, a very fast algorithm exists that passes over the image once. For example, in a left-to-right and top-to-bottom order (Algorithm 8.1). During its operation, the algorithm may determine, in the third if statement, that two regions originally thought to be distinct are, in fact, joined. These events create pairs of equivalent colors. A second pass through the list of these events creates equivalence classes and assigns a unique color to each region.

```
00   algorithm colorBlobs(image f)
01     k ← 1 // initial color
02     scan all pixels left-right, top-bottom
03       if ( f(X_c) = 0) continue
04       else if( f(X_u) = 1 and f(X_l) = 0)
05           color(X_c) ← color(X_u)
06       else if( f(X_l) = 1 and f(X_u) = 0)
07           color(X_c) ← color(X_l)
08       else if( f(X_l) = 1 and f(X_u) = 1)
09           color(X_c) ← color(X_u)
10           color(X_l) equivalent to color(X_u)
11       else if( f(X_l) = 0 and f(X_u) = 0)
12           color(X_c) ← k
13           k ← k + 1
14       endif
15     endscan
16     return
```

	Xu
Xl	Xc

Algorithm 8.1 Binary Blob Coloring. This algorithm finds the four-connected regions of 1's in a binary image very quickly.

The similarity measure, used to detect if pixels are similar, can be anything, and the method generalizes readily to 8-bit (nonbinary) images.

8.1.6.2 Detecting Shapes

Blob coloring can be used with shape descriptors to detect shapes. The following is a simple example. When the environment can be engineered, fiducials can be placed in the scene to aid recognition and localization. They can also be used as features on a calibration fixture, places to rehome the guidance system, or places for the robot to plug in for charging, and so on.

One very effective type of fiducial is based on retroreflective tape. The tape makes them stand out if a light is attached to and aligned with the camera. In this case, they become so bright that they can be found simply by thresholding the image (Figure 8.16).

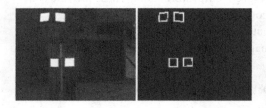

Figure 8.16 Retroreflective Fiducials. Here, squares of retroreflective tape are used to find the legs of parts racks that are to be aligned in order to stack the racks.

Once the blob coloring algorithm has found the four bright regions above, a good set of shape descriptors are the moments of area:

$$I_x = \sum x \qquad\qquad I_y = \sum y$$
$$I_{xx} = \sum x^2 \qquad I_{xy} = \sum xy \qquad I_{yy} = \sum y^2 \tag{8.30}$$

Special combinations of such moments are invariant to scale, translation, and rotation transformations. Hence, they can be found efficiently, anywhere in an image, regardless of where they are in the scene. See [3] for details.

8.1.6.3 Histograms

A histogram (Figure 8.17) of the color values in an image is a valuable tool for purposes of image enhancement – to adjust brightness or perform equalization – but it can also be a good tool for recognition purposes. Whereas moments distill the shape of a region to a few numbers, a histogram can distill the pixel values to a vector of relatively few numbers. If histograms are computed after the image is divided into subimages of equal size, a sense of the spatial variation of color values can be encoded. Histograms are also useful in range imagery.

8.1.6.4 Segmentation: 2D Range Imagery

The earliest known and simplest approaches to segmentation in range imagery are based on using curvature as the basis of similarity measures 9. We usually prefer to represent properties of interest in some manner which is invariant to lighting, scale,

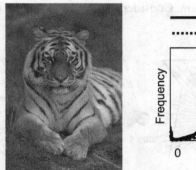 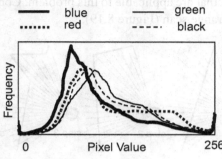

Figure 8.17 Image Histograms. The distribution of pixel values can be a powerful mechanism for recognition.

distortion, foreshortening, and so on. Curvature is invariant to viewpoint so it is a good basis for recognition in range imagery.

Suppose we have a surface patch that can be represented by an equation of the form:

$$z = z(x, y) \tag{8.31}$$

The Hessian matrix is the second derivative of a scalar field in 2D. Recall its definition from Equation 8.8:

$$\frac{\partial^2 z}{\partial x^2} = \begin{bmatrix} \partial^2 z/\partial x^2 & \partial^2 z/\partial x \partial y \\ \partial^2 z/\partial x \partial y & \partial^2 z/\partial y^2 \end{bmatrix} \tag{8.32}$$

Let κ_1 and κ_2 be the eigenvalues of the Hessian, known as the *principal curvatures*. These are the maximum and minimum of the curvatures in any direction on a given surface. The *mean* and *Gaussian* curvatures are defined (respectively) as:

$$H = \frac{\kappa_1 + \kappa_2}{2} \qquad\qquad G = \kappa_1 \kappa_2 \tag{8.33}$$

The 9 possible pairings of $(0,+,-)$ and $(0,+,-)$ for the signs of these two quantities lead to 9 distinct surface shapes (spherical, cylindrical, saddle, etc.). The eigenvalues themselves can be considered to form a plane that can be segmented into different regions to allow different surfaces to be distinguished from each other. Such techniques would make it easy to distinguish a book, from a pipe (Figure 8.18), from a soccer ball, and so on.

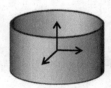

Figure 8.18 Principal Curvatures on a Cylinder. The maximum curvature is oriented axially and the minimum is oriented longitudinally.

8.1.6.5 *Segmentation: 1D Range Imagery*

When a range image contains more than one object it may help to try to segment the image into pieces first. The split and merge algorithm [12] is one of many good approaches that are applicable to this problem. Consider an application of the idea to a simple 1D range scan (Figure 8.19).

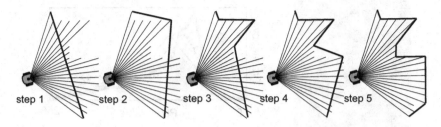

Figure 8.19 Split and Merge. This algorithm finds the lines and corners in the scene very quickly.

The algorithm starts with one line segment joining start and end. Each iteration splits all line segments at the intermediate point that has highest deviation from the line. This is repeated until a termination criterion is met. Occasionally two adjacent line segments must be merged.

8.1.6.6 Other Image Processing Algorithms

Because computer vision is a topic with its own textbooks, it is not feasible in a text on robotics to present all the material that may be of value. This section has deliberately avoided discussion of some core image processing topics such as morphological algorithms, image compression, color models, and optical flow, among others. The interested reader will find they are covered well in the references.

8.1.7 References and Further Reading

Ballard is a classic text that describes some of the algorithms presented here. Forsyth is comprehensive. Both Shapiro and Jain cover image processing as well as 3D vision and Forsyth is a relatively recent and comprehensive text. The image processing community predates that of computer vision. The book by Gonzalez is an example but there are many others including the student oriented book by Petrou. Snyder is a recent source for image analysis material as discussed here as well as pattern recognition.

8.1.7.1 Books

[1]   D. Ballard and C. Brown, *Computer Vision,* Prentice Hall, 1982.

[2]   D. Forsyth and J. Ponce, *Computer Vision – A Modern Approach,* Prentice Hall, 2003.

[3]   R. C. Gonzalez and P. Wintz, *Digital Image Processing,* 2nd ed., Addison-Wessley, 1987.

[4]   R. Jain, R. Kasturi and B. Schunck, *Machine Vision,* McGraw-Hill, 1995.

[5]   A. Low, *Introductory Computer Vision and Image Processing,* McGraw-Hill, 1991.

[6]   M. Petrou and P. Bosdogianni, *Image Processing: The Fundamentals,* Wiley Interscience, 1999.

[7]   L. Shapiro and G. Stockman, *Computer Vision,* Prentice Hall, 2001.

[8]   W. E. Snyder and H. Qi, *Machine Vision,* Cambridge University Press, 2004.

8.1.7.2 Papers

[9] P. J. Besl and R. C. Jain, Segmentation through Variable-Order Surface Fitting, *Transactions on Analysis and Machine Intelligence,* Vol. 10, No. 2, pp. 167–192, 1988.

[10] J. Canny, A Computational Approach To Edge Detection, *IEEE Transactions on Pattern Analysis and Machine Intelligence,* Vol. 8, No. 6, pp. 679–698, 1986.

[11] C. Harris and M. Stephens, A Combined Corner and Edge Detector, Fourth Alvey Vision Conference, pp. 147–151, 1988.

[12] S. L. Horowitz, and T. Pavlidis, Picture Segmentation by a Tree Traversal Algorithm, *Journal of the Association of Computing Machinery,* Vol. 23, No. 2, pp. 368–388, April 1976.

8.1.8 Exercises

8.1.8.1 Image Processing

Every roboticist should write some image processing routines at least once. Using your favorite programming environment, implement the Sobel edge operators and a Gaussian smoothing filter.

8.1.8.2 Signal Matching

Show that minimizing the SSD is equivalent to maximizing the correlation.

8.1.8.3 Box Filter

For a 1D signal, imagine the operator being applied left to right. Essentially, as the mask is moved one step to the right, the algorithm subtracts from the last sum the value of the leftmost pixel *before* moving and adds to the last sum the rightmost pixel *after* moving. Operators of any size require the same amount of processing with this technique. A more straightforward application of the basic operator that did not reuse computations would require computation linear in the mask size.

This idea generalizes readily to 2D spatial problems. The *box filter* is a 2D version of the efficient averaging filter explained above. It is performed in two passes over the image. The first pass computes, for every pixel, $S(i, j)$, which is the sum of all pixel values whose row and column indices are lower than the present pixel. The second pass computes the output image $O(i, j)$ from $S(i, j)$ without overwriting it. Draw a diagram showing:

(i) how $S(i, j)$ is the sum of pixel values in three rectangular regions and how a raster scan of the input image can compute $S(i, j)$ from the three previously computed values of $S(i, j)$.

(ii) how to compute $O(i, j)$ for a window around the pixel (i, j) in the input image from the four corresponding corner values of the $S(i, j)$ image.

8.1.8.4 Separable Operators

A 2D image operator is said to be *separable* if it can be factored into two sequential (and hopefully less intensive operations). The Gaussian filter is implemented using the template

$$f(x, y) = e^{-(x^2/\sigma_x^2 + y^2/\sigma_y^2)}$$

using the properties of double integrals, show that the 2D Gaussian filter is separable. What property must the template have to be separable?

8.2 Physics and Principles of Radiative Sensors

All of the relevant perception sensors can be separated into three categories: contact, noncontact, and inertial. This section considers the principles behind the noncontact (here called *radiative*) sensors that are used for robot perception. Such sensors can be used to present data (e.g., video) to an operator or they may be used by autonomous robots to model, map, recognize, track, or manipulate objects.

8.2.1 Radiative Sensors

Radiative sensors provide the basic capacity to interpret the visible area around the robot (known as the *scene*) without having to make physical contact. Sometimes contact is dangerous, as it is with obstacles. At other times, though not always, there is more information in appearance than in tactile (contact) sensing.

There can be severe difficulties associated with processing radiative sensor data. At times, the required computation is massive, and even when it is available, the problem of true *perception*, of really understanding what the data means, often remains beyond our reach in the same way that duplicating true intelligence does.

Robots can benefit from ambient radiation in the same way that biology does. Many creatures have eyes because the Sun illuminates the planet. Just like humans and bioluminescent creatures, robots can generate their own radiation when necessary. In either case, the complexities of how radiation propagates must be understood in order to understand why many sensors perform in a very nonideal way.

8.2.1.1 Classification of Radiative Sensors

Radiative sensors can be further categorized in useful ways. An *active* sensor emits its own radiation whereas a *passive* sensor relies on ambient radiation. An *imaging* sensor natively produces a vector or array of data whereas a *nonimaging* sensor generates a single piece of data. A *scanning* sensor actively orients the sensing elements – perhaps in order to generate a synthetically wide effective field of view. A *nonscanning* sensor does not orient itself actively. Scanning is the basic mechanism by which a nonimaging sensor is converted into an imaging one. For such sensors, the time it takes to perform the scanning often means that a true projection is not taking place to form the "image."

Some sensors measure *appearance* in the form of color, greyscale intensity or even infrared intensity. Others may measure *proximity* or *range*. A proximity sensor is a binary detector of whether an object is in the field of view. A *ranging* (or simply range) sensor provides a range value to the object or scene elements being sensed. The term *shape* has a specific meaning in computer vision – that of relative or scaled range.

8.2.1.2 Classification of Ranging Sensors

Ranging sensors are of special importance in robotics and they can be further classified [20]. Such sensors include sonar, radar, and laser radar – called either *ladar* or *lidar*. A basic distinction of ranging sensors is the type of radiation used. Sound, light, and other forms of electromagnetic radiation behave very differently in important ways.

Because radiation sensors are ultimately sensitive only to wave properties like intensity, phase, and frequency, range sensors typically include intricate electronics that extract the range value from more fundamental signals. This fact provides the basis for another means of classifying range sensors. Range can be generated either from the principle of time-of-flight and many related concepts or from the principle of triangulation and related concepts (Figure 8.20). Although time-of-flight is necessarily active, triangulation may be used in either active or passive ways.

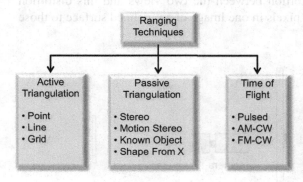

Figure 8.20 Taxonomy of Ranging Techniques. Three major techniques for computing range can be defined.

The next section outlines the details of many of the alternatives.

8.2.2 Techniques for Range Sensing

This section presents some of the principles and tradeoffs associated with the various techniques available for range sensing.

8.2.2.1 Triangulation

In general, triangulation involves solving a triangle. In *stereo triangulation*, the object or point to be ranged is one vertex and two views form the other two vertices. This case involves inverting the parallax or image displacement that is created by the two separated views. The distance between the two views is called the *baseline* and typically, the range accuracy is improved linearly with increases in the baseline.

Stereo triangulation is subject to the *missing parts* problem. The 3D structure of the scene may cause points that are visible in one view to be occluded, and invisible in the second view. When this occurs, ranging is not possible. There is an important tradeoff between range accuracy and missing parts because increasing the baseline to improve accuracy will create more missing parts. Conversely, if the baseline is reduced to almost zero, there will be essentially no missing parts but range accuracy will be very poor.

In *known object triangulation*, the object shape is presumed to be known, so only its pose (including range) relative to the sensor is unknown. Each point on the object that can be identified in the image generates constraints on the pose of the object and relatively few points may be required to solve for the object pose.

The term triangulation often applies when using cameras because they essentially measure angles. If the sensor already measures range, the term *trilateration* is used and the same comments about constraints apply.

8.2.2.1.1 Passive Triangulation. In passive triangulation, ambient radiation is sensed so this means triangulation is not possible in the absence of sufficient ambient radiation (e.g., at night or in shadow). The major practical issue is the determination of corresponding points between the two views, or between the one view and the model.

In stereo, a second important tradeoff occurs (Figure 8.21). Increasing the baseline also increases the perspective distortion between the two views and this distortion makes it harder to match blocks of pixels in one image of an inclined surface to those in the other.

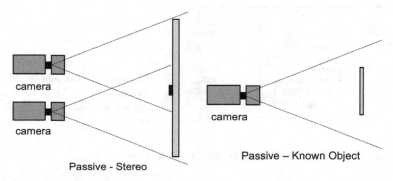

Figure 8.21 Passive Triangulation. (Left) In stereo, ambient radiation is sensed by two separated sensing elements that can measure bearing. (Right) When the object size is known, the size of its projection determines the range.

Passive triangulation also presumes that there is adequate signal variation, loosely called "texture," to permit matching. In plainer terms, if the entire scene is exactly the same color it is not possible to match anything.

8.2.2.1.2 Active Triangulation. Active triangulation, uses an energy generation mechanism of some kind but it cannot be just any energy. It must be recognizable in the view of some sensor. A common approach, called *structured light*, uses a laser to place patterns in the scene and then image them with a camera (Figure 8.22). Many energy patterns can be used including points, lines, grids, and various coded patterns.

One significant disadvantage of active systems is *interference*. For sonars, radars, and lidars, it is quite possible for one robot to sense the energy emitted by the active sensors of another. This situation can lead to essentially random range readings being generated. Also, safety concerns (particularly eye safety for laser energy) limit the levels of power that can be transmitted. Power limits create limits on signal to noise ratios that creative designers try to improve in other ways.

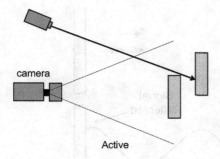

Figure 8.22 Active Triangulation. The missing parts problem is illustrated because the camera cannot see the laser spot on the occluded object.

8.2.2.2 Time of Flight

The time-of-flight (TOF) ranging technique uses the same path for transmitted and received energy so there is no missing parts issue. Of course, the scene can still self-occlude making parts invisible. The active nature of the technique means there is no correspondence problem but as we will see, the signal processing complexity is the cost of making the external interface so straightforward.

In contrast to triangulation, the accuracy of this form of ranging is essentially independent of the range itself. This technique carries its own radiation source with it. This makes it relatively insensitive to ambient radiation but it also makes it easy to detect the presence of the sensor.

8.2.2.2.1 Pulsed Time of Flight. This technique literally sends a very short pulse of energy out and measures how long it takes to come back (Figure 8.23). Of course, if light is used, it travels 30 cm in a nanosecond so processing electronics will have to resolve time of arrival to an astonishing 10-30 picoseconds in order to resolve 1 cm of range difference. The speed of electronics therefore places hard limits on the range resolution of TOF systems but systems exhibiting 1 cm range resolution are feasible and readily available so such devices are more than adequate for most robotics applications.

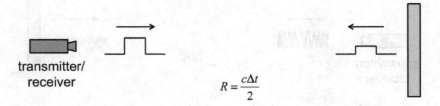

Figure 8.23 Time of Flight Ranging. In its simplest form, time of flight ranging measures half the distance travelled by a pulse of energy that was reflected by the environment.

8.2.2.2.2 AM-CW Modulation. An amplitude modulated continuous wave (AM-CW) sensor sends out an amplitude modulated carrier on a continuous basis and then mixes the returned signal with it in order to measure the phase difference between the two signals. When radiation is reflected from a surface, the wave phase changes continuously (Figure 8.24).

The range to the reflecting surface is proportional to phase difference of the received signal and reference signal. All phase measurements are subject to the *phase*

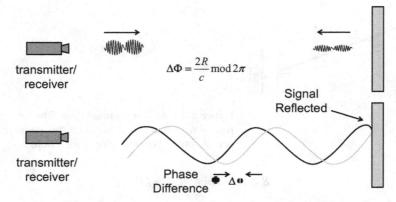

Figure 8.24 AM-CW Ranging. (Top) The range is proportional to the phase difference between the received and reference signals. (Bottom) The wave phase varies continuously across the reflective boundary.

ambiguity problem. In GPS terminology, this is called *integer ambiguity*. This means the phase difference will only include the component of range that remains after all integer half-wavelengths have been subtracted. AM-CW can only determine range modulo a half-wavelength.

Multiple modulation frequencies can be used to resolve the integer ambiguity. A simpler approach is to design the modulation wavelength to be twice the largest range that needs to be measured. There is a tradeoff of range resolution however, because range resolution is proportional to the modulator wavelength.

8.2.2.2.3 FM-CW (Frequency Modulation). A frequency modulated continuous wave (FM-CW) sensor sends out a frequency modulated carrier on a continuous basis and then mixes the returned signal with it (Figure 8.25). The range is proportional to the beat frequency produced when the return is mixed with the reference.

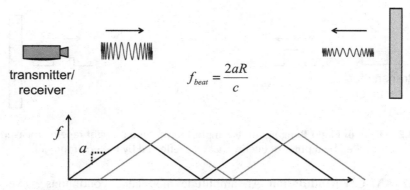

Figure 8.25 FM-CW Ranging. The range is proportional to the beat frequency generated when the return is mixed with the reference signal.

The figure shows a linear frequency modulation signal that generates a signal known as a *chirp*. Clearly, the phase difference between the two signals means the transmit and receive signals are separated by a constant frequency difference. FM-CW sensors involve significant electronics and processing but they achieve comparatively high noise immunity.

8.2.3 Radiation

A number of deficiencies that are traditionally associated with sensors can be traced to more fundamental and uncompromising aspects of physics and engineering. When radiated energy is received by a sensor, whether it is active or passive, the characteristics of the returned signal depend on many factors including the properties of: the transmitted beam and antenna, the medium or object material, any ambient radiation, geometry at multiple scales, and any sensor or object motion.

8.2.3.1 Beam and Antenna Properties

The concentration of radiation into a highly directed beam is accomplished with antennae (interference) or optics (refraction). For an antenna, beamforming is accomplished by exploiting the effect of interference. Energy generated at all points on an antenna is radiated in all directions from all points on the antenna so that the emissions of all of the point sources interfere constructively and destructively to create a *radiation pattern* that is characteristic of the antenna.

The radiation pattern can be visualized as a polar plot whose radius in any direction is proportional to the field strength generated (or the receiver sensitivity) in that direction. A famous radiation pattern is the pattern for a finite, cylindrically symmetric antenna. It takes a characteristic shape defined by the Bessel function Figure 8.26.

Figure 8.26 Beam Radiation Pattern. Side view of a circular antenna. A radiation pattern is a polar graph of emitted power versus each direction.

In practice, the beamwidth is measured as the angle where intensity drops to some percentage of maximum. A narrow beam is said to have high *directivity* and this can be a good thing. It means the gain is high and a lot of power is concentrated in one direction. Angular resolution is a function of beamwidth and a narrow beam has better angular resolution.

It can be shown using diffraction theory that no beam can be narrower than the *diffraction limit* determined by the aperture a, the beamwidth θ and the wavelength λ.

$$\sin\theta = \frac{\lambda}{2a} \qquad (8.34)$$

Spotlight 8.1 Diffraction Limit.

This is why antennae are as big as they are and why beams are as wide as they are. A given beamwidth can be reduced by using a larger antenna or a smaller wavelength and there are always practical limits on both.

It is possible to use sensor motion to synthetically achieve the effects of a large aperture. Reducing wavelength comes at the cost of higher frequencies and increased attenuation.

8.2.3.2 Object and Medium Physical Properties

The distinction between solids, liquids, and gases does not matter much for our purposes in this section. Objects are simply solid media. Properties of the medium affect multiple phenomena including the wave speed and hence refraction, energy attenuation and hence absorption and scattering. Whenever radiation passes through an interface between two media, portions of the energy may be reflected at the interface, transmitted through the second medium, or absorbed by it.

8.2.3.2.1 Wave Speed. For electromagnetic (EM) radiation, including light, the wave speed c depends on the dielectric constant ε and the magnetic permeability μ:

$$c_{light} = \frac{1}{\sqrt{\mu\varepsilon}} \tag{8.35}$$

In a liquid or a gas, the speed of sound depends on the bulk modulus B (a measure of liquid stiffness) and the density ρ:

$$c_{sound} = \sqrt{\frac{B}{\rho}} \tag{8.36}$$

The speed of light is reduced by only 0.03% in air but by 31% in water so light is faster in air. Conversely the speed of sound is about 345 m/s in air and 1500 m/s in water so sound is about five times faster in water.

Any of the medium properties mentioned above may depend on other things. Sound speed is very dependent on temperature. It varies by over 15% over a 100°C temperature range. Speed variation affects calibration accuracy of time of flight sensors.

If any of the above medium properties depend on wavelength, the medium will cause wavelength dependent bending, which is called *dispersion*. Recall that Snell's Law of refraction (Figure 8.29) specifies how a ray bends when it passes through an interface of two media with different wave speeds. This is how a prism works.

8.2.3.2.2 Attenuation. The term *attenuation* refers to the combined effects of absorption and scattering by the medium. Both effects reduce the amount of energy that is transmitted in a given direction. Whereas attenuation of the desired signal is a bad thing, attenuation of noise and unwanted signal is a good thing.

Media tend to absorb a fixed percentage per unit length so attenuation is exponential in distance. Radiation intensity is defined as power per unit area of surface through which the radiation passes. If I_0 is the incident intensity, and α is the absorption coefficient, then the intensity, for both EM radiation and sound, at any other distance r is given by the Beer-Lambert law:

$$I(r) = I_0 e^{-\alpha r} \tag{8.37}$$

This relationship is indicated graphically in Figure 8.27.

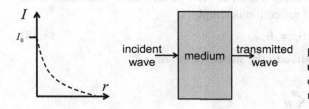

Figure 8.27 Factors Affecting Attenuation in Media. Attenuation is typically exponential in the depth of medium crossed.

The absorption coefficient is related to material properties. For example, for electromagnetic radiation in a conducting medium of conductivity σ:

$$\alpha = c\sigma\mu = \sigma\sqrt{\frac{\mu}{\varepsilon}}$$

Sound absorption increases rapidly with frequency in both water and air. This is why a fog horn has such a low frequency tone. Higher relative humidity in air also causes more absorption.

8.2.3.2.3 Transmission and Transparency. Absorptive and transmissive properties indirectly affect how much energy is transmitted after reflection. A sensor will receive no return if most of the energy incident on a surface is absorbed or transmitted. Soft materials tend to absorb a significant fraction of incident sound energy. Many materials are transparent to radar and light and this may be a problem or an advantage depending on the context. For example, a radar that can see through grass and underbrush to the underlying ground surface would be very useful.

For normal incidence, if E is the electric field amplitude and p is the pressure amplitude, the magnitude of the transmitted K_t and reflected K_r components of electromagnetic or sound energy is given by the following four relationships (Figure 8.28):

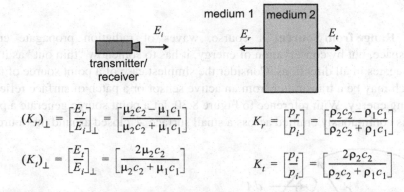

$$(K_r)_\perp = \left[\frac{E_r}{E_i}\right]_\perp = \left[\frac{\mu_2 c_2 - \mu_1 c_1}{\mu_2 c_2 + \mu_1 c_1}\right] \qquad K_r = \left[\frac{p_r}{p_i}\right] = \left[\frac{\rho_2 c_2 - \rho_1 c_1}{\rho_2 c_2 + \rho_1 c_1}\right]$$

$$(K_t)_\perp = \left[\frac{E_t}{E_i}\right]_\perp = \left[\frac{2\mu_2 c_2}{\mu_2 c_2 + \mu_1 c_1}\right] \qquad K_t = \left[\frac{p_t}{p_i}\right] = \left[\frac{2\rho_2 c_2}{\rho_2 c_2 + \rho_1 c_1}\right]$$

Figure 8.28 Reflection and Transmission. At an interface, the fraction of incident energy reflected and transmitted depends on material properties of both media. This is the case for both EM radiation and sound.

8.2.3.2.4 Reflection and Refraction. Non-normal incidence on a surface can give rise to both reflection and bending. Snell's famous laws govern these situations. With reference to Figure 8.29, the law of reflection is simply:

$$\theta_i = \theta_{rfle} \tag{8.38}$$

where the angles are measured relative to the surface normal.

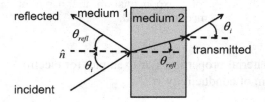

Figure 8.29 Snell's Laws. The reflection law is the basis of mirrors. The reflection law is the basis of prisms and lenses.

The degree to which light rays are bent at an interface depends on the relative wave speed in the two media involved. The index of refraction is defined as:

$$n = \frac{c_{reference}}{c_{medium}} \tag{8.39}$$

Then, the law for refraction is:

$$n_i \sin\theta_i = n_{refr} \sin\theta_{refr} \tag{8.40}$$

Substituting from Equation 8.39 leads to:

$$\frac{\sin\theta_i}{c_i} = \frac{\sin\theta_{rfra}}{c_{rfra}} \tag{8.41}$$

These laws work for both EM and sound. The reference speed for EM is usually the speed in vacuum (sound does not exist in vacuum). The reflected and refracted waves lie in the plane that contains both the incident ray and the surface normal.

8.2.3.3 Geometry

Many aspects of geometry affect how radiation propagates through the environment. Aspects include the relative poses of sensor and object and the surface geometry at all scales.

8.2.3.3.1 Range from Source. Of course, waves of radiation propagate energy through space, but by conservation of energy, it has to somehow "thin out" as it goes if it propagates in all directions. Consider the simplest case of a point source of radiation which may be a transmitter from an active sensor or a patch of surface reflecting or emitting energy. With reference to Figure 8.30, let a point source generate a power P_0 that is continuously emitted across a small surface A closed around the source.

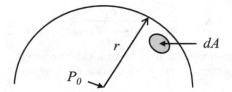

Figure 8.30 Intensity Variation with Range From Sensor. The power emitted through the surface patch dA depends on the radius and its area.

The intensity I is power per unit area emitted. If the surface is a sphere and the power is emitted with equal intensity in all directions, then we must have:

$$P_0 = \int_A I\, dA = IA = 4\pi r^2 I \qquad (8.42)$$

Hence the intensity at radius r is

$$I(r) = P_0/(4\pi r^2) \qquad (8.43)$$

So power falls off as $1/r^2$ if energy is conserved. Power is proportional to amplitude squared for both sound and EM, so amplitude falls off as $1/r$.

8.2.3.3.2 Angle Off Symmetry Axis. A highly *directive* (or *focussed*) source of radiation emits in a narrow beam. Some active sensors are designed to be highly directive. Specular reflections can also be highly focussed. Consider as an example a sonar sensor trying to detect solid objects. The sensor emits and receives energy. With reference to Figure 8.31, a solid object placed on the axis of symmetry will reflect a large amount of energy back to the sensor and one placed along the first sidelobe may be detectable as well. Curiously, an object on the null between the lobes may reflect almost no energy at all.

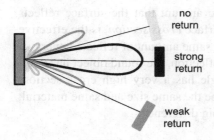

no return

strong return

weak return

Figure 8.31 Return Intensity Variation with Bearing from Sensor Beam. The capacity for a sonar to detect an object depends on where it happens to fall with respect to the axis of symmetry.

8.2.3.3.3 Microscopic Surface Geometry. Waves may be reflected like a mirror does (*specularly*) or may be spread out *diffusely* (Figure 8.32). Real surfaces display both types of reflection to some degree. An ideal diffuse reflector that is uniform in intensity over the entire half sphere regardless of incident angle is called *Lambertian*.

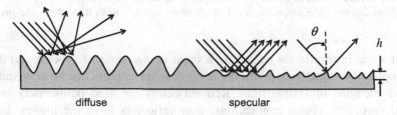

diffuse

specular

θ

h

Figure 8.32 Reflected Intensity Variation with Surface Roughness. As surface roughness is decreased beyond the Rayleigh criterion, reflections change from diffuse to specular.

Specular reflection occurs when the surface roughness is on the order of the wavelength of the wave. The precise criterion for specular reflection also depends on angle of incidence and is known as the *Rayleigh criterion*.

$$h < \frac{\lambda}{8 \sin \theta} \tag{8.44}$$

Spotlight 8.2 Rayleigh Criterion.

This small piece of physics explains why GPS signals (20 cm wavelength) reflect specularly off the ocean and large buildings, and why almost all man-made surfaces are mirrors to sonar.

In the case of light, the criterion explains why everyone in the room can see the laser pointer dot on the wall. However, for non-normal incidence, the laser pointer dot will reflect off of a smooth mirror and return nothing to the viewer. Laser radar sensors may not work well on shiny black ice but they do work well on the rough highly reflective surfaces of snow.

8.2.3.3.4 Macroscopic (Object) Surface Geometry. Macroscopic surface geometry also affects the strength of the returned signal. For a small patch of a surface, the amount of energy incident on it depends on its projected area (which depends on its surface orientation) in the direction of the radiation source. If the surface is diffuse, the amount that the surface reflects back to the sensor is mostly independent of surface orientation.

However, if the surface reflects specularly, the amount that the surface reflects back is a complex function of its geometry. The surface *cross section*, is the effective area of a specular reflector that would generate the same amount of reflected energy.

With reference to Figure 8.33, under specular reflection, the round object has a relatively small cross section whereas the right angle has a very high cross section. Notice that both the ball and the right angle could be the same size and same material, but the effect of only the shape still makes a very big difference.

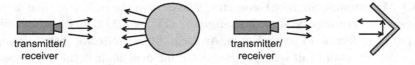

Figure 8.33 Object Cross Section. Under specular reflection, the round object has very low cross section and the right angle has a very high cross section. Both have the same projected area.

The right angle retroreflector occurs with sonar at the corners of rooms and it is the basis of optically reflective tape. In the latter case the corners can be very small due to the wavelengths of visible light. Retroreflectors are used deliberately in many laser and computer vision applications. Retroreflectors have the highest possible cross section since all incident energy is returned coaxially.

8.2.3.3.5 Macroscopic (Scene) Surface Geometry. In the case of specular reflection, the surface geometry of the entire scene matters and there are times when the returned energy is enhanced or diminished due to scene geometric effects (Figure 8.34). Good reflectors can be occluded by bad ones or two surfaces may be at just the right angle to create a strong *multipath* return. In the latter case, the interpretation of the result is likely to be an object positioned somewhere between the two that caused the return.

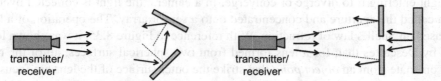

transmitter/
receiver

transmitter/
receiver

Figure 8.34 Scene Geometry Effects. Even the geometric relationships between objects can enhance returns (multipath) or reduce them (occlusion).

8.2.3.4 Sensor Motion

Any effects of sensor motion will be important for a mobile robot. Perhaps the most ubiquitous issue is the need to remember where a moving sensor was when its data was received. It requires effort to be able to read perception sensors and guidance sensors at the same time or to know exactly when each was read to sub-millisecond precision.

Sometimes the raw speed of the sensor interferes with its operation. Rotating sonar sensors (or those on rotating robots) can rotate the receiver away from the return beam before it returns. Sometimes, the raw speed is the quantity of interest. The well-known Doppler effect can be both the principle behind speed measurement (in a groundspeed radar) or the source of a corrupting influence in a target tracking system that expects the sensor to be stationary.

8.2.3.5 Ambient Radiation

For passive sensors, lack of ambient radiation creates the need to carry a source (e.g., headlights) with the robot. There are subtler issues for cameras as well. Shadowed regions can be very difficult to image well if the rest of the scene is brightly lit. Conversely, most inexpensive cameras will bloom if only part of the image is very bright. Imaging the sun early or late in the day is often a source of imaging issues.

Every sensor modality suffers at times from interference generated by ambient radiation. Sonars are sensitive to ambient ultrasound sources and infrared laser rangers are sensitive to sunlight (which can be bright at infrared wavelengths). Radars are, of course, sensitive to radio sources of all kinds and there are more everyday. At times, sensors can hallucinate objects just because they received energy from elsewhere that was unexpected. The effects can also be subtle degradations of fidelity whose sources can be hard to trace. When multiple robots operate in the same area with the same active sensors, problems are likely to occur.

8.2.4 Lenses, Filters and Mirrors

Snell's laws provide sufficient background to understand both lenses and mirrors. Both of these optical devices are commonly used for cameras but some radars and many lidars also use mirrors for scanning the beam over the scene.

8.2.4.1 Thin Lenses

A lens is a device that transmits and refracts light – typically, in order to cause the rays of light entering it to diverge or converge. In a camera, the light is collected over an area called the aperture and concentrated onto a sensor array. The operation of a lens is based on Snell's law of refraction. With reference to Figure 8.35, it was shown long ago by Descartes that, for a lens formed from two spherical surfaces, all of the rays that emanate from an *object point* that strike the outer surface of the lens are focussed at an *image point* behind the lens.

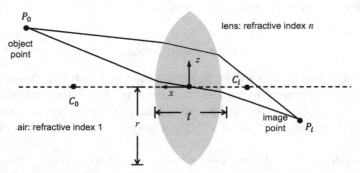

Figure 8.35 Figure for Descartes Lensmaker's Formula. This convex lens is formed from two spherical surfaces of different radii. C_i is the center of curvature of the object side surface etc.

The formula relating the object and image points is:

$$\frac{1}{x_{Po}} - \frac{1}{x_{Pi}} = (n-1)\left(\frac{1}{x_{Co}} - \frac{1}{x_{Ci}}\right) \tag{8.45}$$

Note that $x_{Po} > 0$ and $x_{Pi} < 0$. This formula is valid only when the lens is *thin* (one whose thickness is small relative to the image x_{Pi} and object x_{Po} distances) and the rays are *paraxial* (true when the lens radius is small compared to the image and object distances).

Clearly, as the object point moves around, the image point will move as well. Consider Figure 8.36. The *image focal point* F_i is the image point produced by an object at infinity. It will land on the optical axis because, if P_0 is at infinity, the ray from it through the point O will enter horizontally and be undeflected. Substituting $x_{Po} = \infty$ into the above gives the following result:

$$\frac{1}{x_{Fi}} = -(n-1)\left(\frac{1}{x_{Co}} - \frac{1}{x_{Ci}}\right) \tag{8.46}$$

Spotlight 8.3 Lensmaker's Formula.

Provides the image focal point for an object at infinity for a lens composed of two spherical surfaces of different radii.

Likewise, the *object focal point* F_o is the object point that corresponds to an image point at infinity.

$$\frac{1}{x_{Fo}} = (n-1)\left(\frac{1}{x_{Co}} - \frac{1}{x_{Ci}}\right) \tag{8.47}$$

These have the same numeric value, which is called simply the *focal length f*, but are of opposite signs because they occur on either side of the lens. Substituting Equation 8.46 into Equation 8.45 gives the relationships for a thin lens for an object point at infinity:

$$\frac{1}{x_{P_o}} - \frac{1}{x_{P_i}} = \frac{1}{f}$$

(8.48)

Spotlight 8.4 Thin Lens Formula.

This formula allows us to determine where the image of a point will be formed. In some forms x_{P_i} is considered to be positive and that will change the subtraction to an addition in the formula. We use lenses in cameras because they can collect a lot of light and direct it onto a small sensor with the correct geometry to form an image on the sensor.

With reference to Figure 8.36, we can now use what we know about focal lengths and points at infinity to understand the image formation process for objects that are not at infinity.

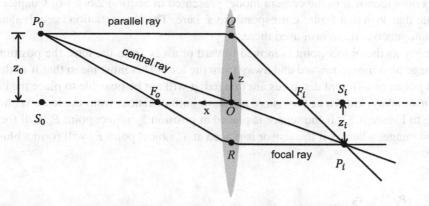

Figure 8.36 Figure for Magnification. The image produced by the lens is scaled and inverted.

The *parallel ray* leaves the object point and travels parallel to the optical axis. Because this ray would be identical if the object point were at infinity, it passes through the image focal point after refraction through the lens. The *central ray* leaves the object and travels right through the center of the lens. For a thin lens, it is undeflected by the lens, so it continues in a straight line. These two rays intersect at the image point. To show that an image is indeed formed, consider the *focal ray* which emanates from the image points and travels parallel to the optical axis back toward the lens. It is refracted and passes through the object focal point (which is also at the focal distance from the lens origin) and arrives at the object point.

By similar triangles $P_i RO$ and $P_o QO$:

$$\frac{z_i}{x_{S_i}} = \frac{z_o}{x_{S_o}}$$

(8.49)

Therefore, the magnification, or ratio of image size to object size, is:

$$M = \frac{z_i}{z_o} = \frac{x_{S_i}}{x_{S_o}} \qquad (8.50)$$

For the two triangles P_iF_iO and P_iQP_o we can also write:

$$\frac{z_i}{z_o - z_i} = \frac{x_{F_i}}{x_{S_o}} = \frac{-f}{x_{S_o}} \qquad (8.51)$$

This can be manipulated to produce:

$$\frac{z_i}{z_o} = \frac{f}{f - x_{S_o}} = \frac{-f}{x_{S_o} - f} \approx \frac{-f}{x_{S_o} + f} \qquad (8.52)$$

because $x_{S_o} \gg f$. If we want to remove the inversion of the image, we can invert it again by replacing z_i by $-z_i$

$$\frac{z_i}{z_o} = \frac{f}{x_{S_o} + f} \qquad (8.53)$$

This is now identical to the camera model presented in Section 2.6.1.1 of Chapter 2 if we note that y in that figure corresponds to x here. The lens equation is equivalent to the homogeneous transform used there.

Clearly as the object point is moved toward or away from the lens, the position of the image also moves toward and away from the lens. This must mean that if multiple object points at different distances are imaged, it will not be possible to place the camera sensor array, known as the *image plane*, at both distances from the lens. With reference to Figure 8.37, if the sensor is placed at position S_i, object point P_p will form a blurred image, whereas if the sensor is placed at S_j, object point P_o will form a blurred image.

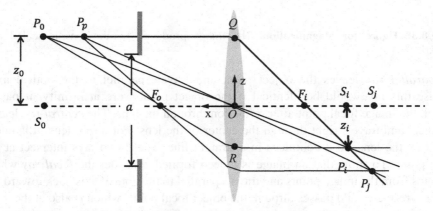

Figure 8.37 Figure for Depth of Field and Aperture. Only one of P_o or P_p can be in perfect focus at a time. Changing the aperture affects the depth of field.

The blurred image of a point is called its *blur circle*. For a given size of blur circle (perhaps one pixel), there is an image plane position both before and after the focussed position that produces such a blur radius. The difference between the farthest position and the nearest position of the image plane with a given blur circle radius is called the *depth of field* of the lens.

The depth of field will increase with a shorter focal length (and wider field of view) lens but this increase will come at the expense of more *lens distortion*. Lens distortion typical bends straight lines in the image plane outward (*barrel distortion*) or inward (*pincushion distortion*) near the center of an image.

The aperture refers to the radius of the circle that admits light to the lens. The depth of field will increase with a reduced aperture but this benefit comes at the expense of less light reaching the image plane.

8.2.4.2 Filters

An optical filter is a device that is used to pass a fraction of the light incident upon it. One form of filter uses compounds embedded in glass in order to absorb unwanted light. Another form reflects unwanted light away and passes the wanted light. The *transmission curve* of a filter is a graph of the fraction of light transmitted as a function of wavelength. A basic filter will pass a band of frequencies of interest and reject all others.

Color CCD cameras typically have an *infrared cut filter* if realistic color response is important to their operations. This filter prevents the sensor from responding to near infrared light. In outdoor robotics applications, sensing IR light can be valuable so there are times when it is useful to remove this filter.

A *Bayer filter* array is a standard component of most single chip cameras. It is an array of tiny elements the size of individual pixels that passes only the colors of interest to the underlying sensing elements.

8.2.4.3 Mirrors

Mirrors can bend or distort the field of view of a camera or a light source and thereby solve some otherwise very difficult problems. A simple use for a mirror is the use of a flat mirror in order to rotate a camera field of view through a fixed angle. This approach can solve a space problem where one or more cameras would otherwise not fit. It can also protect a camera from damage if it can be hidden behind a shield, or bend multiple camera fields of view so they appear to emanate from the same point. If a flat mirror is actuated into motion, it can be the basis for scanning both a laser and a photodiode aperture for a lidar.

A particularly interesting use of mirrors is the use of convex mirrors to distort a standard camera field of view into an omnidirectional one. Ideally, all of the rays will appear to converge at a single center of projection. Mirrors that satisfy this constraint must satisfy a particular differential equation [13]. One mirror shape that satisfies the constraint is a hyperboloid of two sheets where one half is removed (Figure 8.38).

There are several applications for which an omnidirectional field of view is particularly desirable. If a robot needs to change direction regularly, eyes in the back of its

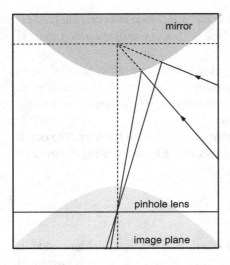

Figure 8.38 Omnicam Constructed From Hyperboloidal Mirror. For the section containing the line of symmetry shown, incoming rays strike the mirror, pass through a pinhole lens and form an image on the image plane. The pinhole must be placed at the second focus of the hyperboloid.

head can be useful. All forms of visual localization usually benefit from omnidirectional views. In visual odometry, for example, it becomes much easier to distinguish rotational motion from translation.

Omnidirectional mirrors can be used to produce synthetic full cylinder panoramic images and even videos (Figure 8.39).

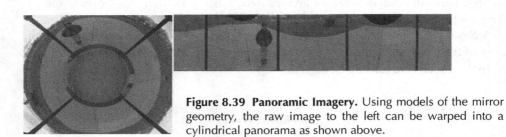

Figure 8.39 Panoramic Imagery. Using models of the mirror geometry, the raw image to the left can be warped into a cylindrical panorama as shown above.

8.2.5 References and Further Reading

The paper by Baker covers mirrors for panoramic imaging. Smith is an authoritative source on range sensor signal processing. Barklay, for example, covers the Rayleigh criterion for surface roughness. Halliday is a joy to read on any topic, including lenses. Ulaby is a good source for material on wave propagation and antennae.

[13] S. Baker and S. K. Nayar, A Theory of Catadioptric Image Formation, in *Proceedings of the 6th International Conference on Computer Vision*, Bombay, India, IEEE Computer Society, 1998.

[14] Les Barklay, ed., *Propagation of Radio Waves,* 2nd ed., Institution of Engineering and Technology, 1996.

[15] D. Halliday, R. Resnick, and J. Walker, *Fundamentals of Physics,* Wiley, New York, 1997.

[16] P. Probert Smith, Active Sensors for Local Planning in Mobile Robotics, *World Scientific Series in Robotics and Intelligent Systems,* Vol. 26, World Scientific Publishing Company, 2001.

[17] F. Ulaby, *Fundamentals of Applied Electromagnetics,* Prentice Hall, 2010.

8.2.6 Exercises

8.2.6.1 Specular Reflection of Ultrasound

The speed of sound 340 meters per second in air. Show that a 50 KHz sonar reflects specularly off most man-made surfaces.

8.2.6.2 Tradeoff of Maximum Range and Beam Width

Comment on the essential tradeoff between maximum range and beam width for both sound and radar antennae.

8.2.6.3 Thins Lens Equation

Use the triangles F_iQO and $F_iP_iS_i$ in Figure 8.36 and Equation 8.50 to derive the thin lens equation from the geometry.

8.3 Sensors for Perception

In order for a robot to respond intelligently to its environment it must be able to sense pertinent aspects of the environment. The engineering aspects of sensor design is a discipline in itself but it is possible, based on the background of the last chapter, to appreciate some of the more important aspects of perception sensors from a users perspective.

Common sensors may sense appearance (including infrared and ultraviolet wavelengths), or range. More esoteric sensors include ground penetrating radar (perhaps used to find buried land mines), ambient sound (to sense traffic or human voices), or chemical sensors (sense of smell).

Without exception, real sensors are often well suited to some applications and poorly suited to others. This section presents some of the most commonly useful non-contact sensors used in mobile robots.

8.3.1 Laser Rangefinders

The technique of LIght Detection and Ranging is called LIDAR (or LADAR) where the second acronym is intended to be analogous to RADAR. Just as for radar, the word lidar has begun to outgrow its status as an acronym and become a word. Lidar sensors have all of the advantages of any active sensor but they are also high resolution in both range and angle and they are typically narrowband so they can be engineered to reject sunlight at the receiver.

Lidars are typically a single range pixel sensor based on any of the time-of-flight ranging principles (TOF, AM, FM), described earlier. Many combinations of multi-sensor arrays and scanning devices have been designed to convert them into 1D and 2D scanning configurations as well.

8.3.1.1 Principles

A discrete laser rangefinder consists of a laser diode that emits light and a photodiode that senses the return. The photodiode is a semiconductor device that operates on the *photoelectric* effect. Light is channelled to a sensitive semiconductor junction that liberates electrons when they are struck by a photon. The resulting current can be sensed to detect the original photon.

As for the laser diode, all lasers are optical oscillators based on the two ingredients of positive optical feedback and frequency filtering. In the case of a semiconductor laser diode (Figure 8.40), the feedback arises from the phenomenon of *stimulated emission* of a photon by an atom that is above its ground state. A hole recombines with a nearby electron in the presence of a photon of a certain frequency and a second identical photon is produced.

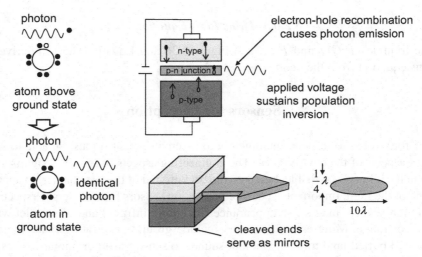

Figure 8.40 Laser Diode Principles. (Left) Stimulated Emission: One photon causes emission of another. (Right) Semiconductor Laser: The cleaved ends of the device serves as mirrors.

Stimulated emission can only be sustained with a *population inversion* – more atoms above ground state than in ground state, and an applied voltage supplies the required energy. The frequency filtering arises because only those photons that meet the *cavity resonance condition* can avoid destructive interference.

In the semiconductor case, the cleaved ends of the device serve as mirrors that create the lasing cavity. The resulting beams are not round and not very well formed, so collimation optics are used to improve the shape of the beam. Infrared wavelengths are typically used in lidar so the beam itself is invisible to the naked eye.

8.3.1.2 Signal Processing

Most contemporary lidars are either pulsed or AM devices. FM devices exist but are more rare. Nominally, the return from the first reflecting surface in the environment is "timed" to find the range. However, when the environment is partially transparent, it is possible for the returned signal to generate several range readings for the same pixel (Figure 8.41). There is some value in recording multiple returns in environments that are dusty or smoke filled, because the first return will be the airborne obscurant. Roughly speaking IR wavelengths are close to visible so if a human can see through

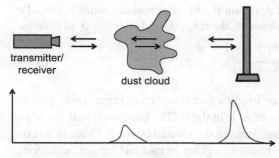

Figure 8.41 Multipulse Processing. Each change in medium generates a return. Here, the front of the dust cloud and the hard surface generate two separate range readings.

the obscurants, a lidar will as well. However whether the sensor ranges to the cloud or beyond it is a matter of signal processing.

A typical image from a 2D scanning lidar is shown in Figure 8.42. Most devices return a measurement of returned signal intensity as well as range, and this signal has many potential uses for uncertainty estimation, terrain typing, recognition, and improved accuracy.

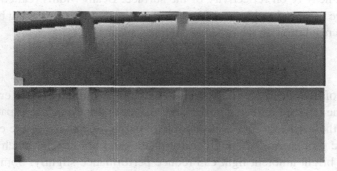

Figure 8.42 Laser Rangefinder Images. Range and reflectance images of AM-CW scanning lidar. (Top) Range image. (Bottom) Intensity image. A tree and a paved walkway are shown. A human is in the top center of the image.

8.3.1.3 Performance

The beamwidth of a scanning lidar is also known as the *instantaneous field of view* (IFOV). We will call the region of the scene that is instantaneously illuminated by the laser the pixel *footprint*.

The precision of lidars used on robots, is typically in the 1 to 5 cm range and it depends on the amount and the structure of the received radiation (Figure 8.43). In most cases, the surfaces encountered reflect diffusely. High incidence angles imply that the distribution of ranges in the footprint is large. High ranges imply that the signal is low, which means the signal to noise ratio will be low.

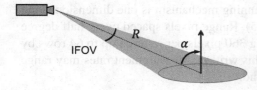

Figure 8.43 Lidar Range Resolution. Range resolution depends on the geometry shown.

One model [18] predicts that the standard deviation σ_R of range measurements is related to the laser wavelength λ, the angle of incidence α, the range R and intensity ρ as follows:

$$\sigma_r \propto \frac{\lambda \cdot R^2}{\rho \cdot \cos\alpha} \qquad (8.54)$$

The finite beamwidth of any real device implies that the correct range value will be ambiguously defined when an occluding edge is in the IFOV. Imagine if half the beam images the side of a tree and the other half images the ground beyond. There is no correct single range and the average range refers to a point in mid air! In such situations, perhaps the best that can be done is to remove the offending range points as outliers.

The laser beam will reflect specularly on some surfaces and virtually no energy will be returned to the receiver. A simple test is that if a surface is optically shiny it is probably also an IR mirror. Signal strengths are typically engineered to be as high as possible without violating eye safety regulations, and this (important) constraint does make it more difficult to construct precision devices. The maximum possible range measurement depends heavily on reflectivity of the surface. Beam widths (called *dispersion*) are in the range 0.1 mrad to 10 mrad. This need not relate to pixel spacing but normally it does. Range resolution on the order of a cm is typical.

8.3.1.4 Advantages and Disadvantages

The accuracy of lidar decreases only slightly with range and most of the error increase is caused by the reduced reflected power and surface orientation. The capacity to measure range in the hardware makes it possible to extract the shape of the environment with very little processing. Although performance does not depend much on ambient lighting, very bright ambient light can reduce performance slightly. Some lidars can operate in the presence of moderate dust, smoke, and fog.

The fact that most lidar systems are physically scanned devices means that a complex scanning mechanism must be designed and its movements must be measured to accuracies of a fraction of a beamwidth. The angular resolution is limited by the minimum beamwidth needed to get an acceptable amount of reflected energy. A minimum surface reflectivity is needed to produce an accurate measurement. Whereas white paper has a reflectivity near 100%, bare wood and concrete are in the neighborhood of 25%. Asphalt is around 15% reflectivity and black rubber is as low as 2%.

8.3.1.5 Scanning Lidar Implementations

The rangefinder module itself typically consists of the transmitter, receiver, collimation optics, and electronics for signal generation, amplification, and time measurement. A time-of-flight design block diagram is shown in Figure 8.44.

Scanning mechanisms may scan in one or two directions. In some cases a mirror oscillates. In others, it rotates. A simple scanning mechanism is one dimensional and rotates continuously in azimuth (Figure 8.45). Range pixels spaced every half degree of rotation are typical and devices producing 360 pixels per rotation up to 64 rows by 3600 columns are available at the time of this writing. Measurement rates may range from 2000 to 500,000 range points per second.

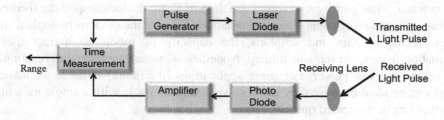

Figure 8.44 Time of Flight Laser Rangefinders. A laser diode/photodiode pair, a clock, and some optics make up the device.

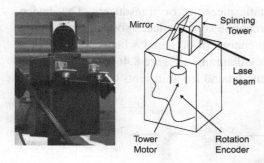

Figure 8.45 Cyclone Laser Rangefinder. A simple custom device for measuring a complete circular field of view.

8.3.1.6 Other Lidars

Recently, *colorized lidars* that also measure the color of the scene pixel have become available. Such sensors hold much promise to enhance the capacity of robots to understand what they see. Custom sensors can be constructed the hard way using camera and lidar and calibrating the mapping between the range and color pixels. Integrated devices employ a single rgb pixel that is coaxial with the laser beam. At the moment, the scanning versions of these devices struggle to operate in low light conditions because the laser receive aperture is scanning so quickly that little light can be collected by the passive color sensor.

Flash lidars have been used for some time for aerial terrain mapping but recently they have become small enough to use on a robot. These sensors project a wide beam "flash" of lidar light that illuminates the entire scene, is reflected from objects in the scene, and is processed by an array of smart pixels in the sensor. Typically, CMOS cameras are used due to the relative ease of associating processing elements with each pixel.

This class of lidar is (uniquely) as immune to motion distortion as a visible light camera and they can use optics for typical cameras to alter their image geometries. Unfortunately, their highly dispersed flash of light leads to very low signal levels in returns. The associated reduced noise immunity presently makes them of limited use outdoors or for indoor imaging beyond a few meters.

8.3.2 Ultrasonic Rangefinders

The technique of SOund Navigation and Ranging (SONAR) was originally developed for underwater applications because high frequency EM radiation does not propagate well in water. Most commercial sonars are time-of-flight devices despite the theoretical availability of more sophisticated alternatives. Despite the obvious biological successes, including bats and dolphins, the capacity of robots to extract useful information from sonar remains limited. Nonetheless, sonars are inexpensive, simple, lightweight and low power. For some applications like (solid) obstacle avoidance, sonars can be ideal because they can resolve a large obstacle with a single measurement that can be processed quickly.

8.3.2.1 Principles

Sonar devices may be based on electrostatic piezoelectric transducers. The device operates as both a loudspeaker and a microphone so it produces sound from electric energy in the transmit phase and electric energy from sound when operating as a receiver. As indicated in the functional block diagram in Figure 8.46, the input amplifier is enabled after the transmit pulse is sent out and any transients have died off.

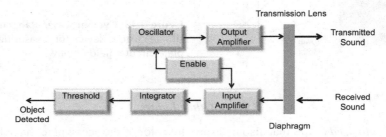

Figure 8.46 Sonar Rangefinder Signal Processing Electronics. The diagram represents the signal flow out to the diaphragm (transmit) and back (receive).

Many devices emit in multiple frequencies in order to reduce the likelihood of destructive interference. The input amplifier is typically programmed to increase its gain over time to account for attenuation and spreading (R^2) loss. This technique permits a fixed threshold to be used to trigger detection of an object.

8.3.2.2 Performance

Difficulties with sonar sensors are caused by many sources including specular reflections, multipath, wide beamwidths, slow wave speed, sidelobes, attenuation, high standoff, reduced maximum range, and environmental interference. Most man-made objects reflect ultrasound specularly at the wavelengths used so indoor environments are composed of many sound mirrors. The strength of the return depends on the angle of incidence. Only an interval of beam azimuth angles smaller than the beamwidth and centered at normal incidence, will reflect significant energy back to the transmitter. Occasionally, corners reflect sidelobes.

Figure 8.47 shows a typical sonar scan in an indoor setting. Often, the right angles at corners of the room produce strong returns whose apparent range is slightly in error. Elsewhere, the sound waves reflect specularly from walls leaving the impression that no walls are present and occasionally the geometry will be just right to cause a multipath

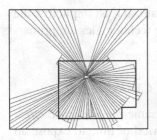

Figure 8.47 Typical Sonar Scan. Sonar distortion is a fact of life. In the room shown, ranges of corners are both over and underestimated. Figure inspired from [24] in Chapter 9.

reflection to cause a hallucination of an object somewhere outside the room. Such errors often contain both systematic pose dependent components and random components. Accumulation of multiple measurements gathered as the sensor moves is an effective technique to potentially remove some systematic sources of error.

Sonar attenuates at about 3 dB/ft so a 60 dB sensor dynamic range is required to measure the range to an object 20 ft away. The *standoff* is the minimum detectable range caused by timesharing the transducer and circuitry. Typically, it takes 1 msec for mechanical damping and pulse widths are 1 msec, so the standoff can be as large as 60 cm. The measurement rate is governed by the speed of sound and maximum range. For a 20 m maximum range, readings can be taken at about 8 Hz. Angular resolutions from 5° to 15° are typical, depending on the width of the primary lobe.

Range accuracy depends primarily on the speed of sound calibration. As a function of temperature T in °C, the speed of sound c in air in m/s is given by:

$$c = 331.4 + 0.607T \tag{8.55}$$

Clearly as T varies over 60°, c will vary by 3.6 m/s or 10%. The range precision for time of flight devices is governed by the carrier wavelength because the detector is likely to trigger when the amplitude of the received signal is highest. However, returned signal strength is also governed by integration of beam energy over world geometry. Hence, a secondary impact of poor angular precision is poor range precision. For example, rounding of corners is common. At longer ranges, range precision is governed by the decreasing signal to noise ratios caused by the spreading and attenuation loss of the sound pulse.

8.3.2.3 Implementations

Commercially available sonar transducers of relevance to robotics operate at ultrasound frequencies ranging from 50-60 KHz. Therefore wavelengths vary from 0.5 to 1 cm and most man-made surfaces are smooth in relative terms. Minimum ranges are as low as 0.25 meters and maximum ranges as high as 20 meters. Beamwidths can vary from 5° to 15°.

8.3.3 Visible Wavelength Cameras

Of course, the digital video camera is now the workhorse of computer vision and such sensors are very valuable components of a robot's suite of perception sensors. As passive sensors, the most significant attribute is their dependence on ambient lighting, but because humans have the same constraint, we often tolerate, at least implicitly, the notion of a robot that cannot see in the dark. Two competing technologies are primarily used today: the CCD and the CMOS sensor.

8.3.3.1 Principles of Operation (CCD and CMOS)

The CCD (charge coupled device) camera is based on the same *photoelectric effect* used in solar arrays. A shutter is opened for a very short period of time to expose an array of sensing elements, called picture elements or *pixels,* to ambient lighting. Each pixel liberates electrons when they are struck by a photon, and the liberated electrons are accumulated in capacitors in each pixel. Periodically, the pixel charges are shifted one at a time to a special capacitor whose voltage (proportional to charge) is read and amplified.

Whereas a monochrome camera operates as described earlier, a color CCD camera generally uses a *Bayer mask* (filter) over the CCD, which amounts to tiny filters that transmit only red, blue, or green light. Each square block of 2 by 2 native pixels is converted to 1 red, 1 blue, and 2 green pixels as a result, and the angular resolution is reduced by a factor of two in order to convert it to a color device.

CMOS (Complementary Metal Oxide Semiconductor) camera technology uses the same manufacturing techniques that are used for integrated circuits. This fact makes it possible to incorporate signal conditioning, and computing, directly into the sensing elements. The signal conditioning may be needed to accommodate the increased noise of CMOS and it limits somewhat the density of pixels that can be achieved. Arrays of many megapixels are common today though.

8.3.3.2 Optics and Sensor Control Features

The passive nature of cameras makes the optics used to gather and focus incident light very important. Many aspects of optics must be mastered to make the right choice. Automatic gain control (AGC) adjusts the electronically controlled ratio of output signal to input light in an attempt to maintain a more-or-less constant output level across the entire image. This feature can be valuable when the images are used for human consumption but it can do more harm than good when a computer is doing the looking.

An *autoiris* lens adjusts optics to maintain image brightness. The iris of a lens is an adjustable diaphragm that controls the amount of light passing through the lens by adjusting the aperture. This is a similar principle to gain control but the iris directly alters the light level incident on the sensor array so it does not amplify noise. A *video autoiris* uses the raw video signal to measure image brightness and drive the aperture whereas a *direct autoiris* permits the aperture to be controlled externally. Conversely, an *electronic iris* mimics an auto iris lens by adjusting the shutter speed rather than the aperture size. Hence, it controls the sensor collection time rather than the area of the aperture.

8.3.3.3 Interface Features

For purposes of stereo vision on a moving vehicle, the ability to synchronize the shutters on both cameras is a critical feature. For lidar data association or merely for accurate pose tagging, it can be useful to be able to externally trigger a camera to take an image at a precise instant.

Although the generated imagery is inherently digital, cameras still sometimes provide analog outputs, which must be converted back to digital with a digitizer, but this is becoming increasingly less common. Some of the more recent camera interface standards are CameraLink (2 Gbps), IEEE 1394 (firewire, 100-3200 Mbps), and Universal Serial Bus (USB) 2.0 (48 Mbps). Gigabit ethernet interfaces are also available.

There are two options for how the image is scanned to produce a serial stream of data. The older *interlaced* standard is derived from television. The image is divided into two fields where odd lines (lower "field") are captured 1/60 second later than even ones. The more modern noninterlaced variant is called *progressive scan*. It uses a single field and is generally preferred for precision work.

8.3.3.4 Performance

CCD cameras have a quantum efficiency of 70%, so they respond to 70% of the incoming light. By contrast, photographic films have an efficiency of only 2%, so CCDs are particularly effective for astronomy and night vision applications. The responsivities of cameras are characterized by response curves, which plot the responsivity as a function of wavelength.

The minimum illumination level for a camera is the minimum level of light needed to achieve 50% or 100% video output level when the camera is set to maximum gain and the lens iris is completely open. Usually illumination is measured in *Lux*, the SI unit of measure for the amount of light intensity at the surface being illuminated. Typical lighting levels can range from 1 at night in a rural setting, to 60 for flood lights on a stone building, to 10,000 on a grey afternoon in Europe and 80,000 on a sunny day at the equator.

The *signal-to-noise ratio* (S/N) is the ratio of the amplitude of the desired signal to the amplitude of the noise signals at a given point in time, usually measured in decibels. A S/N ratio of 60 is considered to have no noise in the image, whereas 50 will correspond to a small amount of noise being apparent.

CCD sensors tend to have higher dynamic ranges, and better signal-to-noise ratios than CMOS cameras. The *responsivity* of the sensor is the amount of signal output per unit of input optical energy. CMOS sensors tend to have slightly better responsivity and significantly better capture speeds than CCDs. CMOS also exhibits particularly low power consumption because power is only used when transistors switch between on and off states.

In addition to the field of view, the *pixel density* will determine the fineness of detail that can be resolved in an image. It is expressed in the number of horizontal and vertical pixels in an image. Standard values include 640×480 (VGA, Television), 800×600 (SVGA), 1024×768 (XVGA), 1280×960 (1 Mpixel) and 2048×1536 (3 Mpixel).

8.3.3.5 Lighting and Motion Issues

A number of cameras with a minimum illumination of 0.05 *Lux* are available but cameras generally do not have sufficient S/N to operate at night. Even in daylight, viewing a scene that includes shadows and bright patches can cause difficulties for cameras with low dynamic ranges. Details in the shadows and bright regions can be lost. More recently, new high dynamic range (HDR) cameras have become available that significantly mitigate this issue.

Techniques for compensating for lighting variation over time include normalization algorithms, which reduce S/N, automatic gain control (AGC), which amplifies noise, and electronic iris, which can slow the shutter to the point of motion blur. Auto-iris is a more effective compensation when it is available.

Blooming refers to the phenomenon of high intensity regions in an image bleeding charges outside their boundaries to adjacent pixels. CMOS sensors are intrinsically highly immune to blooming whereas CCD images can be ruined by streaks that extend across the entire frame due to, for example, a bright light in an otherwise dark scene.

Motion blur is a phenomenon due to motion of the camera or of objects within the scene while the camera is collecting a snapshot. Fast shutter speeds help to ameliorate this problem. Interlaced cameras actually capture the two fields at different times so they are also prone to inter-field blur. It may be feasible to ignore one field of data in some applications. Many CMOS cameras have rolling shutters, which can lead to motion blur that progresses down the frame from top to bottom.

8.3.4 Mid to Far Infrared Wavelength Cameras

The *infrared* region of the EM spectrum is defined as that region with wavelengths longer (frequencies lower) than those of visible light, but shorter (frequencies higher) than those of (microwave) radio waves. Silicon-based (CCD and CMOS) image sensors are equally sensitive to visible and near infrared (NIR) wavelengths up to about 1200 nm. Hence, a camara that is sensitive to near IR can be constructed by simply removing the *IR cut* filter which is normally installed to filter these wavelengths out. Conversely, one can add an *IR filter* to pass only the IR to the sensor array and generate imagery only in the NIR band.

The IR band contains energy in the range of wavelengths closest to the visible, as tabulated in Table 8.1. Midrange and far IR Infrared (IR) cameras are also known as forward looking infrared (FLIR) cameras for historical reasons. Silicon sensors do not sense midrange and far IR energy, so exotic materials are used, including HgCdTe (Mercury-Cadmium-Telluride), InSb (Indium Antimonide) and Platinum Silicide.

Table 8.1 EM Spectrum Around IR

IR Region	nm (10^{-9} meter)
UV	<430
Blue	430 to 500
Green	520 to 565
Red	625 to 740
Near IR	750 to 1300
Mid IR	1300 to 3000
Far IR	3000 nm to 14000
microwave	14000 to 3X10e8

8.3.4.1 Principles

Although visible light cameras are based on the photoelectric effect, IR cameras are based on the *photothermal* effect – the production of heat in response to light absorption. This is the best known EM radiation detector principle in the far-infrared to sub-millimeter wavelength range.

A *bolometer* is a device for measuring thermal (or total) power. They often have at least two components. First, a sensitive thermometer – usually a *thermistor* (a resistor made of semiconductors having resistance that varies rapidly and predictably with temperature). Second, a high cross section absorber for absorbing incident IR energy. The device operates by first absorbing incident IR radiation. The absorber temperature increases rapidly as a result. The temperature is then measured and the heat is then slowly drained to a heat sink to enable the process to start over (Figure 8.48).

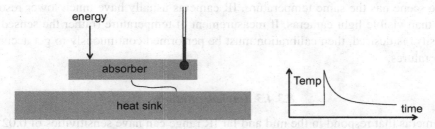

Figure 8.48 Bolometer Principle of Operation. An absorber receives incident energy and its temperature rises in proportion to the absorbed energy. A sensitive thermometer is used to measure the temperature increase.

Microbolometers were developed on a classified MEMS project in the 1980s. Silicon microfabrication techniques are used to make an isolated thermal structure with very little heat capacity. A matrix of such detectors is referred to as a *focal plane array* (FPA).

In the ideal situation, both the absorber and the thermister will experience large changes in temperature or resistance for small changes in their inputs. An important distinction is whether the bolometer is *cooled* or *uncooled*. Cooled sensors are much more sensitive because a small temperature change then produces a big change in resistance. However, cooled devices require a large package and significant power. Uncooled systems can be made very compact and low power.

8.3.4.2 Advantages and Disadvantages

The most striking aspect of IR cameras is their capacity to operate passively in relative darkness because they respond to thermal energy emitted by objects (as opposed to reflected ambient light) (Figure 8.49).

In many situations, the radiant heat sources are the objects of interest (vehicles, people). IR imagery can often provide very good discrimination of living plants (due to presence of chlorophyll) relative to inanimate matter.

Many IR cameras have rolling shutters (like CMOS cameras) so they have similar motion blur issues. Most devices have time constants in the 100 msec range, which is

Figure 8.49 Thermal Imagery. An example of an infrared image taken in total darkness using an uncooled far-infrared camera.

a second cause of motion blur (and associated loss of texture in imagery). Perception algorithms that depend on thermal contrast will have difficulty in an area where the whole scene has the same temperature. IR cameras usually have much lower resolutions than visible light cameras. If measurement of temperature (rather the sensed IR intensity) is desired, then calibration must be performed continuously to get accurate temperatures.

8.3.4.3 Implementations

IR cameras that respond in the mid and far IR range can have sensitivities of 0.02 °C and dynamic range up to 2000 °C. A 640×480 image can be produced at 50Hz where the image integration time is variable and special lenses can produce up to a $40°$ field of view. Volumes on the order of 4000 cubic cm and weights on the order of 4 kg are typical. Pixels may be as deep as 14 bits but the least significant bits may be encoding only noise.

8.3.5 Radars

The technique of RAdio Detection And Ranging (RADAR) predates both sonar and lidar. These sensors can be used for low resolution mapping, obstacle detection, and navigation in mobile robots.

8.3.5.1 Principles

Radars operate according to identical basic principles to those or sonar and lidar. Whereas pulsed TOF systems exist, FM-CW radars are more common due to the simpler circuitry involved. FM-CW radar has the ability to measure the velocity of the target as well as the range. Specifically when c is the speed of light, f_o is the center frequency, f_m is the modulation frequency, f_{b1} and f_{b2} are beat frequencies during upsweep and downsweep respectively, and Δf is the maximum frequency deviation, the range and velocity of the target are given by:

$$R = \frac{(f_{b1} + f_{b2})c}{8 f_m \Delta f} \qquad V = \frac{(f_{b2} - f_{b1})c}{4 f_o} \tag{8.56}$$

8.3.5.2 Performance

The performance of radar systems is similar to sonar in terms of issues. Specularity, and multipath issues are common. The relatively wide beam leads to coarse range and angular resolution. However, like sonar, radar can be the basis of very fast detection of large obstacles.

Angular resolution is dependent on beamwidth. Beamwidths of 10–15° are typical, but some millimeter wave radars are as thin as 2–3°. For TOF devices, range resolution is primarily limited by pulsewidth. A large pulse width signal is easier to generate and detect, but it limits downrange resolution. For FM-CW, range resolution depends on ability to resolve small changes in beat frequencies, which requires a very stable and linear voltage controlled oscillator (VCO) and a low noise receiver.

Frequency is the most important radar parameter because it affects penetration, resolution, and physical antenna size (Table 8.2). Higher frequencies and associated smaller wavelengths lead to better range and angular resolutions and smaller packages at the expense of penetration capability as shown below.

Table 8.2 Radar Performance vs. Frequency

Parameter	300 MHz / 1 m	30 GHz / 1 cm
Solid penetration	some	no
Foliage penetration	excellent	no
Dust/Fog penetration	excellent	some
Beamwidth (small antenna)	large	small
Downrange resolution	not good	excellent

The radar equation, in one form, provides the intensity at the receiver for an object of known cross section. Let P_t be the transmission power, G be the antenna gain, A_e be the antenna aperture, σ be the radar cross section, and S_{min} be the minimum detectable signal. Then, the mean power received for an object at range R is:

$$P_r = \frac{P_t G A_e \sigma}{[4\pi R^2]^2} \tag{8.57}$$

Spotlight 8.5 Radar Equation.

The received power decreased with the fourth power of range and it depends on the antenna aperture, object cross section, and the transmitted power.

Now, if P_{min} is the minimum detectable signal, then the maximum range at which a target can be detected is obtained by solving for R:

$$R_{max} = \left(\frac{P_t G A_e \sigma}{[4\pi]^2 P_{min}} \right)^{1/4} \tag{8.58}$$

The power reflected from a target depends on the two object properties of radar cross section and dielectric ratio. The *dielectric constant* expresses the ability of a material to store or pass on a charge. Radar reflections happen at discontinuities in this property. The signal return ratio is proportional to the ratio of dielectric constants of the two media. Whereas air, soil, glass, and rubber have dielectric constants < 4, water has a value of 80 and metals 10,000. Hence radar works well for detecting metal cars. Most natural scenes do not contain metals, so radar returns in this case tend to be associated with changes in water content. Human tissues may reflect enough signal to be detectable.

8.3.5.3 Advantages and Disadvantages

Radars can do things that no other sensor can do well. Radar can penetrate significant airborne obscurants and hence is a highly relevant sensor for dusty and all-weather applications. Radars can also penetrate the soil to produce a reading of metal objects buried beneath the ground, so ground penetrating radar is suitable for detecting metal mines and other buried metal objects. Radar transducers (antenna) can be made very robust compared to lidar transducers (optics).

Conversely, angular and range resolutions are relatively poor when compared with a lidar. As for sonar, the detection and discrimination capability depends largely on the target's surface orientation and material. Multipath problems can occur if the target geometry is complex. Antennae are relatively large compared to alternative sensors.

8.3.5.4 Implementations

The automotive industry is driving development and production of radar for use in advanced cruise control systems and blind spot monitoring. These systems are low cost and physically robust. A typical automotive radar might operate at 10 GHz, with a relatively wide 30° beam. Range accuracies are on the order of +/–3 cm to 1 m and maximum ranges are on the order of 20 to 120 meters. A radar beam can be steered by rotating a metallic mirror.

8.3.6 References and Further Reading

Everett is a comprehensive survey of sensors of specific relevance to robotics. Besl is an earlier source that concentrates on range imaging. Webster covers sonar and radar and many more topics as well. De Silva is another general and popular reference on sensors. Hornberg covers CCD and CMOS cameras in detail. Rogalski covers bolometers in great detail.

[18]   P. J. Besl, *Range Imaging Sensors,* General Motors Research Publication, GMR-6090, General Motors Research Laboratories, Warren, MI, 1988.

[19]   C. W. de Silva, *Sensors and Actuators,* CRC Press, 2007.

[20]   H. R. Everett, *Sensors for Mobile Robots,* A. K. Peters, 1995.

[21]   Alexander Hornberg, ed., *Handbook of Machine Vision,* Wiley, 2006.

[22]   Antonio Rogalski, *Fundamentals of Infrared Detector Technologies,* CRC Press, 2009.

[23]   J. Fraden, *AIP Handbook of Modern Sensors, Physics, Design, and Applications,* American Institute of Physics, 1993.

[24]   J. G. Webster, *The Measurement, Instrumentation, and Sensors Handbook,* CRC Press, 1999.

8.3.7 Exercises

8.3.7.1 Aperture and Beamwidth

In interference theory, it is the amplitude of a wave that satisfies the superposition principle, and not its power (which is amplitude squared.) Beam forming is accomplished by exploiting this interference phenomenon. Consider a line wave source of length a (the aperture) in a two dimensional world. Recall that two waves that are 180° out of phase completely cancel. Using these ideas, derive the relationship between the wavelength, the aperture, and the beam width at distances from the source which are much greater than the aperture.

8.3.7.2 Lidar Measurement Bandwidth

A mobile robot lidar typically needs to see up to about 20 m maximum range but it may be prudent to wait until any energy returned from as far away as 100 m has subsided before sending out a new pulse. Single shot precision is on the order of 8 mm but 4 samples are averaged to reduce the noise level by half to 4 mm. Compute the maximum possible rate at which measurements could be made.

8.4 Aspects of Geometric and Semantic Computer Vision

This section presents a few more advanced algorithms that are important in mobile robotics.

8.4.1 Pixel Classification

Classification refers to the problem of labelling things in order to place them in a particular class. Pixel classification associates a class with every pixel in an image. In the simplest form, the classes are intended to be disjoint. Some examples of classes that may be appropriate for mobile robots include road/nonroad, vegetation/mineral/animal/man-made, and hazard/nonhazard.

Building a classifier is a two stage process. In the learning phase, labelled example data is processed in order to find the best rules for correctly assigning the test data to the classes provided. In the operational phase, the classifier is executed on new data and it assigns labels based on the rules that have been learned earlier.

See [28] for an introduction to the mathematics of pattern classification. We will cover two straightforward approaches. Some attributes or "features" are associated with each pixel. The features may be as simple as the red, green, and blue values of the pixel, or they may include attributes computed from the neighborhood around the pixel. It is typical to preprocess images to remove effects of shadows, or perhaps to normalize the color to remove the effects of the brightness of the lighting. A simple way to do this is to compute a unit vector in color space:

$$unitPix = \frac{red + grn + blu}{\sqrt{red^2 + grn^2 + blu^2}} \tag{8.59}$$

Many more transformations of color space, including YIQ, HSV, YCBCr, and so on, have their merits. In general, features can be collected into a multidimensional vector and classification is based on the assumption that regions can be found in the space of all feature vectors that correspond to the classes of interest. In Figure 8.50, for example, a classifier has been trained to associate greens with soft vegetation, browns with hard vegetation, and greys with the dirt road.

Figure 8.50 Dirt Road Distinguished from Vegetation. Such a classifier could be used for a trail follower algorithm.

8.4.1.1 Training the Classifier

In *supervised learning*, pixels in the image are labelled (perhaps by drawing a box around a region of grass) to produce *training examples* consisting of the input and desired output of the classifier. This data is used to determine the characteristics of the class. One way to represent a class is in terms of its mean feature vector and its covariance matrix (Figure 8.51).

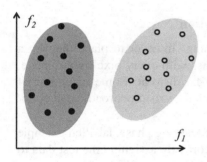

Figure 8.51 Class Ellipses in Feature Space. Each corresponds to some useful class.

8.4.1.2 Decision Surfaces

Once a set of classes is defined, it is possible to ask useful questions about any pixel in the image. For example: What is the probability that this pixel is in class X? What is the class to which it is most likely to belong?

One intuitively appealing way to perform classification for any pixel is to compute its Mahalanobis distance (MD) from each class mean and then choose the class to which the pixel is closest as the classifier output (Figure 8.52).

Recall that the MD is defined as:

$$d^2 = (\underline{x} - \underline{m})^T S^{-1} (\underline{x} - \underline{m}) \tag{8.60}$$

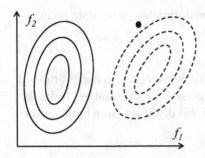

Figure 8.52 Contours of Constant Mahalanobis Distance. The point is clearly closer to the third contour of the right class.

Here, $\underline{x}$ is the feature vector, $\underline{m}$ is the (sample) mean feature vector of the class, and S is the (sample) class covariance matrix. This distance is a deviation from the mean that is normalized by the appropriate standard deviation in each direction.

The computation of MD requires that a matrix be multiplied by a vector and the computation of a vector dot product for each class to be tested. When this is too much computation, simpler decision surfaces can be used as described below.

8.4.1.3 Fisher's Linear Discriminant

In two dimensions, this decision surface is the line which best divides two clusters of points in feature space. A new point is then classified based on which side of the line it occupies.

Let $\underline{m}_1$ and $\underline{m}_2$ denote the means of both sets of points. Let S_1 and S_2 denote the *scatter matrices* of each set of points:

$$S_i = \sum_{i=1, n_i} (\underline{x} - \underline{m}_i)$$

Let $S_W = S_1 + S_2$ denote the *within class* scatter. It is a measure of how spread out all of the data is. Let the rank one matrix:

$$S_B = (\underline{m}_1 - \underline{m}_2)(\underline{m}_1 - \underline{m}_2)^T \tag{8.61}$$

denote the *between class* scatter. It measures how separated the classes are from each other.

The direction $\underline{w}^*$ that maximizes the objective function:

$$J(\underline{w}) = \frac{\underline{w}^T S_B \underline{w}}{\underline{w}^T S_W \underline{w}} \tag{8.62}$$

is the direction that maximizes the ratio of between class scatter to within class scatter.

This is a generalized eigenvalue problem whose solution is:

$$\underline{w}^* = S_W^{-1}(\underline{m}_1 - \underline{m}_2) \tag{8.63}$$

Spotlight 8.6 Fisher's Discriminant.

This is the direction in feature space that best separates the two classes.

Now, to classify a pixel, we will compute a linear transformation of the data point:

$$g(\underline{x}) = \underline{w}^{*T}\underline{x} + w_0 \tag{8.64}$$

where w_0 represents the threshold on $\underline{w}^T\underline{x}$ which must be exceeded to make $g(\underline{x}) > 0$ and thereby cause the choice of class 2 rather than class 1. If we want w_0 to be the point on the w axis in Figure 8.53 where the Mahalanobis distances from both clusters are equal, then:

$$\frac{x - m_1}{s_1} = \frac{x - m_2}{s_2} \tag{8.65}$$

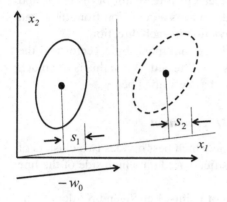

Figure 8.53 Fisher's Linear Discriminant. The technique finds the direction $\underline{w}$ in which the clusters are most separable.

Solving for x, which is also w_0 leads to:

$$w_0 = \left(\frac{m_1}{s_1} + \frac{m_2}{s_2}\right) \Big/ \left(\frac{1}{s_1} + \frac{1}{s_2}\right) \tag{8.66}$$

8.4.2 Computational Stereo Vision

The range, and indeed the entire pose, to a known object can be determined from its camera image as will be discussed later, but at times there is a need to measure the shape of an unknown object. A more general problem specification is that of computing a dense range image – the range to the first surface along the ray through each pixel in the image. There are numerous approaches but the most relevant are computational stereo and structured light. The technique of *structured light* uses an active light source and a camera to triangulate each range pixel. It is relatively straightforward, so it will not be discussed here. Stereo is the preferred method for computing range imagery in a passive manner (i.e., without emitting any energy). Stereo ranging may be performed only at specific feature points (*sparse* stereo) or everywhere in the image (*dense* stereo).

8.4.2.1 Principle of Operation

Whereas two-eyed (*binocular*) stereo is common, there are distinct advantages to having more than two eyes participate in stereo. We will consider the case where the cameras have *parallel* orientations (no *vergence*). The principle of computational stereo is identical to the manner in which many higher animals perceive range using binocular vision. Views from two offset camera poses cause an object to have a slightly different position in each image, as shown in Figure 8.54.

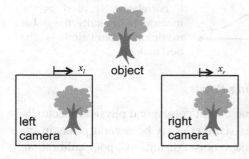

Figure 8.54 Stereo Triangulation. The disparity, $d = x_l - x_r$, is the difference between apparent object positions in two stereo views.

The geometry is such that the point in the right image corresponding to a pixel in the left must occur along a line in the right image called the *epipolar line*. For efficiency, stereo systems are typically engineered to make sure that this line is parallel to the rows or columns of one or both images. The difference between the left and right image coordinates of any pair of corresponding points is called the *disparity* of the pair:

$$d = x_l - x_r$$

Disparity depends on the range to the scene point. Nearer objects will have greater disparity as derived in Section 1.3.10 of Chapter 5. The relationship is exploited in stereo by using disparity d, focal length f, and baseline b to calculate depth X using the geometry of similar triangles. The result is:

$$X = bf/d \tag{8.67}$$

8.4.2.2 Search for Pixel Correspondences

The computationally difficult part of stereo vision is that of computing the correspondences between each point in the reference image and its counterpart in the other (nonreference) image. The rest of the presentation will assume the left image is the reference image and the right is being searched for matches. For now, we will assume that normalized correlation is computed for each pixel, and a finite neighborhood around it, as a measure of similarity. The matching algorithm typically needs to examine the right image only in a finite range of disparities. For each pixel in the left image, the algorithm searches a set of locations (i.e., a range of disparities) along the epipolar line in the right image to find a match. Typically, the search is conducted exhaustively by computing the correlation for every possible disparity.

For each reference image pixel, the maximum of the correlation curve corresponds to the best disparity estimate, d^* as illustrated in Figure 8.55.

After having calculated disparities, a stereo system can then use Equation 8.67 to generate a depth value for each pixel in the left image. The resulting depth image provides distance to the nearest scene surface along each ray projected from the scene point, through the camera lens, to the associated image coordinates.

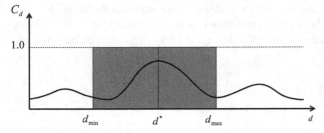

Figure 8.55 Disparity Search. If correlation is used as the measure of similarity, the global maximum correlation is the best match.

8.4.2.3 Matching Points

Spurious matches may occur when regions that do not correspond physically actually look similiar. When such repetitive texture exists, there may be several peaks in the correlation curve as shown in Figure 8.55. Image noise, distortions, poor calibration, and many other error sources make the correlation calculations unreliable.

When the scene surface is not parallel to the image plane, perspective foreshortening will cause corresponding regions in the two images to be different shapes. A square in the left image will typically correspond to a parallelogram in the right image due to the nonzero disparity gradient across the correlation window.

Figure 8.56 shows an appearance and a corresponding stereo depth image of an outdoor scene generated using the tilted horopter technique [25]. This technique distorts the correlation window in the right image based on the assumption that the terrain is flat and level. The resulting disparity image is both denser and more accurate.

Figure 8.56 Dense Stereo on a Natural Scene. (Left) greyscale image of ravine from robot point of view. Center: Disparity image for square correlation window. (Right) Disparity image for warped rectangular correlation window.

8.4.2.4 Advantages and Disadvantages

Stereo ranging has many advantages when compared to alternatives. It is passive, requiring no power to illuminate the scene. The near instantaneous shutter speed of cameras leads to little or no distortion of imagery due to sensor motion. Visible light optics are also relative inexpensive and high in quality. Controllable zoom, autoiris, and panoramic mirror optics are a few examples of what can be accomplished optically.

Stereo depth resolution degrades quadratically with depth and, for realistic baselines and pixel sizes, it cannot compete with time of flight sensing beyond a few meters in range. Like all triangulation systems, stereo is sensitive to occlusion and viewpoint distortion issues. If the baseline is increased in order to improve range resolution, local distortion is increased making correlation more difficult – leading to false matches and more range ambiguity. It also becomes more likely that one camera will not see the same parts of the scene as the other – leading to missing range data.

Although angular resolution may appear to be high for cameras of high pixel densities, correlation windows often need to contain 100 pixels or more for acceptable signal to noise ratios and this means angular resolution of the depth data is reduced by an order of magnitude relative to the appearance data produced natively by the camera. Stereo also fails in regions of no texture or of repetitive texture. At occluding edges or in regions of the scene that are thinner in the image than the correlation window, the depth of the entire region is poorly defined and results are unpredictable.

Stereo requires a high-performance processor just to get the depth data that other sensors produce directly in hardware. Like many other modalities, stereo will fail if levels of airborne obscurants (dust, fog) are high. Infrared cameras may be somewhat immune.

Several attributes of stereo are both advantages and disadvantages. Stereo relies on pixel to pixel alignment of imagery and this is difficult to achieve. However, once it is accomplished, the depth data is intrinsically registered to the appearance data. Passivity is advantageous when there is plenty of ambient lighting and a problem where there is not. Performance can degrade sharply outdoors within a few hours of dawn and dusk due to shadowing effects. Effective exposure and gain control in outdoor environments is mandatory.

8.4.2.5 Data Flow

The typical set of operations for the implementation of a stereo system is shown in Figure 8.57. The images are scaled and normalized in intensity in order to enhance texture. This can be done with a difference of Gaussians operator, statistical normalization, or something similar. Next, the images are rectified – meaning they are warped to remove lens distortion and to create perfect epipolar alignment.

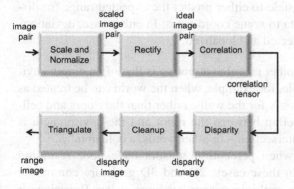

Figure 8.57 Stereo Processing. These steps are typical of dense stereo.

The correlation step is the most expensive so it is often accelerated in some way. On a general purpose processor, the right image can be shifted one pixel at a time relative to the left image and the correlation of the two images can be computed in one step. The output of this process is an array of three indices – row, column, and disparity.

For any (row, column) pair, a correlation curve versus disparity is encoded and it is searched for the disparity of highest correlation. If the correlation score is both high enough and unique, the disparity value can be accepted. Otherwise the pixel is marked to indicate unknown range. Small disconnected regions in the disparity image tend to correspond to erroneous results. These can be removed in a cleanup step if desired. Given the camera parameters, the triangulation step then produces the scene coordinates for each pixel.

8.4.3 Obstacle Detection

This section presents some ideas for detecting objects or regions that represent a collision hazard to a robot. The success achieved in doing so often depends on the difficulty of the environment. It is an easy matter to detect a chair in an office, whereas it may be next to impossible to perceive a large rock hidden under tall grass or a deep hole, far from the sensor, whose near edge occludes the far edge.

It is important to decide whether the environment is assumed to be static – so that the only thing moving is the robot. When this assumption is made incorrectly, moving objects can be smeared in the environmental model and false positive and false negative detections may occur. Collisions may also occur simply because the motions of moving obstacles were not predicted correctly.

8.4.3.1 Evidence of Obstacles

The presence and locations of obstacles can be inferred from many forms of available evidence.

8.4.3.1.1 Deviation from Expectations. When strong assumptions about the nature of the environment can be made, the mere deviation from those assumptions can be a reliable indicator of obstacles. When the environment can be assumed to be flat and level then any matter at all that is detected above the floor can signal an obstacle. For all forms of range imagery, it is possible to either predict the expected range (or disparity) image or to convert range data to scene coordinates. In either case, deviations from the flat model can be easily detected and localized.

8.4.3.1.2 Occupancy/Presence. Another useful assumption is that of an empty environment. Such an approach is possible, for example, when the world can be treated as 2D and the sensors generate returns only for the walls, rather than the floors and ceilings. In this case, any predicted overlap between the robot and the environment is assumed to represent a volumetric intersection – in other words, a collision.

Such an approach is common when perception sensors have poor resolving power – such as sonar and radar. In these cases, 2D and 3D grids are commonly used to accumulate evidence over multiple sensor readings using Bayesian or related techniques

8.4.3.1.3 Color/Composition. At times, color and texture can be a good way to identify obstacles. Tall green things (leaves) are probably not as bad as tall brown things (tree trunks). For a robot golf course mower, it is probably feasible to regard everything larger than a few pixels that is not the color of grass to be an obstacle. The colors of dirt might need to be admitted to allow it to cross the golf cart trail.

More generally, color and texture can be used in a classifier that is trained on what the good and bad classes are. In this way more complicated situations can perhaps be managed. Obstacles in certain environments have characteristic multi spectral signatures, which can be searched. Live vegetation is much easier to detect with infrared sensing and standing water with polarization sensing.

8.4.3.1.4 Density. Sensors like lidar will penetrate foliage, or not, based on precisely where the laser beam is directed. It is possible to estimate (area) density by keeping track of the relative frequency of stops and penetrations of cells by lidar beams in a 3D grid (Figure 8.58).

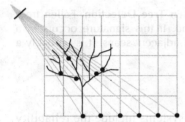

Figure 8.58 Density Accumulation. The average cross section of thin obstacles can be readily estimated given time to accumulate.

When the ratio of *pass-throughs* to *hits* is high, the cell is likely to contain thin vegetation. However, even a soft leaf is more than massive enough to reflect a laser beam so seasonal variation must be figured in the assessment.

8.4.3.1.5 Slope. Slope is the main attribute of interest in some cases. Although slope is a point property of a surface, it can be estimated over regions by fitting planes to range data. A large number of range points can be accumulated in cells and the scatter matrix of the cell can be used to compute the slope of the best fit plane. One way to do this is to fit a plane to the data. The equation of a plane in 3D is:

$$\frac{a}{d}x + \frac{b}{d}y + \frac{c}{d}z = 1 \tag{8.68}$$

Where (a, b, c) encode the normal direction and d is the minimum distance from the origin. For more than three points, this overdetermined system can be solved by the left pseudoinverse. A more refined approach is to find the eigenvalues of the scatter matrix [29] and verify first that only two are of significant magnitudes. This verifies that the data is planar. One large eigenvalue can indicate a thin branch or wire.

8.4.3.1.6 Shape. Surprisingly little research work has gone into the problem of determining which shapes are bad ones for wheels to collide with.

The left obstacle in Figure 8.59 will act as a ramp, whereas the right case may trap the wheel or even shear it off at high speed.

8.4.3.1.7 Class. Sometimes the knowledge that an object fits into a certain (perhaps parameterized) class is enough to declare it an obstacle. For example, in a forested environment, horizontal cylinders on the ground surface are almost certainly fallen trees (Figure 8.60). Prior probabilities can matter a lot. Cylinders of radius >15 inches are highly likely to be rigid and to represent a risk of high centering.

Figure 8.59 Obstacle Shape. The shape of an obstacle can have a large impact on its severity as an obstacle.

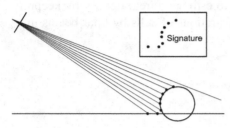

Figure 8.60 Fallen Tree Detection. Fallen trees are mostly round. If this signature occurs in a large number of adjacent scans, it is probably a tree.

8.4.3.2 Performance

Some aspects of the performance of obstacle detection systems include the reliability of detection, the maximum vehicle speed, and the capacity to deal with certain pathological cases.

8.4.3.2.1 Reliability. The most important performance attribute of obstacle detection systems tends to be the *false negative* rate although the *false positive* rate can also be important (Figure 8.61). In the first case, a true obstacle is not detected and a collision could occur. In the second, an imaginary obstacle may be avoided and this may or may not be acceptable depending on the probability of occurrence and the severity of the consequences. These two rates tend to trade off against each other. Algorithms can be configured to detect more obstacles in order to reduce the false negative rate but that will usually increase the false positive rate.

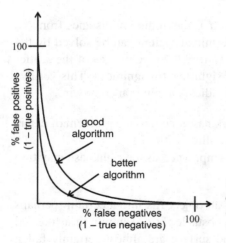

Figure 8.61 Obstacle Detection Trade-Off. Thresholds on obstacles can be made so low that false negatives are rare – but then false positives become more common.

A key decision in the design of an obstacle detection system is whether it should be optimistic or pessimistic. An optimistic system assumes that unknown regions are safe, whereas a pessimistic system does the opposite. In either case, it may be advisable to estimate uncertainty. An object whose density, height, and so on is sufficiently uncertain might be declared an obstacle. Good uncertainty modelling is one way to improve the basic performance of an algorithm.

8.4.3.2.2 Vehicle Speed. Obstacle detection is also a real-time problem. While there may be some time available to accumulate evidence before making a decision, it may not be much and often the best evidence is available only when the vehicle is close to the obstacle, and therefore, almost out of time.

Any system can be made so conservative that it does not move at all. It certainly won't hit anything in this case but it is not useful either. Obstacle detection reliability is often a function of the range at which it must be detected, and if the vehicle must stop if an obstacle is detected at the maximum detection range, this places an upper limit on vehicle speed.

8.4.3.2.3 Pathological Obstacles. There are several situations that can make obstacle detection pathologically hard. Certainly obstacles around the next corner may not be visible and vegetation can hide rocks and other lethal hazards, but there can be obstacles in plain sight that are effectively invisible too. One pathological case is the so-called *negative obstacle*. In range data, the front edge of a negative obstacle occludes most of the information required to determine that it is a negative obstacle. The hole in the surface that supports the robot may only be detected from the absence of any sensor information in the region of the hole. Here, we have a case where absence of information is a clue to the absence of matter to support the robot.

As shown in Figure 8.62, a robot cannot distinguish a downslope from a ledge until it lands a pixel on the downslope. By then, it probably should be moving pretty slowly!

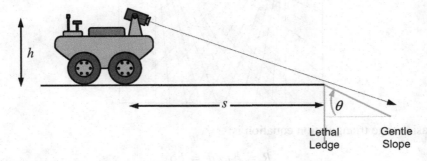

Figure 8.62 Ambiguity in Ledge Detection. The ambiguity between a 30° downslope and a 90° dropoff can not be resolved until the sensor is close enough, regardless of sensor resolution.

Even small wheel-sized negative obstacles can disable a vehicle. It takes only a very small bump to hide a wheel sized hole in its range shadow. Humans seem to use context and higher level intelligence to cope with these situations. We slow down when unsure and we make the assumption of no negative obstacles when appropriate (on most well maintained roads).

8.4.4 References and Further Reading

Ebner covers color normalization and more sophisticated approaches to color constancy. Duda covers Fisher's linear discriminant and better approaches to classification. The papers by Hebert and Roberts are examples of slope-based obstacle detection.

[25] P. Burt, L.Wixson, and G. Salgian, Electronically Directed "Focal" Stereo, *Proceedings of the Fifth International Conference on Computer Vision,* pp. 94–101, June 1995.

[26] Marc Ebner, *Color Constancy,* Wiley, 2007.

[27] Olivier Faugeras, *Three-Dimensional Computer Vision: A Geometric Viewpoint,* MIT Press, 1993.

[28] Richard O. Duda, Peter E. Hart, and D. G. Stock, *Pattern Classification,* Wiley, 2001.

[29] Martial H. Hebert, SMARTY: Point-Based Range Processing for Autonomous Driving, *Intelligent Unmanned Ground Vehicles,* Martial H. Hebert, Charles Thorpe, and Anthony Stentz, ed., Kluwer Academic Publishers, 1997.

[30] J. Roberts and P. Corke, Obstacle Detection for a Mining Vehicle Using a 2-D Laser, in *Proceedings of the Australian Conference on Robotics and Automation,* 2000.

8.4.5 Exercises

8.4.5.1 Stereo Range Resolution

The resolution of stereo is its primary performance limitation when compared to lidar. The following figure illustrates the source of the variation of resolution with distance from the cameras.

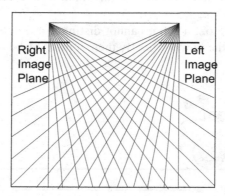

The basic range triangulation equation is:

$$R = bf/d = b\delta$$

where R is the range, f is the focal length, b is the baseline, and d is the disparity. We have defined the normalized disparity (in units of radians):

$$\delta = d/f$$

Differentiate the triangulation equation and show that stereo range resolution is quadratic in range. Develop a formula for crossrange resolution and plot both for a 1 meter baseline and a 1024-pixel-wide image over a 90° field of view.

8.4.5.2 *Complexity of Stereo Vision*

Show that the basic complexity of stereo vision is proportional to the number of rows and columns in the images and the number of disparities searched.

8.4.5.3 *False Detection Rates from Theory*

Suppose an obstacle detector must return true if the height of a step obstacle exceeds 5 cm. Propose a method using marginal probability for computing the false negative rate. That is, the probability of detecting an obstacle when the step is really shorter than 5 cm. Assume you know the conditional sensor model $p(z|x)$ where z is the detected height and x is the true height.

8.4.5.4 *Speed Dependent Resolution*

Obstacles cannot be avoided unless the system can reliably detect them. Reliability in obstacle detection is at least a question of the angular resolution of the sensor. Consider the following figure in which an obstacle appears in the field of view of a sensor.

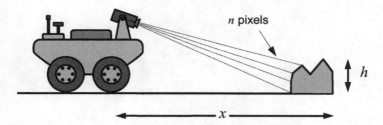

The obstacle is of height h. It is desired that the obstacle be intersected by n pixels in a particular direction. It is possible to define a general requirement for the angular resolution of the sensor as follows:

$$\delta = \frac{[h/x(V)]}{n}$$

where x is the range of the sensor as a function of vehicle velocity. Current sensor technologies provide the following angular resolutions:

Sensor technologies and their angular resolutions

Sensor	Resolution (mrads)
Laser Rangefinder	3 (Typical)
Stereo	80
Radar	10000

Substitute the formula for stopping distance for x and plot the required angular resolution versus speed. How fast can a robot equipped with each sensor reliably drive?

8.4.5.5 Ledge Detection

A robot is driving on flat, level ground. The terrain ahead transitions instantaneously to a (drivable) 30° downslope (Figure 8.62). The slope will fall within a range shadow of the edge of the slope. For a sensor height h derive a relationship for the distance at which the robot can first distinguish the slope from a lethal dropoff. Substitute stopping distance (reaction distance plus braking distance) for this earliest detection distance and solve for the reaction time required as a function of speed. Interpret negative reaction time and note the maximum safe speed of the robot. How can this problem be mitigated?

CHAPTER 9
Localization and Mapping

Figure 9.1 Mars Rovers. The twin Mars rovers *Spirit* and *Opportunity* have driven almost 30 kilometers across the Mars surface. As of this writing, *Opportunity* is still operating. Visual Odometry turned out to be a key technology for driving effectively in the fine Martian soil.

Perception and localization often depend on each other. When building a map, a model of the environment is being constructed and perception and localization cooperate in order to put pieces of the map in the right place relative to each other. When using a map to localize, the robot is determining its location based on matching what it sees to what it expects to see and, in this case, localization depends on perception. More sophisticated approaches can construct a map and localize from it at the same time.

This section will present many aspects of both making and using maps of the environment. Many mobile robots need some kind of map in order to function effectively. Maps are needed when accurate absolute pose is needed. Accurate pose is needed when the robot is told to go to the coordinates of a specific place or when the robot wants to use information of any kind that is located by its position in a second map.

If localization is imperfect, it may be advisable to register data generated at different times and places. This is a more fundamental operation than either localization or mapping. It achieves both the goal of making the map consistent and the goal of refining the estimate of the intervening motion. For this reason, all three topics of mapping, registration, and ego-motion are presented together here.

9.1 Representation and Issues

9.1.1 Introduction

Mapping is the process of making maps. For our purposes, a map is any data structure that implements long term memory of the locations of measurements in raw or processed form. The measurements might have been taken by sensors on the robot, on some other robot, or by any sensors carried by any collection of machines or humans at any time in history.

When maps contain processed data, the maps perform a sensor fusion function in addition to the memory function. Maps encode knowledge beyond whatever can be seen or measured now, and beyond whatever assumptions may be encoded in algorithms. They permit access to this remembered information for purposes like predicting sensor readings (for navigation) or for predicting environment interaction (for planning).

Maps may associate properties with places (e.g., a cost field), or locations with things (e.g., a list of landmarks or obstacles) but in most cases of interest to us, maps will encode some form of spatial information. One ultimate use of maps is for localization (Figure 9.2). Such maps permit a robot to predict sensor readings, compare them to actual ones, and use the difference to resolve the associated pose error. This type of map might be stored as a list of landmarks or a list of range sensor scans.

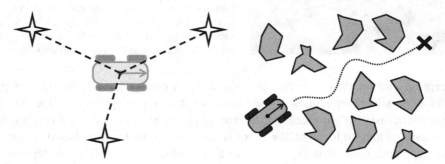

Figure 9.2 Maps. Left) Localization maps encode positions of landmarks, shapes of walls, and so on. They help the robot determine its location. (Right) Planning maps encode such things as positions of obstacles, terrain elevation, volume density, or cost /risk of traversal.

Another form of map is a motion planning map. Its function is to enable prediction of future interaction with the environment – to predict what will happen if the robot decides to go somewhere specific. Such a map might be stored as a 2D or 3D grid or as a list of obstacle locations, roads, and so on, but there are many more options for encoding map information as discussed below.

9.1.2 Representation

The design of map data structures presents a surprising number of decisions, some of which are presented here.

9.1.2.1 Coordinate System Aspects

A key design decision relates to which operations, if any, are to be so favored that they can be performed more easily and/or efficiently. There may be reason to prefer to represent data in one coordinate system or another from this perspective. Common choices include image space (azimuth, elevation), or cartesian coordinates fixed to either the vehicle or the ground.

Consider the case of representing obstacles in the scene around a moving robot. Vehicle-fixed coordinates make it trivial to evaluate how close obstacles are to the robot, whereas ground-fixed coordinates make it trivial to account for motion (Figure 9.3).

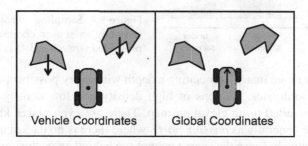

Vehicle Coordinates   Global Coordinates

Figure 9.3 Coordinate Choices for Obstacle Maps. If obstacles are stored in vehicle-fixed coordinates, proximity to the robot is immediate, but all of their positions must be updated when the robot moves. If they are represented in ground-fixed coordinates, only the robot position needs to be updated to account for motion, but then obtaining obstacle proximity requires computation.

9.1.2.2 Objects, Graphs and Fields

There are at least three common, yet distinct ways to represent the environment. An *object view* explicitly represents the discrete physical things that are known, and what is known about them. Conversely, *a field view* explicitly represents all of space and what is known about each piece of space. A *topological view* represents only a network of paths that the robot may move along. Mixtures of these representations are also common.

An object representation (such as in Figure 9.2) is typically implemented as a list. These representations can be very high in resolution but they require more memory for more objects. *Obstacle lists* or *landmark lists* are examples of such representations.

A field representation typically takes the form of an array where memory is allocated to represent regions of space at fixed resolution. Such representations can represent any number of objects but at fixed resolution. An *occupancy* or *evidence grid* is an array encoding the probability that each cell is occupied by part of an obstacle. An *elevation map* is a sampled field of height data that makes it easy to predict vehicle attitude because the height of any point is available in constant time.

A topological representation is typically implemented as a graph. These representations are highly efficient mechanisms to implicitly express many possible options for moving through an area. Efficient search techniques can be used to derive a tree from the graph and thereby find pathways from one place to another in the graph.

9.1.2.3 Sampling Issues and Missing Parts

One motivation for using arrays is the fact that most imaging sensors produce such representations. These representations can induce sampling issues when coordinate transformations are used because coordinate transformations are nonlinear (Figure 9.4).

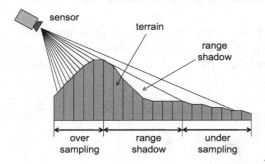

Figure 9.4 Sampling Problem. Uniform sampling in sensor coordinates is seldom preserved when the data is transformed.

A *depth map* is a range image associating a depth with every possible point in azimuth and elevation coordinates. Regions of high density and low density occur when a depth map is converted to an elevation map. There are even places known as *range shadows* or more generally as *missing parts*, where there is no data at all. In this case, the parts are missing because the sensor cannot see behind an occlusion, so the issue is fundamental.

Conversely, if the data is stored in the form of a depth map, it avoids the distortion of information that may occur when data is projected onto a horizontal plane. However, it then becomes more difficult to compute the height of a particular point. Each choice of coordinates has its tradeoffs.

9.1.2.4 Semantic Aspects

One basic decision is what information to store. Object oriented maps could store walls, furniture, or obstacles for planning purposes. They might store point landmarks, lines, image patches, or other features for navigation. Sampled maps might store:

- Terrain shape descriptors: such as elevation. slope, roughness, overhang height.
- Terrain mechanical descriptors: such as stiffness/compressibility, traction, and density (grass and underbrush are low density).
- Terrain classification descriptors: such as wooded, rocky, high grass, deep or shallow water.
- Hazard descriptors: such as cost of traversal, information content (e.g., range shadows have little content).
- Tactical descriptors: such as the relative threat, cover, or communications potential of a location.

9.1.2.5 Meta-Informational Aspects

Another important decision is the degree of data processing or reduction to perform. For example, highly processed data that imposes a semantic interpretation, can be efficient. However, it can also encode an incorrect and even irreversible interpretation if it is generated before all evidence is accumulated. Conversely, the storage of raw sensor readings often implies very high cost in terms of memory and processing but, at least, it allows preliminary interpretations of the data to be reassessed.

Maps may also store a large amount of housekeeping information such as the time (*time tag*) or pose (*pose tag*) of a piece of data or the source (e.g., sensor) associated with the data. When maps are also used to encode search trees for motion planners, the backpointers associated with global planning algorithms may be stored as well. See Chapter 10 for more on backpointers in planning.

9.1.2.6 Uncertainty

For any of the data stored in a map, it may be advisable to store uncertainty information. A simple example is the standard deviation of a height estimate or the probability of occupancy of a cell. If discrete objects are being tracked, it may be advisable to associate uncertainty information with their present and their predicted location. Covariance information for landmarks can be encoded when their location is unknown. Discrete distributions may be used to encode the present belief function over a set of terrain classes.

9.1.3 Timing and Motion Issues

When either the vehicle or parts of the scene are moving, many problems require precision timekeeping and/or segmentation to distinguish what is moving from what is not.

9.1.3.1 Motion Blur

Maps produced from perception data will often become distorted when the robot is moving and the timing of data acquisition is not accurate enough. This kind of *motion blur* error vanishes when the robot stops moving, so it is one of those real time error sources that can be difficult to detect. A classic case is one where the robot hits an obstacle and examination of the map indicates that the robot knew about the obstacle. However, the robot may not have known the correct position of the obstacle when it made the decision causing it to drive over it.

Time tags (or pose tags) are often used to synchronize the perception data stream with the localization data stream to remove these errors. For a time tag, synchronized clocks are read and each piece of pose and perception data has its time of acquisition appended to the data frame. For a pose tag, a low latency link to the position estimation system, perhaps combined with models of remaining latency, makes it possible to associate nearly correct time tags with perception data frames. One way to achieve low latency is to raise an interrupt in the pose estimation system at the instant when perception data is read, and then synchronize the data streams after the pose data arrives.

Angular measurements often matter most and sensitivity to the computed timing of these will be highest when the vehicle is rotating quickly. In order to correctly localize objects at 20 meters range to a precision of 20 cm, timing errors of a fraction of a second will matter when the robot rotates more than 0.01 radians in that time. However, if the map accuracy requirements are modest, some errors may be ignorable.

Latency modelling is a challenging issue for scanning lidar sensors. Precise measurement of the absolute elevation of a laser beam scanned at 120 Hz from a pitching vehicle can be difficult to achieve. Latency in azimuth data can also be important as illustrated in Figure 9.5. Motion blur is less of an issue for FLIR cameras and CMOS cameras. It is usually not an issue at all for CCD cameras unless the lighting requires slow shutter speeds and motion is very fast.

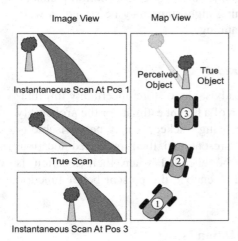

Figure 9.5 Motion Blur. Even over the time required to capture one frame, the cumulative effect of sensor and vehicle attitude and heading changes is quite significant if not accounted for. In this example of a lidar sensor scanning from top to bottom, only the base of the tree is correctly positioned so the robot may drive straight into the tree.

9.1.3.2 Ghosting

A related issue to motion blur occurs in the case when objects in the environments are moving. When the assumption of a static environment is false, and data is accumulated over time, moving objects can create traces in the map. If a map of the underlying static scene is desired then some means to remove the moving content is necessary. This problem occurs when moving people or vehicles are in view, or when one vehicle follows another. In that case, it is important to both see the vehicle in front and to not treat it as an obstacle.

9.1.3.3 Moving Object Detection and Tracking

When objects that are obstacles are moving, their motion must be predicted to avoid them. If the map contains only moving objects, then a certainty grid representation (Figure 9.6) can be updated using tracking algorithms that use measurements to refine estimates of position as well as motion models to account for uncertainty growth between measurements.

When the map contains more than just the moving objects, then *background subtraction* techniques can be used to distinguish the moving parts. The basic idea is to compare two images and assume that regions of large differences correspond to moving objects. If the vehicle is also moving, it is necessary to somehow recognize legitimate differences due to vehicle motion. Computing differences in ground-fixed coordinates in one way to account for vehicle motion.

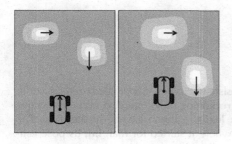

Figure 9.6 Bayesian Object Tracking. It is natural to represent the motion and spread of hypotheses associated with moving obstacles with a probabilistic representation like evidence grids.

9.1.4 Related Localization Issues

Localization data is never perfect, so it is a basic requirement that a robot cope with imperfect localization. When the robot is uncertain of its position and orientation, its capacity to localize objects viewed with its sensors is even more uncertain. This section outlines some of the more prominent issues related to localization in mapping. Computing differences in ground-fixed coordinates is one way to account for vehicle motion.

9.1.4.1 Localization Drift and Local Consistency

Over time and/or distance, dead reckoning error accumulates. This fact is true of any kind of dead reckoning whether it is based on wheel encoders, gyros, or any form of visual odometry, and so on. If the pose solution used to create the map is based only on dead reckoning, the drift of the solution causes viewed objects to become both distorted and mislocated in the map. Although dead reckoning error has special behaviors, the degree of mislocation between two objects under such a solution tends to grow with the distance driven or time elapsed between the robot positions where they were last seen. Hence, maps tend to be *locally consistent* if everything in a local area was viewed over a short period of time.

9.1.4.2 Data Aging and Global Inconsistency

Conversely, if the same object is viewed at two very different times, the accumulated pose error will potentially cause a hallucination of a second copy of the first object located in the map somewhere near the first.

More generally, when the robot returns to a place visited earlier, integrating old and new data can lead to two slightly displaced copies of everything (Figure 9.7). The *accumulation/distortion trade-off* can be a key design driver in sensor fusion. Accumulation of more evidence tends to reduce noise if the data can be correctly aligned or associated, but as soon as alignment fails, the error is raised dramatically.

One effective approach to reducing the problem of inconsistency is to erase objects after a certain time has elapsed or a certain distance has been travelled. This is not always feasible but if the sole purpose of the map is to understand the local context for intelligent control purposes like obstacle avoidance or path tracking, it is an effective approach.

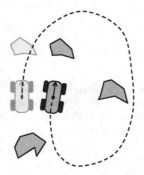

Figure 9.7 Global Inconsistency. When mapping is based on a drifting estimate (e.g., dead reckoning only), merging non-consecutive views of the same area leads to inconsistency in the map. The robot shown returns to where it started for real, but its pose estimate is off. The heading and position error cause a second copy of the same object to be created in the map.

One way to implement this idea efficiently is *data aging* where data is rendered artificially invisible after some time/distance window. There are two aspects to the implementation. First, because data is not explicitly deleted, a mechanism is needed to render older data invisible to map queries. Second, when an attempt is made to merge new data and much older data, the older data must be deleted first.

9.1.4.3 Loop Closure, Revisiting, and Insertion

In planning maps, duplicated data can be a problem whereas in navigation maps, the potential duplication defines a most useful event. Although the problem identified in Figure 9.7 is a problem when the pose solution is drifting, it can also be viewed as the solution to the problem of drifting pose. If the robot can solve the *revisiting problem* of recognizing that is has been here before (perhaps because the object is unique and recognizable), then the accumulated pose error can be removed and the darker robot would realize it is in the same place as the lighter.

Although short-term memory avoids inconsistency, long-term memory is exactly what is required to "close" large loops in the map correctly. If the robot remembers data for a long time, it may traverse a large area, so it becomes necessary for the map to be large. Large maps have their own issues as discussed later. An even harder problem than revisiting is *map insertion*. This is the problem of determining the initial position of the robot based on a map – even one that may have been constructed by some other vehicle (e.g., an aircraft) based on different sensing.

9.1.5 Structural Aspects

The size of the map (in every sense) and how much is remembered are important design decisions. The typical trade-off here is associated with finite available memory in the computer. Eventually the only way to record a larger area is to reduce the resolution, or more generally, the level of detail represented.

9.1.5.1 Structural Aspects

When a region of space is represented, it is necessary to decide if a 2D or 3D representation is required. The underlying data structure could be a 2D array of rectangular *cells* or a 3D array of volume elements – called *voxels*. Most large maps are a 2D overhead projection but 3D representations can be necessary in complex environments or any situation in which a robot must decide if it may collide with an overhanging object, or reconfigure itself (i.e., lower the forks in a forklift) to avoid it.

At the extreme of limited detail, *topological maps* make it easy to determine which parts of the environment are connected to others while omitting much detail. Sometimes connectedness is all that needs to be represented (e.g., a network of traffic signs or intersections) and the robot only needs to know which edge of the underlying graph representation it is on. Edges can be annotated with commands to make a position-based or event-driven motion program. In all topological representations, the distinction between cyclic or acyclic (tree) structure tends to be important. Inferring topology from dense data may not be easy but we will see later that path planning algorithms must accomplish exactly this process when they build their search trees.

9.1.5.2 Extent

When there is too much data to store in memory, there are a few options for how to proceed. The map may be cached to RAM from disk, keeping most of it on disk and moving small pieces in and out of RAM efficiently. A *scrolling map* will continue to shift data in the opposite direction of vehicle motion until the data falls off the end and is deleted (Figure 9.8). A *wrapping map* uses a multidimensional ring buffer to continue to reuse the same memory while always surrounding the vehicle with the nearby data. In this case, data is deleted only when it is overwritten but the special treatment described as data aging above is needed to ensure that old data does not reappear in the map in front of the robot after the robot drives past it.

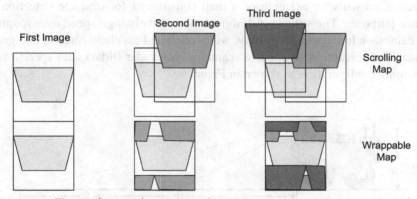

Figure 9.8 Scrolling and Wrapping Maps. The wrapping map continues to reuse the same memory. The scrolling map requires data to be moved to account for motion and any that "falls off the end" is deleted.

In return for the complexity, wrappable maps can be very efficient users of both memory and computation.

9.1.5.3 Hierarchy

Hierarchical representations can permit reasoning at multiple levels of conceptualization, which turns out to be necessary to support more sophisticated behavior. Imagine a three layer map for example, where the highest layer, level 3, is topological, encoding the major pathways through the environment, or at least the major sites that should, or can, be visited.

Level 2 could contain a cost field stored in an array representing a few square kilometers of area, that will be used to plan routes from one site to the next. It could instead be a more detailed graph encoding all the streets in a city. Level 1 could serve as both a local planning map and a localization map. It might be a 3D representation of the objects around the robot.

9.1.5.4 Layers

Instead of, or in addition to hierarchy, it can be useful to maintain redundant representations of the same region of space – and not merge them together. One example of this is keeping the representations of multiple cooperating robots separate from each other in order to support variable weighting, spatial registration, or mechanisms to calibrate one robots' world with the other.

A good example is maintaining one layer that contains processed satellite imagery or aircraft *digital terrain elevation data* (DTED) and another that contains terrain data gathered by a ground-based robot. Once the robot notices that certain perceptual features tend to correspond to trees in satellite imagery, it can instantly know where all the trees are for hundreds of kilometers around.

9.1.6 Example: Unmanned Ground Vehicle (UGV) Terrain Mapping

This section presents an example of a map constructed for obstacle detection and avoidance purposes. The vehicle is designed for relatively high speed over rough terrain. It exhibits a low center of gravity, wide tread, and excellent traction and ground clearance. The perception sensor is a scanning laser radar (lidar) with specifications and mounting configuration as shown in Figure 9.9.

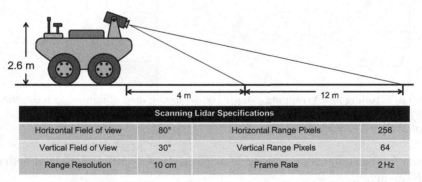

Scanning Lidar Specifications			
Horizontal Field of view	80°	Horizontal Range Pixels	256
Vertical Field of View	30°	Vertical Range Pixels	64
Range Resolution	10 cm	Frame Rate	2 Hz

Figure 9.9 Sensor Configuration and Specifications. The sensor is mounted as shown.

The robot is provided waypoints in latitude-longitude and its job is to visit them in sequence and to make a map of its traverse.

9.1.6.1 Range Imagery and Terrain Map

A *terrain elevation map* (often shortened to just terrain map), representing the supporting surface $z(x, y)$ is constructed in real time as the vehicle drives and makes decisions about how to get to its next waypoint. Such a representation implicitly assumes barren terrain with no overhanging obstacles because it associates a single height with each position.

Each 20 cm by 20 cm cell in the terrain map accumulates the mean and variance of the points that fall within the cell. The mean is used to estimate the height and the variance provides an estimate of the uncertainty. Of course, if a vertical surface falls within a cell, the "variance" will mostly be a measure of the span of the heights of the range points.

The lidar is an AM-CW lidar with a modulation wavelength of 64 ft. Range data is provided to the system in chunks that correspond to one vertical sweep of the scanning mechanism. A typical *range image* is shown in Figure 9.10.

Figure 9.10 Typical Range Image and Terrain Map. (Left) Range image: with intensity proportional to range modulo 64 ft. (Right) The same data in the terrain map viewed from overhead with intensity proportional to elevation. Clearly there is a range shadow behind the hill.

Such an image is not necessarily consistent with a single position of the sensor because the sensor may move significantly during the scanning.

9.1.6.2 Software Data Flow

The most intensive computation is the conversion of coordinates of the 32K of range points produced every second. Each lidar pixel has its coordinates converted from image (polar) coordinates, to the sensor frame, to the body frame, and then to the world frame (Figure 9.11).

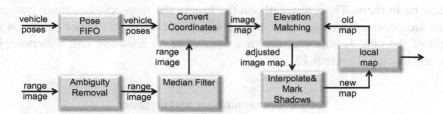

Figure 9.11 Terrain Map Building Data Flow. Range points are converted to world coordinates and placed in a wrapping terrain map.

9.1.6.3 Motion Distortion Removal

When moving at 4.5 m/s, the positioning error of a range pixel due to translation is 2.25 m for a 1/2 second timing error. If the vehicle is turning at 0.5 rads/sec, as much at 5 m of error can be introduced for a range point 20 m from the vehicle. Therefore, achieving a 1 cm error budget for timing errors requires timing accuracy of 1 millisecond. Accurate terrain mapping from scanning lidar at speed requires precise timing for every range pixel processed.

Motion distortion is eliminated by employing a pose FIFO queue into which the immediate history of vehicle poses from the pose estimation system is stored at 200 Hz. Clocks are synchronized with a GPS pulse per second signal. Both poses and the leftmost pixel of each range scanline are time tagged at the instant that the data is acquired.

When the coordinates of a range pixel are to be converted to the world (ground-fixed) frame, the pixel time tag is interpolated from that of the leftmost pixel and the poses of the vehicle before and after the pixel are retrieved from the pose FIFO and the precise vehicle pose for the range pixel is then interpolated.

9.1.6.4 Altitude Drift

The INS-GPS pose estimation system is subject to noticeable drift in altitude if the GPS signal is lost for even a short period of time. If this effect is not removed, a noticeable but hallucinated "step" will exist where the lowest elevation scanline of each image falls in the map. To eliminate this problem, the best fit vertical offset is computed by comparing the height of incoming data to the height of corresponding data already in the map.

Assuming that the pose drift is upward, the drift during the course of a single vertical scan causes a small falloff of the height of the terrain. The scanning is from top to bottom, so the far data is measured earlier and is therefore somewhat lower in height. This drift is removed by assuming that the drift rate is constant over the fraction of a second required to perform one vertical sweep of the laser beam.

9.1.6.5 Sampling Issues

The severity of sampling issues is increased when the terrain is not flat. The solution in this case is to process range data in columns moving from the bottom of the range image to the top. In each column, range pixels are processed in pairs. Both pixels fall in a particular cell and their heights are merged with whatever data may already be in them. Then, any cells on the line in the map between these two endpoints are provided with pseudomeasurements representing an upper bound on the height of the cell. In this way the treatment of range shadows and undersampled areas are unified (Figure 9.12).

9.1.6.6 Computational Stabilization

Depending on the configuration of the sensor, a large fraction of the range data will fall in the region close to the vehicle. When computation is scarce, there are arguments to

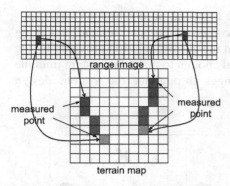

Figure 9.12 Interpolation. Range pixels are processed in pairs of adjacent pixels per column. Missing data on the line between the endpoints is interpolated.

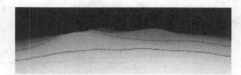

Figure 9.13 Computational Image Stabilization. By processing only the desired range window of data, both far away undersampled and nearby oversampled regions are avoided. Usually, much less than 10% of the image is processed.

support an approach that deliberately does not process this nearby data. First, the currently proximal region was already imaged from far away. Second, if it were not traversable, the robot would already have avoided it. Third, even if it is not traversable, it is too late to respond anyway. Fourth, the increase in perceptual update rate that is achieved by not processing the lower parts of the range image provides more computation to the obstacle avoidance algorithm and thereby increases its competence. From the robot's perspective, spending processing contemplating one's mistakes will actually cause them to occur.

However, it is not necessarily the case that the lower regions of the image are providing data that is close to the vehicle. When cresting a hill for example, the upper parts of the image may be seeing the sky and only the lower parts see any terrain. An elegant solution to the problem is to process only those range pixels that fall between a minimum and a maximum range in the image. After all, the range data is a direct measurement of how far the data is from the vehicle. Provided the sensor height is small relative to the ranges of interest, the range and its projection onto the ground plane are related by the cosine of a small angle.

One final assumption of value is to assume that the range data is monotone in elevation angle – meaning higher pixels in a column are higher ranges. This is a valid assumption on barren terrain, so it is consistent with the choice of a terrain map. On the basis of this assumption, data processing can proceed up each column, skipping all pixels below the minimum desired range and then processing data until the maximum is encountered (Figure 9.13).

9.1.6.7 Dual Pose Estimates

Yet another way in which pose estimation can cause problems is pose fix discontinuities. For example, when GPS signals are lost and then reacquired, the pose solution jumps back to a more correct position and some of the accumulated dead reckoning error is removed. However, when scanning sensors like lidars are used, imaged objects will be split into two pieces when these *pose jumps* occur.

One solution to this problem is to compute a second pose estimate that is optimized for "smoothness." Essentially, this *local pose* estimate is dead reckoning only. It is permitted to drift arbitrarily far from the correct solution provided by the global pose estimate. This approach is powerful enough to make the system immune to pose discontinuities but it requires changes throughout the system design (Figure 9.14).

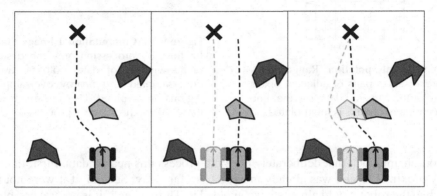

Figure 9.14 Dual Maps and Position Estimates. Darker obstacles were provided in a prior map. The lighter obstacle was sensed by perception and was unexpected. (Left) The robot intends to swerve left to avoid the sensed obstacle. (Center) A GPS jump occurs after the obstacle was seen, to cause the robot to believe it has moved left. It now intends to drive straight but in fact it will run into the obstacle before the obstacle is seen again by perception. (Right) Sensed obstacles are stored in a local map created by perception with a local pose estimate. Both are copied into the global map regularly and the planning system thinks the obstacle has moved, too, so it (correctly) continues to swerve left.

Although motion control, perception, local mapping, and so on use local pose, the higher level route planning and following system uses global pose in order to correctly acquire waypoints. Any fusion of local map data and global map data must be treated with care to account for the constant drift of the local pose estimate.

9.1.7 References and Further Reading

Much of the content of this subchapter is based on the two papers by Kelly that are focussed on robots that operate in natural terrain. The book edited by Buehler presents many interesting solutions for driving in traffic. The book edited by Howard presents many aspects of achieving intelligence for planetary rovers.

[1] M. Buehler et al., ed., The *DARPA Urban Challenge: Autonomous Vehicles in City Traffic,* 1st ed., New York, Springer-Verlag, 2009.

[2] Ayanna Howard and Ed Tunsel, eds., *Intelligence for Space Robotics,* TSI Press, 2006.

[3] A. Kelly, et al., Toward Reliable Off-Road Autonomous Vehicles Operating in Challenging Environments, *The International Journal of Robotics Research,* Vol. 25, No. 5–6, pp. 449–483, June 2006.

[4] A. Kelly, A. Stentz, Rough Terrain Autonomous Mobility – Part 2: An Active Vision, Predictive Control Approach, *Autonomous Robots,* Vol. 5, pp. 163–198, 1998.

9.1.8 Exercises

9.1.8.1 Map Distortion

(i) Derive a simple equation that gives the required frame rate of an imaging laser rangefinder in terms of the maximum range of the sensor and the speed of the vehicle. Justify the derivation in words. Assume images do not overlap, instantaneous digitization, and translational constant velocity motion.

(ii) Propose any rational method of deciding on the required resolution of a grid based environment representation.

(iii) Given a particular resolution for a grid environment representation. Comment on the relationship of vehicle speed and the update rate required of position estimation.

(iv) Propose a metric for evaluating the distortion of an image of a scanning laser rangefinder due to its noninstantaneous capture of a frame of range pixels, nonzero vehicle speed, and the period of time between positioning system updates. Assume zero curvature motion and no interpolation of positioning system updates.

9.2 Visual Localization and Motion Estimation

Whereas the last section presented map construction when the robot pose was known, this section considers three related problems: localizing the robot based on a (localization) map, measuring object positions based on imagery, and measuring motion based on imagery. The last two can be combined to construct maps.

9.2.1 Introduction

All of the ways in which perception sensors can be used to exploit maps and object models, to construct maps and object models, and to estimate sensor motion can be represented in the common framework presented in Figure 9.15.

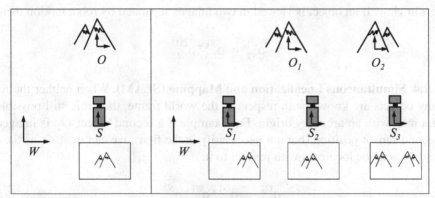

Figure 9.15 Overall Framework. Most of the aspects of visual localization, mapping, and motion estimation can be explained from this figure. The figure suggests a camera but the principles apply to all perception sensors. (Left) The sensor-object-world pose triangle. (Right) The images produced at each sensor location are shown below the sensors.

We will refer to all perception sensor indications here as *images*. It will be useful to refer to the real environment as the *scene* to distinguish it from its representation in the form of a *map* or object *model*. In this section we will use the symbol ρ to indicates poses of sensors, robots, objects, and so on, and reserve x for coordinates in images. The letters O, S, and W designate frames attached to the object in view, the sensor, and the world respectively. Of course, sensors can only make measurements with respect to themselves. However, we will assume that the pose of the sensor on the robot is known so that localizing the sensor in any frame is tantamount to localizing the robot.

9.2.1.1 Canonical Problems

With the above notation, all of the canonical problems of visual localization can now be described.

9.2.1.1.1 Mapping. The problem of mapping is that of determining ρ_O^W. Sensors cannot measure ρ_O^W directly but they can possibly measure ρ_O^S, and if so, and if the robot pose is known, the simplest form of mapping exploits the composition:

$$\rho_O^W = \rho_S^W * \rho_O^S$$

9.2.1.1.2 Localization. The problem of localizing the robot is that of determining ρ_S^W. If the robot pose is not known but ρ_O^W is known, then we have a map, and the robot can be localized with:

$$\rho_S^W = \rho_O^W * \rho_S^W$$

9.2.1.1.3 Visual Motion Estimation. If neither the pose of the object in the world ρ_O^W nor the pose of the robot in the world ρ_S^W is known, then no edges in the pose network (Section 2.7 of Chapter 2) connect to the world frame and nothing can be localized with respect to it. However, it is still possible to measure motion of the sensor relative to objects in view. If an object is viewed in two images separated by robot motion then:

$$\rho_{S2}^{S1} = \rho_{O1}^{S1} * \rho_{S2}^{O1}$$

9.2.1.1.4 Simultaneous Localization and Mapping (SLAM). When neither the robot nor any objects are known with respect to the world frame, then it is still possible to build a map with an arbitrary origin. For example if a second object O_2 is imaged in the second sensor position (but not necessarily in the first), we can treat O_1 as the origin and O_2 can be localized with respect to it:

$$\rho_{O2}^{O1} = \rho_{S1}^{O1} * \rho_{S2}^{S1} * \rho_{O2}^{S2}$$

and so on for subsequent objects. The fact that two poses are composed to localize O_2 suggests that this is a process that accumulates error.

Box 9.1: Localization and Mapping

The canonical problems of localization and mapping can be expressed in terms of compositions of two poses of a single moving sensor and the poses of two distinct objects as follows:

Mapping: $\qquad\qquad\qquad\qquad \underline{\rho}_O^W = \underline{\rho}_S^W * \underline{\rho}_O^S$

Localization: $\qquad\qquad\qquad\quad \underline{\rho}_S^W = \underline{\rho}_O^W * \underline{\rho}_S^O$

Visual Motion Estimation: $\qquad \underline{\rho}_{S2}^{S1} = \underline{\rho}_{O1}^{S1} * \underline{\rho}_{S2}^{O1}$

SLAM: $\qquad\qquad\qquad\qquad\quad \underline{\rho}_{O2}^{O1} = \underline{\rho}_{S1}^{O1} * \underline{\rho}_{S2}^{S1} * \underline{\rho}_{O2}^{S2}$

Because the robot frame will be known relative to the sensor frame, one can also substitute R1 for S1 and R2 for S2 above.

9.2.1.1.5 Consistent Mapping. Now the key issue of consistency is what happens if the robot returns to view an object, say O_2, a second time after significant error has accumulated. It may not recognize this O_{100} to be the same object as O_2 and it is virtually guaranteed that:

$$\underline{\rho}_{O2}^{O1} \neq \underline{\rho}_{100}^{O1}$$

To fix the situation, the objects have to be recognized as the same (known as the *revisiting problem*) and the sequence of poses $\underline{\rho}_{S2}^{S1}$ through $\underline{\rho}_{S100}^{S99}$ will have to be adjusted to make them agree on the position of O_2. This problem of consistent mapping is discussed later in subchapter 9.3 of this chapter.

9.2.1.2 Visual Localization

The process of *visual localization* is based on comparing what the robot sees to what it predicts based on a map or model of some kind. Under such a definition, even GPS is visual localization where the sensor is a multichannel radar and the map is the positions of the satellites in orbit.

9.2.1.2.1 Image Formation. Although the process of predicting the content of lidar imagery was presented in great detail in discussing Kalman filters, camera image formation has not been presented elsewhere. Suppose a model of an object is available and suppose that distinctive points in the model can be identified. Model points are initially known in model coordinates, so the first step is to convert them to sensor coordinates, so if the pose of the object with respect to the sensor $\underline{\rho}_O^S$ is known, the transformation between model frame points and sensor frame points is:

$$\underline{X}^s = T_o^s(\underline{\rho}_O^S)\underline{X}^m \qquad\qquad (9.1)$$

If we express the pose in zxy Euler angles, then we can use Equation 2.55:

$$
\begin{bmatrix} x \\ y \\ z \\ 1 \end{bmatrix}^s = \begin{bmatrix} c\psi c\theta & (c\psi s\theta s\phi - s\psi c\phi) & (c\psi s\theta c\phi + s\psi s\phi) & u \\ s\psi c\theta & (s\psi s\theta s\phi + c\psi c\phi) & (s\psi s\theta c\phi - c\psi s\phi) & v \\ -s\theta & c\theta s\phi & c\theta c\phi & w \\ 0 & 0 & 0 & 1 \end{bmatrix} \begin{bmatrix} x \\ y \\ z \\ 1 \end{bmatrix}^m
$$

The parameters of this transformation are called the *extrinsic* ones. Now, to see where the point falls on the image plane we use a camera projection matrix P:

$$
\underline{x}_i = P\underline{X}^s \tag{9.2}
$$

For the camera, we can use Equation 2.81:

$$
\begin{bmatrix} x_i \\ y_i \\ z_i \\ w_i \end{bmatrix} = \begin{bmatrix} 1 & 0 & 0 & 0 \\ 0 & 0 & 0 & 0 \\ 0 & 0 & 1 & 0 \\ 0 & \dfrac{1}{f} & 0 & 1 \end{bmatrix} \begin{bmatrix} x_s \\ y_s \\ z_s \\ 1 \end{bmatrix}
$$

The parameters of this transformation are called the *intrinsic* ones. In general, a more detailed model will include scaling and radial distortion information.

Therefore, the total transformation from a point on an object to where it appears in a camera image is given by:

$$
\underline{x}_i = P\underline{X}^s = PT_o^s(\underline{\rho}_O^S)\underline{X}^m = T(\underline{\rho}_O^S)\underline{X}^m = \underline{h}(\underline{\rho}_O^S, \underline{X}^m) \tag{9.3}
$$

Spotlight 9.1 Camera Measurement Model and Image Formation.

Generally, we will refer to this sensor model as $h(\underline{\rho}_O^S, \underline{X}^m)$ but occasionally, we will call it $T(\underline{\rho}_O^S)$ to emphasize that, because it is the product of two homogeneous transforms, it is also a homogeneous transform. Note that P is not a rigid transform so neither is T. The result of Equation 9.2 must be divided by w_i to get the true pixel coordinates.

9.2.1.2.2 Localization of Objects. Consider the problem of localizing the object with respect to the sensor. Of course, only the relative pose of the sensor and the object can be measured, so it is equivalent to imagine that the sensor is being localized with respect to the object. If the image of the object contains enough information, it will be possible to compute the relative pose.

The basic representation of the problem starts with our familiar measurement relationship with a few more arguments:

$$
\underline{z}(\underline{x}) = \underline{h}(\underline{x}, \underline{\rho}_O^S, \underline{Z}) \tag{9.4}
$$

Here, $\underline{Z}$ represents the encoding of relevant aspects of the object *model*. The function $\underline{h}$ represents the image formation process, and it depends on the pose relating the object and the sensor $\underline{\rho}_O^S$. It is also necessary to know which parts of the model are visible. The measurement vector $\underline{z}$ represents the image, whatever its form. For localization purposes, the image often contains a relatively significant amount of information. It could be 640×480 color pixels or a lidar range scan consisting of 1024 range values spread equally over $180°$ of azimuth.

The notation $\underline{z}(\underline{x})$ is intended to make explicit the fact that the image is a signal with defined structure. Hence $\underline{x}$ represents coordinates in some kind of image space and signal values $\underline{z}$ vary over the image space. For example, $\underline{x}$ could represent row and column coordinates in a color image and $\underline{z}$ might then be the pixel values in a red, green, and blue color space.

Now, the key point is that the object model can also be represented as a signal defined over a set of coordinates. If $\underline{X}$ represents points in 3D in the scene, then we can write $\underline{Z}(\underline{X})$ to mean that a color can also be assigned to every point in the scene (at least to every point on a visible surface). All of perception based localization is based on the fact that *image and scene coordinates are related by a low dimensional transformation* and once this transformation is known, the entire image becomes predictable from the model. This is computer graphics in a nutshell: given a model, one can synthesize imagery once the camera pose is known. However, the principle applies to other sensors as well.

For example, consider a color camera sensor and suppose that the transformation from scene to image coordinates is a matrix T dependent solely on the relative pose $\underline{\rho}_O^S$:

$$\underline{x} = T(\underline{\rho}_O^S)\underline{X} \tag{9.5}$$

Substituting into the right hand side of Equation 9.4:

$$\underline{z}(\underline{x}) = \underline{z}[T(\underline{\rho}_O^S)\underline{X}] = \underline{Z}(\underline{X}) \tag{9.6}$$

In other words, the imaging process transfers a signal (i.e., some information) from a point in the scene to its corresponding point the image. This process can be predicted if we know the imaging model $T(\underline{\rho}_O^S)$ that transforms coordinates, and we know the content of the model $\underline{Z}(\underline{X})$, meaning the appearance of (e.g., color everywhere on) the object. This information answers the question of what color should be put where in the image. In a more general case, the signal could be range or something else instead of color and the coordinate mapping may be nonlinear (i.e., distorting) and dependent on sensor parameters (e.g., focal length).

9.2.1.2.3 Basic Approaches and Issues. There are two basic approaches to visual localization. The first is based on aligning signals. Here, we search for the pose $\underline{\rho}_O^S$ that reproduces the predicted image given the model (or the map):

$$\underline{z}_{pred}(\underline{x}) = \underline{h}(\underline{x}, \underline{\rho}_O^S, \underline{Z}) \tag{9.7}$$

The second is based on aligning coordinates (or functions of coordinates called *features*).

$$\underline{x}_{pred} = T(\underline{\rho}_O^S)\underline{X} \tag{9.8}$$

Given enough pairs of scene points and image points $(\underline{x}_k, \underline{X}_k)$, the pose, or the entire transform, can be computed. A predictable set of concerns arise when addressing this problem. The first set of questions relate to the *data association* problem. If portions of the image are to be paired with portions of the scene, how are we to know which image feature to pair with which scene feature? We will refer to this problem as *matching*.

The second set of issues relates to the nature of the equations to be solved. Is there a unique pose that explains the image? Is an initial pose estimate available? What is the quality of the sensor data? How much time and computation are available? We will refer to the search for the correct alignment pose as *alignment*.

We have already encountered and solved such problems in the context of optimal estimation and the essential mathematics here is identical. In the final analysis, both approaches amount to inverting the measurement relationship.

9.2.1.2.4 Example: Localizing Pallets. In robotics, a classic case of object localization is that of a material handling robot searching for objects to pick up. Figure 9.16 illustrates the case of finding pallets based on identifying and locating the fork holes.

Figure 9.16 Edge Detection for Forkhole Finding. (Left) Raw image containing pallet. (Center) All detected edges. (Right) Identified fork holes.

In this example, the system first reduces the image to a set of intensity edges (features) and then it matches the edges to a model of the fork holes for which it is searching.

9.2.1.2.5 Robot Localization. The problems of localizing an object with respect to a sensor and a sensor with respect to a map have identical mathematical formulations. The question of whether enough pieces of the object can be recognized to generate enough constraints is equivalent to the question of whether enough landmarks in the environment can be recognized. In the case of localizing the robot, the predicted measurement takes the form.

$$z_{pred}(\underline{x}) = \underline{h}(\underline{x}, \underline{\rho}_S^W, \underline{Z}) \tag{9.9}$$

Now $\underline{Z}$ represents the map (which could be a list of object poses $\underline{\rho}_O^W$), and the pose $\underline{\rho}_O^S$ from the earlier example is replaced with $\underline{\rho}_S^W$. At a fundamental level, the problem of localizing from the image is to determine where the sensor would have to be to see what it is seeing. That is, to invert the measurement relationship to determine the pose $\underline{\rho}_S^W$, which explains the image $\underline{z}$.

9.2.1.2.6 Example: Localizing a Robot with Lidar Occupancy Grid. The map and the image may be very different data structures. For example, a map of a building may be represented by an occupancy grid (an array of binary numbers) whereas a lidar image will be a vector of ranges. In such a case, the predicted image may not be generated explicitly. In the most general case, the problem is solvable so long as we can formulate some measure of alignment error that vanishes more or less uniquely at the desired pose.

Figure 9.17 illustrates the case of trying to determine the pose of a robot based on the content of a lidar range image.

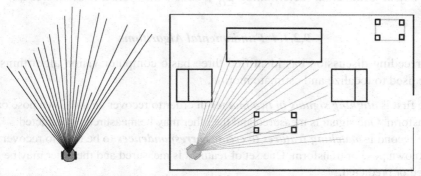

Figure 9.17 Perception Based Localization. The indicated pose of the vacuum cleaning robot is consistent with the range scan.

The two examples provided so far were opposites in many respects. One was a camera looking at a finite object matching edge features derived from video. The other was a range sensor being located inside a large map, matching range signals directly to surfaces and searching for an aligning pose. The differences in the formulations and implementations are substantial, but both can be understood in terms of a more general framework.

9.2.1.3 Visual Motion Estimation

When no map exists, both structure (poses of objects) and relative motion can still potentially be resolved by aligning sensor images to sensor images. The fact that an object appears in both images means that a mapping from one image to another exists. One key question is whether the scene-to-image transform is invertible for the sensor. If so, then the coordinates of the images can be related by inverting one transform:

$$\underline{x}_2 = T(\underline{\rho}_O^{S2})\underline{X} = T(\underline{\rho}_O^{S2})T^{-1}(\underline{\rho}_O^{S1})\underline{x}_1 = T(\underline{\rho}_O^{S1}, \underline{\rho}_O^{S2})\underline{x}_1$$

Once again, this image-to-image transform can be determined by aligning signals from image to image or by matching features. However, this is a potentially simpler problem than visual localization because the signal does not need to be predicted from the map. Often, the above relation can be rewritten in terms of the relative sensor pose:

$$\underline{x}_2 = T(\underline{\rho}_O^{S1}, \underline{\rho}_O^{S2})\underline{x}_1 = T(\underline{\rho}_{S1}^{S2})\underline{x}_1$$

Given enough feature correspondences, the relative pose can be determined. At times, the above image-to-image transform can be written as a function of a pose in image coordinates:

$$\underline{x}_2 = T_S(\underline{\rho}_{S1}^{S2})\underline{x}_1 = T_I(\underline{\rho}_{I1}^{I2})\underline{x}_1$$

This implies that the sensor-to-sensor pose may be derived from the image-to-image pose $\underline{\rho}_{S1}^{S2} = f(\underline{\rho}_{I1}^{I2})$. Once the relative scene motion is computed, the poses of the objects used become known and the objects can be optionally placed in a map data structure. Once again, visual motion estimation (determining $\underline{\rho}_{S2}^{S1}$), combined with visual object localization (determining $\underline{\rho}_O^{S2}$), allows the system to make a map.

9.2.1.4 Fundamental Algorithms

The preceding discussion has identified three basic computer vision algorithms that can be used to localize and estimate motion.

- The first is **aligning signals in two images** in order to recover an unknown pose or transform. One signal is measured and the other may be measured or predicted.
- The second is **matching features to create correspondences** to be used to recover an unknown pose or transform. One set of features is measured and the other may be measured or predicted.
- The third is **computing a relative pose** in the scene from a relative pose in the image.

In the first two cases, if the second image is measured, the unknown pose or transform will encode an image-to-image relationship and in some cases it is possible to formulate the problem in terms of an equivalent scene-to-scene relationship. Likewise if the second image is predicted from a model or map, the unknown pose or transform will encode an image-to-scene relationship. The coordinate frame in the scene that is being related to the image may be an object model or a map.

If the image formation process is modelled in order to find an image-to-scene transform, or a scene-to-scene transform, any signal distortion or transform nonlinearity will automatically be accounted for. Otherwise, the algorithm may need to solve for distortion as part the image-to-image transform. On the basis of this list of fundamental algorithms, the rest of this section will present techniques to align signals and match features, and techniques to search for an optimal pose.

9.2.2 Aligning Signals for Localization and Motion Estimation

This section and the next presents aspects of aligning both video and range imagery. Signal alignment is the most basic tool of visual localization. The transform that is required to cause two signals to agree is used as evidence of a spatial relationship of interest. Signal alignment tends to be used when positional uncertainty is low enough that a brute force search for the aligning transform is feasible. It also tends to be used when there is relatively little information in the signal. In this case, there may be little basis for detecting features that can be matched and all of the information in the raw signal needs to be exploited.

9.2.2.1 Signal-Based Objective Functions

Let us defined the predicted signal:

$$\underline{z}_{pred}(\underline{x}, \underline{\rho}, \underline{Z}) = \underline{h}(\underline{x}, \underline{\rho}, \underline{Z})$$

where $\underline{Z}$ will mean either the map, the object model, or a sequence of one or more prior images and $\underline{\rho}$ means whatever pose we wish to find. The core problem is to solve for the pose that aligns the observed and predicted signals. There is likely to be some systematic error in the model $\underline{h}$, and some noise in the measurements, so it is prudent to formulate the problem as an optimization rather than rootfinding. Consider the residual difference between the image that is observed $\underline{z}_{obs}$ and that which would be predicted based on a pose estimate $\underline{\rho}$:

$$\underline{r}(\underline{x}, \underline{\rho}, \underline{Z}) = \underline{z}_{obs}(\underline{x}) - \underline{z}_{pred}(\underline{x}, \underline{\rho}, \underline{Z}) \tag{9.10}$$

A scalar objective can be formed using the sum of the squared signal residuals over all or some subset of the domain of the signal, and the pose determination problem can then be formulated as nonlinear least squares computed over some window W in image coordinates:

$$\underline{\rho}^* = argmin \left[f(\underline{\rho}) = \frac{1}{2} \sum_{\underline{x} \in W} \underline{r}^T(\underline{x}, \underline{\rho}, \underline{Z}) \underline{r}(\underline{x}, \underline{\rho}, \underline{Z}) \right] \tag{9.11}$$

It is convenient notationally to collect all of the elements in $\underline{z}_{obs}(\underline{x})$, and in all other signals, for all values of $\underline{x}$, into a vector under any convenient prespecified ordering and to indicate this by dropping the argument $\underline{x}$:

$$\underline{z}_{obs} = vec_{\underline{x}}[\underline{z}_{obs}(\underline{x})] \qquad\qquad \underline{z}_{obs} = mat_{\underline{x}}[\underline{z}_{obs}(\underline{x})]$$
$$\underline{z}_{pred}(\underline{\rho}, \underline{Z}) = vec_{\underline{x}}[\underline{z}_{pred}(\underline{x}, \underline{\rho}, \underline{Z})] \quad \underline{z}_{pred}(\underline{\rho}, \underline{Z}) = mat_{\underline{x}}[\underline{z}_{pred}(\underline{x}, \underline{\rho}, \underline{Z})]$$

This allows us to reuse many earlier results. Under this transformation, the nonlinear least squares problem is simply:

$$\underline{\rho} = argmin \left[f(\underline{\rho}) = \frac{1}{2} \underline{r}^T(\underline{\rho}, \underline{Z}) \underline{r}(\underline{\rho}, \underline{Z}) \right]$$

Of course a weighting matrix can be introduced if some parts of the image are more trustworthy than others and a maximum likelihood formulation is also possible. If the measurement model is easily inverted (as it is with range data), the residual can also be computed in scene coordinates. In either case, an alternative formulation is to use crosscorrelation rather than the squared residual:

$$\underline{\rho} = argmax \left[f(\underline{\rho}) = \underline{z}_{obs}^T \underline{z}_{pred}(\underline{\rho}, \underline{Z}) \right] \tag{9.12}$$

In this case, the objective is to be maximized and, in the case of video, it may be advisable to normalize the two images first to remove bias and scale variations.

9.2.2.2 Aligning Video Signals in the Image Plane

Figure 9.18 illustrates a simple case where a monochrome image is searched exhaustively both horizontally and vertically ($\underline{\rho}$ is 2D) in a small region to try to find the best position of a template $\underline{z}_{obs}(\underline{x})$ in the search region in the image. The position of the peak in the correlation surface defines the position of the best alignment.

This simple approach can be generalized to include a warping (distortion) function and to incorporate gradient information in order to align imagery under perspective distortions that occur during motion [16]. We define a warping transformation function

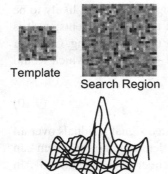

Template

Search Region

Correlation Surface

Figure 9.18 Correlation. A small enough search region can be searched entirely and exhaustively for a match.

$\underline{T}(\underline{x}, \underline{p})$, which depends on a parameter vector $\underline{p}$ and formulate a minimization over the warp parameters instead of just a pose.

In the case above, the warp is simply a (rigid) translation:

$$\underline{y}(\underline{x}, \underline{p}) = \underline{T}(x, \underline{p}) = \begin{bmatrix} x + p_1 \\ y + p_2 \end{bmatrix}$$

but more complicated warps such as affine warps can be used as well. The pixel residuals are now defined as:

$$(\underline{x}, \underline{p}, \underline{Z}) = \underline{z}_{obs}(\underline{x}) - \underline{z}_{pred}(\underline{x}, \underline{p}, \underline{Z}) = \underline{z}_{obs}(\underline{x}) - \underline{Z}[\underline{y}(x, \underline{p})]$$

where $\underline{Z}$ is the other image. As is the case whenever sampled signals are compared, it may be necessary to do interpolation in order to generate a signal value in between the measured samples. Here $\underline{y}(\underline{x}, \underline{p})$ need not be integer-valued.

Vectorizing the signals with the *vec* operator defined above leads to:

$$\underline{p} = argmin \left[f(\underline{p}) = \frac{1}{2} \underline{r}^T(\underline{p}, \underline{Z}) \underline{r}(\underline{p}, \underline{Z}) \right] \tag{9.13}$$

This is a nonlinear least squares problem that can be solved using the algorithms presented in Chapter 3 given some initial estimate of the warp parameters $\underline{p}_0$.

9.2.2.3 Example: Lane Tracking for Cars

Either implicit expectations or explicit models of the appearance of roads constitute a map in the sense that a vehicle can be localized left or right with respect to the road based on where the lane markings appear in imagery. One of the earliest applications of perception to outdoor robots was the use of video to estimate the lateral position of automobiles on roads or in lanes of roads. These applications are good examples of predicting imagery in order to localize. One motivation for this work is the fact that about 15,000 people die each year in just the United States in single vehicle roadway departure accidents [22].

In this example (Figure 9.19), imagery is warped in creative ways to keep your car on the road. The warp is considered known but it is still an important part of the

Figure 9.19 Roadfollowing in Traffic. How might you write a program to find the lane markings?

solution because it makes the rest of the signal matching much simpler. The search for the alignment pose is conducted in an exhaustive manner.

Once lateral offset is estimated in one iteration of the algorithm, it is possible to use steering information and road curvature in order to do prediction of the next image. Such prediction may not be necessary if it is feasible to perform exhaustive search. In any case, once a lane offset is computed, it could be used as the basis of a lane departure warning system or of a visual servo that steers the vehicle autonomously.

A simple approach due to [9] amounts to tracking both the orientation and the curvature of the lane markings. Small regions of the image are warped to remove the expected curvature and lateral offset, the image columns are summed, and an edge detector that is applied to the summed signal produces strong edges at the lane markings (Figure 9.20).

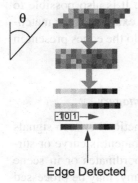

Edge Detected

Figure 9.20 Edge Detection With Strong Predictions. A few columns of data are warped based on the expected orientation and curvature of the edge. Then an efficient filter for edges is as simple as summing the columns and running an edge detector on the summed result.

Later approaches extended this idea to larger portions of the road in view by inverting the perspective mapping of the camera. One system [19] drove 2850 miles across the United States (Figure 9.21). Consider the image produced by a somewhat downward looking camera. For flat terrain, a trapezoid in the image corresponds to a region of constant width that extends forward for some fixed length and that can be adjusted for speed. The pixels in this region are extracted and rearranged to produce a synthetic overhead view of the road.

A hypothesize and test approach is used to find the curvature for which the summed columns in the overhead image have sharpest edges. This is the curvature of the road.

 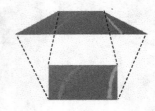

Figure 9.21 Lane Trackers. (Left) The trapezoidal region of interest is sampled to reduce the data processed in RALPH. (Right) Inverse Perspective Mapping.

The summed columns are then aligned with a learned intensity profile in order to find the lateral offset of the lane. A similar approach was used on experimental farming robots [20]. Roadfollowing can be accomplished with range data as well. Range imagery of entry walls was used to control LHD vehicles in mines [10].

9.2.2.4 Other Forms of Maps

Any field of perceptual expectations over the space of robot poses $\underline{h}(\underline{\rho})$ can be used as a map. Visual odometry systems can become visual localization systems if the features encountered the first time a path is followed are remembered in a spatially indexable form. Researchers have demonstrated localization from lidar intensity signatures of roads, and from video of factory floors. Maps constructed from range data of the walls of buildings can be very effectively aligned with new range data as the robot moves, and aerial digital elevation maps produced from flash lidar can be matched with range data produced on a moving ground robot. It is also possible to mix the modalities of mapping sensor and guidance sensor. One example is the matching of vertical planes of buildings that are detected in lidar data to the edges present in satellite video imagery.

9.2.2.5 Aligning Surface Geometry in Range Imagery

Range data is already geometric in character, so making a distinction between signals and features requires more effort. The equivalent of video alignment is curve or surface alignment. The alignment can be conducted in image coordinates or in scene coordinates. As suggested in Figure 9.17, the map or model, if any, may be processed into line segments (2D) or polygonal facets (3D) or any of a number of other representations of geometric surfaces.

Surface alignment is usually based on the assumption that the two surfaces involved are largely undistorted but a search over distortions can also be accomplished. The area between the surfaces is one appropriate measure of the misalignment between them that is similar in principle to intensity residuals in video (Figure 9.22).

One of several alternative methods can be used to estimate this area. Perfect registration occurs when the area is zero but descent algorithms operating on this area will converge only to the nearest local minimum, so the initial guess must be adequately close.

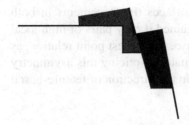

Figure 9.22 Residual of two lidar scans. The area between the two scans is one possible measure of error.

The alignment process described above can be conducted in scene coordinates but aligning the range signals directly can also be an effective approach [8]. Doing so estimates the misregistration area in polar coordinates by using the sum of a number of line lengths to represent the misregistration error between the curves. The basic algorithm is illustrated in Figure 9.23.

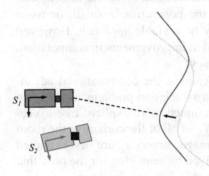

Figure 9.23 Matching Range Data in Image Coordinates. Each point on the light curve is associated with the projectively equivalent point on the dark curve.

Every point in the second scan (image) is converted to the coordinates of the origin of the first scan. Points falling outside the field of view of the first scan are ignored. Those that remain are used to form range residuals with corresponding ranges in the first scan. Interpolation of the first image will lead to faster convergence and better alignment.

Such *projective association* produces highly incorrect matches when the ray-to-surface incidence angle is glancing (Figure 9.24).

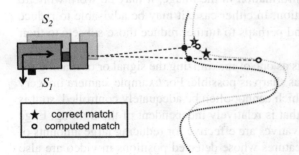

★ correct match
○ computed match

Figure 9.24 Projective Association. An efficient association can be produced by rendering the second image from the perspective of the first. This association is close to exact when the scan misalignment is small and the ray-to-surface incidence angle is small. It is subject to large errors when the incidence is glancing.

One way to express this issue is to notice that points that are close in azimuth need not be close in the scene. Some improvements would be gained above if association was established along the local surface normal. In any case, any form of physical proximity testing cannot guarantee that the chosen pairs actually correspond in the scene. Surface matching is appropriate when the surfaces imaged are smooth but sometimes local geometry is distinct and identifiable on both surfaces. Improvements in both computational efficiency and in robustness might be gained if only pairs of high local curvature or of similar local curvature were paired. Also, the closest point relation, as defined, is not necessarily symmetric at an incorrect match. Noticing this asymmetry would detect the above case. These ideas are moving in the direction of feature-based data association, which is presented next.

9.2.3 Matching Features for Localization and Motion Estimation

We have seen that signal alignment avoids the problem of data association because data at the same position in the two signals is assumed to correspond in an iteration. When aligning the entire measured image z_{obs} to the entire predicted image z_{pred}, the entire signal (vector or image) is compared to the entire signal on an element by element basis. In both video and range data, when the pose error is small, or when exhaustive search for a match is feasible, this may be a viable approach. However, more refined approaches to data association can lead to improvements in computation, radius of convergence, convergence rate, and accuracy.

Once the signals to be aligned are reduced to features, the computational advantages so derived come at the cost of making the data association problem, also known as the *correspondence problem* in computer vision, much more explicit. In our vacuum robot example, consider storing the positions X_k of all of the corners in the room in a (new) feature map. To use the map, the range image corners x_k are first extracted from the range image. Then, the problem can be solved by searching for the pose that causes measured and predicted features to line up best.

9.2.3.1 Segmentation and Features

When proprioceptive sensors like wheel encoders are used to measure movement, the measurement relationship is commonly underdetermined. However, when perception is used, the relationship is often overdetermined. There may be far more information in the image than is absolutely necessary to constrain 6 degrees of freedom of robot pose. Also, if there is little useful information in the image, it may be worthwhile to discard much of it to save computation. In either case, it may be advisable to reduce the image to some useful subsets and perhaps to further reduce those subsets to their most useful form.

One way to think of this process is as one of maximizing the signal or of making the local minimum in the cost function as sharp as possible. For example, camera imagery is dependent on ambient lighting, which cannot often be adequately controlled, so it is useful to reduce imagery to a form that is relatively independent of the lighting. Edge operators and all other forms of derivatives are effective for reducing large amounts of camera imagery to fewer discrete features whose detected positions in video are also fairly invariant to lighting variations. Points of high curvature in range data are the equivalent of edges in video, and both are often called *features*. In contrast to using edges for localization, regions of more or less uniform characteristics can also be useful features for detection. In the forktruck example above, using the moments of area of the dark rectangular forkholes might be an effective approach to the problem of detecting them. Once they are detected, the edges can be used to localize.

9.2.3.2 Objective Function

An image z_{obs} contains more information than its signal amplitudes, because the individual amplitudes occur somewhere in the image. It is not unusual to find that the most useful information is not what the signal amplitudes are, but rather where they occur are in the image. Such *features* may retain some or all of the original measurement signal or they may be stripped of all information other than their positions. For example, for the vacuum cleaner robot in Figure 9.17, one could survey every corner position $\underline{X}_k$ in the living room in world coordinates and then the measurement model might simply produce the position $\underline{x}_k$ of the same corner in the robot frame:

$$\underline{x}_k = \underline{h}(\rho, \underline{X}_k) \tag{9.14}$$

We developed this measurement model in great detail in Section 5.3.4.6 of Chapter 5. At times, systems are engineered by deliberately placing features in the scene that have high signal to noise ratios for both detection and localization. For example, a scanning laser bearing sensor or an omnidirectional camera might record only the angles to reflectors placed in the scene.

9.2.3.3 Feature Attributes

Features can also be augmented with many kinds of information in order to facilitate correct associations. For a scene feature with coordinates $\underline{X}_k$, some of the attributes $\underline{Z}_k$ of the associated scene position or object may be stored in addition to coordinates. Ideally, the objects associated with the features encode their identification information in the data that they generate. Examples include radio frequency identification (RFID) tags which report their id when queried, lidar reflectors with linear bar codes encoding their id, and camera fiducials composed of 2D bar codes (Figure 9.25).

Figure 9.25 Engineered Features. These engineered features identify themselves uniquely when they are sensed. (Left) Camera fiducial. (Right) RFID tag.

Feature attributes can be derived from the nearby signal $\underline{z}_k$ in the image in order to enable signal matching for features. The block of camera pixels surrounding a point feature, or the eigenvalues of Harris corners, may be stored. In range data, principal curvatures or *spin images* [13] can be stored. In all cases, the basic approach is to provide extra information to assist in disambiguating one feature from another. Such disambiguation can be difficult at times as presented below.

9.2.3.4 Typical Features and Objective Functions

When matching features, a new set of issues arise that relate to how information is extracted from correspondences. Strictly speaking, features are pseudomeasurements because the signal itself is the true measurement. In general terms, however, a residual can still be formed:

$$\underline{r}_k(\rho, \underline{X}_k) = \underline{x}_k - \underline{h}(\rho, \underline{X}_k) \tag{9.15}$$

It will be convenient notationally to collect all of the residuals and all of the model features into a single vector and drop the k subscript:

$$\underline{r}(\underline{\rho}, \underline{X}) = \underline{x} - \underline{h}(\underline{\rho}, \underline{X}) \tag{9.16}$$

and the cost function can take any useful form including the residual norm:

$$\underline{\rho} = argmin \left[f(\underline{\rho}) = \frac{1}{2}\underline{r}^T(\underline{\rho}, \underline{Z})\underline{r}(\underline{\rho}, \underline{Z}) \right]$$

When the features are the endpoints of lidar rays or points in a color image, it is feasible to simply compute the distance between corresponding points in any convenient coordinates. However, it can be valuable to correspond points in an image to lines in a model, or to correspond line segments with each other and many more possibilities exist. When correspondences are created, it is important to formulate the observations $\underline{x}_k$ to create the appropriate number of degrees of freedom that contribute to the cost function. Otherwise, the solution will be incorrect.

Some examples of planar correspondences are shown in Figure 9.26. More possibilities exist in 3D. The formulation of the observation is much simplified if they are expressed in the coordinates of a frame attached to the feature such that the distances needed are aligned with the axes. In this case, a *pose Jacobian* (Section 7 of Chapter 2) is generated to linearize the constraint and the appropriate rows are stricken to leave just the valid constraints. An alternative approach is to compute a dot product of the full Jacobian with a unit vector in the direction of interest that is expressed in the same coordinates as the Jacobian. The result is the directional derivative in the direction desired.

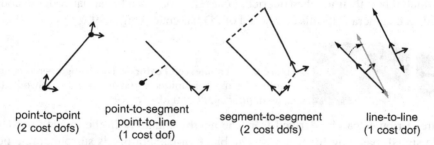

| point-to-point (2 cost dofs) | point-to-segment point-to-line (1 cost dof) | segment-to-segment (2 cost dofs) | line-to-line (1 cost dof) |

Figure 9.26 Planar Feature Correspondences. Different pairings generate residuals of different dimension. If model frames are attached to features as shown, observations can be formulated conveniently in feature coordinates.

9.2.3.5 Search for Associations

When there are multiple predicted features and observed features, we need to know which predicted feature to match with which observed feature in order to assess how they line up. If there are n features in the image and $m > n$ in the map there are m choices for the match to the first image feature, followed by $m - 1$ choices for the second, and so on, so there are many possible associations in the general case. However, the robot pose represents very few degrees of freedom to be constrained so very few noise-free feature associations are needed to constrain it completely. The data association and pose determination problems are coupled. Knowledge of the robot pose constrains the possible associations and knowledge of the associations constrains the pose.

Approaches to data association vary based on how much is known about the pose already. Some approaches to the problem include:

- Richness: Features have enough additional attributes with distinct enough values to tell them apart. Bar codes are one example of this case.
- Pose Estimates: If the pose is already well constrained, a low resolution search in pose space may happen on a pose near the solution for which association becomes easy.
- Spatial Separation: If features are well separated in image coordinates, observed features can be paired to the nearest predicted feature in image coordinates.
- Consensus: If there are enough features that the majority vote is meaningful, generate and test approaches are feasible.
- Conditioning: The problem may be well enough conditioned that it will converge even with (locally) incorrect correspondences. We have seen this approach already with signal alignment.

There are a few issues that may complicate matters further. Self-occlusion of parts of the scene may lead to *missing parts*, meaning a feature that would otherwise be in view is not because it is behind something else. Also the distortions and information loss associated with perspective image formation may make it difficult to record useful feature attributes.

9.2.3.6 RANSAC

One important algorithm for performing data association is RANSAC (short for random sample consensus) [11]. RANSAC is a useful algorithm when a data set contains outliers that do not fit the model. An *outlier* is a data point that really should be ignored because it is not valid data for whatever reason. An *inlier,* by contrast, refers to valid data. It is easy to imagine erroneous associations of features happening in visual data association in cases in which there are two areas in the scene that happen to be near each other, and that happen to have nearly the same geometry or appearance.

Outliers can ruin the accuracy of optimization results because their large errors give them more influence over the solution than inliers. However, outliers are difficult to detect unless the correct answer is already known. Nonetheless, RANSAC provides a mechanism to reject outliers when there are sufficient numbers of inliers relative to outliers to produce a solution in reasonable time. The algorithm is straightforward. It repeats the following process until a termination condition is met:

- Choose a random sample of data of sufficient size to fix all of the parameters of the model. These are a set of hypothetical inliers.
- Test all other data against the hypothetical model and reject as outlier those points that exceed threshold.
- Re-estimate the model from all of the inliers.
- If the number of inliers > minInliers, compute the quality of the fit to the inliers and record this model if it is the best so far.

The algorithm may terminate after a fixed number of iterations, or when a good enough fit has been achieved. The initial inlier test threshold and the acceptable number of inliers must be tuned for specific applications.

9.2.3.6.1 Example RANSAC For Rigid Motion in the Image Plane. RANSAC is a very useful algorithm for associating points in imagery (Figure 9.27). Typically there are many points available for association and only a few are necessary to fit whatever model is used. Suppose 16 features are available to be matched to produce the pose in the image plane that aligns them. There are three degrees of freedom to extract and it only takes two inliers to get it right. If there are 50% outliers in the data, the probability of selecting two inliers in a sample of two points is 25%, so it would only take four random samples on average to find the correct model.

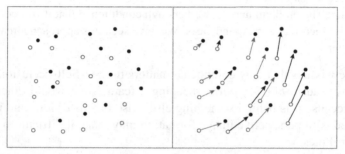

Figure 9.27 RANSAC. (Left) Two sets of points in the plane related by an unknown rigid transformation with 50% outliers. (Right) RANSAC finds the inliers (darker arrows) and the associated transform in four iterations on average.

9.2.3.7 Closest Point Association in Range Data

Some problems can be managed by assuming the closest match is correct. The iterative closest point (ICP) algorithm [7] uses such *nearest neighbor* association for alignment of range data to other range data or to surfaces. The algorithm associates each point in the range image with the closest point, in cartesian coordinates, in the range image or surface being aligned (Figure 9.28).

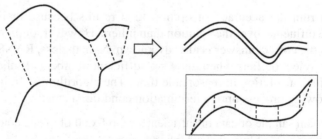

Figure 9.28 Closest Point Association. (Left) Points on the bottom curve are matched with the closest point on the top curve. (Inset) Incorrect matches at endpoints when the curves only partially overlap.

In a straightforward implementation, the association requires n^2 operations so it can become too expensive for large data sets. Of course, associations should be created only in the region of overlap, but that region is often not known. Unless more is done, ICP will find a correspondence even when there isn't one. The fundamental problem is that "closest" does not always imply "corresponding." One approach to mitigation is to use the statistics of the association lengths to implement outlier rejection by guessing which ones should be eliminated.

Interpolation of the data is very important when matching range data to range data (Figure 9.29). Lack of interpolation introduces incorrect components into the cost function that lead to the local minimum occurring somewhere other than the correct alignment. The fundamental reason for this is the fact that points are incorrectly and inconsistently associated so the algorithm ends up pulling the wrong points together. By contrast, association with the closest point measures the distance normal to the surface while permitting tangential motion.

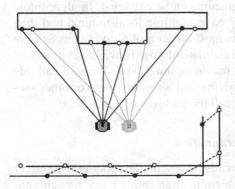

Figure 9.29 Importance of Interpolation. When range scans are matched to range scans, interpolation is crucial. (Top) Range points from two scans are virtually guaranteed not to align. (Bottom) Associating discrete range samples with each other creates a cost for tangential motion.

Figure 9.30 illustrates a straightforward algorithm for finding the closest point on a line segment to another point. If the dot product of the vectors $\vec{v}_1$ and $\vec{v}_2$ is positive, then a point on the line from p_1 to p_2 is closer to p_3. The condition to compute the closest point is:

$$\vec{v}_1 \bullet \vec{v}_2 > 0 \tag{9.17}$$

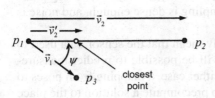

Figure 9.30 Interpolation. The point p_3 on the second scan has been tentatively associated with the point p_1 on the first scan. The point p_2 is further from p_3 than is p_1 or it would have been chosen initially. If the dot product of the vectors v_1 and v_2 is positive, then a point on the line from p_1 to p_2 is closer to p_3.

If this condition is true, then the vector $\vec{v}_2{}'$ points to the new point. It is given by the endpoint of projection of $\vec{v}_1$ onto $\vec{v}_2$. The formula for this projection is:

$$\vec{v}_2{}' = \left|\vec{v}_1\right|\cos\psi\frac{\vec{v}_2}{\left|\vec{v}_2\right|} = \left|\vec{v}_1\right|\frac{\left|\vec{v}_2\right|}{\left|\vec{v}_2\right|}\cos\psi\frac{\vec{v}_2}{\left|\vec{v}_2\right|} = \frac{(\vec{v}_1 \bullet \vec{v}_2)}{(\vec{v}_2 \bullet \vec{v}_2)}\vec{v}_2 \tag{9.18}$$

This algorithm would be invoked on both neighbors of p_1 (left and right). It is possible that if p_1 is an inside corner, both of its neighbors could return a closer point than the associated endpoint.

9.2.4 Searching for the Optimal Pose

This section addresses the problem of finding the pose that best explains the image. The relative difficulty of instances of the problem can be distinguished based on the familiar issues that arise in rootfinding and its derived minimization problems.

If a poor initial estimate of pose is available, or none at all, there may be little basis for distinguishing several potential solutions. Each corner of a room may look the same in lidar data, for example. The solution may be fundamentally ambiguous until the robot moves and enough of a unique place signature can be extracted. In algorithmic terms, the cost (squared residual) surface may have multiple local minima and they may all have similar costs. We will refer to this most difficult of all problems as *pose determination*. When a sufficiently close initial estimate of pose is available, it may be possible to use gradient information to search for the optimal pose. We will call this problem *pose refinement*. When the robot is moving and a measurement or other secondary estimate of motion is available, we will call the problem *pose tracking*.

9.2.4.1 Pose Determination

This problem has also been called *insertion* because it inserts the robot at the correct position in the map. The vision part of the problem is often called *place recognition*. For moving sensors, finding the first pose can be much harder than finding subsequent poses because they can use the last pose as an initial guess. This fact will be familiar to readers with GPS navigation systems in their cars. It takes time to establish the initial lock onto the satellites. Pose determination is the visual equivalent of locking onto the satellites.

As a search for a global minimum, all of the numerical techniques available to solve such problems are potentially available. On the assumption that gradient information is not enough to solve the problem, then sampling may be a viable approach. In this approach, a number of initial guesses $\underline{\rho}_k$ are tried and the nearest local minimum to each is computed. Because pose refinement is really a noisy rootfinding problem, the residual should be small. Provided the sampling is dense enough, and noise is small enough, the global minimum will be found.

However, if a map or object model exists, it may mean that the sensor data used to make the model is available, and even if not, it will be possible to predict measurements given the measurement model $\underline{h}(\underline{\rho}, \underline{X}_k)$. In either case, a mapping from poses to images can be produced and manipulated offline to precompute a solution to the place recognition problem.

Lookup tables can be an effective solution when the map and the region of pose uncertainty is sufficiently small. In this case, the measurement relationship for a dense sampling is inverted offline and stored in a table as a set of pairs $(\underline{z}_k, \underline{\rho}_k)$ or $(\underline{x}_k, \underline{\rho}_k)$. The solution pose for every image or feature set cannot be read directly from the table unless every possible image is stored. Instead, the images are reduced to low resolution keys.

For example, for the vacuum robot, if all positions and orientations in the room are sampled at some resolution, the predicted range image itself at each position can be used as the basis for rapid matching with a measured image. The sample whose range image matches best can be the initial estimate for a local search. Video imagery can often be rich enough in content to permit unambiguous identification of a pose based solely on the content of a single image. When there are too many images in the table to check quickly, a classifier can be constructed that searches them more efficiently than doing so with brute force comparisons to all possibilities.

9.2.4.1.1 Example Place Recognition in Bearing Data. Consider the case of an automated laser guided vehicle that uses a scanning laser bearing sensor to localize itself. The vehicle operates in an area with four retroreflective fiducials arranged in a diamond configuration (Figure 9.31). The insertion problem for this vehicle is to process a single scan of 4 bearings and then determine roughly where the robot is in order to initialize the guidance algorithms. The symmetry of the arrangement means there are 4 potential solutions for any given scan but we will assume that we know the heading is within 45° of East.

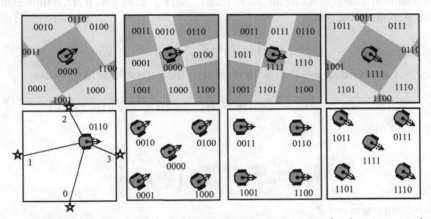

Figure 9.31 AGV Insertion Lookup Table. (Bottom Left) A scan of 4 bearings produces a binary number with bit positions as indicated. The bearings are defined as positive or negative relative to 0,90,180, and 270° counter clockwise respectively. A positive bearing produces a 1 bit. (Top) Partition of space at 4 different headings. (Bottom Right) Only 14 such keys occur and the centroid associated with each is indicated.

A program was written offline to sample robot pose position and orientation at a resolution of 1 cm in position and 1° in orientation. For each such pose, simulated measurements were generated and they were converted into a binary number where the most significant bit comes from the first return whose bearing exceeds (−45°) relative to the forward direction of the robot. Bits are associated with the other bearings in counterclockwise order.

This processes reduces each scan to a 4-bit binary number that will be used as a key in a lookup table. There are nominally 16 possible keys but the numbers 5 (0101) and 10 (1010) do not occur. The offline program computes the centroid of all poses associated with each of the 16 possible keys. This process produces a list of 16 poses. The list is a simple lookup table to support rapid place recognition. To use it, a scan is taken, its key is computed, and the pose centroid associated with the key is provided as the initial guess to a descent algorithm that refines the estimate.

In order this process to work correctly, there must be enough poses in the table to ensure that the initial guess for every scan is within the radius of convergence of the correct pose for the scan. This condition can also be tested offline and if 16 keys are inadequate it is a simple matter to allocate two bits per bearing to produce an 8-bit number and 256 centroids.

9.2.4.2 Pose Refinement

If an initial estimate is available, it may be close enough to justify the use of gradient information. Then the measurement model can be linearized and the problem can be solved as an iterative optimization problem.

9.2.4.2.1 Objective Linearization. The first step is to linearize the objective. In the case of aligning signals, a warping function dependent on parameters $\underline{p}$ may be needed instead of a pose ρ.

In a nonlinear least squares formulation, recall from Equation 3.61 that the (unweighted) Newton step takes the form:

$$\Delta \underline{p} = -[\underline{r}_{\underline{p}}^{T}\underline{r}_{\underline{p}}]^{-1}\underline{r}_{\underline{p}}^{T}\underline{r}(\underline{p}) \tag{9.19}$$

Where $\underline{r}_{\underline{p}}$ is the residual gradient with respect to the parameters. In this case:

$$\underline{r}_{\underline{p}} = \underline{r}_{\underline{p}}(\underline{p}, \underline{Z}) = -\underline{h}_{\underline{p}}(\underline{p}, \underline{Z}) = -\underline{Z}_{\underline{p}}[\underline{y}(\underline{p})] \tag{9.20}$$

By the chain rule:

$$\underline{Z}_{\underline{p}} = \frac{\partial}{\partial \underline{p}}\{\underline{Z}(\underline{y}(\underline{p}))\} = \left(\frac{\partial \underline{Z}}{\partial \underline{y}}\right)\left(\frac{\partial \underline{y}}{\partial \underline{p}}\right)$$

The two components of $\underline{Z}_{\underline{p}}$ are:

- $(\partial \underline{Z}/\partial \underline{y})$, the gradient of the image evaluated at $\underline{y}(\underline{p})$. This is a 1×2 vector for each pixel for monochrome imagery.
- $(\partial \underline{y}/\partial \underline{p})$ the parameter Jacobian of the warp evaluated at $\underline{p}$. A $2 \times n$ matrix for n parameters.

One notable variant on this algorithm [21] uses a trick in computer vision of solving for updates to the warp function directly, rather than for updates to the parameters of the warp function. Note especially that when signals are being aligned, the image gradient appears in the measurement Jacobian.

In the case of matching features, the Newton step is:

$$\Delta \underline{\rho} = -[\underline{r}_{\underline{\rho}}^{T}\underline{r}_{\underline{\rho}}]^{-1}\underline{r}_{\underline{\rho}}^{T}\underline{r}(\underline{\rho})$$

Where $\underline{r}_{\underline{\rho}}$ is the residual gradient with respect to the parameters. With reference to Equation 9.16, the pose gradient is:

$$\underline{r}_{\underline{\rho}} = \underline{r}_{\underline{\rho}}(\underline{\rho}, \underline{X}) = -\underline{h}_{\underline{\rho}}(\underline{\rho}, \underline{X}) \tag{9.21}$$

The Jacobian $\underline{h}_\rho(\underline{\rho}, \underline{X})$ relates changes in the image coordinates of a feature to changes in the pose of the sensor. The Jacobian $\partial \underline{y} / \partial \underline{p}$ in the signal alignment case is very similar. We have seen this kind of Jacobian earlier in Kalman filters. The new aspects are the appearance of the image gradient for aligning signals and the formulation as an optimization problem. Note that for an unknown pose, the Newton step takes the form:

$$\Delta \underline{\rho} = -[\underline{r}_\rho^T \underline{r}_\rho]^{-1} \underline{r}_\rho^T \underline{r}(\underline{p}) = [\underline{h}_\rho^T \underline{h}_\rho]^{-1} \underline{h}_\rho^T \underline{r}(\underline{\rho})$$

This is, of course, a left pseudoinverse solution to Equation 9.21. Another difference from Kalman filters is the fact that these equations are typically very overdetermined so there is no need for a state covariance matrix to generate enough constraints to solve the system.

9.2.4.2.2 Example: Locating a Pallet. When video is used to locate objects, it is common to use features in order counteract many difficult issues. Perspective effects include scale that varies with range and foreshortening that distorts shape. 3D effects include the basic issue that different sides of objects may look very different. When objects are deformable there may even be more degrees of freedom than the motion of the camera. In 3D, only three points in an image and their corresponding positions in the scene are needed to constrain the six degrees of freedom of a rigid body. This "n-point" perspective problem has been well researched [12].

This example provides more details for the simple case of finding forkholes described initially in Figure 9.16. This problem can be reduced to a 2D problem, so it makes a good example. In the plane, only 1-1/2 point correspondences are needed to solve for a pose. This example is also one where an image-to-scene pose is being determined rather than an image-to-image pose.

The system uses geometric pallet models that encode the (scale independent) ratio of hole width to hole separation because this is an invariant quantity under a perspective imaging transformation. The system also exploits the fact that the (vertical fork hole) edges must be principally oriented in the image and they must occur in darkening/lightening pairs (Figure 9.32).

Figure 9.32 Edge Template. Four vertical edges must occur in roughly the right magnitude and separation to signal a pallet. The edge strength per column can be quickly scanned for four strong edges of the correct spatial arrangement.

We will assume that the four edges have been found already and concentrate on finding where the pallet is relative to the camera (Figure 9.33). We will define the camera coordinates the same as we did for a rangefinder in Figure 5.38.

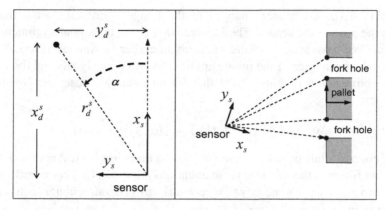

Figure 9.33 Camera Geometry and Scene Relationships. The camera sensor measures the tangent of the bearing to points in the scene. Four vertical edges are imaged to constrain the pose of the pallet in the camera frame.

Let the letter m denote the model frame with respect to which the fork hole geometry is specified and s denotes sensor. Once the scene point (detection point frame d) is known in camera coordinates, the measurement model is simply:

$$y_d^i = (f y_d^s)/x_d^s \tag{9.22}$$

Where y_d^i is clearly proportional to the tangent of the bearing angle α. The Jacobian of this relationship with respect to scene coordinates $\underline{r}_d^s = [x_d^s \ y_d^s]^T$ is:

$$H_{sd}^{id} = \frac{\partial y_d^i}{\partial \underline{r}_d^s} = \left[-\frac{f y_d^s}{(x_d^s)^2} \ \frac{f}{x_d^s} \right] \tag{9.23}$$

Next, we need the transform from the model frame attached to the pallet and its Jacobian:

$$\underline{r}_d^s = T_m^s(\underline{\rho}_m^s) * \underline{r}_d^m \tag{9.24}$$

If we attach a frame to each of the four feature points, it should be clear that the Jacobian in question is a compound-left pose Jacobian, so we can immediately write:

$$H_{sm}^{sd} = \frac{\partial \underline{\rho}_d^s}{\partial \underline{\rho}_m^s} = \begin{bmatrix} 1 & 0 & -(s\psi x_d^m + c\psi y_d^m) \\ 0 & 1 & (c\psi x_d^m - s\psi y_d^m) \\ 0 & 0 & 1 \end{bmatrix} = \begin{bmatrix} 1 & 0 & -(y_d^s - y_m^s) \\ 0 & 1 & (x_d^s - x_m^s) \\ 0 & 0 & 1 \end{bmatrix} \tag{9.25}$$

We will use only the first two lines of this:

$$H_{sm}^{sd} = \frac{\partial \underline{r}_d^s}{\partial \underline{\rho}_m^s} = \begin{bmatrix} 1 & 0 & -(s\psi x_d^m + c\psi y_d^m) \\ 0 & 1 & (c\psi x_d^m - s\psi y_d^m) \end{bmatrix} = \begin{bmatrix} 1 & 0 & -(y_d^s - y_m^s) \\ 0 & 1 & (x_d^s - x_m^s) \end{bmatrix} \tag{9.26}$$

The complete solution for an assumed initial value of $\underline{\rho}_m^s$ is as follows:

$$r_d^s = T_m^s(\underline{\rho}_m^s) * r_d^m$$

$$y_d^i = (f y_d^s)/x_d^s$$

$$H_{sm}^{id} = \left(\frac{\partial y_d^i}{\partial \underline{\rho}_m^s}\right) = \left(\frac{\partial y_d^i}{\partial \underline{\rho}_d^s}\right)\left(\frac{\partial \underline{\rho}_d^s}{\partial \underline{\rho}_m^s}\right) = H_{sd}^{id} H_{sm}^{sd} = \left[-\frac{f y_d^s}{(x_d^s)^2} \quad \frac{f}{x_d^s}\right]\begin{bmatrix} 1 & 0 & -(y_d^s - y_m^s) \\ 0 & 1 & (x_d^s - x_m^s) \end{bmatrix} \quad (9.27)$$

For each of the four features, their model coordinates $\underline{X}_k$ are the points r_d^m in 2D. The predicted measurement $\underline{h}(\underline{\rho}, \underline{X}_k) = y_d^i\big|_{pred}$ and the real measurement $\underline{x}_k = y_d^i$ is a scalar dependent on the sensor-to-model pose $\underline{\rho} = \underline{\rho}_m^s$. The Jacobian is a 3-vector. Four measurements are stacked to form the residual

$$\underline{r}_k(\underline{\rho}, \underline{X}_k) = \underline{x}_k - \underline{h}(\underline{\rho}, \underline{X}_k)$$

Then the Jacobian is $\underline{h}_\rho = H_{sm}^{id}$. This gives enough information to compute the descent direction $\Delta \underline{\rho} = [\underline{h}_\rho^T \underline{h}_\rho]^{-1} \underline{h}_\rho^T \underline{r}(\underline{\rho})$. A line search can then be conducted and the process repeated until convergence.

9.2.4.2.3 Other Object Localization Problems. A large number of interesting problems are similar to the one presented above. Just a few include: indoor robots finding and connecting to electrical outlets for a recharge, soccer robots finding the ball or other teammates, or agricultural robots picking apples. NASA has experimented with this technique as one approach to satellite capture and line replaceable unit (LRU) grappling.

When the problem is overdetermined, it is possible to calibrate the sensor at the same time by adding the unknown calibration parameters to the state vector. In the above example, the focal length can potentially be resolved because there are four constraints.

9.2.4.3 Pose Tracking

This problem is known more classically as *motion estimation*. It can be advantageous to incorporate measurements of the relative motion of the robot when significant motion occurs between pose fixes. There are many ways to do this. One is to use redundant motion sensing like inertial or odometric sensing. Another is to use the velocities of features in image space to derive camera velocity. Another is to use changes in feature positions to determine changes in camera pose. These last two options are discussed below.

9.2.4.3.1 Feature Velocities. Consider the problem of computing camera velocity from feature velocity. We simply linearize Equation 9.14 with respect to sensor motion:

$$\Delta \underline{x}_k = H(\underline{\rho}, \underline{X}_k) \Delta \underline{\rho} \quad (9.28)$$

If we want this result in terms of velocities, we divide by a small Δt and pass to the limit to produce:

$$\dot{\underline{x}}_k = H(\underline{x}, \underline{\rho}, \underline{Z}) \dot{\underline{\rho}} \quad (9.29)$$

If there are enough feature velocities, the sensor velocity can be computed by nonlinear least squares. In the most general case, both prediction and correspondence calculations are necessary and the pose tracking loop takes the form of Figure 9.34:

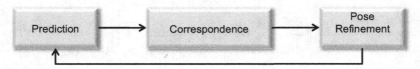

Figure 9.34 Pose Tracking. Features are predicted, possibly based on secondary estimates of motion, and then corresponding features are passed to a pose refinement algorithm that refines the estimate of intervening motion.

A similar technique can be used to relate signal rates to camera velocity. Consider:

$$\Delta \underline{z}(\underline{x}) = H(\underline{x}, \underline{\rho}, \underline{Z})\Delta\underline{\rho} \Rightarrow \dot{\underline{z}}(\underline{x}) = H(\underline{x}, \underline{\rho}, \underline{Z})\dot{\underline{\rho}}$$

9.2.4.3.2 Example: Making and Tracking Floor Mosaics with Odometry Aiding.
This example presents a case where feature tracking is accomplished with the aid of wheel odometry based on [14]. A vehicle has a camera underneath that is only 10 cm above the floor looking straight down. The geometry is ideal in the sense that the surface is both normal and of known distance from the camera. The lighting is ideal because it can be totally controlled. However, a wide field of view is necessary to image a large area from so close to the floor, so the imagery must be corrected for distortion. This is done by imaging a rectangular grid and then solving for a quadratic distortion function which best aligns the corners in the real image with those in the ideal image (Figure 9.35). The corners are found using normalized cross-correlation.

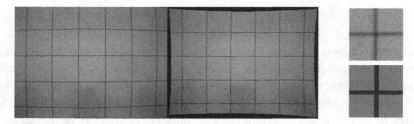

Figure 9.35 Lens Distortion Rectification. (Left) An original distorted image. (Center) Its corrected version. (Right) A block of pixels centered at line intersection and the correlation template used to find it. Line are approximately 1 pixel wide.

Each image covers a rectangular area on the floor of roughly 20 cm on each side. The objective is to rapidly construct a linear mosaic as the vehicle drives and to ultimately construct a globally consistent mosaic that can be used as a map. Vehicle odometry is also used to measure the motion between images. The odometry data is not accurate enough to align images to an accuracy of a pixel, so the relative pose between each two consecutive images is refined by conducting a local search in image coordinates to align the video signals.

Each image is searched for point features of high texture in the region of overlap. For each feature, the alignment algorithm searches a small rectangular window at the predicted position in the next image for the point of highest correlation. Then the image-to-image pose is refined by finding the pose error that best explains the observed displacements between nominal and measured positions of the features (Figure 9.36).

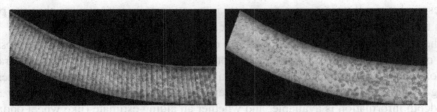

Figure 9.36 1D Image Mosaicking. The 50 or so images left were joined into a single image using point registration.

The alignment (Figure 9.37) is accomplished by writing equations based on the compound-left pose Jacobian for each pair of corresponding features. Only the position components of the pose Jacobian are used because the odometry orientation is good enough for alignment and small orientation errors are resolved by feature displacements:

$$\begin{bmatrix} \Delta a_k^i \\ \Delta b_k^i \end{bmatrix} = \begin{bmatrix} 1 & 0 & -(b_k^i - b_j^i) \\ 0 & 1 & (a_k^i - a_j^i) \end{bmatrix} \begin{bmatrix} \Delta a_j^i \\ \Delta b_j^i \end{bmatrix} \qquad (9.30)$$

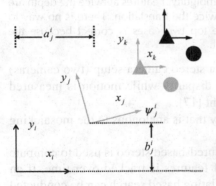

Figure 9.37 Feature Registration in 2D. The light triangle feature fixed to frame k needs to be moved a small amount in order to make it coincident with the dark triangle. The same alignment is needed for the circles. The pose of frame j must be adjusted with respect to frame i to accomplish the alignment.

The left side of each equation is derived from the positions of correlation surface peaks and a set of two or more such equations is inverted using the left pseudoinverse to compute the alignment pose. The rows of the Jacobian are slightly different for each feature due to the appearance of a_k^i and b_k^i.

When making a mosaic, images must overlap, so the vehicle speed is limited. At 10 Hz update rates the speed is limited to about 1/2 an image width in 1/10 second, or 1 m/sec. The value of using odometry to assist in tracking position is more obvious when tracking an existing mosaic. In that case, many features can be tracked successfully by searching uncertainty regions of 10 pixels of size 1cm at 10 Hz. If the odometry error is 1% of distance, that means the vehicle can move 10 m in 1/10 second or 100 m/sec and still track the mosaic! Without odometry, the maximum speed would be 1 m/sec.

9.2.4.3.3 Example: Visual Odometry. The foundation of visual odometry is the generation of correspondences between sequences of sensor readings as the vehicle (camera) changes position. Then, the system solves for the motion that explains the correspondences. If necessary, a secondary integration process computes absolute pose from the sequence of relative pose estimates.

The last example used a simplified form of visual odometry to construct the mosaic. In a more general case, the camera cannot be arranged so favorably and interframe motion must be determined from views of a 3D scene. There are several approaches to doing so. Two important distinctions that separate various approaches are whether feature depth information is available, and whether an aiding estimate (like wheel odometry in the mosaicking example) is available.

For projective sensors in general, the scale of translational pose increments cannot be determined without extra information (Figure 9.38).

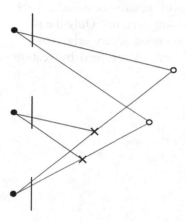

Figure 9.38 Scale Ambiguity in Projective Visual Odometry. The loss of depth information in projective sensing leads to a scale ambiguity. Features at twice the depth are consistent with twice the translation. There is no way to tell which of the top two cases is correct because the image is identical.

In mobile robot applications, it is typical to use a stereo camera setup (two cameras) so that depth can be measured from (left-right) disparity while motion is measured from motion-induced frame to frame displacement [17].

A straightforward approach to visual odometry that is analogous to the mosaicking case is exemplified by (Figure 9.39).

For every pair of frames that is generated, featured-based stereo is used to compute the depth of the features and then the motion of features is tracked over time. If an intermediate motion estimate is available, a correlation based search can be conducted near the predicted locations of features in each new frame. If not, blocks of pixels around each feature location can be compared using correlation or pixel differences to find a match. In either case, once correspondences are available, the remaining problem is one of pose refinement. Higher accuracy is likely to be obtained by forming residuals in image space rather than trying to align the 3D points computed from stereo.

Nominally, the problem can be formulated in terms of a small change in the pose (Equation 9.28):

$$\Delta \underline{x}_k = H(\underline{\rho}, \underline{X}_k)\Delta\underline{\rho}$$

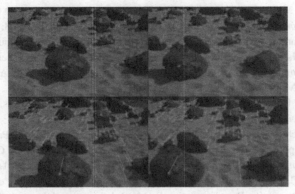

Figure 9.39 Visual Odometry. Tracking feature motion in image space can produce camera motion in the scene as a by-product. (Top Left) Detected features in left camera, (Top Right) Detected features in right camera. (Bottom Left) Feature displacement in left camera. (Bottom Right) Feature displacement in right camera. Figure from [18].

However, higher accuracy will be achieved by iterating until a (numerically) minimum residual relative pose is found. The locations of the same feature in each two images can be expressed as:

$$\underline{x}_{k1} = \underline{h}(\underline{\rho}_1, \underline{X}_k)$$
$$\underline{x}_{k2} = \underline{h}(\underline{\rho}_2, \underline{X}_k)$$

The reprojection error can be formulated as a function of the relative pose:

$$\underline{r}_{12}(\underline{\rho}_2^1, \underline{X}_k) = \underline{x}_{k2} - \underline{x}_{k2} = \underline{h}_{12}(\underline{\rho}_2^1, \underline{X}_k)$$

If not, we can regard $\underline{\rho}_1$ as known and solve for $\underline{\rho}_2$:

$$\underline{r}_{12}(\underline{\rho}_2, \underline{X}_k) = \underline{x}_{k2} - \underline{x}_{k2} = \underline{h}_{12}(\underline{\rho}_2, \underline{X}_k)$$

In either case, we can square this residual to form the objective function, linearize, and iterate until convergence.

9.2.5 References and Further Reading

9.2.5.1 Books

Blake and Szeliski are good sources for the mathematics of pose recovery and other forms of vision based localization.

[5] Andrew Blake and Michael Isard, *Active Contours,* Springer, 1998.
[6] R. Szeliski, *Computer Vision, Algorithms and Applications,* Springer, 2011.

9.2.5.2 Papers

These papers have been referenced in the text.

[7] P. Besl and N. McKay, A Method of Registration of 3-D Shapes, IEEE *Transactions on Pattern Analysis and Machine Intelligence,* Vol. 14, No. 2, pp. 239–256, 1992.

[8]   G. Blais, and M. Levine, Registering Multiview Range Data to Create 3D Computer Objects, *Transactions on Pattern Analysis and Machine Intelligence,* Vol.17, No. 8, 1995.

[9]   E. D. Dickmanns and A. Zapp. Autonomous High Speed Road Vehicle Guidance by Computer Vision. In R. Isermann, ed., Automatic Control-World Congress, 1987: Selected Papers from the 10th Triennial World Congress of the International Federation of Automatic Control, pp. 221–226, Munich, Germany, Pergamon, 1987.

[10] E. Duff and J. Roberts, Wall Following with Constrained Active Contours, in *Proceedings of Field and Service Robots,* 2003.

[11] Martin A. Fischler and Robert C. Bolles, Random Sample Consensus: A Paradigm for Model Fitting with Applications to Image Analysis and Automated Cartography, *Communications of the Association of Computing Machinery,* Vol. 24, pp. 381–339, June 1981.

[12] R. Haralick, C. Lee, K. Ottenberg, and M. Nolle. Review and Analysis of Solutions of the Three Point Perspective Pose Estimation Problem, *International Journal of Computer Vision,* Vol. 13, No. 3, pp. 331–356, 1994.

[13] A. Johnson and M. Hebert. Using Spin Images for Efficient Object Recognition in Cluttered 3D Scenes. *IEEE Transactions on Pattern Analysis and Machine Intelligence,* Vol. 21, No. 5, pp. 433–449, May 1999.

[14] A. Kelly, Mobile Robot Localization From Large Scale Appearance Mosaics, *International Journal of Robotics Research,* Vol. 19, No. 11, pp.1104–1125, 2000.

[15] K. C. Kluge and S. Lakshmanan, "A Deformable-Template Approach to Lane Detection," in *Proceedings of the Intelligence Vehicles Symposion,* Sept. 1995.

[16] B. Lucas, and T. Kanade, An Iterative Image Registration Technique with an Application to Stereo Vision, in *Proceedings of the International Conference on Artificial Intelligence,* pp. 674–679, 1981.

[17] David Nistér, Oleg Naroditsky, and James Bergen, Visual Odometry for Ground Vehicle Applications, *Journal of Field Robotics,* Vol. 23, No. 1, pp. 3–20, January 2006.

[18] C. F. Olsen, L. F. Matthies, M. Schoppers, and M. F. Maimone, Robust Stereo Ego-Motion for Long Distance Navigation, In *Proceedings of the Conference on Computer Vision and Pattern Recognition,* 2000.

[19] D.A. Pomerleau and T. Jochem, Rapidly Adapting Machine Vision for Automated Vehicle Steering, *IEEE Expert, Intelligent Systems and Their Applications,* Vol. 11, No. 2, Apr. 1996.

[20] T. Pilarski et. al., The Demeter System for Autonomous Harvesting, *Autonomous Robots,* Vol. 13, No. 1, pp. 9–20, 2002.

[21] H. Y. Shum and R. Szeliski, Construction of Panoramic Image Mosaics with Global and Local Alignment. *International Journal of Computer Vision,* Vol. 16, No. 1, pp. 63-84, 2000.

[22] J. S. Want and R. R. Knipling, Single Vehicle Roadway Departure Crashes: Problem Size Assessment and Statistical Description, *National Highway Traffic Safety Administration Technical Report,* DTNH-22-91-03121.

9.2.6 Exercises

9.2.6.1 Pose Sensitivity in Camera Based Object Localization

The Jacobian $\partial y_d^i / \partial \underline{\rho}_m^s$ computed in Section 9.2.4.2.2 contains a wealth of information about how to locate objects precisely with a camera. To see this, use the form of $\partial y_d^s / \partial \underline{\rho}_m^s$ that depends explicitly on the object yaw θ and multiply out the Jacobian for a single feature of coordinates $\underline{r}_d^m = \begin{bmatrix} 0 & L \end{bmatrix}$. Next, noting that $\Delta y_d^i / (f / c\alpha) = \Delta \alpha$ is the change in pixel position of the feature in the image, show that the sensitivity of pixel position to i) changes in depth is highest when the object spans the entire field of view of the camera, ii) changes in lateral position is inversely proportional to depth,

iii) changes in object orientation is least when the camera faces the object directly. Also, consider the question of how easy it is to distinguish rotation of the object from changes in depth.

9.3 Simultaneous Localization and Mapping

It may seem unlikely that it is possible to build a map and use it at the same time but, of course, all forms of visual tracking and odometry perform essentially this task. The most common name for this process in robotics is SLAM, for Simultaneous Localization And Mapping. A key event in SLAM is so-called *loop closure* – when something that has not been seen for a while comes back into view. When this happens, the measured innovation provides an opportunity to remove the error that has accumulated since the last time the place or object was seen. However, it may not be easy to determine if a loop has closed and if one has, it may be necessary to update substantial portions of the map. These two problems of updating portions of the map and recognizing when it is time to do so, are presented here.

9.3.1 Introduction

SLAM is akin to visual odometry because the robot uses old features to locate itself and then it uses its updated position to locate new features. It is not possible to determine absolute position from such an arrangement, but it is possible to use statistical modeling to **remove most of the inconsistency** between where a feature is predicted to be, based on measured vehicle motion, and where it now appears to be, based on sensor readings.

However, SLAM algorithms are more ambitious than visual odometry because the landmark and vehicle locations are being measured at the same time. SLAM also differs from motion estimation processes by the depth of its memory of what has been seen to date, and perhaps in the representation of the map produced. SLAM attempts to remember a map of substantially all of what has been seen and, to the extent possible, keep it all consistently positioned. This section will present two of the more straight forward approaches to the SLAM problem.

The measurement relationship $z_{pred} = \underline{h}(\underline{\rho}, \underline{Z})$ constitutes a field of measurement predictions over some space of poses. Even our knowledge of the Earth's magnetic and gravitational fields is a kind of map but we will restrict the presentation below to imagery. It is possible to distinguish map representations in terms of many important properties.

9.3.1.1 Repeatability

The most basic property of a navigation map is its capacity to associate poses with measurements so that a robot can map the measurements onto its pose. Provided the measurement model can be solved for ρ, a robot will be able to use it to navigate.

9.3.1.2 Continuity and Consistency

It is often important that a navigation map support the generation of predicted measurements that are continuous with respect to pose. If the measurement function is continuous, the robot can interpolate using the measurement Jacobian H and track its position continuously. Continuity would be violated in a map if it was constructed using only GPS and the solution jumped 20 meters in an instant while the map was being constructed. The resulting missing or overwritten data would make it difficult to track the map later on.

Maps also become discontinuous if dead reckoning error accumulates to the point where the same physical place can be encountered while mapping but be associated with two different poses. Such a map is often called *inconsistent* and achieving global consistency is a difficult problem. Consistency may not matter if the map is one-dimensional or tree-structured so that there is only one path between any two points. On the other hand, a robot can only range freely in a cyclic map if the map is sufficiently consistent.

9.3.1.3 Accuracy

Even a consistent map need not be everywhere accurate. A consistent map becomes accurate when it is distorted as necessary to force it to agree with some calibration reference for what the correct poses in the map are supposed to be. Accuracy may not matter *if the robot operates as a closed information system*. However, it becomes important when external data must be used and that data is positioned with respect to a different externally derived reference than the one that was used generate the map. A map that is consistent with a CAD drawing, or with guidepaths/ waypoints generated by another position estimation system, or with U.S Geological Survey digital terrain data, will permit the use of any useful data that was generated from that system.

9.3.1.4 Achieving Map Quality

The above aspects of map quality relate to data association on distinct levels. A map becomes *locally smooth* if sequential measurements can be adequately associated by aligning measurements. It becomes *globally consistent* if nonsequential measurements can be adequately associated.

9.3.2 Global Consistency in Cyclic Maps

All maps are constructed from data that is gathered sequentially while a mapping sensor moves through an environment. At times the area to be mapped is a large connected region of space like an open field or a room, and at other times the area to be mapped has a graph structure like a road network, rows in an orchard, or corridors in a building. Hierarchical approaches to resolving cycles in maps can construct maps on the scale of entire university campuses [26][33].

The techniques presented here can be used online or offline to enforce consistency and accuracy in navigation maps. They will work in all cases but it is particularly effective when the map has graph structure.

Suppose that a set of images are available and they are in a form for which simply putting them in the correct place would produce a useful map. They overlap each other and the goal is to align them all so they agree in all the regions of overlap. At least two aspects of this globally consistent mapping problem are important.

- Optimization. Residuals in overlap regions should be as small as possible. Zero residuals are probably not achievable due to distortion and feature localization error.
- Constraint. If cycles exist in the underlying pose network, they should close correctly to produce a consistent map.

There are at least two distinct approaches to solving this problem. If the problem is formulated in terms of the absolute poses of each image in some world frame, then the total residual of all image overlaps can be minimized and the number of unknowns is already minimum (one pose per image) so there is no need to impose additional constraints on them.

If the problem is formulated in terms of relative poses relating each image to its neighbors, then the same total residual can be minimized but there will possibly be more unknowns than the inherent degrees of freedom so additional constraints will need to be formulated. The additional constraints will be loop equations that require relative poses in a close loop to cancel.

9.3.2.1 Absolute Pose Formulation

Suppose that the vector $\underline{\rho}_m^w$ contains the pose describing where the image m is with respect to the world frame w. The positions $\underline{r}^w$ of features in the world frame can be predicted by Figure 9.40:

$$\underline{r}^w = T_m^w(\underline{\rho}_m^w)\underline{r}^m$$

$$\begin{bmatrix} x^w \\ y^w \\ 1 \end{bmatrix} = \begin{bmatrix} c\psi & -s\psi & a \\ s\psi & c\psi & b \\ 0 & 0 & 1 \end{bmatrix} \begin{bmatrix} x^m \\ y^m \\ 1 \end{bmatrix}$$

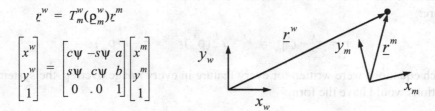

Figure 9.40 Feature Position From Absolute Pose. This diagram and formula give the position of a feature in the world frame.

The residuals in overlap regions can be generated from the differences between positions of the same feature predicted from the poses of two images that contain the feature:

$$\underline{r}^w\big|_m = T_m^w(\underline{\rho}_m^w)\underline{r}^m \qquad \underline{r}^w\big|_k = T_k^w(\underline{\rho}_k^w)\underline{r}^k$$
$$\underline{r} = \underline{r}^w\big|_m - \underline{r}^w\big|_k = T_m^w(\underline{\rho}_m^w)\underline{r}^m - T_k^w(\underline{x}_k^w)\underline{r}^k = h_m(\underline{\rho}_m^w) - h_k(\underline{\rho}_k^w) \tag{9.31}$$

If such equations were written for every feature in every image overlap, the system of equations would have the form:

$$\underline{r} = h_1(\underline{x}) - h_2(\underline{x}) = h(\underline{x}) \tag{9.32}$$

where, $\underline{x}$ contains the absolute (world relative) poses of all of the images that are to be merged into a consistent map. In practice, this set of equations is underconstrained by three degrees of freedom called the *gauge freedom*. As a result, the entire set of images can be moved rigidly in the plane without changing the observations. This issue is solved by fixing one image position and removing it from the unknowns. Otherwise the coefficient matrix is singular.

9.3.2.2 Relative Pose Formulation

Conversely, a formulation based on relative poses is also possible. Suppose that the vector $\underline{\rho}_m^k$ contains the pose describing where the origin of image m is with respect to the origin of image k. The positions of features in frame k corresponding to those in image m can be predicted by Figure 9.41:

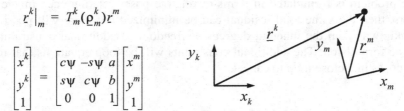

$$\underline{r}^k\big|_m = T_m^k(\underline{\rho}_m^k)\underline{r}^m$$

$$\begin{bmatrix} x^k \\ y^k \\ 1 \end{bmatrix} = \begin{bmatrix} c\psi & -s\psi & a \\ s\psi & c\psi & b \\ 0 & 0 & 1 \end{bmatrix} \begin{bmatrix} x^m \\ y^m \\ 1 \end{bmatrix}$$

Figure 9.41 Feature Position From Relative Pose. This diagram and formula give the position of a feature in the frame of some nearby image.

Again, the residuals in overlap regions can be generated from the differences between positions of the same feature predicted from the poses of two images that contain the feature:

$$\underline{r} = \underline{r}^k - \underline{r}^k\big|_m = \underline{r}^k - T_m^k(\underline{\rho}_m^k)\underline{r}^m = \underline{z} - h(\underline{\rho}_m^k)$$

If such equations were written for every feature in every image overlap, the system of equations would have the form:

$$\underline{r} = \underline{z} - h(\underline{x}) \tag{9.33}$$

where now, $\underline{x}$ contains the *relative poses* of all of the images to be merged into a consistent map. Both cases have now been reduced to the form of a measurement of a state vector that contains absolute or relative poses.

9.3.2.3 Unconstrained Optimization

A map is perfectly consistent when the residual is zero. It is most consistent when the residual is minimized. One way to formulate the minimum residual problem is as a nonlinear least squares problem:

$$minimize:_{\underline{x}} \qquad f(\underline{x}) = \frac{1}{2}\underline{r}(\underline{x})^T\underline{r}(\underline{x}) \tag{9.34}$$

The desired Jacobian is the one used in the linearized observer:

$$\Delta\underline{r} = H\Delta\underline{x} \tag{9.35}$$

Where $\underline{r}$ is the composite vector of residuals in all overlap residuals, and $\Delta \underline{x}$ will be the changes in the composite state vector for all of the images. H is then the composite Jacobian of the entire system. In an ambitious case, the vector $\Delta \underline{x}$ can have 10,000 elements in it and $\Delta \underline{z}$ can be even larger.

For this particular problem, a true minimum may not be worth the computational effort, and it would be acceptable to assume small residuals and "solve" Equation 9.35 with a single iteration of the left pseudoinverse where we attempt to explain all of the residual with an error in the state vector:

$$\underline{r} = H\Delta \underline{x} \tag{9.36}$$

9.3.2.4 Constraint Satisfaction with Relative Poses

Whereas absolute poses are underconstrained unless one pose is removed, a consistency issue is likely to arise if relative poses are used due to the omission of many more constraints. There are R distinct relative poses relating distinct pairs of two images chosen from a set of n, where:

$$R = \sum_i i = 1 + 2 + \dots + n = \frac{n(n-1)}{2}$$

Hence, it is likely that the state vector will become inconsistent if the state vector contains more than $n-1$ relative poses. Such a system would be underconstrained because all of the relative poses are not independent.

There are natural consistency constraints that **should** be imposed on the elements of the state vector. These are of the form:

$$\underline{g}(\underline{x}) = \underline{b} \tag{9.37}$$

The formulation of these constraints relates to loop closure as presented below. These constraints are entirely separate from the feature residual. Given distortion and feature localization error, it is not guaranteed that the minimum feature residual will produce a state vector that satisfies these constraints – unless they are enforced explicitly as hard constraints.

9.3.2.4.1 Loop Constraints: Sparse Case. Most mobile robot mapping problems generate sparse constraints on relative poses due to limited sensor range and/or environmental occlusion (Figure 9.42). Constraints can only be generated for the objects that are common in the views from two locations, so limited range means less objects can be common to two views. Constraint equations are also needed when loops close – when an object is common to two views separated in time by a long intervening motion.

In sparse environments, there are relatively few constraint equations and a highly efficient formulation is possible if relative poses are used. By using relative poses to express the geometry, we can permit a few extra (redundant) degrees of freedom and separately express constraints on them with something like equation Equation 9.37.

9.3.2.4.2 Warping for Constraint Enforcement. It is fundamental to consistent mapping that a large amount of previous decisions need to be reconsidered to remove the effects of localization drift. The problem is somewhat easier if we think in terms of

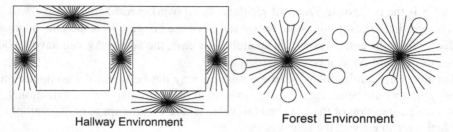

Figure 9.42 Sparsity. Limited sensor range and environmental occlusion both lead to sparse constraint systems. Lidars have limited range and neither cameras nor lidars can see through objects.

relative poses. Suppose we have n poses that relate each of $n + 1$ frames in an ordered sequence to its predecessor.

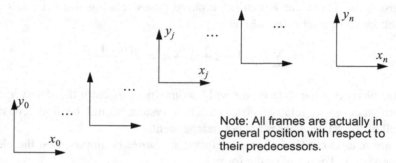

Note: All frames are actually in general position with respect to their predecessors.

Figure 9.43 Setup for Pose Sequence Warping. A number of sequential relative poses compound to produce some overall relative pose between frames 0 and n.

Suppose further that the relationship of the first frame with respect to the last has just been determined to be slightly wrong. The pose sequence warping problem is to change **all** of the intermediate poses in order to fix the compound pose ρ_n^0. We need an expression for how small changes in every one of the degrees of freedom affects the pose of the last frame with respect to the first.

We can write the total differential in terms of the compound-inner pose Jacobian introduced in Chapter 2.

$$\Delta \underline{\rho}_n^0 = \begin{bmatrix} \dfrac{\partial \underline{r}_n^0}{\partial \underline{\rho}_1^0} & \cdots & \dfrac{\partial \underline{r}_n^0}{\partial \underline{\rho}_n^{n-1}} \end{bmatrix} \begin{bmatrix} \Delta \underline{\rho}_1^0 \\ \cdots \\ \Delta \underline{\rho}_n^{n-1} \end{bmatrix} \qquad (9.38)$$

This is an underdetermined system that can be solved with the right pseudoinverse:

$$\Delta \underline{\rho} = J^T [J J^T]^{-1} \Delta \underline{\rho}_n^0 \qquad (9.39)$$

This formulation can be used to force a map to agree with some external calibration standard for where things are supposed to be. A special case of this is most relevant.

When the pose $\underline{\rho}_n^0$ is associated with a loop that is supposed to close, we have a constraint which is something like:

$$\underline{\rho}_1^0 * \underline{\rho}_2^1 \cdots \underline{\rho}_n^{n-1} * \underline{\rho}_0^n = \underline{0} \tag{9.40}$$

Where $\underline{0}$ denotes the identity pose (all of whose elements are zero). For an arbitrary pose $\underline{\rho}$, the pose composition with the identity pose produces the original pose:

$$\underline{\rho} * \underline{0} = \underline{\rho} \tag{9.41}$$

Here, the "*" operator denotes pose composition. What we really mean by this is:

$$T_1^0 T_2^1 \cdots T_n^{n-1} T_0^n = I \tag{9.42}$$

This is of the form of equation Equation 9.37. If multiple loops are to be closed, the equations for all loops can be solved simultaneously although it is often feasible to close one at a time.

In many cases, the original data is so locally smooth that enforcing loop closure is all that is necessary – there is no need to minimize the map residual. On the other hand, the extra computation required for a minimum residual is trivial for large sparse problems.

9.3.2.5 Constrained Optimization

It is possible to perform both optimization and constraint enforcement at the same time [34]. The problem is formulated as simultaneously satisfying both Equation 9.34 and Equation 9.37:

$$\begin{aligned} \textit{minimize:} \quad & f(\underline{x}) = \frac{1}{2} r(\underline{x})^T r(\underline{x}) \\ \textit{subject to:} \quad & \underline{c}(\underline{x}) = \underline{b} \end{aligned} \tag{9.43}$$

Conversely, the residual $z(\underline{x}) = \underline{b} - \underline{c}(\underline{x})$ can be added to the end of the feature residual $f(\underline{x})$ and perhaps weighted in some way so that the solution will try to reduce the constraint residual as well. This would be a *penalty function* approach to the problem.

9.3.2.6 Example: Floor Imagery Mosaics as Maps

An AGV guidance system has been designed based on consistent mosaics of floor imagery. The mechanism for aligning sequentially acquired images was presented earlier in Chapter 9. When the guidepaths followed by the mapping vehicle contain cycles, the loops do not close correctly due to odometry error accumulation. However using the techniques presented above, it is possible to mosaic thousands of images into one consistent map (Figure 9.44).

9.3.2.7 Example: Large Scale Lidar Maps

Lidar scan matching is a very effective technique for computing short term motion and for construction of maps of walls of buildings [31]. A roving kiosk was installed

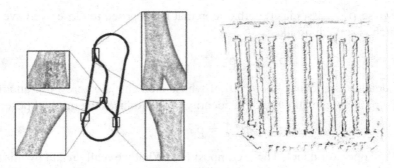

Figure 9.44 Globally Consistent Image Networks. (Left) Thousands of images are mosaicked into one consistent picture. Only three loop constraints are involved. (Right) 10,000 lidar images have been rendered globally consistent in a few seconds of computation. Many more loops had to be closed.

in a grocery store in order to help customers find items. It navigates based on a lidar map of the store produced from about 10,000 images. Lidar data can generate large numbers of overlaps and very dense coefficient matrices. However, the important loops are those that occur at the ends of aisles. Sequential images were aligned and only the major loops resolved to produce the result in Figure 9.44.

9.3.3 Revisiting

The techniques of the previous section can be used to construct an online simultaneous localization and mapping system provided the system can recognize online that it has returned to a position that was visited earlier. This is called the *revisiting problem* and it is central to SLAM. Effective techniques for this problem have been developed in recent years. This section will summarize two of them.

9.3.3.1 Issues

The revisiting problem has a strong connection to *unsupervised* object recognition because there is no training phase to get the system started. Many challenges are related to those of recognition in general. One of the challenges is the reduction of the data associated with any place to a feature signature that is both small enough to be compared rapidly and distinct enough to permit reliable recognition. If place recognition can be performed offline, this tradeoff is less severe.

Solutions potentially have to check every image against every historical image to see if there is a match, so the problem becomes more difficult as the scale over which matches are required increases. Position estimates and their uncertainty can be used to reduce the search for a match.

If multiple places actually look the same (ambiguity), the problem difficulty is increased by another factor. In this case, it may be necessary to match entire submaps of neighborhoods if one image is not unique enough when compared with the place signatures.

The use of invariant features is as important to this problem as it is to recognition in general. In video, crossing an intersection in any of the four cardinal directions may each produce images of entirely different sides of buildings in a forward camera. Omnidirectional sensing can help in this case because then, at least, it is possible to see in all directions while moving in only one.

9.3.3.2 Example Revisting from Lidar

In indoor scenes, a 2D representation of the environment is adequate for many purposes and planar lidar sensors are effective for sensing objects. A horizontal lidar can be used to sense the walls and furniture to build a map. As the robot moves, the detection that a portion of the scene in view was seen before can be performed by regularly comparing recent data to the map that was constructed earlier. Suppose the map is represented as a certainty grid. This is an array of cells $m(i, j)$, which store the probability that the cell is occupied by an object that reflects lidar energy.

A straightforward way to detect a revisit is to convert a few recent scans to a local map $l(i, j)$ and to correlate [29] this local map with the permanent map as it is moved throughout the region of pose uncertainty (see Figure 9.45). An approximation to the probability of a match, for some scale factor k is:

$$p(\rho|l, m) = k \sum_{i \in I} \sum_{j \in J} l[\rho, i, j] m[i, j]$$

There are many mechanisms available to accelerate the process including exploiting special processor instructions for image correlation and the use of log probability to convert the products of probability to a sum. If a very high correlation is computed, a lidar scan matching calculation can be used to compute a refined estimate of the pose that closes the detected loop in the pose network.

In outdoor settings, loops can be much larger and correlation becomes less and less feasible as the pose uncertainty grows with increased loop size. In this case, a feature based approach is more suitable than the signal matching approach above. Lidar data has the property that although sampling of geometry depends on range, the geometry itself is range independent. Hence, descriptions of local shape are good candidates for viewpoint-invariant features.

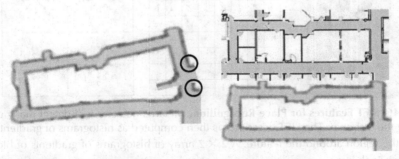

Figure 9.45 Certainty Grid Correlation to Detect Loop Closure. (Left) When the robot returns to the place where it started, a correlation of the recent data with the map will produce a match. (Right) Floor plan and correct map. Figure inspired by [28].

One successful approach has been shown to work well on the scale of tens of kilometers [25]. Lidar scans are first processed to find features called *keypoints,* which can be found repeatably when the same region is viewed from somewhat different positions. For example, points of high curvature are the outdoor equivalent of corners in a room. A weighted (by distance from the keypoint) histogram is computed of the surface normals of all points in the vicinity of each keypoint in order to extract its orientation as the most common orientation of nearby normals.

Keypoints therefore have a position and orientation that can be extracted repeatably from scans, so they establish a local coordinate system. Once a keypoint is found, a square region around it is converted to a grid and all moments up to second order are computed for the points that fall in each grid cell. It is these moments that are compared to the keypoint descriptors of incoming scans to try to detect a loop closure.

9.3.3.3 Example: Revisiting from Video

Although video data typically contains much more information than range data, recognition in video is also more difficult in several ways. Camera imagery suffers from the dependence of apparent size on range to the object, from shape on perspective projection, and from intensity on ambient lighting.

Nonetheless, in recent years, much progress has occurred toward solving the problem of designing features that are invariant to scale, to rotation, and to illumination. The *Scale Invariant Feature Transform* (SIFT) is a recent example [30]. Imagery is reduced to a set of most salient features by first finding the locations and orientations of keypoints and then extracting a descriptor vector from the local neighborhood.

Mobile robots often do not need all of the invariant properties of SIFT because orientation is often essentially fixed and range to features may not vary much from visit to visit. A very effective approach is to locate keypoints with a Harris corner detector [27] and then use the SIFT descriptor vector to encode the signal content. The SIFT descriptor is computed as orientation histograms (eight orientations per histogram) for a $k \times k$ array of blocks of $n \times n$ pixels surrounding the feature ($k = 2$ and $n = 4$ in Figure 9.46). When $k = 4$ this gives a feature vector that is $16 \times 8 = 128$ numbers long

 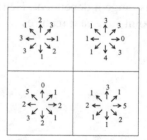

Figure 9.46 SIFT Features for Place Recognition. A Harris detector will detect many corners including the 4 shown. The SIFT descriptor is then computed as histograms of gradient orientation in the region around the feature. A 2 × 2 array of histograms of gradients of blocks of 4 × 4 pixels is shown.

9.3.4 EKF SLAM For Discrete Landmarks

Here we consider the case of discrete landmarks rather than imagery. This section will present a point landmark, extended Kalman filter formulation of SLAM [32]. It is only possible to treat this subject so briefly here because so much has been presented earlier by way of preparation. For generality, we will assume that the sensors can measure both bearing and range to landmark but bearing-only or range-only versions can be developed very similarly. The following presentation picks up where Section 5.3.4.6 of Chapter 5 leaves off.

9.3.4.1 System Model

The system model is similar to what we have seen so far except that *the state vector is augmented to include the landmarks*:

$$\underline{x} = \begin{bmatrix} x & y & \theta & v & \omega & x_1 & y_1 & \dots & x_n & y_n \end{bmatrix}^T \tag{9.44}$$

Let the state vector be partitioned into a vehicle component and a landmark component thus:

$$\underline{x} = \begin{bmatrix} \underline{x}_v^T & \underline{x}_L^T \end{bmatrix}^T \tag{9.45}$$

The subscripts v and L will be used for associated matrices in the following. The system dynamics are then augmented with equations that express the fact that the landmarks are fixed:

$$\dot{\underline{x}}_L = \frac{d}{dt} \left(\begin{bmatrix} x_1 & y_1 & \dots & x_n & y_n \end{bmatrix} \right)^T = \underline{0} \tag{9.46}$$

The transition matrix, derived from the above, includes additional ones on the diagonal to express that the landmarks are stationary. Clearly it would be possible to replace the stationary landmarks with moving objects and track their predicted motions here instead.

9.3.4.2 State Covariance Propagation

Strictly speaking, it is not necessary for the landmark uncertainties to increase with time. A constant small process noise can be placed in the P matrix rather than the Q matrix because elements in Q are added to P every cycle. However, if there are biases in the system there may also be practical reasons to place a small growth factor in Q. The covariance update can be accomplished very efficiently – and this is very important when the number of landmarks is large. The transition matrix is:

$$\Phi = \begin{bmatrix} \Phi_{vv} & 0 \\ 0 & I \end{bmatrix} \tag{9.47}$$

Partitioning similarly, the state covariance can be written as:

$$P = \begin{bmatrix} P_{vv} & P_{vL} \\ P_{Lv} & P_{LL} \end{bmatrix} \tag{9.48}$$

Recall the state covariance update equation:

$$P_{k+1}^- = \Phi_k P_k \Phi_k^T + \Gamma_k Q_k \Gamma_k^T \tag{9.49}$$

The first term in Equation 9.49 is therefore:

$$\Phi_k P_k \Phi_k^T = \begin{bmatrix} \Phi_{vv} & 0 \\ 0 & I \end{bmatrix} \begin{bmatrix} P_{vv} & P_{vL} \\ P_{Lv} & P_{LL} \end{bmatrix} \begin{bmatrix} \Phi_{vv}^T & 0 \\ 0 & I \end{bmatrix} = \begin{bmatrix} \Phi_{vv} P_{vv} \Phi_{vv}^T & \Phi_{vv} P_{vL} I \\ I P_{Lv} \Phi_{vv}^T & I P_{LL} I \end{bmatrix} \tag{9.50}$$

So that the individual elements are:

$$\begin{array}{cc} P_{vv} = \Phi_{vv} P_{vv} \Phi_{vv}^T & P_{vL} = \Phi_{vv} P_{vL} \\ (n \times n)\,(n \times n)\,(n \times n)\,(n \times n) & (n \times m)\,(n \times n)\,(n \times m) \end{array}$$

When the number of landmarks is large, this partitioned form can be orders of magnitude more efficient than Equation 9.49.

The second term in the process noise distribution is partitioned as:

$$\Gamma = \begin{bmatrix} \Gamma_{vv} & 0 \\ 0 & I \end{bmatrix}$$

The process noise is:

$$Q = \begin{bmatrix} Q_{vv} & 0 \\ 0 & 0 \end{bmatrix}$$

The second term in Equation 9.49 is:

$$\Gamma_k Q_k \Gamma_k^T = \begin{bmatrix} \Gamma_{vv} & 0 \\ 0 & I \end{bmatrix} \begin{bmatrix} Q_{vv} & 0 \\ 0 & 0 \end{bmatrix} \begin{bmatrix} \Gamma_{vv}^T & 0 \\ 0 & I \end{bmatrix} = \begin{bmatrix} \Gamma_{vv} Q_{vv} \Gamma_{vv}^T & 0 \\ 0 & 0 \end{bmatrix}$$

This calculation is entirely independent of the number of landmarks. The complete partitioned state covariance update equation is therefore:

$$\begin{aligned} P_{vv} &= \Phi_{vv} P_{vv} \Phi_{vv}^T + \Gamma_{vv} Q_{vv} \Gamma_{vv}^T \\ P_{vL} &= \Phi_{vv} P_{vL} \end{aligned} \tag{9.51}$$

9.3.4.3 Measurement Model

The measurement model was provided in Chapter 5, but it is repeated here for convenience:

$$\underline{r}_d^s = T_b^s * T_w^b(\underline{\rho}_b^w) * T_m^w(\underline{r}_m^w) * \underline{r}_d^m$$

$$z_{sen} = f(\underline{r}_d^s) = \begin{bmatrix} \mathrm{atan}(y_d^s / x_d^s) \\ \sqrt{(x_d^s)^2 + (y_d^s)^2} \end{bmatrix}$$

$$H_x^z = \left(\frac{\partial z}{\partial \underline{\rho}_d^s}\right)\left(\frac{\partial \underline{\rho}_d^s}{\partial \underline{\rho}_d^b}\right)\left(\frac{\partial \underline{\rho}_d^b}{\partial \underline{\rho}_b^w}\right) = H_{sd}^z H_{bd}^{sd} H_x^{bd} \tag{9.52}$$

$$H_{wm}^z = \left(\frac{\partial z}{\partial \underline{\rho}_d^s}\right)\left(\frac{\partial \underline{\rho}_d^s}{\partial \underline{\rho}_d^b}\right)\left(\frac{\partial \underline{\rho}_d^b}{\partial \underline{\rho}_d^w}\right)\left(\frac{\partial \underline{\rho}_d^w}{\partial \underline{\rho}_m^w}\right) = H_{sd}^z H_{bd}^{sd} H_{wd}^{bd} H_{wm}^{wd}$$

9.3.4.4 Efficient Implementation

In SLAM, it is common to observe only one or a few of perhaps hundreds of landmarks in one frame of data. Partitioning can again make the processing much more efficient.

9.3.4.4.1 Prediction Uncertainty. The Kalman gain equation for an EKF is again:

$$K_k = P_k^- H_k^T [H_k P_k^- H_k^T + R_k]^{-1}$$

Let a single measurement arrive for integration with the state estimate. Then, the R matrix is a scalar:

$$R = [r]$$

Let the measurement project onto a a few states with nonzero coefficients. The uncertainty of the predicted measurement is:

$$H_k P_k^- H_k^T$$

For example, suppose there are two nonzero elements in H and rewrite it as the sum of two matrices that project onto one state each:

$$H = H_1 + H_2$$

Then, the uncertainty is:

$$(H_1 + H_2) P_k^- (H_1 + H_2)^T = H_1 P_k^- H_1^T + H_2 P_k^- H_1^T + H_1 P_k^- H_2^T + H_2 P_k^- H_2^T$$

Due to the symmetry of P, the second and third terms are mutual transposes. This result implies that there are four component matrices to the covariance update that have very simple forms. Assuming scalar measurements, if the H_1 matrix is nonzero in the s element and the H_2 matrix is nonzero in the t element, then these four expressions are the scalars:

$$H_1 P_k^- H_1^T = P_{ss}$$
$$H_2 P_k^- H_1^T = H_1 P_k^- H_2^T = P_{st}$$
$$H_1 P_k^- H_1^T = P_{tt}$$

In a more general case of m nonzero coefficients there will be m diagonal elements of P and $m(m-1)$ off diagonal elements (with coefficients of 2) added for a total cost of m^2.

This computation compares favorably with the straightforward application of matrix multiplication. If there are n elements in the state vector, then $P_k^- H_k^T$ generates a column vector in n^2 operations and the product $H_k P_k^- H_k^T$ requires n more operations, for a total of $n(n+1)$ operations. If $m \ll n$ the above technique may be worth the effort.

9.3.4.4.2 Kalman Gain. Computing the Kalman gain from the above result requires the computation of:

$$P_k^- H_k^T = P_k^- (H_1 + H_2)^T$$

Based on the earlier analysis, this computation requires the addition of the sth and tth columns of P_k^- which is an order n operation. For m nonzero coefficients, the cost is mn. A straightforward matrix multiplication would require n^2 operations.

9.3.4.4.3 Uncertainty Propagation. The matrix uncertainty propagation requires the computation of $K(HP)$. If there are m nonzero elements of H, the product HP is a row vector that can be evaluated in mn operations (by adding the relevant m rows of P) rather than n^2. Then, the product $K(HP)$ is an outer product that requires n^2 operations on the assumption both vectors are fully populated.

The final step is to compute $P = P - K(HP)$ which requires n^2 operations unless we have an explicit list of the nonzero elements in $K(HP)$. Such a list of elements (i, j) is those pairs for which K_i and $(HP)_j$ are both nonzero. Both vectors are derived from sums of rows or columns of P so there will be no nonzero elements unless there are uncorrelated states.

9.3.5 Example: Autosurveying of Laser Reflectors

This section presents some pragmatic issues that arise generally in the context of a particular application of SLAM. In its most general form, point landmark SLAM must detect landmarks as well as track them. Depending on the dimension of the measurement vector, one or two measurements of a new landmark will be necessary to generate an estimate of its position, and it may be advisable to observe it several more times to make sure.

Factory AGVs often use laser guidance systems based on deliberately installed reflectors used as landmarks. The reflectors may be presurveyed using a device called a *total station* or some other means but generally speaking surveying is an expense that the factory would rather avoid. It turns out that given accurate positions of two landmarks, the rest can be determined automatically to cm precision using SLAM.

It is possible to drive the robot around in a factory and use the laser guidance system itself to survey the reflector positions. We will assume that the number and approximate location of landmarks is known beforehand.

9.3.5.1 Initialization

SLAM has the **capacity to measure the shape** of the landmark constellation, but not the absolute location of the landmarks in space. It can be shown that the uncertainty of the landmarks in the produced map is bounded from below by the uncertainty of the initial conditions. In other words, the map can never be located better than the error in the initial position of the robot.

There are several ways to manage this situation. One is to use the initial location of the robot as the origin. This may not be feasible when everything else in the factory is known in a building-fixed frame of reference. Alternatively, if three strong constraints can be extracted from the presurveyed landmark positions, the rest of the map can be determined relatively accurately. If such constraints are not available, it can be useful to adjust the landmark uncertainties to establish any two as the origin and the x axis (assuming the distance between them can be measured accurately) and then locate all the others with respect to them. This is what was done for the case shown in Figure 9.47.

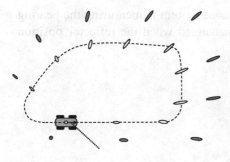

Figure 9.47 Error correlation in SLAM. In bearing-only SLAM, depth to landmarks is not measured so range localization is poor. When the robot gets near landmarks, its downrange uncertainty takes on the character of the nearby landmarks. Pose error and landmark error increase with range from the initial position.

When two landmarks are considered known, the correlations developed in the P matrix can become directly visible as shown. In effect, the uncertainty of each landmark is the same as that of the robot when it was seen, with a slight increase in uncertainty along the line to the origin where the robot position was known very accurately due to sighting two well-known landmarks.

9.3.5.2 Data Association

In the general case, and especially when bearings are the only observations, it can become difficult to ascertain the reflector that is responsible when a return is received. Reasonableness tests on measurement association should include whether the reflective side of a hypothesized landmark is facing the robot or not but this check will not be enough. Any two reflectors define a line between them and the robot may eventually end up on that line.

Uncertainty ellipses that overlap when projected onto the sensor space (bearing) may make it impossible to associate any readings unambiguously, and hence impossible to locate the landmark Figure 9.48.

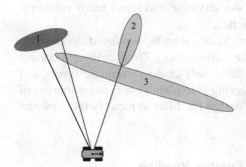

Figure 9.48 Ellipse Occlusion. Landmark 2 above will not to be localized until the uncertainty in the position of landmark 3 is reduced.

However, the validation gate technique discussed in Chapter 5 is very effective at resolving ambiguity or determining when it cannot be resolved. In the latter case the measurement is simply ignored.

9.3.5.3 View Conditioning

For bearing-only sensors, when a reflector is viewed over a narrow range of viewing angles, its position along the (average) direction of the laser cannot be resolved well. However, the lack of a precise position along the laser does not negatively affect the robot pose in these cases because the laser guidance system is measuring the bearing to the reflector and the bearing is relatively unchanged when the reflector position varies along the line of the laser (Figure 9.48).

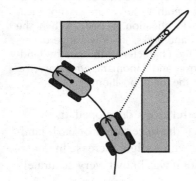

Figure 9.49 Poor View Conditioning. If the angular span of all vehicle positions as viewed form the landmark is small, the capacity to localize it accurately is reduced.

In other words the same insensitivity that makes it difficult to determine landmark position in a certain direction also makes the robot position insensitive to it. These two aspects of sensitivity are two sides of the same coin. Only when the bearing to a reflector of incorrect depth is observed over a large change in view angle can the depth be determined well.

9.3.5.4 Brittleness

Data association is the Achilles heel of the SLAM Kalman filter. The entire algorithm can be likened to a house of cards because one incorrect positive association has great potential to cause divergence. However, false negatives (not using data that could have been used) is much less of a problem when observations are engineered to be frequent, so a practical system can afford to be conservative and reject many measurements, and thereby become very robust in practice.

Recall that the errors in Kalman filters are assumed to be *unbiased*. Systematic errors of any significant size can cause filter divergence. Time delays, incorrect dimensions, wheel radii, and many other effects will cause systematic errors and therefore bias. Part of the art of system engineering is to identify the major sources of such errors are eliminate them beforehand or design the filter to identify them as part of its operation.

9.3.6 References and Further Reading

9.3.6.1 Books

Leonard is perhaps the earliest book on robotic mapping – concentrating on the use of sonar sensing. Castellanos is a more recent source based on more contemporary laser and camera sensing.

[23] José A. Castellanos and Juan D. Tardós, *Mobile Robot Localization and Map Building: A Multisensor Fusion Approach,* Kluwer, 1999.
[24] John J. Leonard and Hugh F. Durrant-Whyte, *Directed Sonar Sensing for Mobile Robot Navigation,* Springer, 1992.

9.3.6.2 Papers

These papers have been referenced in the text.

[25] M. Bosse and R. Zlot, Keypoint Design and Evaluation for Place Recognition in 2D Lidar Maps, in *Robotics: Science and Systems Conference, Inside Data Association Workshop,* 2008.

[26] M Bosse, Paul Newman, John Leonard, and Seth Teller, Simultaneous Localization and Map Building in Large-Scale Cyclic Environments Using the Atlas Framework, *International Journal of Robotics Research,* Vol. 23, No. 12, pp. 1113–1139, Dec. 2004.

[27] M. Cummins and P. Newman, Probabilistic Appearance Based Navigation and Loop Closing, In *Proceeding of the IEEE International Conference on* Robotics and Automation, 2007.

[28] J.S. Gutmann and K. Konolige, Incremental Mapping of Large Cyclic Environments, In *IEEE International Symposium on Computational Intelligence in Robotics and Automation,* pp. 318–325, 1999.

[29] Kurt Konolige, Markov Localization Using Correlation, In *Proceedings of the International Joint Conference on Artificial Intelligence (IJCAI),* 1999.

[30] D. G. Lowe, Object Recognition from Local Scale-Invariant Features, In *International Conference on Computer Vision,* Vol. 2, pp. 1150–1157, 1999.

[31] F. Lu and E. Milios, Globally Consistent Range Scan Alignment for Environment Mapping, *Autonomous Robots,* Vol. 4, No. 4, pp. 333–349, April 1997.

[32] M. W. M. G. Dissanayake, P. Newman, S. Clark, H. F. Durrant-Whyte and M. Csorba, A Solution to the Simultaneous Localization and Map Building (SLAM) Problem, *IEEE Transactions on Automation,* Vol. 17, No. 3, pp. 229–241, June 2001.

[33] S. Thrun and M. Montemerlo, The Graph SLAM Algorithm with Applications to Large-Scale Mapping of Urban Structures, *International Journal of Robotics Research,* Vol. 25, no. 5–6, pp. 403–429, May 2006.

[34] R. Unnikrishnan, and A. Kelly, A Constrained Optimization Approach to Globally Consistent Mapping, in *Proceedings of the International Conference on Intelligent Robots and System,* 2002.

9.3.7 Exercises

9.3.7.1 Efficient Landmark SLAM

Derive a formula for the number of floating point operations (flops) involved in computing $C = AB$ where C is $m \times n$, A is $m \times l$, and B is $l \times n$. Based on this result, show that for five vehicle states and 200 landmarks, Equation 9.50 requires, 1,000 times less processing than the first term of Equation 9.49.

CHAPTER 10

Motion Planning

Figure 10.1 Crusher Robot. The Crusher robot was tested for several years on military bases throughout the United States. Its planner, based on the D* algorithm, regularly plans paths through natural terrain between waypoints separated by a few kilometers.

This section describes the methods used to implement the deliberative autonomy layer that was initially described in Chapter 1. Planning concerns the question of deciding what to do, of which deciding where to go is a special case. Central to planning is the predictive model, which maps candidate actions onto their associated consequences. Equally as important is the mechanism of search because there tend to be many alternative actions to be assessed at any point in time.

Planners think about the future, employing some degree of look ahead and there is a central trade-off between the computational cost of look ahead and the cognitive performance of the system. In addition to perception, planning is where most of what impresses us about robots is located. Given a sufficiently accurate model of the environment, planning technology today can solve, in a comparative instant, problems that we humans would find quite daunting.

10.1 Introduction

Planning refers to processes that *deliberate*, *predict*, and often *optimize*. Respectively these actions will mean:

• Deliberate: Consider many possible sequences of future actions.

- Predict: Predict the outcomes for each sequence.
- Optimize: Pick one, perhaps based on some sense of relative merit.

On real robots, planners are always accompanied by an **executive** element, which is responsible for implementing the plan. Planning processes are the converse of *reactive* processes – those which merely react. Whereas reactive processes use sensing to decide what to do now, planning processes use predictive models to decide what to do now and later. Planning actually **requires models** in order to perform its predictions because it is impossible to sense the future.

Planning concerns the generation of a sequence of actions to perform, usually without considerations of time. The complement of planning is *scheduling*, which concerns the sequence and timing of actions, often without explicit considerations of space. *Task planning* is the problem of generating a sequence of actions that accomplish a larger goal – like assembling a carburetor. *Motion planning* concerns the generation of motions through space.

There are many kinds of motion planning. *Path planning* generates a path from A to B whereas *coverage planning* tries to visit all places exactly once in order to, for example, mow the lawn. *Physical search* is a process whose goal is defined not as a place but as an event and it may not be useful to visit the same place twice – unless the thing searched for is moving. There are many more variations on the problem including reconnaissance, and planning the motions of multiagent formations.

10.1.1 Introducing Path Planning

This chapter concentrates on the most basic motion planning problem – path planning. We have already seen path planning over short time periods – local planning. Obstacle avoidance and trajectory generation were *local path planning* problems. This section addresses path planning over much longer time scales – we will call it *global path planning*.

Global planning techniques tend to "look" well beyond the perceptive horizon – the distance that can be perceived effectively from sensing at the moment. This means that models (maps) of the environment are used, and finite memory considerations often limit the level of detail in those models. Another important consequence of deeper look ahead in time and space is the fact that the topological structure of the environments is more complex on that scale. For example, there will be relatively many ways to weave back and forth to avoid the obstacles to be encountered in the next kilometer, but there may be only two ways, left and right, to avoid the one tree in view of the sensors.

10.1.1.1 Trade-Offs Related to Prediction

Prediction is a basic distinction between planning and reaction. The degree of prediction performed is an important attribute of planning systems. Looking farther ahead in the future corresponds in planning to searching deeper in a search tree, so we will refer to it as *depth* of look ahead. One of the most basic justifications for planning to high depth is avoiding a disastrous decision. As in our everyday experience, it can be valuable to think relatively far ahead into the future. In Figure 10.2, looking farther ahead would have caused the robot to avoid the box canyon to its right.

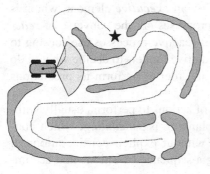

Figure 10.2 Planner Lookahead Depth. Even though it seems easier to go straight, looking farther ahead in the map would tell the robot that the correct answer is to go left.

However, the trade-off is that it will take more time to make a decision if the robot predicts more. Planning is often quite a challenge because it can be very processing intensive, so we often try to preserve the capacity to search deeply by trading off other things.

The processing requirements can be reduced by using simplifying assumptions, but then the decisions are more likely to be wrong. This is a tradeoff between the likelihood of wrong decisions caused by lack of forethought and those caused by imprecise thinking. As always, the choice imposed by finite computation resources is one between fast answers or good answers.

10.1.1.2 Predictive Models for Motion Planning

A third tradeoff worth noting is related to accuracy of predictions. Models are rarely perfect and predictions tend to get less accurate as the robot looks deeper into the future. At some point, predictions are so inaccurate that they add no value.

To predict the consequences of actions for a mobile robot often requires models of the entities involved. These models include those of the robot (volumetric, mass properties, kinematic, dynamic), the environment (slope, traversibility, hazard), and relevant objects (occupancy, shape, motion). Also, models of potential interactions between these entities are needed. These include such considerations as weight support, traction, collision, traversal cost, and so on.

10.1.2 Formulation of Path Planning

For path planning, the alternatives to be considered are candidate paths through space. The paths considered normally have to satisfy a set of constraints:

- Start at one (or one of several) possible start state(s): $\underline{x}(t_0) \in S$ where S is a set of start states.
- Avoid any states that involve intersections with obstacles $\underline{x}(t) \notin O$ where O is a set of states that intersect obstacles. Paths that avoid them are called *admissible* whereas those that do not are *inadmissible*.

- Finish at one (or one of several, or all of several) possible goal state(s): $x(t_f) \in G$ where G is a set of goal states. Perhaps the problem is to get to one point (the *piano movers problem* when obstacles and the robot are polyhedra), to get to any of a number of points (e.g., get to high ground), or to visit all of a set of points in a tour (the *travelling salesman problem*).

The solution path may be expressed as a sequence of actions or a continuous (input) function of time, or it may be expressed as a sequence of states or a continuous (state) function of time. As we have seen, state can usually be derived from inputs but the reverse will not be true if the state trajectory is infeasible.

10.1.2.1 Relationship to Optimal Control

The path planning problem as it has been expressed above can be viewed as an optimal control problem. The problem is essentially a search for an unknown function. Clearly, the "sequence of inputs" is merely a control input, the robot will move as its dynamics dictate, and an objective function can be used to rate alternatives that might otherwise be considered equivalent, so that a winner can be chosen.

At least in path planning problems, we will consider the case where a terminal constraint, like a goal state, is in place, although this is less common in local planning approaches. As is the case elsewhere in optimization, constraints can be converted to cost penalties. In motion planning, it is not uncommon to treat obstacles in terms of their cost of traversal rather than as absolute "no go" regions.

10.1.2.2 Desiderata for Path Planners

Often, we would like planners to have some or all of these properties:

- Soundness: Every solution found is a true solution. There are at least two aspects to soundness: feasibility and admissibility.
- Feasible: Every solution found satisfies motion constraints (vehicle model).
- Admissible: Every solution found does not intersect obstacles.
- Completeness: There are two aspects to completeness.
- If *any* solution exists, it will be found.
- If not, the planner will report failure.
- Optimality. If more than one solution exists, the *best* will be generated.

Achieving any mixture of these goals tends to happen at the expense of computational efficiency.

10.1.3 Obstacle Free Motion Planning

Optimal planning in the absence of obstacles is only trivial if there are no dynamic constraints. When there are no dynamic constraints, a straight line can be drawn from the start to the finish and the problem is solved. For mobile robots, there are almost always dynamic constraints, so the problem of obstacle free motion planning is surprisingly difficult in general [2]. Solutions to the case where there are no obstacles can be very useful as heuristics representing the best possible case when there are obstacles. When a state space model must be respected, optimal trajectories tend to be composed of extremal controls. This section will discuss two examples.

10.1.3.1 Dubins' Car

This vehicle has the capacity to travel only in the forward direction and it can steer at any curvature up to some maximum curvature amplitude [4]. It can be shown that this vehicle can reach any admissible terminal configuration when there are no obstacles to restrict its motion. However, the same is not true when there are obstacles. The optimal control problem for the shortest path between two poses is:

$$minimize: \quad J[\underline{x}, \underline{u}] = \int_0^{s_f} ds = s_f$$

$$where: \quad \underline{x} = \begin{bmatrix} x & y & \theta \end{bmatrix}^T \quad \underline{u} = \begin{bmatrix} \kappa & u \end{bmatrix}^T \qquad (10.1)$$

$$subject\ to: \quad \frac{d\underline{x}}{ds} = \begin{bmatrix} \cos\theta \\ \sin\theta \\ \kappa \end{bmatrix} u \quad \begin{matrix} \underline{x}(s_0) = \underline{x}_0 \quad ; \quad \underline{x}(s_f) = \underline{x}_f \\ u = 1 \quad ; \quad |\kappa| \le \kappa_{max} \end{matrix}$$

The notation used is that $\underline{u}$ is the entire control vector but the scalar u is just the velocity. The objective function is simply the total length of the path. It was shown in [3] that the optimal path between any two configurations has two properties.

- It is composed of no more than three segments.
- Each segment is a primitive motion that is an arc of one of three curvatures $\kappa = -\kappa_{max}$ or $\kappa = 0$ or $\kappa = \kappa_{max}$.

Let's refer to these three primitives as R (right), S (straight), and L (left). Then it was also proven that an optimal trajectory must be of one of six possible forms. These are LRL, RLR, LSL, RSR, LSR, and RSL.

Intuitively, solutions can often be derived graphically by surrounding the start and end poses by circles of minimum radius and searching for the feasible joining segment (an arc or line) that produces the shortest path (Figure 10.3).

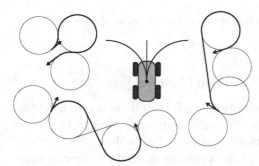

Figure 10.3 Dubins' Car. The Dubins car can turn both directions but it has a finite minimum turn radius. Paths of minimum length between two poses can be understood intuitively as shown.

Given the known structure of the solution, one way to compute a solution is to set up a parameter optimization problem for each of the 6 cases where the parameters are three unknown lengths (some of which can be zero).

For example, we might represent the LSR case as:

$$J[\underline{x}, \underline{u}] = \int_0^{s_1} ds\big|_L + \int_{s_1}^{s_1+s_2} ds\big|_S + \int_{s_1+s2}^{s_1+s_2+s_3} ds\big|_R = s_f$$

The integrals are simply functions of their integration limits, so this is merely:

$$J[\underline{x}, \underline{u}] = s_f = f(s_1, s_2, s_3)$$

10.1.3.2 Reeds-Shepp Car

This vehicle is similar to the Dubins car except that it can drive both forward and backward. It can be shown that this vehicle can reach any terminal configuration in cases where there are no obstacles to restrict its motion.

The optimal control problem for the shortest path between two poses is:

minimize:
$$J[\underline{x}, \underline{u}] = \int_0^{s_f} ds = s_f$$

where:
$$\underline{x} = \begin{bmatrix} x & y & \theta \end{bmatrix}^T \quad \underline{u} = \begin{bmatrix} \kappa & u \end{bmatrix}^T \tag{10.2}$$

subject to:
$$\frac{d\underline{x}}{ds} = \begin{bmatrix} \cos\theta \\ \sin\theta \\ \kappa \end{bmatrix} u \quad \begin{array}{l} \underline{x}(s_0) = \underline{x}_0 \ ; \ \underline{x}(s_f) = \underline{x}_f \\ u \in \{1, -1\} \ |\kappa| \le \kappa_{max} \end{array}$$

In [5], it is proven that optimal solutions are composed once again of paths whose segments are straight lines or curvature extremes (Figure 10.4). In addition to the 6 cases for the Dubins car, there are ten solutions of 4 segments denoted LRLR, RLRL, LRSR, RLSL, LRSL, RLSR, LSLR, RSRL, RSLR, and LSRL. There are also cases with 5 segments denoted LRSLR and RLSRL. For each, the velocity can be either positive or negative in principle but many cases can be eliminated to produce a total of 46 distinct cases. Closed form solutions are available for all 46 controls.

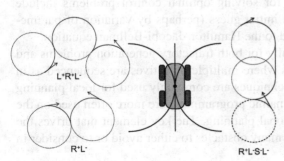

L⁺R⁺L⁻

R⁺L⁻

R⁺L⁻S⁻L⁻

Figure 10.4 Reeds-Shepp Car. The Reeds-Shepp car is a Dubins car that can drive forward or backward.

10.1.4 References and Further Reading

10.1.4.1 Books

Several texts are available that concentrate on path planning. Latombe is perhaps the first book devoted to planning. Laumond's book concentrates on planning when there are differential constraints. Lavalle's book is a recent and comprehensive source.

[1] J. C. Latombe, *Robot Motion Planning,* Kluwer Academic Publishers, Boston, MA, 1991.
[2] J. P. Laumond, *Robot Motion Planning and Control,* Springer-Verlag, New York, 1998.
[3] S. Lavalle, *Planning Algorithms,* Cambridge University Press, 2006.

10.1.4.2 Papers

[4] L. E. Dubins, On Curves of Minimal Length with a Constraint on Average Curvature, and with Prescribed Initial and Terminal Positions and Tangents, *American Journal of Mathematics,* Vol. 79, pp. 497–516, 1957.
[5] J. A. Reeds and L. A. Shepp, Optimal Paths for a Car that Goes Both Forwards and Backwards, *Pacific Journal of Mathematics,* Vol. 145, No. 2, 367–393, 1990.
[6] H. Sussmann and G. Tang, Shortest Paths for the Reeds-Shepp Car: A Worked Out Example of the Use of Geometric Techniques in Nonlinear Optimal Control, Technical Report SYNCON 91-10, Dept. of Mathematics, Rutgers University, Piscataway, NJ, 1991.

10.1.5 Exercises

10.1.5.1 Dubins' Car

Implement Dubins' solution and divide the plane into regions where the solution takes the same form for an initial heading of zero and a terminal heading of π.

10.2 Representation and Search for Global Path Planning

The previous section shows that path planning is essentially an optimal control problem and it even applied this approach to the case of planning problems without obstacles. This section will cover classical techniques for problems when there are obstacles.

Recall that two basic techniques for solving optimal control problems include relaxation approaches that deform an initial guess (perhaps by variation of parameters) or dynamic programming applied to the Hamilton-Jacobi-Bellman equation.

We have used relaxation successfully for both trajectory generation problems and even for trajectory planning problems where multiple primitives are sequenced as in the Dubins car. Whereas relaxation techniques are commonly used for local planning problems, techniques derived from dynamic programming are more often used on the larger scale problems addressed in global planning. The key element that drives the change of approach is the presence of many obstacles to either avoid or to consider in the objective function.

10.2.1 Sequential Motion Planning

Sequential motion planning is an approach that contrasts with the continuum approach used in trajectory generation. In sequential motion planning, the problem is cast in terms of a sequence of decisions (choosing actions that transition between states) that progressively defines the path that solves the problem. For the obstacle free case, the number of possible sequences was sufficiently small that all could be checked exhaustively. However, when there are many obstacles, we will see that there are too many alteratives to check exhaustively.

10.2.1.1 Why Not Continuum Methods?

Consider the path planning problem shown in Figure 10.5. A *homotopy class* of paths is a set of paths with the same start and end that can be continuously deformed one into the other without intersecting obstacles. In the figure, there are four such classes. They could be denoted LR, RL, LL and RR where the first letter denotes the side of the first obstacle on which the path lies, and the second letter denotes the same information for the second obstacle. Because the notation is merely a two digit binary number, it is not hard to see that if there are n such obstacles arranged in a line, there are 2^n homotopy classes and the situation is more complicated if obstacles are arranged throughout the plane.

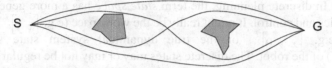

Figure 10.5 Local Minima in Continuum Search. Four possible acyclic path shapes are homotopically distinct in this two obstacle world. They can be denoted LR, RL, LL, RR, where L means avoid to the left and R means avoid to the right.

A relaxation technique slowly deforms paths toward a local solution based on exploiting gradient information. If the cost function used in relaxation treats obstacles as constraints, then deformation to shorten a path will eventually cause it to touch an obstacle and violate the constraint. In such a case, it is not clear how to transition from one class to another in the search for the shortest path – jumping over the obstacle may not decrease the objective function. It seems therefore that all classes may have to be relaxed.

On the other hand, if obstacles are treated in the cost function, then there is likely to be a different local minimum for each homotopy class and once again they will all have to be searched. It seems that, in relaxation techniques, a systematic process that ensures that every possible sequence of decisions is tried would be necessary to find an optimum solution.

Although exhaustive search is still a viable approach when there are few alternatives that need to be checked, it turns out that dynamic programming is a more efficient way to conduct such a search that exploits recursion. It can find the optimum solution without explicitly considering every possible homotopy class. For this reason, it has emerged as the preferred technique when there are many obstacles that induce many constraints or many local minima.

10.2.1.2 Discretization of Search Spaces

The space of all possible paths in the continuum is infinite. Whereas relaxation samples this infinite set by jumping to discrete neighboring paths in each iteration, (discrete) dynamic programming, as it is used in motion planning, searches a finite set of paths that are encoded in a graph that is embedded in (is a subset of) the state space. The problem of planning paths in the continuum is thereby *reduced to a graph search problem*.

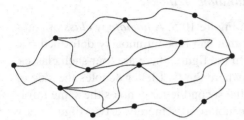

Figure 10.6 Embedded Graph. Discrete states and transitions defined on them leads to a graph embedded in space.

This graph will be known here as the *search graph* (Figure 10.6). It is a discrete subset of the continuum search space. *Nodes* in the graph are associated with *states* of the robot. Each state $\underline{x}$ in the graph can be considered to be a member of a continuous state space X. In discrete planning, the term *state space* has a more general meaning than in dynamics and control. It might really be the workspace (e.g. $\begin{bmatrix} x & y \end{bmatrix}^T$), configuration space (e.g. $\begin{bmatrix} x & y & \theta \end{bmatrix}^T$, or the true dynamical system state space (e.g., $\begin{bmatrix} x & y & \theta & V & \omega \end{bmatrix}^T$) of the robot. The discrete states may or may not be regularly arranged.

It is important to have several edges that leave a given state to connect it to others. *Edges* in the graph are associated with *actions* (also called inputs or *controls*) that move the robot between the states. Each action effects a state transition:

$$x_{k+1} = f(x_k, u) \tag{10.3}$$

The available actions at any state are chosen from the action space $U(\underline{x})$, which may in general depend on the state.

The edges in the graph can be designed to facilitate cost calculations that are necessary in an *optimal* planner. Each may be considered to have some length, or more generally, some cost associated with traversing it. In this way, the optimum path is easily defined as the least cost path in the graph.

Edges can be designed to facilitate obstacle intersection calculations that are necessary in an *admissible* planner. If discrete nontraversable obstacles are considered, then those edges that intersect them (more generally, cause the robot to collide with them) can be eliminated from the graph at the first opportunity. Thereafter, the graph will encode only admissible motions and obstacles can be ignored. If obstacles are encoded as costs, then the edges cannot be removed.

Edges can also be designed to satisfy dynamic constraints that must be satisfied in a *feasible* planner. Each feasible edge encodes a potential real motion of the robot (satisfies kinematic, nonholonomic, power, and other constraints).

Often one or neither of the admissibility and feasibility constraints is imposed in the graph and a second phase of processing may fix a preliminary solution to make it comply with these constraints. On occasion, the design will allow the robot to try to execute infeasible paths and it will become the responsibility of control to do the best it can.

10.2.1.3 Path Planning as a Sequential Decision Process

A search graph can be used to define a sequence of decisions, about which edge to follow at sequentially encountered nodes, in order to ultimately form a path. If the objective is to start somewhere and reach a goal, such a *sequential decision process* becomes equivalent to the original path planning problem expressed in the discrete search space. A path planning algorithm that operates as a sequential decision process is called a *sequential planning algorithm*.

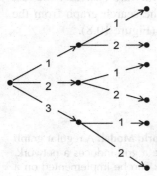

Figure 10.7 Sequential Decision Process. At each state encountered, there are some options for how to proceed. Each one transitions to a new state.

Given a graph to search, the most basic path planning problem is specified in terms of a distinguished start state x_s and a goal state x_g. The problem is to find a sequence of edges, or equivalently, a sequence of states that when traversed in sequence, connect the start state to the goal. Variations on this formulation include multiple goals and even multiple potential start states, and some variations permit start and goal regions rather than states.

As a minimum, we require, at each state encountered, some options for how to proceed, each of which transitions to a new state (Figure 10.7). Each decision considers several edges that define a *path segment* (the continuous trajectory followed during execution of the action) that then serves as a small segment of a candidate path. Path planning proceeds by joining together sequences of path segments. One such sequence of path segments will hopefully generate the solution. During the search process, each path segment is checked for collision or otherwise has its merits evaluated.

Note that the process of generation of the tree in Figure 10.7 is of complexity exponential in the depth of the tree. If there are n options for each decision, then there will be d^n nodes at depth d in the tree, and each new level has n times as many nodes as the last.

10.2.1.4 World Model, C-Space, and Search Graph

For the purpose of representing obstacles or a more general cost field over the work-space, it is useful to partition the volume of the workspace into small cells. Each cell may encode obstacle occupancy information (binary) or more general cost informa-tion (real-valued). In either case, such a representation is a natural way to record pro-cessed perception data in rasterized form, and it is important to have cells that are small enough to resolve the gaps between obstacles sufficiently well to make correct decisions.

Such a world model is typically defined for the purpose of evaluating the cost of paths and/or evaluating collisions. However, the obstacle information is naturally expressed as a field over the robot workspace whereas collision checking (or configu-ration costing) must be computed over the volume occupied by the robot. In the case of a static, known environment, it may be advisable to convert the workspace world model to a C-space world model. Otherwise, it will be necessary to compute the swath occupied by the robot that is generated by each path.

In cases where the motion model of the robot is straightforward (whether the real motion is straightforward or not), it is possible to derive the search graph from the world model or to even use the same data structure for both (Figure 10.8).

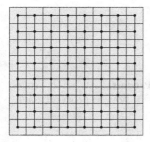

Figure 10.8 Search Graph From World Model. A regular graph can be derived from a grid. Because a grid induces a network, any algorithm defined on a network can be implemented on a grid.

In such a case, the states are identified with the centers of the grid cells and the edges are often implied in the transition function and have no explicit representation in memory. This process merges the search graph into the world model. Small cells have the advantage that they better approximate arbitrary paths but it comes at the cost of higher computational load in planning.

It is also possible to do the reverse – to merge the world model into the search graph. When the environment is static, the cost of edges can be computed once and then the world model is no longer needed in path planning. Whether the environment is static or not, if the states are positioned at the centers of the cells, the cost calculation proceeds as follows. Each edge traverses half the width of two cells when moving from a cell to an immediately adjacent cell. Thus, if $c[\ ]$ denotes cost and there is an edge from x_j to cell x_k, then the cost associated with the edge is computed as the line integral:

$$c[e_{jk}] = \int_{x_j}^{x_k} c[x]ds = \frac{1}{2}(c[x_j] + c[x_k])\Delta s$$

In the case of a binary representation, the edge would be declared to intersect an obstacle if either of the cells involved contained an obstacle. The above example assumes the cost field has already been converted to C-space. In a more general case of an arbitrary search graph unrelated to the world model representation, the cost of a path can still be defined as a line integral.

10.2.1.5 Search Space Design

Many options exist for the design of the search space used in global planning. This section will describe a few of the more distinct options.

10.2.1.5.1 Road Networks. Of course, sometimes the environment has been deliberately structured into a graph of a set of roads and vehicles are normally required to stay on them. Although this is certainly true of the roads we drive our cars on, it is also true of many factories that use mobile robots. For service robots, the hallways of many buildings constitute a road network of sorts as well. In factories, the *guidepaths* (i.e., "robot roads") are also often clearly marked so that people can avoid lingering on them.

10.2.1.5.2 Workspace Lattices. Lattices, of which grids are a special case, are regular (symmetric) arrangements of states. Such a regular state arrangement leads naturally to a common set of actions that can be repeated at each state. A common repeated set of edges makes it easy to avoid storing the entire graph in favor of elaborating it as it is needed during the planning process.

The edges are derived from the states by connecting each cell to its neighbors. In the case of a grid in the plane, there are two clear alternatives for connecting a cell to its immediate neighbors – denoted four-connected and eight-connected. In the first case, edges emanate in the four cardinal directions and in the second case, the four diagonals are added as well.

Note that a search graph representation must approximate all possible paths by those that exist in the graph. A path generated in either the four or eight connected case for a rectangular array of states will not be particularly optimal in general because such a graph cannot represent, for example, a line at 22.5° to any cardinal direction. It is, of course, possible to connect a cell to its neighbors up to two cells away in order to achieve this (Figure 10.9). As we have seen though, the number of edges leaving a cell dramatically affects the cost of planning, so there is a severe practical limit to how large a neighborhood can be used to generate edges.

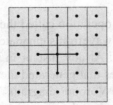 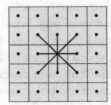 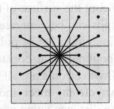

Figure 10.9 Cell Connectedness in Grids. A cell may have 4, 8, or 16 or more neighbors connected by edges. In the last case, note that only half of the cells in the second ring from the center are connected. These missing edges can be composed by repeating existing edges a second time. A planner will do this naturally, so there is less of a need to represent them explicitly.

10.2.1.5.3 State Lattices. Suppose the states used are samples over a configuration space, say $\begin{bmatrix} x & y & \theta \end{bmatrix}^T$. Then it becomes possible to enforce heading continuity in the search graph by requiring that an edge that enters a cell at a certain heading must leave at the same heading [17]. A simple example of this idea is the Dubins' car lattice. If the translational spacing of states is set to the minimum turn radius, then the car can rotate 90° while travelling to a diagonal neighbor as shown in Figure 10.10.

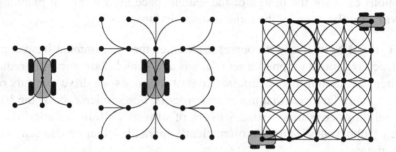

Figure 10.10 A Dubins' Car Lattice. The spatial separation of states is carefully chosen to coincide with the minimum turn radius. Each dot in the graph (right) corresponds to a set of four distinct states with principal headings of 90°, 180°, 270°, and 360°. In this way, the edges are defined to enforce heading continuity when states are traversed. A heading-continuous solution is shown that moves from the bottom left to top right. The vehicle drives in reverse at the top.

State lattices can be defined that are continuous in velocity, curvature, and so on, using the same technique – for any vehicle – given a trajectory generator for the vehicle. The main advantage of such an approach is the potential to encode only feasible motions in the search graph. Higher degrees of continuity of states at the nodes tend to approach full feasibility. For example, heading continuity prevents turning instantaneously but it may permit changing curvature instantaneously.

The symmetry properties of regular lattices make it possible to precompute the world model cells that are intersected by each edge and this technique has similar performance advantages to a C-space obstacle field representation – both perform intersection calculations only once.

10.2.1.5.4 Voronoi Graphs. In binary cost fields or for discrete obstacles, it is possible to derive a special graph from the world model that is called a Voronoi graph [11]. These are easy to visualize in 2D where such a graph is the set of all points that are equidistant from the surface of two or more obstacles.

Such graphs can be generated automatically from an operation called the *distance transform.* Imagine a set of polygonal obstacles and let wavefronts emanate outward from their boundaries at constant speed (Figure 10.11). At any instant in time, the points on all wavefronts are all equidistant from the edges that generated them. Eventually the wavefronts meet and generate a point on the Voronoi diagram. When all points have a distance value or are marked as a Voronoi edge, the process completes.

Each point on a Voronoi edge is equidistant from its two closest obstacles. Two edges can meet at a *meet point,* which is equidistant from three or more obstacles. The edges have the useful property that they constitute a set of paths through the space which are always as far as possible from the obstacles. This is true for a point robot. If the robot is not a point, an effective technique is to grow the obstacles by the radius of the robot's smallest enclosing circle.

10.2.1.5.5 Probabilistic Roadmaps. Approaches to path planning in high dimensional search spaces have tended to avoid the use of a regular sampling of state space in favor of random sampling. One technique is probabilistic roadmaps [14]. The original algorithm was defined on the configuration space but it is easy to see how it generalizes to a dynamical state space. The C-space is randomly sampled for admissible configurations and then each admissible state is connected to some of its neighbors (perhaps the k nearest or all within a radius) using a trajectory generator or other local planner. This process produces a graph (Figure 10.12). The start and goal states can be joined similarly to the graph using a local planner.

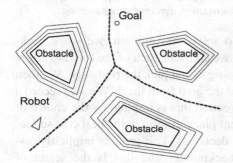

Figure 10.11 Voronoi Diagram. Discrete obstacles induce a roadmap which consists of points farthest from all obstacles.

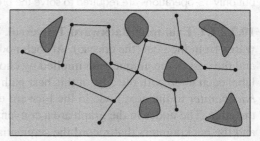

Figure 10.12 Probabilistic Roadmap. Random samples in the search space are verified to be admissible and then joined locally to produce a graph.

10.2.2 Big Ideas in Optimization and Search

Sequential motion planning was reduced above to search in a graph. That graph will turn out to be cyclic and in *cyclic* graphs, there is more than one path between some pairs of nodes. Hence, it becomes necessary to evaluate different path options and there are elegant ways to do this evaluation efficiently.

10.2.2.1 Principle of Optimality

This principle [10] applies to a class of problems known as sequential (also known as Markov) decision processes (SDP). When it is embodied in an algorithm for solving an SDP, the algorithm is known as *dynamic programming*. The principle is stated in Box 7.2 of Chapter 7.

Intuitively, it states that the solution to the entire problem must be composed of optimal solutions to each of its subproblems. Hence, if the optimal path from Pittsburgh to Chicago goes through Toledo, it must be the case that the portion of the optimal path that goes from Toledo to Chicago is optimal as well. This assertion is easy to prove by contradiction.

Consider the example in Figure 10.13. This is an SDP. Starting at the start node, the mouse has to pick one of three and then one of two or three nodes. There are seven possible paths of three edges.

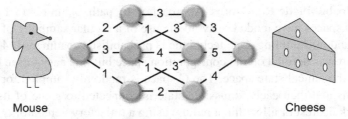

Figure 10.13 Dynamic Programming. If the mouse knows dynamic programming, it can solve this maze very efficiently for the shortest path to the cheese. Edge annotations denote cost of traversal. There are 7 paths of 3 edges each. Enumerating their costs would require 21 operations but only 13 operations are required to solve the problem using dynamic programming.

10.2.2.1.1 Example: Backward Traversal. To solve the problem, we work backwards from the goal (the cheese). At each node we consider each of the forward edges and the cost of the unique path implied by choosing it, and pick the best edge. We then label each node with the cost of this best path to the goal from there. We also record a *backpointer* to the next node in the forward direction that is implied by the choice of the edge. The nodes in the graph are a convenient place to store both "best cost so far" and the backpointers that record the sequential decisions. This process implicitly discards all longer paths to any node with a backpointer and this is the secret of its efficiency.

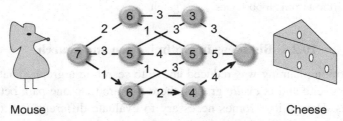

Figure 10.14 Solution Using Backward Traversal. The numbers in the states represent the optimal cost from state to the goal.

Notice that a *partial spanning tree* is being constructed during the graph traversal. It is partial because it includes only the nodes that have been encountered so far in the search process. We will call this tree the *search tree* to distinguish it from the search graph from which it was derived. Both structures contain the same nodes but the edges are different. The edges are also directional in the tree and are typically not so in the graph. In this tree, the single path from any node to the root (goal) is the optimal one and they are constructed recursively as the algorithm proceeds. Each new optimal sub-path is composed of others that are only one edge shorter. This recursive approach is far more efficient on large graphs than more naive alternatives. The process by which the tree grows is called node *expansion*. When a node is expanded, all nodes connected to it in the graph are added to the tree if they are not already in the tree.

The same solution can be generated by searching from the start toward the cheese by recording optimal paths from the start. Any algorithm that finds a path from Start to Goal can in principle be used to find a path in the opposite direction by switching the labels S and G – as we do not care about the order in which the path was generated – we only care about the order of execution.

One direction or the other may be less work if the *indegree* of nodes (number of edges entering) differs from the *outdegree* of nodes. That will not often happen in locally connected graphs like those derived from grids, but we will see later that there can be very good reasons to search backwards in a graph.

10.2.2.2 Branch and Bound

The principle of *branch and bound* [15] provides a way to eliminate entire sections of the search space from consideration. It is based on two notions: a mechanism to split up the search space (branching), and a mechanism to quickly compute bounds on the quality of a solution at a node.

In Figure 10.15, the search is for the shortest path between two points. Bounds on the maximum and minimum length of the resulting path are being computed as the tree evolves. In some cases, the best case for one node (C) is already worse than the worst case for another (B). In the figure, node (C) can be safely neglected without sacrificing optimality.

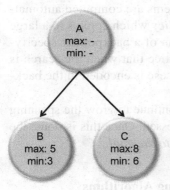

Figure 10.15 Branch and Bound. Because the worst case for node B is better than the best case for node C, node C need never be expanded.

10.2.2.3 Best First Search

The best first search algorithm [16] provides a way to encode arbitrary gradient. It is similar to gradient descent. However, unlike gradient descent, it is systematic, so it will eventually try all options in a finite search space. It may also use more informed evaluation functions than mere local gradients.

The basic mechanism is to maintain all unexplored nodes in a priority queue. Recall that a priority queue is merely a queue whose elements are sorted based on some key value. When it is time to grow the tree, the most promising (Figure 10.16) node is expanded, and "promising" means whatever the designer wants it to mean. It could be closeness to the goal or distance from the nearest obstacle or something else.

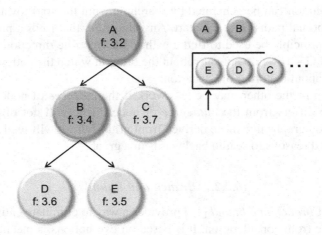

Figure 10.16 Best First Search. Node A is removed from the queue and expanded to produce B & C. Because B has a smaller key, it is removed and expanded, before C, to produce D & E. Because E has the smaller key, it is placed before D in the queue and E is placed before C. Node E is the first in the queue and hence the next to be removed and expanded.

10.2.2.4 Policy Storage

The recursive formulation that makes path planning amenable to dynamic programming also means that the solutions to all subproblems are computed automatically as well. The search tree efficiently encodes a *policy* which applies to a large number of subproblems and the encoding is in the form of a backpointer specifying where to go next for any node. In Figure 10.14, notice that when the search is complete, the optimum path from every node to the cheese is encoded in the backpointers.

When the search space is finite, it can be useful to continue to grow the spanning tree until every node in the search graph has been processed. Once this is done, the tree stores the optimal solution *from every possible start to the goal.*

10.2.3 Uniform Cost Sequential Planning Algorithms

When the cost of all edges in the network is the same, the planning problem is somewhat simpler than otherwise. This case is rich enough, however, that solutions of considerable elegance exist. This section begins a process of presenting important sequential planning algorithms in order from simplest to most complex, and it culminates in an algorithm that is efficient, optimal, and able to rapidly react if the search graph changes.

An inexperienced reader motivated to implement motion planning algorithms would do well to implement these in the order presented so that each new algorithm is a minor change to the one before. Each algorithm reduces the one before to a special case so that when the final one is implemented, there is little need of the others that came before. Yet, little code is deleted along the way so this process is both a tutorial and a way to write a real planner that works.

10.2.3.1 Wandering Motion Planner

Perhaps the simplest planning algorithm defined on a graph is provided in Algorithm 10.1:

```
00    algorithm wanderPlanner()
01        x ← x_s
02        while(true)
03            for some(u ∈ U(x))
04                x ← f(x, u)
05                if(x = x_g) return success
06            endfor
07        endwhile
08    return
```

Algorithm 10.1 Simplest Planner. This planner will wander aimlessly in the *search space*. *Whether and when it reaches the goal is a matter of sheer luck.*

One virtue of this planner is that it remains on the graph. However, it does not necessarily move toward the goal, even when there are no obstacles, so it is clearly not very efficient. It also is not even a planner because it does not remember anything and hence cannot output a plan. It merely tests for whether a path exists, and it does not even do that well because there is no way to know how long it will take for a single execution of this program to terminate, or if it will terminate at all.

Suppose for the rest of this section that the algorithm is augmented to remember a plan in the form of the states it has encountered in sequence before stumbling on the goal. Depending on how the choice of actions is defined, it may not be checking to see that obstacles are avoided, and the actions themselves may not be feasible, so it may not be either *admissible* or *feasible*.

However, a second virtue of this planner is that it discovers the structure of the search space while the planning proceeds, rather than requiring it to be prespecified. The **for** loop at line 3 is said to *expand* each node that it processes. This implicit search space property leads to minimal memory demands. Indeed, the above algorithm uses the same constant memory regardless of the size of the search space. However, we shall see that this lack of memory is really more of a problem than a virtue.

This planner is the simplest of many similar strategies that use only local information to try to find a solution. If, for example, the choice of action was based on preferring the direction to the goal (*gradient descent*) or avoiding nearby obstacles (*potential fields*), the algorithm will still not be guaranteed to find a solution in reasonable time, or even at all. Hence, the algorithm is also not complete. Finally, because it is essentially searching randomly, it will find a random path rather than the optimal one so its is not optimal. Because it is neither optimal, complete, admissible, nor feasible, it is a very bad planner!

10.2.3.2 Systematic Motion Planner

One consequence of the minimal memory used above is that the planner does not even remember where it has been before. Such a basic "planner" does not even try to prevent the generation of a path with a cycle in it. In most realistic situations, with positive edge costs, a path containing a cycle is of higher cost than the same path with the cycle removed (Figure 10.17). Even if that were not the case, a planner that permits one cycle could permit an unlimited number of them and hence, never terminate, depending on how systematically it conducts the search.

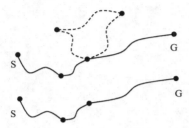

Figure 10.17 Path Cycles. (Top) A path that contains a cycle. (Bottom) In most cases the plan with the cycle removed is best.

The simplest way to implement a strategy of avoiding cycles is to remember every state that has been visited and then prevent repeat visits. The next planner (Algorithm 10.2) partitions the set of visited states into two sets traditionally called "OPEN" and "CLOSED." These are called O and C in the pseudocode. All states that have been visited are either in O or C. One function of the O set is to keep track of a *frontier* of states that are potential sources of new unvisited states. An explicit set of such states is relatively efficient and it also permits easy detection of planner failure when the set becomes empty. O does not contain all visited states by virtue of the removal that occurs in line 4.

```
00   algorithm spanningTree(x_s, x_g)
01       O.insert(x_s)
02       x_s.parent ← null
03       while(O ≠ ∅
04           x ← O.remove( )
05           C.insert(x)
06           if (expandNodeST(x)) return success
07       endwhile
08       return failure
```

Algorithm 10.2 Systematic Planner. This planner will generate a spanning tree for the search graph, up to the point where the goal is encountered, and terminate. If there is no path to the goal, it will return failure after all reachable nodes have been visited.

The node expansion function called at line 6 places all unvisited neighbors of the provided state on O and it detects when the goal is encountered. Algorithm 10.3 is our first version of node expansion.

We can define the parent of any state x_{next} as the state $\underline{x}$ that was expanded in line 2 in order to generate it. Lines 4 and 6 record this information so that the path can be extracted when the goal is reached. Unless it is easy to determine the action given the state transition, it may be useful to record the action here too.

The algorithm permits every state to have only one parent state. Any graph traversal algorithm with this single-parent property generates a *spanning tree* (known here as the *search tree*) and can therefore be described in terms of a traversal of a tree that restrict traversal is discovered during the search process.

```
00    algorithm expandNodeST(x)
01    for each(u ∈ U(x))
02        x_next ← f(x, u)
03        if(x_next = x_g)
04            x_next.parent ← x ;return success
05        else if(x_next ∉ O && x_next ∉ C)
06            x_next.parent ← x
07            O.insert(x_next)
08        endif
09    endfor
10    return failure
```

Algorithm 10.3 Node Expansion for Systematic Planner. All unvisited neighbors of the provided state are placed on OPEN.

In such a tree, the root node is the start state and every other node contains a reference to the parent state encountered on the path through the tree from the node to the root. Hence, these parent pointers can generate the path (in reverse order) to the goal once it is found.

Note that the cost of avoiding cycles is memory. OPEN can easily require a lot of memory for large planning problems. Explicit storage of states, including the CLOSED set can also require significant memory. It can be much faster as well as more memory-efficient to store the information about whether a state is visited in the state itself. In this case, the explicit CLOSED list is not needed. This planner is *complete* over a finite region because eventually every reachable state will be reached and every state that is reached has a path to it.

10.2.3.3 Optimal Motion Planner

Although the previous planner is complete, it is not optimal. Suppose we define the optimal path to mean the shortest one. Here, we are considering the *uniform* or *unweighted edge* case so length of a path is measured as the number of edges in it. A simple way to generate the shortest path to the goal is to generate all paths of length one edge, then all paths that are two edges long, and so on, until the goal is encountered. The first time that the goal is encountered, the path to it must be shortest because all possible shorter paths to anywhere have already been checked and none of them reached the goal.

Let this principle of continuously expanding the unvisited node closest to the start be called the *wavefront optimality principle*. If path length is measured in units of edges in the graph, the implementation is straightforward. The set O above is replaced with a FIFO queue so that its elements become ordered. Nodes are removed from the front of the FIFO and placed at the back. The node expansion algorithm becomes:

```
00    algorithm expandNodeBF(x)
01    for each(u ∈ U(x))
02        x_next ← f(x, u)
03        if(x_next = x_g)
04            x_next.parent ← x ;return success
05        else if(x_next ∉ O && x_next ∉ C)
06            x_next.parent ← x
07            O.insertLast(x_next)
08        endif
09    endfor
10    return failure
```

Algorithm 10.4 Node Expansion for Optimal Planner. All unvisited neighbors of the provided state are placed on the end of a FIFO queue.

The key to the optimality of the algorithm is the FIFO queue O. States are added at the back (Algorithm 10.4) and removed from the front (Algorithm 10.5). As a result, states are processed in order based on the number of node expansions, and hence the number of edges, that were required to reach them.

The first time a node is encountered, it becomes marked as *visited* by virtue of being placed in O. Due to the test at line 5 in Algorithm 10.4, longer paths that encounter it again will not be generated. Hence, every node placed on C has had its optimal path back to the start state computed.

```
00    algorithm breadthFirst(x_s, x_g)
01    O.insertLast(x_s)
02    x_s.parent ← null
03    while(O ≠ ∅)
04        x ← O.removeFirst()
05        C.insert(x)
06        if (expandNodeBF x)) return success
07    endwhile
08    return failure
```

Algorithm 10.5 Optimal Breadth First Planner. This planner will generate a spanning tree for the search graph and produce the path to the goal that requires the least number of edges ("shortest"). It will also report failure if no path exists. Uniform cost edges are assumed

This algorithm is known as *breadth first search*. When the graph generated is associated with a rectangular grid, it is known as the *grassfire* algorithm [10] because the frontier evolves in a manner similar to a fire. Grassfire will produce correct behavior in a grid whether diagonal moves are permitted (eight-connected) or not (four-connected). The algorithm will even produce the correct answer if the cycle prevention step at line 5 in the node expansion, and associated infrastructure (CLOSED set C) are removed, but it will do so at the expense of searching irrelevant cyclic paths.

If the FIFO is converted to a LIFO queue (a stack), the algorithm is called *depth first search*. A depth first algorithm will proceed immediately as deep as possible in the search tree and then move back up the tree ("backtrack") when a node is encountered that has no children. Depth first search can be implemented recursively, in which case the stack used becomes implicit, managed by the programming language. As described, the depth first algorithm is not very useful for planning but a variant called *depth first iterative deepening* is a very powerful trade-off between processing time and memory usage.

10.2.4 Weighted Sequential Planning

So far, we have been able to achieve systematic, optimal search provided the "length" of the path is defined as the number of edges required to traverse it. In a more general situation, each edge has a positive length (or cost) value associated with it and the cost of any path can be considered to be the sum of the costs of all of its component edges. It turns out that a few simple additions can adapt breadth first search to this situation.

Consider three states: the start state x_s, an arbitrary state x on a specific path from the start and the goal state x_g. A useful concept is the *cost-to-come*, denoted $g(x_s, x)$ or simply $g(\ )$ which is the length or cost of the path joining x_s to x. Alternatively, the *cost-to-go*, denoted $h(x, x_g)$ or simply $h(\ )$ is the length or cost of the path joining x to x_g.

10.2.4.1 Optimal Weighted Sequential Planner

If we associate a value of $g(\ )$ with each state, then the wavefront principle can be preserved if the FIFO queue becomes a *priority queue* that is sorted by the cost-to-come $g(\ )$. Provided the cost of edges is nonnegative, the cost of a path $g(\ )$ is monotone increasing in its length, and states placed on O must always be greater than the cost of the node expanded to produce them. Furthermore, the queue is defined to produce the lowest cost state in the queue when one is removed. Hence, the costs of the states expanded will also grow monotonically. With the addition of a priority queue and a few other changes, the algorithm becomes Dijkstra's Algorithm [12] (Algorithm 10.6).

```
00    algorithm Dijkstra(x_s, x_g)
01        x_s.g ← 0
02        O.insertSorted(x_s, x_s.g)
03        x_s.parent ← null
04        while(O ≠ ∅
05            x ← O.removeFirst()
06            C.insert(x)
07            if(x = x_g) return success
08            expandNodeDijkstra(x)
09        endwhile
10    return failure
```

Algorithm 10.6 Dijkstra's Algorithm for Optimal Weighted Graph Search. This planner will generate a spanning tree for the search graph and produce the path to the goal which has least cost. It will also report failure if no path exists.

Unlike the uniform cost case, the cost of the states added to the queue need not grow monotonically because edge costs are arbitrary positive numbers. This means that the apparent cost of nodes may not be optimal at the instant they are **inserted** in the queue O because they may have been discovered first via a relatively high cost edge.

On the other hand, when a node is **removed** from the front of the queue, it can be shown by induction that no shorter path to it can exist. For this reason, the test for the goal has been moved to line 7, effectively delaying the declaration of success until the goal makes its way to the front of the priority queue.

The g values nodes are computed from edge costs and the g values of other nodes (Algorithm 10.7). The net effect is to accumulate the sum of the costs of all edges on the optimal path from the start node to the present node. It is very important to note that this computation is done incrementally as the tree is expanded. The straightforward way to do that is to **store** the g values somewhere (perhaps in the nodes themselves) so that they do not need to be recomputed every time the cost-to-come is needed.

```
00    algorithm calcG(x, x_parent)
01    g ← x_parent . g + edgeCost(x, x_parent)
02    return g
```
Algorithm 10.7 Cumulative cost-to-come. The g value for each node is derived from its parent and the cost of the edge connecting them.

The node expansion part of the algorithm is provided in Algorithm 10.8.

```
00    algorithm expandNodeDijkstra(x)
01    for each(u ∈ U(x))
02        x_next ← f(x, u)
03        gnew = calcG(x_next, x)
04        if(x_next ∉ O && x_next ∉ C)
05            addToODijkstra(x_next, x, gnew)
06        else if (gnew < x . g)
07            O.remove(x_next)
08            addToODijkstra(x_next, x, gnew)
09        endif
10    endfor
11    return
```
Algorithm 10.8 Node Expansion for Dijkstra's Planner. Unvisited neighbors of the provided state are placed on a priority queue.

While a state is still on the OPEN queue, a shorter path to it may be found (Figure 10.18). Lines 6–8 deal with this case. Here, the parent pointer is redirected to the lesser cost parent and the cost-to-come is updated. Due to the change in cost, the state must be repositioned in the queue. One way to accomplish this is to remove and reinsert the state as shown in the pseudocode.

The procedure for adding a node to the priority queue (Algorithm 10.9) uses the g value as the key. The g value was based on the parent that was used when the node was inserted.

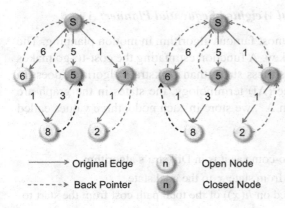

Figure 10.18 Backpointer Update Required. Values of g() are shown in nodes. (Left) When left node of cost 6 is expanded, a new path (of cost 7) is found to the node of cost 8. (Right) The backpointer is updated to reflect the new best path between the start and the node. Its cost is reduced to 7.

```
00    algorithm addToODijkstra(x, x_parent, g)
01        x.g ← g
02        O.insertSorted(x, g)
03        x.parent ← x_parent
04    return
```

Algorithm 10.9 Adding to the Frontier in Dijkstra's Algorithm. This routine computes the priority of a node and places it on the OPEN queue. The node may or may not have been removed from O before being placed back on O here.

Thus, preserving optimality in the weighted edge case involves the additional ingredients of sorting the queue, testing for the goal only upon removal from the queue, and tolerating and resolving multiple visits to the same state. All of this generality comes at an extra cost. The computations necessary to sort the queue during an insertion and the computations to test if a state is in the queue can be significant.

Now that breadth first and Dijkstra's algorithms have been covered, it is worthwhile to note that Dijkstra's algorithm is somewhat more efficient in terms of node expansion than breadth first search even in the case of equal cost edges. The reason is that it advances an equal cost contour rather than an equal depth contour. Figure 10.19 shows the differences in the shape of the frontier (OPEN list) on the same problem. It also shows that even more efficiency is possible using the algorithm discussed next, A*.

Figure 10.19 Search Frontiers for all Algorithms. (Far Left) The planning problem is to go from the bottom left to the top right and there are obstacles in the way. Whereas Dijkstra's algorithm (near right) expands less nodes than breadth first search (near left), the A* algorithm (far right) expands even less nodes than Dijkstra's algorithm. All produce the same solution in the case of equal weight edges, but they do so with varying efficiency.

10.2.4.2 Heuristic Optimal Weighted Sequential Planner: A*

The A* algorithm [13] is perhaps the most famous algorithm in motion planning. The new key ingredient is just that: a new key. A function estimating the cost-to-go makes it possible to be more efficient and visit less states than Dijkstra's algorithm does. In graph theory and artificial intelligence (AI) terminology, the states in the graph are referred to more generally as *nodes*. In A*, we store in each node, three values called f, g, and h where (Spotlight 10.1):

* $g(\underline{x})$ is the exact, known, best cost-to-come as it is in Dijkstra's algorithm.
* $\hat{h}(\underline{x})$ is an estimate of the cost-to-go from state $\underline{x}$ to the goal state.
* $\hat{f}(\underline{x})$ is an estimate (because it's based on $\hat{h}(\underline{x})$) of the total path cost from the start to the goal through state $\underline{x}$.

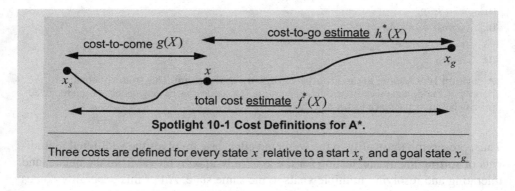

Spotlight 10-1 Cost Definitions for A*.

Three costs are defined for every state x relative to a start x_s and a goal state x_g

The cost estimate $\hat{f}(\underline{x})$ is computed as follows.

$$\hat{f}(\underline{x}) = g(\underline{x}) + \hat{h}(\underline{x}) \tag{10.4}$$

In more detail, the cost estimate algorithm is provided in Algorithm 10.10.

```
00   algorithm calcF(x ,g )
01      f ← g + calcH(x)
02   return f
```

Algorithm 10.10 Astar Cost Function. The *f* includes the known *g* value and an estimate of the cost from here to the goal

The priority queue is now sorted based on $\hat{f}$ rather than g. This change amounts to exploring paths in order of least estimated total cost until the goal is reached. The main algorithm is provided in (Algorithm 10.11):

```
00    algorithm Astar(x_s, x_g)
01    x_s.g ← 0; x_s.f ← calcF(x_s, 0)
02    O.insertSorted(x_s)
03    x_s.parent ← null
04    while(O ≠ ∅)
05        x ← O.removeFirst()
06        C.insert(x)
07        if(x = x_g) return success
08        expandNodeAstar(x)
09    endwhile
10    return failure
```

Algorithm 10.11 A* Algorithm for Heuristic Optimal Weighted Graph Search. This planner will generate a spanning tree for the search graph and produce the path to the goal of least cost. It will also report failure if no path exists.

The node expansion algorithm now has three cases, shown in Algorithm 10.12. As in Dijkstra's algorithm, when a better path to an OPEN node is found, it means that its backpointer must be updated to point to the new best parent. Here though, a better path to a CLOSED node may also be found, because nodes are closed based on $f(\ )$ rather than $g(\ )$. This means that its backpointer must be updated to point to the new best parent. Also, all downstream costs of the updated node must be updated. This is accomplished in the algorithm by simply placing the node back on OPEN.

```
00    algorithm expandNodeAstar(x)
01    for each(u ∈ U(x))
02        x_next ← f(x, u)
03        gnew ← calcG(x_next, x)
04        fnew ← calcF(x_next, gnew)
05        if(x_next ∈ O && fnew < x.f)
06            O.remove(x_next)
07            addToOAstar(x_next, x, fnew, gnew)
08        else if(x_next ∈ C && fnew < x.f)
09            C.remove(x_next)
10            addToOAstar(x_next, x, fnew, gnew)
11        else
12            addToOAstar(x_next, x, fnew, gnew)
13        endif
14    endfor
15    return
```

Algorithm 10.12 Node Expansion for A*. All unvisited neighbors of the provided state are placed on a priority queue.

It will then be removed in the very next step and its downstream costs will be updated in a similar fashion (Figure 10.20).

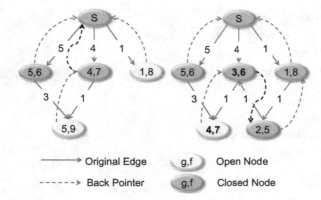

Figure 10.20 Path Update Required. Values shown in nodes are (g,f). (Left) Right node of total cost 8 is expanded. It produces a new node (of cost 5) which is expanded next. (Right) The expansion produces a new path of cost 6 to the central node of former cost 7. The central node backpointer is updated to reflect the new best path between the start and the node. Its cost is reduced to 6. The cost of its child node is also reduced from 9 to 7. This complexity is unnecessary if nodes on CLOSED are optimal.

The routine to place a node on OPEN now stores two costs (Algorithm 10.13). The g value is stored to facilitate downstream nodes computing their g values. The f value is stored to remember the key used to insert the node in OPEN.

```
00    algorithm addToOAstar(x, x_parent, f, g)
01        x.g ← g
02        x.f ← f
03        O.insertSorted(x, f)
04        x.parent ← x_parent
05    return
```

Algorithm 10.13 Adding to the Frontier in Astar. This routine places a node on the OPEN queue. In A*, the node may or may not have been removed from O or C before being placed back on O here.

10.2.4.3 Admissibility of Heuristics

When the heuristic $\hat{h}(\underline{x})$ does not overestimate the true cost-to-go, it is said to be *admissible* – an unrelated use of the same word used to denote obstacle avoidance guarantees. An important fact is that ***when $h(\underline{x})$ is admissible for all $\underline{x}$, the A* algorithm is optimal.***

To see that this claim is true, note that when the goal is removed from the queue $\hat{f}(\underline{x}_{goal}) = g(\underline{x}_{goal})$ because $\hat{h}(\underline{x}_{goal}) = 0$. At that point, some path from the goal back to the start is encoded in the backpointers and its actual cost is known perfectly and given by its f value. Because OPEN is sorted on f, we also know that the (under)estimated total (f) cost of paths to the goal through any of nodes left on OPEN is even higher than this. If we knew that the total costs any new nodes added to OPEN were also higher, we could conclude that the present path was optimal. We will see that new nodes are always of higher cost.

10.2.4.4 Consistency of Heuristics

A heuristic is said to be *consistent* if it is locally admissible. Suppose that a parent state $\underline{x}_p$ is expanded to produce a child state $\underline{x}_c$. Then, we say that the heuristic $h(\underline{x})$ does not over estimate the cost of the edge between them if

$$\hat{h}(\underline{x}_p) - \hat{h}(\underline{x}_c) \le \text{cost}(\underline{x}_p, \underline{x}_c) \qquad (10.5)$$

Under these circumstances, if $\underline{x}_c$ is the goal then $\hat{h}(\underline{x}_p)$ for an arbitrary parent of the goal will not overestimate the cost of the one edge path to the goal. By induction on the above condition, the cost estimate from every possible grandparent of the goal will also be an underestimate, and so on, so a consistent heuristic is not only locally admissible, it is everywhere admissible.

Rearranging the condition:

$$\hat{h}(\underline{x}_p) \le \hat{h}(\underline{x}_c) + \text{cost}(\underline{x}_p, \underline{x}_c) \qquad (10.6)$$

In other words, the estimate of cost to go directly to the goal from $\underline{x}_p$ cannot be higher than the true cost, $\text{cost}(\underline{x}_p, \underline{x}_c)$, to go to $\underline{x}_c$ from $\underline{x}_p$ plus the estimate to continue on from there to the goal. This is the well-known *triangle inequality,* and a heuristic that satisfies it is called a *metric.*

Yet another way to rewrite the condition is:

$$\hat{h}(\underline{x}_c) \ge \hat{h}(\underline{x}_p) - \text{cost}(\underline{x}_p, \underline{x}_c) \qquad (10.7)$$

If we add $g(\underline{x}_c)$ to both sides and rearrange, we have:

$$g(\underline{x}_c) + \hat{h}(\underline{x}_c) \ge g(\underline{x}_c) - \text{cost}(\underline{x}_p, \underline{x}_c) + \hat{h}(\underline{x}_p) = g(\underline{x}_p) + \hat{h}(\underline{x}_p) \qquad (10.8)$$

In other words, the total cost estimate must be *monotone* when moving in the search tree from any parent to any of its child nodes if the heuristic is consistent.

$$\hat{f}(\underline{x}_c) \ge \hat{f}(\underline{x}_p) \qquad (10.9)$$

For this reason, the term *monotone* is used interchangeably with consistent. This consequence of consistency will now be extended to characterize the time sequence of nodes coming off of OPEN, which will turn out to be a second sense in which such a heuristic is monotone.

10.2.4.5 Monotonicity of Total Cost for Consistent Heuristic

Consider what happens when a node $\underline{x}_p$ is removed from the priority queue and expanded to produce children that go back on the queue. All future nodes removed will have to be either higher cost nodes that were in the queue when the parent was removed, or their descendants, or a descendant of $\underline{x}_p$. Provided the edge costs to descendants are always positive, and the heuristic is consistent, all children cost more than their parents so no node that is removed later can have a lower estimated total cost $f(\underline{x})$ than $\underline{x}_p$ had when it was removed. That is, the estimated total cost $f(\underline{x})$ of the nodes coming off the priority queue must also be *monotone in time*.

Therefore, a consistent heuristic also implies that the condition at line 8 of the A* node expansion algorithm will never occur and a node will never have to be moved from CLOSED to OPEN. That implies that nodes are optimal when they are removed from OPEN – meaning their shortest paths back to the start have been computed and both the f and g values are optimal. In particular, the goal is optimal when it is removed from OPEN.

Although all consistent heuristics are admissible, it is not the case that all admissible heuristics are consistent, so consistency is a stronger condition than is necessary for optimality. The test at line 8 of the A* node expansion algorithm is best left in any implementation not only for this reason, but for the reason that it will identify software bugs. There are also occasions where inadmissible heuristics will be deliberately used to enhance efficiency.

10.2.4.6 Informed and Dominant Heuristics

When A* terminates, the goal is removed from OPEN and every other node on OPEN has a higher value of $\hat{f}(\underline{x})$. At that point the value of $\hat{f}(\underline{x})$ associated with the goal is the true cost of the optimal path, which can also be denoted $f^*(\underline{x}_{start})$. For a monotone heuristic, we know that every node whose estimated total cost is less than the cost of the optimal solution will have already been removed from OPEN and hence it will have already been expanded.

Consider two different heuristics $\hat{h}_1(\underline{x})$ and $\hat{h}_2(\underline{x})$. Suppose that $\hat{h}_1(\underline{x}) \geq \hat{h}_2(\underline{x})$ for all states in the search space and that both heuristics are admissible. We say that $\hat{h}_1(\underline{x})$ dominates $\hat{h}_2(\underline{x})$ or that an algorithm using $\hat{h}_1(\underline{x})$ is more informed than one using $\hat{h}_2(\underline{x})$.

The cost of the optimal solution does not depend on the heuristic, but the number of nodes with lower estimated costs does. The $g(\underline{x})$ value of any node is also independent of the heuristic. Therefore, the fact that $\hat{h}_1(\underline{x}) \geq \hat{h}_2(\underline{x})$ means that a wider range of $g(\underline{x})$ values, and hence more nodes, will satisfy the condition $\hat{f}(\underline{x}) \leq f^*(\underline{x}_{start})$ when $\hat{h}_2(\underline{x})$ is used. Hence an algorithm based on $\hat{h}_2(\underline{x})$ will expand all the nodes that one based on $\hat{h}_1(\underline{x})$ will expand—and possibly a lot more depending on the magnitude of the difference in the heuristics.

Two extreme cases are interesting. Search is called unguided or uninformed (i.e., dynamic programming) if $\hat{h}(\underline{x}) = 0$. In this case, more states than necessary may be expanded. Conversely if $\hat{h}(\underline{x}) = \hat{h}^*(\underline{x})$ (meaning the true optimal cost to the goal) then A* expands no unnecessary states at all (if the queue resolves ties in f by favoring a lower h). In practice the presence of obstacles unknown to the heuristic, and the fact that the correct order to process child nodes is unknown means this perfect case is rarely achieved in practice.

If several admissible heuristics are available, then their maximum is also admissible and must be more informed unless they are identical. Thus, if $\hat{h}_1(\underline{x})$ and $\hat{h}_2(\underline{x})$ are distinct and admissible then:

$$\hat{h}_3(\underline{x}) = max[\hat{h}_1(\underline{x}), \hat{h}_2(\underline{x})] \tag{10.10}$$

is more informed. A good example of the use of this rule is a heuristic that is based on the length of a feasible edge at minimum cell cost and the true cost of an infeasible straight line between two states. It can also be shown that if $\hat{h}_1(\underline{x})$ and $\hat{h}_2(\underline{x})$ are consistent, then $\hat{h}_3(\underline{x})$ is consistent.

10.2.4.7 Perfect Heuristics

At least when there are no obstacles, it is possible to precompute the perfect heuristic in A*. When the robot vehicle model must satisfy differential constraints (most do) such a heuristic is potentially much more informed than a straight line between positions. Heuristics can be based on a minimum length curve connecting two states and it may be necessary to convert length to cost by multiplying by some minimum cost per unit length.

For four connected and eight connected grids, perfect heuristics can be computed with simple algorithms. In more complicated cases, the planning algorithm itself can be executed in world models that are free of obstacles in order to compute heuristics. For vehicles that have a minimum turn radius, the Reeds-Shepp solution is often a useful heuristic.

Obstacle-free solution lengths can be stored in lookup tables indexed by the relative position and orientation of the goal and the start. If the table is not large enough to cover all cases, ensuring heuristic consistency across the frontier of the lookup table can become an issue.

In situations where vehicle maneuverability is limited, a heuristic can be computed based on solving the planning problem without the constraints. For example, solving the problem in an eight-connected grid will produce an underestimate of the true cost for a limited maneuverability vehicle but one that does account for the presence of obstacles.

Both the feasible obstacle-free heuristic and the infeasible obstacle-aware heuristic can be combined to produce a new heuristic that is more informed yet still admissible. Once again, the consistency of this composite heuristic can be an issue.

10.2.5 Representation for Sequential Motion Planning

This section covers some of the high-level design issues for implementation of a sequential motion planner. Path planners need to use a representation of the external environment, and a motion model of the vehicle. They also need to implement the data structures used to manage the search process – the search graph and the search tree. This section will present some design issues for these data structures.

10.2.5.1 Vehicle

Depending on the nature of the edge cost function, different aspects of the vehicle may need to be modelled. In the simplest case, the volume of the vehicle, and its pose are needed to compute the volume that it occupies at each point along the edge. In difficult terrain the details of the volume underneath may need to be known to avoid high centering and to permit straddling rises in the terrain that the ground clearance is adequate to avoid. The height may need to be known to avoid collisions with low doorways or tree branches.

A separate matter is the mobility of the vehicle. The design of the edges may or may not attempt to capture realistic motions but if they do, a model of the vehicle dynamics will be needed to generate those motions.

10.2.5.2 Obstacle and Cost Maps

Options for the model of the environment include either a set of discrete obstacles, called an *obstacle map*, or a rasterized *cost field* (also called *cost map*). Discrete obstacles may encode pose, size, shape, and even motion attributes. Cost maps may store continuous or binary cost values in a regular raster pattern implemented, ultimately, as an array. It is sometimes more general to use a cost map, but discrete obstacles may be the preferred implementation for simple representations of objects that are moving. Hybrid representations incorporating both ideas can also be a good approach. In a cost field representation, the world is divided into small finite regions, perhaps square cells, and a cost of traversal is stored in each cell. The computations required to produce the cost information can be very complex in unstructured environments. One approach is to accumulate perception data into a 3D volumetric representation and to derive a 2D cost representation from that. One such 3D representation is a rasterized *point cloud* where voxels in 3D are used to store the statistics of sensed lidar data points.

It is often desirable for the environmental model to be spatially indexed for efficiency in intersection, collision, or overlap calculations. In the case where a prior (to the planning query) model of the environment exists, its value in planning can be sufficient to justify preallocating it entirely in memory or caching it from disk.

The cost map may be defined over C-space, but in either case the cost of a configuration of the robot is naturally a C-space quantity – because rotating the robot changes the occupied volume in the workspace. For discrete obstacles, C-space obstacles can be defined and the cost value of a configuration can be read directly from the C-space cost map. For continuous-valued cost fields in the workspace, an equivalent configuration cost calculation can be performed that determines the set of cells that will be intersected if the vehicle occupies a certain pose in the environment.

Once the configuration calculations are performed, the cost calculation for a path is a line integral of the configuration costs along the C-space path. In the case of binary costs, a single obstacle encountered on the path means the entire path is in collision. When the cost map changes over time due to motion, uncertainty, or discovery of new information, a precomputation of the swath of a path or of the cost of a configuration may not save any effort so a direct calculation in the workspace can be used instead.

10.2.5.3 Search Graph

As we have seen, path planning often constructs a search tree from a search graph. The search graph connects *states* (which possess attributes like position and orientation) via explicit or implicit edges. The basic functionality of a state is to encode spatial coordinates that can be used to generate neighbors and to assess intersections with obstacles/cost maps. The edges of the search graph represent motions, and they have an associated cost of traversal. The edge representation may encode details of how to execute the motion or such information may be completely implicit. For example, every cell in a grid has a neighbor in all four cardinal directions, and that knowledge can be in the code itself rather than represented in data. The cost of an edge between two states is the line integral of the edge over the cost map.

When obstacles are not to be occupied by any part of the robot, they may be encoded topologically by removing all edges through them from the search graph. Another way to perform this operation is to remove edges that enter into obstacles at the time neighbors are generated in the search tree.

The search graph spatial sampling need not be matched to the cost map spatial sampling. Cost map sampling needs to resolve small obstacles and search graph sampling needs to distinguish alterative motions.

Because it is possible that a solution may pass through only a small portion of the region in which planning is to take place, it is potentially desirable to allocate memory for the search graph in a *lazy (only when headed) fashion.* just in case much of the planning space is never touched in the computation.

When the search graph is symmetric (repetitive structure), it is straightforward to generate parts of it as needed by developing a single function that provides the neighbors (predecessors and successors) of a given state. Then, the search graph need not be precomputed. It is important to be able to efficiently find the state that occupies a given location in space. A spatially indexed data structure (like an array) can do this. If the states encode more information than their location, states can be allocated on a lazy basis by creating them when they are first referenced.

10.2.5.4 Search Tree

Conceptually a *planner node* in a search tree data structure is a different entity than a state in a search graph. A planner node needs to store bookkeeping information like f, g, and h values in A* in order to manage the search and it will also store backpointers to assist in path extraction. There typically needs to be exactly one search tree node for every state encountered so keeping them together may simplify memory management. The search tree is generated during search by definition so it need not be preallocated. Likewise, its nodes can be created when they are needed.

10.2.5.5 Lists and Queues

The OPEN queue is either a FIFO or a priority queue in the algorithms presented here. Hence it must at least be a sequence (list, ordered set) and in most cases it is very important that it be efficiently sorted. The efficiency of the priority queue is very important in A*.

The CLOSED set needs no sense of order so it can be implemented as a set. For efficiency in testing for membership, it may be useful to store flags in each search tree *node* to record if it is open or closed or unvisited. This measure makes membership tests very inexpensive. In the case of the CLOSED set, because the only operation desired is to test membership, an explicit data structure is not needed if node flags are used.

10.2.6 References and Further Reading

10.2.6.1 Books

In addition to the books referenced in the last subchapter, the books by Rich and Russel are good introductions to the basics of search as it is taught in computer science. Motion planning has adopted these methods with little change.

[7]   R. E. Bellman, *Dynamic Programming,* Princeton University Press, 2003.

[8]   E. Rich and K. Knight, *Artificial Intelligence,* 2nd ed., McGraw-Hill Science/Engineering/Math, 1991.

[9]   S. Russel and P. Norvig, *Artificial Intelligence: A Modern Approach,* Prentice Hall, 1998.

10.2.6.2 Papers

The following papers were referenced in the text.

[10]   H. Blum, A Transformation for Extracting New Descriptors of Shape, *Models for the Perception of Speech and Visual Form.* MIT Press, pp. 362–380, 1967.

[11]   H. Choset and J. Burdick. Sensor-Based Exploration: The Hierarchical Generalized Voronoi Graph, *The International Journal of Robotics Research* February 2000, Vol. 19, pp. 96–125, 2000.

[12]   E. W. Dijkstra, A Note on Two Problems in Connexion with Graphs, *Numerische Mathematik,* Vol. 1, pp. 269–271, 1959.

[13]   P. E. Hart, N. J. Nilsson, and B. Raphael, A Formal Basis for the Heuristic Determination of Minimum Cost Paths. *IEEE Transactions on Systems Science and Cybernetics,* Vol. 4, No. 2, pp. 100–107, 1968.

[14]   L. E. Kavraki, P. Svestka, J. C. Latombe, M. H. Overmars, Probabilistic Roadmaps for Path Planning in High-Dimensional Configuration Spaces, *IEEE Transactions on Robotics and Automation,* Vol. 12, No. 4, pp. 566–580, 1996.

[15]   A. H. Land and A. G. Doig, An Automatic Method for Solving Discrete Programming Problems, *Econometrica,* Vol. 28, pp. 497–520, 1960.

[16]   Pearl, J. (1984). *Heuristics: Intelligent Search Strategies for Computer Problem Solving.* Addison-Wesley, 1984.

[17]   M. Pivtoraiko, R. Knepper, A. Kelly, Differentially Constrained Mobile Robot Motion Planning in State Lattices. *Journal of Field Robotics,* Vol. 26, No. 3, pp. 308–333, 2009.

10.2.7 Exercises

10.2.7.1 Perfect Heuristics

A perfect heuristic is a solution for the most efficient (typically the shortest) path in the absence of obstacles in particular search space. Write algorithms for perfect heuristics in four and eight connected grids. Do the same for a hexagonal lattice.

10.3 Real-Time Global Motion Planning: Moving in Unknown and Dynamic Environments

10.3.1 Introduction

Of course, the planning approaches presented so far have assumed that the environment is known beforehand. Although building layouts, road networks, and aerial imagery are often both available and very useful, they are typically not enough information. Such *prior map* information is usually not fine enough in detail for obstacle avoidance or other detailed motion planning and it often is geometrically inaccurate or its data is out of date. Even if all those issues did not exist, the moving entities in the environment, including people, animals, vehicles, and other robots will not be represented in these maps.

For our purposes, unknown and dynamic environments can be treated similarly because a dynamic environment is partially unknown. Although the problem of planning in such environments is quite complex, very elegant solutions are known. When the techniques of this section are working, they can create behaviors of astonishing competence. Given a correct map, the capacity of motion planning systems can exceed the competence of humans. Conversely, a (typically myopic) robot that has to discover the environment while navigating in it, can exhibit a level of incompetence that is equally surprising.

The techniques presented in this section are intended to deal with some or all of the following difficulties that occur in more realistic situations:

- real-time: when the robot is moving, there is limited time to decide what to do, so if new plans are needed, they are needed fast.
- unknown environments: when the environment is partially unknown, the only way to continue to learn more is to move, so if new plans are needed, they must start at different places each time.
- uncertain and dynamic environments: even if the environment is "known," its representation may change due to uncertainty or dynamics.
- robot motion: the motion of the robot can render a significant amount of the search tree irrelevant unless the robot returns to a previously visited location.

10.3.1.1 Real-Time Planning in Unknown Environments

This chapter deals with the problem of gathering data, planning, and executing more or less concurrently and continuously. A common scenario is one where a plan is generated and executed until the point is reached where the robot learns something from its sensors that was not known when the original plan was generated. At that point, a new plan can be generated and the process repeated.

A key question is whether the robot must attempt to move more or less continuously. Sometimes it is better to stop and think because more planning time makes better use of available information. At other times, it may be better to move around more to gather more information. In some cases, the robot needs to keep moving in order to get somewhere fast, and stopping every time something new is learned is not an option. This is particularly so when we consider that maps are always inaccurate so a robot can learn something every sensing cycle.

Unknown environments and the desire for continuous motion, create a requirement for real-time planning because the robot needs to move to learn more and it needs to incorporate new knowledge quickly in order to keep moving. In unknown environments, robots often have to commit to actions before their ultimate consequences are known.

Clearly, one piece of information can make a radical difference. If a robot is moving while it is learning its surroundings, it may suddenly learn that the path it is trying to follow is blocked. Conversely, it may learn that a shortcut exists that was not in the original map. In either case, rapid production of a new plan will allow it to keep moving.

It is not an unusual phenomenon to observe a robot continue to change its mind as it learns more information. If each time that the robot sees an area, it may learn more about how bad it is, it may continue to switch strategies and try to make progress elsewhere (Figure 10.21).

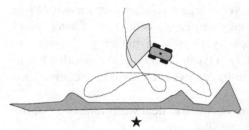

Figure 10.21 Changing Strategy. The robot does not know the extent of the obstruction. It tries to avoid it to the left and finds that it extends further to the left. Then it tries right and finds it is even longer; then left. If the planner is configured to assume obstacles are rare, this behavior may repeat until the extent of the obstacle is fully known.

10.3.1.2 Uncertain Environments

Real sensors have limited maximum range and they are imperfect. These facts lead to an operating mode of continuous imperfect discovery, and unknown environments that remain unknown. Uncertainty in perception is a different order of problem because the system performance may change from being inefficient to being totally nonconvergent. Suppose, for example, that a perceived dead end was a momentary hallucination due to a cloud of dust or a swarm of insects. In this case, the system may make a potentially catastrophic wrong decision, turn around, and never look back. If the frequency of such perception failures is high enough, the robot can wander around aimlessly in an imagined natural or man-made maze and never achieve its goals.

Of course, maps and sensors are never perfect and many interesting applications have moving objects in the robot workspace. Hence, any realistic situation is one where a robot has to move in an unknown environment that is sensed imperfectly and all of the challenges described above occur at once. The rest of this chapter will describe four basic techniques for coping with the challenges of realtime motion planning on the scale of kilometers. They are limited depth search, anytime search, plan repair, and hierarchical planning.

10.3.2 Depth-Limited Approaches

In some cases, the commitment to act must be made even before estimated consequences can be computed, either because there is no time to finish the computation or because the effective range of sensing is limited (it always is). In this case, the question becomes one of how best to use the available computation and the available information.

One approach to dealing with such restrictions is to limit the *planning horizon* – the depth of the search tree that is generated, and to make the best decision possible given the resulting partial plan. Note that such a *depth-limited planning* approach can give new meaning to the word search because the search ends up being conducted for real, on the robot, as it wanders around trying to find a way to the goal.

10.3.2.1 Purely Reactive Planning

The most straightforward limited depth search is to use a completely reactive strategy that simply computes what to do based on locally visible information. No map is constructed on-the-fly because the assumption is that there is no time to search it anyway. This approach is the antithesis of planning and it is only effective in limited situations.

A natural implementation would be to consider multiple options for traversing the environment in view and to then choose an option based on how "promising" it looks from a goal seeking perspective. This is a version of the simplest planner presented earlier, but it is conducted physically with the robot, with obstacle avoidance and a bias toward the goal added.

When obstacles are sparse this can be an effective approach. However, it is easy to construct an environment that will confound this approach because the global structure of the environment (beyond the perception horizon) is such that moving away from the goal is the only way to succeed (Figure 10.22).

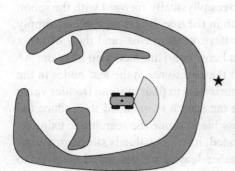

Figure 10.22 Purely Reactive Planner. With no memory, the robot will have a very difficult time finding its way to the goal. A bias to move towards the goal will make matters worse because the right answer is to move away from it for a while.

In any such situation, it may be critical to remember the set of states that have been physically visited on a CLOSED list. Unless some randomization results from either sensor data or changes to the algorithm, the act of revisiting a previously visited state will close a loop, and the robot will then compute and execute the same action as it did the first time it occupied the state. Then it will repeat the entire path again and visit the state a third time, and so on.

10.3.2.2 Depth Limited Planning

Based on the last example, searching deeper in the search tree seems advisable. The motivation is that if the robot can search around obstructions in simulation, it will not have to do so physically. The ***conduct of depth limited planning is the same as receding horizon predictive control.*** The basic idea is to search (in simulation) some limited depth forward in the search tree, choose an edge to follow, execute the edge motion (for real), and then repeat the process.

One way to do this is to search for a limited depth, compute a heuristic $\hat{h}(\underline{x})$ that estimates the remaining cost to the goal, and then pass the cost-of-best-child up the tree to determine the edge that is the first step toward the best leaf node (a horizon node at the depth limit with no children) in the tree (Figure 10.23).

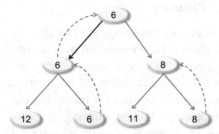

Figure 10.23 Lookahead Search. The heuristic values at the leaves of the tree are passed up the tree, on a best child basis, to find the edge which is the first step toward the best child.

Of course, the robot could execute multiple edges, or even execute all the way to the best leaf node, but that might be imprudent. If the path forward were blocked at a depth of one edge beyond the depth originally searched, then a robot executing all the way will not discover this fact until it is already there and the path is obstructed. The *principle of least commitment* [21] is to execute only one edge on the robot and then to plan again to a limited depth. In this way, every move benefits from the maximum possible deliberation and the search horizon moves physically forward with the robot.

When the cost of a path is equivalent to depth in the tree, it is reasonable to simply plan to some fixed depth. If, however, actions have varying cost (and they will in a cost map), then it can be better to employ a total cost heuristic modelled after the A* algorithm in order to capture information about the cost to reach the leaf nodes in the tree. An alternative to using fixed depth of the horizon is to plan to some frontier value of the cost-to-go $g(x)$. In either case, because the search is intended to produce the leaf node with the lowest value of $f(x)$, it is possible to prune the search tree using α-*pruning*. As soon as the first leaf node is generated, its $\hat{f}(x)$ value is stored in a variable called α and thereafter α is updated as other leaves are generated in order to record the lowest value of $\hat{f}(x)$ at any leaf node. If the heuristic is monotone in depth, the expansion of any nonleaf nodes that already exceed the cost α can be avoided.

A limited depth planner like the one described above will be more informed than the reactive planner, but there is still no guarantee that it will find the goal without mechanisms to prevent cycles, and those mechanism always involve extra memory.

10.3.2.3 Real Time A*

The realtime A* algorithm [21] uses the limited depth search process described above to propagate total path (f) cost information back up the tree to the neighbors of the root (the root is the present state) in a best-child fashion. Moving up the tree, the cost of any node is computed as the lowest value of the cost of any child plus the edge to reach that child. In effect, each node has its cost set to the cost of the best known path based on the amount of search that was performed. These costs can be thought of as heuristics $\hat{h}(x)$ for each node that are informed by the results of the search process as well as the heuristics computed at the leaf nodes.

The edges to the current neighbors of the present state are now evaluated for total path cost $f = g + \hat{h}$ using these more informed heuristics and the edge to the best neighbor is executed. Once this is done, the total path cost of the second best option is stored as the heuristic of the state that was just vacated. It represents the cost of the best known (alternate) path if the robot has to return to that state. At the neighbor state that was just occupied, the limited depth search proceeds again and the process repeats until the goal is found.

The algorithm must also keep the cost information consistent in the search tree if the robot returns to previously visited state via a different path from which it left. If this case is treated correctly, the algorithm becomes complete – guaranteed to eventually find the goal. This concept of storing and repairing the information in the search tree from move to move can be extended to even more efficient levels as described in the following section on plan repair.

10.3.3 Anytime Approaches

An *anytime* approach to motion planning produces solutions of increasing quality as the amount of available computing increases. Some approaches are interruptible at any time, whereas others require a commitment of a fixed amount of time or resources before they can produce a solution. Many approaches require an initial nontrivial computation that may not be interruptible.

Limited depth approaches may be justified on the basis of limited sensor horizon and lack of a map, but if reasonably accurate map information is available, then anytime approaches are likely to be superior because they can eventually find their way to the goal well before the robot moves close to the goal. Anytime approaches are incremental in the sense that each planning iteration improves on the previous solution in some way.

Several anytime approaches present themselves after a little thought. A basic brute force approach is to execute the present plan while a new one is generated in a separate thread of execution. In the case of limited depth search, a second iteration could be used to extend the search tree one or more levels deeper. Typically, the number of nodes is exponential in depth of the tree so the computational demands increase rapidly with depth and this is not a viable approach in the general case. Yet another variant on limited depth is to define a radius around the goal and to search until the first node is found that is within the goal radius. Subsequent iterations can reduce the radius until the goal is reached.

10.3.3.1 Inflated Heuristics

Given the relationship between run-time and the informedness of heuristics, it is not unreasonable to deliberately use an inadmissible heuristic in A* in order to produce a good answer quickly rather than an optimal one more slowly. This strategy allows the algorithm to more quickly direct the search into more promising directions. If the heuristic is inflated by a factor $1 + \varepsilon$ where $\varepsilon > 0$ then the algorithm is called (constant) *weighted A**, or WA*. For WA*, if the original heuristic is admissible, then it can be shown that the solution generated is ε-*admissible*, meaning that no solution generated will have a total cost that exceeds the optimal cost by a factor greater than $1 + \varepsilon$. This idea was originally proposed in [23].

An anytime algorithm can be based on weighted A*. In the first iteration a high inflation factor is used and it can be reduced in subsequent iterations in order to refine the solution. This is a viable approach in practice, but it is potentially wasteful to discard all of the work that is done in one iteration before starting the next. A few techniques are known that reuse the work of previous iterations. These are described in the next two sections.

10.3.3.2 Continued Search

It has been pointed out that there is no need to discontinue the search in WA* once the goal is removed from the OPEN queue [19]. For an inadmissible heuristic, this first path to the goal need not be optimal but the optimal one, and many others, will eventually be generated if WA* is simply allowed to continue execution. The technique of α-*pruning* can be used to reduce the search effort by avoiding expansion of nodes that are higher cost than the lowest cost path encountered so far.

10.3.3.3 Singular Expansion

We have seen that A* may have to expand nodes more than once if the heuristic is not consistent. However, it turns out that the bound of $1 + \varepsilon$ on suboptimality applies even if nodes are expanded only once. The technique of ARA* [22] maintains a list of inconsistent nodes called INCONS. This list contains those nodes that were on CLOSED but needed to be re-expanded more than once in a given planning iteration. Instead of reexpanding these nodes, ARA* delays their reexpansion until the next planning iteration. In that next planning iteration, the nodes in INCONS are moved to OPEN before the iteration starts.

10.3.4 Plan Repair Approach: D* Algorithm

Anytime approaches do not typically deal explicitly with robot motion or with cost changes that occur after a plan is computed. The plan repair approach is based on the fact that the search tree of a second plan is typically not radically different than that of the first, so it ought to be possible to make minor changes to the first plan to produce the second.

The D* algorithm was originally introduced in [25]. Later, a version called D* Lite was introduced [20] that is somewhat easier to understand but the basic principles are the same. This section will refer to both algorithms as D* and it will present a version of D* Lite that is deliberately restructured to be analogous to the algorithms presented so far. One major difference from the original paper is the fact that the version presented here calls the robot position the "goal" state in order for code to be consistent with all algorithms presented so far. The paper [20] calls the node toward which the search is progressing the start state for reason discussed below.

Because a grid is just an implicit graph, D* can be implemented on a grid or a graph. In a grid, it is typical to associate continuous cost values with cells and use the average cost of the two participating cells as the cost of the implicit edge between them. In a graph the costs are associated directly with the edges.

D* starts by producing an initial solution to the planning problem that the robot starts to execute. Thereafter the robot continues to execute the initial plan until something new is learned. For example, the robot may have learned that a pathway that was assumed to be clear is blocked, or vice versa. New information is represented as cost changes in a graph or a cost field and these changes may occur either because something changed for real or because the robot's state of knowledge changed. In either case, the key capability of D* is its capacity to very efficiently replan a new solution to the goal when new information is learned.

10.3.4.1 Search Tree Maintenance

For this presentation, it will be important once again to distinguish the *search graph* from the *search tree*. The former refers to all states and the edges that connect them to adjacent or neighboring states. Let the states that can be reached in one edge from a given state in the search graph be known as the *neighbors* of that state. The search tree is the backpointer data structure that encodes a spanning tree of the search graph. For a given state in the tree, states above it on the path to the root will be called *ancestors* and those below it will be called *descendents*. The immediate ancestor of a node is its *parent* and an immediate descendent its *child*.

Although edges in the search graph, and the search tree possess an inherent cost of traversal, nodes are used to store the cost of the sequence of edges required to reach them from the root. In this way, it is meaningful to speak of the costs of both nodes and edges – with the understanding that nodes store the cost of a sequence of edges. Node costs refer to the estimate total cost (f) values of these paths to the root whereas edge costs refer to the traversal costs from node to node.

Unlike the node lists maintained in realtime A*, D* remembers the entire search tree from one planning cycle to the next and it continues to maintain and repair the search tree as new information is acquired. When a planning cycle (called a *query*) completes, the goal node is ready to go on CLOSED and the path in the tree from the start node to the goal is optimal. For a consistent heuristic, every other node on CLOSED is also optimal, meaning its path to the root is optimal. The information on the OPEN list is still in the process of being optimized but it is already known that the solution to the original query does not go through them so they were not investigated further.

10.3.4.1.1 A* Competition for Parenthood. It is possible to incrementally update the policy in the search tree to repair a plan to the goal if one or more edges in the graph change in cost. Repairing a plan means modifying the search tree minimally to generate the search tree that would have been generated if A* was simply rerun on the new search graph (to produce a new search tree) after the edge was changed. Let this hypothetical second run of A* be called the *virtual rerun* (Figure 10.25).

The key concept required to pinpoint exactly what will happen differently in the virtual rerun is to recognize that while nodes remain on OPEN, nodes on CLOSED *compete to be their parents*. While a node N is on the OPEN list, it is on the frontier of the search. It enters the list with a specific parent P_1 on CLOSED and a cost value $f_{P1}(N) = P1.g + c(P1, N) + N.h$ derived from that parent. While N remains on OPEN, it is possible for another node P_2 to be removed from OPEN, and be expanded to connect to N at a lower total cost. That is, although $f(P_1) < f(P_2)$ by monotonicity, it is still possible for the edge joining N to $P2$ to be such that $f_{P2}(N) < f_{P1}(N)$ This is precisely what line 5 in Algorithm 10.12 is testing for. When N is removed from OPEN, the competition is over and its best parent has already been selected. It is optimal and primed to compete to be the parent of the neighbors it produces when it is expanded.

10.3.4.1.2 Implications of Edge Changes. With the above understanding of the machinery of A*, search tree repair can be understood in terms of how the competition for children would go differently if an edge cost changes and A* was run over again. Consider a single node N and consider the case of a change to the cost of the edge to its parent changes (Figure 10.24). If an edge cost changes, we define a quantity equal to the best possible g value that the node can have after the change occurs.

$$rhs(X) = min_{Y \in neighbors(X)}[g(Y) + c(X, Y)] \tag{10.11}$$

where $c(\ )$ denotes the cost of an edge. This quantity performs a kind of one step lookahead. When $g(N) \neq rhs(N)$ the node is said to be *inconsistent*.

If the edge cost is reduced, then $f(N)$ can be reduced because $g(N)$ can be reduced. We can refer to this case as one where the cost of N is reduced. Recall that A* stores the g value used when a node is placed on OPEN in the node itself. We will refer to this stored value as $g(N)$. When $g(N) > rhs(N)$ we refer to N as an *overconsistent node* meaning its present g is too high. In the virtual rerun of A*, after making N consistent, any of the neighbors of N in the search graph might want to adopt N as their new parent and if so, their costs and those of all of their descendants will be reduced as well (Figure 10.24).

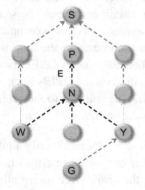 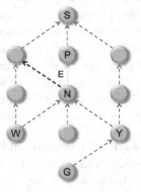

Figure 10.24 Search Tree Repair. (Left) If edge E is reduced in cost, nodes W and Y (which are assumed to be neighbors in the search graph) may want to change their parent to node N. (Right) Conversely, if the cost of edge E is increased, node N itself might choose a new parent.

Conversely, if the cost of the edge from N to its parent is increased, then N might want to adopt a new parent to try to reduce its cost. In either case the cost of N will go up so we can refer to this case as one where the cost of N is increased. When $g(N) < rhs(N)$ we refer to N as an *underconsistent node* meaning its present g value is too low. The cost increase may cause some of its children to adopt a new parent. Whether or not any children change their costs, the increased cost of N must be propagated down to all of its ancestors and any of them may chose to adopt a new parent to improve their costs.

In summary, when a node's cost is raised, the node may lose descendants in the virtual rerun. When a node's cost is lowered, the node may gain descendants. In either case, cost changes have to be propagated down the search tree. In fact, D* operates by placing all inconsistent nodes on OPEN and propagating the associated cost changes down the search tree. The algorithm to start that process when a cost change is detected is shown as Figure 10.25. The nodes whose cost have changed are all placed on OPEN with a special sort key (priority) that is described below.

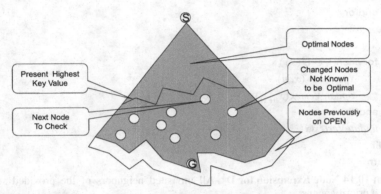

Figure 10.25 Multiple Cost Changes. The highest key value of any changed node defines a cost threshold in the search tree above which all nodes need not be changed. The nodes underneath this boundary must be processed in top to bottom sorted order to repair the tree in one pass.

10.3.4.1.3 Propagating Cost Changes. Suppose that the cost of node N has changed and the plan needs to be repaired. Of course, the A* algorithm already constructs a search tree that propagates costs and computes backpointers, so it seems natural to use A* to repair the plan at N by placing N on OPEN and running A*. However, every node processed in this way will necessarily become a descendant of N, so this process will not allow present descendants to choose new parents that are not also descendants of N. Hence, rerunning A* at N will not repair the plan correctly in general.

When an edge increase is being propagated, the cost of N increases. In this case, the present immediate descendants of N need to be given the option of choosing new parents. If we try to mimic the way A* works, those potential parents, which are the neighbors of N in the search tree, should be placed on OPEN. Furthermore, when an edge reduction is being propagated, the cost of N decreases. In this case, nodes that are neighbors of N, but not presently children, need to be given a chance to select N as a parent. Hence, the rule is that any time the cost of N changes, all of its neighbors in the search graph need to be re-examined. Arguing inductively, this process must be repeated at all nodes encountered as cost updates proceed downward in the tree.

The reexamination of all neighbors will happen automatically provided all of the neighbors of each node encountered are first placed on OPEN. In A*, nodes are sorted based on their f value. This value for any queue is called the sort *key*. D* uses a slightly different key as described below. The node expansion algorithm for D* is provided as Algorithm 10.14. Note in the algorithm how the updateVertex() routine functions like the routine that placed nodes on OPEN in earlier algorithms. In plan repair, however, nodes only go on OPEN if they need repair.

```
00    algorithm expandNodeDstar(x)
01    if( x.g > x.rhs )
02        x.g ← x.rhs
03        for each( u ∈ U(x) )
04            x_next ← f(x, u)
05            updateVertex(x_next)
06        endfor
07    else
08        x.g ← ∞
09        for each( u ∈ U(x) )
10            x_next ← f(x, u)
11            updateVertex(x_next)
12        endfor
13        updateVertex(x)
14    endif
15    return
```

Algorithm 10.14 Node Expansion for D*. All unvisited neighbors of the provided state are placed on a priority queue.

All of the neighbors of the expanded node are updated regardless of other circumstances. If the node itself is overconsistent, its g value is simply corrected. If the node is underconsistent or consistent, its g value is set to infinity and it is updated. As we will see shortly, doing so changes its sort key value to the key it would have had if it were consistent. It still may need to be repaired, but the key value determines when it will be repaired.

One remaining subtlety is the manner by which N and its neighbors are placed on OPEN. After the original and the virtual rerun of A*, two things will be true. First, N will have one parent chosen from its neighbors. Second, N will have zero or more children chosen from its neighbors. If the cost of N goes up, the cost if its children will go up after the increase is propagated down the tree. However, if those children are to be given a chance to adopt new parents, they need to be on the OPEN list when their new parent comes off of OPEN. This means they must be placed on OPEN based on their **former** (not increased) cost. Conversely, if the cost of N goes down, then N may be able to adopt more children. To do that it will have to be placed on the OPEN list based on its **new** (reduced) cost to guarantee that it comes off of OPEN before they do.

It seems that when the search tree is regenerated, nodes need to have a new key value which is the minimum of their old cost and their new cost. This is exactly how D* computes the priority of nodes.

10.3.4.1.4 Propagating Multiple Cost Changes to Termination. Because the above repair algorithm will potentially regenerate a subtree of significant size, running it on every changed edge is bound to be expensive. Ideally it would be possible to place all the changed nodes and their neighbors on OPEN based on the new cost key defined above and then rerun A* in one highly efficient pass committing to cost and back-pointer changes along the way until some termination condition is met. This is exactly how D* works.

The main algorithm for computing the least cost path in D* is very straightforward given the functions defined so far (Algorithm 10.15). The algorithm simply extracts nodes from OPEN and expands them until either the queue is empty, or a termination condition is met.

A* terminates when the goal node is removed from OPEN. In D*, there are clearly cases where the goal will never be placed on OPEN because the processed changes turn out to be irrelevant to the original optimal path to the goal. A more general condition can be generated by once again considering what would happen in a virtual rerun. If the goal is not placed on OPEN, eventually a point is reached where either the OPEN list is empty or the costs of the nodes removed from OPEN are higher than the cost of the goal. The first case terminates naturally. In the second case, the correction wavefront will have passed the goal. Then, there is no need to process the changes any further because the nodes remaining on OPEN are already too high in cost to be on an optimal path to the goal. This is essentially the original A* termination condition but it occurs simultaneously with the goal being removed from OPEN. In practice, it can be important to terminate at a cost slightly higher than the cost of the goal to accommodate roundoff error.

```
00   algorithm computeOptimalPath()
01   while(f[O.peek()] < f(x_g)   or   x_g.g ≠ x_g.rhs)
02       x ← O.removeFirst()
03       expandNodeDstar(x)
04   endwhile
05   return
```
Algorithm 10.15 DStar Plan Repair Main Loop. The main loop runs until the change wavefront passes the goal and the goal is consistent

10.3.4.1.5 Path Extraction. So far backpointers have not been discussed. Path extraction in D* can be accomplished in a manner similar to A*. Each time a new $rhs(\ )$ value is computed for a node, a backpointer can be generated to the parent that generates the minimum g value for the node. After a repair pass completes, the new solution will be encoded in the backpointers.

10.3.4.1.6 Initial Run. D* is designed to be a plan repair algorithm so the question of where the initial plan comes from must be answered. It turns out that by "repairing" an empty plan, it will generate the first plan (Algorithm 10.16) as well.

```
00    algorithm initializeDstar(x_s, x_g)
01    x_s.rhs ← 0
02    O.insertSorted(x_s, calcKey(x_s))
03    x_s.parent ← null
04    computeOptimalPath()
05    return
```

Algorithm 10.16 First Pass of DStar Algorithm. DStar can generate the first plan if it is set up to "repair" an empty plan.

10.3.4.2 Robot Motion

So far, the description of the algorithm has concentrated on edge costs that change over time, and we have avoided the sticky matter of what to do when the robot moves. When the robot moves, it means that the physical start node of the search has moved. Recall that $g(X)$ needs to be stored in the nodes, so that potentially means that the stored $g(X)$ values of all nodes in the search tree become incorrect. Of course, to have to update every node in the search tree every time the robot moves is very bad news indeed, because the point of plan repair is to avoid just such an expensive traversal. This section reveals the clever ways in which D* avoids this computation.

10.3.4.2.1 Search Direction. D* departs from the planners discussed so far in that it reverses the planning direction and plans from the true goal back toward the robot. There are two very good reasons for this reversal. First, the goal is not moving but the robot is. A reversed search direction means that the cost to the start node (true goal node) becomes $g(X)$ rather than $h(X)$. This means the g values of nodes in the search tree remain correct while the robot moves around – until some cost change is discovered that may require a recomputation of the g value of a node.

Second, the changes to the search tree caused by edge cost updates have to be propagated toward the leaves of the tree. The depth change in the tree (and the distance in the world) from the changed edge to the robot can be orders of magnitude smaller than the depth change (or distance) from the changed edge to the goal. Hence, in practice it is far more efficient for the goal node to be the root of the search tree (Figure 10.26).

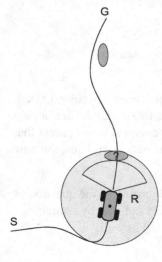

Figure 10.26 Search Direction in D*. The fact that goal distance may exceed sensor range by orders of magnitude means that searching from the goal to the robot will be far more efficient for plan repair.

10.3.4.2.2 Robot Motion. Consider now the second half of the node cost the heuristic. For a reversed search direction, the correct heuristic value $h(X) = h(X, Robot)$ does change as the robot moves. Suppose the robot moves from node N_1 to node N_2 and then detects its first cost change since it was at N_1. The cost change will lead to placing nodes on OPEN but because the search tree is retained from the last planning cycle, the nodes presently on OPEN were sorted based on a different position of the robot. We presumably need at least to ensure that the nodes presently on OPEN are resorted based on the new heuristic computed from the new robot position. One solution is to simply re-sort the OPEN queue, but it is also possible to do the re-sort in a lazy fashion – to fix the node priorities as needed – as described below.

The nodes on OPEN need to be sorted based on an admissible heuristic—an underestimate of the true cost. From the perspective of any arbitrary node N already in OPEN, the worst case is that robot moved directly toward N in the direction of the line from N_2 to N_1. In this case, the heuristic for node N will need to be reduced by $h(N_1, N_2)$ to remain admissible. If this worst case change is subtracted from the heuristic part of the keys of all of the nodes in OPEN, then their heuristics will remain underestimates, and any plan produced will remain optimal.

The next trick is to notice that if the same number is added or subtracted from every key in the search tree, then the relative costs of all nodes remain unchanged and there is no need to resort the nodes on the OPEN list. In fact, we can even avoid updating the keys by noting that instead of subtracting the increment $h(N_1, N_2)$ from nodes that are presently on OPEN, we can instead add it to any new nodes placed on OPEN. We define a quantity to be added to the key of every node, called the *key modifier* k_m and the cost of any new nodes placed on OPEN is computed as:

$$f(X) = g(X) + h(X) + k_m \tag{10.12}$$

If the robot moves again, from N_2 to N_3, then the new increment $h(N_2, N_3)$ is added to the present value of k_m before any new nodes generated at position N_3 are placed on OPEN. The modifier k_m increases monotonically. It is important to realize that when nodes are placed on OPEN, their key values are supposed to be frozen at that point, so when the key of a node on OPEN is queried, the query should return the key that was used to insert the node. Nodes already on OPEN are not updated for robot motion that happens afterward.

With this, ahem, key modification in place, the algorithm needs minimal changes to accommodate robot motion. The approach is to simply check if the key of a node is wrong when it is removed from OPEN, and if it is, it is simply put back on OPEN. This change appears in the main plan repair function (Algorithm 10.17).

10.3.4.3 Pragmatic Information for Plan Repair

Because D* typically deals with cost fields rather than discrete obstacles, it becomes necessary in practice to associate a cost with unknown regions of the workspace. If this cost is unrealistically low, the robot will be more prone to explore in an attempt to avoid crossing high cost regions that it should have crossed. If the cost of unknown areas is unrealistically high, the robot will be prone to crossing high cost regions that it should have looked for a way to avoid.

```
00    algorithm computeOptimalPath()
01    while(f[O.peek( )] < f(x_g)    or    x_g.g ≠ x_g.rhs)
02        x ← O .removeFirst()
03        f_old ← x.f
04        getRhs(x)
05        if(f_old < calcKey(x_s)
06            O.insertSorted(x,calcKey(x))
07        else
08            expandNodeDstar(x)
08        endif
09    endwhile
10    return
```

Algorithm 10.17 DStar Plan Repair Main Loop with Robot Motion. The main loop runs until the change wavefront passes the goal and the goal is consistent.

One of the more important systems-level issues in realtime planning systems is the quality of the pose estimate. Obstacles, and more generally costs, will be placed in the world model at locations that are computed from somewhat erroneous pose estimates. This fact permits all sorts of perverse system failures. For example, a robot planning routes based on a (prior or generated) map can find itself trying to penetrate vegetation on the side of a perfectly good road because the pose estimate (or the map) is shifted sideways and perception is unable to recognize the road.

Furthermore, if the map is accurate but pose estimation is momentarily wrong, it is possible for the system to place two instances of the same obstacle in different places in the map, to erroneously close the only existing issue from an area, or to hallucinate the disappearance of an obstacle that is lethal to the robot.

It can be an effective technique for local planning to define the search graph in vehicle coordinates so that it moves with the robot. However, for plan repair, it is important that the cost of an edge remain the same from one planning iteration to the next unless something changes. Because potentially all graph edges fixed with respect to the robot will change simply due to robot motion (as they move over the obstacles), such a search graph is not conducive to plan repair.

The runtime of D* will vary depending on the amount of changes that need to be processed. When a significant change is noted, it can cause an unusually long plan repair operation. In the worst case, the robot may have to stop moving while this computation completes. Researchers have also developed anytime versions of D* that mitigate this effect.

10.3.5 Hierarchical Planning

For large scale problems, on the scale of kilometers, all of the techniques presented so far may still not be adequate. In such cases, it can be effective to invoke ideas of hierarchical planning. As the term is used here, it means that the planning problem is conducted at more than one conceptual level in order to suppress detail (where possible) and save computation. The level of detail may change with complexity of the environment, with distance from the robot, with time, with robot state, and so on.

Both the environmental model and the search graph can be represented at different levels of detail. Consider first the environmental model. A high resolution raster of cost cells can be usefully reduced to one of lower resolution, to a set of polygonal obstacles, to a set of point obstacles of fixed radius, or to a single scalar representing the cost of regions not in the present scope of the map.

The search graph consists of edges connecting states. It may be reduced in detail by increasing the separation of states. The states can also be reduced in dimensionality. For example, a state space that includes velocity and curvature as well as position and heading is five dimensional. Dramatic reduction of memory and computation is possible if higher derivatives like curvature and velocity can be removed from the search space. Similarly, the outdegree of search graph nodes directly affects the exponent of the exponential growth rate of the search tree, so if the number of edges emanating from nodes is reduced, then the search graph can be reduced in size.

10.3.5.1 Planner Hierarchies

Of course, a literal implementation of hierarchical planning is to have a hierarchy of planners. There are many variations on this theme. Consider the case of two planners. Suppose that one operates on a more "global" scale and another locally. The global planner may run offline on a good map, it may run online on a lower fidelity map, or it could even be a human designating a sequence of subgoals known as *waypoints*.

In this scheme, the local planner tries to follow the global plan while perhaps using local perception and higher fidelity spatial and motion models in order to avoid obstacles or other issues that may not have been known to the global planner. The overall system can function as an optimal controller where deviation from the global plan is discouraged in the cost function and obstacle avoidance is treated as a constraint. Or, the local planner may compute the cost of the portion of a path that is near the robot and the global planner computes the rest (instead of using a relatively uninformed heuristic).

Although this approach has its merits in benign environments, there are failure modes that are fundamental in general (Figure 10.27). If there is a flaw in the global plan like an unforeseen roadblock, then the situation may be resolvable if the global planner can be called upon to replan. If not, the local planner may not be competent to find an alternate route because that function was originally allocated to the global planner for computational reasons. Hence, an offline generated global plan is always risky.

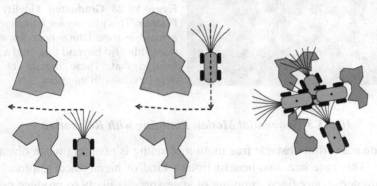

Figure 10.27 Failures of Hierarchical Planners. (Left) The global plan (dotted line) is infeasible and the local planner cannot make the sharp turn. (Center) After missing the turn, the global planner wants the robot to try again. (Right) A feasible multipoint turn is the only way out of the maze.

A more serious failure occurs when the global plan is infeasible on a scale that exceeds the capacity of the local planner to fix. If the global plan is infeasible somewhere along its length, the local planner will be unable to execute the infeasible portion once the robot reaches it and the obvious remedies are all somewhat flawed. First, the local planner can try to deform the path toward feasibility but the plan may then intersect obstacles. Second, the local planner can try to find an alternate route by deviating from the global plan but the global planner will potentially guide the robot right back to the same place unless the local planner ignores it for some (unknown) period of time. Third, the local planner, once again, may not be competent to find an alternate route.

10.3.5.2 Graduated Fidelity

A possibly better approach is one of surrounding the robot by a high-fidelity region (which moves with the robot) and to reduce the fidelity of the representation beyond it, but to use a single planner to search this composite representation [24]. In a sense, limited depth search is such a technique where the low-fidelity region is the region beyond the end of the search tree where the heuristic calculation is used. The heuristic can be argued to be a simplified world model that assumes there are no obstacles.

An example is to use a dynamically feasible search graph near the robot and degrade it to a grid farther away, and perhaps a heuristic beyond that (Figure 10.28). This architecture is an improvement because the planner is now competent to find a new route in difficult areas when perception reveals important new information. If the lower fidelity region of the search space contains edges that are a subset of those used in the high-fidelity region, then plans generated at a distance are guaranteed to be feasible while requiring less computation. The robot may decide on an alternative when it reaches any given place, but at least the original path through the region still exists as an option.

Figure 10.28 Graduated Fidelity Motion Planner. This planner for a Mars rover uses a feasible state lattice near the robot, an infeasible grid beyond that, and a heuristic beyond that. These regions of differing detail move with the robot.

10.3.5.3 Sequential Motion Planning with Relaxation

The opposite case from obstacle free motion planning is planning when obstacles are very dense. This case can also benefit from a kind of hierarchical approach. When obstacles are dense, any fixed sampling of state space is likely to produce nodes and edges that frequently intersect obstacles. Consider, for example, a dense boulder field where the robot can barely fit between the bounders. Although a path through the area may still exist in a regularly sampled search graph, it may not be very optimal. It would be ideal if both the nodes and the edges could be moved around to land in the spaces between the boulders.

Recall that relaxation approaches use the extra information in the cost gradient to deform a path toward a local cost minimum. If an initial guess for a feasible path crosses obstacles (or high cost regions), then a relaxation of the path could potentially cause the path to "fall off" the obstacles into the intervening voids. Whether the environment model uses a cost field or discrete obstacles, it is necessary to formulate a path cost function that varies continuously with path deformations in order for relaxation to work. For discrete obstacles, the degree of penetration could be used for example to generate a gradient that moves the path outside the obstacle.

The strength of relaxation approaches is that they effectively search the continuum of all paths, whereas the weakness is that they can only do so locally. A hybrid technique can be based on the concept of generating an initial path that is low cost and then deforming it to locally (in path space) minimum cost using relaxation. However, it may be the case that the continuum solution is not in the same homotopy class as the initial solution, which was relaxed. Although there may be no way to ensure that the true solution in the continuum is found, it would be prudent to relax many initial guesses that are homotopically distinct.

These observations lead to a desire to automatically produce numerous homotopically distinct paths to seed relaxation. One way to do that is to run a bidirectional search emanating from both the start and the goal that continues until the two search trees connect at multiple, physically separated places. Every point in the joined graph will then have an optimal path toward both the start and the goal encoded in the search tree and samples of such interior points will produce a sampling of all of the homotopy classes that are induced by the obstacles.

10.3.6 References and Further Reading

10.3.6.1 Books

Choset is another book that also covers Dstar.

[18] H. Choset, K. M. Lynch, S. Hutchinson, G. Kantor, W. Burgard, L. E. Kavraki, and S. Thrun, *Principles of Robot Motion: Theory, Algorithms, and Implementations,* MIT Press, 2005.

10.3.6.2 Papers

The following papers were referenced in the text.

[19] E. Hansen and R. Zhou, Anytime Heuristic Search, *Journal of Artificial Intelligence Research,* Vol. 28, pp. 267–297, 2007.

[20] S. Koenig and M. Likhachev, Fast Replanning for Navigation in Unknown Terrain, *IEEE Transactions on Robotics,* Vol. 21, No. 3, pp. 354–363, 2005.

[21] R. Korf, Realtime Heuristic Search, *Artificial Intelligence,* Vol. 42, Nos. 2–3, pp. 189–211, March 1990.

[22] M. Likhachev, G. Gordon, and S. Thrun, ARA*: Anytime A* with Provable Bounds on Sub-Optimality, in *Advances in Neural Information Processing Systems,* MIT Press, 2003.

[23] I. Pohl, Heuristic Search Viewed as Path Planning in a Graph, *Artificial Intelligence*, Vol. 1, No. 3, pp. 193–204, 1970.

[24] M. Pivtoraiko and A. Kelly, Graduated Fidelity: Differentially Constrained Motion Replanning Using State Lattices with Graduated Fidelity, *IROS*, 2008.

[25] A. Stentz, The Focussed D* Algorithm for Real-Time Replanning, Proceedings of IJCAI-95, August 1995.

10.3.7 Exercise

10.3.7.1 Weighted A*

Prove that weighted A* is ε-admissible. That is, if an admissible heuristic is inflated by the factor $1 + \varepsilon$ to produce a new heuristic $h'(X) = (1 + \varepsilon)h(X)$, show that the cost of the computed solution will exceed the optimal by no more than a factor of $1 + \varepsilon$.

Index